Arthur F. Kinney
UNIVERSITY OF MASSACHUSETTS

Kenneth W. Kuiper
CALVIN COLLEGE

Lynn Z. Bloom
FORMERLY OF WESTERN RESERVE UNIVERSITY

Edmund Spenser
arch · · · George Herbert
us · · · John Donne · · · Isaac Watts
re de Ronsard · · · Andrew Marvell · · · Oliver Goldsmith
William Shakespeare
cer · · · Thomas Overbury
Philip Sidney

Molière
John Donne · · · Jonathan Edwards
embo Motoyasu · · · Edward Taylor · Benjamin Franklin
Henry Vaughan
Jacobus Revius · · · Jonathan Swift

Francis Bacon
Miguel de Cervantes · · · Jean Jacques Rousseau
accio · · · Thomas Hobbes · · Cotton Mather
achiavelli · · · John Milton · · · Voltaire · · · Thomas Jefferson
Blaise Pascal · · · Henry Fielding

William Wordsworth
Michel de Montaigne · Andrew Marvell · Alexander Pope
lyot · · · John Smith · · · Matsuo Bashō
Erasmus · · · John Milton · Joseph Addison · · · William Blake
Rabelais · · · Izaak Walton · · · Taniguchi Buson · · · Robert Burns
Kobayashi Issa

Francis Bacon · · · Jonathan Swift
John Locke · · · Samuel Johnson
lore · · · Benjamin Franklin

Philip Sidney
a Vinci
is · · · William Shakespeare
nini · · · John Dryden

Wolfgang Amadeus Mozart

Johann Wolfgang von Goethe

Samuel Taylor Coleridge

SYMPOSIUM

SYMPOSIUM

Houghton Mifflin Company · Boston

NEW YORK   ATLANTA   GENEVA, ILL.   DALLAS   PALO ALTO

CONTENTS *in Order of Appearance*

RELIGION

JUSTICE

NATURE

SCIENCE

THE ARTS

CONTENTS *by Genre*

DRAMA

POETRY

PROSE FICTION

NONFICTION PROSE

PREFACE

IN CLASSIC GREEK, a *symposium* was a drinking party, but because Plato called one of his most moving dialogues by that name, the word has now come to mean a respected method of learning. Plato's *Symposium* depicts a banquet honoring Agathon, who has just won a prize for writing the best tragedy in the annual Attic contest. Agathon's guests, Socrates foremost among them, reject the customary flute girls, wine, and ribald jokes and turn instead to a protracted and perceptive discussion on a single, significant topic: the definition and defense of love. Each of the guests — who include a doctor, a poet, a playwright, a philosopher, and a man-about-town — perceives love through his particular convictions, imagination, and experience. Through dialogue and debate they learn from each other. Thus the meaning of the word *symposium* was changed forever.

This book is indebted to that first symposium in that it presents six such gatherings of thought and opinion. Each of these deals, as Plato's did, with one basic human concern which has compelled the attention of Western man: love, religion, justice, nature, science, and the arts. In the manner of Agathon's guests, the contributors derive their positions from different backgrounds and perspectives. The diversity of their views generates controversy, the heart of *Symposium* — which is based on the conviction that the discovery of truth arises from the heat of debate.

The six sections of *Symposium* share other characteristics. Each is arranged chronologically, tracing its subject from Plato's time to our own. In attempting to define the nature of man and his paramount concerns, they focus on discovery, on demonstration, on argument, and on imaginative interpretation. Moreover, each of the six sections includes quite diverse kinds of distinguished writing: letters, speeches, biographies, essays, poems, stories, novels, and plays. Each selection, like the argument of each of Agathon's guests, contains some portion of the truth we seek, yet perhaps only a portion. So each section of our *Symposium* displays a range of opinion which opens insights not only into the topic at hand, but also into the world, society, and ourselves.

Symposium, then, invites the reader to live, as Socrates lived, a life of inquiry. According to Plato, many Socratic dialogues began by seeking an adequate definition of an idea — love, religion, or justice — or of a field of interest — nature, science, or the arts. Socrates questioned the definition, walked around it, looked at it from all angles. He attacked its assumptions, divided it into issues, quarreled with its implications. Always he kept modifying it. More often than not, in a series of questions and answers bolstered by analogies and syllogisms, he revealed the original definition to be short-sighted, distorted, or patently absurd. This kind of ordeal by examination was not always pleasant. But Socrates and his students sought the eternal truths beyond shifting conventions, false opinions, and easy generalizations. Even if they disproved as often as they proved, they were never total losers. The mere act of participating in the process brought a measurable gain.

It is significant that Socrates did not *write* but *talked*. He enjoyed quoting Homer: " 'When two go together, one sees before the other.' " The gradually sharpened awareness, the organic process of realization which was Socrates' goal, came through dialogue as well as through introspection. He proposed that minds constantly rub against other minds to spark new thoughts. In like manner, we hope that the variety and conflict of ideas presented in our *Symposium* will inspire vigorous, informed discussion both in and out of class. We hope that out of intellectual ferment will come an intensified comprehension of the world, its inhabitants and their concerns. If even through debate we cannot reach an ultimate understanding, the knowledge that we cannot may itself be important. The legacy of critical open-mindedness which Socrates left to his own students was even greater than his other most enduring gift: Plato's academy, the first university in the West.

The six parts of *Symposium* invite the reader to pursue his own thinking as he debates with the contributors to this book. We hope he will also be stimulated to take his reactions into the classroom, into the dormitory, into any open marketplace where, through intellectual bartering, he can finally determine the worth of his ideas. For while each of the six discussions here resembles the symposium which lasted through one spring night in 416 B.C., what is still needed for each is a contemporary Socrates — a gadfly who stings men's beliefs with doubt and spurs them to creative thought and refined knowledge. Each reader of this book can perpetuate the Socratic technique, with others and by himself, remembering that to understand involves the strenuous process of self-discovery and that "Know Thyself" is both the means and end of education.

Acknowledgments and Observations on the Text

In the introductions to the six parts of *Symposium*, we have tried to identify briefly those issues which are important to the topic and recurrent in the selections, but we have made no attempt to suggest any particular way of resolving the issues or reading the selections. The order and method of use would seem best dictated by the reader's temperament and interest. All we have tried to supply, as Socrates himself might have done, are some of the leading questions.

To help us in this as in so much else, a number of colleagues, friends, and students have contributed materially to the comprehensiveness and quality of the book. Lillian Kuiper and Martin Bloom have consistently provided valuable perspectives and helpful suggestions. Useful services have been performed by the staffs of the Houghton and Widener Libraries, Harvard; the Beinecke and Sterling Libraries, Yale; the New York Public Library; and the libraries of Amherst, Calvin, and Smith Colleges; Case Western Reserve University; and the Universities of Massachusetts and Michigan.

Symposium began at the University of Michigan when our students in English composition focused on problems relating to the nature of love and justice. Many students have participated through dialogue and dialectic in the evolution of this book. Those who have read parts of the manuscript or offered suggestions for its contents include Henry Bean, Clifton Cates III, Daniel Chase, Rebecca Coppinger, Thomas Couser, Christine Crowley, Marcia Erush, Ted Giatas, John Gorman, Ann Hadley, John Hamilton, William Harney, Margaret Lindeman, Karl Marlantes, Joseph Maw, Roberta Moore, Stephen O'Brien, James Oliver, Michael Pardee, Neal Plantinga, H. Langdon Reynolds, Arthur Segaloff, Peter Stambler, Richard Teleky, Joseph Tringali, Sheila West, and Emanuel White.

We have taken particular care in selecting editions and translations of texts printed in *Symposium*. Although no rule has been inviolate, we have usually adopted first editions of works by living authors, the last edition published in the lifetime of authors recently dead, and the commonly accepted definitive texts of works by earlier authors. The texts of works in English are usually authoritative, but there are occasional exceptions: we have chosen the original text of D. H. Lawrence's "Christs in the Tirol" rather than the expanded revision, because the earlier version is superior in its immediate tone and direct, simple style. We have kept old spelling without heavy glossing whenever possible, as in Cotton Mather's account of the Goodwin witchcraft case; but we have used Neville Coghill's modernized Chaucer because it is generally easier to read than the Middle English version.

Choosing texts in translation has been considerably more difficult. Most important of our criteria has been fidelity to the sense of the original; a second important consideration has been style insofar as it reflects the style of the original work. Thus while Fitzgerald's translation of the *Oedipus* is remarkably lively, we have selected Kitto's translation because it is closer to the original. And despite some recent and slightly more accurate prose translations of Lucretius, we have used Leonard's because, like the original, it is in poetry.

To help determine the most authoritative and readable texts, we have consulted a number of colleagues and friends who gave willingly of their time and knowledge. Although the catalogue is long, our gratitude is deep and we wish to thank here Charles Chu, John Maki, and Clarence Shute (Oriental); George Dimock, Jr., Cyrus Hamlin, Gilbert Lawall, Lawrence A. Richardson III, Peter Rose, and Eric Segal (classical Greece and Rome); Paul Sanders (Bible); in the ages of English literature, Douglas Cole, E. Talbot Donaldson, John Pope, Harry A. Schroeder, and Eric Stockton (Anglo-Saxon and medieval); Thomas H. Cain, William Elwood, Thomas H. Greene, Davis P. Harding, John A. Hunt, Alvin Kernan, Louis Martz, Michael J.K. O'Loughlin,

Bernard Spivack, Richard Sylvester, and Eugene M. Waith (Renaissance); George deForest Lord, Maynard Mack, Martin Price, Benjamin Nangle, and Howard D. Weinbrot (the Enlightenment); Robert Bagg, Harold Bloom, Michael Cooke, and E. Donald Hirsch (Romanticism); A. Dwight Culler, George S. Fayen, James Hazen, Albert J. Lavalley, Arnold Silver, and Alexander Welsh (Victorian); Russell Alspach, David Clark, Marvin Felheim, John Hagopian, and Mark Spilka (twentieth century); Everett Emerson, Charles Feidelson, James K. Folsom, A. N. Kaul, R.W.B. Lewis, Jay H. Martin, Norman Holmes Pearson, and Roger B. Salomon (American); Cyrus Hamlin and Alex Page (German); Thomas G. Bergin, Thomas Greene, and Michael J.K. O'Loughlin (Italian); Lowrie Nelson, Jr. and A. Regalado (Spanish); Victor Brombert, Jacques Guicharnaud, Joseph McMahon, and Charles Mudge (French); Robert L. Jackson (Slavic); Serge Chermayeff, George A. Kubler, and Vincent Scully (art and architecture); Roland Bainton and Ian Siggins (religion and theology); Dean Albertson, L. P. Curtis, Brooks M. Kelley, Rollin G. Osterweiss, and Alexander White (history); Robert Bailey, Beekman C. Cannon, and Leon Plantinga (music); John Brentlinger, Larry Foster, Patricia James, and T. Kermit Scott (philosophy); and Donald Gallup (textual bibliography). They advised out of kindness; we hope they will be pleased with the result.

Other editorial practices may also be of interest. We have chosen authors' names or pseudonyms most closely identified with their work; thus Eric Blair appears only as George Orwell. We have identified anonymous works as such, listing speculations about authorship in a note and assigning a date derived from internal evidence of content and style. For known authors' dates and identifications, we have consulted *Chambers's Biographical Dictionary*, supplemented with the *Dictionary of National Biography* and *Webster's Biographical Dictionary*. Annotation is always a problem: Dr. Johnson was correct when he remarked that all editors gloss too much for some, too little for others, and please no one, perhaps, but themselves. We have supplied all notes except those specifically credited to editors of the texts we have chosen. Our rule was to gloss only terms and passages not immediately clear or immediately available in a standard college dictionary.

In addition, some of the leading questions of style and content, as well as many of the answers, have been supplied by our editors at Houghton Mifflin — Thomas D. Wittenberg and JoAnne Towell — to whom we are grateful for their unfailing enthusiasm, cooperation, and judgment.

A. F. K.

K. W. K.

L. Z. B.

LOVE

*It is not Love absolutely that is good
or praiseworthy, but only that Love which
impels men to love aright.*

PAUSANIAS, Symposium

LOVE — whether an experience or an emotion, a reality or a fantasy — is a subject on which nearly all of us believe we are experts. And why not? Our atmosphere is saturated with the idea of love. Hippies and ministers preach it; billboards and mass media constantly invoke it; pacifists, militarists, and politicians extol it in the name of patriotism. We could not escape love even if we tried; and usually we do not, for we have come to believe that love is a good and wondrous force which can transport us and transform our experiences.

It is surprising, then, when we come to define love, what a perplexing, demanding task it is. Why the difficulty? Because a feeling cannot be expressed in words? Because love can be manifested in so many ways? Because taboos and prejudices have been formed about attitudes and practices of love? Because love is too universal to capture, too encompassing to compartmentalize?

In the ancient Greek world, men loved each other for their honor and courage, and they loved women for physical satisfaction. This personal devotion was first generalized into love of tribe and then, especially by the Romans, into a love of the state. In medieval times it evolved in the religious into a singular passionate love of God, frequently transforming women into saints, men into mystics, and ordinary practices of love into a tight and sometimes constricting asceticism. Since the Renaissance, however, lovers — and writers about love — have refocused on man, with views of love akin to those of the ancients, though modified by greater equality among classes and between the sexes.

But the historical approach is only one way to understand love. The love of man which Socrates reveals in his *Symposium* is quite opposed to the abject love inherent in the courtly code proposed by the medieval priest Andreas Capellanus; and neither is quite capable of the clever invitation to seduction that governs Marvell's poem, "To His Coy Mistress." To understand love only in terms of time and place is to ignore the perennial, timeless patterns. Love, we are told, improves us; yet lovers are frequently petty, selfish, narcissistic, exploitative. Love, we are told, is pleasurable — its own best reward; yet it causes us pain, doubt, fear, and psychological torment. Love, we are told, is infinite, eternal, abiding. Yet love affairs begin and end in time; some are too brief, others too long, too debilitating. Love, we are told, is all-consuming; yet it can be forgotten, diminished, rejected, sublimated. In his attempt to define love, Lear asks his favorite daughter, Cordelia, for a public proclamation that will forever isolate the character of love and describe its effect; but she can find no appropriate answer. Then what brings about love? he asks her later, in humility born of madness and suffering. "No cause, no cause," she replies. Although love seems to be an emotion which escapes easy definition, those who contribute to the following symposium on love seek to comprehend it and consequently to define it.

The contributors make it clear that love is both a relationship freely begun, as Cordelia implies, and an extension of individual temperament. In most instances, therefore, to understand love we must examine our own needs and responses, as Donne does in "Batter My Heart, Three Person'd God." Nor need we divorce feeling from physical desire, as Rilke asserts.

Symposium's contributors raise other issues as well. If two sorts of love conflict, as they do when Aeneas must choose between Dido and his mission to found a new Troy, what then? What happens when the medieval man, like Peter Abelard, feels as urgent a response toward a woman as toward God? How, indeed, does love turn to hate — a problem examined by Richepin and Meredith? Is it even possible to reject love altogether without becoming a hermit, a misanthrope, or a psychopath?

The lover feels that his own experience is unique; how, therefore, can he communicate it meaningfully to any other person, even his beloved? Why should he try? This section of *Symposium* is predicated on the belief that great literature can communicate the essence of a unique experience, with its complex interweaving of conflicting and transitory moods, attitudes, reactions, behaviors, and values. As readers, we are the judges of whether what is true in the estimation of one person is valid for others, and of how meaningfully an author can convey the universal through the personal. In the following selections we find classic expressions of love which have helped to shape our ideas of love and our behavior as lovers.

Plato (c. 427–c. 347 B.C.)

GREEK PHILOSOPHER

Symposium: On Love

'But now I will leave you in peace, and try to give the account of Love which I once heard from a woman of Mantinea, called Diotima. She had other accomplishments as well — once, before the plague, when the Athenians had been sacrificing to avert it, she succeeded in postponing it for ten years — but what concerns us at present is that she was my instructress in the art of love. I will try, taking the conclusions on which Agathon and I reached agreement as my starting-point, to give the best consecutive account I can of what she told me. As you were so careful to point out to us, Agathon, one must elucidate the essential nature and characteristics of Love before describing his effects. The easiest thing will be to go through the same questions and answers as she did with me. I had used very much the same language to her as Agathon used to me, and had said that Love is a great god and must be reckoned beautiful, but she employed against me the arguments by which I demonstrated to Agathon that to my way of thinking Love is neither beautiful nor good. "What do you mean, Diotima?" I said. "Is Love ugly and bad?" "Don't say such things," she answered; "do you think that anything that is not beautiful is necessarily ugly?" "Of course I do." "And that anything that is not wisdom is ignorance? Don't you know that there is a state of mind half-way between wisdom and ignorance?" "What do you mean?" "Having true convictions without being able to give reasons for them," she replied. "Surely you see that such a state of mind cannot be called understanding, because nothing irrational deserves the name; but it would be equally wrong to call it ignorance; how can one call a state of mind ignorance which hits upon the truth? The fact is that having true convictions is what I called it just now, a condition half-way between knowledge and ignorance." "I grant you that," said I. "Then do not maintain that what is not beautiful is ugly, and what is not good is bad. Do not suppose that because, on your own admission, Love is not good or beautiful, he must on that account be ugly and bad, but rather that he is something between the two." "And yet," I said, "everybody admits that he is a great god." "When you say everybody, do you mean those who don't know him, or do you include those who do?" "I mean absolutely everybody." She burst out laughing, and said: "Well, Socrates, I don't see how he can be admitted to be a great god by those who say that he isn't even a god at all." "Who are they?" I asked. "You are one of them and I'm another." "What can you mean?" "It's per-

Title supplied by editors. From *Symposium* by Plato, translated by W. Hamilton and published by Penguin Books Ltd. Reprinted by permission.

fectly easy; you'd say, wouldn't you, that all gods are happy and beautiful? You wouldn't dare to suggest that any of the gods is not?" "Good heavens, no." "And by happy you mean in secure enjoyment of what is good and beautiful?" "Certainly." "But you have agreed that it is because he lacks what is good and beautiful that Love desires these very things." "Yes, I have." "But a being who has no share of the good and beautiful cannot be a god?" "Obviously not." "Very well then, you see that you are one of the people who believe that Love is not a god."

'"What can Love be then?" I said. "A mortal?" "Far from it." "Well, what?" "As in my previous examples, he is half-way between mortal and immortal." "What sort of being is he then, Diotima?" "He is a great spirit, Socrates; everything that is of the nature of a spirit is half-god and half-man." "And what is the function of such a being?" "To interpret and convey messages to the gods from men and to men from the gods, prayers and sacrifices from the one, and commands and rewards from the other. Being of an intermediate nature, a spirit bridges the gap between them, and prevents the universe from falling into two separate halves. Through this class of being come all divination and the supernatural skill of priests in sacrifices and rites and spells and every kind of magic and wizardry. God does not deal directly with man; it is by means of spirits that all the intercourse and communication of gods with men, both in waking life and in sleep, is carried on. A man who possesses skill in such matters is a spiritual man, whereas a man whose skill is confined to some trade or handicraft is an earthly creature. Spirits are many in number and of many kinds, and one of them is Love."

'"Who are his parents?" I asked. "That is rather a long story," she answered, "but I will tell you. On the day that Aphrodite was born the gods were feasting, among them Contrivance the son of Invention; and after dinner, seeing that a party was in progress, Poverty came to beg and stood at the door. Now Contrivance was drunk with nectar — wine, I may say, had not yet been discovered — and went out into the garden of Zeus, and was overcome by sleep. So Poverty, thinking to alleviate her wretched condition by bearing a child to Contrivance, lay with him and conceived Love. Since Love was begotten on Aphrodite's birthday, and since he has also an innate passion for the beautiful, and so for the beauty of Aphrodite herself, he became her follower and servant. Again, having Contrivance for his father and Poverty for his mother, he bears the following character. He is always poor, and, far from being sensitive and beautiful, as most people imagine, he is hard and weather-beaten, shoeless and homeless, always sleeping out for want of a bed, on the ground, on doorsteps, and in the street. So far he takes after his mother and lives in want. But, being also his father's son, he schemes to get for himself whatever is beautiful and good; he is bold and forward and strenuous, always devising tricks like a cunning huntsman; he yearns after knowledge and is full of resource and is a lover of wisdom all his life, a skilful magician, an alchemist, a true sophist. He is neither mortal nor immortal; but on one and the same day he will live and flourish (when things go well with

him), and also meet his death; and then come to life again through the
vigour that he inherits from his father. What he wins he always loses, and is
neither rich nor poor, neither wise nor ignorant.

' "The truth of the matter is this. No god is a lover of wisdom or desires
to be wise, for he is wise already, and the same is true of other wise persons,
if there be any such. Nor on the other hand do the ignorant love wisdom
and desire to be wise, for the tiresome thing about ignorance is precisely this,
that a man who possesses neither beauty nor goodness nor intelligence is
perfectly well satisfied with himself, and no one who does not believe that he
lacks a thing desires what he does not believe that he lacks."

' "Who then," I said, "are the lovers of wisdom, if they are neither the
wise nor the ignorant!" "A child could answer that question. Obviously
they are the intermediate class, of which Love among others is a member.
Wisdom is one of the most beautiful of things, and Love is love of beauty,
so it follows that Love must be a lover of wisdom, and consequently in a
state half-way between wisdom and ignorance. This too springs from the
circumstances of his birth; his father was wise and fertile in expedients, his
mother devoid of wisdom and helpless. So much for the nature of the spirit,
my dear Socrates. As for your thinking as you did about Love, there is nothing
remarkable in that; to judge by what you said, you identified Love with the
beloved object instead of with what feels love; that is why you thought that
Love is supremely beautiful. The object of love is in all truth beautiful and
delicate and perfect and worthy to be thought happy, but what feels love
has a totally different character such as I have just described."

' "Tell me then, my friend," I said, "for your words carry conviction, what
function Love performs among men, if this is his nature." "That is precisely
what I am going to try to teach you, Socrates. The nature and parentage of
Love are as I have described, and he is also, according to you, love of beauty.
But suppose we were to be asked: 'In what does love of beauty consist, Socrates and Diotima?' or, to put it more plainly, 'What is the aim of the love
which is felt by the lover of beauty?' " "His aim is to attain possession of
beautiful things," I answered. "But that merely raises a further question.
What will have been gained by the man who is in possession of beauty?"
I said that I could supply no ready answer to this question. "Well," she said,
"let us change our terms and substitute good for beautiful. Suppose someone
asked you: 'Now, Socrates, what is the aim of the love felt by the lover of
the good?' " "Possession of the good," I replied. "And what will have been
gained by the man who is in possession of the good?" "I find that an easier
question to answer; he will be happy." "Presumably because happiness consists in the possession of the good, and once one has given that answer, the
inquiry is at an end; there is no need to ask the further question 'Why does
a man desire to be happy?' " "Quite so."

' "Now do you suppose that this desire and this love are characteristics
common to all men, and that all perpetually desire to be in possession of the
good, or what?" "That is exactly what I mean; they are common to all men."

"Why is it then, Socrates, if all men are always in love with the same thing, that we do not speak of all men as being in love, but say that some men are in love and others not?" "I wonder what the reason can be." "There's no need to wonder; the truth is that we isolate a particular kind of love and appropriate for it the name of love, which really belongs to a wider whole, while we employ different names for the other kinds of love." "Can you give me another example of such a usage?" "Yes, here is one. By its original meaning poetry means simply creation, and creation, as you know, can take very various forms. Any action which is the cause of a thing emerging from non-existence into existence might be called poetry, and all the processes in all the crafts are kinds of poetry, and all those who are engaged in them poets." "Yes." "But yet they are not called poets, but have other names, and out of the whole field of poetry or creation one part, which deals with music and metre, is isolated and called by the name of the whole. This part alone is called poetry, and those whose province is this part of poetry are called poets." "Quite true." "It is just the same with love. The generic concept embraces every desire for good and for happiness; that is precisely what almighty and all-ensnaring love is. But this desire expresses itself in many ways, and those with whom it takes the form of love of money or of physical prowess or of wisdom are not said to be in love or called lovers, whereas those whose passion runs in one particular channel usurp the name of lover, which belongs to them all, and are said to be lovers and in love." "There seems to be truth in what you say," I remarked. "There is indeed a theory," she continued, "that lovers are people who are in search of the other half of themselves, but according to my view of the matter, my friend, love is not desire either of the half or of the whole, unless that half or whole happens to be good. Men are quite willing to have their feet or their hands amputated if they believe those parts of themselves to be diseased. The truth is, I think, that people are not attached to what particularly belongs to them, except in so far as they can identify what is good with what is their own, and what is bad with what is not their own. The only object of men's love is what is good. Don't you agree?" "Certainly I do." "May we then say without qualification that men are in love with what is good?" "Yes." "But we must add, mustn't we, that the aim of their love is the possession of the good for themselves?" "Yes." "And not only its possession but its perpetual possession?" "Certainly." "To sum up, then, love is desire for the perpetual possession of the good." "Very true."

' "Now that we have established what love invariably is, we must ask in what way and by what type of action men must show their intense desire if it is to deserve the name of love. What will this function be? Can you tell me?" "If I could, Diotima, I should not be feeling such admiration for your wisdom, or putting myself to school with you to learn precisely this." "Well," she said, "I will tell you. The function is that of procreation in what is beautiful, and such procreation can be either physical or spiritual." "What you say needs an interpreter. I don't understand." "I will put it more plainly.

All men, Socrates, are in a state of pregnancy, both spiritual and physical, and when they come to maturity they feel a natural desire to bring forth, but they can do so only in beauty and never in ugliness. There is something divine about the whole matter; in pregnancy and bringing to birth the mortal creature is endowed with a touch of immortality. But the process cannot take place in disharmony, and ugliness is out of harmony with everything divine, whereas beauty is in harmony with it. That is why Beauty is the goddess who presides over travail, and why, when a person in a state of pregnancy comes into contact with beauty, he has a feeling of serenity and happy relaxation which makes it possible to bring forth and give birth. But, when ugliness is near, the effect is just the opposite; he frowns and withdraws gloomily into himself and recoils and contracts and cannot bring forth, but has painfully to retain the burden of pregnancy. So a person who is pregnant and already great with child is violently attracted towards beauty, because beauty can deliver its possessor from the pains of travail. The object of love, Socrates, is not, as you think, beauty." "What is it then?" "Its object is to procreate and bring forth in beauty." "Really?" "It is so, I assure you. Now, why is procreation the object of love? Because procreation is the nearest thing to perpetuity and immortality that a mortal being can attain. If, as we agreed, the aim of love is the perpetual possession of the good, it necessarily follows that it must desire immortality together with the good, and the argument leads us to the inevitable conclusion that love is love of immortality as well as of the good."

'All this, then, I learnt on the various occasions on which Diotima spoke to me on the subject of love. One day she asked me: "What do you suppose, Socrates, to be the cause of this love and this desire? Look at the behaviour of all animals, both beasts and birds. Whenever the desire to procreate seizes them, they fall a prey to a violent love-sickness. Their first object is to achieve union with one another, their second to provide for their young; for these they are ready to fight however great the odds, and to die if need be, suffering starvation themselves and making any other sacrifice in order to secure the survival of their progeny. With men you might suppose such behaviour to be the result of rational calculation, but what cause is to be ascribed for the occurrence of such love among the beasts? Can you tell me?" I again confessed that I didn't know. "How can you expect ever to become an expert on the subject of love, if you haven't any ideas about this?" "I told you before, Diotima, that this is precisely why I have come to you. I know that I need a teacher. So tell me the cause of this and of all the other phenomena connected with love."

' "Well, if you believe that the natural object of love is what we have more than once agreed that it is, the answer won't surprise you. The same argument holds good in the animal world as in the human, and mortal nature seeks, as far as may be, to perpetuate itself and become immortal. The only way in which it can achieve this is by procreation, which secures the perpetual replacement of an old member of the race by a new. Even during the period for which any living being is said to live and to retain his identity — as a man, for example, is called the same man from boyhood to old age — he does not in fact retain the same attributes, although he is called the same person; he is always becoming a new being and undergoing a process of loss and reparation, which affects his hair, his flesh, his bones, his blood, and his whole body. And not only his body, but his soul as well. No man's character, habits, opinions, desires, pleasures, pains, and fears remain always the same; new ones come into existence and old ones disappear. What happens with pieces of knowledge is even more remarkable; it is not merely that some appear and others disappear, so that we no more retain our identity with regard to knowledge than with regard to the other things I have mentioned, but that each individual piece of knowledge is subject to the same process as we are ourselves. When we use the word recollection we imply by using it that knowledge departs from us; forgetting is the departure of knowledge, and recollection, by implanting a new impression in the place of that which is lost, preserves it, and gives it a spurious appearance of uninterrupted identity. It is in this way that everything mortal is preserved; not by remaining for ever the same, which is the prerogative of divinity, but by undergoing a process in which the losses caused by age are repaired by new acquisitions of a similar kind. This device, Socrates, enables the mortal to partake of immortality, physically as well as in other ways; but the immortal enjoys immortality after another manner. So do not feel surprise that every creature naturally cherishes its own progeny; it is in order to secure immortality that each individual is haunted by this eager desire and love."

'I was surprised at this account and said: "You may be very wise, Diotima, but am I really to believe this?" "Certainly you are," she replied in true professional style; "if you will only reflect you will see that the ambition of men provides an example of the same truth. You will be astonished at its irrationality unless you bear in mind what I have said, and remember that the love of fame and the desire to win a glory that shall never die have the strongest effects upon people. For this even more than for their children they are ready to run risks, spend their substance, endure every kind of hardship, and even sacrifice their lives. Do you suppose that Alcestis[1] would have died to save Admetus, or Achilles to avenge Patroclus,[2] or your Codrus to preserve his kingdom for his sons,[3] if they had not believed that their courage would live for ever in men's memory, as it does in ours? On the contrary; it is desire for immortal renown and a glorious reputation such as theirs that is the

[1] Alcestis consented to die in the place of her husband, Admetus, after Admetus had offended Artemis. Herakles, whom Admetus had treated hospitably, forced Hades to give Alcestis back.
[2] Achilles' sorrow at the death of Patroclus, his best friend, caused him to make up his quarrel with Agamemnon, his leader, and to resume fighting the Trojans and revenge his friend's death.
[3] Codrus, King of Athens, learned that the Dorian invaders would be victorious if his own life were spared; he disguised himself, started a fatal quarrel with the Dorians, and thus saved his land.

incentive of all actions, and the better a man is, the stronger the incentive; he is in love with immortality. Those whose creative instinct is physical have recourse to women, and show their love in this way, believing that by begetting children they can secure for themselves an immortal and blessed memory hereafter for ever; but there are some whose creative desire is of the soul, and who conceive spiritually, not physically, the progeny which it is the nature of the soul to conceive and bring forth. If you ask what that progeny is, it is wisdom and virtue in general; of this all poets and such craftsmen as have found out some new thing may be said to be begetters; but far the greatest and fairest branch of wisdom is that which is concerned with the due ordering of states and families, whose name is moderation and justice. When by divine inspiration a man finds himself from his youth up spiritually pregnant with these qualities, as soon as he comes of due age he desires to bring forth and to be delivered, and goes in search of a beautiful environment for his children; for he can never bring forth in ugliness. In his pregnant condition physical beauty is more pleasing to him than ugliness, and if in a beautiful body he finds also a beautiful and noble and gracious soul, he welcomes the combination warmly, and finds much to say to such a one about virtue and the qualities and actions which mark a good man, and takes his education in hand. By intimate association with beauty embodied in his friend, and by keeping him always before his mind, he succeeds in bringing to birth the children of which he has been long in labour, and once they are born he shares their upbringing with his friend; the partnership between them will be far closer and the bond of affection far stronger than between ordinary parents, because the children that they share surpass human children by being immortal as well as more beautiful. Everyone would prefer children such as these to children after the flesh. Take Homer, for example, and Hesiod, and the other good poets; who would not envy them the children that they left behind them, children whose qualities have won immortal fame and glory for their parents? Or take Lycurgus the lawgiver,[4] and consider the children that he left at Sparta to be the salvation not only of Sparta but one may almost say of Greece. Among you Athenians Solon[5] is honoured for the laws which he produced, and so it is in many other places with other men, both Greek and barbarian, who by their many fine actions have brought forth good fruit of all kinds; not a few of them have even won men's worship on account of their spiritual children, a thing which has never yet happened to anyone by reason of his human progeny.

' "So far, Socrates, I have dealt with love-mysteries into which even you could probably be initiated, but whether you could grasp the perfect revelation to which they lead the pilgrim if he does not stray from the right path, I do not know. However, you shall not fail for any lack of willingness on my part: I will tell you of it, and do you try to follow if you can.

[4] the traditional founder of the Spartan constitution and military system (9th century B.C.).
[5] Athenian statesman (c. 640–560 B.C.) who reformed the constitution so as to assure all citizens some share in the government.

' "The man who would pursue the right way to this goal must begin, when he is young, by applying himself to the contemplation of physical beauty, and, if he is properly directed by his guide, he will first fall in love with one particular beautiful person and beget noble sentiments in partnership with him. Later he will observe that physical beauty in any person is closely akin to physical beauty in any other, and that, if he is to make beauty of outward form the object of his quest, it is great folly not to acknowledge that the beauty exhibited in all bodies is one and the same; when he has reached this conclusion he will become a lover of all physical beauty, and will relax the intensity of his passion for one particular person, because he will realize that such a passion is beneath him and of small account. The next stage is for him to reckon beauty of soul more valuable than beauty of body; the result will be that, when he encounters a virtuous soul in a body which has little of the bloom of beauty, he will be content to love and cherish it and to bring forth such notions as may serve to make young people better; in this way he will be compelled to contemplate beauty as it exists in activities and institutions, and to recognize that here too all beauty is akin, so that he will be led to consider physical beauty taken as a whole a poor thing in comparison. From morals he must be directed to the sciences and contemplate their beauty also, so that, having his eyes fixed upon beauty in the widest sense, he may no longer be the slave of a base and mean-spirited devotion to an individual example of beauty, whether the object of his love be a boy or a man or an activity, but, by gazing upon the vast ocean of beauty to which his attention is now turned, may bring forth in the abundance of his love of wisdom many beautiful and magnificent sentiments and ideas, until at last, strengthened and increased in stature by this experience, he catches sight of one unique science whose object is the beauty of which I am about to speak. And here I must ask you to pay the closest possible attention.

' "The man who has been guided thus far in the mysteries of love, and who has directed his thoughts towards examples of beauty in due and orderly succession, will suddenly have revealed to him as he approaches the end of his initiation a beauty whose nature is marvellous indeed, the final goal, Socrates, of all his previous efforts. This beauty is first of all eternal; it neither comes into being nor passes away, neither waxes nor wanes; next, it is not beautiful in part and ugly in part, nor beautiful at one time and ugly at another, nor beautiful in this relation and ugly in that, nor beautiful here and ugly there, as varying according to its beholders; nor again will this beauty appear to him like the beauty of a face or hands or anything else corporeal, or like the beauty of a thought or a science, or like beauty which has its seat in something other than itself, be it a living thing or the earth or the sky or anything else whatever; he will see it as absolute, existing alone with itself, unique, eternal, and all other beautiful things as partaking of it, yet in such a manner that, while they come into being and pass away, it neither undergoes any increase or diminution nor suffers any change.

‘ "When a man, starting from this sensible world and making his way upward by a right use of his feeling of love for boys, begins to catch sight of that beauty, he is very near his goal. This is the right way of approaching or being initiated into the mysteries of love, to begin with examples of beauty in this world, and using them as steps to ascend continually with that absolute beauty as one's aim, from one instance of physical beauty to two and from two to all, then from physical beauty to moral beauty, and from moral beauty to the beauty of knowledge, until from knowledge of various kinds one arrives at the supreme knowledge whose sole object is that absolute beauty, and knows at last what absolute beauty is.

‘ "This above all others, my dear Socrates," the woman from Mantinea continued, "is the region where a man's life should be spent, in the contemplation of absolute beauty. Once you have seen that, you will not value it in terms of gold or rich clothing or of the beauty of boys and young men, the sight of whom at present throws you and many people like you into such an ecstasy that, provided that you could always enjoy the sight and company of your darlings, you would be content to go without food and drink, if that were possible, and to pass your whole time with them in the contemplation of their beauty. What may we suppose to be the felicity of the man who sees absolute beauty in its essence, pure and unalloyed, who, instead of a beauty tainted by human flesh and colour and a mass of perishable rubbish, is able to apprehend divine beauty where it exists apart and alone? Do you think that it will be a poor life that a man leads who has his gaze fixed in that direction, who contemplates absolute beauty with the appropriate faculty and is in constant union with it? Do you not see that in that region alone where he sees beauty with the faculty capable of seeing it, will he be able to bring forth not mere reflected images of goodness but true goodness, because he will be in contact not with a reflection but with the truth? And having brought forth and nurtured true goodness he will have the privilege of being beloved of God, and becoming, if ever a man can, immortal himself."

‘This, Phaedrus and my other friends, is what Diotima said and what I believe; and because I believe it I try to persuade others that in the acquisition of this blessing human nature can find no better helper than Love. I declare that it is the duty of every man to honour Love, and I honour and practise the mysteries of Love in an especial degree myself, and recommend the same to others, and I praise the power and valour of Love to the best of my ability both now and always. There is my speech, Phaedrus; if you like, you can regard it as a panegyric delivered in honour of Love; otherwise you can give it any name you please.’

Vergil (70–19 B.C.)

ROMAN POET

Dido and Aeneas

Now Dido had felt the heavy slash of care,
the wound that grows in the vein, the lightless flame.
Aeneas' great courage, the glory of his people,
coursed through her mind; fast in her heart lay fixed
his face, his words.[1] She knew no rest or peace.
The next day's lamp of sun was lighting earth,
and Dawn had cleared the sky of dew and dark,
when she, sick soul, spoke to her loving sister:
"Anna! My dreams! They leave me tense with fear!
What strange outsider has come here to our home! 10
How proud his bearing! How brave his heart and
    hand!
I believe — not lightly — he is a child of gods.
Fear proves the soul debased; but he, though battered
by Fate, tells how he fought war after war.
Had I not fixed it firm within my heart
never to yield myself to marriage bond
since that first love[2] left me cheated by death,
did I not sicken at thought of bed and torch,   torch: bridal torch
to this one sin, this once, I might succumb.
No, Anna, I'll speak: Since poor Sychaeus died,   20
since brother drenched my house with husband's
    blood,
Aeneas alone has moved my heart and shaken
resolve. I mark the trace of long-dead flame.
But, oh, may the earth gape wide and deep for me,
or the father almighty blast me down to death,
to the paling ghosts of hell and the pit of night,
before I play honor false or break her laws.

---

[1] The goddess Juno, ever jealous of Venus, has shipwrecked the Trojan Aeneas, son of
Venus and the mortal Anchises. Aeneas, however, finds safety in Carthage, where Queen
Dido reigns. To insure that safety, Venus tricks Dido into falling in love with Aeneas.
She sends her son Cupid, disguised as Aeneas' son Ascanius, to Carthage, and Dido —
already captivated by Aeneas' tales of noble heroism and by his divine mission to found
a new Troy — becomes an easy victim of the little love god.
[2] After Dido's brother Pygmalion, King of Tyre, killed her husband Sychaeus and forced
her to flee Carthage, Dido vowed never to love another.

**Title supplied by editors. Book IV from Vergil: *The Aeneid*, translated by Frank O.
Copley, copyright © 1965, by The Bobbs-Merrill Company, Inc., reprinted by permission
of the Liberal Arts Press Division.**

14

The man who first knew union with me stole
my heart; let him keep and guard it in the tomb."
She spoke; the well of her tears filled and ran over. 30

Then Anna: "Your sister loves you more than life:
why squander youth on endless, lonely grief,
with no sweet sons, without the gifts of love?
You think mere ashes, ghosts in the grave, will care?
So be it! You've mourned; you've turned all suitors
    down
in Libya, and Tyre before. You've scorned Iarbas
and all the chiefs that Africa, proud and rich,
parades: why battle a love that you've found good?
Have you forgotten whose lands you've settled here?
This side, Gaetulians (race untamed by war), 40
savage Numidians, and a barrier sea;
that side, the desert, thirst, the wild nomads
of Barca. Why tell of wars that rise in Tyre
or how your brother threatens?
I'm sure the gods have blessed the Trojan's course,
and Juno favored the wind that blew their ships.
Oh, what a city you'll see, what kingdoms rise,
with such a man! Allied with Trojan arms
Carthage will raise her glory to the sky.
Pray for the gods' forgiveness; give them gifts. 50
Be kind to our guest; weave tissues of delay:
'Winter — the sea is wild — the rains have come —
your ships are damaged — you cannot read the
    skies.'"

Such talk inflamed her heart with uncurbed love,
gave hope to doubt, and let restraint go free.
First they went to altar and shrine to beg
God's peace; they made due rite of sacrifice:
sheep to Ceres, to Phoebus, to Father Bacchus,
and most to Juno, lady of marriage bonds.
Dido the beautiful lifted a cup of wine 60
and poured it between the horns of a pure white cow,
or danced where the gods watch over blood-rich altars.
Each day began with victims; she slit their throats,
and hung over living vitals to read the signs.[3]
But priests are fools! What help from shrine and
    prayer
for her madness? Flames devoured her soft heart's-
    flesh;
the wound in her breast was wordless, but alive.

Iarbas: Dido's chief suitor

Gaetulians, Numidians: fierce inhabitants of a region of North Africa

Juno: wife of Jove and therefore queen of the gods; patron goddess of Dido and Carthage; enemy to Venus and to Venus' son Aeneas

tissues of delay: to hinder Aeneas, who is anxious to continue his mission

victims: sacrifices to propitiate the gods

---

[3] It was thought that the future could be foretold by examining the organs of the sacrificial animals.

Fevered and ill-starred, Dido wandered wild
through all the town, like a doe trailing an arrow
that she, heedless in Cretan forest, caught   70
from a shepherd who shot but never knew his bolt
had flown to the mark; she ranges field and grove
of Dicte; the shaft of death clings to her flank.
Now Dido escorted Aeneas from wall to wall,
showed him her Tyrian wealth, her city all built —
she'd start to speak, but in mid-word fall mute.

Tyrian: Dido was originally Queen of Tyre.

Again, at wane of day, she'd fill her hall
and ask to hear once more of Troy's travail,
and hang once more, madly, upon each word.
Then when they'd parted and the shadowed moon 80
had paled, and fading stars warned men to sleep,
in the empty hall she'd lie where he had lain,
hearing him, seeing him — gone, and she alone;
or hold Ascanius close, caught by his father's
likeness, in hope of eluding a sinful love.
Her towers grew no taller; her army ceased
maneuvers and worked no more to strengthen port
and bastion for war: work hung half-done, walls stood
huge but unsteady; bare scaffolds met the sky.

for war: Dido expects an imminent attack by Pygmalion.

As soon as Jove's dear wife knew Dido gripped   90
by the plague and grown too mad to heed report,
she, daughter of Saturn, spoke harsh words to Venus:
"What glorious praise, what rich return you've
          gained,
you and your son; such might, such fabled power,
now that by godhead twain one woman's conquered!

godhead twain: Venus and Cupid

I'm not deceived: you feared my city, and me,
and hence held Carthage and her halls suspect.
Is there no limit? Why this vast rivalry?
Why not make peace for good, and carry through
the match you planned? You've gained your heart's
          desire: 100
Dido has drawn love's flame deep as her bones.
Why not join hands, join peoples, share the rule
between us? Let Dido serve her Trojan prince
and lay her dower — her Tyrians — in your hand."

Venus knew Juno spoke with veiled intent
to turn Italian power aside to Carthage.
Thus she replied: "To that, who but the mad
could object? Who'd choose to go to war with you?

Italian: the future Roman empire, to be founded by Aeneas

If only success may crown our stratagem!
But I'm not sure of fate: would Jove allow   110
a single city for people of Tyre and Troy?

Approve such mingled blood, such rule conjoint?
You are his wife: seek out his will. You may.
You lead, I'll follow." To her then Juno spoke:
"That shall be my concern. How best to meet
the need of the moment, hear, while I briefly tell.
A hunt is planned. Aeneas, and Dido with him,
are off to the woods soon as tomorrow's sun
rises and with his ray reveals the world.
They'll see the clouds turn black with hail and rain;
then as their beaters rush to encircle a dell,   121
I'll pour down floods and shake all heaven with thun-
     der.
Their men will scatter in darkness and disappear.
Your prince of Troy and Dido both will come
to a cave. I'll be there, too. With your consent,
I'll join them in marriage and name her 'lawful wife.'
Their wedding this shall be." No adverse word
spoke Venus, but nodded. Such tactics made her
     smile.

Meanwhile the Dawn arose and left the sea.
Out from the gates at sunrise young men ran   130
with nets and snares and broad-tipped hunting spears;
out galloped Moors with packs of keen-nosed hounds.   **Moors:** an African tribe
The queen was late; beside her hall the lords
of Carthage waited; there stood her horse, in gold
and purple caparison, nervous, champing the bit.   **caparison:** decorative trappings
At last she came, surrounded by her vast guard,
wrapped in a scarlet cloak broidered with lace.
Gold was her quiver; gold held her plaited hair;
a brooch of gold fastened her purple gown.
In marched a Trojan group, Iulus too,   140   **Iulus:** Julus; alternate name for
smiling and eager. Then, towering over all,   Ascanius
Aeneas joined them and brought their ranks together.
Like Apollo, leaving Lycia and streams of Xanthus,
in winter, to visit Delos, his mother's home!   **Delos:** birthplace of Apollo
He starts the dancing; gathering round his shrine,
islanders, mountaineers, painted plainsmen sing,
while he climbs Cynthus. He braids his flowing hair   **Cynthus:** mountain on Delos where
and hold it in place with laurel and crown of gold;   Apollo had a sanctuary
his arrows clang at his back. So fresh, alive,
was Aeneas, so matchless the glory of his face.   150
They rode to the hills, to the wayless woods and
     marches.
Look! Down from a rocky ridge leaped mountain
     goats
to race downhill; on this side, where the plains
lay open, a line of antelopes flashed past
away from the hillsides, trailing a swirl of dust.

Ascanius — boy on a lively pony — loped
up hill, down dale, with a laugh past these, past those.
Such nerveless beasts! He wished a foam-flecked boar
might come his way, or a lion charge from the hills.

Now thunder roared and rumbled across the sky;   160
soon came black clouds, the hailstorm, and the rain.
The Tyrian people and men of Troy broke ranks,
and with them Venus' grandson ran for shelter —   **Venus' grandson: Ascanius**
anywhere! Rivers in spate rushed down the slopes.
The prince of Troy and Dido both had come
to a cave. The bride's attendant, Earth and Juno,
gave signal: lightning and empyrean flamed
in witness; high in the hills Nymphs made their
        moan.
That was the day, the first of death and first
of evil. Repute, appearance, nothing moved   170
the queen; she laid no plan to hide her love,
but called it marriage, with this word veiled her
        shame.

At once Rumor went out through Libya's towns —
Rumor, than whom no evil thing is faster:
speed is her life; each step augments her strength.
Small, a shiver, at first, she soon rears high.
She walks aground; her head hides in the clouds.
Men say that Earth, in fury at the gods,
bore this last child, a sister to the Giants.
She is swift of foot and nimble on the wing,   180
a horror, misshapen, huge. Beneath each feather
there lies a sleepless eye (wonder to tell!),
and a tongue, and speaking lips, and ears erect.
By night she flies far over the shadowed world
gibbering; sleep never comes to rest her eyes.
By day she sits at watch high on a roof
or lofty tower, and terrifies great cities,
as much a vessel of slander as crier of truth.
This time she filled men's minds with varied gossip,
chuckling and chanting alike both false and true: 190
Aeneas had come, born of the blood of Troy;
Dido had deemed him worthy mate and man.
Now they were warming the winter with rich ex-
        change,
forgetful of thrones, ensnared by shameful lust.
Such tales foul Rumor spread upon men's lips,
then turned her course straight off to King Iarbas,
heaped fire into his heart and raked his wrath.

Iarbas, son of a Nymph by Hammon raped,
had raised in his broad realms a hundred shrines
to Jove, a hundred altars and vigil fires   200
with priests at endless prayer; the blood of beasts
fattened the soil, the doors were decked with flowers.
Maddened at heart, enflamed by bitter rumor
he stood at the altar amid the powers of heaven,
raised hands in suppliance, and prayed aloud:
"Almighty Jove, to whom the Moorish kind
on purple couches serve rich food and wine,
do you see this? Or are we fools to fear
your lightning bolt? Are cloud and fire blind,
that frighten our hearts, mere noise devoid of
    strength?   210
This woman, this immigrant in my bounds, who paid
to build her little town, to whom I granted
tidewater land on terms, rejects my hand
but takes my lord Aeneas to her throne.
And now that Paris and his half-male crew,
with perfumed hair and Persian caps chin-tied,
keeps what he stole, while I bring gifts to shrines —
your shrines — and worship empty shams of glory."

Paris: His theft of Helen brought about the Trojan War.
half-male: effete

As with hand on altar he made this prayer
the almighty heard; his eye turned toward the palace,
toward two in love forgetting their better fame.   221
He spoke to Mercury then with this command:
"Go, son, summon the Zephyrs and take flight.
Our prince of Troy dawdles in Carthage now
and takes no thought for cities assigned by fate.
Fly with the wind, bring him my word, and speak:
'Such not the man his lovely mother promised,
nor such twice saved by her from Argive arms,
but one to rule a country big with power —
Italy, land of the war cry — to pass on   230
the blood of Teucer, and bring worlds under law.'

Teucer: first King of Troy

If none of these great glories fires his heart
and for his own renown he'll spend no toil,
does he begrudge his son a fortress Rome?
What plans, what hopes hold him on foreign soil,
blind to Ausonia and Lavinia's land?
'Sail on!' That is all. Bring him this word from me."

Ausonia: now Italy
Lavinia's land: Latium, where Aeneas has been destined to found Rome, the new Troy, and to marry the princess Lavinia

He ended. Mercury moved to carry out
the father's command. First he put on his sandals
golden, winged, that bear him swift as the wind   240
high over land and high above the sea,
then took his wand. With this he calls the ghosts

pale out of Orcus, or sends them sorrowing down,   **Orcus: the Underworld**
grants sleep, withdraws it, unseals the eyes of death.
With it he drives the winds and sails the clouds.
Now flying he saw the cap and rugged flanks
of Atlas, whose granite shoulders prop the sky —
Atlas: his pine-clad head, forever crowned
with clouds, is buffeted by wind and rain.
A glacier clothes his back, and cascades course   250
down over his face; his beard bristles with ice.
Here Mercury hovering on both wings alike
stopped, then plummeted headlong toward the sea
just like a gull that, round the beaches, round
fish-haunted reefs, skims low across the waves.
So between earth and sky he flew along
toward Libya's sandy shore, cleaving the wind
eastward from Atlas — Mercury, son of Maia.
Soon as his winged feet touched settlement ground,
he saw Aeneas footing down forts and raising   260
new homes. The sword he wore was yellow-starred
with jasper, a cape of glowing Tyrian scarlet
hung from his shoulders — gifts the wealthy queen
had given, and broidered the cloth with thread of
    gold.
Up stepped the god: "Aeneas! In Carthage now
do you lay foundations and plan a handsome town
for a wife? *Your* throne, *your* state — are they for-
    gotten?
From shining Olympus *he* has sent me down —
the king of gods, whose nod makes heaven roll.
He bade me fly with the wind to bring his word: 270
what plans, what hopes hold you at leisure here?
If nothing of promised glory moves your heart,
and for your own renown you'll spend no toil,
what of your son? He's growing! Your heir, Iulus:
what of his hopes? A kingdom — Italy — Rome:
these are his due!" With this, the Cyllenian god   **Cyllenian god: Mercury (born on**
left mortal sight, nor waited for reply;   **Mount Cyllene)**
beyond the eye he vanished into air.

Aeneas was frightened out of speech and mind;
his hair stood up in terror, his voice stuck fast.   280
He burned to go, to flee this pleasant land;
God's word, God's great commands had struck him
    hard.
But what should he do? How dare he tell the queen?
She was mad for love: how could he start his plea?
His mind turned quickly here, turned quickly there,
darting in different ways all round about.

As he weighed the matter this seemed the better
    course:
he called Sergestus, Mnestheus, Serestus the brave:
"Not a word! Prepare to sail! Call out our people!
To battle stations, all: coin some excuse   290
for these new orders." Meanwhile, let gentle Dido
know nothing, suspect no rupture of their love:
he now would test approaches, seek the time
and kindest way to tell her. Quickly all
in joy at his command obeyed his orders.

But still the queen (who can deceive a lover?)
foretold the scheme, caught contemplated moves,
feared even where all was safe. Then Rumor came
to report the fleet outfitted and ready to sail.
Her passion burst control; savage, aflame,   300
she raced through town, as, at an elevation,
the Thyiad who feels the spur of Bacchic hymns
and dances, and hears Cithaeron shout by night.
At last she addressed Aeneas; her words burst forth:

Thyiad: woman follower of Bacchus
Cithaeron: mountain sacred to Bacchus; home of the Furies

"You lied! You thought you could conceal a wrong
so vast, and leave my land without one word?
Our love, your right hand given in pledge that day,
a Dido to suffer and die — are these no check?
What? Fit out your fleet beneath a winter sun,
and hurry across the sea while north winds howl,   310
hard-hearted man? Were it no foreign land,
no unknown home you sought, but Troy still stood,
would you send ships through storms like these to
        Troy?
You run from *me?* In tears, I seize your hand
(what other solace have I left myself?)
and beg you recall our marriage, our wedding day:
if I have served you well, if you have found
delight in me, have mercy! My house is crumbling!
If prayer can still be heard, change, change your
        heart!
You made the Libyan tribes, the Nomad kings,   320
yes, my own Tyrians, hate me; lost for you
were honor and good repute, my only path
to glory. Cast off, fit only to die, who'll have me,
you whom I entertained — no more say, 'married.'
What now? Wait till Pygmalion levels my walls,
or the Moor Iarbas drags me off in chains?
If only before your flight I had conceived
your child, if only a baby Aeneas played
here in my court, whose face might mirror yours,

I'd feel less like one taken and discarded."   330
She finished. Aeneas, strengthened by Jove's words,
gazed steadily at her and suppressed his pain.
At last he briefly replied, "Speak! List them all —
your favors and courtesies! There is not one
I won't confess. I'll think of you with joy
long as I think at all, and live, and breathe.
But now to the point. I did not mean (believe me!)
to slip away by stealth, nor ever feigned
the wedding torch, or made such league with you.
If fate had let me govern my own life   340
and heal my troubles in the way I willed,
I would be living in Troy with what remained
of my people; Priam's halls would still be standing;

Priam's halls: the palace at Troy (where Priam was king)

and we, though beaten, had built our walls anew.
But Apollo Grynean sent me to Italy;
'Find Italy! Win her!' declared the oracles.

Apollo Grynean: epithet for Apollo after his shrine at Gryneum in Mysia

My love, my home, lie there. You are of Tyre,
yet Libyan Carthage holds you, hall and wall:
why take it ill that Trojans look for homes
in Italy? Strange lands we too may seek.   350
Whenever dewy night enshrouds the world
and fiery stars arise, Anchises' ghost,
murky and fearful, warns me in my dreams.

Anchises: Aeneas' father, who died in Sicily before the Trojans reached Carthage

Ascanius, well-loved son: see how I wrong him,
cheating him of Hesperian land and throne!

Hesperian: western

Now comes a messenger from Jove himself
(I swear it!); he sped through air to bring command.
In the clear light of day I saw that god;
he entered these walls; my ears drank in his words.
Cease to enflame my heart and yours with plaints:
not by my choice I go to Italy."   361

Even as he spoke she turned her face away.
Glancing now here, now there, she viewed the man
from head to foot, wordless. Then speech flared out:
"No goddess your mother, no Dardanus sired your
     kind,

Dardanus: founder of Troy; ancestor of Aeneas

you liar! No! Caucasus got you on those cliffs
of jagged granite, and tigers suckled you there!
Dissemble? Why? To await some greater wrong?
I wept; he made no sound, nor turned an eye.
I loved him; where were his tears, his sympathy?   370
What else shall I say? Juno, lady and queen,
Jove, son of Saturn, can be unmoved no longer.
Good faith is folly! I saved him, castaway
and helpless, I made him partner to my power.
He'd lost his ships, his men; I rescued them.
My madness flames like fire: 'Apollo' now,

'the oracles' now; 'sent by Jove himself
a messenger comes through air with dread com-
    mands.'
This is the gods' life work! Such cares disturb   379
their peace! You're free; I'll not refute your claims.
Go! Find your Italian throne by wind and wave!
Midway, I trust, if God has power, you'll drink
requital on a reef and scream for Dido!
There'll be no Dido, but a funeral flame
will follow, and when death sunders soul from flesh
my shade will haunt you till my price is paid.
I'll know! Report will reach my ghost in hell!"
She broke off in mid-speech and, sickened, fled
the light of day — ran from his sight, from him,
while he stood trembling, groping, conning a flood
of words. She fainted. Her people raised her up   391
and bore her to her room and to her bed.

Aeneas the good, though longing to ease her pain
with words of comfort and turn aside her care
(his groans came deep, for love had racked his heart),
obeyed God's orders and sought his fleet again.
Then truly his men fell to; the shore was filled
with hauling of ships. Out swam fresh-painted keels;
men loaded oars still green, and from the woods
brought spars half-hewn in haste.   400
"Move out!" they heard. "All hands!" "Look lively,
    now!"
(As when the ants, mindful of winter, attack
a heap of grain and carry it home across
the fields: black goes the column; they bear their prize
down narrow grassy lanes. Some push big kernels
with heave of shoulders; some close the line of march
and hurry stragglers. The path is a froth of toil.)
Dido! What did you feel to see all this?
What cries did you utter when from tower's top
you saw the shore all seething, saw the sea   410
churned up before your eyes, and heard the shouts!
Shameless love, where do you not drive men's hearts?
Again she went and wept and begged, for try
she must; her pride must bend the knee to love,
lest for failing to move she die in vain.

"Anna, you see them rushing round the shore:
the crews are mustered; the canvas calls the breeze;
the men have cheered as garlands dressed the spar.
Could I have known such sorrow was to come,
I could have borne it; but now in tears I beg   420
one favor, Anna, of you: that faithless man

was always with you, told you his secret thoughts;
you knew, as no one else, his gentler moods.
Go, bring to our heartless guest this humble plea:
I joined no Greeks; I took no oath at Aulis

Aulis: a town where the Greeks
gathered to sail for Troy and war

of death to Trojans, I sent no ships to Troy,
I never harried his father Anchises' ghost.
Why will he lock his ears against my words?
Why haste? Let a broken heart win one last grace:
Await a safer passage and favoring winds!   430
I'll not ask now for the wedlock he betrayed,
or that he resign his darling Latin throne;
I beg for time, an hour of rest from madness,
till fortune teach me how to lose and grieve.
This favor the last your sister asks: be kind!
I'll pay my debt with death to make full measure."

Such was her plea; such sorrows her grieving sister
reported, reported again. But nothing moved him;
no tears nor words could teach his heart to hear. 439
(Fate blocked the way; God closed his ears to pity.)
Like an oak tree, ancient, toughened by the years,
blasted by Alpine winds this way and that
contesting to uproot it; the North Wind howls,
the trunk is shaken, foliage strews the ground.
The tree holds hard; its crown lifts up toward heaven
far as its root grows down toward Tartarus.

Tartarus: lowest part of Hades
where the wicked are punished

Just so Aeneas, by pleas this side and that
assaulted, felt in his heart the thrust of care.
His mind stood firm; tears came, but came in vain.

Then Dido, luckless, by fortune terrified,   450
invited death: to view heaven's vault was pain.
To strengthen her resolve to leave the light,
she saw, when she offered her gifts and censed the
    altars
(dreadful to tell!), the holy water turn black
and the wine pour down in horrid clots of gore.
She told none, not even Anna, what she'd seen.
Besides, in her house there stood a marble shrine
to her former husband, which she kept sacrosanct,
festooned with white wool bands and feast-day
    flowers:
from it she thought she heard her husband's voice 460
calling her, calling, when darkness gripped the world.
And on her roof a lonesome owl sang songs
of death; its mournful cry trailed off in sobs.
Then warnings of seers long dead came crowding
    back
to fill her with fright. She dreamed herself gone mad,

with Aeneas in wild pursuit; then left alone
to travel, forever friendless, a long, long road,
seeking her Tyrians in an empty world,
like maddened Pentheus[4] seeing the rank of Furies,
seeing twin suns and a double Thebes displayed;   470
or like Orestes racing across the stage
to escape a mother armed with torch and serpent —
and at Agamemnon's door the Dirae wait.[5]

Filled with madness and prisoner of her pain,
she determined to die; and now, with how and when
planned in her mind, she addressed her tearful sister
(concealing intent behind a cloudless brow):
"Anna, I've found a way — applaud your sister! —
that will bring him back, or free me from my love.
Near to the ocean's edge and setting sun   480
lies African land's-end, where giant Atlas
bears on his back the spinning star-tricked wheel.
I've found a religious of that place — a Moor;
she served the Hesperides' temple, fed the snake,
and guarded the holy branches on the tree;
with honey and poppy she made the elixir of sleep.
She swears she can release what hearts she will
with spells, and freight still other hearts with care,
can stop the rivers and reverse the stars,
and raise the dead by night: you'll see the earth   490
groan at her feet and trees climb down the hills.
Sister, I tell you, by your life, by all
that's holy, I take to witchcraft against my will.
Slip into our inner courtyard and build there
a pyre; pile on it the arms that perjured man
hung in my house — take all he left, the bed
of marriage that brought me sorrow. I must destroy
his every devilish trace: so says my Moor."
This much, then silence, and her face turned pale.
Yet Anna did not suspect that these strange rites 500
were cover for death; her mind conceived no thought
so mad. Than when Sychaeus died: she feared
no worse, and did as asked.

In the inner court beneath the open sky
the pyre stood huge with pitch pine and with oak.
The queen hung garlands and wreathed the place
          with boughs

Hesperides: three sisters who
guarded a sacred garden of
golden apples

[4] a disbeliever in Bacchus who was punished by madness and was unwittingly murdered
by his mother; a common exemplar for the Romans of the dire fate which overtakes those
who question, defy, or resist the gods.
[5] In Aeschylus' drama *Eumenides*, Orestes killed his mother (Clytemnestra) to avenge
the death of his father (Agamemnon). The Furies (Dirae), urged on by Clytemnestra's
ghost, then hounded Orestes in punishment.

of death; atop, she laid his sword, his garments —
yes, and his image: she knew what she would do.   image: effigy
Ringed by altars the Moor let down her hair,
intoned the gods three hundred, Chaos, and Hell, 510
the Hecates three, Diana the triform virgin.   Hecates three: mysterious goddess
She sprinkled water labeled "from Avernus,"   of sorcery and witchcraft, some-
                                                          times represented in triple form;
selected hairy leaves by moonlight reaped   often confused with Diana, god-
with brazen sickle (their milky juice turns black),   dess of the moon. Avernus: lake
pulled out the membrane torn from a newborn foal   at the entrance to the Underworld
and snatched from its mother's mouth.
Dido stepped to an altar, blessed her hands,
took meal, slipped off one shoe, unlatched her gown,
then, ready to die, begged gods and stars prophetic
to hear her prayer to any power just   520
and mindful, that cares for lovers wrongly matched.

It was night; all over the world the weary flesh
found peace in sleep; forests and savage seas
rested; in middle course the stars rolled on.
No sound from field, from herd, from painted birds
that swarm the liquid lakes or love the thorn
and thicket: they slept in silence of the night,
healing the heart of care, forgetting pain.
But never the broken-hearted, luckless queen
slipped off to sleep or took the night to eyes   530
and heart. Her torment doubled; desire rose
raging; she ebbed and flowed on waves of wrath.
At last she paused and pondered inner thoughts:
"What shall I do? I'm scorned! Shall I turn and try
my earlier suitors, and beg a Nomad's bed?
I have disdained their hand, how many times?
Well, then, to the Trojan fleet? Hurry to catch
their final word? Because they prized my help
and remember that musty favor with gratitude?
Granted the will, who'd let an unloved woman   540
tread his proud deck? You fool! You still don't
        know,
don't see, how the sons of Laomedon can lie?   sons of Laomedon: Trojans; La-
Well — ? Trail his jeering crews, a lovesick girl?   omedon, an early King of Troy,
                                                        lied to both gods and men.
Or board ship with my Tyrians, rank on rank,
around me — men whom just now I saved from
        Sidon: Sidon: Phoenician city
bid them make sail and put to sea once more?
No! Die as you've earned! Take steel and end your
        pains!
You, Anna, hurt by my tears, you topped my folly
with wrongful acts; you tossed me to our foe!
I had not the will to pass my life unwed,   550
unstained, like some wild creature, untouched by
        guilt.

I did not keep my oath to dead Sychaeus."
Such were the sorrows that broke forth from her
        breast.
Aeneas knew he would go; on his tall ship,
his preparations made, he took his rest.
In his dreams a godly form appeared again,
just as before, and seemed to warn once more
(in all like Mercury, in voice, complexion,
in the flaxen hair and graceful limbs of youth):
"Goddess-born, can you sleep at such an hour,   560
and fail to see the dangers that surround you —
madman! — nor hear the favoring West Wind blow?
Dido devises malice and foul crime
(she knows she'll die) and roils her anger's waves.
Run! Leave in haste, while haste's within your
        power.
Soon you will see the ocean churned by ships,
the shore ablaze with savage torch and flames,
if Dawn shall touch you tarrying in this land.
Hurry, now! Ever a various, changeful thing
is woman." He spoke and mingled with black
        night.   570

This apparition terrified Aeneas.
He tore himself from sleep and harried his men
to haste: "Look lively, there, and man the thwarts!
Off buntlines! Quick! A god from heaven's height
again has bid us speed away and cut
our anchor-lines. We come, O sacred presence,
whoever you are! Again we obey your word.
Be with us in peace! Bless us! Show helpful stars   **helpful: guiding**
in heaven!" He spoke, and ripped his flashing sword
from sheath, and with the bared blade slashed the
        lines.   580
Like ardor held them all. They seized, they ran,
they emptied the beach; their vessels hid the sea.
Men heaved, churned up the foam, and swept the
        blue.

And now Aurora brought the dawn's new light
to earth, and left Tithonus' golden couch.   **Tithonus:** Laomedon's son and
Dido was watching, and with the first pale gleam   Priam's brother; loved by Aurora.
she saw the fleet, yards squared and outward bound,   The gods granted him immortality
and marked the emptiness of shore and pier.   but not eternal youth.
Three times and four she beat her lovely breast
and tore her golden hair: "What? Shall he go,"   590
she said, "and mock my power — that foreigner!
There'll be no general muster? No pursuit?
Will no one hurry to launch my ships? Quick, men,
bring torches, hand out arms, lean on your oars!

What's this? Where am I? What madness warps
      my mind?
Fool! Has your sacrilege just struck you now?
It should have, the day you offered a throne! Such
      honor!
And he, they say, brings with him his fathers' gods;
his shoulders carried Anchises, tired and old!
Why couldn't I hack his flesh, tear it, and strew   600
the sea with it? Slaughter his people and his son —
serve up Ascanius at his father's table?
But battle had been uncertain? Grant it so,
why fear, when I meant to die? I'd have thrown fire
and filled their camp with flame: father and son
and people had burned to death to make my pyre.
O Sun, who with your flame light all men's works;
you, Juno, who know my troubles and read them
      true;
Hecate, hailed at night by town and crossroad;
Dirae, gods of a Dido soon to die,   610
receive my prayer; turn sanction meet and right
upon these wrongs; hear me! If touch he must
on promised port and land — that man accursed! —
and so Jove's laws demand, this end is fixed.
But let brave people harass him with war.
Driven from home, torn from Iulus' arms,
let him beg for help, and see his people die
disgraced. Make him surrender under terms
unjust, and know no happy years of rule,
but die untimely, untombed, in miles of sand.   620
This is my final prayer, poured with my blood.
And you, my Tyrians, hate his race, his kind,
all and always. On my remains bestow
this office: no love, no peace between our peoples!
And from my grave let some avenger rise
to harry the Trojan settlers with fire and sword —
now, some day, whenever we have the power.
Shore against shore, I pray, wave against sea,
sword against sword, fight, father and son, forever!"

So said she, and turned her thoughts this way and
      that,   630
seeking how soonest to end an unloved life.
To Barce then she spoke — Sychaeus' nurse
(her own lay buried in the fatherland):
"Dear nurse, bring Anna, my sister, here to me.
Tell her to hurry and wash in a running stream,
then bring the victims and holy things I showed her.
Come, both, with sacred ribbons in your hair.
I wish to do my office to Stygian Jove

carried Anchises: Aeneas carried his old, weakened father out of the burning city of Troy.

serve up Ascanius: as Atreus, who had quarreled with his brother Thyestes, served Thyestes the flesh of his own children at a banquet.

Stygian Jove: Pluto, god of the Underworld

(all duly prepared) to put an end to care
and lay that Trojan soul on funeral flames."   640

This much. In joy, the old nurse hobbled off.
Savage design drove Dido mad with fright.
Her eyes were wild and bloodshot; on her cheek
flush faded to pallor in terror of death so near.
She rushed to the inner court; madly she climbed
up the tall pyre and drew that Trojan sword,
gift that was never meant for such a use.
She saw his Trojan garment and their bed
well-known; then after a moment's tearful thought
lay down on the couch and spoke these final
    words: 650
"Here, trophies that I loved, while God allowed!
Oh, take my life and free me from my sorrow.
I've lived, and run the course that fate assigned;
in glory my shade now goes beneath the earth.
I built a splendid city and saw it walled,
avenged my husband, and made my brother pay —
blessed beyond measure, if only Dardan craft
had never touched upon these shores of mine."
She kissed the couch. "I'll die without revenge,
but die, and pass to darkness undismayed.   660
From shipboard let the heartless Trojan see
my flames! My death ride with him as he sails!"

Dardan: of Dardanus; Trojan

While she yet spoke, her people saw her fall
crumpled upon the sword, the blade all frothed
with blood, her hands spattered. A scream rose high
in the hall; the city was stricken; Rumor ran wild.
Houses were filled with sobs and lamentations,
with keening of women: the din rose to the skies —
as if an enemy had burst in, and all
Carthage or ancient Tyre were falling, while
    flames   670
rolled to the roofs, through homes of gods and men.
Anna, half-dead with fear, came running fast:
her fingers tore her face; she beat her breast.
She pushed through the crowd, calling her sister's
    name:
"Dido, was this what it meant? You lied? to *me*?
Was this the purpose of pyre, altar, and flame?
You left me! What shall I say? You died, but
    scorned
to take me? You might have let me share your death:
one hour, one stroke of pain had served for two.
These hands helped build — this voice of mine
    helped call   680

our gods — oh, cruel! — that I must fail you now!
You've killed yourself and me, your people, the lords
of Sidon, and your own city! Oh, let me wash
your wounds, and if some faltering breath remains,
let my lips take it!" With that, she climbed the pyre
and cradled her dying sister in her arms,
cried as she used her dress to stop the blood.
Dido would open her heavy eyes again,
but failed. The gash hissed in her wounded breast.
Three times she raised herself up on one arm,   690
three times fell back, then with an errant eye
sought light in heaven, and moaned that she had
    found it.

Then Juno in pity for her lingering pain
and laggard death, sent Iris down from heaven

Iris: a messenger of the gods and the personification of the rainbow

to free her struggling soul from limbs entwined.
(For not at her earned and fated hour she died,
but in a flash of fury, before her days:
Proserpina had not yet cut the lock
from her head, nor sentenced her to life below.)

Proserpina: goddess of the Underworld. **cut . . . head:** an offering to Pluto

But Iris flew down, dewy and golden-winged,   700
trailing against the sun a thousand colors.
She stopped over Dido's head: "This sacred lock
I carry to Dis, and from the flesh I free you."

Dis: name for Pluto

With that she cut the wisp; at once all warmth
dispersed, and life retreated to the winds.

Ovid   (43 B.C.–A.D. 17)

ROMAN POET

The Art of Loving

First: be a confident soul, and spread your nets with
    assurance.
    Women can always be caught; that's the first rule
        of the game.
Sooner would birds in the spring be silent, or locusts
    in August,

Title supplied by editors. From *The Art of Love* by Ovid, translated by Rolfe Humphries and published by Indiana University Press. Reprinted by permission.

Sooner would hounds run away when the fierce
    rabbits pursue,
Than would a woman, well-wooed, refuse to succumb
    to a lover;
    She'll make you think she means No! while she is
        planning her Yes!
Love on the sly delights men; it is equally pleasing
    to women.
    Men are poor at pretense; women can hide their
        desire.
It's a convention, no more, that men play the part
    of pursuer.
    Women don't run after us; mousetraps don't run
        after mice.   10
In the soft meadows the heifer lows for the bull to
    come to her,
    Stallions respond, but the mare gives the first
        whinnying call. . . .

Let the tablets of wax prepare the way for your
    coming,
    Let the tablets of wax indicate what's in your
        mind.
Let them carry sweet words, and every device of a
    lover,
    And, whoever you are, do not forget to implore.
Priam's imploring prevailed, and Achilles returned
    Hector's body;
    Even an angry god listens, attentive to prayer.
See that you promise: what harm can there be in
    promising freely?
    There's not a man in the world who can't be rich
        in that coin.   20
Hope endures a long time, if once she has gained
    any credit;
    She is a goddess indeed, useful, though apt to
        deceive.
Once you have made your gift, you can just as well
    be forsaken —
    That's water over the dam, that hasn't cost her a
        cent,
But the gift not made, the gift of the possible future,
    Like the barren field, fooling the husbandman's
        hope,
Like the gambler's bet, made to recover his losses
    When his covetous hands cannot let go of the dice,
That is the toil and the task, to keep her hoping for
    something —
    Keep her giving, lest she think she has given for
        free.   30

tablets of wax: love letters

Priam's . . . body: In Homer's *Iliad*, Achilles lets Priam, the Trojan King, ransom the body of his son Hector, whom Achilles has slain.

So, let your letter be sent, with coaxing words on the
    tablets,
  Make the reconnaissance first, scouting the path-
    ways of love.
Think of Cydippe's vow, and the letter concealed in
    the apple,
  How that maiden was bound, speaking the words
    she had read.

Cydippe's vow: In the temple
of Diana, Cydippe unwittingly
swore to marry Acontius when
she read aloud a marriage vow
written on an apple which he
had thrown at her feet.

Young men of Rome, I advise you to learn the arts
    of the pleader,
  Not so much for the sake of some poor wretch at
    the bar,
But because women are moved, as much as the
    people or Senate,
  Possibly more than a judge, conquered by eloquent
    words,
But dissemble your powers, and don't attempt to
    look learnèd,
  Let your periods shun rancorous terms of abuse. 40

periods: phrases

You would be out of your mind to go and declaim
    to your darling;
  Even in letters beware using litigious terms.
Let the style you employ be natural, easy, familiar,
  Coaxing, also, of course, so that she thinks you are
    there.
If she refuses to read, or sends back a letter un-
    opened,
  Hope that some day she will read, don't be dis-
    couraged. Some day!
Time brings the obdurate ox to submit to the yoke
    and the ploughshare,
  Time brings the fieriest steed under the bridle and
    rein.
Even an iron ring is worn by continual usage,
  Even the hardest ground crumbles at last from the
    plough.   50
What is harder than rock, or what more gentle than
    water?
  Yet the water in time hollows the rigidest stone.
Only persist: you can have more luck than Penelope's
    suitors.
  Though it took a long time, Troy came tumbling
    down.

Penelope's suitors: Men vied for
Penelope's hand in vain for
twenty years; she remained faithful to her husband, Odysseus,
who fought for ten years at Troy
and wandered for another ten
years.

What if she reads, and won't answer? Do not at-
    tempt any pressure.
  Only supply her with more flattering missives to
    read.
What she is willing to read, some day she'll be willing
    to answer —

Every thing in its time, every thing by degrees.
Maybe the first response will make you sad by its
    scolding,
  Saying, "Don't write any more!", saying, "Please
    let me alone!"   60
What she requests, that she fears; what she does not
    ask, she insists on,
  So, go on with your work; some day the day will
    be won.

Meanwhile, if she is borne through the streets on a
    litter with cushions,
  Go to her side, but take care — don't give your
    mission away.
Hide what you really mean in cunning, equivocal
    language,
  Don't let anyone hear words that might cause him
    offense.
Or if she loiters afoot, by the colonnades and the
    porches,
  Dawdle along near by, either ahead or behind,
Or, now and then, cut across, if the columns are
    rising between you,
  With no apparent design, take a few steps at her
    side.   70
Also, be sure to be near when she sits in the theater
    watching;
  You will have something to watch, her shoulders,
    the curve of her dress.
Watch her as much as you please — you may turn
    around to admire her,
  There is a lot you can say, speaking with gesture
    and eye.
Clap and applaud when the star mimics a girl with
    his dancing,
  Favor the lover's cause — that's all that counts in
    the play.
When she rises, you rise; sit still, as long as she's
    seated;
  You have plenty of time, waste it to go with her
    whim. . . .

So, when the wine-god's grace has honored you with
    his blessing,
  And a woman lies sharing a part of your bed,   80
Pray to the god of the night, and all of the spirits of
    night-time,
  Not to permit the gift to go too much to your
    head.

But, before that, you must say words of ambiguous
  meaning,
  Messages meant for her ear; she can interpret the
  code.
Trace on the table in wine the flattering sketch or the
  symbol,
  So she may read and infer you are devoted to her.

Let your eyes gaze into hers, let the gazing be a
  confession:
  Often the silent glance brings more conviction
  than words.
Be the first one to seize the cup that her lips have
  been touching,
  Drink from that edge of the rim which she has
  touched with her lips,   90
Ask her to pass the bread or the fruit she has touched
  with her fingers;
  When she passes it on, manage to touch her hand.
Also, make it your aim to get her husband to like
  you;
  If you can make him your friend, he will be use-
  ful, you'll find.
If you are drinking by lot, and your turn comes first,
  let him have it,
  Give him your garland to wear, say how becoming
  it seems.
No matter where he may sit, be sure that he has the
  first serving;
  If he wants to hold forth, don't interrupt, let him
  talk.
Safe is the way, and well-worn, that takes advantage
  of friendship;
  This is a way of guilt, safe though it be, and well-
  worn.   100
So a caretaker takes great care, and only too often
  Takes more things than care, looks after more than
  his own. . . .

After the party breaks up, draw close to her in the
  confusion,
  Let your foot touch hers, finger the sleeve of her
  dress.
Now is the time for talk! Don't be an oaf of a
  farmer,
  Awkward, abashed, ashamed — Venus favors the
  bold!
Never mind learning the tropes, or the arts of verse
  composition,

Only begin, that's all; eloquence comes as you
 plead.
Play the role of the lover, give the impression of
 heartache;
 No matter what your device, that you must make
 her believe,   110
Nor is it very hard — they all of them think that
 they're lovely,
 Even the ugliest hag dotes on her beauty's appeal.
More than once, you will find, the pretense ends in
 conviction,
 More than once the romance proves, after all, to
 be true.
So, girls, don't be too harsh on the men you suspect
 of pretending:
 Some day the butterfly, Truth, breaks from the
 lying cocoon.
Flattery works on the mind as the waves on the
 bank of a river:
 Praise her face and her hair; praise her fingers and
 toes.
Even honest girls are pleased if you broadcast their
 beauties,
 Even a virgin enjoys thinking herself a delight. 120
Why do you think to this day Juno and Pallas are
 grieving

Pallas: Athena

 Over the verdict they lost on the far Phrygian
 coast?

verdict they lost: when Paris
chose Venus over them as the
most beautiful goddess

Praise the peacock: at once she spreads her plumes in
 her pleasure.
 Watch, but say nothing at all: she'll keep her
 treasure concealed. . . .

Tears are a good thing, too; they move the most
 adamant natures.
 Let her, if possible, see tears on your cheeks, in
 your eyes.
This is not easy: sometimes the eyes will not stream
 at your bidding.
 What can be done about this? — get your hands
 wet, and apply.
If you are wise, with your words include a proportion
 of kisses.
 She may not give in return; take, and pretend that
 she gives.   130
She may fight back at first, and call you all kinds of a
 villain;
 That is the kind of a fight she will be happy to
 lose.

Only don't hurt her too much; be big and strong, but
    be gentle;
    Don't let your roughness supply even the slightest
        excuse.
Once you have taken a kiss, the other things surely
    will follow,
    Or, if they don't, you should lose all you have
        taken before.
How far away is a kiss from the right true end, the
    completion?
    Failure the rest of the way proves you are clumsy,
        not shy.
Force is all right to employ, and women like you to
    use it;
    What they enjoy they pretend they were unwilling
        to give.   140
One who is overcome, and, suddenly, forcefully taken,
    Welcomes the wanton assault, takes it as proof of
        her charm.
But if you let her go untouched when you could have
    compelled her,
    Though she pretends to be glad, she will be
        gloomy at heart. . . .

Oh, of course, it's a shame to be the first one to start
    it,
    Still, when another one starts, isn't it fun to give
        in?
Nevertheless, young man, you'll be conceited and
    foolish
    If you wait till the girl makes the first passes at
        you.
Let the man be the first to make the approach and
    entreaty,
    Let the girl be the one willing to wait and be
        kind.   150
Ask her outright: that's all any girl has been waiting
    for, really,
    Give her a cause, an excuse, just so you give her
        a start.
Jove himself would go and beg the girls for their
    favors:
    He was seducer, in love; no girl solicited Jove.
Yet, if you find that your pleas inspire an arrogant
    coldness,
    Stop what you may have begun, take a few steps
        in retreat.
Many a girl desires the coy and hates the aggressive:
    Take it a little bit slow, don't let her weary of you.

Jove: king of the gods; his amorous escapades were well known.

Don't always show in your talk that you know you
     are going to get her —
   What you are eager to be, tell her, is *Only a
   friend.*   160
I have seen this work, on the most unwilling of
     women —
   Only a friend, who was found more than proficient
   in bed! . . .

So, when hearts grow dull with too much freedom
     from worry,
   They must be given the spur, given incentive to
   love.
Heat her cooling mind, and let her grow anxious
     about you:
   Let her grow pale when she hears evidence you are
   untrue.
Lucky beyond all count is the man whom a woman
     grieves over,
   Pales at the word of his wrong, falls in a faint to
   the ground.
I would not mind, in that case, if she tried to snatch
     me bald-headed,
   Tore at my cheeks with her nails, frantic and weep-
   ing with rage,   170
Gave me her angriest looks, and wanted to do what
     she could not,
   Namely, live without me — what an impossible
   hope!
If you should ask me, "How long is a suitable time
     for resentment?"
   I would say, Not too long; anger flares up with
   delay.
While she is still in tears, put your arms gently
     around her,
   While she is still in tears, hold her close to your
   breast,
Give her, while still in tears, kisses, and something
     much better —
   That is the only way; anger succumbs to that
   peace.
When she has raged her fill, and seems an enemy,
     surely,
   Take her to bed; you will find she will be gentle
   and mild.   180
There the arms are laid down in favor of concord
     and union;
   There, you can take it from me, harmony truly is
   born.

The doves, who were lately at war, join bill to bill in
    affection;
  Soft is the *roucoulade*, murmuring, cooing of
    love. . . .

Only the animals mate where everybody can see
    them —
  Often a modest girl turns her eyes from the sight.
Bedrooms and bolted doors are the place for our
    intimate unions;
  Even there we can lie under the covering sheet,
Even there we prefer, if not an absolute darkness,
  Shadow, half-light, a shade, not the full blaze of
    the sun.   190
In the old primitive days, when the sun and the rain
    were prevented
  Not by the sheltering roof, only by pine-tree and
    oak,
People made love in groves, in caves, not out in the
    open;
  Even the primitive folk recognized decency's claim.
Now we make great boasts of the feats we perform
    in the night-time,
  Prize, more than anything else, loosing extravagant
    talk.
Everyone has to try to make every girl in the city,
  Telling whoever you please, "I have been sleeping
    with her,"
So there will be no lack of girls for a finger to point at,
  So there will be no girl out of the reach of your
    tale.   200
This is a minor offense: some will go very much
    farther,
  Saying there's no one in town they haven't had in
    their time.
Bodies they cannot touch, at least they can handle
    by naming;
  Bodies they could not touch, they can lay claim
    to in talk.
Go now, hateful guard, barricade the doors of a lady,
  On the resolute posts placing your bolts by the
    score!
What is the good of all this, if any concupiscent liar
  Enters in fancy, his wish making adultery true?
I, for my part, believe my affairs are entirely my
    business;
  What I have done in the dark adamant secrecy
    hides.   210

Do not blame a girl for flaws of her nature or person:
  Where's the advantage in that? Better pretend
    them away.
Andromeda, it would seem, was none too fair of
    complexion;
  Perseus, the sandal-winged, never voiced any re-
    proach.
All thought Andromache was much too big for a
    woman;
  Only in Hector's eyes was she of moderate size.
If you like what you get, you will get what you like;
    love is captious
  In our salad days, growing more mellow in time.
While the grafted shoot is new in the green of its
    growing,
  Even the lightest breeze makes it shudder and
    fall,   220
But it will fasten with time, so even a gale cannot
    shake it,
  Bear, on the parent tree, increase after its kind.
Time is a healer, and time removes all faults from
    the body;
  What was a blemish of old comes to be nothing
    at all.
When we are children, we find the odor of leather
    obnoxious,
  Hardly can stand it at all; when we are grown, we
    don't mind.
Words have a magical power to mitigate many short-
    comings:
  If she is blacker than tar, *tanned* is the term to
    employ.
Cross-eyed? She looks like Venus! Albino? Fair as
    Minerva!
  Thin as a rail? What grace lies in her willowy
    charm!   230
If she's a runt, call her *cute*; if fat, *a full-bodied
    woman*:
  Dialectic can make grace out of any defect.

Andromeda: Obeying an oracle,
her father chained her to a rock
as a victim for a sea monster
sent by Poseidon; she was rescued
by Perseus. sandal-winged: Perseus was equipped with winged
sandals to aid him in his search
for the Gorgons. Andromache:
Hector's wife

Martial (c. 40–c. A.D. 104)
ROMAN POET and EPIGRAMMATIST (SPANISH-BORN)

I Do Not Love You

Non amo te, Sabidi, nec possum dicere quare:
hoc tantum possum dicere, non amo te.

I do not love you, Sabidius; and I can't say why.
This only I can say: I do not love you.

Peter Abelard (1079–1142)
FRENCH THEOLOGIAN

Elegy

Low in thy grave with thee
Happy to lie,
Since there's no greater thing left Love to do;
And to live after thee
Is but to die,
For with but half a soul what can Life do?

So share thy victory,
Or else thy grave,
Either to rescue thee, or with thee lie:
Ending that life for thee,
That thou didst save,   10
So Death that sundereth might bring more nigh.

Peace, O my stricken lute!
Thy strings are sleeping.
Would that my heart could still
Its bitter weeping!

Title supplied by editors. "I Do Not Love You" by Martial. From *Epigrams*, translated by Walter C. A. Ker. Reprinted from *The Loeb Classical Library* edition by permission of Harvard University Press.

"Elegy" by Peter Abelard. From *Mediæval Latin Lyrics*, translated by Helen Waddell. Reprinted by permission of Constable Publishers, London.

Andreas Capellanus (12TH CENTURY)

FRENCH CHAPLAIN

The Rules of Courtly Love

    I. Marriage is no real excuse for not loving.

    II. He who is not jealous cannot love.

    III. No one can be bound by a double love.

    IV. It is well known that love is always increasing or decreasing.

    V. That which a lover takes against the will of his beloved has no relish.

    VI. Boys do not love until they arrive at the age of maturity.

    VII. When one lover dies, a widowhood of two years is required of the survivor.

    VIII. No one should be deprived of love without the very best of reasons.

    IX. No one can love unless he is impelled by the persuasion of love.

    X. Love is always a stranger in the home of avarice.

    XI. It is not proper to love any woman whom one would be ashamed to seek to marry.

    XII. A true lover does not desire to embrace in love anyone except his beloved.

    XIII. When made public love rarely endures.

    XIV. The easy attainment of love makes it of little value; difficulty of attainment makes it prized.

    XV. Every lover regularly turns pale in the presence of his beloved.

    XVI. When a lover suddenly catches sight of his beloved his heart palpitates.

    XVII. A new love puts to flight an old one.

    XVIII. Good character alone makes any man worthy of love.

    XIX. If love diminishes, it quickly fails and rarely revives.

    XX. A man in love is always apprehensive.

    XXI. Real jealousy always increases the feeling of love.

    XXII. Jealousy, and therefore love, are increased when one suspects his beloved.

    XXIII. He whom the thought of love vexes eats and sleeps very little.

    XXIV. Every act of a lover ends in the thought of his beloved.

    XXV. A true lover considers nothing good except what he thinks will please his beloved.

    XXVI. Love can deny nothing to love.

    XXVII. A lover can never have enough of the solaces of his beloved.

Title supplied by editors. "The Rules of Courtly Love" by Andreas Capellanus. From *The Art of Courtly Love*, translated and edited by John Jay Parry. Reprinted by permission of Columbia University Press.

XXVIII. A slight presumption causes a lover to suspect his beloved.

XXIX. A man who is vexed by too much passion usually does not love.

XXX. A true lover is constantly and without intermission possessed by the thought of his beloved.

XXXI. Nothing forbids one woman being loved by two men or one man by two women.

Dante Alighieri (1265–1321)

ITALIAN POET

Paolo and Francesca

As the wings of wintering starlings bear them on
 in their great wheeling flights, just so the blast
 wherries these evil souls through time foregone.[1]   **wherries: floats, pushes**

Here, there, up, down, they whirl and, whirling, strain
 with never a hope of hope to comfort them,
 not of release, but even of less pain.

As cranes go over sounding their harsh cry,
 leaving the long streak of their flight in air,
 so come these spirits, wailing as they fly.

And watching their shadows lashed by wind, I
     cried: 10
 "Master, what souls are these the very air
 lashes with its black whips from side to side?"

"The first of these whose history you would know,"
 he answered me, "was Empress of many tongues.
 Mad sensuality corrupted her so

[1] Dante's Inferno is composed of nine concentric circles, descending in order of gravity of sin to the lowest pit of hell. Dante (guided by Vergil) observes all those sinners who have been condemned to an eternal life of suffering: those damned through acts of sensual abandonment are nearer to the entrance of hell; those whose transgressions were more spiritual in nature suffer horrible torments closer to the deepest pit of hell. Here he is passing through Circle 2, where he observes those who have been condemned because of sinful love or lust.

Title supplied by editors. "Paolo and Francesca" by Dante Alighieri. From Canto V of *The Inferno* by Dante, translated by John Ciardi. Copyright © 1954 by John Ciardi. Reprinted by arrangement with The New American Library, Inc., New York.

that to hide the guilt of her debauchery
   she licensed all depravity alike,
   and lust and law were one in her decree.

She is Semiramis[2] of whom the tale is told
   how she married Ninus and succeeded him   20
   to the throne of that wide land the Sultans hold.

The other is Dido[3]; faithless to the ashes
   of Sichaeus, she killed herself for love.
   The next whom the eternal tempest lashes

is sense-drugged Cleopatra. See Helen there,
   from whom such ill arose. And great Achilles,[4]   such ill: the Trojan War
   who fought at last with love in the house of prayer.

And Paris. And Tristan." As they whirled above   Paris: the Trojan whose illicit love
   he pointed out more than a thousand shades   for Helen, wife of the Greek
   of those torn from the mortal life by love.   30   Menelaus, caused the Trojan War
                                            Tristan: medieval hero who shared
I stood there while my Teacher one by one   a passionate and adulterous love
   named the great knights and ladies of dim time;   with Isolde, wife of his king
   and I was swept by pity and confusion.

At last I spoke: "Poet, I should be glad
   to speak a word with those two swept together
   so lightly on the wind and still so sad."[5]

And he to me: "Watch them. When next they pass,
   call to them in the name of love that drives
   and damns them here. In that name they will
      pause."

Thus, as soon as the wind in its wild course   40
   brought them around, I called: "O wearied souls!
   if none forbid it, pause and speak to us."

[2] Queen of Nineveh and mythical founder of the Assyrian Empire. According to legend, she either deserted her first husband to marry Ninus, the King of Assyria, or put Ninus to death and thus gained complete control of the empire.

[3] Dido broke her vow to remain faithful to her dead husband, Sichaeus, and fell in love with Aeneas. Because of the basic inclination of Dido's soul, Dante places her here, among the sinful lovers, rather than in the deeper Circle 7, among those who have committed suicide.

[4] Achilles' passion for the Trojan Polyxena led him to promise Priam, her father and the Trojan King, that he would desert his fellow Greeks on condition of receiving Polyxena in marriage. Priam consented, but at the wedding ceremony Achilles was murdered by the Trojan Prince, Paris.

[5] Francesca da Polenta and Paolo Malatesta; Francesca's affair with Paolo began shortly after her marriage to Paolo's brother, Giovanni. The relationship continued many years until Giovanni surprised and killed the lovers in Francesca's bedroom.

As mating doves that love calls to their nest
   glide through the air with motionless raised wings,
borne by the sweet desire that fills each breast —

Just so those spirits turned on the torn sky
   from the band where Dido whirls across the air;
such was the power of pity in my cry.

"O living creature, gracious, kind, and good,
   going this pilgrimage through the sick night,   50
visiting us who stained the earth with blood,

were the King of Time our friend, we would pray His
      peace
   on you who have pitied us. As long as the wind
will let us pause, ask of us what you please.

The town where I was born lies by the shore
   where the Po descends into its ocean rest
with its attendant streams in one long murmur.

town: Ravenna

Love, which in gentlest hearts will soonest bloom
   seized my lover with passion for that sweet body
from which I was torn unshriven to my doom.   60

unshriven: unforgiven; both Paolo
and Francesca were killed instantly with no opportunity for
confessing their mortal sins.

Love, which permits no loved one not to love,
   took me so strongly with delight in him
that we are one in Hell, as we were above.

Love led us to one death. In the depths of Hell
   Caïna waits for him who took our lives."
This was the piteous tale they stopped to tell.

Caïna: named for Cain; the outer
ring of the pit of Dante's hell,
where lie those who performed
acts of treachery against their kin

And when I had heard those world-offended lovers
   I bowed my head. At last the Poet spoke:
"What painful thoughts are these your lowered
      brow covers?"

When at length I answered, I began: "Alas!   70
   What sweetest thoughts, what green and young
      desire
led these two lovers to this sorry pass." ˋ

Then turning to those spirits once again,
   I said: "Francesca, what you suffer here
melts me to tears of pity and of pain.

But tell me: in the time of your sweet sighs
  by what appearances found love the way
  to lure you to his perilous paradise?"

And she: "The double grief of a lost bliss
  is to recall its happy hour in pain.   80
  Your Guide and Teacher knows the truth of this.

But if there is indeed a soul in Hell
  to ask of the beginning of our love
  out of his pity, I will weep and tell:

On a day for dalliance we read the rhyme
  of Lancelot, how love had mastered him.
  We were alone with innocence and dim time.

Lancelot: the courtly lover of King
Arthur's Round Table

Pause after pause that high old story drew
  our eyes together while we blushed and paled;
  but it was one soft passage overthrew   90

our caution and our hearts. For when we read
  how her fond smile was kissed by such a lover,
  he who is one with me alive and dead

breathed on my lips the tremor of his kiss.
  That book, and he who wrote it, was a pander.
  That day we read no further." As she said this,

the other spirit, who stood by her, wept
  so piteously, I felt my senses reel
  and faint away with anguish. I was swept

by such a swoon as death is, and I fell,   100
as a corpse might fall, to the dead floor of Hell.

Francesco Petrarch   (1304–1374)

ITALIAN POET and SCHOLAR

Laura Rules Me Still

Sennuccio, would you have me, then, confide
My way of life, the tale of my duress?
I burn, I melt, with all the old grievousness,
And Laura rules me still, for, woe betide,
Here she was humble, there she walked in pride,
Now harsh, now gentle; pitiful, pitiless;
Now she was gay; now in her sober dress;
Now scornful; now demure; now angry-eyed;
Here she sang sweetly; here she sat awhile;
And here she turned, and there she held her ground;   10
Her eyes here stabbed my heart with a fatal ray;
And here she spoke; and here I saw her smile;
'Twas here she blushed. — Oh, in this helpless round
Our master, Love, pursues me night and day.

Geoffrey Chaucer   (c. 1345–1400)

ENGLISH POET

The Wife of Bath's Tale

When good King Arthur ruled in ancient days,
A king that every Briton loves to praise,
This was a land brim-full of fairy folk.
The Elf-Queen and her courtiers joined and broke
Their elfin dance on many a green mead,
Or so was the opinion once, I read,

Title supplied by editors. "Laura Rules Me Still" by Francesco Petrarch: Canzioniere CXII. From *Petrarch: Selected Sonnets, Odes and Letters*, translated by Morris Bishop, edited by Thomas Bergin. Reprinted by permission of Morris Bishop.

"The Wife of Bath's Tale" by Geoffrey Chaucer. From *The Canterbury Tales* by Geoffrey Chaucer, translated by Nevill Coghill and published by Penguin Books Ltd. Reprinted by permission.

Hundreds of years ago, in days of yore.
But no one now sees fairies any more,
For now the saintly charity and prayer
Of holy friars seem to have purged the air;   10
They search the countryside through field and stream
As thick as motes that speckle a sun-beam,
Blessing the halls, the chambers, kitchens, bowers,
Cities and boroughs, castles, courts and towers,
Thorpes, barns and stables, outhouses and dairies,
And that's the reason why there are no fairies.
Wherever there was wont to walk an elf
To-day there walks the holy friar himself
As evening falls or when the daylight springs,
Saying his mattins and his holy things,   20
Walking his limit round from town to town.
Women can now go safely up and down,
By every bush or under every tree;
There is no other incubus but he,   *incubus: evil spirit thought to*
So there is really no one else to hurt you   *cause conception*
And he will do no more than take your virtue.
    Now it so happened, I began to say,
Long, long ago in good King Arthur's day,
There was a knight who was a lusty liver.
One day as he came riding from the river   30
He saw a maiden walking all forlorn
Ahead of him, alone as she was born.
And of that maiden, spite of all she said,
By very force he took her maidenhead.
   This act of violence made such a stir,
So much petitioning of the king for her,
That he condemned the knight to lose his head
By course of law. He was as good as dead
(It seems that then the statutes took that view)
But that the queen and other ladies too   40
Implored the king to exercise his grace
So ceaselessly, he gave the queen the case
And granted her his life, and she could choose
Whether to show him mercy or refuse.
    The queen returned him thanks with all her might,
And then she sent a summons to the knight
At her convenience, and expressed her will:
'Sir, your position is precarious still,'
She said, 'you're on the edge of an abyss.
Yet you shall live if you can tell me this.   50
What is the thing that women most desire?
Beware the ax and say as I require.
    'If you can't answer on the moment, though,
I will concede you this: you are to go
A twelvemonth and a day to seek and learn
Sufficient answer, then you shall return.

I shall take gages from you to extort
Surrender of your body to the court.'
    Sad was the knight and sorrowfully sighed,
But there! What option had he? He'd been tried. 60
And in the end he chose to go away
And to return after a year and day
Armed with such answer as there might be sent
To him by God. He took his leave and went.
    He knocked at every house, searched every place,
Yes, anywhere that offered hope of grace.
What could it be that women wanted most?
But all the same he never touched a coast,
Country or town in which there seemed to be
Any two people willing to agree.   70
    Some said that women wanted wealth and treasure,
Honor said some, some jollity and pleasure;
Some gorgeous clothes and others fun in bed
And 'to be widowed and remarried,' said
Yet others. Some the thing that really mattered
Was that we should be gratified and flattered.
That's very near the truth, it seems to me;
A man can win us best with flattery.
Attentiveness and making a great fuss
About a woman, that's what fetches us.   80

fetches us: This tale is told by the sensuous Alice, who has already had five husbands.

    But others said a woman's real passion
Was liberty, behaving in what fashion
Might please her best, and not be corrected
But told she's wise, encouraged and respected.
Truly there's not a woman in ten score
Who has a fault and someone rubs the sore
But she will kick if what he says is true;
You try it out and you will find so too.
However vicious we may be within
We like to be thought wise and void of sin.   90
    Some people said that what we women treasure
Is to be thought dependable in pleasure,
Steadfast in keeping secrets from the jealous,
Not prone to blab the things a man may tell us.
But that opinion isn't worth a rush!

rush: bulrush or common marsh weed

Good Lord, a woman keep a secret? Tush!
Remember Midas? Will you hear the tale?
    Among some other little things now stale,
Ovid relates that Midas, it appears,
Had grown a great big pair of ass's ears   100
Under his flowing locks. As best he might
He kept this foul deformity from sight.
His wife — she was the only one that knew —
Was trusted by him, and he loved her too.
He begged her not to tell a living creature
That he possessed so horrible a feature.

She wouldn't tell for all the world, she swore,
It would be villainy, a sin what's more,
To earn her husband such a filthy name,
Besides it would redound to her own shame.   110
Nevertheless she thought she would have died
Keeping this secret bottled up inside;
It seemed to swell her heart and she, no doubt,
Thought it was on the point of bursting out.

    Fearing to speak of it to woman or man,
Down to a reedy marsh she quickly ran
And reached the sedge. Her heart was all on fire
And, as a bittern bumbles in the mire,
She whispered to the water, near the ground,
'Betray me not, O water, with thy sound!   120
I have told no one yet, but it appears
My husband has a pair of ass's ears!
Ah! My heart's well again, the secret's out!
I couldn't have kept it longer, I don't doubt.'
So, as you see, we women can't keep mum
For very long, but out the secrets come.
For what became of Midas, if you care
To turn up Ovid you will find it there.

    This knight that I am telling you about
Perceived at last he never would find out   130
What it could be that women loved the best.
Faint was the soul within his sorrowful breast
As home he went, he dared no longer stay;
His year was up and now it was the day.

    As he rode home in a dejected mood,
Suddenly, at the margin of a wood,
He saw a dance upon the leafy floor
Of four and twenty ladies, nay, and more.
Eagerly he approached, in hope to learn
Some words of wisdom ere he should return;   140
But lo! Before he came to where they were,
Dancers and dance all vanished into air!
There wasn't a living creature to be seen
Save one old woman crouched upon the green.
A fouler-looking creature I suppose
Could scarcely be imagined. She arose
And said, 'Sir knight, there's no way on from here.
Tell me what you are looking for, my dear,
For peradventure that were best for you;
We old, old women know a thing or two.'   150

    'Dear Mother,' said the knight, 'alack the day!
I am as good as dead if I can't say
What thing it is that women most desire;
If you could tell me I would pay your hire.'
'Give me your hand,' she said, 'and swear to do
Whatever I shall next require of you

Ovid: In Ovid's **Metamorphoses** the marsh reeds whispered Midas' secret to all.

— If so to do should lie within your might —
And you shall know the answer before night.'
'Upon my honor,' he answered, 'I agree.'
'Then,' said the crone, 'I dare to guarantee   160
Your life is safe, I shall make good my claim.
Upon my life the queen will say the same.
Show me the very proudest of them all
In costly coverchief or jeweled caul   caul: headdress
That dare say no to what I have to teach.
Let us go forward without further speech.'
And then she crooned her gospel in his ear
And told him to be glad and not to fear.

    They came to court. This knight, in full array,
Stood forth and said, 'O Queen, I've kept my day 170
And kept my word and have my answer ready.'

    There sat the noble matrons and the heady
Young girls, and widows too, that have the grace
Of wisdom, all assembled in that place,
And there the queen herself was throned to hear
And judge his answer. Then the knight drew near
And silence was commanded through the hall.

    The queen then bade the knight to tell them all
What thing it was that women wanted most.
He stood not silent like a beast or post,   180
But gave his answer with the ringing word
Of a man's voice and the assembly heard:

    'My liege and lady, in general,' said he,
'Women desire the self-same sovereignty
On husbands as they have on those that love them,
And would be set in mastery above them;
That is your greatest wish. Now spare or kill
Me as you please, I stand here at your will.'

    In all the court not one that shook her head
Or contradicted what the knight had said;   190
Maid, wife and widow cried, 'He's saved his life!'

    And on the word up started the old wife,
The one the knight saw sitting on the green,
And cried, 'Your mercy, sovereign lady queen!
Before the court disperses, do me right!
'Twas I who taught this answer to the knight,
For which he swore, and pledged his honor to it,
That the first thing I asked of him he'd do it,
So far as it should lie within his might.
Before this court I ask you then, sir knight,   200
To keep your word and take me for your wife;
For well you know that I have saved your life.
If this be false, deny it on your sword!'

    'Alas!' he said, 'Old lady, by the Lord
I know indeed that such was my behest,
But for God's love think of a new request,

Take all my goods, but leave my body free.'
'A curse on us,' she said, 'if I agree!
I may be foul, I may be poor and old,
Yet will not choose to be, for all the gold   210
That's bedded in the earth or lies above,
Less than your wife, nay, then your very love!'
 'My love?' said he. 'By Heaven, my damnation!
Alas that any of my race and station
Should ever make so foul a misalliance!'
Yet in the end his pleading and defiance
All went for nothing, he was forced to wed.
He takes his ancient wife and goes to bed.
 Now peradventure some may well suspect
A lack of care in me since I neglect   220
To tell of the rejoicings and display
Made at the feast upon their wedding-day.
I have but a short answer to let fall;
I say there was no joy or feast at all,
Nothing but heaviness of heart and sorrow.
He married her in private on the morrow
And all day long stayed hidden like an owl,
It was such torture that his wife looked foul.
 Great was the anguish churning in his head
When he and she were piloted to bed;   230
He wallowed back and forth in desperate style.
His wife lay still and wore a quiet smile;
At last she said, 'Dear husband, bless my soul!
Is this how knights treat wives upon the whole?
Are these the laws of good King Arthur's house?
Is all his knighthood so contemptuous?
I am your own beloved and your wife,
And I am she, indeed, that saved your life;
And certainly I never did you wrong.
Then why, this first of nights, so sad a song?   240
You're carrying on as if you were half-witted!
Say, for God's love, what sin have I committed?
I'll put things right if you will tell me how.'
 'Put right?' he cried. 'That never can be now!
Nothing can ever be put right again!
You're old, and so abominably plain,
So poor to start with, so low-bred to follow;
It's little wonder if I twist and wallow!
God, that my heart would burst within my breast!'
 'Is that,' said she, 'the cause of your unrest?'   250
 'Yes, certainly,' he said, 'and can you wonder?'
 'I could set right what you suppose a blunder,
That's if I cared to, in a day or two,
If I were shown more courtesy by you.
Just now,' she said, 'you spoke of gentle birth,
Such as descends from ancient wealth and worth.

If that's the claim you make for gentlemen
Such arrogance is hardly worth a hen.
Whoever loves to work for virtuous ends,
Public and private, and who most intends   260
To do what deeds of gentleness he can,
Take him to be the greatest gentleman.
Christ wills we take our gentleness from Him,
Not from a wealth of ancestry long dim,
Though they bequeath their whole establishment
By which we claim to be of high descent.
Our fathers cannot make us a bequest
Of all those virtues that became them best
And earned for them the name of gentleman,
But bade us follow them as best we can.   270
    'Thus the wise poet of the Florentines,
Dante by name, has written in these lines,
For such is the opinion Dante launches:
"Seldom arises by these slender branches
Prowess of men, for it is God, no less,
Wills us to claim of Him our gentleness."
For of our parents nothing can we claim
Save temporal things, and these may hurt and maim.
    'But everyone knows this as well as I;
For if gentility were implanted by   280
The natural course of lineage down the line,
Public or not, it could not cease to shine
In doing the fair work of gentle deed.
No vice or villainy could then bear seed.
    'Take fire and carry it to the darkest house
Between this kingdom and the Caucasus,
And shut the doors on it and leave it there.
It will burn on, and it will burn as fair
As if ten thousand men were there to see,
For fire will keep its nature and degree,   290
I can assure you, sir, until it dies.
    'But gentleness, as you will recognize,
Is not annexed in nature to possessions,
Men fail in living up to their professions;
But fire never ceases to be fire.
God knows you'll often find, if you inquire,
Some lording full of villainy and shame.
If you would be esteemed for the mere name
Of having been by birth a gentleman
And stemming from some virtuous, noble clan,   300
And do not live yourself by gentle deed
Or take your fathers' noble code and creed,
You are no gentleman, though duke or earl.
Vice and bad manners are what make a churl.
    'Gentility is only the renown
For bounty that your fathers handed down,

Quite foreign to your person, not your own;
Gentility must come from God alone.
That we are gentle comes to us by grace
And by no means is it bequeathed with place.   310
   'Reflect how noble (says Valerius)
Was Tullius surnamed Hostilius,
Who rose from poverty to nobleness.
And read Boethius, Seneca no less,
Thus they express themselves and are agreed:
"Gentle is he that does a gentle deed."
And therefore, my dear husband, I conclude
That even if my ancestors were rude,
Yet God on high — and so I hope He will —
Can grant me grace to live in virtue still,   320
A gentlewoman only when beginning
To live in virtue and to shrink from sinning.
   'As for my poverty which you reprove,
Almighty God Himself in whom we move,
Believe and have our being, chose a life
Of poverty, and every man or wife
And every child can see our Heavenly King
Would never stoop to choose a shameful thing.
No shame in poverty if the heart is gay,
As Seneca and all the learned say.   330
He who accepts his poverty unhurt
I'd say is rich although he lacked a shirt.
But truly poor are they who whine and fret
And covet what they cannot hope to get.
And he that having nothing covets not
Is rich, though you may think he is a sot.
   'True poverty can find a song to sing.
Juvenal says a pleasant little thing:
"The poor can dance and sing in the relief
Of having nothing that will tempt a thief."   340
Though it be hateful, poverty is good,
A great incentive to a livelihood,
And a great help to our capacity
For wisdom, if accepted patiently.
Poverty is, though wanting in estate,
A kind of wealth that none calumniate.
Poverty often, when the heart is lowly,
Brings one to God and teaches what is holy,
Gives knowledge of oneself and even lends
A glass by which to see one's truest friends.   350
And since it's no offense, let me be plain;
Do not rebuke my poverty again.
   'Lastly you taxed me, sir, with being old.
Yet even if you never had been told
By ancient books, you gentlemen engage
Yourselves in honor to respect old age.

Tullius: Tullus Hostilius, third King of Rome (673–642 B.C.)

Boethius, Seneca: popular Roman philosophers; Boethius was a Neoplatonist, Seneca a Stoic.

Juvenal: Roman satiric poet (c. 100 A.D.)

350   **glass:** eyeglass

To call an old man "father" shows good breeding,
And this could be supported from my reading.
   'You say I'm old and fouler than a fen.
You need not fear to be a cuckold, then.   360
Filth and old age, I'm sure you will agree,
Are powerful wardens upon chastity.
Nevertheless, well knowing your delights,
I shall fulfill your worldly appetites.
   'You have two choices; which one will you try?
To have me old and ugly till I die,
But still a loyal, true and humble wife
That never will displease you all her life,
Or would you rather I were young and pretty
And take your chance what happens in a city   370
Where friends will visit you because of me,
Yes, and in other places too, maybe.
Which would you have? The choice is all your own.'
   The knight thought long, and with a piteous groan
At last he said with all the care in life,
'My lady and my love, my dearest wife,
I leave the matter to your wise decision.
You make the choice yourself, for the provision
Of what may be agreeable and rich
In honor to us both, I don't care which;   380
Whatever pleases you suffices me.'
   'And have I won the mastery?' said she,
'Since I'm to choose and rule as I think fit?'
'Certainly, wife,' he answered her, 'that's it.'
'Kiss me,' she cried. 'No quarrels! On my oath
And word of honor you shall find me both,
That is, both fair and faithful as a wife;
May I go howling mad and take my life
Unless I prove to be as good and true
As ever wife was since the world was new!   390
And if to-morrow when the sun's above
I seem less fair than any lady-love,
Than any queen or empress east or west,
Do with my life and death as you think best.
Cast up the curtain, husband. Look at me!'
   And when indeed the knight had looked to see,
Lo, she was young and lovely, rich in charms.
In ecstasy he caught her in his arms,
His heart went bathing in a bath of blisses
And melted in a hundred thousand kisses,   400
And she responded in the fullest measure
With all that could delight or give him pleasure.
   So they lived ever after to the end
In perfect bliss; and may Christ Jesus send
Us husbands meek and young and fresh in bed,
And grace to overbid them when we wed.

And — Jesu hear my prayer! — cut short the lives
Of those who won't be governed by their wives;
And all old, angry niggards of their pence,
God send them soon a very pestilence!   410

Anonymous (c. 1450)

ENGLISH

Al Only for My Ladies Sake

Now wolde I fayn som myrthes make   fayn: gladly
Al only for my ladies sake,
    When I hire see;   hire: her
But now I am so fer fro hire   fer: far
    It wol not be.

Thogh I be fer out of hir sight,
I am hir man bothe day and nyght,
    And so wol be:
Ther-fore wolde as I love hire
    She lovede me.   10

Whan she is myrie than am I glad,
Whan she is sory than am I sad,
    And cause is why: —
For he lyveth not that loveth hire
    So wel as I.

She seyth that she hath seen it writen
That 'selden seen is soon forgeten.'
    It is not so,
For, in good feith, save only hire
    I love no mo.   20

Wher-fore I preye bothe nyght and day
That she may caste al care awey
    And lyve in reste,
And evermore wher-evere she be
    To love me best;

And I to hire to be so trewe,
And nevere to chaunge for no newe,
   Unto myn ende,
And that I may in hir servise
   Evere to amende.   30

Pierre de Ronsard (1524–1585)

FRENCH POET

For Beauty

"Who," cried the elders on the Trojan wall,
   When Helen passed, "dare of the ills complain
   Which by the beauty have no weight at all,
   Whose single glance outbids a world of pain?
And yet the wrath of Ares to forestall
   Were it not better to yield her up again
   Than see the port besieged, the ramparts fall,
   And all of Troas bloody with the slain?"
But that was old man's rede. King Menelaus
   Asked rightly her return whom rightly Paris   10
   Withheld, since both knew well it was the duty
Of young and old alike, although it slay us,
   To offer and to waste — if all miscarries —
   Country and goods and life itself for beauty.

Helen: Helen, wife of Menelaus, was abducted from her home by Paris, a Trojan; Menelaus and his fellow Greeks attacked and thus brought about the Trojan War.

Troas: Troy

rede: counsel, opinion

Title supplied by editors. "For Beauty" by Pierre de Ronsard, translated by Humbert Wolfe. From *Renaissance and Baroque Lyrics*, edited by Harold Martin Priest and published by Northwestern University Press, 1962, Evanston, Illinois. Reprinted by permission.

Edmund Spenser (1552?–1599)

ENGLISH POET

This Holy Season

This holy season fit to fast and pray,
   Men to devotion ought to be inclynd:
   therefore, I lykewise on so holy day,
   for my sweet Saynt some service fit will find.
Her temple fayre is built within my mind,
   in which her glorious ymage placed is,
   on which my thoughts doo day and night attend
   lyke sacred priests that never thinke amisse.
There I to her as th' author of my blisse,
   will builde an altar to appease her yre: 10
   and on the same my hart will sacrifise,
   burning in flames of pure and chast desyre:
The which vouchsafe O goddesse to accept,
   amongst thy deerest relicks to be kept.

Philip Sidney (1554–1586)

ENGLISH POET, COURTIER, and SOLDIER

Fit Words My Love to Show

Loving in truth, and faine in verse my love to show,
That the deare She might take some pleasure of my
     paine:
Pleasure might cause her reade, reading might make
     her know,

Title supplied by editors. "This Holy Season" by Edmund Spenser: Sonnet XXII from *Amoretti*. From *Spenser's Minor Poems*, edited by Ernest de Selincourt. Reprinted by permission of the Clarendon Press, Oxford.

Title supplied by editors. "Fit Words My Love to Show" by Philip Sidney: Sonnet I from *Astrophel and Stella*. From *The Poems of Sir Philip Sidney*, edited by William A. Ringler, Jr. Reprinted by permission of the Clarendon Press, Oxford.

Knowledge might pitie winne, and pitie grace obtaine,
  I sought fit words to paint the blackest face of woe,
Studying inventions fine, her wits to entertaine:
Oft turning others' leaves, to see if thence would flow
Some fresh and fruitfull showers upon my sunne-
      burn'd braine.
    But words came halting forth, wanting Invention's
      stay,
Invention, Nature's child, fled step-dame Studie's
      blowes,   10
And others' feete still seem'd but strangers in my
      way.
Thus great with child to speake, and helplesse in my
      throwes,
    Biting my trewand pen, beating my selfe for spite,   **trewand: truant**
    'Foole,' said my Muse to me, 'looke in thy heart
      and write.'

William Shakespeare (1564–1616)

ENGLISH DRAMATIST and POET

The Tragedy of King Lear

[DRAMATIS PERSONÆ

LEAR, *King of Britain*	DOCTOR
KING OF FRANCE	FOOL
DUKE OF BURGUNDY	OSWALD, *steward to Goneril*
DUKE OF CORNWALL	AN OFFICER EMPLOYED BY EDMUND
DUKE OF ALBANY	GENTLEMAN ATTENDANT ON CORDELIA
EARL OF KENT	A HERALD
EARL OF GLOUCESTER	SERVANTS TO CORNWALL
EDGAR, *son to Gloucester*	
EDMUND, *bastard son to Gloucester*	GONERIL,
CURAN, *a courtier*	REGAN, ⎬ *daughters to Lear*
OLD MAN, *tenant to Gloucester*	CORDELIA,

Knights of Lear's train, Officers, Messengers, Soldiers, and Attendants

Scene: Britain]

ACT I

SCENE I [*King Lear's palace*]

Enter KENT, GLOUCESTER, *and* EDMUND

KENT. I thought the King had more affected the
    Duke of Albany than Cornwall.   **affected:** liked

GLOUCESTER. It did always seem so to us; but
    now, in the division of the kingdom, it appears
not which of the Dukes he values most; for qualities
are so weigh'd, that curiosity in neither can make   **weigh'd:** balanced. **curiosity:** care-
choice of either's moiety.   ful scrutiny. **moiety:** share

KENT. Is not this your son, my lord?

GLOUCESTER. His breeding, sir, hath been at my
    charge. I have so often blush'd to acknowl-   10
edge him, that now I am braz'd to't.   **braz'd:** brazened, hardened

KENT. I cannot conceive you.

"The Tragedy of King Lear" by William Shakespeare.
From *The Complete Plays and Poems of William Shake-
speare*, edited by William Allan Neilson and Charles
Jarvis Hill (New Cambridge Edition). Brackets indicate
emended readings; minor textual revisions by Arthur F.
Kinney. Reprinted by permission of Houghton Mifflin
Company.

59

GLOUCESTER. Sir, this young fellow's mother
could; whereupon she grew round-womb'd, and
had, indeed, sir, a son for her cradle ere she had a
husband for her bed. Do you smell a fault?

KENT. I cannot wish the fault undone, the issue
of it being so proper.

GLOUCESTER. But I have a son, sir, by order of
law, some year elder than this, who yet is no   20
dearer in my account. Though this knave came something saucily to the world before he was sent for, yet
was his mother fair; there was good sport at his making, and the whoreson must be acknowledged. Do
you know this noble gentleman, Edmund?

account: esteem

EDMUND. No, my lord.

GLOUCESTER. My Lord of Kent. Remember him
hereafter as my honourable friend.

EDMUND. My services to your lordship.

KENT. I must love you, and sue to know you   30
better.

sue: seek

EDMUND. Sir, I shall study deserving.

GLOUCESTER. He hath been out nine years, and
away he shall again. The King is coming.

out: away

Sennet. Enter one bearing a coronet, then KING
LEAR, *then the* DUKES OF ALBANY *and* CORN-
WALL, *next* GONERIL, REGAN, CORDELIA, *with
followers*

Sennet: trumpet call

LEAR. Attend the lords of France and Burgundy,
Gloucester.

GLOUCESTER. I shall, my lord.
            [*Exeunt* [*Gloucester and Edmund*]

LEAR. Meantime we shall express our darker
purpose.
Give me the map there. Know that we have divided
In three our kingdom; and 'tis our fast intent
To shake all cares and business from our age,   40
Conferring them on younger strengths, while we
Unburden'd crawl toward death. Our son of Corn-
wall,
And you, our no less loving son of Albany,
We have this hour a constant will to publish
Our daughters' several dowers, that future strife
May be prevented now. The Princes, France and
Burgundy,
Great rivals in our youngest daughter's love,
Long in our court have made their amorous sojourn,
And here are to be answer'd. Tell me, my daugh-
ters, —
Since now we will divest us both of rule,   50

darker: less known

publish: proclaim

Interest of territory, cares of state, —   **Interest: possession**
Which of you shall we say doth love us most,
That we our largest bounty may extend
Where nature doth with merit challenge? Goneril,
Our eldest-born, speak first.
    GONERIL.   Sir, I love you more than word can
        wield the matter;
Dearer than eye-sight, space, and liberty;
Beyond what can be valued, rich or rare;
No less than life, with grace, health, beauty, honour;
As much as child e'er lov'd, or father found;   60
A love that makes breath poor, and speech unable:
Beyond all manner of so much I love you.
    CORDELIA.   [*Aside*] What shall Cordelia speak?
        Love and be silent.
    LEAR.   Of all these bounds, even from this line to
        this,
With shadowy forests and with champains rich'd,   **champains: plains**
With plenteous rivers and wide-skirted meads,
We make thee lady. To thine and Albany's issues
Be this perpetual. What says our second daughter,
Our dearest Regan, wife of Cornwall? [Speak.]   69
    REGAN.   I am made of that self metal as my sister,
And prize me at her worth. In my true heart
I find she names my very deed of love;
Only she comes too short, that I profess
Myself an enemy to all other joys
Which the most precious square of sense [possesses],   **square: estimate**
And find I am alone felicitate   **felicitate: made happy**
In your dear Highness' love.
    CORDELIA.   [*Aside*] Then poor Cordelia!
And yet not so; since, I am sure, my love's
More ponderous than my tongue.
    LEAR.   To thee and thine hereditary ever   80
Remain this ample third of our fair kingdom;
No less in space, validity, and pleasure,   **validity: value**
Than that conferr'd on Goneril. Now, our joy,
Although our last and least, to whose young love
The vines of France and milk of Burgundy
Strive to be interess'd, what can you say to draw   **be interess'd: establish a claim**
A third more opulent than your sisters? Speak.
    CORDELIA.   Nothing, my lord.
    LEAR.   Nothing?
    CORDELIA.   Nothing.   90
    LEAR.   Nothing will come of nothing. Speak
    again.
    CORDELIA.   Unhappy that I am, I cannot heave
My heart into my mouth. I love your Majesty
According to my bond; no more nor less.   **bond: duty**

LEAR.   How, how, Cordelia! Mend your speech a
   little,
Lest you may mar your fortunes.
   CORDELIA.   Good my lord,
You have begot me, bred me, lov'd me: I
Return those duties back as are right fit;
Obey you, love you, and most honour you.
Why have my sisters husbands, if they say   100
They love you all? Haply, when I shall wed,
That lord whose hand must take my plight shall carry   **plight: troth-plight**
Half my love with him, half my care and duty.
Sure, I shall never marry like my sisters
[To love my father all].
   LEAR.   But goes thy heart with this?
   CORDELIA.   Ay, my good lord.
   LEAR.   So young, and so untender?
   CORDELIA.   So young, my lord, and true.
   LEAR.   Let it be so; thy truth, then, be thy
      dower!
For, by the sacred radiance of the sun,   110
The [mysteries] of Hecate and the night;   **Hecate: goddess of the infernal re-**
By all the operation of the orbs   **gions. operation: influence. orbs:**
From whom we do exist and cease to be;   **planets**
Here I disclaim all my paternal care,
Propinquity and property of blood,
And as a stranger to my heart and me
Hold thee from this for ever. The barbarous
      Scythian,
Or he that makes this generation messes   **generation: children. messes: food**
To gorge his appetite, shall to my bosom
Be as well neighbour'd, piti'd, and reliev'd,   120
As thou my sometime daughter.
   KENT.   Good my liege,
   LEAR.   Peace, Kent!
Come not between the dragon and his wrath.
I lov'd her most, and thought to set my rest   **set my rest: stake my all**
On her kind nursery. [To Cordelia] Hence, and
      avoid my sight! —
So be my grave my peace, as here I give
Her father's heart from her! Call France. — Who
      stirs?
Call Burgundy. Cornwall and Albany,
With my two daughters' dowers digest the third; **digest: absorb**
Let pride, which she calls plainness, marry her.   130
I do invest you jointly with my power,
Pre-eminence, and all the large effects
That troop with majesty. Ourself, by monthly course,
With reservation of an hundred knights
By you to be sustain'd, shall our abode

Make with you by due turn. Only we shall retain
The name, and all th' addition to a king;   **addition: title and honors**
The sway, revenue, execution of the rest,
Beloved sons, be yours; which to confirm,
This coronet part between you.

   KENT.   Royal Lear,   140
Whom I have ever honour'd as my king,
Lov'd as my father, as my master follow'd,
As my great patron thought on in my prayers, —
   LEAR.   The bow is bent and drawn; make from   **The . . . shaft: The deed is done;**
     the shaft.   **step away. The metaphor from**
   KENT.   Let it fall rather, though the fork invade **archery is continued in l.145 and**
The region of my heart: be Kent unmannerly   **ll.159–60. fork: barb**
When Lear is mad. What wouldst thou do, old
     man?
Thinkest thou that duty shall have dread to speak
When power to flattery bows? To plainness hon-
     our's bound
When majesty falls to folly. Reserve thy state;   150 **state: kingly wisdom**
And in thy best consideration check
This hideous rashness. Answer my life my judge-   **my life: with my life**
     ment,
Thy youngest daughter does not love thee least;
Nor are those empty-hearted whose low sounds
Reverb no hollowness.

   LEAR.   Kent, on thy life, no more.
   KENT.   My life I never held but as a pawn
To wage against thine enemies, [nor] fear to lose it,
Thy safety being motive.

   LEAR.   Out of my sight!
   KENT.   See better, Lear; and let me still remain
The true blank of thine eye.   160 **blank: center of the target**
   LEAR.   Now, by Apollo, —
   KENT.   Now, by Apollo, king,
Thou swear'st thy gods in vain.

   LEAR.   O, vassal! miscreant!
     [*Laying his hand on his sword*]
ALBANY. ⎫
CORNWALL. ⎬ Dear sir, forbear.
   KENT.   Kill thy physician, and thy fee bestow
Upon the foul disease. Revoke thy gift,
Or, whilst I can vent clamour from my throat,
I'll tell thee thou dost evil.

   LEAR.   Hear me, recreant!
On thine allegiance, hear me!   168
That thou hast sought to make us break our vows,
Which we durst never yet, and with strain'd pride   **durst: dared. strain'd: exagger-**
To come betwixt our sentence and our power,   **ated**
Which nor our nature nor our place can bear,

Our potency made good, take thy reward.   **Our . . . good: to prove my power**
Five days we do allot thee, for provision
To shield thee from disasters of the world;
And on the sixth to turn thy hated back
Upon our kingdom. If, on the tenth day following,
Thy banish'd trunk be found in our dominions,
The moment is thy death. Away! By Jupiter,
This shall not be revok'd.   180

    KENT.   Fare thee well, king! Sith thus thou wilt   **Sith: since**
    appear,
Freedom lives hence, and banishment is here.
[*To Cordelia*] The gods to their dear shelter take
    thee, maid,
That justly think'st and hast most rightly said!
[*To Regan and Goneril*] And your large speeches may   **approve: justify**
    your deeds approve,
That good effects may spring from words of love.
Thus Kent, O princes, bids you all adieu;
He'll shape his old course in a country new.   188
              [*Exit*

Flourish. Re-enter GLOUCESTER, *with* FRANCE,   **Flourish: with trumpet and/or**
    BURGUNDY, *and Attendants*   **drum**

    GLOUCESTER.   Here's France and Burgundy, my
    noble lord.
    LEAR.   My Lord of Burgundy,
We first address toward you, who with this king
Hath rivall'd for our daughter. What, in the least,
Will you require in present dower with her,
Or cease your quest of love?
    BURGUNDY.   Most royal Majesty,
I crave no more than what your Highness offer'd,
Nor will you tender less.   **tender: offer**
    LEAR.   Right noble Burgundy,
When she was dear to us, we did hold her so;
But now her price is fall'n. Sir, there she stands:
If aught within that little-seeming substance,
Or all of it, with our displeasure piec'd,   200
And nothing more, may fitly like your Grace,   **like: please**
She's there, and she is yours.
    BURGUNDY.   I know no answer.
    LEAR.   Will you, with those infirmities she owes,   **owes: owns**
Unfriended, new-adopted to our hate,
Dower'd with our curse, and stranger'd with our
    oath,
Take her, or leave her?
    BURGUNDY.   Pardon me, royal sir;
    `ion makes not up in such conditions.   **Election . . . conditions: One can-**
        Then leave her, sir; for, by the power that   **not make a choice on these terms.**
      me,

I tell you all her wealth. [*To France*] For you, great
    king,
I would not from your love make such a stray   210   **stray: departure**
To match you where I hate; therefore beseech you
T' avert your liking a more worthier way
Than on a wretch whom Nature is asham'd
Almost t' acknowledge hers.
    FRANCE.   This is most strange,
That she, whom even but now was your [best] object,
The argument of your praise, balm of your age,   **argument: theme**
The best, the dearest, should in this trice of time
Commit a thing so monstrous, to dismantle
So many folds of favour. Sure her offence
Must be of such unnatural degree   220
That monsters it, or your fore-vouch'd affection   **monsters: makes monstrous**
Fallen into taint; which to believe of her,   **Fallen into taint: must have de-**
Must be a faith that reason without miracle   **cayed**
Should never plant in me.
    CORDELIA.   I yet beseech your Majesty, —
If for I want that glib and oily art
To speak and purpose not, since what I [well] intend,
I'll do't before I speak, — that you make known
It is no vicious blot, murder, or foulness,
No unchaste action, or dishonoured step,   229
That hath depriv'd me of your grace and favour;
But even for want of that for which I am richer,
A still-soliciting eye, and such a tongue
That I am glad I have not, though not to have it
Hath lost me in your liking.
    LEAR.   Better thou
Hadst not been born than not t' have pleas'd me
    better.
    FRANCE.   Is it but this, — a tardiness in nature
Which often leaves the history unspoke
That it intends to do? My Lord of Burgundy,
What say you to the lady? Love's not love
When it is mingled with regards that stands   240   **regards: considerations**
Aloof from th' entire point. Will you have her?
She is herself a dowry.
    BURGUNDY.   Royal king,
Give but that portion which yourself propos'd,
And here I take Cordelia by the hand,
Duchess of Burgundy.
    LEAR.   Nothing. I have sworn; I am firm.
    BURGUNDY.   I am sorry, then, you have so lost a
    father
That you must lose a husband.
    CORDELIA.   Peace be with Burgundy!
Since that respect and fortunes are his love,   **respect and: consideration of**
I shall not be his wife.   250

FRANCE.   Fairest Cordelia, that art most rich be-
    ing poor,
Most choice forsaken, and most lov'd despis'd!
Thee and thy virtues here I seize upon,
Be it lawful I take up what 's cast away.
Gods, gods! 'tis strange that from their cold'st neglect
My love should kindle to inflam'd respect.
Thy dowerless daughter, king, thrown to my chance,
Is queen of us, of ours, and our fair France.
Not all the dukes of waterish Burgundy
Can buy this unpriz'd precious maid of me.   260
Bid them farewell, Cordelia, though unkind;   unkind: unnatural
Thou losest here, a better where to find.   where: place
    LEAR.   Thou hast her, France. Let her be thine;
        for we
Have no such daughter, nor shall ever see
That face of hers again. — [To Cordelia] Therefore
        be gone
Without our grace, our love, our benison. —
Come, noble Burgundy.
            [Flourish. Exeunt [all but France, Goneril,
                Regan, and Cordelia]
    FRANCE.   Bid farewell to your sisters.
    CORDELIA.   The jewels of our father, with wash'd   wash'd: tear-washed
        eyes
Cordelia leaves you. I know you what you are;   270
And like a sister am most loath to call
Your faults as they are nam'd. Love well our father.
To your professed bosoms I commit him;   professed: making professions (of
But yet, alas, stood I within his grace,   love)
I would prefer him to a better place.
So, farewell to you both.
    REGAN.   Prescribe not us our duty.
    GONERIL.   Let your study
Be to content your lord, who hath receiv'd you
At fortune's alms. You have obedience scanted,   279   scanted: come short in
And well are worth the want that you have wanted.   want: loss. wanted: lacked
    CORDELIA.   Time shall unfold what plighted cun-
        ning hides;
Who covers faults, at last shame [them] derides.
Well may you prosper!
    FRANCE.   Come, my fair Cordelia.
            [Exeunt [France and Cordelia]
    GONERIL.   Sister, it is not little I have to say of
        what most nearly appertains to us both. I think
our father will hence to-night.
    REGAN.   That's most certain, and with you; next
        month with us.   288
    ˈRIL.   You see how full of changes his age is;

the observation we have made of it hath [not] been little. He always lov'd our sister most; and with what poor judgement he hath now cast her off appears too grossly.

REGAN.   'Tis the infirmity of his age; yet he hath ever but slenderly known himself.

GONERIL.   The best and soundest of his time hath been but rash; then must we look from his age to receive not alone the imperfections of long- 298 engraffed condition, but therewithal the unruly waywardness that infirm and choleric years bring with them.

REGAN.   Such unconstant starts are we like to have from him as this of Kent's banishment.

GONERIL.   There is further compliment of leave-taking between France and him. Pray you, let['s hit] together; if our father carry authority with such disposition as he bears, this last surrender of his will but offend us.

REGAN.   We shall further think of it.   309

GONERIL.   We must do something, and i' th' heat.

[*Exeunt*

grossly: obviously

time: life

unconstant starts: impulsive actions

i' th' heat: while the iron is hot

SCENE II [*The Earl of Gloucester's castle*]

Enter Bastard [EDMUND *with a letter*]

EDMUND.   Thou, Nature, art my goddess; to thy law
My services are bound. Wherefore should I
Stand in the plague of custom, and permit
The curiosity of nations to deprive me,
For that I am some twelve or fourteen moonshines
Lag of a brother? Why bastard? Wherefore base?
When my dimensions are as well compact,
My mind as generous, and my shape as true,
As honest madam's issue? Why brand they us
With base? with baseness? bastardy? base, base? 10
Who, in the lusty stealth of nature, take
More composition and fierce quality
Than doth, within a dull, stale, tired bed,
Go to the creating a whole tribe of fops,
Got 'tween asleep and wake? Well, then,
Legitimate Edgar, I must have your land.
Our father's love is to the bastard Edmund
As to th' legitimate. Fine word, "legitimate!"
Well, my legitimate, if this letter speed
And my invention thrive, Edmund the base   20
Shall [top] th' legitimate. I grow; I prosper.
Now, gods, stand up for bastards!

plague: vexation

curiosity: laws of fine distinction

Lag of: younger than

speed: succeed

Enter GLOUCESTER

GLOUCESTER. Kent banish'd thus! and France in
choler parted!
And the King gone tonight! [subscrib'd] his power!   **subscrib'd: surrendered**
Confin'd to exhibition! All this done   **exhibition: an allowance**
Upon the gad! Edmund, how now! what news?   **gad: spur of the moment**
EDMUND. So please your lordship, none.
[*Putting up the letter*]
GLOUCESTER. Why so earnestly seek you to put
up that letter?
EDMUND. I know no news, my lord.
GLOUCESTER. What paper were you reading?   30
EDMUND. Nothing, my lord.
GLOUCESTER. No? What needed, then, that ter-
rible dispatch of it into your pocket? The qual-
ity of nothing hath not such need to hide itself.
Let's see. Come, if it be nothing, I shall not need
spectacles.
EDMUND. I beseech you, sir, pardon me. It is a
letter from my brother that I have not all o'er-
read; and for so much as I have perus'd, I find it not
fit for your o'er-looking.   40
GLOUCESTER. Give me the letter, sir.
EDMUND. I shall offend either to detain or give it.
The contents, as in part I understand them, are
to blame.
GLOUCESTER. Let's see, let's see.
EDMUND. I hope, for my brother's justification, he
wrote this but as an essay or taste of my virtue.   **essay or taste: trial or test**
GLOUCESTER. (*Reads*) "This policy and reverence   **policy and reverence: policy of**
of age makes the world bitter to the best of our   **revering**
times; keeps our fortunes from us till our oldness   50   **times: lives**
cannot relish them. I begin to find an idle and
fond bondage in the oppression of aged tyranny;   **fond: foolish**
who sways, not as it hath power, but as it is suf-
fer'd. Come to me, that of this I may speak more.
If our father would sleep till I wak'd him, you should
enjoy half his revenue for ever, and live the beloved
of your brother,   EDGAR."
Hum — conspiracy! — "Sleep till I wake him, you
should enjoy half his revenue!" — My son Edgar!
Had he a hand to write this? a heart and brain   60
to breed it in? — When came you to this? Who
brought it?
EDMUND. It was not brought me, my lord; there's
the cunning of it. I found it thrown in at the
casement of my closet.   **closet: private room**
GLOUCESTER. You know the character to be your   **character: handwriting**
brother's?

EDMUND.   If the matter were good, my lord, I
   durst swear it were his; but, in respect of that, I
would fain think it were not.   70

GLOUCESTER.   It is his?

EDMUND.   It is his hand, my lord; but I hope his
   heart is not in the contents.

GLOUCESTER.   Has he never before sounded you in
   this business?

EDMUND.   Never, my lord; but I have heard him
   oft maintain it to be fit that, sons at perfect age
and fathers declin'd, the father should be as ward to   **declin'd: failed**
the son, and the son manage his revenue.

GLOUCESTER.   O villain, villain! His very   80
   opinion in the letter! Abhorred villain! Unnatural, detested, brutish villain! worse than brutish!
Go, sirrah, seek him; I'll apprehend him. Abominable villain! Where is he?

EDMUND.   I do not well know, my lord. If it
   shall please you to suspend your indignation
against my brother till you can derive from him better
testimony of his intent, you should run a certain
course; where if you violently proceed against him,   **where: whereas**
mistaking his purpose, it would make a great gap   90
in your own honour and shake in pieces the heart
of his obedience. I dare pawn down my life for him
that he hath writ this to feel my affection to your   **feel: sound**
honour, and to no other pretence of danger.   **pretence of danger: dangerous in-
                                                       tent**

GLOUCESTER.   Think you so?

EDMUND.   If your honour judge it meet, I will
   place you where you shall hear us confer of this,
and by an auricular assurance have your satisfaction;
and that without any further delay than this very
evening.   100

GLOUCESTER.   He cannot be such a monster —

[EDMUND.   Nor is not, sure.

GLOUCESTER.   To his father, that so tenderly and
   entirely loves him. Heaven and earth!] Ed-
mund, seek him out; wind me into him, I pray you.   **wind . . . him: gain his confidence**
Frame the business after your own wisdom. I would
unstate myself to be in a due resolution.   **unstate . . . resolution: forfeit my
                                                       position to be properly assured**

EDMUND.   I will seek him, sir, presently; convey   **presently: at once. convey: carry
   the business as I shall find means, and acquaint   on**
you withal.   110

GLOUCESTER.   These late eclipses in the sun and
   moon portend no good to us. Though the wisdom of Nature can reason it thus and thus, yet Nature finds itself scourg'd by the sequent effects. Love
cools, friendship falls off, brothers divide: in cities,
mutinies; in countries, discord; in palaces, treason;
and the bond crack'd 'twixt son and father. This vil-

lain of mine comes under the prediction; there's son
against father: the King falls from bias of nature;
there's father against child. We have seen the   120
best of our time; machinations, hollowness, treachery, and all ruinous disorders, follow us disquietly to
our graves. Find out this villain, Edmund; it shall
lose thee nothing; do it carefully. And the noble and
true-hearted Kent banish'd! his offence, honesty! 'Tis
strange.

falls . . . nature: acts against his natural disposition

[*Exit*

EDMUND.   This is the excellent foppery of the
world, that, when we are sick in fortune, —
often the surfeits of our own behaviour, — we make
guilty of our disasters the sun, the moon, and   130
stars, as if we were villains on necessity, fools by heavenly compulsion, knaves, thieves, and treachers by
spherical predominance, drunkards, liars, and adulter-
ers by an enforc'd obedience of planetary influence,
and all that we are evil in, by a divine thrusting on.
An admirable evasion of whoremaster man, to lay his
goatish disposition on the charge of a star! My father
compounded with my mother under the dragon's
tail, and my nativity was under *Ursa major;* so that it
follows, I am rough and lecherous. Fut, I should   140
have been that I am, had the maidenliest star in the
firmament twinkled on my bastardizing. [Edgar —]

foppery: foolishness

treachers: traitors

spherical predominance: influence of the planets

goatish: lecherous

Fut: by God's foot (abbr.)

Enter EDGAR

pat he comes like the catastrophe of the old comedy.
My cue is villanous melancholy, with a sigh like
Tom o' Bedlam. — O, these eclipses do portend
these divisions! *fa, sol, la, mi.*

Tom o' Bedlam: a lunatic beggar

EDGAR.   How now, brother Edmund! what serious
contemplation are you in?

EDMUND.   I am thinking, brother, of a prediction
I read this other day, what should follow   150
these eclipses.

EDGAR.   Do you busy yourself with that?

EDMUND.   I promise you, the effects he writes of
succeed unhappily; [as of unnaturalness between
the child and the parent; death, dearth, dissolutions
of ancient amities; divisions in state, menaces and
maledictions against king and nobles; needless diffidences, banishment of friends, dissipation of cohorts,
nuptial breaches, and I know not what.

diffidences: suspicions

EDGAR.   How long have you been a sectary   160
astronomical?

sectary astronomical: student of astrology

EDMUND.   Come, come;] when saw you my father
last?

EDGAR. The night gone by.

EDMUND. Spake you with him?

EDGAR. Ay, two hours together.

EDMUND. Parted you in good terms? Found you no displeasure in him by word nor countenance?

EDGAR. None at all.

EDMUND. Bethink yourself wherein you may 170 have offended him; and at my entreaty forbear his presence until some little time hath qualified the *qualified: moderated* heat of his displeasure, which at this instant so rageth in him, that with the mischief of your person it *mischief: injury* would scarcely allay.

EDGAR. Some villain hath done me wrong.

EDMUND. That's my fear. I pray you, have a continent forbearance till the speed of his rage goes slower; and, as I say, retire with me to my lodging, from whence I will fitly bring you to hear my 180 *fitly: at a fit time* lord speak. Pray ye, go; there's my key. If you do stir abroad, go arm'd.

EDGAR. Arm'd, brother!

EDMUND. Brother, I advise you to the best; I am no honest man if there be any good meaning toward you. I have told you what I have seen and heard; but faintly, nothing like the image and horror of it. Pray you, away.

EDGAR. Shall I hear from you anon?

EDMUND. I do serve you in this business. 190

[*Exit Edgar*

A credulous father and a brother noble,
Whose nature is so far from doing harms
That he suspects none; on whose foolish honesty
My practices ride easy. I see the business. *practices: plots*
Let me, if not by birth, have lands by wit:
All with me 's meet that I can fashion fit. [*Exit*

SCENE III [*The Duke of Albany's palace*]

Enter GONERIL, *and* [OSWALD, *her*] Steward

GONERIL. Did my father strike my gentleman for chiding of his Fool?

OSWALD. Ay, madam.

GONERIL. By day and night he wrongs me; every hour
He flashes into one gross crime or other
That sets us all at odds. I'll not endure it.
His knights grow riotous, and himself upbraids us
On every trifle. When he returns from hunting
I will not speak with him; say I am sick.

If you come slack of former services,   10
You shall do well; the fault of it I'll answer.

    OSWALD. He's coming, madam; I hear him.

                      [Horns within]

    GONERIL. Put on what weary negligence you
      please,
You and your fellows; I'd have it come to question.   **question: discussion**
If he distaste it, let him to my sister,
Whose mind and mine, I know, in that are one,
[Not to be over-rul'd. Idle old man,
That still would manage those authorities
That he hath given away! Now, by my life,
Old fools are babes again, and must be us'd   20
With checks as flatteries, when they are seen abus'd.]   **as: as well as. abus'd: misled**
Remember what I have said.

    OSWALD.   Well, madam.

    GONERIL. And let his knights have colder looks
      among you;
What grows of it, no matter. Advise your fellows so.
[I would breed from hence occasions, and I shall,
That I may speak.] I'll write straight to my sister
To hold my [very] course. Prepare for dinner.

                        [Exeunt

SCENE IV [*A hall in the same*]

        Enter KENT [*disguised*]

    KENT. If but as well I other accents borrow,
That can my speech defuse, my good intent   **defuse: disguise**
May carry through itself to that full issue   **full issue: final result**
For which I raz'd my likeness. Now, banish'd Kent,   **raz'd my likeness: changed my**
If thou canst serve where thou dost stand con-   **appearance**
    demn'd,
So may it come, thy master, whom thou lov'st,
Shall find thee full of labours.

    Horns within. Enter LEAR, [KNIGHTS] *and*
             Attendants

    LEAR. Let me not stay a jot for dinner; go get it
    ready. [*Exit an attendant*] How now! what art
thou?   10

    KENT. A man, sir.

    LEAR. What dost thou profess? What wouldst
    thou with us?

    KENT. I do profess to be no less than I seem; to
    serve him truly that will put me in trust; to love
him that is honest; to converse with him that is wise
and says little; to fear judgement; to fight when I
cannot choose; and to eat no fish.   **eat no fish: be a Protestant**

LEAR.   What are thou?

KENT.   A very honest-hearted fellow, and as   20
poor as the King.

LEAR.   If thou be'st as poor for a subject as he's
for a king, thou art poor enough. What wouldst
thou?

KENT.   Service.

LEAR.   Who wouldst thou serve?

KENT.   You.

LEAR.   Dost thou know me, fellow?

KENT.   No, sir; but you have that in your countenance which I would fain call master.   30

LEAR.   What's that?

KENT.   Authority.

LEAR.   What services canst thou do?

KENT.   I can keep honest counsel, ride, run, mar
a curious tale in telling it, and deliver a plain
message bluntly. That which ordinary men are fit
for, I am qualified in; and the best of me is diligence.

LEAR.   How old art thou?

KENT.   Not so young, sir, to love a woman for
singing, nor so old to dote on her for any-   40
thing. I have years on my back forty-eight.

LEAR.   Follow me; thou shalt serve me. If I like
thee no worse after dinner, I will not part from
thee yet. Dinner, ho, dinner! Where's my knave?
my Fool? Go you, and call my Fool hither.

                          [Exit an attendant

          Enter Steward [OSWALD].

You, you, sirrah, where's my daughter?

OSWALD.   So please you, —   *[Exit*

LEAR.   What says the fellow there? Call the clot-   **clotpoll: blockhead**
poll back. [*Exit a knight*] Where's my Fool,
ho? I think the world's asleep.   50

         [*Re-enter* KNIGHT]

How now! where's that mongrel?

KNIGHT.   He says, my lord, your daughter is not
well.

LEAR.   Why came not the slave back to me when
I call'd him?

KNIGHT.   Sir, he answered me in the roundest   **roundest: most elaborate**
manner, he would not.

LEAR.   He would not!

KNIGHT.   My lord, I know not what the matter is;
but, to my judgement, your Highness is not   60
entertain'd with that ceremonious affection as you
were wont. There's a great abatement of kindness

appears as well in the general dependants as in the
Duke himself also and your daughter.

LEAR.   Ha! say'st thou so?

KNIGHT.   I beseech you, pardon me, my lord, if I
   be mistaken; for my duty cannot be silent when
I think your Highness wrong'd.

LEAR.   Thou but rememb'rest me of mine own
   conception.   I have perceived a most faint   70
neglect of late, which I have rather blamed as mine
own jealous curiosity than as a very pretence and purpose of unkindness.   I will look further into't.   But
where's my Fool?   I have not seen him this two days.

KNIGHT.   Since my young lady's going into France,
   sir, the Fool hath much pined away.

LEAR.   No more of that; I have noted it well.
Go you, and tell my daughter I would speak with
her.   [Exit an attendant] Go you, call hither my
Fool.   [Exit an attendant]   80

jealous curiosity: suspicious fussi-
ness. *very pretence:* real intention

Re-enter Steward [OSWALD]

O, you sir, you, come you hither, sir.   Who am I,
sir?

OSWALD.   My lady's father.

LEAR.   "My lady's father"!   My lord's knave!   You
   whoreson dog! you slave! you cur!

OSWALD.   I am none of these, my lord; I beseech
   your pardon.

LEAR.   Do you bandy looks with me, you rascal?
                              [Striking him]

OSWALD.   I'll not be strucken, my lord.   89

KENT.   Nor tripp'd neither, you base foot-ball
   player.   [Tripping up his heels]

LEAR.   I thank thee, fellow.   Thou serv'st me, and
   I'll love thee.

KENT.   Come, sir, arise, away!   I'll teach you differences.   Away, away!   If you will measure your
lubber's length again, tarry; but away! go to.   Have
you wisdom?   So.   [Pushes Oswald out]

LEAR.   Now, my friendly knave, I thank thee.
   There's earnest of thy service.   99
                        [Giving Kent money]

differences: propriety

earnest: advance payment

Enter FOOL

FOOL.   Let me hire him too; here's my coxcomb.
                        [Offering Kent his cap]

LEAR.   How now, my pretty knave! how dost
   thou?

FOOL.   Sirrah, you were best take my coxcomb.

[KENT.   Why, Fool?]

FOOL.   Why? For taking one's part that's out of
    favour. Nay, an thou canst not smile as the
wind sits, thou'lt catch cold shortly. There, take my
coxcomb. Why, this fellow has banish'd two   108
on 's daughters, and did the third a blessing against
his will; if thou follow him, thou must needs wear
my coxcomb. — How now, nuncle! Would I had
two coxcombs and two daughters!

LEAR.   Why, my boy?

FOOL.   If I gave them all my living, I'd keep my
    coxcombs myself. There's mine; beg another of
thy daughters.

LEAR.   Take heed, sirrah; the whip.

FOOL.   Truth's a dog must to kennel; he must be
    whipp'd out, when the Lady brach may stand by   **brach: bitch**
the fire and stink.   120

LEAR.   A pestilent gall to me!

FOOL.   Sirrah, I'll teach thee a speech.

LEAR.   Do.

FOOL.   Mark it, nuncle:
        "Have more than thou showest,
        Speak less than thou knowest,
        Lend less than thou owest,   **owest: ownest**
        Ride more than thou goest,   **goest: walkest**
        Learn more than thou trowest,   **trowest: trustest**
        Set less than thou throwest;   130 **Set: stake. throwest: (in dice)**
        Leave thy drink and thy whore,
        And keep in-a-door,
        And thou shalt have more
        Than two tens to a score."

KENT.   This is nothing, Fool.

FOOL.   Then 'tis like the breath of an unfee'd
    lawyer; you gave me nothing for't. Can you
make no use of nothing, nuncle?

LEAR.   Why, no, boy; nothing can be made out
    of nothing.   140

FOOL.   [To Kent] Prithee, tell him so much the
    rent of his land comes to. He will not believe a
Fool.

LEAR.   A bitter fool!

FOOL.   Dost thou know the difference, my boy,
    between a bitter fool and a sweet one?

LEAR.   No, lad; teach me.

[FOOL.   "That lord that counsell'd thee
        To give away thy land,
        Come place him here by me,   150
        Do thou for him stand:

The sweet and bitter fool
   Will presently appear;
The one in motley here,
   The other found out there."

LEAR.   Dost thou call me fool, boy?

FOOL.   All thy other titles thou hast given away;
that thou wast born with.

KENT.   This is not altogether fool, my lord.   159

FOOL.   No, faith, lords and great men will not
let me; if I had a monopoly out, they would
have part on't. And ladies, too, they will not let me
have all the fool to myself; they'll be snatching.]
Nuncle, give me an egg, and I'll give thee two crowns.

LEAR.   What two crowns shall they be?

FOOL.   Why, after I have cut the egg i' th' middle
and eat up the meat, the two crowns of the egg.
When thou clovest thy crown i' th' middle and   168
gav'st away both parts, thou bor'st thine ass on thy
back o'er the dirt. Thou hadst little wit in thy bald
crown when thou gav'st thy golden one away. If I
speak like myself in this, let him be whipp'd that first   **myself: a fool**
finds it so.

   "Fools had ne'er less grace in a year;
      For wise men are grown foppish,
   And know not how their wits to wear,
      Their manners are so apish."

LEAR.   When were you wont to be so full of   178
songs, sirrah?

FOOL.   I have used it, nuncle, e'er since thou
mad'st thy daughters thy mothers; for when
thou gav'st them the rod, and puttest down thine
own breeches,

   "Then they for sudden joy did weep,
      And I for sorrow sung,
   That such a king should play bo-peep,
      And go the fools among."

Prithee, nuncle, keep a schoolmaster that can   188
teach thy Fool to lie. I would fain learn to lie.

LEAR.   And you lie, sirrah, we'll have you whipp'd.

FOOL.   I marvel what kin thou and thy daughters
are. They'll have me whipp'd for speaking true,
thou'lt have me whipp'd for lying; and sometimes I
am whipp'd for holding my peace. I had rather be
any kind o' thing than a Fool; and yet I would not
be thee, nuncle; thou hast pared thy wit o' both sides,
and left nothing i' th' middle. Here comes one o' the
parings.

   Enter GONERIL

LEAR. How now, daughter! what makes that
   frontlet on? [Methinks] you are too much of   **frontlet: frown**
late i' th' frown.   201

   FOOL. Thou wast a pretty fellow when thou
   hadst no need to care for her frowning; now
thou art an O without a figure. I am better than
thou art now; I am a Fool, thou art nothing. [*To
Goneril*] Yes, forsooth, I will hold my tongue; so
your face bids me, though you say nothing. Mum,
mum,

> "He that keeps nor crust nor crumb,
>   Weary of all, shall want some."   210

[*Pointing to Lear*] That's a sheal'd peascod.   **sheal'd: empty**

   GONERIL. Not only, sir, this your all-licens'd Fool,
But other of your insolent retinue
Do hourly carp and quarrel, breaking forth
In rank and not-to-be-endured riots. Sir,
I had thought, by making this well known unto you,
To have found a safe redress; but now grow fearful,
By what yourself, too, late have spoke and done,
That you protect this course and put it on   **put it on: encourage it**
By your allowance; which if you should, the fault 220 **allowance: approval**
Would not scape censure, nor the redresses sleep,
Which, in the tender of a wholesome weal,   **tender of: care for. weal: com-**
Might in their working do you that offence,   **monweal**
Which else were shame, that then necessity   **that then: but**
Will call discreet proceeding.

   FOOL. For, you know, nuncle,
> "The hedge-sparrow fed the cuckoo so long,
>   That it had it head bit off by it young."
So, out went the candle, and we were left darkling. **darkling: in the dark**

   LEAR. Are you our daughter?   230

   GONERIL. [Come, sir,]
I would you would make use of your good wisdom,
Whereof I know you are fraught, and put away   **fraught: furnished with**
These dispositions which of late transport you
From what you rightly are.

   FOOL. May not an ass know when the cart draws
   the horse? "Whoop, Jug! I love thee."

   LEAR. Doth any here know me? This is not
   Lear.
Doth Lear walk thus? speak thus? Where are his
   eyes?
Either his notion weakens, his discernings   240 **notion: mental power**
Are lethargied — Ha! waking? 'Tis not so.
Who is it that can tell me who I am?

FOOL.   Lear's shadow.

[LEAR.   I would learn that; for, by the marks of   by . . . of: tested by
   sovereignty, knowledge, and reason, I should be
false persuaded I had daughters.

FOOL.   Which they will make an obedient father.]

LEAR.   Your name, fair gentlewoman?

GONERIL.   This admiration, sir, is much o' the   admiration: (pretended) surprise
   savour
Of other your new pranks. I do beseech you   250
To understand my purposes aright.
As you are old and reverend, should be wise.
Here do you keep a hundred knights and squires,
Men so disorder'd, so debosh'd and bold,   debosh'd: debauched
That this our court, infected with their manners,
Shows like a riotous inn. Epicurism and lust
Makes it more like a tavern or a brothel
Than a grac'd palace. The shame itself doth speak
For instant remedy. Be then desir'd
By her, that else will take the thing she begs,   260
A little to disquantity your train;   disquantity: reduce
And the remainders that shall still depend   depend: be your dependants
To be such men as may besort your age,   besort: suit
Which know themselves and you.

LEAR.   Darkness and devils!
Saddle my horses; call my train together!
Degenerate bastard! I'll not trouble thee;
Yet have I left a daughter.

GONERIL.   You strike my people; and your disorder'd rabble
Make servants of their betters.

Enter ALBANY

LEAR.   Woe, that too late repents! — [O, sir, are
   you come?]   270
Is it your will? Speak, sir. — Prepare my horses. —
Ingratitude, thou marble-hearted fiend,
More hideous when thou show'st thee in a child
Than the sea-monster!

ALBANY.   Pray, sir, be patient.

LEAR.   [To Goneril]   Detested kite! thou liest.
My train are men of choice and rarest parts,
That all particulars of duty know,
And in the most exact regard support
The worships of their name. O most small fault,   worships . . . name: their honor-
How ugly didst thou in Cordelia show!   280   able reputation
Which, like an engine, wrench'd my frame of nature   engine: rack
From the fix'd place; drew from my heart all love
And added to the gall. O Lear, Lear, Lear!

Beat at this gate, that let thy folly in
                                    [*Striking his head*]
And thy dear judgement out! Go, go, my people.
    ALBANY. My lord, I am guiltless as I am ignorant
Of what hath moved you.
    LEAR.   It may be so, my lord.
Hear, Nature! hear, dear goddess, hear!
Suspend thy purpose, if thou didst intend
To màke this creature fruitful!   290
Into her womb convey sterility!
Dry up in her the organs of increase,
And from her derogate body never spring   **derogate:** debased
A babe to honour her! If she must teem,
Create her child of spleen, that it may live
And be a thwart disnatur'd torment to her!   **thwart:** distorted, perverse. **dis-**
Let it stamp wrinkles in her brow of youth,   **natur'd:** unnatural
With cadent tears fret channels in her cheeks, **cadent:** falling
Turn all her mother's pains and benefits
To laughter and contempt, that she may feel   300
How sharper than a serpent's tooth it is
To have a thankless child! — Away, away!   [*Exit*
    ALBANY. Now, gods that we adore, whereof comes
      this?
    GONERIL. Never afflict yourself to know more
    of it,
But let his disposition have that scope
As dotage gives it.

          Re-enter LEAR

    LEAR. What, fifty of my followers at a clap!
Within a fortnight!
    ALBANY.   What's the matter, sir?
    LEAR. I'll tell thee. [*To Goneril*] Life and death!
    I am asham'd   309
That thou hast power to shake my manhood thus;
That these hot tears, which break from me perforce,
Should make thee worth them. Blasts and fogs upon
    thee!
Th' untented woundings of a father's curse   **untented:** not to be probed
Pierce every sense about thee! Old fond eyes,
Beweep this cause again, I'll pluck ye out,
And cast you, with the waters that you loose,
To temper clay. Ha! [is it come to this?]
Let it be so: I have another daughter,
Who, I am sure, is kind and comfortable.   **comfortable:** comforting
When she shall hear this of thee, with her nails 320
She'll flay thy wolvish visage. Thou shalt find

That I'll resume the shape which thou dost think
I have cast off for ever. [Thou shalt, I warrant thee.]
                 [Exeunt [Lear, Kent, and attendants]
   GONERIL.   Do you mark that?
   ALBANY.   I cannot be so partial, Goneril,
To the great love I bear you, —
   GONERIL.   Pray you, content. — What, Oswald,
     ho!
[To the Fool] You sir, more knave than fool, after
     your master.
   FOOL.   Nuncle Lear, nuncle Lear, tarry! Take the
     Fool with thee.   330
        A fox, when one has caught her,
        And such a daughter,
        Should sure to the slaughter,
        If my cap would buy a halter.
        So the Fool follows after.   [Exit
   GONERIL.   This man hath had good counsel, — a
     hundred knights!
'Tis politic and safe to let him keep
At point a hundred knights; yes, that, on every   **At point: armed**
     dream,
Each buzz, each fancy, each complaint, dislike,
He may enguard his dotage with their powers,   340
And hold our lives in mercy. Oswald, I say!   **in mercy: at his mercy**
   ALBANY.   Well, you may fear too far.
   GONERIL.   Safer than trust too far.
Let me still take away the harms I fear,
Not fear still to be taken. I know his heart.
What he hath utter'd I have writ my sister.
If she sustain him and his hundred knights,
When I have show'd th' unfitness, —

       Re-enter Steward [OSWALD]

             How now, Oswald!
What, have you writ that letter to my sister?
   OSWALD.   Ay, madam.
   GONERIL.   Take you some company, and away to
     horse.   350
Inform her full of my particular fear;
And thereto add such reasons of your own
As may compact it more. Get you gone;   **compact: confirm**
And hasten your return. [Exit Oswald] No, no, my
     lord,
This milky gentleness and course of yours
Though I condemn not, yet, under pardon,
You are much more at task for want of wisdom   **at task: to be blamed**
Than prais'd for harmful mildness.

ALBANY.   How far your eyes may pierce I cannot
   tell.
Striving to better, oft we mar what's well.   360
   GONERIL.   Nay, then —
   ALBANY.   Well, well; th' event.   [*Exeunt*

th' event: (we'll see) the outcome

SCENE V   [*Court before the same*]

Enter LEAR, KENT, *and* FOOL

   LEAR.   Go you before to Gloucester with these letters. Acquaint my daughter no further with anything you know than comes from her demand out of
the letter. If your diligence be not speedy, I shall
be there afore you.
   KENT.   I will not sleep, my lord, till I have delivered your letter.   [*Exit*
   FOOL.   If a man's brains were in 's heels, were't
   not in danger of kibes?

kibes: chilblains

   LEAR.   Ay, boy.   10
   FOOL.   Then, I prithee, be merry; thy wit shall
   not go slip-shod.

slip-shod: in slippers

   LEAR.   Ha, ha, ha!
   FOOL.   Shalt see thy other daughter will use thee
   kindly; for though she's as like this as a crab's
like an apple, yet I can tell what I can tell.

kindly: (1) in friendly fashion, (2) according to her nature

   LEAR.   What canst tell, boy?
   FOOL.   She will taste as like this as a crab does to a
   crab. Thou canst tell why one's nose stands i'
th' middle on 's face?   20
   LEAR.   No.
   FOOL.   Why, to keep one's eyes of either side 's
   nose, that what a man cannot smell out, he may
spy into.
   LEAR.   I did her wrong —
   FOOL.   Canst tell how an oyster makes his shell?
   LEAR.   No.
   FOOL.   Nor I neither; but I can tell why a snail
   has a house.
   LEAR.   Why?   30
   FOOL.   Why, to put 's head in; not to give it away
   to his daughters and leave his horns without a
case.
   LEAR.   I will forget my nature. So kind a father!
   Be my horses ready?
   FOOL.   Thy asses are gone about 'em. The reason
   why the seven stars are no moe than seven is a
pretty reason.

seven stars: the Pleiades

LEAR. Because they are not eight?   39
FOOL. Yes, indeed. Thou wouldst make a good
   Fool.
LEAR. To take 't again perforce! Monster in-   take 't again: resume authority
   gratitude!
FOOL. If thou wert my Fool, nuncle, I'd have
   thee beaten for being old before thy time.
LEAR. How's that?
FOOL. Thou shouldst not have been old till thou
   hadst been wise.
LEAR. O, let me not be mad, not mad, sweet
   heaven!
Keep me in temper; I would not be mad!   50

[Enter GENTLEMAN]

How now! are the horses ready?
GENTLEMAN. Ready, my lord.
LEAR. Come, boy.
FOOL. She that's a maid now, and laughs at my
   departure,
Shall not be a maid long, unless things be cut
   shorter.   [Exeunt

ACT II

SCENE I [The Earl of Gloucester's castle]

Enter Bastard [EDMUND] and CURAN, severally

EDMUND. Save thee, Curan.   Save: God save
CURAN. And you, sir. I have been with your
   father, and given him notice that the Duke of
Cornwall and Regan his duchess will be here with
him this night.
EDMUND. How comes that?
CURAN. Nay, I know not. You have heard of the
   news abroad; I mean the whisper'd ones, for
they are yet but ear-kissing arguments?   ear-kissing arguments: whispered
EDMUND. Not I. Pray you, what are they?   10   topics
CURAN. Have you heard of no likely wars toward, toward: imminent
   'twixt the Dukes of Cornwall and Albany?
EDMUND. Not a word.
CURAN. You may do, then, in time. Fare you
   well, sir.   [Exit
EDMUND. The Duke be here to-night! The bet-
   ter! best!
This weaves itself perforce into my business.
My father hath set guard to take my brother;
And I have one thing, of a queasy question,   of . . . question: requiring deli-
Which I must act. Briefness and Fortune, work! 20 cate handling

Enter EDGAR

Brother, a word; descend. Brother, I say!
My father watches; O sir, fly this place;
Intelligence is given where you are hid;
You have now the good advantage of the night.
Have you not spoken 'gainst the Duke of Cornwall?
He's coming hither, now, i' th' night, i' th' haste,
And Regan with him. Have you nothing said
Upon his party 'gainst the Duke of Albany?
Advise yourself.   **Advise yourself:** consider

    EDGAR.   I am sure on't, not a word.
    EDMUND.   I hear my father coming. Pardon me,   30
In cunning I must draw my sword upon you.
Draw; seem to defend yourself; now quit you well.   **quit you:** acquit yourself
Yield! Come before my father. Light, ho, here! —
Fly, brother. — Torches, torches! — So, farewell
                              [*Exit Edgar*
Some blood drawn on me would beget opinion
                          [*Wounds his arm*]
Of my more fierce endeavour. I have seen drunkards
Do more than this in sport. — Father, father! —
Stop, stop! — No help?

   Enter GLOUCESTER, *and* Servants *with torches*

    GLOUCESTER.   Now, Edmund, where's the villain?
    EDMUND.   Here stood he in the dark, his sharp
    sword out,   40
Mumbling of wicked charms, conjuring the moon
To stand ['s] auspicious mistress, —   **stand . . . mistress:** shed favor-
    GLOUCESTER.   But where is he?   able influence on him
    EDMUND.   Look, sir, I bleed.
    GLOUCESTER.   Where is the villain, Edmund?
    EDMUND.   Fled this way, sir. When by no means
    he could —
    GLOUCESTER.   Pursue him, ho! Go after. [*Exeunt
    some Servants*] By no means what?
    EDMUND.   Persuade me to the murder of your
    lordship;
But that I told him, the revenging gods
'Gainst parricides did all the thunder bend;
Spoke, with how manifold and strong a bond
The child was bound to th' father; sir, in fine,   50   **fine:** brief
Seeing how loathly opposite I stood
To his unnatural purpose, in fell motion,   **in fell motion:** with a fierce stab
With his prepared sword he charges home
My unprovided body, latch'd mine arm;   **unprovided:** unprotected. **latch'd:**
And when he saw my best alarum'd spirits,   caught
Bold in the quarrel's right, rous'd to th' encounter,

Or whether gasted by the noise I made,   gasted: scared
Full suddenly he fled.
    GLOUCESTER.   Let him fly far.
Not in this land shall he remain uncaught;
And found, — dispatch. The noble Duke my mas-
    ter,   60
My worthy arch and patron, comes to-night.   arch: chief
By his authority I will proclaim it,
That he which finds him shall deserve our thanks,
Bringing the murderous coward to the stake;
He that conceals him, death.
    EDMUND.   When I dissuaded him from his intent,   dissuaded: tried to dissuade
And found him pight to do it, with curst speech   pight: pitched, determined. curst:
I threaten'd to discover him; he replied,   angry. discover: reveal
"Thou unpossessing bastard! dost thou think,
If I would stand against thee, would the reposal   70
Of any trust, virtue, or worth in thee
Make thy words faith'd? No! what [I should]   faith'd: trusted
    deny, —
As this I would; [ay,] though thou didst produce
My very character, — I'd turn it all
To thy suggestion, plot, and damned practice;
And thou must make a dullard of the world   world: everyone
If they not thought the profits of my death
Were very pregnant and potential [spurs]
To make thee seek it."
    GLOUCESTER.   O strange and fast'ned villain!   fast'ned: hardened
Would he deny his letter? [I never got him.]   80
                    [Tucket within   Tucket: flourish on a trumpet
Hark, the Duke's trumpets! I know not [why] he
    comes.
All ports I'll bar, the villain shall not scape;   ports: exits
The Duke must grant me that. Besides, his picture
I will send far and near, that all the kingdom
May have due note of him; and of my land,
Loyal and natural boy, I'll work the means
To make thee capable.   capable: able to inherit

      Enter CORNWALL, REGAN, *and Attendants*

    CORNWALL.   How now, my noble friend! since I
    came hither,
Which I can call but now, I have heard [strange
    news].
    REGAN.   If it be true, all vengeance comes too
    short   90
Which can pursue th' offender. How dost, my lord?
    GLOUCESTER.   O, madam, my old heart is crack'd,
    it's crack'd!

REGAN.   What, did my father's godson seek your
    life?
He whom my father nam'd? your Edgar?
    GLOUCESTER.   O, lady, lady, shame would have it
    hid!
    REGAN.   Was he not companion with the riotous
    knights
That tended upon my father?
    GLOUCESTER.   I know not, madam. 'Tis too bad,
    too bad.
    EDMUND.   Yes, madam, he was of that consort.
    REGAN.   No marvel, then, though he were ill
    affected: 100
'Tis they have put him on the old man's death,
To have th' expense and waste of his revenues.   **expense and waste:** power of
                                                            spending and wasting
I have this present evening from my sister
Been well inform'd of them; and with such cautions,
That if they come to sojourn at my house,
I'll not be there.
    CORNWALL.   Nor I, assure thee, Regan.
Edmund, I hear that you have shown your father
A child-like office.   **child-like:** filial
    EDMUND.   'Twas my duty, sir.
    GLOUCESTER.   He did bewray his practice; and   **bewray:** reveal
    receiv'd
This hurt you see, striving to apprehend him.   110
    CORNWALL.   Is he pursued?
    GLOUCESTER.   Ay, my good lord.
    CORNWALL.   If he be taken he shall never more
Be fear'd of doing harm. Make your own purpose,
How in my strength you please. For you, Edmund,   **strength:** authority
Whose virtue and obedience doth this instant
So much commend itself, you shall be ours.
Natures of such deep trust we shall much need;
You we first seize on.
    EDMUND.   I shall serve you, sir,
Truly, however else.
    GLOUCESTER.   For him I thank your Grace.
    CORNWALL.   You know not why we came to visit
    you, —   120
    REGAN.   Thus out of season, threading dark-ey'd
    night?
Occasions, noble Gloucester, of some prize,   **prize:** importance
Wherein we must have use of your advice.
Our father he hath writ, so hath our sister,
Of differences, which I best thought it fit
To answer from our home; the several messengers   **from:** away from
From hence attend dispatch. Our good old friend,

Lay comforts to your bosom; and bestow
Your needful counsel to our businesses,
Which craves the instant use.

GLOUCESTER.   I serve you, madam.   130
Your Graces are right welcome.   [*Exeunt. Flourish*

SCENE II [*Before Gloucester's castle*]

    Enter KENT *and Steward* [OSWALD], *severally*

OSWALD.   Good dawning to thee, friend. Art of
    this house?

KENT.   Ay.

OSWALD.   Where may we set our horses?

KENT.   I' th' mire.

OSWALD.   Prithee, if thou lov'st me, tell me.

KENT.   I love thee not.

OSWALD.   Why, then, I care not for thee.

KENT.   If I had thee in Lipsbury pinfold, I would
    make thee care for me.   10

OSWALD.   Why dost thou use me thus? I know
    thee not.

KENT.   Fellow, I know thee.

OSWALD.   What dost thou know me for?

KENT.   A knave; a rascal; an eater of broken
    meats; a base, proud, shallow, beggarly, three-
suited, hundred-pound, filthy, worsted-stocking knave;
a lily-livered, action-taking, whoreson, glass-gazing,
superserviceable, finical rogue; one-trunk-inheriting
slave; one that wouldst be a bawd in way of   20
good service, and art nothing but the composition
of a knave, beggar, coward, pandar, and the son
and heir of a mongrel bitch; one whom I will beat
into clamorous whining, if thou deni'st the least syllable of thy addition.

OSWALD.   Why, what a monstrous fellow art thou,
thus to rail on one that is neither known of thee nor
knows thee!

KENT.   What a brazen-fac'd varlet art thou, to
    deny thou knowest me! Is it two days since   30
I tripp'd up thy heels, and beat thee before the
King? Draw, you rogue; for, though it be night,
yet the moon shines. I'll make a sop o' th' moon-
shine of you, you whoreson cullionly barber-monger!
Draw!   [*Drawing his sword*]

OSWALD.   Away! I have nothing to do with thee.

KENT.   Draw, you rascal! You come with letters
    against the King; and take Vanity the puppet's

pinfold: pen for enclosing stray animals

broken meats: food scraps

lily-livered: cowardly. **action-taking:** preferring going to law to fighting. **glass-gazing:** vain. **superserviceable:** officious.
composition: combination

thy addition: the titles I have given you

cullionly: rascally. **barber-monger:** frequenter of barber-shops

part against the royalty of her father. Draw, you   39
rogue, or I'll so carbonado your shanks, — draw, you
rascal! Come your ways.

OSWALD.   Help, ho! murder! help!

KENT.   Strike, you slave! Stand, rogue, stand!
You neat slave, strike.   [*Beating him*]

OSWALD.   Help, ho! murder! murder!

Enter Bastard [EDMUND] *with his rapier drawn,*
CORNWALL, REGAN, GLOUCESTER, *and* Servants

EDMUND.   How now! What's the matter? Part.

KENT.   With you, goodman boy, if you please.
Come, I'll flesh ye; come on, young master.

GLOUCESTER.   Weapons! arms! What's the matter here?   50

CORNWALL.   Keep peace, upon your lives!
He dies that strikes again. What is the matter?

REGAN.   The messengers from our sister and the
King.

CORNWALL.   What is your difference? Speak.

OSWALD.   I am scarce in breath, my lord.

KENT.   No marvel, you have so bestirr'd your
valour. You cowardly rascal, Nature disclaims
in thee. A tailor made thee.

CORNWALL.   Thou art a strange fellow. A tailor
make a man?   61

KENT.   A tailor, sir. A stone-cutter or a painter
could not have made him so ill, though they had
been but two years o' th' trade.

CORNWALL.   Speak yet, how grew your quarrel?

OSWALD.   This ancient ruffian, sir, whose life I
have spar'd at suit of his grey beard, —

KENT.   Thou whoreson zed! thou unnecessary
letter! My lord, if you will give me leave, I   69
will tread this unbolted villain into mortar, and daub
the wall of a jakes with him. Spare my grey beard,
you wagtail?

CORNWALL.   Peace, sirrah!
You beastly knave, know you no reverence?

KENT.   Yes, sir; but anger hath a privilege.

CORNWALL.   Why art thou angry?

KENT.   That such a slave as this should wear a
sword,
Who wears no honesty. Such smiling rogues as these,
Like rats, oft bite the holy cords a-twain
Which are too intrinse t' unloose; smooth every
passion   80
That in the natures of their lords rebel;

Glosses (right margin):

carbonado: slash

neat: foppish

goodman: peasant

difference: disagreement

disclaims in: renounces

zed: Z, often omitted in old dictionaries

unbolted: coarse

jakes: privy

holy cords: i.e., of natural affection. intrinse: intricate

[Bring] oil to fire, snow to their colder moods;
[Renege,] affirm, and turn their halcyon beaks
With every gale and vary of their masters,
Knowing nought, like dogs, but following.
A plague upon your epileptic visage!
Smile you my speeches, as I were a fool?
Goose, if I had you upon Sarum Plain,
I'd drive ye cackling home to Camelot.

halcyon: kingfisher, which, if hung up, was believed always to turn with its bill to the wind. vary: variance

Sarum: Salisbury
Camelot: Winchester

    CORNWALL.   What, art thou mad, old fellow?   90
    GLOUCESTER.   How fell you out? Say that.
    KENT.   No contraries hold more antipathy
Than I and such a knave.
    CORNWALL.   Why dost thou call him knave?
      What is his fault?
    KENT.   His countenance likes me not.

likes: pleases

    CORNWALL.   No more, perchance, does mine, nor
      his, nor hers.
    KENT.   Sir, 'tis my occupation to be plain;
I have seen better faces in my time
Than stands on any shoulder that I see
Before me at this instant.

    CORNWALL.   This is some fellow   100
Who, having been prais'd for bluntness, doth affect
A saucy roughness, and constrains the garb
Quite from his nature. He cannot flatter, he;
An honest mind and plain, he must speak truth!
An they will take it, so; if not, he's plain.
These kind of knaves I know, which in this plainness
Harbour more craft and more corrupter ends
Than twenty silly ducking observants
That stretch their duties nicely.

constrains the garb: forces the manner

observants: obsequious attendants
nicely: punctiliously

    KENT.   Sir, in good sooth, in sincere verity,   110
Under the allowance of your great aspect,
Whose influence, like the wreath of radiant fire
On [flickering] Phœbus' front, —
    CORNWALL.   What mean'st by this?
    KENT.   To go out of my dialect, which you dis-
      commend so much. I know, sir, I am no flat-
terer. He that beguil'd you in a plain accent was a
plain knave; which for my part I will not be, though
I should win your displeasure to entreat me to't.
    CORNWALL.   What was th' offence you gave him?
    OSWALD.   I never gave him any.   120
It pleas'd the King his master very late
To strike at me, upon his misconstruction;
When he, compact, and flattering his displeasure,
Tripp'd me behind; being down, insulted, rail'd,
And put upon him such a deal of man
[That 't] worthied him, got praises of the King

compact: taking his side

put . . . man: took such a heroic attitude

For him attempting who was self-subdued;
And, in the fleshment of this [dread] exploit,
Drew on me here again.

  KENT.   None of these rogues and cowards
But Ajax is their fool.

  CORNWALL.   Fetch forth the stocks! 130
You stubborn ancient knave, you reverend braggart,
We'll teach you —

  KENT.   Sir, I am too old to learn.
Call not your stocks for me; I serve the King,
On whose employment I was sent to you.
You shall do small respects, show too bold malice
Against the grace and person of my master,
Stocking his messenger.

  CORNWALL. Fetch forth the stocks! As I have
  life and honour,
There shall he sit till noon.

  REGAN. Till noon! Till night, my lord; and all
  night too. 140

  KENT. Why, madam, if I were your father's dog,
You should not use me so.

  REGAN.   Sir, being his knave, I will.
          [Stocks brought out

  CORNWALL. This is a fellow of the self-same
  colour
Our sister speaks of. Come, bring away the stocks!

  GLOUCESTER. Let me beseech your Grace not to
  do so.
[His fault is much, and the good King his master
Will check him for't. Your purpos'd low correction
Is such as basest and contemned'st wretches
For pilferings and most common trespasses
Are punish'd with.] The King must take it ill 150
That he, so slightly valued in his messenger,
Should have him thus restrain'd.

  CORNWALL.   I'll answer that.

  REGAN. My sister may receive it much more worse
To have her gentleman abus'd, assaulted,
[For following her affairs. Put in his legs.]
      [Kent is put in the stocks.]
[Come, my good] lord, away.
    [Exeunt [all but Gloucester and Kent]

  GLOUCESTER. I am sorry for thee, friend; 'tis the
  Duke's pleasure,
Whose disposition, all the world well knows,
Will not be rubb'd nor stopp'd. I'll entreat for thee.

  KENT. Pray, do not, sir. I have watch'd and
  travell'd hard; 160
Some time I shall sleep out, the rest I'll whistle.

attempting: attacking
fleshment: excitement from first success

Ajax: a foolish counselor

away: out

watch'd: been awake long

A good man's fortune may grow out at heels.   **grow . . . heels:** turn to bad luck
Give you good morrow!
    GLOUCESTER. The Duke's to blame in this; 'twill
        be ill taken.   [*Exit*
    KENT. Good King, that must approve the com-   **approve . . . saw:** prove the prov-
        mon saw,   erb true
Thou out of heaven's benediction com'st   **out . . . sun:** from better to worse
To the warm sun!
Approach, thou beacon to this under globe,
That by thy comfortable beams I may
Peruse this letter! Nothing almost sees miracles   170
But misery. I know 'tis from Cordelia,
Who hath most fortunately been inform'd
Of my obscured course; [*reads*] " — and shall find
    time
From this enormous state — seeking to give
Losses their remedies." — All weary and o'er-watch'd,
Take vantage, heavy eyes, not to behold
This shameful lodging.
Fortune, good-night! Smile once more; turn thy
    wheel!   [*Sleeps*]

[SCENE III   *The same*]

Enter EDGAR

    EDGAR. I heard myself proclaim'd;   **proclaim'd:** called
And by the happy hollow of a tree
Escap'd the hunt. No port is free; no place
That guard and most unusual vigilance
Does not attend my taking. Whiles I may scape   **attend my taking:** wait to capture
I will preserve myself, and am bethought   me
To take the basest and most poorest shape
That ever penury, in contempt of man,
Brought near to beast. My face I'll grime with filth,
Blanket my loins, elf all my hairs in knots,   10   **elf:** tangle as in elf-locks
And with presented nakedness out-face   **presented:** exposed
The winds and persecutions of thy sky.
The country gives me proof and precedent
Of Bedlam beggars, who, with roaring voices,
Strike in their numb'd and mortified arms
Pins, wooden pricks, nails, sprigs of rosemary;
And with this horrible object, from low farms,   **object:** aspect
Poor pelting villages, sheep-cotes, and mills,   **pelting:** petty
Sometimes with lunatic bans, sometimes with prayers,   **bans:** curses
Enforce their charity. Poor Turlygod! poor Tom!   20
That's something yet. Edgar I nothing am.   **Edgar . . . am:** Of Edgar nothing
                                [*Exit*   will remain.

[SCENE IV *The same*]

    Enter LEAR, FOOL, *and* GENTLEMAN [KENT
           in the stocks]

  LEAR. 'Tis strange that they should so depart
from home,
And not send back my messengers.
  GENTLEMAN.   As I learn'd,
The night before there was no purpose in them
Of this remove.
  KENT.   Hail to thee, noble master!
  LEAR. Ha!
Mak'st thou this shame thy pastime?
  KENT.   No, my lord.
  FOOL. Ha, ha! he wears cruel garters. Horses are
tied by the heads, dogs and bears by th' neck,
monkeys by th' loins, and men by th' legs. When a
man's over-lusty at legs, then he wears wooden 10
nether-stocks.

             nether-stocks: stockings

  LEAR. What's he that hath so much thy place
mistook
To set thee here?
  KENT.   It is both he and she;
Your son and daughter.
  LEAR. No.
  KENT. Yes.
  LEAR. No, I say.
  KENT. I say, yea.
  [LEAR. No, no, they would not.
  KENT. Yes, they have.]   20
  LEAR. By Jupiter, I swear, no.
  KENT. By Juno, I swear, ay.
  LEAR.   They durst not do't;
They could not, would not do't. 'Tis worse than
murder
To do upon respect such violent outrage.
Resolve me with all modest haste which way
Thou mightst deserve, or they impose, this usage,
Coming from us.

             upon respect: deliberately
             Resolve: inform

  KENT.   My lord, when at their home
I did commend your Highness' letters to them,
Ere I was risen from the place that show'd
My duty kneeling, came there a reeking post,   30
Stew'd in his haste, half breathless, panting forth
From Goneril his mistress salutations;
Deliver'd letters, spite of intermission,
Which presently they read. On those contents,

             commend: deliver

             post: messenger
             Stew'd: fretting

             **spite of intermission: careless of
interrupting. presently: at once**

They summon'd up their meiny, straight took horse;   meiny: retinue
Commanded me to follow, and attend
The leisure of their answer; gave me cold looks:
And meeting here the other messenger,
Whose welcome, I perceiv'd, had poison'd mine, —
Being the very fellow which of late   40
Display'd so saucily against your Highness, —   Display'd: showed himself
Having more man than wit about me, drew.
He rais'd the house with loud and coward cries.
Your son and daughter found this trespass worth
The shame which here it suffers.
    FOOL. Winter's not gone yet, if the wild geese
      fly that way.
          "Fathers that wear rags
            Do make their children blind;
          But fathers that bear bags   50   bags: moneybags
            Shall see their children kind.
          Fortune, that arrant whore,
          Ne'er turns the key to th' poor."
But, for all this, thou shalt have as many dolours for   dolours: with a pun on dollars
thy daughters as thou canst tell in a year.   tell: count
    LEAR. O, how this mother swells up toward my   mother: hysteria
      heart!
Hysterica passio, down, thou climbing sorrow,   Hysterica passio: hysteria, causing
Thy element's below! — Where is this daughter?   choking
    KENT. With the Earl, sir, here within.
    LEAR.   Follow me not;
Stay here.   [*Exit* 60
    GENTLEMAN. Made you no more offence but
      what you speak of?
    KENT. None.
How chance the King comes with so small a number?
    FOOL. An thou hadst been set i' th' stocks for
      that question, thou'dst well deserv'd it.
    KENT. Why, Fool?
    FOOL. We'll set thee to school to an ant, to
      teach thee there's no labouring i' th' winter.
All that follow their noses are led by their eyes   70
but blind men; and there's not a nose among twenty
but can smell him that's stinking. Let go thy hold
when a great wheel runs down a hill, lest it break
thy neck with following; but the great one that
goes upward, let him draw thee after. When a wise
man gives thee better counsel, give me mine again;
I would have none but knaves follow it, since a fool
gives it.
      "That sir which serves and seeks for gain,
        And follows but for form,   80
      Will pack when it begins to rain,
        And leave thee in the storm.

But I will tarry; the Fool will stay,
    And let the wise man fly.
The knave turns fool that runs away;
    The Fool no knave, perdy."

       perdy: by God (par Dieu, Fr.)

Re-enter LEAR *and* GLOUCESTER

KENT. Where learn'd you this, Fool?

FOOL. Not i' th' stocks, fool.

LEAR. Deny to speak with me? They are sick?
    They are weary?
They have travell'd all the night? Mere fetches; 90   *fetches:* tricks
The images of revolt and flying off.   *images:* signs. **flying off:** deserting
Fetch me a better answer.

GLOUCESTER.   My dear lord,
You know the fiery quality of the Duke;
How unremovable and fix'd he is
In his own course.

LEAR. Vengeance! plague! death! confusion!
"Fiery"? What "quality"? Why, Gloucester, Gloucester,
I'd speak with the Duke of Cornwall and his wife.

GLOUCESTER. Well, my good lord, I have inform'd them so.

LEAR. "Inform'd" them! Dost thou understand
    me, man?   100

GLOUCESTER. Ay, my good lord.

LEAR. The King would speak with Cornwall; the
    dear father
Would with his daughter speak, commands [her]
    service.
Are they "inform'd" of this? My breath and blood!
"Fiery"? The fiery duke? Tell the hot duke that —
No, but not yet; may be he is not well.
Infirmity doth still neglect all office   *office:* duty
Whereto our health is bound; we are not ourselves
When Nature, being oppress'd, commands the mind
To suffer with the body. I'll forbear;   110
And am fallen out with my more headier will,   *headier:* impetuous
To take the indispos'd and sickly fit
For the sound man. — Death on my state! wherefore   [*Looking on Kent*]
Should he sit here? This act persuades me
That this remotion of the Duke and her   *remotion:* removal
Is practice only. Give me my servant forth.   *practice:* trickery
Go tell the Duke and 's wife I'd speak with them,
Now, presently. Bid them come forth and hear me,
Or at their chamber-door I'll beat the drum
Till it cry sleep to death.   120   *cry . . . death:* awakens everyone

GLOUCESTER. I would have all well betwixt you.
                      [*Exit*

LEAR. O me, my heart, my rising heart! But, down!

FOOL.   Cry to it, nuncle, as the cockney did to the eels when she put 'em i' th' paste alive; she knapp'd 'em o' th' coxcombs with a stick, and cried, "Down, wantons, down!" 'Twas her brother that, in pure kindness to his horse, buttered his hay.

Enter CORNWALL, REGAN, GLOUCESTER, *and Servants*

LEAR. Good morrow to you both.

CORNWALL.   Hail to your Grace!
                            [*Kent is set at liberty.*

REGAN. I am glad to see your Highness.   129

LEAR.   Regan, I think you are; I know what reason
I have to think so. If thou shouldst not be glad,
I would divorce me from thy mother's tomb,
Sepulchring an adulteress. [*To Kent*] O, are you free?
Some other time for that. Beloved Regan,
Thy sister's naught. O Regan, she hath tied   **naught: wicked**
Sharp-tooth'd unkindness, like a vulture, here.
                            [*Points to his heart*]
I can scarce speak to thee; thou'lt not believe
With how deprav'd a quality — O Regan!   **quality: manner**

REGAN.   I pray you, sir, take patience. I have hope
You less know how to value her desert   140
Than she to scant her duty.

LEAR.   Say, how is that?

REGAN.   I cannot think my sister in the least
Would fail her obligation. If, sir, perchance
She have restrain'd the riots of your followers,
'Tis on such ground and to such wholesome end
As clears her from all blame.

LEAR.   My curses on her!

REGAN.   O, sir, you are old;
Nature in you stands on the very verge
Of her confine. You should be rul'd and led   **confine: existence**
By some discretion that discerns your state   150
Better than you yourself. Therefore, I pray you,
That to our sister you do make return;
Say you have wrong'd her, sir.

LEAR.   Ask her forgiveness?
Do you but mark how this becomes the house: **house: royal family**
"Dear daughter, I confess that I am old;
Age is unnecessary. [*Kneeling*] On my knees I beg   **Age is unnecessary: Old people are useless.**
That you'll vouchsafe me raiment, bed, and food."

REGAN. Good sir, no more; these are unsightly
  tricks.
Return you to my sister.
  LEAR.   [Rising] Never, Regan:
She hath abated me of half my train;   160
Look'd black upon me; struck me with her tongue,
Most serpent-like, upon the very heart.
All the stor'd vengeances of heaven fall
On her ingrateful top! Strike her young bones,   **top: head. young bones: bones of**
You taking airs, with lameness!   **her unborn child. taking: infec-**
  CORNWALL.   Fie, sir, fie!   **tious**
  LEAR. You nimble lightnings, dart your blinding
    flames
Into her scornful eyes! Infect her beauty,
You fen-suck'd fogs, drawn by the powerful sun,
To fall and [blast her pride!]   169   **fall: humble**
  REGAN. O the blest gods! so will you wish on me,
When the rash mood is on.
  LEAR. No, Regan, thou shalt never have my curse.
Thy tender-hefted nature shall not give   **tender-hefted: gentle**
Thee o'er to harshness. Her eyes are fierce; but thine
Do comfort and not burn. 'Tis not in thee
To grudge my pleasures, to cut off my train,
To bandy hasty words, to scant my sizes,   **scant: reduce. sizes: allowances**
And in conclusion to oppose the bolt   **bolt: door**
Against my coming in. Thou better know'st
The offices of nature, bond of childhood,   180
Effects of courtesy, dues of gratitude.   **Effects: manifestations**
Thy half o' th' kingdom hast thou not forgot,
Wherein I thee endow'd.
  REGAN.   Good sir, to th' purpose.
                              [Tucket within
  LEAR. Who put my man i' th' stocks?

Enter Steward [OSWALD]

  CORNWALL.   What trumpet 's that?
  REGAN. I know 't; my sister's. This approves her
    letter,
That she would soon be here. [To Oswald] Is your
    lady come?
  LEAR. This is a slave whose easy-borrowed pride   **easy-borrowed: not justified by**
Dwells in the [fickle] grace of her he follows.   **his qualities, but on the reflection**
Out, varlet, from my sight!   **of his mistress's position**
  CORNWALL.   What means your Grace?

Enter GONERIL

  LEAR. Who stock'd my servant? Regan, I have
    good hope   190

Thou didst not know on't. — Who comes here? O
   heavens,
If you do love old men, if your sweet sway
Allow obedience, if you yourselves are old,   **Allow:** approve
Make it your cause; send down, and take my part!   **it:** my cause
[*To Goneril*] Art not asham'd to look upon this
   beard?
O Regan, will you take her by the hand?
    GONERIL.   Why not by th' hand, sir? How have I
    offended?
All's not offence that indiscretion finds
And dotage terms so.
    LEAR.   O sides, you are too tough; **199**   **sides:** heart, breast
Will you yet hold? How came my man i' th' stocks?
    CORNWALL.   I set him there, sir; but his own dis-
    orders
Deserv'd much less advancement.   **advancement:** reward
    LEAR.   You! did you?
    REGAN.   I pray you, father, being weak, seem so.
If, till the expiration of your month,
You will return and sojourn with my sister,
Dismissing half your train, come then to me.
I am now from home, and out of that provision
Which shall be needful for your entertainment.
    LEAR.   Return to her, and fifty men dismiss'd!
No, rather I abjure all roofs, and choose   **210**
To wage against the enmity o' th' air;   **wage:** contend
To be a comrade with the wolf and owl, —
Necessity's sharp pinch. Return with her?
Why, the hot-blooded France, that dowerless took
Our youngest born, I could as well be brought
To knee his throne, and, squire-like, pension beg
To keep base life afoot. Return with her?
Persuade me rather to be slave and sumpter   **sumpter:** pack-horse
To this detested groom.   [*Pointing at Oswald*]
    GONERIL.   At your choice, sir.   **219**
    LEAR.   I prithee, daughter, do not make me mad;
I will not trouble thee, my child; farewell!
We'll no more meet, no more see one another.
But yet thou art my flesh, my blood, my daughter;
Or rather a disease that's in my flesh,
Which I must needs call mine; thou art a boil,
A plague-sore, an embossed carbuncle,   **embossed:** swollen
In my corrupted blood. But I'll not chide thee;
Let shame come when it will, I do not call it.
I do not bid the thunder-bearer shoot,
Nor tell tales of thee to high-judging Jove.   **230**
Mend when thou canst; be better at thy leisure.
I can be patient; I can stay with Regan,

I and my hundred knights.

REGAN.   Not altogether so;
I look'd not for you yet, nor am provided
For your fit welcome. Give ear, sir, to my sister;
For those that mingle reason with your passion   with: in response to
Must be content to think you old, and so —
But she knows what she does.

LEAR.   Is this well spoken?

REGAN.   I dare avouch it, sir. What, fifty fol-
    lowers!
Is it not well? What should you need of more?   240
Yea, or so many, sith that both charge and danger   charge: expense
Speak 'gainst so great a number? How, in one house,
Should many people under two commands
Hold amity? 'Tis hard; almost impossible.

GONERIL.   Why might not you, my lord, receive
    attendance
From those that she calls servants or from mine?

REGAN.   Why not, my lord? If then they chanc'd
    to slack ye,   slack: be lacking in their services
We could control them. If you will come to me, —
For now I spy a danger — I entreat you
To bring but five and twenty; to no more   250
Will I give place or notice.

LEAR.   I gave you all.

REGAN.   And in good time you gave it.

LEAR.   Made you my guardians, my depositaries,
But kept a reservation to be followed
With such a number. What, must I come to you
With five and twenty, Regan? Said you so?

REGAN.   And speak 't again, my lord; no more
    with me.

LEAR.   Those wicked creatures yet do look well-
    favour'd
When others are more wicked; not being the worst
Stands in some rank of praise. [To Goneril] I'll go
    with thee.   260
Thy fifty yet doth double five and twenty,
And thou art twice her love.

GONERIL.   Hear me, my lord:
What need you five and twenty, ten, or five,
To follow in a house where twice so many
Have a command to tend you?

REGAN.   What need one?

LEAR.   O, reason not the need! Our basest beggars   reason: examine
Are in the poorest thing superfluous.   Are . . . superfluous: have at the
Allow not nature more than nature needs,   worst more than bare necessities
Man's life is cheap as beast's. Thou art a lady;
If only to go warm were gorgeous,   270

Why, nature needs not what thou gorgeous wear'st,
Which scarcely keeps thee warm. But, for true
    need, —
You heavens, give me that patience, patience I need!
You see me here, you gods, a poor old man,
As full of grief as age; wretched in both!
If it be you that stirs these daughters' hearts
Against their father, fool me not so much   **fool:** humiliate
To bear it tamely; touch me with noble anger,   **To bear:** to force me to accept
And let not women's weapons, water-drops,
Stain my man's cheeks! No, you unnatural hags,   280
I will have such revenges on you both
That all the world shall — I will do such things, —
What they are, yet I know not; but they shall be
The terrors of the earth. You think I'll weep:
No, I'll not weep.
I have full cause of weeping; but this heart
                    (*Storm and tempest*)
Shall break into a hundred thousand flaws,   **flaws:** fragments
Or ere I'll weep. O, Fool! I shall go mad!
        [*Exeunt Lear, Gloucester, Kent, and Fool*
CORNWALL.   Let us withdraw; 'twill be a storm.
REGAN.   This house is little; the old man and 's
    people   290
Cannot be well bestow'd.
GONERIL.   'Tis his own blame; hath put himself
    from rest,
And must needs taste his folly.
REGAN.   For his particular, I'll receive him gladly,   **particular:** own self
But not one follower.
GONERIL.   So am I purpos'd.
Where is my Lord of Gloucester?

            Re-enter GLOUCESTER

CORNWALL.   Follow'd the old man forth. He is
    return'd.
GLOUCESTER.   The King is in high rage.
CORNWALL.   Whither is he going?
GLOUCESTER.   He calls to horse; but will I know
    not whither.
CORNWALL.   'Tis best to give him way; he leads   **leads himself:** does what he wants
    himself.   300
GONERIL.   My lord, entreat him by no means to
    stay.
GLOUCESTER.   Alack, the night comes on, and the
    high winds
Do sorely ruffle; for many miles about   **ruffle:** bluster
There 's scarce a bush.   **bush:** bush not blown
REGAN.   O, sir, to wilful men,

The injuries that they themselves procure
Must be their schoolmasters. Shut up your doors.
He is attended with a desperate train,
And what they may incense him to, being apt
To have his ear abus'd, wisdom bids fear.   abus'd: misled
   CORNWALL.   Shut up your doors, my lord; 'tis a
     wild night: 310
My Regan counsels well. Come out o' th' storm.
                            [*Exeunt*

ACT III

SCENE I [*The open country near Gloucester's castle*]

   Storm still. Enter KENT *and a* GENTLEMAN,
             severally

   KENT.   Who's there, besides foul weather?
   GENTLEMAN.   One minded like the weather, most   minded like: of the same mind as
     unquietly.
   KENT.   I know you. Where's the King?
   GENTLEMAN.   Contending with the fretful ele-
     ments;
Bids the wind blow the earth into the sea,
Or swell the curled waters 'bove the main,   main: mainland
That things might change or cease; [tears his white
   hair,
Which the impetuous blasts with eyeless rage
Catch in their fury, and make nothing of;
Strives in his little world of man to out-scorn   10
The to-and-fro-conflicting wind and rain.
This night, wherein the cub-drawn bear would couch,   cub-drawn: sucked dry
The lion and the belly-pinched wolf
Keep their fur dry, unbonneted he runs,
And bids what will take all.]
   KENT.   But who is with him?
   GENTLEMAN.   None but the Fool, who labours to
     outjest
His heart-struck injuries.
   KENT.   Sir, I do know you,
And dare upon the warrant of my note   note: knowledge (of you)
Commend a dear thing to you. There is division,   dear: important
Although as yet the face of it is cover'd   20
With mutual cunning, 'twixt Albany and Cornwall;
Who have — as who have not, that their great stars   stars: fates
Thron'd and set high? — servants, who seem no less,
Which are to France the spies and speculations   speculations: observers
Intelligent of our state. What hath been seen,   Intelligent: giving information
Either in snuffs and packings of the Dukes,   snuffs: resentments.   packings:
Or the hard rein which both of them have borne   plots

Against the old kind king, or something deeper,
Whereof perchance these are but furnishings —
[But, true it is, from France there comes a power   30   **power:** armed force
Into this scattered kingdom; who already,   **scattered:** divided
Wise in our negligence, have secret feet
In some of our best ports, and are at point   **at point:** ready
To show their open banner. Now to you:
If on my credit you dare build so far   **on my credit:** in trust of me.
To make your speed to Dover, you shall find   **build:** go ahead
Some that will thank you, making just report
Of how unnatural and bemadding sorrow
The King hath cause to plain.   **plain:** complain
I am a gentleman of blood and breeding;   40
And, from some knowledge and assurance, offer
This office to you.]   **office:** responsibility
    GENTLEMAN.   I will talk further with you.
    KENT.   No, do not.
For confirmation that I am much more
Than my out-wall, open this purse and take   **out-wall:** appearance
What it contains. If you shall see Cordelia, —
As fear not but you shall, — show her this ring,
And she will tell you who that fellow is
That yet you do not know. Fie on this storm!
I will go seek the King.   50
    GENTLEMAN.   Give me your hand. Have you no
      more to say?
    KENT.   Few words, but, to effect, more than all   **to effect:** in effect, in importance
      yet;
That, when we have found the King, — in which
      your pain   **pain:** search (is to go)
That way, I'll this, — he that first lights on him
Holla the other.   [*Exeunt* [*severally*]

SCENE II [*The same*] *Storm still*

      Enter LEAR *and* FOOL

    LEAR.   Blow, winds, and crack your cheeks! Rage!
      Blow!
You cataracts and hurricanoes, spout   **hurricanoes:** waterspouts
Till you have drench'd our steeples, drown'd the
    cocks!   **cocks:** weathercocks
You sulph'rous and thought-executing fires,
Vaunt-couriers of oak-cleaving thunderbolts,   **Vaunt-couriers:** forerunners
Singe my white head! And thou, all-shaking thunder,
Strike flat the thick rotundity o' th' world!
Crack nature's moulds, all germens spill at once   **germens,** germs, seeds
That makes ingrateful man!
    FOOL.   O nuncle, court holy-water in a dry   10   **court holy-water:** flattery
      house is better than this rain water out o' door.

Good nuncle, in; ask thy daughters' blessing. Here's
a night pities neither wise men nor fools.

LEAR. Rumble thy bellyful! Spit, fire! Spout,
rain!
Nor rain, wind, thunder, fire are my daughters.
I tax not you, you elements, with unkindness;
I never gave you kingdom, call'd you children;
You owe me no subscription. Then let fall   **subscription:** allegiance
Your horrible pleasure. Here I stand your slave,
A poor, infirm, weak, and despis'd old man;   20
But yet I call you servile ministers,
That will with two pernicious daughters join
Your high-engender'd battles 'gainst a head   **high-engender'd:** produced in the
So old and white as this. Oh! Oh! 'tis foul!   heavens

FOOL. He that has a house to put 's head in has a
good head-piece.
      "The cod-piece that will house
        Before the head has any,
      The head and he shall louse;   **louse:** have lice
        So beggars marry many.   30   **So . . . many:** before either is
      The man that makes his toe   sexually satisfied. **man . . . wake:**
        What he his heart should make   He who disorders the world will
      Shall of a corn cry woe,   suffer for it.
        And turn his sleep to wake."
For there was never yet fair woman but she made   **made mouths:** posed affectedly
mouths in a glass.   **glass:** mirror

Enter KENT

LEAR. No, I will be the pattern of all patience; I
will say nothing.

KENT. Who's there?

FOOL. Marry, here's grace and a cod-piece;   40   **Marry:** by the Virgin Mary
that's a wise man and a fool.

KENT. Alas, sir, are you here? Things that love
night
Love not such nights as these; the wrathful skies
Gallow the very wanderers of the dark,   **Gallow:** frighten
And make them keep their caves. Since I was man,
Such sheets of fire, such bursts of horrid thunder,
Such groans of roaring wind and rain, I never
Remember to have heard. Man's nature cannot carry
Th' affliction nor the fear.

LEAR.   Let the great gods,
That keep this dreadful pudder o'er our heads,   50   **pudder:** turmoil
Find out their enemies now. Tremble, thou wretch
That hast within thee undivulged crimes,
Unwhipp'd of justice! Hide thee, thou bloody hand;
Thou perjur'd, and thou simular of virtue   **simular of:** pretender to
That art incestuous! Caitiff, to pieces shake,

That under covert and convenient seeming

seeming: appearance

Has practis'd on man's life! Close pent-up guilts,
Rive your concealing continents, and cry

continents: disguises.   cry . . .

These dreadful summoners grace. I am a man

grace: ask mercy

More sinn'd against than sinning.

   KENT.   Alack, bare-headed! 60
Gracious my lord, hard by here is a hovel;
Some friendship will it lend you 'gainst the tempest.
Repose you there, while I to this hard house —
More harder than the stones whereof 'tis rais'd,
Which even but now, demanding after you,
Deni'd me to come in — return, and force

Deni'd . . . in: refused to admit me

Their scanted courtesy.

   LEAR.   My wits begin to turn.
Come on, my boy. How dost, my boy? Art cold?
I am cold myself. Where is this straw, my fellow?
The art of our necessities is strange   70

art: state

And can make vile things precious. Come, your
   hovel.
Poor Fool and knave, I have one part in my heart
That's sorry yet for thee.

   FOOL.   [Singing]
      "He that has a little tiny wit, —
         With heigh-ho, the wind and the rain, —
      Must make content with his fortunes fit,
         For the rain it raineth every day."

   LEAR.   True, boy. Come, bring us to this hovel.
             [Exeunt [Lear and Kent]

   FOOL.   This is a brave night to cool a courtezan.

brave: suitable

    I'll speak a prophecy ere I go: 80
   When priests are more in word than matter;
   When brewers mar their malt with water;
   When nobles are their tailors' tutors;
   No heretics burn'd, but wenches' suitors;
   When every case in law is right;
   No squire in debt, nor no poor knight;
   When slanders do not live in tongues;
   Not cutpurses come not to throngs;

cutpurses: thieves

   When usurers tell their gold i' th' field;

tell: count.   i' th' field: openly

   And bawds and whores do churches build;   90

Albion: England

   Then shall the realm of Albion
   Come to great confusion.
   Then comes the time, who lives to see 't,
   That going shall be us'd with feet.

be us'd with feet: proceed correctly and naturally

This prophecy Merlin shall make; for I live before
   his time.   [Exit

SCENE III [*Gloucester's castle*]

Enter GLOUCESTER *and* EDMUND

GLOUCESTER.   Alack, alack, Edmund, I like not
   this unnatural dealing. When I desired their
leave that I might pity him, they took from me the   leave: permission
use of mine own house; charg'd me on pain of per-
petual displeasure neither to speak of him, entreat
for him, or any way sustain him.

EDMUND.   Most savage and unnatural!

GLOUCESTER.   Go to; say you nothing. There is
   division between the Dukes, and a worse matter than that. I have received a letter this night;   10
'tis dangerous to be spoken; I have lock'd the letter in my closet. These injuries the King now bears
will be revenged home; there is part of a power   home: thoroughly.   power: France.
already footed. We must incline to the King. I   footed: landed
will look him and privily relieve him. Go you and
maintain talk with the Duke that my charity be not
of him perceived. If he ask for me, I am ill and
gone to bed. If I die for it, as no less is threat'ned
me, the King my old master must be relieved. There
is strange things toward, Edmund; pray you, be   20
careful.   [*Exit*

EDMUND.   This courtesy, forbid thee, shall the   forbid thee: which you are forbid-
   Duke   den to render
Instantly know; and of that letter too.
This seems a fair deserving, and must draw me   deserving: action by which I shall
That which my father loses; no less than all.   acquire merit
The younger rises when the old doth fall.   [*Exit*

SCENE IV [*The open country. Before a hovel*]

Enter LEAR, KENT, *and* FOOL

KENT.   Here is the place, my lord; good my lord,
   enter.
The tyranny of the open night 's too rough
For nature to endure.   [*Storm still*
LEAR.   Let me alone.
KENT.   Good my lord, enter here.
LEAR.   Wilt break my heart?
KENT.   I had rather break mine own. Good my
   lord, enter.
LEAR.   Thou think'st 'tis much that this conten-
   tious storm
Invades us to the skin; so 'tis to thee;
But where the greater malady is fix'd,   fix'd: situated
The lesser is scarce felt. Thou'dst shun a bear;

But if thy flight lay toward the roaring sea,   10
Thou'dst meet the bear i' th' mouth. When the
      mind 's free,   free: uncontrolled
The body 's delicate; the tempest in my mind   delicate: sensitive
Doth from my senses take all feeling else
Save what beats there. Filial ingratitude!
Is it not as this mouth should tear this hand
For lifting food to't? But I will punish home.
No, I will weep no more. In such a night
To shut me out? Pour on! I will endure.
In such a night as this? O Regan, Goneril!
Your old kind father, whose frank heart gave all, —   20
O, that way madness lies; let me shun that;
No more of that.

      KENT.   Good my lord, enter here.

      LEAR.   Prithee, go in thyself; seek thine own ease.
This tempest will not give me leave to ponder
On things would hurt me more. But I'll go in.
[To the Fool] In, boy; go first. You houseless
      poverty, —   poverty: poor
Nay, get thee in. I'll pray, and then I'll sleep.

                                    [Exit [Fool]
Poor naked wretches, wheresoe'er you are,
That bide the pelting of this pitiless storm,
How shall your houseless heads and unfed sides,   30
Your loop'd and window'd raggedness, defend you   loop'd and window'd: full of holes
From seasons such as these? O, I have ta'en
Too little care of this! Take physic, pomp;   physic, pomp: the right medicine,
Expose thyself to feel what wretches feel,   you men who delight in pomp
That thou mayst shake the superflux to them,   and circumstance
And show the heavens more just.   superflux: superfluous pomp

      EDGAR. [Within] Fathom and half, fathom and
      half! Poor Tom!

                    [The Fool runs out from the hovel]

      FOOL. Come not in here, nuncle, here's a spirit.
      Help me, help me!   40

      KENT. Give me thy hand. Who's there?

      FOOL. A spirit, a spirit! He says his name 's poor
      Tom.

      KENT. What art thou that dost grumble there i'
      th' straw? Come forth.

            [Enter EDGAR, disguised as a madman]

      EDGAR. Away! the foul fiend follows me!
"Through the sharp hawthorn blow the winds."
      Hum! go to thy bed, and warm thee.

      LEAR. Did'st thou give all to thy daughters, and
      art thou come to this?   50

EDGAR.   Who gives anything to poor Tom? whom
the foul fiend hath led through fire and through
flame, and through [ford] and whirlpool, o'er bog
and quagmire; that hath laid knives under his pillow, and halters in his pew; set ratsbane by his
porridge; made him proud of heart, to ride on a
bay trotting-horse over four-inch'd bridges, to course
his own shadow for a traitor. Bless thy five wits!
Tom's a-cold, — O, do de, do de, do de. Bless thee
from whirlwinds, star-blasting, and taking! Do   60
poor Tom some charity, whom the foul fiend vexes.
There could I have him now, — and there, — and
there again, and there.   [*Storm still*

LEAR.   Has his daughters brought him to this
pass?
Couldst thou save nothing? Wouldst thou give 'em
all?

FOOL.   Nay, he reserv'd a blanket, else we had
been all sham'd.

LEAR.   Now, all the plagues that in the pendulous
air
Hang fated o'er men's faults light on thy daughters!

KENT.   He hath no daughters, sir.   70

LEAR.   Death, traitor! nothing could have subdu'd
nature
To such a lowness but his unkind daughters.
Is it the fashion, that discarded fathers
Should have thus little mercy on their flesh?
Judicious punishment! 'Twas this flesh begot
Those pelican daughters.

EDGAR.   "Pillicock sat on Pillicock-hill."
Alow, alow, loo, loo!

FOOL.   This cold night will turn us all to fools
and madmen.   80

EDGAR.   Take heed o' th' foul fiend. Obey thy
parents; keep thy [word justly]; swear not; commit not with man's sworn spouse; set not thy sweet
heart on proud array. Tom 's a-cold.

LEAR.   What hast thou been?

EDGAR.   A serving-man, proud in heart and mind;
that curl'd my hair; wore gloves in my cap;
serv'd the lust of my mistress' heart and did the act
of darkness with her; swore as many oaths as I   89
spake words, and broke them in the sweet face of
heaven: one that slept in the contriving of lust, and
wak'd to do it. Wine lov'd I dearly, dice dearly;
and in woman out-paramour'd the Turk: false of

---

ride . . . bridges: risk his life
course: chase

star-blasting: misfortune caused by the configurations of the stars
taking: infection

pendulous: suspended

pelican: parent-devouring
Pillicock: the phallus

commit: commit adultery

gloves: as his mistress's favors
act of darkness: sexual intercourse

Turk: Sultan

heart, light of ear, bloody of hand; hog in sloth, fox in stealth, wolf in greediness, dog in madness, lion in prey. Let not the creaking of shoes nor the rustling of silks betray thy poor heart to woman. Keep thy foot out of brothels, thy hand out of plackets, thy pen from lenders' books, and defy the foul 99 fiend.

"Still through the hawthorn blows the cold wind." Says suum, mun, nonny. Dolphin my boy, boy, sessa! let him trot by.   [*Storm still*

LEAR.   Thou wert better in a grave than to answer
    with thy uncover'd body this extremity of the skies. Is man no more than this? Consider him well. Thou ow'st the worm no silk, the beast no hide, the sheep no wool, the cat no perfume. Ha! here 's three on 's are sophisticated! Thou art the thing 109 itself; unaccommodated man is no more but such a poor, bare, forked animal as thou art. Off, off, you lendings! come, unbutton here.

                [*Tearing off his clothes*]

Enter GLOUCESTER, *with a torch*

FOOL.   Prithee, nuncle, be contented; 'tis a
    naughty night to swim in. Now a little fire in a wild field were like an old lecher's heart; a small spark, all the rest on 's body cold. Look, here comes a walking fire.

EDGAR.   This is the foul [fiend] Flibbertigib- 118
    bet; he begins at curfew, and walks [till the] first cock; he gives the web and the pin, squints the eye, and makes the hare-lip; mildews the white wheat, and hurts the poor creature of earth.

        "St. Withold footed thrice the 'old;
        He met the night-mare and her ninefold;
            Bid her alight,
            And her troth plight,
        And, aroint thee, witch, aroint thee!"

KENT.   How fares your Grace?
LEAR.   What's he?
KENT.   Who's there? What is't you seek?   130
GLOUCESTER.   What are you there? Your names?
EDGAR.   Poor Tom, that eats the swimming frog,
    the toad, the tadpole, the wall-newt, and the water; that in the fury of his heart, when the foul fiend rages, eats cow-dung for salads; swallows the old rat and the ditch-dog; drinks the green mantle of the standing pool; who is whipp'd from tithing to tithing, and stock'd, punish'd, and imprison'd;

light of ear: credulous

placket: opening in a petticoat

sessa!: go on!

cat: civet cat
on 's: of us
unaccommodated: naked

lendings: clothes, things not really belonging to one

curfew: 9 p.m. **first cock:** midnight. **web . . . pin:** cataract

St. Withold: (Theobald) is supposed to be St. Vitalis. **footed:** walked. **'old:** wold. **ninefold:** offspring

aroint thee: begone

water: water-newt, a lizard

mantle: scum
tithing: district

who hath three suits to his back, six shirts to his
body.   140
    Horse to ride, and weapon to wear;
    But mice and rats, and such small deer,   deer: game
    Have been Tom's food for seven long year.
Beware my follower. Peace, Smulkin; peace, thou   Smulkin: personal demon
    fiend!
    GLOUCESTER.   What, hath your Grace no better
    company?
    EDGAR.   The prince of darkness is a gentleman.
Modo he's called, and Mahu.
    GLOUCESTER.   Our flesh and blood, my lord, is
    grown so vile
That it doth hate what gets it.   gets: begets
    EDGAR.   Poor Tom 's a-cold.   150
    GLOUCESTER.   Go in with me; my duty cannot
    suffer
To obey in all your daughters' hard commands.
Though their injunction be to bar my doors
And let this tyrannous night take hold upon you,
Yet have I ventur'd to come seek you out,
And bring you where both fire and food is ready.
    LEAR.   First let me talk with the philosopher.
What is the cause of thunder?
    KENT.   Good my lord, take his offer; go into th'
    house.
    LEAR.   I'll talk a word with this same learned
    Theban.   160   Theban: Greek philosopher
What is your study?
    EDGAR.   How to prevent the fiend, and to kill   prevent: anticipate
    vermin.
    LEAR.   Let me ask you one word in private.
    KENT.   Importune him once more to go, my lord;
His wits begin t' unsettle.
    GLOUCESTER.   Canst thou blame him?
                  [Storm still
His daughters seek his death. Ah, that good Kent!
He said it would be thus, poor banish'd man!
Thou say'st the King grows mad; I'll tell thee,
    friend,
I am almost mad myself. I had a son,
Now outlaw'd from my blood; he sought my life,   170
But lately, very late. I lov'd him, friend,
No father his son dearer; true to tell thee,
The grief hath craz'd my wits. What a night 's this!
I do beseech your Grace, —
    LEAR.   O, cry you mercy, sir.
Noble philosopher, your company.

EDGAR. Tom 's a-cold.

GLOUCESTER. In, fellow, there, into th' hovel;
keep thee warm.

LEAR. Come, let's in all.

KENT.   This way, my lord.

LEAR.   With him;
I will keep still with my philosopher.   180

KENT. Good my lord, soothe him; let him take
the fellow.

GLOUCESTER. Take him you on.

KENT. Sirrah, come on; go along with us.

LEAR. Come, good Athenian.   **Athenian:** learned philosopher

GLOUCESTER. No words, no words: hush.

EDGAR. "Child Rowland to the dark tower came;
His word was still, 'Fie, foh, and fum,
I smell the blood of a British man.' "

[*Exeunt*

SCENE V [*Gloucester's castle*]

Enter CORNWALL *and* EDMUND

CORNWALL. I will have my revenge ere I depart
his house.

EDMUND. How, my lord, I may be censured that   **censured:** judged
nature thus gives way to loyalty, something fears
me to think of.

CORNWALL. I now perceive, it was not altogether
your brother's evil disposition made him seek his   **his:** Gloucester's
death; but a provoking merit, set a-work by a reprove-   **provoking merit:** good quality
able badness in himself.   that incited him

EDMUND. How malicious is my fortune, that   10
I must repent to be just! This is the letter
which he spoke of, which approves him an intelligent   **intelligent:** informed
party to the advantages of France. O heavens! that
this treason were not, or not I the detector!

CORNWALL. Go with me to the Duchess.

EDMUND. If the matter of this paper be certain,
you have mighty business in hand.

CORNWALL. True or false, it hath made thee Earl
of Gloucester. Seek out where thy father is, that
he may be ready for our apprehension.   20

EDMUND. [*Aside*] If I find him comforting the
King, it will stuff his suspicion more fully. — I   **stuff:** strengthen
will persevere in my course of loyalty, though the
conflict be sore between that and my blood.   **blood:** natural inclination

CORNWALL. I will lay trust upon thee; and thou
shalt find a [dearer] father in my love. [*Exeunt*

Scene VI [*A building attached to Gloucester's castle*]

Enter KENT *and* GLOUCESTER

GLOUCESTER.   Here is better than the open air; take
it thankfully. I will piece out the comfort with
what addition I can. I will not be long from you.
[*Exit*

KENT.   All the power of his wits have given way to
his impatience. The gods reward your kindness!

Enter LEAR, EDGAR, *and* FOOL

EDGAR.   Frateretto calls me; and tells me Nero is
an angler in the lake of darkness. Pray, innocent, and beware of the foul fiend.

Frateretto: Elizabethan demon
innocent: fool

FOOL.   Prithee, nuncle, tell me whether a
madman be a gentleman or a yeoman?   10

LEAR.   A king, a king!

FOOL.   No, he's a yeoman that has a gentleman
to his son; for he's a mad yeoman that sees his
son a gentleman before him.

LEAR.   To have a thousand with red burning spits
Come hissing in upon 'em, —

[EDGAR.   The foul fiend bites my back.

FOOL.   He's mad that trusts in the tameness of a
wolf, a horse's health, a boy's love, or a
whore's oath.   20

LEAR.   It shall be done; I will arraign them
straight.

[*To Edgar*] Come, sit thou here, most learned
justicer;

[*To the Fool*] Thou, sapient sir, sit here. Now, you
she foxes!

EDGAR.   Look, where he stands and glares!
Wantest thou eyes at trial, madam?
    "Come o'er the bourn, Bessy, to me," —

eyes at: eyes to witness your
own. bourn: burn, brook

FOOL.   "Her boat hath a leak,
    And she must not speak
Why she dares not come over to thee."   29

EDGAR.   The foul fiend haunts poor Tom in the
voice of a nightingale. Hopdance cries in Tom's
belly for two white herring. Croak not, black angel;
I have no food for thee.

Hopdance: Elizabethan demon

KENT.   How do you, sir? Stand you not so amaz'd:
Will you lie down and rest upon the cushions?

LEAR.   I'll see their trial first. Bring in their evidence.

[*To Edgar*] Thou robed man of justice, take thy
place;

[*To the Fool*]   And thou, his yoke-fellow of equity,
Bench by his side.   [*To Kent*] You are o' th' com-
   mission,
Sit you too.   40
   EDGAR.   Let us deal justly.
      "Sleepest or wakest thou, jolly shepherd?
         Thy sheep be in the corn;
      And for one blast of thy minikin mouth,   minikin: dainty
         Thy sheep shall take no harm."
Purr! the cat is grey.
   LEAR.   Arraign her first; 'tis Goneril. I here take
      my oath before this honourable assembly, she
kick'd the poor king her father.
   FOOL.   Come hither, mistress. Is your name
      Goneril?   50
   LEAR.   She cannot deny it.
   FOOL.   Cry you mercy, I took you for a joint-   joint-stool: joined stool (a small
      stool.   stool with three legs)
   LEAR.   And here's another, whose warp'd looks
      proclaim
What store her heart is made on. Stop her there!   store: material
Arms, arms, sword, fire! Corruption in the place!
False justicer, why hast thou let her scape?]
   EDGAR.   Bless thy five wits!
   KENT.   O pity! Sir, where is the patience now
That you so oft have boasted to retain?
   EDGAR.   [*Aside*]   My tears begin to take his part
      so much,   60
They mar my counterfeiting.
   LEAR.   The little dogs and all,
Tray, Blanch, and Sweetheart, see, they bark at me.
   EDGAR.   Tom will throw his head at them.
      Avaunt, you curs!
         By thy mouth or black or white,
         Tooth that poisons if it bite;
         Mastiff, greyhound, mongrel grim,
         Hound or spaniel, brach or [lym],   lym: bloodhound
         Or bobtail [tike] or trundle-tail,   70   tike: cur. trundle-tail: curled tail
         Tom will make him weep and wail;
         For, with throwing thus my head,   throwing: jerking about while
         Dogs leapt the hatch, and all are fled.   moaning. hatch: lower half of a
                                                           divided door. wakes: annual par-
Do de, de, de. Sessa! Come, march to wakes and   ish festivals. horn: horn bottle for
fairs and market-towns. Poor Tom, thy horn is dry.   begging a drink
   LEAR.   Then let them anatomize Regan; see what
      breeds about her heart. Is there any cause
in nature that make these hard hearts? [*To Edgar*]
You, sir, I entertain for one of my hundred; only I   entertain: engage
do not like the fashion of your garments. You will
say they are Persian, but let them be chang'd   81   Persian: and thus elaborate

KENT.   Now, good my lord, lie here and rest a
while.

LEAR.   Make no noise, make no noise; draw the
curtains; so, so, so. We'll go to supper i' th'
morning.

FOOL.   And I'll go to bed at noon.

Re-enter GLOUCESTER

GLOUCESTER.   Come hither, friend; where is the
King my master?

KENT.   Here, sir; but trouble him not, his wits are
gone.

GLOUCESTER.   Good friend, I prithee, take him in
thy arms;   90
I have o'erheard a plot of death upon him.
There is a litter ready; lay him in't,
And drive toward Dover, friend, where thou shalt   **Dover: port nearest France**
meet
Both welcome and protection. Take up thy master.
If thou shouldst dally half an hour, his life,
With thine and all that offer to defend him
Stand in assured loss. Take up, take up;
And follow me, that will to some provision
Give thee quick conduct.

KENT.   [Oppressed nature sleeps.
This rest might yet have balm'd thy broken sinews,   **sinews: nerves**
Which, if convenience will not allow,   101
Stand in hard cure. (*To the Fool*) Come, help to
bear thy master;
Thou must not stay behind.]

GLOUCESTER.   Come, come, away.
                    [*Exeunt* [*all but Edgar*]
[EDGAR.   When we our betters see bearing our
woes,
We scarcely think our miseries our foes.
Who alone suffers, suffers most i' th' mind,
Leaving free things and happy shows behind;
But then the mind much sufferance doth o'erskip,
When grief hath mates, and bearing fellowship.   **bearing: suffering**
How light and portable my pain seems now,   110   **portable: bearable**
When that which makes me bend makes the King
bow,
He childed as I fathered! Tom, away!
Mark the high noises; and thyself bewray   **bewray: disclose**
When false opinion, whose wrong thoughts defile
thee,
In thy just proof repeals and reconciles thee.   **repeals: recalls**
What will hap more to-night, safe scape the King!   **What: whatever**
Lurk, lurk.]   [*Exit*]

Scene VII [*Gloucester's castle*]

Enter CORNWALL, REGAN, GONERIL, *Bastard*
[EDMUND], *and* SERVANTS

CORNWALL. [*To Goneril*] Post speedily to my lord
your husband; show him this letter. The army of
France is landed. — Seek out the traitor Gloucester.
                    [*Exeunt some of the Servants*]
REGAN.   Hang him instantly.
GONERIL.   Pluck out his eyes.
CORNWALL.   Leave him to my displeasure. — Edmund, keep you our sister company; the revenges
we are bound to take upon your traitorous father are
not fit for your beholding. Advise the Duke, where
you are going, to a most festinate preparation; we   10   **festinate: speedy**
are bound to the like. Our posts shall be swift and
intelligent betwixt us. Farewell, dear sister; farewell,
my Lord of Gloucester.

Enter Steward [OSWALD]

How now! where's the King?
OSWALD.   My Lord of Gloucester hath convey'd   **Lord of Gloucester: Edmund's new**
him hence.   **title**
Some five or six and thirty of his knights,
Hot questrists after him, met him at gate,   **questrists: searchers**
Who, with some other of the lord's dependants,
Are gone with him toward Dover, where they boast
To have well-armed friends.
CORNWALL.   Get horses for your mistress.   20
GONERIL.   Farewell, sweet lord, and sister.
CORNWALL.   Edmund, farewell.
        [*Exeunt* [*Goneril, Edmund, and Oswald*]
                    Go seek the traitor Gloucester,
Pinion him like a thief, bring him before us.
                    [*Exeunt other Servants*]
Though well we may not pass upon his life
Without the form of justice, yet our power
Shall do a court'sy to our wrath, which men
May blame, but not control.

Enter GLOUCESTER *and* SERVANTS

                    Who's there? The traitor?
REGAN.   Ingrateful fox! 'tis he.
CORNWALL.   Bind fast his corky arms.   **corky: withered**
GLOUCESTER.   What means your Graces? Good
my friends, consider   30
You are my guests. Do me no foul play, friends.
CORNWALL.   Bind him, I say. [*Servants bind him.*]
REGAN.   Hard, hard. O filthy traitor!

GLOUCESTER.   Unmerciful lady as you are, I'm
   none.
CORNWALL.   To this chair bind him. Villain, thou
   shalt find —   [*Regan plucks his beard.*]
GLOUCESTER.   By the kind gods, 'tis most ignobly
   done
To pluck me by the beard.
   REGAN.   So white, and such a traitor!
GLOUCESTER.   Naughty lady,
These hairs, which thou dost ravish from my chin,
Will quicken, and accuse thee. I am your host:
With robber's hands my hospitable favours   40
You should not ruffle thus. What will you do?
   CORNWALL.   Come, sir, what letters had you late
   from France?
REGAN.   Be simple-answer'd, for we know the
   truth.
CORNWALL.   And what confederacy have you with
   the traitors
Late footed in the kingdom?
   REGAN.   To whose hands you have sent the luna-
   tic king,
Speak.
   GLOUCESTER.   I have a letter guessingly set down,
Which came from one that's of a neutral heart,
And not from one oppos'd.
   CORNWALL.   Cunning.
REGAN.   And false.   50
CORNWALL.   Where hast thou sent the King?
GLOUCESTER.   To Dover.
REGAN.   Wherefore to Dover? Wast thou not
   charg'd at peril —
CORNWALL.   Wherefore to Dover? Let him an-
   swer that.
GLOUCESTER.   I am tied to th' stake, and I must
   stand the course.
REGAN.   Wherefore to Dover?
GLOUCESTER.   Because I would not see thy cruel
   nails
Pluck out his poor old eyes; nor thy fierce sister
In his anointed flesh stick boarish fangs.
The sea, with such a storm as his bare head   60
In hell-black night endur'd, would have buoy'd up
And quench'd the stelled fires;
Yet, poor old heart, he holp the heavens to rain.
If wolves had at thy gate howl'd that stern time,
Thou shouldst have said, "Good porter, turn the
   key."
All cruels else subscribe; but I shall see
The winged vengeance overtake such children.

plucks his beard: traditionally a high insult

quicken: become alive
favours: features
ruffle: outrage

course: attack of the dogs (bear-baiting)

anointed: kingly

stelled fires: stars
holp: helped

All . . . subscribe: All cruel creatures but man act otherwise.

CORNWALL. See 't shalt thou never. Fellows,
   hold the chair.
Upon these eyes of thine I'll set my foot.
   GLOUCESTER.   He that will think to live till he be
   old,   70
Give me some help! — O cruel! O you gods!
   REGAN.   One side will mock another; th' other
   too.
   CORNWALL.   If you see vengeance, —
   [1] SERVANT.   Hold your hand, my lord!
I have serv'd you ever since I was a child;
But better service have I never done you
Than now to bid you hold.
   REGAN.   How now, you dog!
   [1] SERVANT.   If you did wear a beard upon your
   chin,
I'd shake it on this quarrel. What do you mean?
   CORNWALL.   My villain!   [*They draw and fight.*]
   [1] SERVANT.   Nay, then, come on, and take the
   chance of anger.   80
   REGAN.   Give me thy sword. A peasant stand up
   thus?
          [*Takes a sword, and runs at him behind*
   [1] SERVANT.   Oh, I am slain! My lord, you have
   one eye left
To see some mischief on him. Oh!   [*Dies*]
   CORNWALL.   Lest it see more, prevent it. Out,
   vile jelly!
Where is thy lustre now?
   GLOUCESTER.   All dark and comfortless. Where's
   my son Edmund?
Edmund, enkindle all the sparks of nature,
To quit this horrid act.
   REGAN.   Out, treacherous villain!
Thou call'st on him that hates thee. It was he
That made the overture of thy treasons to us,   90
Who is too good to pity thee.
   GLOUCESTER.   O my follies! then Edgar was
   abus'd.
Kind gods, forgive me that, and prosper him!
   REGAN.   Go thrust him out at gates, and let him
   smell
His way to Dover.   (*Exit [one] with Gloucester*)
   How is't, my lord? How look you?
   CORNWALL.   I have received a hurt; follow me,
   lady.
Turn out that eyeless villain; throw this slave
Upon the dunghill. Regan, I bleed apace;
Untimely comes this hurt. Give me your arm.   100
          [*Exit Cornwall, led by Regan*]

What . . . mean?: (Probably this should be given to Cornwall or Regan.)

vile jelly: eye (Gloucester is blinded.)

made the overture: disclosed

abus'd: wronged

How look you?: How are you?

[2 SERVANT.   I'll never care what wickedness I do,
If this man come to good.
   3 SERVANT.   If she live long,
And in the end meet the old course of death,   old: usual
Women will all turn monsters.
   2 SERVANT.   Let's follow the old earl, and get the
      Bedlam
To lead him where he would: his roguish madness
Allows itself to anything.
   3 SERVANT.   Go thou: I'll fetch some flax and
      whites of eggs
To apply to his bleeding face. Now, Heaven help
      him!]   [*Exeunt* [*severally*]

ACT IV

SCENE I.   [*The open country nèar Gloucester's*
castle]

Enter EDGAR

EDGAR.   Yet better thus, and known to be con-
     temn'd,
Than, still contemn'd and flatter'd, to be worst.   contemn'd: despised
The lowest and most dejected thing of Fortune
Stands still in esperance, lives not in fear.   esperance: hope
The lamentable change is from the best;
The worst returns to laughter. Welcome, then,   **The worst . . . laughter:** Any
Thou unsubstantial air that I embrace!   change from the worst must be
The wretch that thou hast blown unto the worst   for the better.
Owes nothing to thy blasts.
                                   Owes nothing: cannot be called
                                   on to pay anything more

Enter GLOUCESTER, *led by an* OLD MAN

                  But who comes here?
My father, poorly led? World, world, O world!   10
But that thy strange mutations make us hate thee,
Life would not yield to age.   **Life . . . age:** We should never
   OLD MAN.   O, my good lord, I have been your   live to be old.
tenant, and your father's tenant, these fourscore
years.
   GLOUCESTER.   Away, get thee away! Good friend,
     be gone;
Thy comforts can do me no good at all;
Thee they may hurt.
   OLD MAN.   You cannot see your way.
   GLOUCESTER.   I have no way, and therefore want
     no eyes;
I stumbled when I saw. Full oft 'tis seen,   20
Our means secure us, and our mere defects   secure: make careless
Prove our commodities. O dear son Edgar,   commodities: advantages, re-
The food of thy abused father's wrath!   sources
                                     food: object. abused: deceived

Might I but live to see thee in my touch
I'd say I had eyes again!

OLD MAN.   How now! Who's there?

EDGAR.   [*Aside*] O gods! Who is't can say, "I am
  at the worst"?
I am worse than e'er I was.

OLD MAN.   'Tis poor mad Tom.

EDGAR.   [*Aside*] And worse I may be yet; the worst
  is not
So long as we can say, "This is the worst."   29

OLD MAN.   Fellow, where goest?

GLOUCESTER.   Is it a beggar-man?

OLD MAN.   Madman and beggar too.

GLOUCESTER.   He has some reason, else he could
  not beg.
I' th' last night's storm I such a fellow saw,
Which made me think a man a worm. My son
Came then into my mind, and yet my mind
Was then scarce friends with him. I have heard
    more since.
As flies to wanton boys, are we to th' gods,
They kill us for their sport.

EDGAR.   [*Aside*] How should this be?   **should: can**
Bad is the trade that must play fool to sorrow,
Ang'ring itself and others. — Bless thee, master!   40

GLOUCESTER.   Is that the naked fellow?

OLD MAN.   Ay, my lord.

GLOUCESTER.   [Then, prithee,] get thee away. If,
  for my sake,
Thou wilt o'ertake us hence a mile or twain
I' th' way toward Dover, do it for ancient love;   **ancient: (1) former, (2) traditional,**
And bring some covering for this naked soul,   **natural**
Which I'll entreat to lead me.

OLD MAN.   Alack, sir, he is mad.

GLOUCESTER.   'Tis the time's plague, when mad-
  men lead the blind.
Do as I bid thee, or rather do thy pleasure;
Above the rest, be gone.   **the rest: all**

OLD MAN.   I'll bring him the best 'parel that I
  have.   50
Come on't what will.   [*Exit*

GLOUCESTER.   Sirrah, naked fellow, —

EDGAR.   Poor Tom 's a-cold. [*Aside*] I cannot
  daub it further.   **daub: dissemble**

GLOUCESTER.   Come hither, fellow.

EDGAR.   [*Aside*] And yet I must. — Bless thy sweet
  eyes, they bleed.

GLOUCESTER.   Know'st thou the way to Dover?

EDGAR.   Both stile and gate, horse-way and footpath. Poor Tom hath been scar'd out of his good

wits. Bless thee, good man's son, from the foul 59
fiend! [Five fiends have been in poor Tom at once;
of lust, as Obidicut; Hobbididence, prince of dumbness; Mahu, of stealing; Modo, of murder; Flibber-
t'gibbet, of mopping and mowing, who since possesses chambermaids and waiting-women. So, bless
thee, master!]

dumbness: muteness

mopping and mowing: making faces

GLOUCESTER.   Here, take this purse, thou whom
    the heavens' plagues
Have humbled to all strokes. That I am wretched
Makes thee the happier; heavens, deal so still!
Let the superfluous and lust-dieted man,
That slaves your ordinance, that will not see   70
Because he does not feel, feel your power quickly;
So distribution should undo excess,
And each man have enough. Dost thou know Dover?

strokes: events

superfluous: having too much
lust-dieted: whose every desire is
satisfied. **slaves your ordinance:**
makes your laws subordinate to
his desires

EDGAR.   Ay, master.

GLOUCESTER.   There is a cliff, whose high and
    bending head
Looks fearfully in the confined deep.
Bring me but to the very brim of it,
And I'll repair the misery thou dost bear
With something rich about me. From that place
I shall no leading need.

bending: overhanging

EDGAR.   Give me thy arm;   80
Poor Tom shall lead thee.   [*Exeunt*

SCENE II. [*Before the Duke of Albany's palace*]

Enter GONERIL, *Bastard* [EDMUND], *and Steward* [OSWALD]

GONERIL.   Welcome, my lord! I marvel our mild
    husband
Not met us on the way. — Now, where's your mas-
    ter?

OSWALD.   Madam, within; but never man so
    chang'd.
I told him of the army that was landed;
He smil'd at it. I told him you were coming;
His answer was, "The worse." Of Gloucester's
    treachery,
And of the loyal service of his son,
When I inform'd him, then he call'd me sot,
And told me I had turn'd the wrong side out.   9
What most he should dislike seems pleasant to him;
What like, offensive.

sot: fool

GONERIL.   [*To Edmund*] Then shall you go no
    further.
It is the cowish terror of his spirit,
That dares not undertake; he'll not feel wrongs

cowish: cowardly

Which tie him to an answer. Our wishes on the way
May prove effects. Back, Edmund, to my brother;
Hasten his musters and conduct his powers.
I must change [arms] at home, and give the distaff
Into my husband's hands. This trusty servant
Shall pass between us. Ere long you are like to hear,
If you dare venture in your own behalf,   20
A mistress's command. Wear this; spare speech;
Decline your head. This kiss, if it durst speak,
Would stretch thy spirits up into the air.
Conceive, and fare thee well.
    EDMUND. Yours in the ranks of death.   [*Exit*
    GONERIL.   My most dear Gloucester!
O, the difference of man and man!
To thee a woman's services are due;
My Fool usurps my body.
    OSWALD.   Madam, here comes my lord.
                      [*Exit*

Enter the DUKE OF ALBANY

    GONERIL. I have been worth the whistle.
    ALBANY.   O Goneril!
You are not worth the dust which the rude wind   30
Blows in your face. [I fear your disposition.
That nature which contemns its origin
Cannot be bordered certain in itself.
She that herself will sliver and disbranch
From her material sap, perforce must wither
And come to deadly use.
    GONERIL. No more; the text is foolish.
    ALBANY. Wisdom and goodness to the vile seem
      vile;
Filths savour but themselves. What have you done?
Tigers, not daughters, what have you perform'd?   40
A father, and a gracious aged man,
Whose reverence even the head-lugg'd bear would
    lick,
Most barbarous, most degenerate! have you madded.
Could my good brother suffer you to do it?
A man, a prince, by him so benefited!
If that the heavens do not their visible spirits
Send quickly down to tame these vile offences,
It will come,
Humanity must perforce prey on itself,
Like monsters of the deep.]
    GONERIL.   Milk-liver'd man!   50
That bear'st a cheek for blows, a head for wrongs,
Who hast not in thy brows an eye discerning
Thine honour from thy suffering, [that not know'st
Fools do those villains pity who are punish'd

---

tie him to an answer: force him to retaliate. **prove effects:** be realized

powers: army

arms: Goneril will take the sword.

worth the: worth at least a

bordered certain: kept within bounds

material: essential to life

text: as basis for a sermon

head-lugg'd: baited by dogs

Thine . . . suffering: cruel insults from life's ordinary pains

Ere they have done their mischief, where's thy drum?   **drum:** to announce battle
France spreads his banners in our noiseless land,   **noiseless:** peaceful
With plumed helm thy state begins to threat;
Whiles thou, a moral fool, sits still, and criest,
"Alack, why does he so?"]
    ALBANY.   See thyself, devil!
Proper deformity seems not in the fiend   60   **Proper:** that belongs to him
So horrid as in woman.
    GONERIL.   O vain fool!
    [ALBANY. Thou changed and self-cover'd thing,   **self-cover'd:** whose real self is
    for shame!   hidden
Be-monster not thy feature. Were't my fitness   **Were't my fitness:** were it suitable
To let these hands obey my blood,   for me
   blood: impulse
They are apt enough to dislocate and tear
Thy flesh and bones. Howe'er thou art a fiend,
A woman's shape doth shield thee.
    GONERIL. Marry, your manhood — Mew!   **your . . . Mew!:** hide or retire
   your pretended manhood

         Enter a MESSENGER

    ALBANY. What news?]
    MESSENGER. O, my good lord, the Duke of Corn-
    wall's dead;   70
Slain by his servant, going to put out
The other eye of Gloucester.
    ALBANY.   Gloucester's eyes!
    MESSENGER. A servant that he bred, thrill'd with
    remorse,   **remorse:** pity
Oppos'd against the act, bending his sword
To his great master; who, thereat enrag'd,
Flew on him, and amongst them fell'd him dead;   **amongst them:** with the aid of
But not without that harmful stroke which since   others
Hath pluck'd him after.
    ALBANY.   This shows you are above,
You [justicers,] that these our nether crimes   **nether:** committed here below
So speedily can venge! But, O poor Gloucester!   80
Lost he his other eye?
    MESSENGER.   Both, both, my lord.
This letter, madam, craves a speedy answer.
'Tis from your sister.
    GONERIL. [*Aside*] One way I like this well;
But being widow, and my Gloucester with her,
May all the building in my fancy pluck   **pluck:** pull down
Upon my hateful life. Another way,
The news is not so tart. — I'll read, and answer.
                       [*Exit*
    ALBANY. Where was his son when they did take
    his eyes?
    MESSENGER. Come with my lady hither.
    ALBANY.   He is not here.

MESSENGER. No, my good lord; I met him back
again.   90

back again: returning to his castle

ALBANY. Knows he the wickedness?

MESSENGER. Ay, my good lord; 'twas he inform'd
against him;
And quit the house on purpose that their punishment
Might have the freer course.

ALBANY.   Gloucester, I live
To thank thee for the love thou show'dst the king,
And to revenge thine eyes. Come hither, friend;
Tell me what more thou know'st.   [*Exeunt*

[SCENE III. *The French camp near Dover*

Enter KENT *and a* GENTLEMAN

KENT. Why the King of France is so suddenly
gone back, know you no reason?

GENTLEMAN. Something he left imperfect in the
state, which since his coming forth is thought of;
which imports to the kingdom so much fear and
danger that his personal return was most required
and necessary.

imperfect: unfinished

KENT. Who hath he left behind him General?

GENTLEMAN. The Marshal of France, Monsieur
La Far.   10

KENT. Did your letters pierce the Queen to any
demonstration of grief?

GENTLEMAN. [Ay, sir]; she took them, read them
in my presence;
And now and then an ample tear trill'd down
Her delicate cheek. It seem'd she was a queen
Over her passion, who, most rebel-like,
Sought to be king o'er her.

KENT.   O, then it mov'd her.

GENTLEMAN. Not to a rage; patience and sorrow
[strove]
Who should express her goodliest. You have seen
Sunshine and rain at once: her smiles and tears   20
Were like a better way; those happy smilets
That play'd on her ripe lip seem'd not to know
What guests were in her eyes, which, parted thence,
As pearls from diamonds dropp'd. In brief,
Sorrow would be a rarity most beloved,
If all could so become it.

like a better way: more beautiful
than "sunshine and rain at once"

rarity: something precious

KENT.   Made she no verbal question?

GENTLEMAN. Faith, once or twice she heav'd the
name of "father"
Pantingly forth, as if it press'd her heart;
Cried, "Sisters! sisters! Shame of ladies! sisters!

Kent! father! sisters! What, i' th' storm? i' th'
   night?   30
Let pity not be believ'd!" There she shook
The holy water from her heavenly eyes;
And clamour moistened; then away she started
To deal with grief alone.

KENT.   It is the stars,
The stars above us, govern our conditions;
Else one self mate and make could not beget
Such different issues. You spoke not with her since?

GENTLEMAN.   No.

KENT.   Was this before the King return'd?

GENTLEMAN.   No, since.

KENT.   Well, sir, the poor distressed Lear 's i' th'
   town;   40
Who sometime, in his better tune, remembers
What we are come about, and by no means
Will yield to see his daughter.

GENTLEMAN.   Why, good sir?

KENT.   A sovereign shame so elbows him. His
   own unkindness,
That stripp'd her from his benediction, turn'd her
To foreign casualties, gave her dear rights
To his dog-hearted daughters, — these things sting
His mind so venomously, that burning shame
Detains him from Cordelia.

GENTLEMAN.   Alack, poor gentleman!

KENT.   Of Albany's and Cornwall's powers you
   heard not?   50

GENTLEMAN.   'Tis so, they are afoot.

KENT.   Well, sir, I'll bring you to our master Lear,
And leave you to attend him. Some dear cause
Will in concealment wrap me up a while;
When I am known aright, you shall not grieve
Lending me this acquaintance. I pray you, go
Along with me.]   [*Exeunt*

SCENE [IV *The same. A tent*]

Enter, with drum and colours, CORDELIA, [DOCTOR],
                 and Soldiers

CORDELIA.   Alack, 'tis he! Why, he was met even
   now
As mad as the vex'd sea, singing aloud,
Crown'd with rank fumiter and furrow-weeds,
With hardocks, hemlock, nettles, cuckoo-flowers,
Darnel, and all the idle weeds that grow
In our sustaining corn. A century send forth;
Search every acre in the high-grown field,

Glosses (right margin):

Let pity: for the sake of our pity let it

clamour moistened: Tears followed her outcry (?).

self mate and make: same husband and wife

tune: construction of events

yield: consent

sovereign: over-mastering
elbows: reminds

casualties: risks

dear: important

fumiter: fumitory
hardocks: perhaps for **burdocks** or **harlock**, wild mustard. **Darnel:** a general term for weed; sometimes specifically rye-grass. **century:** body of 100 men

And bring him to our eye. [*Exit an Officer*] What
  can man's wisdom
In the restoring his bereaved sense?   **bereaved: injured**
He that helps him take all my outward worth.   10
  [DOCTOR.]   There is means, madam.
Our foster-nurse of nature is repose,
The which he lacks; that to provoke in him,
Are many simples operative, whose power   **simples: medicinal herbs**
Will close the eye of anguish.
     CORDELIA.   All blest secrets,
All you unpublish'd virtues of the earth,
Spring with my tears! be aidant and remediate   **aidant: helpful. remediate: heal-**
In the good man's [distress]! Seek, seek for him,   **ing**
Lest his ungovern'd rage dissolve the life
That wants the means to lead it.

                   Enter a MESSENGER

   MESSENGER.   News, madam!   20
The British powers are marching hitherward.
   CORDELIA.   'Tis known before; our preparation
     stands
In expectation of them. O dear father,
It is thy business that I go about;
Therefore great France
My mourning and importun'd tears hath pitied.   **importun'd: importunate, urgent**
No blown ambition doth our arms incite,   **blown: puffed up**
But love, dear love, and our ag'd father's right.
Soon may I hear and see him!   [*Exeunt*

SCENE [V *Gloucester's castle*]

        Enter REGAN *and Steward* [OSWALD]

   REGAN.   But are my brother's powers set forth?
   OSWALD.   Ay, madam.
   REGAN.   Himself in person there?
   OSWALD.   Madam, with much ado.   **with much ado: persuaded with**
Your sister is the better soldier.   **difficulty**
   REGAN.   Lord Edmund spake not with your lord
     at home?
   OSWALD.   No, madam.
   REGAN.   What might import my sister's letter to   **import: be contained in**
     him?
   OSWALD.   I know not, lady.
   REGAN.   Faith, he is posted hence on serious mat-
     ter.
It was great ignorance, Gloucester's eyes being out,   **ignorance: foolishness**
To let him live; where he arrives he moves   10
All hearts against us. Edmund, I think, is gone,
In pity of his misery, to dispatch

His nighted life; moreover, to descry   *nighted:* blinded
The strength o' th' enemy.

    OSWALD.   I must needs after him, madam, with
      my letter.

    REGAN.   Our troops set forth to-morrow, stay with
      us;
The ways are dangerous.

    OSWALD.   I may not, madam;
My lady charg'd my duty in this business.

    REGAN.   Why should she write to Edmund?
      Might not you
Transport her purposes by word? Belike   20
Some things — I know not what. I'll love thee
      much —
Let me unseal the letter.

    OSWALD.   Madam, I had rather —

    REGAN.   I know your lady does not love her hus-
      band;
I am sure of that; and at her late being here
She gave strange œillades and most speaking looks   *œillades:* amorous glances
To noble Edmund. I know you are of her bosom.   *of her bosom:* in her confidence

    OSWALD.   I, madam?

    REGAN.   I speak in understanding; y' are, I know 't.
Therefore I do advise you, take this note: *take this note:* note this
My lord is dead; Edmund and I have talk'd;   30
And more convenient is he for my hand
Than for your lady's. You may gather more.
If you do find him, pray you, give him this;   *this:* these words
And when your mistress hears thus much from you,
I pray, desire her call her wisdom to her.   *call:* recall
So, fare you well.
If you do chance to hear of that blind traitor,
Preferment falls on him that cuts him off.

    OSWALD.   Would I could meet him, madam! I
      should show
What party I do follow.

    REGAN.   Fare thee well.   40

                        [*Exeunt*

SCENE [VI *Fields near Dover*]

    Enter GLOUCESTER *and* EDGAR [*dressed like a
               peasant*]

    GLOUCESTER.   When shall I come to th' top of
      that same hill?

    EDGAR.   You do climb up it now; look, how we
      labour.

    GLOUCESTER.   Methinks the ground is even.

    EDGAR.   Horrible steep.

Hark, do you hear the sea?

GLOUCESTER.   No, truly.

EDGAR.   Why, then, your other senses grow im-
        perfect
By your eyes' anguish.

GLOUCESTER.   So may it be, indeed.
Methinks thy voice is alter'd, and thou speak'st
In better phrase and matter than thou didst.

EDGAR.   You're much deceiv'd. In nothing am I
        chang'd
But in my garments.

GLOUCESTER.   Methinks you're better spoken.   10

EDGAR.   Come on, sir, here's the place; stand still.
        How fearful
And dizzy 'tis, to cast one's eyes so low!
The crows and choughs that wing the midway air
Show scarce so gross as beetles. Half way down
Hangs one that gathers samphire, dreadful trade!
Methinks he seems no bigger than his head.
The fishermen, that walk upon the beach,
Appear like mice; and yond tall anchoring bark,
Diminish'd to her cock; her cock, a buoy
Almost too small for sight. The murmuring surge,   20
That on th' unnumb'red idle pebbles chafes,
Cannot be heard so high. I'll look no more,
Lest my brain turn, and the deficient sight
Topple down headlong.

GLOUCESTER.   Set me where you stand.

EDGAR.   Give me your hand; you are now within
        a foot
Of th' extreme verge. For all beneath the moon
Would I not leap upright.

GLOUCESTER.   Let go my hand.
Here, friend, 's another purse; in it a jewel
Well worth a poor man's taking. Fairies and gods
Prosper it with thee! Go thou further off;   30
Bid me farewell, and let me hear thee going.

EDGAR.   Now fare ye well, good sir.

GLOUCESTER.   With all my heart.

EDGAR.   [Aside] Why I do trifle thus with his
        despair
Is done to cure it.

GLOUCESTER.   [Kneeling] O you mighty gods!
This world I do renounce, and in your sights
Shake patiently my great affliction off.
If I could bear it longer, and not fall
To quarrel with your great opposeless wills,
My snuff and loathed part of nature should
Burn itself out. If Edgar live, O bless him!   40

choughs: jackdaws. **midway:** half-
way down the cliff to the sea
gross: big. **samphire:** sea-fennel,
used for pickling

cock: cock-boat

snuff: burnt wick, useless remnant

Now, fellow, fare thee well.   [*He falls.*
    EDGAR.   Gone, sir; farewell!
— And yet I know not how conceit may rob   conceit: imagination
The treasury of life, when life itself
Yields to the theft. Had he been where he thought,
By this had thought been past. Alive or dead? —
Ho, you sir! friend! Hear you, sir! speak! —
Thus might he pass indeed; yet he revives. —   pass: die
What are you, sir?
    GLOUCESTER.   Away, and let me die.
    EDGAR.   Hadst thou been aught but gossamer,
      feathers, air,
So many fathom down precipitating,   50
Thou 'dst shiver'd like an egg: but thou dost breathe;
Hast heavy substance; bleed'st not; speak'st; art
    sound.
Ten masts at each make not the altitude   at each: end to end
Which thou hast perpendicularly fell.
Thy life's a miracle. Speak yet again.
    GLOUCESTER.   But have I fall'n, or no?
    EDGAR.   From the dread summit of this chalky
      bourn.   bourn: boundary
Look up a-height; the shrill-gorg'd lark so far   a-height: on high. shrill-gorg'd:
Cannot be seen or heard. Do but look up.   shrill throated
    GLOUCESTER.   Alack, I have no eyes.   60
Is wretchedness depriv'd that benefit,
To end itself by death? 'Twas yet some comfort,
When misery could beguile the tyrant's rage,   beguile: cheat (through suicide)
And frustrate his proud will.
    EDGAR.   Give me your arm.
Up: so. How is't? Feel you your legs? You stand.
    GLOUCESTER.   Too well, too well.
    EDGAR.   This is above all strangeness.
Upon the crown o' th' cliff, what thing was that
Which parted from you?
    GLOUCESTER.   A poor unfortunate beggar.
    EDGAR.   As I stood here below, methought his
      eyes
Were two full moons; he had a thousand noses,   70
Horns whelk'd and waved like the [enridged] sea.   whelk'd: twisted
It was some fiend; therefore, thou happy father,   happy: fortunate
Think that the clearest gods, who make them hon-   clearest: most pure
    ours
Of men's impossibilities, have preserv'd thee.
    GLOUCESTER.   I do remember now. Henceforth
    I'll bear
Affliction till it do cry out itself
"Enough, enough," and die. That thing you speak
    of,

I took it for a man; often 't would say,
"The fiend, the fiend!" He led me to that place.

EDGAR.   Bear free and patient thoughts.

free: fearless

Enter LEAR [*fantastically dressed with wild
flowers*]

                              But who comes here?   80
The safer sense will ne'er accommodate
His master thus.

safer sense: a sane mind
accommodate: dress up

LEAR.   No, they cannot touch me for [coining];
I am the King himself.

coining: minting coins (the King's
prerogative)

EDGAR.   O thou side-piercing sight!

LEAR.   Nature's above art in that respect. There's
your press-money. That fellow handles his bow
like a crow-keeper; draw me a clothier's yard.
Look, look, a mouse! Peace, peace; this piece of
toasted cheese will do't. There's my gauntlet; I'll 90
prove it on a giant. Bring up the brown bills. O,
well flown, bird! I' th' clout, i' th' clout! Hewgh!
Give the word.

Nature's: inheritance is

press-money: money given to a
conscript. clothier's yard: an arrow a cloth-yard long

prove it: test my challenge against
brown bills: men carrying pikes
stained brown. clout: center of
the target

EDGAR.   Sweet marjoram.

LEAR.   Pass.

GLOUCESTER.   I know that voice.

LEAR.   Ha! Goneril, with a white beard! They
flatter'd me like a dog, and told me I had the white
hairs in my beard ere the black ones were there.
To say "ay" and "no" to everything that I 100
said! "Ay" and "no" too was no good divinity.
When the rain came to wet me once, and the wind
to make me chatter; when the thunder would not
peace at my bidding; there I found 'em, there I
smelt 'em out. Go to, they are not men o' their
words: they told me I was everything; 'tis a lie, I
am not ague-proof.

GLOUCESTER.   The trick of that voice I do well
     remember.

trick: distinctive features

Is't not the King?

LEAR.   Ay, every inch a king!
When I do stare, see how the subject quakes.   110
I pardon that man's life. What was thy cause?
Adultery?

cause: accusation

Thou shalt not die. Die for adultery! No:
The wren goes to't, and the small gilded fly
Does lecher in my sight.
Let copulation thrive; for Gloucester's bastard son
Was kinder to his father than my daughters
Got 'tween the lawful sheets.
To't, luxury, pell-mell! for I lack soldiers.
Behold yond simp'ring dame,   120

luxury: lust

Whose face between her forks presages snow,   **snow:** coldness, chastity
That minces virtue, and does shake the head   **minces:** affects coyly
To hear of pleasure's name, —
The fitchew nor the soiled horse goes to't   **fitchew:** pole-cat. **soiled:** richly
With a more riotous appetite,   fed
Down from the waist they are Centaurs,
Though women all above;
But to the girdle do the gods inherit,   **inherit:** possess
Beneath is all the fiends';
There's hell, there's darkness, there's the sulphurous
     pit,   130
Burning, scalding, stench, consumption; fie, fie, fie!
pah, pah! Give me an ounce of civet; good apothe-   **civet:** perfume
cary, to sweeten my imagination. There's money
for thee.
    GLOUCESTER. O, let me kiss that hand!
    LEAR. Let me wipe it first; it smells of mortality.
    GLOUCESTER. O ruin'd piece of Nature! This
     great world
Shall so wear out to nought. Dost thou know me?
    LEAR. I remember thine eyes well enough. Dost
thou squiny at me? No, do thy worst, blind   140   **squiny:** squint
Cupid; I'll not love. Read thou this challenge; mark
but the penning of it.
    GLOUCESTER. Were all thy letters suns, I could
     not see.
    EDGAR. [*Aside*] I would not take this from report.   **take:** believe
     It is;
And my heart breaks at it.
    LEAR. Read.
    GLOUCESTER. What, with the case of eyes?   **case:** sockets
    LEAR. O, ho, are you there with me? No eyes
in your head, nor no money in your purse? Your
eyes are in a heavy case, your purse in a light; yet   150
you see how this world goes.
    GLOUCESTER. I see it feelingly.
    LEAR. What, art mad? A man may see how this
     world goes with no eyes. Look with thine ears;
see how yond justice rails upon yond simple thief.
Hark, in thine ear: change places, and, handy-
dandy, which is the justice, which is the thief?
Thou hast seen a farmer's dog bark at a beggar?
    GLOUCESTER. Ay, sir.   159
    LEAR. And the creature run from the cur? There
     thou mightst behold the great image of authority:
a dog's obey'd in office.
Thou rascal beadle, hold thy bloody hand!
Why dost thou lash that whore? Strip thy own back;
Thou hotly lusts to use her in that kind   **kind:** act

For which thou whip'st her. The usurer hangs the
    cozener.   **cozener:** petty cheat
Through tatter'd clothes great vices do appear;
Robes and furr'd gowns hide all. [Plate] sins with
    gold,
And the strong lance of justice hurtless breaks;
Arm it in rags, a pigmy's straw does pierce it.   170
None does offend, none, I say, none; I'll able 'em.   **able:** warrant
Take that of me, my friend, who have the power
To seal th' accuser's lips. Get thee glass eyes,
And, like a scurvy politician, seem
To see the things thou dost not. Now, now, now,
    now.
Pull off my boots; harder, harder: so.
    EDGAR. [*Aside*] O, matter and impertinency   **impertinency:** irrelevance
    mix'd!
Reason in madness!
    LEAR. If thou wilt weep my fortunes, take my
    eyes.
I know thee well enough; thy name is Gloucester.   180
Thou must be patient; we came crying hither.
Thou know'st, the first time that we smell the air,
We wawl and cry. I will preach to thee; mark.
    GLOUCESTER. Alack, alack the day!
    LEAR. When we are born, we cry that we are
    come
To this great stage of fools. — This' a good block.   **block:** hat (?)
It were a delicate stratagem, to shoe
A troop of horse with felt. I'll put 't in proof;
And when I have stol'n upon these son-in-laws,
Then, kill, kill, kill, kill, kill, kill!   190

    Enter a GENTLEMAN [*with Attendants*]

    GENTLEMAN. O, here he is! Lay hand upon him.
    Sir,
Your most dear daughter —
    LEAR. No rescue? What, a prisoner? I am even
The natural fool of Fortune. Use me well;
You shall have ransom. Let me have surgeons;
I am cut to th' brains.
    GENTLEMAN.   You shall have anything.
    LEAR. No seconds? All myself?   **seconds:** supporters
Why, this would make a man a man of salt,   **salt:** tears
To use his eyes for garden water-pots,
[Ay, and laying autumn's dust.
    GENTLEMAN.   Good sir, —]   200
    LEAR. I will die bravely, like a smug bridegroom.
    What!
I will be jovial. Come, come; I am a king,
My masters, know you that?

GENTLEMAN.   You are a royal one, and we obey
you.

LEAR.   Then there's life in't. Come, an you get it,
you shall get it by running. Sa, sa, sa, sa.

> Sa: hunting call

[Exit [running; attendants follow]

GENTLEMAN.   A sight most pitiful in the meanest
wretch,
Past speaking of in a king! Thou hast [one] daughter
Who redeems Nature from the general curse
Which twain have brought her to.   210

EDGAR.   Hail, gentle sir.

GENTLEMAN.   Sir, speed you: what's your
will?

> speed: God speed

EDGAR.   Do you hear aught, sir, of a battle toward?

> toward: imminent

GENTLEMAN.   Most sure and vulgar; every one
hears that,

> vulgar: of common knowledge

Which can distinguish sound.

EDGAR.   But, by your favour,
How near's the other army?

GENTLEMAN.   Near and on speedy foot; the main
descry

> the main . . . thought: Every hour we expect to catch sight of the main body.

Stands on the hourly thought.

EDGAR.   I thank you, sir; that's all.

GENTLEMAN.   Though that the Queen on special
cause is here,
Her army is mov'd on.   [Exit

EDGAR.   I thank you, sir.

GLOUCESTER.   You ever-gentle gods, take my
breath from me;   220
Let not my worser spirit tempt me again
To die before you please!

EDGAR.   Well pray you, father.

GLOUCESTER.   Now, good sir, what are you?

EDGAR.   A most poor man, made tame to For-
tune's blows;
Who, by the art of known and feeling sorrows,
Am pregnant to good pity. Give me your hand,
I'll lead you to some biding.

> art: experience
> pregnant: ready
> biding: dwelling

GLOUCESTER.   Hearty thanks;
The bounty and the benison of Heaven
To boot, and boot!

> To boot: also

Enter Steward [OSWALD]

OSWALD.   A proclaim'd prize! Most happy!   230
That eyeless head of thine was first fram'd flesh
To raise my fortunes. Thou old unhappy traitor,
Briefly thyself remember; the sword is out
That must destroy thee.

> proclaim'd prize: criminal sought for a reward

> thyself remember: think on your soul's welfare
> friendly: because Gloucester now wishes to die

GLOUCESTER.   Now let thy friendly hand

Put strength enough to't.   [*Edgar interposes.*]

OSWALD.   Wherefore, bold peasant,
Dar'st thou support a publish'd traitor? Hence;
Lest that the infection of his fortune take
Like hold on thee. Let go his arm.

EDGAR.   'Chill not let go, zir, without vurther
   'casion.   240

OSWALD.   Let go, slave, or thou diest!

EDGAR.   Good gentleman, go your gait, and let
   poor volk pass. An 'chud ha' bin zwagger'd out
of my life, 'twould not ha' bin zo long as 'tis by a
vortnight. Nay, come not near th' old man; keep out,
'che vor ye, or Ise try whether your costard or my
ballow be the harder. 'Chill be plain with you.

OSWALD.   Out, dunghill!

EDGAR.   'Chill pick your teeth, zir. Come, no
   matter vor your foins.   250

         [*They fight, and Edgar knocks him down.*]

OSWALD.   Slave, thou hast slain me. Villain, take
   my purse.
If ever thou wilt thrive, bury my body;
And give the letters which thou find'st about me
To Edmund Earl of Gloucester; seek him out
Upon the English party. O, untimely death!
Death!   [*Dies*

EDGAR.   I know thee well; a serviceable villain,
As duteous to the vices of thy mistress
As badness would desire.

GLOUCESTER.   What, is he dead?

EDGAR.   Sit you down, father; rest you.   260
Let's see these pockets; the letters that he speaks of
May be my friends. He's dead; I am only sorry
He had no other death's-man. Let us see.
Leave, gentle wax; and, manners, blame us not.
To know our enemies' minds, we rip their hearts;
Their papers, is more lawful.

(*Reads the letter*) "Let our reciprocal vows be
rememb'red. You have many opportunities to cut
him off; if your will want not, time and place will
be fruitfully offer'd. There is nothing done, if he   270
return the conqueror; then am I the prisoner, and his
bed my gaol; from the loathed warmth whereof deliver me, and supply the place for your labour.
      "Your — wife, so I would say —
                  "Affectionate servant,
                        "GONERIL."

O indistinguish'd space of woman's will!
A plot upon her virtuous husband's life;
And the exchange my brother! Here, in the sands,
Thee I'll rake up, the post unsanctified   280

'Chill: I will (Edgar takes the part of a peasant and uses Southern dialect.)

volk: folk.   **An 'chud:** if I could

'che vor: I warn.   **Ise:** I shall   **costard:** head.   **ballow:** cudgel

foins: thrusts

death's-man: executioner
Leave: by your leave

servant: lover

indistinguish'd space: unlimited range.   **will:** lust

rake: cover

Of murderous lechers; and in the mature time
With this ungracious paper strike the sight
Of the death-practis'd duke. For him 'tis well

death-practis'd: whose death is plotted

That of thy death and business I can tell.

GLOUCESTER. The King is mad; how stiff is my
vile sense
That I stand up and have ingenious feeling

ingenious: conscious

Of my huge sorrows! Better I were distract;
So should my thoughts be sever'd from my griefs,
And woes by wrong imaginations lose

wrong imaginations: delusions

The knowledge of themselves.   [*Drum afar off*
EDGAR.   Give me your hand.   290
Far off, methinks, I hear the beaten drum.
Come, father, I'll bestow you with a friend. [*Exeunt*]

bestow: lodge

SCENE VII [*A tent in the French camp*]

        Enter CORDELIA, KENT, *and* [DOCTOR]

CORDELIA. O thou good Kent, how shall I live
        and work
To match thy goodness? My life will be too short,
And every measure fail me.
        KENT. To be acknowledg'd, madam, is o'erpaid.
All my reports go with the modest truth;

go: conform

Nor more nor clipp'd, but so.
        CORDELIA.   Be better suited;
These weeds are memories of those worser hours.

weeds: clothes

I prithee, put them off.
        KENT.   Pardon, dear madam;
Yet to be known shortens my made intent.

shortens: interferes with. *made:* prearranged

My boon I make it, that you know me not   10
Till time and I think meet.
        CORDELIA. Then be't so, my good lord. [*To the
        Doctor*] How does the King?
        [DOCTOR] Madam, sleeps still.
        CORDELIA. O you kind gods,
Cure this great breach in his abused nature!
Th' untun'd and jarring senses, O, wind up
Of this child-changed father!

wind up: tune from a stringed instrument. *child-changed:* (1) changed by his children's conduct, (2) changed to a child again

        [DOCTOR]   So please your Majesty
That we may wake the King? He hath slept long.
        CORDELIA. Be govern'd by your knowledge, and
        proceed
I' th' sway of your own will.

I' th' sway of: according to

        Enter LEAR *in a chair carried by* Servants
                [GENTLEMAN *in attendance*]
                        Is he array'd?   20
GENTLEMAN. Ay, madam; in the heaviness of
        sleep
We put fresh garments on him.

[DOCTOR] Be by, good madam, when we do
awake him;
I doubt [not] of his temperance.

temperance: peace of mind

[CORDELIA.   Very well.

[*Music*

DOCTOR. Please you, draw near. — Louder the
music there!]

CORDELIA.   O my dear father! Restoration hang
Thy medicine on my lips; and let this kiss
Repair those violent harms that my two sisters
Have in thy reverence made!

KENT.   Kind and dear princess!

CORDELIA.   Had you not been their father, these
white flakes   30

flakes: hairs

Did challenge pity of them. Was this a face
To be oppos'd against the [warring] winds?
[To stand against the deep dread-bolted thunder?

deep: deep-sounding

In the most terrible and nimble stroke
Of quick, cross lightning? to watch — poor perdu! —

cross: zigzag.   perdu: a sentinel placed in a dangerous station
helm: covering (of hair)

With this thin helm?] Mine enemy's dog,
Though he had bit me, should have stood that night
Against my fire; and wast thou fain, poor father,
To hovel thee with swine and rogues forlorn
In short and musty straw? Alack, alack!   40
'Tis wonder that thy life and wits at once
Had not concluded all. He wakes; speaks to him.

all: altogether

DOCTOR.   Madam, do you; 'tis fittest.

CORDELIA.   How does my royal lord? How fares
your Majesty?

LEAR.   You do me wrong to take me out o' th'
grave.
Thou art a soul in bliss; but I am bound
Upon a wheel of fire, that mine own tears
Do scald like molten lead.

wheel of fire: hellish torture (Lear thinks he is in hell.)

CORDELIA.   Sir, do you know me?

LEAR.   You are a spirit, I know; where did you
die?

CORDELIA.   Still, still, far wide!   50

wide: astray

DOCTOR.   He's scarce awake; let him alone a while.

LEAR.   Where have I been? Where am I? Fair
daylight?
I am mightily abus'd. I should ev'n die with pity,
To see another thus. I know not what to say.
I will not swear these are my hands. Let's see;
I feel this pin prick. Would I were assur'd
Of my condition!

CORDELIA.   O, look upon me, sir,
And hold your hand in benediction o'er me.
[No, sir,] you must not kneel.

LEAR.   Pray, do not mock me.

I am a very foolish fond old man,   60
Fourscore and upward, not an hour more nor less;
And, to deal plainly,
I fear I am not in my perfect mind.
Methinks I should know you, and know this man;
Yet I am doubtful; for I am mainly ignorant   **mainly:** completely
What place this is, and all the skill I have
Remembers not these garments; nor I know not
Where I did lodge last night. Do not laugh at me;
For, as I am a man, I think this lady
To be my child Cordelia.
   CORDELIA.   And so I am, I am.   70
   LEAR. Be your tears wet? Yes, faith. I pray, weep
     not.
If you have poison for me, I will drink it.
I know you do not love me; for your sisters
Have, as I do remember, done me wrong:
You have some cause, they have not.
   CORDELIA   No cause, no cause.
   LEAR. Am I in France?
   KENT.   In your own kingdom, sir.
   LEAR. Do not abuse me.
   DOCTOR. Be comforted, good madam; the great
     rage,
You see, is kill'd in him: [and yet it is danger
To make him even o'er the time he has lost.]   80   **make . . . lost:** calm him by re-
Desire him to go in; trouble him no more   calling what has happened
Till further settling.
   CORDELIA. Will't please your Highness walk?
   LEAR.   You must bear with me.
Pray you now, forget and forgive; I am old and
     foolish.
          [Exeunt [all but Kent and Gentleman]
   [GENTLEMAN. Holds it true, sir, that the Duke
     of Cornwall was so slain?
   KENT. Most certain, sir.
   GENTLEMAN. Who is conductor of his people?
   KENT. As 'tis said, the bastard son of Gloucester.
   GENTLEMAN. They say Edgar, his banish'd   90
     son, is with the Earl of Kent in Germany.
   KENT. Report is changeable. 'Tis time to look   **changeable:** unreliable
     about; the powers of the kingdom approach
apace.
   GENTLEMAN. The arbitrement is like to be   **arbitrement:** decisive battle
     bloody. Fare you well, sir.   *[Exit]*
   KENT. My point and period will be thoroughly   **My . . . period:** the question of
     wrought,   my end
Or well or ill, as this day's battle's fought.]   *[Exit*

ACT V

SCENE I [*The British camp, near Dover*]

Enter, with drum and colours, EDMUND, REGAN,
Officers, *and* Soldiers

EDMUND.   Know of the Duke if his last purpose   last: most recent
hold,
Or whether since he is advis'd by aught
To change the course. He's full of alteration
And self-reproving; bring his constant pleasure.   constant pleasure: fixed decision
                    [*To an Officer, who goes out*]
REGAN.   Our sister's man is certainly miscarried.   is . . . miscarried: has met disaster
EDMUND.   'Tis to be doubted, madam.   doubted: feared
REGAN.   Now, sweet lord,
You know the goodness I intend upon you.
Tell me — but truly — but then speak the truth,
Do you not love my sister?
EDMUND.   In honour'd love.   honour'd: honorable
REGAN.   But have you never found my brother's
way   10
To the forfended place?   forfended: forbidden
[EDMUND.   That thought abuses you.   abuses: (1) deceives, (2) insults
REGAN.   I am doubtful that you have been conjunct
And bosom'd with her, — as far as we call hers.]   bosom'd: intimate. as . . . hers:
                                                     to the utmost limit
EDMUND.   No, by mine honour, madam.
REGAN.   I never shall endure her. Dear my lord,
Be not familiar with her.
EDMUND.   Fear me not.
She and the Duke her husband!

Enter, with drum and colours, ALBANY, GONERIL,
and Soldiers

[GONERIL. [*Aside*] I had rather lose the battle
than that sister
Should loosen him and me.]
ALBANY.   Our very loving sister, well be-met.   20
Sir, this I heard: the King is come to his daughter,
With others whom the rigour of our state
Forc'd to cry out. [Where I could not be honest,
I never yet was valiant. For this business,
It toucheth us, as France invades our land,
Not bolds the King, with others, whom, I fear,
Most just and heavy causes make oppose.
EDMUND.   Sir, you speak nobly.]
REGAN.   Why is this reason'd?   reason'd: discussed
GONERIL.   Combine together 'gainst the enemy;
For these domestic and particular broils   30

Are not the question here.

ALBANY.   Let's then determine

With the ancient of war on our proceeding.   *ancient: veterans*

  [EDMUND. I shall attend you presently at your
    tent.]

  REGAN. Sister, you'll go with us?

  GONERIL. No.

  REGAN. 'Tis most convenient; pray you, go with   *convenient: suitable. us: me,*
    us.   *rather than Edmund.*

  GONERIL. [*Aside*] O, ho, I know the riddle. — I   *riddle: reason for the remark*
    will go.   [*Exeunt both the armies*

[*As they are going out,*] *enter* EDGAR [*disguised.*
        Albany remains]

  EDGAR. If e'er your Grace had speech with man
    so poor,

Hear me one word.

  ALBANY.   I'll overtake you. — Speak.

  EDGAR. Before you fight the battle, ope this
    letter.   40

If you have victory, let the trumpet sound

For him that brought it. Wretched though I seem,

I can produce a champion that will prove

What is avouched there. If you miscarry,

Your business of the world hath so an end,

And machination ceases. Fortune love you!

  ALBANY. Stay till I have read the letter.

  EDGAR.   I was forbid it.

When time shall serve, let but the herald cry,

And I'll appear again.   [*Exit*

  ALBANY. Why, fare thee well; I will o'erlook thy   *o'erlook: look over, peruse*
    paper.   50

        Re-enter EDMUND

  EDMUND. The enemy's in view; draw up your
    powers.

Here is the guess of their true strength and forces

By diligent discovery; but your haste   *discovery: scouting*

Is now urg'd on you.

  ALBANY.   We will greet the time. [*Exit*   *greet the time: meet the occasion*

  EDMUND. To both these sisters have I sworn my
    love;

Each jealous of the other as the stung

Are of the adder. Which of them shall I take?

Both? one? or neither? Neither can be enjoy'd,

If both remain alive. To take the widow

Exasperates, makes mad her sister Goneril;   60

And hardly shall I carry out my side,   *side: purpose*

Her husband being alive. Now then we'll use

His countenance for the battle; which being done,   *countenance: authority*

Let her who would be rid of him devise
His speedy taking off. As for the mercy
Which he intends to Lear and to Cordelia,
The battle done, and they within our power,
Shall never see his pardon; for my state
Stands on me to defend, not to debate.   [*Exit*

Stands on: requires

SCENE II [*A field between the two camps*]

*Alarum within. Enter, with drum and colours, Lear,
    Cordelia, and Soldiers, over the stage; and exeunt*

Enter EDGAR *and* GLOUCESTER

EDGAR.   Here, father, take the shadow of this tree
For your good host; pray that the right may thrive.
If ever I return to you again,
I'll bring you comfort.
    GLOUCESTER.   Grace go with you, sir!
                              [*Exit* [*Edgar*]

father: old man (Edgar has not revealed who he is.) **host:** shelterer

Alarum and retreat within. Re-enter EDGAR

EDGAR.   Away, old man; give me thy hand; away!
King Lear hath lost, he and his daughter ta'en.
Give me thy hand; come on.
    GLOUCESTER.   No further, sir; a man may rot even
        here.
    EDGAR.   What, in ill thoughts again? Men must
        endure
Their going hence even as their coming hither;   10
Ripeness is all. Come on.
    GLOUCESTER.   And that's true too.
                              [*Exeunt*

Ripeness: (1) awareness, (2) maturity

SCENE III [*The British camp near Dover*]

Enter, in conquest, with drum and colours, EDMUND;
        LEAR *and* CORDELIA *as prisoners;* CAPTAIN,
                  Soldiers, *etc.*

EDMUND.   Some officers take them away. Good
        guard,
Until their greater pleasures first be known
That are to censure them.
    CORDELIA   We are not the first
Who with best meaning have incurr'd the worst.
For thee, oppressed king, I am cast down;
Myself could else out-frown false Fortune's frown.
Shall we not see these daughters and these sisters?
    LEAR.   No, no, no, no! Come, let's away to
        prison;

their greater pleasures: the desires of those greater persons. **censure:** judge

We two alone will sing like birds i' th' cage.
When thou dost ask me blessing, I'll kneel down   10
And ask of thee forgiveness. So we'll live,
And pray, and sing, and tell old tales, and laugh
At gilded butterflies, and hear poor rogues   *butterflies: courtiers*
Talk of court news; and we'll talk with them too,
Who loses and who wins; who's in, who's out;
And take upon 's the mystery of things
As if we were God's spies; and we'll wear out,   *God's spies: spies on God's ways*
In a wall'd prison, packs and sects of great ones,   *wear out: outlast*
That ebb and flow by th' moon.
    EDMUND.   Take them away.
    LEAR. Upon such sacrifices, my Cordelia.   20
The gods themselves throw incense. Have I caught   *incense: approval.* **caught:** *won*
  thee?
He that parts us shall bring a brand from heaven,
And fire us hence like foxes. Wipe thine eyes;   *fire us hence: smoke us out*
The good-years shall devour them, flesh and fell,   *good-years: an expression for*
Ere they shall make us weep. We'll see 'em starv'd   *some vague evil influence.* **fell:**
    first.   *skin*
Come.   *[Exeunt [Lear and Cordelia, guarded]*
    EDMUND. Come hither, captain; hark.
Take thou this note [*giving a paper*]; go follow them
    to prison.
One step I have advanc'd thee; if thou dost
As this instructs thee, thou dost make thy way
To noble fortunes. Know thou this, that men   30
Are as the time is; to be tender-minded   *as the time is: opportunistic*
Does not become a sword. Thy great employment   *sword: soldier*
Will not bear question; either say thou'lt do't,
Or thrive by other means.
    CAPTAIN.   I'll do't, my lord.
    EDMUND. About it; and write happy when thou'st   *write happy: call yourself lucky*
    done.
Mark, I say instantly; and carry it so
As I have set it down.
    [CAPTAIN. I cannot draw a cart, nor eat dried oats;
If it be man's work, I'll do't.]   [*Exit*

      Flourish. Enter ALBANY, GONERIL, REGAN,
        [*another* CAPTAIN] *and* Soldiers

    ALBANY. Sir, you have show'd to-day your valiant
    strain,   40
And Fortune led you well. You have the captives
Who were the opposites of this day's strife;
I do require them of you, so to use them
As we shall find their merits and our safety
May equally determine.
    EDMUND.   Sir, I thought it fit

To send the old and miserable king
To some retention [and appointed guard];
Whose age had charms in it, whose title more,
To pluck the common bosom on his side,
And turn our impress'd lances in our eyes   50
Which do command them. With him I sent the
    Queen,
My reason all the same; and they are ready
To-morrow, or at further space, t' appear
Where you shall hold your session. [At this time
We sweat and bleed: the friend hath lost his friend;
And the best quarrels, in the heat, are curs'd
By those that feel their sharpness:
The question of Cordelia and her father
Requires a fitter place.]
    ALBANY.   Sir, by your patience,
I hold you but a subject of this war,   60
Not as a brother.
    REGAN.   That's as we list to grace him.
Methinks our pleasure might have been demanded,
Ere you had spoke so far. He led our powers,
Bore the commission of my place and person;
The which immediacy may well stand up,
And call itself your brother.
    GONERIL.   Not so hot.
In his own grace he doth exalt himself,
More than in your addition.
    REGAN.   In my rights,
By me invested, he compeers the best.
    ALBANY. That were the most, if he should hus-
    band you.   70
    REGAN. Jesters do oft prove prophets.
    GONERIL.   Holla, holla!
That eye that told you so look'd but a-squint.
    REGAN. Lady, I am not well; else I should answer
From a full-flowing stomach. General,
Take thou my soldiers, prisoners, patrimony;
Dispose of them, of me; the walls are thine.
Witness the world, that I create thee here
My lord and master.
    GONERIL.   Mean you to enjoy him?
    ALBANY. The let-alone lies not in your good will.
    EDMUND. Nor in thine, lord.
    ALBANY.   Half-blooded fellow, yes.   80
    REGAN. [To Edmund] Let the drum strike, and
    prove my title thine.
    ALBANY. Stay yet; hear reason. Edmund, I arrest
    thee
On capital treason; and, in thy arrest,

common bosom: affection of the multitude. impress'd lances: weapons of our soldiers who have been pressed into our army

at further space: later
session: trial

list: choose

immediacy: close connection

your addition: what you call him

compeers: equals

stomach: anger. General: Edmund

the walls: I myself

let-alone: power of preventing it

Half-blooded: bastard (half noble)

This gilded serpent. [*Pointing to Goneril*] For your
    claim, fair sister,
I bar it in the interest of my wife.
'Tis she is sub-contracted to this lord,
And I, her husband, contradict your bans.   **bans:** announced intentions to
If you will marry, make your loves to me,   marry. **loves:** love-suits
My lady is bespoke.
    GONERIL.   An interlude!   **interlude:** comedy
    ALBANY.   Thou art arm'd, Gloucester; let the
    trumpet sound.   90
If none appear to prove upon thy person
Thy heinous, manifest, and many treasons,
There is my pledge [*throwing down a glove*]. I'll
    [prove] it on thy heart,
Ere I taste bread, thou art in nothing less
Than I have here proclaim'd thee.
    REGAN.   Sick, O, sick!
    GONERIL. [*Aside*] If not, I'll ne'er trust medicine.   **medicine:** poison
    EDMUND.   There's my exchange [*throwing down a*
    glove]. What in the world he is
/ That names me traitor, villain-like he lies.
Call by the trumpet; — he that dares approach,
On him, on you, who not? I will maintain   100
My truth and honour firmly.
    ALBANY.   A herald, ho!
    [EDMUND.   A herald, ho, a herald!]
    ALBANY.   Trust to thy single virtue; for thy sol-   **single:** unaided. **virtue:** strength
    diers,
All levied in my name, have in my name
Took their discharge.
    REGAN.   My sickness grows upon me.
    ALBANY.   She is not well; convey her to my tent.
                   [*Exit Regan, led*]

         Enter a HERALD

Come hither, herald, — Let the trumpet sound —
And read out this.
    [CAPTAIN.   Sound, trumpet!]
                [*A trumpet sounds.*
    HERALD. (*Reads.*) "If any man of quality or   110
    degree within the lists of the army will maintain
upon Edmund, supposed Earl of Gloucester, that he   **supposed:** pretended
is a manifold traitor, let him appear by the third
sound of the trumpet. He is bold in his defence."
    [EDMUND.   Sound!]   [*First trumpet*
    HERALD.   Again!   [*Second trumpet*
    HERALD.   Again!   [*Third trumpet*
             [*Trumpet answers within*

Enter EDGAR, *at the third sound, armed, with*
a trumpet before him

trumpet: trumpeter, herald

ALBANY.   Ask him his purposes, why he appears
Upon this call o' th' trumpet.
HERALD.   What are you?
Your name, your quality? and why you answer   120
This present summons?
EDGAR.   Know, my name is lost,
By treason's tooth bare-gnawn and canker-bit,
Yet am I noble as the adversary
I come to cope.

canker-bit: worm-eaten

ALBANY.   Which is that adversary?
EDGAR.   What's he that speaks for Edmund Earl
      of Gloucester?
EDMUND.   Himself; what say'st thou to him?
EDGAR.   Draw thy sword.
That, if my speech offend a noble heart,
Thy arm may do thee justice; here is mine.
Behold, it is the privilege of mine honours,
My oath, and my profession. I protest,   130
Maugre thy strength, place, youth, and eminence,
Despite thy victor-sword and fire-new fortune,
Thy valour, and thy heart, thou art a traitor;
False to thy gods, thy brother, and thy father;
Conspirant 'gainst this high illustrious prince;
And, from th' extremest upward of thy head
To the descent and dust below thy foot,
A most toad-spotted traitor. Say thou "No,"
This sword, his arm, and my best spirits are bent
To prove upon thy heart, whereto I speak,   140
Thou liest.

honours: rank
profession: knighthood
Maugre: in spite of
fire-new: brand-new

descent: lowest part
toad-spotted: venomous

EDMUND.   In wisdom I should ask thy name;
But, since thy outside looks so fair and warlike,
And that thy tongue some 'say of breeding breathes,
What safe and nicely I might well delay
By rule of knighthood, I disdain and spurn.
Back do I toss these treasons to thy head;
With the hell-hated lie o'erwhelm thy heart;
Which, for they yet glance by and scarcely bruise,
This sword of mine shall give them instant way
Where they shall rest for ever. Trumpets, speak!   150
            [*Alarums. They fight.* [*Edmund falls.*]
ALBANY.   Save him, save him!
GONERIL.   This is [mere] practice, Gloucester.
By th' law of war thou wast not bound to answer
An unknown opposite. Thou art not vanquish'd,
But cozen'd and beguil'd.
ALBANY.   Shut your mouth, dame,

wisdom: wise practice (since he need not fight with men of lesser rank)
'say: trace
safe and nicely: safely and with technical correctness
treasons: accusations of treason

practice: a plot or trick

Or with this paper shall I stop it. Hold, sir. —
Thou worse than any name, read thine own evil.
No tearing, lady; I perceive you know it.

GONERIL. Say, if I do, the laws are mine, not
    thine.
Who can arraign me for't?

ALBANY.   Most monstrous! oh! —
Know'st thou this paper?

EDMUND.   Ask me not what I know. 160

[*Exit Goneril*]

ALBANY. Go after her; she's desperate; govern her.   **govern: restrain**

EDMUND. What you have charg'd me with, that
    have I done;
And more, much more; the time will bring it out.
'Tis past, and so am I. But what art thou
That hast this fortune on me? If thou'rt noble,   **fortune on: defeat of**
I do forgive thee.

EDGAR.   Let's exchange charity.
I am no less in blood than thou art, Edmund;
If more, the more thou'st wrong'd me.
My name is Edgar, and thy father's son.
The gods are just, and of our pleasant vices,   170   **pleasant: pleasurable**
Make instruments to plague us.
The dark and vicious place where thee he got
Cost him his eyes.

EDMUND.   Thou'st spoken right, 'tis true.
The wheel is come full circle; I am here.   **wheel: wheel of Fortune**

ALBANY. Methought thy very gait did prophesy
A royal nobleness. I must embrace thee.
Let sorrow split my heart, if ever I
Did hate thee or thy father!

EDGAR.   Worthy prince, I know't.

ALBANY. Where have you hid yourself?
How have you known the miseries of your father? 180

EDGAR. By nursing them, my lord. List a brief
    tale;
And when 'tis told, oh, that my heart would burst!
The bloody proclamation to escape,
That follow'd me so near, — oh, our lives' sweetness!
That we the pain of death would hourly die   **hourly die: continually suffer**
Rather than die at once! — taught me to shift
Into a madman's rags, t' assume a semblance
That very dogs disdain'd; and in this habit   **habit: dress**
Met I my father with his bleeding rings,
Their precious stones new lost; became his guide, 190
Led him, begg'd for him, sav'd him from despair;
Never, — O fault! — reveal'd myself unto him,
Until some half-hour past, when I was arm'd.
Not sure, though hoping, of this good success,

I ask'd his blessing, and from first to last
Told him our pilgrimage; but his flaw'd heart,   flaw'd: cracked
Alack, too weak the conflict to support!
'Twixt two extremes of passion, joy and grief,
Burst smilingly.

    EDMUND.   This speech of yours hath mov'd me,
And shall perchance do good. But speak you on;   200
You look as you had something more to say.

    ALBANY.   If there be more, more woeful, hold it in;
For I am almost ready to dissolve,   dissolve: weep
Hearing of this.

    [EDGAR.   This would have seem'd a period
To such as love not sorrow; but another,   but . . . extremity: One more such
To amplify too much, would make much more,   circumstance amplifying what is
And top extremity.   already too much, would increase
Whilst I was big in clamour came there in a man,   it and become humanly unbear-
Who, having seen me in my worst estate,   able. big in clamour: loud in
Shunn'd my abhorr'd society; but then, finding   210   grief
Who 'twas that so endur'd, with his strong arms
He fastened on my neck, and bellowed out
As he'd burst heaven; threw him on my father;
Told the most piteous tale of Lear and him
That ever ear receiv'd; which in recounting,
His grief grew puissant, and the strings of life
Began to crack. Twice then the trumpets sounded,
And there I left him tranc'd.   tranc'd: unconscious

    ALBANY.   But who was this?
    EDGAR.   Kent, sir, the banish'd Kent; who in dis-
guise
Follow'd his enemy king, and did him service   220   enemy: hostile
Improper for a slave.]   Improper: excessive

Enter an OFFICER *with a bloody knife*

    OFFICER.   Help, help, O, help!
    EDGAR.   What kind of help?
    ALBANY.   Speak, man.
    EDGAR.   What means this bloody knife?
    OFFICER.   'Tis hot, it smokes;
It came even from the heart of — O, she's dead!
    ALBANY.   Who dead? Speak, man.
    OFFICER.   Your lady, sir, your lady; and her sister
By her is poison'd; she confesses it.
    EDMUND.   I was contracted to them both. All
    three
Now marry in an instant.
    EDGAR.   Here comes Kent.

Enter KENT

    ALBANY.   Produce the bodies, be they alive or
    dead.   230

This judgement of the heavens, that makes us
   tremble,
Touches us not with pity.   [*Exit Officer*]
                       — O, is this he?
The time will not allow the compliment
Which very manners urges.

compliment: ceremony

very manners: basic graciousness

KENT.   I am come
To bid my king and master aye good-night.
Is he not here?
   ALBANY.   Great thing of us forgot!
Speak, Edmund, where's the King? and where's
   Cordelia?
            [*The bodies of Goneril and Regan are
               brought in.*
See'st thou this object, Kent?
   KENT.   Alack, why thus?
   EDMUND.   Yet Edmund was belov'd!
The one the other poison'd for my sake,   240
And after slew herself.
   ALBANY.   Even so. Cover their faces.
   EDMUND.   I pant for life. Some good I mean to
   do,
Despite of mine own nature. Quickly send,
Be brief in it, to th' castle; for my writ
Is on the life of Lear and on Cordelia.
Nay, send in time.
   ALBANY.   Run, run, O, run!
   EDGAR.   To who, my lord? Who has the office?
   Send
Thy token of reprieve.
   EDMUND.   Well thought on. Take my sword,   250
Give it the captain.
   EDGAR.   Haste thee, for thy life.
                       [*Exit Messenger*]
   EDMUND.   He hath commission from thy wife and
   me
To hang Cordelia in the prison, and
To lay the blame upon her own despair,
That she fordid herself.

fordid: destroyed

   ALBANY.   The gods defend her! Bear him hence a
   while.   [*Edmund is borne off.*]

   Re-enter LEAR *with Cordelia in his arms*
            [OFFICER *following*]

   LEAR.   Howl, howl, howl! O, you are men of
   stones!
Had I your tongues and eyes, I'd use them so
That heaven's vault should crack. She's gone for ever!
I know when one is dead, and when one lives;   260
She's dead as earth. Lend me a looking-glass;

If that her breath will mist or stain the stone,   stone: polished crystal, mirror
Why, then she lives.

KENT.   Is this the promis'd end?   promis'd end: Last Judgment

EDGAR.   Or image of that horror?

ALBANY.   Fall, and cease!

LEAR.   This feather stirs; she lives! If it be so,
It is a chance which does redeem all sorrows
That ever I have felt.

KENT.   [*Kneeling*] O my good master!

LEAR.   Prithee, away.

EDGAR.   'Tis noble Kent, your friend.

LEAR.   A plague upon you, murderers, traitors all!
I might have sav'd her; now she's gone for ever!   270
Cordelia, Cordelia! stay a little. Ha!
What is't thou say'st? Her voice was ever soft,
Gentle, and low; an excellent thing in woman.
I kill'd the slave that was a-hanging thee.

GENTLEMAN.   'Tis true, my lords, he did.

LEAR.   Did I not, fellow?
I have seen the day, with my good biting falchion
I would have made him skip. I am old now,
And these same crosses spoil me. Who are you?   crosses: sufferings
Mine eyes are not o' th' best. I'll tell you straight.   straight: at once

KENT.   If Fortune brag of two she lov'd and
       hated,   280
One of them we behold.

LEAR.   This is a dull sight. Are you not Kent?

KENT.   The same,   Caius: Kent's disguised name
Your servant Kent. Where is your servant Caius?

LEAR.   He's a good fellow, I can tell you that;
He'll strike, and quickly too. He's dead and rotten.

KENT.   No, my good lord; I am the very man, —

LEAR.   I'll see that straight.   that: to that

KENT.   — That, from your first of difference and   first . . . decay: beginning of the
   decay,   change and decay of your fortunes
Have follow'd your sad steps —

LEAR.   You are welcome hither.

KENT.   Nor no man else; All's cheerless, dark, and
   deadly.   290
Your eldest daughters have fordone themselves,
And desperately are dead.

LEAR.   Ay, so I think.

ALBANY.   He knows not what he says; and vain
   is it
That we present us to him.

Enter a MESSENGER

EDGAR.   Very bootless.   bootless: useless

MESSENGER. Edmund is dead, my lord.
ALBANY.   That's but a trifle here. —
You lords and noble friends, know our intent.
What comfort to this great decay may come   *great decay: ruined king*
Shall be appli'd. For us, we will resign,
During the life of this old majesty,
To him our absolute power; [*to Edgar and Kent*]
      you, to your rights,   300
With boot, and such addition as your honours   *boot: good measure*
Have more than merited. All friends shall taste
The wages of their virtue, and all foes
The cup of their deservings. O, see, see!
  LEAR.   And my poor fool is hang'd! No, no, no   *poor fool: Cordelia*
      life!
Why should a dog, a horse, a rat, have life,
And thou no breath at all? Thou'lt come no more,
Never, never, never, never, never!
Pray you, undo this button. Thank you, sir.
Do you see this? Look on her, look, her lips,   310
Look there, look there!   [*Dies*
  EDGAR.   He faints! My lord, my lord!
  KENT.   Break, heart; I prithee, break!
  EDGAR.   Look up, my lord.
  KENT. Vex not his ghost; O, let him pass! He
      hates him
That would upon the rack of this tough world
Stretch him out longer.
  EDGAR.   He is gone, indeed.
  KENT.   The wonder is he hath endur'd so long;
He but usurp'd his life.
  ALBANY.   Bear them from hence. Our present
      business
Is general woe. [*To Kent and Edgar*] Friends of my
      soul, you twain
Rule in this realm, and the gor'd state sustain.   320   *gor'd: wounded*
  KENT.   I have a journey, sir, shortly to go.
My master calls me; I must not say no.
  EDGAR. The weight of this sad time we must obey;
Speak what we feel, not what we ought to say.
The oldest hath borne most; we that are young
Shall never see so much, nor live so long.
            [*Exeunt, with a dead march*

John Donne (1573–1631)

ENGLISH POET and CLERGYMAN

The Indifferent

I can love both faire and browne,
Her whom abundance melts, and her whom want betraies,
Her who loves lonenesse best, and her who maskes and plaies,
　Her whom the country form'd, and whom the town,
　　Her who beleeves, and her who tries,
　　Her who still weepes with spungie eyes,
　And her who is dry corke, and never cries;
　I can love her, and her, and you and you,
　I can love any, so she be not true.

　Will no other vice content you? 　　　　　　　　　　　10
Will it not serve your turn to do, as did your mothers?
Or have you all old vices spent, and now would finde out others?
　Or doth a feare, that men are true, torment you?
　　Oh we are not, be not you so,
　　Let mee and doe you, twenty know.
　Rob mee, but binde me not, and let me goe.
　Must I, who came to travaile thorow you,
　Grow your fixt subject, because you are true?

　Venus heard me sigh this song,
And by Loves sweetest Part, Variety, she swore, 　　　　　20
She heard not this till now; and 't should be so no more.
　She went, examin'd, and return'd ere long,
　　And said, alas, Some two or three
　　Poore Heretiques in love there bee,
　Which thinke to stablish dangerous constancie.
　But I have told them, since you will be true,
　You shall be true to them, who'are false to you.

"The Indifferent" and "A Valediction: forbidding Mourning" by John Donne. From *John Donne: The Elegies and The Songs and Sonnets*, edited by Helen Gardner. Reprinted by permission of the Clarendon Press, Oxford.

A Valediction: forbidding Mourning

As virtuous men passe mildly 'away,
  And whisper to their soules, to goe,
Whilst some of their sad friends doe say,
  The breath goes now, and some say, no:

So let us melt, and make no noise,
  No teare-floods, nor sigh-tempests move,
T'were prophanation of our joyes
  To tell the layetie our love.

Moving of th'earth brings harmes and feares,
  Men reckon what it did and meant,   10
But trepidation of the spheares,
  Though greater farre, is innocent.

trepidation of the spheares: motion of the outermost transparent sphere of the universe (in Ptolemaic, or earth-centered, ı astronomy) which caused the occurrence of the equinox to vary

Dull sublunary lovers love
  (Whose soule is sense) cannot admit
Absence, because it doth remove
  Those things which elemented it.

elemented: composed

But we by a love, so much refin'd,
  That our selves know not what it is,
Inter-assured of the mind,
  Care lesse, eyes, lips, and hands to misse.   20

Our two soules therefore, which are one,
  Though I must goe, endure not yet
A breach, but an expansion,
  Like gold to ayery thinnesse beate.

If they be two, they are two so
  As stiffe twin compasses are two,
Thy soule the fixt foot, makes no show
  To move, but doth, if th'other doe.

And though it in the center sit,
  Yet when the other far doth rome,   30
It leanes, and hearkens after it,
  And growes erect, as it comes home.

Such wilt thou be to mee, who must
  Like th'other foot, obliquely runne;
Thy firmnes makes my circle just,
  And makes me end, where I begunne.

Batter My Heart, Three Person'd God

Batter my heart, three person'd God; for, you
As yet but knocke, breathe, shine, and seeke to mend;
That I may rise, and stand, o'erthrow mee,'and bend
Your force, to breake, blowe, burn and make me new.
I, like an usurpt towne, to'another due,
Labour to'admit you, but Oh, to no end,
Reason your viceroy in mee, mee should defend,
But is captiv'd, and proves weake or untrue.
Yet dearely'I love you, and would be lov'd faine,
But am betroth'd unto your enemie,   10
Divorce mee,'untie, or breake that knot againe,
Take mee to you, imprison mee, for I
Except you'enthrall mee, never shall be free,
Nor ever chast, except you ravish mee.

Thomas Overbury   (1581–1613)

ENGLISH POET, ESSAYIST, and COURTIER

A Good Wife

Is a mans best mooveable, a scien[1] incorporat with the stock, bringing sweet
fruit; one that to her husband is more then a friend, lesse then trouble: an
equall with him in the yoke. Calamities and troubles shee shares alike,
nothing pleaseth her that doth not him. She is relative[2] in all; and hee without her but halfe himselfe. She is his absent hands, eyes, eares, and mouth:
his present and absent All. She frames her nature unto his howsoever, the
Hiacinth followes not the Sunne more willingly. Stubbornnes and obstinacie
are hearbs[3] that grow not in her garden. She leaves tatling to the gossips of
the towne, and is more seene then heard: her houshould is her charge, her care
to that makes her seldome non-resident. Her pride is, but to be cleanly, and

[1] scion, living branch.
[2] A good wife, though opposite by nature to man, is in everything his complement.
[Paylor]
[3] herbs.

"Batter My Heart, Three Person'd God" by John Donne: Holy Sonnet XIV. From *John Donne: The Divine Poems*, edited by Helen Gardner. Reprinted by permission of the Clarendon Press, Oxford.

"A Good Wife" by Thomas Overbury. From *The Overburian Characters*, edited by W. J. Paylor. Reprinted by permission of Basil Blackwell, Publisher, Oxford.

her thrift not to be prodigall. By her discretion she hath children, not wantons; a husband without her is a misery in a mans apparell: none but she hath an aged husband, to whom shee is both a staffe and a chaire. To conclude, she is both wise and religious, which makes her all this.

George Herbert (1593–1633)
ENGLISH POET and CLERGYMAN

Love (III)

Love bade me welcome: yet my soul drew back,
        Guiltie of dust and sinne.
But quick-ey'd Love, observing me grow slack
        From my first entrance in,
Drew nearer to me, sweetly questioning,
        If I lack'd any thing.

A guest, I answer'd, worthy to be here:
        Love said, You shall be he.
I the unkinde, ungratefull? Ah my deare,
        I cannot look on thee.   10
Love took my hand, and smiling did reply,
        Who made the eyes but I?   the: thee

Truth Lord, but I have marr'd them: let my shame
        Go where it doth deserve.
And know you not, sayes Love, who bore the blame?
        My deare, then I will serve.
You must sit down, sayes Love, and taste my meat:
        So I did sit and eat.

"Love (III)" by George Herbert. From *The Works of George Herbert*, edited by F. E. Hutchinson. Reprinted by permission of the Clarendon Press, Oxford.

Andrew Marvell   (1621–1678)

ENGLISH POET and SATIRIST

To His Coy Mistress

Had we but World enough, and Time,
This coyness Lady were no crime.
We would sit down, and think which way
To walk, and pass our long Loves Day.
Thou by the *Indian Ganges* side
Should'st Rubies find: I by the Tide
Of *Humber* would complain. I would
Love you ten years before the Flood:
And you should if you please refuse
Till the Conversion of the *Jews*.   10
My vegetable Love should grow
Vaster then Empires, and more slow.
An hundred years should go to praise
Thine Eyes, and on thy Forehead Gaze.
Two hundred to adore each Breast:
But thirty thousand to the rest.
An Age at least to every part,
And the last Age should show your Heart.
For Lady you deserve this State;
Nor would I love at lower rate.   20
    But at my back I alwaies hear
Times winged Charriot hurrying near:
And yonder all before us lye
Desarts of vast Eternity.
Thy Beauty shall no more be found;
Nor, in thy marble Vault, shall sound
My ecchoing Song: then Worms shall try
That long preserv'd Virginity:
And your quaint Honour turn to dust;
And into ashes all my Lust.   30
The Grave's a fine and private place,
But none I think do there embrace.
    Now therefore, while the youthful hew
Sits on thy skin like morning lew,
And while thy willing Soul transpires
At every pore with instant Fires,

Humber: river between Lincolnshire and Marvell's native Yorkshire. complain: sing sadly of love Flood: at the time of Noah. Conversion of the Jews: to occur just before the Last Judgment. vegetable: proclivity for growth only

Desarts: deserts

quaint: fastidious

lew: warmth; dew

"To His Coy Mistress" by Andrew Marvell. From *The Poems and Letters of Andrew Marvell*, edited by H. M. Margoliouth. Reprinted by permission of the Clarendon Press, Oxford.

Now let us sport us while we may;
And now, like am'rous birds of prey,
Rather at once our Time devour,
Than languish in his slow-chapt pow'r.   40   **slow-chapt:** slowly devouring
Let us roll all our Strength, and all
Our sweetness, up into one Ball:
And tear our Pleasures with rough strife,
Thorough the Iron gates of Life.
Thus, though we cannot make our Sun
Stand still, yet we will make him run.

Isaac Watts (1674–1748)

ENGLISH HYMN-WRITER and CLERGYMAN

The Hazard of Loving the Creatures

Where'er my flattering passions rove,
    I find a lurking snare;
'Tis dangerous to let loose our love
    Beneath the Eternal Fair.

Souls whom the tie of friendship binds
    And partners of our blood,
Seize a large portion of our minds,
    And leave the less for God.

Nature has soft but powerful bands,
    And Reason she controls;   10
While children with their little hands
    Hang closest to our souls.

Thoughtless they act the old serpent's part;
    What tempting things they be!
Lord, how they twine about our heart,
    And draw it off from thee!

Our hasty wills rush blindly on
    Where rising passion rolls,
And thus we make our fetters strong
    To bind our slavish souls.   20

"The Hazard of Loving the Creatures" by Isaac Watts. From *The Collected Works of Isaac Watts*.

> Dear Sovereign, break these fetters off,
>   And set our spirits free;
> God in himself is bliss enough,
>   For we have all in thee.

Oliver Goldsmith (1728–1774)

IRISH ESSAYIST, NOVELIST, and DRAMATIST (IN ENGLAND)

The Man in Black

THE CHARACTER OF THE MAN IN BLACK; WITH
SOME INSTANCES OF HIS INCONSISTENT CONDUCT.

*From Lien Chi Altangi, to Fum Hoam, first president of the Ceremonial
Academy at Pekin, in China.*

Tho' fond of many acquaintances, I desire an intimacy only with a few.
The man in black whom I have often mentioned, is one whose friendship
I cou'd wish to acquire, because he possesses my esteem. His manners, it is
true, are tinctured with some strange inconsistencies; and he may be justly
termed an humourist in a nation of humourists. Tho' he is generous even to
profusion, he affects to be thought a prodigy of parsimony and prudence;
though his conversation be replete with the most sordid and selfish maxims,
his heart is dilated with the most unbounded love. I have known him profess
himself a man hater, while his cheek was glowing with compassion; and while
his looks were softened into pity, I have heard him use the language of the
most unbounded ill nature. Some affect humanity and tenderness; others
boast of having such dispositions from nature; but he is the only man I ever
knew who seemed ashamed of his natural benevolence. He takes as much
pains to hide his feelings as an hypocrite would to conceal his indifference,
but on every unguarded moment the mask drops off, and reveals him to the
most superficial observer.

In one of our late excursions into the country, happening to discourse upon
the provision that was made for the poor in England, he seemed amazed how
any of his countrymen could be so foolishly weak as to relieve occasional

Title supplied by editors. "The Man in Black" by Oliver Goldsmith. Letter XXVI from
*The Citizen of the World; or Letters from a Chinese Philosopher, Residing in London,
to His Friends in the East* (in the *Public Ledger* for Thursday, 3 April 1760). From
Collected Works of Oliver Goldsmith, Vol. II, edited by Arthur Friedman. Reprinted
by permission of the Clarendon Press, Oxford.

objects of charity, when the laws had made such ample provision for their support. In every parish house, says he, the poor are supplied with food, cloaths, fire, and a bed to lie on; they want no more, I desire no more my self; yet still they seem discontented. I'm surprized at the inactivity of our magistrates, in not taking up such vagrants who are only a weight upon the industrious; I'm surprized that the people are found to relieve them, when they must be at the same time sensible that it, in some measure, encourages idleness, extravagance, and imposture. Were I to advise any man for whom I had the least regard, I would caution him by all means not to be imposed upon by their false pretences: let me assure you, Sir, they are impostors, every one of them; and rather merit a prison than relief.

He was proceeding in this strain earnestly, to dissuade me from an imprudence of which I am seldom guilty; when an old man who still had about him the remnants of tattered finery, implored our compassion. He assured us that he was no common beggar, but forced into the shameful profession, to support a dying wife and five hungry children. Being prepossessed against such falshoods, his story had not the least influence upon me; but it was quite otherwise with the man in black; I could see it visibly operate upon his countenance, and effectually interrupt his harangue. I could easily perceive that his heart burned to relieve the five starving children, but he seemed ashamed to discover his weakness to me. While he thus hesitated between compassion and pride, I pretended to look another way, and he seized this opportunity of giving the poor petitioner a piece of silver bidding him at the same time, in order that I should hear, go work for his bread, and not teize passengers with such impertinent falsehoods for the future.

As he had fancied himself quite unperceived, he continued, as we proceeded, to rail against beggars with as much animosity as before; he threw in some episodes on his own amazing prudence and œconomy, with his profound skill in discovering impostors; he explained the manner in which he would deal with beggars were he a magistrate, hinted at enlarging some of the prisons for their reception, and told two stories of ladies that were robbed by beggar men. He was beginning a third to the same purpose, when a sailor with a wooden leg once more crossed our walks, desiring our pity, and blessing our limbs. I was for going on without taking any notice, but my friend looking wishfully upon the poor petitioner, bid me stop, and he would shew me with how much ease he could at any time detect an impostor. He now therefore assumed a look of importance, and in an angry tone began to examine the sailor, demanding in what engagement he was thus disabled and rendered unfit for service. The sailor replied in a tone as angrily as he, that he had been an officer on board a private ship of war, and that he had lost his leg abroad in defence of those who did nothing at home. At this reply, all my friend's importance vanished in a moment; he had not a single question more to ask; he now only studied what method he should take to relieve him unobserved. He had however no easy part to act, as he was obliged to preserve the appearance of ill nature before me, and yet relieve himself by relieving the sailor.

Casting therefore a furious look upon some bundles of chips which the fellow carried in a string at his back, my friend demanded how he sold his matches; but not waiting for a reply, desired, in a surly tone, to have a shilling's worth. The sailor seemed at first surprised at his demand, but soon recollecting himself, and presenting his whole bundle, Here, master, says he, take all my cargo, and a blessing into the bargain.

It is impossible to describe with what an air of triumph my friend marched off with his new purchase, he assured me, that he was firmly of opinion that those fellows must have stolen their goods, who could thus afford to sell them for half value; he informed me of several different uses to which those chips might be applied, he expatiated largely upon the savings that would result from lighting candles with a match instead of thrusting them into the fire. He averred, that he would as soon have parted with a tooth as his money to those vagabonds, unless for some valuable consideration. I cannot tell how long this panegyric upon frugality and matches might have continued, had not his attention been called off by another object more distressful than either of the former. A woman in rags, with one child in her arms, and another on her back, was attempting to sing ballads, but with such a mournful voice that it was difficult to determine whether she was singing or crying. A wretch, who, in the deepest distress still aimed at good humour, was an object my friend was by no means capable of withstanding, his vivacity, and his discourse were instantly interrupted, upon this occasion his very dissimulation had forsaken him. Even, in my presence, he immediately applied his hands to his pockets, in order to relieve her, but guess his confusion, when he found he had already given away all the money he carried about him to former objects. The misery painted in the woman's visage, was not half so strongly expressed as the agony in his. He continued to search for some time, but to no purpose, 'till, at length, recollecting himself, with a face of ineffable good nature, as he had no money, he put into her hands his shilling's worth of matches.

George Gordon, Lord Byron (1788–1824)

ENGLISH POET

Stanzas to Augusta

I.

Though the day of my Destiny's over,
　And the star of my Fate hath declined,
Thy soft heart refused to discover
　The faults which so many could find;
Though thy Soul with my grief was acquainted,
　It shrunk not to share it with me,
And the Love which my Spirit hath painted
　It never hath found but in *Thee*.

II.

Then when Nature around me is smiling,
　The last smile which answers to mine,   10
I do not believe it beguiling,
　Because it reminds me of thine;
And when winds are at war with the ocean,
　As the breasts I believed in with me,
If their billows excite an emotion,
　It is that they bear me from *Thee*.

III.

Though the rock of my last Hope is shivered,
And its fragments are sunk in the wave,
Though I feel that my soul is delivered
　To Pain — it shall not be its slave.   20
There is many a pang to pursue me:
　They may crush, but they shall not contemn;
They may torture, but shall not subdue me;
　'Tis of *Thee* that I think — not of them.

IV.

Though human, thou didst not deceive me,
　Though woman, thou didst not forsake,
Though loved, thou forborest to grieve me,
　Though slander'd, thou never couldst shake;
Though trusted, thou didst not disclaim me,
　Though parted, it was not to fly,   30
Though watchful, 'twas not to defame me,
　Nor, mute, that the world might belie.

Augusta Leigh was Byron's half-sister, with whom he was suspected to have had incest.

From *The Works of Lord Byron*, Poetry, Vol. IV, edited by Ernest Hartley Coleridge. Reprinted by permission of John Murray (Publishers) Ltd., London.

V.

Yet I blame not the World, nor despise it,
    Nor the war of the many with one;
If my Soul was not fitted to prize it,
    'Twas folly not sooner to shun:
And if dearly that error hath cost me,
    And more than I once could foresee,
I have found that, whatever it lost me,
    It could not deprive me of *Thee*.   40

VI.

From the wreck of the past, which hath perished,
    Thus much I at least may recall,
It hath taught me that what I most cherished
    Deserved to be dearest of all:
In the desert a fountain is springing,
    In the wide waste there still is a tree,
And a bird in the solitude singing,
    Which speaks to my spirit of *Thee*.

Alfred Tennyson   (1809–1892)

ENGLISH POET

Saint Agnes' Eve

Deep on the convent-roof the snows
    Are sparkling to the moon;
My breath to heaven like vapour goes;
    May my soul follow soon!
The shadows of the convent-towers
    Slant down the snowy sward,
Still creeping with the creeping hours
    That lead me to my Lord.
Make Thou my spirit pure and clear
    As are the frosty skies,   10
Or this first snowdrop of the year
    That in my bosom lies.

St. Agnes, a Roman virgin, was martyred in about the year 300. According to legend, on St. Agnes' Eve (January 21) a virgin might have a vision of her intended husband.

"Saint Agnes' Eve" by Alfred Tennyson. **From *The Works of Tennyson with Notes by the Author*, edited by Hallam Tennyson.**

As these white robes are soil'd and dark,
    To yonder shining ground;
As this pale taper's earthly spark,
    To yonder argent round;
So shows my soul before the Lamb,
    My spirit before Thee;
So in mine earthly house I am,
    To that I hope to be.   20
Break up the heavens, O Lord! and far,
    Thro' all yon starlight keen,
Draw me, thy bride, a glittering star,
    In raiment white and clean.

He lifts me to the golden doors;
    The flashes come and go;
All heaven bursts her starry floors,
    And strows her lights below,
And deepens on and up! the gates
    Roll back, and far within   30
For me the Heavenly Bridegroom waits,
    To make me pure of sin.
The Sabbaths of Eternity,
    One Sabbath deep and wide —
A light upon the shining sea —
    The Bridegroom with his bride!

George Meredith   (1828–1909)

ENGLISH POET and NOVELIST

Hiding the Skeleton

At dinner, she is hostess, I am host.
Went the feast ever cheerfuller? She keeps
The Topic over intellectual deeps
In buoyancy afloat. They see no ghost.
With sparkling surface-eyes we ply the ball:
It is in truth a most contagious game:
HIDING THE SKELETON, shall be its name.
Such play as this, the devils might appal!

"Hiding the Skeleton" by George Meredith: Sonnet XVII
from *Modern Love.* From *The Poetry and the Philosophy of George Meredith,* edited by G. M. Trevelyan.

But here's the greater wonder; in that we,
Enamoured of an acting nought can tire,   10
Each other, like true hypocrites, admire;
Warm-lighted looks, Love's ephemeriae,   **ephemeriae:** mayflies, insects that
Shoot gaily o'er the dishes and the wine.   live only a few hours
We waken envy of our happy lot.
Fast, sweet, and golden, shows the marriage-knot.
Dear guests, you now have seen Love's corpse-light   **corpse-light:** lights, resembling
    shine.   candleflames, seen in graveyards
                                         or damp places and thought to
                                         portend death

Jean Richepin   (1849–1926)

FRENCH POET, DRAMATIST, and NOVELIST (ALGERIAN-BORN)

A Mother's Heart

There was a young man loved a maid
Who taunted him. "Are you afraid,"
She asked, "to bring to me today
Your mother's heart upon a tray?"

He went and slew his mother dead
Tore from her breast her heart so red
Then toward his lady-love he raced
But tripped and fell in all his haste.

As the heart raced on the ground
It gave forth a plaintive sound.   10
And it spoke, in accents mild:
"Did you hurt yourself, my child?"

Title supplied by editors. "A Mother's Heart" by Jean Richepin, translated by Maria
Pelikan. From *Children and Their Mothers*, published by Hill & Wang, Inc. Reprinted
by permission of Maria Pelikan.

Anton Chekhov (1860–1904)

RUSSIAN SHORT STORY WRITER, NOVELIST,
DRAMATIST, and PHYSICIAN

The Darling

Olenka, the daughter of the retired collegiate assessor, Plemyanniakov, was sitting in her back porch, lost in thought. It was hot, the flies were persistent and teasing, and it was pleasant to reflect that it would soon be evening. Dark rainclouds were gathering from the east, and bringing from time to time a breath of moisture in the air.

Kukin, who was the manager of an open-air theater called the Tivoli, and who lived in the lodge, was standing in the middle of the garden looking at the sky.

"Again!" he observed despairingly. "It's going to rain again! Rain every day, as though to spite me. I might as well hang myself! It's ruin! Fearful losses every day."

He flung up his hands, and went on, addressing Olenka:

"There! That's the life we lead, Olga Semyonovna. It's enough to make one cry. One works and does one's utmost; one wears oneself out, getting no sleep at night, and racks one's brain what to do for the best. And then what happens? To begin with, one's public is ignorant, boorish. I give them the very best operetta, a dainty masque, first rate music-hall artists. But do you suppose that's what they want! They don't understand anything of that sort. They want a clown; what they ask for is vulgarity. And then look at the weather! Almost every evening it rains. It started on the tenth of May, and it's kept it up all May and June. It's simply awful! The public doesn't come, but I've to pay the rent just the same, and pay the artists."

The next evening the clouds would gather again, and Kukin would say with an hysterical laugh:

"Well, rain away, then! Flood the garden, drown me! Damn my luck in this world and the next! Let the artists have me up! Send me to prison! — to Siberia! — the scaffold! ha, ha, ha!"

And next day the same thing.

Olenka listened to Kukin with silent gravity, and sometimes tears came into her eyes. In the end his misfortunes touched her; she grew to love him. He was a small thin man, with a yellow face, and curls combed forward on his forehead. He spoke in a thin tenor; as he talked his mouth worked on one side, and there was always an expression of despair on his face; yet he aroused a deep and genuine affection in her. She was always fond of some one, and could not exist without loving. In earlier days she had loved her papa, who now sat in a darkened room, breathing with difficulty; she had loved her aunt who used to come every other year from Bryansk; and before that, when she was at school, she had loved her French master. She was a gentle, soft-hearted, compassionate girl, with mild, tender eyes and very good health. At the sight of her full rosy cheeks, her soft white neck with a little dark mole on it, and the kind, naïve smile, which came into her face when she listened to anything pleasant, men thought, "Yes, not half bad," and smiled too, while lady visitors could not refrain from seizing her hand in the middle of a conversation, exclaiming in a gush of delight, "You darling!"

The house in which she had lived from her birth upwards, and which was left her in her father's will, was at the extreme end of the town, not far from the Tivoli. In the evenings and at night she could hear the band playing, and the crackling and banging of fireworks, and it seemed to her that it was Kukin struggling with his destiny, storming the entrenchments of his chief foe, the indifferent public; there was a sweet thrill at her heart, she had no desire to sleep, and when he returned home at daybreak, she tapped softly at her bedroom window, and showing him only her face and one shoulder through the curtain, she gave him a friendly smile. . . .

He proposed to her, and they were married. And when he had a closer view of her neck and her plump, fine shoulders, he threw up his hands, and said:

"You darling!"

He was happy, but as it rained on the day and night of his wedding, his face still retained an expression of despair.

They got on very well together. She used to sit in his office, to look after things in the Tivoli, to put down the accounts and pay the wages. And her rosy cheeks, her sweet, naïve, radiant smile, were to be seen now at the office window, now in the refreshment bar or behind the scenes of the theater. And already she used to say to her acquaintances that the theater was the chief and most important thing in life, and that it was only through the drama that one could derive true enjoyment and become cultivated and humane.

"But do you suppose the public understands that?" she used to say. "What they want is a clown. Yesterday we gave *Faust Inside Out*, and almost all the boxes were empty; but if Vanitchka and I had been producing some vulgar thing, I assure you the theater would have been packed. Tomorrow Vanitchka and I are doing *Orpheus in Hell*. Do come."

And what Kukin said about the theater and the actors she repeated. Like him she despised the public for their ignorance and their indifference to art; she took part in the rehearsals, she corrected the actors, she kept an eye on the behavior of the musicians, and when there was an unfavorable notice in the local paper, she shed tears, and then went to the editor's office to set things right.

The actors were fond of her and used to call her "Vanitchka and I," and "the darling"; she was sorry for them and used to lend them small sums of money, and if they deceived her, she used to shed a few tears in private, but did not complain to her husband.

They got on well in the winter too. They took the theater in the town for the whole winter, and let it for short terms to a Little Russian company, or to a conjurer, or to a local dramatic society. Olenka grew stouter, and was always beaming with satisfaction, while Kukin grew thinner and yellower, and continually complained of their terrible losses, although he had not done badly all the winter. He used to cough at night, and she used to give him hot raspberry tea or lime-flower water, to rub him with eau de Cologne and to wrap him in her warm shawls.

"You're such a sweet pet!" she used to say with perfect sincerity, stroking his hair. "You're such a pretty dear!"

Towards Lent he went to Moscow to collect a new troupe, and without him she could not sleep, but sat all night at her window, looking at the stars, and she compared herself to the hens, who are awake all night and uneasy when the cock is not in the henhouse. Kukin was detained in Moscow, and wrote that he would be back at Easter, adding some instructions about the Tivoli. But on the Sunday before Easter, late in the evening, came a sudden ominous knock at the gate; some one was hammering on the gate as though on a barrel — boom, boom boom! The drowsy cook went flopping with her bare feet through the puddles, as she ran to open the gate.

"Please open," said some one outside in a thick bass. "There is a telegram for you."

Olenka had received telegrams from her husband before, but this time for some reason she felt numb with terror. With shaking hands she opened the telegram and read as follows:

> Ivan Petrovitch died suddenly today. Awaiting immate instructions for fufuneral Tuesday.

That was how it was written in the telegram — "fufuneral," and the utterly incomprehensible word "immate." It was signed by the stage manager of the operatic company.

"My darling!" sobbed Olenka. "Vanitchka, my precious, my darling! Why did I ever meet you! Why did I know you and love you! Your poor heart-broken Olenka is all alone without you!"

Kukin's funeral took place on Tuesday in Moscow, Olenka returned home on Wednesday, and as soon as she got indoors she threw herself on her bed and sobbed so loudly that it could be heard next door, and in the street.

"Poor darling!" the neighbors said, as they crossed themselves. "Olga Semyonovna, poor darling! How she does take on!"

Three months later Olenka was coming home from mass, melancholy and in deep mourning. It happened that one of her neighbors, Vassily Andreitch Pustovalov, returning home from church, walked back beside her. He was the manager at Babakayev's, the timber merchant's. He wore a straw hat, a white waistcoat, and a gold watch-chain, and looked more like a country gentleman than a man in trade.

"Everything happens as it is ordained, Olga Semyonovna," he said gravely with a sympathetic note in his voice; "and if any of our dear ones die, it must be because it is the will of God, so we ought to have fortitude and bear it submissively."

After seeing Olenka to her gate, he said good-by and went on. All day afterwards she heard his sedately dignified voice, and whenever she shut her eyes she saw his dark beard. She liked him very much. And apparently she made an impression on him too, for not long afterwards an elderly lady, with whom she was only slightly acquainted, came to drink coffee with her, and as soon as she was seated at table began to talk about Pustovalov, saying that he was an excellent man whom one could thoroughly depend upon, and that any girl would be glad to marry him. Three days later Pustovalov came himself. He did not stay long, only about ten minutes and he did not say much, but when he left, Olenka loved him — loved him so much that she lay awake all night in a perfect fever, and in the morning she sent for the elderly lady. The match was quickly arranged, and then came the wedding.

Pustovalov and Olenka got on very well together when they were married.

Usually he sat in the office till dinnertime,[1] then he went out on business while Olenka took his place, and sat in the office till evening, making up accounts and booking orders.

"Timber gets dearer every year; the price rises twenty per cent," she would say to her customers and friends. "Only fancy we used to sell local timber, and now Vassitchka always has to go for wood to the Mogilev district. And the freight!" she would add, covering her cheeks with her hands in horror. "The freight!"

It seemed to her that she had been in the timber trade for ages and ages, and that the most important and necessary thing in life was timber; and there was something intimate and touching to her in the very sound of words such as "baulk,"[2] "post," "beam," "pole," "scantling," "batten," "lath," "plank," etc.

At night when she was asleep she dreamed of perfect mountains of planks and boards, and long strings of wagons, carting timber somewhere far away. She dreamed that a whole regiment of six-inch beams forty feet high, standing on end, was marching upon the timber-yard; that logs, beams, and boards knocked together with the resounding crash of dry wood, kept falling and getting up again, piling themselves on each other. Olenka cried out in her sleep, and Pustovalov said to her tenderly: "Olenka, what's the matter, darling? Cross yourself!"

Her husband's ideas were hers. If he thought the room was too hot, or that business was slack, she thought the same. Her husband did not care for entertainments, and on holidays he stayed at home. She did likewise.

[1] noon.
[2] rafter.

"You are always at home or in the office," her friends said to her. "You should go to the theater, darling, or to the circus."

"Vassitchka and I have no time to go to theaters," she would answer sedately. "We have no time for nonsense. What's the use of these theaters?"

On Saturdays Pustovalov and she used to go to the evening service; on holidays to early mass, and they walked side by side with softened faces as they came home from church. There was a pleasant fragrance about them both, and her silk dress rustled agreeably. At home they drank tea, with fancy bread and jams of various kinds, and afterwards they ate pie. Every day at twelve o'clock there was a savory smell of beet-root soup and of mutton or duck in their yard, and on fast-days of fish, and no one could pass the gate without feeling hungry. In the office the samovar was always boiling and customers were regaled with tea and cracknels. Once a week the couple went to the baths and returned side by side, both red in the face.

"Yes, we have nothing to complain of, thank God," Olenka used to say to her acquaintances. "I wish every one were as well off as Vassitchka and I."

When Pustovalov went away to buy wood in the Mogilev district, she missed him dreadfully, lay awake and cried. A young veterinary surgeon in the army, called Smirnin, to whom they had let their lodge, used sometimes to come in in the evening. He used to talk to her and play cards with her, and this entertained her in her husband's absence. She was particularly interested in what he told her of his home life. He was married and had a little boy, but was separated from his wife because she had been unfaithful to him, and now he hated her and used to send her forty roubles a month for the maintenance of their son. And hearing of all this, Olenka sighed and shook her head. She was sorry for him.

"Well, God keep you," she used to say to him at parting, as she lighted him down the stairs with a candle. "Thank you for coming to cheer me up, and may the Mother of God give you health."

And she always expressed herself with the same sedateness and dignity, the same reasonableness, in imitation of her husband. As the veterinary surgeon was disappearing behind the door below, she would say:

"You know, Vladimir Platonitch, you'd better make it up with your wife. You should forgive her for the sake of your son. You may be sure the little fellow understands."

And when Pustovalov came back, she told him in a low voice about the veterinary surgeon and his unhappy home life, and both sighed and shook their heads and talked about the boy, who, no doubt, missed his father, and by some strange connection of ideas, they went up to the holy ikons, bowed to the ground before them and prayed that God would give them children.

And so the Pustovalovs lived for six years quietly and peaceably in love and complete harmony.

But behold! one winter day after drinking hot tea in the office, Vassily Andreitch went out into the yard without his cap on to see about sending off some timber, caught cold and was taken ill. He had the best doctors, but he grew worse and died after four months' illness. And Olenka was a widow once more.

"I've nobody, now you've left me, my Darling," she sobbed, after her husband's funeral. "How can I live without you, in wretchedness and misery! Pity me, good people, all alone in the world!"

She went about dressed in black with long "weepers," and gave up wearing hat and gloves for good. She hardly ever went out, except to church, or to her husband's grave, and led the life of a nun. It was not till six months later that she took off the weepers and opened the shutters of the windows. She was sometimes seen in the mornings, going with her cook to market for provisions, but what went on in her house and how she lived now could only be surmised. People guessed, from seeing her drinking tea in her garden with the veterinary surgeon, who read the newspaper aloud to her, and from the fact that, meeting a lady she knew at the post office, she said to her:

"There is no proper veterinary inspection in our town, and that's the cause of all sorts of epidemics. One is always hearing of people's getting infection from the milk supply, or catching diseases from horses and cows. The health of domestic animals ought to be as well cared for as the health of human beings."

She repeated the veterinary surgeon's words, and was of the same opinion as he about everything. It was evident that she could not live a year without some attachment, and had found new happiness in the lodge. In any one else this would have been censured, but no one could think ill of Olenka; everything she did was so natural. Neither she nor the veterinary surgeon said anything to other people of the change in their relations, and tried, indeed, to conceal it, but without success, for Olenka could not keep a secret. When he had visitors, men serving in his regiment, and she poured out tea or served the supper, she would begin talking of the cattle plague, of the foot and mouth disease, and of the municipal slaughter-houses. He was dreadfully embarrassed, and when the guests had gone, he would seize her by the hand and hiss angrily:

"I've asked you before not to talk about what you don't understand. When we veterinary surgeons are talking among ourselves, please don't put your word in. It's really annoying."

And she would look at him with astonishment and dismay, and ask him in alarm: "But, Voloditchka, what *am* I to talk about?"

And with tears in her eyes she would embrace him, begging him not to be angry, and they were both happy.

But this happiness did not last long. The veterinary surgeon departed, departed forever with his regiment, when it was transferred to a distant place to Siberia, it may be. And Olenka was left alone.

Now she was absolutely alone. Her father had long been dead, and his armchair lay in the attic, covered with dust and lame of one leg. She got thinner and plainer, and when people met her in the street they did not look at her as they used to, and did not smile to her; evidently her best years were over and left behind, and now a new sort of life had begun for her, which did not bear thinking about. In the evening Olenka sat in the porch, and heard the band playing and the fireworks popping in the Tivoli, but now the sound stirred no response. She looked into her yard without interest, thought of nothing, wished for nothing, and afterwards, when night came on she went to bed and dreamed of her empty yard. She ate and drank as it were unwillingly.

And what was worst of all, she had no opinions of any sort. She saw the objects about her and understood what she saw, but could not form any opinion about them, and did not know what to talk about. And how awful it is not to have any opinions! One sees a bottle, for instance, or the rain, or a peasant driving in his cart, but what the bottle is for, or the rain, or the peasant, and what is the meaning of it, one can't say, and could not even for a thousand roubles. When she had Kukin, or Pustovalov, or the veterinary surgeon, Olenka could explain everything, and give her opinion about anything you like, but now there was the same emptiness in her brain and in her heart as there was in her yard outside. And it was as harsh and as bitter as wormwood in the mouth.

Little by little the town grew in all directions. The road became a street, and where the Tivoli and the timber-yard had been there was new turnings and houses. How rapidly time passes! Olenka's house grew dingy, the roof got rusty, the shed sank on one side, and the whole yard was overgrown with docks and stinging-nettles. Olenka herself had grown plain and elderly; in summer she sat in the porch, and her soul, as before, was empty and dreary and full of bitterness. In winter she sat at her window and looked at the snow. When she caught the scent of spring, or heard the chime of the church bells, a sudden rush of memories from the past came over her, there was a tender ache in her heart, and her eyes brimmed over with tears; but this was only for a minute, and then came emptiness again and the sense of the futility of life. The black kitten, Briska, rubbed against her and purred softly, but Olenka was not touched by these feline caresses. That was not what she needed. She wanted a love that would absorb her whole being, her whole soul and reason — that would give her ideas and an object in life and would warm her old blood. And she would shake the kitten off her skirt and say with vexation:

"Get along; I don't want you!"

And so it was, day after day and year after year, and no joy, and no opinions. Whatever Mavra, the cook, said she accepted.

One hot July day, towards evening, just as the cattle were being driven away, and the whole yard was full of dust, some one suddenly knocked at the gate. Olenka went to open it herself and was dumbfounded when she looked out: she saw Smirnin, the veterinary surgeon, gray-headed, and dressed as a civilian. She suddenly remembered everything. She could not help crying and letting her head fall on his breast without uttering a word and in the violence of her feeling she did not notice how they both walked into the house and sat down to tea.

"My dear Vladimir Platonitch! What fate has brought you?" she muttered, trembling with joy.

"I want to settle here for good, Olga Semyonovna," he told her. "I have resigned my post, and have come to settle down and try my luck on my own account. Besides, it's time for my boy to go to school. He's a big boy. I am reconciled with my wife, you know."

"Where is she?" asked Olenka.

"She's at the hotel with the boy, and I'm looking for lodgings."

"Good gracious, my dear soul! Lodgings? Why not have my house? Why shouldn't that suit you? Why, my goodness, I wouldn't take any rent!" cried Olenka in a flutter, beginning to cry again. "You live here, and the lodge will do nicely for me. Oh, dear! how glad I am!"

Next day the roof was painted and the walls were whitewashed, and Olenka, with her arms akimbo, walked about the yard giving directions. Her face was beaming with her old smile, and she was brisk and alert as though she had waked from a long sleep. The veterinary's wife arrived — a thin, plain lady, with short hair and a peevish expression. With her was her little Sasha, a boy of ten, small for his age, blue-eyed, chubby, with dimples in his cheeks. And scarcely had the boy walked into the yard when he ran after the cat, and at once there was the sound of his gay, joyous laugh.

"Is that your puss, Auntie?" he asked Olenka. "When she has little ones, do give us a kitten. Mamma is awfully afraid of mice."

Olenka talked to him, and gave him tea. Her heart warmed and there was a sweet ache in her bosom, as though the boy had been her own child. And when he sat at the table in the evening, going over his lessons, she looked at him with deep tenderness and pity as she murmured to herself:

"You pretty pet! . . . my precious! . . . Such a fair little thing, and so clever."

" 'An island is a piece of land which is entirely surrounded by water,' " he read aloud.

"An island is a piece of land," she repeated, and this was the first opinion to which she gave utterance with positive conviction after so many years of silence and dearth of ideas.

Now she had opinions of her own, and at supper she talked to Sasha's parents, saying how difficult the lessons were at the high schools, but that yet the high school was better than a commercial one, since with a high school education all careers were open to one, such as being a doctor or an engineer.

Sacha began going to the high school. His mother departed to Harkov to her sister's and did not return; his father used to go off every day to inspect cattle, and would often be away from home for three days together, and it seemed to Olenka as though Sasha was entirely abandoned, that he was not wanted at home, that he was being starved, and she carried him off to her lodge and gave him a little room there.

And for six months Sasha had lived in the lodge with her. Every morning Olenka came into his bedroom and found him fast asleep, sleeping noiselessly with his hand under his cheek. She was sorry to wake him.

"Sashenka," she would say mournfully, "get up, Darling. It's time for school."

He would get up, dress and say his prayers, and then sit down to breakfast, drink three glasses of tea, and eat two large cracknels and half a buttered roll. All this time he was hardly awake and a little ill-humored in consequence.

"You don't quite know your fable, Sashenka," Olenka would say, looking at him as though he were about to set off on a long journey. "What a lot of trouble I have with you! You must work and do your best, Darling, and obey your teachers."

"Oh, do leave me alone!" Sasha would say.

Then he would go down the street to school, a little figure, wearing a big cap and carrying a satchel on his shoulder. Olenka would follow him noiselessly.

"Sashenka!" she would call after him, and she would pop into his hand a date or a caramel. When he reached the street where the school was, he would feel ashamed of being followed by a tall, stout woman; he would turn round and say:

"You'd better go home, Auntie. I can go the rest of the way alone."

She would stand still and look after him fixedly till he had disappeared at the school gate.

Ah, how she loved him! Of her former attachments not one had been so deep; never had her soul surrendered to any feeling so spontaneously, so disinterestedly, and so joyously as now that her maternal instincts were aroused. For this little boy with the dimple in his cheek and the big school cap she would have given her whole life, she would have given it with joy and tears of tenderness. Why? Who can tell why?

When she had seen the last of Sasha, she returned home, contented and serene, brimming over with love; her face, which had grown younger during the last six months, smiled and beamed; people meeting her looked at her with pleasure.

"Good morning, Olga Semyonovna, Darling. How are you, Darling?"

"The lessons at the high school are very difficult now," she would relate at the market. "It's too much; in the first class yesterday they gave him a fable to learn by heart, and a Latin translation and a problem. You know it's too much for a little chap."

And she would begin talking about the teachers, the lessons, and the school books, saying just what Sasha said.

At three o'clock they had dinner together: in the evening they learned their lessons together and cried. When she put him to bed, she would stay a long time making the cross over him and murmuring a prayer; then she would go to bed and dream of that far-away, misty future when Sasha would finish his studies and become a doctor or an engineer, would have a big house of his own with horses and a carriage, would get married and have children. . . . She would fall asleep still thinking of the same thing and tears would run down her cheeks from her closed eyes, while the black cat lay purring beside her: "Mrr, mrr, mrr."

Suddenly there would come a loud knock at the gate.

Olenka would wake up breathless with alarm, her heart throbbing. Half a minute later would come another knock.

"It must be a telegram from Harkov," she would think, beginning to tremble from head to foot. "Sasha's mother is sending for him from Harkov. Oh, mercy on us!"

She was in despair. Her head, her hands, and her feet would turn chill, and she would feel that she was the most unhappy woman in the world. But another minute would pass, voices would be heard: it would turn out to be the veterinary surgeon coming home from the club.

"Well, thank God!" she would think.

And gradually the load in her heart would pass off, and she would feel at ease. She would go back to bed thinking of Sasha, who lay sound asleep in the next room, sometimes crying out in his sleep:

"I'll give it you! Get away! Shut up!"

William Butler Yeats (1865–1939)

IRISH POET and DRAMATIST

Swift's Epitaph

Ubi saeva indignatio ulterius cor lacerare nequit.[1]

Swift has sailed into his rest;
Savage indignation there
Cannot lacerate his breast.
Imitate him if you dare,
World-besotted traveller; he
Served human liberty.

[1] Where savage indignation can no longer tear the heart.

"Swift's Epitaph" by William Butler Yeats. Reprinted with permission of The Macmillan Company from *The Collected Poems of W. B. Yeats* by William Butler Yeats. Copyright 1933 by The Macmillan Company, renewed 1961 by Bertha Georgie Yeats. Also by permission of Mr. M. B. Yeats and Macmillan & Co. Ltd., London.

Marcel Proust (1871–1922)

FRENCH NOVELIST

The Goodnight

My sole consolation when I went upstairs for the night was that Mamma would come in and kiss me after I was in bed. But this good night lasted for so short a time: she went down again so soon that the moment in which I heard her climb the stairs, and then caught the sound of her garden dress of blue muslin, from which hung little tassels of plaited straw, rustling along the double-doored corridor, was for me a moment of the keenest sorrow. So much did I love that good night that I reached the stage of hoping that it would come as late as possible, so as to prolong the time of respite during which Mamma would not yet have appeared. Sometimes when, after kissing me, she opened the door to go, I longed to call her back, to say to her, "Kiss me just once again," but I knew that then she would at once look displeased, for the concession which she made to my wretchedness and agitation in coming up to me with this kiss of peace always annoyed my father, who thought such ceremonies absurd, and she would have liked to try to induce me to outgrow the need, the custom of having her there at all, which was a very different thing from letting the custom grow up of my asking her for an additional kiss when she was already crossing the threshold. And to see her look displeased destroyed all the sense of tranquillity she had brought me a moment before, when she bent her loving face down over my bed, and held it out to me like a Host, for an act of Communion in which my lips might drink deeply the sense of her real presence, and with it the power to sleep. But those evenings on which Mamma stayed so short a time in my room were sweet indeed compared to those on which we had guests to dinner, and therefore she did not come at all. . . .

I never took my eyes off my mother. I knew that when they were at table I should not be permitted to stay there for the whole of dinner-time, and that Mamma, for fear of annoying my father, would not allow me to give her in public the series of kisses that she would have had in my room. And so I promised myself that in the dining-room, as they began to eat and drink and as I felt the hour approach, I would put beforehand into this kiss, which was bound to be so brief and stealthy in execution, everything that my own efforts could put into it: would look out very carefully first the exact spot on her cheek where I would imprint it, and would so prepare my thoughts that I might be able, thanks to these mental preliminaries, to consecrate the whole of the minute Mamma would allow me to the sensation of her cheek against my lips, as a painter who can have his subject for short sittings only prepares his palette, and from what he remembers and from rough notes does in advance everything which he possibly can do in the sitter's absence. But tonight, before the dinner-bell had sounded, my grandfather said with unconscious cruelty: "The little man looks tired; he'd better go up to bed. Besides, we are dining late to-night."

And my father, who was less scrupulous than my grandmother or mother in observing the letter of a treaty, went on: "Yes, run along; to bed with you."

I would have kissed Mamma then and there, but at that moment the dinner-bell rang.

"No, no, leave your mother alone. You've said good night quite enough. These exhibitions are absurd. Go on upstairs."

And so I must set forth without viaticum;[1] must climb each step of the staircase 'against my heart,' as the saying is, climbing in opposition to my heart's desire, which was to return to my mother, since she had not, by her kiss, given my heart leave to accompany me forth. That hateful staircase, up which I always passed with such dismay, gave out a smell of varnish which had to some extent absorbed, made definite and fixed the special quality of sorrow that I felt each evening, and made it perhaps even more cruel to my sensibility because, when it assumed this olfactory guise, my intellect was powerless to resist it. When we have gone to sleep with a maddening toothache and are conscious of it only as a little girl whom we attempt, time after time, to pull out of the water, or as a line of Molière which we repeat incessantly to ourselves, it is a great relief to wake up, so that our intelligence can disentangle the idea of toothache from any artificial semblance of heroism or rhythmic cadence. It was the precise converse of this relief which I felt when my anguish at having to go up to my room invaded my consciousness in a manner infinitely more rapid, instantaneous almost, a manner at once insidious and brutal as I breathed in — a far more poisonous thing than any moral penetration — the peculiar smell of the varnish upon that staircase.

Once in my room I had to stop every loophole, to close the shutters, to dig my own grave as I turned down the bed-clothes, to wrap myself in the shroud of my nightshirt. But before burying myself in the iron bed which had been placed there because, on summer nights, I was too hot among the rep curtains of the four-poster, I was stirred to revolt, and attempted the desperate stratagem of a condemned prisoner. I wrote to my mother begging her to come upstairs for an important reason which I could not put in writing. My fear was that Françoise, my aunt's cook who used to be put in charge of me when I was at Combray,[2] might refuse to take my note. I had a sus-

[1] in the Catholic Church, extreme unction, or sacrament administered to a dying person; in Roman times, provisions for a journey.
[2] country home of the narrator's family, and the place where he spends spring and summer through adolescence.

picion that, in her eyes, to carry a message to my mother when there was a stranger in the room would appear flatly inconceivable, just as it would be for the door-keeper of a theatre to hand a letter to an actor upon the stage. For things which might or might not be done she possessed a code at once imperious, abundant, subtle, and uncompromising on points themselves imperceptible or irrelevant, which gave it a semblance to those ancient laws which combine such cruel ordinances as the massacre of infants at the breast with prohibitions, of exaggerated refinement, against "seething the kid in his mother's milk," or "eating of the sinew which is upon the hollow of the thigh." This code, if one could judge it by the sudden obstinacy which she would put into her refusal to carry out certain of our instructions, seemed to have foreseen such social complications and refinements of fashion as nothing in Françoise's surroundings or in her career as a servant in a village household could have put into her head; and we were obliged to assume that there was latent in her some past existence in the ancient history of France, noble and little understood, just as there is in those manufacturing towns where old mansions still testify to their former courtly days, and chemical workers toil among delicately sculptured scenes of the Miracle of Theophilus[3] or the Quatre Fils Aymon.[4]

In this particular instance, the article of her code which made it highly improbable that — barring an outbreak of fire — Françoise would go down and disturb Mamma when M. Swann[5] was there for so unimportant a person as myself was one embodying the respect she shewed not only for the family (as for the dead, for the clergy, or for royalty), but also for the stranger within our gates; a respect which I should perhaps have found touching in a book, but which never failed to irritate me on her lips, because of the solemn and gentle tones in which she would utter it, and which irritated me more than usual this evening when the sacred character in which she invested the dinner-party might have the effect of making her decline to disturb its ceremonial. But to give myself one chance of success I lied without hesitation, telling her that it was not in the least myself who had wanted to write to Mamma, but Mamma who, on saying good night to me, had begged me not to forget to send her an answer about something she had asked me to find, and that she would certainly be very angry if this note were not taken to her. I think that Françoise disbelieved me, for, like those primitive men whose senses were so much keener than our own, she could immediately detect, by signs imperceptible by the rest of us, the truth or falsehood of anything that we might wish to conceal from her. She studied the envelope for five minutes as though an examination of the paper itself and the look of my handwriting could enlighten her as to the nature of the contents, or tell her to which article of her code she ought to refer the matter. Then she went out with an air of

[3] legend from 6th century, Asia Minor; Theophilus, a steward, sold his soul to the devil but was saved by the miraculous intervention of the Virgin Mary.

[4] a legendary heroic tale of the exploits of the four Aymon brothers during the time of Charlemagne.

[5] a neighbor of fashion and an intimate of royalty and aristocracy whose ways of life attract the boy.

resignation which seemed to imply: "What a dreadful thing for parents to have a child like this!"

A moment later she returned to say that they were still at the ice stage[6] and that it was impossible for the butler to deliver the note at once, in front of everybody; but that when the finger-bowls were put round he would find a way of slipping it into Mamma's hand. At once my anxiety subsided; it was now no longer (as it had been a moment ago) until to-morrow that I had lost my mother, for my little line was going — to annoy her, no doubt, and doubly so because this contrivance would make me ridiculous in Swann's eyes — but was going all the same to admit me, invisibly and by stealth, into the same room as herself, was going to whisper from me into her ear; for that forbidden and unfriendly dining-room, where but a moment ago the ice itself — with burned nuts in it — and the finger-bowls seemed to me to be concealing pleasures that were mischievous and of a mortal sadness because Mamma was tasting of them and I was far away, had opened its doors to me and, like a ripe fruit which bursts through its skin, was going to pour out into my intoxicated heart the gushing sweetness of Mamma's attention while she was reading what I had written. Now I was no longer separated from her; the barriers were down; an exquisite thread was binding us. Besides, that was not all, for surely Mamma would come.

As for the agony through which I had just passed, I imagined that Swann would have laughed heartily at it if he had read my letter and had guessed its purpose; whereas, on the contrary, as I was to learn in due course, a similar anguish had been the bane of his life for many years, and no one perhaps could have understood my feelings at that moment so well as himself; to him, that anguish which lies in knowing that the creature one adores is in some place of enjoyment where oneself is not and cannot follow — to him that anguish came through Love, to which it is in a sense predestined, by which it must be equipped and adapted; but when, as had befallen me, such an anguish possesses one's soul before Love has yet entered into one's life, then it must drift, awaiting Love's coming, vague and free, without precise attachment, at the disposal of one sentiment to-day, of another to-morrow, of filial piety or affection for a comrade. And the joy with which I first bound myself apprentice, when Françoise returned to tell me that my letter would be delivered; Swann, too, had known well that false joy which a friend can give us, or some relative of the woman we love, when on his arrival at the house or theatre where she is to be found, for some ball or party or 'first-night' at which he is to meet her, he sees us wandering outside, desperately awaiting some opportunity of communicating with her. He recognises us, greets us familiarly, and asks what we are doing there. And when we invent a story of having some urgent message to give to his relative or friend, he assures us that nothing could be more simple, takes us in at the door, and promises to send her down to us in five minutes. How much we love him — as at that

---

[6]Ices (sherbets) were common as dessert.

moment I loved Françoise — the good-natured intermediary who by a single word has made supportable, human, almost propitious the inconceivable, infernal scene of gaiety in the thick of which we had been imagining swarms of enemies, perverse and seductive, beguiling away from us, even making laugh at us, the woman whom we love. If we are to judge of them by him, this relative who has accosted us and who is himself an initiate in those cruel mysteries, then the other guests cannot be so very demoniacal. Those inaccessible and torturing hours into which she had gone to taste of unknown pleasures — behold, a breach in the wall, and we are through it. Behold, one of the moments whose series will go to make up their sum, a moment as genuine as the rest, if not actually more important to ourself because our mistress is more intensely a part of it; we picture it to ourselves, we possess it, we intervene upon it, almost we have created it: namely, the moment in which he goes to tell her that we are waiting there below. And very probably the other moments of the party will not be essentially different, will contain nothing else so exquisite or so well able to make us suffer, since this kind friend has assured us that "Of course, she will be delighted to come down! It will be far more amusing for her to talk to you than to be bored up there." Alas! Swann had learned by experience that the good intentions of a third party are powerless to control a woman who is annoyed to find herself pursued even into a ball-room by a man whom she does not love. Too often, the kind friend comes down again alone.

My mother did not appear, but with no attempt to safeguard my self-respect (which depended upon her keeping up the fiction that she had asked me to let her know the result of my search for something or other) made Françoise tell me, in so many words "There is no answer" — words I have so often, since then, heard the hall-porters in 'mansions' and the flunkeys in gambling-clubs and the like, repeat to some poor girl, who replies in bewilderment: "What! he's said nothing? It's not possible. You did give him my letter, didn't you? Very well, I shall wait a little longer." And just as she invariably protests that she does not need the extra gas which the porter offers to light for her, and sits on there, hearing nothing further, except an occasional remark on the weather which the porter exchanges with a messenger whom he will send off suddenly, when he notices the time, to put some customer's wine on the ice; so, having declined Françoise's offer to make me some tea or to stay beside me, I let her go off again to the servants' hall, and lay down and shut my eyes, and tried not to hear the voices of my family who were drinking their coffee in the garden.

But after a few seconds I realised that, by writing that line to Mamma, by approaching — at the risk of making her angry — so near to her that I felt I could reach out and grasp the moment in which I should see her again, I had cut myself off from the possibility of going to sleep until I actually had seen her, and my heart began to beat more and more painfully as I increased my agitation by ordering myself to keep calm and to acquiesce in my ill-fortune. Then, suddenly, my anxiety subsided, a feeling of intense happiness coursed through me, as when a strong medicine begins to take effect and one's pain vanishes: I had formed a resolution to abandon all attempts to go to sleep without seeing Mamma, and had decided to kiss her at all costs, even with the certainty of being in disgrace with her for long afterwards, when she herself came up to bed. The tranquillity which followed my anguish made me extremely alert, no less than my sense of expectation, my thirst for and my fear of danger.

Noiselessly I opened the window and sat down on the foot of my bed; hardly daring to move in case they should hear me from below. Things outside seemed also fixed in mute expectation, so as not to disturb the moonlight which, duplicating each of them and throwing it back by the extension, forwards, of a shadow denser and more concrete than its substance, had made the whole landscape seem at once thinner and longer, like a map which, after being folded up, is spread out upon the ground. What had to move — a leaf of the chestnut-tree, for instance — moved. But its minute shuddering, complete, finished to the least detail and with utmost delicacy of gesture, made no discord with the rest of the scene, and yet was not merged in it, remaining clearly outlined. Exposed upon this surface of silence, which absorbed nothing from them, the most distant sounds, those which must have come from gardens at the far end of the town, could be distinguished with such exact 'finish' that the impression they gave of coming from a distance seemed due only to their 'pianissimo' execution, like those movements on muted strings so well performed by the orchestra of the Conservatoire that, although one does not lose a single note, one thinks all the same that they are being played somewhere outside, a long way from the concert hall, so that all the old subscribers, and my grandmother's sisters too, when Swann had given them his seats, used to strain their ears as if they had caught the distant approach of an army on the march, which had not yet rounded the corner of the Rue de Trévise.

I was well aware that I had placed myself in a position than which none could be counted upon to involve me in graver consequences at my parents' hands; consequences far graver, indeed, than a stranger would have imagined, and such as (he would have thought) could follow only some really shameful fault. But in the system of education which they had given me faults were not classified in the same order as in that of other children, and I had been taught to place at the head of the list (doubtless because there was no other class of faults from which I needed to be more carefully protected) those in which I can now distinguish the common feature that one succumbs to them by yielding to a nervous impulse. But such words as these last had never been uttered in my hearing; no one had yet accounted for my temptations in a way which might have led me to believe that there was some excuse for my giving in to them, or that I was actually incapable of holding out against them. Yet I could easily recognise this class of transgressions by the anguish of mind which preceded, as well as by the rigour of the punishment which followed them; and I knew that what I had just done was in the same category as certain other sins for which I had been severely chastised, though infinitely more serious than they. When I went out to meet my mother as she herself came up to bed, and when she saw that I had remained up so as to say good night to her again in the passage, I should not be allowed to stay in the house a day longer, I should be packed off to school next morning; so much was certain. Very good: had I been obliged, the next moment, to hurl myself out of the window, I should still have preferred such a fate. For what I wanted now was Mamma, and to say good night to her. I had gone too far along the road which led to the realisation of this desire to be able to retrace my steps.

I could hear my parents' footsteps as they went with Swann; and, when the rattle of the gate assured me that he had really gone, I crept to the window. Mamma was asking my father if he had thought the lobster good, and whether M. Swann had had some of the coffee-and-pistachio ice. "I thought it rather so-so," she was saying; "next time we shall have to try another flavour." . . .

My father and mother were left alone and sat down for a moment; then my father said: "Well, shall we go up to bed?"

"As you wish, dear, though I don't feel in the least like sleeping. I don't know why; it can't be the coffee-ice — it wasn't strong enough to keep me awake like this. But I see a light in the servants' hall: poor Françoise has been sitting up for me, so I will get her to unhook me while you go and undress."

My mother opened the latticed door which led from the hall to the staircase. Presently I heard her coming upstairs to close her window. I went quietly into the passage; my heart was beating so violently that I could hardly move, but at least it was throbbing no longer with anxiety, but with terror and with joy. I saw in the well of the stair a light coming upwards, from Mamma's candle. Then I saw Mamma herself: I threw myself upon her. For an instant she looked at me in astonishment, not realising what could have happened. Then her face assumed an expression of anger. She said not a single word to me; and, for that matter, I used to go for days on end without being spoken to, for far less offences than this. A single word from Mamma would have been an admission that further intercourse with me was within the bounds of possibility, and that might perhaps have appeared to me more terrible still, as indicating that, with such a punishment as was in store for me, mere silence, and even anger, were relatively puerile.

A word from her then would have implied the false calm in which one converses with a servant to whom one has just decided to give notice; the kiss one bestows on a son who is being packed off to enlist, which would have been denied him if it had merely been a matter of being angry with him for a few days. But she heard my father coming from the dressing-room, where he had gone to take off his clothes, and, to avoid the 'scene' which he would make if he saw me, she said, in a voice half-stifled by her anger: "Run away at once. Don't let your father see you standing there like a crazy jane!"

But I begged her again to "Come and say good night to me!" terrified as I saw the light from my father's candle already creeping up the wall, but also making use of his approach as a means of blackmail, in the hope that my mother, not wishing him to find me there, as find me he must if she continued to hold out, would give in to me, and say: "Go back to your room. I will come."

Too late: my father was upon us. Instinctively I murmured, though no one heard me, "I am done for!"

I was not, however. My father used constantly to refuse to let me do things which were quite clearly allowed by the more liberal charters granted me by my mother and grandmother, because he paid no heed to 'Principles,' and because in his sight there were no such things as 'Rights of Man.' For some quite irrelevant reason, or for no reason at all, he would at the last moment prevent me from taking some particular walk, one so regular and so consecrated to my use that to deprive me of it was a clear breach of faith; or again, as he had done this evening, long before the appointed hour he would snap out: "Run along up to bed now; no excuses!" But then again, simply because he was devoid of principles (in my grandmother's sense), so he could not, properly speaking, be called inexorable. He looked at me for a moment with an air of annoyance and surprise, and then when Mamma had told him, not without some embarrassment, what had happened, said to her: "Go along with him, then; you said just now that you didn't feel like sleep, so stay in his room for a little. I don't need anything."

"But dear," my mother answered timidly, "whether or not I feel like sleep is not the point; we must not make the child accustomed . . ."

"There's no question of making him accustomed," said my father, with a shrug of the shoulders; you can see quite well that the child is unhappy. After all, we aren't gaolers.[7] You'll end by making him ill, and a lot of good that will do. There are two beds in his room; tell Françoise to make up the big one for you, and stay beside him for the rest of the night. I'm off to bed, anyhow; I'm not nervous like you. Good night."

It was impossible for me to thank my father; what he called my sentimentality would have exasperated him. I stood there, not daring to move; he was still confronting us, an immense figure in his white nightshirt, crowned with the pink and violet scarf of Indian cashmere in which, since he had begun to suffer from neuralgia, he used to tie up his head, standing like Abraham in the engraving after Benozzo Gozzoli which M. Swann had given me, telling Sarah that she must tear herself away from Isaac. Many years have passed since that night. The wall of the staircase, up which I had watched the light of his candle gradually climb, was long ago demolished. And in myself, too, many things have perished which, I imagined, would last for ever, and new structures have arisen, giving birth to new sorrows and new joys which in those days I could not have foreseen, just as now the old are difficult of comprehension. It is a long time, too, since my father has been

---

[7] jailers.

able to tell Mamma to "Go with the child." Never again will such hours be possible for me. But of late I have been increasingly able to catch, if I listen attentively, the sound of the sobs which I had the strength to control in my father's presence, and which broke out only when I found myself alone with Mamma. Actually, their echo has never ceased: it is only because life is now growing more and more quiet round about me that I hear them afresh, like those convent bells which are so effectively drowned during the day by the noises of the streets that one would suppose them to have been stopped for ever, until they sound out again through the silent evening air.

Mamma spent that night in my room: when I had just committed a sin so deadly that I was waiting to be banished from the household, my parents gave me a far greater concession than I should ever have won as the reward of a good action. Even at the moment when it manifested itself in this crowning mercy, my father's conduct towards me was still somewhat arbitrary, and regardless of my deserts, as was characteristic of him and due to the fact that his actions were generally dictated by chance expediencies rather than based on any formal plan. And perhaps even what I called his strictness, when he sent me off to bed, deserved that title less, really, than my mother's or grandmother's attitude, for his nature, which in some respects differed more than theirs from my own, had probably prevented him from guessing, until then, how wretched I was every evening, a thing which my mother and grandmother knew well; but they loved me enough to be unwilling to spare me that suffering, which they hoped to teach me to overcome, so as to reduce my nervous sensibility and to strengthen my will. As for my father, whose affection for me was of another kind, I doubt if he would have shewn so much courage, for as soon as he had grasped the fact that I was unhappy he had said to my mother: "Go and comfort him."

Mamma stayed all night in my room, and it seemed that she did not wish to mar by recrimination those hours, so different from anything that I had had a right to expect; for when Françoise (who guessed that something extraordinary must have happened when she saw Mamma sitting by my side, holding my hand and letting me cry unchecked) said to her: "But, Madame, what is little Master crying for?" she replied: "Why, Françoise, he doesn't know himself: it is his nerves. Make up the big bed for me quickly and then go off to your own." And thus for the first time my unhappiness was regarded no longer as a fault for which I must be punished, but as an involuntary evil which had been officially recognised a nervous condition for which I was in no way responsible: I had the consolation that I need no longer mingle apprehensive scruples with the bitterness of my tears; I could weep henceforward without sin. I felt no small degree of pride, either, in Françoise's presence at this return to humane conditions which, not an hour after Mamma had refused to come up to my room and had sent the snubbing message that I was to go to sleep, raised me to the dignity of a grown-up person, brought me of a sudden to a sort of puberty of sorrow, to emancipation from tears. I ought then to have been happy; I was not. It struck me that my mother had just made a first concession which must have been painful to her, that it was a first step down from the ideal she had formed for me, and that for the first time she, with all her courage, had to confess herself beaten. It struck me that if I had just scored a victory it was over her; that I had succeeded, as sickness or sorrow or age might have succeeded, in relaxing her will, in altering her judgment; that this evening opened a new era, must remain a black date in the calendar. And if I had dared now, I should have said to Mamma: "No, I don't want you; you mustn't sleep here." But I was conscious of the practical wisdom, of what would be called nowadays the realism with which she tempered the ardent idealism of my grandmother's nature, and I knew that now the mischief was done she would prefer to let me enjoy the soothing pleasure of her company, and not to disturb my father again. Certainly my mother's beautiful features seemed to shine again with youth that evening, as she sat gently holding my hands and trying to check my tears; but, just for that reason, it seemed to me that this should not have happened; her anger would have been less difficult to endure than this new kindness which my childhood had not known; I felt that I had with an impious and secret finger traced a first wrinkle upon her soul and made the first white hair shew upon her head. This thought redoubled my sobs, and then I saw that Mamma, who had never allowed herself to go to any length of tenderness with me, was suddenly overcome by my tears and had to struggle to keep back her own. Then, as she saw that I had noticed this, she said to me, with a smile: "Why, my little buttercup, my little canary-boy, he's going to make Mamma as silly as himself if this goes on. Look, since you can't sleep, and Mamma can't either, we mustn't go on in this stupid way; we must do something; I'll get one of your books." But I had none there. "Would you like me to get out the books now that your grandmother is going to give you for your birthday? Just think it over first, and don't be disappointed if there is nothing new for you then." . . .

Mamma sat down by my bed; she had chosen *François le Champi*, whose reddish cover and incomprehensible title gave it a distinct personality in my eyes and a mysterious attraction. . . .

My agony was soothed; I let myself be borne upon the current of this gentle night on which I had my mother by my side. I knew that such a night could not be repeated; that the strongest desire I had in the world, namely, to keep my mother in my room through the sad hours of darkness, ran too much counter to general requirements and to the wishes of others for such a concession as had been granted me this evening to be anything but a rare and casual exception. To-morrow night I should again be the victim of anguish and Mamma would not stay by my side. But when these storms of anguish grew calm I could no longer realise their existence; besides, to-morrow evening was still a long way off; I reminded myself that I should still have time to think about things, albeit that remission of time could bring me no access of power, albeit the coming event was in no way dependent upon the exercise of my will, and seemed not quite inevitable only because it was still separated from me by this short interval.

Rainer Maria Rilke (1875–1926)

AUSTRIAN POET

Slumbersong

Some day, when I lose you,
will you be able to sleep without
my whispering myself away
like a linden's crown above you?

Without my waking here and laying down
words, almost like eyelids,
upon your breasts, upon your limbs,
upon your mouth?

Without my closing you and leaving
you alone with what is yours,   10
like a garden with a mass
of melissas and star-anise?

Don Marquis (1878–1937)

AMERICAN HUMORIST and JOURNALIST

the lesson of the moth

i was talking to a moth
the other evening
he was trying to break into
an electric light bulb
and fry himself on the wires

why do you fellows
pull this stunt i asked him
because it is the conventional
thing for moths or why

"the lesson of the moth" by Don Marquis. From *The Lives and Times of Archy & Mehitabel* by Don Marquis. Copyright 1927 by Doubleday & Company, Inc. Reprinted by permission of the publisher.

if that had been an uncovered   10
candle instead of an electric
light bulb you would
now be a small unsightly cinder
have you no sense

plenty of it he answered
but at times we get tired
of using it
we get bored with the routine
and crave beauty
and excitement   20
fire is beautiful
and we know that if we get
too close it will kill us
but what does that matter
it is better to be happy
for a moment
and be burned up with beauty
than to live a long time
and be bored all the while
so we wad all our life up   30
into one little roll
and then we shoot the roll
that is what life is for
it is better to be a part of beauty
for one instant and then cease to
exist than to exist forever
and never be a part of beauty
our attitude toward life
is come easy go easy   40
we are like human beings
used to be before they became
too civilized to enjoy themselves

and before i could argue him
out of his philosophy
he went and immolated himself
on a patent cigar lighter
i do not agree with him
myself i would rather have
half the happiness and twice   50
the longevity

but at the same time i wish
there was something i wanted
as badly as he wanted to fry himself

                              archy

Martin Buber (1878–1965)

JEWISH THEOLOGIAN and PHILOSOPHER (AUSTRIAN-BORN)

I and Thou

To man the world is twofold, in accordance with his twofold attitude.

The attitude of man is twofold, in accordance with the twofold nature of the primary words which he speaks.

The primary words are not isolated words, but combined words.

The one primary word is the combination *I–Thou*.

The other primary word is the combination *I–It*; wherein, without a change in the primary word, one of the words *He* and *She* can replace *It*.

Hence the *I* of man is also twofold.

For the *I* of the primary word *I–Thou* is a different *I* from that of the primary word *I–it*.

Primary words do not signify things, but they intimate relations.

Primary words do not describe something that might exist independently of them, but being spoken they bring about existence.

Primary words are spoken from the being.

If *Thou* is said, the *I* of the combination *I–Thou* is said along with it.

If *It* is said, the *I* of the combination *I–It* is said along with it.

The primary word *I–Thou* can only be spoken with the whole being.

The primary word *I–It* can never be spoken with the whole being.

There is no *I* taken in itself, but only the *I* of the primary word *I–Thou* and the *I* of the primary word *I–It*.

When a man says *I* he refers to one or other of these. The *I* to which he refers is present when he says *I*. Further, when he says *Thou* or *It*, the *I* of one of the two primary words is present.

The existence of *I* and the speaking of *I* are one and the same thing.

When a primary word is spoken the speaker enters the word and takes his stand in it.

The life of human beings is not passed in the sphere of transitive verbs alone. It does not exist in virtue of activities alone which have some *thing* for their object.

I perceive something. I am sensible of something. I imagine something. I will something. I feel something. I think something. The life of human beings does not consist of all this and the like alone.

This and the like together establish the realm of *It*.

But the realm of *Thou* has a different basis.

When *Thou* is spoken, the speaker has no thing for his object. For where there is a thing there is another thing. Every *It* is bounded by others; *It* exists only through being bounded by others. But when *Thou* is spoken, there is no thing. *Thou* has no bounds.

When *Thou* is spoken, the speaker has no *thing*; he has indeed nothing. But he takes his stand in relation.

It is said that man experiences his world. What does that mean?

Man travels over the surface of things and experiences them. He extracts knowledge about their constitution from them: he wins an experience from them. He experiences what belongs to the things.

But the world is not presented to man by experiences alone. These present him only with a world composed of *It* and *He* and *She* and *It* again.

I experience something. — If we add "inner" to "outer" experiences, nothing in the situation is changed. We are merely following the uneternal division that springs from the lust of the human race to whittle away the secret of death. Inner things or outer things, what are they but things and things!

I experience something — If we add "secret" to "open" experiences, nothing in the situation is changed. How self-confident is that wisdom which perceives a closed compartment in things, reserved for the initiate and manipulated only with the key. O secrecy without a secret! O accumulation of information! It, always It!

The man who experiences has no part in the world. For it is "in him" and not between him and the world that the experience arises.

The world has no part in the experience. It permits itself to be experienced, but has no concern in the matter. For it does nothing to the experience, and the experience does nothing to it.

As experience, the world belongs to the primary word *I–It*.
The primary word *I–Thou* establishes the world of relation.

The spheres in which the world of relation arises are three.

First, our life with nature. There the relation sways in gloom, beneath the level of speech. Creatures live and move over against us, but cannot come to us, and when we address them as *Thou*, our words cling to the threshold of speech.

Second, our life with men. There the relation is open and in the form of speech. We can give and accept the *Thou*.

Third, our life with spiritual beings. There the relation is clouded, yet it discloses itself; it does not use speech, yet begets it. We perceive no *Thou*, but none the less we feel we are addressed and we answer — forming, thinking, acting. We speak the primary word with our being, though we cannot utter *Thou* with our lips.

But with what right do we draw what lies outside speech into relation with the world of the primary word?

In every sphere in its own way, through each process of becoming that is present to us we look out toward the fringe of the eternal *Thou*: in each we are aware of a breath from the eternal *Thou*; in each *Thou* we address the eternal *Thou*.

I consider a tree.

I can look on it as a picture: stiff column in a shock of light, or splash of green shot with the delicate blue and silver of the background.

I can perceive it as movement: flowing veins on clinging, pressing pith, suck of the roots, breathing of the leaves, ceaseless commerce with earth and air — and the obscure growth itself.

I can classify it in a species and study it as a type in its structure and mode of life.

I can subdue its actual presence and form so sternly that I recognise it only as an expression of law — of the laws in accordance with which a constant opposition of forces is continually adjusted, or of those in accordance with which the component substances mingle and separate.

I can dissipate it and perpetuate it in number, in pure numerical relation.

In all this the tree remains my object, occupies space and time, and has its nature and constitution.

It can, however, also come about, if I have both will and grace, that in considering the tree I become bound up in relation to it. The tree is now no longer *It*. I have been seized by the power of exclusiveness.

To effect this it is not necessary for me to give up any of the ways in which I consider the tree. There is nothing from which I would have to turn my eyes away in order to see, and no knowledge that I would have to forget. Rather is everything, picture and movement, species and type, law and number, indivisibly united in this event.

Everything belonging to the tree is in this: its form and structure, its colours and chemical composition, its intercourse with the elements and with the stars, are all present in a single whole.

The tree is no impression, no play of my imagination, no value depending on my mood; but it is bodied over against me and has to do with me, as I with it — only in a different way.

Let no attempt be made to sap the strength from the meaning of the relation: relation is mutual.

The tree will have a consciousness, then, similar to our own? Of that I have no experience. But do you wish, through seeming to succeed in it with yourself, once again to disintegrate that which cannot be disintegrated? I encounter no soul or dryad of the tree, but the tree itself.

If I face a human being as my *Thou*, and say the primary word I–*Thou* to him, he is not a thing among things, and does not consist of things.

Thus human being is not *He* or *She*, bounded from every other *He* and *She*, a specific point in space and time within the net of the world; nor is he a nature able to be experienced and described, a loose bundle of named qualities. But with no neighbour, and whole in himself, he is *Thou* and fills the heavens. This does not mean that nothing exists except himself. But all else lives in *his* light.

Just as the melody is not made up of notes nor the verse of words nor the statue of lines, but they must be tugged and dragged till their unity has been scattered into these many pieces, so with the man to whom I say *Thou*. I can take out from him the colour of his hair, or of his speech, or of his goodness. I must continually do this. But each time I do it he ceases to be *Thou*.

And just as prayer is not in time but time in prayer, sacrifice not in space but space in sacrifice, and to reverse the relation is to abolish the reality, so with the man to whom I say *Thou*. I do not meet with him at some time and place or other. I can set him in a particular time and place; I must continually do it: but I set only a *He* or a *She*, that is an *It*, no longer my *Thou*.

So long as the heaven of *Thou* is spread out over me the winds of causality cower at my heels, and the whirlpool of fate stays its course.

I do not experience the man to whom I say *Thou*. But I take my stand in relation to him, in the sanctity of the primary word. Only when I step out of it do I experience him once more. In the act of experience *Thou* is far away.

Even if the man to whom I say *Thou* is not aware of it in the midst of his experience, yet relation may exist. For *Thou* is more than *It* realises. No deception penetrates here; here is the cradle of the Real Life.

This is the eternal source of art: a man is faced by a form which desires to be made through him into a work. This form is no offspring of his soul, but is an appearance which steps up to it and demands of it the effective power. The man is concerned with an act of his being. If he carries it through, if he speaks the primary word out of his being to the form which appears, then the effective power streams out, and the work arises.

The act includes a sacrifice and a risk. This is the sacrifice: the endless possibility that is offered up on the altar of the form. For everything which just this moment in play ran through the perspective must be obliterated; nothing of that may penetrate the work. The exclusiveness of what is facing it demands that it be so. This is the risk: the primary word can only be spoken with the whole being. He who gives himself to it may withhold nothing of himself. The work does not suffer me, as do the tree and the man, to turn aside and relax in the world of *It*; but it commands. If I do not serve it aright it is broken, or it breaks me.

I can neither experience nor describe the form which meets me, but only body it forth. And yet I behold it, splendid in the radiance of what confronts me, clearer than all the clearness of the world which is experienced. I do not behold it as a thing among the "inner" things nor as an image of my "fancy," but as that which exists in the present. If test is made of its objectivity the form is certainly not "there." Yet what is actually so much present as it is? And the relation in which I stand to it is real, for it affects me, as I affect it.

To produce is to draw forth, to invent is to find, to shape is to discover. In bodying forth I disclose. I lead the form across — into the world of *It*. The work produced is a thing among things, able to be experienced and described as a sum of qualities. But from time to time it can face the receptive beholder in its whole embodied form.

James Joyce (1882–1941)

IRISH NOVELIST, SHORT STORY WRITER, and DRAMATIST

Araby - dreamed world

North Richmond Street, being blind, was a quiet street except at the hour when the Christian Brothers' School set the boys free. An uninhabited house of two storeys stood at the blind end, detached from its neighbours in a square ground. The other houses of the street, conscious of decent lives within them, gazed at one another with brown imperturbable faces.

The former tenant of our house, a priest, had died in the back drawing-room. Air, musty from having been long enclosed, hung in all the rooms, and the waste room behind the kitchen was littered with old useless papers. Among these I found a few paper-covered books, the pages of which were curled and damp: *The Abbot*, by Walter Scott, *The Devout Communicant* and *The Memoirs of Vidocq*. I liked the last best because its leaves were yellow. The wild garden behind the house contained a central apple-tree and a few straggling bushes under one of which I found the late tenant's rusty bicycle-pump. He had been a very charitable priest; in his will he had left all his money to institutions and the furniture of his house to his sister.

When the short days of winter came dusk fell before we had well eaten our dinners. When we met in the street the houses had grown somber. The space of sky above us was the colour of ever-changing violet and towards it the lamps of the street lifted their feeble lanterns. The cold air stung us and we played till our bodies glowed. Our shouts echoed in the silent street. The career of our play brought us through the dark muddy lanes behind the houses where we ran the gauntlet of the rough tribes from the cottages, to the back doors of the dark dripping gardens where odours arose from the ashpits, to the dark odorous stables where a coachman smoothed and combed the horse or shook music from the buckled harness. When we returned to the street light from the kitchen windows had filled the areas. If my uncle was seen turning the corner we hid in the shadow until we had seen him safely housed. Or if Man-

From *Dubliners* by James Joyce. Originally published by B. W. Huebsch, Inc., in 1916. All Rights Reserved. Reprinted by permission of The Viking Press, Inc.

gan's sister came out on the doorstep to call her brother in to his tea we watched her from our shadow peer up and down the street. We waited to see whether she would remain or go in and, if she remained, we left our shadow and walked up to Mangan's steps resignedly. She was waiting for us, her figure defined by the light from the half-opened door. Her brother always teased her before he obeyed and I stood by the railings looking at her. Her dress swung as she moved her body and the soft rope of her hair tossed from side to side.

Every morning I lay on the floor in the front parlour watching her door. The blind was pulled down to within an inch of the sash so that I could not be seen. When she came out on the doorstep my heart leaped. I ran to the hall, seized my books and followed her. I kept her brown figure always in my eye and, when we came near the point at which our ways diverged, I quickened my pace and passed her. This happened morning after morning. I had never spoken to her, except for a few casual words, and yet her name was like a summons to all my foolish blood.

Her image accompanied me even in places the most hostile to romance. On Saturday evenings when my aunt went marketing I had to go to carry some of the parcels. We walked through the flaring streets, jostled by drunken men and bargaining women, amid the curses of labourers, the shrill litanies of shop-boys who stood on guard by the barrels of pigs' cheeks, the nasal chanting of street-singers, who sang a *come-all-you* about O'Donovan Rossa, or a ballad about the troubles in our native land. These noises converged in a single sensation of life for me: I imagined that I bore my chalice safely through a throng of foes. Her name sprang to my lips at moments in strange prayers and praises which I myself did not understand. My eyes were often full of tears (I could not tell why) and at times a flood from my heart seemed to pour itself out into my bosom. I thought little of the future. I did not know whether I would ever speak to her or not or, if I spoke to her, how I could tell her of my confused adoration. But my body was like a harp and her words and gestures were like fingers running upon the wires.

One evening I went into the back drawing-room in which the priest had died. It was a dark rainy evening and there was no sound in the house. Through one of the broken panes I heard the rain impinge upon the earth, the fine incessant needles of water playing in the sodden beds. Some distant lamp or lighted window gleamed below me. I was thankful that I could see so little. All my senses seemed to desire to veil themselves and, feeling that I was about to slip from them, I pressed the palms of my hands together until they trembled, murmuring: "*O love! O love!*" many times.

At last she spoke to me. When she addressed the first words to me I was so confused that I did not know what to answer. She asked me was I going to *Araby*. I forgot whether I answered yes or no. It would be a splendid bazaar, she said she would love to go.

"And why can't you?" I asked.

While she spoke she turned a silver bracelet round and round her wrist. She could not go, she said, because there would be a retreat that week in her convent. Her brother and two other boys were fighting for their caps and I was alone at the railings. She held one of the spikes, bowing her head towards me. The light from the lamp opposite our door caught the white curve of her neck, lit up her hair that rested there and, falling, lit up the hand upon the railing. It fell over one side of her dress and caught the white border of a petticoat, just visible as she stood at ease.

"It's well for you," she said.

"If I go," I said, "I will bring you something."

What innumerable follies laid waste my waking and sleeping thoughts after that evening! I wished to annihilate the tedious intervening days. I chafed against the work of school. At night in my bedroom and by day in the class-room her image came between me and the page I strove to read. The syllables of the word *Araby* were called to me through the silence in which my soul luxuriated and cast an Eastern enchantment over me. I asked for leave to go to the bazaar on Saturday night. My aunt was surprised and hoped it was not some Freemason[1] affair. I answered few questions in class. I watched my master's face pass from amiability to sternness; he hoped I was not begin-ning to idle. I could not call my wandering thoughts together. I had hardly any patience with the serious work of life which, now that it stood between me and my desire, seemed to me child's play, ugly monotonous child's play.

On Saturday morning I reminded my uncle that I wished to go to the bazaar in the evening. He was fussing at the hallstand, looking for the hat-brush, and answered me curtly:

"Yes, boy, I know."

As he was in the hall I could not go into the front parlour and lie at the window. I left the house in bad humour and walked slowly towards the school. The air was pitilessly raw and already my heart misgave me.

When I came home to dinner my uncle had not yet been home. Still it was early. I sat staring at the clock for some time and, when its ticking began to irritate me, I left the room. I mounted the staircase and gained the upper part of the house. The high cold empty gloomy rooms liberated me and I went from room to room singing. From the front window I saw my companions playing below in the street. Their cries reached me weakened and indistinct and, leaning my forehead against the cool glass, I looked over at the dark house where she lived. I may have stood there for an hour, seeing nothing but the brown-clad figure cast by my imagination, touched discreetly by the lamp-light at the curved neck, at the hand upon the railings and at the border below the dress.

When I came downstairs again I found Mrs. Mercer sitting at the fire. She was an old garrulous woman, a pawnbroker's widow, who collected used stamps for some pious purpose. I had to endure the gossip of the tea-table. The meal was prolonged beyond an hour and still my uncle did not come. Mrs. Mercer stood up to go: she was sorry she couldn't wait any longer, but it was after eight o'clock and she did not like to be out late, as the night air

[1] The Freemasons, a secret society in 18th and 19th century Europe which aimed at brotherhood and benevolence; it was condemned repeatedly by the Catholic Church as a pagan or deistic cult.

was bad for her. When she had gone I began to walk up and down the room, clenching my fists. My aunt said:

"I'm afraid you may put off your bazaar for this night of Our Lord."

At nine o'clock I heard my uncle's latchkey in the halldoor. I heard him talking to himself and heard the hallstand rocking when it had received the weight of his overcoat. I could interpret these signs. When he was midway through his dinner I asked him to give me the money to go to the bazaar. He had forgotten.

"The people are in bed and after their first sleep now," he said.

I did not smile. My aunt said to him energetically:

"Can't you give him the money and let him go? You've kept him late enough as it is."

My uncle said he was very sorry he had forgotten. He said he believed in the old saying: "All work and no play makes Jack a dull boy." He asked me where I was going and, when I had told him a second time he asked me did I know *The Arab's Farewell to his Steed.* When I left the kitchen he was about to recite the opening lines of the piece to my aunt.

I held a florin tightly in my hand as I strode down Buckingham Street towards the station. The sight of the streets thronged with buyers and glaring with gas recalled to me the purpose of my journey. I took my seat in a third-class carriage of a deserted train. After an intolerable delay the train moved out of the station slowly. It crept onward among ruinous houses and over the twinkling river. At Westland Row Station a crowd of people pressed to the carriage doors; but the porters moved them back, saying that it was a special train for the bazaar. I remained alone in the bare carriage. In a few minutes the train drew up beside an improvised wooden platform. I passed out on to the road and saw by the lighted dial of a clock that it was ten minutes to ten. In front of me was a large building which displayed the magical name.

I could not find any sixpenny entrance and, fearing that the bazaar would be closed, I passed in quickly through a turnstile, handing a shilling to a weary-looking man. I found myself in a big hall girdled at half its height by a gallery. Nearly all the stalls were closed and the greater part of the hall was in darkness. I recognized a silence like that which pervades a church after a service. I walked into the centre of the bazaar timidly. A few people were gathered about the stalls which were still open. Before a curtain, over which the words *Café Chantant* were written in coloured lamps, two men were counting money on a salver. I listened to the fall of the coins.

Remembering with difficulty why I had come I went over to one of the stalls and examined porcelain vases and flowered tea-sets. At the door of the stall a young lady was talking and laughing with two young gentlemen. I remarked their English accents and listened vaguely to their conversation.

"O, I never said such a thing!"

"O, but you did!"

"O, but I didn't!"

"Didn't she say that?"

"Yes. I heard her."

— truth, realization, acceptance [handwritten marginalia]

"O, there's a . . . fib!"

Observing me the young lady came over and asked me did I wish to buy anything. The tone of her voice was not encouraging; she seemed to have spoken to me out of a sense of duty. I looked humbly at the great jars that stood like eastern guards at either side of the dark entrance to the stall and murmured:

"No, thank you."

The young lady changed the position of one of the vases and went back to the two young men. They began to talk of the same subject. Once or twice the young lady glanced at me over her shoulder.

I lingered before her stall, though I knew my stay was useless, to make my interest in her wares seem the more real. Then I turned away slowly and walked down the middle of the bazaar. I allowed the two pennies to fall against the sixpence in my pocket. I heard a voice call from one end of the gallery that the light was out. The upper part of the hall was now completely dark.

Gazing up into the darkness I saw myself as a creature driven and derided by vanity; and my eyes burned with anguish and anger. *— Rebirth (painful) learned* [handwritten marginalia]

T. S. Eliot (1888–1965)

ENGLISH POET, CRITIC, and DRAMATIST (AMERICAN-BORN)

The Love Song of J. Alfred Prufrock

chaotic — Prufrock's mind wanders. Life is chaos. No meaning or purpose. [handwritten marginalia]

S'io credesse che mia risposta fosse
A persona che mai tornasse al mondo,
Questa fiamma staria senza piu scosse.
Ma perciocche giammai di questo fondo
Non torno vivo alcun, s'i'odo il vero,
Senza tema d'infamia ti rispondo.[1]

Let us go then, you and I,
When the evening is spread out against the sky
Like a patient etherised upon a table;

[1] If I believed that my answer might belong
To anyone who ever returned to the world,
This flame would leap no more.
But since, however, from these depths
No one ever returns alive, if I know the truth,
Then without fear of infamy I answer you.
(Dante, *Inferno*, xxvii, 58–63). The speaker is Count Guido da Montefeltro, head of Dante's enemies, the Ghibellines; he was placed in hell for giving false counsel.)

Let us go, through certain half-deserted streets,
The muttering retreats
Of restless nights in one-night cheap hotels
And sawdust restaurants with oyster-shells:
Streets that follow like a tedious argument
Of insidious intent
To lead you to an overwhelming question. . .   10
Oh, do not ask, "What is it?"
Let us go and make our visit.

In the room the women come and go
Talking of Michelangelo.   *very symbolic (color)*
    — lack of courage:

The yellow fog that rubs its back upon the window-panes,
The yellow smoke that rubs its muzzle on the window-panes
Licked its tongue into the corners of the evening,
Lingered upon the pools that stand in drains,
Let fall upon its back the soot that falls from chimneys,
Slipped by the terrace, made a sudden leap,   20
And seeing that it was a soft October night,
Curled once about the house, and fell asleep.

And indeed there will be time   *must fill it*
For the yellow smoke that slides along the street,
Rubbing its back upon the window-panes;   *a curse :*
There will be time, there will be time   *up.*
To prepare a face to meet the faces that you meet;
There will be time to murder and create,
And time for all the works and days of hands
That lift and drop a question on your plate;   30
Time for you and time for me,
And time yet for a hundred indecisions,
And for a hundred visions and revisions,
Before the taking of a toast and tea.

In the room the women come and go
Talking of Michelangelo.

And indeed there will be time
appearance To wonder, "Do I dare?" and, "Do I dare?"
Time to turn back and descend the stair,
With a bald spot in the middle of my hair —   40
[They will say: "How his hair is growing thin!"]
My morning coat, my collar mounting firmly to the chin,
My necktie rich and modest, but asserted by a simple pin —
[They will say: "But how his arms and legs are thin!"]
Do I dare
Disturb the universe?
In a minute there is time
For decisions and revisions which a minute will reverse.

For I have known them all already, known them all: —
Have known the evenings, mornings, afternoons,   50
I have measured out my life with coffee spoons;
I know the voices dying with a dying fall
Beneath the music from a farther room.
  So how should I presume?

  And I have known the eyes already, known them all —
The eyes that fix you in a formulated phrase,
And when I am formulated, sprawling on a pin,
When I am pinned and wriggling on the wall,
Then how should I begin
To spit out all the butt-ends of my days and ways?   60
  And how should I presume?

  And I have known the arms already, known them all —
Arms that are braceleted and white and bare
[But in the lamplight, downed with light brown hair!]
Is it perfume from a dress
That makes me so digress?
Arms that lie along a table, or wrap about a shawl.
  And should I then presume?
  And how should I begin?

                . . . . .

Shall I say, I have gone at dusk through narrow streets   70
And watched the smoke that rises from the pipes
Of lonely men in shirt-sleeves, leaning out of windows?

  I should have been a pair of ragged claws _ should have been
Scuttling across the floors of silent seas.

                . . . . .

And the afternoon, the evening, sleeps so peacefully!
Smoothed by long fingers,
Asleep . . . tired . . . or it malingers,
Stretched on the floor, here beside you and me.
Should I, after tea and cakes and ices,
Have the strength to force the moment to its crisis?   80
But though I have wept and fasted, wept and prayed,
Though I have seen my head [grown slightly bald] brought in upon a platter,
I am no prophet — and here's no great matter;
I have seen the moment of my greatness flicker,
And I have seen the eternal Footman hold my coat, and snicker,
And in short, I was afraid.

  And would it have been worth it, after all,
After the cups, the marmalade, the tea,
Among the porcelain, among some talk of you and me,
Would it have been worth while,   90
To have bitten off the matter with a smile,
To have squeezed the universe into a ball

To roll it toward some overwhelming question,
To say: "I am Lazarus, come from the dead,
Come back to tell you all, I shall tell you all" —
If one, settling a pillow by her head,
  Should say: "That is not what I meant at all.
  That is not it, at all."

  And would it have been worth it, after all,
Would it have been worth while,   100
After the sunsets and the dooryards and the sprinkled streets,
After the novels, after the teacups, after the skirts that trail along the floor—
And this, and so much more? —
It is impossible to say just what I mean!
But as if a magic lantern threw the nerves in patterns on a screen:
Would it have been worth while
If one, settling a pillow or throwing off a shawl,
And turning toward the window, should say:
  "That is not it at all,
  That is not what I meant, at all."   110

             .   .   .   .   .

No! I am not Prince Hamlet, nor was meant to be;
Am an attendant lord, one that will do
To swell a progress, start a scene or two,
Advise the prince; no doubt, an easy tool,
Deferential, glad to be of use,
Politic, cautious, and meticulous;
Full of high sentence, but a bit obtuse;
At times, indeed, almost ridiculous —
Almost, at times, the Fool.

  I grow old . . . I grow old . . .   120
I shall wear the bottoms of my trousers rolled.

  Shall I part my hair behind? Do I dare to eat a peach?
I shall wear white flannel trousers, and walk upon the beach.
I have heard the mermaids singing, each to each.

  I do not think that they will sing to me.

  I have seen them riding seaward on the waves
Combing the white hair of the waves blown back
When the wind blows the water white and black.

  We have lingered in the chambers of the sea
By sea-girls wreathed with seaweed red and brown   130
Till human voices wake us, and we drown.

Katherine Anne Porter (b. 1894)

AMERICAN SHORT STORY WRITER and NOVELIST

Flowering Judas

Braggioni sits heaped upon the edge of a straightbacked chair much too small for him, and sings to Laura in a furry, mournful voice. Laura has begun to find reasons for avoiding her own house until the latest possible moment, for Braggioni is there almost every night. No matter how late she is, he will be sitting there with a surly, waiting expression, pulling at his kinky yellow hair, thumbing the strings of his guitar, snarling a tune under his breath. Lupe the Indian maid meets Laura at the door, and says with a flicker of a glance towards the upper room, "He waits."

Laura wishes to lie down, she is tired of her hairpins and the feel of her long tight sleeves, but she says to him, "Have you a new song for me this evening?" If he says yes, she asks him to sing it. If he says no, she remembers his favorite one, and asks him to sing it again. Lupe brings her a cup of chocolate and a plate of rice, and Laura eats at the small table under the lamp, first inviting Braggioni, whose answer is always the same: "I have eaten, and besides, chocolate thickens the voice."

Laura says, "Sing, then," and Braggioni heaves himself into song. He scratches the guitar familiarly as though it were a pet animal, and sings passionately off key, taking the high notes in a prolonged painful squeal. Laura, who haunts the markets listening to the ballad singers, and stops every day to hear the blind boy playing his reed-flute in Sixteenth of September Street, listens to Braggioni with pitiless courtesy, because she dares not smile at his miserable performance. Nobody dares to smile at him. Braggioni is cruel to everyone, with a kind of specialized insolence, but he is so vain of his talents, and so sensitive to slights, it would require a cruelty and vanity greater than his own to lay a finger on the vast cureless wound of his self-esteem. It would require courage, too, for it is dangerous to offend him, and nobody has this courage.

Braggioni loves himself with such tenderness and amplitude and eternal charity that his followers — for he is a leader of men, a skilled revolutionist, and his skin has been punctured in honorable warfare — warm themselves in the reflected glow, and say to each other: "He has a real nobility, a love of humanity raised above mere personal affections." The excess of this self-love has flowed out, inconveniently for her, over Laura, who, with so many others, owes her comfortable situation and her salary to him. When he is in a very good humor, he tells her, "I am tempted to forgive you for being a *gringa.*

Gringita![1] and Laura, burning, imagines herself leaning forward suddenly, and with a sound back-handed slap wiping the suety smile from his face. If he notices her eyes at these moments he gives no sign.

She knows what Braggioni would offer her, and she must resist tenaciously without appearing to resist, and if she could avoid it she would not admit even to herself the slow drift of his intention. During these long evenings which have spoiled a long month for her, she sits in her deep chair with an open book on her knees, resting her eyes on the consoling rigidity of the printed page when the sight and sound of Braggioni singing threaten to identify themselves with all her remembered afflictions and to add their weight to her uneasy premonitions of the future. The gluttonous bulk of Braggioni has become a symbol of her many disillusions, for a revolutionist should be lean, animated by heroic faith, a vessel of abstract virtues. This is nonsense, she knows it now and is ashamed of it. Revolution must have leaders, and leadership is a career for energetic men. She is, her comrades tell her, full of romantic error, for what she defines as cynicism in them is merely "a developed sense of reality." She is almost too willing to say, "I am wrong, I suppose I don't really understand the principles," and afterward she makes a secret truce with herself, determined not to surrender her will to such expedient logic. But she cannot help feeling that she has been betrayed irreparably by the disunion between her way of living and her feeling of what life should be, and at times she is almost contented to rest in this sense of grievance as a private store of consolation. Sometimes she wishes to run away, but she stays. Now she longs to fly out of this room, down the narrow stairs, and into the street where the houses lean together like conspirators under a single mottled lamp, and leave Braggioni singing to himself.

Instead she looks at Braggioni, frankly and clearly, like a good child who understands the rules of behavior. Her knees cling together under sound blue serge, and her round white collar is not purposely nunlike. She wears the uniform of an idea, and has renounced vanities. She was born Roman Catholic, and in spite of her fear of being seen by someone who might make a scandal of it, she slips now and again into some crumbling little church, kneels on the chilly stone, and says a Hail Mary on the gold rosary she bought in Tehuantepec. It is no good and she ends by examining the altar with its tinsel flowers and ragged brocades, and feels tender about the battered doll-shape of some male saint whose white, lace-trimmed drawers hang limply around his ankles below the hieratic[2] dignity of his velvet robe. She had encased herself in a set of principles derived from her early training, leaving no detail of gesture or of personal taste untouched, and for this reason she will not wear lace made on machines. This is her private heresy, for in her special group the machine is sacred, and will be the salvation of the workers. She loves fine lace, and there is a tiny edge of fluted cobweb on this collar, which

[1] pejorative Spanish slang term for *American*. The setting of this story is Mexico.
[2] priestly.

is one of twenty precisely alike, folded in blue tissue paper in the upper drawer of her clothes chest.

Braggioni catches her glance solidly as if he had been waiting for it, leans forward, balancing his paunch between his spread knees, and sings with tremendous emphasis, weighing his words. He has, the song relates, no father and no mother, nor even a friend to console him; lonely as a wave of the sea he comes and goes, lonely as a wave. His mouth opens round and yearns sideways, his balloon cheeks grow oily with the labor of song. He bulges marvelously in his expensive garments. Over his lavender collar, crushed upon a purple necktie, held by a diamond hoop: over his ammunition belt of tooled leather worked in silver, buckled cruelly around his gasping middle: over the tops of his glossy yellow shoes Braggioni swells with ominous ripeness, his mauve silk hose stretched taut, his ankles bound with the stout leather thongs of his shoes.

When he stretches his eyelids at Laura she notes again that his eyes are the true tawny yellow cat's eyes. He is rich, not in money, he tells her, but in power, and this power brings with it the blameless ownership of things, and the right to indulge his love of small luxuries. "I have a taste for the elegant refinements," he said once, flourishing a yellow silk handkerchief before her nose. "Smell that? It is Jockey Club, imported from New York." Nonetheless he is wounded by life. He will say so presently. "It is true everything turns to dust in the hand, to gall on the tongue." He sighs and his leather belt creaks like a saddle girth. "I am disappointed in everything as it comes. Everything." He shakes his head. "You, poor thing, you will be disappointed too. You are born for it. We are more alike than you realize in some things. Wait and see. Some day you will remember what I have told you, you will know that Braggioni was your friend."

Laura feels a slow chill, a purely physical sense of danger, a warning in her blood that violence, mutilation, a shocking death, wait for her with lessening patience. She has translated this fear into something homely, immediate, and sometimes hesitates before crossing the street. "My personal fate is nothing, except as the testimony of a mental attitude," she reminds herself, quoting from some forgotten philosophic primer, and is sensible enough to add, "Anyhow, I shall not be killed by an automobile if I can help it."

"It may be true I am as corrupt, in another way, as Braggioni," she thinks in spite of herself, "as callous, as incomplete," and if this is so, any kind of death seems preferable. Still she sits quietly, she does not run. Where could she go? Uninvited she has promised herself to this place; she can no longer imagine herself as living in another country, and there is no pleasure in remembering her life before she came here.

Precisely what is the nature of this devotion, its true motives, and what are its obligations? Laura cannot say. She spends part of her days in Xochimilco, near by, teaching Indian children to say in English, "The cat is on the mat." When she appears in the classroom they crowd about her with smiles on their wise, innocent, clay-colored faces, crying, "Good morning, my ticher!" in immaculate voices, and they make of her desk a fresh garden of flowers every day.

During her leisure she goes to union meetings and listens to busy important voices quarreling over tactics, methods, internal politics. She visits the prisoners of her own political faith in their cells, where they entertain themselves with counting cockroaches, repenting on their indiscretions, composing their memoirs, writing out manifestoes and plans for their comrades who are still walking about free, hands in pockets, sniffing fresh air. Laura brings them food and cigarettes and a little money, and she brings messages disguised in equivocal phrases from the men outside who dare not set foot in the prison for fear of disappearing into the cells kept empty for them. If the prisoners confuse night and day, and complain, "Dear little Laura, time doesn't pass in this infernal hole, and I won't know when it is time to sleep unless I have a reminder," she brings them their favorite narcotics, and says in a tone that does not wound them with pity, "Tonight will really be night for you," and though her Spanish amuses them, they find her comforting, useful. If they lose patience and all faith, and curse the slowness of their friends in coming to their rescue with money and influence, they trust her not to repeat everything, and if she inquires, "Where do you think we can find money, or influence?" they are certain to answer, "Well, there is Braggioni, why doesn't he do something?"

She smuggles letters from headquarters to men hiding from firing squads in back streets in mildewed houses, where they sit in tumbled beds and talk bitterly as if all Mexico were at their heels, when Laura knows positively they might appear at the band concert in the Alameda on Sunday morning, and no one would notice them. But Braggioni says, "Let them sweat a little. The next time they may be careful. It is very restful to have them out of the way for a while." She is not afraid to knock on any door in any street after midnight, and enter in the darkness, and say to one of these men who is really in danger: "They will be looking for you — seriously — tomorrow morning after six. Here is some money from Vicente. Go to Vera Cruz and wait."

She borrows money from the Roumanian agitator to give to his bitter enemy the Polish agitator. The favor of Braggioni is their disputed territory, and Braggioni holds the balance nicely, for he can use them both. The Polish agitator talks love to her over café tables, hoping to exploit what he believes is her secret sentimental preference for him, and he gives her misinformation which he begs her to repeat as the solemn truth to certain persons. The Roumanian is more adroit. He is generous with his money in all good causes and lies to her with an air of ingenuous candor, as if he were her good friend and confidant. She never repeats anything they may say. Braggioni never asks questions. He has other ways to discover all that he wishes to know about them.

Nobody touches her, but all praise her gray eyes, and the soft, round under lip which promises gayety, yet is always grave, nearly always firmly closed: and they cannot understand why she is in Mexico. She walks back and forth on her errands, with puzzled eyebrows, carrying her little folder of drawings and music and school papers. No dancer dances more beautifully than Laura walks, and she inspires some amusing, unexpected ardors, which cause little gossip, because nothing comes of them. A young captain who had been a soldier in Zapata's[3] army attempted, during a horseback ride near Cuernavaca, to express his desire for her with the noble simplicity befitting a rude folk-hero: but gently, because he was gentle. This gentleness was his defeat, for when he alighted, and removed her foot from the stirrup, and essayed to draw her down into his arms, her horse, ordinarily a tame one, shied fiercely, reared and plunged away. The young hero's horse careered blindly after his stable-mate, and the hero did not return to the hotel until rather late that evening. At breakfast he came to her table in full charro dress,[4] gray buckskin jacket and trousers with strings of silver buttons down the leg, and he was in a humorous, careless mood. "May I sit with you?" and "You are a wonderful rider. I was terrified that you might be thrown and dragged. I should never have forgiven myself. But I cannot admire you enough for your riding!"

"I learned to ride in Arizona," said Laura.

"If you will ride with me again this morning, I promise you a horse that will not shy with you," he said. But Laura remembered that she must return to Mexico City at noon.

Next morning the children made a celebration and spent their playtime writing on the blackboard, "We lov ar ticher," and with tinted chalks they drew wreaths of flowers around the words. The young hero wrote her a letter: "I am a very foolish, wasteful, impulsive man. I should have first said I love you, and then you would not have run away. But you shall see me again." Laura thought, "I must send him a box of colored crayons," but she was trying to forgive herself for having spurred her horse at the wrong moment.

A brown, shock-haired youth came and stood in her patio one night and sang like a lost soul for two hours, but Laura could think of nothing to do about it. The moonlight spread a wash of gauzy silver over the clear spaces of the garden, and the shadows were cobalt blue. The scarlet blossoms of the Judas tree were dull purple, and the names of the colors repeated themselves automatically in her mind, while she watched not the boy, but his shadow, fallen like a dark garment across the fountain rim, trailing in the water. Lupe came silently and whispered expert counsel in her ear: "If you will throw him one little flower, he will sing another song or two and go away." Laura threw the flower, and he sang a last song and went away with the flower tucked in the band of his hat. Lupe said, "He is one of the organizers of the Typog-

---

[3] a Mexican rebel (1877?–1919) who led an army of peasants against a tyrannical government which opposed land reform for the farmers.
[4] horseman's excessively fancy outfit.

raphers Union, and before that he sold corridos[5] in the Merced market, and before that, he came from Guanajuato, where I was born. I would not trust any man, but I trust least those from Guanajuato."

She did not tell Laura that he would be back again the next night, and the next, nor that he would follow her at a certain fixed distance around the Merced market, through the Zócolo, up Francisco I. Madero Avenue, and so along the Paseo de la Reforma to Chapultepec Park, and into the Philosopher's Footpath, still with that flower withering in his hat, and an·indivisible attention in his eyes.

Now Laura is accustomed to him, it means nothing except that he is nineteen years old and is observing a convention with all propriety, as though it were founded on a law of nature, which in the end it might well prove to be. He is beginning to write poems which he prints on a wooden press, and he leaves them stuck like handbills in her door. She is pleasantly disturbed by the abstract, unhurried watchfulness of his black eyes which will in time turn easily towards another object. She tells herself that throwing the flower was a mistake, for she is twenty-two years old and knows better; but she refuses to regret it, and persuades herself that her negation of all external events as they occur is a sign that she is gradually perfecting herself in the stoicism she strives to cultivate against that disaster she fears, though she cannot name it.

She is not at home in the world. Every day she teaches children who remain strangers to her, though she loves their tender round hands and their charming opportunist savagery. She knocks at unfamiliar doors not knowing whether a friend or a stranger shall answer, and even if a known face emerges from the sour gloom of that unknown interior, still it is the face of a stranger. No matter what this stranger says to her, nor what her message to him, the very cells of her flesh reject knowledge and kinship in one monotonous word. No. No. She draws her strength from this one holy talismanic word which does not suffer her to be led into evil. Denying everything, she may walk anywhere in safety, she looks at everything without amazement.

No, repeats this firm unchanging voice of her blood; and she looks at Braggioni without amazement. He is a great man, he wishes to impress this simple girl who covers her great round breasts with thick dark cloth, and who hides long, invaluably beautiful legs under a heavy skirt. She is almost thin except for the incomprehensible fullness of her breasts, like a nursing mother's, and Braggioni, who considers himself a judge of women, speculates again on the puzzle of her notorious virginity, and takes the liberty of speech which she permits without a sign of modesty, indeed, without any sort of sign, which is disconcerting.

"You think you are so cold, *gringita!* Wait and see. You will surprise yourself some day! May I be there to advise you!" He stretches his eyelids at her, and his ill-humored cat's eyes waver in a separate glance for the two points of light marking the opposite ends of a smoothly drawn path between

---

[5] Mexican narrative folk ballads.

the swollen curve of her breasts. He is not put off by that blue serge, nor by her resolutely fixed gaze. There is all the time in the world. His cheeks are bellying with the wind of song. "O girl with the dark eyes," he sings, and reconsiders. "But yours are not dark. I can change all that. O girl with the green eyes, you have stolen my heart away!" then his mind wanders to the song, and Laura feels the weight of his attention being shifted elsewhere. Singing thus, he seems harmless, he is quite harmless, there is nothing to do but sit patiently and say "No," when the moment comes. She draws a full breath, and her mind wanders also, but not far. She dares not wander too far.

Not for nothing has Braggioni taken pains to be a good revolutionist and a professional lover of humanity. He will never die of it. He has the malice, the cleverness, the wickedness, the sharpness of wit, the hardness of heart, stipulated for loving the world profitably. *He will never die of it.* He will live to see himself kicked out from his feeding trough by other hungry world-saviors. Traditionally he must sing in spite of his life which drives him to bloodshed, he tells Laura, for his father was a Tuscany peasant who drifted to Yucatan and married a Maya woman: a woman of race, an aristocrat. They gave him the love and knowledge of music, thus: and under the rip of his thumbnail, the strings of the instrument complain like exposed nerves.

Once he was called Delgadito[6] by all the girls and married women who ran after him; he was so scrawny all his bones showed under his thin cotton clothing, and he could squeeze his emptiness to the very backbone with his two hands. He was a poet and the revolution was only a dream then; too many women loved him and sapped away his youth, and he could never find enough to eat anywhere, anywhere! Now he is a leader of men, crafty men who whisper in his ear, hungry men who wait for hours outside his office for a word with him, emaciated men with wild faces who waylay him at the street gate with a timid, "Comrade, let me tell you . . ." and they blow the foul breath from their empty stomachs in his face.

He is always sympathetic. He gives them handfuls of small coins from his own pocket, he promises them work, there will be demonstrations, they must join the unions and attend the meetings, above all they must be on the watch for spies. They are closer to him than his own brothers, without them he can do nothing — until tomorrow, comrade!

Until tomorrow. "They are stupid, they are lazy, they are treacherous, they would cut my throat for nothing," he says to Laura. He has good food and abundant drink, he hires an automobile and drives in the Paseo on Sunday morning, and enjoys plenty of sleep in a soft bed beside a wife who dares not disturb him, and he sits pampering his bones in easy billows of fat, singing to Laura, who knows and thinks these things about him. When he was fifteen, he tried to drown himself because he loved a girl, his first love, and she laughed at him. "A thousand women have paid for that," and his tight little mouth turns down at the corners. Now he perfumes his hair with

6 literally, "Little Thin One."

Jockey Club, and confides to Laura: "One woman is really as good as another for me, in the dark. I prefer them all."

His wife organizes unions among the girls in the cigarette factories, and walks in picket lines, and even speaks at meetings in the evening. But she cannot be brought to acknowledge the benefits of true liberty. "I tell her I must have my freedom, net. She does not understand my point of view." Laura has heard this many times. Braggioni scratches the guitar and meditates. "She is an instinctively virtuous woman, pure gold, no doubt of that. If she were not, I should lock her up, and she knows it."

His wife, who works so hard for the good of the factory girls, employs part of her leisure lying on the floor weeping because there are so many women in the world, and only one husband for her, and she never knows where nor when to look for him. He told her: "Unless you can learn to cry when I am not here, I must go away for good." That day he went away and took a room at the Hotel Madrid.

It is this month of separation for the sake of higher principles that has been spoiled not only for Mrs. Braggioni, whose sense of reality is beyond criticism, but for Laura, who feels herself bogged in a nightmare. Tonight Laura envies Mrs. Braggioni, who is alone, and free to weep as much as she pleases about a concrete wrong. Laura has just come from a visit to the prison, and she is waiting for tomorrow with a bitter anxiety as if tomorrow may not come, but time may be caught immovably in this hour, with herself transfixed, Braggioni singing on forever, and Eugenio's body not yet discovered by the guard.

Braggioni says: "Are you going to sleep?" Almost before she can shake her head, he begins telling her about the May-day disturbances coming on in Morelia, for the Catholics hold a festival in honor of the Blessed Virgin, and the Socialists celebrate their martyrs on that day. "There will be two independent processions, starting from either end of town, and they will march until they meet, and the rest depends . . . " He asks her to oil and load his pistols. Standing up, he unbuckles his ammunition belt, and spreads it laden across her knees. Laura sits with the shells slipping through the cleaning cloth dipped in oil, and he says again he cannot understand why she works so hard for the revolutionary idea unless she loves some man who is in it. "Are you not in love with someone?" "No," says Laura. "And no one is in love with you?" "No." "Then it is your own fault. No woman need go begging. Why, what is the matter with you? The legless beggar woman in the Alameda has a perfectly faithful lover. Did you know that?"

Laura peers down the pistol barrel and says nothing, but a long, slow faintness rises and subsides in her; Braggioni curves his swollen fingers around the throat of the guitar and softly smothers the music out of it, and when she hears him again he seems to have forgotten her, and is speaking in the hypnotic voice he uses when talking in small rooms to a listening, close-gathered crowd. Some day this world, now seemingly so composed and eternal to the edges of every sea shall be merely a tangle of gaping trenches, of crashing walls and broken bodies. Everything must be torn from its accustomed place where it has rotted for centuries, hurled skyward and distributed, cast down again clean as rain, without separate identity. Nothing shall survive that the stiffened hands of poverty have created for the rich and no one shall be left alive except the elect spirits destined to procreate a new world cleansed of cruelty and injustice, ruled by benevolent anarchy: "Pistols are good, I love them, cannon are even better, but in the end I pin my faith to good dynamite," he concludes, and strokes the pistol lying in her hands. "Once I dreamed of destroying this city, in case it offered resistance to General Ortíz,[7] but it fell into his hands like an overripe pear."

He is made restless by his own words, rises and stands waiting. Laura holds up the belt to him: "Put that on, and go kill somebody in Morelia, and you will be happier," she says softly. The presence of death in the room makes her bold. "Today, I found Eugenio going into a stupor. He refused to allow me to call the prison doctor. He had taken all the tablets I brought him yesterday. He said he took them because he was bored."

"He is a fool, and his death is his own business," says Braggioni, fastening his belt carefully.

"I told him if he had waited only a little while longer, you would have got him set free," says Laura. "He said he did not want to wait."

"He is a fool and we are well rid of him," says Braggioni, reaching for his hat.

He goes away. Laura knows his mood has changed, she will not see him any more for a while. He will send word when he needs her to go on errands into strange streets, to speak to the strange faces that will appear, like clay masks with the power of human speech, to mutter their thanks to Braggioni for his help. Now she is free, and she thinks, I must run while there is time. But she does not go.

Braggioni enters his own house where for a month his wife has spent many hours every night weeping and tangling her hair upon her pillow. She is weeping now, and she weeps more at the sight of him, the cause of all her sorrows. He looks about the room. Nothing is changed, the smells are good and familiar, he is well acquainted with the woman who comes toward him with no reproach except grief on her face. He says to her tenderly: "You are so good, please don't cry any more, you dear good creature." She says, "Are you tired, my angel? Sit here and I will wash your feet." She brings a bowl of water, and kneeling, unlaces his shoes, and when from her knees she raises her sad eyes under her blackened lids, he is sorry for everything, and bursts into tears. "Ah, yes, I am hungry, I am tired, let us eat something together," he says, between sobs. His wife leans her head on his arm and says, "Forgive me!" and this time he is refreshed by the solemn, endless rain of her tears.

Laura takes off her serge dress and puts on a white linen nightgown and goes to bed. She turns her head a little to one side, and lying still, reminds

---

[7] Pascual Ortiz Rubio: Mexican revolutionary, President of Mexico (1930–1932).

herself that it is time to sleep. Numbers tick in her brain like little clocks, soundless doors close of themselves around her. If you would sleep, you must not remember anything, the children will say tomorrow, good morning, my teacher, the poor prisoners who come every day bringing flowers to their jailer. 1-2-3-4-5 it is monstrous to confuse love with revolution, night with day, life with death — ah, Eugenio!

The tolling of the midnight bell is a signal, but what does it mean? Get up, Laura, and follow me: come out of your sleep, out of your bed, out of this strange house. What are you doing in this house? Without a word, without fear she rose and reached for Eugenio's hand, but he eluded her with a sharp, sly smile and drifted away. This is not all, you shall see — Murderer, he said, follow me, I will show you a new country, but it is far away and we must hurry. No, said Laura, not unless you take my hand, no; and she clung first to the stair rail, and then to the topmost branch of the Judas tree that bent down slowly and set her upon the earth, and then to the rocky ledge of a cliff, and then to the jagged wave of a sea that was not water but a desert of crumbling stone. Where are you taking me, she asked in wonder but without fear. To death, and it is a long way off, and we must hurry, said Eugenio. No, said Laura, not unless you take my hand. Then eat these flowers, poor prisoner, said Eugenio in a voice of pity, take and eat: and from the Judas tree he stripped the warm bleeding flowers, and held them to her lips. She saw that his hand was fleshless, a cluster of small white petrified branches, and his eye sockets were without light, but she ate the flowers greedily for they satisfied both hunger and thirst. Murderer! said Eugenio, and Cannibal! This is my body and my blood. Laura cried No! and at the sound of her own voice, she awoke trembling, and was afraid to sleep again.

James Agee   (1909–1955)

AMERICAN NOVELIST, JOURNALIST, and SCENARIO WRITER

A Visit to Grandma's

After dinner the babies and all the children except Rufus were laid out on the beds to take their naps, and his mother thought he ought to lie down too, but his father said no, why did he need to, so he was allowed to stay up. He stayed out on the porch with the men. They were so full up and sleepy they hardy even tried to talk, and he was so full up and sleepy that he could hardly see or hear, but half dozing between his father's knees in the thin shade, trying to keep his eyes open, he could just hear the mild, lazy rumbling of their voices, and the more talkative voices of the women back in the kitchen, talking more easily, but keeping their voices low, not to wake the children, and the rattling of the dishes they were doing, and now and then their walking here or there along the floor; and mused with half-closed eyes which went in and out of focus with sleepiness, upon the slow twinkling of the millions of heavy leaves on the trees and the slow flashing of the blades of the corn, and nearer at hand, the hens dabbing in the pocked dirt yard and the ragged edge of the porch floor, and everything hung dreaming in a shining silver haze, and a long, low hill of blue silver shut off everything against a blue-white sky, and he leaned back against his father's chest and he could hear his heart pumping and his stomach growling and he could feel the hard knees against his sides, and the next thing he knew his eyes opened and he was looking up into his mother's face and he was lying on a bed and she was saying it was time to wake up because they were going on a call and see his great-great-grandmother and she would most specially want to see him because he was her oldest great-great-grandchild. And he and his father and mother and Catherine got in the front seat and his Granpa Follet and Aunt Jessie and her baby and Jim-Wilson and Ettie Lou and Aunt Sadie and her baby got in the back seat and Uncle Ralph stood on the running board because he was sure he could remember the way, and that was all there was room for, and they started off very carefully down the lane, so nobody would be jolted, and even before they got out to the road his mother asked his father to stop a minute, and she insisted on taking Ettie Lou with them in front, to make a little more room in back, and after she insisted for a while, they gave in, and then they all got started again, and his father guided the auto so very carefully across the deep ruts into the road, the other way from LaFollette as Ralph told him to ("Yeah, I know," his father said, "I remember *that* much anyhow."), that they were hardly joggled at all, and his mother commented on how very nicely and carefully his father always drove when he didn't just forget and go too fast, and his father blushed, and after a few minutes his mother began to look uneasy, as if she had to go to the bathroom but didn't want to say anything about it, and after a few minutes more she said, "Jay, I'm awfully sorry but now I really think you *are* forgetting."

"Forgetting what?" he said.

"I mean a little too fast, dear," she said.

"Good road along here," he said. "Got to make time while the road's good." He slowed down a little. "Way I remember it," he said, "there's some stretches you can't hardly ever get a mule through, we're coming to, ain't they Ralph?"

"Oh, mercy," his mother said.

"We are just raggin you," he said. "They're not all *that* bad. But all the same we better make time while we can." And he sped up a little.

After another two or three miles Uncle Ralph said, "Now around this bend you run through a branch and you turn up sharp to the right," and they ran through the branch and turned into a sandy woods road and his father went a little slower and a cool breeze flowed through them and his mother said how lovely this shade was after that terrible hot sun, wasn't it, and all the older people murmured that it sure was, and almost immediately they broke out of the woods and ran through two miles of burned country with stumps and sometimes whole tree trunks sticking up out of it sharp and cruel, and blackberry and honeysuckle all over the place, and a hill and its shadow ahead. And when they came within the shadow of the hill, Uncle Ralph said in a low voice, "Now you get to the hill, start along the base of it to your left till you see your second right and then you take that," but when they got there, there was only the road to the left and none to the right and his father took it and nobody said anything, and after a minute Uncle Ralph said, "Reckon they wasn't much to choose from there, was they?" and laughed unhappily.

"That's right," his father said, and smiled.

"Reckon my memory ain't so sharp as I bragged," Ralph said.

"You're doin fine," his father said, and his mother said so too.

"I could a swore they was a road both ways there," Ralph said, "but it was nigh on twenty years since I was out here." Why for goodness sake, his mother said, then she *certainly* thought he had a wonderful memory.

"How long since *you* were here, Jay?" He did not say anything. "Jay?"

"I'm a-studyin it," he said.

"There's your turn," Ralph said suddenly, and they had to back the auto to turn into it.

They began a long, slow, winding climb, and Rufus half heard and scarcely understood their disjointed talking. His father had not been there in nearly thirteen years; the last time was just before he came to Knoxville. He was always her favorite, Ralph said. Yes, his grandfather said, he reckoned that was a fact, she always seemed to take a shine to Jay. His father said quietly that he always did take a shine to her. It turned out he was the last of those in the auto who had seen her. They asked how she was, as if it had been within a month or two. He said she was failing lots of ways, specially getting around, her rheumatism was pretty bad, but in the mind she was bright as a dollar, course that wasn't saying how they might find her by now, poor old soul; no *use* saying. Nope, Uncle Ralph said, *that* was a fact; time sure did fly, didn't it; seemed like before you knew it, this year was last year. She had never yet seen Jay's children, or Ralph's, or Jessie's or Sadie's, it was sure going to be a treat for her. A treat *and* a surprise. Yes it sure would be that, his father said, always supposing she could still recognize them. Mightn't she even have died? his mother wanted to know. *Oh* no, all the Follets said, they'd have heard for sure if she'd died. Matter of fact they *had* heard she had failed a good bit. Sometimes her memory slipped up and she got confused, poor old soul. His mother said well she should *think* so, poor old lady.

She asked, carefully, if she was taken good care of. Oh, yes, they said. That she was. Sadie's practically giving her life to her. That was Grandpa Follet's oldest sister and young Sadie was named for her. Lived right with her tending to her wants, day and night. Well, isn't that just wonderful, his mother said. Wasn't anybody else could do it, they agreed with each other. All married and gone, and she wouldn't come live with any of them, they all offered, over and over, but she wouldn't leave her home. I raised my family here, she said, I lived here all my life from fourteen years on and I aim to die here, that must be a good thirty-five, most, a good near forty year ago, Grampaw died. Goodness sake, his mother said, and she was an old *old* woman *then!* His father said soberly, "She's a hundred and three years old. Hundred and three or hundred and four. She never could remember for sure which. But she knows she wasn't born later than eighteen-twelve. And she always reckoned it might of been eighteen-eleven."

"*Great heavens*, Jay! Do you *mean* that?" He just nodded, and kept his eyes on the road. "Just *imagine that*, Rufus," she said. "Just *think* of *that!*"

"She's an old, old lady," his father said gravely; and Ralph gravely and proudly concurred.

"The things she must have seen!" Mary said, quietly. "Indians. Wild animals." Jay laughed. "I mean *man*-eaters, Jay. Bears, and wildcats — terrible things."

"There were cats back in these mountains, Mary — we called em painters, that's the same as a panther — they were around here still when *I* was a boy. And there is still bear, they claim."

"Gracious Jay, did you ever *see* one? A panther?"

"Saw one'd been shot."

"Goodness," Mary said.

"A mean-lookin varmint."

"I know," she said. "I mean, I *bet* he was. I just can't get over — why she's almost as old as the country, Jay."

"*Oh*, no," he laughed. "Ain't nobody *that* old. Why I read somewhere, that just these mountains here are the oldest . . ."

"Dear, I meant the nation," she said. "The United States, I mean. Why let me see, why it was hardly as old as I am when she was born." They all calculated for a moment. "Not even as old," she said triumphantly.

"By golly," his father said. "I never thought of it like that." He shook his head. "By golly," he said, "that's a fact."

"Abraham Lincoln was just two years old," she murmured. "Maybe three," she said grudgingly. "Just try to *imagine* that, Rufus," she said after a moment. "Over a hundred years." But she could see that he couldn't comprehend it. "You know what she is?" she said, "she's Granpa Follet's *grandmother!*"

"That's a fact, Rufus," his grandfather said from the back seat, and Rufus looked around, able to believe it but not to imagine it, and the old man smiled and winked. "Woulda never believed you'd hear *me* call nobody 'Granmaw,' now would you?"

"No sir," Rufus said.

"Well, yer goana," his grandfather said, "quick's I see her."

Ralph was beginning to mutter and to look worried and finally his brother said, "What's eaten ye, Ralph? Lost the way?" And Ralph said he didn't know for sure as he had lost it exactly, no, he wouldn't swear to that yet, but by golly he was damned if he was sure this was *hit* anymore, all the same.

"Oh *dear*, Ralph how *too bad*," Mary said, "but don't you mind. Maybe we'll find it. I mean maybe soon you'll recognize landmarks and set us all straight again."

But his father, looking dark and painfully patient, just slowed the auto down and then came to a stop in a shady place. "Maybe we better figure it out right now," he said.

"Nothin round hyer I know," Ralph said, miserably. "What I mean, maybe we ought to start back while we still know the *way* back. Try it another Sunday."

"Oh, Jay."

"I hate to but we got to get back in town tonight, don't forget. We could try it another Sunday. Make an early start." But the upshot of it was that they decided to keep on ahead awhile, anyway. They descended into a long, narrow valley through the woods of which they could only occasionally see the dark ridges and the road kept bearing in a direction Ralph was almost sure was wrong, and they found a cabin, barely even cut out of the woods, they commented later, hardly even a corn patch, big as an ordinary barnyard; but the people there, very glum and watchful, said they had never even heard of her; and after a long while the valley opened out a little and Ralph began to think that perhaps he recognized it, only it sure didn't look like itself if it *was* it, and all of a sudden a curve opened into half-forested meadow and there were glimpses of a gray house through swinging vistas of saplings and Ralph said, "By golly," and again, "By golly, that is *hit*. That's hit all right. Only we come on it from behind!" And his father began to be sure too, and the house grew larger, and they swung around where they could see the front of it, and his father and his Uncle Ralph and his Grandfather all said, "Why sure enough," and sure enough it was: and, "There she is," and there she was: it was a great, square-logged gray cabin closed by a breezeway, with a frame second floor, and an enormous oak plunging from the packed dirt in front of it, and a great iron ring, the rim of a wagon wheel, hung by a chain from a branch of the oak which had drunk the chains into itself, and in the shade of the oak, which was as big as the whole corn patch they had seen, an old woman was standing up from a kitchen chair as they swung slowly in onto the dirt and under the edge of the shade, and another old woman continued to sit very still in her chair.

The younger of the two old women was Great Aunt Sadie, and she knew them the minute she laid eyes on them and came right on up to the side of the auto before they could even get out. "Lord God," she said in a low, hard voice, and she put her hands on the edge of the auto and just looked from one to the other of them. Her hands were long and narrow and as big as a man's and every knuckle was swollen and split. She had hard black eyes, and there was a dim purple splash all over the left side of her face. She looked at them so sharply and silently from one to another that Rufus thought she must be mad at them, and then she began to shake her head back and forth. "Lord God," she said again. "Howdy, John Henry," she said.

"Howdy, Sadie," his grandfather said.

"Howdy, Aunt Sadie," his father and his Aunt Sadie said.

"Howdy, Jay," she said, looking sternly at his father, "howdy, Ralph," and she looked sternly at Ralph. "Reckon you must be Jess, and yore Sadie. Howdy, Sadie."

"This is Mary, Aunt Sadie," his father said. "Mary, this is Aunt Sadie."

"I'm proud to know you," the old woman said, looking very hard at his mother. "I figured it must be you," she said, just as his mother said, "I'm awfully glad to know you too." "And this is Rufus and Catherine and Ralph's Jim-Wilson and Ettie Lou and Jessie's Charlie after his daddy and Sadie's Jessie after her Granma and her Aunt Jessie," his father said.

"Well, Lord God," the old woman said. "Well, file on out."

"How's Granmaw?" his father asked, in a low voice, without moving yet to get out.

"Good as we got any right to expect," she said, "but don't feel put out if she don't know none-a-yews. She mought and she mought not. Half the time she don't even know me."

Ralph shook his head and clucked his tongue. "Pore old soul," he said, looking at the ground. His father let out a slow breath, puffing his cheeks.

"So if I was you-all I'd come up on her kind of easy," the old woman said. "Bin a coon's age since she seen so many folks at onct. Me either. Mought skeer her if ye all come a whoopin up at her in a flock."

"Sure," his father said.

"Ayy," his mother whispered.

His father turned and looked back. "Whyn't you go see her the first, Paw?" he said very low. "Yore the eldest."

"Tain't me she wants to see," Grandfather Follet said. "Hit's the younguns ud tickle her most."

"Reckon that's the truth, if she can take notice," the old woman said. "She shore like to cracked her heels when she heared *yore* boy was born," she said to Jay, "Mary or no Mary.[1] Proud as Lucifer. Cause that was the first," she told Mary.

"Yes, I know," Mary said. "Fifth generation, that made."

"Did you get her postcard, Jay?"

"What postcard?"

"Why no," Mary said.

"She tole me what to write on one a them postcards and put hit in the mail to both a yews so I done it. Didn't ye never get it?"

Jay shook his head. "First I ever heard tell of it," he said.

---

[1] Mary, a Roman Catholic, has married into a Protestant family, some of whose members disapprove of her religion.

"Well I shore done give hit to the mail. Ought to remember. Cause I went all the way into Polly to buy it and all the way in again to put it in the mail."

"We never did get it," Jay said.

"What street did you send it, Aunt Sadie?" Mary asked. "Because we moved not long be . . ."

"Never sent it to no street," the old woman said. "Never knowed I needed to, Jay working for the post office."

"Why, I quit working for the post office a long time back, Aunt Sadie. Even before that."

"Well I reckon that's how come then. Cause I just sent hit to 'Post Office, Cristobal, Canal Zone, Panama,' and I spelt hit right, too. C-r-i . . ."

"Oh," Mary said.

"Aw," Jay said. "Why, Aunt Sadie, I thought you'd a known. We been living in Knoxvul since pert near two years before Rufus was born."

She looked at him keenly and angrily, raising her hands slowly from the edge of the auto, and brought them down so hard that Rufus jumped. Then she nodded, several times, and still she did not say anything. At last she spoke, coldly, "Well, they might as well just put me out to grass," she said. "Lay me down and give me both barls threw the head."

"Why, Aunt Sadie," Mary said gently, but nobody paid any attention.

After a moment the old woman went on solemnly, staring hard into Jay's eyes: "I knowed that like I know my own name and it plumb slipped my mind."

"Oh what a shame," Mary said sympathetically.

"Hit ain't shame I feel," the old woman said, "hit's sick in the stummick."

"Oh I didn't m . . ."

"Right hyer!" and she slapped her hand hard against her stomach and laid her hand back on the edge of the auto. "If I git like that too," she said to Jay, "*then* who's agonna look out fer her?"

"Aw, tain't so bad, Aunt Sadie," Jay said. "Everybody slips up nown then. Do it myself an I ain't half yer age. And you just ought see Mary."

"Gracious, yes," Mary said. "I'm just a perfect scatterbrain."

The old woman looked briefly at Mary and then looked back at Jay. "Hit ain't the only time," she said, "not by a long chalk. Twarn't three days ago I . . ." she stopped. "Takin on about yer troubles ain't never holp nobody," she said. "You just set hyer a minute."

She turned and walked over to the older woman and leaned deep over against her ear and said, quite loudly, but not quite shouting, "Granmaw, ye got company." And they watched the old woman's pale eyes, which had been on them all this time in the light shadow of the sunbonnet, not changing, rarely ever blinking, to see whether they would change now, and they did not change at all, she didn't even move her head or her mouth. "Ye hear me, Granmaw?" The old woman opened and shut her sunken mouth, but not as if she were saying anything. "Hit's Jay and his wife and younguns, come up from Knoxvul to see you," she called, and they saw the hands crawl in her lap and the face turned towards the younger woman and they could hear a thin, dry crackling, no words.

"She can't talk any more," Jay said, almost in a whisper.

"Oh *no*," Mary said.

But Sadie turned to them and her hard eyes were bright. "She knows ye," she said quietly. "Come on over." And they climbed slowly and shyly out onto the swept ground. "I'll tell her about the rest a yuns in a minute," Sadie said.

"Don't want to mix her up," Ralph explained, and they all nodded.

It seemed to Rufus like a long walk over to the old woman because they were all moving so carefully and shyly; it was almost like church. "Don't holler," Aunt Sadie was advising his parents, "hit only skeers her. Just talk loud and plain right up next her ear."

"I know," his mother said. "My mother is very deaf, too."

"Yeah," his father said. And he bent down close against her ear. "Granmaw?" he called, and he drew a little away, where she could see him, while his wife and his children looked on, each holding one of the mother's hands. She looked straight into his eyes and her eyes and her face never changed, a look as if she were gazing at some small point at a great distance, with complete but idle intensity, as if what she was watching was no concern of hers. His father leaned forward again and gently kissed her on the mouth, and drew back again where she could see him well, and smiled a little, anxiously. Her face restored itself from his kiss like grass that has been lightly stepped on; her eyes did not alter. Her skin looked like brown-marbled stone over which water has worked for so long that it is as smooth and blind as soap. He leaned to her ear again. "I'm Jay," he said. "John Henry's boy." Her hands crawled in her skirt: every white bone and black vein showed through the brown-splotched skin; the wrinkled knuckles were like pouches; she wore a red rubber guard ahead of her wedding ring. Her mouth opened and shut and they heard her low, dry croaking, but her eyes did not change. They were bright in their thin shadow, but they were as impersonally bright as two perfectly shaped eyes of glass.

"I figure she knows you," Sadie said quietly.

"She can't talk, can she?" Jay said, and now that he was not looking at her, it was as if they were talking over a stump.

"Times she can," Sadie said. "Times she can't. Ain't only so seldom call for talk, reckon she loses the hang of it. But I figger she knows ye and I am tickled she does."

His father looked all around him in the shade and he looked sad, and unsure, and then he looked at him. "Come here, Rufus," he said.

"Go to him," his mother whispered for some reason, and she pushed his hand gently as she let it go.

"Just call her Granmaw," his father said quietly. "Get right up by her ear like you do to Granmaw Lynch and say, 'Granmaw, I'm Rufus.' "

He walked over to her as quietly as if she were asleep, feeling strange to be by himself, and stood on tiptoe beside her and looked down into her sunbonnet towards her ear. Her temple was deeply sunken as if a hammer had struck it and frail as a fledgling's belly. Her skin was crosshatched with the razor-fine slashes of innumerable square wrinkles and yet every slash was like smooth stone; her ear was just a fallen intricate flap with a small gold ring in it; her smell was faint yet very powerful, and she smelled like new mushrooms and old spices and sweat, like his fingernail when it was coming off. "Granmaw, I'm Rufus," he said carefully, and yellow-white hair stirred beside her ear. He could feel coldness breathing from her cheek.

"Come out where she can see you," his father said, and he drew back and stood still further on tiptoe and leaned across her, where she could see. "I'm Rufus," he said, smiling, and suddenly her eyes darted a little and looked straight into his, but they did not in any way change their expression. They were just color: seen close as this, there was color through a dot at the middle, dim as blue-black oil, and then a circle of blue so pale it was almost white, that looked like glass, smashed into a thousand dimly sparkling pieces, smashed and infinitely old and patient, and then a ring of dark blue, so fine and sharp no needle could have drawn it, and then a clotted yellow full of tiny squiggles of blood, and then a wrong-side furl of red-bronze, and little black lashes. Vague light sparkled in the crackled blue of the eye like some kind of remote ancestor's anger, and the sadness of time dwelt in the blue-breathing, oily center, lost and alone and far away, deeper than the deepest well. His father was saying something, but he did not hear and now he spoke again, careful to be patient, and Rufus heard, "Tell her 'I'm Jay's boy.' Say, 'I'm Jay's boy Rufus.'"

And again he leaned into the cold fragrant cavern next her ear and said, "I'm Jay's boy Rufus," and he could feel her face turn towards him.

"Now kiss her," his father said, and he drew out of the shadow of her bonnet and leaned far over and again entered the shadow and kissed her paper mouth, and the mouth opened, and the cold sweet breath of rotting and of spice broke from her with the dry croaking, and he felt the hands take him by the shoulders like knives and forks of ice through his clothes. She drew him closer and looked at him almost glaring, she was so filled with grave intensity. She seemed to be sucking on her lower lip and her eyes filled with light, and then, as abruptly as if the two different faces had been joined without transition in a strip of moving-picture film, she was not serious any more but smiling so hard that her chin and her nose almost touched and her deep little eyes giggled for joy. And again the croaking gurgle came, making shapes which were surely words but incomprehensible words, and she held him even more tightly by the shoulders, and looked at him even more keenly and incredulously with her giggling, all but hidden eyes, and smiled and smiled, and cocked her head to one side, and with sudden love he kissed her again. And he could hear his mother's voice say, "Jay," almost whispering, and his father say, "Let her be," in a quick, soft, angry voice, and when at length they gently disengaged her hands, and he was at a little distance, he could see that there was water crawling along the dust from under her chair, and his father and his Aunt Sadie looked gentle and sad and dignified, and his mother was trying not to show that she was crying, and the old lady sat there aware only that something had been taken from her, but growing quickly calm, and nobody said anything about it.

Dylan Thomas (1914–1953)

WELSH POET

Do Not Go Gentle into That Good Night

Do not go gentle into that good night,
Old age should burn and rave at close of day;
Rage, rage against the dying of the light.

Though wise men at their end know dark is right
Because their words had forked no lightning they
Do not go gentle into that good night.

Good men, the last wave by, crying how bright
Their frail deeds might have danced in a green bay,
Rage, rage against the dying of the light.

Wild men who caught and sang the sun in flight,   10
And learn, too late, they grieved it on its way,
Do not go gentle into that good night.

Grave men, near death, who see with blinding sight
Blind eyes could blaze like meteors and be gay,
Rage, rage against the dying of the light.

And you, my father, there on the sad height,
Curse, bless, me now with your fierce tears, I pray.
Do not go gentle into that good night.
Rage, rage against the dying of the light.

Max Shulman   (b. 1919)

AMERICAN NOVELIST and DRAMATIST

Love Is a Fallacy

Cool was I and logical. Keen, calculating, perspicacious, acute and astute — I was all of these. My brain was as powerful as a dynamo, as precise as a chemist's scales, as penetrating as a scalpel. And — think of it! — I was only eighteen.

It is not often that one so young has such a giant intellect. Take, for example, Petey Bellows, my roommate at the university. Same age, same background, but dumb as an ox. A nice enough fellow, you understand, but nothing upstairs. Emotional type. Unstable. Impressionable. Worst of all, a faddist. Fads, I submit, are the very negation of reason. To be swept up in every new craze that comes along, to surrender yourself to idiocy just because everybody else is doing it — this, to me, is the acme of mindlessness. Not, however, to Petey.

One afternoon I found Petey lying on his bed with an expression of such distress on his face that I immediately diagnosed appendicitis. "Don't move," I said. "Don't take a laxative. I'll get a doctor."

"Raccoon," he mumbled thickly.

"Raccoon?" I said, pausing in my flight.

"I want a raccoon coat," he wailed.

I perceived that his trouble was not physical, but mental. "Why do you want a raccoon coat?"

"I should have known it," he cried, pounding his temples. "I should have known they'd come back when the Charleston came back. Like a fool I spent all my money for textbooks, and now I can't get a raccoon coat."

"Can you mean," I said incredulously, "that people are actually wearing raccoon coats again?"

"All the Big Men on Campus are wearing them. Where've you been?"

"In the library," I said, naming a place not frequented by Big Men on Campus.

He leaped from the bed and paced the room. "I've got to have a raccoon coat," he said passionately. "I've got to!"

"Petey, why? Look at it rationally. Raccoon coats are unsanitary. They shed. They smell bad. They weigh too much. They're unsightly. They ——"

"You don't understand," he interrupted impatiently. "It's the thing to do. Don't you want to be in the swim?"

"No," I said truthfully.

212

"Well, I do," he declared. "I'd give anything for a raccoon coat. Anything!"

My brain, that precision instrument, slipped into high gear. "Anything?" I asked, looking at him narrowly.

"Anything," he affirmed in ringing tones.

I stroked my chin thoughtfully. It so happened that I knew where to get my hands on a raccoon coat. My father had had one in his undergraduate days; it lay now in a trunk in the attic back home. It also happened that Petey had something I wanted. He didn't *have* it exactly, but at least he had first rights on it. I refer to his girl, Polly Espy.

I had long coveted Polly Espy. Let me emphasize that my desire for this young woman was not emotional in nature. She was, to be sure, a girl who excited the emotion, but I was not one to let my heart rule my head. I wanted Polly for a shrewdly calculated, entirely cerebral reason.

I was a freshman in law school. In a few years I would be out in practice. I was well aware of the importance of the right kind of wife in furthering a lawyer's career. The successful lawyers I had observed were, almost without exception, married to beautiful, gracious, intelligent women. With one omission, Polly fitted these specifications perfectly.

Beautiful she was. She was not yet of pin-up proportions, but I felt sure that time would supply the lack. She already had the makings.

Gracious she was. By gracious I mean full of graces. She had an erectness of carriage, an ease of bearing, a poise that clearly indicated the best of breeding. At table her manners were exquisite. I had seen her at the Kozy Kampus Korner eating the specialty of the house — a sandwich that contained scraps of pot roast, gravy, chopped nuts, and a dipper of sauerkraut — without even getting her fingers moist.

Intelligent she was not. In fact, she veered in the opposite direction. But I believed that under my guidance she would smarten up. At any rate, it was worth a try. It is, after all, easier to make a beautiful dumb girl smart than to make an ugly smart girl beautiful.

"Petey," I said, "are you in love with Polly Espy?"

"I think she's a keen kid," he replied, "but I don't know if you'd call it love. Why?"

"Do you," I asked, "have any kind of formal arrangement with her? I mean are you going steady or anything like that?"

"No. We see each other quite a bit, but we both have other dates. Why?"

"Is there," I asked, "any other man for whom she has a particular fondness?"

"Not that I know of. Why?"

I nodded with satisfaction. "In other words, if you were out of the picture, the field would be open. Is that right?"

"I guess so. What are you getting at?"

"Nothing, nothing," I said innocently, and took my suitcase out of the closet.

"Where you going?" asked Petey.

"Home for the week end." I threw a few things into the bag.

"Listen," he said, clutching my arm eagerly, "while you're home, you couldn't get some money from your old man, could you, and lend it to me so I can buy a raccoon coat?"

"I may do better than that," I said with a mysterious wink and closed my bag and left.

"Look," I said to Petey when I got back Monday morning. I threw open the suitcase and revealed the huge, hairy, gamy object that my father had worn in his Stutz Bearcat in 1925.

"Holy Toledo!" said Petey reverently. He plunged his hands into the raccoon coat and then his face. "Holy Toledo!" he repeated fifteen or twenty times.

"Would you like it?" I asked.

"Oh yes!" he cried, clutching the greasy pelt to him. Then a canny look came into his eyes. "What do you want for it?"

"Your girl," I said, mincing no words.

"Polly?" he said in a horrified whisper. "You want Polly?"

"That's right."

He flung the coat from him. "Never," he said stoutly.

I shrugged. "Okay. If you don't want to be in the swim, I guess it's your business."

I sat down in a chair and pretended to read a book, but out of the corner of my eye I kept watching Petey. He was a torn man. First he looked at the coat with the expression of a waif at a bakery window. Then he turned away and set his jaw resolutely. Then he looked back at the coat, with even more longing in his face. Then he turned away, but with not so much resolution this time. Back and forth his head swiveled, desire waxing, resolution waning. Finally he didn't turn away at all; he just stood and stared with mad lust at the coat.

"It isn't as though I was in love with Polly," he said thickly. "Or going steady or anything like that."

"That's right," I murmured.

"What's Polly to me, or me to Polly?"

"Not a thing," said I.

"It's just been a casual kick — just a few laughs, that's all."

"Try on the coat," said I.

He complied. The coat hunched high over his ears and dropped all the way down to his shoe tops. He looked like a mound of dead raccoons. "Fits fine," he said happily.

I rose from my chair. "Is it a deal?" I asked, extending my hand.

He swallowed. "It's a deal," he said and shook my hand.

I had my first date with Polly the following evening. This was in the nature of a survey; I wanted to find out just how much work I had to do to get her mind up to the standard I required. I took her first to dinner. "Gee, that was a delish dinner," she said as we left the restaurant. Then I took her to a movie. "Gee, that was a marvy movie," she said as we left the theater. And then I took her home. "Gee, I had a sensaysh time," she said as she bade me good night.

I went back to my room with a heavy heart. I had gravely underestimated the size of my task. This girl's lack of information was terrifying. Nor would it be enough merely to supply her with information. First she had to be taught to *think*. This loomed as a project of no small dimensions, and at first I was tempted to give her back to Petey. But then I got to thinking about her abundant physical charms and about the way she entered a room and the way she handled a knife and fork, and I decided to make an effort.

I went about it, as in all things, systematically. I gave her a course in logic. It happened that I, as a law student, was taking a course in logic myself, so I had all the facts at my finger tips. "Polly," I said to her when I picked her up on our next date, "tonight we are going over to the Knoll and talk."

"Oo, terrif," she replied. One thing I will say for this girl: you would go far to find another so agreeable.

We went to the Knoll, the campus trysting place, and we sat down under an old oak, and she looked at me expectantly. "What are we going to talk about?" she asked.

"Logic."

She thought this over for a minute and decided she liked it. "Magnif," she said.

"Logic," I said, clearing my throat, "is the science of thinking. Before we can think correctly, we must first learn to recognize the common fallacies of logic. These we will take up tonight."

"Wow-dow!" she cried, clapping her hands delightedly.

I winced, but went bravely on. "First let us examine the fallacy called Dicto Simpliciter."

"By all means," she urged, batting her lashes eagerly.

"Dicto Simpliciter means an argument based on an unqualified generalization. For example: Exercise is good. Therefore everybody should exercise."

"I agree," said Polly earnestly. "I mean exercise is wonderful. I mean it builds the body and everything."

"Polly," I said gently, "the argument is a fallacy. *Exercise is good* is an unqualified generalization. For instance, if you have heart disease, exercise is bad, not good. Many people are ordered by their doctors *not* to exercise. You must *qualify* the generalization. You must say exercise is *usually* good, or exercise is good *for most people*. Otherwise you have committed a Dicto Simpliciter. Do you see?"

"No," she confessed. "But this is marvy. Do more! Do more!"

"It will be better if you stop tugging at my sleeve," I told her, and when she desisted, I continued. "Next we take up a fallacy called Hasty Generalization. Listen carefully: You can't speak French. I can't speak French. Petey Bellows can't speak French. I must therefore conclude that nobody at the University of Minnesota can speak French."

"Really?" said Polly, amazed. "*Nobody?*"

I hid my exasperation. "Polly, it's a fallacy. The generalization is reached too hastily. There are too few instances to support such a conclusion."

"Know any more fallacies?" she asked breathlessly. "This is more fun than dancing even."

I fought off a wave of despair. I was getting nowhere with this girl, absolutely nowhere. Still, I am nothing if not persistent. I continued. "Next comes Post Hoc. Listen to this: Let's not take Bill on our picnic. Every time we take him out with us, it rains."

"I know somebody just like that," she exclaimed. "A girl back home — Eula Becker, her name is. It never fails. Every single time we take her on a picnic — "

"Polly," I said sharply, "it's a fallacy. Eula Becker doesn't *cause* the rain. She has no connection with the rain. You are guilty of Post Hoc if you blame Eula Becker."

"I'll never do it again," she promised contritely. "Are you mad at me?"

I sighed. "No, Polly, I'm not mad."

"Then tell me some more fallacies."

"All right. Let's try Contradictory Premises."

"Yes, let's," she chirped, blinking her eyes happily.

I frowned, but plunged ahead. "Here's an example of Contradictory Premises: If God can do anything, can He make a stone so heavy that He won't be able to lift it?"

"Of course," she replied promptly.

"But if He can do anything, He can lift the stone," I pointed out.

"Yeah," she said thoughtfully. "Well, then I guess He can't make the stone."

"But He can do anything," I reminded her.

She scratched her pretty, empty head. "I'm all confused," she admitted.

"Of course you are. Because when the premises of an argument contradict each other, there can be no argument. If there is an irresistible force, there can be no immovable object. If there is an immovable object, there can be no irresistible force. Get it?"

"Tell me some more of this keen stuff," she said eagerly.

I consulted my watch. "I think we'd better call it a night. I'll take you home now, and you go over all the things you've learned. We'll have another session tomorrow night."

I deposited her at the girls' dormitory, where she assured me that she had had a perfectly terrif evening, and I went glumly home to my room. Petey lay snoring in his bed, the raccoon coat huddled like a great hairy beast at his feet. For a moment I considered waking him and telling him that he could have his girl back. It seemed clear that my project was doomed to failure. The girl simply had a logic-proof head.

But then I reconsidered. I had wasted one evening; I might as well waste another. Who knew? Maybe somewhere in the extinct crater of her mind a few embers still smoldered. Maybe somehow I could fan them into flame. Admittedly it was not a prospect fraught with hope, but I decided to give it one more try.

Seated under the oak the next evening I said, "Our first fallacy tonight is called Ad Misericordiam."[1]

She quivered with delight.

"Listen closely," I said. "A man applies for a job. When the boss asks him what his qualifications are, he replies that he has a wife and six children at home, the wife is a helpless cripple, the children have nothing to eat, no clothes to wear, no shoes on their feet, there are no beds in the house, no coal in the cellar, and winter is coming."

A tear rolled down each of Polly's pink cheeks. "Oh, this is awful, awful," she sobbed.

"Yes, it's awful," I agreed, "but it's no argument. The man never answered the boss's question about his qualifications. Instead he appealed to the boss's sympathy. He committed the fallacy of Ad Misericordiam. Do you understand?"

"Have you got a handkerchief?" she blubbered.

I handed her a handkerchief and tried to keep from screaming while she wiped her eyes. "Next," I said in a carefully controlled tone, "we will discuss False Analogy. Here is an example: Students should be allowed to look at their textbooks during examinations. After all, surgeons have X-rays to guide them during an operation, lawyers have briefs to guide them during a trial, carpenters have blueprints to guide them when they are building a house. Why, then, shouldn't students be allowed to look at their textbooks during an examination?"

"There now," she said enthusiastically, "is the most marvy idea I've heard in years."

"Polly," I said testily, "the argument is all wrong. Doctors, lawyers, and carpenters aren't taking a test to see how much they have learned, but students are. The situations are altogether different, and you can't make an analogy between them."

"I still think it's a good idea," said Polly.

"Nuts," I muttered. Doggedly I pressed on. "Next we'll try Hypothesis Contrary to Fact."

"Sounds yummy," was Polly's reaction.

"Listen: If Madame Curie had not happened to leave a photographic plate in a drawer with a chunk of pitchblende, the world today would not know about radium."

"True, true," said Polly, nodding her head. "Did you see the movie? Oh, it just knocked me out. That Walter Pidgeon is so dreamy. I mean he fractures me."

"If you can forget Mr. Pidgeon for a moment," I said coldly, "I would like

---

[1] [to move] to compassion, pity.

to point out that the statement is a fallacy. Maybe Madame Curie would have discovered radium at some later date. Maybe somebody else would have discovered it. Maybe any number of things would have happened. You can't start with a hypothesis that is not true and then draw any supportable conclusions from it."

"They ought to put Walter Pidgeon in more pictures," said Polly. "I hardly ever see him any more."

One more chance, I decided. But just one more. There is a limit to what flesh and blood can bear. "The next fallacy is called Poisoning the Well."

"How cute!" she gurgled.

"Two men are having a debate. The first one gets up and says, 'My opponent is a notorious liar. You can't believe a word that he is going to say.' . . . Now, Polly, think. Think hard. What's wrong?"

I watched her closely as she knit her creamy brow in concentration. Suddenly a glimmer of intelligence — the first I had seen — came into her eyes. "It's not fair," she said with indignation. "It's not a bit fair. What chance has the second man got if the first man calls him a liar before he even begins talking?"

"Right!" I cried exultantly. "One hundred per cent right. It's not fair. The first man has *poisoned the well* before anybody could drink from it. He has hamstrung his opponent before he could even start. . . . Polly, I'm proud of you."

"Pshaw," she murmured, blushing with pleasure.

"You see, my dear, these things aren't so hard. All you have to do is concentrate. Think — examine — evaluate. Come now, let's review everything we have learned."

"Fire away," she said with an airy wave of her hand.

Heartened by the knowledge that Polly was not altogether a cretin, I began a long, patient review of all I had told her. Over and over and over again I cited instances, pointed out flaws, kept hammering away without letup. It was like digging a tunnel. At first everything was work, sweat, and darkness. I had no idea when I would reach the light, or even *if* I would. But I persisted. I pounded and clawed and scraped, and finally I was rewarded. I saw a chink of light. And then the chink got bigger and the sun came pouring in and all was bright.

Five grueling nights this took, but it was worth it. I had made a logician out of Polly; I had taught her to think. My job was done. She was worthy of me at last. She was a fit wife for me, a proper hostess for my many mansions, a suitable mother for my well-heeled children.

It must not be thought that I was without love for this girl. Quite the contrary. Just as Pygmalion loved the perfect woman he had fashioned, so I loved mine. I decided to acquaint her with my feelings at our very next meeting. The time had come to change our relationship from academic to romantic.

"Polly," I said when next we sat beneath our oak, "tonight we will not discuss fallacies."

"Aw, gee," she said, disappointed.

"My dear," I said, favoring her with a smile, "we have now spent five evenings together. We have gotten along splendidly. It is clear that we are well matched."

"Hasty Generalization," said Polly brightly.

"I beg your pardon," said I.

"Hasty Generalization," she repeated. "How can you say that we are well matched on the basis of only five dates?"

I chuckled with amusement. The dear child had learned her lessons well. "My dear," I said, patting her hand in a tolerant manner, "five dates is plenty. After all, you don't have to eat a whole cake to know that it's good."

"False Analogy," said Polly promptly. "I'm not a cake. I'm a girl."

I chuckled with somewhat less amusement. The dear child had learned her lessons perhaps too well. I decided to change tactics. Obviously the best approach was a simple, strong, direct declaration of love. I paused for a moment while my massive brain chose the proper words. Then I began:

"Polly, I love you. You are the whole world to me, and the moon and the stars and the constellations of outer space. Please, my darling, say that you will go steady with me, for if you will not, life will be meaningless. I will languish. I will refuse my meals. I will wander the face of the earth, a shambling, hollow-eyed hulk."

There, I thought, folding my arms, that ought to do it.

"Ad Misercordiam," said Polly.

I ground my teeth. I was not Pygmalion; I was Frankenstein, and my monster had me by the throat. Frantically I fought back the tide of panic surging through me. At all costs I had to keep cool.

"Well, Polly," I said, forcing a smile, "you certainly have learned your fallacies."

"You're darn right," she said with a vigorous nod.

"And who taught them to you, Polly?"

"You did."

"That's right. So you do owe me something, don't you, my dear? If I hadn't come along you never would have learned about fallacies."

"Hypothesis Contrary to Fact," she said instantly.

I dashed perspiration from my brow. "Polly," I croaked, "you mustn't take all these things so literally. I mean this is just classroom stuff. You know that the things you learn in school don't have anything to do with life."

"Dicto Simpliciter," she said, wagging her finger at me playfully.

That did it. I leaped to my feet, bellowing like a bull. "Will you or will you not go steady with me?"

"I will not," she replied.

"Why not?" I demanded.

"Because this afternoon I promised Petey Bellows that I would go steady with him."

I reeled back, overcome with the infamy of it. After he promised, after he made a deal, after he shook my hand! "The rat!" I shrieked, kicking up great chunks of turf. "You can't go with him, Polly. He's a liar. He's a cheat. He's a rat."

"Poisoning the Well," said Polly, "and stop shouting. I think shouting must be a fallacy too."

With an immense effort of will, I modulated my voice. "All right," I said. "You're a logician. Let's look at this thing logically. How could you choose Petey Bellows over me? Look at me — a brilliant student, a tremendous intellectual, a man with an assured future. Look at Petey — a knothead, a jitterbug, a guy who'll never know where his next meal is coming from. Can you give me one logical reason why you should go steady with Petey Bellows?"

"I certainly can," declared Polly. "He's got a raccoon coat."

Donald Hall (b. 1928)

AMERICAN POET

My Son, My Executioner

My son, my executioner,
 I take you in my arms,
Quiet and small and just astir,
 And whom my body warms.

Sweet death, small son, our instrument
 Of immortality,
Your cries and hungers document
 Our bodily decay.

We twenty-five and twenty-two,
 Who seemed to live forever,   10
Observe enduring life in you
 And start to die together.

Evgenii Yevtushenko (b. 1933)

RUSSIAN POET

Party Card

A shot-up forest full of black holes.
Mind-crushing explosions.
He wants some berries, he wants some berries:
the young lieutenant, lying in his blood.
I was a smallish boy,
who crawled in the long grass till it was dark
and brought him back a cap of strawberries,
and when they came there was no use for them.
The rain of July lightly falling.
He was lying in remoteness and silence   10
among the ruined tanks and the dead.
The rain glistened on his eyelashes.
There were sadness and worry in his eyes.
I waited saying nothing and soaking,
like waiting for an answer to something
he couldn't answer. Passionate with silence
unable to see when he asked me,
I took his party card from his pocket.   party card: for membership
And small and tired and without understanding   in the Communist Party
wandering in the flushed and smoking dark,   20
met up with refugees moving east
and somehow through the terribly flashing night
we travelled without a map, the priest
with his long grey hair and his rucksack,
and me and a sailor with a wounded arm.
Child crying. Horse whinnying.
And answered to with love and with courage
and white, white, the bell-towers rang out
speaking to Russia with a tocsin voice.
Wheatfields blackened round their villages.   30
In the woman's coat I wore at that time.
I felt for the party card close to my heart.

"Party Card" by Evgenii Yevtushenko, translated by Robin Milner-Gullard and Peter Levi, S.J., and published by Penguin Books Ltd. Reprinted by permission.

RELIGION

*Divination is the craft which establishes
good-will between gods and men,
because it understands the principles of
love which, in human life, issue in
virtuous and god-fearing behaviour.*

ERYXIMACHUS, *Symposium*

RELIGION, we are told, is regaining the influence once lost on a generation of post-Darwinian skeptics. The local atheist has become an anachronism, but so has undeviating adherence to ritual. Liturgy is spoken in the vernacular; sermons involve cinema and sculpture; the pipe organ harmonizes with the guitar. Seekers of answers to the ultimate questions, customarily the young, are now joined by the generations over thirty as they consult gurus, Eastern mystics, Western theologians, local clergymen — and psychiatrists. This questioning is considered not only desirable but necessary, for whether or not one eventually accepts some faith or tradition, he becomes fully a person in time and society only after he has considered various fundamental issues and tried to resolve them.

Because the issues are fundamental, the questions themselves are both timely and timeless. When the Greeks offered sacrifices of burnt cattle and goats, they were acknowledging an ultimate power in praise, gratitude, and requests for direction. They sought direction from the events that occurred subsequent to their supplications, often quarreling over interpretations of these events or projecting on them what they most wished to observe. These offerings, like the medieval Mass and our more personal, contemporary prayers, are attempts to search out advice or solace; they are often based on the concept of a purposeful, orderly, responsive force which is powerful and understanding.

The nature of this force and of man's relation to it forms the basis for much of our religion and our best literature. Literary works have become particularly meaningful in the current search for beliefs and values. But they also raise a number of basic questions.

Some of these questions are cosmological. How does man relate to the known world? What is the nature of the universe? What is the nature of human existence? Can man survive in a universe that is conceived to be without purpose, a universe that seems at best puzzling?

Other questions are theological. Dostoevsky's Ivan Karamazov considers, among other things, whether there is — or was — a God and, if so, why man might choose to ignore or reject Him. Vaughan and Taylor attempt to provide individual definitions of God, while Swift and Browning explore, through satire and negative examples, the question of how religion functions and how it affects those who subscribe to it. *Abraham and Isaac* dramatizes the believer's relation to God; Larkin writes of the unbeliever's relation to religion. Stace attempts to understand religion by examining conditions of its absence, while through

"The Perennial Philosophy" Huxley considers the fundamental similarities and differences between Eastern and Western religions.

Religious questions are sometimes sociological in perspective. Matters of faith or ethics shape patterns of behavior and help to define the nature of a man's relation to his fellow man, to groups, and to society as a whole. What happens, for example, if one attempts (under the guise of religion) to manipulate others? Has one a responsibility or even a right to communicate his faith or to impose it on others? Can politics mix with religion? Can religion be a means of attaining power in society? Does society tolerate religious positions of importance or prestige?

Approaches to the fundamental questions may be philosophical. The modern existentialists Kafka and Camus examine, through legend and parable, the meaning of the self — fundamentally and in isolation. From a Jewish perspective Malamud examines the apprehension of religious experience during a period of extreme trial, while Hawthorne's Goodman Brown, ostensibly a Puritan, finds that faith is not a matter of outward form but of inner spirit.

Each of these perspectives raises questions, the complexities and nuances of which are explored in the following selections. Symbol and metaphor, fact and analogue are often used as means of making the abstract communicable. And, like the complexities of love, the complexities of religion are expressed through many moods: denial and doubt, pain and pride, fear and faith. In these literary writings, monologue becomes dialogue which invites the reader to question, confirm, or deny. But who is to answer these questions? No matter which answers satisfy, according to whatever criteria, there are other criteria, other answers, other questions.

In this section we explore in many voices, many modes, those questions that have plagued man since his first belief that there exists some supreme authority.

Moses (c. 14th CENTURY B.C.)

HEBREW PROPHET and LAWGIVER

Lord, Thou Hast Been Our Dwelling Place

90 LORD, thou hast been our dwelling place in all generations.

2 Before the mountains were brought forth, or ever thou hadst formed the earth and the world, even from everlasting to everlasting, thou *art* God.

3 Thou turnest man to destruction; and sayest, Return, ye children of men.

4 For a thousand years in thy sight *are but* as yesterday when it is past, and *as* a watch in the night.

5 Thou carriest them away as with a flood; they are *as* a sleep: in the morning *they are* like grass *which* groweth up.

6 In the morning it flourisheth, and groweth up; in the evening it is cut down, and withereth.

7 For we are consumed by thine anger, and by thy wrath are we troubled.

8 Thou hast set our iniquities before thee, our secret *sins* in the light of thy countenance.

9 For all our days are passed away in thy wrath: we spend our years as a tale *that is told*.

10 The days of our years *are* threescore years and ten; and if by reason of strength *they be* fourscore years, yet *is* their strength labour and sorrow; for it is soon cut off, and we fly away.

11 Who knoweth the power of thine anger? even according to thy fear, *so is* thy wrath.

12 So teach *us* to number our days, that we may apply *our* hearts unto wisdom.

13 Return, O LORD, how long? and let it repent thee concerning thy servants.

14 O satisfy us early with thy mercy; that we may rejoice and be glad all our days.

15 Make us glad according to the days *wherein* thou hast afflicted us, *and* the years *wherein* we have seen evil.

16 Let thy work appear unto thy servants, and thy glory unto their children.

17 And let the beauty of the LORD our God be upon us: and establish thou the work of our hands upon us; yea, the work of our hands establish thou it.

The authorship of this psalm is disputed, but most scholars attribute it to Moses. The dates of Moses' life are disputed also, with estimates ranging from the 12th to the 16th centuries B.C.

Title supplied by editors. "Lord, Thou Hast Been Our Dwelling Place" attributed to Moses. From the King James Version of The Bible, Psalm 90.

David   (1013?–?973 B.C.)

KING OF JUDAH and ISRAEL

The Lord Is My Shepherd

23   The LORD *is* my shepherd; I shall not want.

2 He maketh me to lie down in green pastures: he leadeth me beside the still waters.

3 He restoreth my soul: he leadeth me in the paths of righteousness for his name's sake.

4 Yea, though I walk through the valley of the shadow of death, I will fear no evil: for thou *art* with me; thy rod and thy staff they comfort me.

5 Thou preparest a table before me in the presence of mine enemies: thou anointest my head with oil; my cup runneth over.

6 Surely goodness and mercy shall follow me all the days of my life: and I will dwell in the house of the LORD for ever.

The King James Version of The Bible

23   The Lord to mee a shepheard is, want therefore shall not I.

2 Hee in the folds of tender-grasse, doth cause mee downe to lie:
To waters calme me gently leads (3) Restore my soule doth hee:
he doth in paths of righteousnes: for his names sake leade mee.

4 Yea though in valley of deaths shade I walk, none ill I'le feare:
because thou art with mee, thy rod, and staffe my comfort are.

5 For mee a table thou hast spread, in presence of my foes:
thou dost annoynt my head with oyle, my cup it over-flowes.

6 Goodnes & mercy surely shall all my dayes follow mee:
and in the Lords house I shall dwell so long as dayes shall bee.

The Bay Psalm Book

Title supplied by editors. "The Lord Is My Shepherd" by David: Psalm 23. The second version is from the *Bay Psalm Book* (A *Facsimile Reprint of the First Edition of 1640*) by Zoltán Haraszti, published by The University of Chicago Press. © 1956 by The University of Chicago. Published 1956; Composed and printed by The University of Chicago Press, Chicago, Illinois, U.S.A. Reprinted by permission.

23   The LORD is my shepherd, I shall not want;
  2 he makes me lie down in green pastures.
He leads me beside still waters;
  3 he restores my soul.
He leads me in paths of righteousness
      for his name's sake.

  4 Even though I walk through the valley of the shadow of death,
      I fear no evil;
for thou art with me;
      thy rod and thy staff,
      they comfort me.

  5 Thou preparest a table before me in the presence of my enemies;
thou anointest my head with oil,
      my cup overflows.
  6 Surely goodness and mercy shall follow me
      all the days of my life;
and I shall dwell in the house of the LORD
      for ever.

The Revised Standard Version of The Bible

Yahwist School (codified c. 950 B.C.)

Eastward in Eden

8 And the LORD God planted a garden eastward in Eden; and there he put the man whom he had formed.

9 And out of the ground made the LORD God to grow every tree that is pleasant to the sight, and good for food; the tree of life also in the midst of the garden, and the tree of knowledge of good and evil.

10 And a river went out of Eden to water the garden; and from thence it was parted, and became into four heads.

11 The name of the first is Pison: that *is* it which compasseth the whole land of Havilah, where *there is* gold;

This ascription assumes composite authorship of the Pentateuch. Many reputable scholars hold to the view that Moses was the author of *Genesis*.

Title supplied by editors. From the King James Version of The Bible, *Genesis* 2:8–3:24.

12 And the gold of that land *is* good: there *is* bdellium and the onyx stone.

13 And the name of the second river is Gihon: the same *is* it that compasseth the whole land of Ethiopia.

14 And the name of the third river *is* Hiddekel: that *is* it which goeth toward the east of Assyria. And the fourth river *is* Euphrates.

15 And the Lord God took the man, and put him into the garden of Eden to dress it and to keep it.

16 And the Lord God commanded the man, saying, Of every tree of the garden thou mayest freely eat:

17 But of the tree of the knowledge of good and evil, thou shalt not eat of it: for in the day that thou eatest thereof thou shalt surely die.

18 And the Lord God said, *It is* not good that the man should be alone; I will make him an help meet for him.

19 And out of the ground the Lord God formed every beast of the field, and every fowl of the air; and brought *them* unto Adam to see what he would call them: and whatsoever Adam called every living creature, that *was* the name thereof.

20 And Adam gave names to all cattle, and to the fowl of the air, and to every beast of the field; but for Adam there was not found an help meet for him.

21 And the Lord God caused a deep sleep to fall upon Adam, and he slept: and he took one of his ribs, and closed up the flesh instead thereof;

22 And the rib, which the Lord God had taken from man, made he a woman, and brought her unto the man.

23 And Adam said, This *is* now bone of my bones, and flesh of my flesh: she shall be called Woman, because she was taken out of Man.

24 Therefore shall a man leave his father and his mother, and shall cleave unto his wife: and they shall be one flesh.

25 And they were both naked, the man and his wife, and were not ashamed.

3   Now the serpent was more subtil than any beast of the field which the Lord God had made. And he said unto the woman, Yea, hath God said, Ye shall not eat of every tree of the garden?

2 And the woman said unto the serpent, We may eat of the fruit of the trees of the garden:

3 But of the fruit of the tree which *is* in the midst of the garden, God hath said, Ye shall not eat of it, neither shall ye touch it, lest ye die.

4 And the serpent said unto the woman, Ye shall not surely die:

5 For God doth know that in the day ye eat thereof, then your eyes shall be opened, and ye shall be as gods, knowing good and evil.

6 And when the woman saw that the tree *was* good for food, and that it *was* pleasant to the eyes, and a tree to be desired to make *one* wise, she took of the fruit thereof, and did eat, and gave also unto her husband with her; and he did eat.

7 And the eyes of them both were opened, and they knew that they *were* naked; and they sewed fig leaves together, and made themselves aprons.

8 And they heard the voice of the Lord God walking in the garden in the cool of the day: and Adam and his wife hid themselves from the presence of the Lord God amongst the trees of the garden.

9 And the Lord God called unto Adam, and said unto him, Where *art* thou?

10 And he said, I heard thy voice in the garden, and I was afraid, because I *was* naked; and I hid myself.

11 And he said, Who told thee that thou *wast* naked? Hast thou eaten of the tree, whereof I commanded thee that thou shouldest not eat?

12 And the man said, The woman whom thou gavest *to be* with me, she gave me of the tree, and I did eat.

13 And the Lord God said unto the woman, What *is* this *that* thou hast done? And the woman said, The serpent beguiled me, and I did eat.

14 And the Lord God said unto the serpent, Because thou hast done this, thou *art* cursed above all cattle, and above every beast of the field; upon thy belly shalt thou go, and dust shalt thou eat all the days of thy life:

15 And I will put enmity between thee and the woman, and between thy seed and her seed; it shall bruise thy head, and thou shalt bruise his heel.

16 Unto the woman he said, I will greatly multiply thy sorrow and thy conception; in sorrow thou shalt bring forth children; and thy desire *shall be* to thy husband, and he shall rule over thee.

17 And unto Adam he said, Because thou hast hearkened unto the voice of thy wife, and hast eaten of the tree, of which I commanded thee, saying, Thou shalt not eat of it: cursed *is* the ground for thy sake; in sorrow shalt thou eat *of* it all the days of thy life;

18 Thorns also and thistles shall it bring forth to thee; and thou shalt eat the herb of the field;

19 In the sweat of thy face shalt thou eat bread, till thou return unto the ground; for out of it wast thou taken: for dust thou *art*, and unto dust shalt thou return.

20 And Adam called his wife's name Eve; because she was the mother of all living.

21 Unto Adam also and to his wife did the Lord God make coats of skins, and clothed them.

22 And the Lord God said, Behold, the man is become as one of us, to know good and evil: and now, lest he put forth his hand, and take also of the tree of life, and eat, and live for ever:

23 Therefore the Lord God sent him forth from the garden of Eden, to till the ground from whence he was taken.

24 So he drove out the man; and he placed at the east of the garden of Eden Cherubims, and a flaming sword which turned every way, to keep the way of the tree of life.

Polybius (c. 205–c. 123 B.C.)

GREEK HISTORIAN

Religion and the Public Morality

. . . The quality in which the Roman commonwealth is most distinctly superior is in my opinion the nature of their religious convictions. I believe that it is the very thing which among other peoples is an object of reproach, I mean superstition, which maintains the cohesion of the Roman State. These matters are clothed in such pomp and introduced to such an extent into their public and private life that nothing could exceed it, a fact which will surprise many. My own opinion at least is that they have adopted this course for the sake of the common people. It is a course which perhaps would not have been necessary had it been possible to form a state composed of wise men, but as every multitude is fickle, full of lawless desires, unreasoned passion, and violent anger, the multitude must be held in by invisible terrors and suchlike pageantry. For this reason I think, not that the ancients acted rashly and at haphazard in introducing among the people notions concerning the gods and beliefs in the terrors of hell, but that the moderns are most rash and foolish in banishing such beliefs. The consequence is that among the Greeks, apart from other things, members of the government, if they are entrusted with no more than a talent, though they have ten copyists and as many seals and twice as many witnesses, cannot keep their faith; whereas among the Romans those who as magistrates and legates are dealing with large sums of money maintain correct conduct just because they have pledged their faith by oath. Whereas elsewhere it is a rare thing to find a man who keeps his hands off public money, and whose record is clean in this respect, among the Romans one rarely comes across a man who has been detected in such conduct. . . .

Title supplied by editors. "Religion and the Public Morality" by Polybius. From *The Histories*, Book VI, translated by W. R. Paton. Reprinted from *The Loeb Classical Library* edition, Vol. III, by permission of Harvard University Press.

Anonymous (14th CENTURY)

ENGLISH

Abraham and Isaac

CHARACTERS

ABRAHAM
ISAAC
AN ANGEL
DOCTOR, OR TEACHER

Scene: A hilly landscape. Abraham and Isaac
are kneeling on a level piece of ground.

ABRAHAM.   Father of Heaven, omnipotent
    With all my heart to thee I call,
Thou has given me both land and rent.
And my livelihood thou hast me sent,
    I thank thee highly evermore for all.

First of the earth thou madest Adam,
    And Eve also to be his wife;
All other creatures from these two came.
And now thou hast granted to me, Abraham,
    Here in this land to lead my life.   10

In my age thou has granted me this
    That this young child with me shall dwell.
I love nothing so much in this,
Except thine own self, dear Father of Bliss,
    As Isaac here, my own sweet son.

I who have many children mo'
    Love them not as half so well.
This fair sweet child he cheers me so
In every place wherever I do go,
    That of no affliction may I tell.   20

And therefore, Father of Heaven, I thee pray
    For his health and also for his grace.

"Abraham and Isaac," the Brome version. Original stage
directions appear in quotation marks; all others have been
interpolated by John Gassner. From *Medieval and Tudor
Drama*, edited by John Gassner. Copyright © 1935, 1940,
1950, 1951, 1963, by Simon & Schuster, Inc. Reprinted
by permission of Mrs. John Gassner.

Now, Lord, keep him both night and day
That never discomfort nor dismay
  Come to my child in any place.
    (*Rising*)
Now come on, Isaac, my own sweet child,
  Go we home and take our rest.

ISAAC. Abraham, mine own father so mild,
To follow you I am full pleased,
  Both early and late.   **30**

 ABRAHAM. Come on, sweet child. I love thee best
  Of all the children that ever I begot.

(ABRAHAM *and* ISAAC *start on their homeward
journey.* GOD *and an* ANGEL *appear.*)

 GOD. Mine angel, fast hie thee thy way,
  And unto middle-earth anon thou go —
Abram's heart now will I assay,
  Whether that he be steadfast or no.

Say I commanded him for to take
  Isaac, his young son that he loves so well,
And with his blood sacrifice he make,
  If any of my friendship he would feel. **40**

Show him the way unto the hill
  Where that his sacrifice shall be.
I shall assay now his good will,
  Whether he loveth better his child or me.
All men shall take example by him
  My commandments how to keep.

(*As the* ANGEL *descends,* ABRAHAM, *moved in
spirit, kneels again.*)

 ABRAHAM. Now, Father of Heaven, that formed
  everything,
  My prayers I make to thee again,
For this day a tender offering
  Here must I give to thee certain. **50**
Ah, Lord God, almighty King,
  What manner of beast would'st thou fain?
If I had thereof true knowing,
  It should be done with all my main
    Full soon by me.
To do thy pleasure on a hill,
Verily, it is my will,
  Dear Father, God in Trinity!

(*The* ANGEL *reaches* ABRAHAM, *while* ISAAC *has wandered off.*)

ANGEL.   Abraham, Abraham, be at rest!
      Our Lord commandeth thee to take   60
Isaac, thy young son whom thou lovest best,
      And with his blood that sacrifice thou make.

Into the Land of Vision do thou go,
      And offer thy child unto thy Lord;
I shall thee lead and also show.
      To God's behest, Abraham, accord,

And follow me upon this green!

ABRAHAM.   Welcome to me be my Lord's com-
    mand!
      And his word I will not withstand
      Yet Isaac, my young son in hand,   70
A full dear child to me has been.

I had rather, if God had been pleased,
      To have forborne all the goods that I have,
Than Isaac, my son, should be deceased, —
      So God in heaven my soul may save!

I have loved never a thing so much on earth,
      And now I must the child go kill!
Ah, Lord God, my conscience lacketh mirth!
And yet, my dear Lord, I am sore afeared
      To grudge anything against thy will.   80

I love my child as my life,
      But yet I love my God much more
For though my heart should make any strife
Yet will I not spare for child or wife,
      But do after my dread Lord's lore.

Though I love my son never so well,
      Yet smite off his head soon I shall.
Ah, Father of Heaven! to thee I kneel —
A hard death my son shall feel,
      To honor thee, Lord, withal!   90

ANGEL.   Abraham, Abraham, this is well said,
      And all these commandments look that thou
        keep, —

But in thy heart be nothing dismayed.

ABRAHAM.   Nay, nay, forsooth. I hold me well
   repaid
     To please my God to the best that I may.
For though my heart be heavily set
     To see the blood of my own dear son,
Yet for all that I will not let,
But Isaac, my son, I will go get,
     And come as fast as ever we can.   100

(*The* ANGEL *departs and* ABRAHAM *looks for his son.*)

ABRAHAM.   Now, Isaac, my own son dear.
     Where art thou, child? Speak to me.

ISAAC.   My father, sweet father, I am here,
     And make my prayers to the Trinity.

ABRAHAM.   Rise up, my child, and fast come
   hither,
     My gentle bairn that art so wise,
For we, too, child, must go together,
     And unto my Lord make sacrifice.

(ISAAC *rises and goes to him.*)

ISAAC.   I am full ready, my father, lo!
     Given to your hands, I stand right here;   110
And whatsoever ye bid me do, even so
     It shall be done with glad cheer,
       Full well and fine.

ABRAHAM.   Ah, Isaac, my own son so dear,
     God's blessing I give thee, and mine.

Hold this faggot upon thy back,
     And I myself fire shall bring.

ISAAC.   Father, all this here will I pack;
     I am full fain to do your bidding.   **fain: willing**
ABRAHAM.   Ah, Lord of Heaven!   120
(ABRAHAM *looks up to heaven, and wrings his hands.*)
This child's words all do wound my heart!
    (*Controlling himself and turning to* ISAAC)
Now, Isaac, son, go we on our way
     Unto yon mount with all our main.

ISAAC.   Go we, my dear father, as fast as I may;
     To follow you I am full fain,
       Although I be slender.

(ABRAHAM *stops as they arrive at the mountain, his
eyes fixed on heaven.*)

ABRAHAM.   Ah, Lord, my heart breaketh in twain
    This child's words, they be so tender!
       (*Again controlling himself.*)
Ah, Isaac son, anon lay it down,
    No longer upon thy back it hold,   130
For I must make ready prayer soon
    To honor my Lord God as I was told.

      (ISAAC *drops the faggots.*)

ISAAC.   Lo, my dear father, here it is.
    (*Moving close to him tenderly.*)
    To cheer you always I draw me near.
But, father, I marvel sore at this,
    Why ye make this heavy cheer,

And also, father, even more dread I —
    Where is quick beast that ye should kill?   **quick: living**
Both fire and wood we have ready nigh,
    But quick beast have we none on this hill. 140
      (*Anxiously*)
A quick beast, I wot well, must be slain,   **wot: know**
    Your sacrifice to make.

ABRAHAM.   Dread thee nought, my child, I would
    fain;
Our Lord will send me unto this place
    Some manner of beast for to take
    Through his command.

ISAAC.   Yea, father, but my heart beginneth to
    quake
    To see that sharp sword in your hand.

Why bear ye your sword drawn so?
    Of your countenance I have much wonder. 150

ABRAHAM (*aside*).   Ah, Father of Heaven! such is
    my woe,
    This child here breaks my heart in sunder.

ISAAC.   Tell me, my dear father, so that ye cease —
    Bear ye your sword drawn for me?

ABRAHAM.   Ah, Isaac! sweet son, peace, peace!
    For in truth thou break'st my heart in three!

ISAAC.   Now truly, on something, father, ye think,
    That ye mourn thus more and more.

ABRAHAM.   Ah, Lord of Heaven, let thy grace sink,
    For my heart was never half so sore!   160

ISAAC.   I pray ye, father, that ye will let me know
    Whether I shall have any harm or no.

ABRAHAM.   Alas, sweet son, I may not tell thee yet,
    My heart is now so full of woe.

ISAAC.   Dear father, I pray you, hide it not from
    me,
    But some of your thought, I pray tell me.

ABRAHAM.   Ah, Isaac, Isaac, I must kill thee!

ISAAC.   Kill me, father? Alas, what have I done?

If I have trespassed against you aught,
    With a rod ye may make me full mild;   170
And with your sharp sword kill me naught,
    For in truth, father, I am but a child.

ABRAHAM.   I am full sorry, son, thy blood for to
    spill,
But truly, child, I may not as I please.

ISAAC.   Now I would to God my mother were here
    on this hill.
She would kneel for me on both her knees
        To save my life.
And since that my mother is not here,
I pray you, father, change your cheer,
        And kill me not with your knife.   180

ABRAHAM.   Forsooth, my son, save I thee kill,
    I should grieve God right sore, I dread,
It is his commandment and also his will
    That I should do this same deed.

He commanded me, son, for certain,
    To make my sacrifice with thy blood.

ISAAC.   And is it God's will that I should be slain?

ABRAHAM.   Yea, truly, Isaac, my son so good;
    And therefore my hands I wring!

ISAAC.   Now father, against my Lord's will,   190
      I will never grouch, loud or still.
He might a-sent me a better destiny,
      If it had been his pleasure.

ABRAHAM.   Forsooth, son, but that this deed I did,
      Grievously displeased our Lord would be.

ISAAC.   Nay, nay, father, God forbid
      That ever ye should grieve him for me!

Ye have other children, one or two,
      Which ye should love well in natural kind.
I pray you, father, make you no woe;   200
For, be I once dead and from you go,
      I shall be soon out of your mind.

Therefore do our Lord's bidding,
      And when I am dead, then pray for me.
But, good father, tell ye my mother nothing,
Say that I am in another country dwelling.

ABRAHAM.   Ah, Isaac, Isaac, blessed mayest thou
   be!

My heart beginneth wildly to rise
      To see the blood of thy blessed body!

ISAAC.   Father, since it may be no other wise,   210
      Let it pass over as well as I.

But, father, ere I go unto my death,
      I pray you bless me with your hand.

(ISAAC *kneels*; ABRAHAM *places his hand on the
lad's head.*)

ABRAHAM.   Now Isaac, with all my breath
      My blessing I give thee upon this land,
      And may God also thereto add his.
Isaac, Isaac, son, up thou stand,
      Thy fair sweet mouth that I may kiss.

ISAAC.   Now farewell, my own father so fine,
      And greet well my mother on earth,   220
But I pray you, father, to hide my eyne   eyne: eyes
      That I see not the stroke of your sharp sword
         That my flesh shall defile.

ABRAHAM.   Son, thy words make me to weep full
  sore;
Now, my dear son Isaac, speak no more.

ISAAC.   Ah, my own dear father! wherefore?
    We shall speak together here but a while.

And since that I must needs be dead,
    Yet, my dear father, to you I pray,
Smite but few strokes at my head   230
      And make an end as soon as ye may,
        And tarry not too long.

ABRAHAM.   Thy meek words, child, bring me dismay;
    So "wellaway" must be my song,

Except alone for God's good will.
    Ah! Isaac's, my own sweet child,
Kiss me yet again upon this hill;
    In all the world, is none so mild!

ISAAC.   Now, truly, father, all this tarrying,
    It doth my heart but harm —   240
I pray you, father, make an ending.

ABRAHAM.   Come up, sweet son, unto my arm.
      (*He binds him.*)
I must bind thy hands too
    Although thou be never so mild.

ISAAC.   Ah, mercy, father! Why should ye so do?

ABRAHAM.   That thou should'st not stay me, my
  child.

ISAAC.   Indeed nay, father, I will not stay you.
    Do on, for me, your will;
And on the purpose that ye have set you,
    For God's love, keep it steadfast still.   250

I am full sorry this day to die,
    But yet I will not cause my God to grieve.
Do your desire for me hardily;
    My fair sweet father, I do give you leave.

But, father, I pray you ever more,
    Nothing to my mother tell,
If she wist it, she would weep full sore,   **wist: knew**
    Indeed she loves me, father, well,
      God's good blessing may she have!

Now farewell, my mother so sweet,   260
We two are like no more to meet.

ABRAHAM.   Ah! Isaac, Isaac, son, thou makest me
    grieve,
       And with thy words thou so distemperest me.

ISAAC.   Indeed, sweet father, I am sorry to grieve
    you;
       I cry you mercy for what I have done,
And for all trespass ever I did so.
Now, dear father, forgive all I have done. —
       God of Heaven be with me!

ABRAHAM.   Ah! dear child, leave off thy moans!
In all thy life thou grieved men ever once.   270
Now blessed be thou, body and bones,
       That ever thou were bred and born;
Thou hast been to me child full good.
       But in truth, child, though I mourn never so
          fast,
       Yet must I needs here at the last
In this place shed all thy blood;

Therefore, my dear son, here shalt thou lie, —
       (*He places him on the altar.*)
       Unto my work I must proceed.
In truth, I had as lief myself to die
       If God were pleased with the deed   280
       That I my own body should offer.

ISAAC.   Ah, mercy, father, mourn ye no more;
Your weeping maketh my heart sore
       That mine own death I am to suffer.

Your kerchief, father, about my eyes wind.

ABRAHAM.   So I shall, my sweetest child on earth.
ISAAC.   Now yet, good father, have this in mind,
       And smite me not often with your sharp
          sword,
       But hastily that it be sped.   289

("*Here* ABRAHAM *laid a cloth on* ISAAC'*s face, thus
saying:*")

ABRAHAM.   Now farewell, my child so full of grace.

ISAAC.   Ah, father, turn downward my face,
       For of your sharp sword I am ever adread!

(ABRAHAM *looks up to heaven resignedly.*)

ABRAHAM.   To do this deed I am full sorry,
    But, Lord, thine behest I will not withstand.

ISAAC.   Ah! Father of Heaven, to thee I cry;
    Lord, receive me thou into thy hand!

(ABRAHAM *falters and pleads again.*)

ABRAHAM.   Lo, now is the time come for certain,
    That my sword in his neck shall bite.
Ah, Lord! my heart riseth there again,
    I may not find it in my heart to smite.   300
      My heart will not now thereto!
Ah, fain I would work my Lord's will,
But this young innocent lies so still,
I may not find it in my heart him to kill.
    Oh, Father of Heaven! what shall I do?

ISAAC.   Ah, mercy, father, why tarry ye so,
    And let me lie there so long on this heath?
Now I would God the stroke were done also;
Father, heartily I pray you, shorten my woe.
    And let me not wait thus for my death.   310

ABRAHAM.   Now, heart, why would'st thou not
    break in three?
    Yet shalt thou not make me to my God un-
      mild.
I will no longer stay for thee,
For that my God aggrieved would be.
    Now have thy stroke, my own dear child.

("Here ABRAHAM *drew his stroke, and the* ANGEL
took the sword in his hand suddenly")

ANGEL.   I am an angel, thou mayest see blithe,
    That from heaven to thee is sent.
Our Lord thanketh thee a hundred time
    For the keeping of his commandment.

He knoweth thy will, and also thy heart,   320
    That thou dreadst him above all thing;
And some of thy heaviness for to depart
    A fair ram yonder I did bring;

He standeth, lo, among the briars tied.
    Now, Abraham, amend thy mood,
For Isaac, thy young son, here by thy side
    This day shall not shed his blood.

Go, make thy sacrifice with yon ram.
Now farewell, blessed Abraham,
For unto heaven I go now home, —   330
      The way is full straight. . . .
      Take up thy son now free!

                     (*Exit*)

ABRAHAM. Ah, Lord! I thank thee for thy great
   grace,
      Now am I eased in diverse wise.
      Arise up, Isaac, my dear son, arise,
Arise up, sweet child, and come to me!

ISAAC. Ah, mercy, father, why smite ye naught?
      Ah, smite on, father, once with your knife.

ABRAHAM. Peace, my sweet son, and take no
   thought,   339
      For our Lord of Heaven hath granted life
      By his angel now,
That thou shalt not die this day, son, truly.

ISAAC. Ah, father, full glad then were I;
      In truth, father — I say, I — wis,   **wis: know**
      That this tale were true!

ABRAHAM. A hundred times, my son fair of hue,
      For joy thy mouth now will I kiss.

ISAAC. Ah, my dear father Abraham,
      Will not God be wroth that we do thus?

ABRAHAM. No, no! hardly, my sweet son!   350
      For yon same ram he hath now sent
      Hither down to us.
Yon beast shall die here in thy stead,
      In the worship of our Lord, alone.
Go fetch him hither, my child, indeed.

ISAAC. Father I will go seize him by the head,
      And bring yon beast with me anon.
         (ISAAC *gets the ram.*)
Ah, sheep, sheep, blessed may thou be,
      That ever thou wert sent down hither!
Thou shalt this day die for me,   360
In worship of the Holy Trinity.
      Now come fast and go we together,
        To my father of Heaven.

Though thou be never so gentle and good,
Yet I had liefer thou shed thy blood   liefer: rather
    In truth, sheep, than I!
      (*He leads it to* ABRAHAM.)
Lo, father, I have brought here, full smart,
    This gentle sheep, and him to you I give.
      (*With a sigh of relief*)
But, Lord God, I thank thee with all my heart!
    For I am glad that I shall live,   370
      And kiss once more my dear mother!

    ABRAHAM.   Now be right merry, my sweet child,
For this quick beast, that is so mild,
    Here I shall offer before all other.

    ISAAC.   And I will fast begin to blow;
    This fire shall burn a full good speed.
      (*Hesitating, however.*)
But, father, if I stoop down low,
Ye will not kill me with your sword, I trow?   trow: trust

    ABRAHAM.   No, hardly, sweet son; have no
    dread.
      My mourning is past!   380

    ISAAC.   Yea, but would that sword were sped —
    For, father, it doth make me yet full ill aghast.

(*"Here* ABRAHAM *made his offering, kneeling and
saying thus:"*)

    ABRAHAM.   Now, Lord God of Heaven in Trinity,
    Almighty God omnipotent,
My offering I make in the worship of thee,
    And with this quick beast I thee present.
    Lord, receive thou mine intent,
As thou art God and ground of our grace.

    GOD.   Abraham, Abraham, well mayest thou
    speed,
    And Isaac, thy young son, thee by!   390
Truly, Abraham, for this deed,
    I shall multiply both your seed
    As thick as stars be in the sky,
      Both of bigger and less.
And as thick as gravel in the sea,
So thick multiplied your seed shall be;
    This grant I you for your goodness.

Of you shall come fruit unknown,
       And ever be in bliss without end,
For ye dread me as God alone   400
And keep my commandments, every one.
       My blessing I give wheresoever ye wend!

ABRAHAM.   Lo, Isaac my son, how think ye
       Of this work that we have wrought?
Full glad and blithe may we be
       That 'gainst the will of God we muttered
           nought
       On this fair heath.

ISAAC.   Ah, father, I thank our Lord every deal   **deal:** day
That my wit served me so weel   **weel:** well
       For God to fear more than my death.   410

ABRAHAM.   Why, dear-worthy son, wert thou
   afraid?
       Boldly, child, tell me thy lore.

ISAAC.   Yea! by my faith, father, be it said,
       I was never so afraid before,
       As I have been on yon hill!
Ah, by my faith, father, I swear
I will nevermore come there,
       Except it be against my will!

ABRAHAM.   Yea, come on with me, my own sweet
   son,
       And homeward fast let us be gone.   420

ISAAC.   By my faith, father, thereto I agree!
I had never such good will to go home,
And to speak with my dear mother!

ABRAHAM.   Ah, Lord of Heaven, I thank thee,
       For now I may lead home with me
       Isaac, my young son so free,
The gentlest child above all other, —
       This may avowed be.
Now, go we forth, my blessed son.

ISAAC.   I grant, father, let us be gone,   430
For, by my troth, were I home then,
I would never go out as thus again.
I pray God give us grace evermore true,
And all those that we be beholden to!

(ABRAHAM *and* ISAAC *go out. The* DOCTOR *enters.*)

DOCTOR.   Lo, now sovereigns and sirs, thus did we
    show
       This solemn story to great and small.
It is a good lesson for both learned and low,
       And even for the wisest of us all,
       Without any barring.
For this story showeth you deep   440
How to our best power we should keep
       God's commandments without doubting.

Think ye, sirs, if God sent an angel,
       And commanded you your child to slay,
By your truth, is there any of you
       That would balk or gainsay?
How think ye now, sirs, thereby?

There be three or four or more, I trow.
And those women that weep so sorrowfully
       When that their children from them die   450
       As nature takes of our kind,
It is folly, as I may well avow,
Against God to grudge or to grieve so low;
For ye shall never see them mischiefed, well I know,
       By land or water, — have this in mind!

And grudge not against our Lord God.
       In wealth or woe whatever he you send,
Though ye be never so hard bestead;
       For when he willeth, he may it amend,   459
His commandments truly if ye keep with good soul,
       As this story hath now showed you before,
And faithfully serve him, while ye be whole,
       That ye may please God both even and morn.
Now Jesu, that wore the crown of thorn,
       Bring us all to heaven's bliss!

Komparu Zembo Motoyasu (1453–1532)

JAPANESE DRAMATIST

Early Snow

Persons

EVENING MIST, *a servant girl*
A LADY, *the Abbot's daughter*
TWO NOBLE LADIES
THE SOUL OF THE BIRD HATSUYUKI (*"Early Snow"*)
CHORUS

Scene: The Great Temple at Izumo

SERVANT. I am a servant at the Nyoroku Shrine in the Great Temple of Izumo. My name is Evening Mist. You must know that the Lord Abbot has a daughter, a beautiful lady and gentle as can be. And she keeps a tame bird that was given her a year ago, and because it was a lovely white bird she called it Hatsuyuki, Early Snow; and she loves it dearly.

I have not seen the bird to-day. I think I will go to the bird-cage and have a look at it.

(*She goes to the cage.*)

Mercy on us, the bird is not there! Whatever 10 shall I say to my lady? But I shall have to tell her. I think I'll tell her now. Madam, madam, your dear Snow-bird is not here!

LADY. What is that you say? Early Snow is not there? It cannot be true.

(*She goes to the cage.*)

It is true. Early Snow has gone! How can that be? How can it be that my pretty one that was so tame should vanish and leave no trace?

> Oh bitterness of snows
> That melt and disappear! 20
> Now do I understand
> The meaning of a midnight dream
> That lately broke my rest.
> A harbinger it was
> Of Hatsuyuki's fate.

(*She bursts into tears.*)

CHORUS.   Though for such tears and sighs
There be no cause,
Yet came her grief so suddenly,
Her heart's fire is ablaze;
And all the while   30
Never a moment are her long sleeves dry.
They say that written letters first were traced
By feet of birds in sand
Yet Hatsuyuki leaves no testament.

(*They mourn.*)

CHORUS (*"kuse" chant, irregular verse accompanied
by dancing*). How sad to call to mind
When first it left the breeding-cage
So fair of form
And coloured white as snow.
We called it Hatsuyuki, "Year's First Snow."
And where our mistress walked   40
It followed like the shadow at her side.
But now alas! it is a bird of parting
Though not in Love's dark lane.
   LADY.   There's no help now.

(*She weeps bitterly.*)

CHORUS.   Still there is one way left. Stop weep-
      ing, Lady,
And turn your heart to him who vowed to hear.
The Lord Amida, if a prayer be said —
Who knows but he can bring
Even a bird's soul into Paradise
And set it on the Lotus Pedestal?   50
   LADY.   Evening Mist, are you not sad that Hatsu-
yuki has gone? . . . But we must not cry any more.
Let us call together the noble ladies of this place and
for seven days sit with them praying behind barred
doors. Go now and do my bidding.

(EVENING MIST *fetches the* NOBLE LADIES *of the
place.*)

TWO NOBLE LADIES (*together*).   A solemn Mass
      we sing
A dirge for the Dead;
At this hour of heart-cleansing
We beat on Buddha's gong.

(*They pray.*)

NAMU AMIDA BUTSU
NAMU NYORAI
      Praise to Amida Buddha,   60
      Praise to Mida our Saviour!

(*The prayers and gong-beating last for some time
and form the central ballet of the play.*)

bird of parting: "Wakare no tori," the bird which warns lovers of the approach of day

set . . . Pedestal: turn it into a Buddha

CHORUS (*the bird's soul appears as a white speck in the sky*). Look! Look! A cloud in the clear mid-sky!
But it is not a cloud.
With pure white wings beating the air
The Snow-bird comes!
Flying towards our lady
Lovingly he hovers,
Dances before her.
    THE BIRD'S SOUL. Drawn by the merit of your prayers and songs
    CHORUS. Straightway he was reborn in Paradise. 70
By the pond of Eight Virtues he walks abroad:
With the Phœnix and Fugan his playtime passing.
He lodges in the sevenfold summit of the trees of Heaven.
No hurt shall harm him
For ever and ever.

Now like the tasselled doves we loose
From battlements on holy days
A little while he flutters;
Flutters a little while and then is gone
We know not where. 80

John Donne (1573–1631)

ENGLISH POET and CLERGYMAN

A Hymne to God the Father

I

Wilt thou forgive that sinne where I begunne,
   Which is my sin, though it were done before?
Wilt thou forgive those sinnes through which I runne,
   And doe them still: though still I doe deplore?
     When thou hast done, thou hast not done,
       For, I have more.

"A Hymne to God the Father" by John Donne. From *John Donne: The Divine Poems*, edited by Helen Gardner. Reprinted by permission of the Clarendon Press, Oxford.

II

Wilt thou forgive that sinne by which I wonne
  Others to sinne? and, made my sinne their doore?
Wilt thou forgive that sinne which I did shunne
  A yeare, or two: but wallowed in, a score?   10
    When thou hast done, thou hast not done,
        For, I have more.

III

I have a sinne of feare, that when I have spunne
  My last thred, I shall perish on the shore;
Sweare by thy selfe, that at my death thy Sunne
  Shall shine as it shines now, and heretofore;
    And, having done that, Thou hast done,
        I have no more.

Jacobus Revius   (1586–1658)

DUTCH CLERGYMAN and POET

Mary

  Most blessed is this maid, all virgins' crown,
The temple of God's Son and inmost might,
The dawn through which the long-awaited light
Of heaven's rising Sun comes smiling down.
  Most blessed she, the sister of her child,
Daughter of him whom she herself gave birth,
The bride of him who from her womb came forth —
That womb where heaven and earth were reconciled.
  Most blessed are those breasts from which the spring
Of life itself lay thirsting for a drink,   10
Most blessed is that lap in which he lay;
  But blessed above all are those who live
(As Mary did) for him, who gladly give
Their lives to him by walking in his way.

"Mary" by Jacobus Revius, translated by Henrietta Ten Harmsel. Reprinted from *Selected Poems of Jacobus Revius*, 1968, by Henrietta Ten Harmsel, by permission of the Wayne State University Press.

Molière (1622–1673)

FRENCH DRAMATIST

Tartuffe

CHARACTERS

MME PERNELLE, *Orgon's mother*
ORGON, *Elmire's husband*
ELMIRE, *Orgon's wife*
DAMIS, *Orgon's son, Elmire's stepson*
MARIANE, *Orgon's daughter, Elmire's stepdaughter,
    in love with Valère*
VALERE, *in love with Mariane*
CLEANTE, *Orgon's brother-in-law*
TARTUFFE, *a hypocrite*
DORINE, *Mariane's lady's-maid*
M. LOYAL, *a bailiff*
A POLICE OFFICER
FLIPOTE, *Mme Pernelle's maid*

The Scene throughout: Orgon's house in Paris

ACT 1

SCENE I. MADAME PERNELLE *and* FLIPOTE, *her
maid*, ELMIRE, MARIANE, DORINE, DAMIS, *and* CLEANTE

MADAME PERNELLE. Come, come, Flipote; it's
    time I left this place.
ELMIRE. I can't keep up, you walk at such a pace.
MADAME PERNELLE. Don't trouble, child; no need
    to show me out.
It's not your manners I'm concerned about.

ELMIRE.   We merely pay you the respect we owe.
But, Mother, why this hurry? Must you go?
MADAME PERNELLE.   I must. This house appals
    me. No one in it
Will pay attention for a single minute.
Children, I take my leave much vexed in spirit.
I offer good advice, but you won't hear it.   10
You all break in and chatter on and on.
It's like a madhouse with the keeper gone.
DORINE.   If . . .
MADAME PERNELLE.   Girl, you talk too much, and
    I'm afraid
You're far too saucy for a lady's-maid.
You push in everywhere and have your say.
DAMIS.   But . . .
MADAME PERNELLE.   You, boy, grow more foolish
    every day.
To think my grandson should be such a dunce!
I've said a hundred times, if I've said it once,
That if you keep the course on which you've started,
You'll leave your worthy father broken-hearted.   20
MARIANE.   I think . . .
MADAME PERNELLE.   And you, his sister, seem
    so pure,
So shy, so innocent, and so demure.
But you know what they say about still waters.
I pity parents with secretive daughters.
ELMIRE.   Now, Mother . . .
MADAME PERNELLE.   And as for you,
    child, let me add
That your behavior is extremely bad,
And a poor example for these children, too.
Their dear, dead mother did far better than you.
You're much too free with money, and I'm distressed
To see you so elaborately dressed.   30
When it's one's husband that one aims to please,
One has no need of costly fripperies.
CLEANTE.   Oh, Madam, really . . .
MADAME PERNELLE.   You are her brother, Sir,
And I respect and love you; yet if I were
My son, this lady's good and pious spouse,
I wouldn't make you welcome in my house.
You're full of worldly counsels which, I fear,
Aren't suitable for decent folk to hear.
I've spoken bluntly, Sir; but it behooves us
Not to mince words when righteous fervor moves
    us.   40

DAMIS.   Your man Tartuffe is full of holy
    speeches . . .
MADAME PERNELLE.   And practises precisely what
    he preaches.
He's a fine man, and should be listened to.
I will not hear him mocked by fools like you.
    DAMIS.   Good God! Do you expect me to submit
To the tyranny of that carping hypocrite?
Must we forgo all joys and satisfactions
Because that bigot censures all our actions?
    DORINE.   To hear him talk — and he talks all the
    time —
There's nothing one can do that's not a crime.   50
He rails at everything, your dear Tartuffe.
    MADAME PERNELLE.   Whatever he reproves de-
    serves reproof.
He's out to save your souls, and all of you
Must love him, as my son would have you do.
    DAMIS.   Ah no, Grandmother, I could never take
To such a rascal, even for my father's sake.
That's how I feel, and I shall not dissemble.
His every action makes me seethe and tremble
With helpless anger, and I have no doubt
That he and I will shortly have it out.   60
    DORINE.   Surely it is a shame and a disgrace
To see this man usurp the master's place —
To see this beggar who, when first he came,
Had not a shoe or shoestring to his name
So far forget himself that he behaves
As if the house were his, and we his slaves.
    MADAME PERNELLE.   Well, mark my words, your
    souls would fare far better
If you obeyed his precepts to the letter.
    DORINE.   You see him as a saint. I'm far less
    awed;
In fact, I see right through him. He's a fraud.   70
    MADAME PERNELLE.   Nonsense!
    DORINE.   His man Laurent's
    the same, or worse;
I'd not trust either with a penny purse.
    MADAME PERNELLE.   I can't say what his servant's
    morals may be;
His own great goodness I can guarantee.
You all regard him with distaste and fear
Because he tells you what you're loath to hear,
Condemns your sins, points out your moral flaws,
And humbly strives to further Heaven's cause.

DORINE.   If sin is all that bothers him, why is it
He's so upset when folk drop in to visit?   80
Is Heaven so outraged by a social call
That he must prophesy against us all?
I'll tell you what I think: if you ask me,
He's jealous of my mistress' company.
    MADAME PERNELLE.   Rubbish! (*To Elmire*) He's
        not alone, child, in complaining
Of all of your promiscuous entertaining.
Why, the whole neighborhood's upset, I know,
By all these carriages that come and go,
With crowds of guests parading in and out
And noisy servants loitering about.   90
In all of this, I'm sure there's nothing vicious;
But why give people cause to be suspicious?
    CLEANTE.   They need no cause; they'll talk in any
        case.
Madam, this world would be a joyless place
If, fearing what malicious tongues might say,
We locked our doors and turned our friends away.
And even if one did so dreary a thing,
D'you think those tongues would cease their chat-
        tering?
One can't fight slander; it's a losing battle;
Let us instead ignore their tittle-tattle.   100
Let's strive to live by conscience' clear decrees,
And let the gossips gossip as they please.
    DORINE.   If there is talk against us, I know the
        source:
It's Daphne and her little husband, of course.
Those who have greatest cause for guilt and shame
Are quickest to besmirch a neighbor's name.
When there's a chance for libel, they never miss it;
When something can be made to seem illicit
They're off at once to spread the joyous news,
Adding to fact what fantasies they choose.   110
By talking up their neighbor's indiscretions
They seek to camouflage their own transgressions,
Hoping that others' innocent affairs
Will lend a hue of innocence to theirs,
Or that their own black guilt will come to seem
Part of a general shady color-scheme.
    MADAME PERNELLE.   All that is quite irrelevant.
        I doubt
That anyone's more virtuous and devout
Than dear Orante; and I'm informed that she
Condemns your mode of life most vehemently.   120

DORINE.   Oh, yes, she's strict, devout, and has no
      taint
Of worldliness; in short, she seems a saint.
But it was time which taught her that disguise;
She's thus because she can't be otherwise.
So long as her attractions could enthrall,
She flounced and flirted and enjoyed it all,
But now that they're no longer what they were
She quits a world which fast is quitting her,
And wears a veil of virtue to conceal
Her bankrupt beauty and her lost appeal.   130
That's what becomes of old coquettes today:
Distressed when all their lovers fall away,
They see no recourse but to play the prude,
And so confer a style on solitude.
Thereafter, they're severe with everyone,
Condemning all our actions, pardoning none,
And claiming to be pure, austere, and zealous
When, if the truth were known, they're merely
      jealous,
And cannot bear to see another know
The pleasures time has forced them to forgo.   140
MADAME PERNELLE (*Initially to Elmire*).   That
      sort of talk is what you like to hear;
Therefore you'd have us all keep still, my dear,
While Madam rattles on the livelong day.
Nevertheless, I mean to have my say.
I tell you that you're blest to have Tartuffe
Dwelling, as my son's guest, beneath this roof;
That Heaven has sent him to forestall its wrath
By leading you, once more, to the true path;
That all he reprehends is reprehensible,
And that you'd better heed him, and be sensible. 150
These visits, balls, and parties in which you revel
Are nothing but inventions of the Devil.
One never hears a word that's edifying:
Nothing but chaff and foolishness and lying,
As well as vicious gossip in which one's neighbor
Is cut to bits with epee, foil, and saber.
People of sense are driven half-insane
At such affairs, where noise and folly reign
And reputations perish thick and fast.
As a wise preacher said on Sunday last,   160
Parties are Towers of Babylon, because   **Babylon: Babel**
The guests all babble on with never a pause;
And then he told a story which, I think . . .
(*To Cléante*) I heard that laugh, Sir, and I saw that
      wink!

Go find your silly friends and laugh some more!
Enough; I'm going; don't show me to the door.
I leave this household much dismayed and vexed;
I cannot say when I shall see you next.
(*Slapping Flipote*) Wake up, don't stand there gap-
    ing into space!
I'll slap some sense into that stupid face.   170
Move, move, you slut.

SCENE II. CLEANTE *and* DORINE

    CLEANTE.   I think I'll stay behind;
I want no further pieces of her mind.
How that old lady . . .
    DORINE.   Oh, what wouldn't she say
If she could hear you speak of her that way!
She'd thank you for the *lady*, but I'm sure
She'd find the *old* a little premature.
    CLEANTE.   My, what a scene she made, and what
    a din!
And how this man Tartuffe has taken her in!
    DORINE.   Yes, but her son is even worse deceived;
His folly must be seen to be believed.   10
In the late troubles, he played an able part
And served his king with wise and loyal heart,
But he's quite lost his senses since he fell
Beneath Tartuffe's infatuating spell.
He calls him brother, and loves him as his life,
Preferring him to mother, child, or wife.
In him and him alone will he confide;
He's made him his confessor and his guide;
He pets and pampers him with love more tender
Than any pretty maiden could engender,   20
Gives him the place of honor when they dine,
Delights to see him gorging like a swine,
Stuffs him with dainties till his guts distend,
And when he belches, cries "God bless you, friend!"
In short, he's mad; he worships him; he dotes;
His deeds he marvels at, his words he quotes,
Thinking each act a miracle, each word
Oracular as those that Moses heard.
Tartuffe, much pleased to find so easy a victim,
Has in a hundred ways beguiled and tricked him,   30
Milked him of money, and with his permission
Established here a sort of Inquisition.
Even Laurent, his lackey, dares to give
Us arrogant advice on how to live;
He sermonizes us in thundering tones
And confiscates our ribbons and colognes.

late troubles: an armed rebellion, by landed nobility against royal authority, which was crushed by the time Louis XIV came of age and assumed the throne in 1643

Last week he tore a kerchief into pieces
Because he found it pressed in a *Life of Jesus:*
He said it was a sin to juxtapose
Unholy vanities and holy prose.   **40**

SCENE III. ELMIRE, MARIANE, DAMIS, CLEANTE, *and*
     DORINE

   ELMIRE (*To Cléante*). You did well not to fol-
     low; she stood in the door
And said *verbatim* all she'd said before.
I saw my husband coming. I think I'd best
Go upstairs now, and take a little rest.
   CLEANTE. I'll wait and greet him here; then I
     must go.
I've really only time to say hello.
   DAMIS. Sound him about my sister's wedding,
     please.
I think Tartuffe's against it, and that he's
Been urging Father to withdraw his blessing.
As you well know, I'd find that most distressing.   **10**
Unless my sister and Valère can marry,
My hopes to wed *his* sister will miscarry,
And I'm determined . . .
   DORINE.   He's coming.

SCENE IV. ORGON, CLEANTE, *and* DORINE

   ORGON.   Ah, Brother, good-day.
   CLEANTE. Well, welcome back. I'm sorry I can't
     stay.
How was the country? Blooming, I trust, and green?
   ORGON. Excuse me, Brother; just one moment.
(*To Dorine*)   Dorine . . .
(*To Cléante*) To put my mind at rest, I always learn
The household news the moment I return.
(*To Dorine*) Has all been well, these two days I've
     been gone?
How are the family? What's been going on?
   DORINE. Your wife, two days ago, had a bad fever,
And a fierce headache which refused to leave her.   **10**
   ORGON. Ah. And Tartuffe?
   DORINE.   Tartuffe? Why, he's round and red,
Bursting with health, and excellently fed.
   ORGON. Poor fellow!
   DORINE.   That night, the mistress was unable
To take a single bite at the dinner-table.
Her headache-pains, she said, were simply hellish.
   ORGON. Ah. And Tartuffe?
   DORINE.   He ate his meal with relish,

And zealously devoured in her presence
A leg of mutton and a brace of pheasants.
    ORGON.   Poor fellow!
    DORINE.   Well, the pains continued strong,
And so she tossed and tossed the whole night long, 20
Now icy-cold, now burning like a flame.
We sat beside her bed till morning came.
    ORGON.   Ah. And Tartuffe?
    DORINE.   Why, having eaten, he rose
And sought his room, already in a doze,
Got into his warm bed, and snored away
In perfect peace until the break of day.
    ORGON.   Poor fellow!
    DORINE.   After much ado, we talked her
Into dispatching someone for the doctor.
He bled her, and the fever quickly fell.   29
    ORGON.   Ah. And Tartuffe?
    DORINE.   He bore it very well.
To keep his cheerfulness at any cost,
And make up for the blood *Madame* had lost,
He drank, at lunch, four beakers full of port.
    ORGON.   Poor fellow!
    DORINE.   Both are doing well, in short.
I'll go and tell *Madame* that you've expressed
Keen sympathy and anxious interest.

SCENE V. ORGON *and* CLEANTE

    CLEANTE.   That girl was laughing in your face, and
      though
I've no wish to offend you, even so
I'm bound to say that she had some excuse.
How can you possibly be such a goose?
Are you so dazed by this man's hocus-pocus
That all the world, save him, is out of focus?
You've given him clothing, shelter, food, and care;
Why must you also . . .
    ORGON.   Brother, stop right there.
You do not know the man of whom you speak.
    CLEANTE.   I grant you that. But my judgment's
      not so weak   10
That I can't tell, by his effect on others . . .
    ORGON.   Ah, when you meet him, you two will be
      like brothers!
There's been no loftier soul since time began.
He is a man who . . . a man who . . . an excellent
    man.
To keep his precepts is to be reborn,
And view this dunghill of a world with scorn.

Yes, thanks to him I'm a changed man indeed.
Under his tutelage my soul's been freed
From earthly loves, and every human tie:
My mother, children, brother, and wife could die,   20
And I'd not feel a single moment's pain.

    CLEANTE.   That's a fine sentiment, Brother; most
      humane.

    ORGON.   Oh, had you seen Tartuffe as I first knew
      him,
Your heart, like mine, would have surrendered to
      him.
He used to come into our church each day
And humbly kneel nearby, and start to pray.
He'd draw the eyes of everybody there
By the deep fervor of his heartfelt prayer;
He'd sigh and weep, and sometimes with a sound
Of rapture he would bend and kiss the ground;   30
And when I rose to go, he'd run before
To offer me holy-water at the door.
His serving-man, no less devout than he,
Informed me of his master's poverty;
I gave him gifts, but in his humbleness
He'd beg me every time to give him less.
"Oh, that's too much," he'd cry, "too much by twice!
I don't deserve it. The half, Sir, would suffice."
And when I wouldn't take it back, he'd share
Half of it with the poor, right then and there.   40
At length, Heaven prompted me to take him in
To dwell with us, and free our souls from sin.
He guides our lives, and to protect my honor
Stays by my wife, and keeps an eye upon her;
He tells me whom she sees, and all she does,
And seems more jealous than I ever was!
And how austere he is! Why, he can detect
A mortal sin where you would least suspect;
In smallest trifles, he's extremely strict.
Last week, his conscience was severely pricked   50
Because, while praying, he had caught a flea
And killed it, so he felt, too wrathfully.

    CLEANTE.   Good God, man! Have you lost your
      common sense —
Or is this all some joke at my expense?
How can you stand there and in all sobriety . . .

    ORGON.   Brother, your language savors of impiety.
Too much free-thinking's made your faith unsteady,
And as I've warned you many times already,
'Twill get you into trouble before you're through.

    CLEANTE.   So I've been told before by dupes like
     you: 60

free thinking: (1) deism (2) loose
questioning of traditional faith

Being blind, you'd have all others blind as well;
The clear-eyed man you call an infidel,
And he who sees through humbug and pretense
Is charged, by you, with want of reverence.
Spare me your warnings, Brother; I have no fear
Of speaking out, for you and Heaven to hear,
Against affected zeal and pious knavery.
There's true and false in piety, as in bravery,
And just as those whose courage shines the most
In battle, are the least inclined to boast,   70
So those whose hearts are truly pure and lowly
Don't make a flashy show of being holy.
There's a vast difference, so it seems to me,
Between true piety and hypocrisy:
How do you fail to see it, may I ask?
Is not a face quite different from a mask?
Cannot sincerity and cunning art,
Reality and semblance, be told apart?
Are scarecrows just like men, and do you hold
That a false coin is just as good as gold?   80
Ah, Brother, man's a strangely fashioned creature
Who seldom is content to follow Nature,
But recklessly pursues his inclination
Beyond the narrow bounds of moderation,
And often, by transgressing Reason's laws,
Perverts a lofty aim or noble cause.
A passing observation, but it applies.
     ORGON.   I see, dear Brother, that you're profoundly
          wise;
You harbor all the insight of the age.
You are our one clear mind, our only sage,   90
The era's oracle, its Cato too,
And all mankind are fools compared to you.

> Cato: Roman statesman (234–149 B.C.) who tried to restore earlier integrity of morals by strict censorship

     CLEANTE.   Brother, I don't pretend to be a sage,
Nor have I all the wisdom of the age.
There's just one insight I would dare to claim:
I know that true and false are not the same;
And just as there is nothing I more revere
Than a soul whose faith is steadfast and sincere,
Nothing that I more cherish and admire
Than honest zeal and true religious fire,   100
So there is nothing that I find more base
Than specious piety's dishonest face —
Than these bold mountebanks, these histrios

> histrios: actors

Whose impious mummeries and hollow shows
Exploit our love of Heaven, and make a jest
Of all that men think holiest and best;
These calculating souls who offer prayers
Not to their Maker, but as public wares,

And seek to buy respect and reputation
With lifted eyes and sighs and exaltation; 110
These charlatans, I say, whose pilgrim souls
Proceed, by way of Heaven, toward earthly goals,
Who weep and pray and swindle and extort,
Who preach the monkish life, but haunt the court,
Who make their zeal the partner of their vice —
Such men are vengeful, sly, and cold as ice,
And when there is an enemy to defame
They cloak their spite in fair religion's name,
Their private spleen and malice being made
To seem a high and virtuous crusade, 120
Until, to mankind's reverent applause,
They crucify their foe in Heaven's cause.
Such knaves are all too common; yet, for the wise,
True piety isn't hard to recognize,
And, happily, these present times provide us
With bright examples to instruct and guide us.
Consider Ariston and Périandre;
Look at Oronte, Alcidamas, Clitandre;
Their virtue is acknowledged; who could doubt it?
But you won't hear them beat the drum about it. 130
They're never ostentatious, never vain,
And their religion's moderate and humane;
It's not their way to criticize and chide:
They think censoriousness a mark of pride,
And therefore, letting others preach and rave,
They show, by deeds, how Christians should behave.
They think no evil of their fellow man,
But judge of him as kindly as they can.
They don't intrigue and wangle and conspire;
To lead a good life is their one desire; 140
The sinner wakes no rancorous hate in them;
It is the sin alone which they condemn;
Nor do they try to show a fiercer zeal
For Heaven's cause than Heaven itself could feel.
These men I honor, these men I advocate
As models for us all to emulate.
Your man is not their sort at all, I fear:
And, while your praise of him is quite sincere,
I think that you've been dreadfully deluded.
    ORGON. Now then, dear Brother, is your speech
    concluded? 150
    CLEANTE. Why, yes.
    ORGON.   Your servant, Sir. (*He turns to go.*)
    CLEANTE.   No, Brother; wait.
There's one more matter. You agreed of late
That young Valère might have your daughter's hand.
    ORGON. I did.
    CLEANTE.   And set the date, I understand.

Ariston . . . Clitandre: ironic reference to characters in other plays by Molière

ORGON. Quite so.

CLEANTE.   You've now postponed it; is
that true?

ORGON. No doubt.

CLEANTE.   The match no longer pleases you?

ORGON. Who knows?

CLEANTE.   D'you mean to go back on
your word?

ORGON. I won't say that.

CLEANTE.   Has anything occurred
Which might entitle you to break your pledge?

ORGON. Perhaps.

CLEANTE.   Why must you hem, and haw,
and hedge?   **160**
The boy asked me to sound you in this affair . . .

ORGON. It's been a pleasure.

CLEANTE.   But what shall I tell Valère?

ORGON. Whatever you like.

CLEANTE.   But what have you decided?
What are your plans?

ORGON.   I plan, Sir, to be guided
By Heaven's will.

CLEANTE.   Come, Brother, don't talk rot.
You've given Valère your word; will you keep it, or
not?

ORGON. Good day.

CLEANTE.   This looks like poor Valère's
undoing;
I'll go and warn him that there's trouble brewing.

ACT 2

Scene I. ORGON *and* MARIANE

ORGON. Mariane.

MARIANE.   Yes, Father?

ORGON.   A word with you; come here.

MARIANE. What are you looking for?

ORGON (*Peering into a small closet*). Eavesdrop-
pers, dear.
I'm making sure we shan't be overheard.
Someone in there could catch our every word.
Ah, good, we're safe. Now, Mariane, my child,
You're a sweet girl who's tractable and mild,
Whom I hold dear, and think most highly of.

MARIANE. I'm deeply grateful, Father, for your
love.

ORGON. That's well said, Daughter; and you can
repay me
If, in all things, you'll cheerfully obey me.   **10**

MARIANE.   To please you, Sir, is what delights me
best.

ORGON.   Good, good. Now, what d'you think of
Tartuffe, our guest?

MARIANE.   I, Sir?

ORGON.   Yes. Weigh your answer; think
it through.

MARIANE.   Oh, dear. I'll say whatever you wish
me to.

ORGON.   That's wisely said, my Daughter. Say of
him, then,
That he's the very worthiest of men,
And that you're fond of him, and would rejoice
In being his wife, if that should be my choice.
Well?

MARIANE.   What?

ORGON.   What's that?

MARIANE.   I . . .

ORGON.   Well?

MARIANE.   Forgive me, pray.

ORGON.   Did you not hear me?

MARIANE.   Of *whom*, Sir, must I say
That I am fond of him, and would rejoice   21
In being his wife, if that should be your choice?

ORGON.   Why, of Tartuffe.

MARIANE.   But, Father, that's false, you know.
Why would you have me say what isn't so?

ORGON.   Because I am resolved it shall be true.
That it's my wish should be enough for you.

MARIANE.   You can't mean, Father . . .

ORGON.   Yes, Tartuffe shall be
Allied by marriage to this family,
And he's to be your husband, is that clear?
It's a father's privilege . . .

SCENE II. DORINE, ORGON, *and* MARIANE

ORGON (*To Dorine*).   What are you doing in
here?
Is curiosity so fierce a passion
With you, that you must eavesdrop in this fashion?

DORINE.   There's lately been a rumor going
about —
Based on some hunch or chance remark, no doubt —
That you mean Mariane to wed Tartuffe.
I've laughed it off, of course, as just a spoof.

ORGON.   You find it so incredible?

DORINE.   Yes, I do.
I won't accept that story, even from you.

ORGON.   Well, you'll believe it when the thing is
   done.   10
DORINE.   Yes, yes, of course. Go on and have your
   fun.
ORGON.   I've never been more serious in my life.
DORINE.   Ha!
ORGON.   Daughter, I mean it; you're to be
   his wife.
DORINE.   No, don't believe your father; it's all a
   hoax.
ORGON.   See here, young woman . . .
DORINE.   Come, Sir, no more jokes;
You can't fool us.
   ORGON.   How dare you talk that way?
DORINE.   All right, then: we believe you, sad to
   say.
But how a man like you, who looks so wise
And wears a moustache of such splendid size,
Can be so foolish as to . . .
   ORGON.   Silence, please!   20
My girl, you take too many liberties.
I'm master here, as you must not forget.
   DORINE.   Do let's discuss this calmly; don't be
      upset.
You can't be serious, Sir, about this plan.
What should that bigot want with Mariane?
Praying and fasting ought to keep him busy.
And then, in terms of wealth and rank, what is he?
Why should a man of property like you
Pick out a beggar son-in-law?
   ORGON.   That will do.
Speak of his poverty with reverence.   30
His is a pure and saintly indigence
Which far transcends all worldly pride and pelf.
He lost his fortune, as he says himself,
Because he cared for Heaven alone, and so
Was careless of his interests here below.
I mean to get him out of his present straits
And help him to recover his estates —
Which, in his part of the world, have no small fame.
Poor though he is, he's a gentleman just the same.
   DORINE.   Yes, so he tells us; and, Sir, it seems to
      me   40
Such pride goes very ill with piety.
A man whose spirit spurns this dungy earth
Ought not to brag of lands and noble birth;
Such worldly arrogance will hardly square
With meek devotion and the life of prayer.
. . . But this approach, I see, has drawn a blank;
Let's speak, then, of his person, not his rank.

Doesn't it seem to you a trifle grim
To give a girl like her to a man like him?
When two are so ill-suited, can't you see   50
What the sad consequence is bound to be?
A young girl's virtue is imperilled, Sir,
When such a marriage is imposed on her;
For if one's bridegroom isn't to one's taste,
It's hardly an inducement to be chaste,
And many a man with horns upon his brow   horns: sign of a cuckold
Has made his wife the thing that she is now.
It's hard to be a faithful wife, in short,
To certain husbands of a certain sort,
And he who gives his daughter to a man she hates 60
Must answer for her sins at Heaven's gates.
Think, Sir, before you play so risky a role.

> ORGON. This servant-girl presumes to save my
> soul!
> DORINE. You would do well to ponder what I've
> said.
> ORGON. Daughter, we'll disregard this dunder-
> head.

Just trust your father's judgment. Oh, I'm aware
That I once promised you to young Valère;
But now I hear he gambles, which greatly shocks me;
What's more, I've doubts about his orthodoxy.
His visits to church, I note, are very few.   70

> DORINE. Would you have him go at the same
> hours as you,

And kneel nearby, to be sure of being seen?

> ORGON. I can dispense with such remarks, Dorine.

(To Mariane) Tartuffe, however, is sure of Heaven's
blessing,
And that's the only treasure worth possessing.
This match will bring you joys beyond all measure;
Your cup will overflow with every pleasure;
You two will interchange your faithful loves
Like two sweet cherubs, or two turtle-doves.
No harsh word shall be heard, no frown be seen,   80
And he shall make you happy as a queen.

> DORINE. And she'll make him a cuckold, just
> wait and see.
> ORGON. What language!
> DORINE.   Oh, he's a man of destiny;

He's *made* for horns, and what the stars demand
Your daughter's virtue surely can't withstand.

> ORGON. Don't interrupt me further. Why can't
> you learn

That certain things are none of your concern?

DORINE.   It's for your own sake that I interfere.
*(She repeatedly interrupts Orgon just as he is
turning to speak to his daughter.)*

ORGON.   Most kind of you. Now, hold your
tongue, d'you hear?   89

DORINE.   If I didn't love you . . .

ORGON.   Spare me your affection.

DORINE.   I'll love you, Sir, in spite of your objection.

ORGON.   Blast!

DORINE.   I can't bear, Sir, for your honor's sake,
To let you make this ludicrous mistake.

ORGON.   You mean to go on talking?

DORINE.   If I didn't protest
This sinful marriage, my conscience couldn't rest.

ORGON.   If you don't hold your tongue, you little
shrew . . .

DORINE.   What, lost your temper? A pious man
like you?

ORGON.   Yes! Yes! You talk and talk. I'm maddened by it.
Once and for all, I tell you to be quiet.

DORINE.   Well, I'll be quiet. But I'll be thinking
hard.   100

ORGON.   Think all you like, but you had better
guard
That saucy tongue of yours, or I'll . . .
(Turning back to Mariane)   Now, child,
I've weighed this matter fully.

DORINE *(Aside)*.   It drives me wild
That I can't speak.

             (Orgon turns his head, and she is silent.)

ORGON.   Tartuffe is no young dandy,
But, still, his person . . .

DORINE *(Aside)*.   Is as sweet as candy.

ORGON.   Is such that, even if you shouldn't care
For his other merits . . .
   (He turns and stands facing Dorine, arms crossed.)

DORINE *(Aside)*.   They'll make a lovely pair.
If I were she, no man would marry me
Against my inclination, and go scot-free.
He'd learn, before the wedding-day was over,   110
How readily a wife can find a lover.

ORGON *(To Dorine)*.   It seems you treat my orders as a joke.

DORINE.   Why, what's the matter? 'Twas not to
you I spoke.

ORGON.   What *were* you doing?

DORINE.   Talking to myself, that's all.

ORGON.   Ah! (*Aside*) One more bit of impudence
and gall,

And I shall give her a good slap in the face.

(*He puts himself in position to slap her; Dorine,
whenever he glances at her, stands immobile and
silent.*)

Daughter, you shall accept, and with good grace,

The husband I've selected . . . Your wedding day . . .

(*To Dorine*). Why don't you talk to yourself?

DORINE.   I've nothing to say.

ORGON.   Come, just one word.

DORINE.   No thank you, Sir. I pass.

ORGON.   Come, speak; I'm waiting.

DORINE.   I'd not be such an ass.

ORGON (*Turning to Mariane*). In short, dear
Daughter, I mean to be obeyed,   122

And you must bow to the sound choice I've made.

DORINE (*Moving away*). I'd not wed such a
monster, even in jest.

(*Orgon attempts to slap her, but misses.*)

ORGON.   Daughter, that maid of yours is a thorough pest;

She makes me sinfully annoyed and nettled.

I can't speak further; my nerves are too unsettled.

She's so upset me by her insolent talk,

I'll calm myself by going for a walk.

SCENE III. DORINE *and* MARIANE

DORINE (*Returning*). Well, have you lost your
tongue, girl? Must I play

Your part, and say the lines you ought to say?

Faced with a fate so hideous and absurd,

Can you not utter one dissenting word?

MARIANE.   What good would it do? A father's
power is great.

DORINE.   Resist him now, or it will be too late.

MARIANE.   But . . .

DORINE.   Tell him one cannot love at
a father's whim;

That you shall marry for yourself, not him;

That since it's you who are to be the bride,

It's you, not he, who must be satisfied;   10

And that if his Tartuffe is so sublime,

He's free to marry him at any time.

MARIANE.   I've bowed so long to Father's strict
   control,
I couldn't oppose him now, to save my soul.
   DORINE.   Come, come, Mariane. Do listen to
      reason, won't you?
Valère has asked your hand. Do you love him, or
   don't you?
   MARIANE.   Oh, how unjust of you! What can you
      mean
By asking such a question, dear Dorine?
You know the depth of my affection for him;
I've told you a hundred times how I adore him.   20
   DORINE.   I don't believe in everything I hear;
Who knows if your professions were sincere?
   MARIANE.   They were, Dorine, and you do me
      wrong to doubt it;
Heaven knows that I've been all too frank about it.
   DORINE.   You love him, then?
   MARIANE.   Oh, more than I can express.
   DORINE.   And he, I take it, cares for you no less?
   MARIANE.   I think so.
   DORINE.   And you both, with equal fire,
Burn to be married?
   MARIANE.   That is our one desire.
   DORINE.   What of Tartuffe, then? What of your
      father's plan?
   MARIANE.   I'll kill myself, if I'm forced to wed
      that man.   30
   DORINE.   I hadn't thought of that recourse. How
      splendid!
Just die, and all your troubles will be ended!
A fine solution. Oh, it maddens me
To hear you talk in that self-pitying key.
   MARIANE.   Dorine, how harsh you are! It's most
      unfair.
You have no sympathy for my despair.
   DORINE.   I've none at all for people who talk drivel
And, faced with difficulties, whine and snivel.
   MARIANE.   No doubt I'm timid, but it would be
      wrong . . .
   DORINE.   True love requires a heart that's firm
      and strong.   40
   MARIANE.   I'm strong in my affection for Valère,
But coping with my father is his affair.
   DORINE.   But if your father's brain has grown so
      cracked
Over his dear Tartuffe that he can retract

His blessing, though your wedding-day was named,
It's surely not Valère who's to be blamed.

MARIANE.   If I defied my father, as you suggest,
Would it not seem unmaidenly, at best?
Shall I defend my love at the expense
Of brazenness and disobedience?   50
Shall I parade my heart's desires, and flaunt . . .

DORINE.   No, I ask nothing of you. Clearly you
    want
To be Madame Tartuffe, and I feel bound
Not to oppose a wish so very sound.
What right have I to criticize the match?
Indeed, my dear, the man's a brilliant catch.
Monsieur Tartuffe! Now, there's a man of weight!
Yes, yes, Monsieur Tartuffe, I'm bound to state,
Is quite a person; that's not to be denied;
'Twill be no little thing to be his bride.   60
The world already rings with his renown;
He's a great noble — in his native town;
His ears are red, he has a pink complexion,
And all in all, he'll suit you to perfection.

MARIANE.   Dear God!

DORINE.   Oh, how triumphant you will feel
At having caught a husband so ideal!

MARIANE.   Oh, do stop teasing, and use your
    cleverness
To get me out of this appalling mess.
Advise me, and I'll do whatever you say.

DORINE.   Ah no, a dutiful daughter must obey   70
Her father, even if he weds her to an ape.
You've a bright future; why struggle to escape?
Tartuffe will take you back where his family lives,
To a small town aswarm with relatives —
Uncles and cousins whom you'll be charmed to meet.
You'll be received at once by the elite,
Calling upon the bailiff's wife, no less —
Even, perhaps, upon the mayoress,
Who'll sit you down in the *best* kitchen chair.
Then, once a year, you'll dance at the village fair 80
To the drone of bagpipes — two of them, in fact —
And see a puppet-show, or an animal act.
Your husband . . .

MARIANE.   Oh, you turn my blood to ice!
Stop torturing me, and give me your advice.

DORINE (*Threatening to go*). Your servant, Madam.

MARIANE.   Dorine, I beg of you . . .

DORINE.   No, you deserve it; this marriage must
    go through.

MARIANE.   Dorine!

DORINE.   No.

MARIANE.   Not Tartuffe! You know I
think him . . .

DORINE.   Tartuffe's your cup of tea, and you shall
drink him.

MARIANE.   I've always told you everything, and
relied . . .

DORINE.   No. You deserve to be tartuffified.   90

MARIANE.   Well, since you mock me and refuse
to care,
I'll henceforth seek my solace in despair:
Despair shall be my counsellor and friend,
And help me bring my sorrows to an end.
                    (*She starts to leave.*)

DORINE.   There now, come back; my anger has
subsided.
You do deserve some pity, I've decided.

MARIANE.   Dorine, if Father makes me undergo
This dreadful martyrdom, I'll die, I know.

DORINE.   Don't fret; it won't be difficult to discover
Some plan of action . . . But here's Valère, your lover.

SCENE IV. VALERE, MARIANE, *and* DORINE

VALERE.   Madam, I've just received some wondrous news
Regarding which I'd like to hear your views.

MARIANE.   What news?

VALERE.   You're marrying Tartuffe.

MARIANE.   I find
That Father does have such a match in mind.

VALERE.   Your father, Madam . . .

MARIANE.   . . . has just this minute said
That it's Tartuffe he wishes me to wed.

VALERE.   Can he be serious?

MARIANE.   Oh, indeed he can;
He's clearly set his heart upon the plan.

VALERE.   And what position do you propose to
take,   9
Madam?

MARIANE.   Why — I don't know.

VALERE.   For heaven's sake —
You don't know?

MARIANE.   No.

VALERE.   Well, well!

MARIANE.   Advise me, do.

VALERE.   Marry the man. That's my advice to
you.

MARIANE.   That's your advice?

VALERE.   Yes.

MARIANE.   Truly?

VALERE.   Oh, absolutely.
You couldn't choose more wisely, more astutely.

MARIANE.   Thanks for this counsel; I'll follow it,
   of course.

VALERE.   Do, do; I'm sure 'twill cost you no
   remorse.

MARIANE.   To give it didn't cause your heart to
   break.

VALERE.   I gave it, Madam, only for your sake.

MARIANE.   And it's for your sake that I take it,
   Sir.

DORINE (*Withdrawing to the rear of the stage*).
   Let's see which fool will prove the stubborner. 20

VALERE.   So! I am nothing to you, and it was flat
Deception when you . . .

MARIANE.   Please, enough of that.
You've told me plainly that I should agree
To wed the man my father's chosen for me,
And since you've deigned to counsel me so wisely,
I promise, Sir, to do as you advise me.

VALERE.   Ah, no, 'twas not by me that you were
   swayed.
No, your decision was already made;
Though now, to save appearances, you protest
That you're betraying me at my behest.   30

MARIANE.   Just as you say.

VALERE.   Quite so. And I now see
That you were never truly in love with me.

MARIANE.   Alas, you're free to think so if you
   choose.

VALERE.   I choose to think so, and here's a bit of
   news:
You've spurned my hand, but I know where to turn
For kinder treatment, as you shall quickly learn.

MARIANE.   I'm sure you do. Your noble qualities
Inspire affection . . .

VALERE.   Forget my qualities, please.
They don't inspire you overmuch, I find.
But there's another lady I have in mind   40
Whose sweet and generous nature will not scorn
To compensate me for the loss I've borne.

MARIANE.   I'm no great loss, and I'm sure that
   you'll transfer
Your heart quite painlessly from me to her.

VALERE.   I'll do my best to take it in my stride.
The pain I feel at being cast aside

Time and forgetfulness may put an end to.
Or if I can't forget, I shall pretend to.
No self-respecting person is expected
To go on loving once he's been rejected.   50
    MARIANE.   Now, that's a fine, high-minded senti-
    ment.
    VALERE.   One to which any sane man would
    assent.
Would you prefer it if I pined away
In hopeless passion till my dying day?
Am I to yield you to a rival's arms
And not console myself with other charms?
    MARIANE.   Go then; console yourself; don't hesi-
    tate.
I wish you to; indeed, I cannot wait.
    VALERE.   You wish me to?
    MARIANE.   Yes.
    VALERE.   That's the final straw.
Madam, farewell. Your wish shall be my law.   60
    (*He starts to leave, and then returns; this
    repeatedly*)
    MARIANE.   Splendid.
    VALERE (*Coming back again*).   This breach, re-
    member, is of your making;
It's you who've driven me to the step I'm taking.
    MARIANE.   Of course.
    VALERE (*Coming back again*).   Remember, too,
    that I am merely
Following your example.
    MARIANE.   I see that clearly.
    VALERE.   Enough. I'll go and do your bidding,
    then.
    MARIANE.   Good.
    VALERE (*Coming back again*).   You shall never
    see my face again.
    MARIANE.   Excellent.
    VALERE (*Walking to the door, then turning
    about*).   Yes?
    MARIANE.   What?
    VALERE.   What's that? What did you say?
    MARIANE.   Nothing. You're dreaming.
    VALERE.   Ah. Well, I'm on my way.
Farewell, *Madame*.   (*He moves slowly away.*)
    MARIANE.   Farewell.
    DORINE (*To Mariane*).   If you ask me,
Both of you are as mad as mad can be.   70
Do stop this nonsense, now. I've only let you
Squabble so long to see where it would get you.

Whoa there, Monsieur Valère!
> (*She goes and seizes Valère by the arm; he*
> *makes a great show of resistance.*)

VALERE.   What's this, Dorine?

DORINE.   Come here.

VALERE.   No, no, my heart's too full
> of spleen.

Don't hold me back; her wish must be obeyed.

DORINE.   Stop!

VALERE.   It's too late now; my decision's
> made.

DORINE.   Oh, pooh!

MARIANE (*Aside*).   He hates the sight of me,
> that's plain.

I'll go, and so deliver him from pain.

DORINE (*Leaving Valère, running after Mariane*).

And now *you* run away! Come back.

MARIANE.   No, no.

Nothing you say will keep me here. Let go!   80

VALERE (*Aside*).   She cannot bear my presence, I
> perceive.

To spare her further torment, I shall leave.

DORINE (*Leaving Mariane, running after Valère*).

Again! You'll not escape, Sir; don't you try it.

Come here, you two. Stop fussing, and be quiet.
> (*She takes Valère by the hand, then Mariane,*
> *and draws them together.*)

VALERE (*To Dorine*).   What do you want of me?

MARIANE (*To Dorine*).   What is the point of this?

DORINE.   We're going to have a little armistice.

(*To Valère*) Now, weren't you silly to get so over-
> heated?

VALERE.   Didn't you see how badly I was treated?

DORINE (*To Mariane*).   Aren't you a simpleton,
> to have lost your head?

MARIANE.   Didn't you hear the hateful things he
> said?   90

DORINE (*To Valère*).   You're both great fools.
> Her sole desire, Valère,

Is to be yours in marriage. To that I'll swear.

(*To Mariane*) He loves you only, and he wants no
> wife

But you, Mariane. On that I'll stake my life.

MARIANE (*To Valère*).   Then why you advised
> me so, I cannot see.

VALERE (*To Mariane*).   On such a question, why
> ask advice of *me*?

DORINE. Oh, you're impossible. Give me your
   hands, you two.
(*To Valère*) Yours first.
   VALERE (*Giving Dorine his hand*). But why?
   DORINE (*to Mariane*).   And
      now a hand from you.
   MARIANE (*Also giving Dorine her hand*). What
      are you doing?
   DORINE.   There: a perfect fit.
You suit each other better than you'll admit.   100
      (*Valère and Mariane hold hands for some time
      without looking at each other.*)
   VALERE (*Turning toward Mariane*). Ah, come,
      don't be so haughty. Give a man
A look of kindness, won't you, Mariane?
            (*Mariane turns toward Valère and smiles.*)
   DORINE. I tell you, lovers are completely mad!
   VALERE (*To Mariane*). Now come, confess that
      you were very bad
To hurt my feelings as you did just now.
I have a just complaint, you must allow.
   MARIANE. *You* must allow that you were most
      unpleasant . . .
   DORINE. Let's table that discussion for the
      present;
Your father has a plan which must be stopped.
   MARIANE. Advise us, then; what means must we
      adopt?   110
   DORINE. We'll use all manner of means, and all
      at once.
(*To Mariane*) Your father's addled; he's acting like
   a dunce.
Therefore you'd better humor the old fossil.
Pretend to yield to him, be sweet and docile,
And then postpone, as often as necessary,
The day on which you have agreed to marry.
You'll thus gain time, and time will turn the trick.
Sometimes, for instance, you'll be taken sick,
And that will seem good reason for delay;
Or some bad omen will make you change the
      day —   120
You'll dream of muddy water, or you'll pass
A dead man's hearse, or break a looking-glass.
If all else fails, no man can marry you
Unless you take his ring and say "I do."
But now, let's separate. If they should find
Us talking here, our plot might be divined.
(*To Valère*) Go to your friends, and tell them what's
      occurred,
And have them urge her father to keep his word.

Meanwhile, we'll stir her brother into action,
And get Elmire, as well, to join our faction.   130
Good-bye.
    VALERE (*To Mariane*).   Though each of us will
      do his best,
It's your true heart on which my hopes shall rest.
    MARIANE (*To Valère*).   Regardless of what Father
      may decide,
None but Valère shall claim me as his bride.
    VALERE.   Oh, how those words content me!
      Come what will . . .
    DORINE.   Oh, lovers, lovers! Their tongues are
      never still.
Be off, now.
    VALERE (*Turning to go, then turning back*).   One
      last word . . .
    DORINE.   No time to chat:
You leave by this door; and *you* leave by that.
    (*Dorine pushes them, by the shoulders, toward
    opposing doors.*)

ACT 3

SCENE I. DAMIS *and* DORINE

    DAMIS.   May lightning strike me even as I speak,
May all men call me cowardly and weak,
If any fear or scruple holds me back
From settling things, at once, with that great quack!
    DORINE.   Now, don't give way to violent emotion.
Your father's merely talked about this notion,
And words and deeds are far from being one.
Much that is talked about is never done.
    DAMIS.   No, I must stop that scoundrel's machina-
    tions;
I'll go and tell him off; I'm out of patience.   10
    DORINE.   Do calm down and be practical. I had
    rather
My mistress dealt with him — and with your father.
She has some influence with Tartuffe, I've noted.
He hangs upon her words, seems most devoted,
And may, indeed, be smitten by her charm.
Pray Heaven it's true! 'Twould do our cause no
    harm.
She sent for him, just now, to sound him out
On this affair you're so incensed about;
She'll find out where he stands, and tell him, too,
What dreadful strife and trouble will ensue   20
If he lends countenance to your father's plan.
I couldn't get in to see him, but his man

Says that he's almost finished with his prayers.
Go, now. I'll catch him when he comes downstairs.

DAMIS.   I want to hear this conference, and I will.

DORINE.   No, they must be alone.

DAMIS.   Oh, I'll keep still.

DORINE.   Not you. I know your temper. You'd
start a brawl,

And shout and stamp your foot and spoil it all.
Go on.

DAMIS.   I won't; I have a perfect right . . .

DORINE.   Lord, you're a nuisance! He's coming;
get out of sight.   30
(*Damis conceals himself in a closet at the rear of
the stage.*)

SCENE II. TARTUFFE *and* DORINE

TARTUFFE (*Observing Dorine, and calling to his
man-servant offstage*). Hang up my hair-shirt,
put my scourge in place,

And pray, Laurent, for Heaven's perpetual grace.
I'm going to the prison now, to share
My last few coins with the poor wretches there.

DORINE (*Aside*). Dear God, what affectation!
What a fake!

TARTUFFE.   You wished to see me?

DORINE.   Yes . . .

TARTUFFE (*Taking a handkerchief from his
pocket*).   For mercy's sake,

Please take this handkerchief, before you speak.

DORINE.   What?

TARTUFFE.   Cover that bosom, girl. The
flesh is weak,

And unclean thoughts are difficult to control.
Such sights as that can undermine the soul.   10

DORINE.   Your soul, it seems, has very poor
defenses,

And flesh makes quite an impact on your senses.
It's strange that you're so easily excited;
My own desires are not so soon ignited,
And if I saw you naked as a beast,
Not all your hide would tempt me in the least.

TARTUFFE.   Girl, speak more modestly; unless you
do,

I shall be forced to take my leave of you.

DORINE.   Oh, no, it's I who must be on my way;
I've just one little message to convey.   20
Madame is coming down, and begs you, Sir,
To wait and have a word or two with her.

TARTUFFE.   Gladly.

DORINE (*Aside*).   *That* had a softening effect!
I think my guess about him was correct.

TARTUFFE.   Will she be long?

DORINE.   No: that's her step I hear.
Ah, here she is, and I shall disappear.

SCENE III.   ELMIRE *and* TARTUFFE

TARTUFFE.   May Heaven, whose infinite goodness
    we adore,
Preserve your body and soul forevermore,
And bless your days, and answer thus the plea
Of one who is its humblest votary.

ELMIRE.   I thank you for that pious wish. But
    please,
Do take a chair and let's be more at ease.
                            (*They sit down.*)

TARTUFFE.   I trust that you are once more well
    and strong?

ELMIRE.   Oh, yes: the fever didn't last for long.

TARTUFFE.   My prayers are too unworthy, I am
    sure,
To have gained from Heaven this most gracious
    cure;   10
But lately, Madam, my every supplication
Has had for object your recuperation.

ELMIRE.   You shouldn't have troubled so, I don't
    deserve it.

TARTUFFE.   Your health is priceless, Madam, and
    to preserve it
I'd gladly give my own, in all sincerity.

ELMIRE.   Sir, you outdo us all in Christian charity.
You've been most kind. I count myself your debtor.

TARTUFFE.   'Twas nothing, Madam. I long to
    serve you better.

ELMIRE.   There's a private matter I'm anxious to
    discuss.
I'm glad there's no one here to hinder us.   20

TARTUFFE.   I too am glad; it floods my heart with
    bliss
To find myself alone with you like this.
For just this chance I've prayed with all my power —
But prayed in vain, until this happy hour.

ELMIRE.   This won't take long, Sir, and I hope
    you'll be
Entirely frank and unconstrained with me.

TARTUFFE.   Indeed, there's nothing I had rather
    do
Than bare my inmost heart and soul to you.

First, let me say that what remarks I've made
About the constant visits you are paid   30
Were prompted not by any mean emotion,
But rather by a pure and deep devotion,
A fervent zeal . . .

    ELMIRE.   No need for explanation.
Your sole concern, I'm sure, was my salvation.

    TARTUFFE (*Taking Elmire's hand and pressing her
        fingertips*). Quite so; and such great fervor do
        I feel . . .

    ELMIRE. Ooh! Please! You're pinching!

    TARTUFFE.   'Twas from excess of zeal.
I never meant to cause you pain, I swear.
I'd rather . . .

              (*He places his hand on Elmire's knee.*)

    ELMIRE.   What can your hand be doing there?

    TARTUFFE. Feeling your gown: what soft, fine-
      woven stuff!

    ELMIRE. Please, I'm extremely ticklish. That's
      enough.   40
      (*She draws her chair away; Tartuffe pulls his
      after her.*)

    TARTUFFE (*Fondling the lace collar of her gown*).
      My, my, what lovely lacework on your dress!
The workmanship's miraculous, no less.
I've not seen anything to equal it.

    ELMIRE. Yes, quite. But let's talk business for a
      bit.
They say my husband means to break his word
And give his daughter to you, Sir. Had you heard?

    TARTUFFE. He did once mention it. But I confess
I dream of quite a different happiness.
It's elsewhere, Madam, that my eyes discern
The promise of that bliss for which I yearn.   50

    ELMIRE. I see: you care for nothing here
      below.

    TARTUFFE. Ah, well — my heart's not made of
      stone, you know.

    ELMIRE. All your desires mount heavenward, I'm
      sure,
In scorn of all that's earthly and impure.

    TARTUFFE. A love of heavenly beauty does not
      preclude
A proper love for earthly pulchritude;
Our senses are quite rightly captivated
By perfect works our Maker has created.
Some glory clings to all that Heaven has made;
In you, all Heaven's marvels are displayed.   60

On that fair face, such beauties have been lav-
    ished,
The eyes are dazzled and the heart is ravished;
How could I look on you, O flawless creature,
And not adore the Author of all Nature,
Feeling a love both passionate and pure
For you, his triumph of self-portraiture?
At first, I trembled lest that love should be
A subtle snare that Hell had laid for me;
I vowed to flee the sight of you, eschewing
A rapture that might prove my soul's undoing;   70
But soon, fair being, I became aware
That my deep passion could be made to square
With rectitude, and with my bounden duty.
I thereupon surrendered to your beauty.
It is, I know, presumptuous on my part
To bring you this poor offering of my heart,
And it is not my merit, Heaven knows,
But your compassion on which my hopes repose.
You are my peace, my solace, my salvation;
On you depends my bliss — or desolation;   80
I bide your judgment and, as you think best,
I shall be either miserable or blest.
    ELMIRE.   Your declaration is most gallant, Sir,
But don't you think it's out of character?
You'd have done better to restrain your passion
And think before you spoke in such a fashion.
It ill becomes a pious man like you . . .
    TARTUFFE.   I may be pious, but I'm human too:
With your celestial charms before his eyes,
A man has not the power to be wise.   90
I know such words sound strangely,' coming from
    me,
But I'm no angel, nor was meant to be,
And if you blame my passion, you must needs
Reproach as well the charms on which it feeds.
Your loveliness I had no sooner seen
Than you became my soul's unrivalled queen;
Before your seraph glance, divinely sweet,
My heart's defenses crumbled in defeat,
And nothing fasting, prayer, or tears might do
Could stay my spirit from adoring you.   100
My eyes, my sighs have told you in the past
What now my lips make bold to say at last,
And if, in your great goodness, you will deign
To look upon your slave, and ease his pain, —
If, in compassion for my soul's distress,
You'll stoop to comfort my unworthiness,

I'll raise to you, in thanks for that sweet manna,
An endless hymn, an infinite hosanna.
With me, of course, there need be no anxiety,
No fear of scandal or of notoriety.   110
These young court gallants, whom all the ladies
      fancy,
Are vain in speech, in action rash and chancy;
When they succeed in love, the world soon knows it;
No favor's granted them but they disclose it
And by the looseness of their tongues profane
The very altar where their hearts have lain.
Men of my sort, however, love discreetly,
And one may trust our reticence completely.
My keen concern for my good name insures
The absolute security of yours;   120
In short, I offer you, my dear Elmire,
Love without scandal, pleasure without fear.
      ELMIRE.   I've heard your well-turned speeches to
         the end,
And what you urge I clearly apprehend.
Aren't you afraid that I may take a notion
To tell my husband of your warm devotion,
And that, supposing he were duly told,
His feelings toward you might grow rather cold?
      TARTUFFE.   I know, dear lady, that your exceeding
         charity
Will lead your heart to pardon my temerity;   130
That you'll excuse my violent affection
As human weakness, human imperfection;
And that — O fairest! — you will bear in mind
That I'm but flesh and blood, and am not blind.
      ELMIRE.   Some women might do otherwise, per-
         haps,
But I shall be discreet about your lapse;
I'll tell my husband nothing of what's occurred
If, in return, you'll give your solemn word
To advocate as forcefully as you can
The marriage of Valère and Mariane,   140
Renouncing all desire to dispossess
Another of his rightful happiness,
And . . .

SCENE IV. DAMIS, ELMIRE, *and* TARTUFFE

      DAMIS (*Emerging from the closet where he has
         been hiding*).   No! We'll not hush up this vile
         affair;
I heard it all inside that closet there,
Where Heaven, in order to confound the pride
Of this great rascal, prompted me to hide.

Ah, now I have my long-awaited chance
To punish his deceit and arrogance,
And give my father clear and shocking proof
Of the black character of his dear Tartuffe.
   ELMIRE. Ah no, Damis; I'll be content if he
Will study to deserve my leniency.   **10**
I've promised silence — don't make me break my
    word;
To make a scandal would be too absurd.
Good wives laugh off such trifles, and forget them;
Why should they tell their husbands, and upset
    them?
   DAMIS. You have your reasons for taking such a
    course,
And I have reasons, too, of equal force.
To spare him now would be insanely wrong.
I've swallowed my just wrath for far too long
And watched this insolent bigot bringing strife
And bitterness into our family life.   **20**
Too long he's meddled in my father's affairs,
Thwarting my marriage-hopes, and poor Valère's.
It's high time that my father was undeceived,
And now I've proof that can't be disbelieved —
Proof that was furnished me by Heaven above.
It's too good not to take advantage of.
This is my chance, and I deserve to lose it
If, for one moment, I hesitate to use it.
   ELMIRE. Damis . . .
   DAMIS.   No, I must do what I think right.
Madam, my heart is bursting with delight,   **30**
And, say whatever you will, I'll not consent
To lose the sweet revenge on which I'm bent.
I'll settle matters without more ado;
And here, most opportunely, is my cue.

SCENE V. ORGON, DAMIS, TARTUFFE, *and* ELMIRE

   DAMIS. Father, I'm glad you've joined us. Let us
    advise you
Of some fresh news which doubtless will surprise you.
You've just now been repaid with interest
For all your loving-kindness to our guest.
He's proved his warm and grateful feelings toward
    you;
It's with a pair of horns he would reward you.
Yes, I surprised him with your wife, and heard
His whole adulterous offer, every word.
She, with her all too gentle disposition,
Would not have told you of his proposition;   **10**

But I shall not make terms with brazen lechery,
And feel that not to tell you would be treachery.
　　ELMIRE.　And I hold that one's husband's peace
　　　　of mind
Should not be spoilt by tattle of this kind.
One's honor doesn't require it: to be proficient
In keeping men at bay is quite sufficient.
These are my sentiments, and I wish, Damis,
That you had heeded me and held your peace.

SCENE VI.　ORGON, DAMIS, *and* TARTUFFE

　　ORGON.　Can it be true, this dreadful thing I hear?
　　TARTUFFE.　Yes, Brother, I'm a wicked man, I
　　　　fear:
A wretched sinner, all depraved and twisted,
The greatest villain that has ever existed.
My life's one heap of crimes, which grows each
　　　　minute;
There's naught but foulness and corruption in it;
And I perceive that Heaven, outraged by me,
Has chosen this occasion to mortify me.
Charge me with any deed you wish to name;
I'll not defend myself, but take the blame.　　　　10
Believe what you are told, and drive Tartuffe
Like some base criminal from beneath your roof;
Yes, drive me hence, and with a parting curse:
I shan't protest, for I deserve far worse.
　　ORGON (*To Damis*).　Ah, you deceitful boy, how
　　　　dare you try
To stain his purity with so foul a lie?
　　DAMIS.　What! Are you taken in by such a bluff?
Did you not hear . . . ?
　　ORGON.　　　　　　　　Enough, you rogue, enough!
　　TARTUFFE.　Ah, Brother, let him speak: you're
　　　　being unjust.
Believe his story; the boy deserves your trust.　　20
Why, after all, should you have faith in me?
How can you know what I might do, or be?
Is it on my good actions that you base
Your favor? Do you trust my pious face?
Ah, no, don't be deceived by hollow shows;
I'm far, alas, from being what men suppose;
Though the world takes me for a man of worth,
I'm truly the most worthless man on earth.
(*To Damis*) Yes, my dear son, speak out now: call
　　　　me the chief
Of sinners, a wretch, a murderer, a thief;　　　　30

Load me with all the names men most abhor;
I'll not complain; I've earned them all, and more;
I'll kneel here while you pour them on my head
As a just punishment for the life I've led.
    ORGON (*To Tartuffe*). This is too much, dear
        Brother.
(*To Damis*) Have you no heart?
    DAMIS. Are you so hoodwinked by this rascal's
        art . . . ?
    ORGON. Be still, you monster.
(*To Tartuffe*)   Brother, I pray you, rise.
(*To Damis*) Villain!
    DAMIS.   But . . .
    ORGON.   Silence!
    DAMIS.   Can't you realize . . . ?
    ORGON. Just one word more, and I'll tear you
        limb from limb.
    TARTUFFE. In God's name, Brother, don't be
        harsh with him.   40
I'd rather far be tortured at the stake
Than see him bear one scratch for my poor sake.
    ORGON (*To Damis*). Ingrate!
    TARTUFFE.   If I must beg you,
        on bended knee,
To pardon him . . .
    ORGON (*Falling to his knees, addressing Tartuffe*).
                Such goodness cannot be!
(*To Damis*) Now, *there's* true charity!
    DAMIS.   What, you . . . ?
    ORGON.   Villain, be still!
I know your motives; I know you wish him ill:
Yes, all of you — wife, children, servants, all —
Conspire against him and desire his fall,
Employing every shameful trick you can
To alienate me from this saintly man.   50
Ah, but the more you seek to drive him away,
The more I'll do to keep him. Without delay,
I'll spite this household and confound its pride
By giving him my daughter as his bride.
    DAMIS. You're going to force her to accept his
        hand?
    ORGON. Yes, and this very night, d'you under-
        stand?
I shall defy you all, and make it clear
That I'm the one who gives the orders here.
Come, wretch, kneel down and clasp his blessed
    feet,
And ask his pardon for your black deceit.   60

DAMIS. I ask that swindler's pardon? Why, I'd
rather . . .

ORGON.   So! You insult him, and defy your
father!

A stick! A stick! (*To Tartuffe*) No, no — release
me, do.

(*To Damis*) Out of my house this minute! Be off
with you,

And never dare set foot in it again.

DAMIS. Well, I shall go, but . . .

ORGON.   Well, go quickly, then.

I disinherit you; an empty purse

Is all you'll get from me — except my curse!

SCENE VII. ORGON *and* TARTUFFE

ORGON. How he blasphemed your goodness!
What a son!

TARTUFFE. Forgive him, Lord, as I've already
done.

(*To Orgon*) You can't know how it hurts when
someone tries

To blacken me in my dear Brother's eyes.

ORGON. Ahh!

TARTUFFE. The mere thought of such ingratitude

Plunges my soul into so dark a mood . . .

Such horror grips my heart . . . I gasp for breath,

And cannot speak, and feel myself near death.

ORGON. (*He runs, in tears, to the door through
which he has just driven his son.*) You black-
guard! Why did I spare you? Why did I not

Break you in little pieces on the spot?   10

Compose yourself, and don't be hurt, dear friend.

TARTUFFE. These scenes, these dreadful quarrels,
have got to end.

I've much upset your household, and I perceive

That the best thing will be for me to leave.

ORGON. What are you saying!

TARTUFFE.   They're all against me here;

They'd have you think me false and insincere.

ORGON. Ah, what of that? Have I ceased believing in you?

TARTUFFE. Their adverse talk will certainly continue,

And charges which you now repudiate

You may find credible at a later date.   20

ORGON. No, Brother, never.

TARTUFFE.   Brother, a wife can sway

Her husband's mind in many a subtle way.

ORGON.   No, no.

TARTUFFE.   To leave at once is the solution;
Thus only can I end their persecution.

ORGON.   No, no, I'll not allow it; you shall remain.

TARTUFFE.   Ah, well; 'twill mean much martyrdom
    and pain,
But if you wish it . . .

ORGON.   Ah!

TARTUFFE.   Enough; so be it.
But one thing must be settled, as I see it.
For your dear honor, and for our friendship's sake,
There's one precaution I feel bound to take.   30
I shall avoid your wife, and keep away . . .

ORGON.   No, you shall not, whatever they may say.
It pleases me to vex them, and for spite
I'd have them see you with her day and night.
What's more, I'm going to drive them to despair
By making you my only son and heir;
This very day, I'll give to you alone
Clear deed and title to everything I own.
A dear, good friend and son-in-law-to-be
Is more than wife, or child, or kin to me.   40
Will you accept my offer, dearest son?

TARTUFFE.   In all things, let the will of Heaven
    be done.

ORGON.   Poor fellow! Come, we'll go draw up the
    deed.
Then let them burst with disappointed greed!

ACT 4

SCENE I.   CLEANTE *and* TARTUFFE

CLEANTE.   Yes, all the town's discussing it, and
    truly,
Their comments do not flatter you unduly.
I'm glad we've met, Sir, and I'll give my view
Of this sad matter in a word or two.
As for who's guilty, that I shan't discuss;
Let's say it was Damis who caused the fuss;
Assuming, then, that you have been ill-used
By young Damis, and groundlessly accused,
Ought not a Christian to forgive, and ought
He not to stifle every vengeful thought?   10
Should you stand by and watch a father make
His only son an exile for your sake?
Again I tell you frankly, be advised:
The whole town, high and low, is scandalized;

This quarrel must be mended, and my advice is
Not to push matters to a further crisis.
No, sacrifice your wrath to God above,
And help Damis regain his father's love.

    TARTUFFE.   Alas, for my part I should take great
        joy
In doing so. I've nothing against the boy.   20
I pardon all, I harbor no resentment;
To serve him would afford me much contentment.
But Heaven's interest will not have it so:
If he comes back, then I shall have to go.
After his conduct — so extreme, so vicious —
Our further intercourse would look suspicious.
God knows what people would think! Why, they'd
    describe
My goodness to him as a sort of bribe;
They'd say that out of guilt I made pretense
Of loving-kindness and benevolence —   30
That, fearing my accuser's tongue, I strove
To buy his silence with a show of love.

    CLEANTE.   Your reasoning is badly warped and
      stretched,
And these excuses, Sir, are most far-fetched.
Why put yourself in charge of Heaven's cause?
Does Heaven need our help to enforce its laws?
Leave vengeance to the Lord, Sir; while we live,
Our duty's not to punish, but forgive;
And what the Lord commands, we should obey
Without regard to what the world may say.   40
What! Shall the fear of being misunderstood
Prevent our doing what is right and good?
No, no: let's simply do what Heaven ordains,
And let no other thoughts perplex our brains.

    TARTUFFE.   Again, Sir, let me say that I've
      forgiven
Damis, and thus obeyed the laws of Heaven;
But I am not commanded by the Bible
To live with one who smears my name with libel.

    CLEANTE.   Were you commanded, Sir, to indulge
      the whim
Of poor Orgon, and to encourage him   50
In suddenly transferring to your name
A large estate to which you have no claim?

    TARTUFFE.   'Twould never occur to those who
      know me best
To think I acted from self-interest.
The treasures of this world I quite despise;
Their specious glitter does not charm my eyes;
And if I have resigned myself to taking
The gift which my dear Brother insists on making,

I do so only, as he well understands,
Lest so much wealth fall into wicked hands,   60
Lest those to whom it might descend in time
Turn it to purposes of sin and crime,
And not, as I shall do, make use of it
For Heaven's glory and mankind's benefit.
   CLEANTE.   Forget these trumped-up fears. Your
     argument
Is one the rightful heir might well resent;
It *is* a moral burden to inherit
Such wealth, but give Damis a chance to bear it.
And would it not be worse to be accused
Of swindling, than to see that wealth misused?   70
I'm shocked that you allowed Orgon to broach
This matter, and that you feel no self-reproach;
Does true religion teach that lawful heirs
May freely be deprived of what is theirs?
And if the Lord has told you in your heart
That you and young Damis must dwell apart,
Would it not be the decent thing to beat
A generous and honorable retreat,
Rather than let the son of the house be sent,
For your convenience, into banishment?   80
Sir, if you wish to prove the honesty
Of your intentions . . .
   TARTUFFE.   Sir, it is half-past three.
I've certain pious duties to attend to,
And hope my prompt departure won't offend you.
   CLEANTE (*Alone*).   Damn.

SCENE II.   ELMIRE, MARIANE, CLEANTE, *and* DORINE
   DORINE.   Stay, Sir, and help
     Mariane, for Heaven's sake!
She's suffering so, I fear her heart will break.
Her father's plan to marry her off tonight
Has put the poor child in a desperate plight.
I hear him coming. Let's stand together, now,
And see if we can't change his mind, somehow,
About this match we all deplore and fear.

SCENE III.   ORGON, ELMIRE, MARIANE, CLEANTE, *and*
DORINE

   ORGON.   Hah! Glad to find you all assembled here.
(*To Mariane*) This contract, child, contains your
     happiness,
And what it says I think your heart can guess.
   MARIANE (*Falling to her knees*). Sir, by that
     Heaven which sees me here distressed,
And by whatever else can move your breast,

Do not employ a father's power, I pray you,
To crush my heart and force it to obey you,
Nor by your harsh commands oppress me so
That I'll begrudge the duty which I owe —
And do not so embitter and enslave me   10
That I shall hate the very life you gave me.
If my sweet hopes must perish, if you refuse
To give me to the one I've dared to choose,
Spare me at least — I beg you, I implore —
The pain of wedding one whom I abhor;
And do not, by a heartless use of force,
Drive me to contemplate some desperate course.
  ORGON (*Feeling himself touched by her*). Be
   firm, my soul. No human weakness, now.
  MARIANE. I don't resent your love for him. Allow
Your heart free rein, Sir; give him your property,   20
And if that's not enough, take mine from me;
He's welcome to my money; take it, do,
But don't, I pray, include my person too.
Spare me, I beg you; and let me end the tale
Of my sad days behind a convent veil.
  ORGON. A convent! Hah! When crossed in their
   amours,
All lovesick girls have the same thought as yours.
Get up! The more you loathe the man, and dread
   him,
The more ennobling it will be to wed him.
Marry Tartuffe, and mortify your flesh!   30
Enough; don't start that whimpering afresh.
  DORINE. But why . . . ?
  ORGON.   Be still, there. Speak
   when you're spoken to.
Not one more bit of impudence out of you.
  CLEANTE. If I may offer a word of counsel
   here . . .
  ORGON. Brother, in counselling you have no peer;
All your advice is forceful, sound, and clever;
I don't propose to follow it, however.
  ELMIRE (*To Orgon*). I am amazed, and don't
   know what to say;
Your blindness simply takes my breath away.
You are indeed bewitched, to take no warning   40
From our account of what occurred this morning.
  ORGON. Madam, I know a few plain facts, and
   one
Is that you're partial to my rascal son;
Hence, when he sought to make Tartuffe the victim
Of a base lie, you dared not contradict him.

Ah, but you underplayed your part, my pet;
You should have looked more angry, more upset.
    ELMIRE. When men make overtures, must we
      reply
With righteous anger and a battle-cry?
Must we turn back their amorous advances   50
With sharp reproaches and with fiery glances?
Myself, I find such offers merely amusing,
And make no scenes and fusses in refusing;
My taste is for good-natured rectitude,
And I dislike the savage sort of prude
Who guards her virtue with her teeth and claws,
And tears men's eyes out for the slightest cause:
The Lord preserve me from such honor as that,
Which bites and scratches like an alley-cat!
I've found that a polite and cool rebuff   60
Discourages a lover quite enough.
    ORGON. I know the facts, and I shall not be
      shaken.
    ELMIRE. I marvel at your power to be mistaken.
Would it, I wonder, carry weight with you
If I could *show* you that our tale was true?
    ORGON. Show me?
    ELMIRE.   Yes.
    ORGON.   Rot.
    ELMIRE.   Come, what if I found a way
To make you see the facts as plain as day?
    ORGON. Nonsense.
    ELMIRE.   Do answer me; don't be absurd.
I'm not now asking you to trust our word.
Suppose that from some hiding place in here   70
You learned the whole sad truth by eye and ear —
What would you say of your good friend, after that?
    ORGON. Why, I'd say . . . nothing, by Jehosha-
      phat!
It can't be true.
    ELMIRE.   You've been too long deceived,
And I'm quite tired of being disbelieved.
Come now: let's put my statements to the test,
And you shall see the truth made manifest.
    ORGON. I'll take that challenge. Now do your
      uttermost.
We'll see how you make good your empty boast.   79
    ELMIRE (*To Dorine*). Send him to me.
    DORINE.   He's crafty; it may be hard
To catch the cunning scoundrel off his guard.
    ELMIRE. No, amorous men are gullible. Their
      conceit
So blinds them that they're never hard to cheat.

Have him come down (*To Cléante and Mariane*)
    Please leave us, for a bit.

SCENE IV. ELMIRE *and* ORGON

    ELMIRE.   Pull up this table, and get under it.
    ORGON.   What?
    ELMIRE.   It's essential that you be well-hidden.
    ORGON.   Why there?
    ELMIRE.   Oh, Heaven! Just do as you
    are bidden.
I have my plans; we'll soon see how they fare.
Under the table, now; and once you're there,
Take care that you are neither seen nor heard.
    ORGON.   Well, I'll indulge you, since I gave my
    word
To see you through this infantile charade.
    ELMIRE.   Once it is over, you'll be glad we played.
(*To her husband, who is now under the table*) I'm
    going to act quite strangely, now, and you   10
Must not be shocked at anything I do.
Whatever I may say, you must excuse
As part of that deceit I'm forced to use.
I shall employ sweet speeches in the task
Of making that impostor drop his mask;
I'll give encouragement to his bold desires,
And furnish fuel to his amorous fires.
Since it's for your sake, and for his destruction,
That I shall seem to yield to his seduction,
I'll gladly stop whenever you decide   20
That all your doubts are fully satisfied.
I'll count on you, as soon as you have seen
What sort of man he is, to intervene,
And not expose me to his odious lust
One moment longer than you feel you must.
Remember: you're to save me from my plight
Whenever . . . He's coming! Hush! Keep out of
    sight!

SCENE V. TARTUFFE, ELMIRE, *and* ORGON

    TARTUFFE.   You wish to have a word with me,
    I'm told.
    ELMIRE.   Yes. I've a little secret to unfold.
Before I speak, however, it would be wise
To close that door, and look about for spies.
        (*Tartuffe goes to the door, closes it, and re-
        turns.*)
The very last thing that must happen now
Is a repetition of this morning's row.

I've never been so badly caught off guard.
Oh, how I feared for you! You saw how hard
I tried to make that troublesome Damis
Control his dreadful temper, and hold his peace.   10
In my confusion, I didn't have the sense
Simply to contradict his evidence;
But as it happened, that was for the best,
And all has worked out in our interest.
This storm has only bettered your position;
My husband doesn't have the least suspicion,
And now, in mockery of those who do,
He bids me be continually with you.
And that is why, quite fearless of reproof,
I now can be alone with my Tartuffe.   20
And why my heart — perhaps too quick to yield —
Feels free to let its passion be revealed.

    TARTUFFE.   Madam, your words confuse me. Not
       long ago,
You spoke in quite a different style, you know.

    ELMIRE.   Ah, Sir, if that refusal made you smart,
It's little that you know of woman's heart,
Or what that heart is trying to convey
When it resists in such a feeble way!
Always, at first, our modesty prevents
The frank avowal of tender sentiments;   30
However high the passion which inflames us,
Still, to confess its power somehow shames us.
Thus we reluct, at first, yet in a tone   **reluct: show reluctance**
Which tells you that our heart is overthrown,
That what our lips deny, our pulse confesses,
And that, in time, all noes will turn to yesses.
I fear my words are all too frank and free,
And a poor proof of woman's modesty;
But since I'm started, tell me, if you will —
Would I have tried to make Damis be still,   40
Would I have listened, calm and unoffended,
Until your lengthy offer of love was ended,
And been so very mild in my reaction,
Had your sweet words not given me satisfaction?
And when I tried to force you to undo
The marriage-plans my husband has in view,
What did my urgent pleading signify
If not that I admired you, and that I
Deplored the thought that someone else might own
Part of a heart I wished for mine alone?   50

    TARTUFFE.   Madam, no happiness is so complete
As when, from lips we love, come words so sweet;
Their nectar floods my every sense, and drains
In honeyed rivulets through all my veins.

To please you is my joy, my only goal;
Your love is the restorer of my soul;
And yet I must beg leave, now, to confess
Some lingering doubts as to my happiness.
Might this not be a trick? Might not the catch
Be that you wish me to break off the match   60
With Mariane, and so have feigned to love me?
I shan't quite trust your fond opinion of me
Until the feelings you've expressed so sweetly
Are demonstrated somewhat more concretely,
And you have shown, by certain kind concessions,
That I may put my faith in your professions.
    ELMIRE (*She coughs, to warn her husband*).
      Why be in such a hurry? Must my heart
Exhaust its bounty at the very start?
To make that sweet admission cost me dear,
But you'll not be content, it would appear,   70
Unless my store of favors is disbursed
To the last farthing, and at the very first.
    TARTUFFE.   The less we merit, the less we dare to
      hope,
And with our doubts, mere words can never cope.
We trust no promised bliss till we receive it;
Not till a joy is ours can we believe it.
I, who so little merit your esteem,
Can't credit this fulfillment of my dream,
And shan't believe it, Madam, until I savor
Some palpable assurance of your favor.   80
    ELMIRE.   My, how tyrannical your love can be,
And how it flusters and perplexes me!
How furiously you take one's heart in hand,
And make your every wish a fierce command!
Come, must you hound and harry me to death?
Will you not give me time to catch my breath?
Can it be right to press me with such force,
Give me no quarter, show me no remorse,
And take advantage, by your stern insistence,
Of the fond feelings which weaken my resistance?   90
    TARTUFFE.   Well, if you look with favor upon my
      love,
Why, then, begrudge me some clear proof thereof?
    ELMIRE.   But how can I consent without offense
To Heaven, toward which you feel such reverence?
    TARTUFFE.   If Heaven is all that holds you back,
      don't worry.
I can remove that hindrance in a hurry.
Nothing of that sort need obstruct our path.
    ELMIRE.   Must one not be afraid of Heaven's
      wrath?

TARTUFFE. Madam, forget such fears, and be my
    pupil,
And I shall teach you how to conquer scruple. 100
Some joys, it's true, are wrong in Heaven's eyes;
Yet Heaven is not averse to compromise;
There is a science, lately formulated,
Whereby one's conscience may be liberated,
And any wrongful act you care to mention
May be redeemed by purity of intention.
I'll teach you, Madam, the secrets of that science;
Meanwhile, just place on me your full reliance.
Assuage my keen desires, and feel no dread:
The sin, if any, shall be on my head. 110
      (*Elmire coughs, this time more loudly.*)
You've a bad cough.

ELMIRE. Yes, yes. It's bad indeed.

TARTUFFE (*Producing a little paper bag*). A bit
    of licorice may be what you need.

ELMIRE. No, I've a stubborn cold, it seems. I'm
    sure it
Will take much more than licorice to cure it.

TARTUFFE. How aggravating.

ELMIRE. Oh, more than I can say.

TARTUFFE. If you're still troubled, think of things
    this way:
No one shall know our joys, save us alone,
And there's no evil till the act is known;
It's scandal, Madam, which makes it an offense,
And it's no sin to sin in confidence. 120

ELMIRE (*Having coughed once more*). Well,
    clearly I must do as you require,
And yield to your importunate desire.
It is apparent, now, that nothing less
Will satisfy you, and so I acquiesce.
To go so far is much against my will;
I'm vexed that it should come to this; but still,
Since you are so determined on it, since you
Will not allow mere language to convince you,
And since you ask for concrete evidence, I
See nothing for it, now, but to comply. 130
If this is sinful, if I'm wrong to do it,
So much the worse for him who drove me to it.
The fault can surely not be charged to me.

TARTUFFE. Madam, the fault is mine, if fault
    there be,
And . . .

ELMIRE. Open the door a little, and peek out;
I wouldn't want my husband poking about.

TARTUFFE.   Why worry about the man? Each
    day he grows
More gullible; one can lead him by the nose.
To find us here would fill him with delight,
And if he saw the worst, he'd doubt his sight.   140
    ELMIRE.   Nevertheless, do step out for a minute
Into the hall, and see that no one's in it.

SCENE VI. ORGON *and* ELMIRE

ORGON (*Coming out from under the table*). That
    man's a perfect monster, I must admit!
I'm simply stunned. I can't get over it.
    ELMIRE.   What, coming out so soon? How pre-
    mature!
Get back in hiding, and wait until you're sure.
Stay till the end, and be convinced completely;
We mustn't stop till things are proved concretely.
    ORGON.   Hell never harbored anything so vicious!
    ELMIRE.   Tut, don't be hasty. Try to be judicious.
Wait, and be certain that there's no mistake.
No jumping to conclusions, for Heaven's sake!   10
(*She places Orgon behind her, as Tartuffe re-enters.*)

SCENE VII. TARTUFFE, ELMIRE, *and* ORGON

TARTUFFE (*Not seeing Orgon*). Madam, all things
    have worked out to perfection;
I've given the neighboring rooms a full inspection;
No one's about; and now I may at last . . .
    ORGON (*intercepting him*). Hold on, my passion-
    ate fellow, not so fast!
I should advise a little more restraint.
Well, so you thought you'd fool me, my dear saint!
How soon you wearied of the saintly life —
Wedding my daughter, and coveting my wife!
I've long suspected you, and had a feeling
That soon I'd catch you at your double-dealing.   10
Just now, you've given me evidence galore;
It's quite enough; I have no wish for more.
    ELMIRE (*To Tartuffe*). I'm sorry to have treated
    you so slyly,
But circumstances forced me to be wily.
    TARTUFFE.   Brother, you can't think . . .
    ORGON.   No more talk from you;
Just leave this household, without more ado.
    TARTUFFE.   What I intended . . .
    ORGON.   That seems fairly clear.
Spare me your falsehoods and get out of here.

TARTUFFE.   No, I'm the master, and you're the
    one to go!
This house belongs to me, I'll have you know,   20
And I shall show you that you can't hurt *me*
By this contemptible conspiracy,
That those who cross me know not what they do,
And that I've means to expose and punish you,
Avenge offended Heaven, and make you grieve
That ever you dared order me to leave.

SCENE VIII.   ELMIRE *and* ORGON

ELMIRE.   What was the point of all that angry
    chatter?
ORGON.   Dear God, I'm worried. This is no laugh-
    ing matter.
ELMIRE.   How so?
ORGON.   I fear I understood his drift.
I'm much disturbed about that deed of gift.
ELMIRE.   You gave him . . . ?
ORGON.   Yes, it's all been drawn and signed.
But one thing more is weighing on my mind.
ELMIRE.   What's that?
ORGON.   I'll tell you; but first let's
    see if there's
A certain strong-box in his room upstairs.

ACT 5

SCENE I.   ORGON *and* CLEANTE

CLEANTE.   Where are you going so fast?
ORGON.   God knows!
CLEANTE.   Then wait;
Let's have a conference, and deliberate
On how this situation's to be met.
ORGON.   That strong-box has me utterly upset;
This is the worst of many, many shocks.
CLEANTE.   Is there some fearful mystery in that
    box?
ORGON.   My poor friend Argas brought that box
    to me
With his own hands, in utmost secrecy;
'Twas on the very morning of his flight.
It's full of papers which, if they came to light,   10
Would ruin him — or such is my impression.
CLEANTE.   Then why did you let it out of your
    possession?

ORGON.   Those papers vexed my conscience, and it
    seemed best
To ask the counsel of my pious guest.
The cunning scoundrel got me to agree
To leave the strong-box in his custody,
So that, in case of an investigation,
I could employ a slight equivocation
And swear I didn't have it, and thereby,
At no expense to conscience, tell a lie.   **20**
    CLEANTE.   It looks to me as if you're out on a
    limb.
Trusting him with that box, and offering him
That deed of gift, were actions of a kind
Which scarcely indicate a prudent mind.
With two such weapons, he has the upper hand,
And since you're vulnerable, as matters stand,
You erred once more in bringing him to bay.
You should have acted in some subtler way.
    ORGON.   Just think of it: behind that fervent face,
A heart so wicked, and a soul so base!   **30**
I took him in, a hungry beggar, and then . . .
Enough, by God! I'm through with pious men:
Henceforth I'll hate the whole false brotherhood,
And persecute them worse than Satan could.
    CLEANTE.   Ah, there you go — extravagant as ever!
Why can you not be rational? You never
Manage to take the middle course, it seems,
But jump, instead, between absurd extremes.
You've recognized your recent grave mistake
In falling victim to a pious fake;   **40**
Now, to correct that error, must you embrace
An even greater error in its place,
And judge our worthy neighbors as a whole
By what you've learned of one corrupted soul?
Come, just because one rascal made you swallow
A show of zeal which turned out to be hollow,
Shall you conclude that all men are deceivers,
And that, today, there are no true believers?
Let atheists make that foolish inference;
Learn to distinguish virtue from pretense,   **50**
Be cautious in bestowing admiration,
And cultivate a sober moderation.
Don't humor fraud, but also don't asperse
True piety; the latter fault is worse,
And it is best to err, if err one must,
As you have done, upon the side of trust.

SCENE II. DAMIS, ORGON, *and* CLEANTE

DAMIS. Father, I hear that scoundrel's uttered
   threats
Against you; that he pridefully forgets
How, in his need, he was befriended by you,
And means to use your gifts to crucify you.
   ORGON. It's true, my boy. I'm too distressed for
   tears.
   DAMIS. Leave it to me, Sir; let me trim his ears.
Faced with such insolence, we must not waver.
I shall rejoice in doing you the favor
Of cutting short his life, and your distress.
   CLEANTE. What a display of young hotheaded-
   ness!   10
Do learn to moderate your fits of rage.
In this just kingdom, this enlightened age,
One does not settle things by violence.

SCENE III. MADAME PERNELLE, MARIANE, ELMIRE,
DAMIS, ORGON, *and* CLEANTE

MADAME PERNELLE. I hear strange tales of very
   strange events.
   ORGON. Yes, strange events which these two eyes
   beheld.
The man's ingratitude is unparalleled.
I save a wretched pauper from starvation,
House him, and treat him like a blood relation,
Shower him every day with my largesse,
Give him my daughter, and all that I possess;
And meanwhile the unconscionable knave
Tries to induce my wife to misbehave;
And not content with such extreme rascality,   10
Now threatens me with my own liberality,
And aims, by taking base advantage of
The gifts I gave him out of Christian love,
To drive me from my house, a ruined man,
And make me end a pauper, as he began.
   DORINE. Poor fellow!
   MADAME PERNELLE. No, my son, I'll never bring
Myself to think him guilty of such a thing.
   ORGON. How's that?
   MADAME PERNELLE. The righteous always were
   maligned.
   ORGON. Speak clearly, Mother. Say what's on
   your mind.

MADAME PERNELLE.   I mean that I can smell a
 rat, my dear.   20
You know how everybody hates him, here.
 ORGON.   That has no bearing on the case at all.
MADAME PERNELLE.   I told you a hundred times,
 when you were small,
That virtue in this world is hated ever;
Malicious men may die, but malice never.
 ORGON.   No doubt that's true, but how does it
 apply?
MADAME PERNELLE.   They've turned you against
 him by a clever lie.
 ORGON.   I've told you, I was there and saw it done.
MADAME PERNELLE.   Ah, slanderers will stop at
 nothing, Son.
 ORGON.   Mother, I'll lose my temper . . . For the
 last time,   30
I tell you I was witness to the crime.
 MADAME PERNELLE.   The tongues of spite are
 busy night and noon,
And to their venom no man is immune.
 ORGON.   You're talking nonsense. Can't you real-
 ize
I saw it; saw it; saw it with my eyes?
Saw, do you understand me? Must I shout it
Into your ears before you'll cease to doubt it?
 MADAME PERNELLE.   Appearances can deceive, my
 son. Dear me,
We cannot always judge by what we see.
 ORGON.   Drat! Drat!
MADAME PERNELLE.   One often interprets things
 awry;   40
Good can seem evil to a suspicious eye.
 ORGON.   Was I to see his pawing at Elmire
As an act of charity?
 MADAME PERNELLE.   Till his guilt is clear,
A man deserves the benefit of the doubt.
You should have waited, to see how things turned
 out.
 ORGON.   Great God in Heaven, what more proof
 did I need?
Was I to sit there, watching, until he'd . . .
You drive me to the brink of impropriety.
 MADAME PERNELLE.   No, no, a man of such sur-
 passing piety
Could not do such a thing. You cannot shake me. 50
I don't believe it, and you shall not make me.

ORGON.   You vex me so that, if you weren't my
    mother,
I'd say to you . . . some dreadful thing or other.
    DORINE.   It's your turn now, Sir, not to be listened
        to;
You'd not trust us, and now she won't trust you.
    CLEANTE.   My friends, we're wasting time which
        should be spent
In facing up to our predicament.
I fear that scoundrel's threats weren't made in sport.
    DAMIS.   Do you think he'd have the nerve to go
        to court?
    ELMIRE.   I'm sure he won't: they'd find it all too
        crude   60
A case of swindling and ingratitude.
    CLEANTE.   Don't be too sure. He won't be at a
        loss
To give his claims a high and righteous gloss;
And clever rogues with far less valid cause
Have trapped their victims in a web of laws.
I say again that to antagonize
A man so strongly armed was most unwise.
    ORGON.   I know it; but the man's appalling cheek
Outraged me so, I couldn't control my pique.
    CLEANTE.   I wish to Heaven that we could
        devise   70
Some truce between you, or some compromise.
    ELMIRE.   If I had known what cards he held, I'd
        not
Have roused his anger by my little plot.
    ORGON (*To Dorine, as M. Loyal enters*).   What
        is that fellow looking for? Who is he?
Go talk to him — and tell him that I'm busy.

SCENE IV.   MONSIEUR LOYAL, MADAME PERNELLE,
ORGON, DAMIS, MARIANE, DORINE, ELMIRE, *and*
CLEANTE

    MONSIEUR LOYAL.   Good day, dear sister. Kindly
        let me see
Your master.
    DORINE.   He's involved with company,
And cannot be disturbed just now, I fear.
    MONSIEUR LOYAL.   I hate to intrude; but what has
        brought me here
Will not disturb your master, in any event.
Indeed, my news will make him most content.

DORINE.   Your name?

MONSIEUR LOYAL.   Just say that I bring greetings from

Monsieur Tartuffe, on whose behalf I've come.

DORINE (*To Orgon*). Sir, he's a very gracious
man, and bears

A message from Tartuffe, which, he declares,   10

Will make you most content.

CLEANTE.   Upon my word,

I think this man had best be seen, and heard.

ORGON.   Perhaps he has some settlement to suggest.

How shall I treat him? What manner would be best?

CLEANTE.   Control your anger, and if he should
mention

Some fair adjustment, give him your full attention.

MONSIEUR LOYAL.   Good health to you, good Sir.
May Heaven confound

Your enemies, and may your joys abound.

ORGON (*Aside, to Cléante*).   A gentle salutation:
it confirms

My guess that he is here to offer terms.   20

MONSIEUR LOYAL.   I've always held your family
most dear;

I served your father, Sir, for many a year.

ORGON.   Sir, I must ask your pardon; to my shame,

I cannot now recall your face or name.

MONSIEUR LOYAL.   Loyal's my name; I come from
Normandy,

And I'm a bailiff, in all modesty.

For forty years, praise God, it's been my boast

To serve with honor in that vital post,

And I am here, Sir, if you will permit

The liberty, to serve you with this writ . . .   30

ORGON.   To — *what?*

MONSIEUR LOYAL.   Now, please, Sir, let us have
no friction:

It's nothing but an order of eviction.

You are to move your goods and family out

And make way for new occupants, without

Deferment or delay, and give the keys . . .

ORGON.   I? Leave this house?

MONSIEUR LOYAL.   Why yes, Sir, if you
please.

This house, Sir, from the cellar to the roof,

Belongs now to the good Monsieur Tartuffe,

And he is lord and master of your estate

By virtue of a deed of present date,   40

Drawn in due form, with clearest legal phrasing . . .
   DAMIS. Your insolence is utterly amazing!
   MONSIEUR LOYAL. Young man, my business here
    is not with you,
But with your wise and temperate father, who,
Like every worthy citizen, stands in awe
Of justice, and would never obstruct the law.
   ORGON. But . . .
   MONSIEUR LOYAL. Not for a million, Sir, would
    you rebel
Against authority; I know that well.
You'll not make trouble, Sir, or interfere
With the execution of my duties here.   50
   DAMIS. Someone may execute a smart tattoo
On that black jacket of yours, before you're through.
   MONSIEUR LOYAL. Sir, bid your son be silent. I'd
    much regret
Having to mention such a nasty threat
Of violence, in writing my report.
   DORINE (*Aside*). This man Loyal's a most dis-
    loyal sort!
   MONSIEUR LOYAL. I love all men of upright char-
    acter,
And when I agreed to serve these papers, Sir,
It was your feelings that I had in mind.
I couldn't bear to see the case assigned   60
To someone else, who might esteem you less
And so subject you to unpleasantness.
   ORGON. What's more unpleasant than telling a
    man to leave
His house and home?
   MONSIEUR LOYAL. You'd like a short reprieve?
If you desire it, Sir, I shall not press you,
But wait until tomorrow to dispossess you.
Splendid. I'll come and spend the night here, then,
Most quietly, with half a score of men.
For form's sake, you might bring me, just before
You go to bed, the keys to the front door.   70
My men, I promise, will be on their best
Behavior, and will not disturb your rest.
But bright and early, Sir, you must be quick
And move out all your furniture, every stick:
The men I've chosen are both young and strong,
And with their help it shouldn't take you long.
In short, I'll make things pleasant and convenient,
And since I'm being so extremely lenient,
Please show me, Sir, a like consideration,
And give me your entire cooperation.   80

ORGON (*Aside*).   I may be all but bankrupt, but I
vow
I'd give a hundred louis, here and now,
Just for the pleasure of landing one good clout
Right on the end of that complacent snout.
CLEANTE.   Careful; don't make things worse.
DAMIS.   My bootsole itches
To give that beggar a good kick in the breeches.
DORINE.   Monsieur Loyal, I'd love to hear the
whack
Of a stout stick across your fine broad back.
MONSIEUR LOYAL.   Take care: a woman too may
go to jail if
She uses threatening language to a bailiff.   90
CLEANTE.   Enough, enough, Sir. This must not
go on.
Give me that paper, please, and then begone.
MONSIEUR LOYAL.   Well, *au revoir*. God give you
all good cheer!
ORGON.   May God confound you, and him who
sent you here!

SCENE V.   ORGON, CLEANTE, MARIANE, ELMIRE,
MADAME PERNELLE, DORINE, *and* DAMIS

ORGON.   Now, Mother, was I right or not? This
writ
Should change your notion of Tartuffe a bit.
Do you perceive his villainy at last?
MADAME PERNELLE.   I'm thunderstruck. I'm ut-
terly aghast.
DORINE.   Oh, come, be fair. You mustn't take
offense
At this new proof of his benevolence.
He's acting out of selfless love, I know.
Material things enslave the soul, and so
He kindly has arranged your liberation
From all that night endanger your salvation.   10
ORGON.   Will you not ever hold your tongue, you
dunce?
CLEANTE.   Come, you must take some action, and
at once.
ELMIRE.   Go tell the world of the low trick he's
tried.
The deed of gift is surely nullified
By such behavior, and public rage will not
Permit the wretch to carry out his plot.

SCENE VI. VALERE, ORGON, CLEANTE, ELMIRE, MAR-
IANE, MADAME PERNELLE, DAMIS, *and* DORINE

VALERE. Sir, though I hate to bring you more bad
    news,
Such is the danger that I cannot choose.
A friend who is extremely close to me
And knows my interest in your family
Has, for my sake, presumed to violate
The secrecy that's due to things of state,
And sends me word that you are in a plight
From which your one salvation lies in flight.
That scoundrel who's imposed upon you so
Denounced you to the King an hour ago   10
And, as supporting evidence, displayed
The strong-box of a certain renegade
Whose secret papers, so he testified,
You had disloyally agreed to hide.
I don't know just what charges may be pressed,
But there's a warrant out for your arrest;
Tartuffe has been instructed, furthermore,
To guide the arresting officer to your door.
    CLEANTE. He's clearly done this to facilitate
His seizure of your house and your estate.   20
    ORGON. That man, I must say, is a vicious beast!
    VALERE. You can't afford to delay, Sir, in the
        least.
My carriage is outside, to take you hence;
This thousand louis should cover all expense.
Let's lose no time, or you shall be undone;
The sole defense, in this case, is to run.
I shall go with you all the way, and place you
In a safe refuge to which they'll never trace you.
    ORGON. Alas, dear boy, I wish that I could show
        you
My gratitude for everything I owe you.   30
But now is not the time; I pray the Lord
That I may live to give you your reward.
Farewell, my dears; be careful . . .
    CLEANTE.   Brother, hurry.
We shall take care of things; you needn't worry.

SCENE VII. THE OFFICER, TARTUFFE, VALERE, OR-
GON, ELMIRE, MARIANE, MADAME PERNELLE, DORINE,
CLEANTE, *and* DAMIS

TARTUFFE. Gently, Sir, gently; stay right where
    you are.
No need for haste; your lodging isn't far.

You're off to prison, by order of the Prince.

ORGON.   This is the crowning blow, you wretch;
and since
It means my total ruin and defeat,
Your villainy is now at last complete.

TARTUFFE.   You needn't try to provoke me; it's
no use.
Those who serve Heaven must expect abuse.

CLEANTE.   You are indeed most patient, sweet,
and blameless.

DORINE.   How he exploits the name of Heaven!
It's shameless.   10

TARTUFFE.   Your taunts and mockeries are all for
naught;
To do my duty is my only thought.

MARIANE.   Your love of duty is most meritorious,
And what you've done is little short of glorious.

TARTUFFE.   All deeds are glorious, Madam, which
obey
The sovereign prince who sent me here today.

ORGON.   I rescued you when you were destitute;
Have you forgotten that, you thankless brute?

TARTUFFE.   No, no, I well remember everything;
But my first duty is to serve my King.   20
That obligation is so paramount
That other claims, beside it, do not count;
And for it I would sacrifice my wife,
My family, my friend, or my own life.

ELMIRE.   Hypocrite!

DORINE.   All that we most revere, he uses
To cloak his plots and camouflage his ruses.

CLEANTE.   If it is true that you are animated
By pure and loyal zeal, as you have stated,
Why was this zeal not roused until you'd sought
To make Orgon a cuckold, and been caught?   30
Why weren't you moved to give your evidence
Until your outraged host had driven you hence?
I shan't say that the gift of all his treasure
Ought to have damped your zeal in any measure;
But if he is a traitor, as you declare,
How could you condescend to be his heir?

TARTUFFE (To the Officer).   Sir, spare me all this
clamor; it's growing shrill.
Please carry out your orders, if you will.

OFFICER.   Yes, I've delayed too long, Sir. Thank
you kindly.
You're just the proper person to remind me.   40
Come, you are off to join the other boarders
In the King's prison, according to his orders.

TARTUFFE.   Who? I, Sir?

OFFICER.   Yes.

TARTUFFE.   To prison? This can't be true!

OFFICER.   I owe an explanation, but not to you.
(*To Orgon*) Sir, all is well; rest easy, and be grateful.
We serve a Prince to whom all sham is hateful,
A Prince who sees into our inmost hearts,
And can't be fooled by any trickster's arts.
His royal soul, though generous and human,
Views all things with discernment and acumen;   50
His sovereign reason is not lightly swayed,
And all his judgments are discreetly weighed.
He honors righteous men of every kind,
And yet his zeal for virtue is not blind,
Nor does his love of piety numb his wits
And make him tolerant of hypocrites.
'Twas hardly likely that this man could cozen
A King who's foiled such liars by the dozen.
With one keen glance, the King perceived the whole
Perverseness and corruption of his soul,   60
And thus high Heaven's justice was displayed:
Betraying you, the rogue stood self-betrayed.
The King soon recognized Tartuffe as one
Notorious by another name, who'd done
So many vicious crimes that one could fill
Ten volumes with them, and be writing still.
But to be brief: our sovereign was appalled
By this man's treachery toward you, which he called
The last, worst villainy of a vile career,
And bade me follow the impostor here   70
To see how gross his impudence could be,
And force him to restore your property.
Your private papers, by the King's command,
I hereby seize and give into your hand.
The King, by royal order, invalidates
The deed which gave this rascal your estates,
And pardons, furthermore, your grave offense
In harboring an exile's documents.
By these decrees, our Prince rewards you for
Your loyal deeds in the late civil war,   80
And shows how heartfelt is his satisfaction
In recompensing any worthy action,
How much he prizes merit, and how he makes
More of men's virtues than of their mistakes.

DORINE.   Heaven be praised!

MADAME PERNELLE.   I breathe again, at last.

ELMIRE.   We're safe.

MARIANE.   I can't believe the danger's past.

ORGON (*To Tartuffe*). Well, traitor, now you
    see . . .
    CLEANTE.   Ah, Brother, please.
Let's not descend to such indignities.
Leave the poor wretch to his unhappy fate,
And don't say anything to aggravate   90
His present woes; but rather hope that he
Will soon embrace an honest piety,
And mend his ways, and by a true repentance
Move our just King to moderate his sentence.
Meanwhile, go kneel before your sovereign's throne
And thank him for the mercies he has shown.
    ORGON.   Well said: let's go at once and, gladly
        kneeling,
Express the gratitude which all are feeling.
Then, when that first great duty has been done,
We'll turn with pleasure to a second one,   100
And give Valère, whose love has proven so true,
The wedded happiness which is his due.

Henry Vaughan   (1622–1695)

ENGLISH POET and MYSTIC

The Retreate

Happy those early dayes, when I
Shin'd in my Angell-infancy!
Before I understood this place
Appointed for my second race,
Or taught my soul to fancy ought   ought: anything
But a white, celestiall thought;
When yet I had not walkt above
A mile or two from my first Love,
And looking back, at that short space,
Could see a glimpse of his bright face;   10
When on some *gilded Cloud* or *Flowre*
My gazing soul would dwell an houre,
And in those weaker glories spy
Some shadows of eternity;

"The Retreate" by Henry Vaughan. From *The Works of
Henry Vaughan*, edited by Leonard Cyril Martin. Reprinted by permission of the Clarendon Press, Oxford.

Before I taught my tongue to wound
My conscience with a sinfull sound,
Or had the black art to dispence
A sev'rall sinne to ev'ry sense,   sev'rall: separate
But felt through all this fleshly dresse
Bright *shootes* of everlastingnesse.   20
    O how I long to travell back,
And tread again that ancient track!
That I might once more reach that plaine,
Where first I left my glorious traine;
From whence th' inlightened spirit sees
That shady City of Palme trees.   City: Jericho
But ah! my soul with too much stay
Is drunk, and staggers in the way!
Some men a forward motion love,
But I by backward steps would move;   30
And, when this dust falls to the urn,
In that state I came, return.

Edward Taylor (1645?–1729)

AMERICAN CLERGYMAN, POET, and PHYSICIAN

Huswifery

Make me, O Lord, thy Spin[n]ing Wheele compleat;
    Thy Holy Worde my Distaff make for mee.
Make mine Affections thy Swift Flyers neate,
    And make my Soule thy holy Spoole to bee.
My Conversation make to be thy Reele,
    And reele the yarn thereon spun of thy Wheele.

Make me thy Loome then, knit therein this Twine:
    And make thy Holy Spirit, Lord, winde quills: quills: bobbins
Then weave the Web thyselfe. The yarn is fine.
    Thine Ordinances make my Fulling Mills.   10
    Then dy the same in Heavenly Colours Choice,
    All pinkt with Varnish't Flowers of Paradise.

"Huswifery" by Edward Taylor. From *The Poetical Works of Edward Taylor*, edited by Thomas H. Johnson. Reprinted by permission of Princeton University Press. Copyright Rockland Editions, 1939; Princeton University Press, 1943.

Then cloath therewith mine Understanding, Will,
  Affections, Judgment, Conscience, Memory;
My Words and Actions, that their shine may fill
  My wayes with glory and thee glorify.
  Then mine apparell shall display before yee
  That I am Cloathd in Holy robes for glory.

Jonathan Swift (1667–1745)

ENGLISH SATIRIST and CLERGYMAN (IRISH-BORN)

An Argument against Abolishing Christianity

I am very sensible what a Weakness and Presumption it is, to reason against the general Humour and Disposition of the World. I remember it was with great Justice, and a due Regard to the Freedom both of the Publick and the Press, forbidden upon severe Penalties to write or discourse, or lay Wagers against the *Union*,[1] even before it was confirmed by Parliament: Because that was looked upon as a Design to oppose the Current of the People; which besides the Folly of it, is a manifest Breach of the Fundamental Law, that makes this Majority of Opinion the Voice of God. In like Manner, and for the very same Reasons, it may perhaps be neither safe nor prudent to argue against the Abolishing of Christianity, at a Juncture when all Parties appear so unanimously determined upon the Point; as we cannot but allow from their Actions, their Discourses, and their Writings. However, I know not how, whether from the Affectation of Singularity, or the Perverseness of human Nature; but so it unhappily falls out, that I cannot be entirely of this Opinion. Nay, although I were sure an Order were issued out for my immediate Prosecution by the Attorney-General; I should still confess, that in the present Posture of our Affairs at home or abroad, I do not yet see the absolute Necessity of extirpating the Christian Religion from among us.

This perhaps may appear too great a Paradox, even for our wise and paradoxical Age to endure: Therefore I shall handle it with all Tenderness, and with the utmost Deference to that great and profound Majority, which is of another Sentiment.

And yet the Curious may please to observe, how much the Genius of a

---

[1] the union of Scotland and England completed the previous year (1707).

"An Argument against Abolishing Christianity" by Jonathan Swift. Swift's title, "An Argument To prove, That the Abolishing of Christianity in England, May, as Things now Stand, be attended with some Inconveniencies, and perhaps, not produce those many good Effects proposed thereby." From the *Bickerstaff Papers*, edited by Herbert Davis. Reprinted by permission of Basil Blackwell, Publisher, Oxford.

Nation is liable to alter in half an Age: I have heard it affirmed for certain by some very old People, that the contrary Opinion was even in their Memories as much in Vogue as the other is now; and, that a Project for the Abolishing of Christianity would then have appeared as singular, and been thought as absurd, as it would be at this Time to write or discourse in its Defence.

Therefore I freely own, that all Appearances are against me. The System of the Gospel, after the Fate of other Systems is generally antiquated and exploded; and the Mass or Body of the common People, among whom it seems to have had its latest Credit, are now grown as much ashamed of it as their Betters: Opinions, like Fashions always descending from those of Quality to the middle Sort, and thence to the Vulgar, where at length they are dropt and vanish.

But here I would not be mistaken; and must therefore be so bold as to borrow a Distinction from the Writers on the other Side, when they make a Difference between nominal and real *Trinitarians*. I hope, no Reader imagines me so weak to stand up in the Defence of *real* Christianity; such as used in primitive Times (if we may believe the Authors of those Ages) to have an Influence upon Mens Belief and Actions: To offer at the Restoring of that, would indeed be a wild Project; it would be to dig up Foundations; to destroy at one Blow *all* the Wit, and *half* the Learning of the Kingdom; to break the entire Frame and Constitution of Things; to ruin Trade, extinguish Arts and Sciences with the Professors of them; in short, to turn our Courts, Exchanges and Shops into Desarts: And would be full as absurd as the Proposal of *Horace*,[2] where he advises the *Romans*, all in a Body, to leave their City, and seek a new Seat in some remote Part of the World, by Way of Cure for the Corruption of their Manners.

Therefore, I think this Caution was in it self altogether unnecessary, (which I have inserted only to prevent all Possibility of cavilling) since every candid Reader will easily understand my Discourse to be intended only in Defence of *nominal* Christianity; the other having been for some Time wholly laid aside by general Consent, as utterly inconsistent with our present Schemes of Wealth and Power.

But why we should therefore cast off the Name and Title of Christians, although the general Opinion and Resolution be so violent for it; I confess I cannot (with Submission) apprehend the Consequence necessary. However, since the Undertakers propose such wonderful Advantages to the Nation by this Project; and advance many plausible Objections against the System of Christianity; I shall briefly consider the Strength of both; fairly allow them their greatest Weight, and offer such Answers as I think most reasonable. After which I will beg leave to shew what Inconveniencies may possibly happen by such an Innovation, in the present Posture of our Affairs.

First, One great Advantage proposed by the Abolishing of Christianity is, That it would very much enlarge and establish Liberty of Conscience, that

[2] Roman poet (65–8 B.C.) who extolled the joys of simple, rural life.

great Bulwark of our Nation, and of the *Protestant* Religion, which is still too much limited by *Priest-Craft*, notwithstanding all the good Intentions of the Legislature; as we have lately found by a severe Instance. For it is confidently reported, that two young Gentlemen of great Hopes, bright Wit, and profound Judgment, who upon a thorough Examination of Causes and Effects, and by the meer Force of natural Abilities, without the least Tincture of Learning; having made a Discovery, that there was no God, and generously communicating their Thoughts for the Good of the Publick; were some Time ago, by an unparalleled Severity, and upon I know not what *obsolete* Law, broke *only* for *Blasphemy*. And as it hath been wisely observed; if Persecution once begins, no Man alive knows how far it may reach, or where it will end.

In Answer to all which, with Deference to wiser Judgments; I think this rather shews the Necessity of a *nominal* Religion among us. Great Wits love to be free with the highest Objects; and if they cannot be allowed a *God* to revile or renounce; they will *speak Evil of Dignities*, abuse the Government, and reflect upon the Ministry; which I am sure, few will deny to be of much more pernicious Consequence; according to the Saying of *Tiberius*; *Deorum offensa Diis curæ*.[3] As to the particular Fact related, I think it is not fair to argue from one Instance; perhaps another cannot be produced; yet (to the Comfort of all those, who may be apprehensive of Persecution) Blasphemy we know is freely spoke a Million of Times in every Coffee-House and Tavern, or where-ever else *good Company* meet. It must be allowed indeed, that to break an *English Free-born* Officer only for Blasphemy, was, to speak the gentlest of such an Action, a very high Strain of absolute Power. Little can be said in Excuse for the General; perhaps he was afraid it might give Offence to the Allies, among whom, for ought I know, it may be the Custom of the Country to believe a God. But if he argued, as some have done, upon a mistaken Principle, that an Officer who is guilty of speaking Blasphemy, may, some Time or other, proceed so far as to raise a Mutiny; the Consequence is, by no Means, to be admitted: For, surely the Commander of an *English* Army is like to be but ill obeyed, whose Soldiers fear and reverence him as little as they do a Deity.

It is further objected against the Gospel System, that it obliges Men to the Belief of Things too difficult for Free-Thinkers,[4] and such who have shaken off the Prejudices that usually cling to a confined Education. To which I answer, that Men should be cautious how they raise Objections, which reflect upon the Wisdom of the Nation. Is not every Body freely allowed to believe whatever he pleaseth; and to publish his Belief to the World whenever he thinks fit; especially if it serve to strengthen the Party which is in the Right? Would any indifferent Foreigner, who should read the Trumpery lately written by *Asgill*, *Tindall*, *Toland*, *Coward*,[5] and Forty more, imagine the Gospel to be our Rule of Faith, and confirmed by Parliaments? Does any

---

3 "The insults to the gods must be their own worry" (correctly, from Tacitus, *Annals* I, 63).
4 Deists.
5 Deists whose criticism provoked State censure.

Man either believe, or say he believes, or desire to have it thought that he says he believes one Syllable of the Matter? And is any Man worse received upon that Score; or does he find his Want of *Nominal* Faith a Disadvantage to him, in the Pursuit of any Civil, or Military Employment? What if there be an old dormant Statute or two against him? Are they not now obsolete, to a Degree, that *Empson* and *Dudley*[6] themselves, if they were now alive, would find it impossible to put them in Execution?

It is likewise urged, that there are, by Computation, in this Kingdom, above ten Thousand Parsons; whose Revenues added to those of my Lords the Bishops, would suffice to maintain, at least, two Hundred young Gentlemen of Wit and Pleasure, and Free-thinking; Enemies to Priest-craft, narrow Principles, Pedantry, and Prejudices; who might be an Ornament to the Court and Town: And then again, so great a Number of able (bodied) Divines might be a Recruit to our Fleet and Armies. This, indeed, appears to be a Consideration of some Weight: But then, on the other Side, several Things deserve to be considered likewise: As, First, Whether it may not be thought necessary, that in certain Tracts of Country, like what we call Parishes, there should be *one* Man at least, of Abilities to read and write. Then, it seems a wrong Computation, that the Revenues of the Church throughout this Island, would be large enough to maintain two Hundred young Gentlemen, or even Half that Number, after the present refined Way of Living; that is, to allow each of them such a Rent, as, in the modern Form of Speech, would make them *easy.* But still, there is in this Project a greater Mischief behind; and we ought to beware of the Woman's Folly, who killed the Hen, that every Morning laid her a Golden Egg. For, pray, what would become of the Race of Men in the next Age, if we had nothing to trust to, besides the scrophulous consumptive Productions furnished by our Men of Wit and Pleasure; when having squandered away their Vigour, Health, and Estates; they are forced, by some disagreeable Marriage, to piece up their broken Fortunes, and entail Rottenness and Politeness on their Posterity? Now, here are ten Thousand Persons reduced by the wise Regulations of *Henry* the Eighth,[7] to the Necessity of a low Diet, and moderate Exercise, who are the only great Restorers of our Breed; without which, the Nation would, in an Age or two, become but one great Hospital.

Another Advantage proposed by the abolishing of Christianity, is, the clear Gain of one Day in Seven, which is now entirely lost, and consequently the Kingdom one Seventh less considerable in Trade, Business, and Pleasure; beside the Loss to the Publick of so many stately Structures now in the Hands of the Clergy; which might be converted into Theatres, Exchanges, Market-houses, common Dormitories, and other publick Edifices.

I hope I shall be forgiven a hard Word, if I call this a perfect Cavil. I readily own there hath been an old Custom, Time out of Mind, for People to assemble in the Churches every *Sunday,* and that Shops are still frequently

[6] Officers of Henry VII who were executed by Henry VIII for illegal collection of taxes.
[7] Henry seized monastic lands for state taxes and rights.

shut; in order, as it is conceived, to preserve the Memory of that antient Practice; but how this can prove a Hindrance to Business, or Pleasure, is hard to imagine. What if the Men of Pleasure are forced, one Day in the Week, to game at home, instead of the *Chocolate-House?* Are not the *Taverns* and *Coffee-Houses* open? Can there be a more convenient Season for taking a Dose of Physick? Are fewer Claps got upon *Sundays* than other Days? Is not that the chief Day for Traders to sum up the Accounts of the Week; and for Lawyers to prepare their Briefs? But I would fain know how it can be pretended, that the Churches are misapplied. Where are more Appointments and Rendezvouzes of Gallantry? Where more Care to appear in the foremost Box with greater Advantage of Dress? Where more Meetings[8] for Business? Where more Bargains driven of all Sorts? And where so many Conveniences, or Incitements to sleep?

There is one Advantage, greater than any of the foregoing, proposed by the abolishing of Christianity; that it will utterly extinguish Parties among us, by removing those factious Distinctions of High and Low Church, of *Whig* and *Tory, Presbyterian* and *Church-of-England;* which are now so many grievous Clogs upon publick Proceedings, and dispose Men to prefer the gratifying themselves, or depressing their Adversaries, before the most important Interest of the State.

I confess, if it were certain that so great an Advantage would redound to the Nation by this Expedient, I would submit and be silent: But, will any Man say, that if the Words *Whoring, Drinking, Cheating, Lying, Stealing,* were, by Act of Parliament, ejected out of the *English* Tongue and Dictionaries; we should all awake next Morning chaste and temperate, honest and just, and Lovers of Truth. Is this a fair Consequence? Or if the Physicians would forbid us to pronounce the Words *Pox, Gout, Rheumatism,* and *Stone;* would that Expedient serve like so many *Talismans* to destroy the Diseases themselves? Are Party and Faction rooted in Mens Hearts no deeper than Phrases borrowed from Religion; or founded upon no firmer Principles? And is our Language so poor, that we cannot find other Terms to express them? Are Envy, Pride, Avarice and Ambition, such ill Nomenclators, that they cannot furnish Appellations for their Owners? Will not *Heydukes* and *Mamalukes, Mandarins,* and *Potshaws,*[9] or any other Words formed at Pleasure, serve to distinguish those who are in the *Ministry* from others, who *would be in* it *if they could?* What, for Instance, is easier than to vary the Form of Speech; and instead of the Word *Church,* make it a Question in Politicks, Whether the *Monument* be in Danger? Because Religion was nearest at Hand to furnish a few convenient Phrases; is our Invention so barren, we can find no others? Suppose, for Argument Sake, that the *Tories* favoured *Margarita,* the *Whigs* Mrs. *Tofts,* and the *Trimmers*[10] *Valentini;*[11] would not *Margaritians, Toftians,* and *Valentinians,* be very tolerable Marks

---

8 Churchyards — even church aisles — were frequently used for business on Sundays.
9 various foreign titles or epithets.
10 those who incline both ways politically, as interest dictates.
11 well-known opera singers.

of Distinction? The *Prasini* and *Veneti*,[12] two most virulent Factions in *Italy*, began (if I remember right) by a Distinction of Colours in Ribbonds; which we might do, with as good a Grace, about the Dignity of the *Blue* and the *Green*; and would serve as properly to divide the Court, the Parliament, and the Kingdom between them, as any Terms of Art whatsoever, borrowed from Religion. Therefore, I think there is little Force in this Objection against *Christianity*; or Prospect of so great an Advantage as is proposed in the Abolishing of it.

It is again objected, as a very absurd, ridiculous Custom, that a Set of Men should be suffered, much less employed, and hired to bawl one Day in Seven, against the Lawfulness of those Methods most in Use towards the Pursuit of Greatness, Riches, and Pleasure; which are the constant Practice of all Men alive on the other Six. But this Objection is, I think, a little unworthy so refined an Age as ours. Let us argue this Matter calmly. I appeal to the Breast of any polite Free-Thinker, whether in the Pursuit of gratifying a predominant Passion, he hath not always felt a wonderful Incitement, by reflecting it was a Thing forbidden: And therefore we see, in order to cultivate this Taste, the Wisdom of the Nation hath taken special Care, that the Ladies should be furnished with prohibited Silks, and the Men with prohibited Wine: And, indeed, it were to be wished, that some other Prohibitions were promoted, in order to improve the Pleasures of the Town; which, for want of such Expedients, begin already, as I am told, to flag and grow languid; giving way daily to cruel Inroads from the Spleen.

It is likewise proposed, as a great Advantage to the Publick, that if we once discard the System of the Gospel, all Religion will, of Course, be banished for ever; and consequently along with it, those grievous Prejudices of Education; which, under the Names of Virtue, Conscience, Honour, Justice, and the like, are so apt to disturb the Peace of human Minds; and the Notions whereof are so hard to be eradicated by right Reason, or Free-thinking, sometimes during the whole Course of our Lives.

Here, first, I observe how difficult it is to get rid of a Phrase, which the World is once grown fond of, although the Occasion that first produced it, be entirely taken away. For several Years past, if a Man had but an ill-favoured Nose, the Deep-Thinkers of the Age would, some way or other, contrive to impute the Cause to the Prejudice of his Education. From this Fountain are said to be derived all our foolish Notions of Justice, Piety, Love of our Country; all our Opinions of God, or a future State, Heaven, Hell, and the like: And there might formerly, perhaps, have been some Pretence for this Charge. But so effectual Care hath been since taken, to remove those Prejudices by an entire Change in the Methods of Education; that (with Honour I mention it to our polite Innovators) the young Gentlemen, who are now on the Scene, seem to have not the least Tincture left of those Infusions, or String of those Weeds; and, by Consequence, the Reason for abolishing *Nominal* Christianity upon that Pretext, is wholly ceased.

---

[12] major parties in the Roman civil war against Justinian (532 A.D.).

For the rest, it may perhaps admit a Controversy, whether the Banishing all Notions of Religion whatsoever, would be convenient for the Vulgar. Not that I am in the least of Opinion with those, who hold Religion to have been the Invention of Politicians, to keep the lower Part of the World in Awe, by the Fear of invisible Powers; unless Mankind were then very different from what it is now: For I look upon the Mass, or Body of our People here in *England*, to be as Free-Thinkers, that is to say, as stanch Unbelievers, as any of the highest Rank. But I conceive some scattered Nòtions about a superior Power to be of singular Use for the common People, as furnishing excellent Materials to keep Children quiet, when they grow peevish; and providing Topicks of Amusement in a tedious Winter Night.

Lastly, It is proposed as a singular Advantage, that the Abolishing of Christianity, will very much contribute to the uniting of *Protestants*, by enlarging the Terms of Communion, so as to take in all Sorts of *Dissenters*; who are now shut out of the Pale upon Account of a few Ceremonies, which all Sides confess to be Things indifferent: That this alone will effectually answer the great Ends of a Scheme for Comprehension, by opening a large noble Gate, at which all Bodies may enter; whereas the chaffering with *Dissenters*, and dodging about this or the other Ceremony, is but like opening a few Wickets, and leaving them at jar, by which no more than one can get in at a Time, and that not without stooping and sideling, and squeezing his Body.

To all this I answer, That there is one darling Inclination of Mankind, which usually affects to be a Retainer to Religion, although she be neither its Parent, its Godmother, or its Friend; I mean the Spirit of Opposition, that lived long before Christianity, and can easily subsist without it. Let us, for Instance, examine wherein the Opposition of Sectaries among us consists; we shall find Christianity to have no Share in it at all. Does the Gospel anywhere prescribe a starched squeezed Countenance, a stiff formal Gait, a Singularity of Manners and Habit, or any affected Modes of Speech, different from the reasonable Part of Mankind? Yet, if Christianity did not lend its Name, to stand in the Gap, and to employ or divert these Humours, they must of Necessity be spent in Contraventions to the Laws of the Land, and Disturbance of the publick Peace. There is a Portion of Enthusiasm assigned to every Nation, which if it hath not proper Objects to work on, will burst out, and set all in a Flame. If the Quiet of a State can be bought by only flinging Men a few Ceremonies to devour, it is a Purchase no wise Man would refuse. Let the Mastiffs amuse themselves about a Sheep-skin stuffed with Hay, provided it will keep them from worrying the Flock. The Institution of Convents abroad, seems in one Point a Strain of great Wisdom; there being few Irregularities in human Passions, that may not have recourse to vent themselves in some of those Orders; which are so many Retreats for the Speculative, the Melancholy, the Proud, the Silent, the Politick and the Morose, to spend themselves, and evaporate the noxious Particles; for each of whom, we in this Island are forced to provide a several Sect of Religion, to keep them quiet. And whenever Christianity shall be abolished, the Legislature must find some other Expedient to employ and entertain them. For what imports it, how large a Gate you open, if there will be always left a Number, who place a Pride and a Merit in refusing to enter?

Having thus considered the most important Objections against Christianity, and the chief Advantages proposed by the Abolishing thereof; I shall now with equal Deference and Submission to wiser Judgments as before, proceed to mention a few Inconveniences that may happen, if the Gospel should be re-pealed; which perhaps the Projectors may not have sufficiently considered.

And first, I am very sensible how much the Gentlemen of Wit and Pleasure are apt to murmur, and be choqued[13] at the sight of so many daggled-tail[14] Parsons, who happen to fall in their Way, and offend their Eyes: But at the same Time these wise Reformers do not consider what an Advantage and Felicity it is, for great Wits to be always provided with Objects of Scorn and Contempt, in order to exercise and improve their Talents, and divert their Spleen from falling on each other, or on themselves; especially when all this may be done without the least imaginable *Danger to their Persons.*

And to urge another Argument of a parallel Nature: If Christianity were once abolished, how would the Free-Thinkers, the strong Reasoners, and the Men of profound Learning be able to find another Subject so calculated in all Points whereon to display their Abilities. What wonderful Productions of Wit should we be deprived of, from those whose Genius, by continual Prac-tice hath been wholly turned upon Raillery and Invectives against Religion; and would therefore never be able to shine or distinguish themselves upon any other Subject. We are daily complaining of the great Decline of Wit among us; and would we take away the greatest, perhaps the only Topick we have left? Who would ever have suspected *Asgill* for a Wit, or *Toland* for a Philoso-pher, if the inexhaustible Stock of Christianity had not been at hand to provide them with Materials? What other Subject through all Art or Nature could have produced *Tindal* for a profound Author, or furnished him with Readers? It is the wise Choice of the Subject that alone adorns and distin-guishes the Writer. For had an hundred such Pens as these been employed on the Side of Religion, they would have immediately sunk into Silence and Oblivion.

Nor do I think it wholly groundless, or my Fears altogether imaginary; that the Abolishing of Christianity may perhaps bring the Church in Danger; or at least put the Senate to the Trouble of another Securing Vote. I desire, I may not be mistaken; I am far from presuming to affirm or think, that the Church is in Danger at present, or as Things now stand; but we know not how soon it may be so, when the Christian Religion is repealed. As plausible as this Project seems, there may a dangerous Design lurk under it. Nothing can be more notorious, than that the *Atheists, Deists, Socinians, Anti-Trini-tarians,* and other Subdivisions of Free-Thinkers, are Persons of little Zeal for the present Ecclesiastical Establishment: Their declared Opinion is for repeal-

---

[13] choked (deliberately affected spelling).
[14] long-robed (and hence muddy-robed). The term was slang for prostitutes.

ing the Sacramental Test;[15] they are very indifferent with regard to Ceremonies; nor do they hold the *Jus Divinum*[16] of Episcopacy. Therefore this
may be intended as one politick Step towards altering the Constitution of the
Church Established, and setting up *Presbytery* in the stead; which I leave to
be further considered by those at the Helm.

In the last Place, I think nothing can be more plain, than that by this
Expedient, we shall run into the Evil we chiefly pretend to avoid; and that
the Abolishment of the Christian Religion, will be the readiest Course we can
take to introduce Popery. And I am the more inclined to this Opinion,
because we know it hath been the constant Practice of the *Jesuits* to send over
Emissaries, with Instructions to personate themselves Members of the several
prevailing Sects amongst us. So it is recorded, that they have at sundry Times
appeared in the Guise of *Presbyterians, Anabaptists, Independents,* and
Quakers, according as any of these were most in Credit: So, since the Fashion
hath been taken up of exploding Religion, the *Popish* Missionaries have not
been wanting to mix with the Free-Thinkers; among whom, *Toland,* the great
Oracle of the *Anti-Christians,* is an *Irish* Priest, the Son of an *Irish* Priest; and
the most learned and ingenious Author of a Book, called the *Rights of the
Christian Church,* was, in a proper Juncture, reconciled to the *Romish* Faith;
whose true Son, as appears by an Hundred Passages in his Treatise, he still
continues. Perhaps I could add some others to the Number; but the Fact
is beyond Dispute; and the Reasoning they proceed by, is right: For, supposing
Christianity to be extinguished, the People will never be at Ease, till they
find out some other Method of Worship; which will as infallibly produce
Superstition, as this will end in *Popery.*

And therefore, if, notwithstanding all I have said, it shall still be thought
necessary to have a Bill brought in for repealing Christianity; I would humbly
offer an Amendment, that instead of the Word *Christianity,* may be put
Religion in general; which I conceive, will much better answer all the good
Ends proposed by the Projectors of it. For, as long as we leave in Being a
God, and his Providence, with all the necessary Consequences, which curious
and inquisitive Men will be apt to draw from such Premises; we do not strike
at the Root of the Evil, although we should ever so effectually annihilate
the present Scheme of the Gospel. For, of what Use is Freedom of Thought,
if it will not produce Freedom of Action; which is the sole End, how remote
soever, in Appearance, of all Objections against Christianity? And therefore,
the Free-Thinkers consider it as a Sort of Edifice, wherein all the Parts have
such a mutual Dependance on each other, that if you happen to pull out one
single Nail, the whole Fabrick must fall to the Ground. This was happily
expressed by him, who had heard of a Text brought for Proof of the Trinity,
which in an antient Manuscript was differently read; he thereupon immediately took the Hint, and by a sudden Deduction of a long *Sorites,* most

---

[15] from the Test Act of 1667, which required taking of the Holy Sacrament in the Church
of England as a prerequisite to holding important governmental positions.
[16] divine law, by which Anglican bishops claimed authority.

logically concluded; Why, if it be as you say, I may safely whore and drink on, and defy the Parson. From which, and many the like Instances easy to be produced, I think nothing can be more manifest, than that the Quarrel is not against any particular Points of hard Digestion in the Christian System; but against Religion in general; which, by laying Restraints on human Nature, is supposed the great Enemy to the Freedom of Thought and Action.

Upon the whole; if it shall still be thought for the Benefit of Church and State, that Christianity be abolished; I conceive, however, it may be more convenient to defer the Execution to a Time of Peace; and not venture in this Conjuncture to disoblige our Allies; who, as it falls out, are all Christians; and many of them, by the Prejudices of their Education, so bigotted, as to place a Sort of Pride in the Appellation. If, upon being rejected by them, we are to trust to an Alliance with the *Turk*, we shall find our selves much deceived: For, as he is too remote, and generally engaged in War with the *Persian* Emperor; so his People would be more scandalized at our Infidelity, than our Christian Neighbours. Because, the *Turks* are not only strict Observers of religious Worship; but, what is worse, believe a God; which is more than is required of us, even while we preserve the Name of Christians.

To conclude: Whatever some may think of the great Advantages to Trade, by this favourite Scheme; I do very much apprehend, that in six Months Time, after the Act is past for the Extirpation of the Gospel, the Bank and *East-India* Stock may fall, at least, One *per Cent*. And, since that is Fifty Times more than ever the Wisdom of our Age thought fit to venture for the *Preservation* of Christianity, there is no Reason we should be at so great a Loss, meerly for the Sake of *destroying* it.

Jonathan Edwards (1703–1758)

AMERICAN CLERGYMAN and THEOLOGIAN

A *Spiritual Autobiography*

I had a variety of concerns and exercises about my soul from my childhood; but had two more remarkable seasons of awakening, before I met with that change by which I was brought to those new dispositions, and that new sense of things, that I have since had. The first time was when I was a boy, some years before I went to college, at a time of remarkable awakening in my

Title supplied by editors. From "Personal Narrative" in *Jonathan Edwards*, edited by Clarence H. Faust and Thomas H. Johnson. Reprinted by permission of Hill & Wang, Inc.

father's congregation,[1] I was then very much affected for many months, and concerned about the things of religion, and my soul's salvation; and was abundant in duties. I used to pray five times a day in secret, and to spend much time in religious talk with other boys; and used to meet with them to pray together. I experienced I know not what kind of delight in religion. My mind was much engaged in it, and had much selfrighteous pleasure; and it was my delight to abound in religious duties. I with some of my schoolmates joined together, and built a booth in a swamp, in a very retired spot, for a place of prayer. And besides, I had particular secret places of my own in the woods, where I used to retire by myself; and was from time to time much affected. My affections seemed to be lively and easily moved, and I seemed to be in my element when engaged in religious duties. And I am ready to think, many are deceived with such affections, and such a kind of delight as I then had in religion, and mistake it for grace.

But in process of time, my convictions and affections wore off; and I entirely lost all those affections and delights and left off secret prayer, at least as to any constant performance of it; and returned like a dog to his vomit, and went on in the ways of sin. Indeed I was at times very uneasy, especially towards the latter part of my time at college; when it pleased God, to seize me with a pleurisy; in which he brought me nigh to the grave, and shook me over the pit of hell. And yet, it was not long after my recovery, before I fell again into my old ways of sin. But God would not suffer me to go on with any quietness; I had great and violent inward struggles, till, after many conflicts with wicked inclinations, repeated resolutions, and bonds that I laid myself under by a kind of vows to God, I was brought wholly to break off all former wicked ways, and all ways of known outward sin; and to apply myself to seek salvation, and practise many religious duties; but without that kind of affection and delight which I had formerly experienced. My concern now wrought more by inward struggles and conflicts, and selfreflections. I made seeking my salvation the main business of my life. But yet, it seems to me, I sought after a miserable manner; which has made me sometimes since to question, whether ever it issued in that which was saving; being ready to doubt, whether such miserable seeking ever succeeded. I was indeed brought to seek salvation in a manner that I never was before; I felt a spirit to part with all things in the world, for an interest in Christ. My concern continued and prevailed, with many exercising thoughts and inward struggles; but yet it never seemed to be proper to express that concern by the name of terror.

From my childhood up, my mind had been full of objections against the doctrine of God's sovereignty, in choosing whom he would to eternal life, and rejecting whom he pleased;[2] leaving them eternally to perish, and be everlastingly tormented in hell. It used to appear like a horrible doctrine to me. But I remember the time very well, when I seemed to be convinced, and fully satisfied, as to this sovereignty of God, and his justice in thus eternally dis-

---

[1] Edwards' father and grandfather were both ministers.
[2] The Puritan belief in predestination (from Calvin).

posing of men, according to his sovereign pleasure. But never could give an account, how, or by what means, I was thus convinced, not in the least imagining at the time, nor a long time after, that there was any extraordinary influence of God's Spirit in it; but only that now I saw further, and my reason apprehended the justice and reasonableness of it. However, my mind rested in it; and it put an end to all those cavils and objections. And there has been a wonderful alteration in my mind, in respect to the doctrine of God's sovereignty, from that day to this; so that I scarce ever have found so much as the rising of an objection against it, in the most absolute sense, in God's shewing mercy to whom he will shew mercy, and hardening whom he will. God's absolute sovereignty and justice, with respect to salvation and damnation, is what my mind seems to rest assured of, as much as of any thing that I see with my eyes; at least it is so at times. But I have often, since that first conviction, had quite another kind of sense of God's sovereignty than I had then. I have often since had not only a conviction, but a delightful conviction. The doctrine has very often appeared exceeding pleasant, bright, and sweet. Absolute sovereignty is what I love to ascribe to God. But my first conviction was not so.

The first instance that I remember of that sort of inward, sweet delight in God and divine things that I have lived much in since, was on reading those words, I Tim. i. 17. *Now unto the King eternal, immortal, invisible, the only wise God, be honor and glory for ever and ever, Amen.* As I read the words, there came into my soul, and was as it were diffused through it, a sense of the glory of the Divine Being; a new sense, quite different from any thing I ever experienced before. Never any words of scripture seemed to me as these words did. I thought with myself, how excellent a Being that was, and how happy I should be, if I might enjoy that God, and be rapt up to him in heaven, and be as it were swallowed up in him for ever! I kept saying, and as it were singing over these words of scripture to myself; and went to pray to God that I might enjoy him, and prayed in a manner quite different from what I used to do; with a new sort of affection. But it never came into my thought, that there was any thing spiritual, or of a saving nature in this.

From about that time, I began to have a new kind of apprehensions and ideas of Christ, and the work of redemption, and the glorious way of salvation by him. An inward, sweet sense of these things, at times, came into my heart; and my soul was led away in pleasant views and contemplations of them. And my mind was greatly engaged to spend my time in reading and meditating on Christ, on the beauty and excellency of his person, and the lovely way of salvation by free grace in him. I found no books so delightful to me, as those that treated of these subjects. Those words Cant. ii. 1, used to be abundantly with me, *I am the Rose of Sharon, and the Lilly of the valleys.* The words seemed to me, sweetly to represent the loveliness and beauty of Jesus Christ. The whole book of Canticles used to be pleasant to me, and I used to be much in reading it, about that time; and found, from time to time, an inward sweetness, that would carry me away, in my contemplations. This I know not how to express otherwise, than by a calm, sweet abstraction of soul from all the concerns of this world; and sometimes a kind of vision, or fixed ideas and imaginations, of being alone in the mountains, or some solitary wilderness, far from all mankind, sweetly conversing with Christ, and wrapt and swallowed up in God. The sense I had of divine things, would often of a sudden kindle up, as it were, a sweet burning in my heart; an ardor of soul, that I know not how to express.

Not long after I first began to experience these things, I gave an account to my father of some things that had passed in my mind. I was pretty much affected by the discourse we had together; and when the discourse was ended, I walked abroad alone, in a solitary place in my father's pasture, for contemplation. And as I was walking there, and looking up on the sky and clouds, there came into my mind so sweet a sense of the glorious *majesty* and *grace* of God, that I know not how to express. I seemed to see them both in a sweet conjunction; majesty and meekness joined together; it was a sweet, and gentle, and holy majesty; and also a majestic meekness; an awful sweetness; a high, and great, and holy gentleness.

After this my sense of divine things gradually increased, and became more and more lively, and had more of that inward sweetness. The appearance of every thing was altered; there seemed to be, as it were, a calm, sweet cast, or appearance of divine glory, in almost every thing. God's excellency, his wisdom, his purity and love, seemed to appear in every thing; in the sun, moon, and stars; in the clouds, and blue sky; in the grass, flowers, trees; in the water, and all nature; which used greatly to fix my mind. I often used to sit and view the moon for continuance; and in the day, spent much time in viewing the clouds and sky, to behold the sweet glory of God in these things; in the mean time, singing forth, with a low voice my contemplations of the Creator and Redeemer. And scarce any thing, among all the works of nature, was so sweet to me as thunder and lightning; formerly, nothing had been so terrible to me. Before, I used to be uncommonly terrified with thunder, and to be struck with terror when I saw a thunder storm rising; but now, on the contrary, it rejoiced me. I felt God, so to speak, at the first appearance of a thunder storm; and used to take the opportunity, at such times, to fix myself in order to view the clouds, and see the lightnings play, and hear the majestic and awful voice of God's thunder, which oftentimes was exceedingly entertaining, leading me to sweet contemplations of my great and glorious God. While thus engaged, it always seemed natural to me to sing, or chant for my meditations; or, to speak my thoughts in soliloquies with a singing voice.

I felt then great satisfaction, as to my good state; but that did not content me. I had vehement longings of soul after God and Christ, and after more holiness, wherewith my heart seemed to be full, and ready to break; which often brought to my mind the words of the Psalmist, Psal. cxix. 28. *My soul breaketh for the longing it hath.* I often felt a mourning and lamenting in my heart, that I had not turned to God sooner, that I might have had more time to grow in grace. My mind was greatly fixed on divine things; almost perpetually in the contemplation of them. I spent most of my time in thinking of divine things, year after year; often walking alone in the woods, and solitary places, for meditation, soliloquy, and prayer, and converse with God; and it was always my manner, at such times, to sing forth my contemplations. I was almost constantly in ejaculatory prayer, wherever I was. Prayer seemed to be natural to me, as the breath by which the inward burnings of my heart had vent. The delights which I now felt in the things of religion, were of an exceeding different kind from those before mentioned, that I had when a boy; and what I then had no more notion of, than one born blind has of pleasant and beautiful colors. They were of a more inward, pure, soul animating and refreshing nature. Those former delights never reached the heart; and did not arise from any sight of the divine excellency of the things of God; or any taste of the soul satisfying and life-giving good there is in them.

My sense of divine things seemed gradually to increase, until I went to preach at Newyork, which was about a year and a half after they began; and while I was there, I felt them, very sensibly, in a much higher degree than I had done before. My longings after God and holiness, were much increased. Pure and humble, holy and heavenly Christianity, appeared exceeding amiable to me. I felt a burning desire to be in every thing a complete Christian; and conformed to the blessed image of Christ; and that I might live, in all things, according to the pure, sweet and blessed rules of the gospel. I had an eager thirsting after progress in these things; which put me upon pursuing and pressing after them. It was my continual strife day and night, and constant inquiry, how I should *be* more holy, and *live* more holily, and more becoming a child of God, and a disciple of Christ. I now sought an increase of grace and holiness, and a holy life, with much more earnestness, than ever I sought grace before I had it. I used to be continually examining myself, and studying and contriving for likely ways and means, how I should live holily, with far greater diligence and earnestness, than ever I pursued any thing in my life; but yet with too great a dependence on my own strength; which afterwards proved a great damage to me. My experience had not then taught me, as it has done since, my extreme feebleness and impotence, every manner of way; and the bottomless depths of secret corruption and deceit there was in my heart. However, I went on with my eager pursuit after more holiness, and conformity to Christ.

The heaven I desired was a heaven of holiness; to be with God, and to spend my eternity in divine love, and holy communion with Christ. My mind was very much taken up with contemplations on heaven, and the enjoyments there; and living there in perfect holiness, humility and love: And it used at that time to appear a great part of the happiness of heaven, that there the saints could express their love to Christ. It appeared to me a great clog and burden, that what I felt within, I could not express as I desired. The inward ardor of my soul, seemed to be hindered and pent up, and could not freely flame out as it would. I used often to think, how in heaven this principle should freely and fully vent and express itself. Heaven appeared exceedingly delightful, as a world of love; and that all happiness consisted in living in pure, humble, heavenly, divine love.

I remember the thoughts I used then to have of holiness; and said sometimes to myself, "I do certainly know that I love holiness, such as the gospel prescribes." It appeared to me, that there was nothing in it but what was ravishingly lovely; the highest beauty and amiableness . . . a *divine* beauty; far purer than any thing here upon earth; and that every thing else was like mire and defilement, in comparison of it.

Holiness, as I then wrote down some of my contemplations on it, appeared to me to be of a sweet, pleasant, charming, serene, calm nature; which brought an inexpressible purity, brightness, peacefulness and ravishment to the soul. In other words, that it made the soul like a field or garden of God, with all manner of pleasant flowers; all pleasant, delightful, and undisturbed; enjoying a sweet calm, and the gently vivifying beams of the sun. The soul of a true Christian, as I then wrote my meditations, appeared like such a little white flower as we see in the spring of the year; low and humble on the ground, opening its bosom to receive the pleasant beams of the sun's glory; rejoicing as it were in a calm rapture; diffusing around a sweet fragrancy; standing peacefully and lovingly, in the midst of other flowers round about; all in like manner opening their bosoms, to drink in the light of the sun. There was no part of creature holiness, that I had so great a sense of its loveliness, as humility, brokenness of heart and poverty of spirit; and there was nothing that I so earnestly longed for. My heart panted after this, to lie low before God, as in the dust; that I might be nothing, and that God might be ALL, that I might become as a little child.

Benjamin Franklin (1706–1790)

AMERICAN STATESMAN and SCIENTIST

A Serviceable Religion

Before I enter upon my public Appearance in Business it may be well to let you know the then State of my Mind, with regard to my Principles and Morals, that you may see how far those influenc'd the future Events of my Life. My Parents had early given me religious Impressions, and brought me

Title supplied by editors. From *The Autobiography of Benjamin Franklin*, edited by Leonard W. Labaree *et al.*, based on *Benjamin Franklin's Memoirs Parallel Text Edition*, edited by Max Farrand. Reprinted by permission of the University of California Press and Yale University Press.

through my Childhood piously in the Dissenting Way. But I was scarce 15 when, after doubting by turns of several Points as I found them disputed in the different Books I read, I began to doubt of Revelation it self. Some Books against Deism fell into my Hands; they were said to be the Substance of Sermons preached at Boyle's Lectures.[1] It happened that they wrought an Effect on me quite contrary to what was intended by them: For the Arguments of the Deists which were quoted to be refuted, appeared to me much stronger than the Refutations. In short I soon became a thorough Deist. My Arguments perverted some others, particularly Collins and Ralph:[2] but each of them having afterwards wrong'd me greatly without the least Compunction and recollecting Keith's[3] Conduct towards me, (who was another Freethinker) and my own towards Vernon[4] and Miss Read[5] which at Times gave me great Trouble, I began to suspect that this Doctrine tho' it might be true, was not very useful. My London Pamphlet, which had for its Motto those Lines of Dryden

—— Whatever is, is right. ——
Tho' purblind Man
Sees but a Part of the Chain, the nearest Link,
His Eyes not carrying to the equal Beam,
That poizes all, above.[6]

And from the Attributes of God, his infinite Wisdom, Goodness and Power concluded that nothing could possibly be wrong in the World, and that Vice and Virtue were empty Distinctions, no such Things existing: appear'd now not so clever a Performance as I once thought it; and I doubted whether some Error had not insinuated itself unperceiv'd into my Argument, so as to infect all that follow'd, as is common in metaphysical Reasonings. I grew convinc'd that *Truth, Sincerity and Integrity* in Dealings between Man and Man, were of the utmost Importance to the Felicity of Life, and I form'd written Resolutions, (which still remain in my Journal Book) to practice them ever while I lived. Revelation had indeed no weight with me as such; but I entertain'd an Opinion, that tho' certain Actions might not be bad *because* they were forbidden by it, or good *because* it commanded them; yet probably those Actions might be forbidden *because* they were bad for us, or commanded *because* they were beneficial to us, in their own Natures, all the Circumstances of things considered. And this Persuasion, with the kind hand

[1] Robert Boyle (1627–1691), English physicist and chemist, endowed lectures in defense of Christianity.
[2] John Collins and James Ralph, boyhood friends who failed to pay debts to Franklin.
[3] Sir William Keith, Governor of Pennsylvania, who disappointed Franklin by not setting him up in a Philadelphia printing business as promised.
[4] a friend of Franklin's older brother; Franklin collected a debt for Vernon and then foolishly used the money to support Collins' dissipations.
[5] When in England Franklin broke off his engagement to her; she married in his absence but after she was widowed married Franklin.
[6] Franklin is partly right. The first of these lines is from Pope, *Essay on Man,* i, 294; the remaining lines are a slightly inaccurate quotation from Dryden, *Oedipus,* iii, 288–291.

of Providence, or some guardian Angel, or accidental favourable Circumstances and Situations, or all together, preserved me (thro' this dangerous Time of Youth and the hazardous Situations I was sometimes in among Strangers, remote from the Eye and Advice of my Father) without any *wilful* gross Immorality or Injustice that might have been expected from my Want of Religion. I say *wilful*, because the Instances I have mentioned, had something of *Necessity* in them, from my Youth, Inexperience, and the Knavery of others. I had therefore a tolerable Character to begin the World with, I valued it properly, and determin'd to preserve it. . . .

I had been religiously educated as a Presbyterian,[7] and tho' some of the Dogmas of that Persuasion, such as the Eternal Decrees of God, Election, Reprobation, &c. appear'd to me unintelligible, others doubtful, and I early absented myself from the Public Assemblies of the Sect, Sunday being my Studying-Day, I never was without some religious Principles; I never doubted, for instance, the Existance of the Deity, that he made the World, and govern'd it by his Providence; that the most acceptable Service of God was the doing Good to Man; that our Souls are immortal; and that all Crime will be punished and Virtue rewarded either here or hereafter; these I esteem'd the Essentials of every Religion, and being to be found in all the Religions we had in our Country I respected them all, tho' with different degrees of Respect as I found them more or less mix'd with other Articles which without any Tendency to inspire, promote or confirm Morality, serv'd principally to divide us and make us unfriendly to one another. This Respect to all, with an Opinion that the worst had some good Effects, induc'd me to avoid all Discourse that might tend to lessen the good Opinion another might have of his own Religion; and as our Province increas'd in People and new Places of worship were continually wanted, and generally erected by voluntary Contribution, my Mite for such purpose, whatever might be the Sect, was never refused.

Tho' I seldom attended any Public Worship, I had still an Opinion of its Propriety, and of its Utility when rightly conducted, and I regularly paid my annual Subscription for the Support of the only Presbyterian Minister or Meeting we had in Philadelphia. He us'd to visit me sometimes as a Friend, and admonish me to attend his Administrations, and I was now and then prevail'd on to do so, once for five Sundays successively. Had he been, *in my Opinion*, a good Preacher perhaps I might have continued, notwithstanding the occasion I had for the Sunday's Leisure in my Course of Study: But his Discourses were chiefly either polemic Arguments, or Explications of the peculiar Doctrines of our Sect, and were all to me very dry, uninteresting and unedifying, since not a single moral Principle was inculcated or enforc'd, their Aim seeming to be rather to make us Presbyterians than good Citizens. At length he took for his Text that Verse of the 4th Chapter of Philippians, *Finally, Brethren, Whatsoever Things are true, honest, just, pure, lovely, or of good report, if there be any virtue, or any praise, think on these Things;*

[7] Strictly speaking, Franklin had been baptized and educated in what was coming to be called the Congregational Church, not the Presbyterian. [Labaree, abridged]

and I imagin'd in a Sermon on such a Text, we could not miss of having some Morality: But he confin'd himself to five Points only as meant by the Apostle, viz. 1. Keeping holy the Sabbath Day. 2. Being diligent in Reading the Holy Scriptures. 3. Attending duly the Publick Worship. 4. Partaking of the Sacrament. 5. Paying a due Respect to God's Ministers. These might be all good Things, but as they were not the kind of good Things that I expected from that Text, I despaired of ever meeting with them from any other, was disgusted, and attended his Preaching no more. I had some Years before compos'd a little Liturgy or Form of Prayer for my own private Use, viz, in 1728. entitled, *Articles of Belief and Acts of Religion*. I return'd to the Use of this, and went no more to the public Assemblies. My Conduct might be blameable, but I leave it without attempting farther to excuse it, my present purpose being to relate Facts, and not to make Apologies for them.

It was about this time that I conceiv'd the bold and arduous Project of arriving at moral Perfection. I wish'd to live without committing any Fault at any time; I would conquer all that either Natural Inclination, Custom, or Company might lead me into. As I knew, or thought I knew, what was right and wrong, I did not see why I might not *always* do the one and avoid the other. But I soon found I had undertaken a Task of more Difficulty than I had imagined. While my *Attention was taken up* in guarding against one Fault, I was often surpriz'd by another. Habit took the Advantage of Inattention. Inclination was sometimes too strong for Reason. I concluded at length, that the mere speculative Conviction that it was our Interest to be compleatly virtuous, was not sufficient to prevent our Slipping, and that the contrary Habits must be broken and good ones acquired and established, before we can have any Dependance on a steady uniform Rectitude of Conduct. For this purpose I therefore contriv'd the following Method.

In the various Enumerations of the moral Virtues I had met with in my Reading, I found the Catalogue more or less numerous, as different Writers included more or fewer Ideas under the same Name. Temperance, for Example, was by some confin'd to Eating and Drinking, while by others it was extended to mean the moderating every other Pleasure, Appetite, Inclination or Passion, bodily or mental, even to our Avarice and Ambition. I propos'd to myself, for the sake of Clearness, to use rather more Names with fewer Ideas annex'd to each, than a few Names with more Ideas; and I included under Thirteen Names of Virtues all that at that time occurr'd to me as necessary or desirable, and annex'd to each a short Precept, which fully express'd the Extent I gave to its Meaning.

These Names of Virtues with their Precepts were

1. TEMPERANCE.

Eat not to Dulness.
Drink not to Elevation.

2. SILENCE.

Speak not but what may benefit others or yourself. Avoid trifling Conversation.

3. ORDER.

Let all your Things have their Places. Let each Part of your Business have its Time.

4. RESOLUTION.

Resolve to perform what you ought. Perform without fail what you resolve.

5. FRUGALITY.

Make no Expence but to do good to others or yourself: i.e. Waste nothing.

6. INDUSTRY.

Lose no Time. Be always employ'd in something useful. Cut off all unnecessary Actions.

7. SINCERITY.

Use no hurtful Deceit.
Think innocently and justly; and, if you speak, speak accordingly.

8. JUSTICE.

Wrong none, by doing Injuries or omitting the Benefits that are your Duty.

9. MODERATION.

Avoid Extreams. Forbear resenting Injuries so much as you think they deserve.

10. CLEANLINESS.

Tolerate no Uncleanness in Body, Cloaths or Habitation.

11. TRANQUILITY.

Be not disturbed at Trifles, or at Accidents common or unavoidable.

12. CHASTITY.

Rarely use Venery but for Health or Offspring; Never to Dulness, Weakness, or the Injury of your own or another's Peace or Reputation.

13. HUMILITY.

Imitate Jesus and Socrates. . . .

It will be remark'd that, tho' my Scheme was not wholly without Religion there was in it no Mark of any of the distinguishing Tenets of any particular Sect. I had purposely avoided them; for being fully persuaded of the Utility and Excellency of my Method, and that it might be serviceable to People in all Religions, and intending some time or other to publish it, I would not have any thing in it that should prejudice any one of any Sect against it. I purposed writing a little Comment on each Virtue, in which I would have shown the Advantages of possessing it, and the Mischiefs attending its opposite Vice; and I should have called my Book the ART of Virtue, because it would have shown the Means and Manner of obtaining Virtue, which would have distinguish'd it from the mere Exhortation to be good, that does not instruct and indicate the Means; but is like the Apostle's Man of verbal Charity, who only, without showing to the Naked and the Hungry how or where they might get Cloaths or Victuals, exhorted them to be fed and clothed. James II, 15, 16. . . .

Having mentioned a great and extensive Project which I had conceiv'd, it seems proper that some Account should be here given of that Project and its Object. Its first Rise in my Mind appears in the following little Paper, accidentally preserved, viz

OBSERVATIONS on my Reading History in Library, May 9. 1731.

"That the great Affairs of the World, the Wars, Revolutions, &c. are carried on and effected by Parties.

"That the View of these Parties is their present general Interest, or what they take to be such.

"That the different Views of these different Parties, occasion all Confusion.

"That while a Party is carrying on a general Design, each Man has his particular private Interest in View.

"That as soon as a Party has gain'd its general Point, each Member becomes Intent upon his particular Interest, which thwarting others, breaks that Party into Divisions, and occasions more Confusion.

"That few in Public Affairs act from a meer View of the Good of their Country, whatever they may pretend; and tho' their Actings bring real Good to their Country, yet Men primarily consider'd that their own and their Country's Interest was united, and did not act from a Principle of Benevolence.

"That fewer still in public Affairs act with a View to the Good of Mankind.

"There seems to me at present to be great Occasion for raising an united Party for Virtue, by forming the Virtuous and good Men of all Nations into a regular Body, to be govern'd by suitable good and wise Rules, which good and wise Men may probably be more unanimous in their Obedience to, than common People are to common Laws.

"I at present think, that whoever attempts this aright, and is well qualified, cannot fail of pleasing God, and of meeting with Success.   B.F."

Revolving this Project in my Mind, as to be undertaken hereafter when my Circumstances should afford me the necessary Leisure, I put down from time to time on Pieces of Paper such Thoughts as occur'd to me respecting it. Most of these are lost; but I find one purporting to be the Substance of an intended Creed, containing as I thought the Essentials of every known Religion, and being free of every thing that might shock the Professors of any Religion. It is express'd in these Words. viz

"That there is one God who made all things.

"That he governs the World by his Providence.

"That he ought to be worshipped by Adoration, Prayer and Thanksgiving.

"But that the most acceptable Service of God is doing Good to Man.

"That the Soul is immortal.

"And that God will certainly reward Virtue and punish Vice either here or hereafter."

My Ideas at that time were, that the Sect should be begun and spread at first among young and single Men only; that each Person to be initiated should not only declare his Assent to such Creed, but should have exercis'd himself with the Thirteen Weeks Examination and Practice of the Virtues as in the before-mention'd Model; that the Existence of such a Society should be kept a Secret till it was become considerable, to prevent Solicitations for the Admission of improper Persons; but that the Members should each of them search among his Acquaintance for ingenuous well-disposed Youths, to whom with prudent Caution the Scheme should be gradually communicated: That the Members should engage to afford their Advice Assistance and Support to each other in promoting one another's Interest, Business and Advancement in Life: That for Distinction, we should be call'd the Society of the *Free and Easy*; Free, as being by the general Practice and Habit of the Virtues, free from the Dominion of Vice, and particularly by the Practice of Industry and Frugality, free from Debt, which exposes a Man to Confinement and a Species of Slavery to his Creditors. This is as much as I can now recollect of the Project. . . .

Nathaniel Hawthorne (1804–1864)

AMERICAN NOVELIST and SHORT STORY WRITER

Young Goodman Brown

Young Goodman Brown came forth at sunset into the street at Salem village; but put his head back, after crossing the threshold, to exchange a parting kiss with his young wife. And Faith, as the wife was aptly named, thrust her own pretty head into the street, letting the wind play with the pink ribbons of her cap while she called to Goodman Brown.

"Dearest heart," whispered she, softly and rather sadly, when her lips were close to his ear, "prithee put off your journey until sunrise and sleep in your own bed to-night. A lone woman is troubled with such dreams and such

From *Mosses from an Old Manse* in the *Complete Works of Nathaniel Hawthorne*, Vol. II, edited by George Parsons Lathrop. Reprinted by permission of Houghton Mifflin Company.

thoughts that she's afeard of herself sometimes. Pray tarry with me this night, dear husband, of all nights in the year."

"My love and my Faith," replied young Goodman Brown, "of all nights in the year, this one night must I tarry away from thee. My journey, as thou callest it, forth and back again, must needs be done 'twixt now and sunrise. What, my sweet, pretty wife, dost thou doubt me already, and we but three months married?"

"Then God bless you!" said Faith, with the pink ribbons; "and may you find all well when you come back."

"Amen!" cried Goodman Brown. "Say thy prayers, dear Faith, and go to bed at dusk, and no harm will come to thee."

So they parted; and the young man pursued his way until, being about to turn the corner by the meeting-house, he looked back and saw the head of Faith still peeping after him with a melancholy air, in spite of her pink ribbons.

"Poor little Faith!" thought he, for his heart smote him. "What a wretch am I to leave her on such an errand! She talks of dreams, too. Methought as she spoke there was trouble in her face, as if a dream had warned her what work is to be done tonight. But no, no; 't would kill her to think it. Well, she's a blessed angel on earth; and after this one night I'll cling to her skirts and follow her to heaven."

With this excellent resolve for the future, Goodman Brown felt himself justified in making more haste on his present evil purpose. He had taken a dreary road, darkened by all the gloomiest trees of the forest, which barely stood aside to let the narrow path creep through, and closed immediately behind. It was all as lonely as could be; and there is this peculiarity in such a solitude, that the traveller knows not who may be concealed by the innumerable trunks and the thick boughs overhead; so that with lonely footsteps he may yet be passing through an unseen multitude.

"There may be a devilish Indian behind every tree," said Goodman Brown to himself; and he glanced fearfully behind him as he added, "What if the devil himself should be at my very elbow!"

His head being turned back, he passed a crook of the road, and, looking forward again, beheld the figure of a man, in grave and decent attire, seated at the foot of an old tree. He arose at Goodman Brown's approach and walked onward side by side with him.

"You are late, Goodman Brown," said he. "The clock of the Old South was striking as I came through Boston, and that is full fifteen minutes agone."

"Faith kept me back a while," replied the young man, with a tremor in his voice, caused by the sudden appearance of his companion, though not wholly unexpected.

It was now deep dusk in the forest, and deepest in that part of it where these two were journeying. As nearly as could be discerned, the second traveller was about fifty years old, apparently in the same rank of life as Goodman Brown, and bearing a considerable resemblance to him, though perhaps more in expression than features. Still they might have been taken for father and son. And yet, though the elder person was as simply clad as the younger, and as simple in manner too, he had an indescribable air of one who knew the world, and who would not have felt abashed at the governor's dinner table or in King William's court, were it possible that his affairs should call him thither. But the only thing about him that could be fixed upon as remarkable was his staff, which bore the likeness of a great black snake, so curiously wrought that it might almost be seen to twist and wriggle itself like a living serpent. This, of course, must have been an ocular deception, assisted by the uncertain light.

"Come, Goodman Brown," cried his fellow-traveller, "this is a dull pace for the beginning of a journey. Take my staff, if you are so soon weary."

"Friend," said the other, exchanging his slow pace for a full stop, "having kept covenant by meeting thee here, it is my purpose now to return whence I came. I have scruples touching the matter thou wot'st[1] of."

"Sayest thou so?" replied he of the serpent, smiling apart. "Let us walk on, nevertheless, reasoning as we go; and if I convince thee not thou shalt turn back. We are but a little way in the forest yet."

"Too far! too far!" exclaimed the goodman, unconsciously resuming his walk. "My father never went into the woods on such an errand, nor his father before him. We have been a race of honest men and good Christians since the days of the martyrs; and shall I be the first of the name of Brown that ever took this path and kept" —

"Such company, thou wouldst say," observed the elder person, interpreting his pause. "Well said, Goodman Brown! I have been as well acquainted with your family as with ever a one among the Puritans; and that's no trifle to say. I helped your grandfather, the constable, when he lashed the Quaker woman so smartly through the streets of Salem; and it was I that brought your father a pitch-pine knot, kindled at my own hearth, to set fire to an Indian village, in King Philip's war. They were my good friends, both; and many a pleasant walk have we had along this path, and returned merrily after midnight. I would fain be friends with you for their sake."

"If it be as thou sayest," replied Goodman Brown, "I marvel they never spoke of these matters; or, verily, I marvel not, seeing that the least rumor of the sort would have driven them from New England. We are a people of prayer, and good works to boot, and abide no such wickedness."

"Wickedness or not," said the traveller with the twisted staff, "I have a very general acquaintance here in New England. The deacons of many a church have drunk the communion wine with me; the selectmen of divers towns make me their chairman; and a majority of the Great and General Court are firm supporters of my interest. The governor and I, too — But these are state secrets."

"Can this be so?" cried Goodman Brown, with a stare of amazement at his undisturbed companion. "Howbeit, I have nothing to do with the gov-

---

[1] know.

ernor and council; they have their own ways, and are no rule for a simple husbandman like me. But, were I to go on with thee, how should I meet the eye of that good old man, our minister, at Salem village? Oh, his voice would make me tremble both Sabbath day and lecture day."

Thus far the elder traveller had listened with due gravity; but now burst into a fit of irrepressible mirth, shaking himself so violently that his snake-like staff actually seemed to wriggle in sympathy.

"Ha! ha! ha!" shouted he again and again; then composing himself, "Well, go on, Goodman Brown, go on; but, prithee, don't kill me with laughing."

"Well, then, to end the matter at once," said Goodman Brown, considerably nettled, "there is my wife, Faith. It would break her dear little heart; and I'd rather break my own."

"Nay, if that be the case," answered the other, "e'en go thy ways, Goodman Brown. I would not for twenty old women like the one hobbling before us that Faith should come to any harm."

As he spoke he pointed his staff at a female figure on the path, in whom Goodman Brown recognized a very pious and exemplary dame, who had taught him his catechism in youth, and was still his moral and spiritual adviser, jointly with the minister and Deacon Gookin.

"A marvel, truly, that Goody Cloyse should be so far in the wilderness at nightfall," said he. "But with your leave, friend, I shall take a cut through the woods until we have left this Christian woman behind. Being a stranger to you, she might ask whom I was consorting with and whither I was going." .

"Be it so," said his fellow-traveller. "Betake you to the woods, and let me keep the path."

Accordingly the young man turned aside, but took care to watch his companion, who advanced softly along the road until he had come within a staff's length of the old dame. She, meanwhile, was making the best of her way, with singular speed for so aged a woman, and mumbling some indistinct words — a prayer, doubtless — as she went. The traveller put forth his staff and touched her withered neck with what seemed the serpent's tail.

"The devil!" screamed the pious old lady.

"Then Goody Cloyse knows her old friend?" observed the traveller, confronting her and leaning on his writhing stick.

"Ah, forsooth, and is it your worship indeed?" cried the good dame. "Yea, truly is it, and in the very image of my old gossip, Goodman Brown, the grandfather of the silly fellow that now is. But — would your worship believe it? — my broomstick hath strangely disappeared, stolen, as I suspect, by that unhanged witch, Goody Cory, and that, too, when I was all anointed with the juice of smallage, and cinquefoil, and wolf's bane"[2] —

"Mingled with fine wheat and the fat of a new-born babe," said the shape of old Goodman Brown.

"Ah, your worship knows the recipe," cried the old lady, cackling aloud.

[2] wild flowers and herbs sometimes used for medicinal purposes.

"So, as I was saying, being all ready for the meeting, and no horse to ride on, I made up my mind to foot it; for they tell me there is a nice young man to be taken into communion to-night. But now your good worship will lend me your arm, and we shall be there in a twinkling."

"That can hardly be," answered her friend. "I may not spare you my arm, Goody Cloyse; but here is my staff, if you will."

So saying, he threw it down at her feet, where, perhaps, it assumed life, being one of the rods which its owner had formerly lent to the Egyptian magi. Of this fact, however, Goodman Brown could not take cognizance. He had cast up his eyes in astonishment, and, looking down again, beheld neither Goody Cloyse nor the serpentine staff, but his fellow-traveller alone, who waited for him as calmly as if nothing had happened.

"That old woman taught me my catechism," said the young man; and there was a world of meaning in this simple comment.

They continued to walk onward, while the elder traveller exhorted his companion to make good speed and persevere in the path, discoursing so aptly that his arguments seemed rather to spring up in the bosom of his auditor than to be suggested by himself. As they went, he plucked a branch of maple to serve for a walking stick, and began to strip it of the twigs and little boughs, which were wet with evening dew. The moment his fingers touched them they became strangely withered and dried up as with a week's sunshine. Thus the pair proceeded, at a good free pace, until suddenly, in a gloomy hollow of the road, Goodman Brown sat himself down on the stump of a tree and refused to go any farther.

"Friend," said he, stubbornly, "my mind is made up. Not another step will I budge on this errand. What if a wretched old woman do choose to go to the devil when I thought she was going to heaven: is that any reason why I should quit my dear Faith and go after her?"

"You will think better of this by and by," said his acquaintance, composedly. "Sit here and rest yourself a while; and when you feel like moving again, there is my staff to help you along."

Without more words, he threw his companion the maple stick, and was as speedily out of sight as if he had vanished into the deepening gloom. The young man sat a few moments by the roadside, applauding himself greatly, and thinking with how clear a conscience he should meet the minister in his morning walk, nor shrink from the eye of good old Deacon Gookin. And what calm sleep would be his that very night, which was to have been spent so wickedly, but so purely and sweetly now, in the arms of Faith! Amidst these pleasant and praiseworthy meditations, Goodman Brown heard the tramp of horses along the road, and deemed it advisable to conceal himself within the verge of the forest, conscious of the guilty purpose that had brought him thither, though now so happily turned from it.

On came the hoof tramps and the voices of the riders, two grave old voices, conversing soberly as they drew near. These mingled sounds appeared to pass along the road, within a few yards of the young man's hiding-place; but, owing doubtless to the depth of the gloom at that particular spot, neither the travellers nor their steeds were visible. Though their figures brushed the small boughs by the wayside, it could not be seen that they intercepted, even, for a moment, the faint gleam from the strip of bright sky athwart which they must have passed. Goodman Brown alternately crouched and stood on tiptoe, pulling aside the branches and thrusting forth his head as far as he durst without discerning so much as a shadow. It vexed him the more, because he could have sworn, were such a thing possible, that he recognized the voices of the minister and Deacon Gookin, jogging along quietly, as they were wont to do, when bound to some ordination or ecclesiastical council. While yet within hearing, one of the riders stopped to pluck a switch.

"Of the two, reverend sir," said the voice like the deacon's, "I had rather miss an ordination dinner than to-night's meeting. They tell me that some of our community are to be here from Falmouth and beyond, and others from Connecticut and Rhode Island, besides several of the Indian powwows, who, after their fashion, know almost as much deviltry as the best of us. Moreover, there is a goodly young woman to be taken into communion."

"Mighty well, Deacon Gookin!" replied the solemn old tones of the minister. "Spur up, or we shall be late. Nothing can be done, you know, until I get on the ground."

The hoofs clattered again; and the voices, talking so strangely in the empty air, passed on through the forest, where no church had ever been gathered or solitary Christian prayed. Whither, then, could these holy men be journeying so deep into the heathen wilderness? Young Goodman Brown caught hold of a tree for support, being ready to sink down on the ground, faint and over-burdened with the heavy sickness of his heart. He looked up to the sky, doubting whether there really was a heaven above him. Yet there was the blue arch, and the stars brightening in it.

"With heaven above and Faith below, I will yet stand firm against the devil!" cried Goodman Brown.

While he still gazed upward into the deep arch of the firmament and had lifted his hands to pray, a cloud, though no wind was stirring, hurried across the zenith and hid the brightening stars. The blue sky was still visible, except directly overhead, where this black mass of cloud was sweeping swiftly northward. Aloft in the air, as if from the depths of the cloud, came a confused and doubtful sound of voices. Once the listener fancied that he could distinguish the accents of towns-people of his own, men and women, both pious and ungodly, many of whom he had met at the communion table, and had seen others rioting at the tavern. The next moment, so indistinct were the sounds, he doubted whether he had heard aught but the murmur of the old forest, whispering without a wind. Then came a stronger swell of those familiar tones, heard daily in the sunshine at Salem village, but never until now from a cloud of night. There was one voice, of a young woman, uttering lamentations, yet with an uncertain sorrow, and entreating for some favor, which, perhaps, it would grieve her to obtain; and all the unseen multitude, both saints and sinners, seemed to encourage her onward.

"Faith!" shouted Goodman Brown, in a voice of agony and desperation; and the echoes of the forest mocked him, crying, "Faith! Faith!" as if bewildered wretches were seeking her all through the wilderness.

The cry of grief, rage, and terror was yet piercing the night, when the unhappy husband held his breath for a response. There was a scream, drowned immediately in a louder murmur of voices, fading into far-off laughter, as the dark cloud swept away, leaving the clear and silent sky above Goodman Brown. But something fluttered lightly down through the air and caught on the branch of a tree. The young man seized it, and beheld a pink ribbon.

"My Faith is gone!" cried he, after one stupefied moment. "There is no good on earth; and sin is but a name. Come, devil; for to thee is this world given."

And, maddened with despair, so that he laughed loud and long, did Goodman Brown grasp his staff and set forth again, at such a rate that he seemed to fly along the forest path rather than to walk or run. The road grew wilder and drearier and more faintly traced, and vanished at length, leaving him in the heart of the dark wilderness, still rushing onward with the instinct that guides mortal man to evil. The whole forest was peopled with frightful sounds — the creaking of the trees, the howling of wild beasts, and the yell of Indians; while sometimes the wind tolled like a distant church bell, and sometimes gave a broad roar around the traveller, as if all Nature were laughing him to scorn. But he was himself the chief horror of the scene, and shrank not from its other horrors.

"Ha! ha! ha!" roared Goodman Brown when the wind laughed at him. "Let us hear which will laugh loudest. Think not to frighten me with your deviltry. Come witch, come wizard, come Indian powwow, come devil himself, and here comes Goodman Brown. You may as well fear him as he fear you."

In truth, all through the haunted forest there could be nothing more frightful than the figure of Goodman Brown. On he flew among the black pines, brandishing his staff with frenzied gestures, now giving vent to an inspiration of horrid blasphemy, and now shouting forth such laughter as set all the echoes of the forest laughing like demons around him. The fiend in his own shape is less hideous than when he rages in the breast of man. Thus sped the demoniac on his course, until, quivering among the trees, he saw a red light before him, as when the felled trunks and branches of a clearing have been set on fire, and throw up their lurid blaze against the sky, at the hour of midnight. He paused, in a lull of the tempest that had driven him onward, and heard the swell of what seemed a hymn, rolling solemnly from a distance with the weight of many voices. He knew the tune; it was a familiar one in the choir of the village meeting-house. The verse died heavily away, and was lengthened by a chorus, not of human voices, but of all the sounds of the benighted wilderness pealing in awful harmony together. Goodman Brown cried out, and his cry was lost to his own ear by its unison with the cry of the desert.

In the interval of silence he stole forward until the light glared full upon his eyes. At one extremity of an open space, hemmed in by the dark wall of the forest, arose a rock, bearing some rude, natural resemblance either to an altar or a pulpit, and surrounded by four blazing pines, their tops aflame, their stems untouched, like candles at an evening meeting. The mass of foliage that had overgrown the summit of the rock was all on fire, blazing high into the night and fitfully illuminating the whole field. Each pendent twig and leafy festoon was in a blaze. As the red light arose and fell, a numerous congregation alternately shone forth, then disappeared in shadow, and again grew, as it were, out of the darkness, peopling the heart of the solitary woods at once.

"A grave and dark-clad company," quoth Goodman Brown.

In truth they were such. Among them, quivering to and fro between gloom and splendor, appeared faces that would be seen next day at the council board of the province, and others which, Sabbath after Sabbath, looked devoutly heavenward, and benignantly over the crowded pews, from the holiest pulpits in the land. Some affirm that the lady of the governor was there. At least there were high dames well known to her, and wives of honored husbands, and widows, a great multitude, and ancient maidens, all of excellent repute, and fair young girls, who trembled lest their mothers should espy them. Either the sudden gleams of light flashing over the obscure field bedazzled Goodman Brown, or he recognized a score of the church members of Salem village famous for their especial sanctity. Good old Deacon Gookin had arrived, and waited at the skirts of that venerable saint, his revered pastor. But, irreverently consorting with these grave, reputable, and pious people, these elders of the church, these chaste dames and dewy virgins, there were men of dissolute lives and women of spotted fame, wretches given over to all mean and filthy vice, and suspected even of horrid crimes. It was strange to see that the good shrank not from the wicked, nor were the sinners abashed by the saints. Scattered also among their pale-faced enemies were the Indian priests, or powwows, who had often scared their native forest with more hideous incantations than any known to English witchcraft.

"But where is Faith?" thought Goodman Brown; and, as hope came into his heart, he trembled.

Another verse of the hymn arose, a slow and mournful strain, such as the pious love, but joined to words which expressed all that our nature can conceive of sin, and darkly hinted at far more. Unfathomable to mere mortals is the lore of fiends. Verse after verse was sung; and still the chorus of the desert swelled between like the deepest tone of a mighty organ; and with the final peal of that dreadful anthem there came a sound, as if the roaring wind, the rushing streams, the howling beasts, and every other voice of the unconcerted wilderness were mingling and according with the voice of guilty man in homage to the prince of all. The four blazing pines threw up a loftier flame, and obscurely discovered shapes and visages of horror on the smoke wreaths above the impious assembly. At the same moment the fire on the rock shot redly forth and formed a glowing arch above its base, where now appeared a figure. With reverence be it spoken, the figure bore no slight similitude, both in garb and manner, to some grave divine of the New England churches.

"Bring forth the converts!" cried a voice that echoed through the field and rolled into the forest.

At the word, Goodman Brown stepped forth from the shadow of the trees and approached the congregation, with whom he felt a loathful brotherhood by the sympathy of all that was wicked in his heart. He could have well-nigh sworn that the shape of his own dead father beckoned him to advance, looking downward from a smoke wreath, while a woman, with dim features of despair, threw out her hand to warn him back. Was it his mother? But he had no power to retreat one step, nor to resist, even in thought, when the minister and good old Deacon Gookin seized his arms and led him to the blazing rock. Thither came also the slender form of a veiled female, led between Goody Cloyse, that pious teacher of the catechism, and Martha Carrier,[3] who had received the devil's promise to be queen of hell. A rampant hag was she. And there stood the proselytes beneath the canopy of fire.

"Welcome, my children," said the dark figure, "to the communion of your race. Ye have found thus young your nature and your destiny. My children, look behind you!"

They turned; and flashing forth, as it were, in a sheet of flame, the fiend worshippers were seen; the smile of welcome gleamed darkly on every visage.

"There," resumed the sable form, "are all whom ye have reverenced from youth. Ye deemed them holier than yourselves, and shrank from your own sin, contrasting it with their lives of righteousness and prayerful aspirations heavenward. Yet here are they all in my worshipping assembly. This night it shall be granted you to know their secret deeds: how hoary-bearded elders of the church have whispered wanton words to the young maids of their households; how many a woman, eager for widows' weeds, has given her husband a drink at bedtime and let him sleep his last sleep in her bosom; how beardless youths have made haste to inherit their fathers' wealth; and how fair damsels — blush not, sweet ones — have dug little graves in the garden, and bidden me, the sole guest, to an infant's funeral. By the sympathy of your human hearts for sin ye shall scent out all the places — whether in church, bed-chamber, street, field, or forest — where crime has been committed, and shall exult to behold the whole earth one stain of guilt, one mighty blood spot. Far more than this. It shall be yours to penetrate, in every bosom, the deep mystery of sin, the fountain of all wicked arts, and which

[3] women sentenced to death as witches by Hawthorne's great-great-grandfather in 1692.

inexhaustibly supplies more evil impulses than human power — than my power at its utmost — can make manifest in deeds. And now, my children, look upon each other."

They did so; and, by the blaze of the hell-kindled torches, the wretched man beheld his Faith, and the wife her husband, trembling before that unhallowed altar.

"Lo, there ye stand, my children," said the figure, in a deep and solemn tone, almost sad with its despairing awfulness, as if his once angelic nature could yet mourn for our miserable race. "Depending upon one another's hearts, ye had still hoped that virtue were not all a dream. Now are ye undeceived. Evil is the nature of mankind. Evil must be your only happiness. Welcome again, my children, to the communion of your race."

"Welcome," repeated the fiend worshippers, in one cry of despair and triumph.

And there they stood, the only pair, as it seemed, who were yet hesitating on the verge of wickedness in this dark world. A basin was hollowed, naturally, in the rock. Did it contain water, reddened by the lurid light? or was it blood? or, perchance, a liquid flame? Herein did the shape of evil dip his hand and prepare to lay the mark of baptism upon their foreheads, that they might be partakers of the mystery of sin, more conscious of the secret guilt of others, both in deed and thought, than they could now be of their own. The husband cast one look at his pale wife, and Faith at him. What polluted wretches would the next glance show them to each other, shuddering alike at what they disclosed and what they saw!

"Faith! Faith!" cried the hubsand, "look up to heaven, and resist the wicked one."

Whether Faith obeyed he knew not. Hardly had he spoken when he found himself amid calm night and solitude, listening to a roar of the wind which died heavily away through the forest. He staggered against the rock, and felt it chill and damp; while a hanging twig, that had been all on fire, besprinkled his cheek with the coldest dew.

The next morning young Goodman Brown came slowly into the street of Salem village, staring around him like a bewildered man. The good old minister was taking a walk along the graveyard to get an appetite for breakfast and meditate his sermon, and bestowed a blessing, as he passed, on Goodman Brown. He shrank from the venerable saint as if to avoid an anathema. Old Deacon Gookin was at domestic worship, and the holy words of his prayer were heard through the open window. "What God doth the wizard pray to?" quoth Goodman Brown. Goody Cloyse, that excellent old Christian, stood in the early sunshine at her own lattice, catechizing a little girl who had brought her a pint of morning's milk. Goodman Brown snatched away the child as from the grasp of the fiend himself. Turning the corner by the meeting-house, he spied the head of Faith, with the pink ribbons, gazing anxiously forth, and bursting into such joy at sight of him that she skipped along the street and almost kissed her husband before the whole village. But Goodman Brown looked sternly and sadly into her face, and passed on without a greeting.

Had Goodman Brown fallen asleep in the forest and only dreamed a wild dream of a witch-meeting?

Be it so if you will; but, alas! it was a dream of evil omen for young Goodman Brown. A stern, a sad, a darkly meditative, a distrustful, if not a desperate man did he become from the night of that fearful dream. On the Sabbath day, when the congregation were singing a holy psalm, he could not listen because an anthem of sin rushed loudly upon his ear and drowned all the blessed strain. When the minister spoke from the pulpit with power and fervid eloquence, and, with his hand on the open Bible, of the sacred truths of our religion, and of saint-like lives and triumphant deaths, and of future bliss or misery unutterable, then did Goodman Brown turn pale, dreading lest the roof should thunder down upon the gray blasphemer and his hearers. Often, awaking suddenly at midnight, he shrank from the bosom of Faith; and at morning or eventide, when the family knelt down at prayer, he scowled and muttered to himself, and gazed sternly at his wife, and turned away. And when he had lived long, and was borne to his grave a hoary corpse, followed by Faith, an aged woman, and children and grandchildren, a goodly procession, besides neighbors not a few, they carved no hopeful verse upon his tombstone, for his dying hour was gloom.

Robert Browning   (1812–1889)

ENGLISH POET

The Bishop Orders His Tomb at Saint Praxed's Church

Rome, 15 —

Vanity, saith the preacher, vanity!
Draw round my bed: is Anselm keeping back?
Nephews — sons mine . . . ah God, I know not!
    Well —
She, men would have to be your mother once,
Old Gandolf envied me, so fair she was!
What's done is done, and she is dead beside,
Dead long ago, and I am Bishop since,

Vanity . . . vanity: loose quote from Ecclesiastes 1:2

From *Poems of Robert Browning*, edited by Donald Smalley (Riverside Edition). Reprinted by permission of Houghton Mifflin Company.

And as she died so must we die ourselves,
And thence ye may perceive the world's a dream.
Life, how and what is it? As here I lie   10
In this state-chamber, dying by degrees,
Hours and long hours in the dead night, I ask
"Do I live, am I dead?" Peace, peace seems all.
Saint Praxed's ever was the church for peace;
And so, about this tomb of mine. I fought
With tooth and nail to save my niche, ye know:
— Old Gandolf cozened me, despite my care;
Shrewd was that snatch from out the corner South
He graced his carrion with, God curse the same!
Yet still my niche is not so cramped but thence   20
One sees the pulpit o' the epistle-side,
And somewhat of the choir, those silent seats,
And up into the aery dome where live
The angels, and a sunbeam's sure to lurk:
And I shall fill my slab of basalt there,
And 'neath my tabernacle take my rest,
With those nine columns round me, two and two,
The odd one at my feet where Anselm stands:
Peach-blossom marble all, the rare, the ripe
As fresh-poured red wine of a mighty pulse.   30
— Old Gandolf with his paltry onion-stone,
Put me where I may look at him! True peach,
Rosy and flawless: how I earned the prize!
Draw close: that conflagration of my church
— What then? So much was saved if aught were
     missed!
My sons, ye would not be my death? Go dig
The white-grape vineyard where the oil-press stood,
Drop water gently till the surface sink,
And if ye find . . . Ah God, I know not, I! . . .
Bedded in store of rotten fig-leaves soft,   40
And corded up in a tight olive-frail,
Some lump, ah God, of *lapis lazuli*,
Big as a Jew's head cut off at the nape,
Blue as a vein o'er the Madonna's breast . . .
Sons, all have I bequeathed you, villas, all,
That brave Frascati villa with its bath,
So, let the blue lump poise between my knees,
Like God the Father's globe on both his hands
Ye worship in the Jesu Church so gay,
For Gandolf shall not choose but see and burst!   50
Swift as a weaver's shuttle fleet our years:
Man goeth to the grave, and where is he?
Did I say basalt for my slab, sons? Black —
'Twas ever antique-black I meant! How else
Shall ye contrast my frieze to come beneath?

Saint Praxed's: a small church in Rome named for the charitable daughter of a Roman senator

epistle-side: right side of the altar where the Epistles are read during Mass

tabernacle: stone canopy

onion-stone: inexpensive marble that disintegrates in layers

olive-frail: basket

Frascati: town in the Alban Hills near Rome

The bas-relief in bronze ye promised me,
Those Pans and Nymphs ye wot of, and perchance
Some tripod, thyrsus, with a vase or so,
The Saviour at his sermon on the mount,
Saint Praxed in a glory, and one Pan   60
Ready to twitch the Nymph's last garment off,
And Moses with the tables . . . but I know
Ye mark me not! What do they whisper thee,
Child of my bowels, Anselm? Ah, ye hope
To revel down my villas while I gasp
Bricked o'er with beggar's mouldy travertine
Which Gandolf from his tomb-top chuckles at!
Nay, boys, ye love me — all of jasper, then!
'Tis jasper ye stand pledged to, lest I grieve
My bath must needs be left behind, alas!   70
One block, pure green as a pistachio-nut,
There's plenty jasper somewhere in the world —
And have I not Saint Praxed's ear to pray
Horses for ye, and brown Greek manuscripts,
And mistresses with great smooth marbly limbs?
— That's if ye carve my epitaph aright,
Choice Latin, picked phrase, Tully's every word,
No gaudy ware like Gandolf's second line —
Tully, my masters? Ulpian serves his need!
And then how I shall lie through centuries,   80
And hear the blessed mutter of the mass,
And see God made and eaten all day long,
And feel the steady candle-flame, and taste
Good strong thick stupefying incense-smoke!
For as I lie here, hours of the dead night,
Dying in state and by such slow degrees,
I fold my arms as if they clasped a crook,
And stretch my feet forth straight as stone can point,
And let the bedclothes, for a mortcloth, drop
Into great laps and folds of sculptor's-work: 90
And as yon tapers dwindle, and strange thoughts
Grow, with a certain humming in my ears,
About the life before I lived this life,
And this life too, popes, cardinals and priests,
Saint Praxed at his sermon on the mount,
Your tall pale mother with her talking eyes,
And new-found agate urns as fresh as day,
And marble's language, Latin pure, discreet,
— Aha, ELUCESCEBAT quoth our friend?
No Tully, said I, Ulpian at the best!   100
Evil and brief hath been my pilgrimage.
All *lapis*, all, sons! Else I give the Pope
My villas! Will ye ever eat my heart?

wot: know

tripod: three-legged stool which was a symbol of the Delphic oracle and a favorite offering to Apollo. thyrsus: staff decorated with vines or grapes; attribute of Bacchus and others engaging in bacchic rites. tables: Ten Commandments

travertine: limestone

Tully's: of Marcus Tullius Cicero, Roman orator and statesman (106–43 B.C.)
Ulpian: Domitius Ulpianus, whose Latin was less pure than Cicero's classic prose

made and eaten: the Eucharist

mortcloth: funeral pall

ELUCESCEBAT: "he was illustrious" (correctly, "elucebat")

Ever your eyes were as a lizard's quick,
They glitter like your mother's for my soul,
Or ye would heighten my impoverished frieze,
Piece out its starved design, and fill my vase
With grapes, and add a vizor and a Term,
And to the tripod ye would tie a lynx
That in his struggle throws the thyrsus down,   110
To comfort me on my entablature
Whereon I am to lie till I must ask
"Do I live, am I dead?" There, leave me, there!
For ye have stabbed me with ingratitude
To death — ye wish it — God, ye wish it! Stone —
Gritstone, a-crumble! Clammy squares which sweat
As if the corpse they keep were oozing through —
And no more *lapis* to delight the world!
Well go! I bless ye. Fewer tapers there,
But in a row: and, going, turn your backs   120
— Ay, like departing altar-ministrants,
And leave me in my church, the church for peace,
That I may watch at leisure if he leers —
Old Gandolf, at me, from his onion-stone,
As still he envied me, so fair she was!

vizor: mask. Term: pillar adorned with a figure of a head or bust (originally of the Roman god Terminus)

Walt Whitman (1819–1892)

AMERICAN POET and JOURNALIST

A Noiseless Patient Spider

A noiseless patient spider,
I mark'd where on a little promontory it stood isolated,
Mark'd how to explore the vacant vast surrounding,
It launch'd forth filament, filament, filament, out of itself,
Ever unreeling them, ever tirelessly speeding them.

And you O my soul where you stand,
Surrounded, detached, in measureless oceans of space,
Ceaselessly musing, venturing, throwing, seeking the spheres to connect them,
Till the bridge you will need be form'd, till the ductile anchor hold,
Till the gossamer thread you fling catch somewhere, O my soul.

"A Noiseless Patient Spider" by Walt Whitman. From *Complete Poetry and Selected Prose of Walt Whitman*, edited by James E. Miller (Riverside Edition). Reprinted by permission of Houghton Mifflin Company.

Fyodor Dostoevsky (1821–1881)

RUSSIAN NOVELIST and SHORT STORY WRITER

The Grand Inquisitor

"Even this must have a preface — that is, a literary preface," laughed Ivan, "and what kind of *littérateur* am I? You see, the action takes place in the sixteenth century, and at that time, as you probably learnt at school, it was customary in poetry to bring down heavenly powers on earth. Not to speak of Dante, in France, court clerks, as well as the monks in the monasteries, used to give regular performances in which the Madonna, the saints, the angels, Christ, and God Himself were brought on the stage. In those days it was done in all simplicity. In Victor Hugo's 'Notre Dame de Paris' an edifying and gratuitous spectacle was provided for the people in the Hôtel de Ville[1] of Paris in the reign of Louis XI in honour of the birth of the dauphin. It was called *Le bon jugement de la très sainte et gracieuse Vierge Marie*,[2] and she appears in person on the stage and pronounces her *bon jugement*. Similar plays, chiefly from the Old Testament, were occasionally performed in Moscow, too, up to the time of Peter the Great. But besides dramatic spectacles there were current in the world all sorts of tales and songs, in which the holy angels and all the powers of heaven took part when required. In our monasteries the monks busied themselves in translating, copying, and even composing such poems — and as far back as the time of the Tatars.[3] There is, for instance, one monastic poem (of course, from the Greek), 'The Wanderings of Our Lady through Hell,' with descriptions as bold as Dante's. Our Lady visits hell, and the Archangel Michael guides her through the torments. She sees the sinners and their tortures. There is there among others one very entertaining set of sinners in a burning lake; some of them sink so deep in the lake that they can't swim out, and 'these God forgets' — an expression

[1] town hall.
[2] "The good judgment of the most holy and gracious Virgin Mary."
[3] a Turkic people, allied with the Mongol hordes of Ghengis Khan, who overran and imposed tribute on the Russians from the 13th to the 16th century.

In this scene from *The Brothers Karamazov* two of the brothers, Ivan and Alyosha, discuss the nature of God. Acknowledging that God exists, Ivan does not like God's way of doing things, since the world is filled with suffering. Ivan is not satisfied that those who cause the suffering be punished, inasmuch as that would merely cause more suffering. He knows that forgiveness is no solution either, because no one has the power to forgive so much evil. Then Alyosha suggests that Christ can and will forgive the evil and bear the punishment by dying on the cross. In response to that suggestion Ivan tells the story of the Grand Inquisitor.

"The Grand Inquisitor" by Fyodor Dostoevsky. From the Heritage Press edition of *The Brothers Karamazov*, in the Constance Garnett translation revised by Avrahm Yarmolinsky, reproduced by permission of The George Macy Companies, Inc., copyright 1933, renewed 1961.

of extraordinary depth and force. And so Our Lady, overcome and weeping, falls before the throne of God and begs for mercy for all in hell — for all she has seen there, indiscriminately. Her conversation with God is immensely interesting. She beseeches Him, she will not desist, and when God points to the hands and feet of her Son, nailed to the Cross, and asks, 'How can I forgive His tormentors?' she bids all the saints, all the martyrs, all the angels and archangels to kneel down with her and pray for mercy on all without distinction. It ends by her winning from God a respite from suffering every year from Good Friday till Trinity day, and the sinners at once raise a cry of gratitude from hell, chanting, 'Thou are just, O Lord, in this judgment.' Well, my poem would have been of the same sort if it had appeared at that time. In my poem He comes on the scene, but He says nothing, only appears and passes on. Fifteen centuries have passed since He promised to come in His glory, fifteen centuries since His prophet wrote, 'Behold, I come quickly'; 'Of that day and that hour knoweth no man, neither the Son, but the Father,' as He himself said on earth. But humanity awaits him with the same faith and with the same emotion. Oh, with greater faith, for it is fifteen centuries since man has ceased to see signs from Heaven.

> Believe but what the heart doth say
> No signs from Heaven come to-day.

There was nothing left but faith in what the heart doth say. It is true there were many miracles in those days. There were saints who performed miraculous cures; some holy people, according to their 'Lives,'[4] were visited by the Queen of Heaven herself. But the devil does not slumber, and doubts were already arising among men regarding the truth of these miracles. And just then there appeared in the north, in Germany, a terrible new heresy. 'A great star like unto a torch' (that is, a church) 'fell upon the fountains of the waters and they were made bitter.' These heretics began blasphemously denying miracles. But those who remained faithful were all the more ardent in their faith. Humanity poured out its tears to Him as before, awaited His coming, loved Him, hoped for Him, yearned to suffer and die for Him as before. And so many ages mankind had prayed with faith and fervour, 'O Lord our God, hasten Thy coming,' so many ages called upon Him, that in His infinite mercy He conceived the desire to descend to His worshippers. Before that day He had come down, He had visited some holy men, martyrs and hermits, as is written in their 'Lives.' Among us, Tyutchev,[5] with absolute faith in the truth of his words, bore witness that

> Bearing the Cross, in slavish dress
> Weary and worn, the Heavenly King
> Our mother, Russia, came to bless,
> And through our land went wandering.

And that certainly was so, I assure you.

[4] popular collections of brief biographies of saints.
[5] Russian poet (1803–1873).

"And behold, He desired to appear, if only for a moment, to the people, to the tortured, suffering people, sunk in foul iniquity, but loving Him like children. My story is laid in Spain, in Seville, in the most terrible time of the Inquisition, when fires were lighted every day to the glory of God, and 'in magnificent *autos-da-fé*[6] the wicked heretics were burnt.' Oh, of course, this was not the coming in which He will appear according to His promise at the end of time in all His heavenly glory, and which will be sudden 'as lightning flashing from east to west.' No, He desired to visit His children only for a moment, and just there where the flames were crackling round the heretics. In His infinite mercy He walks once more among men in that human shape in which He walked among men for three years fifteen centuries ago. He descends upon the 'torrid plazas' of the southern town in which on the day before almost a hundred heretics had, *ad majorem gloriam Dei*,[7] been burnt by monseigneur, the Grand Inquisitor, in a magnificent *auto-da-fé*, in the presence of the king, the court, the knights, the cardinals, the most charming ladies of the court, and the whole population of Seville.

"He came softly, unobserved, and yet, strange to say, every one recognised Him. That might be one of the best passages in the poem. I mean, why they recognised Him. The people are irresistibly drawn to Him, they surround Him, they flock about Him, follow Him. He moves silently in their midst with a gentle smile of infinite compassion. The sun of love burns in His heart, light and power shine from His eyes, and their radiance, shed on the people, stirs their hearts with responsive love. He stretches out His hands to them, blesses them, and a healing virtue comes from contact with Him, even with His garments. An old man in the crowd, blind since childhood, cries out, 'O Lord, heal me and I shall see Thee!' and, as it were, scales fall from his eyes and the blind man sees Him. The crowd weeps and kisses the earth under His feet. Children throw flowers before Him, sing, and cry hosannah. 'It is He — it is He!' all repeat. 'It must be He, it can be no one but He!' He stops at the steps of the Seville cathedral at the moment when the weeping mourners are bringing in a little open white coffin. In it lies a child of seven, the only daughter of a prominent citizen. The dead child lies covered with flowers. 'He will raise your child,' people in the crowd shout to the weeping mother. The priest, coming to meet the coffin, looks perplexed, and frowns, but the mother of the dead child throws herself at His feet with a wail. 'If it be Thou, raise my child!' she cries, stretching out her hands to Him. The procession halts, the coffin is laid on the steps at His feet. He looks with compassion, and His lips once more softly pronounce, '*Talitha cumi!*'[8] — 'and the damsel rose up.'

"The little girl sits up in the coffin and looks round, smiling with wide-open wondering eyes, holding a bunch of white roses they had put in her hand.

[6] literally, "act of faith": the public declaration of judgement passed by the courts of the Spanish Inquisition, followed by the execution of such judgement.
[7] "to the greater glory of God."
[8] "Maiden arise!"

"There are cries, sobs, confusion among the people, and at that moment the monseigneur himself, the Grand Inquisitor, passes by the cathedral. He is an old man, almost ninety, tall and erect, with a withered face and sunken eyes, in which there is still a gleam of light. He is not dressed in the gorgeous pontifical robes, which he had flaunted before the people the previous day, when the enemies of the Roman Church were being burned — no, at this moment he is wearing his coarse, old, monk's cassock. At a distance behind him come his gloomy assistants and his slaves and the 'sacred guard.' He stops at the sight of the crowd and watches it from a distance. He had seen everything; he had seen them set the coffin down at His feet, seen the child rise up. His face darkens. He knits his thick grey brows and his eyes gleam with a sinister fire. He holds out his finger and bids the guards take Him. And such is his power, so completely are the people cowed into submission and trembling obedience to him, that the crowd immediately makes way for the guards, and in the midst of deathlike silence they lay hands on Him and lead Him away. The crowd instantly bows down to the earth, like one man, before the old Inquisitor. He blesses the people in silence and passes on. The guards lead their Prisoner to the close, gloomy, vaulted prison in the ancient palace of the Holy Inquisition and shut Him in it. The day passes and is followed by the black, hot, 'breathless' night of Seville. The air is 'fragrant with laurel and lemon.' In the pitch darkness the iron door of the prison is suddenly opened and the Grand Inquisitor himself comes in with a lantern in his hand. He is alone; the door is closed at once behind him. He stands in the doorway and for a minute or two gazes into His face. At last he goes up slowly, sets the lantern on the table and speaks.

" 'Is is Thou? Thou?' but receiving no answer, he adds at once. 'Don't answer, be silent. What canst Thou say, indeed? I know too well what Thou wouldst say. And Thou hast no right to add anything to what Thou didst say of old. Why, then, art Thou come to hinder us? For Thou hast come to hinder us, and Thou knowest that. But dost Thou know what will be to-morrow? I know not who Thou art and care not to know whether it is Thou or only a semblance of Thee, but to-morrow I shall condemn Thee and burn Thee at the stake as the worst of heretics. And the very people who have to-day kissed Thy feet, tomorrow at the faintest sign from me will rush to heap up the embers of Thy fire. Knowest Thou that? Yes, maybe Thou knowest it,' he added with thoughtful penetration, never for a moment taking his eyes off the Prisoner."

"I don't quite understand, Ivan. What does it mean?" Alyosha, who had been listening in silence, said with a smile. "Is it simply a wild fantasy, or a mistake on the part of the old man — some impossible *qui pro quo?*"[9]

"Take it as the last," said Ivan, laughing, "if you are so corrupted by modern realism and can't stand anything fantastic. If you like it to be a case of mistaken identity, let it be so. It is true," he went on, laughing, "the old man was ninety, and he may well have gone crazy over his set idea. He might have

---

[9] correctly, 'quid pro quo': "one thing in return for another."

been struck by the appearance of the Prisoner. It might, in fact, be simply his ravings, the delusion of an old man of ninety, over-excited by the *auto-da-fé* of a hundred heretics the days before. But does it matter to us after all whether it was a mistake of identity or a wild fantasy? All that matters is that the old man should speak out, should speak openly of what he has thought in silence for ninety years."

"And the Prisoner, too, is silent? Does He look at him and not say a word?"

"That's inevitable in any case." Ivan laughed again. "The old man has told Him He hasn't the right to add anything to what He has said of old. One may say it is the most fundamental feature of Roman Catholicism, in my opinion at least. 'All has been transmitted by Thee to the Pope,' they say, 'and all, therefore, is now in the Pope's hands, and there is no need for Thee to come now at all. Thou must not meddle for the time, at least.' That's how they speak and write too — the Jesuits, at any rate, I have read it myself in the works of their theologians. 'Hast Thou the right to reveal to us one of the mysteries of that world from which Thou hast come?' my old man asks Him, and answers the question for Him. 'No, Thou hast not; that Thou mayest not add to what has been said of old, and mayest not take from men the freedom which Thou didst uphold when Thou wast on earth. Whatsoever Thou revealest anew will encroach on men's freedom of faith; for it will be manifest as a miracle, and the freedom of their faith was dearer to Thee than anything in those days fifteen hundred years ago. Didst Thou not often say then, "I would make you free"? But now Thou hast seen these "free" men,' the old man adds suddenly, with pensive irony. 'Yes, we've paid dearly for it,' he goes on, looking sternly at Him, 'but at last we have completed that work in Thy name. For fifteen centuries we have been wrestling with Thy freedom, but now it is ended and over for good. Dost Thou not believe that it's over for good? Thou lookest meekly at me and deignest not even to be wroth with me. But let me tell Thee that now, to-day, people are more convinced than ever that they have perfect freedom, yet they have brought their freedom to us and laid it humbly at our feet. But that has been our doing. Was this what Thou didst desire? Was this Thy freedom?' "

"I don't understand again," Alyosha broke in. "Is he ironical, is he jesting?"

"Not a bit of it! He claims it as a merit for himself and his Church that at last they have vanquished freedom and have done so to make men happy. 'For now' (he is speaking of the Inquisition, of course) 'for the first time it has become possible to think of the happiness of men. Man was created a rebel; and how can rebels be happy? Thou wast warned,' he says to Him. 'Thou hast had no lack of signs and warnings, but Thou didst not listen to those warnings; Thou didst reject the only way by which men might be made happy. But, fortunately, departing, Thou didst hand on the work to us. Thou hast promised, Thou hast established by Thy word, Thou hast given to us the right to bind and to unbind, and now, of course, Thou canst not think of taking it away. Why, then, hast Thou come to hinder us?' "

"And what's the meaning of 'no lack of signs and warnings'?" asked Alyosha.

"Why, that's the chief part of what the old man must say.

" 'The wise and dread spirit, the spirit of self-destruction and non-existence,' the old man goes on, 'the great spirit talked with Thee in the wilderness, and we are told in the books that he "tempted" Thee. Is that so? And could anything truer be said than what he revealed to Thee in three questions and what Thou didst reject, and what in the books is called "the temptation"? And yet if there has ever been on earth a real stupendous miracle, it took place on that day, on the day of the three temptations. The statement of those three questions was itself the miracle. If it were possible to imagine simply for the sake of argument that those three questions of the dread spirit had perished utterly from the books, and that we had to restore them and to invent them anew, in order to restore them to the books, and to do so had gathered together all the wise men of the earth — rulers, chief priests, learned men, philosophers, poets — and had set them the task of inventing three questions, such as would not only fit the occasion, but express in three words, three human phrases, the whole future history of the world and of humanity — dost Thou believe that all the combined wisdom of the earth could have invented anything in depth and force equal to the three questions which were actually put to Thee then by the wise and mighty spirit in the wilderness? From those questions alone, from the miracle of their statement, we can see that we have here to do not with the fleeting human intelligence, but with the absolute and eternal. For in those three questions the whole subsequent history of mankind is, as it were, brought together into one whole, and fore-told, and in them are united all the unsolved historical contradictions of human nature. At the time it could not be so clear, since the future was unknown; but now that fifteen hundred years have passed, we see that every-thing in those three questions was so justly divined and foretold, and has been so truly fulfilled, that nothing can be added to them or taken from them.

" 'Judge Thyself who was right — Thou or he who questioned Thee then? Remember the first question; its meaning, though not its letter, was this: "Thou wouldst go into the world, and art going with empty hands, with some promise of freedom which men in their simplicity and their native unruliness cannot even understand, which they fear and dread — for nothing has ever been more insupportable for man and human society than freedom. But seest Thou these stones in this parched and barren wilderness? Turn them into bread, and mankind will run after Thee like a flock of sheep, grateful and obedient, though for ever trembling, lest Thou withdraw Thy hand and deny them Thy bread." But Thou didst not will to deprive man of freedom and didst reject the offer, thinking, what is that freedom worth, if obedience is bought with bread? Thou didst reply that man lives not by bread alone. But dost Thou know that for the sake of that earthly bread the spirit of the earth will rise up against Thee and will strive with Thee and overcome Thee and all will follow him, crying, "Who is like unto this beast?

He has given us fire from heaven!" Dost Thou know that ages will pass, and humanity will proclaim by the lips of their sages and men of science that there is no crime, and therefore no sin; there is only hunger? "Feed men, and then ask of them virtue!" that's what they'll write on the banner, which they will raise against Thee, and with which Thy temple will be destroyed. Where Thy temple stood will rise a new building; the terrible tower of Babel will be built again, and though, like the one of old, it will not be finished, yet Thou mightest have prevented that new tower and have cut short the sufferings of men by a thousand years; for they will come back to us after a thousand years of agony with their tower. They will seek us again, hidden underground in the catacombs, for we shall be again persecuted and tortured. They will find us and cry to us, "Feed us, for those who have promised us fire from heaven haven't given it!" And then we shall finish building their tower, for he will finish the building who will feed them. And we alone shall feed them in Thy name, declaring falsely that it is in Thy name. Oh, never, never can they feed themselves without us! No science will give them bread so long as they remain free. In the end they will lay their freedom at our feet, and say to us, "Make us your slaves, but feed us." They will understand themselves, at last, that freedom and bread enough for all are inconceivable together, for never, never will they be able to share between them! They will be convinced, too, that they can never be free, for they are weak, vicious, worthless, and rebellious. Thou didst promise them the bread of Heaven, but, I repeat again, can it compare with earthly bread in the eyes of the weak, ever sinful and ignoble race of man? And if for the sake of the bread of Heaven thousands and tens of thousands shall follow Thee, what is to become of the millions and tens of thousands of millions of creatures who will not have the strength to forego the earthly bread for the sake of the heavenly? Or dost Thou care only for the tens of thousands of the great and strong, while the millions, numerous as the sands of the sea, who are weak but love Thee, must exist only to serve as raw material for the great and strong? No, we cherish the weak, too. They are sinful and rebellious, but in the end they, too, will become obedient. They will marvel at us and look on us as gods, because we are ready to endure the freedom which they have found so dreadful and to rule over them — so awful will they find it in the end to be free. But we shall tell them that we obey Thee and rule in Thy name. We shall deceive them again, for we will not let Thee come to us again. That deception will be our suffering, for we shall be forced to lie.

" 'This is the meaning of the first question in the wilderness, and this is what Thou hast rejected in the name of that freedom which Thou hast exalted above everything. Yet in this question lay hid the great mystery of this world. Choosing "bread," Thou wouldst have satisfied the universal and everlasting craving of each man and of humanity as a whole — to find some one to bow down to. Having remained free, man strives for nothing so incessantly and so painfully as to find some one to bow down to. But man seeks to bow down to what is established beyond dispute, so that all men would agree at once to bow down to it. For these pitiful creatures are concerned not only to find what one or the other can bow down to, but to find something that all would believe in and bow down to; and it is essential that they all do it *together*. This craving for *community* of worship is the chief torment of every man individually and of all humanity from the beginning of time. For the sake of common worship they've slain each other with the sword. They have set up gods and challenged one another, "Put away your gods and come and worship ours, or we will kill you and your gods!" And so it will be to the end of the world, even when gods disappear from the earth; they will fall down before idols just the same. Thou didst know, Thou couldst not but have known, this fundamental secret of human nature, but Thou didst reject the one infallible banner which was offered Thee to make all men bow down to Thee alone — the banner of earthly bread; and Thou hast rejected it for the sake of freedom and the bread of Heaven. Behold what Thou didst further. And all again in the name of freedom! I tell Thee that man is tormented by no greater anxiety than to find some one quickly to whom he can hand over that gift of freedom with which the ill-fated creature is born. But only he will take possession of their freedom who can appease their conscience. In bread there was offered Thee an infallible token; give bread, and man will worship thee, for nothing is more certain than bread. But if some one else, apart from Thee, will gain possession of his conscience — oh! then he will cast away Thy bread and follow after him who has ensnared his conscience. In that Thou wast right. For the secret of man's being is not only to live but to have something to live for. Without a stable conception of the object of life, man would not consent to go on living, and would rather destroy himself than remain on earth, though he had bread in abundance. That is true. But what happened? Instead of taking men's freedom from them, Thou didst make it greater than ever! Didst Thou forget that man prefers peace, and even death, to freedom of choice in the knowledge of good and evil? Nothing is more seductive for man than his freedom of conscience, but nothing is more painful. And behold, instead of furnishing a firm foundation for setting the conscience of man at rest for ever, Thou didst choose all that is extraordinary, vague, and conjectural; Thou didst choose what was utterly beyond the strength of men, acting as though Thou didst not love them at all — Thou who didst come to give Thy life for them! Instead of taking possession of men's freedom, Thou didst increase it and burdened the spiritual kingdom of mankind with its sufferings for ever. Thou didst desire man's free love, that he should follow Thee freely, enticed and captivated by Thee. In place of the firm ancient law, man must hereafter with free heart decide for himself what is good and what is evil, having only Thy image before him as his guide. But did it not occur to Thee that he would at last question and indeed reject even Thy image and Thy truth, if he were weighed down with such a fearful burden as freedom of choice?

They will cry aloud at last that the truth is not in Thee, for they could not have been left in greater confusion and suffering than Thou hast caused, laying upon them so many cares and insoluble problems.

" 'So that, in truth, Thou didst Thyself lay the foundation for the destruction of Thy kingdom, and no one is more to blame for it. And yet was that what was offered Thee? There are three powers on earth, three powers alone, able to conquer and to hold captive for ever the conscience of these impotent rebels for their happiness — those powers are miracle, mystery, and authority. Thou hast rejected all three and hast set the example for doing so. When the wise and dread spirit set Thee on the pinnacle of the temple and said to Thee, "If Thou wouldst know whether Thou art the Son of God, cast Thyself down from hence, for it is written: the angels shall bear him up lest haply he dash his foot against a stone, and Thou shalt know then whether Thou art the Son of God and shalt prove then how great is Thy faith in Thy Father." But Thou didst refuse and wouldst not cast Thyself down. Oh! of course, Thou didst proudly and splendidly, like God; but the weak, unruly race of men, are they gods? Oh, Thou didst know then that in taking one step, in making one movement to cast Thyself down, Thou wouldst be tempting God and wouldst have lost all Thy faith in Him, and wouldst have been dashed to pieces against that earth which Thou didst come to save. And the wise spirit that tempted Thee would have rejoiced. But I ask again, are there many like Thee? And couldst Thou believe for one moment that men, too, could face such a temptation? Is the nature of men such, that they can reject miracle, and at the great moments of life, the moments of their deepest, most agonising spiritual difficulties, cling only to the free verdict of the heart? Oh, Thou didst know that Thy deed would be recorded in the books, would be handed down to remote times and reach the utmost ends of the earth, and Thou didst hope that man, following Thee, would cling to God without needing a miracle. But Thou didst not know that when man rejects miracle he rejects God, too; for man seeks not so much God as miracles. And as man cannot bear to be without the miracle, he will create new miracles of his own for himself, and will worship deeds of sorcery and witchcraft, though he might be a hundred times over a rebel, a heretic, and an atheist. Thou didst not come down from the Cross when they shouted to Thee, mocking and reviling Thee, "Come down from the cross and we will believe that Thou art He." Thou didst not come down, for again Thou wouldst not enslave man by a miracle, and didst crave faith given freely, not based on miracle. Thou didst crave free love and not the base raptures of the slave before the might that has overawed him for ever. But Thou didst think too highly of men therein, for they are slaves, of course, though rebellious by nature. Look round and judge; fifteen centuries have passed, look upon them. Whom hast Thou raised up to Thyself? I swear, man is weaker and baser by nature than Thou hast believed him! Can he, can he do what Thou didst? By showing him so much respect, Thou didst, as it were, cease to compassionate him, for Thou didst ask far too much from him — Thou who hast loved him more than Thyself! Respecting him less, Thou wouldst have asked less of him. That would have been more like love, for his burden would have been lighter. He is weak and vile. What though he is everywhere now rebelling against our power, and proud of his rebellion? It is the pride of a child and a school-boy. They are little children rioting and barring out the teacher at school. But their childish delight will end; it will cost them dear. They will cast down temples and drench the earth with blood. But they will see at last, the foolish children, that, though they are rebels, they are impotent rebels, unable to keep up their own rebellion. Bathed in their foolish tears, they will recognise at last that He who created them rebels must have meant to mock at them. They will say this in despair, and their utterance will be a blasphemy which will make them more unhappy still, for man's nature cannot bear blasphemy, and in the end always avenges it on itself. And so unrest, confusion, and unhappiness — that is the present lot of men after Thou didst suffer so much for their freedom! Thy great prophet tells in vision and in allegory, that he saw all those who took part in the first resurrection and that there were of each tribe twelve thousand. But if there were so many of them, they must have been not men but gods. They had borne Thy cross, they had endured scores of years in the barren, hungry wilderness, living upon locusts and roots — and Thou mayest indeed point with pride at those children of freedom, of free love, of free and splendid sacrifice in Thy name. But remember that they were only some thousands; and what of the rest? And how are the other weak ones to blame, because they could not endure what the strong have endured? How is the weak soul to blame that it is unable to receive such terrible gifts? Canst Thou have simply come to the elect and for the elect? But if so, it is a mystery and we cannot understand it. And if it is a mystery, we, too, have a right to preach a mystery, and to teach them that it's not the free judgment of their hearts, not love that matters, but a mystery which they must follow blindly, even against their conscience. So we have done. We have corrected Thy work and have founded it upon *miracle, mystery,* and *authority.* And men rejoiced that they were again led like sheep, and that the terrible gift that had brought them such suffering was, at last, lifted from their hearts. Were we right teaching them this? Speak! Did we not love mankind, so meekly acknowledging their feebleness, lovingly lightening their burden, and permitting their weak nature even sin with our sanction? Why hast Thou come now to hinder us? And why dost Thou look silently and searchingly at me with Thy meek eyes? Show anger. I don't want Thy love, for I love Thee not. And what use is it for me to hide anything from Thee? Don't I know to Whom I am speaking? All that I can say is known to Thee already, I read it in Thy eyes. And is it for me to conceal from Thee our secret? Perhaps it is Thy will to hear it from my lips. Listen, then. We are not with Thee, but with *him* — that is our secret. It's a long time — eight centuries — since we have been not with Thee but with *him.* Just eight centuries ago, we took from him what Thou didst reject with scorn, that last gift he offered Thee, showing Thee all the kingdoms of the earth. We took from him Rome and the sword of Cæsar, and proclaimed ourselves sole rulers of the earth, though hitherto we have not been able to bring our work to full completion. But whose fault is that? Oh, the work is only beginning, but it has begun. We have long to wait for completion and the earth has yet much to suffer, but we shall triumph and shall be Cæsars, and then we shall plan the universal happiness of man. But Thou mightest have taken even then the sword of Cæsar. Why didst Thou reject that last gift? Hadst Thou accepted that last counsel of the mighty spirit, Thou wouldst have accomplished all that man seeks on earth — that is, some one to bow down to, some one to hand his conscience to, and some means of uniting all in one unanimous and harmonious ant-heap, for the craving for universal unity is the third and last anguish of men. Mankind as a whole has always striven to organise a universal state. There have been many great nations with great histories, but the more highly they were developed the more unhappy they were, for they felt more acutely than other people the craving for world-wide union. The great conquerors, Timours and Genghis-Khans,[10] whirled like hurricanes over the face of the earth striving to conquer the universe, but even they, though unconsciously, expressed the same great craving of mankind for universal unity. Hadst Thou taken the world and Cæsar's purple,[11] Thou wouldst have founded the universal state and have given universal peace. For who can rule men if not he who holds their conscience and their bread in his hands. We have taken the sword of Cæsar, and in taking it, of course, have rejected Thee and followed *him.* Oh, there will yet be ages of the confusion of free thought, ages of their science and cannibalism. For having begun to build their tower of Babel without us, they will end, of course, with cannibalism. But then the beast will crawl to us and lick our feet and spatter them with tears of blood. And we shall sit upon the beast and raise the cup, and on it will be written, "Mystery." But then, and only then, the reign of peace and happiness will come for men. Thou art proud of Thine elect, but Thou hast only the elect, while we shall give rest to all. And besides, how many of those elect, those mighty ones who could become elect, have grown weary waiting for Thee, and have carried and will carry the powers of their spirit and the ardour of their heart to the other camp, and will end by raising their *free* banner against Thee. Thou didst Thyself lift up that banner. But with us all will be happy and will neither rebel nor destroy one another any more as under Thy freedom. Oh, we shall persuade them that they will become free only when they renounce their freedom in our favour and submit to us. And shall we be right or shall we be lying? They will be convinced that we are right, for they will remember the horrors of slavery and confusion to which Thy freedom brought them. Freedom, free thought and science, will lead them into such straits and will bring them face to face with such marvels and insoluble mysteries, that some of

[10] Tamerlane (1336–1405), Tatar conqueror; Genghis Khan (1162–1227), Mongol conqueror.
[11] imperial robe.

them, the fierce and rebellious, will destroy themselves, others, rebellious but weak, will destroy one another, while the rest, weak and unhappy, will crawl fawning to our feet and cry to us: "Yes, you were right, you alone possess His mystery, and we come back to you: save us from ourselves!"

" 'Receiving bread from us, they will see clearly that we take the bread made by their hands from them, to give it to them, without any miracle. They will see that we do not change the stones to bread, but in truth they will be more thankful for taking it from our hands than for the bread itself! For they will remember only too well that in old days, without our help, even the bread they made turned to stones in their hands, while since they have come back to us, the very stones have turned to bread in their hands. Too, too well will they know the value of complete submission! And until men know that, they will be unhappy. Who is most to blame for their not knowing it? Speak! Who scattered the flock and sent it astray on unknown paths? But the flock will come together again and will submit once more, and then it will be for all time. Then we shall give them the quiet humble happiness of weak creatures such as they are by nature. Oh, we shall persuade them at last not to be proud, for Thou didst lift them up and thereby taught them pride. We shall show them that they are weak, that they are only pitiful children, but that childlike happiness is the sweetest of all. They will become timid and will look to us and huddle close to us in fear, as chicks to the hen. They will marvel at us and will be awe-stricken before us, and will be proud of our being so powerful and clever that we have been able to subdue such a turbulent flock of thousands of millions. They will tremble impotently before our wrath, their minds will grow timid, they will become as tearful as women and children, but they will be just as ready at a sign from us to pass to laughter and rejoicing, to happy mirth and childish song. Yes, we shall set them to work, but in their leisure hours we shall make their life like a child's game, with children's songs and innocent dances. Oh, we shall allow them even sin, they are weak and helpless, and they will love us like children because we allow them to sin. We shall tell them that every sin will be expiated, if it is committed with our permission, that we allow them to sin because we love them, and the punishment for these sins we take upon ourselves. And we shall take it upon ourselves, and they will adore us as their saviours who have taken on themselves their sins before God. And they will have no secrets from us. We shall allow or forbid them to live with their wives and mistresses, to have or not to have children — according to whether they have been obedient or disobedient — and they will submit to us gladly and cheerfully. The most painful secrets of their conscience, all, all they will bring to us, and we shall absolve all. And they will be glad to accept our absolution, for it will save them from the great anxiety and terrible agony they endure at present in making a free decision for themselves. And all will be happy, all the millions of creatures except the hundred thousand who rule over them. For only we, we who guard the mystery, shall be unhappy. There will be thousands of millions of happy babes, and a hundred thousand sufferers who have taken upon themselves the curse of the knowledge of good and evil. Peacefully they will die, peacefully they will expire in Thy name, and beyond the grave they will find nothing but death. But we shall keep the secret, and for their happiness we shall allure them with the reward of heaven and eternity. For if there were anything in the other world, it certainly would not be for such as they. It is prophesied that Thou wilt come again victorious, Thou wilt come with Thy chosen, the proud and strong, but we will say that they have only saved themselves, but we have saved all. We are told that the harlot who sits upon the beast, and holds in her hands *mystery*, shall be put to shame, that the weak will rise up again, and will rend her royal purple and will strip naked her loathsome body. But I will then stand up and point out to Thee the thousand millions of happy babes who knew no sin. And we who have taken their sins upon us for the sake of their happiness will stand up before Thee and say: "Judge us if Thou canst and darest." Know that I fear Thee not. Know that I, too, have been in the wilderness, I, too, have lived on roots and locusts, I, too, prized the freedom with which Thou hast blessed men, and I, too, was striving to stand among Thy elect, among the strong and powerful, thirsting "to complete the number." But I awakened and would not serve madness. I turned back and joined the ranks of those *who have corrected Thy work*. I left the proud and went back to the humble, for the happiness of the humble. What I say to Thee will come to pass, and our Kingdom will be built. I repeat, to-morrow Thou shalt see that obedient flock who at a sign from me will hasten to heap up the hot embers about the pile on which I shall burn Thee for coming to hinder us. For if there ever was one who more than all others deserved our fires, it is Thou. To-morrow I shall burn Thee. *Dixi.*' "[12]

Ivan stopped. He was carried away as he talked and spoke with excitement; when he had finished, he suddenly smiled.

Alyosha, who had listened in silence, towards the end was greatly moved and seemed several times on the point of interrupting, but restrained himself. Now his words came with a rush.

"But . . . that's absurd!" he cried, flushing. "Your poem is in praise of Jesus, it does not blame Him — as you meant it to do. And who will believe you about freedom? Is that the way to understand it? That's not the idea of it in the Orthodox Church. . . . That's Rome, and not even the whole of Rome, it's false — those are the worst of the Catholics, the Inquisitors, the Jesuits! . . . And there could not be such a fantastic creature as your Inquisitor. What are these sins of mankind they take on themselves? Who are these keepers of the mystery who have taken some curse upon themselves for the happiness of mankind? When have they ever been seen? We know the Jesuits, they are spoken ill of, but are they really what you describe? They are not that at all, not at all. . . . They are simply the Romish army of the future universal earthly kingdom, with the Pontiff of Rome for Emperor . . .

[12] "I have spoken."

that's their ideal, but there's no sort of mystery or lofty melancholy about it. . . . It's simple lust for power, for filthy earthly goods, for domination — something like a universal serfdom with them as masters — that's all they stand for. They don't even believe in God perhaps. Your suffering Inquisitor is a mere fantasy."

"Stop, stop," laughed Ivan, "how hot you are! A fantasy you say, let it be so! Of course it's a fantasy. But allow me to say: do you really think that the Roman Catholic movement of the last centuries is actually nothing but the lust for power, for filthy goods? Is that what Father Païssy teaches you?"

"No, no, on the contrary, Father Païssy did once say something rather like what you said . . . but of course it's not that, not that at all," Alyosha hastily corrected himself.

"A precious admission, in spite of your 'not that at all.' I ask you why your Jesuits and Inquisitors have united simply for vile material gain? Why can there not be among them one martyr oppressed by great sorrow and loving humanity? You see, only suppose that there was one such man among all those who desire nothing but filthy material goods — if there's only one like my old Inquisitor, who had himself eaten roots in the desert and made frenzied efforts to subdue his flesh to make himself free and perfect. But yet all his life he loved humanity, and suddenly his eyes were opened, and he saw that it is no great moral blessedness to attain perfection and freedom, if at the same time one gains the conviction that millions of God's creatures have remained a mockery, that they will never be capable of using their freedom, that these poor rebels can never turn into giants to complete the tower, that it was not for such geese that the great idealist dreamt his dream of harmony. Seeing all that he turned back and joined — the clever people. Surely that could have happened?"

"Joined whom, what clever people?" cried Alyosha, almost in a frenzy. "They have no such great cleverness and no mysteries and secrets. . . . Perhaps nothing but atheism, that's all their secret. Your Inquisitor does not believe in God, that's his whole secret!"

"What if it is so! At last you have guessed it. It's perfectly true, it's true that that's the whole secret, but isn't that suffering, at least for a man like that, who has wasted his whole life in the desert and yet could not shake off his incurable love of humanity? In his declining days he reaches the clear conviction that nothing but what the great dread spirit advised could make any tolerable sort of life for the feeble, unruly, 'incomplete, experimental creatures fashioned in jest.' And so, convinced of this, he sees that he must follow the counsel of the wise spirit, the dread spirit of death and destruction, and therefore accept falsehood and deception, and lead men consciously to death and destruction, and yet deceive them all the way so that they may not notice where they are being led, that the poor blind creatures may at least on the way think themselves happy. And note, the deception is in the name of Him in Whose ideal the old man had so fervently believed all his life long. Isn't that a misfortune? And if only one such found himself at the head of the whole army 'filled with the lust for power only for the sake of filthy goods' — would not one such be enough to make a tragedy? More than that, one such standing at the head is enough to create the actual leading idea of the Roman Church with all its armies and Jesuits, its highest idea. I tell you frankly that I firmly believe that there has always been such a man among those who stood at the head of the movement. Who knows, there may have been some such even among the Roman Popes. Who knows, perhaps the spirit of that accursed old man who loves mankind so obstinately in his own way is to be found even now in a whole multitude of such old men, existing not by chance but by agreement, as a secret league formed long ago for the guarding of the mystery, to keep it from the weak and the unhappy, so as to make them happy. No doubt it is so, and so it must be indeed. I fancy that even among the Masons[13] there's something of the same mystery at the bottom, and that that's why the Catholics so detest the Masons as their rivals breaking up the unity of the idea, while it is so essential that there should be one flock and one shepherd. . . . But from the way I defend my idea I might be an author impatient of your criticism. Enough of it."

"You are perhaps a Mason yourself!" broke suddenly from Alyosha. "You don't believe in God," he added, speaking this time very sorrowfully. He fancied besides that his brother was looking at him ironically. "How does your poem end?" he asked, suddenly looking down. "Or was it the end?"

"I meant to end it like this. When the Inquisitor ceased speaking he waited some time for his Prisoner to answer him. The Prisoner's silence weighs down upon him. He saw that the Prisoner had listened intently all the time, looking gently in his eyes and evidently not wishing to reply. The old man longs for Him to say something, however bitter and terrible. But He suddenly approaches the old man in silence and gently kisses him on his bloodless aged lips. That is his whole answer. The old man shudders. The corners of his lips tremble. He goes to the door, opens it, and says to Him: 'Go, and come no more . . . come not at all, never, never!' And he lets Him out into the dark streets of the town. The Prisoner goes away."

"And the old man?"

"The kiss burns in his heart, but the old man adheres to his idea."

"And you with him, you too?" cried Alyosha mournfully.

Ivan laughed.

"Why, it's all nonsense, Alyosha. It's only a silly poem by a silly student, who could never write two lines of verse. Why do you take it so seriously? Surely you don't suppose I am going straight off to the Jesuits, to join the men who are correcting His work? Good Lord, it's no business of mine. I told you, all I want is to live on till I'm thirty, and then . . . dash the cup to the ground!"

"But the little sticky leaves, and the precious graves, and the blue sky, and the woman you love! How will you live, how will you love them?" Alyosha

[13] the Freemasons, a secret society prevalent in Europe in the 18th and 19th centuries, having for its aim mutual assistance and brotherly love.

cried sorrowfully. "With such a hell in your heart and your head, how can you? No, that's just what you are going away for, to join them . . . if not, you will kill yourself, you can't endure it!"

"There is a strength to endure everything," Ivan said with a cold smile.

"What strength?"

"The strength of the Karamazovs — the strength of the Karamazov baseness."

"To sink into debauchery, to stifle your soul with corruption, yes?"

"Possibly even that . . . only perhaps till I am thirty I shall escape it, and then . . ."

"How will you escape it? By what means will you escape it? That's impossible with your ideas."

"In the Karamazov way, again."

" 'Everything is permitted,' you mean? Everything is permitted, is that it?"

Ivan scowled, and all at once turned strangely pale.

"Ah, you've caught up yesterday's phrase, which so offended Miüsov — and which Dmitri pounced upon so naïvely and paraphrased!" he smiled queerly. "Yes, if you like, 'everything is lawful' since the word has been said. I won't deny it. And Mitya's version isn't bad."

Alyosha looked at him in silence.

"I thought that going away from here I have you at least," Ivan said suddenly, with unexpected feeling; "but now I see that there is no place for me even in your heart, my dear hermit. The formula, 'everything is permitted,' I won't renounce — will you renounce me for that, yes?"

Alyosha got up, went to him and gently kissed him on the lips.

"That's plagiarism," cried Ivan, highly delighted. "You stole that from my poem. Thank you though. Get up, Alyosha, it's time we were going, both of us."

They went out, but stopped when they reached the entrance of the restaurant.

"Listen, Alyosha," Ivan began in a resolute voice, "if I am really able to care for the sticky little leaves I shall only love them, remembering you. It's enough for me that you are somewhere here, and I shan't lose my desire for life yet. Is that enough for you? Take it as a declaration of love if you like. And now you go to the right and I to the left. And it's enough, do you hear, enough. I mean even if I don't go away to-morrow (I think I certainly shall go) and we meet again, don't say a word more on these subjects. I beg that particularly. And about Dmitri, too, I ask you specially never speak to me again," he added, with sudden irritation; "it's all done with, it has all been said over and over again, hasn't it? And I'll make you one promise in return for it. When, at thirty, I am ready to 'dash the cup to the ground,' wherever I may be I'll come to have one more talk with you, even though it were from America, you may be sure of that. I'll come on purpose. It will be very interesting to have a look at you, to see what you'll be by that time. It's rather a solemn promise, you see. And we really may be parting for seven years or ten. Come, go now to your Pater Seraphicus,[14] he is dying. If he dies without you, you will be angry with me for having kept you. Good-bye, kiss me once more; that's right, now go."

Ivan turned suddenly and went his way without looking back. . . .

Matthew Arnold   (1822–1888)

ENGLISH POET and CRITIC

Dover Beach

The sea is calm to-night.
The tide is full, the moon lies fair
Upon the straits; — on the French coast the light
Gleams and is gone; the cliffs of England stand,
Glimmering and vast, out in the tranquil bay.
Come to the window, sweet is the night-air!
Only, from the long line of spray
Where the sea meets the moon-blanch'd land,
Listen! you hear the grating roar
Of pebbles which the waves draw back, and fling,   10
At their return, up the high strand,
Begin, and cease, and then again begin,
With tremulous cadence slow, and bring
The eternal note of sadness in.

Sophocles long ago
Heard it on the Ægæan, and it brought
Into his mind the turbid ebb and flow
Of human misery; we
Find also in the sound a thought,
Hearing it by this distant northern sea.   20

The Sea of Faith
Was once, too, at the full, and round earth's shore
Lay like the folds of a bright girdle furl'd.
But now I only hear
Its melancholy, long, withdrawing roar,
Retreating, to the breath
Of the night-wind, down the vast edges drear
And naked shingles of the world.

[14] Angelic Father; Alyosha is temporarily out visiting from the monastery where he is a novitiate.

From *Poetry and Criticism of Matthew Arnold*, edited by A. Dwight Culler (Riverside Edition). Reprinted by permission of Houghton Mifflin Company.

Ah, love, let us be true
To one another! for the world, which seems   30
To lie before us like a land of dreams,
So various, so beautiful, so new,
Hath really neither joy, nor love, nor light,
Nor certitude, nor peace, nor help for pain;
And we are here as on a darkling plain
Swept with confused alarms of struggle and·flight,
Where ignorant armies clash by night.

Thomas Hardy (1840–1928)

ENGLISH NOVELIST, POET, and DRAMATIST

The Oxen

Christmas Eve, and twelve of the clock.
 "Now they are all on their knees,"
An elder said as we sat in a flock
 By the embers in hearthside ease.

We pictured the meek mild creatures where
 They dwelt in their strawy pen,
Nor did it occur to one of us there
 To doubt they were kneeling then.

So fair a fancy few would weave
 In these years! Yet, I feel,   10
If someone said on Christmas Eve,
 "Come; see the oxen kneel,

"In the lonely barton by yonder coomb   **barton:** farmyard. **coomb:** valley
 Our childhood used to know,"
I should go with him in the gloom,
 Hoping it might be so.

Gerard Manley Hopkins (1844–1889)

ENGLISH POET and CLERGYMAN

God's Grandeur

The world is charged with the grandeur of God.
  It will flame out, like shining from shook foil;
  It gathers to a greatness, like the ooze of oil
Crushed. Why do men then now not reck his rod?
Generations have trod, have trod, have trod;
  And all is seared with trade; bleared, smeared with toil;
  And wears man's smudge and shares man's smell: the soil
Is bare now, nor can foot feel, being shod.

And for all this, nature is never spent;
  There lives the dearest freshness deep down things;   10
And though the last lights off the black West went
  Oh, morning, at the brown brink eastward, springs —
Because the Holy Ghost over the bent
  World broods with warm breast and with ah! bright wings.

William Butler Yeats (1865–1939)

IRISH POET and DRAMATIST

The Second Coming

Turning and turning in the widening gyre
The falcon cannot hear the falconer;
Things fall apart; the centre cannot hold;
Mere anarchy is loosed upon the world,
The blood-dimmed tide is loosed, and everywhere
The ceremony of innocence is drowned;
The best lack all conviction, while the worst
Are full of passionate intensity.

gyre: spiral of bird's flight; for Yeats history is composed of two interlocking gyres, one inverted, so that the moment of greatest destruction is the moment of greatest hope.

"God's Grandeur" by Gerard Manley Hopkins. From *Poems of Gerard Manley Hopkins,* Third Edition, edited by W. H. Gardner. Copyright 1948 by Oxford University Press, Inc. Reprinted by permission.

"The Second Coming" by William Butler Yeats. Reprinted with permission of The Macmillan Company from *The Collected Poems of W. B. Yeats* by William Butler Yeats. Copyright 1924 by The Macmillan Company, renewed 1952 by Bertha Georgie Yeats. Also by permission of Mr. M. B. Yeats and Macmillan & Co. Ltd., London.

Surely some revelation is at hand;
Surely the Second Coming is at hand.   10
The Second Coming! Hardly are those words out
When a vast image out of *Spiritus Mundi*
Troubles my sight: somewhere in sands of the desert
A shape with lion body and the head of a man,
A gaze blank and pitiless as the sun,
Is moving its slow thighs, while all about it
Reel shadows of the indignant desert birds.
The darkness drops again; but now I know
That twenty centuries of stony sleep
Were vexed to nightmare by a rocking cradle,   20
And what rough beast, its hour come round at last,
Slouches towards Bethlehem to be born?

Spiritus Mundi: world's collective spirit or memory

shape . . . man: Sphinx

V. I. Lenin   (1870–1924)

RUSSIAN REVOLUTIONARY LEADER

Socialism and Religion

Modern society is based entirely on the exploitation of the enormous masses of the working-class by an insignificant minority of the population — the landowning and capitalist classes. This society is a slave society, for the "free" workers, who work all their lives for the benefit of capital, have a "right" only to so much of the means of existence as is essential to sustain them as slaves while producing profit for the capitalists — or, in short, sufficient to secure and perpetuate capitalist slavery.

This economic oppression of the workers inevitably causes and breeds all forms of political oppression and social degradation: it renders the spiritual and moral life of the masses coarser and more sordid. The workers may acquire a greater or less degree of political freedom to fight for their economic emancipation, but so long as the domination of capital is not overthrown, no amount of freedom will rid them of destitution, unemployment and oppression. Religion is one of the forms of spiritual oppression which everywhere weigh upon the masses who are crushed by continuous toil for others, by poverty and loneliness. The helplessness of the exploited classes in their struggle against the exploiters inevitably generates a belief in a better life after death, even as the helplessness of the savage in his struggle with nature gives rise to a belief in gods, devils, miracles, etc.

Title supplied by editors. "Socialism and Religion" by V. I. Lenin. From *Religion* (Little Lenin Library, Vol. 7). Reprinted by permission of International Publishers Co., Inc.

Religion teaches those who toil in poverty all their lives to be resigned and patient in this world, and consoles them with the hope of reward in heaven. As for those who live upon the labour of others, religion teaches them to be charitable in earthly life, thus providing a cheap justification for their whole exploiting existence and selling them at a reasonable price tickets to heavenly bliss. Religion is the opium of the people.[1] Religion is a kind of spiritual intoxicant, in which the slaves of capital drown their humanity and their desires for some sort of decent human existence.

But a slave who has become conscious of his slavery, and who has risen to the height of fighting for his emancipation, has half ceased to be a slave. The class-conscious worker of to-day, brought up in big industry and enlightened by town life, rejects religious prejudices with contempt. He leaves heaven to the priests and bourgeois hypocrites and fights for a better life for himself, here on earth. The modern proletariat ranges itself on the side of Socialism, which, with the help of science, is dispersing the fog of religion and is liberating the workers from their faith in a life after death, by rallying them to the present-day struggle for a better life here upon earth.

"Religion must be regarded as a private matter"; in these words the attitude of Socialists to religion is usually expressed. But we must define the meaning of these words precisely so as to avoid misunderstanding. We demand that religion be regarded as a private matter as far as the state is concerned, but under no circumstances can we consider it a private matter with regard to our own Party.

The state must not concern itself with religion; religious societies must not be bound to the state. Every one must be absolutely free to profess whatever religion he likes, or to profess no religion, i.e., to be an atheist, as every Socialist is. There must be no discrimination whatever in the rights of citizens on religious grounds. Even particulars concerning the religion of citizens on official documents must be completely done away with. No subsidies must be paid to the established church, and no grants from state funds made to the church or religious societies. These must become independent of the state, voluntary associations of citizens of one faith.

Only the thorough fulfilment of these demands can put an end to that shameful and accursed past when the church was in feudal dependence on the state, and Russian citizens were in feudal dependence on the established church; when inquisitorial, mediæval laws (which are still in our statute books and in our legal codes) were actively in force. These laws laid down penalties for the profession or non-profession of a particular religion. They violated the conscience of the individual, and connected the distribution of official posts and revenues with the distribution of this or that state church intoxicant. Complete separation of the church and the state — this is the demand made on the present-day state and church by the socialist proletariat.

The Russian revolution must realise this demand, as a necessary integral

---

[1] The phrase is properly Marx's.

part of political freedom. The Russian revolution is in fact in a particularly favourable position for doing this, since the disgusting red tape of the politically feudal autocracy has stirred up discontent, ferment and indignation even among the clergy. Cowed and ignorant as the Russian orthodox clergy is, even it has been aroused by the thundering collapse of the old mediæval Russian régime. Even the clergy endorses the demand for liberty, protests against bureaucracy and the tyranny of officials, against the police inquisition forced on the "Servants of God." We, Socialists, must support this movement, carrying the demands of the honest and sincere people among the clergy to their logical conclusion, taking them at their word when they talk about liberty, demanding that they completely sever all connection between religion and the police. Either you are sincere, in which case you must stand for a complete separation of the church from the state and of the school from the church, and insist that religion be regarded entirely and unconditionally as a private matter. Or you do not accept these consistent demands of liberty, in which case it means that you are still a slave to inquisitorial traditions, that you are still hankering after government posts and the revenues attached to them, that you do not believe in the spiritual force of your weapon, and that you still wish to take bribes from the government. If this is so, the class-conscious Russian workers will declare ruthless war on you.

To the party of the Socialist proletariat, however, religion is not a private matter. Our Party is a league of class-conscious, progressive fighters for the liberation of the working-class. Such a league cannot and must not be indifferent to lack of class-consciousness, to ignorance or insanity in the shape of religious beliefs. We demand entire separation of the state from the church, in order to disperse the fog of religion by purely intellectual, and only intellectual, weapons, by our press and oral persuasion. One of the objects of our organisation, the Russian Social-Democratic Labour Party,[2] is precisely to fight against all religious deception of the workers. For us, the ideological struggle is not a private matter but one that concerns the whole Party, the whole proletariat.

If so, why do we not declare in our programme that we are atheists? Why do we not debar Christians and believers in god from joining our Party?

The answer to this question reveals a very important difference between the bourgeois-democratic, and the Social-Democratic attitude towards religion.

Our programme is based entirely on scientific — to be more precise — upon a *materialist* world conception. In explaining our programme, therefore, we must necessarily explain the actual historical and economic roots of the religious fog. Our programme necessarily includes the propaganda of atheism. The publication of related scientific literature (which up till now has been strictly forbidden and persecuted by the autocratic feudal government) must now form one of the items of our party work. We shall now, probably, have

---

[2] The original name of the party of which (after 1903) the Bolsheviks became the left-wing. Ultimately the division became a complete split and the Bolsheviks went forward to become the Communist Party of the U.S.S.R. [Ed.]

to follow the advice which Engels once gave to the German Socialists — to translate and spread among the masses the enlightening atheist literature of the eighteenth century.

But, in this connection, we must under no circumstances allow ourselves to be sidetracked into a treatment of the religious question in the abstract — idealistically — as a matter of "pure reason," detached from the class struggle, a presentation often given by radical bourgeois democrats. It would be absurd to imagine in a society based upon the unlimited oppression and degradation of the working masses that it is possible to dispel religious prejudices by mere preaching. It would be bourgeois narrow-mindedness to lose sight of the fact that the oppression exercised by religion on humanity is only a product and reflection of the economic oppression in society. No books, no preaching, can possibly enlighten the proletariat, unless it is enlightened by its own struggle against the dark forces of capitalism. The unity of that genuinely revolutionary struggle of the oppressed class to set up a heaven on earth is more important to us than a unity in proletarian opinion about the imaginary paradise in the sky.

That is why we do not declare, and must not declare in our programme that we are atheists; that is why we do not forbid and must not forbid proletarians who still cling to the remnants of old prejudices to come into closer contact with our Party. We shall always preach a scientific world conception; we must fight against the inconsistencies of the "Christians"; but this does not mean that the religious question must be pushed into the foreground where it does not belong. We must not allow the forces waging a genuinely revolutionary economic and political struggle to be broken up for the sake of opinions and dreams that are of third-rate importance, which are rapidly losing all political significance, and which are being steadily relegated to the rubbish heap by the normal course of economic development.

The reactionary bourgeoisie, here as elsewhere, always takes pains to fan religious animosities in order to divert the attention of the masses to religion and away from those really important and fundamental questions, economic and political, which the All-Russian proletariat, actually uniting in the revolutionary struggle, is now deciding. This reactionary tactic of splitting the proletarian forces, which to-day manifests itself mainly by Black-Hundred pogroms,[3] may to-morrow express itself in more subtle forms. We will in any case oppose to it a calm, sustained and patient advocacy of proletarian solidarity and scientific world conception, which will avoid provoking secondary differences.

The revolutionary proletariat will see to it that religion does really become a private matter as far as the state is concerned. And then, under a régime cleaned of mediæval mustiness, the proletariat will wage a great open struggle for the abolition of economic slavery, the real source of the religious deception of humanity.

[3] widespread organized massacres, especially of Jews, around the turn of the century in Russia.

Franz Kafka (1883–1924)

AUSTRIAN NOVELIST and SHORT STORY WRITER

The Hunter Gracchus

Two boys were sitting on the harbor wall playing with dice. A man was reading a newspaper on the steps of the monument, resting in the shadow of a hero who was flourishing his sword on high. A girl was filling her bucket at the fountain. A fruitseller was lying beside his scales, staring out to sea. Through the vacant window and door openings of a café one could see two men quite at the back drinking their wine. The proprietor was sitting at a table in front and dozing. A bark was silently making for the little harbor, as if borne by invisible means over the water. A man in a blue blouse climbed ashore and drew the rope through a ring. Behind the boatman two other men in dark coats with silver buttons carried a bier, on which, beneath a great flower-patterned tasselled silk cloth, a man was apparently lying.

Nobody on the quay troubled about the newcomers; even when they lowered the bier to wait for the boatman, who was still occupied with his rope, nobody went nearer, nobody asked them a question, nobody accorded them an inquisitive glance.

The pilot was still further detained by a woman who, a child at her breast, now appeared with loosened hair on the deck of the boat. Then he advanced and indicated a yellowish two-storeyed house that rose abruptly on the left beside the sea; the bearers took up their burden and bore it to the low but gracefully pillared door. A little boy opened a window just in time to see the party vanishing into the house, then hastily shut the window again. The door too was now shut; it was of black oak, and very strongly made. A flock of doves which had been flying round the belfry alighted in the street before the house. As if their food were stored within, they assembled in front of the door. One of them flew up to the first storey and pecked at the window-pane. They were bright-hued, well-tended, beautiful birds. The woman on the boat flung grain to them in a wide sweep; they ate it up and flew across to the woman.

A man in a top hat tied with a band of crêpe now descended one of the narrow and very steep lanes that led to the harbor. He glanced round vigilantly, everything seemed to displease him, his mouth twisted at the sight of some offal in a corner. Fruit skins were lying on the steps of the monument; he swept them off in passing with his stick. He rapped at the house door, at the same time taking his top hat from his head with his black-gloved hand.

The door was opened at once, and some fifty little boys appeared in two rows in the long entry-hall, and bowed to him.

The boatman descended the stairs, greeted the gentleman in black, conducted him up to the first storey, led him round the bright and elegant loggia which encircled the courtyard, and both of them entered, while the boys pressed after them at a respectful distance, a cool spacious room looking towards the back, from whose window no habitation, but only a bare, blackish grey rocky wall was to be seen. The bearers were busied in setting up and lighting several long candles at the head of the bier, yet these did not give light, but only scared away the shadows which had been immobile till then, and made them flicker over the walls. The cloth covering the bier had been thrown back. Lying on it was a man with wildly matted hair, who looked somewhat like a hunter. He lay without motion and, it seemed, without breathing, his eyes closed; yet only his trappings indicated that this man was probably dead.

The gentleman stepped up to the bier, laid his hand on the brow of the man lying upon it, then kneeled down and prayed. The boatman made a sign to the bearers to leave the room; they went out, drove away the boys who had gathered outside, and shut the door. But even that did not seem to satisfy the gentleman; he glanced at the boatman; the boatman understood, and vanished through a side door into the next room. At once the man on the bier opened his eyes, turned his face painfully towards the gentleman, and said: "Who are you?" Without any mark of surprise the gentleman rose from his kneeling posture and answered: "The Burgomaster of Riva."

The man on the bier nodded, indicated a chair with a feeble movement of his arm, and said, after the Burgomaster had accepted his invitation: "I knew that, of course, Burgomaster, but in the first moments of returning consciousness I always forget, everything goes round before my eyes, and it is best to ask about anything even if I know. You too probably know that I am the hunter Gracchus."

"Certainly," said the Burgomaster. "Your arrival was announced to me during the night. We had been asleep for a good while. Then towards midnight my wife cried: 'Salvatore' — that's my name — 'look at that dove at the window.' It was really a dove, but as big as a cock. It flew over me and said in my ear: 'Tomorrow the dead hunter Gracchus is coming; receive him in the name of the city.'"

The hunter nodded and licked his lips with the tip of his tongue: "Yes, the doves flew here before me. But do you believe, Burgomaster, that I shall remain in Riva?"

"I cannot say that yet," replied the Burgomaster. "Are you dead?"

"Yes," said the hunter, "as you see. Many years ago, yes, it must be a great many years ago, I fell from a precipice in the Black Forest — that is in Germany — when I was hunting a chamois. Since then I have been dead."

"But you are alive too," said the Burgomaster.

"In a certain sense," said the hunter, "in a certain sense I am alive too. My death ship lost its way; a wrong turn of the wheel, a moment's absence of mind on the pilot's part, a longing to turn aside towards my lovely native country, I cannot tell what it was; I only know this, that I remained on earth and that ever since my ship has sailed earthly waters. So I, who asked for nothing better than to live among my mountains, travel after my death through all the lands of the earth."

"And you have no part in the other world?" asked the Burgomaster, knitting his brow.

"I am forever," replied the hunter, "on the great stair that leads up to it. On that infinitely wide and spacious stair I clamber about, sometimes up, sometimes down, sometimes on the right, sometimes on the left, always in motion. The hunter has been turned into a butterfly. Do not laugh."

"I am not laughing," said the Burgomaster in self-defense.

"That is very good of you," said the hunter. "I am always in motion. But when I make a supreme flight and see the gate actually shining before me I awaken presently on my old ship, still stranded forlornly in some earthly sea or other. The fundamental error of my one-time death grins at me as I lie in my cabin. Julia, the wife of the pilot, knocks at the door and brings me on my bier the morning drink of the land whose coasts we chance to be passing. I lie on a wooden pallet, I wear — it cannot be a pleasure to look at me — a filthy winding sheet, my hair and beard, black tinged with grey, have grown together inextricably, my limbs are covered with a great flower-patterned woman's shawl with long fringes. A sacramental candle stands at my head and lights me. On the wall opposite me is a little picture, evidently of a Bushman who is aiming his spear at me and taking cover as best he can behind a beautifully painted shield. On shipboard one is often a prey to stupid imaginations, but that is the stupidest of them all. Otherwise my wooden case is quite empty. Through a hole in the side wall come in the warm airs of the southern night, and I hear the water slapping against the old boat.

"I have lain here ever since the time when, as the hunter Gracchus living in the Black Forest, I followed a chamois and fell from a precipice. Everything happened in good order. I pursued, I fell, bled to death in a ravine, died, and this ship should have conveyed me to the next world. I can still remember how gladly I stretched myself out on this pallet for the first time. Never did the mountains listen to such songs from me as these shadowy walls did then.

"I had been glad to live and I was glad to die. Before I stepped aboard, I joyfully flung away my wretched load of ammunition, my knapsack, my hunting rifle that I had always been proud to carry, and I slipped into my winding sheet like a girl into her marriage dress. I lay and waited. Then came the mishap."

"A terrible fate," said the Burgomaster, raising his hand defensively. "And you bear no blame for it?"

"None," said the hunter. "I was a hunter; was there any sin in that? I followed my calling as a hunter in the Black Forest, where there were still wolves in those days. I lay in ambush, shot, hit my mark, flayed the skins from my victims: was there any sin in that? My labors were blessed. 'The great hunter of the Black Forest' was the name I was given. Was there any sin in that?"

"I am not called upon to decide that," said the Burgomaster, "but to me also there seems to be no sin in such things. But, then, whose is the guilt?"

"The boatman's," said the hunter. "Nobody will read what I say here, no one will come to help me; even if all the people were commanded to help me, every door and window would remain shut, everybody would take to bed and draw the bedclothes over his head, the whole earth would become an inn for the night. And there is sense in that, for nobody knows of me, and if anyone knew he would not know where I could be found, and if he knew where I could be found, he would not know how to deal with me, he would not know how to help me. The thought of helping me is an illness that has to be cured by taking to one's bed.

"I know that, and so I do not shout to summon help, even though at moments — when I lose control over myself, as I have done just now, for instance — I think seriously of it. But to drive out such thoughts I need only look round me and verify where I am, and — I can safely assert — have been for hundreds of years."

"Extraordinary," said the Burgomaster, "extraordinary. — And now do you think of staying here in Riva with us?"

"I think not," said the hunter with a smile, and, to excuse himself, he laid his hand on the Burgomaster's knee. "I am here, more than that I do not know, further than that I cannot go. My ship has no rudder, and it is driven by the wind that blows in the undermost regions of death."

Walter T. Stace   (1886–1967)

AMERICAN PHILOSOPHER

Man against Darkness

I

The Catholic bishops of America recently issued a statement in which they said that the chaotic and bewildered state of the modern world is due to man's loss of faith, his abandonment of God and religion. For my part I believe in no religion at all. Yet I entirely agree with the bishops. It is no doubt an over-simplification to speak of *the* cause of so complex a state of affairs as the tortured condition of the world today. Its causes are doubtless multitudinous. Yet allowing for some element of oversimplification, I say that the bishops' assertion is substantially true.

M. Jean-Paul Sartre, the French existentialist philosopher, labels himself an atheist. Yet his views seem to me plainly to support the statement of the bishops. So long as there was believed to be a God in the sky, he says, men could regard him as the source of their moral ideals. The universe, created and governed by a fatherly God, was a friendly habitation for man. We could be sure that, however great the evil in the world, good in the end would triumph and the forces of evil would be routed. With the disappearance of God from the sky all this has changed. Since the world is not ruled by a spiritual being, but rather by blind forces, there cannot be any ideals, moral or otherwise, in the universe outside us. Our ideals, therefore, must proceed only from our own minds; they are our own inventions. Thus the world which surrounds us is nothing but an immense spiritual emptiness. It is a dead universe. We do not live in a universe which is on the side of our values. It is completely indifferent to them.

Years ago Mr. Bertrand Russell, in his essay *A Free Man's Worship*, said much the same thing.

> Such in outline, but even more purposeless, more void of meaning, is the world which Science presents for our belief. Amid such a world, if anywhere, our ideals henceforward must find a home. . . . Blind to good and evil, reckless of destruction, omnipotent matter rolls on its relentless way; for man, condemned today to lose his dearest, tomorrow himself to pass through the gate of darkness, it remains only to cherish, ere yet the blow falls, the lofty thoughts that ennoble his little day; . . . to worship at the shrine his own hands have built; . . . to sustain alone, a weary but unyielding Atlas, the world that his own ideals have fashioned despite the trampling march of unconscious power.

It is true that Mr. Russell's personal attitude to the disappearance of religion is quite different from either that of M. Sartre or the bishops or myself. The bishops think it a calamity. So do I. M. Sartre finds it "very distressing." And he berates as shallow the attitude of those who think that without God the world can go on just the same as before, as if nothing had happened. This creates for mankind, he thinks, a terrible crisis. And in this I agree with him. Mr. Russell, on the other hand, seems to believe that religion has done more harm than good in the world, and that its disappearance will be a blessing. But his picture of the world, and of the modern mind, is the same as that of M. Sartre. He stresses the *purposelessness* of the universe, the facts that man's ideals are his own creations, that the universe outside him in no way supports them, that man is alone and friendless in the world.

Mr. Russell notes that it is science which has produced this situation. There is no doubt that this is correct. But the way in which it has come about is not generally understood. There is a popular belief that some particular scientific discoveries or theories, such as the Darwinian theory of evolution, or the views of geologists about the age of the earth, or a series of such discoveries, have done the damage. It would be foolish to deny that these discoveries have had a great effect in undermining religious dogmas. But this account does not at all go to the root of the matter. Religion can probably outlive any scientific discoveries which could be made. It can accommodate itself to them. The root cause of the decay of faith has not been any particular discovery of science, but rather the general spirit of science and certain basic assumptions upon which modern science, from the seventeenth century onwards, has proceeded.

II

It was Galileo and Newton — notwithstanding that Newton himself was a deeply religious man — who destroyed the old comfortable picture of a friendly universe governed by spiritual values. And this was effected, not by Newton's discovery of the law of gravitation nor by any of Galileo's brilliant investigations, but by the general picture of the world which these men and others of their time made the basis of the science, not only of their own day, but of all succeeding generations down to the present. That is why the century immediately following Newton, the eighteenth century, was notoriously an age of religious skepticism. Skepticism did not have to wait for the discoveries of Darwin and the geologists in the nineteenth century. It flooded the world immediately after the age of the rise of science.

Neither the Copernican hypothesis nor any of Newton's or Galileo's particular discoveries were the real causes. Religious faith might well have accommodated itself to the new astronomy. The real turning point between the medieval age of faith and the modern age of unfaith came when the scientists of the seventeenth century turned their backs upon what used to be called "final causes." The final cause of a thing or event meant the purpose which it was supposed to serve in the universe, its cosmic purpose. What lay back of this was the presupposition that there is a cosmic order or plan and that everything which exists could in the last analysis be explained in terms of its place in this cosmic plan, that is, in terms of its purpose.

Plato and Aristotle believed this, and so did the whole medieval Christian world. For instance, if it were true that the sun and the moon were created and exist for the purpose of giving light to man, then this fact would explain why the sun and the moon exist. We might not be able to discover the purpose of everything, but everything must have a purpose. Belief in final causes thus amounted to a belief that the world is governed by purposes, presumably the purposes of some overruling mind. This belief was not the invention of Christianity. It was basic to the whole of Western civilization, whether in the ancient pagan world or in Christendom, from the time of Socrates to the rise of science in the seventeenth century.

The founders of modern science — for instance, Galileo, Kepler, and Newton — were mostly pious men who did not doubt God's purposes. Nevertheless they took the revolutionary step of consciously and deliberately expelling the idea of purpose as controlling nature from their new science of nature. They did this on the ground that inquiry into purposes is useless for what science aims at: namely, the prediction and control of events. To predict an eclipse, what you have to know is not its purpose but its causes. Hence science from the seventeenth century onwards became exclusively an inquiry into causes. The conception of purpose in the world was ignored and frowned on. This, though silent and almost unnoticed, was the greatest revolution in human history, far outweighing in importance any of the political revolutions whose thunder has reverberated through the world.

For it came about in this way that for the past three hundred years there has been growing up in men's minds, dominated as they are by science, a new imaginative picture of the world. The world, according to this new picture, is purposeless, senseless, meaningless. Nature is nothing but matter in motion. The motions of matter are governed, not by any purpose, but by blind forces and laws. Nature on this view, says Whitehead[1] — to whose writings I am indebted in this part of my paper — is "merely the hurrying of material, endlessly, meaninglessly." You can drew a sharp line across the history of Europe dividing it into two epochs of very unequal length. The line passes through the lifetime of Galileo. European man before Galileo — whether ancient pagan or more recent Christian — thought of the world as controlled by plan and purpose. After Galileo European man thinks of it as utterly purposeless. This is the great revolution of which I spoke.

It is this which has killed religion. Religion could survive the discoveries that the sun, not the earth, is the center; that men are descended from simian ancestors; that the earth is hundreds of millions of years old. These discoveries may render out of date some of the details of older theological dogmas, may force their restatement in new intellectual frameworks. But they do not touch the essence of the religious vision itself, which is the faith that there is plan and purpose in the world, that the world is a moral order, that in the end all things are for the best. This faith may express itself through many different intellectual dogmas, those of Christianity, of Hinduism, of Islam. All and any of these intellectual dogmas may be destroyed without destroying the essential religious spirit. But that spirit cannot survive destruction of belief in a plan and purpose of the world, for that is the very heart of it. Religion can get on with any sort of astronomy, geology, biology, physics. But it cannot get on with a purposeless and meaningless universe.

If the scheme of things is purposeless and meaningless, then the life of man is purposeless and meaningless too. Everything is futile, all effort is in the end worthless. A man may, of course, still pursue disconnected ends, money,

[1] Alfred North Whitehead (1861–1947), British mathematician and philosopher.

fame, art, science, and may gain pleasure from them. But his life is hollow at the center. Hence the dissatisfied, disillusioned, restless spirit of modern man.

The picture of a meaningless world, and a meaningless human life, is, I think, the basic theme of much modern art and literature. Certainly it is the basic theme of modern philosophy. According to the most characteristic philosophies of the modern period from Hume in the eighteenth century to the so-called positivists of today, the world is just what it is, and that is the end of all inquiry. There is no reason for its being what it is. Everything might just as well have been quite different, and there would have been no reason for that either. When you have stated what things are, what things the world contains, there is nothing more which could be said, even by an omniscient being. To ask any question about *why* things are thus, or what purpose their being so serves, is to ask a senseless question, because they serve no purpose at all. For instance, there is for modern philosophy no such thing as the ancient problem of evil. For this once famous question presupposes that pain and misery, though they seem so inexplicable and irrational to us, must ultimately subserve some rational purpose, must have their places in the cosmic plan. But this is nonsense. There is no such overruling rationality in the universe. Belief in the ultimate irrationality of everything is the quintessence of what is called the modern mind.

It is true that, parallel with these philosophies which are typical of the modern mind, preaching the meaninglessness of the world, there has run a line of idealistic philosophies whose contention is that the world is after all spiritual in nature and that moral ideals and values are inherent in its structure. But most of these idealisms were simply philosophical expressions of romanticism, which was itself no more than an unsuccessful counterattack of the religious against the scientific view of things. They perished, along with romanticism in literature and art, about the beginning of the present century, though of course they still have a few adherents.

At the bottom these idealistic systems of thought were rationalizations of man's wishful thinking. They were born of the refusal of men to admit the cosmic darkness. They were comforting illusions within the warm glow of which the more tender-minded intellectuals sought to shelter themselves from the icy winds of the universe. They lasted a little while. But they are shattered now, and we return once more to the vision of a purposeless world.

III

Along with the ruin of the religious vision there went the ruin of moral principles and indeed of all values. If there is a cosmic purpose, if there is in the nature of things a drive towards goodness, then our moral systems will derive their validity from this. But if our moral rules do not proceed from something outside us in the nature of the universe — whether we say it is God or simply the universe itself — then they must be our own inventions. Thus it came to be believed that moral rules must be merely an expression of our own likes and dislikes. But likes and dislikes are notoriously variable. What pleases one man, people, or culture displeases another. Therefore morals are wholly relative.

This obvious conclusion from the idea of a purposeless world made its appearance in Europe immediately after the rise of science, for instance in the philosophy of Hobbes.[2] Hobbes saw at once that if there is no purpose in the world there are no values either. "Good and evil," he writes, "are names that signify our appetites and aversions; which in different tempers, customs, and doctrines of men are different. . . . Every man calleth that which pleaseth him, good; and that which displeaseth him, evil."

This doctrine of the relativity of morals, though it has recently received an impetus from the studies of anthropologists, was thus really implicit in the whole scientific mentality. It is disastrous for morals because it destroys their entire traditional foundation. That is why philosophers who see the danger signals, from the time at least of Kant,[3] have been trying to give to morals a new foundation, that is, a secular or nonreligious foundation. This attempt may very well be intellectually successful. Such a foundation, independent of the religious view of the world, might well be found. But the question is whether it can ever be a *practical* success, that is, whether apart from its logical validity and its influence with intellectuals, it can ever replace among the masses of men the lost religious foundation. On that question hangs perhaps the future of civilization. But meanwhile disaster is overtaking us.

The widespread belief in "ethical relativity" among philosophers, psychologists, ethnologists, and sociologists is the theoretical counterpart of the repudiation of principle which we see all around us, especially in international affairs, the field in which morals have always had the weakest foothold. No one any longer effectively believes in moral principles except as the private prejudices either of individual men or of nations or cultures. This is the inevitable consequence of the doctrine of ethical relativity, which in turn is the inevitable consequence of believing in a purposeless world.

Another characteristic of our spiritual state is loss of belief in the freedom of the will. This also is a fruit of the scientific spirit, though not of any particular scientific discovery. Science has been built up on the basis of determinism, which is the belief that every event is completely determined by a chain of causes and is therefore theoretically predictable beforehand. It is true that recent physics seems to challenge this. But so far as its practical consequences are concerned, the damage has long ago been done. A man's actions, it was argued, are as much events in the natural world as is an eclipse of the sun. It follows that men's actions are as theoretically predictable as an eclipse. But if it is certain now that John Smith will murder Joseph Jones at 2.15 P.M. on January 1, 1963, what possible meaning can it have to say that

[2] Thomas Hobbes, English philosopher (1588–1679), attempted to examine man and society without theological or ethical preconceptions, using scientific methods of observation.
[3] Immanuel Kant, German philosopher (1724–1804), investigated the forms of human understanding and aimed at disclosing the conditions which make valid knowledge possible.

when that time comes John Smith will be *free* to choose whether he will commit the murder or not? And if he is not free, how can he be held responsible?

It is true that the whole of this argument can be shown by a competent philosopher to be a tissue of fallacies — or at least I claim that it can. But the point is that the analysis required to show this is much too subtle to be understood by the average entirely unphilosophical man. Because of this, the argument against free will is generally swallowed whole by the unphilosophical. Hence the thought that man is not free, that he is the helpless plaything of forces over which he has no control, has deeply penetrated the modern mind. We hear of economic determinism, cultural determinism, historical determinism. We are not responsible for what we do because our glands control us, or because we are the products of environment or heredity. Not moral self-control, but the doctor, the psychiatrist, the educationist, must save us from doing evil. Pills and injections in the future are to do what Christ and the prophets have failed to do. Of course I do not mean to deny that doctors and educationists can and must help. And I do not mean in any way to belittle their efforts. But I do wish to draw attention to the weakening of moral controls, the greater or less repudiation of personal responsibility which, in the popular thinking of the day, result from these tendencies of thought.

IV

What, then, is to be done? Where are we to look for salvation from the evils of our time? All the remedies I have seen suggested so far are, in my opinion, useless. Let us look at some of them.

Philosophers and intellectuals generally can, I believe, genuinely do something to help. But it is extremely little. What philosophers can do is to show that neither the relativity of morals nor the denial of free will really follows from the grounds which have been supposed to support them. They can also try to discover a genuine secular basis for morals to replace the religious basis which has disappeared. Some of us are trying to do these things. But in the first place philosophers unfortunately are not agreed about these matters, and their disputes are utterly confusing to the non-philosophers. And in the second place their influence is practically negligible because their analyses necessarily take place on a level on which the masses are totally unable to follow them.

The bishops, of course, propose as remedy a return to belief in God and in the doctrines of the Christian religion. Others think that a new religion is what is needed. Those who make these proposals fail to realize that the crisis in man's spiritual condition is something unique in history for which there is no sort of analogy in the past. They are thinking perhaps of the collapse of the ancient Greek and Roman religions. The vacuum then created was easily filled by Christianity, and it might have been filled by Mithraism[4]

---

[4] Indo-Iranian religion centered around the worship of Mithra, god of light, which spread throughout Asia Minor and the Roman Empire and finally gave way to Christianity.

if Christianity had not appeared. By analogy they think that Christianity might now be replaced by a new religion, or even that Christianity itself, if revivified, might bring back health to men's lives.

But I believe that there is no analogy at all between our present state and that of the European peoples at the time of the fall of paganism. Men had at that time lost their belief only in particular dogmas, particular embodiments of the religious view of the world. It had no doubt become incredible that Zeus and the other gods were living on the top of Mount Olympus. You could go to the top and find no trace of them. But the imaginative picture of a world governed by purpose, a world driving towards the good — which is the inner spirit of religion — had at that time received no serious shock. It had merely to re-embody itself in new dogmas, those of Christianity or some other religion. Religion itself was not dead in the world, only a particular form of it.

But now the situation is quite different. It is not merely that particular dogmas, like that of the virgin birth, are unacceptable to the modern mind. That is true, but it constitutes a very superficial diagnosis of the present situation of religion. Modern skepticism is of a wholly different order from that of the intellectuals of the ancient world. It has attacked and destroyed not merely the outward forms of the religious spirit, its particularized dogmas, but the very essence of that spirit itself, belief in a meaningful and purposeful world. For the founding of a new religion a new Jesus Christ or Buddha would have to appear, in itself a most unlikely event and one for which in any case we cannot afford to sit and wait. But even if a new prophet and a new religion did appear, we may predict that they would fail in the modern world. No one for long would believe in them, for modern men have lost the vision, basic to all religion, of an ordered plan and purpose of the world. They have before their minds the picture of a purposeless universe, and such a world-picture must be fatal to any religion at all, not merely to Christianity.

We must not be misled by occasional appearances of a revival of the religious spirit. Men, we are told, in their disgust and disillusionment at the emptiness of their lives, are turning once more to religion, or are searching for a new message. It may be so. We must expect such wistful yearnings of the spirit. We must expect men to wish back again the light that is gone, and to try to bring it back. But however they may wish and try, the light will not shine again — not at least in the civilization to which we belong.

Another remedy commonly proposed is that we should turn to science itself, or the scientific spirit, for our salvation. Mr. Russell and Professor Dewey[5] both make this proposal, though in somewhat different ways. Professor Dewey seems to believe that discoveries in sociology, the application of scientific method to social and political problems, will rescue us. This seems to me to be utterly naïve. It is not likely that science, which is basically the cause of our spiritual troubles, is likely also to produce the cure for them. Also it lies in the nature of science that, though it can teach us the best means

[5] John Dewey (1859–1952), American philosopher and educator who believed in teaching by experience rather than by precept.

for achieving our ends, it can never tell us what ends to pursue. It cannot give us any ideals. And our trouble is about ideals and ends, not about the means for reaching them.

V

No civilization can live without ideals, or to put it in another way, without a firm faith in moral ideas. Our ideals and moral ideas have in the past been rooted in religion. But the religious basis of our ideals has been undermined, and the superstructure of ideals is plainly tottering. None of the commonly suggested remedies on examination seems likely to succeed. It would therefore look as if the early death of our civilization were inevitable.

Of course we know that it is perfectly possible for individual men, very highly educated men, philosophers, scientists, intellectuals in general, to live moral lives without any religious convictions. But the question is whether a whole civilization, a whole family of peoples, composed almost entirely of relatively uneducated men and women, can do this.

It follows, of course, that if we could make the vast majority of men as highly educated as the very few are now, we might save the situation. And we are already moving slowly in that direction through the techniques of mass education. But the critical question seems to concern the time-lag. Perhaps in a few hundred years most of the population will, at the present rate, be sufficiently highly educated and civilized to combine high ideals with an absence of religion. But long before we reach any such stage, the collapse of our civilization may have come about. How are we to live through the intervening period?

I am sure that the first thing we have to do is to face the truth, however bleak it may be, and then next we have to learn to live with it. Let me say a word about each of these two points. What I am urging as regards the first is complete honesty. Those who wish to resurrect Christian dogmas are not, of course, consciously dishonest. But they have that kind of unconscious dishonesty which consists in lulling oneself with opiates and dreams. Those who talk of a new religion are merely hoping for a new opiate. Both alike refuse to face the truth that there is, in the universe outside man, no spirituality, no regard for values, no friend in the sky, no help or comfort for man of any sort. To be perfectly honest in the admission of this fact, not to seek shelter in new or old illusions, not to indulge in wishful dreams about this matter, this is the first thing we shall have to do.

I do not urge this course out of any special regard for the sanctity of truth in the abstract. It is not self-evident to me that truth is the supreme value to which all else must be sacrificed. Might not the discoverer of a truth which would be fatal to mankind be justified in suppressing it, even in teaching men a falsehood? Is truth more valuable than goodness and beauty and happiness? To think so is to invent yet another absolute, another religious delusion in which Truth with a capital T is substituted for God. The reason why we must now boldly and honestly face the truth that the universe is non-spiritual and indifferent to goodness, beauty, happiness, or truth is not that it would be wicked to suppress it, but simply that it is too late to do so, so that in the end we cannot do anything else but face it. Yet we stand on the brink, dreading the icy plunge. We need courage. We need honesty.

Now about the other point, the necessity of learning to live with the truth. This means learning to live virtuously and happily, or at least contentedly, without illusions. And this is going to be extremely difficult because what we have now begun dimly to perceive is that human life in the past, or at least human happiness, has almost wholly depended upon illusions. It has been said that man lives by truth, and that the truth will make us free. Nearly the opposite seems to me to be the case. Mankind has managed to live only by means of lies, and the truth may very well destroy us. If one were a Bergsonian[6] one might believe that nature deliberately puts illusions into our souls in order to induce us to go on living.

The illusions by which men have lived seem to be of two kinds. First, there is what one may perhaps call the Great Illusion — I mean the religious illusion that the universe is moral and good, that it follows a wise and noble plan, that it is gradually generating some supreme value, that goodness is bound to triumph in it. Secondly, there is a whole host of minor illusions on which human happiness nourishes itself. How much of human happiness notoriously comes from the illusions of the lover about his beloved? Then again we work and strive because of the illusions connected with fame, glory, power, or money. Banners of all kinds, flags, emblems, insignia, ceremonials, and rituals are invariably symbols of some illusion or other. The British Empire, the connection between mother country and dominions, is partly kept going by illusions surrounding the notion of kingship. Or think of the vast amount of human happiness which is derived from the illusion of supposing that if some nonsense syllable, such as "sir," or "count" or "lord," is pronounced in conjunction with our names, we belong to a superior order of people.

There is plenty of evidence that human happiness is almost wholly based upon illusions of one kind or another. But the scientific spirit, or the spirit of truth, is the enemy of illusions and therefore the enemy of human happiness. That is why it is going to be so difficult to live with the truth.

There is no reason why we should have to give up the host of minor illusions which render life supportable. There is no reason why the lover should be scientific about the loved one. Even the illusions of fame and glory may persist. But without the Great Illusion, the illusion of a good, kindly, and purposeful universe, we shall *have* to learn to live. And to ask this is really no more than to ask that we become genuinely civilized beings and not merely sham civilized beings.

I can best explain the difference by a reminiscence. I remember a fellow student in my college days, an ardent Christian, who told me that if he did

6 Henri Bergson, French philosopher (1859–1941), was concerned with the importance of intuition and perception in man's knowledge.

not believe in a future life, in heaven and hell, he would rape, murder, steal, and be a drunkard. That is what I call being a sham civilized being. On the other hand, not only could a Huxley,[7] a John Stuart Mill, a David Hume,[8] live great and fine lives without any religion, but a great many others of us, quite obscure persons, can at least live decent lives without it.

To be genuinely civilized means to be able to walk straightly and to live honorably without the props and crutches of one or another of the childish dreams which have so far supported men. That such a life is likely to be ecstatically happy I will not claim. But that it can be lived in quiet content, accepting resignedly what cannot be helped, not expecting the impossible, and thankful for small mercies, this I would maintain. That it will be difficult for men in general to learn this lesson I do not deny. But that it will be impossible I would not admit since so many have learned it already.

Man has not yet grown up. He is not adult. Like a child he cries for the moon and lives in a world of fantasies. And the race as a whole has perhaps reached the great crisis of its life. Can it grow up as a race in the same sense as individual men grow up? Can man put away childish things and adolescent dreams? Can he grasp the real world as it actually is, stark and bleak, without its romantic or religious halo, and still retain his ideals, striving for great ends and noble achievements? If he can, all may yet be well. If he cannot, he will probably sink back into the savagery and brutality from which he came, taking a humble place once more among the lower animals.

[7] Thomas Henry Huxley, English biologist (1825–1895), advocated agnosticism and the subordination of belief to evidence and reason.
[8] English philosophers.

E. E. Cummings   (1894–1962)

AMERICAN POET, NOVELIST, and PAINTER

Jehovah buried,Satan dead

Jehovah buried,Satan dead,
do fearers worship Much and Quick;
badness not being felt as bad,
itself thinks goodness what is meek;
obey says toc,submit says tic,
Eternity's a Five Year Plan:
if Joy with Pain shall hang in hock
who dares to call himself a man?

go dreamless knaves on Shadows fed,
your Harry's Tom,your Tom is Dick;   10
while Gadgets murder squawk and add,
the cult of Same is all the chic;
by instruments,both span and spic,
are justly measured Spic and Span:
to kiss the mike if Jew turn kike
who dares to call himself a man?

loudly for Truth have liars pled,
their heels for Freedom slaves will click;
where Boobs are holy,poets mad,
illustrious punks of Progress shriek;   20
when Souls are outlawed,Hearts are sick,
Hearts being sick,Minds nothing can:
if Hate's a game and Love's a φυκ
who dares to call himself a man?

φυκ: fuck (phony Greek, apparently used phonetically to avoid the taboo word)

King Christ,this world is all aleak;
and lifepreservers there are none:
and waves which only He may walk
Who dares to call Himself a man.

Aldous Huxley (1894–1963)

ENGLISH NOVELIST and ESSAYIST

The Perennial Philosophy

More than twenty-five centuries have passed since that which has been called the Perennial Philosophy was first committed to writing; and in the course of those centuries it has found expression, now partial, now complete, now in this form, now in that, again and again. In Vedanta and Hebrew prophecy, in the Tao Teh King[1] and the Platonic dialogues, in the Gospel according to St. John and Mahayana theology,[2] in Plotinus[3] and the Areopagite,[4] among the Persian Sufis and the Christian mystics of the Middle Ages

[1] a book of Taoist philosophical verse by Lao-Tzu.
[2] one of the two major schools of Buddhism, which teaches the path to salvation through faith and love for all creatures.
[3] Roman philosopher (205–270) and founder of the Neoplatonist school, which concerned itself with religious questions.
[4] Dionysius the Areopagite, an Athenian converted by St. Paul.

Title supplied by editors. "The Perennial Philosophy" by Aldous Huxley. Introduction to *The Song of God: Bhagavad-Gita* by Aldous Huxley, translated by Swami Prabhavananda and Christopher Isherwood. Originally published by Harper & Brothers. Copyright, 1944, 1951, by the Vedanta Society of Southern California. Reprinted by permission.

and the Renaissance — the Perennial Philosophy has spoken almost all the languages of Asia and Europe and has made use of the terminology and traditions of every one of the higher religions. But under all this confusion of tongues and myths, of local histories and particularist doctrines, there remains a Highest Common Factor, which is the Perennial Philosophy in what may be called its chemically pure state. This final purity can never, of course, be expressed by any verbal statement of the philosophy, however undogmatic that statement may be, however deliberately syncretistic. The very fact that it is set down at a certain time by a certain writer, using this or that language, automatically imposes a certain sociological and personal bias on the doctrines so formulated. It is only in the act of contemplation, when words and even personality are transcended, that the pure state of the Perennial Philosophy can actually be known. The records left by those who have known it in this way make it abundantly clear that all of them, whether Hindu, Buddhist, Hebrew, Taoist, Christian or Mohammedan, were attempting to describe the same essentially indescribable Fact.

The original scriptures of most religions are poetical and unsystematic. Theology, which generally takes the form of a reasoned commentary on the parables and aphorisms of the scriptures, tends to make its appearance at a later stage of religious history. The Bhagavad-Gita[5] occupies an intermediate position between scripture and theology; for it combines the poetical qualities of the first with the clear-cut methodicalness of the second. The book may be described, writes Ananda K. Coomaraswamy in his admirable *Hinduism and Buddhism*, 'as a compendium of the whole Vedic doctrine to be found in the earlier Vedas, Brahmanas and Upanishads, and being therefore the basis of all the later developments, it can be regarded as the focus of all Indian religion.' But this 'focus of Indian religion' is also one of the clearest and most comprehensive summaries of the Perennial Philosophy ever to have been made. Hence its enduring value, not only for Indians, but for all mankind.

At the core of the Perennial Philosophy we find four fundamental doctrines.

First: the phenomenal world of matter and of individualized consciousness — the world of things and animals and men and even gods — is the manifestation of a Divine Ground within which all partial realities have their being, and apart from which they would be non-existent.

Second: human beings are capable not merely of knowing *about* the Divine Ground by inference; they can also realize its existence by a direct intuition, superior to discursive reasoning. This immediate knowledge unites the knower with that which is known.

Third: man possesses a double nature, a phenomenal ego and an eternal Self, which is the inner man, the spirit, the spark of divinity within the soul. It is possible for a man, if he so desires, to identify himself with the spirit and therefore with the Divine Ground, which is of the same or like nature with the spirit.

Fourth: man's life on earth has only one end and purpose: to identify

[5] part of a long Indian epic, and one of the great religious classics of the world.

himself with his eternal Self and so to come to unitive knowledge of the Divine Ground.

In Hinduism the first of these four doctrines is stated in the most categorical terms. The Divine Ground is Brahman, whose creative, sustaining and transforming aspects are manifested in the Hindu trinity. A hierarchy of manifestations connects inanimate matter with man, gods, High Gods and the undifferentiated Godhead beyond.

In Mahayana Buddhism the Divine Ground is called Mind or the Pure Light of the Void; the place of the High Gods is taken by the Dhyani-Buddhas.[6]

Similar conceptions are perfectly compatible with Christianity and have in fact been entertained, explicitly or implicitly, by many Catholic and Protestant mystics, when formulating a philosophy to fit facts observed by super-rational intuition. Thus, for Eckhart and Ruysbroeck,[7] there is an Abyss of Godhead underlying the Trinity, just as Brahman underlies Brahma, Vishnu and Shiva.[8] Suso[9] has even left a diagrammatic picture of the relations subsisting between Godhead, triune God and creatures. In this very curious and interesting drawing a chain of manifestation connects the mysterious symbol of the Divine Ground with the three Persons of the Trinity, and the Trinity in turn is connected in a descending scale with angels and human beings. These last, as the drawing vividly shows, may make one of two choices. They can either lead the life of the outer man, the life of separative selfhood; in which case they are lost (for, in the words of the Theologia Germanica, 'nothing burns in hell but the self'). Or else they can identify themselves with the inner man, in which case it became possible for them, as Suso shows, to ascend again, through unitive knowledge, to the Trinity and even, beyond the Trinity, to the ultimate Unity of the Divine Ground.

Within the Mohammedan tradition such a rationalization of the immediate mystical experience would have been dangerously unorthodox. Nevertheless, one has the impression, while reading certain Sufi texts, that their authors did in fact conceive of *al haqq*, the Real, as being the Divine Ground or Unity of Allah, underlying the active and personal aspects of the Godhead.

The second doctrine of the Perennial Philosophy — that it is possible to know the Divine Ground by a direct intuition higher than discursive reasoning — is to be found in all the great religions of the world. A philosopher who is content merely to know about the ultimate Reality — theoretically and by hearsay — is compared by Buddha to a herdsman of other men's cows. Mohammed uses an even homelier barnyard metaphor. For him the philosopher who has not realized his metaphysics is just an ass bearing a load of books. Christian, Hindu and Taoist teachers wrote no less emphatically about the absurd pretensions of mere learning and analytical reasoning. In the words

[6] a Mahayana school of Buddhism which relies on meditation as the chief means for Enlightenment.

[7] Meister Eckhart (1260?–1328?), German mystic; Jan van Ruysbroeck (1293–1381), Flemish mystic and writer.

[8] also Siva; Hindu god of destruction and reproduction.

[9] Heinrich Suso (1295–1366), German mystic, Dominican monk, and a disciple of Eckhart.

of the Anglican Prayer Book, our eternal life, now and hereafter, 'stands in the knowledge of God;' and this knowledge is not discursive but 'of the heart,' a super-rational intuition, direct, synthetic and timeless.

The third doctrine of the Perennial Philosophy, that which affirms the double nature of man, is fundamental in all the higher religions. The unitive knowledge of the Divine Ground has, as its necessary condition, self-abnegation and charity. Only by means of self-abnegation and charity can we clear away the evil, folly and ignorance which constitute the thing we call our personality and prevent us from becoming aware of the spark of divinity illuminating the inner man. But the spark within is akin to the Divine Ground. By identifying ourselves with the first we can come to unitive knowledge of the second. These empirical facts of the spiritual life have been variously rationalized in terms of the theologies of the various religions. The Hindus categorically affirm that thou art That — that the indwelling Atman[10] is the same as Brahman. For orthodox Christianity there is not an identity between the spark and God. Union of the human spirit with God takes place — union so complete that the word 'deification' is applied to it; but it is not the union of identical substances. According to Christian theology the saint is 'deified,' not because Atman *is* Brahman, but because God has assimilated the purified human spirit into the divine substance by an act of grace. Islamic theology seems to make a similar distinction. The Sufi, Mansur, was executed for giving to the words 'union' and 'deification' the literal meaning which they bear in the Hindu tradition. For our present purposes, however, the significant fact is that these words are actually used by Christians and Mohammedans to describe the empirical facts of metaphysical realization by means of direct, super-rational intuition.

In regard to man's final end, all the higher religions are in complete agreement. The purpose of human life is the discovery of Truth, the unitive knowledge of the Godhead. The degree to which this unitive knowledge is achieved here on earth determines the degree to which it will be enjoyed in the posthumous state. Contemplation of truth is the end, action the means. In India, in China, in ancient Greece, in Christian Europe, this was regarded as the most obvious and axiomatic piece of orthodoxy. The invention of the steam engine produced a revolution, not merely in industrial techniques, but also and much more significantly in philosophy. Because machines could be made progressively more and more efficient, Western man came to believe that men and societies would automatically register a corresponding moral and spiritual improvement. Attention and allegiance came to be paid, not to Eternity, but to the Utopian future. External circumstances came to be regarded as more important than states of mind about external circumstances, and the end of human life was held to be action, with contemplation as a means to that end. These false and, historically, aberrant and heretical doctrines are now systematically taught in our schools and repeated, day in, day

10 soul, or principle of life.

out, by those anonymous writers of advertising copy who, more than any other teachers, provide European and American adults with their current philosophy of life. And so effective has been the propaganda that even professing Christians accept the heresy unquestioningly and are quite unconscious of its complete incompatibility with their own or anybody else's religion.

These four doctrines constitute the Perennial Philosophy in its minimal and basic form. A man who can practise what the Indians call Jnana yoga (the metaphysical discipline of discrimination between the real and the apparent) asks for nothing more. The simple working hypothesis is enough for his purposes. But such discrimination is exceedingly difficult and can hardly be practised, at any rate in the preliminary stages of the spiritual life, except by persons endowed with a particular kind of mental constitution. That is why most statements of the Perennial Philosophy have included another doctrine, affirming the existence of one or more human Incarnations of the Divine Ground, by whose mediation and grace the worshipper is helped to achieve his goal — that unitive knowledge of the Godhead, which is man's eternal life and beatitude. The Bhagavad-Gita is one such statement. Here, Krishna is an Incarnation of the Divine Ground in human form. Similarly, in Christian and Buddhist theology, Jesus and Gotama[11] are Incarnations of divinity. But whereas in Hinduism and Buddhism more than one Incarnation of the Godhead is possible (and is regarded as having in fact taken place), for Christians there has been and can be only one.

An Incarnation of the Godhead and, to a lesser degree, any theocentric saint, sage or prophet is a human being who knows Who he is and can therefore effectively remind other human beings of what they have allowed themselves to forget: namely, that if they choose to become what potentially they already are, they too can be eternally united with the Divine Ground.

Worship of the Incarnation and contemplation of his attributes are for most men and women the best preparation for unitive knowledge of the Godhead. But whether the actual knowledge itself can be achieved by this means is another question. Many Catholic mystics have affirmed that, at a certain stage of that contemplative prayer in which, according to the most authoritative theologians, the life of Christian perfection ultimately consists, it is necessary to put aside all thoughts of the Incarnation as distracting from the higher knowledge of that which has been incarnated. From this fact have arisen misunderstandings in plenty and a number of intellectual difficulties. Here, for example, is what Abbot John Chapman[12] writes in one of his admirable Spiritual Letters: 'The problem of *reconciling* (not merely uniting) mysticism with Christianity is more difficult. The Abbot (Abbot Marmion)[13] says that St John of the Cross[14] is like a sponge full of Christianity. You can

---

[11] Gautama Buddha (563–483 B.C.), founder of the Buddhist religion.
[12] English monk (1865–1933).
[13] Irish-born Abbot (1858–1923) of the Belgian monastery of Maredsous.
[14] Juan de Yepes (1542–1591), Spanish monk, mystic and poet, and co-founder of the Discalced (i.e., unshod) Carmelites.

squeeze it all out, and the full mystical theory remains. Consequently, for fifteen years or so, I hated St John of the Cross and called him a Buddhist. I loved St Teresa,[15] and read her over and over again. She is first a Christian, only secondarily a mystic. Then I found that I had wasted fifteen years, so far as prayer was concerned.' And yet, he concludes, in spite of its 'Buddhistic' character, the practice of mysticism (or, to put it in other terms, the realization of the Perennial Philosophy) makes good Christians. He might have added that it also makes good Hindus, good Buddhists, good Taoists, good Moslems and good Jews.

The solution to Abbot Chapman's problem must be sought in the domain, not of philosophy, but of psychology. Human beings are not born identical. There are many different temperaments and constitutions; and within each psycho-physical class one can find people at very different stages of spiritual development. Forms of worship and spiritual discipline which may be valuable for one individual may be useless or even positively harmful for another belonging to a different class and standing, within that class, at a lower or higher level of development. All this is clearly set forth in the Gita, where the psychological facts are linked up with general cosmology by means of the postulate of the *gunas*.[16] Krishna, who is here the mouthpiece of Hinduism in all its manifestations, finds it perfectly natural that different men should have different methods and even apparently different objects of worship. All roads lead to Rome — provided, of course, that it is Rome and not some other city which the traveller really wishes to reach. A similar attitude of charitable inclusiveness, somewhat surprising in a Moslem, is beautifully expressed in the parable of Moses and the Shepherd, told by Jalaluddin Rumi[17] in the second book of the Masnavi. And within the more exclusive Christian tradition these problems of temperament and degree of development have been searchingly discussed in their relation to the way of Mary and the way of Martha in general, and in particular to the vocation and private devotion of individuals.

We now have to consider the ethical corollaries of the Perennial Philosophy. 'Truth,' says St Thomas Aquinas, 'is the last end for the entire universe, and the contemplation of truth is the chief occupation of wisdom.' The moral virtues, he says in another place, belong to contemplation, not indeed essentially, but as a necessary predisposition. Virtue, in other words, is not the end, but the indispensable means to the knowledge of divine reality. Shankara, the greatest of the Indian commentators on the Gita, holds the same doctrine. Right action is the way to knowledge; for it purifies the mind, and it is only to a mind purified from egotism that the intuition of the Divine Ground can come.

Self-abnegation, according to the Gita, can be achieved by the practice of two all-inclusive virtues — love and non-attachment. The latter is the same

15 St. Teresa of Avila (1515–1582), Spanish Carmelite nun, author of "The Way of Perfection" and other spiritual works.
16 a Sankhya or Vedantic experience culminating in *satori*.
17 Persian poet (1207–1373), author of the *Masnavi,* a series of stories with moral maxims.

thing as that 'holy indifference,' on which St François de Sales[18] is never tired of insisting. 'He who refers every action to God,' writes Camus, summarizing his master's teaching, 'and has no aims save His Glory, will find rest everywhere, even amidst the most violent commotions.' So long as we practise this holy indifference to the fruits of action, 'no lawful occupation will separate us from God; on the contrary, it can be made a means of closer union.' Here the word 'lawful' supplies a necessary qualification to a teaching which, without it, is incomplete and even potentially dangerous. Some actions are intrinsically evil or inexpedient; and no good intentions, no conscious offering of them to God, no renunciation of the fruits can alter their essential character. Holy indifference requires to be taught in conjunction not merely with a set of commandments prohibiting crimes, but also with a clear conception of what in Buddha's Eightfold Path is called 'right livelihood.' Thus, for the Buddhist, right livelihood was incompatible with the making of deadly weapons and of intoxicants; for the mediæval Christian, with the taking of interest and with various monopolistic practices which have since come to be regarded as legitimate good business. John Woolman, the American Quaker, provides a most enlightening example of the way in which a man may live in the world, while practising perfect non-attachment and remaining acutely sensitive to the claims of right livelihood. Thus, while it would have been profitable and perfectly lawful for him to sell West Indian sugar and rum to the customers who came to his shop, Woolman refrained from doing so, because these things were the products of slave labour. Similarly, when he was in England, it would have been both lawful and convenient for him to travel by stage coach. Nevertheless, he preferred to make his journeys on foot. Why? Because the comforts of rapid travel could only be bought at the expense of great cruelty to the horses and the most atrocious working conditions for the post-boys. In Woolman's eyes, such a system of transportation was intrinsically undesirable, and no amount of personal non-attachment could make it anything but undesirable. So he shouldered his knapsack and walked.

In the preceding pages I have tried to show that the Perennial Philosophy and its ethical corollaries constitute a Highest Common Factor, present in all the major religions of the world. To affirm this truth has never been more imperatively necessary than at the present time. There will never be enduring peace unless and until human beings come to accept a philosophy of life more adequate to the cosmic and psychological facts than the insane idolatries of nationalism and the advertising man's apocalyptic faith in Progress towards a mechanized New Jerusalem. All the elements of this philosophy are present, as we have seen, in the traditional religions. But in existing circumstances there is not the slightest chance that any of the traditional religions will obtain universal acceptance. Europeans and Americans will see no reason for being converted to Hinduism, say, or Buddhism. And the people of Asia can hardly be expected to renounce their own traditions for the Christianity professed,

[18] St. Francis of Sales (1567–1622), Bishop of Geneva, taught that perfection is possible for all.

often sincerely, by the imperialists who, for four hundred years and more, have been systematically attacking, exploiting and oppressing, and are now trying to finish off the work of destruction by 'educating' them. But happily there is the Highest Common Factor of all religions, the Perennial Philosophy which has always and everywhere been the metaphysical system of the prophets, saints and sages. It is perfectly possible for people to remain good Christians, Hindus, Buddhists or Moslems and yet to be united in full agreement on the basic doctrines of the Perennial Philosophy. . . .

C. S. Lewis (1898–1963)

ENGLISH WRITER and CHRISTIAN APOLOGIST

What Christians Believe

I

I have been asked to tell you what Christians believe, and I am going to begin by telling you one thing that Christians don't need to believe. If you are a Christian you don't have to believe that all the other religions are simply wrong all through. If you are an atheist you do have to believe that the main point in all the religions of the whole world is simply one huge mistake. If you are a Christian, you are free to think that all these religions, even the queerest ones, contain at least some hint of the truth. When I was an atheist I had to try to persuade myself that the whole human race were pretty good fools until about one hundred years ago; when I became a Christian I was able to take a more liberal view. But, of course, being a Christian does mean thinking that where Christianity differs from other religions, Christianity is right and they are wrong. Like in arithmetic — there's only one right answer to a sum, and all other answers are wrong: but some of the wrong answers are much nearer being right than others.

The first big division of humanity is into the majority, who believe in some kind of God or gods, and the minority who don't. On this point, Christianity lines up with the majority — lines up with ancient Greeks and Romans, modern savages, Stoics, Platonists, Hindoos, Mohammedans, etc., against the modern Western European materialist. There are all sorts of different reasons for believing in God, and here I'll mention only one. It is this. Supposing there was no intelligence behind the universe, no creative mind. In that case

Reprinted with permission of The Macmillan Company from *The Case for Christianity*, Part II, by C. S. Lewis. First published in the United States of America in 1943. Also by permission of Geoffrey Bles Ltd., Publishers, London.

nobody designed my brain for the purpose of thinking. It is merely that when the atoms inside my skull happen for physical or chemical reasons to arrange themselves in a certain way, this gives me, as a bye-product, the sensation I call thought. But if so, how can I trust my own thinking to be true? It's like upsetting a milk-jug and hoping that the way the splash arranges itself will give you a map of London. But if I can't trust my own thinking, of course I can't trust the arguments leading to atheism, and therefore have no reason to be an atheist, or anything else. Unless I believe in God, I can't believe in thought: so I can never use thought to disbelieve in God.

Now I go on to the next big division. People who all believe in God can be divided according to the sort of God they believe in. There are two very different ideas on this subject. One of them is the idea that He is beyond good and evil. We call one thing good and another thing bad. But according to some people that's merely our human point of view. These people would say that the wiser you become the less you'd want to call anything good or bad, and the more clearly you'd see that everything is good in one way and bad in another, and that nothing could have been different. Consequently, these people think that long before you got anywhere near the divine point of view the distinction would have disappeared altogether. We call a cancer bad, they'd say, because it kills a man; but you might just as well call a successful surgeon bad because he kills a cancer. It all depends on the point of view. The other and opposite idea is that God is quite definitely "good" or "righteous," a God who take sides, who loves love and hates hatred, who wants us to behave in one way and not in another. The first of these views — the one that thinks God beyond good and evil — is called Pantheism. It was held by the great Prussian philosopher Hegel and, as far as I can understand them, by the Hindoos. The other view is held by Jews, Mohammedans, and Christians.

And with this big difference between Pantheism and the Christian idea of God, there usually goes another. Pantheists usually believe that God, so to speak, animates the universe as you animate your body: that the universe almost *is* God, so that if it didn't exist He wouldn't exist either, and anything you find in the universe is a part of God. The Christian idea is quite different. They think God *made* the universe — like a man making a picture or composing a tune. A painter isn't a picture, and he doesn't die if his picture is destroyed. You may say, "He's put a lot of himself into it," but that only means that all its beauty and interest has come out of his head. His skill isn't in the picture in the same way that it's in his head, or even in his hands. I expect you see how this difference between Pantheists and Christians hangs together with the other one. If you don't take the distinction between good and bad very seriously, then it's easy to say that anything you find in this world is a part of God. But, of course, if you think some things really bad, and God really good, then you can't talk like that. You must believe that God is separate from the world and that some of the things we see in it are contrary to His will. Confronted with a cancer or a slum the Pantheist can say, "If you could only see it from the divine point of view, you would realise that this also is God." The Christian replies, "Don't talk damned nonsense."[1] For Christianity is a fighting religion. It thinks God made the world — that space and time, heat and cold, and all the colours and tastes, and all the animals and vegetables, are things that God "made up out of His head" as a man makes up a story. But it also thinks that a great many things have gone wrong with the world that God made and that God insists, and insists very loudly, on our putting them right again.

And, of course, that raises a very big question. If a good God made the world why has it gone wrong? And for many years I simply wouldn't listen to the Christian answers to this question, because I kept on feeling "whatever you say, and however clever your arguments are, isn't it much simpler and easier to say that the world was *not* made by any intelligent power? Aren't all your arguments simply a complicated attempt to avoid the obvious?" But then that threw me back into those difficulties about atheism which I spoke of a moment ago. And soon I saw another difficulty.

My argument against God was that the universe seemed so cruel and unjust. But how had I got this idea of *just* and *unjust?* A man doesn't call a line crooked unless he has some idea of a straight line. What was I comparing this universe with when I called it unjust? If the whole show was bad and senseless from A to Z, so to speak, why did I, who was supposed to be part of the show, find myself in such violent reaction against it? A man feels wet when he falls into water, because man isn't a water animal: a fish wouldn't feel wet. Of course I could have given up my idea of justice by saying it was nothing but a private idea of my own. But if I did that then my argument against God collapsed too — for the argument depended on saying that the world was really unjust, not that it just didn't happen to please my private fancies. Thus in the very act of trying to prove that God didn't exist — in other words, that the whole of reality was senseless — I found I was forced to assume that one part of reality — namely my idea of justice — was full of sense. Consequently atheism turns out to be too simple. If the whole universe has no meaning, we should never have found out that it has no meaning: just as if there were no light in the universe and therefore no creatures with eyes we should never know it was dark. *Dark* would be a word without meaning.

II

Very well then, atheism is too simple. And I'll tell you another view that is also too simple. It's the view I call Christianity-and-water, the view that just says there's a good God in Heaven and everything is all right — leaving out all the difficult and terrible doctrines about sin and hell and the devil, and the redemption. Both these are boys' philosophies.

---

[1] "One listener [to this talk] complained of the word *damned* as frivolous swearing. But I mean exactly what I say — nonsense that *is damned* is under God's curse, and will (apart from God's grace) lead those who believe to eternal death." (Lewis' note)

It is no good asking for a simple religion. After all, real things *aren't* simple. They *look* simple, but they're not. The table I'm sitting at looks simple: but ask a scientist to tell you what it's really made of — all about the atoms and how the light waves rebound from them and hit my eye and what they do to the optic nerve and what it does to my brain — and, of course, you find that what we call "seeing a table" lands you in mysteries and complications which you can hardly get to the end of. A child, saying a child's prayer, looks simple. And if you're content to stop there, well and good. But if you're not — and the modern world usually isn't — if you want to go on and ask what's really happening — then you must be prepared for something difficult. If we ask for something more than simplicity, it's silly then to complain that the something more isn't simple. Another thing I've noticed about reality is that, besides being difficult, it's odd: it isn't neat, it isn't what you expect. I mean, when you've grasped that the earth and the other planets all go round the sun, you'd naturally expect that all the planets were made to match — all at equal distances from each other, say, or distances that regularly increased, or all the same size, or else getting bigger or smaller as you go further from the sun. In fact, you find no rhyme or reason (that we can see) about either the sizes or the distances; and some of them have one moon, one has four, one has two, some have none, and one has a ring.

Reality, in fact, is always something you couldn't have guessed. That's *one* of the reasons I believe Christianity. It's a religion you couldn't have guessed. If it offered us just the kind of universe we'd always expected, I'd feel we were making it up. But, in fact, it's not the sort of thing anyone would have made up. It has just that queer twist about it that real things have. So let's leave behind all these boys' philosophies — these over-simple answers. The problem isn't simple and the answer isn't going to be simple either.

What is the problem? A universe that contains much that is obviously bad and apparently meaningless, but containing creatures like ourselves who know that it is bad and meaningless. There are only two views that face all the facts. One is the Christian view that this is a good world that has gone wrong, but still retains the memory of what it ought to have been. The other is the view called Dualism.[2] Dualism means the belief that there are two equal and independent powers at the back of everything, one of them good and the other bad, and that this universe is the battlefield in which they fight out an endless war. I personally think that next to Christianity Dualism is the manliest and most sensible creed on the market. But it has a catch in it.

The two powers, or spirits, or gods — the good one and the bad one — are supposed to be quite independent. They both existed from all eternity. Neither of them made the other, neither of them has any more right than the other to call itself God. Each presumably thinks it is good and thinks the other bad. One of them likes hatred and cruelty, the other likes love and mercy, and each backs its own view. Now what do we mean when we call

[2] properly, "Manicheanism."

one of them the Good Power and the other the Bad Power? Either we're merely saying that we happen to prefer the one to the other — like preferring beer to cider — or else we're saying that, whatever *they* say about it, and whichever *we* happen to like, one of them is actually wrong, actually mistaken, in regarding itself as good. Now if we mean merely that we happen to prefer the first, then we must give up talking about good and evil at all. For good means what you ought to prefer quite regardless of what you happen to like at any given moment. If "being good" meant simply joining the side you happened to fancy, for no real reason, then good wouldn't *be* good. So we must mean that one of the two powers is actually wrong and the other actually right.

But the moment you say that, you are putting into the universe a third thing in addition to the two Powers: some law or standard or rule of good which one of the powers conforms to and the other fails to conform to. But since the two powers are judged by this standard, then this standard, or the being who made this standard, is farther back and higher up than either of them, and He will be the real God. In fact, what we meant by calling them good and bad turns out to be that one of them is in a right relation to the real ultimate God and the other in a wrong relation to Him.

The same point can be made in a different way. If Dualism is true, then the Bad Power must be a being who likes badness for its own sake. But in reality we have no experience of anyone liking badness just because it is bad. The nearest we can get to it is in cruelty. But in real life people are cruel for one of two reasons — either because they are sadists, that is, because they have a sexual perversion which makes cruelty a cause of sensual pleasure to them, or else for the sake of something they are going to get out of it — money, or power, or safety. But pleasure, money, power, and safety are all, as far as they go, good things. The badness consists in pursuing them by the wrong method, or in the wrong way, or too much. I don't mean, of course, that the people who do this aren't desperately wicked. I do mean that wickedness, when you examine it, turns out to be the pursuit of some good in the wrong way. You can be good for the mere sake of goodness: you can't be bad for the mere sake of badness. You can do a kind action when you're not feeling kind and when it gives you no pleasure, simply because kindness is right; but no one ever did a cruel action simply because cruelty is wrong — only because cruelty was pleasant or useful to him. In other words badness can't succeed even in being bad *in the same way* in which goodness is good. Goodness is, so to speak, itself: badness is only spoiled goodness. And there must be something good first before it can be spoiled. We called Sadism a sexual perversion; but you must first have the idea of a normal sexuality before you can talk of it being perverted; and you can see which is the perversion, because you can explain the perverted from the normal, and can't explain the normal from the perverted. It follows that the Bad Power, who is supposed to be on an equal footing with the Good Power, and to love badness in the same way as the good one loves goodness, is a mere bogey. In order to be bad he must have good things to want and then to pursue in the wrong way: he must have impulses which were originally good in order to be able to pervert them. But if he is bad he can't supply himself either with good things to desire or with good impulses to pervert. He must be getting both from the Good Power. And if so, then he is not independent. He is part of the Good Power's world: he was made either by the Good Power or by some power above them both.

Put it more simply still. To be bad, he must exist and have intelligence and will. But existence, intelligence, and will are in themselves good. Therefore he must be getting them from the Good Power: even to be bad he must borrow or steal from his opponent. And do you now begin to see why Christianity has always said that the devil is a fallen angel? That isn't a mere story for the children. It's a real recognition of the fact that evil is a parasite, not an original thing. The powers which enable evil to carry on are powers given it by goodness. All the things which enable a bad man to be effectively bad are in themselves good things — resolution, cleverness, good looks, existence itself. That's why Dualism, in a strict sense, won't work.

But I want to say that real Christianity (as distinct from Christianity-and-water) goes much nearer to Dualism than people think. One of the things that surprised me when I first read the New Testament seriously was that it was always talking about a Dark Power in the universe — a mighty evil spirit who was held to be the Power behind death and disease, and sin. The difference is that Christianity thinks this Dark Power was created by God, and was good when he was created, and went wrong. Christianity agrees with Dualism that this universe is at war. But it doesn't think this is a war between independent powers. It thinks it's a civil war, a rebellion, and that we are living in a part of the universe occupied by the rebel.

Enemy-occupied territory — that's what this world is. Christianity is the story of how the rightful king has landed, you might say landed in disguise, and is calling us all to take part in a great campaign of sabotage. When you go to church you're really listening in to the secret wireless from our friends: that's why the enemy is so anxious to prevent us going. He does it by playing on our conceit and laziness and intellectual snobbery. I know someone will ask me, "Do you really mean, at this time of day, to re-introduce our old friend the devil — hoofs and horns and all?" Well, what the time of day has to do with it I don't know. And I'm not particular about the hoofs and horns. But in other respects my answer is, "Yes, I do." I don't claim to know anything about his personal appearance. If anybody really wants to know him better I'd say to that person, "Don't worry. If you really want to, you will. Whether you'll like it when you do is another question."

III

Christians, then, believe that an evil power has made himself for the present the Prince of this World. And, of course, that raises problems. Is this state of affairs in accordance with God's will or not? If it is, He's a strange God, you'll say: and if it isn't, how *can* anything happen contrary to the will of a being with absolute power?

But anyone who has been in authority knows how a thing can be in accordance with your will in one way and not in another. It may be quite sensible for a mother to say to the children, "I'm not going to go and make you tidy the schoolroom every night. You've got to learn to keep it tidy on your own." Then she goes up one night and finds the Teddy bear and the ink and the French Grammar all lying in the grate. That's against her will. She would prefer the children to be tidy. But on the other hand, it is her will which has left the children free to be untidy. The same thing arises in any regiment, or trades union, or school. You make a thing voluntary and then half the people don't do it. That isn't what you willed, but your will has made it possible.

It's probably the same in the universe. God created things which had free will. That means creatures which can go wrong *or* right. Some people think they can imagine a creature which was free but had no possibility of going wrong, but I can't. If a thing is free to be good it's also free to be bad. And free will is what has made evil possible. Why, then, did God give them free will? Because free will, though it makes evil possible, is also the only thing that makes possible any love or goodness or joy worth having. A world of automata — of creatures that worked like machines — would hardly be worth creating. The happiness which God designs for His higher creatures is the happiness of being freely, voluntarily united to Him and to each other in an ecstasy of love and delight compared with which the most rapturous love between a man and a woman on this earth is *mere milk and water*. And for that they've got to be free.

Of course God knew that would happen if they used their freedom the wrong way: apparently He thought it worth the risk. Perhaps we feel inclined to disagree with Him. But there's a difficulty about disagreeing with God. He is the source from which all your reasoning power comes: you couldn't be right and He wrong any more than a stream can rise higher than its own source. When you are arguing against Him you're arguing against the very power that makes you able to argue at all: it's like cutting off the branch you're sitting on. If God thinks this state of war in the universe a price worth paying for free will — that is, for making a *real* world in which creatures can do real good or harm and something of real importance can happen, instead of a toy world which only moves when He pulls the strings — then we may take it it *is* worth paying.

When we've understood about free will, we shall see how silly it is to ask, as somebody once asked me: "Why did God make a creature of such rotten stuff that it went wrong?" The better stuff a creature is made of — the cleverer and stronger and freer it is — then the better it will be if it goes right, but also the worse it will be if it goes wrong. A cow can't be very good or very bad; a dog can be both better and worse; a child better and worse still; an ordinary man, still more so; a man of genius, still more so; a superhuman spirit best — or worst — of all.

How did the Dark Power go wrong? Well, the moment you have a self at all, there is a possibility of putting yourself first — wanting to be the centre — wanting to *be* God, in fact. That was the sin of Satan: and that was the sin he taught the human race. Some people think the fall of man had something to do with sex, but that's a mistake. What Satan put into the heads of our remote ancestors was the idea that they could "be like gods" — could set up on their own as if they had created themselves — be their own masters — invent some sort of happiness for themselves outside God, apart from God. And out of that hopeless attempt has come nearly all that we call human history — money, poverty, ambition, war, prostitution, classes, empires, slavery — the long terrible story of man trying to find something other than God which will make him happy.

The reason why it can never succeed is this. God made us: invented us as a man invents an engine. A car is made to run on petrol, and won't run properly on anything else. Now God designed the human machine to run on Himself. He Himself is the fuel our spirits were designed to burn, or the food our spirits were designed to feed on. There isn't any other. That's why it's just no good asking God to make us happy in our own way without bothering about religion. God can't give us a happiness and peace apart from Himself, because it isn't there. There's no such thing.

That is the key to history. Terrific energy is expended — civilisations are built up — excellent institutions devised; but each time something goes wrong. Some fatal flaw always brings the selfish and cruel people to the top and it all slides back into misery and ruin. In fact, the machine konks. It seems to start up all right and runs a few yards, and then it breaks down. They're trying to run it on the wrong juice. That's what Satan has done to us humans.

And what did God do? First of all He left us conscience, the sense of right and wrong: and all through history there have been people trying (some of them very hard) to obey it. None of them ever quite succeeded. Secondly, He sent the human race what I call good dreams: I mean those queer stories scattered all through the heathen religions about a god who dies and comes to life again and, by his death, has somehow given new life to men. Thirdly, He selected one particular people and spent several centuries hammering into their heads the sort of God He was — that there was only one of Him and that He cared about right conduct. Those people were the Jews, and the Old Testament gives an account of the hammering process.

Then comes the real shock. Among these Jews there suddenly turns up a man who goes about talking as if He was God. He claims to forgive sins. He says He has always existed. He says He is coming to judge the world at the end of time. Now let us get this clear. Among Pantheists, like the Indians, anyone might say that he was a part of God, or one with God: there'd be nothing very odd about it. But this man, since He was a Jew, couldn't mean that kind of God. God, in their language, meant the Being outside the world Who had made it and was infinitely different from anything else. And when you've grasped that, you will see that what this man said was, quite simply, the most shocking thing that has ever been uttered by human lips.

I'm trying here to prevent anyone from saying the really silly thing that people often say about Him: "I'm ready to accept Jesus as a great moral teacher, but I don't accept His claim to be God." That's the one thing we mustn't say. A man who was merely a man and said the sort of things Jesus said wouldn't be a great moral teacher. He'd either be a lunatic — on a level with the man who says he's a poached egg — or else he'd be the Devil of Hell. You must make your choice. Either this man was, and is, the Son of God: or else a madman or something worse. You can shut Him up for a fool, you can spit at Him and kill Him as a demon; or you can fall at His feet and call Him Lord and God. But don't let us come with any patronising nonsense about His being a great human teacher. He hasn't left that open to us. He didn't intend to.

IV

We are faced, then, with a frightening alternative. This man we're talking about either was (and is) just what He said or else a lunatic, or something worse. Now it seems to me obvious that He wasn't either a lunatic or a fiend: and consequently, however strange or terrifying or unlikely it may seem, I have to accept the view that He was and is God. God has landed on this enemy-occupied world in human form.

And now, what was the purpose of it all? What did He come to do? Well, to teach, of course; but as soon as you look into the New Testament or any other Christian writing you'll find they're constantly talking about something different — about His death and His coming to life again. It's obvious that Christians think the whole point of the story lies there. They think the main thing He came to earth to do was to suffer and be killed.

Now before I became a Christian I was under the impression that the main thing Christians had to believe was one particular theory as to what the point of this dying was. According to that theory God wanted to punish men for having deserted and joined the Great Rebel, but Christ volunteered to be punished instead, and so God let us off. Now I admit that even this theory doesn't seem to me quite so immoral and so silly as it used to; but that isn't the point I want to make. What I came to see later on was that neither this theory nor any other *is* Christianity. The central Christian belief is that Christ's death has somehow put us right with God and given us a fresh start. Theories as to *how* it did this are another matter. A good many different theories have been held as to how it works; what all Christians are agreed on is that it does work. I'll tell you what I think it's like. All sensible people know that if you're tired and hungry a meal will do you good. But the modern theory of nourishment — all about the vitamins and proteins — is a different thing. People ate their dinners and felt better long before the theory of vitamins was ever heard of: and if the theory of vitamins is some day abandoned they'll go on eating their dinners just the same. Theories about Christ's death aren't Christianity: they're explanations about how it works. Christians wouldn't all agree as to how important these theories are. My own church — the Church of England — doesn't lay down any one of them as the right one. The Church of Rome goes a bit further. But I think they'll all agree that the thing itself is infinitely more important than any explanations that theologians have produced. I think they'd probably admit that no explanation will ever be quite adequate to the reality. But as I said in the preface to this book, I'm only a layman, and at this point we're getting into deep water. So I'll just tell you, for what it's worth, how I personally look at the matter.

On my view the theories are not themselves the thing you're asked to accept. I wonder have many of you read Jeans[3] or Eddington?[4] What they do when they want to explain the atom, or something of that sort, is to give you a description out of which you can make a mental picture. But then they warn you that this picture is not what the scientists actually believe. What the scientists believe is a mathematical formula. The pictures are there only to help you to understand the formula. They are not really true in the way the formula is; they don't give you the real thing but only something more or less like it. They're only meant to help, and if they don't help you can drop them. The thing itself *can't* be pictured, it can only be expressed mathematically. Now we're in the same boat here. We believe that the death of Christ is just that point in history at which something absolutely unimaginable from outside shows through into our own world. And if we can't picture even the atoms of which our own world is built, of course we're not going to be able to picture this. Indeed, if we found that we could fully understand it, that very fact would show it wasn't what it professes to be — the inconceivable, the uncreated, the thing from beyond nature, striking down into nature like lightning. You may ask what good will it be to us if we don't understand it. But that's an easy one. A man can eat his dinner without understanding exactly how food nourishes him. A man can accept what Christ has done without knowing how it works: indeed, he certainly won't know how it works *until* he's accepted it.

We are told that Christ was killed for us, that His death has washed out our sins, and that by dying He disabled death itself. That's the formula. That's Christianity. That's what has to be believed. Any theories we build up as to how Christ's death did all this are, in my view, quite secondary: mere

---

[3] Sir James Jeans (1877–1946), English mathematician and physicist who wrote popular books on science.
[4] Sir Arthur Eddington (1882–1944), British astronomer whose writings stimulated other scientists' thought and research.

plans or diagrams to be left alone if they don't help us, and, even if they do help us, not to be confused with the thing itself. All the same, some of these theories are worth looking at.

The one most people have heard is the one I mentioned before — the one about our being let off because Christ had volunteered to bear a punishment instead of us. Now on the face of it that's a very silly theory. If God was prepared to let us off, why on earth didn't He do so? And what possible point could there be in punishing an innocent person instead? None at all that I can see if you're thinking of punishment in the police-court sense. On the other hand, if you think of a debt, there's plenty of point in a person who has some assets paying it on behalf of someone who hasn't. Or if you take "paying the penalty," not in the sense of being punished, but in the more general sense of standing the racket or footing the bill, then, of course, it's a matter of common experience that, when one person has got himself into a hole, the trouble of getting him out usually falls on a kind friend.

Now what was the sort of "hole" man had got himself into? He had tried to set up on his own, to behave as if he belonged to himself. In other words, fallen man isn't simply an imperfect creature who needs improvement: he's a rebel who must lay down his arms. Laying down your arms, surrendering, saying you're sorry, realising that you've been on the wrong track and getting ready to start life over again from the ground floor — that's the only way out of our "hole." This process of surrender — this movement full speed astern — is what Christians call repentance. Now repentance isn't any fun at all. It's something much harder than just eating humble pie. It means unlearning all the self-conceit and self-will that we've been training ourselves into for thousands of years. It means *killing* part of yourself, undergoing a kind of death. In fact it needs a good man to repent. And here comes the catch. Only a bad person *needs* to repent: only a good person *can* repent. The worse you are the more you need it and the less you can do it. The only person who could do it perfectly would be a perfect person — and he wouldn't need it.

Remember, this repentance, this willing submission to humiliation and a kind of death, isn't something God demands of you before He'll take you back and which He could let you off if He chose: it's simply a description of what going back to Him is like. If you ask God to take you back without it, you're really asking Him to let you go back without going back. It can't happen. Very well, then, we've got to go through with it. But the same badness which makes us need it, makes us unable to do it. Can we do it if God helps us? Yes, but what do we mean when we talk of God helping us? We mean God putting into us a bit of Himself, so to speak. He lends us a little of His reasoning powers and that's how we think: He puts a little of His love into us and that's how we love one another. When you teach a child writing, you hold its hand while it forms the letters: that is, it forms the letters because you are forming them. We love and reason because God loves and reasons and holds our hand while we do it. Now if we hadn't fallen, that would be all plain sailing. But unfortunately we now need God's help in order to do something which God, in His own nature, never does at all — to surrender, to suffer, to submit, to die. Nothing in God's nature corresponds to this process at all. So that the one road for which we now need God's leadership most of all is a road God, in His own nature, has never walked. God can share only what He has: this thing, in His own nature, He has not.

But supposing God became a man — suppose our human nature which can suffer and die was amalgamated with God's nature in one person — then that person could help us. He could surrender His will, and suffer and die, because He was man; and He could do it perfectly because He was God. You and I can go through this process only if God does it in us; but God can do it only if He becomes man. Our attempts at this dying will succeed only if we men share in God's dying, just as our thinking can succeed only because it is a drop out of the ocean of His intelligence: but we can't share God's dying unless God dies; and He can't die except by being a man. That is the sense in which He pays our debt, and suffers for us what He Himself needn't suffer at all.

At least that's how I see it. But remember this is only one more picture. Don't mistake it for the thing itself: and if it doesn't help you, drop it.

v

The perfect surrender and humiliation was undergone by Christ: perfect because He was God, surrender and humiliation because He was man. Now the Christian belief is that if we somehow share the humility and suffering of Christ we shall also share in His conquest of death and find a new life after we have died and in it become perfect, and perfectly happy, creatures. This means something much more than our trying to follow His teaching. People often ask when the next step in evolution — the step to something beyond man — will happen. Well, on the Christian view, it has happened already. In Christ, a new kind of man appeared: and the new kind of life which began in Him is to be put into us.

How is this to be done? Now, please remember how we acquired the old, ordinary kind of life. We derived it from others, from our father and mother and all our ancestors, without our consent — and by a very curious process, involving pleasure, pain, and danger. A process you'd never have guessed. Most of us spend a good many years in childhood trying to guess it: and some children, when they're first told, don't believe it — and I'm not sure that I blame them, for it *is* very odd. Now the God who arranged that process is the same God who arranges how the new kind of life — the Christ life — is to be spread. So you must be prepared for it being odd too. He didn't consult us when He invented sex: He hasn't consulted us either when He invented this.

There are three things that spread the Christ life to us: baptism, belief, and that mysterious action which different Christians call by different names — Holy Communion, the Mass, the Lord's Supper. At least, those are the three ordinary methods. I'm not saying there may not be special cases where it is spread without one or more of these. I haven't time to go into special cases, and I don't know enough. If you're trying in a few minutes to tell a man how to get to Edinburgh you'll tell him the trains: he *can* get there by boat or by a plane, but you'd hardly bring that in. And I'm not saying anything about which of these three things is the most essential. My Methodist friend would like me to say a lot more about belief and a lot less (in proportion) about the other two. But I'm not going into that. Anyone who professes to teach you Christian doctrine will, in fact, tell you to use all three, and that's good enough for our present purpose.

I can't myself see why these things should be the conductors of the new kind of life. But then, if one didn't happen to know, I should never have seen any connection between a particular physical pleasure and the appearance of a new human being in the world. We've got to take reality as it comes to us: there's no good jabbering about what it ought to be like or what we'd have expected it to be like. But though I can't see why it *should* be so, I can tell you why I believe it *is* so. I've explained why I have to believe that Jesus was (and is) God. And it seems plain as a matter of history that He taught His followers that the new life was communicated in this way. In other words, I believe it on His authority. Don't be scared by the word authority. Believing things on authority only means believing them because you've been told them by someone you think trustworthy. Ninety-nine per cent. of the things you believe are believed on authority. I believe there is such a place as New York. I haven't seen it myself. I couldn't prove by abstract reasoning that there must be such a place. I believe it because reliable people have told me so. The ordinary man believes in the Solar System, atoms, evolution, and the circulation of the blood on authority — because the scientists say so. Every historical statement in the world is believed on authority. None of us has seen the Norman Conquest or the defeat of the Armada. None of us could prove them by pure logic as you prove a thing in mathematics. We believe them simply because people who did see them have left writings that tell us about them: in fact, on authority. A man who jibbed at authority in other things as some people do in religion would have to be content to know nothing all his life.

Don't think I'm setting up baptism and belief and the Holy Communion as things that will do instead of your own attempts to copy Christ. Your natural life is derived from your parents; that doesn't mean it will stay there if you do nothing about it. You can lose it by neglect, or you can drive it away by committing suicide. You've got to feed it and look after it: but remember, all the time you're not making it you're only keeping up a life you got from someone else. In the same way a Christian can lose the Christ-life which has been put into him, and he has to make efforts to keep it. But even the best Christian that ever lived is not acting on his own steam — he is only nourishing or protecting a life he could never have acquired by his own efforts. And that has practical consequences. As long as the natural life is in your body, it will do a lot towards repairing that body. Cut it, and up to a point it will heal, as a dead body wouldn't. A live body isn't one that never gets hurt, but one that can to some extent repair itself. In the same way a Christian isn't a man who never goes wrong, but a man who is enabled to repent and pick himself up and begin over again after each stumble — because the Christ-life is inside him, repairing him all the time, enabling him to repeat (in some degree) the kind of voluntary death which Christ Himself carried out.

That is why the Christian is in a different position from other people who are trying to be good. They hope, by being good, to please God if there is one; or — if they think there isn't — at least they hope to deserve approval from good men. But the Christian thinks any good he does comes from the Christ-life inside him. He doesn't think God will love us because we're good, but that God will make us good because He loves us; just as the roof of a greenhouse doesn't attract the sun because it's bright, but becomes bright because the sun shines on it.

And let me make it quite clear that when Christians say the Christ-life is in them, they don't mean simply something mental or moral. This isn't simply a way of saying that we are thinking about Christ or copying Him. They mean that Christ is actually operating through them; that the whole mass of Christians are literally the physical organism through which Christ acts — that we are His fingers and muscles, the cells of His body. And perhaps that explains one or two things. It explains why this new life is spread not only by purely mental acts like belief, but by bodily acts like baptism and Holy Communion. It's not merely the spreading of an idea; it's more like evolution — a biological or super-biological fact. There's no good trying to be more spiritual than God. God never meant man to be a purely spiritual creature. That's why He uses material things like bread and wine to put the new life into us. We may think this rather crude and unspiritual. God doesn't: He *invented* eating. He likes matter. He invented it.

Then there's another thing that used to puzzle me. Isn't it frightfully unfair that this new life should be confined to people who have heard of Christ and been able to believe in Him? Well, the truth is God hasn't told us what His arrangements about the other people are. We do know that no man can be saved except through Christ; we don't know that only those who know Him can be saved through Him. But in the meantime, if you're worried about the people outside, the most unreasonable thing you can do is to remain outside yourself. Christians are Christ's body, the organism through which He works. Every addition to that body enables Him to do more. If you want to help those outside you must add your own little cell to the body of Christ who *can* help them. Cutting off a man's fingers would be an odd way of getting him to do more work.

Another possible objection is this: Why is God landing in this enemy-occupied world in disguise and starting a sort of secret society to undermine the devil? Why isn't he landing in force, invading it? Is it that He isn't strong enough? Well, Christians think He's going to land in force; we don't know when. But we can guess why He's delaying. He wants to give us the chance of joining His side freely. I don't suppose you and I would think much of a Frenchman who waited till the Allies were marching into Berlin and then announced he was on our side. God will invade. But I wonder whether people who ask God to interfere openly and directly in our world quite realise what it will be like when He does. When that happens, it's the end of the world. When the author walks on to the stage the play's over. God's going to invade, all right: but what's the good of saying you're on His side *then*, when you see the whole natural universe melting away like a dream and something else — something it never entered your head to conceive — comes crashing in; something so beautiful to some of us and so terrible to others that none of us will have any choice left? For this time it will be God *without* disguise; something so overwhelming that it will strike either irresistible love or irresistible horror into every creature. It will be too late then to *choose* your side. There's no good saying you choose to lie down when it has become impossible to stand up. That won't be the time for choosing: it will be the time when we discover which side we really have chosen, whether we realised it before or not. *Now* is our chance to choose the right side. God is holding back to give us that chance. It won't last for ever. We must take it or leave it.

Albert Camus   (1913–1960)

FRENCH WRITER (ALGERIAN-BORN)

The Myth of Sisyphus

The gods had condemned Sisyphus to ceaselessly rolling a rock to the top of a mountain, whence the stone would fall back of its own weight. They had thought with some reason that there is no more dreadful punishment than futile and hopeless labor.

If one believes Homer, Sisyphus was the wisest and most prudent of mortals. According to another tradition, however, he was disposed to practice the profession of highwayman. I see no contradiction in this. Opinions differ as to the reasons why he became the futile laborer of the underworld. To begin with, he is accused of a certain levity in regard to the gods. He stole their secrets. Ægina, the daughter of Æsopus, was carried off by Jupiter. The father was shocked by that disappearance and complained to Sisyphus. He, who knew of the abduction, offered to tell about it on condition that

Æsopus would give water to the citadel of Corinth. To the celestial thunder-bolds he preferred the benediction of water. He was punished for this in the underworld. Homer tells us also that Sisyphus had put Death in chains. Pluto could not endure the sight of his deserted, silent empire. He dispatched the god of war, who liberated Death from the hands of her conqueror.

It is said also that Sisyphus, being near to death, rashly wanted to test his wife's love. He ordered her to cast his unburied body into the middle of the public square. Sisyphus woke up in the underworld. And there, annoyed by an obedience so contrary to human love, he obtained from Pluto permission to return to earth in order to chastise his wife. But when he had seen again the face of this world, enjoyed water and sun, warm stones and the sea, he no longer wanted to go back to the infernal darkness. Recalls, signs of anger, warnings were of no avail. Many years more he lived facing the curve of the gulf, the sparkling sea, and the smiles of earth. A decree of the gods was necessary. Mercury came and seized the impudent man by the collar and, snatching him from his joys, led him forcibly back to the underworld, where his rock was ready for him.

You have already grasped that Sisyphus is the absurd hero. He *is*, as much through his passions as through his torture. His scorn of the gods, his hatred of death, and his passion for life won him that unspeakable penalty in which the whole being is exerted toward accomplishing nothing. This is the price that must be paid for the passions of this earth. Nothing is told us about Sisyphus in the underworld. Myths are made for the imagination to breathe life into them. As for this myth, one sees merely the whole effort of a body straining to raise the huge stone, to roll it and push it up a slope a hundred times over; one sees the face screwed up, the cheek tight against the stone, the shoulder bracing the clay-covered mass, the foot wedging it, the fresh start with arms outstretched, the wholly human security of two earth-clotted hands. At the very end of his long effort measured by skyless space and time without depth, the purpose is achieved. Then Sisyphus watches the stone rush down in a few moments toward that lower world whence he will have to push it up again toward the summit. He goes back down to the plain.

It is during that return, that pause, that Sisyphus interests me. A face that toils so close to stones is already stone itself! I see that man going back down with a heavy yet measured step toward the torment of which he will never know the end. That hour like a breathing-space which returns as surely as his suffering, that is the hour of consciousness. At each of those moments when he leaves the heights and gradually sinks toward the lairs of the gods, he is superior to his fate. He is stronger than his rock.

If this myth is tragic, that is because its hero is conscious. Where would his torture be, indeed, if at every step the hope of succeeding upheld him? The workman of today works every day in his life at the same tasks, and this fate is no less absurd. But it is tragic only at the rare moments when it be-comes conscious. Sisyphus, proletarian of the gods, powerless and rebellious, knows the whole extent of his wretched condition: it is what he thinks of during his descent. The lucidity that was to constitute his torture at the same time crowns his victory. There is no fate that cannot be surmounted by scorn.

If the descent is thus sometimes performed in sorrow, it can also take place in joy. This word is not too much. Again I fancy Sisyphus returning toward his rock, and the sorrow was in the beginning. When the images of earth cling too tightly to memory, when the call of happiness becomes too insistent, it happens that melancholy rises in man's heart: this is the rock's victory, this is the rock itself. The boundless grief is too heavy to bear. These are our nights of Gethsemane. But crushing truths perish from being acknowledged. Thus, Œdipus[1] at the outset obeys fate without knowing it. But from the moment he knows, his tragedy begins. Yet at the same moment, blind and desperate, he realizes that the only bond linking him to the world is the cool hand of a girl.[2] Then a tremendous remark rings out: "Despite so many ordeals, my advanced age and the nobility of my soul make me conclude that all is well." Sophocles' Œdipus, like Dostoevsky's Kirilov,[3] thus gives the recipe for the absurd victory. Ancient wisdom confirms modern heroism.

One does not discover the absurd without being tempted to write a manual of happiness. "What! by such narrow ways —?" There is but one world, however. Happiness and the absurd are two sons of the same earth. They are inseparable. It would be a mistake to say that happiness necessarily springs from the absurd discovery. It happens as well that the feeling of the absurd springs from happiness. "I conclude that all is well," says Œdipus, and that remark is sacred. It echoes in the wild and limited universe of man. It teaches that all is not, has not been, exhausted. It drives out of this world a god who had come into it with dissatisfaction and a preference for futile sufferings. It makes of fate a human matter, which must be settled among men.

All Sisyphus' silent joy is contained therein. His fate belongs to him. His rock is his thing. Likewise, the absurd man, when he contemplates his torment, silences all the idols. In the universe suddenly restored to its silence, the myriad wondering little voices of the earth rise up. Unconscious, secret calls, invitations from all the faces, they are the necessary reverse and price of victory. There is no sun without shadow, and it is essential to know the night. The absurd man says yes and his effort will henceforth be unceasing. If there is a personal fate, there is no higher destiny, or at least there is but one which he concludes is inevitable and despicable. For the rest, he knows himself to be the master of his days. At that subtle moment when man glances backward over his life, Sisyphus returning toward his rock, in that slight pivoting he contemplates that series of unrelated actions which becomes his fate,

---

[1] the hero of a dramatic trilogy by Sophocles; as an oracle predicted, Oedipus unknowingly kills his father and marries his mother.

[2] Antigone, in *Œdipus at Colonus*.

[3] a character in Dostoevsky's novel *The Possessed*; Kirilov commits suicide, convinced that if one man were to kill himself purely as an exercise of free will, the world would be changed.

created by him, combined under his memory's eye and soon sealed by his death. Thus, convinced of the wholly human origin of all that is human, a blind man eager to see who knows that the night has no end, he is still on the go. The rock is still rolling.

I leave Sisyphus at the foot of the mountain! One always finds one's burden again. But Sisyphus teaches the higher fidelity that negates the gods and raises rocks. He too concludes that all is well. This universe henceforth without a master seems to him neither sterile nor futile. Each atom of that stone, each mineral flake of that night-filled mountain, in itself forms a world. The struggle itself toward the heights is enough to fill a man's heart. One must imagine Sisyphus happy.

William Barrett (b. 1913)

AMERICAN PHILOSOPHER and ESSAYIST

Zen for the West

I

Zen Buddhism[1] presents a surface so bizarre and irrational, yet so colorful and striking, that some Westerners who approach it for the first time fail to make sense of it, while others, attracted by this surface, take it up in a purely frivolous and superficial spirit. Either response would be unfortunate. The fact is that Zen . . . is an essential expression of Buddhism, and Buddhism is one of the most tremendous spiritual achievements in human history — an achievement which we Westerners probably have not yet fully grasped. We have to remember how recent it is that we have sought out any knowledge of the East. Only a century separates us from Schopenhauer, the first Western philosopher who attempted a sympathetic interpretation of Buddhism, a brilliant and sensational misunderstanding on the basis of meagre translations. Since then great strides have been made in Oriental studies, but a curiously paradoxical provincialism still haunts the West: the civilization which has battered its way into every corner of the globe has been very tardy in examining its own prejudices by the wisdom of the non-Western peoples. Even

[1] Zen from Japanese *zazen*, to sit and meditate, a translation of the Chinese *ch'an*, which in turn was the translation of the Indian *Dhyana* (meditation). Thus Zen begins as a particular sect of Buddhism, an essentially meditative one, but in its development it radically transforms the traditional Buddhist discipline of meditation: the dualism between meditation and activity is abolished. (Barrett's note, abridged)

From *Zen Buddhism: The Selected Writings of D. T. Suzuki*, edited by William Barrett. Copyright © 1956 by William Barrett. Reprinted by permission of Doubleday & Company, Inc.

today when the slogan "One World!" is an incessant theme of Sunday journalism and television, we tend to interpret it in a purely Western sense to mean merely that the whole planet is now bound together in the net of modern technology and communications. That the phrase may imply a necessity for coming to terms with our Eastern opposite and brother seems to pass publicly unnoticed. . . .

But do these ancient Oriental masters have anything to say to us who belong to the present-day West? Very much so, I think; and the reason is that we Westerners have only recently come to face certain realities of life with which the Oriental has been living for centuries. This is a large claim, and requires some itemized documentation.

What we call the Western tradition is formed by two major influences, Hebraic and Greek, and both these influences are profoundly dualistic in spirit. That is, they divide reality into two parts and set one part off against the other. The Hebrew makes his division on religious and moral grounds: God absolutely transcends the world, is absolutely separate from it; hence there follow the dualisms of God and creature, the Law and the erring members, spirit and flesh. The Greek, on the other hand, divides reality along intellectual lines. Plato, who virtually founded Western philosophy single-handed — Whitehead has remarked that 2500 years of Western philosophy is but a series of footnotes to Plato — absolutely cleaves reality into the world of the intellect and the world of the senses. The great achievement of the Greeks was to define the ideal of rationality for man; but in doing so, Plato and Aristotle not only made reason the highest and most valued function, they also went so far as to make it the very center of our personal identity. The Orientals never succumbed to this latter error; favoring intuition over reason, they grasped intuitively a center of the personality which held in unity the warring opposites of reason and unreason, intellect and senses, morality and nature. So far as we are Westerners, we inherit these dualisms, they are part of us: an irrationally nagging conscience from the Hebrews, an excessively dividing rational mind from the Greeks. Yet the experience of modern culture, in the most diverse fields, makes them less and less acceptable.

Medieval Christianity still lives in the rational world of the Greeks. The universe of St. Thomas Aquinas is the same bandbox universe of Aristotle, a tight tiny tidy rational whole, where all is in apple-pie order, and everything occupies its logical and meaningful place in the absolute hierarchy of Being. When we turn from such humanized universes to Indian thought, we are at first staggered by the vision of vast spaces, endless aeons of time, universe upon universe, against which man looks very small and meaningless; then we realize these are the spaces and times of modern astronomy, and the Indian idea is therefore closer to us. The distinguished Protestant theologian Paul Tillich has described the essential experience of modern man as an encounter with "meaninglessness": lost in the vastness of the universe, man begins to think that his own existence and that of the universe are "meaningless." The God of Theism, says Tillich echoing Nietzsche, is dead, and Western man must find a God beyond the God of Theism: the God offered us by rational theology is no longer acceptable. From the point of view of the medieval Catholic (and many still survive) the very premises of Buddhist thinking would look "meaningless"; they are also more difficult and grim, but they look much closer to what we moderns may have to swallow.

In science itself, modern developments have combined to make our inherited rationalism more shaky. Physics and mathematics, the two most advanced of Western sciences, have in our time become paradoxical: that is, arrived at the state where they breed paradoxes for reason itself. One hundred fifty years ago the philosopher Kant attempted to show that there were ineluctable limits to reason, but the Western mind, positivistic to the core, could be expected to take such a conclusion seriously only when it showed up in science itself. Well, science in this century has at last caught up with Kant: almost simultaneously Heisenberg in physics, and Godel in mathematics, have shown ineluctable limits to human reason. Heisenberg's Principle of Indeterminacy shows essential limits to our ability to know and predict physical states of affairs, and opens up to us the glimpse of a nature irrational and chaotic at bottom. Godel's results would seem to have even more far-reaching consequences when one reflects that in the Western tradition, from the Pythagoreans and Plato onward, mathematics has inspired the most absolute claims of rationalism. Now it turns out that even in his most precise science — in the province where his reason had seemed omnipotent — man cannot escape his essential finitude: every system of mathematics that he constructs is doomed to incompleteness. Mathematics is like a ship in mid-ocean that has sprung leaks (paradoxes) which have been temporarily plugged, but our reason can never guarantee that the ship will not spring other leaks. That this human insecurity should manifest itself in what had hitherto been the very citadel of reason, mathematics, marks a new turn in Western thinking. The next step would be to recognize the essentially paradoxical nature of reason itself.

This step has been taken by some modern philosophers. The most original and influential philosopher now alive on the European continent is the German Existentialist Martin Heidegger.[2] A German friend of Heidegger told me that one day when he visited Heidegger he found him reading one of Suzuki's books; "If I understand this man correctly," Heidegger remarked, "this is what I have trying to say in all my writings." This remark may be the slightly exaggerated enthusiasm of a man under the impact of a book in which he recognizes some of his own thoughts; certainly Heidegger's philosophy in its tone and temper and sources is Western to its core, and there is much in him that is not in Zen, but also very much more in Zen that is not in Heidegger; and yet the points of correspondence between the two, despite their disparate sources, are startling enough. For what, after all, is Heidegger's

[2] German philosopher (b. 1889), who investigated the nature of human existence and believed it to be founded on the fear of nothingness and death.

final message but that Western philosophy is a great error, the result of the dichotomizing intellect that has cut man off from unity with Being itself and from his own Being. This error begins (in Plato) with locating truth in the intellect; the world of nature thereby becomes a realm of objects set over against the mind, eventually objects to be manipulated by scientific and practical calculation. Twenty-five hundred years of Western metaphysics move from Plato's intellectualism to Nietzsche's Will to Power, and concurrently man does become in fact the technological master of the whole planet; but the conquest of nature merely estranges him from Being itself and from his own Being and delivers him over to an ever ascending, ever more frantic will to power. "Divide and conquer" might thus be said to be the motto which Western man has adopted toward Being itself; but this of course is the counsel of power not of wisdom. Heidegger repeatedly tells us that this tradition of the West has come to the end of its cycle; and as he says this, one can only gather that he himself has already stepped beyond that tradition. Into the tradition of the Orient? I should say at least that he has come pretty close to Zen.

If these happenings in science and philosophy indicate changed ways of thinking in the West, our modern art would seem to indicate very new ways of feeling. Whatever may be said on the thorny subject of modern art, the one fact that is clear is that to the artistic conservative it represents a scandal and a break with the tradition. Our modern art presents a surface so irrational, bizarre, and shocking that it must be considered a break with the older more rational canons of Western art. That Western painters and sculptors in this century have gone outside their tradition to nourish themselves with the art of the rest of the world — Oriental, African, Melanesian — signifies that what we knew as *the* tradition is no longer able to nourish its most creative members; its confining mould has broken, under pressures from within. Our painting has detached itself from three-dimensional space, the arena of Western man's power and mobility; detached itself from the object, the supreme fixation of Western man's extroversion; and it has become subjective, contrary to the whole tenor of our Western life. Is all this merely malaise and revolt, or prophecy of a different spirit to come? In the past, new styles in painting have often been thus prophetic. In the art of literature, of course, the writer can be vocal about the new and revolutionary thing, and we find a novelist like D. H. Lawrence preaching against the bloodless rationalism of his culture. Lawrence urged the necessity of something he called "mindlessness," of becoming "mindless," if the meddlesome and self-conscious intellect were not in the end to cut off Western man irreparably from nature and even the possibility of real sexual union. Oddly enough, this "mindlessness" of Lawrence is a groping intuition after the doctrine of "no-mind" which Zen Buddhism had elaborated a thousand years before. . . . Unlike Lawrence, however, the Zen masters developed this doctrine without falling into primitivism and the worship of the blood. In Lawrence's behalf it must be remembered that his culture gave him no help at all on these matters, and he had to grope in the dark pretty much on his own. And to change to one final literary example that involves no preaching or thesis whatsoever: the most considerable work of prose in English in this century is probably James Joyce's *Ulysses*, and this is so profoundly Oriental a book that the psychologist C. G. Jung recommended it as a long-needed bible for the white-skinned peoples. Joyce shattered the aesthetic of the Georgians[3] that would divide reality into a compartment of the Beautiful forever separate from the opposite compartments of the Ugly or Sordid. *Ulysses*, like the Oriental mind, succeeds in holding the opposites together: light and dark, beautiful and ugly, sublime and banal. The spiritual premise of this work is an acceptance of life that no dualism — whether puritanical or aesthetic — could ever possibly embrace.

Admittedly, all these happenings I have cited — from science, philosophy, art — make up a very selective list; this list could be expanded greatly; nevertheless even as it stands, these instances make up a body of "coincidence" so formidable that they must make us pause. When events run parallel this way, when they occur so densely together in time and in such diverse fields, they can no longer be considered as mere meaningless "coincidence" but as very meaningful symptoms; in this case symptoms that the West in its own depths begins to experience new things, begins in fact to experience its own opposite. In this new climate a concern with something like Zen Buddhism can no longer be taxed as idle exoticism, for it has to do with the practical daily bread of the spirit.

The really somber paradox about all these changes is that they have happened in the deep and high parts of our culture, while in the areas in between everything goes on as usual. Despite the discoveries of its artists, philosophers, theoretical scientists, the West, in its public and external life at any rate, is just as Western as ever, if not more so. Gadgets and traffic accumulate, the American way of life (or else the Russian) spreads all over the globe, the techniques for externalizing life become year by year more slick and clever. All of which may only show what a creature of contradictions Western man has become. And now that at last his technology has put in his hands the hydrogen bomb, this fragmented creature has the power to blow himself and his planet to bits. Plain common sense would seem to advise that he turn to look inward a little.

II

None of the above considerations has to do with Zen itself. Or rather — to put it abruptly as Zen likes to do — Zen has nothing at all to do with them. They deal with the complicated abstractions of the intellect — philosophy, culture, science, and the rest — and what Zen seeks above all is the concrete and the simple that lie beyond the snarled tangles of intellectualization. Zen *is* the concrete itself. Zen eschews abstractions, or uses them only

[3] the period of the reigns of George I, II, and III of England, 1714–1820.

to get beyond them. Even when Zen declares against abstractions, it has to put the matter concretely: thus when the great Master Tokusan has his enlightenment, he does not merely say in pallid fashion that concepts are not enough; no, he burns all his philosophic texts, declaring, "All our understanding of the abstractions of philosophy is like a single hair in the vastness of space." Let the Western reader fasten upon this image and he will find it harder to miss the point. Or when another Master remarks on the difficulty of solving one of the Zen questions — which is equivalent to answering the riddle of existence itself — he does not merely say that it is difficult or so very very difficult that it is well-nigh impossible, but this: "It is like a mosquito trying to bite into an iron bull." The image lives because the image suggests the meaning beyond conceptualization.

Now it is just this concreteness of expression, this extraordinary profusion of images and examples, that can make Zen most helpful to the Westerner, who in fact derives from a more highly abstract culture. But it would be a mistake for the Western reader to imagine that these are merely so many literary devices or adornments adopted by the Zen masters. On the contrary, the language of Zen is of the essence, the manner of expression is one with the matter. Zen expresses itself concretely because Zen is above all interested in facts not theories, in realities and not those pallid counters for reality which we know as concepts. "Fact" may suggest to the Western mind something merely quantitative or statistical — therefore also a lifeless and abstract thing. Zen wants, rather, the facts as living and concrete. In this sense, Zen might be described as Radical Intuitionism — if the Westerner wishes a handle by which to lay hold of it. This does not mean that it is merely a philosophy of intuition like Bergson's, though it agrees with Bergson that the conceptualizing intellect does not reach reality; rather, it is radical intuition in the act itself. Radical Intuitionism means that Zen holds that thinking and sensing live, move, and have their being within the vital medium of intuition. We see with the two eyes only insofar as we are also seeing (though we may not know it) with the third eye — the eye of intuition. Hence, any sensory facts will do for Zen provided they serve to awaken the third eye, and we encounter in the Zen writings the most extraordinary incidents of illumination in connection with the most humble objects. In the end all language is pointing: we use language to point beyond language, beyond concepts to the concrete. The monk asks the Master, "How may I enter in the Way?", and the Master, pointing to the mountain spring, responds, "Do you hear the sound of that torrent? There you may enter." Another time Master and monk are walking upon the mountain, and the Master asks, "Do you smell the mountain laurel?" "Yes." "There, I have held nothing back from you."

In its emphasis upon the living fact over the mere idea, Zen is true to the essential teaching of Buddha. Buddha cared very little for the philosophers; there were said to be already some 63 schools in existence in his time, and he had occasion to observe from their wrangling how imprisoned in the labyrinths of the intellect the human spirit can become. Thus Zen itself is not a philosophy (the Western reader must be warned here), though there lie behind it some of the great philosophies of Mahayana Buddhism.[4] Though Buddha began by opposing the philosophers, nevertheless in the course of its history Buddhism evolved one of the greatest and most profound philosophies ever created. Is this a contradiction of the original spirit of the founder? No; for Buddhist philosophy is activated by an altogether different purpose from that of Western philosophy: Buddhism takes up philosophy only as a device to save the philosopher from his conceptual prison; its philosophy is, as it were, a non-philosophy, a philosophy to undo philosophy. A comparison of the mind of Buddha and Plato — probably the greatest intellects of East and West — may make us understand how sharply East and West diverge on this crucial point. For Plato philosophy is a discipline that leads us from the lower to the higher world, from the world of the senses to the world of ideas, to leave us abiding in this latter world as much as is humanly possible; for the Buddhist, philosophy should lead us beyond the intellect back into the one real world that was always there in its undivided wholeness. Zen presupposes this view of philosophy, but goes beyond the mere restatement of it to make actual use of it in its practical and concrete Chinese fashion.

This passion for the living fact accounts for that quality in the Zen masters which must seem most amazing to the Westerner: their supreme matter-of-factness. "What is the Tao (the way, the truth)?" asks the disciple. "Your everyday mind," replies the Master; and he goes on to amplify: "When I am hungry, I eat; when tired, I sleep." The disciple is puzzled, and asks whether this is not what everybody else does too. No, the Master replies; most people are never wholly in what they are doing; when eating, they may be absent-mindedly preoccupied with a thousand different fantasies; when sleeping, they are not sleeping. The supreme mark of the thoroughly integrated man is to be without a divided mind. This matter-of-fact spirit of Zen is expressed in another paradoxical statement: "Before you have studied Zen, mountains are mountains and rivers are rivers; while you are studying it, mountains are no longer mountains and rivers no longer rivers; but once you have had Enlightenment, mountains are once again mountains and rivers are rivers." The stories of their arduous struggles for Enlightenment teach us that this matter-of-fact spirit of the Zen masters is not a thing easily come by: they are indeed awesome figures who have crossed the mountains and rivers, floods and fires of the spirit in order to come back sole and whole to the most banal things of daily life. The nearest thing to this, so far as I know, that the West has produced is Kierkegaard's wonderful comparison of the Knight of Resignation and the Knight of Faith: the former all fidgets and romanticism, aspiring after the infinite but never at home with the finite, while the Knight of Faith sits so solidly in his existence that from without he looks as prosaic and matter-of-fact as a tax-collector. But this ideal of being in direct and unmediated relation to ordinary reality was something that poor Kierkegaard,

[4] one of the two major schools of Buddhism; it teaches the path to salvation through faith and compassion.

who waged a feverish lifelong struggle against the mediating and devouring power of his intelligence, could only aspire after but never realize.

In this striving for an unmediated relation to reality, as well as in its doctrine of an enlightenment (satori) that goes beyond reason, Zen would seem to be a form of Mysticism. But Zen is not mysticism as the West understands mysticism. The mystic, as defined by William James in *Varieties of Religious Experience* (James did not know about Zen), is one who pierces the veil of the natural or sensuous world in order to experience direct union with the higher reality. This formula holds for most of the great Western mystics from Plotinus onward, but it would not hold of Zen, which would reject this kind of mysticism as dualistic through and through, since it divides reality into lower and higher worlds. For Zen, higher and lower are one world; and in the records of Zen enlightenment which Suzuki sets before us there does not seem to occur anywhere the blurring of consciousness, the trancelike or semi-hallucinated state, which you will find among Western mystics. Even where it seems to move closest to mysticism, Zen remains supremely matter-of-fact. Nor is Zen to be confused with anything like pantheism, even though the Zen writings abound in statements that the Buddha-nature is to be found everywhere, in the dried up dirt-scraper, the cypress tree in the courtyard, etc., etc. Pantheism involves a division between the God who penetrates nature and nature itself as the phenomenal garment of God. But this too is a dualism that Zen leaves behind.

Neither a philosophy, then, in the Western sense, nor a mysticism, not Pantheism and not Theism, Zen might seem to the reader at this point so much a matter of subtlety and nuance as to be devoid of all practical value. On the contrary; for the greatest contemporary tribute to the practicality of Zen comes not from philosophers or artists, but from two prominent *practicing* psychiatrists, C. C. Jung and Karen Horney, who became passionately interested in Zen for its therapeutic possibilities. Jung has written about Zen, and before her death Karen Horney visited Japan to observe the life of a Zen monastery at first hand. What attracted Jung to Zen was its remarkable pursuit of psychological wholeness. Horney saw something similar, but in terms of her own psychology: namely, the search for self-realization without either the false image of an idealized self ("We are saved such as we are," says the Zen master), or without the resigned and dependent clinging to external props like family, social group, or church (after his enlightenment the disciple slaps the Master Obaku's face, remarking "There is not, after all, very much in the Buddhism of Obaku," and the master is pleased, for the disciple shows he can now stand on his own two feet). Certainly the Zen masters, as we read of them in Suzuki's pages, give us the powerful impression of fully individuated individuals, carved out of one whole and solid block. What is most incredible to the Westerner is that this demand for the individuation of the disciple should be made by a *religion!* Western religions have always been willing to settle for less, very much less, from the believer

— his filial obedience or docility, let him be a miserable psychological fragment otherwise. The reason is that Western religion has always placed the weight of emphasis upon the religious object outside the individual — God beyond the world, the Mosaic Law, the Church, the divine personality of Jesus. One can hardly imagine a Western religion producing a saying like the Zen Master's to his monks, "When you utter the name of Buddha, wash your mouth out." Zen is individualistic, and so iconoclastic and antinomian in its individualism that it will seem irreverent to many Westerners; but this is only because Zen wishes to strip the individual naked in order to return him to himself; in the end he cannot lean even upon the image of Buddha. Here precisely is the aspect of Zen Buddhism which is the greatest challenge to Western religions, and which needs to be studied most by us Westerners; for the march of our own history, as the great world of medieval religious images recedes ever further from our grasp and an increasingly secularized society engulfs us, has stripped Western man naked and left no rocklike security anywhere to lean upon. Here there looms before the frightened eyes of the Westerner what Buddhism calls the Great Emptiness; but if he does not run away in fear, this great void may bloom with all manner of miracles, and heaven and earth, in consort once again, engender effortlessly all their ancient marvels.

As to what Zen is, I leave the reader to discover . . . ; what I have provided have been but a few negative warnings, signposts not to stray off the road, which come out of my own earlier failures of understanding. But there is one final misgiving I imagine taking shape in the reader's mind, because it has been taking shape in mine as I write, which needs to be faced before we are done; and it is this: Must not Buddhism forever remain an alien form to the Westerner? something he cannot appropriate and make his own? Are not the conditions that make ourselves and our lives what they are such that something like Zen could never be lived here? The question cannot be shirked; Zen itself would insist upon it, since Zen holds that it is not the abstract or bookish truth but the lived truth that counts. Indeed, the question looms so intensely before my mind that it seems almost to take on the imaginary body of some Zen master shaking his stick, threatening thirty blows and crying, "Speak quick, quick!" Well then, quickly: I would agree with Suzuki when he holds that Zen is the living fact in all religions East or West; or, a little more modestly, that Zen touches what is the living fact in all religions. For the readers of this books the question will hardly arise of becoming a Buddhist, but that does not lessen the importance of Zen to them: for however small the fragment of Zen that makes live contact with the Westerner, its influence is bound to work through, and he will never be quite the same again. In the beautiful words of the Master Hoyen: *When water is scooped up in the hands, the moon is reflected in them; when flowers are handled, the scent soaks into the robe.*

Bernard Malamud (b. 1914)

AMERICAN NOVELIST and SHORT STORY WRITER

Angel Levine

Manischevitz, a tailor, in his fifty-first year suffered many reverses and indignities. Previously a man of comfortable means, he overnight lost all he had, when his establishment caught fire and, after a metal container of cleaning fluid exploded, burned to the ground. Although Manischevitz was insured against fire, damage suits by two customers who had been hurt in the flames deprived him of every penny he had collected. At almost the same time, his son, of much promise, was killed in the war, and his daughter, without so much as a word of warning, married a lout and disappeared with him as off the face of the earth. Thereafter Manischevitz was victimized by excruciating backaches and found himself unable to work even as a presser — the only kind of work available to him — for more than an hour or two daily, because beyond that the pain from standing became maddening. His Fanny, a good wife and mother, who had taken in washing and sewing, began before his eyes to waste away. Suffering shortness of breath, she at last became seriously ill and took to her bed. The doctor, a former customer of Manischevitz, who out of pity treated them, at first had difficulty diagnosing her ailment but later put it down as hardening of the arteries at an advanced stage. He took Manischevitz aside, prescribed complete rest for her, and in whispers gave him to know there was little hope.

Throughout his trials Manischevitz had remained somewhat stoic, almost unbelieving that all this had descended upon his head, as if it were happening, let us say, to an acquaintance or some distant relative; it was in sheer quantity of woe incomprehensible. It was also ridiculous, unjust, and because he had always been a religious man, it was in a way an affront to God. Manischevitz believed this in all his suffering. When his burden had grown too crushingly heavy to be borne he prayed in his chair with shut hollow eyes: "My dear God, sweetheart, did I deserve that this should happen to me?" Then recognizing the worthlessness of it, he put aside the complaint and prayed humbly for assistance: "Give Fanny back her health, and to me for myself that I shouldn't feel pain in every step. Help now or tomorrow is too late. This I don't have to tell you." And Manischevitz wept.

Manischevitz's flat, which he had moved into after the disastrous fire, was a meager one, furnished with a few sticks of chairs, a table, and bed, in one of the poorer sections of the city. There were three rooms: a small, poorly-papered living room; an apology for a kitchen, with a wooden icebox; and the comparatively large bedroom where Fanny lay in a sagging secondhand bed, gasping for breath. The bedroom was the warmest room of the house and it was here, after his outburst to God, that Manischevitz, by the light of two small bulbs overhead, sat reading his Jewish newspaper. He was not truly reading, because his thoughts were everywhere; however the print offered a convenient resting place for his eyes, and a word or two, when he permitted himself to comprehend them, had the momentary effect of helping him forget his troubles. After a short while he discovered, to his surprise, that he was actively scanning the news, searching for an item of great interest to him. Exactly what he thought he would read he couldn't say — until he realized, with some astonishment, that he was expecting to discover something about himself. Manischevitz put his paper down and looked up with the distinct impression that someone had entered the apartment, though he could not remember having heard the sound of the door opening. He looked around: the room was very still, Fanny sleeping, for once, quietly. Half-frightened, he watched her until he was satisfied she wasn't dead; then, still disturbed by the thought of an unannounced visitor, he stumbled into the living room and there had the shock of his life, for at the table sat a Negro reading a newspaper he had folded up to fit into one hand.

"What do you want here?" Manischevitz asked in fright.

The Negro put down the paper and glanced up with a gentle expression. "Good evening." He seemed not to be sure of himself, as if he had got into the wrong house. He was a large man, bonily built, with a heavy head covered by a hard derby, which he made no attempt to remove. His eyes seemed sad, but his lips, above which he wore a slight mustache, sought to smile; he was not otherwise prepossessing. The cuffs of his sleeves, Manischevitz noted, were frayed to the lining and the dark suit was badly fitted. He had very large feet. Recovering from his fright, Manischevitz guessed he had left the door open and was being visited by a case worker from the Welfare Department — some came at night — for he had recently applied for relief. Therefore he lowered himself into a chair opposite the Negro, trying, before the man's uncertain smile, to feel comfortable. The former tailor sat stiffly but patiently at the table, waiting for the investigator to take out his pad and pencil and begin asking questions; but before long he became convinced the man intended to do nothing of the sort.

"Who are you?" Manischevitz at last asked uneasily.

"If I may, insofar as one is able to, identify myself, I bear the name of Alexander Levine."

In spite of all his troubles Manischevitz felt a smile growing on his lips. "You said Levine?" he politely inquired.

The Negro nodded. "That is exactly right."

Carrying the jest farther, Manischevitz asked, "You are maybe Jewish?"

"All my life I was, willingly."

The tailor hesitated. He had heard of black Jews but had never met one. It gave an unusual sensation.

Recognizing in afterthought something odd about the tense of Levine's remark, he said doubtfully, "You ain't Jewish anymore?"

Levine at this point removed his hat, revealing a very white part in his black hair, but quickly replaced it. He replied, "I have recently been disincarnated into an angel. As such, I offer you my humble assistance, if to offer is within my province and ability — in the best sense." He lowered his eyes in apology. "Which calls for added explanation: I am what I am granted to be, and at present the completion is in the future."

"What kind of angel is this?" Manischevitz gravely asked.

"A bona fide angel of God, within prescribed limitations," answered Levine, "not to be confused with the members of any particular sect, order, or organization here on earth operating under a similar name."

Manischevitz was thoroughly disturbed. He had been expecting something but not this. What sort of mockery was it — provided Levine was an angel — of a faithful servant who had from childhood lived in the synagogues, always concerned with the word of God?

To test Levine he asked, "Then where are your wings?"

The Negro blushed as well as he was able. Manischewitz understood this from his changed expression. "Under certain circumstances we lose privileges and prerogatives upon returning to earth, no matter for what purpose, or endeavoring to assist whosoever."

"So tell me," Manischevitz said triumphantly, "how did you get here?"

"I was transmitted."

Still troubled, the tailor said, "If you are a Jew, say the blessing for bread."

Levine recited it in sonorous Hebrew.

Although moved by the familiar words Manischevitz still felt doubt that he was dealing with an angel.

"If you are an angel," he demanded somewhat angrily, "give me the proof."

Levine wet his lips. "Frankly, I cannot perform either miracles or near miracles, due to the fact that I am in a condition of probation. How long that will persist or even consist, I admit, depends on the outcome."

Manischevitz racked his brains for some means of causing Levine positively to reveal his true identity, when the Negro spoke again:

"It was given me to understand that both your wife and you require assistance of a salubrious nature?"

The tailor could not rid himself of the feeling that he was the butt of a jokester. Is this what a Jewish angel looks like? he asked himself. This I am not convinced.

He asked a last question. "So if God sends to me an angel, why a black? Why not a white that there are so many of them?"

"It was my turn to go next," Levine explained.

Manischevitz could not be persuaded. "I think you are a faker."

Levine slowly rose. His eyes showed disappointment and worry. "Mr. Manischevitz," he said tonelessly, "if you should desire me to be of assistance

to you any time in the near future, or possibly before, I can be found" —
he glanced at his fingernails — "in Harlem."

He was by then gone.

The next day Manischevitz felt some relief from his backache and was
able to work four hours at pressing. The day after, he put in six hours; and
the third day four again. Fanny sat up a little and asked for some halvah[1] to
suck. But on the fourth day the stabbing, breaking ache afflicted his back,
and Fanny again lay supine, breathing with blue-lipped difficulty.

Manischevitz was profoundly disappointed at the return of his active pain
and suffering. He had hoped for a longer interval of easement, long enough
to have some thought other than of himself and his troubles. Day by day,
hour by hour, minute after minute, he lived in pain, pain his only memory,
questioning the necessity of it, inveighing against it, also, though with affection, against God. Why *so much*, Gottenyu? If He wanted to teach His
servant a lesson for some reason, some cause — the nature of His nature —
to teach him, say, for reasons of his weakness, his pride, perhaps, during his
years of prosperity, his frequent neglect of God — to give him a little lesson,
why then any of the tragedies that had happened to him, any *one* would
have sufficed to chasten him. But *all together* — the loss of both his children,
his means of livelihood, Fanny's health and his — that was too much to ask
one frail-boned man to endure. Who, after all, was Manischevitz that he had
been given so much to suffer? A tailor. Certainly not a man of talent. Upon
him suffering was largely wasted. It went nowhere, into nothing: into more
suffering. His pain did not earn him bread, nor fill the cracks in the wall, nor
lift, in the middle of the night, the kitchen table; only lay upon him, sleepless,
so sharply oppressively that he could many times have cried out yet not
heard himself through this thickness of misery.

In this mood he gave no thought to Mr. Alexander Levine, but at moments
when the pain wavered, slightly diminishing, he sometimes wondered if he
had been mistaken to dismiss him. A black Jew and angel to boot — very
hard to believe, but suppose he *had* been sent to succor him, and he, Manischevitz, was in his blindness too blind to comprehend? It was this thought
that put him on the knife-point of agony.

Therefore the tailor, after much self-questioning and continuing doubt,
decided he would seek the self-styled angel in Harlem. Of course he had
great difficulty, because he had not asked for specific directions, and movement was tedious to him. The subway took him to 116th Street, and from
there he wandered in the dark world. It was vast and its lights lit nothing.
Everywhere were shadows, often moving. Manischevitz hobbled along with
the aid of a cane, and not knowing where to seek in the blackened tenement
buildings, looked fruitlessly through store windows. In the stores he saw peo-

[1] candy made of crushed sesame seeds.

ple and *everybody* was black. It was an amazing thing to observe. When he was too tired, too unhappy to go farther, Manischevitz stopped in front of a tailor's store. Out of familiarity with the appearance of it, with some sadness he entered. The tailor, an old skinny Negro with a mop of woolly gray hair, was sitting cross-legged on his workbench, sewing a pair of full-dress pants that had a razor slit all the way down the seat.

"You'll excuse me, please, gentleman," said Manischevitz, admiring the tailor's deft, thimbled fingerwork, "but you know maybe somebody by the name Alexander Levine?"

The tailor, who Manischevitz thought, seemed a little antagonistic to him, scratched his scalp.

"Cain't say I ever heard dat name."

"Alex-ander Lev-ine," Manischevitz repeated it.

The man shook his head. "Cain't say I heared."

About to depart, Manischevitz remembered to say: "He is an angel, maybe."

"Oh *him*," said the tailor clucking. "He hang out in dat honky tonk down here a ways." He pointed with his skinny finger and returned to the pants.

Manischevitz crossed the street against a red light and was almost run down by a taxi. On the block after the next, the sixth store from the corner was a cabaret, and the name in sparkling lights was Bella's. Ashamed to go in, Manischevitz gazed through the neon-lit window, and when the dancing couples had parted and drifted away, he discovered at a table on the side, towards the rear, Levine.

He was sitting alone, a cigarette butt hanging from the corner of his mouth, playing solitaire with a dirty pack of cards, and Manischevitz felt a touch of pity for him, for Levine had deteriorated in appearance. His derby was dented and had a gray smudge on the side. His ill-fitting suit was shabbier, as if he had been sleeping in it. His shoes and trouser cuffs were muddy, and his face was covered with an impenetrable stubble the color of licorice. Manischevitz, though deeply disappointed, was about to enter, when a big-breasted Negress in a purple evening gown appeared before Levine's table, and with much laughter through many white teeth, broke into a vigorous shimmy. Levine looked straight at Manischevitz with a haunted expression, but the tailor was too paralyzed to move or acknowledge it. As Bella's gyrations continued, Levine rose, his eyes lit in excitement. She embraced him with vigor, both his hands clasped around her big restless buttocks and they tangoed together across the floor, loudly applauded by the noisy customers. She seemed to have lifted Levine off his feet and his large shoes hung limp as they danced. They slid past the windows where Manischevitz, white-faced, stood staring in. Levine winked slyly and the tailor left for home.

Fanny lay at death's door. Through shrunken lips she muttered concerning her childhood, the sorrows of the marriage bed, the loss of her children, yet wept to live. Manischevitz tried not to listen, but even without ears he would have heard. It was not a gift. The doctor panted up the stairs, a broad but bland, unshaven man (it was Sunday) and soon shook his head. A day at most, or two. He left at once, not without pity, to spare himself Manischevitz's multiplied sorrow; the man who never stopped hurting. He would someday get him into a public home.

Manischevitz visited a synagogue and there spoke to God, but God had absented himself. The tailor searched his heart and found no hope. When she died he would live dead. He considered taking his life although he knew he wouldn't. Yet it was something to consider. Considering, you existed. He railed against God — Can you love a rock, a broom, an emptiness? Baring his chest, he smote the naked bones, cursing himself for having believed.

Asleep in a chair that afternoon, he dreamed of Levine. He was standing before a faded mirror, preening small decaying opalescent wings. "This means," mumbled Manischevitz, as he broke out of sleep, "that it is possible he could be an angel." Begging a neighbor lady to look in on Fanny and occasionally wet her lips with a few drops of water, he drew on his thin coat, gripped his walking stick, exchanged some pennies for a subway token, and rode to Harlem. He knew this act was the last desperate one of his woe: to go without belief, seeking a black magician to restore his wife to invalidism. Yet if there was no choice, he did at least what was chosen.

He hobbled to Bella's but the place had changed hands. It was now, as he breathed, a synagogue in a store. In the front, towards him, were several rows of empty wooden benches. In the rear stood the Ark, it portals of rough wood covered with rainbows of sequins; under it a long table on which lay the sacred scroll unrolled, illuminated by the dim light from a bulb on a chain overhead. Around the table, as if frozen to it and the scroll, which they all touched with their fingers, sat four Negroes wearing skullcaps. Now as they read the Holy Word, Manischevitz could, through the plate glass window, hear the singsong chant of their voices. One of them was old, with a gray beard. One was bubble-eyed. One was humpbacked. The fourth was a boy, no older than thirteen. Their heads moved in rhythmic swaying. Touched by this sight from his childhood and youth, Manischevitz entered and stood silent in the rear.

"Neshoma," said bubble eyes, pointing to the word with a stubby finger. "Now what dat mean?"

"That's the word that means soul," said the boy. He wore glasses.

"Let's git on wid de commentary," said the old man.

"Ain't necessary," said the humpback. "Souls is immaterial substance. That's all. The soul is derived in that manner. The immateriality is derived from the substance, and they both, causally an' otherwise, derived from the soul. There can be no higher."

"That's the highest."

"Over de top."

"Wait a minute," said bubble eyes. "I don't see what is dat immaterial substance. How come de one gits hitched up to de odder?" He addressed the humpback.

"Ask me something hard. Because it is substanceless immateriality. It couldn't be closer together, like all the parts of the body under one skin — closer."

"Hear now," said the old man.

"All you done is switched de words."

"It's the primum mobile, the substanceless substance from which comes all things that were incepted in the idea — you, me and everything and body else."

"Now how did all dat happen? Make it sound simple."

"It de speerit," said the old man. "On de face of de water moved de speerit. An' dat was good. It say so in de Book. From de speerit ariz de man."

"But now listen here. How come it become substance if it all de time a spirit?"

"God alone done dat."

"Holy! Holy! Praise His Name."

"But has dis spirit got some kind of a shade or color?" asked bubble eyes, deadpan.

"Man, of course not. A spirit is a spirit."

"Then how come we is colored?" he said with a triumphant glare.

"Ain't got nothing to do wid dat."

"I still like to know."

"God put the spirit in all things," answered the boy. "He put it in the green leaves and the yellow flowers. He put it with the gold in the fishes and the blue in the sky. That's how come it came to us."

"Amen."

"Praise Lawd and utter loud His speechless name."

"Blow de bugle till it bust the sky."

They fell silent, intent upon the next word. Manischevitz approached them.

"You'll excuse me," he said. "I am looking for Alexander Levine. You know him maybe?"

"That's the angel," said the boy.

"Oh, *him*," snuffed bubble eyes.

"You'll find him at Bella's. It's the establishment right across the street," the humpback said.

Manischevitz said he was sorry that he could not stay, thanked them, and limped across the street. It was already night. The city was dark and he could barely find his way.

But Bella's was bursting with the blues. Through the window Manischevitz recognized the dancing crowd and among them sought Levine. He was sitting loose-lipped at Bella's side table. They were tippling from an almost empty whiskey fifth. Levine had shed his old clothes, wore a shiny new checkered suit, pearl-gray derby, cigar, and big, two-tone button shoes. To the tailor's dismay, a drunken look had settled upon his formerly dignified face. He leaned toward Bella, tickled her ear lobe with his pinky, while whispering words that sent her into gales of raucous laughter. She fondled his knee.

Manischevitz, girding himself, pushed open the door and was not welcomed.

"This place reserved."

"Beat it, pale puss."

"Exit, Yankel, Semitic trash."

But he moved towards the table where Levine sat, the crowd breaking before him as he hobbled forward.

"Mr. Levine," he spoke in a trembly voice. "Is here Manischevitz."

Levine glared blearily. "Speak yo' piece, son."

Manischevitz shuddered. His back plagued him. Cold tremors tormented his crooked legs. He looked around, everybody was all ears.

"You'll excuse me. I would like to talk to you in a private place."

"Speak, Ah is a private pusson."

Bella laughed piercingly. "Stop it, boy, you killin' me."

Manischevitz, no end disturbed, considered fleeing but Levine addressed him:

"Kindly state the pu'pose of yo' communication with yo's truly."

The tailor wet cracked lips. "You are Jewish. This I am sure."

Levine rose, nostrils flaring. "Anythin' else yo' got to say?"

Manischevitz's tongue lay like stone.

"Speak now or fo'ever hold off."

Tears blinded the tailor's eyes. Was ever man so tried? Should he say he believed a half-drunken Negro to be an angel?

The silence slowly petrified.

Manischevitz was recalling scenes of his youth as a wheel in his mind whirred: believe, do not, yes, no, yes, no. The pointer pointed to yes, to between yes and no, to no, no it was yes. He sighed. It moved but one had still to make a choice.

"I think you are an angel from God." He said it in a broken voice, thinking, If you said it it was said. If you believed it you must say it. If you believed, you believed.

The hush broke. Everybody talked but the music began and they went on dancing. Bella, grown bored, picked up the cards and dealt herself a hand.

Levine burst into tears. "How you have humiliated me."

Manischevitz apologized.

"Wait'll I freshen up." Levine went to the men's room and returned in his old clothes.

No one said goodbye as they left.

They rode to the flat via subway. As they walked up the stairs Manischevitz pointed with his cane at his door.

"That's all been taken care of," Levine said. "You best go in while I take off."

Disappointed that it was so soon over but torn by curiosity, Manischevitz followed the angel up three flights to the roof. When he got there the door was already padlocked.

Luckily he could see through a small broken window. He heard an odd noise, as though of a whirring of wings, and when he strained for a wider view, could have sworn he saw a dark figure borne aloft on a pair of magnificent black wings.

A feather drifted down. Manischevitz gasped as it turned white, but it was only snowing.

He rushed downstairs. In the flat Fanny wielded a dust mop under the bed and then upon the cobwebs on the wall.

"A wonderful thing, Fanny," Manischevitz said. "Believe me, there are Jews everywhere."

Philip Larkin (b. 1922)

ENGLISH POET and LIBRARIAN

Church Going

Once I am sure there's nothing going on
I step inside, letting the door thud shut.
Another church: matting, seats, and stone,
And little books; sprawlings of flowers, cut
For Sunday, brownish now; some brass and stuff
Up at the holy end; the small neat organ;
And a tense, musty, unignorable silence,
Brewed God knows how long. Hatless, I take off
My cycle-clips in awkward reverence,

Move forward, run my hand around the font.   10
From where I stand, the roof looks almost new —
Cleaned, or restored? Someone would know: I don't.
Mounting the lectern, I peruse a few
Hectoring large-scale verses, and pronounce
'Here endeth' much more loudly than I'd meant.
The echoes snigger briefly. Back at the door
I sign the book, donate an Irish sixpence,
Reflect the place was not worth stopping for.

Yet stop I did: in fact I often do,
And always end much at a loss like this, 20
Wondering what to look for; wondering, too,
When churches fall completely out of use
What we shall turn them into, if we shall keep
A few cathedrals chronically on show,
Their parchment, plate and pyx in locked cases,
And let the rest rent-free to rain and sheep.
Shall we avoid them as unlucky places?

Or, after dark, will dubious women come
To make their children touch a particular stone;
Pick simples for a cancer; or on some 30   simples: medicinal herbs
Advised night see walking a dead one?
Power of some sort or other will go on
In games, in riddles, seemingly at random;
But superstition, like belief, must die,
And what remains when disbelief has gone?
Grass, weedy pavement, brambles, buttress, sky,

A shape less recognisable each week,
A purpose more obscure. I wonder who
Will be the last, the very last, to seek
This place for what it was; one of the crew 40
That tap and jot and know what rood-lofts were?   rood-loft: gallery over the screen
Some ruin-bibber, randy for antique,   which separates nave from choir
Or Christmas- addict, counting on a whiff   in a church
Of gown-and-bands and organ-pipes and myrrh?
Or will he be my representative,

Bored, uninformed, knowing the ghostly silt
Dispersed, yet tending to this cross of ground
Through suburb scrub because it held unspilt
So long and equably what since is found
Only in separation — marriage, and birth, 50
And death, and thoughts of these — for whom was
      built
This special shell? For, though I've no idea
What this accoutred frowsty barn is worth,
It pleases me to stand in silence here;

A serious house on serious earth it is,
In whose blent air all our compulsions meet,
Are recognised, and robed as destinies.
And that much never can be obsolete,
Since someone will forever be surprising
A hunger in himself to be more serious, 60
And gravitating with it to this ground,
Which, he once heard, was proper to grow wise in,
If only that so many dead lie round.

X. J. Kennedy (b. 1929)

AMERICAN POET

First Confession

Blood thudded in my ears. I scuffed,
   Steps stubborn, to the telltale booth
Beyond whose curtained portal coughed
   The robed repositor of truth.

The slat shot back. The universe
   Bowed down his cratered dome to hear
Enumerated my each curse,
   The sip snitched from my old man's beer,

My sloth pride envy lechery,
   The dime held back from Peter's Pence   10
With which I'd bribed my girl to pee
   That I might spy her instruments.

Hovering scale-pans when I'd done
   Settled their balance slow as silt
While in the restless dark I burned
   Bright as a brimstone in my guilt

Until as one feeds birds he doled
   Seven Our Fathers and a Hail
Which I to double-scrub my soul
   Intoned twice at the altar rail   20

Where Sunday in seraphic light
   I knelt, as full of grace as most,
And stuck my tongue out at the priest:
   A fresh roost for the Holy Ghost.

John Updike (b. 1932)

AMERICAN POET, NOVELIST, and SHORT STORY WRITER

Seven Stanzas at Easter

Make no mistake: if He rose at all
it was as His body;
if the cells' dissolution did not reverse, the molecules
  reknit, the amino acids rekindle,
the Church will fall.

It was not as the flowers,
each soft Spring recurrent;
it was not as His Spirit in the mouths and fuddled
  eyes of the eleven apostles;
it was as His flesh: ours.   10

The same hinged thumbs and toes,
the same valved heart
that — pierced — died, withered, paused, and then
  regathered out of enduring Might
new strength to enclose.

Let us not mock God with metaphor,
analogy, sidestepping, transcendence;
making of the event a parable, a sign painted in the
  faded credulity of earlier ages:
let us walk through the door.   20

The stone is rolled back, not papier-mâché,
not a stone in a story,
but the vast rock of materiality that in the slow
  grinding of time will eclipse for each of us
the wide light of day.

And if we will have an angel at the tomb,
make it a real angel,
weighty with Max Planck's quanta, vivid with hair,
  opaque in the dawn light, robed in real linen
spun on a definite loom.   30

Let us not seek to make it less monstrous,
for our own convenience, our own sense of beauty,
lest, awakened in one unthinkable hour, we are
  embarrassed by the miracle,
and crushed by remonstrance.

JUSTICE

*But far the greatest and fairest branch
of wisdom is that which is concerned with
the due ordering of states and families,
whose name is moderation and justice.*

Diotima to Socrates, *Symposium*

JUSTICE is a maze, complex and convoluted. We cheer when robbers are caught, yet we cheat on our income taxes; we scorn the betrayers of atomic secrets, yet we support the CIA; we have as a personal credo "Do unto others," yet our motto in business is "Caveat emptor." Recent decisions of the United States Supreme Court illustrate intricate and pervasive applications of justice to many aspects of human life — to the personal, cultural, political, and criminal. Yet legal justice is rarely absolute or irrevocable: it does not necessarily indicate judicial unanimity or represent popular sentiment.

And, as daily experience tells us, justice is not necessarily a matter of law or the courts at all. The best man may not always win; merit may not always be rewarded; grades may not always represent ability.

What is justice? In the writings which follow, this and other complex questions about justice are asked and examined. Sophocles considers, in part, whether actions modify justice and whether justice alters actions. Fielding explores the question whether the punishment should fit the crime, the criminal, or the demands of the public. Hesiod's proposal of "an eye for an eye" may yield to Paul's "love thy neighbor" or to Tolstoy's "rehabilitate thy neighbor"; and these concepts may operate simultaneously in different situations. But do guides for individual morality, such as "Do unto others," apply equally to the moral codes of groups and nations? Cervantes examines, among other concerns, whether the just society is composed of many, several, or a single just man.

What are the standards of justice? They may be absolute, as the Old Testament sets forth and Sophocles demonstrates, or relative, as Pascal and Voltaire contend. For instance, perhaps the law should not be applied uniformly to murderers or alleged murderers such as Adolf Hitler, Lee Harvey Oswald, Jack Ruby, and Sirhan Bishara Sirhan. How one decides standards of justice and evaluates situations are basic issues in Faulkner's "Dry September" and Camus' "The Guest."

What is the source of justice? It may be from the divine, the natural, or the human. Justice, as Machiavelli shows, may be based on power, wealth, expediency, or personality. It may or may not be rational. Thoreau and the late Martin Luther King, Jr. discuss on what grounds civil disobedience is justified and how one can decide which principles to obey when his conscience or conception of a higher morality conflicts with human law.

How are justice and morality related? As implied by Emily Dickinson and Robert Graves, does the amorality of the natural world carry over to the human realm? Can seeming injustice be accounted for? Unlike the workings of justice in real life, poetic justice is more satisfying because it guarantees the victory of the "good guy." Moreover, except in literature, complete justice may not be possible as long as witnesses are unreliable and, as "In a Grove" illustrates, there is ambiguity, absence, or conflict of testimony and evidence. Granted human fallibility, how can we ever locate the truth? Who finally is to judge the judges?

The chronological arrangement of the following selections reveals that the idea of justice has shifted from an early belief in the authority of divine law to a current belief in the efficacy of human law. Formerly simple and rigid applications of the law have become more subtle and flexible. If medieval man saw little distinction between moral law and civil law, the "enlightened" man of the eighteenth century believed in the ability of human reason to construct fair, pragmatic codes to govern each separate society. Yet whether we deal with Old Testament Mosaic law or try to accommodate the relativistic laws outlined by Voltaire, nearly all questions ever asked about law and justice have impressive contemporary relevance. How we apply them may depend on our own religious, social, economic, and political backgrounds — or on our own implicit innocence or guilt.

Hesiod (c. 8th century b.c.)

GREEK POET

The Reason for Justice

The man who does evil to another does evil to himself,
and the evil counsel is most evil for him who counsels it.
The eye of Zeus sees everything. His mind understands all.
He is watching us right now, if he wishes to, nor does he fail
to see what kind of justice this community keeps inside it.
Now, otherwise I would not myself be righteous among men
nor have my son be so; for it is a hard thing for a man
to be righteous, if the unrighteous man is to have the greater right.
But I believe that Zeus of the counsels will not let it end thus.

You, Perses, should store away in your mind all that I tell you,   10
and listen to justice, and put away all notions of violence.
Here is the law, as Zeus established it for human beings;
as for fish, and wild animals, and the flying birds,
they feed on each other, since there is no idea of justice among them;
but to men he gave justice, and she in the end is proved the best thing
they have. If a man sees what is right and is willing to argue it,
Zeus of the wide brows grants him prosperity.
But when one, knowingly, tells lies and swears an oath on it,
when he is so wild as to do incurable damage against justice,
this man is left a diminished generation hereafter,   20
but the generation of the true-sworn man grows stronger.

Elohist School (codified c. 750 b.c.)

Hebraic Law: Ten Commandments

20 And God spake all these words, saying,
2 I *am* the Lord thy God, which have brought thee out of the land of Egypt,
out of the house of bondage.
3 Thou shalt have no other gods before me.

Title supplied by editors. "The Reason for Justice" by Hesiod. Reprinted from *The Works and Days* in *Hesiod*, translated by Richmond Lattimore, by permission of The University of Michigan Press. Copyright © by the University of Michigan, 1959.

Title supplied by editors. "Hebraic Law: Ten Commandments" by the Elohist School. From the King James Version of The Bible, *Exodus* 20 and 21.

429

4 Thou shalt not make unto thee any graven image, or any likeness *of any thing* that *is* in heaven above, or that *is* in the earth beneath, or that *is* in the water under the earth:

5 Thou shalt not bow down thyself to them, nor serve them: for I the LORD thy God *am* a jealous God, visiting the iniquity of the fathers upon the children unto the third and fourth *generation* of them that hate me;

6 And shewing mercy unto thousands of them that love me, and keep my commandments.

7 Thou shalt not take the name of the LORD thy God in vain; for the LORD will not hold him guiltless that taketh his name in vain.

8 Remember the sabbath day, to keep it holy.

9 Six days shalt thou labour, and do all thy work:

10 But the seventh day *is* the sabbath of the LORD thy God: *in it* thou shalt not do any work, thou, nor thy son, nor thy daughter, thy manservant, nor thy maidservant, nor thy cattle, nor thy stranger that *is* within thy gates:

11 For *in* six days the LORD made heaven and earth, the sea, and all that in them *is*, and rested the seventh day: wherefore the LORD blessed the sabbath day, and hallowed it.

12 Honour thy father and thy mother: that thy days may be long upon the land which the LORD thy God giveth thee.

13 Thou shalt not kill.

14 Thou shalt not commit adultery.

15 Thou shalt not steal.

16 Thou shalt not bear false witness against thy neighbour.

17 Thou shalt not covet thy neighbour's house, thou shalt not covet thy neighbour's wife, nor his manservant, nor his maidservant, nor his ox, nor his ass, nor any thing that *is* thy neighbour's.

18 And all the people saw the thunderings, and the lightnings, and the noise of the trumpet, and the mountain smoking: and when the people saw *it*, they removed, and stood afar off.

19 And they said unto Moses, Speak thou with us, and we will hear: but let not God speak with us, lest we die.

20 And Moses said unto the people, Fear not: for God is come to prove you, and that his fear may be before your faces, that ye sin not.

21 And the people stood afar off, and Moses drew near unto the thick darkness where God *was*.

22 And the LORD said unto Moses, Thus thou shalt say unto the children of Israel, Ye have seen that I have talked with you from heaven.

23 Ye shall not make with me gods of silver, neither shall ye make unto you gods of gold.

24 An altar of earth thou shalt make unto me, and shalt sacrifice thereon thy burnt offerings, and thy peace offerings, thy sheep, and thine oxen: in all places where I record my name I will come unto thee, and I will bless thee.

25 And if thou wilt make me an altar of stone, thou shalt not build it of hewn stone: for if thou lift up thy tool upon it, thou hast polluted it.

26 Neither shalt thou go up by steps unto mine altar, that thy nakedness be not discovered thereon.

21 Now these *are* the judgments which thou shalt set before them.

2 If thou buy an Hebrew servant, six years he shall serve: and in the seventh he shall go out free for nothing.

3 If he came in by himself, he shall go out by himself: if he were married, then his wife shall go out with him.

4 If his master have given him a wife, and she have borne him sons or daughters; the wife and her children shall be her master's, and he shall go out by himself.

5 And if the servant shall plainly say, I love my master, my wife, and my children; I will not go out free:

6 Then his master shall bring him unto the judges; he shall also bring him to the door, or unto the door post; and his master shall bore his ear through with an aul; and he shall serve him for ever.

7 And if a man sell his daughter to be a maidservant, she shall not go out as the menservants do.

8 If she please not her master, who hath betrothed her to himself, then shall he let her be redeemed: to sell her unto a strange nation he shall have no power, seeing he hath dealt deceitfully with her.

9 And if he have betrothed her unto his son, he shall deal with her after the manner of daughters.

10 If he take him another *wife*; her food, her raiment, and her duty of marriage, shall he not diminish.

11 And if he do not these three unto her, then shall she go out free without money.

12 He that smiteth a man, so that he die, shall be surely put to death.

13 And if a man lie not in wait, but God deliver *him* into his hand; then I will appoint thee a place whither he shall flee.

14 But if a man come presumptuously upon his neighbour, to slay him with guile; thou shalt take him from mine altar, that he may die.

15 And he that smiteth his father, or his mother, shall be surely put to death.

16 And he that stealeth a man, and selleth him, or if he be found in his hand, he shall surely be put to death.

17 And he that curseth his father, or his mother, shall surely be put to death.

18 And if men strive together, and one smite another with a stone, or with *his* fist, and he die not, but keepeth *his* bed:

19 If he rise again, and walk abroad upon his staff, then shall he that smote *him* be quit: only he shall pay *for* the loss of his time, and shall cause *him* to be thoroughly healed.

20 And if a man smite his servant, or his maid, with a rod, and he die under his hand; he shall be surely punished.

21 Notwithstanding, if he continue a day or two, he shall not be punished: for he *is* his money.

22 If men strive, and hurt a woman with child, so that her fruit depart *from her,* and yet no mischief follow: he shall be surely punished, according as the woman's husband will lay upon him; and he shall pay as the judges *determine.*

23 And if *any* mischief follow, then thou shalt give life for life,

24 Eye for eye, tooth for tooth, hand for hand, foot for foot,

25 Burning for burning, wound for wound, stripe for stripe.

Sophocles (c. 496–405 B.C.)

GREEK DRAMATIST

Oedipus the King

DRAMATIS PERSONAE

OEDIPUS, *King of Thebes*
PRIEST OF ZEUS
CREON, *brother of Iocasta*
TEIRESIAS, *a Seer*
IOCASTA, *Queen of Thebes*
A CORINTHIAN SHEPHERD
A THEBAN SHEPHERD
A MESSENGER
CHORUS *of Theban citizens*
Priests, Attendants, etc.

Scene: Thebes, before the royal palace

OEDIPUS. My children, latest brood of ancient
    Cadmus,
What purpose brings you here, a multitude
Bearing the boughs that mark the suppliant?
Why is our air so full of frankincense,
So full of hymns and prayers and lamentations?
This, children, was no matter to entrust
To others: therefore I myself am come
Whose fame is known to all — I, Oedipus.
— You, Sir, are pointed out by length of years
To be the spokesman: tell me, what is in   10
Your hearts? What fear? What sorrow? Count on
    all
That I can do, for I am not so hard
As not to pity such a supplication.
    PRIEST. Great King of Thebes, and sovereign
    Oedipus,
Look on us, who now stand before the altars —
Some young, still weak of wing; some bowed with
    age —
The priests, as I, of Zeus; and these, the best
Of our young men; and in the market-place,
And by Athena's temples and the shrine
Of fiery divination, there is kneeling,   20
Each with his suppliant branch, the rest of Thebes.

Cadmus: legendary king who, on the advice of the oracle at Delphi, founded Thebes

Athena: protector of Cadmus; here also goddess of wisdom, law and order

From *Sophocles: Three Tragedies: Antigone, Oedipus the King, Electra,* translated by H. D. F. Kitto. © 1962 by Oxford University Press. Reprinted by permission.

433

The city, as you see yourself, is now
Storm-tossed, and can no longer raise its head
Above the waves and angry surge of death.
The fruitful blossoms of the land are barren,
The herds upon our pastures, and our wives
In childbirth, barren. Last, and worst of all,
The withering god of fever swoops on us
To empty Cadmus' city and enrich
Dark Hades with our groans and lamentations.   30
No god we count you, that we bring our prayers,
I and these children, to your palace-door,
But wise above all other men to read
Life's riddles,[1] and the hidden ways of Heaven;
For it was you who came and set us free
From the blood-tribute that the cruel Sphinx
Had laid upon our city; without our aid
Or our instruction, but, as we believe,
With god as ally, you gave us back our life.
So now, most dear, most mighty Oedipus,   40
We all entreat you on our bended knees,
Come to our rescue, whether from the gods
Or from some man you can find means to save.
For I have noted, *that* man's counsel is
Of best effect, who has been tried in action.
Come, noble Oedipus! Come, save our city.
Be well advised; for that past service given
This city calls you Saviour; of your kingship
Let not the record be that first we rose
From ruin, then to ruin fell again.   50
No, save our city, let it stand secure.
You brought us gladness and deliverance
Before; now do no less. You rule this land;
Better to rule it full of living men
Than rule a desert; citadel or ship
Without its company of men is nothing.
    OEDIPUS.   My children, what you long for, that I
      know
Indeed, and pity you. I know how cruelly
You suffer; yet, though sick, not one of you
Suffers a sickness half as great as mine.   60
Yours is a single pain; each man of you
Feels but his own. My heart is heavy with
The city's pain, my own, and yours together.
You come to me not as to one asleep

---

[1] The Sphinx, sent to punish the city of Thebes, demanded of the Thebans the answer to her riddle: "What goes on four legs in the morning, two legs at noon, and three legs at night?" An inhabitant was devoured at each unsuccessful try until Oedipus said correctly that it is man, who crawls as a baby, walks as a grown man, and uses a cane as an old man. Oedipus thus caused the Sphinx to kill herself, and Thebes was saved.

And needing to be wakened; many a tear
I have been shedding, every path of thought
Have I been pacing; and what remedy,
What single hope my anxious thought has found
That I have tried. Creon, Menoeceus' son,
My own wife's brother, I have sent to Delphi   70
To ask in Phoebus' house what act of mine,
What word of mine, may bring deliverance.
Now, as I count the days, it troubles me
What he is doing; his absence is prolonged
Beyond the proper time. But when he comes
Then write me down a villain, if I do
Not each particular that the god discloses.

> Delphi: site of a temple to Phoebus Apollo, god of prophecy and wisdom, and of an oracle who foretold the future and solved puzzling questions

    PRIEST.   You give us hope. — And here is more, for they
Are signalling that Creon has returned.
    OEDIPUS.   O Lord Apollo, even as Creon smiles, 80
Smile now on us, and let it be deliverance!
    PRIEST.   The news is good; or he would not be wearing
That ample wreath of richly-berried laurel.
    OEDIPUS.   We soon shall know; my voice will reach so far:
Creon my lord, my kinsman, what response
Do you bring with you from the god of Delphi?

Enter CREON

    CREON.   Good news! Our sufferings, if they are guided right,
Can even yet turn to a happy issue.
    OEDIPUS.   This only leaves my fear and confidence
In equal balance: what did Phoebus say?   90
    CREON.   Is it your wish to hear it now, in public,
Or in the palace? I am at your service.
    OEDIPUS.   Let them all hear! Their sufferings distress
Me more than if my own life were at stake.
    CREON.   Then I will tell you what Apollo said —
And it was very clear. There is pollution
Here in our midst, long-standing. This must we
Expel, nor let it grow past remedy.
    OEDIPUS.   What has defiled us? and how are we to purge it?
    CREON.   By banishing or killing one who murdered,   100
And so called down this pestilence upon us.
    OEDIPUS.   Who is the man whose death the god denounces?

CREON.   Before the city passed into your care,
My lord, we had a king called Laius.
    OEDIPUS.   So have I often heard. — I never saw
    him.
CREON.   His death, Apollo clearly charges us,
We must avenge upon his murderers.
    OEDIPUS.   Where are they now? And where shall
    we disclose
The unseen traces of that ancient crime?
    CREON.   The god said, Here. — A man who hunts
    with care   110
May often find what other men will miss.
    OEDIPUS.   Where was he murdered? In the palace
    here?
Or in the country? Or was he abroad?
    CREON.   He made a journey to consult the god,
He said — and never came back home again.
    OEDIPUS.   But was there no report? no fellow
    traveller
Whose knowledge might have helped you in your
    search?
    CREON.   All died, except one terror-stricken man,
And he could tell us nothing — next to nothing.
    OEDIPUS.   And what was that? One thing might
    lead to much,   120
If only we could find one ray of light.
    CREON.   He said they met with brigands — not
    with one,
But a whole company; they killed Laius.
    OEDIPUS.   A brigand would not *dare* — unless
    perhaps
Conspirators in Thebes had bribed the man.
    CREON.   There *was* conjecture; but disaster came
And we were leaderless, without our king.
    OEDIPUS.   Disaster? With a king cut down like
    that
You did not seek the cause? Where was the hin-
    drance?
    CREON.   The Sphinx. *Her* riddle pressed us harder
    still;   130
For Laius — out of sight was out of mind.
    OEDIPUS.   I will begin again; I'll find the truth.
The dead man's cause has found a true defender
In Phoebus, and in you. And I will join you
In seeking vengeance on behalf of Thebes
And Phoebus too; indeed, I must: if I
Remove this taint, it is not for a stranger,
But for myself: the man who murdered him
Might make the same attempt on me; and so,

Avenging him, I shall protect myself. — 140
    Now you, my sons, without delay, arise,
Take up your suppliant branches. — Someone, go
And call the people here, for I will do
What can be done; and either, by the grace
Of God we shall be saved — or we shall fall.
    PRIEST. My children, we will go; the King has
        promised
All that we came to ask. — O Phoebus, thou
Hast given us an answer: give us too
Protection! grant remission of the plague!
      [*Exeunt* CREON, PRIESTS, *etc.* OEDIPUS *remains*]
Enter the CHORUS *representing the citizens of Thebes*

STROPHE 1

    CHORUS. Sweet is the voice of the god, that
(*mainly dactyls:* $\frac{4}{4}$)   sounds in the
Golden shrine of Delphi. 151
What message has it sent to Thebes? My trembling
Heart is torn with anguish.
Thou god of Healing, Phoebus Apollo,
How do I fear! What hast thou in mind
To bring upon us now? what is to be fulfilled
From days of old?
Tell me this, O Voice divine,
Thou child of golden Hope.

Healing: Apollo was god of medicine as well as of prophecy.

ANTISTROPHE 1

First on the Daughter of Zeus I call for 160
Help, divine Athene;
And Artemis, whose throne is all the earth, whose
Shrine is in our city;
Apollo too, who shoots from afar:
Trinity of Powers, come to our defence!
If ever in the past, when ruin threatened us,
You stayed its course
And turned aside the flood of Death,
O then, protect us now!

Artemis: twin sister of Apollo and a goddess of forests, earth, and hunting

STROPHE 2

(*agitated:* $\frac{3}{8}$) Past counting are the woes we suf-
    fer; 170
Affliction bears on all the city, and
Nowhere is any defence against destruction.
The holy soil can bring no increase,
Our women suffer and cry in childbirth

But do not bring forth living children.
The souls of those who perish, one by one,
Unceasingly, swift as raging fire,
Rise and take their flight to the dark realms of the
    dead.

ANTISTROPHE 2

Past counting, those of us who perish:
They lie upon the ground, unpitied,   180
Unburied, infecting the air with deadly pollution.
Young wives, and grey-haired mothers with them,
From every quarter approach the altars
And cry aloud in supplication.
The prayer for healing, the loud wail of lament,
Together are heard in dissonance:
O thou golden Daughter of Zeus, grant thy aid!

STROPHE 3

(*mainly iambic*: $\frac{3}{8}$) The fierce god of War has laid
    aside
His spear; but yet his terrible cry
Rings in our ears; he spreads death and destruc-
    tion.   190
Ye gods, drive him back to his distant home!
    For what the light of day has spared,
    That the darkness of night destroys.
    Zeus our father! All power is thine:
The lightning-flash is thine: hurl upon him
Thy thunderbolt, and quell this god of War!

ANTISTROPHE 3

We pray, Lord Apollo: draw thy bow
In our defence. Thy quiver is full of
Arrows unerring: shoot! slay the destroyer!
And thou, radiant Artemis, lend thy aid!   200
    Thou whose hair is bound in gold,
Bacchus, lord of the sacred dance,
    Theban Bacchus! Come, show thyself!
Display thy blazing torch; drive from our midst
The savage god, abhorred by other gods!
    OEDIPUS. Would you have answer to these pray-
        ers? Then hear
My words; give heed; your help may bring
Deliverance, and the end of all our troubles.
Here do I stand before you all, a stranger
Both to the deed and to the story. — What   210

Bacchus: god of festivities, including those at which this play
was first performed, about 425
B.C.

Could I have done alone, without a clue?
But I was yet a foreigner; it was later
That I became a Theban among Thebans.
So now do I proclaim to all the city:
If any Theban knows by what man's hand
He perished, Laius, son of Labdacus,
Him I command to tell me all he can;
And if he is afraid, let him annul
Himself the charge he fears; no punishment
Shall fall on him, save only to depart   220
Unharmed from Thebes. Further, if any knows
The slayer to be a stranger from abroad,
Let him speak out; I will reward him, and
Besides, he will have all my gratitude.
But if you still keep silent, if any man
Fearing for self or friend shall disobey me,
This will I do — and listen to my words:
Whoever he may be, I do forbid
All in this realm, of which I am the King
And high authority, to shelter in their houses   230
Or speak to him, or let him be their partner
In prayers or sacrifices to the gods, or give
Him lustral water; I command you all   **lustral: purifying**
To drive him from your doors; for he it is
That brings this plague upon us, as the god
Of Delphi has but now declared to me. —
So stern an ally do I make myself
Both of the god and of our murdered king. —
And for the man that slew him, whether he
Slew him alone, or with a band of helpers,   240
I lay this curse upon him, that the wretch
In wretchedness and misery may live.
And more: if with my knowledge he be found
To share my hearth and home, then upon me
Descend that doom that I invoke on him.
This charge I lay upon you, to observe
All my commands: to aid myself, the god,
And this our land, so spurned of Heaven, so ravaged.
For such a taint we should not leave unpurged —
The death of such a man, and he your king —   250
Even if Heaven had not commanded us,
But we should search it out. Now, since 'tis I
That wear the crown that he had worn before me,
And have his Queen to wife, and common children
Were born to us, but that his own did perish,
And sudden death has carried him away —
Because of this, I will defend his cause
As if it were my father's; nothing I
Will leave undone to find the man who killed

The son of Labdacus, and offspring of   260
Polydorus, Cadmus, and of old Agênor.
On those that disobey, this is my curse:
May never field of theirs give increase, nor
Their wives have children; may our present plagues,
And worse, be ever theirs, for their destruction.
But for the others, all with whom my words
Find favour, this I pray: Justice and all
The gods be ever at your side to help you.

    CHORUS-LEADER. Your curse constrains me; there-
      fore will I speak.
I did not kill him, neither can I tell   270
Who did. It is for Phoebus, since he laid
The task upon us, to declare the man.

    OEDIPUS. True; but to force the gods against their
      will —
That is a thing beyond all human power.

    CHORUS-LEADER. All I could say is but a second
      best.

    OEDIPUS. Though it were third best, do not hold
      it back.

    CHORUS-LEADER. I know of none that reads Apol-
      lo's mind
So surely as the lord Teiresias;
Consulting him you best might learn the truth.

    OEDIPUS. Not even this have I neglected:
      Creon   280
Advised me, and already I have sent
Two messengers. — Strange he has not come.

    CHORUS-LEADER. There's nothing else but old and
      idle gossip.

    OEDIPUS. And what was that? I clutch at any
      straw.

    CHORUS-LEADER. They said that he was killed by
      travellers.

    OEDIPUS. So I have heard; but no one knows a
      witness.

    CHORUS-LEADER. But if he is not proof against
      all fear
He'll not keep silent when he hears your curse.

    OEDIPUS. And will they fear a curse, who dared to
      kill?

    CHORUS-LEADER. Here is the one to find him, for
      at last   290
They bring the prophet here. He is inspired,
The only man whose heart is filled with truth.

    Enter TEIRESIAS, *led by a boy*

    OEDIPUS. Teiresias, by your art you read the signs
And secrets of the earth and of the sky;

Therefore you know, although you cannot see,
The plague that is besetting us; from this
No other man but you, my lord, can save us.
Phoebus has said — you may have heard already —
In answer to our question, that this plague
Will never cease unless we can discover   300
What men they were who murdered Laius,
And punish them with death or banishment.
Therefore give freely all that you have learned
From birds or other form of divination;
Save us; save me, the city, and yourself,
From the pollution that his bloodshed causes.
No finer task, than to give all one has
In helping others; we are in your hands.

> TEIRESIAS.   Ah! what a burden knowledge is, when
>   knowledge

Can be of no avail! I knew this well,   310
And yet forgot, or I should not have come.

> OEDIPUS.   Why, what is this? Why are you so
>   despondent?

> TEIRESIAS.   Let me go home! It will be best for
>   you,

And best for me, if you will let me go.

> OEDIPUS.   But to withhold your knowledge! This
>   is wrong,

Disloyal to the city of your birth.

> TEIRESIAS.   I know that what you say will lead you
>   on

To ruin; therefore, lest the same befall me too . . .

> OEDIPUS.   No, by the gods! Say all you know, for
>   we

Go down upon our knees, your suppliants.   320

> TEIRESIAS.   Because *you* do *not* know! I never
>   shall

Reveal my burden — I will not say *yours*.

> OEDIPUS.   You know, and will not tell us? Do you
>   wish

To ruin Thebes and to destroy us all?

> TEIRESIAS.   *My* pain, and yours, will not be caused
>   by me.

Why these vain questions? — for I will not speak.

> OEDIPUS.   You villain! — for you would provoke
>   a stone

To anger: you'll not speak, but show yourself
So hard of heart and so inflexible?

> TEIRESIAS.   You heap the blame on me; but what
>   is yours   330

You do not know — therefore *I* am the villain!

> OEDIPUS.   And who would not be angry, finding
>   that

You treat our people with such cold disdain?

   TEIRESIAS.   The truth will come to light, without
     my help.

   OEDIPUS.   If it is bound to come, you ought to
     speak it.

   TEIRESIAS.   I'll say no more, and you, if so you
     choose,

May rage and bluster on without restraint.

   OEDIPUS.   Restraint? Then I'll show none! I'll
     tell you all

That I can see in you: I do believe

This crime was planned and carried out by you,   340

All but the killing; and were you not blind

I'd say your hand alone had done the murder.

   TEIRESIAS.   So? Then I tell you this: submit your-
     self

To that decree that you have made; from now

Address no word to these men nor to me:

You are the man whose crimes pollute our city.

   OEDIPUS.   What, does your impudence extend
     thus far?

And do you hope that it will go scot-free?

   TEIRESIAS.   It will. I have a champion — the
     truth.

   OEDIPUS.   Who taught you that? For it was not
     your art.   350

   TEIRESIAS.   No; you! You made me speak, against
     my will.

   OEDIPUS.   Speak what? Say it again, and say it
     clearly.

   TEIRESIAS.   Was I not clear? Or are you tempting
     me?

   OEDIPUS.   Not clear enough for me. Say it again.

   TEIRESIAS.   You are yourself the murderer you
     seek.

   OEDIPUS.   You'll not affront me twice and go un-
     punished!

   TEIRESIAS.   Then shall I give you still more cause
     for rage?

   OEDIPUS.   Say what you will; you'll say it to no
     purpose.

   TEIRESIAS.   I know, *you* do not know, the hideous
     life

Of shame you lead with those most near to you.   360

   OEDIPUS.   You'll pay most dearly for this inso-
     lence!

   TEIRESIAS.   No, not if Truth is strong, and can
     prevail.

   OEDIPUS.   It is — except in you; for you are blind

In eyes and ears and brains and everything.

TEIRESIAS.   You'll not forget these insults that you throw
At me, when all men throw the same at you.
    ODEIPUS.   You live in darkness; you can do no harm
To me or any man who has his eyes.
    TEIRESIAS.   No; I am not to bring you down, because
Apollo is enough; he'll see to it.   370
    OEDIPUS.   Creon, or you? Which of you made this plot?
    TEIRESIAS.   Creon's no enemy of yours; you are your own.
    OEDIPUS.   O Wealth! O Royalty! whose commanding art
Outstrips all other arts in life's contentions!
How great a store of envy lies upon you,
If for this sceptre, that the city gave
Freely to me, unasked — if now my friend,
The trusty Creon, burns to drive me hence
And steal it from me! So he has suborned
This crafty schemer here, this mountebank,   380
Whose purse alone has eyes, whose art is blind. —
Come, prophet, show your title! When the Sphinx
Chanted her music here, why did not *you*   **music: riddle**
Speak out and save the city? Yet such a question
Was one for augury, not for mother wit.
You were no prophet then; your birds, your voice
From Heaven, were dumb. But I, who came by chance,
I, knowing nothing, put the Sphinx to flight,
Thanks to my wit — no thanks to divination!
And now you try to drive me out; you hope   390
When Creon's king to bask in Creon's favour.
You'll expiate the curse? Ay, and repent it,
Both you and your accomplice. But that you
Seem old, I'd teach you what you gain by treason!
    CHORUS-LEADER.   My lord, he spoke in anger; so, I think,
Did you. What help in angry speeches? Come,
This is the task, how we can best discharge
The duty that the god has laid on us.
    TEIRESIAS.   King though you are, I claim the privilege
Of equal answer. No, I have the right;   400
I am no slave of yours — I serve Apollo,
And therefore am not listed *Creon's* man.
Listen — since you have taunted me with blindness!
You have your sight, and yet you cannot see
Where, nor with whom, you live, nor in what horror.

Your parents — do you know them? or that you
Are enemy to your kin, alive or dead?
And that a father's and a mother's curse
Shall join to drive you headlong out of Thebes
And change the light that now you see to dark-
        ness?   410
Your cries of agony, where will they not reach?
Where on Cithaeron will they not re-echo?
When you have learned what meant the marriage-
        song
Which bore you to an evil haven here
After so fair a voyage? And you are blind
To other horrors, which shall make you one
With your own children. Therefore, heap your scorn
On Creon and on me, for no man living
Will meet a doom more terrible than yours.
    OEDIPUS. What? Am I to suffer words like this
        from him?   420
Ruin, damnation seize you! Off at once
Out of our sight! Go! Get you whence you came!
    TEIRESIAS. Had you not called me, I should not
        be here.
    OEDIPUS. And had I known that you would talk
        such folly,
I'd not have called you to a house of mine.
    TEIRESIAS. To you I seem a fool, but to your
        parents,
To those who did beget you, I was wise.
    OEDIPUS. Stop! Who were they? Who *were* my
        parents? Tell me!
    TEIRESIAS. This day will show your birth and
        your destruction.
    OEDIPUS. You are too fond of dark obscurities. 430
    TEIRESIAS. But do you not excel in reading
        riddles?
    OEDIPUS. I scorn your taunts; my skill has
        brought me glory.
    TEIRESIAS. And this success brought you to ruin
        too.
    OEDIPUS. I am content, if so I saved this city.
    TEIRESIAS. Then I will leave you. Come, boy,
        take my hand.
    OEDIPUS. Yes, let him take it. You are nothing
        but
Vexation here. Begone, and give me peace!
    TEIRESIAS. When I have had my say. No frown
        of yours
Shall frighten *me*; you cannot injure me.
Here is my message: that man whom you seek   440

With threats and proclamations for the death
Of Laius, he is living here; he's thought
To be a foreigner, but shall be found
Theban by birth — and little joy will this
Bring *him*; when, with his eyesight turned to blind-
            ness,
His wealth to beggary, on foreign soil
With staff in hand he'll tap his way along,
His children with him; and he will be known
Himself to be their father and their brother,
The husband of the mother who gave him birth,   450
Supplanter of his father, and his slayer.
— There! Go, and think on this; and if you find
That I'm deceived, say then — and not before —
That I am ignorant in divination.
            [*Exeunt severally* TEIRESIAS *and* OEDIPUS

STROPHE 1

CHORUS. The voice of god rang out in the holy
      cavern,
Denouncing one who has killed a King — the crime
      of crimes.
      Who is the man? Let him begone in
      Headlong flight, swift as a horse!

(*anapaests*) For the terrible god, like a warrior armed,
Stands ready to strike with a lightning-flash: 460
      The Furies who punish crime, and never fail,
      Are hot in their pursuit.

Furies: avenging goddesses who punished through mental and physical anguish

ANTISTROPHE 1

The snow is white on the cliffs of high Parnassus.
It has flashed a message: Let every Theban join the
      hunt!
      Lurking in caves among the mountains,
      Deep in the woods — where is the man?

Parnassus: mountain near which Delphi was located

(*anapaests*) In wearisome flight, unresting, alone,
An outlaw, he shuns Apollo's shrine;
      But ever the living menace of the god
      Hovers around his head.   470

STROPHE 2

(*choriambics*) Strange, disturbing, what the wise
Prophet has said. What can he mean?
Neither can I believe, nor can I disbelieve;

I do not know what to say.
I look here, and there; nothing can I find —
No strife, either now or in the past,
Between the kings of Thebes and Corinth.
A hand unknown struck down the King;
Though I would learn who it was dealt the blow,
That *he* is guilty whom all revere —   480
How can I believe this with no proof?

ANTISTROPHE 2

Zeus, Apollo — they have knowledge;
They understand the ways of life.
Prophets are men, like me; that they can understand
More than is revealed to me —
Of that, I can find nowhere certain proof,
Though one man is wise, another foolish.
Until the charge is manifest
I will not credit his accusers.
I saw myself how the Sphinx challenged him: 490
He proved his wisdom; he saved our city;
Therefore how can I now condemn him?

Enter CREON

CREON.   They tell me, Sirs, that Oedipus the King
Has made against me such an accusation
That I will not endure. For if he thinks
That in this present trouble I have done
Or said a single thing to do him harm,
Then let me die, and not drag out my days
With such a name as that. For it is not
One injury this accusation does me;   500
It touches my whole life, if you, my friends,
And all the city are to call me traitor.
CHORUS-LEADER.   The accusation may perhaps
   have come
From heat of temper, not from sober judgement.
CREON.   What was it made him think contrivances
Of mine suborned the seer to tell his lies?
CHORUS-LEADER.   Those were his words; I do not
   know his reasons.
CREON.   Was he in earnest, master of himself,
When he attacked me with this accusation?
CHORUS-LEADER.   I do not closely scan what kings
   are doing.—   510
But here he comes in person from the palace.

Enter OEDIPUS

OEDIPUS.   What, *you?* You dare come here? How
   can you find

The impudence to show yourself before
My house, when you are clearly proven
To have sought my life and tried to steal my crown?
Why, do you think me then a coward, or
A fool, that you should try to lay this plot?
Or that I should not see what you were scheming,
And so fall unresisting, blindly, to you?
But you were mad, so to attempt the throne,   520
Poor and unaided; this is not encompassed
Without the strong support of friends and money!

    CREON. This you must do: now you have had
      your say
Hear my reply; then yourself shall judge.

    OEDIPUS. A ready tongue! But I am bad at
      listening —
To you. For I have found how much you hate me.

    CREON. One thing: first listen to what I have to
      say.

    OEDIPUS. One thing: do not pretend you're not
      a villain.

    CREON. If you believe it is a thing worth having,
Insensate stubbornness, then you are wrong.   530

    OEDIPUS. If you believe that one can harm a
      kinsman
Without retaliation, you are wrong.

    CREON. With this I have no quarrel; but explain
What injury you say that I have done you.

    OEDIPUS. Did you advise, or did you not, that I
Should send a man for that most reverend prophet?

    CREON. I did, and I am still of that advice.

    OEDIPUS. How long a time is it since Laius . . .

    CREON. Since Laius did *what?* How can I say?

    OEDIPUS. Was seen no more, but met a violent
      death?   540

    CREON. It would be many years now past and
      gone.

    OEDIPUS. And had this prophet learned his art
      already?

    CREON. Yes; his repute was great — as it is now.

    OEDIPUS. Did he make any mention then of me?

    CREON. He never spoke of you within my hearing.

    OEDIPUS. Touching the murder: did you make no
      search?

    CREON. No search? Of course we did; but we
      found nothing.

    OEDIPUS. And why did this wise prophet not
      speak *then?*

    CREON. Who knows? Where I know nothing I
      say nothing.

OEDIPUS.   This much you know — and you'll do
well to answer: 550

CREON.   What is it? If I know, I'll tell you freely.

OEDIPUS.   That if he had not joined with you,
he'd not
Have said that I was Laius' murderer.

CREON.   If he said this, I did not know. — But I
May rightly question you, as you have me.

OEDIPUS.   Ask what you will. You'll never prove
I killed him.

CREON.   Why then: are you not married to my
sister?

OEDIPUS.   I am indeed; it cannot be denied.

CREON.   You share with her the sovereignty of
Thebes?

OEDIPUS.   She need but ask, and anything is
hers.   560

CREON.   And am I not myself conjoined with you?

OEDIPUS.   You are; not rebel therefore, but a
traitor!

CREON.   Not so, if you will reason with yourself,
As I with you. This first: would any man,
To gain no increase of authority,
Choose kingship, with its fears and sleepless nights?
Not I. What I desire, what every man
Desires, if he has wisdom, is to take
The substance, not the show, of royalty.
For now, through you, I have both power and
ease,   570
But were I king, I'd be oppressed with cares.
Not so: while I have ample sovereignty
And rule in peace, why should I want the crown?
I am not yet so mad as to give up
All that which brings me honour and advantage.
Now, every man greets me, and I greet him;
Those who have need of you make much of me,
Since I can make or mar them. Why should I
Surrender this to load myself with that?
A man of sense was never yet a traitor;   580
I have no taste for that, nor could I force
Myself to aid another's treachery.
    But you can test me: go to Delphi; ask
If I reported rightly what was said.
And further: if you find that I had dealings
With that diviner, you may take and kill me
Not with your single vote, but yours and mine,
But not on bare suspicion, unsupported.
How wrong it is, to use a random judgement
And think the false man true, the true man false!   590

To spurn a loyal friend, that is no better
Than to destroy the life to which we cling.
This you will learn in time, for Time alone
Reveals the upright man; a single day
Suffices to unmask the treacherous.

    CHORUS-LEADER.   My lord, he speaks with caution,
        to avoid
Grave error. Hasty judgement is not sure.

    OEDIPUS.   But when an enemy is quick to plot
And strike, I must be quick in answer too.
If I am slow, and wait, then I shall find   600
That he has gained his end, and I am lost.

    CREON.   What do you wish? To drive me into
        exile?

    OEDIPUS.   No, more than exile: I will have your
        life.

    CREON.   [When will it cease, this monstrous rage
        of yours?]

    OEDIPUS.   When your example shows what comes
        of envy.

    CREON.   Must you be stubborn? Cannot you be-
        lieve me?

    OEDIPUS.   [You speak to me as if I were a fool!]

    CREON.   Because I know you're wrong.

    OEDIPUS.   Right, for myself!

    CREON.   It is not right for me!

    OEDIPUS.   But you're a traitor.

    CREON.   What if your charge is false?

    OEDIPUS.   I have to govern.   610

    CREON.   Not govern badly!

    OEDIPUS.   Listen to him, Thebes!

    CREON.   You're not the city! I am Theban too.

    CHORUS-LEADER.   My lords, no more! Here comes
        the Queen, and not
Too soon, to join you. With her help, you must
Compose the bitter strife that now divides you.

Enter IOCASTA

    IOCASTA.   You frantic men! What has aroused
        this wild
Dispute? Have you no shame, when such a plague
Afflicts us, to indulge in private quarrels?
Creon, go home, I pray. You, Oedipus,
Come in; do not make much of what is nothing.

    CREON.   My sister: Oedipus, your husband
        here,   620
Has thought it right to punish me with one
Of two most awful dooms: exile, or death.

When . . . yours: Brackets indicate reconstructed lines that are
garbled in the manuscript.

OEDIPUS.   I have: I have convicted him, Iocasta,
Of plotting secretly against my life.
    CREON.   If I am guilty in a single point
Of such a crime, then may I die accursed.
    IOCASTA.   O, by the gods, believe him, Oedipus!
Respect the oath that he has sworn, and have
Regard for me, and for these citizens.

*(In what follows, the parts given to the chorus are
sung, the rest, presumably, spoken. The rhythm of
the music and dance is either dochmiac, 5-time, or a
combination of 3- and 5-time.)*

STROPHE

    CHORUS.   My lord, I pray, give consent.   **630**
Yield to us; ponder well.
    OEDIPUS.   What is it you would have me yield?
    CHORUS.   Respect a man ripe in years,
Bound by this mighty oath he has sworn.
    OEDIPUS.   Your wish is clear?
    CHORUS.   It is.
    OEDIPUS.   Then tell it me.
    CHORUS.   Not to repel, and drive out of our midst
    a friend,
Scorning a solemn curse, for uncertain cause.
    OEDIPUS.   I tell you this: your prayer will mean
    for me
My banishment from Thebes, or else my death.
    CHORUS.   No, no! by the Sun, the chief of
    gods,   **640**
Ruin and desolation and all evil come upon me
If I harbour thoughts such as these!
No; our land racked with plague breaks my heart.
    Do not now deal a new wound on Thebes to crown
    the old!
    OEDIPUS.   Then let him be, though I must die
    twice over,
Or be dishonoured, spurned and driven out.
It's your entreaty, and not his, that moves
My pity; he shall have my lasting hatred.
    CREON.   You yield ungenerously; but when your
    wrath
Has cooled, how it will prick you! Natures such   **650**
As yours give most vexation to themselves.
    OEDIPUS.   O, let me be! Get from my sight.
    CREON.   I go,
Misjudged by you — but these will judge me better
    [*indicating* CHORUS].
                          [*Exit* CREON

ANTISTROPHE

CHORUS. My lady, why now delay?
Let the King go in with you.
 IOCASTA. When you have told me what has
  passed.
 CHORUS. Suspicion came. — Random words, un-
  deserved,
Will provoke men to wrath.
 IOCASTA. It was from both?
 CHORUS.   It was.
 IOCASTA.   And what was said?
 CHORUS. It is enough for me, more than enough,
  when I   660
Think of our ills, that this should rest where it lies.
 OEDIPUS. You and your wise advice, blunting my
  wrath,
Frustrated me — and it has come to this!
 CHORUS. This, O my King, I said, and say again:
  I should be mad, distraught,
  I should be a fool, and worse,
  If I sought to drive you away.
  Thebes was near sinking; you brought her safe
Through the storm. Now again we pray that you
  may save us.
 IOCASTA. In Heaven's name, my lord, I too must
  know   670
What was the reason for this blazing anger.
 OEDIPUS. There's none to whom I more defer;
  and so,
I'll tell you: Creon and his vile plot against me.
 IOCASTA. What has he done, that you are so
  incensed?
 OEDIPUS. He says that I am Laius' murderer.
 IOCASTA. From his own knowledge? Or has some-
  one told him?
 OEDIPUS. No; that suspicion should not fall upon
Himself, he used a tool — a crafty prophet.
 IOCASTA. Why, have no fear of *that*. Listen to
  me,
And you will learn that the prophetic art   680
Touches our human fortunes not at all.
I soon can give you proof. — An oracle
Once came to Laius — from the god himself
I do not say, but from his ministers:
His fate it was, that should he have a son
By me, that son would take his father's life.
But he was killed — or so they said — by strangers,
By brigands, at a place where three ways meet.
As for the child, it was not three days old

When Laius fastened both its feet together   690
And had it cast over a precipice.
Therefore Apollo failed; for neither did
His son kill Laius, nor did Laius meet
The awful end he feared, killed by his son.
So much for what prophetic voices uttered.
Have no regard for them. The god will bring
To light himself whatever thing he chooses.

   OEDIPUS.   Iocasta, terror seizes me, and shakes
My very soul, at one thing you have said.

    IOCASTA.   Why so? What have I said to frighten
      you?   700

    OEDIPUS.   I think I heard you say that Laius
Was murdered at a place where three ways meet?

    IOCASTA.   So it was said — indeed, they say it still.

    OEDIPUS.   Where is the place where this en-
      counter happened?

    IOCASTA.   They call the country Phokis, and a
      road
From Delphi joins a road from Daulia.

    OEDIPUS.   Since that was done, how many years
      have passed?

    IOCASTA.   It was proclaimed in Thebes a little
      time
Before the city offered you the crown.

    OEDIPUS.   O Zeus, what fate hast thou ordained
      for me?   710

    IOCASTA.   What is the fear that so oppresses you?

    OEDIPUS.   One moment yet: tell me of Laius.
What age was he? and what was his appearance?

    IOCASTA.   A tall man, and his hair was touched
      with white;
In figure he was not unlike yourself.

    OEDIPUS.   O God! Did I, then, in my ignorance,
Proclaim that awful curse against myself?

    IOCASTA.   What are you saying? How you frighten
      me!

    OEDIPUS.   I greatly fear that prophet was not
      blind.
But yet one question; that will show me more.   720

    IOCASTA.   For all my fear, I'll tell you what I can.

    OEDIPUS.   Was he alone, or did he have with him
A royal bodyguard of men-at-arms?

    IOCASTA.   The company in all were five; the King
Rode in a carriage, and there was a Herald.

    OEDIPUS.   Ah God! How clear the picture is! . . .
      But who,
Iocasta, brought report of this to Thebes?

    IOCASTA.   A slave, the only man that was not
      killed.

OEDIPUS.   And is he round about the palace now?

IOCASTA.   No, he is not. When he returned, and   **730**
   saw
You ruling in the place of the dead King,
He begged me, on his bended knees, to send him
Into the hills as shepherd, out of sight,
As far as could be from the city here.
I sent him, for he was a loyal slave;
He well deserved this favour — and much more.

OEDIPUS.   Could he be brought back here — at
   once — to see me?

IOCASTA.   He could; but why do you desire his
   coming?

OEDIPUS.   I fear I have already said, Iocasta,
More than enough; and therefore I will see him.   **740**

IOCASTA.   Then he shall come. But, as your wife,
   I ask you,
What is the terror that possesses you?

OEDIPUS.   And you shall know it, since my fears
   have grown
So great; for who is more to me than you,
That I should speak to *him* at such a moment?
   My father, then, was Polybus of Corinth;
My mother, Merope. My station there
Was high as any man's — until a thing
Befell me that was strange indeed, though not
Deserving of the thought I gave to it.   **750**
A man said at a banquet — he was full
Of wine — that I was not my father's son.
It angered me; but I restrained myself
That day. The next I went and questioned both
My parents. They were much incensed with him
Who had let fall the insult. So, from them,
I had assurance. Yet the slander spread
And always chafed me. Therefore secretly,
My mother and my father unaware,
I went to Delphi. Phoebus would return   **760**
No answer to my question, but declared
A thing most horrible: he foretold that I
Should mate with my own mother, and beget
A brood that men would shudder to behold,
And that I was to be the murderer
Of my own father.
           Therefore, back to Corinth
I never went — the stars alone have told me
Where Corinth lies — that I might never see
Cruel fulfilment of that oracle.
So journeying, I came to that same spot   **770**
Where, as you say, this King was killed. And now,
This is the truth, Iocasta: when I reached

The place where three ways meet, I met a herald,
And in a carriage drawn by colts was such
A man as you describe. By violence
The herald and the older man attempted
To push me off the road, I, in my rage,
Struck at the driver, who was hustling me.
The old man, when he saw me level with him,
Taking a double-goad, aimed at my head   780   **double-goad:** two-headed spear
A murderous blow. He paid for that, full measure.
Swiftly I hit him with my staff; he rolled
Out of his carriage, flat upon his back.
I killed them all. — But if, between this stranger
And Laius there was any bond of kinship,
Who could be in more desperate plight than I?
Who more accursèd in the eyes of Heaven?
For neither citizen nor stranger may
Receive me in his house, nor speak to me,
But he must bar the door. And it was none   790
But I invoked this curse on my own head!
And I pollute the bed of him I slew
With my own hands! Say, am I vile? Am I
Not all impure? Seeing I must be exiled,
And even in my exile must not go
And see my parents, nor set foot upon
My native land; or, if I do, I must
Marry my mother, and kill Polybus
My father, who engendered me and reared me.
If one should say it was a cruel god   800
Brought this upon me, would he not speak right?
    No, no, you holy powers above! Let me
Not see that day! but rather let me pass
Beyond the sight of men, before I see
The stain of such pollution come upon me!
    CHORUS-LEADER.   My lord, this frightens me. But
        you must hope,
Until we hear the tale from him that saw it.
    OEDIPUS.   That is the only hope that's left to me;
We must await the coming of the shepherd.
    IOCASTA.   What do you hope from him, when he
        is here?   810
    OEDIPUS.   I'll tell you: if his story shall be found
The same as yours, then I am free of guilt.
    IOCASTA.   But what have I said of especial note?
    OEDIPUS.   You said that he reported it was
        brigands
Who killed the King. If he still speaks of 'men',
It was not I; a single man, and 'men',
Are not the same. But if he says it was
A traveller journeying alone, why then,
The burden of the guilt must fall on me.

IOCASTA.   But that *is* what he said, I do assure
　　you!   820
He cannot take it back again! Not I
Alone, but the whole city heard him say it!
But even if he should revoke the tale
He told before, not even so, my lord,
Will he establish that the King was slain
According to the prophecy. For that was clear:
His son, and mine, should slay him. — He, poor
　　thing,
Was killed himself, and never killed his father.
Therefore, so far as divination goes,
Or prophecy, I'll take no notice of it.   830
　　OEDIPUS.   And that is wise. — But send a man to
　　　　bring
The shepherd; I would not have that neglected.
　　IOCASTA.   I'll send at once. — But come with me;
　　　　for I
Would not do anything that could displease you.
　　　　　　　　　　　[*Exeunt* OEDIPUS *and* IOCASTA

STROPHE 1

　　CHORUS.   I pray that I may pass my life
(*in a steady rhythm*) In reverent holiness of word
　　and deed.
For there are laws enthroned above;
Heaven created them,
Olympus was their father,
And mortal men had no part in their birth;   840
Nor ever shall their power pass from sight
In dull forgetfulness;
A god moves in them; he grows not old.

ANTISTROPHE 1

Pride makes the tyrant — pride of wealth
And power, too great for wisdom and restraint;
For Pride will climb the topmost height;
Then is the man cast down
To uttermost destruction.
There he finds no escape, no resource.
But high contention for the city's good   850
May the gods preserve.
For me — may the gods be my defence!

STROPHE 2

If there is one who walks in pride
Of word or deed, and has no fear of Justice,

No reverence for holy shrines —
May utter ruin fall on him!
So may his ill-starred pride be given its reward.
Those who seek dishonourable advantage
And lay violent hands on holy things
And do not shun impiety —   860
Who among these will secure himself from the wrath
    of God?
If deeds like these are honoured,
Why should I join in the sacred dance?

ANTISTROPHE 2

No longer shall Apollo's shrine,
The holy centre of the Earth, receive my worship;
No, nor his seat at Abae, nor   **Abae: a city in Greece**
The temple of Olympian Zeus,
If what the god foretold does not come to pass.
Mighty Zeus — if so I should address Thee —
O great Ruler of all things, look on this!   870
Now are thy oracles falling into contempt, and men
Deny Apollo's power.
Worship of the gods is passing away.

> *Enter* IOCASTA, *attended by a girl carrying
> a wreath and incense*

IOCASTA.   My lords of Thebes, I have bethought
    myself
To approach the altars of the gods, and lay
These wreaths on them, and burn this frankincense.
For every kind of terror has laid hold
On Oedipus; his judgement is distracted.
He will not read the future by the past
But yields himself to any who speaks fear.   880
Since then no words of mine suffice to calm him
I turn to Thee, Apollo — Thou art nearest —
Thy suppliant, with these votive offerings.
Grant us deliverance and peace, for now
Fear is on all, when we see Oedipus,
The helmsman of the ship, so terrified.

(*A reverent silence, while* IOCASTA *lays the wreath at
the altar and sets fire to the incense. The wreath will
remain and the incense smoke during the rest of the
play.*)

> *Enter a* SHEPHERD FROM CORINTH

CORINTHIAN.   Might I inquire of you where I may
    find

The royal palace of King Oedipus?
Or, better, where himself is to be found?
   CHORUS-LEADER.   There is the palace; himself, Sir,
     is within,   890
But here his wife and mother of his children.
   CORINTHIAN.   Ever may happiness attend on her,
And hers, the wedded wife of such a man.
   IOCASTA.   May you enjoy the same; your gentle
     words
Deserve no less. — Now, Sir, declare your purpose;
With what request, what message have you come?
   CORINTHIAN.   With good news for your husband
     and his house.
   IOCASTA.   What news is this? And who has sent
     you here?
   CORINTHIAN.   I come from Corinth, and the news
     I bring
Will give you joy, though joy be crossed with
     grief.   900
   IOCASTA.   What is this, with its two-fold influence?
   CORINTHIAN.   The common talk in Corinth is that
     they
Will call on Oedipus to be their king.
   IOCASTA.   What? Does old Polybus no longer
     reign?
   CORINTHIAN.   Not now, for Death has laid him in
     his grave.
   IOCASTA.   Go quickly to your master, girl; give him
The news. — You oracles, where are you now?
This is the man whom Oedipus so long
Has shunned, fearing to kill him; now he's dead,
And killed by Fortune, not by Oedipus.   910

      Enter OEDIPUS, *very nervous*

   OEDIPUS.   My dear Iocasta, tell me, my dear wife,
Why have you sent to fetch me from the palace?
   IOCASTA.   Listen to *him*, and as you hear, reflect
What has become of all those oracles.
   OEDIPUS.   Who is this man? — What has he to
     tell me?
   IOCASTA.   He is from Corinth, and he brings you
     news
About your father. Polybus is dead.
   OEDIPUS.   What say you, sir? Tell me the news
     yourself.
   CORINTHIAN.   If you would have me first report
     on this,
I tell you; death has carried him away.   920

OEDIPUS. By treachery? Or did sickness come to
him?

CORINTHIAN. A small mischance will lay an old
man low.

OEDIPUS. Poor Polybus! He died, then, of a sickness?

CORINTHIAN. That, and the measure of his many
years.

OEDIPUS. Ah me! Why then, Iocasta, should a
man
Regard the Pythian house of oracles,
Or screaming birds, on whose authority
I was to slay my father? But he is dead;
The earth has covered him; and here am I,
My sword undrawn — unless perchance *my* loss   930
Has killed him; so might I be called his slayer.
But for those oracles about my father,
Those he has taken with him to the grave
Wherein he lies, and they are come to nothing.

IOCASTA. Did I not say long since it would be so?

OEDIPUS. You did; but I was led astray by fear.

IOCASTA. So none of this deserves another
thought.

OEDIPUS. Yet how can I not fear my mother's
bed?

IOCASTA. Why should we fear, seeing that man is
ruled
By chance, and there is room for no clear fore-
thought?   940
No; live at random, live as best one can.
So do not fear this marriage with your mother;
Many a man has suffered this before —
But only in his dreams. Whoever thinks
The least of this, he lives most comfortably.

OEDIPUS. Your every word I do accept, if she
That bore me did not live; but as she does —
Despite your wisdom, how can I but tremble?

IOCASTA. Yet there is comfort in your father's
death.

OEDIPUS. Great comfort, but still fear of her who
lives.   950

CORINTHIAN. And who is this who makes you so
afraid?

OEDIPUS. Meropê, my man, the wife of Polybus.

CORINTHIAN. And what in *her* gives cause of fear
in *you*?

OEDIPUS. There was an awful warning from the
gods.

CORINTHIAN. Can it be told, or must it be kept
secret?

Pythia: priestess of Apollo who
pronounced the oracles at Delphi
screaming birds: Ravens, hawks
and crows were sacred to Apollo.

OEDIPUS.   No secret. Once Apollo said that I
Was doomed to lie with my own mother, and
Defile my own hands with my father's blood.
Wherefore has Corinth been, these many years,
My home no more. My fortunes have been
      fair. —   960
But it is good to see a parent's face.
   CORINTHIAN.   It was for fear of *this* you fled the
      city?
   OEDIPUS.   This, and the shedding of my father's
      blood.
   CORINTHIAN.   Why then, my lord, since I am
      come in friendship,
I'll rid you here and now of that misgiving.
   OEDIPUS.   Be sure, your recompense would be in
      keeping.
   CORINTHIAN.   It was the chief cause of my coming
      here
That your return might bring me some advantage.
   OEDIPUS.   Back to my parents I will never go.
   CORINTHIAN.   My son, it is clear, you know not
      what you do. . . .   970
   OEDIPUS.   Not know? What is this? Tell me
      what you mean.
   CORINTHIAN.   If for this reason you avoid your
      home.
   OEDIPUS.   Fearing Apollo's oracle may come true.
   CORINTHIAN.   And you incur pollution from your
      parents?
   OEDIPUS.   That is the thought that makes me live
      in terror.
   CORINTHIAN.   I tell you then, this fear of yours is
      idle.
   OEDIPUS.   How? Am I not their child, and they
      my parents?
   CORINTHIAN.   Because there's none of Polybus in
      you.
   OEDIPUS.   How can you say so? Was he not my
      father?
   CORINTHIAN.   I am your father just as much as
      he!   980
   OEDIPUS.   A stranger equal to the father? How?
   CORINTHIAN.   Neither did he beget you, nor did I.
   OEDIPUS.   Then for what reason did he call me
      son?
   CORINTHIAN.   He had you as a gift — from my
      own hands.
   OEDIPUS.   And showed such love to me? Me, not
      his own?

CORINTHIAN.   Yes; his own childlessness so worked on him.

OEDIPUS.   You, when you gave me: had you bought, or found me?

CORINTHIAN.   I found you in the woods upon Cithaeron.

OEDIPUS.   Why were you travelling in that neighbourhood?

CORINTHIAN.   I tended flocks of sheep upon the mountain.   990

OEDIPUS.   You were a shepherd, then, wandering for hire?

CORINTHIAN.   I was, my son; but that day, your preserver.

OEDIPUS.   How so? What ailed me when you took me up?

CORINTHIAN.   For that, your ankles might give evidence.

OEDIPUS.   Alas! why speak of this, my life-long trouble?

CORINTHIAN.   I loosed the fetters clamped upon your feet.

OEDIPUS.   A pretty gift to carry from the cradle!

CORINTHIAN.   It was for this they named you Oedipus.

OEDIPUS.   Who did, my father or my mother? Tell me.

Oedipus: etymologically, "swollen foot"

CORINTHIAN.   I cannot; he knows more, from whom I had you.   1000

OEDIPUS.   It was another, not yourself, that found me?

CORINTHIAN.   Yes, you were given me by another shepherd.

OEDIPUS.   Who? Do you know him? Can you name the man?

CORINTHIAN.   They said that he belonged to Laius.

OEDIPUS.   What — him who once was ruler here in Thebes?

CORINTHIAN.   Yes, he it was for whom this man was shepherd.

OEDIPUS.   And is he still alive, that I can see him?

CORINTHIAN [*turning to the Chorus*].   You that are native here would know that best.

OEDIPUS.   Has any man of you now present here
Acquaintance with this shepherd, him he speaks of?   1010
Has any seen him, here, or in the fields?
Speak; on this moment hangs discovery.

CHORUS-LEADER.   It is, I think, the man that you
　　have sent for,
The slave now in the country. But who should
　　know
The truth of this more than Iocasta here?
　　OEDIPUS.   The man he speaks of: do you think,
　　Iocasta,
He is the one I have already summoned?
　　IOCASTA.   What matters who he is? Pay no re-
　　gard. —
The tale is idle; it is best forgotten.　　　　1020
　　OEDIPUS.   It cannot be that I should have this
　　clue
And then not find the secret of my birth.
　　IOCASTA.   In God's name stop, if you have any
　　thought
For your own life! My ruin is enough.
　　OEDIPUS.   Be not dismayed; nothing can prove
　　you base.
Not though I find my mother thrice a slave.
　　IOCASTA.   O, I beseech you, do not! Seek no
　　more!
　　OEDIPUS.   You cannot move me. I *will* know the
　　truth.
　　IOCASTA.   I know that what I say is for the best.
　　OEDIPUS.   This 'best' of yours! I have no patience
　　with it.
　　IOCASTA.   O may you never learn what man you
　　are!　　　　　　　　　　　　　　　　1030
　　OEDIPUS.   Go, someone, bring the herdsman here
　　to me,
And leave her to enjoy her pride of birth.
　　IOCASTA.   O man of doom! For by no other name
Can I address you now or evermore.
　　　　　　　　　　　　　　[*Exit* IOCASTA
　　CHORUS-LEADER.   The Queen has fled, my lord, as
　　if before
Some driving storm of grief. I fear that from
Her silence may break forth some great disaster.
　　OEDIPUS.   Break forth what will! My birth, how-
　　ever humble,
I am resolved to find. But she, perhaps,
Is proud, as women will be; is ashamed　　1040
Of my low birth. But I do rate myself
The child of Fortune, giver of all good,
And I shall not be put to shame, for I
Am born of Her; the Years who are my kinsmen
Distinguished my estate, now high, now low;
So born, I could not make me someone else,
And not do all to find my parentage.

STROPHE 1

CHORUS.   If I have power of prophecy,
(*animated rhythm*) If I have judgement wise and
      sure, Cithaeron
(I swear by Olympus),   1050
Thou shalt be honoured when the moon
Next is full, as mother and foster-nurse
And birth-place of Oedipus, with festival and danc-
      ing,
For thou hast given great blessings to our King.
To Thee, Apollo, now we raise our cry:
O grant our prayer find favour in thy sight!

ANTISTROPHE

Who is thy mother, O my son?
Is she an ageless nymph among the mountains,
That bore thee to Pan?
Or did Apollo father thee?   1060
For dear to him are the pastures in the hills.
Or Hermes, who ruleth from the summit of Kyllene?
Or Dionysus on the mountain-tops,
Did he receive thee from thy mother's arms,
A nymph who follows him on Helicon?
      OEDIPUS.   If I, who never yet have met the man,
May risk conjecture, I think I see the herdsman
Whom we have long been seeking. In his age
He well accords; and more, I recognize
Those who are with him as of my own house-
      hold.   1070
But as for knowing, you will have advantage
Of me, if you have seen the man before.
      CHORUS-LEADER.   'Tis he, for certain — one of
      Laius' men,
One of the shepherds whom he trusted most.

Enter the THEBAN SHEPHERD

      OEDIPUS.   You first I ask, you who have come
      from Corinth:
Is that the man you mean?
      CORINTHIAN.   That very man.
      OEDIPUS.   Come here, my man; look at me; an-
      swer me
My questions. Were you ever Laius' man?
      THEBAN.   I was; his slave — born in the house,
      not bought.
      OEDIPUS.   What was your charge, or what your
      way of life?   1080

THEBAN. Tending the sheep, the most part of
my life.

OEDIPUS. And to what regions did you most
resort?

THEBAN. Now it was Cithaeron, now the country
round.

OEDIPUS. And was this man of your acquaintance
there?

THEBAN. In what employment? Which is the
man you mean?

OEDIPUS. Him yonder. Had you any dealings
with him?

THEBAN. Not such that I can quickly call to
mind.

CORINTHIAN. No wonder, Sir, but though he has
forgotten

I can remind him. I am very sure,

He knows the time when, round about Cithaeron, 1090

He with a double flock, and I with one,

We spent together three whole summer seasons,

From spring until the rising of Arcturus.   **rising of Arcturus:** (in September)

Then, with the coming on of winter, I

Drove my flocks home, he his, to Laius' folds.

Is this the truth? or am I telling lies?

THEBAN. It is true, although it happened long
ago.

CORINTHIAN. Then tell me: do you recollect a
baby

You gave me once to bring up for my own?

THEBAN. Why this? Why are you asking me this
question?

CORINTHIAN. My friend, *here* is the man who was
that baby!   1100

THEBAN. O, devil take you! Cannot you keep
silent?

OEDIPUS. Here, Sir! This man needs no reproof
from you.

Your tongue needs chastisement much more than his.

THEBAN. O best of masters, how am I offending?

OEDIPUS. Not telling of the child of whom he
speaks.

THEBAN. He? He knows nothing. He is wasting
time.

OEDIPUS [*threatening*]. If you'll not speak from
pleasure, speak from pain.

THEBAN. No, no, I pray! Not torture an old man!

OEDIPUS. Here, someone, quickly! Twist this fellow's arms!

THEBAN.   Why, wretched man? What would you
know besides?   1110

OEDIPUS.   That child: you gave it him, the one he
speaks of?

THEBAN.   I did. Ah God, would I had died instead!

OEDIPUS.   And die you shall, unless you speak the
truth.

THEBAN.   And if I do, then death is still more
certain.

OEDIPUS.   This man, I think, is trying to delay me.

THEBAN.   Not I! I said I gave the child — just
now.

OEDIPUS.   And got it — where? Your own? or
someone else's?

THEBAN.   No, not my own. Someone had given
it me.

OEDIPUS.   Who? Which of these our citizens?
From what house?

THEBAN.   No, I implore you, master! Do not
ask!   1120

OEDIPUS.   You die if I must question you again.

THEBAN.   Then, 'twas a child of one in Laius'
house.

OEDIPUS.   You mean a slave? Or someone of his
kin?

THEBAN.   God! I am on the verge of saying it.

OEDIPUS.   And I of hearing it, but hear I must.

THEBAN.   His own, or so they said. But she within
Could tell you best — your wife — the truth of it.

OEDIPUS.   What, did she give you it?

THEBAN.   She did, my lord.

OEDIPUS.   With what intention?

THEBAN.   That I should destroy it.

OEDIPUS.   Her own? — How could she?

THEBAN.   Frightened by oracles. 1130

OEDIPUS.   What oracles?

THEBAN.   That it would kill its parents.

OEDIPUS.   Why did you let it go to this man here?

THEBAN.   I pitied it, my lord. I thought to send
The child abroad, whence this man came. And he
Saved it, for utter doom. For if you are
The man he says, then you were born for ruin.

OEDIPUS.   Ah God! Ah God! This is the truth, at
last!
O Sun, let me behold thee this once more,
I who am proved accursed in my conception,
And in my marriage, and in him I slew.   1140

   [*Exeunt severally* OEDIPUS, CORINTHIAN, THEBAN

STROPHE 1

CHORUS.   Alas! you generations of men!
(*glyconics*) Even while you live you are next to
    nothing!
Has any man won for himself
More than the shadow of happiness,
A shadow that swiftly fades away?
Oedipus, now as I look on you,
See your ruin, how can I say that
Mortal man can be happy?

ANTISTROPHE 1

For who won greater prosperity?
Sovereignty and wealth beyond all desiring?   1150
The crooked-clawed, riddling Sphinx,
Maiden and bird, you overcame;
You stood like a tower of strength to Thebes.
So you received our crown, received the
Highest honours that we could give —
King in our mighty city.

STROPHE 2

Who more wretched, more afflicted now,
With cruel misery, with fell disaster,
Your life in dust and ashes?
    O noble Oedipus!   1160
    How could it be? to come again
A bridegroom of her who gave you birth!
How could such a monstrous thing
Endure so long, unknown?

ANTISTROPHE 2

Time sees all, and Time, in your despite,
Disclosed and punished your unnatural marriage —
A child, and then a husband.
    O son of Laius,
    Would I had never looked on you!
I mourn you as one who mourns the dead.   1170
First you gave me back my life,
And now, that life is death.

Enter, from the palace, a MESSENGER

MESSENGER.   My Lords, most honoured citizens of
    Thebes,
What deeds am I to tell of, you to see!

What heavy grief to bear, if still remains
Your native loyalty to our line of kings.
For not the Ister, no, nor Phasis' flood
Could purify this house, such things it hides,
Such others will it soon display to all,
Evils self-sought. Of all our sufferings   1180
Those hurt the most that we ourselves inflict.
    CHORUS-LEADER.   Sorrow enough — too much —
      in what was known
Already. What new sorrow do you bring?
    MESSENGER.   Quickest for me to say and you to
      hear:
It is the Queen, Iocasta — she is dead.
    CHORUS-LEADER.   Iocasta, dead? But how? What
      was the cause?
    MESSENGER.   By her own hand. Of what has
      passed, the worst
Cannot be yours: that was, to see it.
But you shall hear, so far as memory serves,
The cruel story. — In her agony   1190
She ran across the courtyard, snatching at
Her hair with both her hands. She made her way
Straight to her chamber; she barred fast the doors
And called on Laius, these long years dead,
Remembering their by-gone procreation.
'Through this did you meet death yourself, and leave
To me, the mother, child-bearing accursed
To my own child.' She cried aloud upon
The bed where she had borne a double brood,
Husband from husband, children from a child.   1200
And thereupon she died, I know not how;
For, groaning, Oedipus burst in, and we,
For watching him, saw not *her* agony
And how it ended. He, ranging through the palace,
Came up to each man calling for a sword,
Calling for her whom he had called his wife,
Asking where was she who had borne them all,
Himself and his own children. So he raved.
And then some deity showed him the way,
For it was none of us that stood around;   1210
He cried aloud, as if to someone who
Was leading him; he leapt upon the doors,
Burst from their sockets the yielding bars, and fell
Into the room; and there, hanged by the neck,
We saw his wife, held in a swinging cord.
He, when he saw it, groaned in misery
And loosed her body from the rope. When now
She lay upon the ground, awful to see
Was that which followed: from her dress he tore

Ister, Phasis: rivers in what are now Austria and southwest Russia

The golden brooches that she had been wearing, 1220
Raised them, and with their points struck his own
    eyes,
Crying aloud that they should never see
What he had suffered and what he had done,
But in the dark henceforth they should behold
Those whom they ought not; nor should recognize
Those whom he longed to see. To such refrain
He smote his eyeballs with the pins, not once,
Nor twice; and as he smote them, blood ran down
His face, not dripping slowly, but there fell
Showers of black rain and blood-red hail to-
    gether. 1230
    Not on his head alone, but on them both,
Husband and wife, this common storm has broken.
Their ancient happiness of early days
Was happiness indeed; but now, today,
Death, ruin, lamentation, shame — of all
The ills there are, not one is wanting here.
    CHORUS-LEADER.   Now is there intermission in his
      agony?
    MESSENGER.   He shouts for someone to unbar the
      gates,
And to display to Thebes the parricide, —
His mother's — no, I cannot speak the words; 1240
For, by the doom he uttered, he will cast
Himself beyond our borders, nor remain
To be a curse at home. But he needs strength,
And one to guide him; for these wounds are greater
Than he can bear — as you shall see; for look!
They draw the bolts. A sight you will behold
To move the pity even of an enemy.

    The doors open. OEDIPUS *slowly advances*

    CHORUS.   O horrible, dreadful sight. More dread-
      ful far
(*These verses sung or chanted in a slow march-time.*)
    Than any I have yet seen. What cruel frenzy
Came over you? What spirit with superhuman
    leap 1250
Came to assist your grim destiny?
Ah, most unhappy man!
But no! I cannot bear even to look at you,
Though there is much that I would ask and see and
    hear.
But I shudder at the very sight of you.
    OEDIPUS. [*sings in the dochmiac rhythm*].   Alas!
      alas! and woe for my misery!
Where are my steps taking me?

My random voice is lost in the air.
O God! how hast thou crushed me!

    CHORUS-LEADER [*spoken*].   Too terribly for us to
      hear or see.   1260

    OEDIPUS [*sings*].   O cloud of darkness abominable,
My enemy unspeakable,
In cruel onset insuperable.
Alas! alas! Assailed at once by pain
Of pin-points and of memory of crimes.

    CHORUS-LEADER.   In such tormenting pains you
      well may cry
A double grief and feel a double woe.

    OEDIPUS [*sings*].   Ah, my friend!
Still at my side? Still steadfast?
Still can you endure me?   1270
Still care for me, a blind man?
[*speaks*] For it is you, my friend; I know 'tis you;
Though all is darkness, yet I know your voice.

    CHORUS-LEADER.   O, to destroy your sight! How
      could you bring
Yourself to do it? What god incited you?

    OEDIPUS [*sings*].   It was Apollo, friends, Apollo.
He decreed that I should suffer what I suffer;
But the hand that struck, alas! was my own,
And not another's.
For why should I have sight,   1280
When sight of nothing could give me pleasure?

    CHORUS.   It was even as you say.

    OEDIPUS.   What have I left, my friends, to see,
To cherish, whom to speak with, or
To listen to, with joy?
Lead me away at once, far from Thebes;
Lead me away, my friends!
I have destroyed; I am accursed, and, what is more,
Hateful to Heaven, as no other.

    CHORUS-LEADER [*speaks*].   Unhappy your inten-
      tion, and unhappy   1290
Your fate. O would that I had never known you!

    OEDIPUS [*sings*].   Curses on him, whoever he was,
Who took the savage fetters from my feet,
  Snatched me from death, and saved me.
  No thanks I owe him,
  For had I died that day
Less ruin had I brought on me and mine.

    CHORUS.   That wish is my wish too.

    OEDIPUS.   I had not then come and slain my
      father.
Nor then would men have called me   1300
Husband of her that bore me.

Now am I God's enemy, child of the guilty,
And she that bore me has borne too my children;
And if there is evil surpassing evil,
    That has come to Oedipus.
    CHORUS-LEADER. How can I say that you have
        counselled well?
Far better to be dead than to be blind.
    OEDIPUS. That what is done was not done for the
      best
Seek not to teach me: counsel me no more.
I know not how I could have gone to Hades   1310
And with these eyes have looked upon my father
Or on my mother; such things have I done
To them, death is no worthy punishment.
Or could I look for pleasure in the sight
Of my own children, born as they were born?
Never! No pleasure there, for eyes of mine,
Nor in this city, nor its battlements
Nor sacred images. From these — ah, miserable! —
I, the most nobly born of any Theban
Am banned for ever by my own decree   1320
That the defiler should be driven forth,
The man accursed of Heaven and Laius' house.
Was I to find such taint in me, and then
With level eyes to look *them* in the face?
Nay more: if for my ears I could have built
Some dam to stay the flood of sound, that I
Might lose both sight and hearing, and seal up
My wretched body — that I would have done.
How good to dwell beyond the reach of pain!
    Cithaeron! Why did you accept me? Why   1330
Did you not take and kill me? Never then
Should I have come to dwell among the Thebans.
    O Polybus! Corinth! and that ancient home
I thought my father's — what a thing you nurtured!
How fair, how foul beneath! For I am found
Foul in myself and in my parentage.
    O you three ways, that in a hidden glen
Do meet: you narrow branching roads within
The forest — you, through my own hands, did drink
My father's blood, that was my own. — Ah! do
      you   1340
Remember what you saw me do? And what
I did again in Thebes? You marriages!
You did beget me: then, having begotten,
Bore the same crop again, and brought to light
Commingled blood of fathers, brothers, sons,
Brides, mothers, wives; all that there can be
Among the human kind most horrible!

But that which it is foul to do, it is
Not fair to speak of. Quick as you can, I beg,
Banish me, hide me, slay me! Throw me forth   1350
Into the sea, where I may sink from view.
I pray you, deign to touch one so afflicted
And do not fear: there is no man alive
Can bear this load of evil but myself.

    CHORUS-LEADER.   To listen to your prayers, Creon
    is here,
For act or guidance opportune; for he,
In your defection, is our champion.

Enter CREON

    OEDIPUS.   Alas! alas! How can I speak to him?
What word of credit find? In all my commerce
With him aforetime I am proven false.   1360
    CREON.   No exultation, Oedipus, and no reproach
Of injuries inflicted brings me here;
But if the face of men moves not your shame,
Then reverence show to that all-nurturing fire,
The holy Sun, that he be not polluted
By such accursèd sight, which neither Earth
Nor rain from Heaven nor sunlight can endure.
    Take him within, and quickly: it is right
His kinsmen only should behold and hear
Evils that chiefly on his kinsmen fall.   1370
    OEDIPUS.   In Heaven's name — since you cheat
    my expectation,
So noble towards my baseness — grant me this:
It is for you I ask it, not myself.
    CREON.   What is this supplication that you make?
    OEDIPUS.   Drive me at once beyond your bounds,
    where I
Shall be alone, and no one speak to me.
    CREON.   I would have done it; but I first desired
To ask the God what he would have me do.
    OEDIPUS.   No, his command was given in full, to
    slay
Me, the polluter and the parricide.   1380
    CREON.   Those were his words; but in our present
    need
It would be wise to ask what we should do.
    OEDIPUS.   You will inquire for such a wretch as I?
    CREON.   I will; for now *you* may believe the god.
    OEDIPUS.   Yes; and on you I lay this charge and
    duty:
Give burial, as you will, to her who lies
Within — for she is yours, and this is proper;
And, while I live, let not my father's city

Endure to have me as a citizen.
My home must be the mountains — on Cithae-
    ron,   1390
Which, while they lived, my parents chose to be   *— acceptance*
My tomb: they wished to slay me; now they shall.
For this I know: sickness can never kill me,
Nor any other evil; I was not saved
That day from death, except for some strange doom.
My fate must take the course it will. — Now, for my
    sons,
Be not concerned for them: they can, being men,
Fend for themselves, wherever they may be:
But my unhappy daughters, my two girls,
Whose chairs were always set beside my own   1400
At table — they who shared in every dish
That was prepared for me — oh Creon! these
Do I commend to you. And grant me this:
To take them in my arms, and weep for them.
My lord! most noble Creon! could I now
But hold them in my arms, then I should think
I had them as I had when I could see them.
Ah! what is this?
Ah Heaven! do I not hear my dear ones, sobbing?
Has Creon, in his pity, sent to me   1410
My darling children? Has he? Is it true?
    CREON.   It is; they have been always your delight;
So, knowing this, I had them brought to you.
    OEDIPUS.   Then Heaven reward you, and for this
    kind service
Protect you better than it protected me!
    Where are you, children? Where? O come to me!
Come, let me clasp you with a brother's arms,
These hands, which helped your father's eye, once
    bright,
To look upon you as they see you now —
Your father who, not seeing, nor inquiring,   1420
Gave you for mother her who bore himself.
See you I cannot; but I weep for you,
For the unhappiness that must be yours,
And for the bitter life that you must lead.
What gathering of the citizens, what festivals,
Will you have part in? Your high celebrations
Will be to go back home, and sit in tears.
And when the time for marriage comes, what man
Will stake upon the ruin and the shame
That I am to my parents and to you?   1430
Nothing is wanting there: your father slew
His father, married her who gave him birth,
And then, from that same source whence he himself

Had sprung, got you. — With these things they will
    taunt you;
And who will take you then in marriage? — Nobody;
But you must waste, unwedded and unfruitful.
    Ah, Creon! Since they have no parent now
But you — for both of us who gave them life
Have perished — suffer them not to be cast out
Homeless and beggars; for they are your kin.   1440
Have pity on them, for they are so young,
So desolate, except for you alone.
Say 'Yes', good Creon! Let your hand confirm it.
    And now, my children, for my exhortation
You are too young; but you can pray that I
May live henceforward — where I should; and you
More happily than the father who begot you.

CREON.   Now make an end of tears, and go within.

OEDIPUS.   Then I must go — against my will.

CREON.   There is a time for everything.   1450

OEDIPUS.   You know what I would have you do?

CREON.   If you will tell me, I shall know.

OEDIPUS.   Send me away, away from Thebes.

CREON.   The God, not I, must grant you this.

OEDIPUS.   The gods hate no man more than me!

CREON.   Then what you ask they soon will give.

OEDIPUS.   You promise this?

CREON.   Ah no! When I
    Am ignorant, I do not speak.

OEDIPUS.   Then lead me in; I say no more.

CREON.   Release the children then, and come. 1460

OEDIPUS.   What? Take these children from me?
    No!

CREON.   Seek not to have your way in all things:
Where you had your way before,
Your mastery broke before the end.

(*There was no doubt a short concluding utterance
from the Chorus. What stands in the MSS. appears
to be spurious.*)

Herodotus (c. 485–425 B.C.)

GREEK HISTORIAN

What Manner of Rule?

And now when five days were gone, and the hubbub[1] had settled down, the conspirators met together to consult about the situation of affairs. At this meeting speeches were made, to which many of the Greeks give no credence, but they were made nevertheless. Otanes recommended that the management of public affairs should be entrusted to the whole nation. "To me," he said, "it seems advisable, that we should no longer have a single man to rule over us — the rule of one is neither good nor pleasant. You cannot have forgotten to what lengths Cambyses went in his haughty tyranny, and the haughtiness of the Magi you have experienced. How indeed is it possible that monarchy should be a well-adjusted thing, when it allows a man to do as he likes without being answerable? Such licence is enough to stir strange and unwonted thoughts in the heart of the worthiest of men. Give a person this power, and straightway his manifold good things puff him up with pride, while envy is so natural to human kind that it cannot but arise in him. But pride and envy together include all wickedness; both leading on to deeds of savage violence. True it is that kings, possessing as they do all that heart can desire, ought to be void of envy, but the contrary is seen in their conduct towards the citizens. They are jealous of the most virtuous among their subjects, and wish their death; while they take delight in the meanest and basest, being ever ready to listen to the tales of slanderers. A king, besides, is beyond all other men inconsistent with himself. Pay him court in moderation, and he is angry because you do not show him more profound respect—show him profound respect, and he is offended again, because (as he says) you fawn on him. But the worst of all is, that he sets aside the laws of the land, puts men to death without trial, and rapes women. The rule of the many, on the other hand, has, in the first place, the fairest of names, equality before the law; and further it is free from all those outrages which a king is wont to commit. There, places are given by lot, the magistrate is answerable for what he does, and measures rest with the commonalty. I vote, therefore, that we do away with monarchy, and raise the people to power. For the people are all in all."

Such were the sentiments of Otanes. Megabyzus spoke next, and advised the setting up of an oligarchy. "In all that Otanes has said to persuade you to put down monarchy," he observed, "I fully concur; but his recommendation

---

[1] Otanes, a Persian nobleman of 5th century B.C., has, with six other conspirators, just killed the False Smerdis who tried to succeed Cambyses to the Persian throne.

Title supplied by editors. From *Herodotus: The Persian Wars*, translated by George Rawlinson. Reprinted by permission of Random House, Inc.

that we should call the people to power seems to me not the best advice. For there is nothing so void of understanding, nothing so full of wantonness as the unwieldy rabble. It were folly not to be borne for men, while seeking to escape the wantonness of a tyrant, to give themselves up to the wantonness of a rude unbridled mob. The tyrant, in all his doings, at least knows what he is about, but a mob is altogether devoid of knowledge; for how should there be any knowledge in a rabble, untaught, and with no natural sense of what is right and fit? It rushes wildly into state affairs with all the fury of a stream swollen in the winter, and confuses everything. Let the enemies of the Persians be ruled by democracies; but let us choose out from the citizens a certain number of the worthiest, and put the government into their hands. For thus both we ourselves shall be among the governors, and power being entrusted to the best men, it is likely that the best counsels will prevail in the state."

This was the advice which Megabyzus gave, and after him Darius came forward, and spoke as follows, "All that Megabyzus said against democracy was well said, I think; but about oligarchy he did not speak advisedly; for take these three forms of government, democracy, oligarchy, and monarchy, and let them each be at their best, I maintain that monarchy far surpasses the other two. What government can possibly be better than that of the very best man in the whole state? The counsels of such a man are like himself, and so he governs the mass of the people to their heart's content; while at the same time his measures against evil-doers are kept more secret than in other states. Contrariwise, in oligarchies, where men vie with each other in the service of the commonwealth, fierce enmities are apt to arise between man and man, each wishing to be leader, and to carry his own measures; whence violent quarrels come, which lead to open strife, often ending in bloodshed. Then monarchy is sure to follow; and this too shows how far that rule surpasses all others. Again, in a democracy, it is impossible but that there will be malpractices: these malpractices, however, do not lead to enmities, but to close friendships, which are formed among those engaged in them, who must hold well together to carry on their villanies. And so things go on until a man stands forth as champion of the commonalty, and puts down the evil-doers. Straightway the author of so great a service is admired by all, and from being admired soon comes to be appointed king; so that here too it is plain that monarchy is the best government. Lastly, to sum up all in a word, whence, I ask, was it that we got the freedom which we enjoy? — did democracy give it us, or oligarchy, or a monarch? As a single man recovered our freedom for us, my sentence is that we keep to the rule of one. Even apart from this, we ought not to change the laws of our forefathers when they work fairly; for to do so, is not well."

Such were the three opinions brought forward at this meeting; the four other Persians voted in favour of the last. Otanes, who wished to give his countrymen a democracy, when he found the decision against him, arose a second time, and spoke thus before the assembly, "Brother conspirators, it is plain that the king who is to be chosen will be one of ourselves, whether we make the choice by casting lots for the prize, or by letting the people decide which of us they will have to rule over them, or in any other way. Now, as I have neither a mind to rule nor to be ruled, I shall not enter the lists with you in this matter. I withdraw, however, on one condition — none of you shall claim to exercise rule over me or my seed for ever." The six agreed to these terms, and Otanes withdrew and stood aloof from the contest. And still to this day the family of Otanes continues to be the only free family in Persia; those who belong to it submit to the rule of the king only so far as they themselves choose; they are bound, however, to observe the laws of the land like the other Persians.

After this the six took counsel together, as to the fairest way of setting up a king: and first, with respect to Otanes, they resolved, that if any of their own number got the kingdom, Otanes and his seed after him should receive year by year, as a mark of special honour, a Median robe, and all such other gifts as are accounted the most honourable in Persia. And these they resolved to give him, because he was the man who first planned the outbreak, and who brought the seven together. These privileges, therefore, were assigned specially to Otanes. The following were made common to them all: It was to be free to each, whenever he pleased, to enter the palace unannounced, unless the king were sleeping with a woman; and the king was to be bound to marry into no family excepting those of the conspirators. Concerning the appointment of a king, the resolve to which they came was the following: They would ride out together next morning into the skirts of the city, and he whose steed first neighed after the sun was up should have the kingdom.

Cicero (106–43 B.C.)

ROMAN ORATOR, STATESMAN, and MAN OF LETTERS

Justice, Expedience, and Right Rule

Is there, then, any object of such value or any advantage so worth the winning that, to gain it, one should sacrifice the name of a "good man" and the lustre of his reputation? What is there that your so-called expediency can bring to you that will compensate for what it can take away, if it steals from you the name of a "good man" and causes you to lose your sense of honour and justice? For what difference does it make whether a man is actually transformed into a beast or whether, keeping the outward appearance of a man, he has the savage nature of a beast within?

Title supplied by editors. Reprinted by permission of the publishers from Cicero: *De Officiis*, translated by Walter Miller. Cambridge, Mass.: Harvard University Press.

Again, when people disregard everything that is morally right and true, if only they may secure power thereby, are they not pursuing the same course as he[1] who wished to have as a father-in-law the man by whose effrontery he might gain power for himself? He thought it advantageous to secure supreme power while the odium of it fell upon another; and he failed to see how unjust to his country this was, and how wrong morally. But the father-in-law himself used to have continually upon his lips the Greek verses from the Phoenissae, which I will reproduce as well as I can — awkwardly, it may be, but still so that the meaning can be understood:

> "If wrong may e'er be right, for a throne's sake
> Were wrong most right: — be God in all else feared!"

Our tyrant[2] deserved his death for having made an exception of the one thing that was the blackest crime of all. Why do we gather instances of petty crime — legacies criminally obtained and fraudulent buying and selling? Behold, here you have a man who was ambitious to be king of the Roman People and master of the whole world; and he achieved it! The man who maintains that such an ambition is morally right is a madman; for he justifies the destruction of law and liberty and thinks their hideous and detestable suppression glorious. But if anyone agrees that it is not morally right to be king in a state that once was free and that ought to be free now, and yet imagines that it is advantageous for him who can reach that position, with what remonstrance or rather with what appeal should I try to tear him away from so strange a delusion? For, oh ye immortal gods! can the most horrible and hideous of all murders — that of fatherland — bring advantage to anybody, even though he who has committed such a crime receives from his enslaved fellow-citizens the title of "Father of his Country"? Expediency, therefore, must be measured by the standard of moral rectitude, and in such a way, too, that these two words shall seem in sound only to be different but in real meaning to be one and the same.

What greater advantage one could have, according to the standard of popular opinion, than to be a king, I do not know; when, however, I begin to bring the question back to the standard of truth, then I find nothing more disadvantageous for one who has risen to that height by injustice. For can occasions for worry, anxiety, fear by day and by night, and a life all beset with plots and perils be of advantage to anybody?

> "Thrones have many foes and friends untrue, but few devoted friends,"

says Accius.[3] But of what sort of throne was he speaking? Why, one that was held by right, handed down from Tantalus and Pelops.[4] Aye, but how many more foes, think you, had that king who with the Roman People's army brought the Roman People themselves into subjection and compelled a state

---

1 Pompey, who married Caesar's daughter.
2 Caesar.
3 Roman tragic poet and prose writer (c. 170 B.C.–c. 86 B.C.).
4 ancestors of Agamemnon, King of Mycenae, and Menelaus, his brother.

that not only had been free but had been mistress of the world to be his slave? What stains do you think he had upon his conscience, what scars upon his heart? But whose life can be advantageous to himself, if that life is his on the condition that the man who takes it shall be held in undying gratitude and glory? But if these things which seem so very advantageous are not advantageous because they are full of shame and moral wrong, we ought to be quite convinced that nothing can be expedient that is not morally right.

And yet this very question has been decided on many occasions before and since; but in the war with Pyrrhus the decision rendered by Gaius Fabricius, in his second consulship, and by our senate was particularly striking. Without provocation King Pyrrhus had declared war upon the Roman People; the struggle was against a generous and powerful prince, and the supremacy of power was the prize; a deserter came over from him to the camp of Fabricius and promised, if Fabricius would assure him of a reward, to return to the camp of Pyrrhus as secretly as he had come, administer poison to the king, and bring about his death. Fabricius saw to it that this fellow was taken back to Pyrrhus; and his action was commended by the senate. And yet, if the mere show of expediency and the popular conception of it are all we want, this one deserter would have put an end to that wasting war and to a formidable foe of our supremacy; but it would have been a lasting shame and disgrace to us to have overcome not by valour but by crime the man with whom we had a contest for glory.

Which course, then, was more expedient for Fabricius, who was to our city what Aristides[5] was to Athens, or for our senate, who never divorced expediency from honour — to contend against the enemy with the sword or with poison? If supremacy is to be sought for the sake of glory, crime should be excluded, for there can be no glory in crime; but if it is power for its own sake that is sought, whatever the price, it cannot be expedient if it is linked with shame.

That well-known measure, therefore, introduced by Philippus, the son of Quintus, was not expedient. With the authority of the senate, Lucius Sulla had exempted from taxation certain states upon receipt of a lump sum of money from them. Philippus proposed that they should again be reduced to the condition of tributary states, without repayment on our part of the money that they had paid for their exemption. And the senate accepted his proposal. Shame upon our government! The pirates' sense of honour is higher than the senate's. "But," some one will say, "the revenues were increased, and therefore it was expedient." How long will people venture to say that a thing that is not morally right can be expedient? Furthermore, can hatred and shame be expedient for any government? For government ought to be founded upon fair fame and the loyalty of allies?

On this point I often disagreed even with my friend Cato; it seemed to me that he was too rigorous in his watchful care over the claims of the treasury

[5] Athenian statesman and soldier (c. 520–468 B.C.).

and the revenues; he refused everything that the farmers of the revenue asked for and much that the allies desired; whereas, as I insisted, it was our duty to be generous to the allies and to treat the publicans as we were accustomed individually to treat our tenants — and all the more, because harmony between the orders was essential to the welfare of the republic.[6] Curio,[7] too, was wrong, when he pleaded that the demands of the people beyond the Po were just, but never failed to add "Let expediency prevail." He ought rather to have proved that the claims were not just, because they were not expedient for the republic, than to have admitted that they were just, when, as he maintained, they were not expedient.

The sixth book of Hecaton's "Moral Duties" is full of questions like the following: "Is it consistent with a good man's duty to let his slaves go hungry when provisions are at famine prices?"

Hecaton[8] gives the arguments on both sides of the question; but still in the end it is by the standard of expediency, as he conceives it, rather than by one of human feeling, that he decides the question of duty.

Then he raises this question: supposing a man had to throw part of his cargo overboard in a storm, should he prefer to sacrifice a high-priced horse or a cheap and worthless slave? In this case regard for his property interest inclines him one way, human feeling the other.

"Suppose that a foolish man has seized hold of a plank from a sinking ship, shall a wise man wrest it away from him if he can?"

"No," says Hecaton; "for that would be unjust."

"But how about the owner of the ship? Shall he take the plank away because it belongs to him?"

"Not at all; no more than he would be willing when far out at sea to throw a passenger overboard on the ground that the ship was his. For until they reach the place for which the ship is chartered, she belongs to the passengers, not to the owner."

"Again; suppose there were two to be saved from the sinking ship — both of them wise men — and only one small plank, should both seize it to save themselves? Or should one give place to the other?"

"Why of course, one should give place to the other, but that other must be the one whose life is more valuable either for his own sake or for that of his country."

"But what if these considerations are of equal weight in both?"

6 The publicans, farmers of the revenue, were the moneyed men of the times and belonged to the equestrian order. They purchased from the senate the farming of the revenues and then sublet their contract to the collectors. Sometimes they found that they had agreed to pay too high a rate and petitioned the senate to release them from their contract or reduce their obligations, as on this occasion (B.C. 61). The opposition of Cato [the Younger] and others strained the relations between the senate, who had control of the business, and the equestrian order, driving many of the equites over to Caesar's side. Complete harmony between the senate and the knights, as Cicero says, was the only thing that could have saved Rome from the popular party and Caesar. [Miller]

7 probably Curio the Elder (d. 53 B.C.), consul and proconsul in Macedonia.

8 a Platonizing Stoic of Rhodes; Cicero gives our only account of him.

"Then there will be no contest, but one will give place to the other, as if the point were decided by lot or at a game of odd and even."

"Again, suppose a father were robbing temples or making underground passages to the treasury, should a son inform the officers of it?"

"Nay; that were a crime; rather should he defend his father, in case he were indicted."

"Well, then, are not the claims of country paramount to all other duties?"

"Aye, verily; but it is to our country's interest to have citizens who are loyal to their parents."

"But once more — if the father attempts to make himself king, or to betray his country, shall the son hold his peace?"

"Nay, verily; he will plead with his father not to do so. If that accomplishes nothing, he will take him to task; he will even threaten; and in the end, if things point to the destruction of the state, he will sacrifice his father to the safety of his country."

Again, he raises the question: "If a wise man should inadvertently accept counterfeit money for good, will he offer it as genuine in payment of a debt after he discovers his mistake?" Diogenes says "Yes"; Antipater, "No," and I agree with him.

[If a] man knowingly offers for sale wine that is spoiling, ought he tell his customers? Diogenes thinks that it is not required; Antipater holds that an honest man would do so. These are like so many points of the law disputed among the Stoics. "In selling a slave, should his faults be declared — not those only which the seller is bound by the civil law to declare or have the slave returned to him, but also the fact that he is untruthful, or disposed to gamble, or steal, or get drunk?" The one thinks such facts should be declared, the other does not.

"If a man thinks that he is selling brass, when he is actually selling gold, should an upright man inform him that his stuff is gold, or go on buying for [about one denarius] what is worth a thousand?"

It is clear enough by this time what my views are on these questions, and what are the grounds of dispute between the above-named philosophers.

The question arises also whether agreements and promises must always be kept, "when," in the language of the praetors' edicts, "they have not been secured through force or criminal fraud."

If one man gives another a remedy for the dropsy, with the stipulation that, if he is cured by it, he shall never make use of it again; suppose the patient's health is restored by the use of it but some years later he contracts the same disease once more; and suppose he cannot secure from the man with whom he made the agreement permission to use the remedy again, what should he do? That is the question. Since the man is unfeeling in refusing the request, and since no harm could be done to him by his friend's using the remedy, the sick man is justified in doing what he can for his own life and health.

Again: suppose that a millionaire is making some wise man his heir and leaving him in his will a hundred million sesterces; and suppose that he has asked the wise man, before he enters upon his inheritance, to dance publicly in broad daylight in the forum; and suppose that the wise man has given his promise to do so, because the rich man would not leave him his fortune on any other condition; should he keep his promise or not? I wish he had made no such promise; that, I think, would have been in keeping with his dignity. But seeing that he has made it, it will be mortally better for him, if he believes it morally wrong to dance in the forum, to break his promise and refuse to accept his inheritance rather than to keep his promise and accept it — unless, perhaps, he contributes the money to the state to meet some grave crisis. In that case, to promote thereby the interests of one's country, it would not be morally wrong even to dance, if you please, in the forum.

No more binding are those promises which are inexpedient for the persons themselves to whom they have been given. To go back to the realm of story, the sungod promised his son Phaëthon to do for him whatever he should wish. His wish was to be allowed to ride in his father's chariot. It was granted. And before he came back to the ground he was consumed by a stroke of lightning. How much better had it been, if in his case the father's promise had not been kept. And what of that promise, the fulfilment of which Theseus required from Neptune? When Neptune offered him three wishes, he wished for the death of his son Hippolytus, because the father was suspicious of the son's relations with his step-mother. And when this wish was granted, Theseus was overwhelmed with grief. And once more; when Agamemnon had vowed to Diana the most beautiful creature born that year within his realm, he was brought to sacrifice Iphigenia;[9] for in that year nothing was born more beautiful than she. He ought to have broken his vow rather than commit so horrible a crime.

Promises are, therefore, sometimes not to be kept; and trusts are not always to be restored. Suppose that a person leaves his sword with you when he is in his right mind, and demands it back in a fit of insanity; it would be criminal to restore it to him; it would be your duty not to do so. Again, suppose that a man who has entrusted money to you proposes to make war upon your common country, should you restore the trust? I believe you should not; for you would be acting against the state, which ought to be the dearest thing in the world to you. Thus there are many things which in and of themselves seem morally right, but which under certain circumstances prove to be not morally right: to keep a promise, to abide by an agreement, to restore a trust may, with a change of expediency, cease to be morally right.

With this I think I have said enough about those actions which masquerade as expedient under the guise of prudence, while they are really contrary to justice.

[9] Agamemnon's own daughter.

Paul (1ST CENTURY A.D.)

ROMAN MISSIONARY

Bless Them Which Persecute You

12 I beseech you therefore, brethren, by the mercies of God, that ye present your bodies a living sacrifice, holy, acceptable unto God, *which is* your reasonable service.

2 And be not conformed to this world, but be ye transformed by the renewing of your mind, that ye may prove what *is* that good, and acceptable, and perfect, will of God.

3 For I say, through the grace given unto me, to every man that is among you, not to think *of himself* more highly than he ought to think; but to think soberly, according as God hath dealt to every man the measure of faith.

4 For as we have many members in one body, and all members have not the same office:

5 So we, *being* many, are one body in Christ, and every one members one of another. . . .

14 Bless them which persecute you: bless, and curse not.

15 Rejoice with them that do rejoice, and weep with them that weep.

16 *Be* of the same mind one toward another. Mind not high things, but condescend to men of low estate. Be not wise in your own conceits.

17 Recompense to no man evil for evil. Provide things honest in the sight of all men.

18 If it be possible, as much as lieth in you, live peaceably with all men.

19 Dearly beloved, avenge not yourselves, but *rather* give place unto wrath: for it is written, Vengeance *is* mine; I will repay, saith the Lord.

20 Therefore if thine enemy hunger, feed him; if he thirst, give him drink: for in so doing thou shalt heap coals of fire on his head.

21 Be not overcome of evil, but overcome evil with good.

Title supplied by editors. "Bless Them Which Persecute You" by Paul. From the King James Version of The Bible, *Romans* 12.

Plutarch (c. A.D. 46–c. 120)

GREEK HISTORIAN, BIOGRAPHER, and PHILOSOPHER

The Basis of Good Rule

Of all Aristides'[1] virtues it was his justice which most impressed itself on the masses, since it was this which he practised most consistently and which affected most people. For this reason, although he was poor and had no standing but that of a popular leader, he won that most royal and godlike title of The Just. That is an epithet which was never sought after by kings or tyrants: some of them delighted in being styled The Besieger of Cities, The Thunderbolt, or The Conqueror, and others The Eagle or The Hawk, but all of them, apparently, preferred a renown which was founded on power or violence rather than on virtue. And yet the divine nature, with which these men strive to be associated and to resemble, is believed to be distinguished by three superior attributes, immortality, power, and virtue, and of these the noblest and the most truly divine is virtue. The void and the elements are, in a sense, immortal, and earthquakes, thunderbolts, floods, and hurricanes can overwhelm by their power, but justice belongs only to those beings who are capable of reason and the knowledge of the divine.

So when we consider the three sentiments, admiration, fear, and reverence, which divinity inspires among mankind, we find that men appear to admire the gods and think them blessed because they are immortal and unchangeable; to stand in fear and awe of them because of their power and authority; and to love, honour, and reverence them because of their justice. At the same time men long for immortality, to which no flesh can attain, and for power, which remains for the most part in the hands of fortune, while they give virtue, the only divine excellence of which we are capable, the last place in their scheme of values. But here they show themselves fools, since a life that is spent in the midst of power and great fortune and authority still needs justice to make it divine, for injustice renders it merely brutish.

---

[1] Athenian statesman and soldier (c. 520–468 B.C.) renowned for his honesty.

Title supplied by editors. "The Basis of Good Rule" by Plutarch. From "The Life of Aristides" in *Parallel Lives* by Plutarch. Reprinted from *The Rise and Fall of Athens: Nine Greek Lives by Plutarch*, translated by Ian Scott-Kilvert and published by Penguin Books Ltd. Reprinted by permission.

Epictetus (c. 50–c. 135)

GREEK PHILOSOPHER

The Power of Man

There are things which are within our power, and there are things which are beyond our power. Within our power are opinion, aim, desire, aversion, and, in one word, whatever affairs are our own. Beyond our power are body, property, reputation, office, and, in one word, whatever are not properly our own affairs.

Now the things within our power are by nature free, unrestricted, unhindered; but those beyond our power are weak, dependent, restricted, alien. Remember, then, that if you attribute freedom to things by nature dependent and take what belongs to others for your own, you will be hindered, you will lament, you will be disturbed, you will find fault both with gods and men. But if you take for your own only that which is your own and view what belongs to others just as it really is, then no one will ever compel you, no one will restrict you; you will find fault with no one, you will accuse no one, you will do nothing against your will; no one will hurt you, you will not have an enemy, nor will you suffer any harm.

Aiming, therefore, at such great things, remember that you must not allow yourself any inclination, however slight, toward the attainment of the others; but that you must entirely quit some of them, and for the present postpone the rest. But if you would have these, and possess power and wealth likewise, you may miss the latter in seeking the former; and you will certainly fail of that by which alone happiness and freedom are procured.

Seek at once, therefore, to be able to say to every unpleasing semblance, "You are but a semblance and by no means the real thing." And then examine it by those rules which you have; and first and chiefly by this: whether it concerns the things which are within our own power or those which are not; and if it concerns anything beyond our power, be prepared to say that it is nothing to you. . . .

Marcus Aurelius (121–180)

ROMAN EMPEROR and PHILOSOPHER

Whatever Happens Is Just

Consider that everything which happens, happens justly, and if thou observest carefully, thou wilt find it to be so. I do not say only with respect to the continuity of the series of things, but with respect to what is just, and as if it were done by one who assigns to each thing its value. Observe then as thou hast begun; and whatever thou doest, do it in conjunction with this, the being good, and in the sense in which a man is properly understood to be good. Keep to this in every action.

Do not have such an opinion of things as he has who does thee wrong, or such as he wishes thee to have, but look at them as they are in truth.

A man should always have these two rules in readiness; the one, to do only whatever the reason of the ruling and legislating faculty may suggest for the use of men; the other, to change thy opinion, if there is any one at hand who sets thee right and moves thee from any opinion. But this change of opinion must proceed only from a certain persuasion, as of what is just or of common advantage, and the like, not because it appears pleasant or brings reputation.

Augustine (353–430)

EARLY CHRISTIAN CHURCH FATHER and PHILOSOPHER

The Source of Law and Justice

For though the soul may seem to rule the body admirably, and the reason the vices, if the soul and reason do not themselves obey God, as God has commanded them to serve Him, they have no proper authority over the body and the vices. For what kind of mistress of the body and the vices can that

Title supplied by editors. "Whatever Happens Is Just" from *Meditations* by Marcus Aurelius. From *The Stoic and Epicurean Philosophers*, edited by Whitney J. Oates. Copyright 1940 by Random House, Inc. Reprinted by permission.

Title supplied by editors. "The Source of Law and Justice" from *City of God* by St. Augustine, in *Fathers of the Church* series, Vol. 24. Reprinted by permission of The Catholic University of America Press.

mind be which is ignorant of the true God, and which, instead of being subject to His authority, is prostituted to the corrupting influences of the most vicious demons? It is for this reason that the virtues which it seems to itself to possess, and by which it restrains the body and the vices that it may obtain and keep what it desires, are rather vices than virtues so long as there is no reference to God in the matter. For although some suppose that virtues which have a reference only to themselves and are desired only on their own account, are yet true and genuine virtues, the fact is that even then they are inflated with pride and are therefore to be reckoned vices rather than virtues. For as that which gives life to the flesh is not derived from flesh, but is above it, so that which gives blessed life to man is not derived from man, but is something above him; and what I say of man is true of every celestial power and virtue whatsoever.

Thomas Aquinas (1226–1274)

ITALIAN SCHOLASTIC THEOLOGIAN

Whether Human Law Binds a Man in Conscience

Objection 1. It would seem that human law does not bind a man in conscience. For an inferior power has no jurisdiction in a court of higher power. But the power of man, which frames human law, is beneath the Divine power. Therefore human law cannot impose its precept in a Divine court, such as is the court of conscience.

Obj. 2. Further, the judgment of conscience depends chiefly on the commandments of God. But sometimes God's commandments are made void by human laws, according to Matth. xv. 6: *You have made void the commandment of God for your tradition.* Therefore human law does not bind a man in conscience.

Obj. 3. Further, human laws often bring loss of character and injury on man, according to Isa. x. 1 *et seq.*: *Woe to them that make wicked laws, and when they write, write injustice; to oppress the poor in judgment, and do violence to the cause of the humble of My people.* But it is lawful for anyone to avoid oppression and violence. Therefore human laws do not bind man in conscience.

On the contrary, It is written (1 Pet. ii. 19): *This is thanksworthy, if for conscience . . . a man endure sorrows, suffering wrongfully.*

Title supplied by editors. "Whether Human Law Binds a Man in Conscience" from the *Summa Theologica* of St. Thomas Aquinas. Reprinted by permission of Benziger Brothers, Inc., and Burns & Oates Ltd., London.

I answer that, Laws framed by man are either just or unjust. If they be just, they have the power of binding in conscience, from the eternal law whence they are derived, according to Prov. viii. 15: *By Me kings reign, and lawgivers decree just things.* Now laws are said to be just, both from the end, when, to wit, they are ordained to the common good, — and from their author, that is to say, when the law that is made does not exceed the power of the lawgiver, — and from their form, when, to wit, burdens are laid on the subjects, according to an equality of proportion and with a view to the common good. For, since one man is a part of the community, each man, in all that he is and has, belongs to the community; just as a part, in all that it is, belongs to the whole; wherefore nature inflicts a loss on the part, in order to save the whole: so that on this account, such laws as these, which impose proportionate burdens, are just and binding in conscience, and are legal laws.

On the other hand laws may be unjust in two ways; first, by being contrary to human good, through being opposed to the things mentioned above: — either in respect of the end, as when an authority imposes on his subjects burdensome laws, conducive, not to the common good, but rather to his own cupidity or vainglory; — or in respect of the author, as when a man makes a law that goes beyond the power committed to him; — or in respect of the form, as when burdens are imposed unequally on the community, although with a view to the common good. The like are acts of violence rather than laws; because, as Augustine says (*De Lib. Arb.* i. 5), *a law that is not just, seems to be no law at all.* Wherefore such laws do not bind in conscience, except perhaps in order to avoid scandal or disturbance, for which cause a man should even yield his right, according to Matth. v. 40, 41: *If a man . . . take away thy coat, let go thy cloak also unto him; and whosoever will force thee one mile, go with him other two.*

Secondly, laws may be unjust through being opposed to the Divine good: such are the laws of tyrants inducing to idolatry, or to anything else contrary to the Divine law: and laws of this kind must nowise be observed, because, as stated in Acts v. 29, *we ought to obey God rather than men.*

Reply Obj. 1.   As the Apostle says (Rom. xiii. 1, 2), all human power is from God . . . *therefore he that resisteth the power,* in matters that are within its scope, *resisteth the ordinance of God;* so that he becomes guilty according to his conscience.

Reply Obj. 2.   This argument is true of laws that are contrary to the commandments of God, which is beyond the scope of (human) power. Wherefore in such matters human law should not be obeyed.

Reply Obj. 3.   This argument is true of a law that inflicts unjust hurt on its subjects. The power that man holds from God does not extend to this: wherefore neither in such matters is man bound to obey the law, provided he avoid giving scandal or inflicting a more grievous hurt.

Anonymous (c. 14TH CENTURY)

SCOTTISH

Edward

"Why dois your brand sae drap wi bluid,
               Edward, Edward,   brand: sword   sae: so
Why dois your brand sae drap wi bluid,   drap: drip
  And why sae sad gang yee O?"   gang: go
"O I hae killed my hauke sae guid,   guid: good
               Mither, mither,
O I hae killed my hauke sae guid,
  And I had nae mair bot hee O."   bot: but

"Your haukis bluid was nevir sae reid,
               Edward, Edward,   10
Your haukis bluid was nevir sae reid,
  My deir son I tell thee O."
"O I hae killed my reid-roan steid,
               Mither, mither,
O I hae killed my reid-roan steid,
  That erst was sae fair and frie O."   frie: lively

Your steid was auld, and ye hae gat mair,
               Edward, Edward,
Your steid was auld, and ye hae gat mair,
  Sum other dule ye drie O."   20   dule: grief   drie: suffer
"O I hae killed my fadir deir,
               Mither, mither,
O I hae killed my fadir deir,
  Alas, and wae is mee O!"   wae: woe

"And whatten penance wul ye drie for that,
               Edward, Edward?
And whatten penance will ye drie for that?
  My deir son, now tell me O."
"Ile set my feit in yonder boat,
               Mither, mither,   30
Ile set my feit in yonder boat,
  And Ile fare ovir the sea O."

From *Traditional British Ballads*, edited by Bartlett Jere
Whiting.

"And what wul ye doe wi your towirs and your ha,
            Edward, Edward?   **ha: hall**
And what wul ye doe wi your towirs and your ha,
  That were sae fair to see O?"
"Ile let thame stand tul they doun fa,   **fa: fall**
            Mither, mither,
Ile let thame stand tul they doun fa,
  For here nevir mair maun I bee O."   40   **maun: must**

"And what wul ye leive to your bairns and your wife,
            Edward, Edward?
And what wul ye leive to your bairns and your wife,
  Whan ye gang ovir the sea O?"
"The warldis room, late them beg thrae life,   **warldis: world's   late: let**
            Mither, mither,   **thrae: through**
The warldis room, late them beg thrae life,
  For thame nevir mair wul I see O."

"And what wul ye leive to your ain mither deir,
            Edward, Edward?   50
And what wul ye leive to your ain mither deir?
  My deir son, now tell me O."
"The curse of hell frae me sall ye beir,   **frae: from**
            Mither, mither,
The curse of hell frae me sall ye beir,
  Sic counseils ye gave to me O."   **Sic: such**

Giovanni Boccaccio (1313–1375)

ITALIAN STORYTELLER and POET

The Clever Monk

Dioneo, without waiting for the queen's command, began as follows:

If I have understood your intention rightly, amorous ladies, we are here to amuse ourselves by telling stories.[1] So long as we achieve that, I think each of

[1] Dioneo and his friends have been driven from Florence to neighboring villas during a plague epidemic.

Title supplied by editors. "The First Day: Fourth Tale" from *The Decameron of Giovanni Boccaccio*, translated by Richard Aldington. Reprinted by permission of Rosica Colin Ltd., London.

us should be allowed to tell the story he thinks most likely to be amusing; and just now the queen said that we could do this. . . . So, without any fear of censure from you, I am going to tell you briefly how a monk's prudence saved his hide from serious punishment.

In Lunigiana, a district not far from here, there was a monastery which in the past abounded more in monks and sanctity than it does today. Among them was a young monk, whose virility and youth were unsubdued by fasts and vigils. One day he chanced to go out about noon when the other monks were asleep. He was walking round the church by himself — it was in a rather isolated spot — when he saw a very pretty girl, probably the daughter of one of the peasants, who was picking flowers in the meadows. As soon as he saw her, he was violently attacked by carnal desire.

He went up and began talking to her; he got on so well that they came to an understanding, and he took her up to his cell without anyone seeing them. Carried away by overmuch good will, he was enjoying her too vigorously when the Abbot arose from sleep and, as he passed softly by the cell, heard the noise they were making together. To make certain of the voices, the Abbot stopped outside the cell to listen, and realised that a woman was there. At first, he was tempted to make them open the door; then he changed his mind and decided to act differently. So he went back to his own cell to wait until the monk came out.

Now, although the monk was extremely preoccupied with his pleasure, and delight in the girl, he thought he heard a shuffling of feet in the dormitory. He looked through a crack and plainly saw the Abbot there listening, which meant that the Abbot knew he had a girl in his cell. This troubled him greatly, for he knew quite well he would be severely punished. However, he did not let the girl see his anxiety but at once tried to think how he could escape. He hit upon a new scheme, which exactly achieved the end he wanted.

He pretended that he thought he had been long enough with the girl, and said:

"I must go and find some means for you to get away without being seen, so stay here quietly till I get back."

He went out, locking the cell behind him, and went straight to the Abbot's room, as every monk does when he wants to go out. He presented himself to the Abbot, and, putting a good face on things, said:

"Messer, this morning I couldn't get in all the logs needed, so with your permission I am going to the wood to fetch them."

The Abbot thought the monk did not know he had been seen and, glad of the opportunity to enquire more closely into the monk's offence, gave him the key and permission to go out. When the monk had gone, the Abbot began to wonder what he should do next. Should he open the cell in the presence of all the monks for them to see the crime and thereby prevent them from grumbling about him when he punished the monk? Or should he first go and ask the girl how it had happened? It then occurred to him that she might be the wife or daughter of some respectable man, whom he would prefer not to hold up to shame before all the monks; so he thought he would see her first, and then decide what to do. He went stealthily to the cell, opened it, went in, and shut the door.

The girl was frightened when she saw the Abbot, felt she would be shamed, and began to cry. Messer Abbot cast his eye upon her, and saw that she was fresh and pretty. Although he was an old man, he suddenly felt the warm stings of the flesh, just as the young monk had, and said to himself:

"Ah now, why shouldn't I take a little pleasure when I can get it? I have enough worry and trouble every day, without adding this. She's a pretty girl, and no one knows she's here. If I can persuade her to pleasure me, I don't know why I shouldn't do so. Who's to know? Nobody will ever know it — and sin hidden is half forgiven. This chance may never happen again. I think him a wise man who can pick his own pleasure from what God sends to others."

Having entirely changed his mind in this way, he went nearer to the girl, gently comforted her and begged her not to cry. So, going from one thing to another, he finally expressed his desires.

The girl was not made of iron or adamant, and willingly yielded to the Abbot's pleasure. When he had fondled and kissed her, he lay down on the monk's bed. It may be that he thought of the weight of his own dignity, and the girl's tender age, and was afraid to lay too much weight on her; in any case, he did not lie on her breast but made her lie on his, and for a long time enjoyed himself with her.

Meanwhile the monk, after pretending to go to the wood, had hidden himself in the dormitory, and saw the Abbot enter the cell alone. Completely reassured, he felt that his little plan would succeed; and when he heard the Abbot lock the door, he was quite sure of it. He left his hiding-place, and through a crack heard and saw all the Abbot said and did.

When the Abbot thought he had had enough of the girl, he locked her in the cell and went back to his own room. A little later he saw the monk and thought he had come back from the wood. The Abbot's plan was to reprimand him severely, and imprison him, to enjoy the well-earned prize all to himself. Therefore he called the monk up, frowned on him, severely reprimanded him, and ordered him to be imprisoned. But the monk promptly replied:

"Messer, I have not been long enough in the Order of Saint Benedict to know every particular connected with it; you did not tell me that monks should humble themselves beneath women, as with fasts and vigils. But now you have showed me, I promise you, if I am forgiven this time, that I will not go wrong again here, but will always do exactly as I saw you do."

The Abbot was a sharp fellow and saw at once that the monk was smarter than he was, and moreover had seen what he did. Remorseful at his own slip, he was ashamed to give the monk a punishment he deserved himself. So he pardoned him and told him to say nothing about what he had seen. He had the girl secretly sent out of the monastery, and it may be well supposed that he often had her brought back.

Niccolo Machiavelli (1469–1527)

ITALIAN STATESMAN and WRITER

Advice for the Successful Prince

... A prince should want to have a reputation for compassion rather than for cruelty: nonetheless, he should be careful that he does not make bad use of compassion. Cesare Borgia was accounted cruel; nevertheless, this cruelty of his reformed the Romagna, brought it unity, and restored order and obedience. On reflection, it will be seen that there was more compassion in Cesare than in the Florentine people, who, to escape being called cruel, allowed Pistoia to be devastated.[1] So a prince should not worry if he incurs reproach for his cruelty so long as he keeps his subjects united and loyal. By making an example or two he will prove more compassionate than those who, being too compassionate, allow disorders which lead to murder and rapine. These nearly always harm the whole community, whereas executions ordered by a prince only affect individuals. A new prince, of all rulers, finds it impossible to avoid a reputation for cruelty, because of the abundant dangers inherent in a newly won state. Vergil, through the mouth of Dido, says:

> Res dura, et regni novitas me talia cogunt
> Moliri, et late fines custode tueri.[2]

Nonetheless, a prince should be slow to take action, and should watch that he does not come to be afraid of his own shadow; his behaviour should be tempered by humanity and prudence so that over-confidence does not make him rash or excessive distrust make him unbearable.

[1] Pistoia was a subject-city of Florence, which forcibly restored order there when conflict broke out between two rival factions in 1501–2. Machiavelli was concerned with this business at first hand. [Bull]

[2] 'Harsh necessity, and the newness of my kingdom, force me to do such things and to guard my frontiers everywhere.' *Aeneid*, i, 563. [Bull]

Title supplied by editors. From *The Prince* by Niccolo Machiavelli, translated by George Bull and published by Penguin Books Ltd. Reprinted by permission.

From this arises the following question: whether it is better to be loved than feared, or the reverse. The answer is that one would like to be both the one and the other; but because it is difficult to combine them, it is far better to be feared than loved if you cannot be both. One can make this generalization about men: they are ungrateful, fickle, liars, and deceivers, they shun danger and are greedy for profit; while you treat them well, they are yours. They would shed their blood for you, risk their property, their lives, their children, so long, as I said above, as danger is remote; but when you are in danger they turn against you. Any prince who has come to depend entirely on promises and has taken no other precautions ensures his own ruin; friendship which is bought with money and not with greatness and nobility of mind is paid for, but it does not last and it yields nothing. Men worry less about doing an injury to one who makes himself loved than to one who makes himself feared. The bond of love is one which men, wretched creatures that they are, break when it is to their advantage to do so; but fear is strengthened by a dread of punishment which is always effective.

The prince should nonethless make himself feared in such a way that, if he is not loved, at least he escapes being hated. For fear is quite compatible with an absence of hatred; and the prince can always avoid hatred if he abstains from the property of his subjects and citizens and from their women. If, even so, it proves necessary to execute someone, this should be done only when there is proper justification and manifest reason for it. But above all a prince should abstain from the property of others; because men sooner forget the death of their father than the loss of their patrimony. It is always possible to find pretexts for confiscating someone's property; and a prince who starts to live by rapine always finds pretexts for seizing what belongs to others. On the other hand, pretexts for executing someone are harder to find and they are less easily sustained.

However, when a prince is campaigning with his soldiers and is in command of a large army then he need not worry about having a reputation for cruelty; because, without such a reputation, he can never keep his army united and disciplined. Among the admirable achievements of Hannibal[3] is included this: that although he led a huge army, made up of countless different races, on foreign campaigns, there was never any dissension, either among the troops themselves or against their leader, whether things were going well or badly. For this, his inhuman cruelty was wholly responsible. It was this, along with his countless other qualities, which made him feared and respected by his soldiers. If it had not been for his cruelty, his other qualities would not have been enough. The historians, having given little thought to this, on the one hand admire what Hannibal achieved, and on the other condemn what made his achievements possible.

That his other qualities would not have been enough by themselves can

[3] the great Carthaginian general (247–182 B.C.) who invaded Italy by crossing the Alps. He was considered one of the world's greatest soldiers and leaders.

be proved by looking at Scipio,[4] a man unique in his own time and through all recorded history. His armies mutinied against him in Spain, and the only reason for this was his excessive leniency, which allowed his soldiers more licence than was good for military discipline. Fabius Maximus reproached him for this in the Senate and called him a corrupter of the Roman legions. Again, when the Locri were plundered by one of Scipio's officers, he neither gave them satisfaction nor punished his officer's insubordination; and this was all because of his having too lenient a nature. By way of excuse for him some senators argued that many men were better at not making mistakes themselves than at correcting them in others. But in time Scipio's lenient nature would have spoilt his fame and glory had he continued to indulge it during his command; when he lived under orders from the Senate, however, this fatal characteristic of his was not only concealed but even brought him glory.

So, on this question of being loved or feared, I conclude that since some men love as they please but fear when the prince pleases, a wise prince should rely on what he controls, not on what he cannot control. He should only endeavour, as I said, to escape being hated. . . .

You should understand, therefore, that there are two ways of fighting: by law or by force. . . .

[As] a prince is forced to know how to act like a beast, he should learn from the fox and the lion; because the lion is defenceless against traps and a fox is defenceless against wolves. Therefore one must be a fox in order to recognize traps, and a lion to frighten off wolves. Those who simply act lions are stupid. So it follows that a prudent ruler cannot, and should not, honour his word when it places him at a disadvantage and when the reasons for which he made his promise no longer exist. If all men were good, this precept would not be good; but because men are wretched creatures who would not keep their word to you, you need not keep your word to them. And a prince will never lack good excuses to colour his bad faith. . . .

There is one fresh example I do not want to omit. Alexander VI[5] was always, and he thought only of, deceiving people; and he always found victims for his deceptions. There never was a man capable of such convincing asseverations, or so ready to swear to the truth of something, who would honour his word less. Nonetheless his deceptions always had the result he intended, because he was a past master in the art.

A prince, therefore, need not necessarily have all the good qualities . . . but he should certainly appear to have them. He should appear to be compassionate, faithful to his word, guileless, and devout. And indeed he should be so. But his disposition should be such that, if he needs to be the opposite, he knows how. You must realize this: that a prince, and especially a new prince, cannot observe all those things which give men a reputation for virtue, because in order to maintain his state he is often forced to act in defiance of good faith, of charity, of kindness, of religion. And so he should have a flexible

[4] Scipio Africanus, the Roman general (236–184 B.C.) who defeated Hannibal.
[5] Pope (1492–1503); a Borgia and a prince whom Machiavelli particularly wished to please.

disposition, varying as fortune and circumstances dictate. As I said above, he should not deviate from what is good, if that is possible, but he should know how to do evil, if that is necessary. . . .

. . . Men in general judge by their eyes rather than by their hands; because everyone is in a position to watch, few are in a position to come in close touch with you. Everyone sees what you appear to be, few experience what you really are. And those few dare not gainsay the many who are backed by the majesty of the state. In the actions of all men, and especially of princes, where there is no court of appeal, one judges by the result. So let a prince set about the task of conquering and maintaining his state; his methods will always be judged honourable and will be universally praised. The common people are always impressed by appearances and results. In this context, there are only common people, and there is no room for the few when the many are supported by the state. A certain contemporary ruler, whom it is better not to name, never preaches anything except peace and good faith; and he is an enemy of both one and the other, and if he had ever honoured either of them he would have lost either his standing or his state many times over.

Miguel de Cervantes (1547–1616)

SPANISH STORYTELLER and POET

Governor Sancho Panza

The Duke and Duchess . . . decided to carry on with their jests, seeing how apt a subject they had to take them in earnest. So having outlined the plot and given their servants and tenants instructions how they were to act towards Sancho in the matter of the governorship of the promised isle,[1] the day after Clavileño's[2] flight the Duke told Sancho to prepare and put himself in readiness to go and be governor, for his islesmen were longing for him as for water in May. Sancho made his bow and said:

'Ever since my journey through the sky, when from its lofty height I gazed on the earth and saw it so small, my very great desire to be a governor has partly cooled. For what greatness is there in governing on a mustard seed? What dignity or power in commanding half a dozen men the size of hazel

[1] As a reward for loyalty and service to Don Quixote, the Duke has made Sancho governor of an island.

[2] the wooden horse on which the blindfolded Don and Sancho thought they flew, because the Duke and Duchess tricked them.

Title supplied by editors. From *Don Quixote* by Miguel de Cervantes, translated by J. M. Cohen and published by Penguin Books Ltd. Reprinted by permission.

nuts — for as far as I could see there were no more on the whole earth? If your Lordship would be so kind as to give me ever so small a bit of the sky, even a mile would do, and I would rather have it than the best isle in the world.'

'See here, friend Sancho,' answered the Duke. 'I cannot give anyone a portion of the sky, not even so much as a finger-nail of it, for such favours and rewards are in God's hands alone. What I can give you I will, and that is an isle, right and straight, round and well proportioned, exceedingly fertile and fruitful; and there, if you know how to manage things, from the riches of earth you can gain the riches of heaven.'

'Well now,' replied Sancho, 'let the isle come. For I'll try to be such a governor that I'll get to Heaven, despite all rogues. And it's not out of greed that I want to leave my poor huts and rise to greater things, but from my desire to find out what it tastes like to be a governor.'

'If once you try it, Sancho,' said the Duke, 'you will take to governing like a duck to water, for it is the sweetest thing to give orders and be obeyed. I am pretty sure that when your master comes to be an Emperor — which no doubt he will, by the way his affairs are going — they will not tear his office away from him at their pleasure, and he will be vexed and grieved from the bottom of his heart for the time lost before he became one.'

'Sir,' replied Sancho, 'it's a good thing to command, I imagine, even if it's only a herd of cattle.'

'Let me be buried alongside you, Sancho,' said the Duke; 'you know everything, and I expect you will be just such a governor as your wisdom promises. But here let it rest. Remember that tomorrow, for certain, you are to go to the governorship of the isle, and this evening you shall be fitted with suitable dress and everything necessary for your departure.'

'Let them dress me as they will,' said Sancho, 'for whatever way I go dressed I shall be Sancho Panza.'

'That is true,' said the Duke, 'but clothes have to suit the office or dignity occupied. It would not be right for a lawyer to be dressed like a soldier, nor a soldier like a priest. You will go, Sancho, dressed as part lawyer, part captain, because in the isle I am giving you arms are as necessary as learning and learning as arms.'

'Learning,' answered Sancho, 'I've little of that, for I don't even know my A.B.C., though I have the big Christ-cross in my memory, and that's enough to make me a good governor.'

'With a memory like his,' said the Duke, 'Sancho cannot go wrong.'

At this moment Don Quixote came up, and when he learned what was happening and how soon Sancho was to leave for his governorship, by the Duke's permission he took his squire by the hand and led him to his apartment to give him advice as to his behaviour in office. Then, having entered, he shut the door after him and, almost forcing Sancho to sit down beside him, addressed him with great deliberation:

'I give infinite thanks to Heaven, Sancho my friend, that first and foremost, before I strike any good luck myself, prosperity has come out to meet and receive you. I who had staked the payment for your services on my own success find myself at the beginning of my advancement; while you find yourself rewarded with your heart's desire before your time and contrary to all reasonable expectations. Some bribe, importune, solicit, rise early, entreat, pester, and yet fail to achieve their aims; then there comes another, and without knowing how or why he finds himself with the place and office which many others have sought for. Here the proverb comes in pat, that there is good and bad luck in petitionings. You are, in my opinion, most certainly a dullard. Yet without rising early or working late or putting yourself to great pains, with only the breath of knight errantry which has touched you, you find yourself without more ado governor of an isle, as if that were nothing. I say all this, Sancho, so that you shall not attribute this favour to your own merits, but shall give thanks to God, who disposes things so kindly, and afterwards to the greatness implicit in the profession of knight errantry.

'With your heart disposed to believe my words, be attentive, my son, to this your Cato,[3] who will advise you and be the pole-star and guide to direct you and bring you to a safe port, out of this stormy sea in which you are likely to drown. For offices and great places are nothing but a deep gulf of confusion.

'Firstly, my son, you must fear God; for in fearing Him is wisdom and, being wise, you can make no mistake.

'Secondly, you must consider what you are, seeking to know yourself, which is the most difficult task conceivable. From self-knowledge you will learn not to puff yourself up, like the frog who wanted to be as big as an ox. If you achieve this, the memory that you kept hogs in your own country will come to be like the peacock's ugly feet to the tail of your folly.'

'True enough,' answered Sancho, 'but that was when I was a boy. Afterwards, when I was more of a man, it was geese I kept, not hogs. But this doesn't seem to me to the point, for not all governors come from royal stock.'

'True,' replied Don Quixote, 'and therefore those who are not of noble origin must accompany the gravity of the office they exercise with a mild suavity which, guided by prudence, may save them from malicious slanderers, from whom no station is free.

'Rejoice, Sancho, in the humbleness of your lineage, and do not think it a disgrace to say you come of peasants; for, seeing that you are not ashamed, no one will attempt to shame you. Consider it more meritorious to be virtuous and poor than noble and a sinner. Innumerable men there are, born of low stock, who have mounted to the highest dignities, pontifical and imperial; and of this truth I could weary you with examples.

'Remember, Sancho, that if you take virtue for your means, and pride your-

[3] Cato 'Censorius' (234–149 B.C.), whose advice to Valerius Flaccus helped to settle the Roman administration in Spain and who aimed at establishing social solidarity at home and security abroad. His writings also greatly influenced Cicero.

self on performing virtuous deeds, you will have no reason to envy those who were born princes and lords. For blood is inherited but virtue acquired, and virtue has an intrinsic worth, which blood has not.

'This being so, if any of your relations should chance to come and visit you when you are in your isle, do not reject them or insult them. On the contrary, you must receive them, make much of them and entertain them. In that way you will please God, who would have no one disdain His creation; and what is more, you will be complying with your duty to the order of nature.

'If you should take your wife with you — for it is not right that those engaged in government should be for long without wives of their own — instruct her, indoctrinate her and pare her of her native rudeness; for often everything a wise governor gains is lost and wasted by an ill-mannered and foolish wife.

'If you should chance to be widowed — a thing which may happen — and wish to make a better match to suit your office, do not choose a wife to serve you as a bait and a fishing-rod and take bribes in her hood; for I tell you truly that whatever a judge's wife receives her husband will have to account for at the Last Judgment, where he will have to pay fourfold in death for the statutes of which he has taken no account in his lifetime.

'Never be guided by arbitrary law, which has generally great influence with the ignorant who set up to be clever.

'Let the poor man's tears find more compassion in you, but not more justice, than the pleadings of the rich.

'Try to discover the truth behind the rich man's promises and gifts, as well as behind the poor man's sobbings and importunities.

'Where equity may justly temper the rigour of the law do not pile the whole force of it on to the delinquent; for the rigorous judge has no higher reputation than the merciful.

'If you should chance to bend the rod of justice, do not let it be with the weight of a bribe, but with that of pity.

'When you happen to judge the case of some enemy of yours, turn your mind away from your injury and apply it to the truth of the case.

'Do not let personal passion blind you in another's case, for most of the errors you make will be irremediable, and if you should find a remedy it will cost you your reputation, or even your fortune.

'If a beautiful woman comes to beg you for justice, turn your eyes from her tears and your ears from her groans, and consider the substance of her plea at leisure, if you do not want your reason to be drowned in her sobs and your honour in her sighs.

'Do not revile with words the man you must punish with deeds, since the pain of the punishment is sufficient for the wretch without adding ill-language.

'Consider the culprit who comes before you for judgment as a wretched man, subject to the conditions of our depraved nature, and so far as in you lies without injury to the contrary party, show yourself pitiful and lenient; for although all godlike attributes are equal, mercy is more precious and resplendent in our sight than justice.

'If you follow these precepts and rules, Sancho, your days will be long, your fame eternal, your rewards abundant, your happiness indescribable. You will marry your children as you wish to; they and your grandchildren will have titles; you will live in peace and good-will among men, and in your life's last stages you will arrive at the hour of death in a mild and ripe old age, and the tender and delicate hands of your great-grandchildren will close your eyes. . . .

I must tell you then that Sancho Panza with all his escort arrived at a village of about a thousand inhabitants, which was one of the best in the Duke's dominions. They gave him to understand that this was called the Isle Barataria,[4] either because the town's name was *Baratario*, or because of the '*barato*', or low price, at which he had got the government. When they reached the gates of the place, which was walled, the town-council came out to receive him. They rang the bells, and all the inhabitants demonstrated their general rejoicing and conducted him in great pomp to the principal church to give thanks to God. Then with some comical ceremonies they delivered him the keys of the town, and admitted him as perpetual governor of the Isle Barataria. The new governor's apparel, his beard, his fatness and his smallness surprised everyone who was not in the secret, and even those many who were. Next they bore him from the church to the judge's throne and seated him upon it, where the Duke's steward thus addressed him:

'It is an ancient custom in this famous isle, Lord Governor, that everyone who comes to take possession of it is obliged to reply to a question, and this must be a rather intricate and difficult one. By this reply the town touches and feels the pulse of its new governor's understanding and, accordingly, is either glad or grieved at his coming.'

Whilst the steward was thus addressing him, Sancho was gazing at a number of large letters inscribed on the wall facing his seat. Now, as he could not read, he asked what those paintings were on that wall, and the answer came: 'Sir, yonder is written and recorded the day on which your Lordship took possession of this isle, and the inscription says: "*This day, such a date of such a month in such a year, there took possession of the isle the Lord Don Sancho Panza; may he enjoy it for many years.*"'

'Who are they calling Don Sancho Panza?' asked Sancho.

'Your Lordship,' answered the steward, 'for no other Panza has entered this isle but the one seated on that seat.'

'Then take notice, brother,' said Sancho, 'that I'm no Don, and there has never been a Don in my whole family. Plain Sancho Panza's my name, and Sancho my father was called, and Sancho my grandfather, and they were all Panzas without the addition of Dons or Doñas. I fancy there are more Dons than stones in this isle. But enough. God knows my meaning, and perhaps

[4] The "island" the Duke offers is merely a section of his own inland province.

if my government lasts four days I may weed out these Dons, for judging by their numbers they must be as tiresome as gnats. Go on with your question, Master Steward, for I'll reply as best I can, whether the town be sorry or rejoice.'

At this moment two men came into the judgment-hall, one dressed as a labourer and the other as a tailor with scissors in his hand, the latter crying: 'My lord Governor, here's why I and this countryman have come before your worship. That fellow came to my shop yesterday — I, saving your presence, am a licensed tailor, God be praised! — and put a piece of cloth into my hands, and asked me: "Would there be enough here, sir, to make a cap?" I measured the stuff and answered him yes. I suppose he must have suspected that I intended to rob him of part of the cloth, basing his belief on his own roguery and the bad reputation of tailors. And he was quite right. Then he asked me to examine it again and see if there was enough for two. I guessed his drift, and said yes. Then, persisting in his damned idea, he went on adding caps, and I added more yeses till we came to five. And he has just come this very moment for his caps, and I've offered them to him. And he won't pay me for the making, but demands that I shall pay him instead or return him his cloth.'

'Is all this true, brother?' asked Sancho.

'Yes, sir,' answered the fellow, 'but make him show you the five caps he has made me, your worship.'

'With pleasure,' said the tailor.

And taking his hands suddenly from under his cloak, he displayed five caps, one on the tip of each finger, and said: 'Here are the five caps this good man ordered and, by God and my conscience, there wasn't a scrap of cloth over, and I'll submit the work to be examined by the inspectors of the trade.'

Everyone present laughed at the number of caps and the novel nature of the case. But Sancho set himself to consider a little and said: 'There seems to me no need for long delays in this suit; it can be decided on the spot by a wise man's judgment. My sentence, therefore, is that the tailor shall lose his making and the countryman his cloth, the caps to be given to the prisoners in the jail, and let that be an end of the matter.'

This judgment moved the audience to laughter, but the governor's orders were carried out.

Next there came before him two old men, one of them carrying a cane for a walking stick. 'Sir,' said the one without the stick, 'Some time ago I lent this fellow ten crowns in gold, as a favour and a service to him, on condition that he should repay me on demand. I didn't ask him for them for a long time, so as not to put him into greater difficulties through repaying than he was in when I lent him them. But as he didn't seem to me to be troubling about his debt, I asked him for them, not once but many times. Now not only does he not repay me but he denies the debt, saying that I never lent him these ten crowns, or that if I did he has returned them. I have no witnesses of the loan — nor he of the repayment, for he never made it. So I want your worship to put him under oath, and if he swears that he has repaid me I will let him off the debt here, before God.'

'What do you say to this, you fellow with the stick?' asked Sancho.

'I confess that he lent them to me, sir,' answered the old man. 'Hold down your wand of justice, your worship, and since he leaves it to my oath, I'll swear that I really and truly returned them to him.'

The Governor lowered his wand, and at the same time this old man gave his stick, as if it were very much in his way, to the other old man to hold whilst he took his oath. Then he put his hand on the cross of the wand and declared that he had truly borrowed the ten crowns demanded of him, but that he had returned them into the plaintiff's own hands, and that it was only the other man's forgetfulness that made him continually demand them back.

At this the great Governor asked the creditor what answer he had to give to his adversary. For beyond all doubt the debtor must be speaking the truth since, in his opinon, he was an honest man and a good Christian. It must, in fact, have been the plaintiff who had forgotten how and when the money had been returned, and thenceforward he must never ask for repayment again. The debtor took back his stick, bowed and went out of the court. Now when Sancho saw the defendant also depart without more ado and observed the plaintiff's resignation, he bowed his head on his breast and, placing the first finger of his right hand over his brows and his nose, remained as if in thought for a short while. Then he raised his head and ordered the old man with the stick, who had already left the building, to be recalled; and when he was brought back into his presence, Sancho said: 'Give me that stick, my fellow. I've need of it.'

'With great pleasure,' replied the old man, putting it into Sancho's hand. 'Here it is, sir.' Sancho then took it and, handing it to the other old man, said to him: 'Go, in God's name. You're repaid now.'

'What, sir?' replied the old man. 'Is this stick worth ten gold crowns then?'

'Yes,' said the Governor. 'If it isn't I'm the greatest dolt in the world. And now you'll see whether I haven't the gumption to govern a whole kingdom.'

Then he ordered the cane to be broken open in the presence of everyone; and when this was done they found ten gold crowns inside. Whereupon everyone expressed astonishment, and hailed the governor as a new Solomon. And when asked how he had deduced that the ten crowns were inside the cane, he answered that he had watched the defendant give the stick to the plaintiff whilst he took his oath that he had really and truly returned the money; and when the fellow had completed his oath and asked for the stick back, it had occurred to him that the sum in dispute must be inside. From this, he added, they might see that sometimes God directs the judgments of governors, even if some of them are fools. Besides, he had heard the priest of his village tell of a similar case, and he had so good a memory that, if it weren't that he forgot everything he wanted to remember, there would not be a better in the whole isle. Finally they departed, one abashed and the other satisfied. The audience was flabbergasted, and the secretary who noted down Sancho's words, acts and gestures was unable to decide whether to write him down a wise man or a fool.

But no sooner was this case over than a woman came into the court, stoutly clinging to a man dressed like a rich herdsman, and crying out loudly as she came: 'Justice, Lord Governor! Justice! If I don't find it on earth, I'll go and seek it in Heaven! Sweet governor, this wicked man sprang on me in the middle of a field, and abused my body like a dirty dish-rag and, poor wretch that I am, he robbed me of a treasure I've kept for more than twenty-three-years, and defended from Moors and Christians, natives and foreigners. I've always been as resistant as a cork-tree and preserved myself as pure as the salamander in the fire, or as wool on the briars, for this fellow now to come and handle me with his clean hands!'

'We have still to discover whether this fine fellow has clean hands or not,' said Sancho.

Then, turning to the man, he asked him what answer he had to offer to the woman's complaint. And the man replied in great confusion: 'Sirs, I am a poor herdsman with a herd of swine, and this morning I left this place to sell — saving your presence — four pigs, and what with dues and exactions they took from me very nearly their full value. Now as I was coming back to my village I met this good woman on the way, and the Devil, the author of all mischief, made us couple together. I paid her sufficient, but she wasn't content and caught hold of me and wouldn't let me go until she had dragged me to this place. She says I forced her, and that's a lie, as I'll swear on oath; and that's the whole truth, to the last crumb.'

Then the Governor asked him if he had any silver money on him, and he replied he had about twenty ducats inside his shirt in a leather purse. This the governor ordered him to take out and hand over to the plaintiff just as it was. He obeyed trembling, and the woman took it, making a thousand curtseys to the company, and praying God for the life and health of the good governor, who thus looked after needy orphans and maidens. With this she left the court, grasping the purse tightly with both hands, although she looked first to see if the money in it was really silver. Then, no sooner was she gone than Sancho said to the herdsman, who was on the point of tears, for his eyes and his heart yearned after his purse, 'Run after that woman, my good fellow, and take the purse away from her, whether she likes it or not. Then come back here with her.'

It was not a fool or a deaf man he spoke to, for the man dashed out at once like lightning and ran to obey. All the audience were in suspense as they awaited the outcome of the case. Then shortly afterwards the man and woman came back, more closely entwined and locked together than before, she with her skirt tucked up and the purse in the fold, and the man struggling to get it away from her. But it was impossible, so stoutly did she defend it, crying out loudly: 'Justice, in God's name! Justice! See, Lord worshipful Governor, the shamelessness of this bold, godless fellow. In the middle of the town, in the middle of the street, he's been trying to rob me of the purse your worship made him give me.'

'And did he rob you?' asked the Governor.

'How rob me?' replied the woman. 'I had rather lose my life than this purse. A pretty babe I should be! You must set other cats at my chin than this miserable, filthy fellow. Pincers and hammers, mallets and chisels, won't be enough to get it out of my clutches, nor lion's claws either. They shall sooner have my soul from the very heart of my body!'

'She's right,' said the man. 'I'm beaten, I admit, and tired out. I confess I haven't the strength to take it from her. I give up.'

Then the Governor said to the woman: 'Show me that purse, honest and valiant woman.'

She gave it to him at once, and the Governor returned it to the man, saying to the forcible but unforced woman: 'Sister, if you'd shown the same valorous spirit you've displayed in defending that purse, or even half as much, in defending your body, the strength of Hercules couldn't have forced you. Get out, confound you, and ill luck go with you. Don't stay anywhere in this isle, nor within twenty miles of it, under pain of two hundred lashes. Get out at once, I say, you loose-tongued, shameless swindler.'

The woman was thrown into confusion, and went off hanging her head, in high dudgeon, and the Governor said to the man: 'Good fellow, go back home, in God's name, with your money, and in future, if you don't want to lose it, try not to get a fancy for coupling with anyone.'

The man thanked him with the worst possible grace and departed, and the audience were once more astonished at their new governor's judicious decisions. All this, duly recorded by his chronicler, was straightway written down for the Duke, who was most eagerly waiting for news. But here let good Sancho rest. . . .

Francis Bacon   (1561–1626)

ENGLISH PHILOSOPHER and STATESMAN

Of Judicature

Judges ought to remember that their office is *jus dicere*, and not *jus dare*; to interpret law, and not to make law, or give law. Else will it be like the authority claimed by the church of Rome, which under pretext of exposition

From *The Works of Francis Bacon*, edited by James Spedding, Robert Ellis, and Douglas Heath.

of Scripture doth not stick[1] to add and alter; and to pronounce that which they do not find; and by shew[2] of antiquity to introduce novelty. Judges ought to be more learned than witty, more reverend than plausible, and more advised than confident. Above all things, integrity is their portion and proper virtue. *Cursed* (saith the law) *is he that removeth the landmark.* The mislayer of a mere-stone is to blame. But it is the unjust judge that is the capital remover of landmarks, when he defineth amiss of lands and property. One foul sentence doth more hurt than many foul examples. For these do but corrupt the stream, the other corrupteth the fountain. So saith Salomon, *Fons turbatus, et vena corrupta, est justus cadens in causâ suâ coram adversario:* [A righteous man falling down before the wicked is as a troubled fountain or a corrupt spring.] The office of judges may have reference unto the parties that sue, unto the advocates that plead, unto the clerks and ministers of justice underneath them, and to the sovereign or state above them.

First, for the causes or parties that sue. *There be* (saith the Scripture) *that turn judgment into wormwood*; and surely there be also that turn it into vinegar; for injustice maketh it bitter, and delays make it sour. The principal duty of a judge is to suppress force and fraud; whereof force is the more pernicious when it is open, and fraud when it is close and disguised. Add thereto contentious suits, which ought to be spewed out, as the surfeit of courts. A judge ought to prepare his way to a just sentence, as God useth to prepare his way, by raising valleys and taking down hills: so when there appeareth on either side an high hand, violent prosecution, cunning advantages taken, combination, power, great counsel, then is the virtue of a judge seen, to make inequality equal; that he may plant his judgment as upon an even ground. *Qui fortiter emungit, elicit sanguinem*; [Violent blowing makes the nose bleed;] and where the wine-press is hard wrought, it yields a harsh wine, that tastes of the grape-stone. Judges must beware of hard constructions and strained inferences; for there is no worse torture than the torture of laws. Specially in case of laws penal, they ought to have care that that which was meant for terror be not turned into rigour; and that they bring not upon the people that shower whereof the Scripture speaketh, *Pluet super eos laqueos*; for penal laws pressed are a *shower of snares* upon the people. Therefore let penal laws, if they have been sleepers of long, or if they be grown unfit for the present time, be by wise judges confined in the execution: *Judicis officium est, ut res, ita tempora rerum, &c.* [A judge must have regard to the time as well as to the matter.] In causes of life and death, judges ought (as far as the law permitteth) in justice to remember mercy; and to cast a severe eye upon the example, but a merciful eye upon the person.

Secondly, for the advocates and counsel that plead. Patience and gravity of hearing is an essential part of justice; and an overspeaking judge is no well-tuned cymbal. It is no grace to a judge first to find that which he might have heard in due time from the bar; or to show quickness of conceit in cutting

[1] hesitate.
[2] show.

off evidence or counsel too short; or to prevent information by questions, though pertinent. The parts of a judge in hearing are four: to direct the evidence; to moderate length, repetition, or impertinency of speech; to recapitulate, select, and collate the material points of that which hath been said; and to give the rule or sentence. Whatsoever is above these is too much; and proceedeth either of glory and willingness to speak, or of impatience to hear, or of shortness of memory, or of want of a staid and equal attention. It is a strange thing to see that the boldness of advocates should prevail with judges; whereas they should imitate God, in whose seat they sit; who *represseth the presumptuous, and giveth grace to the modest.* But it is more strange, that judges should have noted favourites; which cannot but cause multiplication of fees, and suspicion of bye-ways. There is due from the judge to the advocate some commendation and gracing, where causes are well handled and fair pleaded; especially towards the side which obtaineth not; for that upholds in the client the reputation of his counsel, and beats down in him the conceit of his cause. There is likewise due to the public a civil represension of advocates, where there appeareth cunning counsel, gross neglect, slight information, indiscreet pressing, or an over-bold defence. And let not the counsel at the bar chop[3] with the judge, nor wind himself into the handling of the cause anew after the judge hath declared his sentence; but on the other side, let not the judge meet the cause half way, nor give occasion for the party to say his counsel or proofs were not heard.

Thirdly, for that that concerns clerks and ministers. The place of justice is an hallowed place; and therefore not only the bench, but the foot-pace[4] and precincts and purprise[5] thereof, ought to be preserved without scandal and corruption. For certainly *Grapes* (as the Scripture saith) *will not be gathered of thorns or thistles;* neither can justice yield her fruit with sweetness amongst the briars and brambles of catching and polling[6] clerks and ministers. The attendance of courts is subject to four bad instruments. First, certain persons that are sowers of suits; which make the court swell, and the country pine. The second sort is of those that engage courts in quarrels of jurisdiction, and are not truly *amici curiæ*, but *parasiti curiæ*,[7] in puffing a court up beyond her bounds, for their own scraps and advantage. The third sort is of those that may be accounted the left hands of courts; persons that are full of nimble and sinister tricks and shifts, whereby they pervert the plain and direct courses of courts, and bring justice into oblique lines and labyrinths. And the fourth is the poller and exacter of fees; which justifies the common resemblance of the courts of justice to the bush whereunto while the sheep flies for defence in weather, he is sure to lose part of his fleece. On the other side, an ancient clerk, skilful in precedents, wary in proceeding, and understanding in the busi-

---

[3] split hairs, bicker.
[4] dais, platform.
[5] surroundings.
[6] arresting and seizing.
[7] friends of the court, but parasites of the court.

ness of the court, is an excellent finger of a court; and doth many times point the way to the judge himself.

Fourthly, for that which may concern the sovereign and estate. Judges ought above all to remember the conclusion of the Roman Twelve Tables; *Salus populi suprema lex*; [The supreme law of all is the weal of the people;] and to know that laws, except they be in order to that end, are but things captious, and oracles not well inspired. Therefore it is an happy thing in a state when kings and states do often consult with judges; and again when judges do often consult with the king and state: the one, when there is matter of law intervenient in business of state; the other, when there is some consideration of state intervenient in matter of law. For many times the things deduced to judgment may be *meum* and *tuum*,[8] when the reason and consequence thereof may trench to point[9] of estate: I call matter of estate, not only the parts of sovereignty, but whatsoever introduceth any great alteration or dangerous precedent; or concerneth manifestly any great portion of people. And let no man weakly conceive that just laws and true policy have any antipathy; for they are like the spirits and sinews, that one moves with the other. Let judges also remember, that Salomon's throne was supported by lions on both sides: let them be lions, but yet lions under the throne; being circumspect that they do not check or oppose any points of sovereignty. Let not judges also be so ignorant of their own right, as to think there is not left to them, as a principal part of their office, a wise use and application of laws. For they may remember what the apostle saith of a greater law than theirs; *Nos scimus quia lex bona est, modo quis eâ utatur legitime.* [We know that the law is good, if a man use it lawfully.]

Thomas Hobbes (1588–1679)

ENGLISH PHILOSOPHER

The Foundation of Justice

From that law of nature, by which we are obliged to transfer to another, such rights, as being retained, hinder the peace of mankind, there followeth a third; which is this, *that men perform their covenants made*: without which,

[8] mine and thine.
[9] approach some affair.

Title supplied by editors. From Leviathan or the Matter, Forme and Power of a Commonwealth Ecclesiasticall and Civil by Thomas Hobbes in Hobbes: Leviathan, edited by Michael Oakeshott. Reprinted by permission of Basil Blackwell, Publisher, Oxford.

covenants are in vain, and but empty words; and the right of all men to all things remaining, we are still in the condition of war.

And in this law of nature, consisteth the fountain and original of JUSTICE. For where no covenant hath preceded, there hath no right been transferred, and every man has right to every thing; and consequently, no action can be unjust. But when a covenant is made, then to break it is *unjust:* and the definition of INJUSTICE, is no other than *the not performance of covenant.* And whatsoever is not unjust, is *just.*

But because covenants of mutual trust, where there is a fear of not performance on either part, as hath been said in the former chapter, are invalid; though the original of justice be the making of covenants; yet injustice actually there can be none, till the cause of such fear be taken away; which while men are in the natural condition of war, cannot be done. Therefore before the names of just, and unjust can have place, there must be some coercive power, to compel men equally to the performance of their covenants, by the terror of some punishment, greater than the benefit they expect by the breach of their covenant; and to make good that propriety, which by mutual contract men acquire, in recompense of the universal right they abandon: and such power there is none before the erection of a commonwealth. And this is also to be gathered out of the ordinary definition of justice in the Schools: for they say, that *justice is the constant will of giving to every man his own.* And therefore where there is no *own,* that is no propriety, there is no injustice; and where there is no coercive power erected, that is, where there is no commonwealth, there is no propriety; all men having right to all things: therefore where there is no commonwealth, there nothing is unjust. So that the nature of justice, consisteth in keeping of valid covenants: but the validity of covenants begins not but with the constitution of a civil power, sufficient to compel men to keep them: and then it is also that propriety begins.

John Milton   (1608–1674)

ENGLISH POET and ESSAYIST

When I Consider How My Light Is Spent

When I consider how my light is spent,
  Ere half my days, in this dark world and wide,
  And that one Talent which is death to hide,
  Lodg'd with me useless, though my Soul more bent

Talent: (1) ability, (2) Roman coin

"When I Consider How My Light Is Spent" by John Milton. From *John Milton: Complete Poems and Major Prose,* edited by Merritt Y. Hughes and published by the Odyssey Press, Inc., New York, 1958. Reprinted by permission.

To serve therewith my Maker, and present
  My true account, lest he returning chide;
  "Doth God exact day-labor, light denied,"
  I fondly ask; But patience to prevent
That murmur, soon replies, "God doth not need
  Either man's work or his own gifts; who best   10
  Bear his mild yoke, they serve him best; his State
Is Kingly. Thousands at his bidding speed
  And post o'er Land and Ocean without rest:
  They also serve who only stand and wait."

fondly: foolishly. *prevent:* anticipate

Blaise Pascal (1623–1662)

FRENCH MATHEMATICIAN, PHYSICIST, THEOLOGIAN,
and MAN OF LETTERS

Observations on Justice

. . . On what shall a man base the economy[1] of the world that he wants to rule? Will it be on the whim of each individual? What chaos! Will it be on justice? He does not know the meaning of the word.

Certainly, if he had known it, he would not have prescribed this rubric which is the commonest of all those known to men: that each should conform to the customs of his own country; the light of true equity would have brought all nations under its rule, and legislators would not have replaced an enduring conception of justice by taking the whims and fancies of the Persians and the Germans as their models. We should see a model system of justice established in every country in the world in every age, instead of which we see no system of justice or injustice which does not vary from one country to another like the climate. If the temperature at the pole went up by three degrees, it would turn jurisprudence upside down; a meridian determines truth; after a few years' possession, fundamental laws undergo sweeping changes; right has its periods; the entry of Saturn into Leo marks the origin of some crime or other.[2] A comic sort of justice that has a river for its boundary! Truth on this side of the Pyrenees, error on the other.

They admit that justice is not to be sought in custom, but in natural laws which are common to all countries. Certainly, they would stick obstinately

[1] organization.
[2] reference to astrological study, which interprets the planets' influence on men's lives.

Title supplied by editors. "Observations on Justice" from pp. 139–141 *Pascal's Pensées* by Blaise Pascal, translated by Martin Turnell. Copyright © in Martin Turnell's translation with the Harvill Press, 1962. Reprinted by permission of Harper & Row, Publishers, and William Collins Sons & Co. Ltd., London.

to their view if the boldness of chance, which is responsible for human laws, had hit on one that was universal; but the joke is such that human whim is so various that there is none. Robbery, incest, the slaughter of children and fathers have in their time all been regarded as virtuous actions. Can anything be more preposterous than the fact that a man has the right to kill me because he lives on the other side of the ocean and because his prince has a grievance against mine, though I have none against him? There are no doubt natural laws; but once right reason was corrupted, it corrupted everything: *Nihil amplius nostrum est; quod nostrum dicimus, artis est. Ex senatus consultis et plebiscitis crimina exercentur. Ut olim vitiis, sic nunc legibus laboramus.*[3]

This confusion leads one man to declare that the essence of justice is the authority of the lawgiver; a second, that it is the comfort of the sovereign; a third, present custom; and that is the safest: according to reason, nothing is just in itself; everything changes with the times. Custom is the whole of equity for the sole reason that it is accepted; that is the mystic foundation of its authority. Anyone who tries to trace it back to its first principles will destroy it. Nothing is so faulty as laws which purport to redress wrongs; anyone who obeys them because they are just, obeys a justice which is the product of his imagination, but not the essence of the law; it is entirely contained within itself; it is law and nothing more. Anyone who wants to examine its structure will find that it is so weak and frivolous that, unless he is in the habit of contemplating the prodigies of human imagination, he will be surprised that in the course of a century it has acquired so much pomp and circumstance. The art of opposition and rebellion lies in undermining established customs by tracing them back to their origins in order to reveal their lack of authority and justice. 'We must,' it is said, 'go back to the primitive and fundamental laws of the State which have been abolished by unjust custom.' It is the surest way of losing everything; nothing will appear just when subjected to a test of that kind. . . .

---

[3] There is no longer anything that is ours; what we call ours is a work of convention (Cicero: *De finibus*, v, 21). It is in virtue of the senatus consultus and the plebiscites that crimes are committed (Seneca: *Epistles*, xcv). We suffered long ago for our vices: today we suffer for our laws (Tacitus: *Annals*, III, 25). [Turnell]

Cotton Mather (1663–1728)

AMERICAN DIVINE

An Account of the Goodwin Witchcraft Case

WITCHCRAFTS AND POSSESSIONS.
THE FIRST EXEMPLE.

Section I.   There dwells at this time, in the south part of Boston, a sober and pious man, whose Name is John Goodwin, whose Trade is that of a Mason, and whose Wife (to which a Good Report gives a share with him in all the Characters of Vertue) `has made him the Father of six (now living) Children. Of these Children, all but the Eldest, who works with his Father at his Calling, and the Youngest, who lives yet upon the Breast of its mother, have laboured under the direful effects of a (no less palpable than) stupendous *Witchcraft*. Indeed that exempted Son had also, as was thought, some lighter touches of it, in unaccountable stabbs and pains now and then upon him; as indeed every person in the Family at some time or other had, except the godly Father, and the sucking Infant, who never felt any impressions of it. But these Four Children mentioned, were handled in so sad and strange a manner, as has given matter of Discourse and Wonder to all the Countrey, and of History not unworthy to be considered by more than all the serious or the curious Readers in the New-English World.

Sect. II.   The four Children (whereof the Eldest was about Thirteen, and the youngest was perhaps about a third part so many years of age[1]) had enjoyed a Religious Education, and answered it with a very towardly Ingenuity.[2] They had an observable Affection unto Divine and Sacred things; and those of them that were capable of it, seem'd to have such a Resentment[3] of their eternal Concernments as is not altogether usual. Their Parents also kept them to a continual Employment, which did more than deliver them from the Temptations of Idleness, and as young as they were, they took a delight in it, it may be as much as they should have done. In a word, Such was the whole Temper and Carriage of the Children, that there cannot easily be any thing more unreasonable, than to imagine that a Design to Dissemble could cause

---

[1] Martha was 13, John 11, Mercy 7, Benjamin 5, the elder son (Nathaniel) 15, the baby (Hannah) six months old, when the narrative opens (midsummer, 1688). (Savage, *Genealogical Dictionary*, and Boston records.)
[2] with encouraging promise. [eds.]
[3] realization. [eds.]

Title supplied by editors. From *Memorable Providences relating to Witchcraft and Possessions* in *Narratives of the Witchcraft Cases 1648–1706*, by Cotton Mather, edited and annotated by George Lincoln Burr. Reprinted by permission of Barnes & Noble, Inc.

them to fall into any of their odd Fits; though there should not have happened,[4] as there did, a thousand Things, wherein it was perfectly impossible for any Dissimulation of theirs to produce what scores of spectators were amazed at.

Sect. III.   About Midsummer, in the year 1688, the Eldest of these Children, who is a Daughter, saw cause to examine their Washerwoman, upon their missing of some Linnen, which twas fear'd she had stollen from them; and of what use this linnen might bee to serve the Witchcraft intended, the Theef's Tempter knows! This Laundress was the Daughter of an ignorant and a scandalous old Woman in the Neighbourhood; whose miserable Husband before he died, had sometimes complained of her, that she was undoubtedly a Witch, and that whenever his Head was laid, she would quickly arrive unto the punishments due to such an one. This Woman in her daughters Defence bestow'd very bad Language upon the Girl that put her to the Question; immediately upon which, the poor child became variously indisposed in her health, and visited with strange Fits, beyond those that attend an Epilepsy, or a Catalepsy, or those that they call The Diseases of Astonishment.[5]

Sect. IV.   It was not long before one of her Sisters, and two of her Brothers, were seized, in Order one after another, with Affects[6] like those that molested her. Within a few weeks, they were all four tortured every where in a manner so very grievous, that it would have broke an heart of stone to have seen their Agonies. Skilful Physicians were consulted for their Help, and particularly our worthy and prudent Friend Dr. Thomas Oakes,[7] who found himself so affronted[8] by the Distempers of the children, that he concluded nothing but an hellish Witchcraft could be the Original[9] of these Maladies. And that which yet more confirmed such Apprehension was, That for one good while, the children were tormented just in the same part of their bodies all at the same time together; and tho they saw and heard not one anothers complaints, tho likewise their pains and sprains were swift like Lightening, yet when (suppose) the Neck, or the Hand, or the Back of one was Rack't, so it was at that instant with t'other too.

Sect. V.   The variety of their tortures increased continually; and tho about Nine or Ten at Night they alwaies had a Release from their miseries, and ate and slept all night for the most part indifferently well, yet in the day time they were handled with so many sorts of Ails, that it would require of us almost as much time to Relate them all, as it did of them to Endure them. Sometimes they would be Deaf, sometimes Dumb, and sometimes Blind, and often, all this at once. One while their Tongues would be drawn down their

---

[4] even if there had not. [eds.]

[5] *i.e.*, stupefaction: diseases that rob one of his wits. The author had once, while his stammering seemed to bar him from the ministry, begun the study of medicine. [abridged]

[6] affections, ailments.

[7] Dr. Oakes (1644–1719) was the locally eminent physician who in 1689 became speaker of the legislature and in 1690 was sent as a colonial deputy to England.

[8] nonplussed, dumbfounded.

[9] origin.

Throats; another-while they would be pull'd out upon their Chins, to a prodigious length. They would have their Mouths opened unto such a Wideness,
that their Jaws went out of joint; and anon they would clap together again
with a Force like that of a strong Spring-Lock. The same would happen to
their Shoulder-Blades, and their Elbows, and Hand-wrists, and several of their
joints. They would at times ly in a benummed condition; and be drawn together as those that are ty'd Neck and Heels;[10] and presently be stretched out,
yea, drawn Backwards, to such a degree that it was fear'd the very skin of their
Bellies would have crack'd. They would make most pitteous out-cries, that
they were cut with Knives, and struck with Blows that they could not bear.
Their Necks would be broken, so that their Neck-bone would seem dissolved
unto them that felt after it; and yet on the sudden, it would become again so
stiff that there was no stirring of their Heads; yea, their Heads would be
twisted almost round; and if main Force at any time obstructed a dangerous
motion which they seem'd to be upon, they would roar exceedingly. Thus
they lay some weeks most pittiful Spectacles; and this while as a further Demonstration of Witchcraft in these horrid Effects, when I went to Prayer by
one of them, that was very desireous to hear what I said, the Child utterly
lost her Hearing till our Prayer was over.

Sect. VI.   It was a Religious Family that these Afflictions happened unto;
and none but a Religious Contrivance to obtain Releef, would have been welcome to them. Many superstitious proposals were made unto them, by persons that were I know not who, nor what, with Arguments fetch't from I
know not how much Necessity and Experience; but the distressed Parents rejected all such counsils, with a gracious Resolution, to oppose Devils with no
other weapons but Prayers and Tears, unto Him that has ne Chaining of
them; and to try first whether Graces were not the best things to encounter
Witchcrafts with. Accordingly they requested the four Ministers of Boston,
with the Minister of Charlstown, to keep a Day of Prayer at their thus haunted
house; which they did in the Company of some devout people there. Immediately upon this Day, the youngest of the four children was delivered, and
never felt any trouble as afore. But there was yet a greater Effect of these our
Applications unto our God!

Sect. VII.   The Report of the Calamities of the Family for which we were
thus concerned, arrived now unto the ears of the Magistrates, who presently
and prudently apply'd themselves, with a just vigour, to enquire into the story.
The Father of the Children complained of his Neighbour, the suspected ill
woman, whose name was Glover; and she being sent for by the Justices, gave
such a wretched Account of her self, that they saw cause to commit her unto
the Gaolers[11] Custody. Goodwin had no proof that could have done her any
Hurt; but the Hag had not power to deny her interest in the Enchantment of

[10] "Tied neck and heels" was doubtless at first only a phrase for the securest method of
fettering; but it had now become a name for what was (in defiance of English law) a
method of torture. [abridged]
[11] jailer's. [eds.]

the Children; and when she was asked, Whether she believed there was a God? her Answer was too blasphemous and horrible for any Pen of mine to mention. An Experiment was made, Whether she could recite the Lords Prayer; and it was found, that tho clause after clause was most carefully repeated unto her, yet when she said it after them that prompted her, she could not possibly avoid making Nonsense of it, with some ridiculous Depravations. This Experiment I had the curiosity since to see made upon two more, and it had the same Event. Upon the Commitment of this extraordinary Woman, all the Children had some present ease; until one (related unto her) accidentally meeting one or two of them, entertain'd them with her Blessing, that is, Railing; upon which Three of them fell ill again, as they were before.

  Sect. VIII.   It was not long before the Witch thus in the Trap, was brought upon her Tryal; at which, thro' the Efficacy of a Charm, I suppose, used upon her, by one or some of her Crue,[12] the Court could receive Answers from her in none but the Irish, which was her Native Language; altho she understood the English very well, and had accustomed her whole Family to none but that Language in her former Conversation; and therefore the Communication between the Bench and the Bar,[13] was now cheefly convey'd by two honest and faithful men that were interpreters. It was long before she could with any direct Answers plead unto her Indictment; and when she did plead, it was with Confession rather than Denial of her Guilt. Order was given to search the old womans house, from whence there were brought into the Court, several small Images, or Puppets, or Babies, made of Raggs, and stuff't with Goat's hair, and other such Ingredients. When these were produced, the vile Woman acknowledged, that her way to torment the Objects of her malice, was by wetting of her Finger with her Spittle, and stroaking of those little Images. The abused Children were then present, and the Woman still kept stooping and shrinking as one that was almost prest to Death with a mighty Weight upon her. But one of the Images being brought unto her, immediately she started up after an odd manner, and took it into her hand; but she had no sooner taken it, than one of the Children fell into sad Fits, before the whole Assembly. This the Judges had their just Apprehensions at; and carefully causing the Repetition of the Experiment, found again the same event of it. They asked her, Whether she had any[14] to stand by her: She replied, She had; and looking very pertly in the Air; she added, No, He's gone. And she then confessed, that she had One, who was her Prince, with whom she maintain'd, I know not what Communion. For which cause, the night after, she was heard expostulating with a Devil, for his thus deserting her; telling him that Because he had served her so basely and falsly, she had confessed all. However to make all clear, The Court appointed five or six Physicians one evening to examine her very strictly, whether she were not craz'd in her Intellectuals, and had not procured to her self by Folly and Madness the Reputation of a Witch.

---

12 crew.
13 *i.e.,* between the judges and the prisoner at the bar.
14 attending spirits or "familiars" (who performed favors for witches). [eds.]

Diverse hours did they spend with her; and in all that while no Discourse came from her, but what was pertinent and agreeable: particularly, when they asked her, What she thought would become of her soul? she reply'd "You ask me a very solemn Question, and I cannot well tell what to say to it." She own'd her self a Roman Catholick; and could recite her Pater Noster in Latin very readily; but there was one Clause or two alwaies too hard for her, whereof she said, "She could not repeat it, if she might have all the world." In the up-shot, the Doctors returned her Compos Mentis;[15] and Sentence of Death was pass'd upon her.

[15] in sound mind.

Voltaire (1694–1778)

FRENCH SATIRIST, SHORT STORY WRITER,
POET, and DRAMATIST

Candide Meets the Oreillons

. . . Candide and his valet were beyond the barriers and no one in the camp yet knew of the death of the German Jesuit.[1] The vigilant Cacambo had taken care to refill his bag with bread, chocolate, ham, fruits, and several bottles of wine. On their Andalusian horses they plunged into an unknown country where they discovered no road whatever. At last a beautiful prairie cross-cut by streams appeared before them. Our two travelers fed their mounts. Cacambo suggests to his master that they eat, and sets him an example. "How do you expect me to eat ham," said Candide, "when I have killed the son of Monsieur the Baron, and when I see myself condemned not to see the beautiful Cunégonde[2] as long as I live? What good will it do me to prolong my miserable days, since I must drag them out far from her in remorse and despair? And what will the *Journal de Trévoux*[3] say?"

While speaking this way, he did not fail to eat. The sun was setting. The two wanderers heard several little cries which seemed to be uttered by women. They did not know whether these cries were of pain or of joy; but they arose hastily with that anxiety and alarm which everything inspires in an unknown

[1] killed, in self-defense, by Candide.
[2] Candide's first love, lost and presumably dead.
[3] a celebrated Jesuit journal known for its scrupulous accuracy; it was consistently hostile to Voltaire.

Title supplied by editors. From *Candide* by Voltaire, translated by Peter Gay. Reprinted by permission of St. Martin's Press, Inc.

country. These clamors came from two stark naked girls, who were running lightly along the edge of the prairie, while two monkeys followed them biting their behinds. Candide was moved by pity; among the Bulgarians he had learned to shoot, and he could have knocked down a nut from a bush without touching the leaves. He takes his double-barreled Spanish rifle, shoots, and kills the two monkeys. "God be praised, my dear Cacambo! I have delivered these two poor creatures from a great peril; if I have committed a sin in killing an Inquisitor and a Jesuit, I have thoroughly made it up by saving the lives of two girls. These are perhaps two young ladies of quality, and this adventure may secure us great advantages in this country."

He was about to go on, but his tongue was paralyzed when he saw these two girls tenderly embrace the two monkeys, burst into tears over their bodies, and fill the air with the most pitiful cries. "I had not expected so much goodness of soul," he finally said to Cacambo; who replied: "You have performed a masterpiece there, my master; you have killed the two lovers of these ladies." — "Their lovers! Can it be possible? You are making fun of me, Cacambo; how can I believe you?" — "My dear master," returned Cacambo, "you're always astonished at everything; why do you find it so strange that in some countries there should be monkeys who obtain ladies' favors? They are one-quarter men just as I am one-quarter Spanish." — "Alas!" returned Candide, "I remember hearing Master Pangloss[4] say that in earlier times similar accidents had happened and that these mixtures had produced Aigypans,[5] fauns, satyrs; that many great personages of antiquity had seen them; but I had taken this for fables." — "Now you ought to be convinced," said Cacambo, "that it is the truth, and you see how people behave who have not received a certain education; all I fear is that these ladies may get us into trouble."

These solid reflections led Candide to leave the prairie and to plunge into the woods. There he dined with Cacambo; and the two, after they had cursed the Inquisitor of Portugal, the governor of Buenos Aires, and the Baron, fell asleep on moss. When they woke up, they found that they could not move; the reason for that was that during the night, the Oreillons,[6] the inhabitants of the country, to whom the two ladies had denounced them, had tied them up with cords made of bark. They were surrounded by about fifty stark naked Oreillons, armed with arrows, clubs, and stone hatchets; some were bringing a big cauldron to a boil, others were preparing spits, and all shouted: "It's a Jesuit, it's a Jesuit! We'll be avenged, and we'll eat well; let's eat Jesuit, let's eat Jesuit!"[7]

"I told you, my dear master," Cacambo sadly exclaimed, "that these two girls would play us a bad trick." Candide, seeing the cauldron and the spits,

[4] Candide's tutor, a foolish disciple of Leibnitz, the German philosopher (1646–1716) who attempted to reconcile the existence of evil with the premise that this is the best possible world.
[5] Egipans, fictional creatures.
[6] literally, "Big Ears."
[7] Candide has escaped after the murder by donning the dead priest's habit.

exclaimed: "We're surely going to be roasted or boiled. Ah! What would Master Pangloss say,[8] if he saw how pure nature[9] is made? All is well; granted; but I confess that it is very cruel to have lost Mademoiselle Cunégonde and to be put on the spit by Oreillons." Cacambo never lost his head. "Don't despair of anything," he said to the disconsolate Candide; "I understand a little of the jargon of this nation, I'll talk to them." — "Don't fail to point out to them," said Candide, "what dreadful inhumanity it is to cook men, and how un-Christian it is."

"Gentlemen," said Cacambo, "so you're counting on eating a Jesuit today? Well done; nothing is juster than to treat your enemies this way. In fact natural law teaches us to kill our neighbor, and this is how everyone acts everywhere. If we don't exercise the right of eating him, that's because we have other things to make a good meal with; but you don't have the same resources as we do; certainly it is better to eat your enemy than to abandon the fruits of your victory to crows and ravens. But, gentlemen, you would not want to eat your friends. You think you're about to put a Jesuit on a spit, and it is your defender, it is the enemy of your enemies whom you are about to roast. As for myself, I was born in your country; the gentleman you see is my master, and far from being a Jesuit, he has just killed a Jesuit, he is wearing his spoils; that's the reason for your misunderstanding. To confirm what I am telling you, take his robe, carry it to the first barrier of the kingdom of Los Padres[10] and find out if my master has not killed a Jesuit officer. It will take you little time; you can still eat us if you have found I have lied to you. But if I have told you the truth, you know the principles of international law, its uses and regulations too well, not to pardon us."

The Oreillons found this speech very reasonable; they deputized two notables to go with speed to discover the truth; the two deputies fulfilled their commission like men of intelligence, and soon returned bringing the good news. The Oreillons untied their two prisoners, paid them all kind of courtesies, offered them girls, gave them refreshments, and guided them all the way to the borders of their state, shouting with joy: "He's not a Jesuit, he's not a Jesuit!"

Candide did not cease wondering at the reason for his deliverance. "What a nation!" he said. "What men! What customs! If I had not had the good luck of giving a big sword thrust through the body of Mademoiselle Cunégonde's brother I would have been eaten without mercy. But after all pure nature is good, because these people here, instead of eating me, have given me a thousand courtesies as soon as they found out that I was not a Jesuit."

---

[8] The tutor's premise is that man lives in "the best of all possible worlds."
[9] i.e., uncivilized man.
[10] The Fathers.

Henry Fielding (1707–1754)

ENGLISH NOVELIST and DRAMATIST

The Gypsy Governor

. . . They now discovered a light at some distance, to the great pleasure of Jones, and to the no small terror of Partridge, who firmly believed himself to be bewitched, and that this light was a Jack-with-a-lantern, or somewhat more mischievous.

But how were these fears increased when, as they approached nearer to this light (or lights as they now appeared), they heard a confused sound of human voices; of singing, laughing, and hallooing together with a strange noise that seemed to proceed from some instrument — but could hardly be allowed the name of music! indeed, to favour a little the opinion of Partridge, it might very well be called music bewitched.

It is impossible to conceive a much greater degree of horror than what now seized on Partridge, the contagion of which had reached the post-boy, who had been very attentive to many things that the other had uttered. He now, therefore, joined in petitioning Jones to return, saying he firmly believed what Partridge had just before said, that though the horses seemed to go on, they had not moved a step forwards during at least the last half-hour.

Jones could not help smiling, in the midst of his vexation, at the fears of these poor fellows. 'Either we advance,' says he, 'towards the lights, or the lights have advanced towards us; for we are now at a very little distance from them; but how can either of you be afraid of a set of people who appear only to be merry-making?'

'Merry-making, sir!' cries Partridge; 'who could be merry-making at this time of night, and in such a place, and such weather? They can be nothing but ghosts or witches, or some evil spirits or other, that's certain.'

'Let them be what they will,' cries Jones, 'I am resolved to go up to them and inquire the way to Coventry. All witches, Partridge, are not such ill-natured hags as that we had the misfortune to meet with last.'

'Oh, Lord, sir,' cries Partridge, 'there is no knowing what humour they will be in; to be sure, it is always best to be civil to them; but what if we should meet with something worse than witches, with evil spirits themselves? —— Pray, sir, be advised; pray, sir, do. If you had read so many terrible accounts as I have of these matters, you would not be so foolhardy. —— The Lord knows whither we have got already, or whither we are going; for, sure, such darkness was never seen upon earth, and I question it can be darker in the other world.'

Title supplied by editors. From *The History of Tom Jones A Foundling*. Reprinted by permission of Random House, Inc.

Jones put forwards as fast as he could, notwithstanding all these hints and cautions, and poor Partridge was obliged to follow; for though he hardly dared to advance, he dared still less to stay behind by himself.

At length they arrived at the place whence the lights and different noises had issued. This Jones perceived to be no other than a barn, where a great number of men and women were assembled, and diverting themselves with much apparent jollity.

Jones no sooner appeared before the great doors of the barn, which were open, than a masculine and very rough voice from within demanded, who was there? — To which Jones gently answered, 'A friend'; and immediately asked the road to Coventry.

'If you are a friend,' cries another of the men in the barn, 'you had better alight till the storm is over' (for indeed it was now more violent than ever); 'you are very welcome to put up your horse, for there is sufficient room for him at the end of the barn.'

'You are very obliging,' returned Jones; 'and I will accept your offer for a few minutes whilst the rain continues; and here are two more who will be glad of the same favour.' This was accorded with more good-will than it was accepted; for Partridge would rather have submitted to the utmost inclemency of the weather than have trusted to the clemency of those whom he took for hobgoblins, and the poor post-boy was now infected with the same apprehensions; but they were both obliged to follow the example of Jones, — the one because he durst not leave his horse, and the other because he feared nothing so much as being left by himself.

Had this history been writ in the days of superstition, I should have had too much compassion for the reader to have left him so long in suspense, whether Beelzebub or Satan was about actually to appear in person, with all his hellish retinue; but as these doctrines are at present very unfortunate, and have but few, if any believers, I have not been much aware of conveying any such terrors. To say truth, the whole furniture of the infernal regions hath long been appropriated by the managers of playhouses, who seem lately to have laid them by as rubbish, capable only of affecting the upper gallery[1] a place in which few of our readers ever sit.

However, though we do not suspect raising any great terror on this occasion, we have reason to fear some other apprehensions may here arise in our reader, into which we would not willingly betray him; I mean that we are going to take a voyage into fairyland, and introduce a set of beings into our history which scarce any one was ever childish enough to believe, though many have been foolish enough to spend their time in writing and reading their adventures.

To prevent, therefore, any such suspicions so prejudicial to the credit of an historian, who professes to draw his materials from nature only, we shall now proceed to acquaint the reader who these people were, whose sudden appear-

[1] the most expensive seats.

ance had struck such terrors into Partridge, had more than half-frightened the post-boy, and had a little surprised even Mr. Jones himself.

The people then assembled in this barn were no other than a company of Egyptians or, as they are vulgarly called, gypsies, and they were now celebrating the wedding of one of their society.

It is impossible to conceive a happier set of people than appeared here to be met together. The utmost mirth, indeed, showed itself in every countenance; nor was their ball totally void of all order and decorum. Perhaps it had more than a country assembly is sometimes conducted with; for these people are subject to a formal government and laws of their own, and all pay obedience to one great magistrate, whom they call their king.

Greater plenty, likewise, was nowhere to be seen than what flourished in this barn. Here was indeed no nicety nor elegance, nor did the keen appetite of the guests require any. Here was good store of bacon, fowls, and mutton, to which every one present provided better sauce himself than the best and dearest French cook can prepare.

Æneas is not described under more consternation in the temple of Juno,

Dum stupet obtutuque hæret defixus in uno,[2]

than was our hero at what he saw in this barn. While he was looking everywhere round him with astonishment, a venerable person approached him with many friendly salutations, rather of too hearty a kind to be called courtly. This was no other than the king of the gypsies himself. He was very little distinguished in dress from his subjects, nor had he any regalia of majesty to support his dignity; and yet there seemed (as Mr. Jones said) to be somewhat in his air which denoted authority, and inspired the beholders with an idea of awe and respect; though all this was perhaps imaginary in Jones; and the truth may be that such ideas are incident to power, and almost inseparable from it.

There was somewhat in the open countenance and courteous behavior of Jones which, being accompanied with much comeliness of person, greatly recommended him at first sight to every beholder. These were, perhaps, a little heightened in the present instance by that profound respect which he paid to the king of the gypsies the moment he was acquainted with his dignity, and which was the sweeter to his gypseian majesty as he was not used to receive such homage from any but his own subjects.

The king ordered a table to be spread with the choicest of their provisions for his accommodation; and, having placed himself at his right hand, his majesty began to discourse with our hero in the following manner: —

'Me doubt not, sir, but you have often seen some of my people, who are what you call de parties detache, for dey go about everywhere; but me fancy you imagine not we be so considerable body as we be; and may be you will be surprise more when you hear de gypsy be as orderly and well govern people as any upon face of de earth.

---

[2] "While astonished he stood with his gaze on this single view." (*Aeneid,* I, 511)

'Me have honour, as me say, to be deir king, and no monarch can do boast of more dutiful subject, ne no more affectionate. How far me deserve deir good-will me no say; but dis me can say, dat me never design anyting but to do dem good. Me sall no do boast of dat neider; for what can me do oderwise dan consider of de good of dose poor people who go about all day to give me always the best of what dey get. Dey love and honour me darefore, because me do love and take care of dem; dat is all, me know no oder reason.

'About a tousand or two tousand year ago, me cannot tell to a year or two, as can neider write nor read, dere was a great what you call — a volution among de gypsy; for dere was de lord gypsy in dose days; and dese lord did quarrel vid one anoder about de place; but de king of de gypsy did demolish dem all, and made all his subject equal vid each oder; and since dat time dey have agree very well, for dey no tink of being king; and may be it be better for dem as dey be, for me assure you it be ver troublesome ting to be king and always to do justice; me have often wish to be de private gypsy when me have been forced to punish my dear friend and relation; for dough we never put to death, our punishments be ver severe. Dey make de gypsy ashamed of demselves, and dat be ver terrible punishment; me 'ave scarce ever known de gypsy so punish do harm any more.'

The king then proceeded to express some wonder that there was no such punishment as shame in other governments. Upon which Jones assured him to the contrary; for that there were many crimes for which shame was inflicted by the English laws, and that it was indeed one consequence of all punishment. 'Dat be ver strange,' said the king; 'for me know and hears good deal of your people, dough me no live among dem; and me have often hear dat sham is de consequence and de cause too of many of your rewards. Are your rewards and punishments den de same ting?'

While his majesty was thus discoursing with Jones, a sudden uproar arose in the barn, and, as it seems, upon this occasion: — the courtesy of these people had by degrees removed all the apprehensions of Partridge, and he was prevailed upon not only to stuff himself with their food, but to taste some of their liquors, which by degrees entirely expelled all fear from his composition, and in its stead introduced much more agreeable sensations.

A young female gypsy, more remarkable for her wit than her beauty, had decoyed the honest fellow aside, pretending to tell his fortune. Now, when they were alone together in a remote part of the barn, whether it proceeded from the strong liquor, which is never so apt to inflame inordinate desire as after moderate fatigue, or whether the fair gypsy herself threw aside the delicacy and decency of her sex, and tempted the youth Partridge with express solicitations; but they were discovered in a very improper manner by the husband of the gypsy, who, from jealousy it seems, had kept a watchful eye over his wife, and had dogged her to the place, where he found her in the arms of her gallant.

To the great confusion of Jones, Partridge was now hurried before the king; who heard the accusation, and likewise the culprit's defence, which was indeed very trifling; for the poor fellow was confounded by the plain evidence which appeared against him, and had very little to say for himself. His majesty, then turning towards Jones, said, 'Sir, you have hear what dey say; what punishment do you tink your man deserve?'

Jones answered, he was sorry for what had happened, and that Partridge should make the husband all the amends in his power: he said he had very little money about him at that time; and, putting his hand into his pocket, offered the fellow a guinea. To which he immediately answered, 'He hoped his honour would not think of giving him less than five.'

This sum, after some altercation, was reduced to two; and Jones, having stipulated for the full forgiveness of both Partridge and the wife, was going to pay the money, when his majesty, restraining his hand, turned to the witness and asked him at what time he had discovered the criminals. To which he answered that he had been desired by the husband to watch the motions of his wife from her first speaking to the stranger, and that he had never lost sight of her afterwards till the crime had been committed. The king then asked if the husband was with him all that time in his lurking-place. To which he answered in the affirmative. His Egyptian majesty then addressed himself to the husband as follows: 'Me be sorry to see any gypsy dat have no more honour dan to sell de honour of his wife for money. If you had de love for your wife, you would have prevented dis matter, and not endeavour to make her de whore dat you might discover her. Me do order dat you have no money given you, for you deserve punishment, not reward; me do order, derefore, dat you be de infamous gypsy, and do wear pair of horns[3] upon your forehead for one month, and dat your wife be called de whore, and pointed at all dat time; for you be de infamous gypsy, but she be no less de infamous whore.'

The gypsies immediately proceeded to execute the sentence, and left Jones and Partridge alone with his majesty.

Jones greatly applauded the justice of the sentence; upon which the king, turning to him, said, 'Me believe you be surprise; for me suppose you have ver bad opinion of my people; me suppose you tink us all de tieves.'

'I must confess, sir,' said Jones, 'I have not heard so favourable an account of them as they seem to deserve.'

'Me vil tell you,' said the king, 'how the difference is between you and us. My people rob your people, and your people rob one anoder.'

Jones afterwards proceeded very gravely to sing forth the happiness of those subjects who live under such a magistrate.

Indeed their happiness appears to have been so complete, that we are aware lest some advocate for arbitrary power should hereafter quote the case of those people as an instance of the great advantages which attend that government above all others.

And here we will make a concession, which would not perhaps have been

[3] sign of a cuckold.

expected from us, that no limited form of government is capable of rising to the same degree of perfection, or of producing the same benefits to society, with this. Mankind have never been so happy as when the greatest part of the then known world was under the dominion of a single master; and this state of their felicity continued during the reigns of five successive princes.[4] This was the true era of the Golden Age, and the only Golden Age which ever had any existence, unless in the warm imaginations of the poets, from the expulsion from Eden down to this day.

In reality, I know but of one solid objection to absolute monarchy. The only defect in which excellent constitution seems to be, the difficulty of finding any man adequate to the office of an absolute monarch; for this indispensably requires three qualities very difficult, as it appears from history, to be found in princely natures: first, a sufficient quantity of moderation in the prince, to be contented with all the power which is possible for him to have; secondly, enough of wisdom to know his own happiness; and, thirdly, goodness sufficient to support the happiness of others, when not only compatible with, but instrumental to his own.

Now if an absolute monarch, with all these great and rare qualifications, should be allowed capable of conferring the greatest good on society, it must be surely granted, on the contrary, that absolute power, vested in the hands of one who is deficient in them all, is likely to be attended with no less a degree of evil.

In short, our own religion furnishes us with adequate ideas of the blessing, as well as curse, which may attend absolute power. The pictures of heaven and of hell will place a very lively image of both before our eyes; for though the prince of the latter can have no power but what he originally derives from the omnipotent Sovereign in the former, yet it plainly appears from Scripture that absolute power in his infernal dominions is granted to their diabolical ruler. This is indeed the only absolute power which can by Scripture be derived from heaven. If, therefore, the several tyrannies upon earth can prove any title to a Divine authority, it must be derived from this original grant to the prince of darkness; and these subordinate deputations must consequently come immediately from him whose stamp they so expressly bear.

To conclude, as the examples of all ages show us that mankind in general desire power only to do harm, and, when they obtain it, use it for no other purpose, it is not consonant with even the least degree of prudence to hazard an alteration, where our hopes are poorly kept in countenance by only two or three exceptions out of a thousand instances to alarm our fears. In this case it will be much wiser to submit to a few inconveniences arising from the dispassionate deafness of laws, than to remedy them by applying to the passionate open ears of a tyrant.

Nor can the example of the gypsies, though possibly they may have long been happy under this form of government, be here urged; since we must

[4] The Roman emperors Nerva, Trajan, Adrian, and the two Antonini.

remember the very material respect in which they differ from all other people, and to which perhaps this their happiness is entirely owing, namely, that they have no false honours among them, and that they look on shame as the most grievous punishment in the world.

Jean Jacques Rousseau (1712–1778)

FRENCH POLITICAL PHILOSOPHER and ESSAYIST

The Right of the Strongest

The strongest is never strong enough to be always the master, unless he transforms strength into right, and obedience into duty. Hence the right of the strongest, which, though to all seeming meant ironically, is really laid down as a fundamental principle. But are we never to have an explanation of this phrase? Force is a physical power, and I fail to see what moral effect it can have. To yield to force is an act of necessity, not of will — at the most, an act of prudence. In what sense can it be a duty?

Suppose for a moment that this so-called "right" exists. I maintain that the sole result is a mass of inexplicable nonsense. For, if force creates right, the effect changes with the cause: every force that is greater than the first succeeds to its right. As soon as it is possible to disobey with impunity, disobedience is legitimate; and, the strongest being always in the right, the only thing that matters is to act so as to become the strongest. But what kind of right is that which perishes when force fails? If we must obey perforce, there is no need to obey because we ought; and if we are not forced to obey, we are under no obligation to do so. Clearly, the word "right" adds nothing to force: in this connection, it means absolutely nothing.

Obey the powers that be. If this means yield to force, it is a good precept, but superfluous: I can answer for its never being violated. All power comes from God, I admit; but so does all sickness: does that mean that we are forbidden to call in the doctor? A brigand surprises me at the edge of a wood: must I not merely surrender my purse on compulsion; but, even if I could withhold it, am I in conscience bound to give it up? For certainly the pistol he holds is also a power.

Let us then admit that force does not create right, and that we are obliged to obey only legitimate powers. . . .

Title supplied by editors. "The Right of the Strongest" from *The Social Contract and Discourses* by Jean Jacques Rousseau. Translated by G. D. H. Cole. Everyman's Library Edition. Reprinted by permission of E. P. Dutton & Co., Inc., and J. M. Dent & Sons Ltd., London.

Thomas Jefferson (1743–1826)

AMERICAN STATESMAN, WRITER,
and THIRD PRESIDENT OF THE UNITED STATES

Declaration of Independence

THE UNANIMOUS DECLARATION OF THE THIRTEEN UNITED STATES OF AMERICA

When in the Course of human events, it becomes necessary for one people to dissolve the political bands which have connected them with another, and to assume among the powers of the earth, the separate and equal station to which the Laws of Nature and of Nature's God entitle them, a decent respect to the opinions of mankind requires that they should declare the causes which impel them to the separation.

We hold these truths to be self-evident, that all men are created equal, that they are endowed by their Creator with certain unalienable Rights, that among these are Life, Liberty and the pursuit of Happiness. That to secure these rights, Governments are instituted among Men, deriving their just powers from the consent of the governed, That whenever any Form of Government becomes destructive to these ends, it is the Right of the People to alter or to abolish it, and to institute new Government, laying its foundation on such principles and organizing its powers in such form, as to them shall seem most likely to effect their Safety and Happiness. Prudence, indeed, will dictate that Governments long established should not be changed for light and transient causes; and accordingly all experience hath shewn that mankind are more disposed to suffer, while evils are sufferable, than to right themselves by abolishing the forms to which they are accustomed. But when a long train of abuses and usurpations, pursuing invariably the same Object evinces a design to reduce them under absolute Despotism, it is their right, it is their duty, to throw off such Government, and to provide new Guards for their future security. Such has been the patient sufferance of these Colonies; and such is now the necessity which constrains them to alter their former Systems of Government. The history of the present King of Great Britain is a history of repeated injuries and usurpations, all having in direct object the establishment of an absolute Tyranny over these States. To prove this, let Facts be submitted to a candid world.

He has refused his Assent to Laws, the most wholesome and necessary for the public good.

He has forbidden his Governors to pass Laws of immediate and pressing

"Declaration of Independence" (in Congress, July 4, 1776).

importance, unless suspended in their operation till his Assent should be obtained; and when so suspended, he has utterly neglected to attend to them.

He has refused to pass other Laws for the accommodation of large districts of people, unless those people would relinquish the right of Representation in the Legislature, a right inestimable to them and formidable to tyrants only.

He has called together legislative bodies at places unusual, uncomfortable, and distant from the depository of their public Records, for the sole purpose of fatiguing them into compliance with his measures.

He has dissolved Representative Houses repeatedly, for opposing with manly firmness his invasions on the rights of the people.

He has refused for a long time, after such dissolutions, to cause others to be elected; whereby the Legislative powers, incapable of Annihilation, have returned to the People at large for their exercise; the State remaining in the mean time exposed to all the dangers of invasion from without, and convulsions within.

He has endeavoured to prevent the population of these States; for that purpose obstructing the Laws for Naturalization of Foreigners; refusing to pass others to encourage their migrations hither, and raising the conditions of new Appropriations of Lands.

He has obstructed the Administration of Justice, by refusing his Assent to Laws for establishing Judiciary powers.

He has made Judges dependent on his Will alone, for the tenure of their offices, and the amount and payment of their salaries.

He has erected a multitude of New Offices, and sent hither swarms of Officers to harass our people, and eat out their substance.

He has kept among us, in times of peace, Standing Armies without the Consent of our legislatures.

He has affected to render the Military independent of and superior to the Civil power.

He has combined with others to subject us to a jurisdiction foreign to our constitution, and unacknowledged by our laws; giving his Assent to their Acts of pretended Legislation:

For quartering large bodies of armed troops among us:

For protecting them, by a mock Trial, from punishment for any Murders which they should commit on the Inhabitants of these States:

For cutting off our Trade with all parts of the world:

For imposing Taxes on us without our Consent:

For depriving us in many cases, of the benefits of Trial by Jury:

For transporting us beyond Seas to be tried for pretended offences:

For abolishing the free System of English Laws in a neighbouring Province, establishing therein an Arbitrary government, and enlarging its Boundaries so as to render it at once an example and fit instrument for introducing the same absolute rule into these Colonies:

For taking away our Charters, abolishing our most valuable Laws, and altering fundamentally the Forms of our Governments:

For suspending our own Legislatures, and declaring themselves invested with power to legislate for us in all cases whatsoever.

He has abdicated Government here, by declaring us out of his Protection and waging War against us.

He has plundered our seas, ravaged our Coasts, burnt our towns, and destroyed the lives of our people.

He is at this time transporting large Armies of foreign Mercenaries to compleat the works of death, desolation and tyranny, already begun with circumstances of Cruelty & perfidy scarcely paralleled in the most barbarous ages, and totally unworthy the Head of a civilized nation.

He has constrained our fellow Citizens taken Captive on the high Seas to bear Arms against their Country, to become the executioners of their friends and Brethren, or to fall themselves by their Hands.

He has excited domestic insurrections amongst us, and has endeavoured to bring on the inhabitants of our frontiers, the merciless Indian Savages, whose known rule of warfare is an undistinguished destruction of all ages, sexes and conditions.

In every stage of these Oppressions We have Petitioned for Redress in the most humble terms: Our repeated Petitions have been answered only by repeated injury. A Prince, whose character is thus marked by every act which may define a Tyrant, is unfit to be the ruler of a free people.

Nor have We been wanting in attentions to our British brethren. We have warned them from time to time of attempts by their legislature to extend an unwarrantable jurisdiction over us. We have reminded them of the circumstances of our emigration and settlement here. We have appealed to their native justice and magnanimity, and we have conjured them by the ties of our common kindred to disavow these usurpations, which would inevitably interrupt our connections and correspondence. They too have been deaf to the voice of justice and of consanguinity. We must, therefore, acquiesce in the necessity, which denounces our Separation, and hold them, as we hold the rest of mankind. Enemies in War, in Peace Friends.

WE, THEREFORE, the REPRESENTATIVES OF THE UNITED STATES OF AMERICA, IN GENERAL CONGRESS, Assembled, appealing to the Supreme Judge of the world for the rectitude of our intentions, do, in the Name, and by authority of the good People of these Colonies, solemnly PUBLISH and DECLARE, That these United Colonies are, and of Right ought to be FREE AND INDEPENDENT STATES; that they are Absolved from all Allegiance to the British Crown, and that all political connection between them and the State of Great Britain, is and ought to be totally dissolved; and that as FREE AND INDEPENDENT STATES, they have full Power to levy War, conclude Peace, contract Alliances, establish Commerce, and to do all other Acts and Things which INDEPENDENT STATES may of right do. And for the support of this Declaration, with a firm reliance on the protection of divine Providence, we mutually pledge to each other our Lives, our Fortunes and our sacred Honor.

John Greenleaf Whittier (1807–1892)

AMERICAN POET and ABOLITIONIST

Skipper Ireson's Ride

Of all the rides since the birth of time,
Told in story or sung in rhyme, —
On Apuleius's Golden Ass,
Or one-eyed Calendar's horse of brass,
Witch astride of a human back,
Islam's prophet on Al-Borák, —
The strangest ride that ever was sped
Was Ireson's, out from Marblehead!
    Old Floyd Ireson, for his hard heart,
      Tarred and feathered and carried in a cart   10
    By the women of Marblehead!

Golden Ass: a novel (c. A.D. 115), in which the hero is transformed into an ass. **one-eyed . . . brass:** confusion of two horses: one, of brass, belonging to a Tatar prince, the other the mount of a one-eyed king in **The Arabian Nights**

Body of turkey, head of owl,
Wings a-droop like a rained-on fowl,
Feathered and ruffled in every part,
Skipper Ireson stood in the cart.
Scores of women, old and young,
Strong of muscle, and glib of tongue,
Pushed and pulled up the rocky lane,
Shouting and singing the shrill refrain:

In the valuable and carefully prepared *History of Marblehead*, published in 1879 by Samuel Roads, Jr., it is stated that the crew of Captain Ireson, rather than himself, were responsible for the abandonment of the disabled vessel. To screen themselves they charged their captain with the crime. In view of this the writer of the ballad addressed the following letter to the historian: —

Oak Knoll, Danvers, 5 *mo.* 18, 1880.

My Dear Friend; I heartily thank thee for a copy of thy *History of Marblehead*. I have read it with great interest and think good use has been made of the abundant material. No town in Essex County has a record more honorable than Marblehead; no one has done more to develop the industrial interests of our New England seaboard; and certainly none have given such evidence of self-sacrificing patriotism. I am glad the story of it has been at last told, and told so well. I have now no doubt that thy version of Skipper Ireson's ride is the correct one. My verse was founded solely on a fragment of rhyme which I heard from one of my early schoolmates, a native of Marblehead.

I suppose the story to which it referred dated back at least a century. I knew nothing of the participators, and the narrative of the ballad was pure fancy. I am glad for the sake of truth and justice that the real facts are given in thy book. I certainly would not knowingly do injustice to any one, dead or living.

I am very truly thy friend,
John G. Whittier.
(Whittier's note)

From the *Complete Poetical Works of John Greenleaf Whittier*, edited by Horace E. Scudder (Cambridge edition). Reprinted by permission of Houghton Mifflin Company.

"Here's Flud Oirson, fur his horrd horrt,   20
Torr'd an' futherr'd an' corr'd in a corrt
    By the women o' Morble'ead!"

Wrinkled scolds with hands on hips,
Girls in bloom of cheek and lips,
Wild-eyed, free-limbed, such as chase
Bacchus round some antique vase,
Brief of skirt, with ankles bare,
Loose of kerchief and loose of hair,
With conch-shells blowing and fish-horns' twang,
Over and over the Mænads sang: 30
    "Here's Flud Oirson, fur his horrd horrt,
    Torr'd an' furtherr'd an' corr'd in a corrt
        By the women o' Morble'ead!"

Small pity for him! — He sailed away
From a leaking ship in Chaleur Bay, —
Sailed away from a sinking wreck,
With his own town's-people on her deck!
"Lay by! lay by!" they called to him.
Back he answered, "Sink or swim!
Brag of your catch of fish again!"   40
And off he sailed through the fog and rain!
    Old Floyd Ireson, for his hard heart,
    Tarred and feathered and carried in a cart
        By the women of Marblehead!

Fathoms deep in dark Chaleur
That wreck shall lie forevermore.
Mother and sister, wife and maid,
Looked from the rocks of Marblehead
Over the moaning and rainy sea, —
Looked for the coming that might not be!   50
What did the winds and the sea-birds say
Of the cruel captain who sailed away? —
    Old Floyd Ireson, for his hard heart,
    Tarred and feathered and carried in a cart
        By the women of Marblehead!

Through the street, on either side,
Up flew windows, doors swung wide;
Sharp-tongued spinsters, old wives gray,
Treble lent the fish-horn's bray.
Sea-worn grandsires, cripple-bound,   60
Hulks of old sailors run aground,
Shook head, and fist, and hat, and cane,
And cracked with curses the hoarse refrain:

"Here's Flud Oirson, fur his horrd horrt,
Torr'd an' furtherr'd an' corr'd in a corrt
    By the women o' Morble'ead!"

Sweetly along the Salem road
Bloom of orchard and lilac showed.
Little the wicked skipper knew
Of the fields so green and the sky so blue.   70
Riding there in his sorry trim,
Like an Indian idol glum and grim,
Scarcely he seemed the sound to hear
Of voices shouting, far and near:
    "Heres Flud Oirson, fur his horrd horrt,
    Torr'd an' furtherr'd an' corr'd in a corrt
        By the women o' Morble'ead!"

"Hear me, neighbors!" at last he cried, —
"What to me is this noisy ride?
What is the shame that clothes the skin   80
To the nameless horror that lives within?
Waking or sleeping, I see a wreck,
And hear a cry from a reeling deck!
Hate me and curse me, — I only dread
The hand of God and the face of the dead!"
    Said old Floyd Ireson, for his hard heart,
    Tarred and feathered and carried in a cart
        By the women of Marblehead!

Then the wife of the skipper lost at sea
Said, "God has touched him! why should we!"   90
Said an old wife mourning her only son,
"Cut the rogue's tether and let him run!"
So with soft relentings and rude excuse,
Half scorn, half pity, they cut him loose,
And gave him a cloak to hide him in,
And left him alone with his shame and sin.
    Poor Floyd Ireson, for his hard heart,
    Tarred and feathered and carried in a cart
        By the women of Marblehead!

Henry David Thoreau (1817–1862)

AMERICAN ESSAYIST and POET

Concerning Civil Disobedience

I heartily accept the motto, — "That government is best which governs least;" and I should like to see it acted up to more rapidly and systematically. Carried out, it finally amounts to this, which also I believe, — "That government is best which governs not at all;" and when men are prepared for it, that will be the kind of government which they will have. Government is at best but an expedient; but most governments are usually, and all governments are sometimes, inexpedient. The objections which have been brought against a standing army, and they are many and weighty, and deserve to prevail, may also at last be brought against a standing government. The standing army is only an arm of the standing government. The government itself, which is only the mode which the people have chosen to execute their will, is equally liable to be abused and perverted before the people can act through it. Witness the present Mexican war, the work of comparatively a few individuals using the standing government as their tool; for, in the outset, the people would not have consented to this measure.

This American government, — what is it but a tradition, though a recent one, endeavoring to transmit itself unimpaired to posterity, but each instant losing some of its integrity? It has not the vitality and force of a single living man; for a single man can bend it to his will. It is a sort of wooden gun to the people themselves. But it is not the less necessary for this; for the people must have some complicated machinery or other, and hear its din, to satisfy that idea of government which they have. Governments show thus how successfully men can be imposed on, even impose on themselves, for their own advantage. It is excellent, we must all allow. Yet this government never of itself furthered any enterprise, but by the alacrity with which it got out of its way. *It* does not keep the country free. *It* does not settle the West. *It* does not educate. The character inherent in the American people has done all that has been accomplished; and it would have done somewhat more, if the government had not sometimes got in its way. For government is an expedient by which men would fain succeed in letting one another alone; and, as has been said, when it is most expedient, the governed are most let alone by it. Trade and commerce, if they were not made of India-rubber, would never manage to bounce over the obstacles which legislators are continually putting in their way; and, if one were to judge these men wholly by the effects of their actions and not partly by their intentions, they would deserve to be classed

Title supplied by editors. From "Civil Disobedience" in *Miscellanies* in *The Writings of Henry David Thoreau*. Reprinted by permission of Houghton Mifflin Company.

529

and punished with those mischievous persons who put obstructions on the railroads.

But, to speak practically and as a citizen, unlike those who call themselves no-government men, I ask for, not at once no government, but *at once* a better government. Let every man make known what kind of government would command his respect, and that will be one step toward obtaining it.

After all, the practical reason why, when the power is once in the hands of the people, a majority are permitted, and for a long period continue, to rule is not because they are most likely to be in the right, nor because this seems fairest to the minority, but because they are physically the strongest. But a government in which the majority rule in all cases cannot be based on justice, even as far as men understand it. Can there not be a government in which majorities do not virtually decide right and wrong, but conscience? — in which majorities decide only those questions to which the rule of expediency is applicable? Must the citizen ever for a moment, or in the least degree, resign his conscience to the legislator? Why has every man a conscience, then? I think that we should be men first, and subjects afterward. It is not desirable to cultivate a respect for the law, so much as for the right. The only obligation which I have a right to assume is to do at any time what I think right. It is truly enough said, that a corporation has no conscience; but a corporation of conscientious men is a corporation *with* a conscience. Law never made men a whit more just; and, by means of their respect for it, even the well-disposed are daily made the agents of injustice. A common and natural result of an undue respect for law is, that you may see a file of soldiers, colonel, captain, corporal, privates, powder-monkeys, and all, marching in admirable order over hill and dale to the wars, against their wills, ay, against their common sense and consciences, which makes it very steep marching indeed, and produces a palpitation of the heart. They have no doubt that it is a damnable business in which they are concerned; they are all peaceably inclined. Now, what are they? Men at all? or small movable forts and magazines, at the service of some unscrupulous man in power? Visit the Navy-Yard, and behold a marine, such a man as an American government can make, or such as it can make a man with its black arts, — a mere shadow and reminiscence of humanity, a man laid out alive and standing, and already, as one may say, buried under arms with funeral accompaniments, though it may be, —

> "Not a drum was heard, not a funeral note,
>   As his corse to the rampart we hurried;
> Not a soldier discharged his farewell shot
>   O'er the grave where our hero we buried."

The mass of men serve the state thus, not as men mainly, but as machines, with their bodies. They are the standing army, and the militia, jailers, constables, posse comitatus,[1] etc. In most cases there is no free exercise whatever of the judgment or of the moral sense; but they put themselves on a level

[1] posse; literally, "power or authority of the country."

with wood and earth and stones; and wooden men can perhaps be manufactured that will serve the purpose as well. Such command no more respect than men of straw or a lump of dirt. They have the same sort of worth only as horses and dogs. Yet such as these even are commonly esteemed good citizens. Others — as most legislators, politicians, lawyers, ministers, and office-holders — serve the state chiefly with their heads; and, as they rarely make any moral distinctions, they are as likely to serve the Devil, without *intending* it, as God. A very few, as heroes, patriots, martyrs, reformers in the great sense, and *men*, serve the state with their consciences also, and so necessarily resist it for the most part; and they are commonly treated as enemies by it. A wise man will only be useful as a man, and will not submit to be "clay," and "stop a hole to keep the wind away," but leave that office to his dust at least: —

> "I am too high-born to be propertied,
> To be a secondary at control,
> Or useful serving-man and instrument
> To any sovereign state throughout the world."

He who gives himself entirely to his fellow-men appears to them useless and selfish; but he who gives himself partially to them is pronounced a benefactor and philanthropist.

How does it become a man to behave toward this American government to-day? I answer, that he cannot without disgrace be associated with it. I cannot for an instant recognize that political organization as *my* government which is the *slave's* government also. . . .

It is not a man's duty, as a matter of course, to devote himself to the eradication of any, even the most enormous wrong; he may still properly have other concerns to engage him; but it is his duty, at least, to wash his hands of it, and, if he gives it no thought longer, not to give it practically his support. If I devote myself to other pursuits and contemplations, I must first see, at least, that I do not pursue them sitting upon another man's shoulders. I must get off him first, that he may pursue his contemplations too. See what gross inconsistency is tolerated. I have heard some of my townsmen say, "I should like to have them order me out to help put down an insurrection of the slaves, or to march to Mexico; — see if I would go;" and yet these very men have each, directly by their allegiance, and so indirectly, at least, by their money, furnished a substitute. The soldier is applauded who refuses to serve in an unjust war by those who do not refuse to sustain the unjust government which makes the war; is applauded by those whose own act and authority he disregards and sets at naught; as if the state were penitent to that degree that it hired one to scourge it while it sinned, but not to that degree that it left off sinning for a moment. Thus, under the name of Order and Civil Government, we are all made at last to pay homage to and support our own meanness. After the first blush of sin comes its indifference; and from immoral it becomes, as it were, *un*moral, and not quite unnecessary to that life which we have made. . . .

I have paid no poll-tax for six years. I was put into a jail once on this account, for one night; and, as I stood considering the walls of solid stone, two or three feet thick, the door of wood and iron, a foot thick, and the iron grating which strained the light, I could not help being struck with the foolishness of that institution which treated me as if I were mere flesh and blood and bones, to be locked up. I wondered that it should have concluded at length that this was the best use it could put me to, and had never thought to avail itself of my services in some way. I saw that, if there was a wall of stone between me and my townsmen, there was a still more difficult one to climb or break through before they could get to be as free as I was. I did not for a moment feel confined, and the walls seemed a great waste of stone and mortar. I felt as if I alone of all my townsmen had paid my tax. They plainly did not know how to treat me, but behaved like persons who are underbred. In every threat and in every compliment there was a blunder; for they thought that my chief desire was to stand the other side of that stone wall. I could not but smile to see how industriously they locked the door on my meditations, which followed them out again without let or hindrance, and they were really all that was dangerous. As they could not reach me, they had resolved to punish my body; just as boys, if they cannot come at some person against whom they have a spite, will abuse his dog. I saw that the State was half-witted, that it was timid as a lone woman with her silver spoons, and that it did not know its friends from its foes, and I lost all my remaining respect for it, and pitied it.

Thus the State never intentionally confronts a man's sense, intellectual or moral, but only his body, his senses. It is not armed with superior wit or honesty, but with superior physical strength. I was not born to be forced. I will breathe after my own fashion. Let us see who is the strongest. What force has a multitude? They only can force me who obey a higher law than I. They force me to become like themselves. I do not hear of men being forced to live this way or that by masses of men. What sort of life were that to live? When I meet a government which says to me, "Your money or your life," why should I be in haste to give it my money? It may be in a great strait, and not know what to do: I cannot help that. It must help itself; do as I do. It is not worth the while to snivel about it. I am not responsible for the successful working of the machinery of society. I am not the son of the engineer. I perceive that, when an acorn and a chestnut fall side by side, the one does not remain inert to make way for the other, but both obey their own laws, and spring and grow and flourish as best they can, till one, perchance, overshadows and destroys the other. If a plant cannot live according to its nature, it dies; and so a man.

Leo Tolstoy (1828–1910)

RUSSIAN WRITER, AESTHETIC PHILOSOPHER,
MORALIST, and MYSTIC

A Matter of Justice

Returning from his journey through South Russia in the happiest state of mind, Pierre carried out an intention he had long had of visiting his friend Bolkónski, whom he had not seen for two years.

Boguchárovo lay in a flat uninteresting part of the country among fields and forests of fir and birch, which were partly cut down. The house lay behind a newly dug pond filled with water to the brink and with banks still bare of grass. It was at the end of a village that stretched along the highroad in the midst of a young copse in which were a few fir trees.

The homestead consisted of a threshing floor, outhouses, stables, a bathhouse, a lodge, and a large brick house with semicircular façade still in course of construction. Round the house was a garden newly laid out. The fences and gates were new and solid; two fire pumps and a water cart, painted green, stood in a shed; the paths were straight, the bridges were strong and had handrails. Everything bore an impress of tidiness and good management. Some domestic serfs Pierre met, in reply to inquiries as to where the prince lived, pointed out a small newly built lodge close to the pond. Antón, a man who had looked after Prince Andrew in his boyhood, helped Pierre out of his carriage, said that the prince was at home, and showed him into a clean little anteroom.

Pierre was struck by the modesty of the small though clean house after the brilliant surroundings in which he had last met his friend in Petersburg.

He quickly entered the small reception room with its still-unplastered wooden walls redolent of pine, and would have gone farther, but Antón ran ahead on tiptoe and knocked at a door.

"Well, what is it?" came a sharp, unpleasant voice.

"A visitor," answered Antón.

"Ask him to wait," and the sound was heard of a chair being pushed back.

Pierre went with rapid steps to the door and suddenly came face to face with Prince Andrew, who came out frowning and looking old. Pierre embraced him and lifting his spectacles kissed his friend on the cheek and looked at him closely.

"Well, I did not expect you, I am very glad," said Prince Andrew.

Pierre said nothing; he looked fixedly at his friend with surprise. He was struck by the change in him. His words were kindly and there was a smile

Title supplied by editors. From *War and Peace* by Leo Tolstoy, translated by Louise and Aylmer Maude, published by Oxford University Press. Reprinted by permission.

on his lips and face, but his eyes were dull and lifeless and in spite of his evident wish to do so he could not give them a joyous and glad sparkle. Prince Andrew had grown thinner, paler, and more manly-looking, but what amazed and estranged Pierre till he got used to it were his inertia and a wrinkle on his brow indicating prolonged concentration on some one thought.

As is usually the case with people meeting after a prolonged separation, it was long before their conversation could settle on anything. They put questions and gave brief replies about things they knew ought to be talked over at length. At last the conversation gradually settled on some of the topics at first lightly touched on: their past life, plans for the future, Pierre's journeys and occupations, the war,[1] and so on. The preoccupation and despondency which Pierre had noticed in his friend's look was now still more clearly expressed in the smile with which he listened to Pierre, especially when he spoke with joyful animation of the past or the future. It was as if Prince Andrew would have liked to sympathize with what Pierre was saying, but could not. The latter began to feel that it was in bad taste to speak of his enthusiasms, dreams, and hopes of happiness or goodness, in Prince Andrew's presence. He was ashamed to express his new Masonic views, which had been particularly revived and strengthened by his late tour. He checked himself, fearing to seem naïve, yet he felt an irresistible desire to show his friend as soon as possible that he was now a quite different, and better, Pierre than he had been in Petersburg.

"I can't tell you how much I have lived through since then. I hardly know myself again."

"Yes, we have altered much, very much, since then," said Prince Andrew.

"Well, and you? What are your plans?"

"Plans!" repeated Prince Andrew ironically. "My plans?" he said, as if astonished at the word. "Well, you see, I'm building. I mean to settle here altogether next year. . . ."

Pierre looked silently and searchingly into Prince Andrew's face, which had grown much older.

"No, I meant to ask . . ." Pierre began, but Prince Andrew interrupted him.

"But why talk of me? . . . Talk to me, yes, tell me about your travels and all you have been doing on your estates."

Pierre began describing what he had done on his estates, trying as far as possible to conceal his own part in the improvements that had been made. Prince Andrew several times prompted Pierre's story of what he had been doing, as though it were all an old-time story, and he listened not only without interest but even as if ashamed of what Pierre was telling him.

Pierre felt uncomfortable and even depressed in his friend's company and at last became silent.

"I'll tell you what, my dear fellow," said Prince Andrew, who evidently also felt depressed and constrained with his visitor, "I am only bivouacking here and have just come to look round. I am going back to my sister today.

---

[1] Napoleon's invasion of Russia in 1812.

I will introduce you to her. But of course you know her already," he said, evidently trying to entertain a visitor with whom he now found nothing in common. "We will go after dinner. And would you now like to look round my place?"

They went out and walked about till dinnertime, talking of the political news and common acquaintances like people who do not know each other intimately. Prince Andrew spoke with some animation and interest only of the new homestead he was constructing and its buildings, but even here, while on the scaffolding, in the midst of a talk explaining the future arrangements of the house, he interrupted himself:

"However, this is not at all interesting. Let us have dinner, and then we'll set off."

At dinner, conversation turned on Pierre's marriage.

"I was very much surprised when I heard of it," said Prince Andrew.

Pierre blushed, as he always did when it was mentioned, and said hurriedly: "I will tell you some time how it all happened. But you know it is all over, and forever."

"Forever?" said Prince Andrew. "Nothing's forever."

"But you know how it all ended, don't you? You heard of the duel?"

"And so you had to go through that too!"

"One thing I thank God for is that I did not kill that man," said Pierre.

"Why so?" asked Prince Andrew. "To kill a vicious dog is a very good thing really."

"No, to kill a man is bad — wrong."

"Why is it wrong?" urged Prince Andrew. "It is not given to man to know what is right and what is wrong. Men always did and always will err, and in nothing more than in what they consider right and wrong."

"What does harm to another is wrong," said Pierre, feeling with pleasure that for the first time since his arrival Prince Andrew was roused, had begun to talk, and wanted to express what had brought him to his present state.

"And who has told you what is bad for another man?" he asked.

"Bad! Bad!" exclaimed Pierre. "We all know what is bad for ourselves."

"Yes, we know that, but the harm I am conscious of in myself is something I cannot inflict on others," said Prince Andrew, growing more and more animated and evidently wishing to express his new outlook to Pierre. He spoke in French. "I only know two very real evils in life: remorse and illness. The only good is the absence of those evils. To live for myself avoiding those two evils is my whole philosophy now."

"And love of one's neighbor, and self-sacrifice?" began Pierre. "No, I can't agree with you! To live only so as not to do evil and not to have to repent is not enough. I lived like that, I lived for myself and ruined my life. And only now when I am living, or at least trying" (Pierre's modesty made him correct himself) "to live for others, only now have I understood all the happiness of life. No, I shall not agree with you, and you do not really believe what you are saying."

Prince Andrew looked silently at Pierre with an ironic smile.

"When you see my sister, Princess Mary, you'll get on with her," he said. "Perhaps you are right for yourself," he added after a short pause, "but everyone lives in his own way. You lived for yourself and say you nearly ruined your life and only found happiness when you began living for others. I experienced just the reverse. I lived for glory. — And after all what is glory? The same love of others, a desire to do something for them, a desire for their approval. — So I lived for others, and not almost, but quite, ruined my life. And I have become calmer since I began to live only for myself."

"But what do you mean by living only for yourself?" asked Pierre, growing excited. "What about your son, your sister, and your father?"

"But that's just the same as myself — they are not *others*," explained Prince Andrew. "The others, one's neighbors, *le prochain*,[2] as you and Princess Mary call it, are the chief source of all error and evil. *Le prochain* — your Kiev peasants to whom you want to do good."

And he looked at Pierre with a mocking, challenging expression. He evidently wished to draw him on.

"You are joking," replied Pierre, growing more and more excited. "What error or evil can there be in my wishing to do good, and even doing a little — though I did very little and did it very badly? What evil can there be in it if unfortunate people, our serfs, people like ourselves, were growing up and dying with no idea of God and truth beyond ceremonies and meaningless prayers and are now instructed in a comforting belief in future life, retribution, recompense, and consolation? What evil and error are there in it, if people were dying of disease without help while material assistance could so easily be rendered, and I supplied them with a doctor, a hospital, and an asylum for the aged? And is it not a palpable, unquestionable good if a peasant, or a woman with a baby, has no rest day or night and I give them rest and leisure?" said Pierre, hurrying and lisping. "And I have done that though badly and to a small extent; but I have done something toward it and you cannot persuade me that it was not a good action, and more than that, you can't make me believe that you do not think of yourself. And the main thing is," he continued, "that I know, and know for certain, that the enjoyment of doing this good is the only sure happiness in life."

"Yes, if you put it like that it's quite a different matter," said Prince Andrew. "I build a house and lay out a garden, and you build hospitals. The one and the other may serve as a pastime. But what's right and what's good must be judged by one who knows all, but not by us. Well, you want an argument," he added, "come on then."

They rose from the table and sat down in the entrance porch which served as a veranda.

"Come, let's argue then," said Prince Andrew. "You talk of schools," he went on, crooking a finger, "education and so forth; that is, you want to raise him" (pointing to a peasant who passed by them taking off his cap) "from

[2] mankind.

his animal condition and awaken in him spiritual needs, while it seems to me that animal happiness is the only happiness possible, and that is just what you want to deprive him of. I envy him, but you want to make him what I am, without giving him my means. Then you say, 'lighten his toil.' But as I see it, physical labor is as essential to him, as much a condition of his existence, as mental activity is to you or me. You can't help thinking. I go to bed after two in the morning, thoughts come and I can't sleep but toss about till dawn, because I think and can't help thinking, just as he can't help plowing and mowing; if he didn't, he would go to the drink shop or fall ill. Just as I could not stand his terrible physical labor but should die of it in a week, so he could not stand my physical idleness, but would grow fat and die. The third thing — what else was it you talked about?" and Prince Andrew crooked a third finger. "Ah, yes, hospitals, medicine. He has a fit, he is dying, and you come and bleed him and patch him up. He will drag about as a cripple, a burden to everybody, for another ten years. It would be far easier and simpler for him to die. Others are being born and there are plenty of them as it is. It would be different if you grudged losing a laborer — that's how I regard him — but you want to cure him from love of him. And he does not want that. And besides, what a notion that medicine ever cured anyone! Killed them, yes!" said he, frowning angrily and turning away from Pierre.

Prince Andrew expressed his ideas so clearly and distinctly that it was evident he had reflected on this subject more than once, and he spoke readily and rapidly like a man who has not talked for a long time. His glance became more animated as his conclusions became more hopeless.

"Oh, that is dreadful, dreadful!" said Pierre. "I don't understand how one can live with such ideas. I had such moments myself not long ago, in Moscow and when traveling, but at such times I collapse so that I don't live at all — everything seems hateful to me . . . myself most of all. Then I don't eat, don't wash . . . and how is it with you? . . ."

"Why not wash? That is not cleanly," said Prince Andrew; "on the contrary one must try to make one's life as pleasant as possible. I'm alive, that is not my fault, so I must live out my life as best I can without hurting others."

"But with such ideas what motive have you for living? One would sit without moving, undertaking nothing. . . ."

"Life as it is leaves one no peace. I should be thankful to do nothing, but here on the one hand the local nobility have done me the honor to choose me to be their marshal;[3] it was all I could do to get out of it. They could not understand that I have not the necessary qualifications for it — the kind of good-natured, fussy shallowness necessary for the position. Then there's this house, which must be built in order to have a nook of one's own in which to be quiet. And now there's this recruiting."

"Why aren't you serving in the army?"

"After Austerlitz!" said Prince Andrew gloomily. "No, thank you very

[3] Marshal of the nobility, *Maréchal de la noblesse*; the official representative of the nobility and landed gentry of a district. [A. Maude]

much! I have promised myself not to serve again in the active Russian army. And I won't — not even if Bonaparte were here at Smolénsk threatening Bald Hills — even then I wouldn't serve in the Russian army! Well, as I was saying," he continued, recovering his composure, "now there's this recruiting. My father is chief in command of the Third District, and my only way of avoiding active service is to serve under him."

"Then you are serving?"

"I am."

He paused a little while.

"And why do you serve?"

"Why, for this reason! My father is one of the most remarkable men of his time. But he is growing old, and though not exactly cruel he has too energetic a character. He is so accustomed to unlimited power that he is terrible, and now he has this authority of a commander in chief of the recruiting, granted by the Emperor. If I had been two hours late a fortnight ago he would have had a paymaster's clerk at Yúkhnovna hanged," said Prince Andrew with a smile. "So I am serving because I alone have any influence with my father, and now and then can save him from actions which would torment him afterwards."

"Well, there you see!"

"Yes, but it is not as you imagine," Prince Andrew continued. "I did not, and do not, in the least care about that scoundrel of a clerk who had stolen some boots from the recruits; I should even have been very glad to see him hanged, but I was sorry for my father — that again is for myself."

Prince Andrew grew more and more animated. His eyes glittered feverishly while he tried to prove to Pierre that in his actions there was no desire to do good to his neighbor.

"There now, you wish to liberate your serfs," he continued; "that is a very good thing, but not for you — I don't suppose you ever had anyone flogged or sent to Siberia — and still less for your serfs. If they are beaten, flogged, or sent to Siberia, I don't suppose they are any the worse off. In Siberia they lead the same animal life, and the stripes on their bodies heal, and they are happy as before. But it is a good thing for proprietors who perish morally, bring remorse upon themselves, stifle this remorse and grow callous, as a result of being able to inflict punishments justly and unjustly. It is those people I pity, and for their sake I should like to liberate the serfs. You may not have seen, but I have seen, how good men brought up in those traditions of unlimited power, in time when they grow more irritable, become cruel and harsh, are conscious of it, but cannot restrain themselves and grow more and more miserable."

Prince Andrew spoke so earnestly that Pierre could not help thinking that these thoughts had been suggested to Prince Andrew by his father's case.

He did not reply.

"So that's what I'm sorry for — human dignity, peace of mind, purity, and not the serfs' backs and foreheads, which, beat and shave[4] as you may, always remain the same backs and foreheads."

"No, no! A thousand times no! I shall never agree with you," said Pierre.

Emily Dickinson (1830–1886)

AMERICAN POET

Apparently with No Surprise

Apparently with no surprise
To any happy Flower
The Frost beheads it at it's play —
In accidental power —
The blonde Assassin passes on —
The Sun proceeds unmoved
To measure off another Day
For an Approving God.

William James (1842–1910)

AMERICAN PSYCHOLOGIST and PHILOSOPHER

The Aesthetics of Justice

The æsthetic principles are at bottom such axioms as that a note sounds good with its third and fifth, or that potatoes need salt. We are once for all so made that when certain impressions come before our mind, one of them

---

[4] A proprietor could send any of his serfs as exiles to Siberia, and when going there one side of the head was shaved, that the man might more easily be recaptured should he run away. [A. Maude]

"Apparently with No Surprise" by Emily Dickinson. Reprinted by permission of the publishers and the Trustees of Amherst College from Thomas H. Johnson, Editor, *The Poems of Emily Dickinson*, Cambridge, Mass.: The Belknap Press of Harvard University Press, Copyright, 1951, 1955, by The President and Fellows of Harvard College.

Title supplied by editors. "The Aesthetics of Justice" by William James. From *The Principles of Psychology* by William James, published by Holt, Rinehart and Winston, Inc. Reprinted by permission.

will seem to call for or repel the others as its companions. To a certain extent the principle of habit will explain these æsthetic connections. When a conjunction is repeatedly experienced, the cohesion of its terms grows grateful, or at least their disruption grows unpleasant. But to explain *all* æsthetic judgments in this way would be absurd; for it is notorious how seldom natural experiences come up to our æsthetic demands. Many of the so-called metaphysical principles are at bottom only expressions of æsthetic feeling. Nature is simple and invariable; makes no leaps, or makes nothing but leaps; is rationally intelligible; neither increases nor diminishes in quantity; flows from one principle, etc., etc., — what do all such principles express save our sense of how pleasantly our intellect would feel if it had a Nature of that sort to deal with? The subjectivity of which feeling is of course quite compatible with Nature also turning out objectively to be of that sort, later on.

The *moral* principles which our mental structure engenders are quite as little explicable *in toto* by habitual experiences having bred inner cohesions. Rightness is not *mere* usualness, wrongness not *mere* oddity, however numerous the facts which might be invoked to prove such identity. Nor are the moral judgments those most invariably and emphatically impressed on us by public opinion. The most characteristically and peculiarly moral judgments that a man is ever called on to make are in unprecedented cases and lonely emergencies, where no popular rhetorical maxims can avail, and the hidden oracle alone can speak; and it speaks often in favor of conduct quite unusual, and suicidal as far as gaining popular approbation goes. The forces which conspire to this resultant are subtle harmonies and discords between the elementary ideas which form the data of the case. Some of these harmonies, no doubt, have to do with habit; but in respect to most of them our sensibility must assuredly be a phenomenon of supernumerary order, correlated with a brain-function quite as secondary as that which takes cognizance of the diverse excellence of elaborate musical compositions. No more than the higher musical sensibility can the higher moral sensibility be accounted for by the frequency with which outer relations have cohered.[1] Take judgments of justice or equity, for example. Instinctively, one judges everything differently, according as it pertains to one's self or to some one else. Empirically one notices that everybody else does the same. But little by little there dawns in one the judgment "nothing can be right for me which would not be right for another similarly placed;" or "the fulfilment of my desires is intrinsically no more imperative than that of anyone else's;" or "what it is reasonable that

[1] As one example out of a thousand of exceptionally delicate idiosyncrasy in this regard, take this: "I must quit society. I would rather undergo twice the danger from beasts and ten times the danger from rocks. It is not pain, it is not death, that I dread, — it is the hatred of a man; there is something in it so shocking that I would rather submit to any injury than incur or increase the hatred of a man by revenging it. . . . Another sufficient reason for suicide is that I was this morning out of temper with Mrs. Douglas (for no fault of hers). I did not betray myself in the least, but I reflected that to be exposed to the possibility of such an event once a year, was evil enough to render life intolerable. The disgrace of using an impatient word is to me overpowering." (Elton Hammond, quoted in Henry Crabb Robinson's Diary, vol. I. p. 424.) (James' note)

another should do for me, it is also reasonable that I should do for him;"[2] and forthwith the whole mass of the habitual gets overturned. It gets *seriously* overturned only in a few fanatical heads. But its overturning is due to a back-door and not to a front-door process. Some minds are preternaturally sensitive to logical consistency and inconsistency. When they have ranked a thing under a kind, they *must* treat it as of that kind's kind, or feel all out of tune. In many respects we do class ourselves with other men, and call them and ourselves by a common name. They agree with us in having the same Heavenly Father, in not being consulted about their birth, in not being themselves to thank or blame for their natural gifts, in having the same desires and pains and pleasures, in short in a host of fundamental relations. Hence, *if these things be our essence*, we should be substitutable for other men, and they for us, in any proposition in which either of us is involved. The more fundamental and common the essence chosen, and the more simple the reasoning,[3] the more wildly radical and unconditional will the justice be which is aspired to. Life is one long struggle between conclusions based on abstract ways of conceiving cases, and opposite conclusions prompted by our instinctive perception of them as individual facts. The logical stickler for justice always seems pedantic and mechanical to the man who goes by tact and the particular instance, and who usually makes a poor show at argument. Sometimes the abstract conceiver's way is better, sometimes that of the man of instinct. But just as in our study of reasoning we found it impossible to lay down any mark whereby to distinguish right conception of a concrete case from *confusion*, so here we can give no general rule for deciding when it is morally useful to treat a concrete case as *sui generis*,[4] and when to lump it with others in an abstract class.[5]

[2] Compare H. Sidgwick, Methods of Ethics, bk. III, chap. XIII. §3. (James' note)

[3] A gentleman told me that he had a conclusive argument for opening the Harvard Medical School to women. It was this: "Are not women human?" — which major premise of course had to be granted. "Then are they not entitled to all the rights of humanity?" My friend said that he had never met anyone who could successfully meet this reasoning. (James' note)

[4] in a class by itself.

[5] You reach the Mephistophelian point of view as well as the point of view of justice by treating cases as if they belonged rigorously to abstract classes. Pure rationalism, complete immunity from prejudice, consists in refusing to see that the case before one is absolutely unique. It is always possible to treat the country of one's nativity, the house of one's fathers, the bed in which one's mother died, nay, the mother herself if need be, on a naked equality with all other specimens of so many respective genera. It shows the world in a clear frosty light from which all fuliginous mists of affection, all swamp-lights of sentimentality, are absent. Straight and immediate action becomes easy then — witness a Napoleon's or a Frederick's career. But the question always remains, "Are not the mists and vapors *worth* retaining?" The illogical refusal to treat certain concretes by the mere law of their genus has made the drama of human history. The obstinate insisting that tweedledum is *not* tweedledee is the bone and marrow of life. Look at the Jews and the Scots, with their miserable factions and sectarian disputes, their loyalties and patriotisms and exclusions, — their annals now become a classic heritage, because men of genius took part and sang in them. A thing is important if any one *think* it important. The process of history consists in certain folks becoming possessed of the mania that certain special things are important infinitely, whilst other folks cannot agree in the belief. The Shah of Persia refused to be

An adequate treatment of the way in which we come by our aesthetic and moral judgments which require a separate chapter, which I cannot conveniently include in this book. Suffice it that these judgments express inner harmonies and discords between objects of thought; and that whilst outer cohesions frequently repeated will often seem harmonious, all harmonies are not thus engendered, but our feeling of many of them is a secondary and incidental function of the mind. Where harmonies are asserted of the real world, they are obviously mere postulates of rationality, so far as they transcend experience. Such postulates are exemplified by the ethical propositions that the individual and universal good are one, and that happiness and goodness are bound to coalesce in the same subject.

---

taken to the Derby Day, saying "It is already known to me that one horse can run faster than another. He made the question *"which* horse?" immaterial. Any question can be made immaterial by subsuming all its answers under a common head. Imagine what college ball-games and races would be if the teams were to forget the absolute distinctness of Harvard from Yale and think of both as One in the higher genus College. The sovereign road to indifference, whether to evils or to goods, lies in the thought of the higher genus. "When we have meat before us," says Marcus Aurelius, seeking indifference to *that* kind of good, "we must receive the impression that this is the dead body of a fish, and this is the dead body of a bird or of a pig; and again that this Falernian is only a little grape-juice, and this purple robe some sheep's wool dyed with the blood of a shell-fish. Such, then, are these impressions, and they reach the things themselves and penetrate them, and we see what kind of things they are. Just in the same way ought we to act through life, and where there are things which appear most worthy of our approbation, we ought to lay them bare and look at their worthlessness and strip them of all the words by which they are exalted." (Long's Translation, VI. 13.) (James' note)

Gerard Manley Hopkins (1844–1889)

ENGLISH POET and CLERGYMAN

Thou Art Indeed Just, Lord

*Justus quidem tu es, Domine, si disputem tecum: verumtamen
justa loquar ad te: Quare via impiorum prosperatur? &c.*[1]

Thou art indeed just, Lord, if I contend
With thee; but, sir, so what I plead is just.
Why do sinners' ways prosper? and why must
Disappointment all I endeavour end?
  Wert thou my enemy, O thou my friend,
How wouldst thou worse, I wonder, than thou dost
Defeat, thwart me? Oh, the sots and thralls of lust
Do in spare hours more thrive than I that spend,
Sir, life upon thy cause. See, banks and brakes
Now, leavèd how thick! lacèd they are again   10
With fretty chervil, look, and fresh wind shakes
Them; birds build — but not I build; no, but strain,
Time's eunuch, and not breed one work that wakes.
Mine, O thou lord of life, send my roots rain.

Edwin Arlington Robinson (1869–1935)

AMERICAN POET

Richard Cory

Whenever Richard Cory went down town,
We people on the pavement looked at him:
He was a gentleman from sole to crown,
Clean favored, and imperially slim.

And he was always quietly arrayed,
And he was always human when he talked;
But still he fluttered pulses when he said,
"Good-morning," and he glittered when he walked.

And he was rich — yes, richer than a king —
And admirably schooled in every grace: 10
In fine, we thought that he was everything
To make us wish that we were in his place.

So on we worked, and waited for the light,
And went without the meat, and cursed the bread;
And Richard Cory, one calm summer night,
Went home and put a bullet through his head.

Akutagawa Ryūnosuke (1892–1927)

JAPANESE NOVELIST, SHORT STORY WRITER, and POET

In a Grove

The Testimony of a Woodcutter Questioned by a High Police Commissioner

Yes, sir. Certainly, it was I who found the body. This morning, as usual, I went to cut my daily quota of cedars, when I found the body in a grove in a hollow in the mountains. The exact location? About 150 meters off the Yamashina stage road. It's an out-of-the-way grove of bamboo and cedars.

The body was lying flat on its back dressed in a bluish silk kimono and a wrinkled head-dress of the Kyoto style. A single sword-stroke had pierced the breast. The fallen bamboo-blades around it were stained with bloody blossoms. No, the blood was no longer running. The wound had dried up, I believe. And also, a gad-fly was stuck fast there, hardly noticing my footsteps.

You ask me if I saw a sword or any such thing?

No, nothing, sir. I found only a rope at the root of a cedar near by. And . . . well, in addition to a rope, I found a comb. That was all. Apparently he must have made a battle of it before he was murdered, because the grass and fallen bamboo-blades had been trampled down all around.

"A horse was near by?"

No, sir. It's hard enough for a man to enter, let alone a horse.

THE TESTIMONY OF A TRAVELING BUDDHIST PRIEST QUESTIONED BY A HIGH POLICE COMMISSIONER

The time? Certainly, it was about noon yesterday, sir. The unfortunate man was on the road from Sekiyama to Yamashina. He was walking toward Sekiyama with a woman accompanying him on horseback, who I have since learned was his wife. A scarf hanging from her head hid her face from view. All I saw was the color of her clothes, a lilac-colored suit. Her horse was a sorrel with a fine mane. The lady's height? Oh, about four feet five inches. Since I am a Buddhist priest, I took little notice about her details. Well, the man was armed with a sword as well as a bow and arrows. And I remember that he carried some twenty odd arrows in his quiver.

Little did I expect that he would meet such a fate. Truly human life is as evanescent as the morning dew or a flash of lightning. My words are inadequate to express my sympathy for him.

THE TESTIMONY OF A POLICEMAN QUESTIONED BY A HIGH POLICE COMMISSIONER

The man that I arrested? He is a notorious brigand called Tajomaru. When I arrested him, he had fallen off his horse. He was groaning on the bridge at Awataguchi. The time? It was in the early hours of last night. For the record, I might say that the other day I tried to arrest him, but unfortunately he escaped. He was wearing a dark blue silk kimono and a large plain sword. And, as you see, he got a bow and arrows somewhere. You say that this bow and these arrows look like the ones owned by the dead man? Then Tajomaru must be the murderer. The bow wound with leather strips, the black lacquered quiver, the seventeen arrows with hawk feathers — these were all in his possession I believe. Yes, sir, the horse is, as you say, a sorrel with a fine mane. A little beyond the stone bridge I found the horse grazing by the roadside, with his long rein dangling. Surely there is some providence in his having been thrown by the horse.

Of all the robbers prowling around Kyoto, this Tajomaru has given the most grief to the women in town. Last autumn a wife who came to the mountain back of the Pindora of the Toribe Temple, presumably to pay a visit, was murdered, along with a girl. It has been suspected that it was his doing. If this criminal murdered the man, you cannot tell what he may have done with the man's wife. May it please your honor to look into this problem as well.

The Testimony of an Old Woman Questioned
by a High Police Commissioner

Yes, sir, that corpse is the man who married my daughter. He does not come from Kyoto. He was a samurai in the town of Kokufu in the province of Wakasa. His name was Kanazawa no Takehiko, and his age was twenty-six. He was of a gentle disposition, so I am sure he did nothing to provoke the anger of others.

My daughter? Her name is Masago, and her age is nineteen. She is a spirited, fun-loving girl, but I am sure she has never known any man except Takehiko. She has a small, oval, dark-complected face with a mole at the corner of her left eye.

Yesterday Takehiko left for Wakasa with my daughter. What bad luck it is that things should have come to such a sad end! What has become of my daughter? I am resigned to giving up my son-in-law as lost, but the fate of my daughter worries me sick. For heaven's sake leave no stone unturned to find her. I hate that robber Tajomaru, or whatever his name is. Not only my son-in-law, but my daughter . . . (Her later words were drowned in tears.)

Tajomaru's Confession

I killed him, but not her. Where's she gone? I can't tell. Oh, wait a minute. No torture can make me confess what I don't know. Now things have come to such a head, I won't keep anything from you.

Yesterday a little past noon I met that couple. Just then a puff of wind blew, and raised her hanging scarf, so that I caught a glimpse of her face. Instantly it was again covered from my view. That may have been one reason; she looked like a Bodhisattva. At that moment I made up my mind to capture her even if I had to kill her man.

Why? To me killing isn't a matter of such great consequence as you might think. When a woman is captured, her man has to be killed anyway. In killing, I use the sword I wear at my side. Am I the only one who kills people? You, you don't use your swords. You kill people with your power, with your money. Sometimes you kill them on the pretext of working for their good. It's true they don't bleed. They are in the best of health, but all the same you've killed them. It's hard to say who is a greater sinner, you or me. (An ironical smile.)

But it would be good if I could capture a woman without killing her man. So, I made up my mind to capture her, and do my best not to kill him. But it's out of the question on the Yamashina stage road. So I managed to lure the couple into the mountains.

It was quite easy. I became their traveling companion, and I told them there was an old mound in the mountain over there, and that I had dug it open and found many mirrors and swords. I went on to tell them I'd buried the things in a grove behind the mountain, and that I'd like to sell them at a low price to anyone who would care to have them. Then . . . you see, isn't greed terrible? He was beginning to be moved by my talk before he knew it. In less than half an hour they were driving their horse toward the mountain with me.

When he came in front of the grove, I told them that the treasures were buried in it, and I asked them to come and see. The man had no objection — he was blinded by greed. The woman said she would wait on horseback. It was natural for her to say so, at the sight of a thick grove. To tell you the truth, my plan worked just as I wished, so I went into the grove with him, leaving her behind alone.

The grove is only bamboo for some distance. About fifty yards ahead there's a rather open clump of cedars. It was a convenient spot for my purpose. Pushing my way through the grove, I told him a plausible lie that the treasures were buried under the cedars. When I told him this, he pushed his laborious way toward the slender cedar visible through the grove. After a while the bamboo thinned out, and we came to where a number of cedars grew in a row. As soon as we got there, I seized him from behind. Because he was a trained, sword-bearing warrior, he was quite strong, but he was taken by surprise, so there was no help for him. I soon tied him up to the root of a cedar. Where did I get a rope? Thank heaven, being a robber, I had a rope with me, since I might have to scale a wall at any moment. Of course it was easy to stop him from calling out by gagging his mouth with fallen bamboo leaves.

When I disposed of him, I went to his woman and asked her to come and see him, because he seemed to have been suddenly taken sick. It's needless to say that this plan also worked well. The woman, her sedge hat off, came into the depths of the grove, where I led her by the hand. The instant she caught sight of her husband, she drew a small sword. I've never seen a woman of such violent temper. If I'd been off guard, I'd have got a thrust in my side. I dodged, but she kept on slashing at me. She might have wounded me deeply or killed me: But I'm Tajomaru. I managed to strike down her small sword without drawing my own. The most spirited woman is defenseless without a weapon. At last I could satisfy my desire for her without taking her husband's life.

Yes, . . . without taking his life. I had no wish to kill him. I was about to run away from the grove, leaving the woman behind in tears, when she frantically clung to my arm. In broken fragments of words, she asked that either her husband or I die. She said it was more trying than death to have her shame known to two men. She gasped out that she wanted to be the wife of whichever survived. Then a furious desire to kill him seized me. (Gloomy excitement.)

Telling you in this way, no doubt I seem a crueler man than you. But that's because you didn't see her face. Especially her burning eyes at that moment. As I saw her eye to eye, I wanted to make her my wife even if I were to be struck by lightning. I wanted to make her my wife . . . this single desire filled my mind. This was not only lust, as you might think. At that time if I'd had no other desire than lust, I'd surely not have minded knocking her down and running away. Then I wouldn't have stained my sword with his blood. But the moment I gazed at her face in the dark grove, I decided not to leave there without killing him.

But I didn't like to resort to unfair means to kill him. I untied him and told him to cross swords with me. (The rope that was found at the root of the cedar is the rope I dropped at the time.) Furious with anger, he drew his thick sword. And quick as thought, he sprang at me ferociously, without speaking a word. I needn't tell you how our fight turned out. The twenty-third stroke . . . please remember this. I'm impressed with this fact still. Nobody under the sun has ever clashed swords with me twenty strokes. (A cheerful smile.)

When he fell, I turned toward her, lowering my blood-stained sword. But to my great astonishment she was gone. I wondered to where she had run away. I looked for her in the clump of cedars. I listened, but heard only a groaning sound from the throat of the dying man.

As soon as we started to cross swords, she may have run away through the grove to call for help. When I thought of that, I decided it was a matter of life and death to me. So, robbing him of his sword, and bow and arrows, I ran out to the mountain road. There I found her horse still grazing quietly. It would be a mere waste [of] words to tell you the later details, but before I entered town I had already parted with the sword. That's all my confession. I know that my head will be hung in chains anyway, so put me down for the maximum penalty. (A defiant attitude.)

The Confession of a Woman Who Has Come to the *Shimizu* Temple[1]

That man in the blue silk kimono, after forcing me to yield to him, laughed mockingly as he looked at my bound husband. How horrified my husband must have been! But no matter how hard he struggled in agony, the rope cut into him all the more tightly. In spite of myself I ran stumblingly toward his side. Or rather I tried to run toward him, but the man instantly knocked me down. Just at that moment I saw an indescribable light in my husband's eyes. Something beyond expression . . . his eyes make me shudder even now. That instantaneous look of my husband, who couldn't speak a word, told me all his heart. The flash in his eyes was neither anger nor sorrow . . . only a cold light, a look of loathing. More struck by the look in his eyes than by the blow of the thief, I called out in spite of myself and fell unconscious.

---

[1] Buddhist temple in Kyoto.

In the course of time I came to, and found that the man in blue silk was gone. I saw only my husband still bound to the root of the cedar. I raised myself from the bamboo-blades with difficulty, and looked into his face; but the expression in his eyes was just the same as before.

Beneath the cold contempt in his eyes, there was hatred. Shame, grief, and anger . . . I don't know how to express my heart at that time. Reeling to my feet, I went up to my husband.

"Takejiro," I said to him, "since things have come to this pass, I cannot live with you. I'm determined to die, . . . but you must die, too. You saw my shame. I can't leave you alive as you are."

This was all I could say. Still he went on gazing at me with loathing and contempt. My heart breaking, I looked for his sword. It must have been taken by the robber. Neither his sword nor his bow and arrows were to be seen in the grove. But fortunately my small sword was lying at my feet. Raising it over head, once more I said, "Now give me your life. I'll follow you right away."

When he heard these words, he moved his lips with difficulty. Since his mouth was stuffed with leaves, of course his voice could not be heard at all. But at a glance I understood his words. Despising me, his look said only, "Kill me." Neither conscious nor unconscious, I stabbed the small sword through the lilac-colored kimono into his breast.

Again at this time I must have fainted. By the time I managed to look up, he had already breathed his last — still in bonds. A streak of sinking sunlight streamed through the clump of cedars and bamboos, and shone on his pale face. Gulping down my sobs, I untied the rope from his dead body. And . . . and what has become of me since I have no more strength to tell you. Anyway I hadn't the strength to die. I stabbed my own throat with the small sword, I threw myself into a pond at the foot of the mountain, and I tried to kill myself in many ways. Unable to end my life, I am still living in dishonor. (A lonely smile.) Worthless as I am, I must have been forsaken even by the most merciful Kwannon. I killed my own husband. I was violated by the robber. Whatever can I do? Whatever can I . . . I . . . (Gradually, violent sobbing.)

The Story of the Murdered Man, as Told
through a Medium

After violating my wife, the robber, sitting there, began to speak comforting words to her. Of course I couldn't speak. My whole body was tied fast to the root of a cedar. But meanwhile I winked at her many times, as much as to say "Don't believe the robber." I wanted to convey some such meaning to her. But my wife, sitting dejectedly on the bamboo leaves, was looking hard at her lap. To all appearance, she was listening to his words. I was agonized by jealousy. In the meantime the robber went on with his clever talk, from one subject to another. The robber finally made his bold, brazen proposal. "Once your virtue is stained, you won't get along well with your husband, so won't you be my wife instead? It's my love for you that made me be violent toward you."

While the criminal talked, my wife raised her face as if in a trance. She had never looked so beautiful as at that moment. What did my beautiful wife say in answer to him while I was sitting bound there? I am lost in space, but I have never thought of her answer without burning with anger and jealousy. Truly she said, . . . "Then take me away with you wherever you go."

This is not the whole of her sin. If that were all, I would not be tormented so much in the dark. When she was going out of the grove as if in a dream, her hand in the robber's, she suddenly turned pale, and pointed at me tied to the root of the cedar, and said, "Kill him! I cannot marry you as long as he lives." "Kill him!" she cried many times, as if she had gone crazy. Even now these words threaten to blow me headlong into the bottomless abyss of darkness. Has such a hateful thing come out of a human mouth ever before? Have such cursed words ever struck a human ear, even once? Even once such a . . . (A sudden cry of scorn.) At these words the robber himself turned pale. "Kill him," she cried, clinging to his arms. Looking hard at her, he answered neither yes nor no. . . . but hardly had I thought about his answer before she had been knocked down into the bamboo leaves. (Again a cry of scorn.) Quietly folding his arms, he looked at me and said, "What will you do with her? Kill her or save her? You have only to nod. Kill her?" For these words alone I would like to pardon his crime.

While I hesitated, she shrieked and ran into the depths of the grove. The robber instantly snatched at her, but he failed even to grasp her sleeve.

After she ran away, he took up my sword, and my bow and arrows. With a single stroke he cut one of my bonds. I remember his mumbling, "My fate is next." Then he disappeared from the grove. All was silent after that. No, I heard someone crying. Untying the rest of my bonds, I listened carefully, and I noticed that it was my own crying. (Long silence.)

I raised my exhausted body from the root of the cedar. In front of me there was shining the small sword which my wife had dropped. I took it up and stabbed it into my breast. A bloody lump rose to my mouth, but I didn't feel any pain. When my breast grew cold, everything was as silent as the dead in their graves. What profound silence! Not a single bird-note was heard in the sky over this grave in the hollow of the mountains. Only a lonely light lingered on the cedars and mountain. By and by the light gradually grew fainter, till the cedars and bamboo were lost to view. Lying there, I was enveloped in deep silence.

Then someone crept up to me. I tried to see who it was. But darkness had already been gathering round me. Someone . . . that someone drew the small sword softly out of my breast in its invisible hand. At the same time once more blood flowed into my mouth. And once and for all I sank down into the darkness of space.

Robert Graves (b. 1895)

ENGLISH POET, NOVELIST, and ANTHROPOLOGIST

The Blue-Fly

Five summer days, five summer nights,
The ignorant, loutish, giddy blue-fly
Hung without motion on the cling peach,
Humming occasionally: 'O my love, my fair one!'
    As in the *Canticles.*

Magnified one thousand times, the insect
Looks farcically human; laugh if you will!
Bald head, stage-fairy wings, blear eyes,
A caved-in chest, hairy black mandibles,
    Long spindly thighs.   10

The crime was detected on the sixth day.
What then could be said or done? By anyone?
It would have been vindictive, mean and what-not
To swat that fly for being a blue-fly,
    For debauch of a peach.

Is it fair, either, to bring a microscope
To bear on the case, even in search of truth?
Nature, doubtless, has some compelling cause
To glut the carriers of her epidemics —
    Nor did the peach complain.   20

William Faulkner (1897–1963)

AMERICAN NOVELIST and SHORT STORY WRITER

Dry September

I

Through the bloody September twilight, aftermath of sixty-two rainless days, it had gone like a fire in dry grass — the rumor, the story, whatever it was. Something about Miss Minnie Cooper and a Negro. Attacked, insulted, frightened: none of them, gathered in the barber shop on that Saturday evening where the ceiling fan stirred, without freshening it, the vitiated air, sending back upon them, in recurrent surges of stale pomade and lotion, their own stale breath and odors, knew exactly what had happened.

"Except it wasn't Will Mayes," a barber said. He was a man of middle age; a thin, sand-colored man with a mild face, who was shaving a client. "I know Will Mayes. He's a good nigger. And I know Miss Minnie Cooper, too."

"What do you know about her?" a second barber said.

"Who is she?" the client said. "A young girl?"

"No," the barber said. "She's about forty, I reckon. She ain't married. That's why I don't believe — "

"Believe, hell!" a hulking youth in a sweat-stained silk shirt said. "Wont you take a white woman's word before a nigger's?"

"I dont believe Will Mayes did it," the barber said. "I know Will Mayes."

"Maybe you know who did it, then. Maybe you already got him out of town, you damn niggerlover."

"I dont believe anybody did anything. I don't believe anything happened. I leave it to you fellows if them ladies that get old without getting married dont have notions that a man cant — "

"Then you are a hell of a white man," the client said. He moved under the cloth. The youth had sprung to his feet.

"You dont?" he said. "Do you accuse a white woman of lying?"

The barber held the razor poised above the half-risen client. He did not look around.

"It's this durn weather," another said. "It's enough to make a man do anything. Even to her."

Nobody laughed. The barber said in his mild, stubborn tone: "I aint accusing nobody of nothing. I just know and you fellows know how a woman that never — "

"You damn niggerlover!" the youth said.

"Shut up, Butch," another said. "We'll get the facts in plenty of time to act."

"Who is? Who's getting them?" the youth said. "Facts, hell! I — "

"You're a fine white man," the client said. "Aint you?" In his frothy beard he looked like a desert rat in the moving pictures. "You tell them, Jack," he said to the youth. "If there aint any white men in this town, you can count on me, even if I aint only a drummer[1] and a stranger."

"That's right, boys," the barber said. "Find out the truth first. I know Will Mayes."

"Well, by God!" the youth shouted. "To think that a white man in this town — "

"Shut up, Butch," the second speaker said. "We got plenty of time."

The client sat up. He looked at the speaker. "Do you claim that anything excuses a nigger attacking a white woman? Do you mean to tell me you are a white man and you'll stand for it? You better go back North where you came from. The South dont want your kind here."

"North what?" the second said. "I was born and raised in this town."

"Well, by God!" the youth said. He looked about with a strained, baffled gaze, as if he was trying to remember what it was he wanted to say or to do. He drew his sleeve across his sweating face. "Damn if I'm going to let a white woman — "

"You tell them, Jack," the drummer said. "By God, if they — "

The screen door crashed open. A man stood in the floor, his feet apart and his heavy-set body poised easily. His white shirt was open at the throat; he wore a felt hat. His hot, bold glance swept the group. His name was McLendon. He had commanded troops at the front in France and had been decorated for valor.

"Well," he said, "are you going to sit there and let a black son rape a white woman on the streets of Jefferson?"

Butch sprang up again. The silk of his shirt clung flat to his heavy shoulders. At each armpit was a dark halfmoon. "That's what I been telling them! That's what I — "

"Did it really happen?" a third said. "This aint the first man scare she ever had, like Hawkshaw says. Wasn't there something about a man on the kitchen roof, watching her undress, about a year ago?"

"What?" the client said. "What's that?" The barber had been slowly forcing him back into the chair; he arrested himself reclining, his head lifted, the barber still pressing him down.

McLendon whirled on the third speaker. "Happen? What the hell difference does it make? Are you going to let the black sons get away with it until one really does it?"

"That's what I'm telling them!" Butch shouted. He cursed, long and steady, pointless.

[1] traveling salesman.

"Here, here," a fourth said. "Not so loud. Dont talk so loud."

"Sure," McLendon said; "no talking necessary at all. I've done my talking. Who's with me?" He poised on the balls of his feet, roving his gaze.

The barber held the drummer's face down, the razor poised. "Find out the facts first, boys. I know Willy Mayes. It wasn't him. Let's get the sheriff and do this thing right."

McLendon whirled upon him his furious, rigid face. The barber did not look away. They looked like men of different races. The other barbers had ceased also above their prone clients. "You mean to tell me," McLendon said, "that you'd take a nigger's word before a white woman's? Why, you damn niggerloving — "

The third speaker rose and grasped McLendon's arm; he too had been a soldier. "Now, now. Let's figure this thing out. Who knows anything about what really happened?"

"Figure out hell!" McLendon jerked his arm free. "All that're with me get up from there. The ones that aint — " He roved his gaze, dragging his sleeve across his face.

Three men rose. The drummer in the chair sat up. "Here," he said, jerking at the cloth about his neck; "get this rag off me. I'm with him. I dont live here, but by God, if our mothers and wives and sisters — " He smeared the cloth over his face and flung it to the floor. McLendon stood in the floor and cursed the others. Another rose and moved toward him. The remainder sat uncomfortable, not looking at one another, then one by one they rose and joined him.

The barber picked the cloth from the floor. He began to fold it neatly. "Boys, dont do that. Will Mayes never done it. I know."

"Come on," McLendon said. He whirled. From his hip pocket protruded the butt of a heavy automatic pistol. They went out. The screen door crashed behind them reverberant in the dead air.

The barber wiped the razor carefully and swiftly, and put it away, and ran to the rear, and took his hat from the wall. "I'll be back as soon as I can," he said to the other barbers. "I cant let — " He went out, running. The two other barbers followed him to the door and caught it on the rebound, leaning out and looking up the street after him. The air was flat and dead. It had a metallic taste at the base of the tongue.

"What can he do?" the first said. The second one was saying "Jees Christ, Jees Christ" under his breath. "I'd just as lief be Will Mayes as Hawk, if he gets McLendon riled."

"Jees Christ, Jees Christ," the second whispered.

"You reckon he really done it to her?" the first said.

II

She was thirty-eight or thirty-nine. She lived in a small frame house with her invalid mother and a thin, sallow, unflagging aunt, where each morning between ten and eleven she would appear on the porch in a lace-trimmed boudoir cap, to sit swinging in the porch swing until noon. After dinner she lay down for a while, until the afternoon began to cool. Then, in one of the three or four new voile dresses which she had each summer, she would go downtown to spend the afternoon in the stores with the other ladies, where they would handle the goods and haggle over the prices in cold, immediate voices, without any intention of buying.

She was of comfortable people — not the best in Jefferson, but good people enough — and she was still on the slender side of ordinary looking, with a bright, faintly haggard manner and dress. When she was young she had had a slender, nervous body and a sort of hard vivacity which had enabled her for a time to ride upon the crest of the town's social life as exemplified by the high school party and church social period of her contemporaries while still children enough to be unclassconscious.

She was the last to realize that she was losing ground; that those among whom she had been a little brighter and louder flame than any other were beginning to learn the pleasure of snobbery — male — and retaliation — female. That was when her face began to wear that bright, haggard look. She still carried it to parties on shadowy porticoes and summer lawns, like a mask or a flag, with that bafflement of furious repudiation of truth in her eyes. One evening at a party she heard a boy and two girls, all schoolmates, talking. She never accepted another invitation.

She watched the girls with whom she had grown up as they married and got homes and children, but no man ever called on her steadily until the children of the other girls had been calling her "aunty" for several years, the while their mothers told them in bright voices about how popular Aunt Minnie had been as a girl. Then the town began to see her driving on Sunday afternoons with the cashier in the bank. He was a widower of about forty — a high-colored man, smelling always faintly of the barber shop or of whisky. He owned the first automobile in town, a red runabout; Minnie had the first motoring bonnet and veil the town ever saw. Then the town began to say: "Poor Minnie." "But she is old enough to take care of herself," others said. That was when she began to ask her old schoolmates that their children call her "cousin" instead of "aunty."

It was twelve years now since she had been relegated into adultery by public opinion, and eight years since the cashier had gone to a Memphis bank, returning for one day each Christmas, which he spent at an annual bachelors' party at a hunting club on the river. From behind their curtains the neighbors would see the party pass, and during the over-the-way Christmas day visiting they would tell her about him, about how well he looked, and how they heard that he was prospering in the city, watching with bright, secret eyes her haggard, bright face. Usually by that hour there would be the scent of whisky on her breath. It was supplied her by a youth, a clerk at the soda fountain: "Sure; I buy it for the old gal. I reckon she's entitled to a little fun."

Her mother kept to her room altogether now; the gaunt aunt ran the house. Against that background Minnie's bright dresses, her idle and empty days, had a quality of furious unreality. She went out in the evenings only with women now, neighbors, to the moving pictures. Each afternoon she dressed in one of the new dresses and went downtown alone, where her young "cousins" were already strolling in the late afternoons with their delicate, silken heads and thin, awkward arms and conscious hips, clinging to one another or shrieking and giggling with paired boys in the soda fountain when she passed and went on along the serried store fronts, in the doors of which the sitting and lounging men did not even follow her with their eyes any more.

III

The barber went swiftly up the street where the sparse lights, insect-swirled, glared in rigid and violent suspension in the lifeless air. The day had died in a pall of dust; above the darkened square, shrouded by the spent dust, the sky was as clear as the inside of a brass bell. Below the east was a rumor of the twice-waxed moon.

When he overtook them McLendon and three others were getting into a car parked in an alley. McLendon stooped his thick head, peering out beneath the top. "Changed your mind, did you?" he said. "Damn good thing; by God, tomorrow when this town hears about how you talked tonight — "

"Now, now," the other ex-soldier said. "Hawkshaw's all right. Come on, Hawk; jump in."

"Will Mayes never done it, boys," the barber said. "If anybody done it. Why, you all know well as I do there aint any town where they got better niggers than us. And you know how a lady will kind of think things about men when there aint any reason to, and Miss Minnie anyway — "

"Sure, sure," the soldier said. "We're just going to talk to him a little; that's all."

"Talk hell!" Butch said. "When we're through with the — "

"Shut up, for God's sake!" the soldier said. "Do you want everybody in town — "

"Tell them, by God!" McLendon said. "Tell every one of the sons that'll let a white woman — "

"Let's go; let's go: here's the other car." The second car slid squealing out of a cloud of dust at the alley mouth. McLendon started his car and took the lead. Dust lay like fog in the street. The street lights hung nimbused as in water. They drove on out of town.

A rutted lane turned at right angles. Dust hung above it too, and above all the land. The dark bulk of the ice plant, where the Negro Mayes was night watchman, rose against the sky. "Better stop here, hadn't we?" the soldier said. McLendon did not reply. He hurled the car up and slammed to a stop, the headlights glaring on the blank wall.

"Listen here, boys," the barber said; "if he's here, dont that prove he never done it? Dont it? If it was him, he would run. Dont you see he would?" The second car came up and stopped. McLendon got down; Butch sprang down beside him. "Listen, boys," the barber said.

"Cut the lights off!" McLendon said. The breathless dark rushed down. There was no sound in it save their lungs as they sought air in the parched dust in which for two months they had lived; then the diminishing crunch of McLendon's and Butch's feet, and a moment later McLendon's voice:

"Will! . . . Will!"

Below the east the wan hemorrhage of the moon increased. It heaved above the ridge, silvering the air, the dust, so that they seemed to breathe, live, in a bowl of molten lead. There was no sound of nightbird nor insect, no sound save their breathing and a faint ticking of contracting metal about the cars. Where their bodies touched one another they seemed to sweat dryly, for no more moisture came. "Christ!" a voice said; "let's get out of here."

But they didn't move until vague noises began to grow out of the darkness ahead; then they got out and waited tensely in the breathless dark. There was another sound: a blow, a hissing expulsion of breath and McLendon cursing in undertone. They stood a moment longer, then they ran forward. They ran in a stumbling clump, as though they were fleeing something. "Kill him, kill the son," a voice whispered. McLendon flung them back.

"Not here," he said. "Get him into the car." "Kill him, kill the black son!" the voice murmured. They dragged the Negro to the car. The barber had waited beside the car. He could feel himself sweating and he knew he was going to be sick at the stomach.

"What is it, captains?" the Negro said. "I aint done nothing. 'Fore God, Mr John." Someone produced handcuffs. They worked busily about the Negro as though he were a post, quiet, intent, getting in one another's way. He submitted to the handcuffs, looking swiftly and constantly from dim face to dim face. "Who's here, captains?" he said, leaning to peer into the faces until they could feel his breath and smell his sweaty reek. He spoke a name or two. "What you all say I done, Mr John?"

McLendon jerked the car door open. "Get in!" he said.

The Negro did not move. "What you all going to do with me, Mr John? I aint done nothing. White folks, captains, I aint done nothing: I swear 'fore God." He called another name.

"Get in!" McLendon said. He struck the Negro. The others expelled their breath in a dry hissing and struck him with random blows and he whirled and cursed them, and swept his manacled hands across their faces and slashed the barber upon the mouth, and the barber struck him also. "Get him in there," McLendon said. They pushed at him. He ceased struggling and got in and sat quietly as the others took their places. He sat between the barber and the soldier, drawing his limbs in so as not to touch them, his eyes going swiftly and constantly from face to face. Butch clung to the running board. The car moved on. The barber nursed his mouth with his handkerchief.

"What's the matter, Hawk?" the soldier said.

"Nothing," the barber said. They regained the highroad and turned away from town. The second car dropped back out of the dust. They went on, gaining speed; the final fringe of houses dropped behind.

"Goddamn, he stinks!" the soldier said.

"We'll fix that," the drummer in front beside McLendon said. On the running board Butch cursed into the hot rush of air. The barber leaned suddenly forward and touched McLendon's arm.

"Let me out, John," he said.

"Jump out, niggerlover," McLendon said without turning his head. He drove swiftly. Behind them the sourceless lights of the second car glared in the dust. Presently McLendon turned into a narrow road. It was rutted with disuse. It led back to an abandoned brick kiln — a series of reddish mounds and weed- and vine-choked vats without bottom. It had been used for pasture once, until one day the owner missed one of his mules. Although he prodded carefully in the vats with a long pole, he could not even find the bottom of them.

"John," the barber said.

"Jump out, then," McLendon said, hurling the car along the ruts. Beside the barber the Negro spoke:

"Mr. Henry."

The barber sat forward. The narrow tunnel of the road rushed up and past. Their motion was like an extinct furnace blast: cooler, but utterly dead. The car bounded from rut to rut.

"Mr Henry," the Negro said.

The barber began to tug furiously at the door. "Look out, there!" the soldier said, but the barber had already kicked the door open and swung onto the running board. The soldier leaned across the Negro and grasped at him, but he had already jumped. The car went on without checking speed.

The impetus hurled him crashing through dust-sheathed weeds, into the ditch. Dust puffed about him, and in a thin, vicious crackling of sapless stems he lay choking and retching until the second car passed and died away. Then he rose and limped on until he reached the highroad and turned toward town, brushing at his clothes with his hands. The moon was higher, riding high and clear of the dust at last, and after a while the town began to glare beneath the dust. He went on, limping. Presently he heard cars and the glow of them grew in the dust behind him and he left the road and crouched again in the weeds until they passed. McLendon's car came last now. There were four people in it and Butch was not on the running board.

They went on; the dust swallowed them; the glare and the sound died away. The dust of them hung for a while, but soon the eternal dust absorbed it again. The barber climbed back onto the road and limped on toward town.

IV

As she dressed for supper on that Saturday evening, her own flesh felt like fever. Her hands trembled among the hooks and eyes, and her eyes had a feverish look, and her hair swirled crisp and crackling under the comb. While she was still dressing the friends called for her and sat while she donned her sheerest underthings and stockings and a new voile dress. "Do you feel strong enough to go out?" they said, their eyes bright too, with a dark glitter. "When you have had time to get over the shock, you must tell us what happened. What he said and did; everything."

In the leafed darkness, as they walked toward the square, she began to breathe deeply, something like a swimmer preparing to dive, until she ceased trembling, the four of them walking slowly because of the terrible heat and out of solicitude for her. But as they neared the square she began to tremble again, walking with her head up, her hands clenched at her sides, their voices about her murmurous, also with that feverish, glittering quality of their eyes.

They entered the square, she in the center of the group, fragile in her fresh dress. She was trembling worse. She walked slower and slower, as children eat ice cream, her head up and her eyes bright in the haggard banner of her face, passing the hotel and the coatless drummers in chairs along the curb looking around at her: "That's the one: see? The one in pink in the middle." "Is that her? What did they do with the nigger? Did they — ?" "Sure. He's all right." "All right, is he?" "Sure. He went on a little trip." Then the drug store, where even the young men lounging in the doorway tipped their hats and followed with their eyes the motion of her hips and legs when she passed.

They went on, passing the lifted hats of the gentlemen, the suddenly ceased voices, deferent, protective. "Do you see?" the friends said. Their voices sounded like long, hovering sighs of hissing exultation. "There's not a Negro on the square. Not one."

They reached the picture show. It was like a miniature fairyland with its lighted lobby and colored lithographs of life caught in its terrible and beautiful mutations. Her lips began to tingle. In the dark, when the picture began, it would be all right; she could hold back the laughing so it would not waste away so fast and so soon. So she hurried on before the turning faces, the undertones of low astonishment, and they took their accustomed places where she could see the aisle against the silver glare and the young men and girls coming in two and two against it.

The lights flicked away; the screen glowed silver, and soon life began to unfold, beautiful and passionate and sad, while still the young men and girls entered, scented and sibilant in the half dark, their paired backs in silhouette delicate and sleek, their slim, quick bodies awkward, divinely young, while beyond them the silver dream accumulated, inevitably on and on. She began to laugh. In trying to suppress it, it made more noise than ever; heads began to turn. Still laughing, her friends raised her and led her out, and she stood at the curb, laughing on a high, sustained note, until the taxi came up and they helped her in.

They removed the pink voile and the sheer underthings and the stockings, and put her to bed, and cracked ice for her temples, and sent for the doctor. He was hard to locate, so they ministered to her with hushed ejaculations, renewing the ice and fanning her. While the ice was fresh and cold she stopped laughing and lay still for a time, moaning only a little. But soon the laughing welled again and her voice rose screaming.

"Shhhhhhhhhhh! Shhhhhhhhhhhhhhh!" they said, freshening the icepack, smoothing her hair, examining it for gray; "poor girl!" Then to one another: "Do you suppose anything really happened?" their eyes darkly aglitter, secret and passionate. "Shhhhhhhhhh! Poor girl! Poor Minnie!"

V

It was midnight when McLendon drove up to his neat new house. It was trim and fresh as a birdcage and almost as small, with its clean, green-and-white paint. He locked the car and mounted the porch and entered. His wife rose from a chair beside the reading lamp. McLendon stopped in the floor and stared at her until she looked down.

"Look at that clock," he said, lifting his arm, pointing. She stood before him, her face lowered, a magazine in her hands. Her face was pale, strained, and weary-looking. "Haven't I told you about sitting up like this, waiting to see when I come in?"

"John," she said. She laid the magazine down. Poised on the balls of his feet, he glared at her with his hot eyes, his sweating face.

"Didn't I tell you?" He went toward her. She looked up then. He caught her shoulder. She stood passive, looking at him.

"Don't, John. I couldn't sleep . . . The heat; something. Please, John. You're hurting me."

"Didn't I tell you?" He released her and half struck, half flung her across the chair, and she lay there and watched him quietly as he left the room.

He went on through the house, ripping off his shirt, and on the dark, screened porch at the rear he stood and mopped his head and shoulders with the shirt and flung it away. He took the pistol from his hip and laid it on the table beside the bed, and sat on the bed and removed his shoes, and rose and slipped his trousers off. He was sweating again already, and he stooped and hunted furiously for the shirt. At last he found it and wiped his body again, and, with his body pressed against the dusty screen, he stood panting. There was no movement, no sound, not even an insect. The dark world seemed to lie stricken beneath the cold moon and the lidless stars.

Lionel Trilling (b. 1905)

AMERICAN NOVELIST, SHORT STORY WRITER, and CRITIC

Of This Time, Of That Place

It was a fine September day. By noon it would be summer again, but now it was true autumn with a touch of chill in the air. As Joseph Howe stood on the porch of the house in which he lodged, ready to leave for his first class of the year, he thought with pleasure of the long indoor days that were coming. It was a moment when he could feel glad of his profession.

On the lawn the peach tree was still in fruit and young Hilda Aiken was taking a picture of it. She held the camera tight against her chest. She wanted the sun behind her, but she did not want her own long morning shadow in the foreground. She raised the camera, but that did not help, and she lowered it, but that made things worse. She twisted her body to the left, then to the right. In the end she had to step out of the direct line of the sun. At last she snapped the shutter and wound the film with intense care.

Howe, watching her from the porch, waited for her to finish and called good morning. She turned, startled, and almost sullenly lowered her glance. In the year Howe had lived at the Aikens', Hilda had accepted him as one of her family, but since his absence of the summer she had grown shy. Then suddenly she lifted her head and smiled at him, and the humorous smile confirmed his pleasure in the day. She picked up her bookbag and set off for school.

The handsome houses on the streets to the college were not yet fully awake, but they looked very friendly. Howe went by the Bradby house where he would be a guest this evening at the first dinner party of the year. When he had gone the length of the picket fence, the whitest in town, he turned back. Along the path there was a fine row of asters and he went through the gate and picked one for his buttonhole. The Bradbys would be pleased if they happened to see him invading their lawn and the knowledge of this made him even more comfortable.

He reached the campus as the hour was striking. The students were hurrying to their classes. He himself was in no hurry. He stopped at his dim cubicle of an office and lit a cigarette. The prospect of facing his class had suddenly presented itself to him and his hands were cold; the lawful seizure of power he was about to make seemed momentous. Waiting did not help. He put out his cigarette, picked up a pad of theme paper, and went to his classroom.

As he entered, the rattle of voices ceased, and the twenty-odd freshmen settled themselves and looked at him appraisingly. Their faces seemed gross, his heart sank at their massed impassivity, but he spoke briskly.

'My name is Howe,' he said, and turned and wrote it on the blackboard. The carelessness of the scrawl confirmed his authority. He went on, 'My office is 412 Slemp Hall, and my office-hours are Monday, Wednesday and Friday from eleven-thirty to twelve-thirty.'

He wrote, 'M., W., F., 11:30–12:30.' He said, 'I'll be very glad to see any of you at that time. Or if you can't come then, you can arrange with me for some other time.'

He turned again to the blackboard and spoke over his shoulder. 'The text for the course is Jarman's *Modern Plays*, revised edition. The Co-op has it in stock.' He wrote the name, underlined 'revised edition' and waited for it to be taken down in the new notebooks.

When the bent heads were raised again he began his speech of prospectus. 'It is hard to explain —' he said, and paused as they composed themselves. 'It is hard to explain what a course like this is intended to do. We are going to try to learn something about modern literature and something about prose composition.'

As he spoke, his hands warmed and he was able to look directly at the class. Last year on the first day the faces had seemed just as cloddish, but as the term wore on they became gradually alive and quite likable. It did not seem possible that the same thing could happen again.

'I shall not lecture in this course,' he continued. 'Our work will be carried on by discussion and we will try to learn by an exchange of opinion. But you will soon recognize that my opinion is worth more than anyone else's here.'

He remained grave as he said it, but two boys understood and laughed. The rest took permission from them and laughed too. All Howe's private ironies protested the vulgarity of the joke, but the laughter made him feel benign and powerful.

When the little speech was finished, Howe picked up the pad of paper he had brought. He announced that they would write an extemporaneous theme. Its subject was traditional, 'Who I am and why I came to Dwight College.' By now the class was more at ease and it gave a ritualistic groan of protest. Then there was a stir as fountain pens were brought out and the writing-arms of the chairs were cleared, and the paper was passed about. At last, all the heads bent to work, and the room became still.

Howe sat idly at his desk. The sun shone through the tall clumsy windows. The cool of the morning was already passing. There was a scent of autumn and varnish and the stillness of the room was deep and oddly touching. Now and then a student's head was raised and scratched in the old, elaborate students' pantomime that calls the teacher to witness honest intellectual effort.

Suddenly a tall boy stood within the frame of the open door. 'Is this,' he said, and thrust a large nose into a college catalogue, 'is this the meeting place of English 1A? The section instructed by Dr. Joseph Howe?'

He stood on the very sill of the door, as if refusing to enter until he was perfectly sure of all his rights. The class looked up from work, found him absurd and gave a low mocking cheer.

The teacher and the new student, with equal pointedness, ignored the disturbance. Howe nodded to the boy, who pushed his head forward and then jerked it back in a wide elaborate arc to clear his brow of a heavy lock of hair. He advanced into the room and halted before Howe, almost at attention. In a loud, clear voice he announced, 'I am Tertan, Ferdinand R., reporting at the direction of Head of Department Vincent.'

The heraldic formality of this statement brought forth another cheer. Howe looked at the class with a sternness he could not really feel, for there was indeed something ridiculous about this boy. Under his displeased regard the rows of heads dropped to work again. Then he touched Tertan's elbow, led him up to the desk and stood so as to shield their conversation from the class.

'We are writing an extemporaneous theme,' he said. 'The subject is, "Who I am and why I came to Dwight College." '

He stripped a few sheets from the pad and offered them to the boy. Tertan hesitated and then took the paper, but he held it only tentatively. As if with the effort of making something clear, he gulped, and a slow smile fixed itself on his face. It was at once knowing and shy.

'Professor,' he said, 'to be perfectly fair to my classmates' — he made a large gesture over the room — 'and to you' — he inclined his head to Howe — 'this would not be for me an extemporaneous subject.'

Howe tried to understand. 'You mean you've already thought about it — you've heard we always give the same subject? That doesn't matter.'

Again the boy ducked his head and gulped. It was the gesture of one who wishes to make a difficult explanation with perfect candor. 'Sir,' he said, and made the distinction with great care, 'the topic I did not expect, but I have given much ratiocination to the subject.'

Howe smiled and said, 'I don't think that's an unfair advantage. Just go ahead and write.'

Tertan narrowed his eyes and glanced sidewise at Howe. His strange mouth smiled. Then in quizzical acceptance, he ducked his head, threw back the heavy, dank lock, dropped into a seat with a great loose noise and began to write rapidly.

The room fell silent again and Howe resumed his idleness. When the bell rang, the students who had groaned when the task had been set now groaned again because they had not finished. Howe took up the papers, and held the class while he made the first assignment. When he dismissed it, Tertan bore down on him, his slack mouth held ready for speech.

'Some professors,' he said, 'are pedants. They are Dryasdusts.[1] However, some professors are free souls and creative spirits. Kant, Hegel and Nietzsche

[1] name for a pedantic scholar who occupies himself with dry details; derived from the name of a fictitious person who wrote prefaces to some of the novels of Sir Walter Scott (1771–1832).

were all professors.' With this pronouncement he paused. 'It is my opinion,' he continued, 'that you occupy the second category.'

Howe looked at the boy in surprise and said with good-natured irony, 'With Kant, Hegel and Nietzsche?'

Not only Tertan's hand and head but his whole awkward body waved away the stupidity. 'It is the kind and not the quantity of the kind,' he said sternly.

Rebuked, Howe said as simply and seriously as he could, 'It would be nice to think so.' He added, 'Of course I am not a professor.'

This was clearly a disappointment but Tertan met it. 'In the French sense,' he said with composure. 'Generically, a teacher.'

Suddenly he bowed. It was such a bow, Howe fancied, as a stage-director might teach an actor playing a medieval student who takes leave of Abelard[2] — stiff, solemn, with elbows close to the body and feet together. Then, quite as suddenly, he turned and left.

A queer fish, and as soon as Howe reached his office, he sifted through the batch of themes and drew out Tertan's. The boy had filled many sheets with his unformed headlong scrawl. 'Who am I?' he had begun. 'Here, in a mundane, not to say commercialized academe, is asked the question which from time long immemorably out of mind has accreted doubts and thoughts in the psyche of man to pester him as a nuisance. Whether in St. Augustine[3] (or Austin as sometimes called) or Miss Bashkirtsieff[4] or Frederic Amiel[5] or Empedocles,[6] or in less lights of the intellect than these, this posed question has been ineluctable.'

Howe took out his pencil. He circled 'academe' and wrote 'vocab.' in the margin. He underlined 'time long immemorably out of mind' and wrote 'Diction!' But this seemed inadequate for what was wrong. He put down his pencil and read ahead to discover the principle of error in the theme. 'Today as ever, in spite of gloomy prophets of the dismal science (economics) the question is uninvalidated. Out of the starry depths of heaven hurtles this spear of query demanding to be caught on the shield of the mind ere it pierces the skull and the limbs be unstrung.'

Baffled but quite caught, Howe read on. 'Materialism, by which is meant the philosophic concept and not the moral idea, provides no aegis against the question which lies beyond the tangible (metaphysics). Existence without alloy is the question presented. Environment and heredity relegated aside, the rags and old clothes of practical life discarded, the name and the instrumentality of livelihood do not, as the prophets of the dismal science insist

[2] a French theologian and philosopher (1079–1142); condemned by the Church for his intellectual probings into orthodox doctrines but much loved by his students.
[3] (353–430); one of the most important fathers of Christian theology and author of the *City of God* and *Confessions*.
[4] Maria Konstantinovna Bashkirtseva (1860–1884), a Russian aristocrat and artist whose *Journal* and *Letters* caused a sensation because of their sincerity and frankness.
[5] Henri Frederic Amiel (1821–1881), a poet and professor of ethics and aesthetics at the Geneva Academy in Switzerland.
[6] (c. 490–430 B.C.); influential in Greece in his own time as a Pythagorean philosopher, democratic statesman, and eloquent poet.

on in this connection, give solution to the interrogation which not from the professor merely but veritably from the cosmos is given. I think, therefore I am (cogito etc.)[7] but who am I? Tertan I am, but what is Tertan? Of this time, of that place, of some parentage, what does it matter?'

Existence without alloy: the phrase established itself. Howe put aside Tertan's paper and at random picked up another. 'I am Arthur J. Casebeer, Jr.,' he read. 'My father is Arthur J. Casebeer and my grandfather was Arthur J. Casebeer before him. My mother is Nina Wimble Casebeer. Both of them are college graduates and my father is in insurance. I was born in St. Louis eighteen years ago and we still make our residence there.'

Arthur J. Casebeer, who knew who he was, was less interesting than Tertan, but more coherent. Howe picked up Tertan's paper again. It was clear that none of the routine marginal comments, no 'sent. str.' or 'punct.' or 'vocab.' could cope with this torrential rhetoric. He read ahead, contenting himself with underscoring the errors against the time when he should have the necessary 'conference' with Tertan.

It was a busy and official day of cards and sheets, arrangements and small decisions, and it gave Howe pleasure. Even when it was time to attend the first of the weekly Convocations he felt the charm of the beginning of things when intention is still innocent and uncorrupted by effort. He sat among the young instructors on the platform, and joined in their humorous complaints at having to assist at the ceremony, but actually he got a clear satisfaction from the ritual of prayer, and prosy speech, and even from wearing his academic gown. And when the Convocation was over the pleasure continued as he crossed the campus, exchanging greetings with men he had not seen since the spring. They were people who did not yet, and perhaps never would, mean much to him, but in a year they had grown amiably to be part of his life. They were his fellow-townsmen.

The day had cooled again at sunset, and there was a bright chill in the September twilight. Howe carried his voluminous gown over his arm, he swung his doctoral hood by its purple neckpiece, and on his head he wore his mortarboard with its heavy gold tassel bobbing just over his eye. These were the weighty and absurd symbols of his new profession and they pleased him. At twenty-six Joseph Howe had discovered that he was neither so well off nor so bohemian as he had once thought. A small income, adequate when supplemented by a sizable cash legacy, was genteel poverty when the cash was all spent. And the literary life — the room at the Lafayette,[8] or the small apartment without a lease, the long summers on the Cape,[9] the long afternoons and the social evenings — began to weary him. His writing filled his mornings, and should perhaps have filled his life, yet it did not. To the amusement of his friends, and with a certain sense that he was betraying his

---

[7] reference to the focal point of Descartes' (1596–1650) philosophy as expressed in *Meditations: Cogito, ergo sum* ('I think, therefore I am').

[8] hotel in Greenwich Village.

[9] Cape Cod.

own freedom, he had used the last of his legacy for a year at Harvard. The small but respectable reputation of his two volumes of verse had proved useful — he continued at Harvard on a fellowship and when he emerged as Doctor Howe he received an excellent appointment, with prospects, at Dwight.

He had his moments of fear when all that had ever been said of the dangers of the academic life had occurred to him. But after a year in which he had tested every possibility of corruption and seduction he was ready to rest easy. His third volume of verse, most of it written in his first years of teaching, was not only ampler but, he thought, better than its predecessors.

There was a clear hour before the Bradby dinner party, and Howe looked forward to it. But he was not to enjoy it, for lying with his mail on the hall table was a copy of this quarter's issue of *Life and Letters*, to which his land-lord subscribed. Its severe cover announced that its editor, Frederic Woolley, had this month contributed an essay called 'Two Poets,' and Howe, picking it up, curious to see who the two poets might be, felt his own name start out at him with cabalistic power — Joseph Howe. As he continued to turn the pages his hand trembled.

Standing in the dark hall, holding the neat little magazine, Howe knew that his literary contempt for Frederic Woolley meant nothing, for he suddenly understood how he respected Woolley in the way of the world. He knew this by the trembling of his hand. And of the little world as well as the great, for although the literary groups of New York might dismiss Woolley, his name carried high authority in the academic world. At Dwight it was even a revered name, for it had been here at the college that Frederic Woolley had made the distinguished scholarly career from which he had gone on to literary journalism. In middle life he had been induced to take the editorship of *Life and Letters*, a literary monthly not widely read but heavily endowed, and in its pages he had carried on the defense of what he sometimes called the older values. He was not without wit; he had great knowledge and considerable taste, and even in the full movement of the 'new' literature he had won a certain respect for his refusal to accept it. In France, even in England, he would have been connected with a more robust tradition of conservatism, but America gave him an audience not much better than genteel. It was known in the college that to the subsidy of *Life and Letters* the Bradbys contributed a great part.

As Howe read, he saw that he was involved in nothing less than an event. When the Fifth Series of *Studies in Order and Value* came to be collected, this latest of Frederic Woolley's essays would not be merely another step in the old direction. Clearly and unmistakably, it was a turning point. All his literary life Woolley had been concerned with the relation of literature to morality, religion, and the private and delicate pieties, and he had been unalterably opposed to all that he had called 'inhuman humanitarianism.' But here, suddenly, dramatically late, he had made an about-face, turning to the public life and to the humanitarian politics he had so long despised. This was the kind of incident the histories of literature make much of. Frederic Woolley was opening for himself a new career and winning a kind of new youth. He contrasted the two poets, Thomas Wormser, who was admirable, Joseph Howe, who was almost dangerous. He spoke of the 'precious subjectivism' of Howe's verse. 'In times like ours,' he wrote, 'with millions facing penury and want, one feels that the qualities of the *tour d'ivoire* are well-nigh inhuman, nearly insulting. The *tour d'ivoire*[10] becomes the *tour d'ivresse*,[11] and it is not self-intoxicated poets that our people need.' The essay said more: 'The problem is one of meaning. I am not ignorant that the creed of the esoteric poets declares that a poem does not and should not *mean* anything, that it *is* something. But poetry is what the poet makes it, and if he is a true poet he makes what his society needs. And what is needed now is the tradition in which Mr. Wormser writes, the true tradition of poetry. The Howes do no harm, but they do no good when positive good is demanded of all responsible men. Or do the Howes indeed do no harm? Perhaps Plato would have said they do, that in some ways theirs is the Phrygian music that turns men's minds from the struggle. Certainly it is true that Thomas Wormser writes in the lucid Dorian mode[12] which sends men into battle with evil.'

It was easy to understand why Woolley had chosen to praise Thomas Wormser. The long, lilting lines of *Corn Under Willows* hymned, as Woolley put it, the struggle for wheat in the Iowa fields, and expressed the real lives of real people. But why out of the dozen more notable examples he had chosen Howe's little volume as the example of 'precious subjectivism' was hard to guess. In a way it was funny, this multiplication of himself into 'the Howes.' And yet this becoming the multiform political symbol by whose creation Frederic Woolley gave the sign of a sudden new life, this use of him as a sacrifice whose blood was necessary for the rites of rejuvenation, made him feel oddly unclean.

Nor could Howe get rid of a certain practical resentment. As a poet he had a special and respectable place in the college life. But it might be another thing to be marked as the poet of a willful and selfish obscurity.

As he walked to the Bradbys', Howe was a little tense and defensive. It seemed to him that all the world knew of the 'attack' and agreed with it. And, indeed, the Bradbys had read the essay but Professor Bradby, a kind and pretentious man, said, 'I see my old friend knocked you about a bit, my boy,' and his wife Eugenia looked at Howe with her child-like blue eyes and said, 'I shall *scold* Frederic for the untrue things he wrote about you. You aren't the least obscure.' They beamed at him. In their genial snobbery they seemed to feel that he had distinguished himself. He was the leader of Howeism. He enjoyed the dinner party as much as he had thought he would.

And in the following days, as he was more preoccupied with his duties, the

---

[10] ivory tower.

[11] tower of intoxication, or madness.

[12] tonal orientations derived from the ancient Greeks for use in ecclesiastical music: the Phrygian mode was lively and bright, whereas the Doric was serious and somber.

incident was forgotten. His classes had ceased to be mere groups. Student after student detached himself from the mass and required or claimed a place in Howe's awareness. Of them all it was Tertan who first and most violently signaled his separate existence. A week after classes had begun Howe saw his silhouette on the frosted glass of his office door. It was motionless for a long time, perhaps stopped by the problem of whether or not to knock before entering. Howe called, 'Come in!' and Tertan entered with his shambling stride.

He stood beside the desk, silent and at attention. When Howe asked him to sit down, he responded with a gesture of head and hand, as if to say that such amenities were beside the point. Nevertheless, he did take the chair. He put his ragged, crammed briefcase between his legs. His face, which Howe now observed fully for the first time, was confusing, for it was made up of florid curves, the nose arched in the bone and voluted in the nostril, the mouth loose and soft and rather moist. Yet the face was so thin and narrow as to seem the very type of asceticism. Lashes of unusual length veiled the eyes and, indeed, it seemed as if there were a veil over the whole countenance. Before the words actually came, the face screwed itself into an attitude of preparation for them.

'You can confer with me now?' Tertan said.

'Yes, I'd be glad to. There are several things in your two themes I want to talk to you about.' Howe reached for the packet of themes on his desk and sought for Tertan's. But the boy was waving them away.

'These are done perforce,' he said. 'Under the pressure of your requirement. They are not significant; mere duties.' Again his great hand flapped vaguely to dismiss his themes. He leaned forward and gazed at his teacher.

'You are,' he said, 'a man of letters? You are a poet?' It was more declaration than question.

'I should like to think so,' Howe said.

At first Tertan accepted the answer with a show of appreciation, as though the understatement made a secret between himself and Howe. Then he chose to misunderstand. With his shrewd and disconcerting control of expression, he presented to Howe a puzzled grimace. 'What does that mean?' he said.

Howe retracted the irony. 'Yes. I am a poet.' It sounded strange to say.

'That,' Tertan said, 'is a wonder.' He corrected himself with his ducking head. 'I mean that is wonderful.'

Suddenly, he dived at the miserable briefcase between his legs, put it on his knees, and began to fumble with the catch, all intent on the difficulty it presented. Howe noted that his suit was worn thin, his shirt almost unclean. He became aware, even, of a vague and musty odor of garments worn too long in unaired rooms. Tertan conquered the lock and began to concentrate upon a search into the interior. At last he held in his hand what he was after, a torn and crumpled copy of *Life and Letters*.

'I learned it from here,' he said, holding it out.

Howe looked at him sharply, his hackles a little up. But the boy's face was not only perfectly innocent, it even shone with a conscious admiration. Apparently nothing of the import of the essay had touched him except the wonderful fact that his teacher was a 'man of letters.' Yet this seemed too stupid, and Howe, to test it, said, 'The man who wrote that doesn't think it's wonderful.'

Tertan made a moist hissing sound as he cleared his mouth of saliva. His head, oddly loose on his neck, wove a pattern of contempt in the air. 'A critic,' he said, 'who admits *prima facie* that he does not understand.' Then he said grandly, 'It is the inevitable fate.'

It was absurd, yet Howe was not only aware of the absurdity but of a tension suddenly and wonderfully relaxed. Now that the 'attack' was on the table between himself and this strange boy, and subject to the boy's funny and absolutely certain contempt, the hidden force of his feeling was revealed to him in the very moment that it vanished. All unsuspected, there had been a film over the world, a transparent but discoloring haze of danger. But he had no time to stop over the brightened aspect of things. Tertan was going on. 'I also am a man of letters. Putative.'

'You have written a good deal?' Howe meant to be no more than polite, and he was surprised at the tenderness he heard in his words.

Solemnly the boy nodded, threw back the dank lock, and sucked in a deep, anticipatory breath. 'First, a work of homiletics, which is a defense of the principles of religious optimism against the pessimism of Schopenhauer and the humanism of Nietzsche.'

'Humanism? Why do you call it humanism?'

'It is my nomenclature for making a deity of man,' Tertan replied negligently. 'Then three fictional works, novels. And numerous essays in science, combating materialism. Is it your duty to read these if I bring them to you?'

Howe answered simply, 'No, it isn't exactly my duty, but I shall be happy to read them.'

Tertan stood up and remained silent. He rested his bag on the chair. With a certain compunction — for it did not seem entirely proper that, of two men of letters, one should have the right to blue-pencil the other, to grade him or to question the quality of his 'sentence structure' — Howe reached for Tertan's papers. But before he could take them up, the boy suddenly made his bow-to-Abelard, the stiff inclination of the body with the hands seeming to emerge from the scholar's gown. Then he was gone.

But after his departure something was still left of him. The timbre of his curious sentences, the downright finality of so quaint a phrase as 'It is the inevitable fate' still rang in the air. Howe gave the warmth of his feeling to the new visitor who stood at the door announcing himself with a genteel clearing of the throat.

'Doctor Howe, I believe?' the student said. A large hand advanced into the room and grasped Howe's hand. 'Blackburn, sir, Theodore Blackburn, vice-president of the Student Council. A great pleasure, sir.'

Out of a pair of ruddy cheeks a pair of small eyes twinkled good-naturedly. The large face, the large body were not so much fat as beefy and suggested something 'typical' — monk, politician, or innkeeper.

Blackburn took the seat beside Howe's desk. 'I may have seemed to introduce myself in my public capacity, sir,' he said. 'But it is really as an individual that I came to see you. That is to say, as one of your students to be.'

He spoke with an English intonation and he went on, 'I was once an English major, sir.'

For a moment Howe was startled, for the roast-beef look of the boy and the manner of his speech gave a second's credibility to one sense of his statement. Then the collegiate meaning of the phrase asserted itself, but some perversity made Howe say what was not really in good taste even with so forward a student, 'Indeed? What regiment?'

Blackburn stared and then gave a little pouf-pouf of laughter. He waved the misapprehension away. 'Very good, sir. It certainly is an ambiguous term.' He chuckled in appreciation of Howe's joke, then cleared his throat to put it aside. 'I look forward to taking your course in the romantic poets, sir,' he said earnestly. 'To me the romantic poets are the very crown of English literature.'

Howe made a dry sound, and the boy, catching some meaning in it, said, 'Little as I know them, of course. But even Shakespeare who is so dear to us of the Anglo-Saxon tradition is in a sense but the preparation for Shelley, Keats and Byron. And Wadsworth.'

Almost sorry for him, Howe dropped his eyes. With some embarrassment, for the boy was not actually his student, he said softly, 'Wordsworth.'

'Sir?'

'Wordsworth, not Wadsworth. You said Wadsworth.'

'Did I, sir?' Gravely he shook his head to rebuke himself for the error. 'Wordsworth, of course — slip of the tongue.' Then, quite in command again, he went on. 'I have a favor to ask of you, Doctor Howe. You see, I began my college course as an English major,' — he smiled — 'as I said.'

'Yes?'

'But after my first year I shifted. I shifted to the social sciences. Sociology and government — I find them stimulating and very real.' He paused, out of respect for reality. 'But now I find that perhaps I have neglected the other side.'

'The other side?' Howe said.

'Imagination, fancy, culture. A well-rounded man.' He trailed off as if there were perfect understanding between them. 'And so, sir, I have decided to end my senior year with your course in the romantic poets.'

His voice was filled with an indulgence which Howe ignored as he said flatly and gravely, 'But that course isn't given until the spring term.'

'Yes, sir, and that is where the favor comes in. Would you let me take your romantic prose course? I can't take it for credit, sir, my program is full, but just for background it seems to me that I ought to take it. I do hope,' he concluded in a manly way, 'that you will consent.'

'Well, it's no great favor, Mr. Blackburn. You can come if you wish, though there's not much point in it if you don't do the reading.'

The bell rang for the hour and Howe got up.

'May I begin with this class, sir?' Blackburn's smile was candid and boyish.

Howe nodded carelessly and together, silently, they walked to the class-room down the hall. When they reached the door Howe stood back to let his student enter, but Blackburn moved adroitly behind him and grasped him by the arm to urge him over the threshold. They entered together with Blackburn's hand firmly on Howe's biceps, the student inducting the teacher into his own room. Howe felt a surge of temper rise in him and almost violently he disengaged his arm and walked to the desk, while Blackburn found a seat in the front row and smiled at him.

II

The question was, At whose door must the tragedy be laid?

All night the snow had fallen heavily and only now was abating in sparse little flurries. The windows were valanced high with white. It was very quiet; something of the quiet of the world had reached the class, and Howe found that everyone was glad to talk or listen. In the room there was a comfortable sense of pleasure in being human.

Casebeer believed that the blame for the tragedy rested with heredity. Picking up the book he read, 'The sins of the fathers are visited on their children.' This opinion was received with general favor. Nevertheless, Johnson ventured to say that the fault was all Pastor Manders' because the Pastor had made Mrs. Alving[13] go back to her husband and was always hiding the truth. To this Hibbard objected with logic enough, 'Well then, it was really all her husband's fault. He *did* all the bad things.' DeWitt, his face bright with an impatient idea, said that the fault was all society's. 'By society I don't mean upper-crust society,' he said. He looked around a little defiantly, taking in any members of the class who might be members of upper-crust society. 'Not in that sense. I mean the social unit.'

Howe nodded and said, 'Yes, of course.'

'If the society of the time had progressed far enough in science,' DeWitt went on, 'then there would be no problem for Mr. Ibsen to write about. Captain Alving plays around a little, gives way to perfectly natural biological urges, and he gets a social disease, a venereal disease. If the disease is cured, no problem. Invent salvarsan[14] and the disease is cured. The problem of heredity disappears and li'l Oswald just doesn't get paresis. No paresis, no problem — no problem, no play.'

This was carrying the ark into battle, and the class looked at De Witt with

[13] two of the main characters in *Ghosts* by Henrik Ibsen (1828–1906).
[14] an arsenic compound used in the treatment of syphilis.

respectful curiosity. It was his usual way and on the whole they were sympathetic with his struggle to prove to Howe that science was better than literature. Still, there was something in his reckless manner that alienated them a little.

'Or take birth-control, for instance,' De Witt went on. 'If Mrs. Alving had some knowledge of contraception, she wouldn't have had to have li'l Oswald at all. No li'l Oswald, no play.'

The class was suddenly quieter. In the back row Stettenhover swung his great football shoulders in a righteous sulking gesture, first to the right, then to the left. He puckered his mouth ostentatiously. Intellect was always ending up by talking dirty.

Tertan's hand went up, and Howe said, 'Mr. Tertan.' The boy shambled to his feet and began his long characteristic gulp. Howe made a motion with his fingers, as small as possible, and Tertan ducked his head and smiled in apology. He sat down. The class laughed. With more than half the term gone, Tertan had not been able to remember that one did not rise to speak. He seemed unable to carry on the life of the intellect without this mark of respect for it. To Howe the boy's habit of rising seemed to accord with the formal shabbiness of his dress. He never wore the casual sweaters and jackets of his classmates. Into the free and comfortable air of the college classroom he brought the stuffy sordid strictness of some crowded, metropolitan high school.

'Speaking from one sense,' Tertan began slowly, 'there is no blame ascribable. From the sense of determinism, who can say where the blame lies? The preordained is the preordained and it cannot be said without rebellion against the universe, a palpable absurdity.'

In the back row Stettenhover slumped suddenly in his seat, his heels held out before him, making a loud, dry, disgusted sound. His body sank until his neck rested on the back of his chair. He folded his hands across his belly and looked significantly out of the window, exasperated not only with Tertan, but with Howe, with the class, with the whole system designed to encourage this kind of thing. There was a certain insolence in the movement and Howe flushed. As Tertan continued to speak, Howe stalked casually toward the window and placed himself in the line of Stettenhover's vision. He stared at the great fellow, who pretended not to see him. There was so much power in the big body, so much contempt in the Greek-athlete face under the crisp Greek-athlete curls, that Howe felt almost physical fear. But at last Stettenhover admitted him to focus and under his disapproving gaze sat up with slow indifference. His eyebrows raised high in resignation, he began to examine his hands. Howe relaxed and turned his attention back to Tertan.

'Flux of existence,' Tertan was saying, 'produces all things, so that judgment wavers. Beyond the phenomena, what? But phenomena are adumbrated and to them we are limited.'

Howe saw it for a moment as perhaps it existed in the boy's mind — the world of shadows which are cast by a great light upon a hidden reality as in the old myth of the Cave.[15] But the little brush with Stettenhover had tired him, and he said irritably, 'But come to the point, Mr. Tertan.'

He said it so sharply that some of the class looked at him curiously. For three months he had gently carried Tertan through his verbosities, to the vaguely respectful surprise of the other students, who seemed to conceive that there existed between this strange classmate and their teacher some special understanding from which they were content to be excluded. Tertan looked at him mildly, and at once came brilliantly to the point. 'This is the summation of the play,' he said and took up his book and read, ' "Your poor father never found any outlet for the overmastering joy of life that was in him. And I brought no holiday into his home, either. Everything seemed to turn upon duty and I am afraid I made your poor father's home unbearable to him, Oswald." Spoken by Mrs. Alving.'

Yes, that was surely the 'summation' of the play and Tertan had hit it, as he hit, deviously and eventually, the literary point of almost everything. But now, as always, he was wrapping it away from sight. 'For most mortals,' he said, 'there are only joys of biological urgings, gross and crass, such as the sensuous Captain Alving. For certain few there are the transmutations beyond these to a contemplation of the utter whole.'

Oh, the boy was mad. And suddenly the word, used in hyperbole, intended almost for the expression of exasperated admiration, became literal. Now that the word was used, it became simply apparent to Howe that Tertan was mad.

It was a monstrous word and stood like a bestial thing in the room. Yet it so completely comprehended everything that had puzzled Howe, it so arranged and explained what for three months had been perplexing him that almost at once its horror became domesticated. With this word Howe was able to understand why he had never been able to communicate to Tertan the value of a single criticism or correction of his wild, verbose themes. Their conferences had been frequent and long but had done nothing to reduce to order the splendid confusion of the boy's ideas. Yet, impossible though its expression was, Tertan's incandescent mind could always strike for a moment into some dark corner of thought.

And now it was suddenly apparent that it was not a faulty rhetoric that Howe had to contend with. With his new knowledge he looked at Tertan's face and wondered how he could have so long deceived himself. Tertan was still talking, and the class had lapsed into a kind of patient unconsciousness, a coma of respect for words which, for all that most of them knew, might be profound. Almost with a suffusion of shame, Howe believed that in some dim way the class had long ago had some intimation of Tertan's madness. He reached out as decisively as he could to seize the thread of Tertan's discourse before it should be entangled further.

[15] from the *Republic* (VII) by Plato (c. 427–c. 347 B.C.); the myth describes man's sudden turning away from the shadow-world of material existence to enter the sunlit world of true forms.

'Mr. Tertan says that the blame must be put upon whoever kills the joy of living in another. We have been assuming that Captain Alving was a wholly bad man, but what if we assume that he became bad only because Mrs. Alving, when they were first married, acted toward him in the prudish way she says she did?'

It was a ticklish idea to advance to freshmen and perhaps not profitable. Not all of them were following.

'That would put the blame on Mrs. Alving herself, whom most of you admire. And she herself seems to think so.' He glanced at his watch. The hour was nearly over. 'What do you think, Mr. De Witt?'

De Witt rose to the idea, he wanted to know if society couldn't be blamed for educating Mrs. Alving's temperament in the wrong way. Casebeer was puzzled, Stettenhover continued to look at his hands until the bell rang.

Tertan, his brows louring in thought, was making as always for a private word. Howe gathered his books and papers to leave quickly. At this moment of his discovery and with the knowledge still raw, he could not engage himself with Tertan. Tertan sucked in his breath to prepare for speech and Howe made ready for the pain and confusion. But at that moment Casebeer detached himself from the group with which he had been conferring and which he seemed to represent. His constituency remained at a tactful distance. The mission involved the time of an assigned essay. Casebeer's presentation of the plea — it was based on the freshmen's heavy duties at the fraternities during Carnival Week — cut across Tertan's preparations for speech. 'And so some of us fellows thought,' Casebeer concluded with heavy solemnity, 'that we could do a better job, give our minds to it more, if we had more time.'

Tertan regarded Casebeer with mingled curiosity and revulsion. Howe not only said that he would postpone the assignment but went on to talk about the Carnival, and even drew the waiting constituency into the conversation. He was conscious of Tertan's stern and astonished stare, then of his sudden departure.

Now that the fact was clear, Howe knew he must act on it. His course was simple enough. He must lay the case before the Dean. Yet he hesitated. His feeling for Tertan must now, certainly, be in some way invalidated. Yet could he, because of a word, hurry to assign to official and reasonable solicitude what had been, until this moment, so various and warm? He could at least delay and, by moving slowly, lend a poor grace to the necessary, ugly act of making his report.

It was with some notion of keeping the matter in his own hands that he went to the Dean's office to look up Tertan's records. In the outer office the Dean's secretary greeted him brightly, and at his request brought him the manila folder with the small identifying photograph pasted in the corner. She laughed. 'He was looking for the birdie in the wrong place,' she said.

Howe leaned over her shoulder to look at the picture. It was as bad as all the Dean's-office photographs were, but it differed from all that Howe had ever seen. Tertan, instead of looking into the camera, as no doubt he had been bidden, had, at the moment of exposure, turned his eyes upward. His mouth, as though conscious of the trick played on the photographer, had the sly superior look that Howe knew.

The secretary was fascinated by the picture. 'What a funny boy,' she said. 'He looks like Tartuffe!'[16]

And so he did, with the absurd piety of the eyes and the conscious slyness of the mouth and the whole face bloated by the bad lens.

'Is he *like* that?' the secretary said.

'Like Tartuffe? No.'

From the photograph there was little enough comfort to be had. The records themselves gave no clue to madness, though they suggested sadness enough. Howe read of a father, Stanislaus Tertan, born in Budapest and trained in engineering in Berlin, once employed by the Hercules Chemical Corporation — this was one of the factories that dominated the south end of the town — but now without employment. He read of a mother Erminie (Youngfellow) Tertan, born in Manchester, educated at a Normal School at Leeds, now housewife by profession. The family lived on Greenbriar Street which Howe knew as a row of once elegant homes near what was now the factory district. The old mansion had long ago been divided into small and primitive apartments. Of Ferdinand himself there was little to learn. He lived with his parents, had attended a Detroit high school and had transferred to the local school in his last year. His rating for intelligence, as expressed in numbers, was high, his scholastic record was remarkable, he held a college scholarship for his tuition.

Howe laid the folder on the secretary's desk. 'Did you find what you wanted to know?' she asked.

The phrases from Tertan's momentous first theme came back to him. 'Tertan I am, but what is Tertan? Of this time, of that place, of some parentage, what does it matter?'

'No, I didn't find it,' he said.

Now that he had consulted the sad, half-meaningless record he knew all the more firmly that he must not give the matter out of his own hands. He must not release Tertan to authority. Not that he anticipated from the Dean anything but the greatest kindness for Tertan. The Dean would have the experience and skill which he himself could not have. One way or another the Dean could answer the question, 'What is Tertan?' Yet this was precisely what he feared. He alone could keep alive — not forever but for a somehow important time — the question, 'What is Tertan?' He alone could keep it still a question. Some sure instinct told him that he must not surrender the question to a clean official desk in a clear official light to be dealt with, settled and closed.

He heard himself saying, 'Is the Dean busy at the moment? I'd like to see him.'

[16] a religious hypocrite and charlatan who temporarily dupes others into supporting his lusts, in a play of the same name by Molière (1622–1673).

His request came thus unbidden, even forbidden, and it was one of the surprising and startling incidents of his life. Later when he reviewed the events, so disconnected in themselves, or so merely odd, of the story that unfolded for him that year, it was over this moment, on its face the least notable, that he paused longest. It was frequently to be with fear and never without a certainty of its meaning in his own knowledge of himself that he would recall this simple, routine request, and the feeling of shame and freedom it gave him as he sent everything down the official chute. In the end, of course, no matter what he did to 'protect' Tertan, he would have had to make the same request and lay the matter on the Dean's clean desk. But it would always be a landmark of his life that, at the very moment when he was rejecting the official way, he had been, without will or intention, so gladly drawn to it.

After the storm's last delicate flurry, the sun had come out. Reflected by the new snow, it filled the office with a golden light which was almost musical in the way it made all the commonplace objects of efficiency shine with a sudden sad and noble significance. And the light, now that he noticed it, made the utterance of his perverse and unwanted request even more momentous.

The secretary consulted the engagement pad. 'He'll be free any minute. Don't you want to wait in the parlor?'

She threw open the door of the large and pleasant room in which the Dean held his Committee meetings, and in which his visitors waited. It was designed with a homely elegance on the masculine side of the eighteenth-century manner. There was a small coal fire in the grate and the handsome mahogany table was strewn with books and magazines. The large windows gave on the snowy lawn, and there was such a fine width of window that the white casements and walls seemed at this moment but a continuation of the snow, the snow but an extension of casement and walls. The outdoors seemed taken in and made safe, the indoors seemed luxuriously freshened and expanded.

Howe sat down by the fire and lighted a cigarette. The room had its intended effect upon him. He felt comfortable and relaxed, yet nicely organized, some young diplomatic agent of the eighteenth century, the newly fledged Swift carrying out Sir William Temple's business.[17] The rawness of Tertan's case quite vanished. He crossed his legs and reached for a magazine.

It was that famous issue of *Life and Letters* that his idle hand had found and his blood raced as he sifted through it, and the shape of his own name, Joseph Howe, sprang out at him, still cabalistic in its power. He tossed the magazine back on the table as the door of the Dean's office opened and the Dean ushered out Theodore Blackburn.

'Ah, Joseph!' the Dean said.

[17] statesman and author (1628–1699) who employed Jonathan Swift (1667–1745) as his secretary.

Blackburn said, 'Good morning, Doctor.' Howe winced at the title and caught the flicker of amusement over the Dean's face. The Dean stood with his hand high on the door-jamb and Blackburn, still in the doorway, remained standing almost under the long arm.

Howe nodded briefly to Blackburn, snubbing his eager deference. 'Can you give me a few minutes?' he said to the Dean.

'All the time you want. Come in.' Before the two men could enter the office, Blackburn claimed their attention with a long full 'er.' As they turned to him, Blackburn said, 'Can *you* give *me* a few minutes, Doctor Howe?' His eyes sparkled at the little audacity he had committed, the slightly impudent play with hierarchy. Of the three of them Blackburn kept himself the lowest, but he reminded Howe of his subaltern relation to the Dean.

'I mean, of course,' Blackburn went on easily, 'when you've finished with the Dean.'

'I'll be in my office shortly,' Howe said, turned his back on the ready 'Thank you, sir,' and followed the Dean into the inner room.

'Energetic boy,' said the Dean. 'A bit beyond himself but very energetic. Sit down.'

The Dean lighted a cigarette, leaned back in his chair, sat easy and silent for a moment, giving Howe no signal to go ahead with business. He was a young Dean, not much beyond forty, a tall handsome man with sad, ambitious eyes. He had been a Rhodes scholar. His friends looked for great things from him, and it was generally said that he had notions of education which he was not yet ready to try to put into practice.

His relaxed silence was meant as a compliment to Howe. He smiled and said, 'What's the business, Joseph?'

'Do you know Tertan — Ferdinand Tertan, a freshman?'

The Dean's cigarette was in his mouth and his hands were clasped behind his head. He did not seem to search his memory for the name. He said, 'What about him?'

Clearly the Dean knew something, and he was waiting for Howe to tell him more. Howe moved only tentatively. Now that he was doing what he had resolved not to do, he felt more guilty at having been so long deceived by Tertan and more need to be loyal to his error.

'He's a strange fellow,' he ventured. He said stubbornly, 'In a strange way he's very brilliant.' He concluded, 'But very strange.'

The springs of the Dean's swivel chair creaked as he came out of his sprawl and leaned forward to Howe. 'Do you mean he's so strange that it's something you could give a name to?'

Howe looked at him stupidly. 'What do you mean?' he said.

'What's his trouble?' the Dean said more neutrally.

'He's very brilliant, in a way. I looked him up and he has a top intelligence rating. But somehow, and it's hard to explain just how, what he says is always on the edge of sense and doesn't quite make it.'

The Dean looked at him and Howe flushed up. The Dean had surely read Woolley on the subject of 'the Howes' and the *tour d'ivresse*. Was that quick glance ironical?

The Dean picked up some papers from his desk, and Howe could see that they were in Tertan's impatient scrawl. Perhaps the little gleam in the Dean's glance had come only from putting facts together.

'He sent me this yesterday,' the Dean said. 'After an interview I had with him. I haven't been able to do more than glance at it. When you said what you did, I realized there was something wrong.'

Twisting his mouth, the Dean looked over the letter. 'You seem to be involved,' he said without looking up. 'By the way, what did you give him at mid-term?'

Flushing, setting his shoulders, Howe said firmly, 'I gave him A-minus.'

The Dean chuckled. 'Might be a good idea if some of our nicer boys went crazy — just a little.' He said, 'Well,' to conclude the matter and handed the papers to Howe. 'See if this is the same thing you've been finding. Then we can go into the matter again.'

Before the fire in the parlor, in the chair that Howe had been occupying, sat Blackburn. He sprang to his feet as Howe entered.

'I said my office, Mr. Blackburn.' Howe's voice was sharp. Then he was almost sorry for the rebuke, so clearly and naively did Blackburn seem to relish his stay in the parlor, close to authority.

'I'm in a bit of a hurry, sir,' he said, 'and I did want to be sure to speak to you, sir.'

He was really absurd, yet fifteen years from now he would have grown up to himself, to the assurance and mature beefiness. In banks, in consular offices, in brokerage firms, on the bench, more seriously affable, a little sterner, he would make use of his ability to be administered by his job. It was almost reassuring. Now he was exercising his too-great skill on Howe. 'I owe you an apology, sir,' he said.

Howe knew that he did, but he showed surprise.

'I mean, Doctor, after your having been so kind about letting me attend your class, I stopped coming.' He smiled in deprecation. 'Extracurricular activities take up so much of my time. I'm afraid I undertook more than I could perform.'

Howe had noticed the absence and had been a little irritated by it after Blackburn's elaborate plea. It was an absence that might be interpreted as a comment on the teacher. But there was only one way for him to answer. 'You've no need to apologize,' he said. 'It's wholly your affair.'

Blackburn beamed. 'I'm so glad you feel that way about it, sir. I was worried you might think I had stayed away because I was influenced by — ' he stopped and lowered his eyes.

Astonished, Howe said, 'Influenced by what?'

'Well, by — ' Blackburn hesitated and for answer pointed to the table on which lay the copy of *Life and Letters*. Without looking at it, he knew where to direct his hand. 'By the unfavorable publicity, sir.' He hurried on. 'And that brings me to another point, sir. I am secretary of Quill and Scroll, sir, the student literary society, and I wonder if you would address us. You could read your own poetry, sir, and defend your own point of view. It would be very interesting.'

It was truly amazing. Howe looked long and cruelly into Blackburn's face, trying to catch the secret of the mind that could have conceived this way of manipulating him, this way so daring and inept — but not entirely inept — with its malice so without malignity. The face did not yield its secret. Howe smiled broadly and said, 'Of course I don't think you were influenced by the unfavorable publicity.'

'I'm still going to take — regularly, for credit — your romantic poets course next term,' Blackburn said.

'Don't worry, my dear fellow, don't worry about it.'

Howe started to leave and Blackburn stopped him with, 'But about Quill, sir?'

'Suppose we wait until next term? I'll be less busy then.'

And Blackburn said, 'Very good, sir, and thank you.'

In his office the little encounter seemed less funny to Howe, was even in some indeterminate way disturbing. He made an effort to put it from his mind by turning to what was sure to disturb him more, the Tertan letter read in the new interpretation. He found what he had always found, the same florid leaps beyond fact and meaning, the same headlong certainty. But as his eye passed over the familiar scrawl it caught his own name, and for the second time that hour he felt the race of his blood.

'The Paraclete,' Tertan had written to the Dean, 'from a Greek word meaning to stand in place of, but going beyond the primitive idea to mean traditionally the helper, the one who comforts and assists, cannot without fundamental loss be jettisoned. Even if taken no longer in the supernatural sense, the concept remains deeply in the human consciousness inevitably. Humanitarianism is no reply, for not every man stands in the place of every other man for this other comrade's comfort. But certain are chosen out of the human race to be the consoler of some other. Of these, for example, is Joseph Barker Howe, Ph.D. Of intellects not the first yet of true intellect and lambent instructions, given to that which is intuitive and irrational, not to what is logical in the strict word, what is judged by him is of the heart and not the head. Here is one chosen, in that he chooses himself to stand in the place of another for comfort and consolation. To him more than another I give my gratitude, with all respect to our Dean who reads this, a noble man, but merely dedicated, not consecrated. But not in the aspect of the Paraclete only is Dr. Joseph Barker Howe established, for he must be the Paraclete to another aspect of himself, that which is driven and persecuted by the lack of understanding in the world at large, so that he in himself embodies the full history of man's tribulations and, overflowing upon others, notably the present writer, is the ultimate end.'

This was love. There was no escape from it. Try as Howe might to remember that Tertan was mad and all his emotions invalidated, he could not destroy the effect upon him of his student's stern, affectionate regard. He had betrayed not only a power of mind but a power of love. And, however firmly he held before his attention the fact of Tertan's madness, he could do nothing to banish the physical sensation of gratitude he felt. He had never thought of himself as 'driven and persecuted' and he did not now. But still he could not make meaningless his sensation of gratitude. The pitiable Tertan sternly pitied him, and comfort came from Tertan's never-to-be-comforted mind.

III

In an academic community, even an efficient one, official matters move slowly. The term drew to a close with no action in the case of Tertan, and Joseph Howe had to confront a curious problem. How should he grade his strange student, Tertan?

Tertan's final examinnation had been no different from all his other writing, and what did one 'give' such a student? De Witt must have his A, that was clear. Johnson would get a B. With Casebeer it was a question of a B-minus or a C-plus, and Stettenhover, who had been crammed by the team tutor to fill half a blue-book with his thin feminine scrawl, would have his C-minus which he would accept with mingled indiffence and resentment. But with Tertan it was not so easy.

The boy was still in the college process and his name could not be omitted from the grade sheet. Yet what should a mind under suspicion of madness be graded? Until the medical verdict was given, it was for Howe to continue as Tertan's teacher and to keep his judgment pedagogical. Impossible to give him an F: he had not failed. B was for Johnson's stolid mediocrity. He could not be put on the edge of passing with Stettenhover, for he exactly did not pass. In energy and richness of intellect he was perhaps even De Witt's superior, and Howe toyed grimly with the notion of giving him an A, but that would lower the value of the A De Witt had won with his beautiful and clear, if still arrogant, mind. There was a notation which the Registrar recognized — Inc., for Incomplete, and in the horrible comedy of the situation, Howe considered that. But really only a mark of M for Mad would serve.

In his perplexity, Howe sought the Dean, but the Dean was out of town. In the end, he decided to maintain the A-minus he had given Tertan at mid-term. After all, there had been no falling away from that quality. He entered it on the grade sheet with something like bravado.

Academic time moves quickly. A college year is not really a year, lacking as it does three months. And it is endlessly divided into units which, at their beginning, appear larger than they are — terms, half-terms, months, weeks.

And the ultimate unit, the hour, is not really an hour, lacking as it does ten minutes. And so the new term advanced rapidly, and one day the fields about the town were all brown, cleared of even the few thin patches of snow which had lingered so long.

Howe, as he lectured on the romantic poets, became conscious of Blackburn emanating wrath. Blackburn did it well, did it with enormous dignity. He did not stir in his seat, he kept his eyes fixed on Howe in perfect attention, but he abstained from using his notebook, there was no mistaking what he proposed to himself as an attitude. His elbow on the writing-wing of the chair, his chin on the curled fingers of his hand, he was the embodiment of intellectual indignation. He was thinking his own thoughts, would give no public offense, yet would claim his due, was not to be intimidated. Howe knew that he would present himself at the end of the hour.

Blackburn entered the office without invitation. He did not smile; there was no cajolery about him. Without invitation he sat down beside Howe's desk. He did not speak until he had taken the blue-book from his pocket. He said, "What does this mean, sir?"

It was a sound and conservative student tactic. Said in the usual way it meant, 'How could you have so misunderstood me?' or 'What does this mean for my future in the course?' But there were none of the humbler tones in Blackburn's way of saying it.

Howe made the established reply, 'I think that's for you to tell me.'

Blackburn continued icy. 'I'm sure I can't, sir.'

There was a silence between them. Both dropped their eyes to the blue-book on the desk. On its cover Howe had penciled: 'F. This is very poor work.'

Howe picked up the blue-book. There was always the possibility of injustice. The teacher may be bored by the mass of papers and not wholly attentive. A phrase, even the student's handwriting, may irritate him unreasonably. 'Well,' said Howe, 'Let's go through it.'

He opened the first page. 'Now here: you write, "In *The Ancient Mariner*, Coleridge lives in and transports us to a honey-sweet world where all is rich and strange, a world of charm to which we can escape from the humdrum existence of our daily lives, the world of romance. Here, in this warm and honey-sweet land of charming dreams we can relax and enjoy ourselves."'

Howe lowered the paper and waited with a neutral look for Blackburn to speak. Blackburn returned the look boldly, did not speak, sat stolid and lofty. At last Howe said, speaking gently, 'Did you mean that, or were you just at a loss for something to say?'

'You imply that I was just "bluffing"?' The quotation marks hung palpable in the air about the word.

'I'd like to know. I'd prefer believing that you were bluffing to believing that you really thought this.'

Blackburn's eyebrows went up. From the height of a great and firm-based idea he looked at his teacher. He clasped the crags for a moment and then pounced, craftily, suavely. 'Do you mean, Doctor Howe, that there aren't two opinions possible?'

It was superbly done in its air of putting all of Howe's intellectual life into the balance. Howe remained patient and simple. 'Yes, many opinions are possible, but not this one. Whatever anyone believes of *The Ancient Mariner*, no one can in reason believe that it represents a — a honey-sweet world in which we can relax.'

'But that is what I *feel*, sir.'

This was well-done, too. Howe said, 'Look, Mr. Blackburn. Do you really relax with hunger and thirst, the heat and the sea-serpents, the dead men with staring eyes, Life in Death and the skeletons? Come now, Mr. Blackburn.'

Blackburn made no answer, and Howe pressed forward. 'Now, you say of Wordsworth, "Of peasant stock himself, he turned from the effete life of the salons and found in the peasant the hope of a flaming revolution which would sweep away all the old ideas. This is the subject of his best poems." '

Beaming at his teacher with youthful eagerness, Blackburn said, 'Yes, sir, a rebel, a bringer of light to suffering mankind. I see him as a kind of Prothemeus.'

'A kind of what?'

'Prothemeus, sir.'

'Think, Mr. Blackburn. We were talking about him only today and I mentioned his name a dozen times. You don't mean Prothemeus. You mean — ' Howe waited, but there was no response.

'You mean Prometheus.'

Blackburn gave no assent, and Howe took the reins. 'You've done a bad job here, Mr. Blackburn, about as bad as could be done.' He saw Blackburn stiffen and his genial face harden again. 'It shows either a lack of preparation or a complete lack of understanding.' He saw Blackburn's face begin to go to pieces and he stopped.

'Oh, sir,' Blackburn burst out, 'I've never had a mark like this before, never anything below a B, never. A thing like this has never happened to me before.'

It must be true, it was a statement too easily verified. Could it be that other instructors accepted such flaunting nonsense? Howe wanted to end the interview. 'I'll set it down to lack of preparation,' he said. 'I know you're busy. That's not an excuse, but it's an explanation. Now, suppose you really prepare, and then take another quiz in two weeks. We'll forget this one and count the other.'

Blackburn squirmed with pleasure and gratitude. 'Thank you, sir. You're really very kind, very kind.'

Howe rose to conclude the visit. 'All right, then — in two weeks.'

It was that day that the Dean imparted to Howe the conclusion of the case of Tertan. It was simple and a little anti-climatic. A physician had been called in, and had said the word, given the name.

'A classic case, he called it,' the Dean said. 'Not a doubt in the world,' he said. His eyes were full of miserable pity, and he clutched at a word. 'A classic case, a classic case.' To his aid and to Howe's there came the Parthenon[18] and the form of the Greek drama, the Aristotelian logic, Racine[19] and the Well-Tempered Clavichord,[20] the blueness of the Aegean and its clear sky. Classic — that is to say, without a doubt, perfect in its way, a veritable model, and, as the Dean had been told, sure to take a perfectly predictable and inevitable course to a foreknown conclusion.

It was not only pity that stood in the Dean's eyes. For a moment there was fear too. 'Terrible,' he said, 'it is simply terrible.'

Then he went on briskly. 'Naturally, we've told the boy nothing. And, naturally, we won't. His tuition's paid by his scholarship, and we'll continue him on the rolls until the end of the year. That will be kindest. After that the matter will be out of our control. We'll see, of course, that he gets into the proper hands. I'm told there will be no change, he'll go on like this, be as good as this, for four to six months. And so we'll just go along as usual.'

So Tertan continued to sit in Section 5 of English 1A, to his classmates still a figure of curiously dignified fun, symbol to most of them of the respectable but absurd intellectual life. But to his teacher he was now very different. He had not changed — he was still the greyhound casting for the scent of ideas, and Howe could see that he was still the same Tertan, but he could not feel it. What he felt as he looked at the boy sitting in his accustomed place was the hard blank of a fact. The fact itself was formidable and depressing. But what Howe was chiefly aware of was that he had permitted the metamorphosis of Tertan from person to fact.

As much as possible he avoided seeing Tertan's upraised hand and eager eye. But the fact did not know of its mere factuality, it continued its existence as if it were Tertan, hand up and eye questioning, and one day it appeared in Howe's office with a document.

'Even the spirit who lives egregiously, above the herd, must have its relations with the fellowman,' Tertan declared. He laid the document on Howe's desk. It was headed 'Quill and Scroll Society of Dwight College. Application for Membership.'

'In most ways these are crass minds,' Tertan said, touching the paper. 'Yet as a whole, bound together in their common love of letters, they transcend their intellectual lacks since it is not a paradox that the whole is greater than the sum of its parts.'

[18] a Doric temple built in Athens during the 5th century B.C. to honor the goddess Athena; probably the most beautiful example of classical architecture in the world.
[19] Jean Baptiste Racine (1639–1699), a great French playwright who was one of the few able to adapt Greek tragedies successfully to the strict alexandrine form of the French classical period.
[20] the title given by Johann Sebastian Bach (1685–1750) to two originally separate sets of preludes and fugues written in all the major and minor keys.

'When are the elections?' Howe asked.

'They take place tomorrow.'

'I certainly hope you will be successful.'

'Thank you. Would you wish to implement that hope? A rather dirty finger pointed to the bottom of the sheet. 'A faculty recommender is necessary,' Tertan said stiffly, and waited.

'And you wish me to recommend you?'

'It would be an honor.'

'You may use my name.'

Tertan's finger pointed again. 'It must be a written sponsorship, signed by the sponsor.' There was a large blank space on the form under the heading, 'Opinion of Faculty Sponsor.'

This was almost another thing and Howe hesitated. Yet there was nothing else to do and he took out his fountain pen. He wrote, 'Mr. Ferdinand Tertan is marked by his intense devotion to letters and by his exceptional love of all things of the mind.' To this he signed his name, which looked bold and assertive on the white page. It disturbed him, the strange affirming power of a name. With a businesslike air, Tertan whipped up the paper, folding it with decision, and put it into his pocket. He bowed and took his departure, leaving Howe with the sense of having done something oddly momentous.

And so much now seemed odd and momentous to Howe that should not have seemed so. It was odd and momentous, he felt, when he sat with Blackburn's second quiz before him, and wrote in an excessively firm hand the grade of C-minus. The paper was a clear, an indisputable failure. He was carefully and consciously committing a cowardice. Blackburn had told the truth when he had pleaded his past record. Howe had consulted it in the Dean's office. It showed no grade lower than a B-minus. A canvass of some of Blackburn's previous instructors had brought vague attestations to the adequate powers of a student imperfectly remembered, and sometimes surprise that his abilities could be questioned at all.

As he wrote the grade, Howe told himself that his cowardice sprang from an unwillingness to have more dealings with a student he disliked. He knew it was simpler than that. He knew he feared Blackburn; that was the absurd truth. And cowardice did not solve the matter after all. Blackburn, flushed with a first success, attacked at once. The minimal passing grade had not assuaged his feelings and he sat at Howe's desk and again the blue-book lay between them. Blackburn said nothing. With an enormous impudence, he was waiting for Howe to speak and explain himself.

At last Howe said sharply and rudely, 'Well?' His throat was tense and the blood was hammering in his head. His mouth was tight with anger at himself for his disturbance.

Blackburn's glance was almost baleful. 'This is impossible, sir.'

'But there it is,' Howe answered.

'Sir?' Blackburn had not caught the meaning but his tone was still haughty.

Impatiently Howe said, 'There it is, plain as day. Are you here to complain again?'

'Indeed I am, sir.' There was surprise in Blackburn's voice that Howe should ask the question.

'I shouldn't complain if I were you. You did a thoroughly bad job on your first quiz. This one is a little, only a very little, better.' This was not true. If anything, it was worse.

'That might be a matter of opinion, sir.'

'It is a matter of opinion. Of my opinion.'

'Another opinion might be different, sir.'

'You really believe that?' Howe said.

'Yes.' The omission of the 'sir' was monumental.

'Whose, for example?'

'The Dean's, for example.' Then the fleshy jaw came forward a little. 'Or a certain literary critic's, for example.'

It was colossal and almost too much for Blackburn himself to handle. The solidity of his face almost crumpled under it. But he withstood his own audacity and went on. 'And the Dean's opinion might be guided by the knowledge that the person who gave me this mark is the man whom a famous critic, the most eminent judge of literature in this country, called a drunken man. The Dean might think twice about whether such a man is fit to teach Dwight students.'

Howe said in quiet admonition, 'Blackburn, you're mad,' meaning no more than to check the boy's extravagance.

But Blackburn paid no heed. He had another shot in the locker. 'And the Dean might be guided by the information, of which I have evidence, documentary evidence,' — he slapped his breast pocket twice — 'that this same person personally recommended to the college literary society, the oldest in the country, that he personally recommended a student who is crazy, who threw the meeting into an uproar — a psychiatric case. The Dean might take that into account.'

Howe was never to learn the details of that 'uproar.' He had always to content himself with the dim but passionate picture which at that moment sprang into his mind, of Tertan standing on some abstract height and madly denouncing the multitude of Quill and Scroll who howled him down.

He sat quiet a moment and looked at Blackburn. The ferocity had entirely gone from the student's face. He sat regarding his teacher almost benevolently. He had played a good card and now, scarcely at all unfriendly, he was waiting to see the effect. Howe took up the blue-book and negligently sifted through it. He read a page, closed the book, struck out the C-minus and wrote an F.

'Now you may take the paper to the Dean,' he said. 'You may tell him that after reconsidering it, I lowered the grade.'

The gasp was audible. 'Oh, sir!' Blackburn cried. 'Please!' His face was agonized. 'It means my graduation, my livelihood, my future. Don't do this to me.'

'It's done already.'

Blackburn stood up. 'I spoke rashly, sir, hastily. I had no intention, no real intention, of seeing the Dean. It rests with you — entirely, entirely. I *hope* you will restore the first mark.'

'Take the matter to the Dean or not, just as you choose. The grade is what you deserve and it stands.'

Blackburn's head dropped. 'And will I be failed at mid-term, sir?'

'Of course.'

From deep out of Blackburn's great chest rose a cry of anguish. 'Oh, sir, if you want me to go down on my knees to you, I will, I will.'

Howe looked at him in amazement.

'I will, I will. On my knees, sir. This mustn't, mustn't happen.'

He spoke so literally, meaning so very truly that his knees and exactly his knees were involved and seeming to think that he was offering something of tangible value to his teacher, that Howe, whose head had become icy clear in the nonsensical drama, thought, 'The boy is mad,' and began to speculate fantastically whether something in himself attracted or developed aberration. He could see himself standing absurdly before the Dean and saying, 'I've found another. This time it's the vice-president of the Council, the manager of the debating team and secretary of Quill and Scroll.'

One more such discovery, he thought, and he himself would be discovered! And there, suddenly, Blackburn was on his knees with a thump, his huge thighs straining his trousers, his hand outstretched in a great gesture of supplication.

With a cry, Howe shoved back his swivel chair and it rolled away on its casters half across the little room. Blackburn knelt for a moment to nothing at all, then got to his feet.

Howe rose abruptly. He said, 'Blackburn, you will stop acting like an idiot. Dust your knees off, take your paper and get out. You've behaved like a fool and a malicious person. You have half a term to do a decent job. Keep your silly mouth shut and try to do it. Now get out.'

Blackburn's head was low. He raised it and there was a pious light in his eyes. 'Will you shake hands, sir?' he said. He thrust out his hand.

'I will not,' Howe said.

Head and hand sank together. Blackburn picked up his blue-book and walked to the door. He turned and said, 'Thank you, sir.' His back, as he departed, was heavy with tragedy and stateliness.

IV

After years of bad luck with the weather, the College had a perfect day for Commencement. It was wonderfully bright, the air so transparent, the wind so brisk that no one could resist talking about it.

As Howe set out for the campus he heard Hilda calling from the back yard. She called, 'Professor, professor,' and came running to him.

Howe said, 'What's this "professor" business?'

'Mother told me,' Hilda said. 'You've been promoted. And I want to take your picture.'

'Next year,' said Howe. 'I won't be a professor until next year. And you know better than to call anybody "professor." '

'It was just in fun,' Hilda said. She seemed disappointed.

'But you can take my picture if you want. I won't look much different next year.' Still, it was frightening. It might mean that he was to stay in this town all his life.

Hilda brightened. 'Can I take it in this?' she said, and touched the gown he carried over his arm.

Howe laughed. 'Yes, you can take it in this.'

'I'll get my things and meet you in front of Otis,' Hilda said. 'I have the background all picked out.'

On the campus the Commencement crowd was already large. It stood about in eager, nervous little family groups. As he crossed, Howe was greeted by a student, capped and gowned, glad of the chance to make an event for his parents by introducing one of his teachers. It was while Howe stood there chatting that he saw Tertan.

He had never seen anyone quite so alone, as though a circle had been woven about him to separate him from the gay crowd on the campus. Not that Tertan was not gay, he was the gayest of all. Three weeks had passed since Howe had last seen him, the weeks of examination, the lazy week before Commencement, and this was now a different Tertan. On his head he wore a panama hat, broad-brimmed and fine, of the shape associated with South American planters. He wore a suit of raw silk, luxurious, but yellowed with age and much too tight, and he sported a whangee cane. He walked sedately, the hat tilted at a devastating angle, the stick coming up and down in time to his measured tread. He had, Howe guessed, outfitted himself to greet the day in the clothes of that ruined father whose existence was on record in the Dean's office. Gravely and arrogantly he surveyed the scene — in it, his whole bearing seemed to say, but not of it. With his haughty step, with his flashing eye, Tertan was coming nearer. Howe did not wish to be seen. He shifted his position slightly. When he looked again, Tertan was not in sight.

The chapel clock struck the quarter hour. Howe detached himself from his chat and hurried to Otis Hall at the far end of the campus. Hilda had not yet come. He went up into the high portico and, using the glass of the door for a mirror, put on his gown, adjusted the hood on his shoulders and set the mortarboard on his head. When he came down the steps, Hilda had arrived.

Nothing could have told him more forcibly that a year had passed than the development of Hilda's photographic possessons from the box camera of the previous fall. By a strap about her neck was hung a leather case, so thick and strong, so carefully stitched and so molded to its contents that it could only hold a costly camera. The appearance was deceptive, Howe knew, for he had been present at the Aikens' pre-Christmas conference about its purchase. It was only a fairly good domestic camera. Still, it looked very impressive. Hilda carried another leather case from which she drew a collapsible tripod. Decisively she extended each of its gleaming legs and set it up on the path. She removed the camera from its case and fixed it to the tripod. In its compact efficiency the camera almost had a life of its own, but Hilda treated it with easy familiarity, looked into its eye, glanced casually at its gauges. Then from a pocket she took still another leather case and drew from it a small instrument through which she looked first at Howe, who began to feel inanimate and lost, and then at the sky. She made some adjustment on the instrument, then some adjustment on the camera. She swept the scene with her eye, found a spot and pointed the camera in its direction. She walked to the spot, stood on it and beckoned to Howe. With each new leather case, with each new instrument, and with each new adjustment she had grown in ease and now she said, 'Joe, will you stand here?'

Obediently Howe stood where he was bidden. She had yet another instrument. She took out a tape-measure on a mechanical spool. Kneeling down before Howe, she put the little metal ring of the tape under the tip of his shoe. At her request, Howe pressed it with his toe. When she had measured her distance, she nodded to Howe who released the tape. At a touch, it sprang back into the spool. 'You have to be careful if you're going to get what you want,' Hilda said. 'I don't believe in all this snap-snap-snapping,' she remarked loftily. Howe nodded in agreement, although he was beginning to think Hilda's care excessive.

Now at last the moment had come. Hilda squinted into the camera, moved the tripod slightly. She stood to the side, holding the plunger of the shutter-cable. 'Ready,' she said. 'Will you relax, Joseph, please?' Howe realized that he was standing frozen. Hilda stood poised and precise as a setter, one hand holding the little cable, the other extended with curled dainty fingers like a dancer's, as if expressing to her subject the precarious delicacy of the moment. She pressed the plunger and there was the click. At once she stirred to action, got behind the camera, turned a new exposure. 'Thank you,' she said. 'Would you stand under that tree and let me do a character study with light and shade?'

The childish absurdity of the remark restored Howe's ease. He went to the little tree. The pattern the leaves made on his gown was what Hilda was after. He had just taken a satisfactory position when he heard in the unmistakable voice, 'Ah, Doctor! Having your picture taken?'

Howe gave up the pose and turned to Blackburn who stood on the walk, his hands behind his back, a little too large for his bachelor's gown. Annoyed that Blackburn should see him posing for a character study in light and shade, Howe said irritably, 'Yes, having my picture taken.'

Blackburn beamed at Hilda. 'And the little photographer?' he said. Hilda fixed her eyes on the ground and stood closer to her brilliant and aggressive camera. Blackburn, teetering on his heels, his hands behind his back, wholly prelatical and benignly patient, was not abashed at the silence. At last Howe said, "If you'll excuse us, Mr. Blackburn, we'll go on with the picture.'

'Go right ahead, sir. I'm running along.' But he only came closer. 'Doctor Howe,' he said fervently, 'I want to tell you how glad I am that I was able to satisfy your standards at last.'

Howe was surprised at the hard, insulting brightness of his own voice, and even Hilda looked up curiously as he said, 'Nothing you have ever done has satisfied me, and nothing you could ever do would satisfy me, Blackburn.'

With a glance at Hilda, Blackburn made a gesture as if to hush Howe — as though all his former bold malice had taken for granted a kind of under-standing between himself and his teacher, a secret which must not be be-trayed to a third person. 'I only meant, sir,' he said, 'that I was able to pass your course after all.'

Howe said, 'You didn't pass my course. I passed you out of my course. I passed you without even reading your paper. I wanted to be sure the college would be rid of you. And when all the grades were in and I did read your paper, I saw I was right not to have read it first.'

Blackburn presented a stricken face. 'It was very bad, sir?'

But Howe had turned away. The paper had been fantastic. The paper had been, if he wished to see it so, mad. It was at this moment that the Dean came up behind Howe and caught his arm. 'Hello, Joseph,' he said. 'We'd better be getting along, it's almost late.'

He was not a familiar man, but when he saw Blackburn, who approached to greet him, he took Blackburn's arm, too. 'Hello, Theodore,' he said. Lean-ing forward on Howe's arm and on Blackburn's, he said, 'Hello, Hilda dear.' Hilda replied quietly, 'Hello, Uncle George.'

Still clinging to their arms, still linking Howe and Blackburn, the Dean said, 'Another year gone, Joe, and we've turned out another crop. After you've been here a few years, you'll find it reasonably upsetting — you wonder how there can be so many graduating classes while you stay the same. But of course, you don't stay the same.' Then he said, 'Well,' sharply, to dismiss the thought. He pulled Blackburn's arm and swung him around to Howe. 'Have you heard about Teddy Blackburn?' he asked. 'He has a job already, before graduation — the first man of his class to be placed.' Ex-pectant of congratulations, Blackburn beamed at Howe. Howe remained silent.

'Isn't that good?' the Dean said. Still Howe did not answer and the Dean, puzzled and put out, turned to Hilda. 'That's a very fine-looking camera, Hilda.' She touched it with affectionate pride.

'Instruments of precision,' said a voice. 'Instruments of precision.' Of the three with joined arms, Howe was the nearest to Tertan, whose gaze took in all the scene except the smile and the nod which Howe gave him. The boy leaned on his cane. The broad-brimmed hat, canting jauntily over his eye, confused the image of his face that Howe had established, suppressed the rigid lines of the ascetic and brought out the baroque curves. It made an effect of perverse majesty.

'Instruments of precision,' said Tertan for the last time, addressing no one, making a casual comment to the universe. And it occurred to Howe that Tertan might not be referring to Hilda's equipment. The sense of the thrice-woven circle of the boy's loneliness smote him fiercely. Tertan stood in majestic jauntiness, superior to all the scene, but his isolation made Howe ache with a pity of which Tertan was more the cause than the object, so general and indiscriminate was it.

Whether in his sorrow he made some unintended movement toward Tertan which the Dean checked, or whether the suddenly tightened grip on his arm was the Dean's own sorrow and fear, he did not know. Tertan watched them in the incurious way people watch a photograph being taken, and suddenly the thought that, to the boy, it must seem that the three were posing for a picture together made Howe detach himself almost rudely from the Dean's grasp.

'I promised Hilda another picture,' he announced — needlessly, for Tertan was no longer there, he had vanished in the last sudden flux of visitors who, now that the band had struck up, were rushing nervously to find seats.

'You'd better hurry,' the Dean said. 'I'll go along, it's getting late for me.' He departed and Blackburn walked stately by his side.

Howe again took his position under the little tree which cast its shadow over his face and gown. 'Just hurry, Hilda, won't you?' he said. Hilda held the cable at arm's length, her other arm crooked and her fingers crisped. She rose on her toes and said 'Ready,' and pressed the release. 'Thank you,' she said gravely and began to dismantle her camera as he hurried off to join the procession.

Albert Camus   (1913–1960)

FRENCH WRITER (ALGERIAN-BORN)

The Guest

The schoolmaster was watching the two men climb toward him. One was on horseback, the other on foot. They had not yet tackled the abrupt rise leading to the schoolhouse built on the hillside. They were toiling onward, making slow progress in the snow, among the stones, on the vast expanse of the high, deserted plateau. From time to time the horse stumbled. Without hearing anything yet, he could see the breath issuing from the horse's nostrils. One of the men, at least, knew the region. They were following the trail although it had disappeared days ago under a layer of dirty white snow. The schoolmaster calculated that it would take them half an hour to get onto the hill. It was cold; he went back into the school to get a sweater.

He crossed the empty, frigid classroom. On the blackboard the four rivers of France,[1] drawn with four different colored chalks, had been flowing toward their estuaries for the past three days. Snow had suddenly fallen in mid-October after eight months of drought without the transition of rain, and the twenty pupils, more or less, who lived in the villages scattered over the plateau had stopped coming. With fair weather they would return. Daru now heated only the single room that was his lodging, adjoining the classroom and giving also onto the plateau to the east. Like the class windows, his window looked to the south too. On that side the school was a few kilometers from the point where the plateau began to slope toward the south. In clear weather could be seen the purple mass of the mountain range where the gap opened onto the desert.

Somewhat warmed, Daru returned to the window from which he had first seen the two men. They were no longer visible. Hence they must have tackled the rise. The sky was not so dark, for the snow had stopped falling during the night. The morning had opened with a dirty light which had scarcely become brighter as the ceiling of clouds lifted. At two in the afternoon it seemed as if the day were merely beginning. But still this was better than those three days when the thick snow was falling amidst unbroken darkness with little gusts of wind that rattled the double door of the classroom. Then Daru had spent long hours in his room, leaving it only to go to the shed and feed the chickens or get some coal. Fortunately the delivery truck from Tadjid, the nearest village to the north, had brought his supplies two days before the blizzard. It would return in forty-eight hours.

Besides, he had enough to resist a siege, for the little room was cluttered with bags of wheat that the administration left as a stock to distribute to those of his pupils whose families had suffered from the drought. Actually they had all been victims because they were all poor. Every day Daru would distribute a ration to the children. They had missed it, he knew, during these bad days. Possibly one of the fathers or big brothers would come this afternoon and he could supply them with grain. It was just a matter of carrying them over to the next harvest. Now shiploads of wheat were arriving from France and the worst was over. But it would be hard to forget that poverty, that army of ragged ghosts wandering in the sunlight, the plateaus burned to a cinder month after month, the earth shriveled up little by little, literally scorched, every stone bursting into dust under one's foot. The sheep had died then by thousands and even a few men, here and there, sometimes without anyone's knowing.

In contrast with such poverty, he who lived almost like a monk in his remote schoolhouse, nonetheless satisfied with the little he had and with the

[1] The setting is Algeria, a protectorate of France when the story was written.

rough life, had felt like a lord with his whitewashed walls, his narrow couch, his unpainted shelves, his well, and his weekly provision of water and food. And suddenly this snow, without warning, without the foretaste of rain. This is the way the region was, cruel to live in, even without men — who didn't help matters either. But Daru had been born here. Everywhere else, he felt exiled.

He stepped out onto the terrace in front of the schoolhouse. The two men were now halfway up the slope. He recognized the horseman as Balducci, the old gendarme he had known for a long time. Balducci was holding on the end of a rope an Arab who was walking behind him with hands bound and head lowered. The gendarme waved a greeting to which Daru did not reply, lost as he was in contemplation of the Arab dressed in a faded blue jellaba, his feet in sandals but covered with socks of heavy raw wool, his head surmounted by a narrow, short *chèche*. They were approaching. Balducci was holding back his horse in order not to hurt the Arab, and the group was advancing slowly.

Within earshot, Balducci shouted: "One hour to do the three kilometers from El Ameur!" Daru did not answer. Short and square in his thick sweater, he watched them climb. Not once had the Arab raised his head. "Hello," said Daru when they got up onto the terrace. "Come in and warm up." Balducci painfully got down from his horse without letting go the rope. From under his bristling mustache he smiled at the schoolmaster. His little dark eyes, deep-set under a tanned forehead, and his mouth surrounded with wrinkles made him look attentive and studious. Daru took the bridle, led the horse to the shed, and came back to the two men, who were now waiting for him in the school. He led them into his room. "I am going to heat up the classroom," he said. "We'll be more comfortable there." When he entered the room again, Balducci was on the couch. He had undone the rope tying him to the Arab, who had squatted near the stove. His hands still bound, the *chèche* pushed back on his head, he was looking toward the window. At first Daru noticed only his huge lips, fat, smooth, almost Negroid; yet his nose was straight, his eyes were dark and full of fever. The *chèche* revealed an obstinate forehead and, under the weathered skin now rather discolored by the cold, the whole face had a restless and rebellious look that struck Daru when the Arab, turning his face toward him, looked him straight in the eyes. "Go into the other room," said the schoolmaster, "and I'll make you some mint tea." "Thanks," Balducci said. "What a chore! How I long for retirement." And addressing his prisoner in Arabic: "Come on, you." The Arab got up and, slowly, holding his bound wrists in front of him, went into the classroom.

With the tea, Daru brought a chair. But Balducci was already enthroned on the nearest pupil's desk and the Arab had squatted against the teacher's platform facing the stove, which stood between the desk and the window. When he held out the glass of tea to the prisoner, Daru hesitated at the sight of his bound hands. "He might perhaps be untied." "Sure," said Balducci. "That was for the trip." He started to get to his feet. But Daru, setting the glass on the floor, had knelt beside the Arab. Without saying anything, the Arab watched him with his feverish eyes. Once his hands were free, he rubbed his swollen wrists against each other, took the glass of tea, and sucked up the burning liquid in swift little sips.

"Good," said Daru. "And where are you headed?"

Balducci withdrew his mustache from the tea. "Here, son."

"Odd pupils! And you're spending the night?"

"No. I'm going back to El Ameur. And you will deliver this fellow to Tinguit. He is expected at police headquarters."

Balducci was looking at Daru with a friendly little smile.

"What's this story?" asked the schoolmaster. "Are you pulling my leg?"

"No, son. Those are the orders."

"The orders? I'm not . . ." Daru hesitated, not wanting to hurt the old Corsican. "I mean, that's not my job."

"What! What's the meaning of that? In wartime people do all kinds of jobs."

"Then I'll wait for the declaration of war!"

Balducci nodded.

"O.K. But the orders exist and they concern you too. Things are brewing, it appears. There is talk of a forthcoming revolt. We are mobilized, in a way."

Daru still had his obstinate look.

"Listen, son," Balducci said. "I like you and you must understand. There's only a dozen of us at El Ameur to patrol throughout the whole territory of a small department and I must get back in a hurry. I was told to hand this guy over to you and return without delay. He couldn't be kept there. His village was beginning to stir; they wanted to take him back. You must take him to Tinguit tomorrow before the day is over. Twenty kilometers shouldn't faze a husky fellow like you. After that, all will be over. You'll come back to your pupils and your comfortable life."

Behind the wall the horse could be heard snorting and pawing the earth. Daru was looking out the window. Decidedly, the weather was clearing and the light was increasing over the snowy plateau. When all the snow was melted, the sun would take over again and once more would burn the fields of stone. For days, still, the unchanging sky would shed its dry light on the solitary expanse where nothing had any connection with man.

"After all," he said, turning around toward Balducci, "what did he do?" And, before the gendarme had opened his mouth, he asked: "Does he speak French?"

"No, not a word. We had been looking for him for a month, but they were hiding him. He killed his cousin."

"Is he against us?"

"I don't think so. But you can never be sure."

"Why did he kill?"

"A family squabble, I think. One owed the other grain, it seems. It's not at all clear. In short, he killed his cousin with a billhook. You know, like a sheep, *kreezk!*"

Balducci made the gesture of drawing a blade across his throat and the Arab, his attention attracted, watched him with a sort of anxiety. Daru felt a sudden wrath against the man, against all men with their rotten spite, their tireless hates, their blood lust.

But the kettle was singing on the stove. He served Balducci more tea, hesitated, then served the Arab again, who, a second time, drank avidly. His raised arms made the jellaba fall open and the schoolmaster saw his thin, muscular chest.

"Thanks, kid," Balducci said. "And now, I'm off."

He got up and went toward the Arab, taking a small rope from his pocket.

"What are you doing?" Daru asked dryly.

Balducci, disconcerted, showed him the rope.

"Don't bother."

The old gendarme hesitated. "It's up to you. Of course, you are armed?"

"I have my shotgun."

"Where?"

"In the trunk."

"You ought to have it near your bed."

"Why? I have nothing to fear."

"You're crazy, son. If there's an uprising, no one is safe, we're all in the same boat."

"I'll defend myself. I'll have time to see them coming."

Balducci began to laugh, then suddenly the mustache covered the white teeth.

"You'll have time? O.K. That's just what I was saying. You have always been a little cracked. That's why I like you, my son was like that."

At the same time he took out his revolver and put it on the desk.

"Keep it; I don't need two weapons from here to El Ameur."

The revolver shone against the black paint of the table. When the gendarme turned toward him, the schoolmaster caught the smell of leather and horseflesh.

"Listen, Balducci," Daru said suddenly, "every bit of this disgusts me, and first of all your fellow here. But I won't hand him over. Fight, yes, if I have to. But not that."

The old gendarme stood in front of him and looked at him severely.

"You're being a fool," he said slowly. "I don't like it either. You don't get used to putting a rope on a man even after years of it, and you're even ashamed — yes, ashamed. But you can't let them have their way."

"I won't hand him over," Daru said again.

"It's an order, son, and I repeat it."

"That's right. Repeat to them what I've said to you: I won't hand him over."

Balducci made a visible effort to reflect. He looked at the Arab and at Daru. At last he decided.

"No, I won't tell them anything. If you want to drop us, go ahead; I'll not denounce you. I have an order to deliver the prisoner and I'm doing so. And now you'll just sign this paper for me."

"There's no need. I'll not deny that you left him with me."

"Don't be mean with me. I know you'll tell the truth. You're from hereabouts and you are a man. But you must sign, that's the rule."

Daru opened his drawer, took out a little square bottle of purple ink, the red wooden penholder with the "sergeant-major" pen he used for making models of penmanship, and signed. The gendarme carefully folded the paper and put it into his wallet. Then he moved toward the door.

"I'll see you off," Daru said.

"No," said Balducci. "There's no use being polite. You insulted me."

He looked at the Arab, motionless in the same spot, sniffed peevishly, and turned away toward the door. "Good-by, son," he said. The door shut behind him. Balducci appeared suddenly outside the window and then disappeared. His footsteps were muffled by the snow. The horse stirred on the other side of the wall and several chickens fluttered in fright. A moment later Balducci reappeared outside the window leading the horse by the bridle. He walked toward the little rise without turning around and disappeared from sight with the horse following him. A big stone could be heard bouncing down. Daru walked back toward the prisoner, who, without stirring, never took his eyes off him. "Wait," the schoolmaster said in Arabic and went toward the bedroom. As he was going through the door, he had a second thought, went to the desk, took the revolver, and stuck it in his pocket. Then, without looking back, he went into his room.

For some time he lay on his couch watching the sky gradually close over, listening to the silence. It was this silence that had seemed painful to him during the first days here, after the war. He had requested a post in the little town at the base of the foothills separating the upper plateaus from the desert. There, rocky walls, green and black to the north, pink and lavender to the south, marked the frontier of eternal summer. He had been named to a post farther north, on the plateau itself. In the beginning, the solitude and the silence had been hard for him on these wastelands peopled only by stones. Occasionally, furrows suggested cultivation, but they had been dug to uncover a certain kind of stone good for building. The only plowing here was to harvest rocks. Elsewhere a thin layer of soil accumulated in the hollows would be scraped out to enrich paltry village gardens. This is the way it was: bare rock covered three quarters of the region. Towns sprang up, flourished, then disappeared; men came by, loved one another or fought bitterly, then died. No one in this desert, neither he nor his guest, mattered. And yet, outside this desert neither of them, Daru knew, could have really lived.

When he got up, no noise came from the classroom. He was amazed at the unmixed joy he derived from the mere thought that the Arab might have fled and that he would be alone with no decision to make. But the prisoner was there. He had merely stretched out between the stove and the desk. With eyes open, he was staring at the ceiling. In that position, his thick lips were particularly noticeable, giving him a pouting look. "Come," said Daru. The Arab got up and followed him. In the bedroom, the schoolmaster pointed to a chair near the table under the window. The Arab sat down without taking his eyes off Daru.

"Are you hungry?"

"Yes," the prisoner said.

Daru set the table for two. He took flour and oil, shaped a cake in a frying-pan, and lighted the little stove that functioned on bottled gas. While the cake was cooking, he went out to the shed to get cheese, eggs, dates, and condensed milk. When the cake was done he set it on the window sill to cool, heated some condensed milk diluted with water, and beat up the eggs into an omelette. In one of his motions he knocked against the revolver stuck in his right pocket. He set the bowl down, went into the classroom, and put the revolver in his desk drawer. When he came back to the room, night was falling. He put on the light and served the Arab. "Eat," he said. The Arab took a piece of the cake, lifted it eagerly to his mouth, and stopped short.

"And you?" he asked.

"After you. I'll eat too."

The thick lips opened slightly. The Arab hesitated, then bit into the cake determinedly.

The meal over, the Arab looked at the schoolmaster. "Are you the judge?"

"No, I'm simply keeping you until tomorrow."

"Why do you eat with me?"

"I'm hungry."

The Arab fell silent. Daru got up and went out. He brought back a folding bed from the shed, set it up between the table and the stove, perpendicular to his own bed. From a large suitcase which, upright in a corner, served as a shelf for papers, he took two blankets and arranged them on the camp bed. Then he stopped, felt useless, and sat down on his bed. There was nothing more to do or to get ready. He had to look at this man. He looked at him, therefore, trying to imagine his face bursting with rage. He couldn't do so. He could see nothing but the dark yet shining eyes and the animal mouth.

"Why did you kill him?" he asked in a voice whose hostile tone surprised him.

The Arab looked away.

"He ran away. I ran after him."

He raised his eyes to Daru again and they were full of a sort of woeful interrogation. "Now what will they do to me?"

"Are you afraid?"

He stiffened, turning his eyes away.

"Are you sorry?"

The Arab stared at him openmouthed. Obviously he did not understand. Daru's annoyance was growing. At the same time he felt awkward and self-conscious with his big body wedged between the two beds.

"Lie down there," he said impatiently. "That's your bed."

The Arab didn't move. He called to Daru:

"Tell me!"

The schoolmaster looked at him.

"Is the gendarme coming back tomorrow?"

"I don't know."

"Are you coming with us?"

"I don't know. Why?"

The prisoner got up and stretched out on top of the blankets, his feet toward the window. The light from the electric bulb shone straight into his eyes and he closed them at once.

"Why?" Daru repeated, standing beside the bed.

The Arab opened his eyes under the blinding light and looked at him, trying not to blink.

"Come with us," he said.

In the middle of the night, Daru was still not asleep. He had gone to bed after undressing completely; he generally slept naked. But when he suddenly realized that he had nothing on, he hesitated. He felt vulnerable and the temptation came to him to put his clothes back on. Then he shrugged his shoulders; after all, he wasn't a child and, if need be, he could break his adversary in two. From his bed he could observe him, lying on his back, still motionless with his eyes closed under the harsh light. When Daru turned out the light, the darkness seemed to coagulate all of a sudden. Little by little, the night came back to life in the window where the starless sky was stirring gently. The schoolmaster soon made out the body lying at his feet. The Arab still did not move, but his eyes seemed open. A faint wind was prowling around the schoolhouse. Perhaps it would drive away the clouds and the sun would reappear.

During the night the wind increased. The hens fluttered a little and then were silent. The Arab turned over on his side with his back to Daru, who thought he heard him moan. Then he listened for his guest's breathing, become heavier and more regular. He listened to that breath so close to him and mused without being able to go to sleep. In this room where he had been sleeping alone for a year, this presence bothered him. But it bothered him also by imposing on him a sort of brotherhood he knew well but refused to accept in the present circumstances. Men who share the same rooms, soldiers or prisoners, develop a strange alliance as if, having cast off their armor with their clothing, they fraternized every evening, over and above their differences, in the ancient community of dream and fatigue. But Daru shook himself; he didn't like such musings, and it was essential to sleep.

A little later, however, when the Arab stirred slightly, the schoolmaster was still not asleep. When the prisoner made a second move, he stiffened, on the alert. The Arab was lifting himself slowly on his arms with almost the motion of a sleepwalker. Seated upright in bed, he waited motionless without turning his head toward Daru, as if he were listening attentively. Daru did not stir; it had just occurred to him that the revolver was still in the drawer of his desk. It was better to act at once. Yet he continued to observe the prisoner, who, with the same slithery motion, put his feet on the ground, waited again, then began to stand up slowly. Daru was about to call out to him when the Arab began to walk, in a quite natural but extraordinarily silent way. He was heading toward the door at the end of the room that opened into the shed. He lifted the latch with precaution and went out, pushing the door behind him but without shutting it. Daru had not stirred. "He is running away," he merely thought. "Good riddance!" Yet he listened attentively. The hens were not fluttering; the guest must be on the plateau. A faint sound of water reached him, and he didn't know what it was until the Arab again stood framed in the doorway, closed the door carefully, and came back to bed without a sound. Then Daru turned his back on him and fell asleep. Still later he seemed, from the depths of his sleep, to hear furtive steps around the schoolhouse. "I'm dreaming! I'm dreaming!" he repeated to himself. And he went on sleeping.

When he awoke, the sky was clear; the loose window let in a cold, pure air. The Arab was asleep, hunched up under the blankets now, his mouth open, utterly relaxed. But when Daru shook him, he started dreadfully, staring at Daru with wild eyes as if he had never seen him and such a frightened expression that the schoolmaster stepped back. "Don't be afraid. It's me. You must eat." The Arab nodded his head and said yes. Calm had returned to his face, but the expression was vacant and listless.

The coffee was ready. They drank it seated together on the folding bed as they munched their pieces of the cake. Then Daru led the Arab under the shed and showed him the faucet where he washed. He went back into the room, folded the blankets and the bed, made his own bed and put the room in order. Then he went through the classroom and out onto the terrace. The sun was already rising in the blue sky; a soft, bright light was bathing the deserted plateau. On the ridge the snow was melting in spots. The stones were about to reappear. Crouched on the edge of the plateau, the schoolmaster looked at the deserted expanse. He thought of Balducci. He had hurt him, for he had sent him off in a way as if he didn't want to be associated with him. He could still hear the gendarme's farewell and, without knowing why, he felt strangely empty and vulnerable. At that moment, from the other side of the schoolhouse, the prisoner coughed. Daru listened to him almost despite himself and then, furious, threw a pebble that whistled through the air before sinking into the snow. That man's stupid crime revolted him, but to hand him over was contrary to honor. Merely thinking of it made him smart with humiliation. And he cursed at one and the same time his own people who had sent him this Arab and the Arab too who had dared to kill and not managed to get away. Daru got up, walked in a circle on the terrace, waited motionless, and then went back into the schoolhouse.

The Arab, leaning over the cement floor of the shed, was washing his teeth with two fingers. Daru looked at him and said: "Come." He went back into the room ahead of the prisoner. He slipped a hunting-jacket on over his sweater and put on walking-shoes. Standing, he waited until the Arab had put on his *chèche* and sandals. They went into the classroom and the schoolmaster pointed to the exit, saying: "Go ahead." The fellow didn't budge. "I'm coming," said Daru. The Arab went out. Daru went back into the room and made a package of pieces of rusk, dates, and sugar. In the classroom, before going out, he hesitated a second in front of his desk, then crossed the threshold and locked the door. "That's the way," he said. He started toward the east, followed by the prisoner. But, a short distance from the schoolhouse, he thought he heard a slight sound behind them. He retraced his steps and examined the surroundings of the house; there was no one there. The Arab watched him without seeming to understand. "Come on," said Daru.

They walked for an hour and rested beside a sharp peak of limestone. The snow was melting faster and faster and the sun was drinking up the puddles at once, rapidly cleaning the plateau, which gradually dried and vibrated like the air itself. When they resumed walking, the ground rang under their feet. From time to time a bird rent the space in front of them with a joyful cry. Daru breathed in deeply the fresh morning light. He felt a sort of rapture before the vast familiar expanse, now almost entirely yellow under its dome of blue sky. They walked an hour more, descending toward the south. They reached a level height made up of crumbly rocks. From there on, the plateau sloped down, eastward, toward a low plain where there were a few spindly trees and, to the south, toward outcroppings of rock that gave the landscape a chaotic look.

Daru surveyed the two directions. There was nothing but the sky on the horizon. Not a man could be seen. He turned toward the Arab, who was looking at him blankly. Daru held out the package to him. "Take it," he said. "There are dates, bread, and sugar. You can hold out for two days. Here are a thousand francs too." The Arab took the package and the money but kept his full hands at chest level as if he didn't know what to do with what was being given him. "Now look," the schoolmaster said as he pointed in the direction of the east, "there's the way to Tinguit. You have a two-hour walk. At Tinguit you'll find the administration and the police. They are expecting you." The Arab looked toward the east, still holding the package and the money against his chest. Daru took his elbow and turned him rather roughly toward the south. At the foot of the height on which they stood could be seen a faint path. "That's the trail across the plateau. In a day's walk from here you'll find pasturelands and the first nomads. They'll take you in and shelter you according to their law." The Arab had now turned toward Daru and a sort of panic was visible in his expression. "Listen," he said. Daru shook his head: "No, be quiet. Now I'm leaving you." He turned his back on him, took two long steps in the direction of the school, looked hesitantly at the motionless Arab, and started off again. For a few minutes he heard nothing but his own step resounding on the cold ground and did not turn his head. A moment later, however, he turned around. The Arab was still there on the edge of the hill, his arms hanging now, and he was looking at the schoolmaster. Daru felt something rise in his throat. But he swore with impatience, waved vaguely, and started off again. He had already gone some distance when he again stopped and looked. There was no longer anyone on the hill.

Daru hesitated. The sun was now rather high in the sky and was beginning to beat down on his head. The schoolmaster retraced his steps, at first somewhat uncertainly, then with decision. When he reached the little hill, he was bathed in sweat. He climbed it as fast as he could and stopped, out of breath, at the top. The rock-fields to the south stood out sharply against the blue sky, but on the plain to the east a steamy heat was already rising. And in that slight haze, Daru, with heavy heart, made out the Arab walking slowly on the road to prison.

A little later, standing before the window of the classroom, the schoolmaster was watching the clear light bathing the whole surface of the plateau, but he hardly saw it. Behind him on the blackboard, among the winding French rivers, sprawled the clumsily chalked-up words he had just read: "You handed over our brother. You will pay for this." Daru looked at the sky, the plateau, and, beyond, the invisible lands stretching all the way to the sea. In this vast landscape he had loved so much, he was alone.

Martin Luther King, Jr. (1929–1968)

AMERICAN CLERGYMAN and CIVIL RIGHTS LEADER

Letter from Birmingham Jail

Martin Luther King, Jr.
Birmingham City Jail
April 16, 1963

Bishop C. C. J. Carpenter
Bishop Joseph A. Durick
Rabbi Milton L. Grafman
Bishop Paul Hardin
Bishop Nolan B. Harmon
The Rev. George M. Murray
The Rev. Edward V. Ramage
The Rev. Earl Stallings

My dear Fellow Clergymen,

While confined here in the Birmingham City Jail, I came across your recent statement calling our present activities "unwise and untimely." Seldom, if ever, do I pause to answer criticism of my work and ideas. If I sought to answer all of the criticisms that cross my desk, my secretary would be engaged in little else in the course of the day and I would have no time for constructive work. But since I feel that you are men of genuine good will and your criticisms are sincerely set forth, I would like to answer your statement in what I hope will be patient and reasonable terms.

I think I should give the reason for my being in Birmingham, since you have been influenced by the argument of "outsiders coming in." I have the honor of serving as president of the Southern Christian Leadership Conference, an organization operating in every Southern state with headquarters in Atlanta, Georgia. We have some eighty-five affiliate organizations all across the South — one being the Alabama Christian Movement for Human Rights. Whenever necessary and possible we share staff, educational, and financial resources with our affiliates. Several months ago our local affiliate here in

Jailed for his role in the 1963 civil rights demonstrations in Birmingham, Alabama, the late Dr. King wrote his now-famous "Letter from Birmingham Jail" in reply to a published statement by eight Alabama clergymen. They objected to these demonstrations as "unwise and untimely" and maintained that "When rights are consistently denied, a cause should be pressed in the courts and in negotiations among local leaders, and not in the streets."

Birmingham invited us to be on call to engage in a nonviolent direct action program if such were deemed necessary. We readily consented and when the hour came we lived up to our promises. So I am here, along with several members of my staff, because we were invited here. I am here because I have basic organizational ties here. Beyond this, I am in Birmingham because injustice is here. Just as the eighth century prophets left their little villages and carried their "thus saith the Lord" far beyond the boundaries of their home town, and just as the Apostle Paul left his little village of Tarsus and carried the gospel of Jesus Christ to practically every hamlet and city of the Graeco-Roman world, I too am compelled to carry the gospel of freedom beyond my particular home town. Like Paul, I must constantly respond to the Macedonian call for aid.

Moreover, I am cognizant of the interrelatedness of all communities and states. I cannot sit idly by in Atlanta and not be concerned about what happens in Birmingham. Injustice anywhere is a threat to justice everywhere. We are caught in an inescapable network of mutuality tied in a single garment of destiny. Whatever affects one directly affects all indirectly. Never again can we afford to live with the narrow, provincial "outside agitator" idea. Anyone who lives inside the United States can never be considered an outsider anywhere in this country.

You deplore the demonstrations that are presently taking place in Birmingham. But I am sorry that your statement did not express a similar concern for the conditions that brought the demonstrations into being. I am sure that each of you would want to go beyond the superficial social analyst who looks merely at effects, and does not grapple with underlying causes. I would not hesitate to say that it is unfortunate that so-called demonstrations are taking place in Birmingham at this time, but I would say in more emphatic terms that it is even more unfortunate that the white power structure of this city left the Negro community with no other alternative.

In any nonviolent campaign there are four basic steps: (1) collection of the facts to determine whether injustices are alive; (2) negotiation; (3) self-purification; and (4) direct action. We have gone through all of these steps in Birmingham. There can be no gainsaying of the fact that racial injustice engulfs this community. Birmingham is probably the most thoroughly segregated city in the United States. Its ugly record of police brutality is known in every section of this country. Its unjust treatment of Negroes in the courts is a notorious reality. There have been more unsolved bombings of Negro homes and churches in Birmingham than any city in this nation. These are the hard, brutal, and unbelievable facts. On the basis of these conditions Negro leaders sought to negotiate with the city fathers. But the political leaders consistently refused to engage in good faith negotiation.

Then came the opportunity last September to talk with some of the leaders of the economic community. In these negotiating sessions certain promises were made by the merchants — such as the promise to remove the humiliating racial signs from the stores. On the basis of these promises Rev. Shuttlesworth and the leaders of the Alabama Christian Movement for Human Rights agreed to call a moratorium on any type of demonstrations. As the weeks and months unfolded we realized that we were the victims of a broken promise. The signs remained. As in so many experiences of the past we were confronted with blasted hopes, and the dark shadow of a deep disappointment settled upon us. So we had no alternative except that of preparing for direct action, whereby we would present our very bodies as a means of laying our case before the conscience of the local and national community. We were not unmindful of the difficulties involved. So we decided to go through a process of self-purification. We started having workshops on nonviolence and repeatedly asked ourselves the questions, "Are you able to accept blows without retaliating?" "Are you able to endure the ordeals of jail?"

We decided to set our direct action program around the Easter season, realizing that with the exception of Christmas, this was the largest shopping period of the year. Knowing that a strong economic withdrawal program would be the by-product of direct action, we felt that this was the best time to bring pressure on the merchants for the needed changes. Then it occurred to us that the March election was ahead, and so we speedily decided to postpone action until after election day. When we discovered that Mr. Connor was in the run-off, we decided again to postpone action so that the demonstrations could not be used to cloud the issues. At this time we agreed to begin our nonviolent witness the day after the run-off.

This reveals that we did not move irresponsibly into direct action. We too wanted to see Mr. Connor defeated; so we went through postponement after postponement to aid in this community need. After this we felt that direct action could be delayed no longer.

You may well ask, "Why direct action? Why sit-ins, marches, etc.? Isn't negotiation a better path?" You are exactly right in your call for negotiation. Indeed, this is the purpose of direct action. Nonviolent direct action seeks to create such a crisis and establish such creative tension that a community that has constantly refused to negotiate is forced to confront the issue. It seeks so to dramatize the issue that it can no longer be ignored. I just referred to the creation of tension as a part of the work of the nonviolent resister. This may sound rather shocking. But I must confess that I am not afraid of the word tension. I have earnestly worked and preached against violent tension, but there is a type of constructive nonviolent tension that is necessary for growth. Just as Socrates felt that it was necessary to create a tension in the mind so that individuals could rise from the bondage of myths and half-truths to the unfettered realm of creative analysis and objective appraisal, we must see the need of having nonviolent gadflies to create the kind of tension in society that will help men rise from the dark depths of prejudice and racism to the majestic heights of understanding and brotherhood. So the purpose of the direct action is to create a situation so crisis-packed that it will inevitably open the door to negotiation. We, therefore, concur with you in your call for negotiation. Too long has our beloved Southland been bogged down in the tragic attempt to live in monologue rather than dialogue.

One of the basic points in your statement is that our acts are untimely. Some have asked, "Why didn't you give the new administration time to act?" The only answer that I can give to this inquiry is that the new administration must be prodded about as much as the outgoing one before it acts. We will be sadly mistaken if we feel that the election of Mr. Boutwell will bring the millennium to Birmingham. While Mr. Boutwell is much more articulate and gentle than Mr. Connor, they are both segregationists dedicated to the task of maintaining the status quo. The hope I see in Mr. Boutwell is that he will be reasonable enough to see the futility of massive resistance to desegregation. But he will not see this without pressure from the devotees of civil rights. My friends, I must say to you that we have not made a single gain in civil rights without determined legal and nonviolent pressure. History is the long and tragic story of the fact that privileged groups seldom give up their privileges voluntarily. Individuals may see the moral light and voluntarily give up their unjust posture; but as Reinhold Niebuhr has reminded us, groups are more immoral than individuals.

We know through painful experience that freedom is never voluntarily given by the oppressor; it must be demanded by the oppressed. Frankly I have never yet engaged in a direct action movement that was "well timed," according to the timetable of those who have not suffered unduly from the disease of segregation. For years now I have heard the word "Wait!" It rings in the ear of every Negro with a piercing familiarity. This "wait" has almost always meant "never." It has been a tranquilizing thalidomide, relieving the emotional stress for a moment, only to give birth to an ill-formed infant of frustration. We must come to see with the distinguished jurist of yesterday that "justice too long delayed is justice denied." We have waited for more than three hundred and forty years for our constitutional and God-given rights. The nations of Asia and Africa are moving with jet-like speed toward the goal of political independence, and we still creep at horse and buggy pace toward the gaining of a cup of coffee at a lunch counter.

I guess it is easy for those who have never felt the stinging darts of segregation to say wait. But when you have seen vicious mobs lynch your mothers and fathers at will and drown your sisters and brothers at whim; when you have seen hate filled policemen curse, kick, brutalize, and even kill your black brothers and sisters with impunity; when you see the vast majority of your twenty million Negro brothers smothering in an air-tight cage of poverty in the midst of an affluent society; when you suddenly find your tongue twisted and your speech stammering as you seek to explain to your six-year-old daughter why she can't go to the public amusement park that has just been advertised on television, and see tears welling up in her little eyes when she is told that Funtown is closed to colored children, and see the depressing clouds of inferiority begin to form in her little mental sky, and see her begin to distort her little personality by unconsciously developing a bitterness toward white people; when you have to concoct an answer for a five-year-old son asking in agonizing pathos: "Daddy, why do white people treat colored people so mean?"; when you take a cross country drive and find it necessary to sleep night after night in the uncomfortable corners of your automobile because no motel will accept you; when you are humiliated day in and day out by nagging signs reading "white" men and "colored"; when your first name becomes "nigger" and your middle name becomes "boy" (however old you are) and your last name becomes "John," and when your wife and mother are never given the respected title "Mrs."; when you are harried by day and haunted by night by the fact that you are a Negro, living constantly at tip-toe stance never quite knowing what to expect next, and plagued with inner fears and outer resentments; when you are forever fighting a degenerating sense of "nobodiness"; — then you will understand why we find it difficult to wait. There comes a time when the cup of endurance runs over, and men are no longer willing to be plunged into an abyss of injustice where they experience the bleakness of corroding despair. I hope, sirs, you can understand our legitimate and unavoidable impatience.

You express a great deal of anxiety over our willingness to break laws. This is certainly a legitimate concern. Since we so diligently urge people to obey the Supreme Court's decision of 1954 outlawing segregation in the public schools, it is rather strange and paradoxical to find us consciously breaking laws. One may well ask, "How can you advocate breaking some laws and obeying others?" The answer is found in the fact that there are two types of laws. There are *just* laws and there are *unjust* laws. I would be the first to advocate obeying just laws. One has not only a legal but moral responsibility to obey just laws. Conversely, one has a moral responsibility to disobey unjust laws. I would agree with Saint Augustine that "An unjust law is no law at all."

Now what is the difference between the two? How does one determine when a law is just or unjust? A just law is a man-made code that squares with the moral law or the law of God. An unjust law is a code that is out of harmony with the moral law. To put it in the terms of Saint Thomas Aquinas, an unjust law is a human law that is not rooted in eternal and natural law. Any law that uplifts human personality is just. Any law that degrades human personality is unjust. All segregation statutes are unjust because segregation distorts the soul and damages the personality. It gives the segregator a false sense of superiority and the segregated a false sense of inferiority. To use the words of Martin Buber, the great Jewish philosopher, segregation substitutes an "I-it" relationship for the "I-thou" relationship, and ends up relegating persons to the status of things. So segregation is not only politically, economically, and sociologically unsound, but it is morally wrong and sinful. Paul Tillich has said that sin is separation. Isn't segregation an existential expression of man's tragic separation, an expression of his awful estrangement, his terrible sinfulness? So I can urge men to obey the

1954 decision of the Supreme Court because it is morally right, and I can urge them to disobey segregation ordinances because they are morally wrong.

Let us turn to a more concrete example of just and unjust laws. An unjust law is a code that a majority inflicts on a minority that is not binding on itself. This is *difference* made legal. On the other hand a just law is a code that a majority compels a minority to follow that it is willing to follow itself. This is *sameness* made legal.

Let me give another explanation. An unjust law is a code inflicted upon a minority which that minority had no part in enacting or creating because they did not have the unhampered right to vote. Who can say the legislature of Alabama which set up the segregation laws was democratically elected? Throughout the state of Alabama all types of conniving methods are used to prevent Negroes from becoming registered voters and there are some counties without a single Negro registered to vote despite the fact that the Negro constitutes a majority of the population. Can any law set up in such a state be considered democratically structured?

These are just a few examples of unjust and just laws. There are some instances when a law is just on its face but unjust in its application. For instance, I was arrested Friday on a charge of parading without a permit. Now there is nothing wrong with an ordinance which requires a permit for a parade, but when the ordinance is used to preserve segregation and to deny citizens the First Amendment privilege of peaceful assembly and peaceful protest, then it becomes unjust.

I hope you can see the distinction I am trying to point out. In no sense do I advocate evading or defying the law as the rabid segregationist would do. This would lead to anarchy. One who breaks an unjust law must do it *openly, lovingly* (not hatefully as the white mothers did in New Orleans when they were seen on television screaming "nigger, nigger, nigger") and with a willingness to accept the penalty. I submit that an individual who breaks a law that conscience tells him is unjust, and willingly accepts the penalty by staying in jail to arouse the conscience of the community over its injustice, is in reality expressing the very highest respect for law.

Of course there is nothing new about this kind of civil disobedience. It was seen sublimely in the refusal of Shadrach, Meshach, and Abednego to obey the laws of Nebuchadnezzar because a higher moral law was involved. It was practiced superbly by the early Christians who were willing to face hungry lions and the excruciating pain of chopping blocks, before submitting to certain unjust laws of the Roman Empire. To a degree academic freedom is a reality today because Socrates practiced civil disobedience.

We can never forget that everything Hitler did in Germany was "legal" and everything the Hungarian freedom fighters did in Hungary was "illegal." It was "illegal" to aid and comfort a Jew in Hitler's Germany. But I am sure that, if I had lived in Germany during that time, I would have aided and comforted my Jewish brothers even though it was illegal. If I lived in a communist country today where certain principles dear to the Christian faith are suppressed, I believe I would openly advocate disobeying these antireligious laws.

I must make two honest confessions to you, my Christian and Jewish brothers. First I must confess that over the last few years I have been gravely disappointed with the white moderate. I have almost reached the regrettable conclusion that the Negroes' great stumbling block in the stride toward freedom is not the White Citizens' "Counciler" or the Ku Klux Klanner, but the white moderate who is more devoted to "order" than to justice; who prefers a negative peace which is the absence of tension to a positive peace which is the presence of justice; who constantly says "I agree with you in the goal you seek, but I can't agree with your methods of direct action"; who paternalistically feels that he can set the time-table for another man's freedom; who lives by the myth of time and who constantly advises the Negro to wait until a "more convenient season." Shallow understanding from people of good will is more frustrating than absolute misunderstanding from people of ill will. Lukewarm acceptance is much more bewildering than outright rejection.

I had hoped that the white moderate would understand that law and order exist for the purpose of establishing justice, and that when they fail to do this they become the dangerously structured dams that block the flow of social progress. I had hoped that the white moderate would understand that the present tension in the South is merely a necessary phase of the transition from an obnoxious negative peace, where the Negro passively accepted his unjust plight, to a substance-filled positive peace, where all men will respect the dignity and worth of human personality. Actually, we who engage in nonviolent direct action are not the creators of tension. We merely bring to the surface the hidden tension that is already alive. We bring it out in the open where it can be seen and dealt with. Like a boil that can never be cured as long as it is covered up but must be opened with all its pus-flowing ugliness to the natural medicines of air and light, injustice must likewise be exposed, with all of the tension its exposing creates, to the light of human conscience and the air of national opinion before it can be cured.

In your statement you asserted that our actions, even though peaceful, must be condemned because they precipitate violence. But can this assertion be logically made? Isn't this like condemning the robbed man because his possession of money precipitated the evil act of robbery? Isn't this like condemning Socrates because his unswerving commitment to truth and his philosophical delvings precipitated the misguided popular mind to make him drink the hemlock? Isn't this like condemning Jesus because His unique God consciousness and never-ceasing devotion to His will precipitated the evil act of crucifixion? We must come to see, as federal courts have consistently affirmed, that it is immoral to urge an individual to withdraw his efforts to gain his basic constitutional rights because the quest precipitates violence. Society must protect the robbed and punish the robber.

I had also hoped that the white moderate would reject the myth of time.

I received a letter this morning from a white brother in Texas which said: "All Christians know that the colored people will receive equal rights eventually, but is it possible that you are in too great of a religious hurry? It has taken Christianity almost 2000 years to accomplish what it has. The teachings of Christ take time to come to earth." All that is said here grows out of a tragic misconception of time. It is the strangely irrational notion that there is something in the very flow of time that will inevitably cure all ills. Actually time is neutral. It can be used either destructively or constructively. I am coming to feel that the people of ill will have used time much more effectively than the people of good will. We will have to repent in this generation not merely for the vitriolic words and actions of the bad people, but for the appalling silence of the good people. We must come to see that human progress never rolls in on wheels of inevitability. It comes through the tireless efforts and persistent work of men willing to be co-workers with God, and without this hard work time itself becomes an ally of the forces of social stagnation.

We must use time creatively, and forever realize that the time is always ripe to do right. Now is the time to make real the promise of democracy, and transform our pending national elegy into a creative psalm of brotherhood. Now is the time to lift our national policy from the quicksand of racial injustice to the solid rock of human dignity.

You spoke of our activity in Birmingham as extreme. At first I was rather disappointed that fellow clergymen would see my nonviolent efforts as those of the extremist. I started thinking about the fact that I stand in the middle of two opposing forces in the Negro community. One is a force of complacency made up of Negroes who, as a result of long years of oppression, have been so completely drained of self-respect and a sense of "somebodiness" that they have adjusted to segregation, and of a few Negroes in the middle class who, because of a degree of academic and economic security, and because at points they profit by segregation, have unconsciously become insensitive to the problems of the masses. The other force is one of bitterness and hatred and comes periously close to advocating violence. It is expressed in the various black nationalist groups that are springing up over the nation, the largest and best known being Elijah Muhammad's Muslim movement. This movement is nourished by the contemporary frustration over the continued existence of racial discrimination. It is made up of people who have lost faith in America, who have absolutely repudiated Christianity, and who have concluded that the white man is an incurable "devil." I have tried to stand between these two forces saying that we need not follow the "do-nothingism" of the complacent or the hatred and despair of the black nationalist. There is the more excellent way of love and nonviolent protest. I'm grateful to God that, through the Negro church, the dimension of nonviolence entered our struggle. If this philosophy had not emerged I am convinced that by now many streets of the South would be flowing with floods of blood. And I am further convinced that if our white brothers dismiss us as "rabble rousers" and "outside agitators" — those of us who are working through the channels of nonviolent direct action — and refuse to support our nonviolent efforts, millions of Negroes, out of frustration and despair, will seek solace and security in black nationalist ideologies, a development that will lead inevitably to a frightening racial nightmare.

Oppressed people cannot remain oppressed forever. The urge for freedom will eventually come. This is what has happened to the American Negro. Something within has reminded him of his birthright of freedom; something without has reminded him that he can gain it. Consciously and unconsciously, he has been swept in by what the Germans call the *Zeitgeist*,[1] and with his black brothers of Africa, and his brown and yellow brothers of Asia, South America, and the Caribbean, he is moving with a sense of cosmic urgency toward the promised land of racial justice. Recognizing this vital urge that has engulfed the Negro community, one should readily understand public demonstrations. The Negro has many pent-up resentments and latent frustrations. He has to get them out. So let him march sometimes; let him have his prayer pilgrimages to the city hall; understand why he must have sit-ins and freedom rides. If his repressed emotions do not come out in these nonviolent ways, they will come out in ominous expressions of violence. This is not a threat; it is a fact of history. So I have not said to my people, "Get rid of your discontent." But I have tried to say that this normal and healthy discontent can be channeled through the creative outlet of nonviolent direct action. Now this approach is being dismissed as extremist. I must admit that I was initially disappointed in being so categorized.

But as I continued to think about the matter I gradually gained a bit of satisfaction from being considered an extremist. Was not Jesus an extremist in love? "Love your enemies, bless them that curse you, pray for them that despitefully use you." Was not Amos an extremist for justice — "Let justice roll down like waters and righteousness like a mighty stream." Was not Paul an extremist for the gospel of Jesus Christ — "I bear in my body the marks of the Lord Jesus." Was not Martin Luther an extremist — "Here I stand; I can do none other so help me God." Was not John Bunyan an extremist — "I will stay in jail to the end of my days before I make a butchery of my conscience." Was not Abraham Lincoln an extremist — "This nation cannot survive half slave and half free." Was not Thomas Jefferson an extremist — "We hold these truths to be self evident that all men are created equal." So the question is not whether we will be extremist but what kind of extremist will we be. Will we be extremists for hate or will we be extremists for love? Will we be extremists for the preservation of injustice — or will we be extremists for the cause of justice? In that dramatic scene on Calvary's hill three men were crucified. We must never forget that all three were crucified

[1] spirit of the times.

for the same crime — the crime of extremism. Two were extremists for immorality, and thus fell below their environment. The other, Jesus Christ, was an extremist for love, truth, and goodness, and thereby rose above His environment. So, after all, maybe the South, the nation, and the world are in dire need of creative extremists.

I had hoped that the white moderate would see this. Maybe I was too optimistic. Maybe I expected too much. I guess I should have realized that few members of a race that has oppressed another race can understand or appreciate the deep groans and passionate yearnings of those that have been oppressed, and still fewer have the vision to see that injustice must be rooted out by strong, persistent, and determined action. I am thankful, however, that some of our white brothers have grasped the meaning of this social revolution and committed themselves to it. They are still all too small in quantity, but they are big in quality. Some like Ralph McGill, Lillian Smith, Harry Golden, and James Dabbs have written about our struggle in eloquent, prophetic, and understanding terms. Others have marched with us down nameless streets of the South. They have languished in filthy, roach-infested jails, suffering the abuse and brutality of angry policemen who see them as "dirty nigger lovers." They, unlike so many of their moderate brothers and sisters, have recognized the urgency of the moment and sensed the need for powerful "action" antidotes to combat the disease of segregation.

Let me rush on to mention my other disappointment. I have been so greatly disappointed with the white Church and its leadership. Of course there are some notable exceptions. I am not unmindful of the fact that each of you has taken some significant stands on this issue. I commend you, Rev. Stallings, for your Christian stand on this past Sunday, in welcoming Negroes to your worship service on a non-segregated basis. I commend the Catholic leaders of this state for integrating Springhill College several years ago.

But despite these notable exceptions I must honestly reiterate that I have been disappointed with the Church. I do not say that as one of those negative critics who can always find something wrong with the Church. I say it as a minister of the gospel, who loves the Church; who was nurtured in its bosom; who has been sustained by its spiritual blessings and who will remain true to it as long as the cord of life shall lengthen.

I had the strange feeling when I was suddenly catapulted into the leadership of the bus protest in Montgomery several years ago that we would have the support of the white Church. I felt that the white ministers, priests, and rabbis of the South would be some of our strongest allies. Instead, some have been outright opponents, refusing to understand the freedom movement and misrepresenting its leaders; all too many others have been more cautious than courageous and have remained silent behind the anesthetizing security of stained glass windows.

In spite of my shattered dreams of the past, I came to Birmingham with the hope that the white religious leadership of this community would see the justice of our cause and, with deep moral concern, serve as the channel through which our just grievances could get to the power structure. I had hoped that each of you would understand. But again I have been disappointed.

I have heard numerous religious leaders of the South call upon their worshippers to comply with a desegregation decision because it is the law, but I have longed to hear white ministers say follow this decree because integration is morally right and the Negro is your brother. In the midst of blatant injustices inflicted upon the Negro, I have watched white churches stand on the sideline and merely mouth pious irrelevancies and sanctimonious trivalities. In the midst of a mighty struggle to rid our nation of racial and economic injustice, I have heard so many ministers say, "Those are social issues with which the Gospel has no real concern," and I have watched so many churches commit themselves to a completely other-worldly religion which made a strange distinction between body and soul, the sacred and the secular.

So here we are moving toward the exit of the twentieth century with a religious community largely adjusted to the status quo, standing as a tail light behind other community agencies rather than a headlight leading men to higher levels of justice.

I have travelled the length and breadth of Alabama, Mississippi, and all the other Southern states. On sweltering summer days and crisp autumn mornings I have looked at her beautiful churches with their spires pointing heavenward. I have beheld the impressive outlay of her massive religious education buildings. Over and over again I have found myself asking: "Who worships here? Who is their God? Where were their voices when the lips of Governor Barnett dripped with words of interposition and nullification? Where were they when Governor Wallace gave the clarion call for defiance and hatred? Where were their voices of support when tired, bruised, and weary Negro men and women decided to rise from the dark dungeons of complacency to the bright hills of creative protest?"

Yes, these questions are still in my mind. In deep disappointment, I have wept over the laxity of the Church. But be assured that my tears have been tears of love. There can be no deep disappointment where there is not deep love. Yes, I love the Church; I love her sacred walls. How could I do otherwise? I am in the rather unique position of being the son, the grandson, and the great grandson of preachers. Yes, I see the Church as the body of Christ. But, oh! How we have blemished and scarred that body through social neglect and fear of being nonconformist.

There was a time when the Church was very powerful. It was during that period when the early Christians rejoiced when they were deemed worthy to suffer for what they believed. In those days the Church was not merely a thermometer that recorded the ideas and principles of popular opinion; it was a thermostat that transformed the mores of society. Wherever the early Christians entered a town the power structure got disturbed and immediately sought to convict them for being "disturbers of the peace" and "outside agitators." But they went on with the conviction that they were a "colony of heaven" and had to obey God rather than man. They were small in number but big in commitment. They were too God-intoxicated to be "astronomically intimidated." They brought an end to such ancient evils as infanticide and gladiatorial contest.

Things are different now. The contemporary Church is so often a weak, ineffectual voice with an uncertain sound. It is so often the arch-supporter of the status quo. Far from being disturbed by the presence of the Church, the power structure of the average community is consoled by the Church's silent and often vocal sanction of things as they are.

But the judgment of God is upon the Church as never before. If the Church of today does not recapture the sacrificial spirit of the early Church, it will lose its authentic ring, forfeit the loyalty of millions, and be dismissed as an irrelevant social club with no meaning for the twentieth century. I am meeting young people every day whose disappointment with the Church has risen to outright disgust.

Maybe again I have been too optimistic. Is organized religion too inextricably bound to the status quo to save our nation and the world? Maybe I must turn my faith to the inner spiritual Church, the church within the Church, as the true *ecclesia*[1] and the hope of the world. But again I am thankful to God that some noble souls from the ranks of organized religion have broken loose from the paralyzing chains of conformity and joined us as active partners in the struggle for freedom. They have left their secure congregations and walked the streets of Albany, Georgia, with us. They have gone through the highways of the South on torturous rides for freedom. Yes, they have gone to jail with us. Some have been kicked out of their churches and lost the support of their bishops and fellow ministers. But they have gone with the faith that right defeated is stronger than evil triumphant. These men have been the leaven in the lump of the race. Their witness has been the spiritual salt that has preserved the true meaning of the Gospel in these troubled times. They have carved a tunnel of hope through the dark mountain of disappointment.

I hope the Church as a whole will meet the challenge of this decisive hour. But even if the Church does not come to the aid of justice, I have no despair about the future. I have no fear about the outcome of our struggle in Birmingham, even if our motives are presently misunderstood. We will reach the goal of freedom in Birmingham and all over the nation, because the goal of America is freedom. Abused and scorned though we may be, our destiny is tied up with the destiny of America. Before the pilgrims landed at Plymouth, we were here. Before the pen of Jefferson etched across the pages of history the majestic words of the Declaration of Independence, we were here. For more than two centuries our fore-parents labored in this country without wages; they made cotton "king"; and they built the homes of their masters

---

[1] congregation, church.

in the midst of brutal injustice and shameful humiliation — and yet out of a bottomless vitality they continued to thrive and develop. If the inexpressible cruelties of slavery could not stop us, the opposition we now face will surely fail. We will win our freedom because the sacred heritage of our nation and the eternal will of God are embodied in our echoing demands.

I must close now. But before closing I am impelled to mention one other point in your statement that troubled me profoundly. You warmly commended the Birmingham police force for keeping "order" and "preventing violence." I don't believe you would have so warmly commended the police force if you had seen its angry violent dogs literally biting six unarmed, nonviolent Negroes. I don't believe you would so quickly commend the policemen if you would observe their ugly and inhuman treatment of Negroes here in the city jail; if you would watch them push and curse old Negro women and young Negro girls; if you would see them slap and kick old Negro men and young Negro boys; if you will observe them, as they did on two occasions, refuse to give us food because we wanted to sing our grace together. I'm sorry that I can't join you in your praise for the police department.

It is true that they have been rather disciplined in their public handling of the demonstrators. In this sense they have been rather publicly "nonviolent." But for what purpose? To preserve the evil system of segregation. Over the last few years I have consistently preached that nonviolence demands that the means we use must be as pure as the ends we seek. So I have tried to make it clear that it is wrong to use immoral means to attain moral ends. But now I must affirm that it is just as wrong, or even more so, to use moral means to preserve immoral ends. Maybe Mr. Connor and his policemen have been rather publicly nonviolent, as Chief Prichett was in Albany, Georgia, but they have used the moral means of nonviolence to maintain the immoral end of flagrant racial injustice. T. S. Eliot has said that there is no greater treason than to do the right deed for the wrong reason.

I wish you had commended the Negro sit-inners and demonstrators of Birmingham for their sublime courage, their willingness to suffer, and their amazing discipline in the midst of the most inhuman provocation. One day the South will recognize its real heroes. They will be the James Merediths, courageously and with a majestic sense of purpose, facing jeering and hostile mobs and the agonizing loneliness that characterizes the life of the pioneer. They will be old, oppressed, battered Negro women, symbolized in a seventy-two year old woman of Montgomery, Alabama, who rose up with a sense of dignity and with her people decided not to ride the segregated buses, and responded to one who inquired about her tiredness with ungrammatical profundity: "My feets is tired, but my soul is rested." They will be young high school and college students, young ministers of the gospel and a host of the elders, courageously and nonviolently sitting in at lunch counters and willingly going to jail for conscience sake. One day the South will know that when these disinherited children of God sat down at lunch counters they were in reality standing up for the best in the American dream and the most sacred values in our Judeo-Christian heritage, and thus carrying our whole nation back to great wells of democracy which were dug deep by the founding fathers in the formulation of the Constitution and the Declaration of Independence.

Never before have I written a letter this long (or should I say a book?). I'm afraid that it is much too long to take your precious time. I can assure you that it would have been much shorter if I had been writing from a comfortable desk, but what else is there to do when you are alone for days in the dull monotony of a narrow jail cell other than write long letters, think strange thoughts, and pray long prayers?

If I have said anything in this letter that is an overstatement of the truth and is indicative of an unreasonable impatience, I beg you to forgive me. If I have said anything in this letter that is an understatement of the truth and is indicative of my having a patience that makes me patient with anything less than brotherhood, I beg God to forgive me.

I hope this letter finds you strong in the faith. I also hope that circumstances will soon make it possible for me to meet each of you, not as an integrationist or a civil rights leader, but as a fellow clergyman and a Christian brother. Let us all hope that the dark clouds of racial prejudice will soon pass away and the deep fog of misunderstanding will be lifted from our fear-drenched communities and in some not too distant tomorrow the radiant stars of love and brotherhood will shine over our great nation with all of their scintillating beauty.

Yours for the cause of
Peace and Brotherhood

MARTIN LUTHER KING, JR.

NATURE

*When the elements . . . hot and cold
and dry and wet, are bound together in
love which is orderly, and combined
harmoniously in due proportions, man and
the other animals and plants thrive and
are healthy and take no harm.*

ERYXIMACHUS, *Symposium*

NATURE and the American people are not yet completely divorced, but the process of separation and estrangement continues. The great majority of our population now lives in cities or in ever-sprawling suburbia where nature is both controlled and corrupted by man: animals are either domesticated or exterminated; air and water are artificially purified — and polluted. On the one hand, man sentimentalizes nature, customarily depicting love scenes and cigarette commercials against backdrops of brooks, blue skies, and majestic forests, real or painted; on the other hand, he synthesizes nature, manufacturing aerosol scents of "fresh air," artificial diamonds, and laboratory-produced DNA, the physical basis of life itself. Still, a few people continue to explore the natural world, from the depths of the sea to the outermost reaches of the universe, partly for the sake of knowledge and discovery, partly for exploitation. At the same time, many more people destroy nature by cutting it down, digging it up, paving it over.

From earliest times, when nature was thought to be the home of gods, to medieval times, when God infused nature with His divine spirit, to the Renaissance, when the countryside often served as a sanctuary for undisturbed meditation, the process of civilization has involved a progressive turning away from the natural. The emphasis of the city has displaced the country and nature generally. Man has come to think about nature in ways relating to himself, and it is these relationships that the following selections explore. By understanding such relationships as they have been interpreted in the past and present, we can, hopefully, gain some understanding of the meaning of nature for ourselves and some notion of what we shall lose if we become completely isolated from our natural environment.

Nature has assumed many roles. Its least complicated function, perhaps, has been simply a phenomenon to be observed and understood. What can we learn from examining it? Are we content to understand natural phenomena for their own sake, or must we continually interpret their relevance to the human condition? To what extent is the human condition similar or even identical to the natural?

Nature may be interpreted paradoxically. On the one hand, the natural world is ideal; its physical harmony and perfection contrast with a materialistic and morally corrupt civilization. In this perspective nature becomes a teacher or a noble model to be emulated, as the poems of Burns, Wordsworth, and Keats suggest. Even if nature does not teach us, it may help us by providing inspiration, companionship, recreation,

616

solace, or relaxation; nature is all of these for Izaak Walton. Or nature may exist for our physical or economic exploitation, as Captain John Smith contends.

On the other hand, the natural world is "red in tooth and claw," full of conflict and hostile or indifferent to human activity and aspiration. Nature not only resists human control; its violent forces hold man at their pleasure and mercy. Homer suggests this violence through his personification of the sea as Poseidon, while Stephen Crane's sea emphasizes a cosmic indifference toward man. According to such views, art and artifact, contrived and controlled, are infinitely more durable and preferable to the natural world, nasty and brutish. So says Addison in "The Aesthetics of Nature."

Whether hero or villain, nature is often used in literature as a metaphor to represent the human condition, physical, spiritual, or psychological. The natural world is thus an "objective correlative" of various human experiences: Huck Finn's island in part symbolizes his naturalness and his physical and moral isolation from society; Hopkins's windhover swoops and flames as an analogue of the narrator's religious state.

Which of these conceptions of nature is most relevant, most meaningful for contemporary readers? Perhaps modern man has been influenced by the absence of nature. Perhaps a return to the land or to the ideals attributed to nature is no longer possible or even desirable. Nature may in fact have been all but destroyed by estrangement or exploitation. But if nature is dead, then what happens to literature about nature? Does it become merely a quaint paean to the past? Or does its abundant existence indicate that what has been so intensely meaningful for centuries cannot be abandoned, that vital new relationships between man and nature will emerge in the future? The following symposium not only suggests ways in which nature or the idea of nature relates to man, but also helps to suggest what facts or concepts concerning our natural environment are still worth preserving as we continue to annihilate much of the world around us.

Homer (c. 850–800 B.C.)

GREEK POET

Poseidon's Revenge

When Dawn spread out her finger tips of r
Odysseus pulled his tunic and his cloak on
while the sea nymph dressed in a silvery gown
of subtle tissue, drew about her waist
a golden belt, and veiled her head, and then
took thought for the great-hearted hero's voyage.
A brazen axehead first she had to give him,
two-bladed, and agreeable to the palm
with a smooth-fitting haft of olive wood;
next a well-polished adze; and then she led him   10
to the island's tip where bigger timber grew —
besides the alder and poplar, tall pine trees,
long dead and seasoned, that would float him high.
Showing him in that place her stand of timber
the loveliest of nymphs took her way home.
Now the man fell to chopping; when he paused
twenty tall trees were down. He lopped the branches,
split the trunks, and trimmed his puncheons true.
Meanwhile Kalypso brought him an auger tool
with which he drilled through all his planks, then
        drove   20
stout pins to bolt them, fitted side by side.
A master shipwright, building a cargo vessel,
lays down a broad and shallow hull; just so
Odysseus shaped the bottom of his craft.
He made his decking fast to close-set ribs
before he closed the side with longer planking,
then cut a mast pole, and a proper yard,
and shaped a steering oar to hold her steady.
He drove long strands of willow in all the seams
to keep out waves, and ballasted with logs.   30
As for a sail, the lovely nymph Kalypso
brought him a cloth so he could make that, too.
Then he ran up his rigging — halyards, braces —
and hauled the boat on rollers to the water.

sea nymph: Kalypso, with whom
he has stayed seven years

Title supplied by editors. From *Homer: The Odyssey*
translated by Robert Fitzgerald. Copyright © 1961 by
Robert Fitzgerald. Reprinted by permission of Doubleday
& Company, Inc.

This was the fourth day when he had all ready;
on the fifth day, she sent him out to sea.
But first she bathed him, gave him a scented cloak,
and put on board a skin of dusky wine
with water in a bigger skin, and stores —
boiled meats and other victuals — in a bag.   40
Then she conjured a warm land breeze to blowing —
joy for Odysseus when he shook out sail!
Now the great seaman, leaning on his oar,
steered all the night unsleeping, and his eyes
picked out the Pleiadês, the laggard Ploughman,
and the Great Bear, that some have called the Wain,
pivoting in the sky before Orion;
of all the night's pure figures, she alone
would never bathe or dip in the Ocean stream.
These stars the beautiful Kalypso bade him   50
hold on his left hand as he crossed the main.
Seventeen nights and days in the open water
he sailed, before a dark shoreline appeared;
Skhería then came slowly into view
like a rough shield of bull's hide on the sea.

But now the god of earthquake, storming home
over the mountains of Asia from the Sunburned land,
sighted him far away. The god grew sullen
and tossed his great head, muttering to himself:

"Here is a pretty cruise! While I was gone   60
the gods have changed their minds about Odysseus.
Look at him now, just offshore of that island
that frees him from the bondage of his exile!
Still I can give him a rough ride in, and will."

Brewing high thunderheads, he churned the deep
with both hands on his trident — called up wind
from every quarter, and sent a wall of rain
to blot out land and sea in torrential night.
Hurricane winds now struck from the South and East
shifting North West in a great spume of seas,   70
on which Odysseus' knees grew slack, his heart
sickened, and he said within himself:

"Rag of man that I am, is this the end of me?
I fear the goddess told it all too well —
predicting great adversity at sea
and far from home. Now all things bear her out:
the whole rondure of heaven hooded so
by Zeus in woeful cloud, and the sea raging
under such winds. I am going down, that's sure.

Ploughman: Boötes, northern constellation. **Great Bear:** constellation near the North Pole

Skhería: possibly Corfu

god of earthquake: Poseidon, god of the sea and brother of Zeus; father of Polyphemus, the cyclops, whom Odysseus blinded

the goddess: Athena, goddess of wisdom and protectress of Odysseus

How lucky those Danaans were who perished   80
on Troy's wide seaboard, serving the Atreidai!
Would God I, too, had died there — met my end
that time the Trojans made so many casts at me
when I stood by Akhilleus after death.
I should have had a soldier's burial
and praise from the Akhaians — not this choking
waiting for me at sea, unmarked and lonely."

A great wave drove at him with toppling crest
spinning him round, in one tremendous blow,
and he went plunging overboard, the oar-haft   90
wrenched from his grip. A gust that came on howling
at the same instant broke his mast in two,
hurling his yard and sail far out to leeward.
Now the big wave a long time kept him under,
helpless to surface, held by tons of water,
tangled, too, by the seacloak of Kalypso.
Long, long, until he came up spouting brine,
with streamlets gushing from his head and beard;
but still bethought him, half-drowned as he was,
to flounder for the boat and get a handhold   100
into the bilge — to crouch there, foiling death.
Across the foaming water, to and fro,
the boat careered like a ball of tumbleweed
blown on the autumn plains, but intact still.
So the winds drove this wreck over the deep,
East Wind and North Wind, then South Wind and
    West,
coursing each in turn to the brutal harry.

But Ino saw him — Ino, Kadmos' daughter,
slim-legged, lovely, once an earthling girl,
now in the seas a nereid, Leukothea.   110
Touched by Odysseus' painful buffeting
she broke the surface, like a diving bird,
to rest upon the tossing raft and say:

"O forlorn man, I wonder
why the Earthshaker, Lord Poseidon, holds
this fearful grudge — father of all your woes.
He will not drown you, though, despite his rage.
You seem clear-headed still; do what I tell you.
Shed that cloak, let the gale take your craft,
and swim for it — swim hard to get ashore   120
upon Skhería, yonder,
where it is fated that you find a shelter.
Here: make my veil your sash; it is not mortal;
you cannot, now, be drowned or suffer harm.

Danaans: Greeks

Atreidai: Agamemnon and Menelaus (sons of Atreus); the Greek
chiefs whom Odysseus served in
the Trojan War

Akhaians: Greeks

Only, the instant you lay hold of earth,
discard it, cast it far, far out from shore
in the winedark sea again, and turn away."

After she had bestowed her veil, the nereid
dove like a gull to windward
where a dark waveside closed over her whiteness.   130
But in perplexity Odysseus
said to himself, his great heart laboring:

"O damned confusion! Can this be a ruse
to trick me from the boat for some god's pleasure?
No, I'll not swim; with my own eyes I saw
how far the land lies that she called my shelter.
Better to do the wise thing, as I see it.
While this poor planking holds, I stay aboard;
I may ride out the pounding of the storm,
or if she cracks up, take to the water then;   140
I cannot think it through a better way."

But even while he pondered and decided,
the god of earthquake heaved a wave against him
high as a rooftree and of awful gloom.
A gust of wind, hitting a pile of chaff,
will scatter all the parched stuff far and wide;
just so, when this gigantic billow struck
the boat's big timbers flew apart. Odysseus
clung to a single beam, like a jockey riding,
meanwhile stripping Kalypso's cloak away;   150
then he slung round his chest the veil of Ino
and plunged headfirst into the sea. His hands
went out to stroke, and he gave a swimmer's kick.
But the strong Earthshaker had him under his eye,
and nodded as he said:

                 "Go on, go on;
wander the high seas this way, take your blows,
before you join that race the gods have nurtured.
Nor will you grumble, even then, I think,
for want of trouble."

              Whipping his glossy team
he rode off to his glorious home at Aigai.   160
But Zeus's daughter Athena countered him:
she checked the course of all the winds but one,
commanding them, "Be quiet and go to sleep."
Then sent a long swell running under a norther
to bear the prince Odysseus, back from danger,
to join the Phaiákians, people of the sea.

Phaiákians: (Phaeacians) descendants of Poseidon who emigrated
to Skhería; extraordinary mariners
and navigators, traditionally very
hospitable to seafarers

Two nights, two days, in the solid deep-sea swell
he drifted, many times awaiting death,
until with shining ringlets in the East
the dawn confirmed a third day, breaking clear   170
over a high and windless sea; and mounting
a rolling wave he caught a glimpse of land.
What a dear welcome thing life seems to children
whose father, in the extremity, recovers
after some weakening and malignant illness:
his pangs are gone, the gods have delivered him.
So dear and welcome to Odysseus
the sight of land, of woodland, on that morning.
It made him swim again, to get a foothold
on solid ground. But when he came in earshot   180
he heard the trampling roar of sea on rock,
where combers, rising shoreward, thudded down
on the sucking ebb — all sheeted with salt foam.
Here were no coves or harborage or shelter,
only steep headlands, rockfallen reefs and crags.
Odysseus' knees grew slack, his heart faint,
a heaviness came over him, and he said:
"A cruel turn, this. Never had I thought
to see this land, but Zeus has let me see it —
and let me, too, traverse the Western Ocean —   190
only to find no exit from these breakers.
Here are sharp rocks off shore, and the sea a smother
rushing around them; rock face rising sheer
from deep water; nowhere could I stand up
on my two feet and fight free of the welter.
No matter how I try it, the surf may throw me
against the cliffside; no good fighting there.
If I swim down the coast, outside the breakers,
I may find shelving shore and quiet water —
but what if another gale comes on to blow?   200
Then I go cursing out to sea once more.
Or then again, some shark of Amphitritê's
may hunt me, sent by the genius of the deep.
I know how he who makes earth tremble hates me."

During this meditation a heavy surge
was taking him, in fact, straight on the rocks.
He had been flayed there, and his bones broken,
had not grey-eyed Athena instructed him:
he gripped a rock-ledge with both hands in passing
and held on, groaning, as the surge went by,   210
to keep clear of its breaking. Then the backwash
hit him, ripping him under and far out.
An octopus, when you drag one from his chamber,
comes up with suckers full of tiny stones:

Amphitritê: a nereid, goddess of the sea, who governed the waves and sea animals

Odysseus left the skin of his great hands
torn on that rock-ledge as the wave submerged him.
And now at last Odysseus would have perished,
battered inhumanly, but he had the gift
of self-possession from grey-eyed Athena.
So, when the backwash spewed him up again,   220
he swam out and along, and scanned the coast
for some landspit that made a breakwater.
Lo and behold, the mouth of a calm river
at length came into view, with level shores
unbroken, free from rock, shielded from wind —
by far the best place he had found.
But as he felt the current flowing seaward
he prayed in his heart:

            "O hear me, lord of the stream:
how sorely I depend upon your mercy!
derelict as I am by the sea's anger.   230
Is he not sacred, even to the gods,
the wandering man who comes, as I have come,
in weariness before your knees, your waters?
Here is your servant; lord, have mercy on me."

lord of the stream: Each river had
its own particular local deity.

Now even as he prayed the tide at ebb
had turned, and the river god made quiet water,
drawing him into safety in the shallows.
His knees buckled, his arms gave way beneath him,
all vital force now conquered by the sea.
Swollen from head to foot he was, and seawater   240
gushed from his mouth and nostrils. There he lay,
scarce drawing breath, unstirring, deathly spent.
In time, as air came back into his lungs
and warmth around his heart, he loosed the veil,
letting it drift away on the estuary
downstream to where a white wave took it under
and Ino's hands received it. Then the man
crawled to the river bank among the reeds
where, face down, he could kiss the soil of earth.

Plato (c. 427–c. 347 B.C.)

GREEK PHILOSOPHER

The Allegory of the Cave

Next, said I, here is a parable to illustrate the degrees in which our nature may be enlightened or unenlightened. Imagine the condition of men living is a sort of cavernous chamber underground, with an entrance open to the light and a long passage all down the cave. Here they have been from childhood, chained by the leg and also by the neck, so that they cannot move and can see only what is in front of them, because the chains will not let them turn their heads. At some distance higher up is the light of a fire burning behind them; and between the prisoners and the fire is a track[1] with a parapet built along it, like the screen at a puppet-show, which hides the performers while they show their puppets over the top.

I see, said he.

Now behind this parapet imagine persons carrying along various artificial objects, including figures of men and animals in wood or stone or other materials, which project above the parapet. Naturally, some of these persons will be talking, others silent.[2]

It is a strange picture, he said, and a strange sort of prisoners.

Like ourselves, I replied; for in the first place prisoners so confined would have seen nothing of themselves or of one another, except the shadows thrown by the fire-light on the wall of the Cave facing them, would they?

Not if all their lives they had been prevented from moving their heads.

And they would have seen as little of the objects carried past.

Of course.

Now, if they could talk to one another, would they not suppose that their words referred only to those passing shadows which they saw?

Necessarily.

And suppose their prisoner had an echo from the wall facing them? When one of the people crossing behind them spoke, they could only suppose that the sound came from the shadow passing before their eyes.

[1] The track crosses the passage into the cave at right angles, and is *above* the parapet built along it.

[2] A modern Plato would compare his Cave to an underground cinema, where the audience watch the play of shadows thrown by the film passing before a light at their backs. The film itself is only an image of 'real' things and events in the world outside the cinema. For the film Plato has to substitute the clumsier apparatus of a procession of artificial objects carried on their heads by persons who are merely part of the machinery, providing for the movement of the objects and the sounds whose echo the prisoners hear. The parapet prevents these persons' shadows from being cast on the wall of the Cave.

Title supplied by editors. From *The Republic of Plato*, translated and annotated by F. N. Cornford. First American edition, 1945. Reprinted by permission of Oxford University Press.

No doubt.

In every way, then, such prisoners would recognize as reality nothing but the shadows of those artificial objects.

Inevitably.

Now consider what would happen if their release from the chains and the healing of their unwisdom should come about in this way. Suppose one of them set free and forced suddenly to stand up, turn his head, and walk with eyes lifted to the light; all these movements would be painful, and he would be too dazzled to make out the objects whose shadows he had been used to see. What do you think he would say, if someone told him that what he had formerly seen was meaningless illusion, but now, being somewhat nearer to reality and turned towards more real objects, he was getting a truer view? Suppose further that he were shown the various objects being carried by and were made to say, in reply to questions, what each of them was. Would he not be perplexed and believe the objects now shown him to be not so real as what he formerly saw?

Yes, not nearly so real.

And if he were forced to look at the fire-light itself, would not his eyes ache, so that he would try to escape and turn back to the things which he could see distinctly, convinced that they really were clearer than these other objects now being shown to him?

Yes.

And suppose someone were to drag him away forcibly up the steep and rugged ascent and not let him go until he had hauled him out into the sunlight, would he not suffer pain and vexation at such treatment, and, when he had come out into the light, find his eyes so full of its radiance that he could not see a single one of the things that he was now told were real?

Certainly he would not see them all at once.

He would need, then, to grow accustomed before he could see things in that upper world. At first it would be easiest to make out shadows, and then the images of men and things reflected in water, and later on the things themselves. After that, it would be easier to watch the heavenly bodies and the sky itself by night, looking at the light of the moon and stars rather than the Sun and the Sun's light in the day-time.

Yes, surely.

Last of all, he would be able to look at the Sun and contemplate its nature, not as it appears when reflected in water or any alien medium, but as it is in itself in its own domain.

No doubt.

And now he would begin to draw the conclusion that it is the Sun that produces the seasons and the course of the year and controls everything in the visible world, and moreover is in a way the cause of all that he and his companions used to see.

Clearly he would come at last to that conclusion.

He spoke to me, while laughter still played about his
  lips: 20
  'Whither by noon, Simichidas, are you toiling
    along thus,
When even the very lizard in the stone wall is asleep,
And the tomb-crested larks[1] no more are flitting to
    and fro?
Are you bidden to a banquet, that you stride along so
    fast?
Or else to tread some neighbour's vintage? For your
    speed is such,
That all the stones in the road are ringing stricken by
    your boot.'
  'Dear Lycidas,' I answered him, ' 'tis you that all
    men say
Among herdsmen and harvesters have far the greatest
    skill
In playing on the pan-pipes: and it delights my heart
To hear this said. Yet to my thinking I should have
    some claim   30
To be your rival. Now our journey leads to a harvest-
    home,
Where friends are making festival to the fair-robed
    Demeter
From the first-fruits of their increase; for with wealth
    of barley grain
The Goddess in rich measure has filled their thresh-
    ing-floor.
But come, since we are sharers alike of road and morn,
Let us sing pastoral lays: perchance each will delight
    the other.
For I too serve the Muses; their clear-voiced mouth
    am I.
All call me best of minstrels; but I am not credulous;
No, by the Earth, for to my mind I cannot conquer
    yet
In song that rare Sikelides of Samos, nor Philetas,   40
But vainly like a frog against cicalas I contend.'
  Thus did I speak to gain my end: and with a
    kindly laugh
The goatherd said: 'I offer you this crook, because I
    know
You are a sapling Zeus has moulded wholly in truth's
    mould.

Sikelides, Philetas: Greek poets
cicalas: cicadas

---

[1] According to fable, the lark was created first of the birds, and before earth. Therefore
when the lark died, his son, having no land in which to bury him, was obliged to entomb
him on his own head.

Even as I loathe your builder who strives to raise a
   house
As lofty as the topmost peak of Mount Oromedon,   Mount Oromedon: a mountain on
So all birds of the Muses do I loathe, that croak and   Cos
   cackle
Against the Chian minstrel, wasting their toil in vain.   Chian minstrel: Homer
But come let us begin forthwith our pastoral melodies,
Simichidas: and I first — well, friend, see if this
   chance to please you,   50
This ditty which I worked out not long since on the
   hills.

He sings
   Fair voyage to Mytilene shall befall Ageänax,   Mytilene: chief city of Lesbos
When the Kids are in the Western sky, and the   Kids: the constellation Capricorn,
   South wind is chasing   which is low in the western sky
The wet waves, and Orion stands with his feet on   in November, as is Orion
   the sea,
If he will but save Lycidas, who in Aphrodite's fire
Is scorched; for burning is the love that consumes me
   for him.
The halcyons[2] will calm the ocean waves and lull the
   winds
Of South and East, that stir the sea-weed far up on
   the shore,
The halcyons that are dearest to the green-haired
   Nereïds
Of all the birds that from the salt sea waters take
   their prey.   60
Thus may the season smile upon Ageänax as he sails
To Mytilene, and may his ship come safely home to
   port.
And I upon that day will set a garland on my head
Of anise, or of roses, or of white violets,
And the best wine of Ptelea will I pour forth from
   the bowl,
As I lie before the fire, where beans are roasting in
   the embers.
And high as to the elbow thick-strewn shall be my
   couch
With sweet fleabane and asphodel and curling parsley
   leaves.
Thus will I drink luxuriously with Ageänax in my
   thoughts

[2] The halcyon, a legendary bird identified with the kingfisher, was supposed to lay its eggs
in nests that floated on the sea about the time of the winter solstice. While the nests
floated, the bird had the power to calm the waves and produce good weather.

Draining each wine-cup with firm lip even to the very
    dregs.   70
    Two shepherds, from Acharnae one, the other from
    Lykōpe,

Acharnae, Lykōpe: areas in Attica
(Greece)

Shall be my flute-players; and beside me Tityrus shall
    sing
How once Daphnis the herdsman loved Xenia the
    nymph,
And how the mountain grieved for him, and the oak-
    trees sang his dirge
(The oaks that grow along the banks of the river
    Himeras),

Himeras: a river in Sicily

When he lay wasting like a streak of snow beneath
    tall Haimos,

Haimos . . . Caucasus: mountains

Or Rhodope, or Athos, or far-off Caucasus.
    And he shall sing how once the goatherd was
    enclosed alive[3]
In a great coffer by his lord's outrage and cruel spite;
And how the blunt-faced bees, as from the meadows
    they flew home   80
To the fragrant chest of cedar-wood, fed him with
    tender flowers,
Because with sweet nectar the Muse had steeped his
    lips.
    O fortunate Komatas, such joys indeed were thine;
Yea, prisoned in the coffer, by the bees thou wast fed
With honey-comb, and didst endure thy bondage a
    whole year.
Would that thou hadst been numbered with the
    living in my days,
That so I might have grazed thy pretty she-goats on
    the hills,
Listening to thy voice, whilst thou under the oaks or
    pines
Hadst lain, divine Komatas, singing sweet melodies.'
    So far he sang, then made an end; and after him
    in turn   90
Thus did I speak: 'Dear Lycidas, many things else
    the Nymphs
Have taught me too, while I was pasturing kine
    among the hills,
Good songs, that fame perchance has brought even
    to the throne of Zeus.

[3] Comatus sacrificed his master's cattle to the Muses; in revenge his lord locked him in a
chest. When the chest was opened after a year, Comatus was found alive, having been
miraculously fed by bees.

But one there is, the best of all, which now to do you
honour
I'll sing. Do you then listen, since the Muses love
you well.

He sings
    On Simichidas the Loves have sneezed: for truly
    the poor wretch
Loves Myrto just as dearly as the goats love the
Spring.
But Arātos, whom Simichidas holds best of all his
friends,
Hides in his heart the longing for a boy. Aristis
knows
(That best and worthiest man, whom Phoebus' self
would joy to see   100
Standing beside his tripods and singing lyre in hand),

tripod: three-legged stool; a symbol of the Delphic oracle and a
favorite offering to Apollo

He knows how love for a boy is burning Arātos to the
bone.
O Pan, lord of the pleasant pastures of Mount
Homole,
I pray thee, bring him unbidden to my friend's long-
ing arms,
Whether it be the delicate Philinos, or some other.
And if thou wilt do this, O darling Pan, may never-
more
The Arcadian children whip thee with squills about
thy ribs
And shoulders, when too little meat is left them on
thy altar.
But if otherwise thou shouldst decree, then may bites
set thy nails
Scratching thy skin all over, and on nettles mayst
thou couch.   110
On the Edonian mountains in midwinter mayst thou
dwell

Edonian, Hebros: in Thrace

Lodging beside the river Hebros near to the Great
Bear.
But mid the farthest Aethiops in summer mayst thou
range,

Aethiops: Ethiopia

Beneath the Blemyan mountain cliff, whence Nile is
seen no more.

Blemyan: in Ethiopia

    But ye, leaving the pleasant fount of Hyetis and
    Byblis,

Hyetis, Byblis, Oikeus: mountains
and springs near Miletus, in Asia
Minor.   Dione: mother of Aphrodite; here probably referring to
Aphrodite herself

And Oikeus' hill, the lofty shrine of golden-tressed
Dione,
O ye winged Loves, rosy as blushing apples, hither
come,
Pierce, I pray, with your arrows Philinos the desired,

Pierce him, that miserable wretch, who pities not my
    friend.
And yet he's but a pear that's over-ripe, and the girls
    cry,   120
"Ah welaway Philinos! fading is thy fair bloom!"
Come then, Arātos, let's no more stand watching at
    his gates,
Nor wear our feet away; but let the cock that crows
    at dawn
Give others over to be chilled by numbing misery.
Alone let Molon wrestle, friend, with anguish such
    as that.
But our concern be peace of mind: some old crone
    let us seek,
To spit on us for luck and keep unlovely things afar.'
    Thus I sang; and the goatherd, with the same
    kindly laugh,
Gave me the crook, in token of our brotherhood in
    the Muses.
Then slanting off towards the left he took the road
    to Pyxa,   130
While with the pretty boy Amyntas, Eukritos and I
Turned to the farm of Phrasidemos; and arriving
    there
We soon were lying joyously couched upon soft deep
    beds
Heaped with scented rushes and vine-leaves newly
    stripped.
And high above our heads there swayed and quivered
    many a branch
Of poplar and of elm-tree, while close beside us
    welled
The sacred water gushing from the cavern of the
    Nymphs.
Amid the shadowing foliage the brown cicalas
    chirped
And chattered busily without pause; and far away was
    heard
From the dense bramble thicket the tree-frog's fluted
    note.   140
Larks and thistle-finches sang, the turtle dove was
    moaning:
About the running water hovered the tawny bees.
All things breathed the scent of teeming summer and
    ripe fruits.
Pears at our feet lay fallen, and apples at our sides
Were rolling in abundance; and the plum-tree's ten-
    der boughs

Drooped overburdened with their load of damsons to
    the earth;
And mouth of jars, for four years sealed with resin,
    were unstopped.
   Ye Nymphs of Castaly, that haunt the steep Par-
    nassian hill,
Did ever aged Cheiron[4] in Pholos'[5] rocky cave
Set before Herakles a bowl with such a vintage
    filled?   150
Did ever such a draught of nectar beguile that
    shepherd lout
Who dwelt beside Anāpos, and pelted ships with
    crags,
Strong Polypheme,[6] and set his feet capering about
    his folds? —
Such a draught as ye Nymphs that day made stream
    for us beside
Harvest Demeter's altar, upon whose mound of corn
May it be mine once more to plant the great fan,[7]
    while she sits
And smiles upon us, holding sheaves and poppies in
    each hand.

Castaly: Castalia, a fountain on Mount Parnassus sacred to Apollo and the Muses, and thought to possess powers of inspiration

Ovid   (43 B.C.–A.D. 17)

ROMAN POET

Echo and Narcissus

Now Narcissus
Was sixteen years of age, and could be taken
Either for boy or man; and boys and girls
Both sought his love, but in that slender stripling
Was pride so fierce no boy, no girl, could touch him.
He was out hunting one day, driving deer
Into the nets, when a nymph named Echo saw him,

[4] a wise centaur, learned in music and medicine, who tutored Herakles (Hercules).
[5] a centaur, guardian of the wine of Dionysus, who entertained Herakles; the smell of the wine attracted and maddened many neighboring centaurs, and a fierce fight ensued.
[6] Polyphemus, a one-eyed giant who held Odysseus captive and threw huge stones at his ships when he escaped.
[7] The usual image of Demeter, goddess of vegetation and harvest, showed her holding spikes of corn and poppies, emblems of fertility and plenty.

Title supplied by editors. From Metamorphoses by Ovid, translated by Rolfe Humphries and published by Indiana University Press. Reprinted by permission.

A nymph whose way of talking was peculiar
In that she could not start a conversation
Nor fail to answer other people talking.   10
Up to this time Echo still had a body,
She was not merely voice. She liked to chatter,
But had no power of speech except the power
To answer in the words she last had heard.
Juno had done this: when she went out looking
For Jove on top of some nymph among the mountains,
Echo would stall the goddess off by talking
Until the nymphs had fled. Sooner or later
Juno discovered this and said to Echo:
"The tongue that made a fool of me will shortly   20
Have shorter use, the voice be brief hereafter."
Those were not idle words; now Echo always
Says the last thing she hears, and nothing further.
She saw Narcissus roaming through the country,
Saw him, and burned, and followed him in secret,
Burning the more she followed, as when sulphur
Smeared on the rim of torches, catches fire
When other fire comes near it. Oh, how often
She wanted to come near with coaxing speeches,
Make soft entreaties to him! But her nature   30
Sternly forbids; the one thing not forbidden
Is to make answers. She is more than ready
For words she can give back. By chance Narcissus
Lost track of his companions, started calling
"Is anybody here?" and "Here!" said Echo.
He looked around in wonderment, called louder
"Come to me!" "Come to me!" came back the answer.
He looked behind him, and saw no one coming;
"Why do you run from me?" and heard his question
Repeated in the woods. "Let us get together!"   40
There was nothing Echo would ever say more gladly,
"Let us get together!" And, to help her words,
Out of the woods she came, with arms all ready
To fling around his neck. But he retreated:
"Keep your hands off," he cried, "and do not touch me!
I would die before I give you a chance at me."
"I give you a chance at me," and that was all
She ever said thereafter, spurned and hiding,
Ashamed, in the leafy forests, in lonely caverns.
But still her love clings to her and increases   50
And grows on suffering; she cannot sleep,
She frets and pines, becomes all gaunt and haggard,
Her body dries and shrivels till voice only
And bones remain, and then she is voice only
For the bones are turned to stone. She hides in woods
And no one sees her now along the mountains,
But all may hear her, for her voice is living.

She was not the only one on whom Narcissus
Had visited frustration; there were others,
Naiads or Oreads, and young men also   60
Till finally one rejected youth, in prayer,
Raised up his hands to Heaven: "May Narcissus
Love one day, so, himself, and not win over
The creature whom he loves!" Nemesis heard him,
Goddess of Vengeance, and judged the plea was righteous.
There was a pool, silver with shining water,
To which no shepherds came, no goats, no cattle,
Whose glass no bird, no beast, no falling leaf
Had ever troubled. Grass grew all around it,
Green from the nearby water, and with shadow   70
No sum burned hotly down on. Here Narcissus,
Worn from the heat of hunting, came to rest
Finding the place delightful, and the spring
Refreshing for the thirsty. As he tried
To quench his thirst, inside him, deep within him,
Another thirst was growing, for he saw
An image in the pool, and fell in love
With that unbodied hope, and found a substance
In what was only shadow. He looks in wonder,
Charmed by himself, spell-bound, and no more moving   80
Than any marble statue. Lying prone
He sees his eyes, twin stars, and locks as comely
As those of Bacchus or the god Apollo,
Smooth cheeks, and ivory neck, and the bright beauty
Of countenance, and a flush of color rising
In the fair whiteness. Everything attracts him
That makes him so attractive. Foolish boy,
He wants himself; the loved becomes the lover,
The seeker sought, the kindler burns. How often
He tries to kiss the image in the water,   90
Dips in his arms to embrace the boy he sees there,
And finds the boy, himself, elusive always,
Not knowing what he sees, but burning for it,
The same delusion mocking his eyes and teasing.
Why try to catch an always fleeing image,
Poor credulous youngster? What you seek is nowhere,
And if you turn away, you will take with you
The boy you love. The vision is only shadow,
Only reflection, lacking any substance.
It comes with you, it stays with you, it goes   100
Away with you, if you go away.
No thought of food, no thought of rest, can make him
Forsake the place. Stretched on the grass, in shadow,
He watches, all unsatisfied, that image
Vain and illusive, and he almost drowns
In his own watching eyes. He rises, just a little,

Enough to lift his arms in supplication
To the trees around him, crying to the forest:
"What love, whose love, has ever been more cruel?
You woods should know: you have given many lovers   110
Places to meet and hide in; has there ever,
Through the long centuries, been anyone
Who has pined away as I do? He is charming,
I see him, but the charm and sight escape me.
I love him and I cannot seem to find him!
To make it worse, no sea, no road, no mountain,
No city-wall, no gate, no barrier, parts us
But a thin film of water. He is eager
For me to hold him. When my lips go down
To kiss the pool, his rise, he reaches toward me.   120
You would think that I could touch him — almost nothing
Keeps us apart. Come out, whoever you are!
Why do you tease me so? Where do you go
When I am reaching for you? I am surely
Neither so old or ugly as to scare you,
And nymphs have been in love with me. You promise,
I think, some hope with a look of more than friendship.
You reach out arms when I do, and your smile
Follows my smiling; I have seen your tears
When I was tearful; you nod and beckon when I do;   130
Your lips, it seems, answer when I am talking
Though what you say I cannot hear. I know
The truth at last. He is myself! I feel it,
I know my image now. I burn with love
Of my own self; I start the fire I suffer.
What shall I do? Shall I give or take the asking?
What shall I ask for? What I want is with me,
My riches make me poor. If I could only
Escape from my own body! if I could only —
How curious a prayer from any lover —   140
Be parted from my love! And now my sorrow
Is taking all my strength away; I know
I have not long to live, I shall die early,
And death is not so terrible, since it takes
My trouble from me; I am sorry only
The boy I love must die: we die together."
He turned again to the image in the water,
Seeing it blur through tears, and the vision fading,
And as he saw it vanish, he called after:
"Where are you going? Stay: do not desert me,   150
I love you so. I cannot touch you; let me
Keep looking at you always, and in looking
Nourish my wretched passion!" In his grief
He tore his garment from the upper margin,
Beat his bare breast with hands as pale as marble,

And the breast took on a glow, a rosy color,
As apples are white and red, sometimes, or grapes
Can be both green and purple. The water clears,
He sees it all once more, and cannot bear it.
As yellow wax dissolves with warmth around it,   160
As the white frost is gone in morning sunshine,
Narcissus, in the hidden fire of passion,
Wanes slowly, with the ruddy color going,
The strength and hardihood and comeliness,
Fading away, and even the very body
Echo had loved. She was sorry for him now,
Though angry still, remembering; you could hear her
Answer "Alas!" in pity, when Narcissus
Cried out "Alas!" You could hear her own hands beating
Her breast when he beat his. "Farewell, dear boy,   170
Beloved in vain!" were his last words, and Echo
Called the same words to him. His weary head
Sank to the greensward, and death closed the eyes
That once had marveled at their owner's beauty.
And even in Hell, he found a pool to gaze in,
Watching his image in the Stygian water.
While in the world above, his naiad sisters
Mourned him, and dryads wept for him, and Echo
Mourned as they did, and wept with them, preparing
The funeral pile, the bier, the brandished torches,   180
But when they sought his body, they found nothing,
Only a flower with a yellow center
Surrounded with ~~white petals~~.

↓ Pearls

Anonymous   (c. 1070)

ENGLISH

The Seafarer

A song I sing   of my sea-adventure,
The strain of peril,   the stress of toil,
Which oft I endured   in anguish of spirit
Through weary hours   of aching woe.
My bark was swept   by the breaking seas;
Bitter the watch   from the bow by night

From *An Anthology of Old English Poetry*, translated by Charles W. Kennedy. Copyright © 1960 by Oxford University Press, Inc. Reprinted by permission.

As my ship drove on   within sound of the rocks.
My feet were numb   with the nipping cold,
Hunger sapped   a sea-weary spirit,
And care weighed heavy   upon my heart.   10
  Little the landlubber,   safe on shore,
Knows what I've suffered   in icy seas
Wretched and worn   by the winter storms,
Hung with icicles,   stung by hail,
Lonely and friendless   and far from home.
In my ears no sound   but the roar of the sea,
The icy combers,   the cry of the swan;
In place of the mead-hall   and laughter of men
My only singing   the sea-mew's call,
The scream of the gannet,   the shriek of the gull;   20
Through the wail of the wild gale   beating the bluffs
The piercing cry   of the ice-coated petrel,
The storm-drenched eagle's echoing scream.
In all my wretchedness,   weary and lone,
I had no comfort   of comrade or kin.
  Little indeed can he credit,   whose town-life
Pleasantly passes   in feasting and joy,
Sheltered from peril,   what weary pain
Often I've suffered   in foreign seas.
Night shades darkened   with driving snow   30
From the freezing north,   and the bonds of frost
Firm-locked the land,   while falling hail,
Coldest of kernels,   encrusted earth.
  Yet still, even now,   my spirit within me
Drives me seaward   to sail the deep,
To ride the long swell   of the salt sea-wave.
Never a day   but my heart's desire
Would launch me forth   on the long sea-path,
Fain of far harbors   and foreign shores.
Yet lives no man   so lordly of mood,   40
So eager in giving,   so ardent in youth,
So bold in his deeds,   or so dear to his lord,
Who is free from dread   in his far sea-travel,
Or fear of God's purpose   and plan for his fate.
The beat of the harp,   and bestowal of treasure,
The love of woman,   and worldly hope,
Nor other interest   can hold his heart
Save only the sweep   of the surging billows;
His heart is haunted   by love of the sea.
  Trees are budding   and towns are fair,   50
Meadows kindle   and all life quickens,
All things hasten   the eager-hearted,
Who joyeth therein,   to journey afar,
Turing seaward   to distant shores.
The cuckoo stirs him   with plaintive call,

The herald of summer,   with mournful song,
Foretelling the sorrow   that stabs the heart.
Who liveth in luxury,   little he knows
What woe men endure   in exile's doom.
   Yet still, even now,   my desire outreaches,   60
My spirit soars   over tracts of sea,
O'er the home of the whale,   and the world's expanse.
Eager, desirous,   the lone sprite returneth;
It cries in my ears   and it urges my heart
To the path of the whale   and the plunging sea.

Anonymous (c. 1100)

ENGLISH

The Lion

Leo the Lion, mightiest of beasts, will stand up to anybody.

The word 'beasts' should properly be used about lions, leopards, tigers, wolves, foxes, dogs, monkeys and others which rage about with tooth and claw — with the exception of snakes. They are called Beasts because of the violence with which they rage, and are known as 'wild' (*ferus*) because they are accustomed to freedom by nature and are governed (*ferantur*) by their own wishes. They wander hither and thither, fancy free, and they go wherever they want to go.

The name 'Lion' (*leo*) has been turned into Latin from a Greek root, for it is called '*leon*' in Greek — but this is a muddled name, partly corrupted, since '*leon*' has also been translated as 'king' from Greek into Latin, owing to the fact that he is the Prince of All Animals.

They say that the litters of these creatures come in threes. The short ones with curly manes are peaceful: the tall ones with plain hair are fierce.

The nature of their brows and tail-tufts is an index to their disposition. Their courage is seated in their hearts, while their constancy is in their heads. They fear the creaking of wheels, but are frightened by fires even more so.

A lion, proud in the strength of his own nature, knows not how to mingle his ferocity with all and sundry, but, like the king he is, disdains to have a lot of different wives.

Scientists say that Leo has three principal characteristics.

From *The Bestiary* (*A Book of Beasts*) by T. H. White. Reprinted by permission of G. P. Putnam's Sons and Jonathan Cape Ltd., London.

His first feature is that he loves to saunter on the tops of mountains. Then, if he should happen to be pursued by hunting men, the smell of the hunters reaches up to him, and he disguises his spoor behind him with his tail. Thus the sportsmen cannot track him.

It was in this way that our Saviour (i.e. the Spiritual Lion of the Tribe of Judah, the Rod of Jesse,[1] the Lord of Lords, the Son of God) once hid the spoor of his love in the high places, until, being sent by the Father, he came down into the womb of the Virgin Mary and saved the human race which had perished. Ignorant of the fact that his spoor could be concealed, the Devil (i.e. the hunter of humankind) dared to pursue him with temptations like a mere man. Even the angels themselves who were on high, not recognizing his spoor, said to those who were going up with him when he ascended to his reward: 'Who is this King of Glory?'

The Lion's second feature is, that when he sleeps, he seems to keep his eyes open.

In this very way, Our Lord also, while sleeping in the body, was buried after being crucified — yet his Godhead was awake. As it is said in the *Song of Songs*, 'I am asleep and my heart is awake,'[2] or, in the Psalm, 'Behold, he that keepeth Israel shall neither slumber nor sleep.'[3]

The third feature is this, that when a lioness gives birth to her cubs, she brings them forth dead and lays them up lifeless for three days — until their father, coming on the third day, breathes in their faces and makes them alive.

Just so did the Father Omnipotent raise Our Lord Jesus Christ from the dead on the third day. Quoth Jacob: 'He shall sleep like a lion, and the lion's whelp shall be raised.'[4]

So far as their relations with men are concerned, the nature of lions is that they do not get angry unless they are wounded.

Any decent human ought to pay attention to this. For men do get angry when they are not wounded, and they oppress the innocent although the law of Christ bids them to let even the guilty go free.

The compassion of lions, on the contrary, is clear from innumerable examples — for they spare the prostrate; they allow such captives as they come across to go back to their own country; they prey on men rather than on women, and they do not kill children except when they are very hungry.

Furthermore, lions abstain from over-eating: in the first place, because they only take food and drink on alternate days — and frequently, if digestion has not followed, they are even in the habit of putting off the day for dinner.

[1] See *Isaiah* 11.
[2] *Song of Solomon* 5:2.
[3] *Psalms* 121:4.
[4] cf. *Genesis* 49:9.

In the second place, they pop their paws carefully into their mouths and pull out the meat of their own accord, when they have eaten too much. Indeed, when they have to run away from somebody, they perform the same action if they are full up.

Lack of teeth is a sign of old age in lions.

They copulate the backward way. Nor are they the only ones, but also Lynxes, Camels, Elephants, Rhinoceroses, Tigers and Hyaenas.

When they first have babies, they produce five whelps. Then, one by one, they reduce the number in succeeding years. Finally, when they have come down to one, the maternal fertility disappears and they become sterile for ever afterward.

A lion turns up its nose at yesterday's dinner, and will go away hungry from food which has been left over.

What creature dares declare himself an enemy to this beast, in whose roar there is such natural terribleness that many animals, which could escape its charge by their speed, fail to get away from the very sound of its voice — as if dumbfounded and overcome by brute force!

A sick lion searches for a monkey to eat, by which means he can be cured.

A lion fears a cock, especially a white one.

A lion, although he is the king of beasts, gets harassed by the tiny sting of a scorpion, and snake poison kills him.

We read about certain creatures of moderate size, called Leontophontes, which people burn when they get them. They burn them so that they may kill lions with meat which has been tainted by a sprinkling of their ash, and thrown down at crossroads between converging tracks, should the lions eat the least little bit of it. Consequently lions instinctively pursue these creatures with hatred, and, when they get a chance, they do not actually bite them, but they lacerate and kill them with the weight of their paws.

Desiderius Erasmus (1466–1536)

DUTCH HUMANIST, SCHOLAR, and THEOLOGIAN

In Praise of Nature

Isn't it true that the happiest creatures are those which are least artificial and most natural? What could be happier than the bees, or more wonderful? They lack some of the senses, but what architect has equalled their construc-

Title supplied by editors. "In Praise of Nature" by Desiderius Erasmus. From *The Praise of Folly,* translated by Leonard F. Dean (New York: Hendricks House, Inc. 1946). Reprinted by permission of and arrangement with the publisher.

tive skill, or what philosopher has framed a republic to match theirs? Now the horse, who does have some of the human senses and who travels around with men, suffers also from human ills. He feels ashamed if he loses a race. While seeking military glory, he is run through and bites the dust along with his rider. Think, too, of the hard bit, the sharp spurs, the prison-like stable, the whips, sticks, and straps, the rider himself — in short, all the tragedy of servitude to which he exposes himself when he imitates men of honor and zealously seeks vengeance against the enemy. How much more desirable, except for the interference of men, is the lot of flies and birds, who live for the moment and by the light of nature. Everyone has noticed how a bird loses its natural beauty when it is shut up in a cage and taught to speak. In every sphere, what is natural is happier than what is falsified by art.

Thomas Elyot (1490–1546)
ENGLISH WRITER and PHILOSOPHER

The Estates of Animal and Man

Behold . . . the order that God hath put generally in all his creatures, beginning at the most inferior or base and ascending upward: he made nat only herbs to garnish the earth, but also trees of a more eminent stature than herbs, and yet in the one and the other be degrees of qualities; some pleasant to behold, some delicate or good in taste, other wholesome and medicinable, some commodious and necessary. Semblably in birds, beasts, and fishes, some be good for the sustenance of man, some bear things profitable to sundry uses, other be apt to occupation and labor; in diverse is strength and fierceness only; in many is both strength and commodity; some other serve for pleasure; none of them hath all these qualities; few have the more part or many, specially beauty, strength, and profit. But where any is found that hath many of the said properties, he is more set by than all the other, and by that estimation the order of his place and degree evidently appeareth; so that every kind of trees, herbs, birds, beasts, and fishes, beside their diversity of fourms, have (as who saith) a peculiar disposition appropered unto them by God their creator. So that in everything is order, and without order may be nothing stable or permanent; and it may nat be called order except it do contain in it degrees, high and base, according to the merit or estimation of the thing that is ord'red.

Title supplied by editors. "The Estates of Animal and Man" by Thomas Elyot. From *The Boke Named the Governour* in *The Renaissance in England*, edited by Hyder E. Rollins and Herschel Baker.

Now to retourn to the astate of mankind, for whose use all the said creatures were ordained of God, and also excelleth them all by prerogatife of knowledge and wisdom, hit seemeth that in him should be no lass providence of God declared than in the inferior creatures, but rather with a more perfect order and disposition. And therefore hit appeareth that God giveth nat to every man like gifts of grace or of nature, but to some more, some less, as it liketh his divine majesty.

Ne they be nat in commune (as fantastical fools would have all things), nor one man hath nat all virtues and good qualities. Natwithstanding, forasmuch as understanding is the most excellent gift that man can receive in his creation, whereby he doth approach most nigh unto the similitude of God, which understanding is the principal part of the soul; it is therefore congruent and according that as one excelleth another in that influence, as thereby being next to the similitude of his Maker, so should the astate of his person be avanced in degree or place where understanding may profit: which is also distributed into sundry uses, faculties, and offices, necessary for the living and governance of mankind. And like as the angels which be most fervent in contemplation be highest exalted in glory (after the opinion of holy doctors), and also the fire which is the most pure of elements, and also doth clarify the other inferior elements, is deputed to the highest sphere or place, so in this world they which excel other in this influence of understanding, and do imploy it to the detaining of other within the bounds of reason, and shew them how to provide for their necessary living; such ought to be set in a more high place than the residue where they may see and also be seen, that by the beams of their excellent wit, shewed through the glass of auctority,[1] other of inferior understanding may be directed to the way of virtue and commodious living.

[1] authority.

François Rabelais (1494?–1553)

FRENCH SATIRIST, MONK, and PHYSICIAN

The Fable of the Horse and the Ass

After we[1] had feasted our fill, Æditus[2] led us into a well-furnished room, hung with fine tapestry and all smothered with gilt. Here he had us served with myrobalan plums and green preserved ginger, with plenty of mulled sack and delicious wine. With these restoratives, as with a drink of sweet Lethe water, he invited us to forget the toils we had suffered on the sea, and to dismiss them from our minds. He also had a generous quantity of victuals carried aboard our ships, which were lying in the harbour. But we could not sleep, on account of the everlasting jangling of the bells.

At midnight Æditus woke us up to drink; and he himself drank first, saying: You people from the other world say that ignorance is the mother of all evils, and you are right. But all the same you do not banish it from your minds for a single moment. You live in it, with it, and by it. That is why so many evils afflict you day by day. You are always complaining and lamenting. You are never satisfied. I can see it at this present moment. For ignorance keeps you here, tied to your beds, as the great god of battles was by Vulcan's art,[3] and you do not understand that it is your duty to be sparing of your sleep, and not to be sparing of the good things of this famous island. You should have consumed three meals already. What is more, you can take it from me that to eat the food of Ringing Island you have to rise very early in the morning. Eaters multiply, but those who are sparing waste away. Plough the field in due season, and the grass will spring up again thicker and richer for the manger. But if you don't mow it, in a few years it will be carpeted with nothing but moss. Let's drink, my friends. Let's drink, one and all. The skinniest of our birds are now singing, and all for us. We will drink to them, if you please. Let's drink, I beg of you. You'll only spit the better for it. Let's drink, one, two, three, nine bumpers, *non zelus, sed charitas.*'[4]

---

[1] a dialectical pair of protagonists for Rabelais' overview of the world: Panurge is a fool who looks at the world with wonder and hopes to find himself by discovering an ideal land; Pantagruel, his mentor, is a learned commentator who knows that to understand the world means to understand oneself.

[2] the Sacristan of "Ringing Island" and the host and guide for Panurge and Pantagruel during their visit there.

[3] Mars, the Roman god of war, was caught in bed with Venus and trapped there by her husband, Vulcan, the god of fire and metalworking.

[4] "not out of duty, but out of kindness to yourself." [Cohen]

Title supplied by editors. From *The Histories of Gargantua and Pantagruel* by François Rabelais, translated by J. M. Cohen and published by Penguin Books Ltd. Reprinted by permission.

At daybreak he woke us again to drink the early morning soups; and after that we ate only one meal, which lasted all day. We did not know whether it was dinner or supper, luncheon or bed-time snacks. Merely by way of pastime, we took a turn or two about the island to hear the joyous songs of those pretty birds.

In the evening, Panurge said to Æditus: 'I hope you don't mind if I tell you a little story about something that happened in the district of Châtellerault some twenty-three months ago. One morning in the month of April a gentleman's groom was exercising his steeds on some fallow land, and there he saw a gay little shepherd girl

A-keeping of her lambs
In the shadow of a wood

and with them an ass and several goats. After a little chat, he persuaded her to mount behind him on the crupper, and come to his stable to take a country snack with him. Now, as they were talking, his horse went up to the ass and whispered in his ear — for animals could talk all that year in one place and another: "You poor, miserable moke,⁵ I feel pity and compassion for you. You must work very hard every day, I can see that by the marks of your crupper. But that's as it should be, for God created you for the service of man. You are an honest moke. But that you shouldn't be rather better rubbed down and combed and caparisoned⁶ and fed, that does seem to me somewhat tyrannical — indeed most unreasonable — treatment. You're all rough-coated and dirty and beaten, and here you eat nothing but reeds, thorns, and tough thistles. So my advice to you, moke, is to pace it along with me, and see how those of us are treated and fed whom Nature has bred for war. I promise you a taste of my ordinary fodder."

' "Thank you," answered the ass. "I'll come most willingly, Master Horse."

' "Master Charger to you, moke," observed the steed.

' "Excuse me, Master Charger," replied the ass, "we country folk from the villages are not very good at our language. We haven't been well taught. But I'll obey you willingly and follow you at a distance, through fear of blows — my hide is all criss-crossed with them — since you're so good as to do me this honour and kindness."

'When the shepherdess was mounted, the ass followed the horse, firmly resolved to get a good meal. But when they came to the stable and the groom saw him, he told the stable-boys to welcome him with a fork and give him a good thrashing. On hearing this, the ass commended himself to the god Neptune, and began to scamper off at a lively pace, thinking and reasoning to himself like this: "He is quite right. I'm not of the rank to attend the courts of the great. Nature bred me only to be a help to the poor. Aesop warned me of that clearly enough in one of his fables. This has been presumption on my part, and there's no help for it but to scamper off cheerfully,

⁵ donkey, dolt (slang).
⁶ bedecked with ornamental trappings.

and in less time than it takes to cook asparagus." With that the ass made off with a trot and a fart and a bound, a rush, a gallop, and another volley.

'When the shepherdess saw the ass make off she told the groom that he was her beast and insisted that he should be well treated, or else she would not come in at all, but would go straight away. So the groom ordered that all the horses should go without oats for a week rather than the ass fail to get his bellyful. But the difficulty was to coax him back. For it was no good the boys calling: "Here, here, moke, good moke, come up!" "I'm not coming," said the ass. "I'm shy." The more wheedlingly they called him, the more stubbornly he made off, galloping and farting the while. They would have been at it still, in fact, if the shepherdess had not told them to toss the oats high in a sieve and call him then. This they did, and the ass suddenly turned back. "Fodder," he cried; "by God the Father, but none of your fork! I'm none of your card-players. I don't say, I pass." So he went back to them, singing melodiously. For, as you know, the melodious voices of these beasts from Arcady[7] are a joy to hear.

"When he got there he was taken into a stable beside the great steed. Then he was rubbed, wiped down, and combed. Fresh litter was thrown to him belly-high and the rack was piled full of hay, the manger was filled with oats also, and as the stable-boys were sifting them he pricked up his ears, as much as to say that he would eat them gladly enough without sifting, and that this was too much of an honour for him. Now, after they had both taken their fill, the horse turned to the ass and asked: "Well, how are you getting along now, my poor moke? How do you like this reception? And yet you did not want to come. What do you say now?"

' "By the fig which one of our ancestors ate," replied the ass, "which made Philemon die of laughing, this is balm to me, Master Charger. But, after all, it's only half cheer. Do you never have a leaping match here, you worthy and horsy gentlemen?"

' "What kind of leaping do you mean, ass?" demanded the horse; "the glanders take you, moke, do you think I'm a donkey?"

' "Ha, ha," answered the ass. "I'm a bit slow in learning the courtly language of you horses. What I mean is, don't you play the stallion here, you noble chargers?"

' "Speak quietly, ass," said the horse. "If the stable-boys were to hear you they'd give you such a mighty hard battering with their forks that you'd have no stomach for a leaping match. We daren't stiffen our pizzles here, even to piss, for fear of a beating. But for the rest, we're as happy as kings."

' "By the pommel of the pack-saddle on my back," said the ass, "you're welcome. You can keep your litter and your hay and your oats. Long live the thistles of the field, for there you can play the stallion to your heart's content. Eat less and always leap your fill, that's my motto. Leaping's hay and fodder to us. Oh, Master Charger, my friend, if you had only seen us at

---

[7] a pastoral region in Greece which came to be represented as a paradise in Greek, Roman and Renaissance literature.

the fairs, when we hold our provincial chapter, how we stallionize all out while our mistresses sell their goslings and pullets!" Such was their parting, and my tale is done.'

Here Panurge ceased, and uttered no further sound. Pantagruel urged him to finish his argument, but Æditus replied: 'One word is enough for a good listener. I perfectly understand the moral you intend to convey by your fable of the ass and the horse. But you *are* a bashful fellow. Let me tell you, however, that there's nothing for you here. Don't mention the matter again.'

'Yet,' said Panurge, 'I saw a white-plumed abbeygess[8] here not long ago, who would be nicer to ride than to lead by the hand. If the rest of them are game-birds, she seems to me a game hen. Pretty and dainty I say, and well worth a sin or two. God forgive me, I mean no harm. But may all the harm I do mean befall me very promptly.'

Michel de Montaigne (1533–1592)

FRENCH ESSAYIST and PHILOSOPHER

The Natural Superiority of Cannibals

...I think there is nothing barbarous and savage in that nation,[1] from what I have been told, except that each man calls barbarism whatever is not his own practice; for indeed it seems we have no other test of truth and reason than the example and pattern of the opinions and customs of the country we live in. *There* is always the perfect religion, the perfect government, the perfect and accomplished manners in all things. Those people are wild, just as we call wild the fruits that Nature has produced by herself and in her normal course; whereas really it is those that we have changed artificially and led astray from the common order, that we should rather call wild. The former retain alive and vigorous their genuine, their most useful and natural, virtues and properties, which we have debased in the latter in adapting them to gratify our corrupted taste. And yet for all that, the savor and delicacy of some uncultivated fruits of those countries is quite as excellent, even to our taste, as that of our own. It is not reasonable that art should win the place of honor over our great and powerful mother Nature. We have so overloaded the beauty and richness

---

[8] The birds of Ringing Island are named after positions in the church; "abbeygess" might suggest "abbess."

[1] Brazil; Montaigne learned about the country from an acquaintance who lived there.

Title supplied by editors. From *Montaigne's Essays and Selected Writings*, translated by Donald M. Frame. Reprinted by permission of St. Martin's Press, Inc.

of her works by our inventions that we have quite smothered her. Yet wherever her purity shines forth, she wonderfully puts to shame our vain and frivolous attempts:

> Ivy comes readier without our care;
> In lonely caves the arbutus grows more fair;
> No art with artless bird song can compare.[2]

All our efforts cannot even succeed in reproducing the nest of the tiniest little bird, its contexture, its beauty and convenience; or even the web of the puny spider. All things, says Plato, are produced by nature, by fortune, or by art; the greatest and most beautiful by one or the other of the first two, the least and most imperfect by the last.

These nations,[3] then, seem to me barbarous in this sense, that they have been fashioned very little by the human mind, and are still very close to their original naturalness. The laws of nature still rule them, very little corrupted by ours; and they are in such a state of purity that I am sometimes vexed that they were unknown earlier, in the days when there were men able to judge them better than we. I am sorry that Lycurgus[4] and Plato did not know of them; for it seems to me that what we actually see in these nations surpasses not only all the pictures in which poets have idealized the golden age and all their inventions in imagining a happy state of man, but also the conceptions and the very desire of philosophy. They could not imagine a naturalness so pure and simple as we see by experience; nor could they believe that our society could be maintained with so little artifice and human solder. This is a nation, I should say to Plato,[5] in which there is no sort of traffic, no knowledge of letters, no science of numbers, no name for a magistrate or for political superiority, no custom of servitude, no riches or poverty, no contracts, no successions, no partitions, no occupations but leisure ones, no care for any but common kinship, no clothes, no agriculture, no metal, no use of wine or wheat. The very words that signify lying, treachery, dissimulation, avarice, envy, belittling, pardon — unheard of. How far from this perfection would he find the republic that he imagined: *Men fresh sprung from the gods.*[6]

> These manners nature first ordained.[7]

For the rest, they live in a country with a very pleasant and temperate climate, so that according to my witnesses it is rare to see a sick man there; and they have assured me that they never saw one palsied, bleary-eyed, toothless, or bent with age. They are settled along the sea and shut in on the land

---

[2] Propertius, *Elegies*, i, ii, 10–12.
[3] the Americas, then being explored.
[4] reformer and traditional lawgiver of Sparta (c. 9th century B.C.).
[5] referring to Plato's account, in the *Timaeus* and the *Critias*, of Atlantis, a legendary island in the Atlantic Ocean which was characterized by an ideal commonwealth.
[6] Seneca, *Epistles*, xc, 44. [Frame]
[7] Virgil, *Georgics*, ii, 20. [Frame]

side by great high mountains, with a stretch about a hundred leagues wide in between. They have a great abundance of fish and flesh which bear no resemblance to ours, and they eat them with no other artifice than cooking. The first man who rode a horse there, though he had had dealings with them on several other trips, so horrified them in this posture that they shot him dead with arrows before they could recognize him.

Their buildings are very long, with a capacity of two or three hundred souls; they are covered with the bark of great trees, the strips reaching to the ground at one end and supporting and leaning on one another at the top, in the manner of some of our barns, whose covering hangs down to the ground and acts as a side. They have wood so hard that they cut with it and make of it their swords and grills to cook their food. Their beds are of a cotton weave, hung from the roof like those in our ships, each man having his own; for the wives sleep apart from their husbands.

They get up with the sun, and eat immediately upon rising, to last them through the day; for they take no other meal than that one. Like some other Eastern peoples, of whom Suidas[8] tells us, who drank apart from meals, they do not drink then; but they drink several times a day, and to capacity. Their drink is made of some root, and is of the color of our claret wines. They drink it only lukewarm. This beverage keeps only two or three days; it has a slightly sharp taste, is not at all heady, is good for the stomach, and has a laxative effect upon those who are not used to it; it is a very pleasant drink for any one who is accustomed to it. In place of bread they use a certain white substance like preserved coriander. I have tried it; it tastes sweet and a little flat.

The whole day is spent in dancing. The younger men go to hunt animals with bows. Some of the women busy themselves meanwhile with warming their drink, which is their chief duty. Some one of the old men, in the morning before they begin to eat, preaches to the whole barnful in common, walking from one end to the other, and repeating one single sentence several times until he has completed the circuit (for the buildings are fully a hundred paces long). He recommends to them only two things: valor against the enemy and love for their wives. And they never fail to point out this obligation, as their refrain, that it is their wives who keep their drink warm and seasoned.

There may be seen in several places, including my own house, specimens of their beds, of their ropes, of their wooden swords and the bracelets with which they cover their wrists in combats, and of the big canes, open at one end, by whose sound they keep time in their dances. They are close shaven all over, and shave themselves much more cleanly than we, with nothing but a wooden or stone razor. They believe that souls are immortal, and that those who have deserved well of the gods are lodged in that part of heaven where the sun rises, and the damned in the west.

[8] the name of an encyclopedia (not of its author) compiled in the 10th century A.D.

They have some sort of priests and prophets, but they rarely appear before the people, having their home in the mountains. On their arrival there is a great feast and solemn assembly of several villages — each barn, as I have described it, makes up a village, and they are about one French league from each other. The prophet speaks to them in public, exhorting them to virtue and their duty; but their whole ethical science contains only these two articles: resoluteness in war and affection for their wives. He prophesies to them things to come and the results they are to expect from their undertakings, and urges them to war or holds them back from it; but this is on the condition that when he fails to prophesy correctly, and if things turn out otherwise than he has predicted, he is cut into a thousand pieces if they catch him, and condemned as a false prophet. For this reason, the prophet who has once been mistaken is never seen again.

Divination is a gift of God; that is why its abuse should be punished as imposture. Among the Scythians,[9] when the soothsayers failed to hit the mark, they were laid, chained hand and foot, on carts full of heather and drawn by oxen, on which they were burned. Those who handle matters subject to the control of human capacity are excusable if they do the best they can. But these others, who come and trick us with assurances of an extraordinary faculty that is beyond our ken, should they not be punished for not making good their promise, and for the temerity of their imposture?

They have their wars with the nations beyond the mountains, further inland, to which they go quite naked, with no other arms than bows or wooden swords ending in a sharp point, in the manner of the tongues of our boar spears. It is astonishing what firmness they show in their combats, which never end but in slaughter and bloodshed; for as to routs and terror, they know nothing of either.

Each man brings back as his trophy the head of the enemy he has killed, and sets it up at the entrance to his dwelling. After they have treated their prisoners well for a long time with all the hospitality they can think of, each man who has a prisoner calls a great assembly of his acquaintances. He ties a rope to one of the prisoner's arms, by the end of which he holds him, a few steps away, for fear of being hurt, and gives his dearest friend the other arm to hold in the same way; and these two, in the presence of the whole assembly, kill him with their swords. This done, they roast him and eat him in common and send some pieces to their absent friends. This is not, as people think, for nourishment, as of old the Scythians used to do; it is to betoken an extreme revenge. And the proof of this came when they saw the Portuguese, who had joined forces with their adversaries, inflict a different kind of death on them when they took them prisoner, which was to bury them up to the waist, shoot the rest of their body full of arrows, and afterward hang

[9] inhabitants of southeastern Europe in the 7th century B.C.; the Greeks regarded them as utter barbarians.

them. They thought that these people from the other world, being men who had sown the knowledge of many vices among their neighbors and were much greater masters than themselves in every sort of wickedness, did not adopt this sort of vengeance without some reason, and that it must be more painful than their own; so they began to give up their old method and to follow this one.

I am not sorry that we notice the barbarous horror of such acts, but I am heartily sorry that, judging their faults rightly, we should be so blind to our own. I think there is more barbarity in eating a man alive than in eating him dead; and in tearing by tortures and the rack a body still full of feeling, in roasting a man bit by bit, in having him bitten and mangled by dogs and swine (as we have not only read but seen within fresh memory, not among ancient enemies, but among neighbors and fellow citizens, and what is worse, on the pretext of piety and religion), than in roasting and eating him after he is dead.

John Smith (1580–1631)

ENGLISH COLONIST

Gotte from the Rude Earth

In the moneth of Aprill, 1614. with two Ships from *London,* of a few Marchants, I chanced to ariue in *New-England,* a parte of *Ameryca,* at the Ile of *Monahiggan,*[1] in 43½ of Northerly latitude: our plot was there to take Whales and make tryalls of a Myne of Gold and Copper. If those failed, Fish and Furres was then our refuge, to make our selues sauers howsoeuer[2]: we found this Whalefishing a costly conclusion: we saw many, and spent much time in chasing them; but could not kill any: They beeing a kinde of Iubartes,[3] and not the Whale that yeeldes Finnes and Oyle as wee expected. For our Golde, it was rather the Masters deuice to get a voyage that proiected it, then any knowledge hee had at all of any such matter. Fish and Furres

[1] off the coast of Maine.
[2] to make up for our losses.
[3] a 17th century term for the Rorqual whale or Fin whale.

Title supplied by editors. From "A Description of *New England*: OR The Observations, and Discoveries of Captain *Iohn Smith* (Admirall of that Country) in the North of America, in the year of our Lord 1614: *with the successe of sixe Ships, that went the next yeare* 1615; *and the accidents befell him among the French men of warre.*" In *Tracts and Other Papers, Relating Principally to the Origin, Settlement, and Progress of the Colonies in North America, From the Discovery of the Country to the Year 1776,* collected by Peter Force.

was now our guard: and by our late arriual, and long lingring about the Whale, the prime of both those seasons were past ere wee perceiued it; we thinking that their seasons serued at all times: but wee found it otherwise; for by the midst of Iune, the fishing failed. Yet in Iuly and August some was taken, but not sufficient to defray so great a charge as our stay required. Of dry fish we made about 40000. of Cor fish[4] about 7000. Whilest the sailers fished, my selfe with eight or nine others of them might best bee spared; Ranging the coast in a small boat, wee got for trifles neer 1100 Beuer skinnes, 100 Martins, and neer as many Otters; and the most of them within the distance of twenty leagues.[5] We ranged the Coast both East and West much furder,[6] but Eastwards our commodities were not esteemed, they were so neare the French who affords them better: and right against vs in the Main was a Ship of Sir *Frances Popphames*, that had there such acquaintance, hauing many yeares vsed onely that porte, that the most parte there was had by him. And 40 leagues westwards were two French Ships, that had made there a great voyage by trade, during the time wee tryed those conclusions, not knowing the Coast, nor Saluages[7] habitation. With these Furres, the Traine, and Cor-fish I returned for *England* in the Bark: where within six months after our departure from the *Downes*, we safe arriued back. The best of this fish was solde for fiue pound the hundreth, the rest by ill vsage betwixt three pound and fifty shillings. The other Ship staied to fit herselfe for *Spaine* with the dry fish which was sould, by the Sailers reporte that returned, at forty ryalls[8] the quintall, each hundred weighing two quintalls and a halfe. . . .

[OF *New* ENGLAND]

. . . Heer nature and liberty affords vs that freely, which in *England* we want, or it costeth vs dearely. What pleasure can be more, then (being tired with any occasion a-shore) in planting Vines, Fruits, or Hearbs, in contriuing their owne Grounds, to the pleasure of their owne mindes, their Fields, Gardens, Orchards, Buildings, Ships, and other works, &c. to recreate themselues before their owne doores, in their owne boates vpon the Sea, where man, woman and childe, with a small hooke and line, by angling, may take diuerse sorts of excellent fish, at their pleasures? And is it not pretty sport, to pull vp two pence, six pence, and twelue pence, as fast as you can hale and veare[9] a line? He is a very bad fisher, cannot kill in one day with his hooke and line, one, two, or three hundred Cods: which dressed and dryed, if they be sould there for ten shillings the hundred, though in *England* they will giue more then twentie; may not both the seruant, the master, and marchant, be well content with this gaine? If a man worke but three dayes in seauen,

---

[4] salted fish (cod).
[5] sixty nautical miles.
[6] farther.
[7] savages; Indians.
[8] forty reals (former monetary unit of Spain).
[9] pull in and let out.

he may get more then hee can spend, vnlesse he will be excessiue. Now that Carpenter, Mason, Gardiner, Taylor, Smith, Sailer, Forgers, or what other, may they not make this a pretty recreation though they fish but an houre in a day, to take more then they eate in a weeke: or? if they will not eate it, because there is so much better choise; yet sell it, or change it, with the fisher men, or marchants, for any thing they want. And what sport doth yeeld a more pleasing content, and lesse hurt or charge then angling with a hooke, and crossing the sweete ayre from Ile to Ile, ouer the silent streames of a calme Sea? wherein the most curious may finde pleasure, profit, and content. Thus, though all men be not fishers: yet all men, whatsoeuer, may in other matters doe as well. For necessity doth in these cases so rule a Commonwealth, and each in their seuerall functions, as their labours in their qualities may be as profitable, because there is a necessary mutuall vse of all.

For Gentlemen, what exercise should more delight them, then ranging dayly those vnknowne parts, vsing fowling and fishing, for hunting and hauking? and yet you shall see the wilde haukes giue you some pleasure, in seeing them stoope (six or seauen after one another) an houre or two together, at the skuls of fish in the faire harbours, as those a-shore at a foule; and neuer trouble nor torment your selues, with watching, mewing,[10] feeding, and attending them: nor kill horse and man with running and crying, *See you not a hauk?* For hunting also: the woods, lakes, and riuers, affoord not onely chase sufficient, for any that delights in that kinde of toyle, or pleasure; but such beasts to hunt, that besides the delicacy of their bodies for food, their skins are so rich, as may well recompence thy dayly labour, with a Captains pay.

For labourers, if those that sowe hemp, rape, turnips, parsnips, carrats, cabidge, and such like; giue 20, 30, 40, 50 shillings yearely for an acre of ground, and meat, drinke, and wages to vse it, and yet grow rich; when better, or at least as good ground, may be had and cost nothing but labour; it seemes strange to me, any such should there grow poore.

My purpose is not to perswade children from their parents; men from their wiues; nor seruants from their masters: onely, such as with free consent may be spared: But that each parish, or village, in Citie, or Countrey, that will but apparell[11] their fatherlesse children, of thirteene or fourteen years of age, or young maried people, that haue small wealth to liue on; heere by their labour may liue exceeding well: prouided alwaies that first there bee a sufficient power to command them, houses to receiue them, meanes to defend them, and meet prouisions for them; for, any place may bee ouerlain[12]: and it is most necessarie to haue a fortresse (ere this grow to practice) and sufficient masters (as, Carpenters, Masons, Fishers, Fowlers, Gardiners, Husbandmen, Sawyers, Smiths, Spinsters, Taylors, Weauers, and such like) to take ten,

---

[10] caging.
[11] outfit, equip.
[12] overloaded, overcrowded.

twelue, or twentie, or as their is occasion, for Apprentises. The Masters by this may quicklie growe rich; these may learne their trades themselues, to doe the like; to a generall and an incredible benefit, for King, and Countrey, Master, and Seruant. . . .

Izaak Walton (1593–1683)

ENGLISH NATURALIST and BIOGRAPHER

The Gallant Trout

Viator.[1] Good Master, as we walk towards the water, wil you be pleased to make the way seeme shorter by telling me first the nature of the ,*Trout,* and then how to catch him.

Piscator.[2] My honest Scholer, I wil do it freely: The *Trout* (for which I love to angle above any fish) may be justly said (as the ancient Poets say of Wine, and we English say of Venson) to be a generous fish, because he has his seasons, a fish that comes in, and goes out with the *Stag* or *Buck:* and you are to observe, that as there be some *barren Does,* that are good in Summer; so there be some *barren Trouts,* that are good in Winter; but there are not many that are so, for usually they be in their perfection in the month of *May,* and decline with the *Buck:* Now you are to take notice, that in several Countries, as in *Germany* and in other parts compar'd to ours, they differ much in their bigness, shape and other wayes, and so do *Trouts;* 'tis wel known that in the Lake *Lemon,* the Lake of *Geneva,* there are *Trouts* taken, of three Cubits long, as is affirmed by *Gesner,* a Writer of good credit: and *Mercator* sayes, the *Trouts* that are taken in the Lake of *Geneva,* are a great part of the Merchandize of that famous City. And you are further to know, that there be certaine waters that breed *Trouts* remarkable, both for their number and smalness — I know a little Brook in *Kent* that breeds them to a number incredible, and you may take them twentie or fortie in an hour, but none greater then about the size of a *Gudgion.* There are also in divers Rivers, especially that relate to, or be near to the Sea, (as *Winchester,* or the Thames about *Windsor*) a little *Trout* called a *Samlet* or *Skegger Trout* (in both which places I have caught twentie or fortie at a standing) that will

[1] Traveler.
[2] Fisherman.

Title supplied by editors. From *The Compleat Angler; Or, The Contemplative Man's Recreation.*

bite as fast and as freely as *Minnows*; these be by some taken to be young *Salmons*, but in those waters they never grow to bee bigger then a *Herring*.

There is also in *Kent*, neer to *Canterbury*, a *Trout* (called there a *Fordig Trout*) a *Trout* (that bears the name of the Town where 'tis usually caught) that is accounted rare meat, many of them near the bigness of a *Salmon*, but knowne by their different colour, and in their best season cut very white; and none have been known to be caught with an Angle, unless it were one that was caught by honest Sir *George Hastings*, an excellent Angler (and now with God) and he has told me, he thought that *Trout* bit not for hunger, but wantonness; and 'tis the rather to be believed, because both he then, and many others before him have been curious to search into their bellies what the food was by which they lived; and have out nothing by which they might satisfie their curiositie.

Concerning which you are to take notice, that it is reported, there is a fish that hath not any mouth, but lives by taking breath by the porinss[3] of her gils, and feeds and is nourish'd by no man knows what; and this may be believed of the *Fordig Trout*, which (as it is said of the *Stork*, that he knowes his season, so he) knows his times (I think almost his day) of coming into that River out of the Sea, where he lives (and it is like feeds) nine months of the year, and about three in the River of *Fordig*.

And now for some confirmation of this; you are to know, that this *Trout* is thought to eat nothing in the fresh water; and it may be the better believed, because it is well known, that *Swallowes*, which are not seen to flye in *England* for six months in the year, but about *Michaelmas*[4] leave us for a hotter climate; yet some of them, that have been left behind their fellows, have been found (many thousand at a time) in hollow trees, where they have been observed to live and sleep out the whole winter without meat;[5] and so *Albertus*[6] observes that there is one kind of *Frog* that hath her mouth naturally shut up about the end of *August*, and that she lives so all the Winter, and though it be strange to some, yet it is known to too many amongst us to bee doubted.

And so much for these *Fordidg Trouts*, which never afford an *Angler* sport, but either live their time of being in the fresh water by their meat formerly gotten in the Sea, (not unlike the *Swallow* or *Frog*) or by the vertue of the fresh water only, as the *Camelion* is said to live by the air.

There is also in *Northumberland*, a *Trout*, called a *Bull Trout*, of a much greater length and bignesse then any in these Southern parts; and there is in many Rivers that relate to the Sea, *Salmon Trouts* as much different one from another, both in shape and in their spots, as we see Sheep differ one from another in their shape and bigness, and in the finess of their wool: and

---

[3] pores.
[4] September 29.
[5] Walton is quoting Topsel's *Bestiary*, held to be scientific in Walton's day.
[6] St. Albertus Magnus (1193?–1280), German theologian.

certainly as some Pastures do breed larger Sheep, so do some Rivers, by reason of the ground over which they run, breed larger *Trouts*.

Now the next thing that I will commend to your consideration is, That the *Trout* is of a more sudden growth then other fish: concerning which you are also to take notice, that he lives not so long as the *Pearch* and divers other fishes do, as Sir *Francis Bacon* hath observed in his History of life and death.

And next, you are to take notice, that after hee is come to his full growth, he declines in his bodie, but keeps his bigness or thrives in his head till his death. And you are to know that he wil about (especially before) the time of his Spawning, get almost miraculously through *Weires* and *Floud-Gates* against the stream, even through such high and swift places as is almost incredible. Next, that the *Trout* usually Spawns about *October* or *November*, but in some Rivers a little sooner or later; which is the more observable, because most other fish Spawne in the Spring or Summer, when the Sun hath warmed both the earth and water, and made it fit for generation.

And next, you are to note, that till the Snn [Sun] gets to such a height as to warm the earth and the water, the *Trout* is sick, and lean, and lowsie, and unwholsome: for you shall in winter find him to have a big head, and then to be lank, and thin, & lean; at which time many of them have sticking on them Sugs, or *Trout* lice, which is a kind of a worm, in shape like a Clove or a Pin, with a big head, and sticks close to him and sucks his moisture; those I think the *Trout* breeds himselfe, and never thrives til he free himself from them, which is till warm weather comes, and then as he growes stronger, he gets from the dead, still water, into the sharp streames and the gravel, and there rubs off these worms or lice: and then as he grows stronger, so he gets him into swifter and swifter streams, and there lies at the watch for any flie or Minow that comes neer to him; and he especially loves the *May* flie, which is bred of the *Cod-worm* or *Caddis*; and these make the *Trout* bold and lustie, and he is usually fatter, and better meat at the end of that month, then at any time of the year.

Now you are to know, that it is observed, that usually the best *Trouts* are either red or yellow, though some be white and yet good; but that is not usual; and it is a note observable that the female *Trout* hath usually a less head and a deeper body then the male *Trout*; and a little head to any fish, either *Trout*, *Salmon*, or other fish, is a sign that that fish is in season.

But yet you are to note, that as you see some Willows or Palm trees bud and blossome sooner then others do, so some *Trouts* be in some Rivers sooner in season; and as the Holly or Oak are longer before they cast their Leaves, so are some *Trouts* in some Rivers longer before they go out of season.

John Milton (1608–1674)

ENGLISH POET and ESSAYIST

Lycidas

In this Monody the Author bewails a learned Friend,[1] unfortunately drown'd in his Passage from *Chester* on the *Irish* Seas, 1637. And by occasion foretells the ruin of our corrupted Clergy then in their height.

Yet once more, O ye Laurels, and once more
Ye Myrtles brown, with Ivy never sere,
I come to pluck your Berries harsh and crude,
And with forc'd fingers rude,
Shatter your leaves before the mellowing year.
Bitter constraint, and sad occasion dear,
Compels me to disturb your season due:
For *Lycidas* is dead, dead ere his prime,
Young *Lycidas*, and hath not left his peer:
Who would not sing for *Lycidas?* he knew   10
Himself to sing, and build the lofty rhyme.
He must not float upon his wat'ry bier
Unwept, and welter to the parching wind,
Without the meed of some melodious tear.
  Begin then, Sisters of the sacred well,
That from beneath the seat of Jove doth spring,
Begin, and somewhat loudly sweep the string.
Hence with denial vain, and coy excuse,
So may some gentle Muse
With lucky words favor my destin'd Urn,   20
And as he passes turn,
And bid fair peace be to my sable shroud.
For we were nurst upon the self-same hill,
Fed the same flock, by fountain, shade, and rill.
  Together both, ere the high Lawns appear'd
Under the opening eyelids of the morn,
We drove afield, and both together heard
What time the Gray-fly winds her sultry horn,

Laurels, Myrtle, Ivy: evergreens symbolizing immortality and associated with poetic inspiration and achievement. **harsh and crude:** unripe

Sisters: the Muses. **sacred well:** perhaps the Pierian Spring on Mount Olympus, sacred to the Muses and thought to be a source of poetic inspiration

Muse: poet

self-same hill: Cambridge

Gray-fly . . . horn: insects buzz (at midday)

[1] Edward King, a former Cambridge schoolmate who was a promising poet studying for the priesthood.

From *John Milton: Complete Poems and Major Prose*, edited by Merritt Y. Hughes and published by the Odyssey Press, Inc., New York, 1958. Reprinted by permission.

Batt'ning our flocks with the fresh dews of night,
Oft till the Star that rose, at Ev'ning, bright   30
Toward Heav'n's descent had slop'd his westering
    wheel.
Meanwhile the Rural ditties were not mute,
Temper'd to th'Oaten Flute;
Rough *Satyrs* danc'd, and *Fauns* with clov'n heel
From the glad sound would not be absent long,
And old *Damaetas* lov'd to hear our song.
    But O the heavy change, now thou art gone,
Now thou, art gone, and never must return!
Thee Shepherd, thee the Woods, and desert Caves,
With wild Thyme and the gadding Vine o'ergrown,   40
And all their echoes mourn.
The Willows and the Hazel Copses green
Shall now no more be seen,
Fanning their joyous Leaves to thy soft lays.
As killing as the Canker to the Rose,
Or Taint-worm to the weanling Herds that graze,
Or Frost to Flowers, that their gay wardrobe wear,
When first the White-thorn blows;
Such, *Lycidas*, thy loss to Shepherd's ear.
    Where were ye Nymphs when the remorseless
        deep   50
Clos'd o'er the head of your lov'd *Lycidas*?
For neither were ye playing on the steep,
Where your old *Bards*, the famous *Druids*, lie,
Nor on the shaggy top of *Mona* high,
Nor yet where *Deva* spreads her wizard stream:
Ay me, I fondly dream!
Had ye been there — for what could that have done?
What could the Muse herself that *Orpheus* bore,
The Muse herself, for her enchanting son
Whom Universal nature did lament,   60
When by the rout that made the hideous roar,
His gory visage down the stream was sent,
Down the swift *Hebrus* to the *Lesbian* shore?
    Alas! What boots it with uncessant care
To tend the homely slighted Shepherd's trade,
And strictly meditate the thankless Muse?
Were it not better done as others use,
To sport with *Amaryllis* in the shade,
Or with the tangles of *Neaera's* hair?
Fame is the spur that the clear spirit doth raise   70
(That last infirmity of Noble mind)
To scorn delights, and live laborious days;
But the fair Guerdon when we hope to find,
And think to burst out into sudden blaze,

Star: Hesperus

Toward . . . wheel: began to set

Damaetas: a common pastoral name; perhaps a Cambridge tutor

gadding: wandering

Canker: cankerworm

Taint-worm: worm that attacks oxen

steep: Holyhead on the Welsh coast

Mona: an island off Wales

Deva: Welsh river Dee. **wizard:** Its changing waters were thought to indicate future good or evil in the land.

the Muse herself: Calliope, muse of epic poetry and mother of Orpheus. **Orpheus:** Greek poet who charmed all of nature with his song

gory visage . . . sent: Women maddened by a Bacchic rite tore Orpheus to pieces; his head floated to Lesbos where it made the land sacred to poetry. **boots:** profits

Amaryllis, Neaera: conventional names for nymphs

Comes the blind *Fury* with th'abhorred shears,
And slits the thin-spun life. "But not the praise,"
Phoebus repli'd, and touch'd my trembling ears;
"*Fame* is no plant that grows on mortal soil,
Nor in the glistering foil
Set off to th'world, nor in broad rumor lies,   80
But lives and spreads aloft by those pure eyes
And perfect witness of all-judging *Jove*;
As he pronounces lastly on each deed,
Of so much fame in Heav'n expect thy meed."
    O Fountain *Arethuse*, and thou honor'd flood,
Smooth-sliding *Mincius*; crown'd with vocal reeds,
That strain I heard was of a higher mood:
But now my Oat proceeds,
And listens to the Herald of the Sea
That came in *Neptune's* plea.   90
He ask'd the Waves, and ask'd the Felon winds,
What hard mishap hath doom'd this gentle swain?
And question'd every gust of rugged wings
That blows from off each beaked Promontory.
They knew not of his story,
And sage *Hippotades* their answer brings,
That not a blast was from his dungeon stray'd,
The Air was calm, and on the level brine,
Sleek *Panope* with all her sisters play'd.
It was that fatal and perfidious Bark   100
Built in th'eclipse, and rigg'd with curses dark,
That sunk so low that sacred head of thine.
    Next *Camus*, reverend Sire, went footing slow,
His Mantle hairy, and his Bonnet sedge,
Inwrought with figures dim, and on the edge
Like to that sanguine flower inscrib'd with woe.
"Ah! Who hath reft" (quoth he) "my dearest
      pledge?"
Last came, and last did go,
The Pilot of the *Galilean* lake.
Two massy Keys he bore of metals twain   110
(The Golden opes, the Iron shuts amain).
He shook his Mitred locks, and stern bespake:
"How well could I have spar'd for thee, young swain,
Enough of such as for their bellies' sake,
Creep and intrude and climb into the fold?
Of other care they little reck'ning make,
Than how to scramble at the shearers' feast,
And shove away the worthy bidden guest;
Blind mouths! that scarce themselves know how to
    hold
A Sheep-hook, or have learn'd aught else the least   120

Fury: agent of vengeance; here coalesced with the Fate Atropos who normally cuts the thread of life
Phoebus: Apollo, god of inspiration and poetry. **glistering foil:** metal used to enhance brilliance of gems; tinsel

Arethuse: Sicilian fountain; convention for pastoral poetry and associated with the pastorals of Theocritus. The nymph Arethusa, pursued by Alpheus, was changed into a fountain by Diana, divine protectress of chastity.
Mincius: river in northern Italy; connected with pastoral poetry of Vergil. **Oat:** pipe, or the song itself. **Herald of the Sea:** Triton, son of Neptune (god of the sea)

Hippotades: Aeolus, god of the winds

Panope . . . sisters: sea nymphs

th'eclipse: i.e., King's ship was doomed.

Camus: god of the river Cam; represents Cambridge. **Mantle . . . sedge:** refers to the abundant reeds on the edge of the Cam **sanguine flower:** hyacinth; the flower which sprang from the blood of a boy loved, but accidentally killed, by Apollo. Its markings recall the Greek word "Alas". **reft:** taken. **pledge:** child. **Pilot:** St. Peter, keeper of the keys of Heaven.

Mitred locks: hair covered by a miter, or bishop's hat

That to the faithful Herdman's art belongs!
What recks it them? What need they? They are
    sped;
And when they list, their lean and flashy songs
Grate on their scrannel Pipes of wretched straw.
The hungry Sheep look up, and are not fed,
But swoln with wind, and the rank mist they draw,
Rot inwardly, and foul contagion spread:
Besides what the grim Wolf with privy paw
Daily devours apace, and nothing said;
But that two-handed engine at the door   130
Stands ready to smite once, and smite no more."
    Return *Alpheus*, the dread voice is past
That shrunk thy streams; Return *Sicilian* Muse,
And call the Vales, and bid them hither cast
Their Bells and Flowrets of a thousand hues.
Ye valleys low where the mild whispers use
Of shades and wanton winds and gushing brooks,
On whose fresh lap the swart Star sparely looks,
Throw hither all your quaint enamell'd eyes,
That on the green turf suck the honied showers,   140
And purple all the ground with vernal flowers.
Bring the rathe Primrose that forsaken dies,
The tufted Crow-toe, and pale Jessamine,
The white Pink, and the Pansy freakt with jet,
The glowing Violet,
The Musk-rose, and the well-attir'd Woodbine,
With Cowslips wan that hang the pensive head,
And every flower that sad embroidery wears:
Bid *Amaranthus* all his beauty shed,
And Daffadillies fill their cups with tears,   150
To strew the Laureate Hearse where *Lycid* lies.
For so to interpose a little ease,
Let our frail thoughts dally with false surmise.
Ay me! Whilst thee the shores and sounding Seas
Wash far away, where'er thy bones are hurl'd,
Whether beyond the stormy *Hebrides*,
Where thou perhaps under the whelming tide
Visit'st the bottom of the monstrous world;
Or whether thou to our moist vows denied,
Sleep'st by the fable of *Bellerus* old,   160
Where the great vision of the guarded Mount
Looks toward *Namancos* and *Bayona's* hold;
Look homeward Angel now, and melt with ruth:
And, O ye *Dolphins*, waft the hapless youth.
    Weep no more, woeful Shepherds weep no more,
For *Lycidas* your sorrow is not dead,
Sunk though he be beneath the wat'ry floor,

---

sped: provided for
songs: sermons

two-handed engine: Many definitions for this cryptic machine have been attempted; most probably it refers to some vehicle of divine justice. **Alpheus:** a river god **Sicilian Muse:** associated with pastoral poetry

swart Star: Sirius, the Dog Star, which appears in late summer and was thought to blacken vegetation

rathe: early (archaic)
Crow-toe: perhaps the hyacinth
freakt: streaked

monstrous world: world of sea monsters
moist vows: tearful prayers
Bellerus: Land's End, in Cornwall, named after Bellerus, a mythical giant. **Mount:** St. Michael's Mount, which looks south toward Namancos and Bayona in Spain, is off the coast of Cornwall. **Angel:** St. Michael. **Dolphins:** These animals rescued Arion, a poet, from the sea; they also carried to shore the body of Melicertes (Palaemon), later transformed into a sea god.

So sinks the day-star in the Ocean bed,   day-star: sun
And yet anon repairs his drooping head,
And tricks his beams, and with new-spangled Ore, 170   tricks: adorns. Ore: gold
Flames in the forehead of the morning sky:
So *Lycidas*, sunk low, but mounted high,
Through the dear might of him that walk'd the   him: Christ
     waves,
Where other groves, and other streams along,
With *Nectar* pure his oozy Locks he laves,
And hears the unexpressive nuptial Song,   unexpressive: inexpressible
In the blest Kingdoms meek of joy and love.
There entertain him all the Saints above,
In solemn troops, and sweet Societies
That sing, and singing in their glory move, 180
And wipe the tears for ever from his eyes.
Now *Lycidas*, the Shepherds weep no more;
Henceforth thou art the Genius of the shore,   Genius: protecting spirit
In thy large recompense, and shalt be good
To all that wander in that perilous flood.

    Thus sang the uncouth Swain to th'Oaks and rills,
While the still morn went out with Sandals gray;
He touch't the tender stops of various Quills,   Quills: hollow stems of reeds con-
With eager thought warbling his *Doric* lay: stituting a Pan's pipe. Doric:
And now the Sun had stretch't out all the hills, 190   rustic, pastoral
And now was dropt into the Western bay;
At last he rose, and twitch't his Mantle blue: twitch't: threw on
Tomorrow to fresh Woods, and Pastures new.

Andrew Marvell (1621–1678)

ENGLISH POET and SATIRIST

The Garden

I

How vainly men themselves amaze
To win the Palm, the Oke, or Bayes;   Palm . . . Bayes: military, civil,
And their uncessant Labours see   and poetic — earthly — awards
Crown'd from some single Herb or Tree.

From *The Poems and Letters of Andrew Marvell*, edited
by H. M. Margoliouth. Reprinted by permission of the
Clarendon Press, Oxford.

Whose short and narrow verged Shade
Does prudently their Toyles upbraid;
While all Flow'rs and all Trees do close
To weave the Garlands of repose.

II

Fair quiet, have I found thee here,
And Innocence thy Sister dear!   10
Mistaken long, I sought you then
In busie Companies of Men.
Your sacred Plants, if here below,
Only among the Plants will grow.
Society is all but rude,   all but: only
To this delicious Solitude.

III

No white nor red was ever seen
So am'rous as this lovely green.
Fond Lovers, cruel as their Flame,
Cut in these Trees their Mistress name.   20
Little, Alas, they know, or heed,
How far these Beauties Hers exceed!
Fair Trees! where s'eer your barkes I wound,
No Name shall but your own be found.

IV

When we have run our Passions heat,
Love hither makes his best retreat.
The *Gods*, that mortal Beauty chase,
Still in a Tree did end their race.
Apollo hunted *Daphne* so,
Only that She might Laurel grow.   30
And *Pan* did after *Syrinx* speed,   Syrinx: a mountain nymph pur-
Not as a Nymph, but for a Reed.   sued by Pan and transformed into
                                                  reeds from which Pan then made
                                                  his Pan-pipes (syrinx)

V

What wond'rous Life is this I lead!
Ripe Apples drop about my head;
The Luscious Clusters of the Vine
Upon my Mouth do crush their Wine;
The Nectaren, and curious Peach,   curious: exquisite
Into my hands themselves do reach;
Stumbling on Melons, as I pass,
Insnar'd with Flow'rs, I fall on Grass.   40

VI

Mean while the Mind, from pleasure less,
Withdraws into its happiness:
The Mind, that Ocean where each kind
Does streight its own resemblance find;   resemblance: corresponding form

Yet it creates, transcending these,
Far other Worlds, and other Seas;
Annihilating all that 's made
To a green Thought in a green Shade.

other Worlds: its own microcosm

VII

Here at the Fountains sliding foot,
Or at some Fruit-trees mossy root,   50
Casting the Bodies Vest aside,
My Soul into the boughs does glide:
There like a Bird it sits, and sings,
Then whets, and combs its silver Wings;
And, till prepar'd for longer flight,
Waves in its Plumes the various Light.

whets: preens

VIII

Such was that happy Garden-state,
While Man there walk'd without a Mate:
After a Place so pure, and sweet,
What other Help could yet be meet!   60
But 'twas beyond a Mortal's share
To wander solitary there:
Two Paradises 'twere in one
To live in Paradise alone.

IX

How well the skilful Gardner drew
Of flow'rs and herbes this Dial new;
Where from above the milder Sun
Does through a fragrant Zodiack run;
And, as it works, th' industrious Bee
Computes its time as well as we.   70
How could such sweet and wholsome Hours
Be reckon'd but with herbs and flow'rs!

Dial: flowers arranged as a sundial

Bashō, Buson, Issa, Shiki

JAPANESE POETS

A Garland of Haiku

THE CAMELLIA

As it fell,
    water poured out —
      the camellia-bell.

THE UNKNOWN FLOWER

To bird and butterfly
    unknown, a flower blooms:
      the autumn sky.

PERSISTENCE

Did it yell
    till it became *all* voice?
      Cicada-shell!

                    Matsuo Bashō (*c.* 1644–1694)

The Camellia: Fall-way/ in/ water/ spill-out *keri* [untranslatable]/ flower-camellia
The Unknown Flower: Butterfly/ bird's/ not-known/ flower/ there-is [i.e., one word in Japanese]/ autumn-sky
Persistence: Voice/ to/ all/ crying-out/ ?/ cicada-shell

SPRING BREEZE

These morning airs —
    one can see them stirring
      caterpillar hairs!

THE PORTENT

There is no stir,
    not even one leaf; awesome
      is the summer grove.

Spring Breeze: Morning-breeze's/ hairs/ *wo* [makes hairs accusative]/ blowing-is-seen/ caterpillar/ *kana* [untranslatable]
The Portent: Moving/ leaf/ even/ not-exist/ frightening/ summer-grove

It is impossible for any seventeen-syllable translation of Japanese haiku to carry the precise flavor and meaning of the original. For this reason, Harold Henderson's transliterations of these selections are included.

Title supplied by editors. From *An Introduction to Haiku* translated by Harold G. Henderson. Copyright © 1958 by Harold G. Henderson. Reprinted by permission of Doubleday & Company, Inc.

THE RED PEONY

It falls, the peony —
    and upon each other lie
        petals, two or three.

                Taniguchi Buson (1715–1783)

The Red Peony: Peony/ scattering/ have-piled-up/ two-three-petals

A MEETING

Right at my feet —
    and when did you get here,
        snail?

THE VISION

In its eye
    are mirrored far-off mountains —
        dragonfly!

MOOR HENS

The moor hens sing,
    and to their tempo — look! — the clouds
        are hurrying.

                Kobayashi Issa (1763–1828)

A Meeting: Foot-base/ to/ when/ did-arrive/ ?!/ snail
The Vision: Distant-mountains'/ eye-jewels/ in/ reflect/ dragonfly/ *kana* [untranslatable]
Moor Hens: Moor hens/ sing/ tempo/ to/ clouds'/ hurrying/ ! [look] !

THE MOOR

Spring moor:
    for what do people go, for what
        do they return?

AFTER THE STORM

The thunderstorm goes by;
    on one tree evening sunlight —
        a cicada cry.

SUMMER EVENING

The moon begins to rise
    behind the grasses; a wind stirs them;
        and a cuckoo cries.

                Masaoka Shiki (1867–1902)

The Moor: Spring-moor/ :/ what-for/ people/ go/ people/ return
After the Storm: Thunder/ clearing-up/ one-tree's/ evening-sun/ locust's/ voice
Summer Evening: Moon's/ out-coming's/ grasses/ in/ wind/ blow/ cuckoo

Joseph Addison (1672–1719)

ENGLISH ESSAYIST and DRAMATIST

The Aesthetics of Nature

> . . . *Alterius sic*
> *Altera poscit opem res & conjurat amicè.*
> Hor.[1]

If we consider the Works of *Nature* and *Art,* as they are qualified to entertain the Imagination, we shall find the last very defective, in Comparison of the former; for though they may sometimes appear as Beautiful or Strange, they can have nothing in them of that Vastness and Immensity, which afford so great an Entertainment to the Mind of the Beholder. The one may be as Polite and Delicate as the other, but can never shew her self so August and Magnificent in the Design. There is something more bold and masterly in the rough careless Strokes of Nature, than in the nice Touches and Embellishments of Art. The Beauties of the most stately Garden or Palace lie in a narrow Compass, the Imagination immediately runs them over, and requires something else to gratifie her; but, in the wide Fields of Nature, the Sight wanders up and down without Confinement, and is fed with an infinite variety of Images, without any certain Stint or Number. For this Reason we always find the Poet in love with a Country-Life, where Nature appears in the greatest Perfection, and furnishes out all those Scenes that are most apt to delight the Imagination.

> *Scriptorum chorus omnis amat nemus & fugit Urbes.* Hor.[2]

> *Hic Secura quies, & nescia fallere vita,*
> *Dives opum variarum; hic latis otia fundis,*
> *Speluncæ, vivique lacus, hic frigida Tempe,*
> *Mugitusque boum, mollesque sub arbore somni.* Vir.[3]

[1] *Motto.* Horace, *Ars poetica,* 410:11:
  Each by it self is vain, I'm sure, but join'd,
  Their Force is strong, each proves the others Friend. (Creech)
[2] Horace, *Epistles,* 2. 2. 77.
  Each Writer hates the Town and Woods approves. (Creech)
[3] Virgil, *Georgics,* 2. 467–70.
  Unvex'd with Quarrels, undisturb'd with Noise,
  The Country King his peaceful Realm enjoys:
  Cool Grots, and living Lakes, the Flow'ry Pride
  Of Meads, and Streams that thro' the Valley glide;
  And shady Groves that easie Sleep invite,
  And after toilsome Days, a soft repose at Night. (Dryden)

Title supplied by editors. In *The Spectator,* No. 414 (for Wednesday, June 25, 1712), by Richard Steele and Joseph Addison. This selection is attributed to Joseph Addison. From *The Spectator,* Vol. III, edited and annotated by Donald F. Bond. Reprinted by permission of the Clarendon Press, Oxford.

But tho' there are several of these wild Scenes, that are more delightful than any artificial Shows; yet we find the Works of Nature still more pleasant, the more they resemble those of Art: For in this case our Pleasure arises from a double Principle; from the Agreeableness of the Objects to the Eye, and from their Similitude to other Objects: We are pleased as well with comparing their Beauties, as with surveying them, and can represent them to our Minds, either as Copies or Originals. Hence it is that we take Delight in a Prospect which is well laid out, and diversified with Fields and Meadows, Woods and Rivers, in those accidental Landskips of Trees, Clouds and Cities, that are sometimes found in the Veins of Marble, in the curious Fret-work of Rocks and Grottos, and, in a Word, in any thing that hath such a Variety or Regularity as may seem the Effect of Design, in what we call the Works of Chance.

If the Products of Nature rise in Value, according as they more or less resemble those of Art, we may be sure that artificial Works receive a greater Advantage from their Resemblance of such as are natural; because here the Similitude is not only pleasant, but the Pattern more perfect. The prettiest Landskip[4] I ever saw, was one drawn on the Walls of a dark Room, which stood opposite on one side to a navigable River, and on the other to a Park. The Experiment is very common in Opticks. Here you might discover the Waves and Fluctuations of the Water in strong and proper Colours, with the Picture of a Ship entering at one end, and sailing by Degrees through the whole Piece. On another there appeared the Green Shadows of Trees, waving to and fro with the Wind, and Herds of Deer among them in Miniature, leaping about upon the Wall. I must confess, the Novelty of such a sight may be one occasion of its Pleasantness to the Imagination, but certainly the chief Reason is its near Resemblance to Nature, as it does not only, like other Pictures, give the Colour and Figure, but the Motion of the Things it represents.

We have before observed, that there is generally in Nature something more Grand and August, than what we meet with in the Curiosities of Art. When, therefore, we see this imitated in any measure, it gives us a nobler and more exalted kind of Pleasure than what we receive from the nicer and more accurate Productions of Art. On this Account our *English* Gardens are not so entertaining to the Fancy as those in *France* and *Italy*, where we see a large Extent of Ground covered over with an agreeable mixture of Garden and Forest, which represent every where an artificial Rudeness, much more charming than that Neatness and Elegancy which we meet with in those of our own Country. It might, indeed, be of ill Consequence to the Publick, as well as unprofitable to private Persons, to alienate so much Ground from Pasturage, and the Plow, in many Parts of a Country that is so well peopled, and cultivated to a far greater Advantage. But why may not a whole Estate be thrown into a kind of Garden by frequent Plantations, that may turn as much

---

4 Addison probably has in mind the scene obtained by a camera obscura, or possibly that produced by the projection of two on opposite walls. There was such a camera obscura at Greenwich Park. [abridged]

to the Profit, as the Pleasure of the Owner? A Marsh overgrown with Willows, or a Mountain shaded with Oaks, are not only more beautiful, but more beneficial, than when they lie bare and unadorned. Fields of Corn make a pleasant Prospect, and if the Walks were a little taken care of that lie between them, if the natural Embroidery of the Meadows were helpt and improved by some small Additions of Art, and the several Rows of Hedges set off by Trees and Flowers, that the Soil was capable of receiving, a Man might make a pretty Landskip of his own Possessions.

Writers, who have given us an Account of *China*, tell us, the Inhabitants of that Country laugh at the Plantations of our *Europeans*, which are laid out by the Rule and Line; because they say, any one may place Trees in equal Rows and uniform Figures. They chuse rather to shew a Genius in Works of this Nature, and therefore always conceal the Art by which they direct themselves. They have a Word, it seems, in their Language, by which they express the particular Beauty of a Plantation that thus strikes the Imagination at first Sight, without discovering what it is that has so agreeable an Effect. Our *British* Gardeners, on the contrary, instead of humouring Nature, love to deviate from it as much as possible. Our Trees rise in Cones, Globes, and Pyramids. We see the Marks of the Scissars upon every Plant and Bush. I do not know whether I am singular in my Opinion, but, for my own part, I would rather look upon a Tree in all its Luxuriancy and Diffusion of Boughs and Branches, than when it is thus cut and trimmed into a Mathematical Figure; and cannot but fancy that an Orchard in Flower looks infinitely more delightful, than all the little Labyrinths of the most finished Parterre. But as our great Modellers of Gardens have their Magazines of Plants to dispose of, it is very natural for them to tear up all the Beautiful Plantations of Fruit Trees, and contrive a Plan that may most turn to their own Profit, in taking off their Evergreens, and the like Moveable Plants, with which their Shops are plentifully stocked.

Alexander Pope (1688–1744)

ENGLISH POET

Nature and the Social State of Man

Here then we rest: 'The Universal Cause
Acts to one end, but acts by various laws.'
In all the madness of superfluous health,
The trim of pride, the impudence of wealth,
Let this great truth be present night and day;
But most be present, if we preach or pray.
    Look round our World; behold the chain of Love
Combining all below and all above.
See plastic Nature working to this end,
The single atoms each to other tend,   10
Attract, attracted to, the next in place
Form'd and impell'd its neighbour to embrace.
See Matter next, with various life endu'd,
Press to one centre still, the gen'ral Good.
See dying vegetables life sustain,
See life dissolving vegetate again:
All forms that perish other forms supply,
(By turns we catch the vital breath, and die)
Like bubbles on the sea of Matter born,
They rise, they break, and to that sea return.   20
Nothing is foreign: Parts relate to whole;
One all-extending all-preserving Soul
Connects each being, greatest with the least;
Made Beast in aid of Man, and Man of Beast;
All serv'd, all serving! nothing stands alone;
The chain holds on, and where it ends, unknown.
    Has God, thou fool! work'd solely for thy good,
Thy joy, thy pastime, thy attire, thy food?
Who for thy table feeds the wanton fawn,
For him as kindly spread the flow'ry lawn.   30
Is it for thee the lark ascends and sings?
Joy tunes his voice, joy elevates his wings:
Is it for thee the linnet pours his throat?
Loves of his own and raptures swell the note:
The bounding steed you pompously bestride,
Shares with his lord the pleasure and the pride:

plastic Nature: the informing and forming power of God, as manifested in the creativity of nature [Mack]

Press . . . centre: alluding to the supposed movement of matter to earth's centre [Mack]

Title supplied by editors. Epistle III from *An Essay on Man*, edited by Maynard Mack, in *The Poems of Alexander Pope (Twickenham Edition)*. Reprinted by permission of Yale University Press and Methuen & Company, Ltd., London.

Is thine alone the seed that strews the plain?
The birds of heav'n shall vindicate their grain:
Thine the full harvest of the golden year?
Part pays, and justly, the deserving steer: 40
The hog, that plows not nor obeys thy call,
Lives on the labours of this lord of all.
    Know, Nature's children all divide her care;
The fur that warms a monarch, warm'd a bear.
While Man exclaims, 'See all things for my use!'
'See man for mine!' replies a pamper'd goose;
And just as short of Reason he must fall,
Who thinks all made for one, not one for all.
    Grant that the pow'rful still the weak controul,
Be Man the Wit and Tyrant of the whole: 50
Nature that Tyrant checks; he only knows,
And helps, another creature's wants and woes.
Say, will the falcon, stooping from above,
Smit with her varying plumage, spare the dove?   **Smit: smitten**
Admires the jay the insect's gilded wings?
Or hears the hawk when Philomela sings?
Man cares for all: to birds he gives his woods,   **Man . . . all: the traditional belief that man alone has sense of beauty [Mack]**
To beasts his pastures, and to fish his floods;
For some his Int'rest prompts him to provide,
For more his pleasure, yet for more his pride;   60
All feed on one vain Patron, and enjoy
Th'extensive blessing of his luxury.
That very life his learned hunger craves,
He saves from famine, from the savage saves;
Nay, feasts the animal he dooms his feast,
And, 'till he ends the being, makes it blest;
Which sees no more the stroke, or feels the pain,
Than favour'd Man by touch etherial slain.   **etherial: celestial**
The creature had his feast of life before;
Thou too must perish, when thy feast is o'er!   70
    To each unthinking being, Heav'n a friend,
Gives not the useless knowledge of its end:
To Man imparts it; but with such a view
As, while he dreads it, makes him hope it too:
The hour conceal'd, and so remote the fear,
Death still draws nearer, never seeming near.
Great standing miracle! that Heav'n assign'd
Its only thinking thing this turn of mind.
    II. Whether with Reason, or with Instinct blest,
Know, all enjoy that pow'r which suits them best;   80
To bliss alike by that direction tend,
And find the means proportion'd to their end.
Say, where full Instinct is th'unerring guide,   **Council: the Roman Catholic council, which claims to be infallible [Mack]**
What Pope or Council can they need beside?

Reason, however able, cool at best,
Cares not for service, or but serves when prest,
Stays 'till we call, and then not often near;
But honest Instinct comes a volunteer;
Sure never to o'er-shoot, but just to hit,
While still too wide or short is human Wit;   90
Sure by quick Nature happiness to gain,
Which heavier Reason labours at in vain.
This too serves always, Reason never long;
One must go right, the other may go wrong.
See then the acting and comparing pow'rs
One in their nature, which are two in ours,
And Reason raise o'er Instinct as you can,
In this 'tis God directs, in that 'tis Man.

　　Who taught the nations of the field and wood
To shun their poison, and to chuse their food?   100
Prescient, the tides or tempests to withstand,
Build on the wave, or arch beneath the sand?[1]
Who made the spider parallels design,
Sure as De-moivre,[2] without rule or line?
Who bid the stork, Columbus-like, explore
Heav'ns not his own, and worlds unknown before?
Who calls the council, states the certain day,
Who forms the phalanx, and who points the way?

　　iii. God, in the nature of each being, founds
Its proper bliss, and sets its proper bounds: 110
But as he fram'd a Whole, the Whole to bless,
On mutual Wants built mutual Happiness:
So from the first eternal ORDER ran,
And creature link'd to creature, man to man.
Whate'er of life all-quick'ning æther keeps,
Or breathes thro' air, or shoots beneath the deeps,
Or pours profuse on earth; one nature feeds
The vital flame, and swells the genial seeds.
Not Man alone, but all that roam the wood,
Or wing the sky, or roll along the flood,   120
Each loves itself, but not itself alone,
Each sex desires alike, 'till two are one.
Nor ends the pleasure with the fierce embrace;
They love themselves, a third time, in their race.
Thus beast and bird their common charge attend,
The mothers nurse it, and the sires defend;

[1] evidently an allusion, in the first instance, to the supposed nesting habits of the halcyon, 'on the wave,' and in the second, to the reported nesting habits, 'beneath the sand,' of the kingfisher, with which the halcyon was usually identified. [Mack]
[2] an eminent mathematician (1667–1754), who contributed significantly to the theory of probability and to trigonometry.

The young dismiss'd to wander earth or air,
There stops the Instinct, and there ends the care;
The link dissolves, each seeks a fresh embrace,
Another love succeeds, another race.   130
A longer care Man's helpless kind demands;
That longer care contracts more lasting bands:
Reflection, Reason, still the ties improve,
At once extend the int'rest, and the love;
With choice we fix, with sympathy we burn;
Each Virtue in each Passion takes its turn;
And still new needs, new helps, new habits rise,
That graft benevolence on charities.
Still as one brood, and as another rose,
These nat'ral love maintain'd, habitual those: 140
The last, scarce ripen'd into perfect Man,
Saw helpless him from whom their life began:
Mem'ry and fore-cast just returns engage,
That pointed back to youth, this on to age:
While pleasure, gratitude, and hope, combin'd,
Still spread the int'rest, and preserv'd the kind.
    iv. Nor think, in NATURE'S STATE they blindly
        trod;
The state of Nature was the reign of God:
Self-love and Social at her birth began,
Union the bond of all things, and of Man.   150
Pride then was not; nor arts, that Pride to aid;
Man walk'd with beast, joint tenant of the shade;
The same his table, and the same his bed;
No murder cloath'd him, and no murder fed.
In the same temple, the resounding wood,
All vocal beings hymn'd their equal God.
The shrine with gore unstain'd, with gold undrest,
Unbrib'd, unbloody, stood the blameless priest:
Heav'n's attribute was Universal Care,
And Man's prerogative to rule, but spare.   160
Ah! how unlike the man of times to come!
Of half that live the butcher and the tomb;
Who, foe to Nature, hears the gen'ral groan,
Murders their species, and betrays his own.
But just disease to luxury succeeds,
And ev'ry death its own avenger breeds;
The Fury-passions from that blood began,
And turn'd on Man a fiercer savage, Man.
    See him from Nature rising slow to Art!
To copy Instinct then was Reason's part;   170
Thus then to Man the voice of Nature spake —
'Go, from the Creatures thy instructions take:
Learn from the birds what food the thickets yield;
Learn from the beasts the physic of the field;   physic: medicine

Thy arts of building from the bee receive;
Learn of the mole to plow, the worm to weave;
Learn of the little Nautilus to sail,
Spread the thin oar, and catch the driving gale.
Here too all forms of social union find,
And hence let Reason, late, instruct Mankind: 180
Here subterranean works and cities see;
There towns aerial on the waving tree.
Learn each small People's genius, policies,
The Ant's republic, and the realm of Bees;
How those in common all their wealth bestow,
And Anarchy without confusion know;
And these for ever, tho' a Monarch reign,
Their sep'rate cells and properties maintain.
Mark what unvary'd laws preserve each state,
Laws wise as Nature, and as fix'd as Fate.   190
In vain thy Reason finer webs shall draw,
Entangle Justice in her net of Law,
And right, too rigid, harden into wrong;
Still for the strong too weak, the weak too strong.
Yet go! and thus o'er all the creatures sway,
Thus let the wiser make the rest obey,
And for those Arts mere Instinct could afford,
Be crown'd as Monarchs, or as Gods ador'd.'
    v. Great Nature spoke; observant Men obey'd;
Cities were built, Societies were made: 200
Here rose one little state; another near
Grew by like means, and join'd, thro' love or fear.
Did here the trees with ruddier burdens bend,
And there the streams in purer rills descend?
What War could ravish, Commerce could bestow,
And he return'd a friend, who came a foe.
Converse and Love mankind might strongly draw,
When Love was Liberty, and Nature Law.
Thus States were form'd; the name of King unknown,
'Till common int'rest plac'd the sway in one.   210
'Twas VIRTUE ONLY (or in arts or arms,
Diffusing blessings, or averting harms)
The same which in a Sire the Sons obey'd,
A Prince the Father of a People made.
    vi. 'Till then, by Nature crown'd, each Patriarch
        sate,
King, priest, and parent of his growing state;
On him, their second Providence, they hung,
Their law his eye, their oracle his tongue.
He from the wond'ring furrow call'd the food,
Taught to command the fire, controul the flood,   220
Draw forth the monsters of th'abyss profound,
Or fetch th'aerial eagle to the ground.

subterranean works and cities: referring especially to ant-hills and bee-hives [Mack]

'Till drooping, sick'ning, dying, they began
Whom they rever'd as God to mourn as Man:
Then, looking up from sire to sire, explor'd
One great first father, and that first ador'd.
Or plain tradition that this All begun,
Convey'd unbroken faith from sire to son,
The worker from the work distinct was known,
And simple Reason never sought but one: 230
Ere Wit oblique had broke that steddy light,
Man, like his Maker, saw that all was right,
To Virtue, in the paths of Pleasure, trod,
And own'd a Father when he own'd a God.
Love all the faith, and all th'allegiance then;
For Nature knew no right divine in Men,
No ill could fear in God; and understood
A sov'reign being but a sov'reign good.
True faith, true policy, united ran,
That was but love of God, and this of Man.   240
    Who first taught souls enslav'd, and realms un-
        done,
Th' enormous faith of many made for one;
That proud exception to all Nature's laws,
T'invert the world, and counter-work its Cause?
Force first made Conquest, and that conquest, Law;
'Till Superstition taught the tyrant awe,
Then shar'd the Tyranny, then lent it aid,
And Gods of Conqu'rors, Slaves of Subjects made:
She, 'midst the light'ning's blaze, and thunder's
        sound,
When rock'd the mountains, and when groan'd the
        ground,   250
She taught the weak to bend, the proud to pray,
To Pow'r unseen, and mightier far than they:
She, from the rending earth and bursting skies,
Saw Gods descend, and fiends infernal rise:
Here fix'd the dreadful, there the blest abodes;
Fear made her Devils, and weak Hope her Gods;
Gods partial, changeful, passionate, unjust,
Whose attributes were Rage, Revenge, or Lust;
Such as the souls of cowards might conceive,
And, form'd like tyrants, tyrants would believe.   260
Zeal then, not charity, became the guide,
And hell was built on spite, and heav'n on pride.
Then sacred seem'd th'etherial vault no more;
Altars grew marble then, and reek'd with gore:
Then first the Flamen tasted living food;   **Flamen: pagan priest**
Next his grim idol smear'd with human blood;
With Heav'n's own thunders shook the world below,
And play'd the God an engine on his foe.   **engine: destructive weapon**

So drives Self-love, thro' just and thro' unjust,
To one Man's pow'r, ambition, lucre, lust: 270
The same Self-love, in all, becomes the cause
Of what restrains him, Government and Laws.
For, what one likes if others like as well,
What serves one will, when many wills rebel?
How shall he keep, what, sleeping or awake,
A weaker may surprise, a stronger take?
His safety must his liberty restrain:
All join to guard what each desires to gain.
Forc'd into virtue thus by Self-defence,
Ev'n Kings learn'd justice and benevolence: 280
Self-love forsook the path it first pursu'd,
And found the private in the public good.
    'Twas then, the studious head or gen'rous mind,
Follow'r of God or friend of human-kind,
Poet or Patriot, rose but to restore
The Faith and Moral, Nature gave before;   **Moral: equivalent to 'ethical principles' [Mack]**
Re-lum'd her ancient light, not kindled new:
If not God's image, yet his shadow drew:
Taught Pow'r's due use to People and to Kings,
Taught nor to slack, nor strain its tender strings,   290
The less, or greater, set so justly true,
That touching one must strike the other too;
'Till jarring int'rests of themselves create
Th'according music of a well-mix'd State.
Such is the World's great harmony, that springs
From Order, Union, full Consent of things!
Where small and great, where weak and mighty, made
~~To serve, not suffer, strengthen, not invade,~~
More pow'rful each as needful to the rest,
And, in proportion as its blesses, blest,   300
Draw to one point, and to one centre bring
Beast, Man, or Angel, Servant, Lord, or King.
    For Forms of Government let fools contest;
Whate'er is best administer'd is best:
For Modes of Faith, let graceless zealots fight;
His can't be wrong whose life is in the right:
In Faith and Hope the world will disagree,
But all Mankind's concern is Charity:
All must be false that thwart this One great End,
And all of God, that bless Mankind or mend.   310
    Man, like the gen'rous vine, supported lives;
The strength he gains is from th'embrace he gives.
On their own Axis as the Planets run,
Yet make at once their circle round the Sun:
So two consistent motions act the Soul;
And one regards Itself, and one the Whole.
    Thus God and Nature link'd the gen'ral frame,
And bade Self-love and Social be the same.

William Blake (1757–1827)

ENGLISH POET, PAINTER, and MYSTIC

The Tyger

Tyger! Tyger! burning bright
In the forests of the night,
What immortal hand or eye
Could frame thy fearful symmetry?

In what distant deeps or skies
Burnt the fire of thine eyes?
On what wings dare he aspire?
What the hand dare sieze the fire?

And what shoulder, & what art,
Could twist the sinews of thy heart?   10
And when thy heart began to beat,
What dread hand? & what dread feet?

What the hammer? what the chain?
In what furnace was thy brain?
What the anvil? what dread grasp
Dare its deadly terrors clasp?

When the stars threw down their spears,
And water'd heaven with their tears,
Did he smile his work to see?
Did he who made the Lamb make thee?   20

Tyger! Tyger! burning bright
In the forests of the night,
What immortal hand or eye
Dare frame thy fearful symmetry?

A Poison Tree

I was angry with my friend:
I told my wrath, my wrath did end.
I was angry with my foe:
I told it not, my wrath did grow.

"The Tyger" and "A Poison Tree" from *The Complete Writings of William Blake,* edited by Geoffrey Keynes.

And I water'd it in fears,
Night & morning with my tears;
And I sunned it with smiles,
And with soft deceitful wiles.

And it grew both day and night,
Till it bore an apple bright;   10
And my foe beheld it shine,
And he knew that it was mine,

And into my garden stole
When the night had veil'd the pole:
In the morning glad I see
My foe outstretch'd beneath the tree.

Robert Burns (1759–1796)

SCOTTISH POET

To a Mouse

ON TURNING HER UP IN HER NEST,
WITH THE PLOUGH, NOVEMBER, 1785.

Wee, sleeket, cowran, tim'rous *beastie*,   sleeket: sleek. cowran: cowering
O, what a panic's in thy breastie!
Thou need na start awa sae hasty,   na: not. awa: away. sae: so
      Wi' bickering brattle!   bickering: noisy. brattle: hurry
I wad be laith to rin an' chase thee,   wad: would. laith: loath. rin: run
      Wi' murd'ring *pattle!*

I'm truly sorry Man's dominion
Has broken Nature's social union,
An' justifies that ill opinion,
      Which makes thee startle,   10
At me, thy poor, earth-born companion,
      An' *fellow-mortal!*

"To a Mouse" by Robert Burns. From *Selected Poetry and Prose of Robert Burns*, edited by Robert D. Thornton (Riverside Edition). Reprinted by permission of Houghton Mifflin Company.

I doubt na, whyles, but thou may *thieve;*
What then? poor beastie, thou maun live!
A *daimen-icker* in a *thrave*
       'S a sma' request:
I'll get a blessin wi' the lave,
       An' never miss 't!

Thy wee-bit *housie*, too, in ruin!
Its silly wa's the win's are strewin!
An' naething, now, to big a new ane,
       O' foggage green!
An' bleak *December's winds* ensuin,
       Baith snell an' keen!

Thou saw the fields laid bare an' wast,
An' weary *Winter* comin fast,
An' cozie here, beneath the blast,
       Thou thought to dwell,
Till crash! the cruel *coulter* past
       Out thro' thy cell.

That wee-bit heap o' leaves an' stibble,
Has cost thee monie a weary nibble!
Now thou's turn'd out, for a' thy trouble,
       But house or hald,
To thole the Winter's *sleety dribble,*
       An' *cranreuch* cauld!

But Mousie, thou art no thy-lane,
In proving *foresight* may be vain:
The best laid schemes o' *Mice* an' *Men,*
       Gang aft agley,
An' lea'e us nought but grief an' pain,
       For promis'd joy!

Still, thou art blest, compar'd wi' *me!*
The *present* only toucheth thee:
But Och! I *backward* cast my e'e,
       On prospects drear!
An' *forward*, tho' I canna *see,*
       I *guess* an' *fear!*

Glosses:

whyles: sometimes
maun: must
daimen-icker: occasional ear of corn. thrave: two shocks of corn
'S: is. sma': small. lave: rest

20   wa's: walls. win's: winds
naething: nothing. ane: one. foggage: second crop of grass (after hay)

Baith: both. snell: biting

coulter: blade of the plow
30

stibble: stubble
monie: many

But: without. hald: abode
thole: suffer
cranreuch: frozen dew. cauld: cold

no thy-lane: not alone

40   Gang aft agley: go often awry, amiss. lea'e: leave

e'e: eye

William Wordsworth (1770–1850)

ENGLISH POET

Lines Composed a Few Miles above Tintern Abbey

ON REVISITING THE BANKS OF THE WYE DURING A TOUR, JULY 13, 1798

Five years have past; five summers, with the length
Of five long winters! and again I hear
These waters, rolling from their mountain-springs
With a soft inland murmur. — Once again
Do I behold these steep and lofty cliffs,
That on a wild secluded scene impress
Thoughts of more deep seclusion; and connect
The landscape with the quiet of the sky.
The day is come when I again repose
Here, under this dark sycamore, and view   10
These plots of cottage-ground, these orchard-tufts,
Which at this season, with their unripe fruits,
Are clad in one green hue, and lose themselves
'Mid groves and copses. Once again I see
These hedge-rows, hardly hedge-rows, little lines
Of sportive wood run wild: these pastoral farms,
Green to the very door; and wreaths of smoke
Sent up, in silence, from among the trees!
With some uncertain notice, as might seem
Of vagrant dwellers in the houseless woods,   20
Or of some Hermit's cave, where by his fire
The Hermit sits alone.
                              These beauteous forms,
Through a long absence, have not been to me
As is a landscape to a blind man's eye:
But oft, in lonely rooms, and 'mid the din
Of towns and cities, I have owed to them
In hours of weariness, sensations sweet,
Felt in the blood, and felt along the heart;
And passing even into my purer mind,
With tranquil restoration: — feelings too   30
Of unremembered pleasure: such, perhaps,
As have no slight or trivial influence
On that best portion of a good man's life,

From *Selected Poems and Prefaces* by William Wordsworth, edited by Jack Stillinger (Riverside Edition). Reprinted by permission of Houghton Mifflin Company.

His little, nameless, unremembered, acts
Of kindness and of love. Nor less, I trust,
To them I may have owed another gift,
Of aspect more sublime; that blessed mood,
In which the burthen of the mystery,
In which the heavy and the weary weight
Of all this unintelligible world,   40
Is lightened: — that serene and blessed mood,
In which the affections gently lead us on, —
Until, the breath of this corporeal frame
And even the motion of our human blood
Almost suspended, we are laid asleep
In body, and become a living soul:
While with an eye made quiet by the power
Of harmony, and the deep power of joy,
We see into the life of things.

                                                     If this
Be but a vain belief, yet, oh! how oft —   50
In darkness and amid the many shapes
Of joyless daylight; when the fretful stir
Unprofitable, and the fever of the world,
Have hung upon the beatings of my heart —
How oft, in spirit, have I turned to thee,
O sylvan Wye! thou wanderer thro' the woods,
How often has my spirit turned to thee!

    And now, with gleams of half-extinguished thought,
With many recognitions dim and faint,
And somewhat of a sad perplexity,   60
The picture of the mind revives again:
While here I stand, not only with the sense
Of present pleasure, but with pleasing thoughts
That in this moment there is life and food
For future years. And so I dare to hope,
Though changed, no doubt, from what I was when first
I came among these hills; when like a roe
I bounded o'er the mountains, by the sides
Of the deep rivers, and the lonely streams,
Wherever nature led: more like a man   70
Flying from something that he dreads, than one
Who sought the thing he loved. For nature then
(The coarser pleasures of my boyish days,
And their glad animal movements all gone by)
To me was all in all. — I cannot paint
What then I was. The sounding cataract
Haunted me like a passion: the tall rock,
The mountain, and the deep and gloomy wood,
Their colours and their forms, were then to me
An appetite; a feeling and a love,   80

That had no need of a remoter charm,
By thought supplied, nor any interest
Unborrowed from the eye. — That time is past,
And all its aching joys are now no more,
And all its dizzy raptures. Not for this
Faint I, nor mourn nor murmur; other gifts
Have followed; for such loss, I would believe,
Abundant recompense. For I have learned
To look on nature, not as in the hour
Of thoughtless youth; but hearing oftentimes   90
The still, sad music of humanity,
Nor harsh nor grating, though of ample power
To chasten and subdue. And I have felt
A presence that disturbs me with the joy
Of elevated thoughts; a sense sublime
Of something far more deeply interfused,
Whose dwelling is the light of setting suns,
And the round ocean and the living air,
And the blue sky, and in the mind of man:
A motion and a spirit, that impels   100
All thinking things, all objects of all thought,
And rolls through all things. Therefore am I still
A lover of the meadows and the woods,
And mountains; and of all that we behold
From this green earth; of all the mighty world
Of eye, and ear, — both what they half create,
And what perceive; well pleased to recognise
In nature and the language of the sense,
The anchor of my purest thoughts, the nurse,
The guide, the guardian of my heart, and soul   110
Of all my moral being.
                                    Nor perchance,
If I were not thus taught, should I the more
Suffer my genial spirits to decay:
For thou art with me here upon the banks
Of this fair river; thou my dearest Friend,
My dear, dear Friend; and in thy voice I catch
The language of my former heart, and read
My former pleasures in the shooting lights
Of thy wild eyes. Oh! yet a little while
May I behold in thee what I was once,   120
My dear, dear Sister![1] and this prayer I make,
Knowing that Nature never did betray
The heart that loved her; 'tis her privilege,
Through all the years of this our life, to lead
From joy to joy: for she can so inform
The mind that is within us, so impress

[1] Wordsworth's sister Dorothy, one year younger than he.

With quietness and beauty, and so feed
With lofty thoughts, that neither evil tongues,
Rash judgments, nor the sneers of selfish men,
Nor greetings where no kindness is, nor all   130
The dreary intercourse of daily life,
Shall e'er prevail against us, or disturb
Our cheerful faith, that all which we behold
Is full of blessings. Therefore let the moon
Shine on thee in thy solitary walk;
And let the misty mountain-winds be free
To blow against thee: and, in after years,
When these wild ecstasies shall be matured
Into a sober pleasure; when thy mind
Shall be a mansion for all lovely forms,   140
Thy memory be as a dwelling-place
For all sweet sounds and harmonies; oh! then,
If solitude, or fear, or pain, or grief,
Should be thy portion, with what healing thoughts
Of tender joy wilt thou remember me,
And these my exhortations! Nor, perchance —
If I should be where I no more can hear
Thy voice, nor catch from thy wild eyes these gleams
Of past existence — wilt thou then forget
That on the banks of this delightful stream   150
We stood together; and that I, so long
A worshipper of Nature, hither came
Unwearied in that service; rather say
With warmer love — oh! with far deeper zeal
Of holier love. Nor wilt thou then forget,
That after many wanderings, many years
Of absence, these steep woods and lofty cliffs,
And this green pastoral landscape, were to me
More dear, both for themselves and for thy sake!

John Keats (1795–1821)

ENGLISH POET

To Autumn

I

Season of mists and mellow fruitfulness,
    Close bosom-friend of the maturing sun;
Conspiring with him how to load and bless
    With fruit the vines that round the thatch-eves run;
To bend with apples the moss'd cottage-trees,
    And fill all fruit with ripeness to the core;
        To swell the gourd, and plump the hazel shells
With a sweet kernel; to set budding more,
    And still more, later flowers for the bees,
        Until they think warm days will never cease,   10
        For Summer has o'er-brimm'd their clammy cells.

II

Who hath not seen thee oft amid thy store?
    Sometimes whoever seeks abroad may find
Thee sitting careless on a granary floor,
    Thy hair soft-lifted by the winnowing wind;
Or on a half-reap'd furrow sound asleep,
    Drows'd with the fume of poppies, while thy hook
        Spares the next swath and all its twined flowers:
And sometimes like a gleaner thou dost keep
    Steady thy laden head across a brook;   20
    Or by a cyder-press, with patient look,
        Thou watchest the last oozings hours by hours.

III

Where are the songs of Spring? Ay, where are they?
    Think not of them, thou hast thy music too, —
While barred clouds bloom the soft-dying day,
    And touch the stubble-plains with rosy hue;
Then in a wailful choir the small gnats mourn
    Among the river sallows, borne aloft
        Or sinking as the light wind lives or dies;
And full-grown lambs loud bleat from hilly bourn;   30
    Hedge-crickets sing; and now with treble soft
    The red-breast whistles from a garden-croft;
        And gathering swallows twitter in the skies.

"To Autumn" by John Keats. From *Selected Poems and Letters* by John Keats, edited by Douglas Bush (Riverside Edition). Reprinted by permission of Houghton Mifflin Company.

Charles Darwin (1809–1882)

ENGLISH NATURALIST

The Struggle for Existence

Nothing is easier than to admit in words the truth of the universal struggle for life, or more difficult — as least I have found it so — than constantly to bear this conclusion in mind. Yet unless it be thoroughly engrained in the mind, the whole economy of nature, with every fact on distribution, rarity, abundance, extinction, and variation, will be dimly seen or quite misunderstood. We behold the face of nature bright with gladness, we often see superabundance of food; we do not see or we forget, that the bids which are idly singing round us mostly live on insects or seeds, and are thus constantly destroying life; or we forget how largely these songsters, or their eggs, or their nestlings, are destroyed by birds and beasts of prey; we do not always bear in mind, that, though food may be now superabundant, it is not so at all seasons of each recurring year.

The Term, Struggle for Existence, used in a large sense

I should premise that I use this term in a large and metaphorical sense including dependence of one being on another, and including (which is more important) not only the life of the individual, but success in leaving progeny. Two canine animals, in a time of dearth, may be truly said to struggle with each other which shall get food and live. But a plant on the edge of a desert is said to struggle for life against the drought, though more properly it should be said to be dependent on the moisture. A plant which annually produces a thousand seeds, of which only one on an average comes to maturity, may be more truly said to struggle with the plants of the same and other kinds which already clothe the ground. The misletoe is dependent on the apple and a few other trees, but can only in a far-fetched sense be said to struggle with these trees, for, if too many of these parasites grow on the same tree, it languishes and dies. But several seedling misletoes, growing close together on the same branch, may more truly be said to struggle with each other. As the misletoe is disseminated by birds, its existence depends on them; and it may metaphorically be said to struggle with other fruit-bearing plants, in tempting the birds to devour and thus disseminate its seeds. In these several senses, which pass into each other, I use for convenience' sake the general term of Struggle for Existence.

Title supplied by editors. "The Struggle for Existence" by Charles Darwin. From *The Origin of Species By Means of Natural Selection, Or the Preservation of Favoured Races in the Struggle for Life.*

GEOMETRICAL RATIO OF INCREASE

A struggle for existence inevitably follows from the high rate at which all organic beings tend to increase. Every being, which during its natural lifetime produces several eggs or seeds, must suffer destruction during some period of its life, and during some season or occasional year, otherwise, on the principle of geometrical increase, its numbers would quickly become so inordinately great that no country could support the product. Hence, as more individuals are produced than can possibly survive, there must in every case be a struggle for existence, either one individual with another of the same species, or with the individuals of distinct species, or with the physical conditions of life. It is the doctrine of Malthus[1] applied with manifold force to the whole animal and vegetable kingdoms; for in this case there can be no artificial increase of food, and no prudential restraint from marriage. Although some species may be now increasing, more or less rapidly, in numbers, all cannot do so, for the world would not hold them.

There is no exception to the rule that every organic being naturally increases at so high a rate, that, if not destroyed, the earth would soon be covered by the progeny of a single pair. Even slow-breeding man has doubled in twenty-five years, and at this rate, in less than a thousand years, there would literally not be standing-room for his progeny. Linnæus has calculated that if an annual plant produced only two seeds — and there is no plant so unproductive as this — and their seedlings next year produced two, and so on, then in twenty years there would be a million plants. The elephant is reckoned the slowest breeder of all known animals, and I have taken some pains to estimate its probable minimum rate of natural increase; it will be safest to assume that it begins breeding when thirty years old, and goes on breeding till ninety years old, bringing forth six young in the interval, and surviving till one hundred years old; if this be so, after a period of from 740 to 750 years there would be nearly nineteen million elephants alive, descended from the first pair.

But we have better evidence on this subject than mere theoretical calculations, namely, the numerous recorded cases of the astonishingly rapid increase of various animals in a state of nature, when circumstances have been favourable to them during two or three following seasons. Still more striking is the evidence from our domestic animals of many kinds which have run wild in several parts of the world; if the statements of the rate of increase of slow-breeding cattle and horses in South America, and latterly in Australia, had not been well authenticated, they would have been incredible. So it is with plants; cases could be given of introduced plants which have become common throughout whole islands in a period of less than ten years. Several of the

---

[1] Thomas Robert Malthus (1766–1834), English political economist who proposed that since parents can and do often bear more than two children, only such factors as war, disease, and famine keep population in check.

of game animals are now annually shot. On the other hand, in some cases, as with the elephant, none are destroyed by beasts of prey; for even the tiger in India most rarely dares to attack a young elephant protected by its dam.

Climate plays an important part in determining the average numbers of a species, and periodical seasons of extreme cold or drought seem to be the most effective of all checks. I estimated (chiefly from the greatly reduced numbers of nests in the spring) that the winter of 1854–5 destroyed four-fifths of the birds in my own grounds; and this is a tremendous destruction, when we remember that ten per cent is an extraordinarily severe mortality from epidemics with man. The action of climate seems at first sight to be quite independent of the struggle for existence; but in so far as climate chiefly acts in reducing food, it brings on the most severe struggle between the individuals, whether of the same or of distinct species, which subsist on the same kind of food. Even when climate, for instance extreme cold, acts directly, it will be the least vigorous individuals, or those which have got least food through the advancing winter, which will suffer most. When we travel from south to north, or from a damp region to a dry, we invariably see some species gradually getting rarer and rarer, and finally disappearing; and the change of climate being conspicuous, we are tempted to attribute the whole effect to its direct action. But this is a false view; we forget that each species, even where it most abounds, is constantly suffering enormous destruction at some period of its life, from enemies or from competitors for the same place and food; and if these enemies or competitors be in the least degree favoured by any slight change of climate, they will increase in numbers; and as each area is already fully stocked with inhabitants, the other species must decrease. When we travel southward and see a species decreasing in numbers, we may feel sure that the cause lies quite as much in other species being favoured, as in this one being hurt. So it is when we travel northward, but in a somewhat lesser degree, for the number of species of all kinds, and therefore of competitors, decreases northwards; hence in going northwards, or in ascending a mountain, we far oftener meet with stunted forms, due to the *directly* injurious action of climate, than we do in proceeding southwards or in descending a mountain. When we reach the Arctic regions, or snow-capped summits, or absolute deserts, the struggle for life is almost exclusively with the elements.

That climate acts in main part indirectly by favouring other species, we clearly see in the prodigious number of plants which in our gardens can perfectly well endure our climate, but which never become naturalised, for they cannot compete with our native plants nor resist destruction by our native animals.

When a species, owing to highly favourable circumstances, increases inordinately in numbers in a small tract, epidemics — at least, this seems generally to occur with our game animals — often ensue; and here we have a limiting check independent of the struggle for life. But even some of these so-called epidemics appear to be due to parasitic worms, which have from some cause, possibly in part through facility of diffusion amongst the crowded animals, been disproportionally favoured: and here comes in a sort of struggle between the parasite and its prey.

On the other hand, in many cases, a large stock of individuals of the same species, relatively to the numbers of its enemies, is absolutely necessary for its preservation. Thus we can easily raise plenty of corn and rape-seed, &c., in our fields, because the seeds are in great excess compared with the number of birds which feed on them; nor can the birds, though having a superabundance of food at this one season, increase in number proportionally to the supply of seed, as their numbers are checked during winter; but any one who has tried, knows how troublesome it is to get seed from a few wheat or other such plants in a garden: I have in this case lost every single seed. This view of the necessity of a large stock of the same species for its preservation, explains, I believe, some singular facts in nature such as that of very rare plants being sometimes extremely abundant, in the few spots where they do exist; and that of some social plants being social, that is abounding in individuals, even on the extreme verge of their range. For in such cases, we may believe, that a plant could exist only where the conditions of its life were so favourable that many could exist together, and thus save the species from utter destruction. I should add that the good effects of intercrossing, and the ill effects of close interbreeding, no doubt come into play in many of these cases; but I will not here enlarge on this subject.

COMPLEX RELATIONS OF ALL ANIMALS AND PLANTS TO EACH OTHER IN THE STRUGGLE FOR EXISTENCE

Many cases are on record showing how complex and unexpected are the checks and relations between organic beings, which have to struggle together in the same country. I will give only a single instance, which, though a simple one, interested me. In Staffordshire, on the estate of a relation, where I had ample means of investigation, there was a large and extremely barren heath, which had never been touched by the hand of man; but several hundred acres of exactly the same nature had been enclosed twenty-five years previously and planted with Scotch fir. The change in the native vegetation of the planted part of the heath was most remarkable, more than is generally seen in passing from one quite different soil to another; not only the proportional numbers of the heath-plants were wholly changed, but twelve species of plants (not counting grasses and carices[4]) flourished in the plantations, which could not be found on the heath. The effect on the insects must have been still greater, for six insectivorous birds were very common in the plantations, which were not to be seen on the heath; and the heath was frequented by two or three distinct insectivorous birds. Here we see how potent has been the effect of the introduction of a single tree, nothing whatever else having been done, with the exception of the land having been enclosed, so that cattle could not

---

[4] grassy-looking plants similar to sedge.

enter. But how important an element enclosure is, I plainly saw near Farn-ham, in Surrey. Here there are extensive heaths, with a few clumps of old Scotch firs on the distant hilltops: within the last ten years large spaces have been enclosed, and self-sown firs are now springing up in multitudes, so close together that all cannot live. When I ascertained that these young trees had not been sown or planted, I was so much surprised at their numbers that I went to several points of view, whence I could examine hundreds of acres of the unenclosed heath, and literally I could not see a single Scotch fir, except the old planted clumps. But on looking closely between the stems of the heath, I found a multitude of seedlings and little trees which had been perpetually browsed down by the cattle. In one square yard, at a point some hundred yards distant from one of the old clumps, I counted thirty-two little trees; and one of them, with twenty-six rings of growth, had, during many years tried to raise its head above the stems of the heath, and had failed. No wonder that, as soon as the land was enclosed, it became thickly clothed with vigorously growing young firs. Yet the heath was so extremely barren and so extensive that no one would ever have imagined that cattle would have so closely and effectually searched it for food.

Here we see that cattle absolutely determine the existence of, the Scotch fir; but in several parts of the world insects determine the existence of cattle. Perhaps Paraguay offers the most curious instance of this; for here neither cattle nor horses nor dogs have ever run wild, though they swarm southward and northward in a feral state; and Azara and Rengger[5] have shown that this is caused by the greater number in Paraguay of a certain fly, which lays its eggs in the navels of these animals when first born. The increase of these flies, numerous as they are, must be habitually checked by some means, probably by other parasitic insects. Hence, if certain insectivorous birds were to decrease in Paraguay, the parasitic insects would probably increase; and this would lessen the number of the navel-frequenting flies — then cattle and horses would become feral, and this would certainly greatly alter (as indeed I have observed in parts of South America) the vegetation: this again would largely affect the insects; and this, as we have just seen in Staffordshire, the insectivorous birds, and so onwards in ever-increasing circles of complexity. Not that under nature the relations will ever be as simple as this. Battle within battle must be continually recurring with varying success; and yet in the long-run the forces are so nicely balanced, that the face of nature remains for long periods of time uniform, though assuredly the merest trifle would give the victory to one organic being over another. Nevertheless, so profound is our ignorance, and so high our presumption, that we marvel when we hear of the extinction of an organic being; and as we do not see the cause, we invoke cataclysms to desolate the world, or invent laws on the duration of the forms of life! . . .

The dependency of one organic being on another, as of a parasite on its

5 Felix d'Azara (1764–1811), Spanish naturalist and traveller; John R. Rengger (1795–1832), Swiss naturalist and traveller.

prey, lies generally between beings remote in the scale of nature. This is likewise sometimes the case with those which may be strictly said to struggle with each other for existence, as in the case of locusts and grass-feeding quadrupeds. But the struggle will almost invariably be most severe between the individuals of the same species, for they frequent the same districts, require the same food, and are exposed to the same dangers. In the case of varieties of the same species, the struggle will generally be almost equally severe, and we sometimes see the contest soon decided; for instance, if several varieties of wheat be sown together, and the mixed seed be resown, some of the varieties which best suit the soil or climate, or are naturally the most fertile, will beat the others and so yield more seed, and will consequently in a few years supplant the other varieties. To keep up a mixed stock of even such extremely close varieties as the variously-coloured sweet-peas, they must be each year harvested separately, and the seed then mixed in due proportion, otherwise the weaker kinds will steadily decrease in number and disappear. So again with the varieties of sheep: it has been asserted that certain mountain-varieties will starve out other mountain-varieties, so that they cannot be kept together. The same result has followed from keeping together different varieties of the medicinal leech. It may even be doubted whether the varieties of any of our domestic plants or animals have so exactly the same strength, habits, and constitution, that the original proportions of a mixed stock (crossing being prevented) could be kept up for half-a-dozen generations, if they were allowed to struggle together, in the same manner as beings in a state of nature, and if the seed or young were not annually preserved in due proportion.

STRUGGLE FOR LIFE MOST SEVERE BETWEEN INDIVIDUALS AND VARIETIES OF THE SAME SPECIES

As the species of the same genus usually have, though by no means invariably, much similarity in habits and constitution, and always in structure, the struggle will generally be more severe between them, if they come into competition with each other, than between the species of distinct genera. We see this in the recent extension over parts of the United States of one species of swallow having caused the decrease of another species. The recent increase of the missel-thrush in parts of Scotland has caused the decrease of the song-thrush. How frequently we hear of one species of rat taking the place of another species under the most different climates! In Russia the small Asiatic cockroach has everywhere driven before it its great congener. In Australia the imported hive-bee is rapidly exterminating the small, stingless native bee. One species of charlock has been known to supplant another species; and so in other cases. We can dimly see why the competition should be most severe between allied forms, which fill nearly the same place in the economy of nature; but probably in no one case could we precisely say why one species has been victorious over another in the great battle of life.

A corollary of the highest importance may be deduced from the foregoing remarks, namely, that the structure of every organic being is related, in the most essential yet often hidden manner, to that of all the other organic beings, with which it comes into competition for food or residence, or from which it has to escape, or on which it preys. This is obvious in the structure of the teeth and talons of the tiger; and in that of the legs and claws of the parasite which clings to the hair on the tiger's body. But in the beautifully plumed seed of the dandelion, and in the flattened and fringed legs of the water-beetle, the relation seems at first confined to the elements of air and water. Yet the advantage of plumed seeds no doubt stands in the closest relation to the land being already thickly clothed with other plants; so that the seeds may be widely distributed and fall on unoccupied ground. In the water-beetle, the structure of its legs, so well adapted for diving, allows it to compete with other aquatic insects, to hunt for its own prey, and to escape serving as prey to other animals.

The store of nutriment laid up within the seeds of many plants seems at first sight to have no sort of relation to other plants. But from the strong growth of young plants produced from such seeds, as peas and beans, when sown in the midst of long grass, it may be suspected that the chief use of the nutriment in the seed is to favour the growth of the seedlings, whilst struggling with other plants growing vigorously all around.

Look at a plant in the midst of its range, why does it not double or quadruple its numbers? We know that it can perfectly well withstand a little more heat or cold, dampness or dryness, for elsewhere it ranges into slightly hotter or colder, damper or drier districts. In this case we can clearly see that if we wish in imagination to give the plant the power of increasing in number, we should have to give it some advantage over its competitors, or over the animals which prey on it. On the confines of its geographical range, a change of constitution with respect to climate would clearly be an advantage to our plant; but we have reason to believe that only a few plants or animals range so far, that they are destroyed exclusively by the rigour of the climate. Not until we reach the extreme confines of life, in the Arctic regions or on the borders of an utter desert, will competition cease. The land may be extremely cold or dry, yet there will be competition between some few species, or between the individuals of the same species, for the warmest or dampest spots.

Hence we can see that when a plant or animal is placed in a new country amongst new competitors, the conditions of its life will generally be changed in an essential manner, although the climate may be exactly the same as in its former home. If its average numbers are to increase in its new home, we should have to modify it in a different way to what we should have had to do in its native country; for we should have to give it some advantage over a different set of competitors or enemies.

It is good thus to try in imagination to give to any one species an advantage over another. Probably in no single instance should we know what to do.

This ought to convince us of our ignorance on the mutual relations of all organic beings; a conviction as necessary, as it is difficult to acquire. All that we can do, is to keep steadily in mind that each organic being is striving to increase in a geometrical ratio; that each at some period of its life, during some season of the year; during each generation or at intervals, has to struggle for life and to suffer great destruction. When we reflect on this struggle, we may console ourselves with the full belief, that the war of nature is not incessant, that no fear is felt, that death is generally prompt, and that the vigorous, the healthy, and the happy survive and multiply.

Herman Melville (1819–1891)

AMERICAN NOVELIST and POET

The Grand Armada

The long and narrow peninsula of Malacca, extending southeastward from the territories of Birmah,[1] forms the most southerly point of all Asia. In a continuous line from that peninsula stretch the long islands of Sumatra, Java, Bally,[2] and Timor; which, with many others, form a vast mole, or rampart, lengthwise connecting Asia with Australia, and dividing the long unbroken Indian ocean from the thickly studded oriental archipelagoes. This rampart is pierced by several sally-ports[3] for the convenience of ships and whales; conspicuous among which are the straits of Sunda and Malacca. By the straits of Sunda, chiefly, vessels bound to China from the west, emerge into the China seas.

Those narrow straits of Sunda divide Sumatra from Java; and standing midway in that vast rampart of islands, buttressed by that bold green promontory, known to seamen as Java Head; they not a little correspond to the central gateway opening into some vast walled empire: and considering the inexhaustible wealth of spices, and silks, and jewels, and gold, and ivory, with which the thousand islands of that oriental sea are enriched, it seems a significant provision of nature, that such treasures, by the very formation of the land, should at least bear the appearance, however ineffectual, of being guarded from the all-grasping western world. The shores of the Straits of Sunda are unsupplied with those domineering fortresses which guard the

[1] Burma. [Feidelson]
[2] Bali. [Feidelson]
[3] openings for landing in a fortification.

entrances to the Mediterranean, the Baltic, and the Propontis.[4] Unlike the Danes, these Orientals do not demand the obsequious homage of lowered top-sails from the endless procession of ships before the wind, which for centuries past, by night and by day, have passed between the islands of Sumatra and Java, freighted with the costliest cargoes of the east. But while they freely waive a ceremonial like this, they do by no means renounce their claim to more solid tribute.

Time out of mind the piratical proas[5] of the Malays, lurking among the low shaded coves and islets of Sumatra, have sallied out upon the vessels sailing through the straits, fiercely demanding tribute at the point of their spears. Though by the repeated bloody chastisements they have received at the hands of European cruisers, the audacity of these corsairs has of late been somewhat repressed; yet, even at the present day, we occasionally hear of English and American vessels, which, in those waters, have been remorselessly boarded and pillaged.

With a fair, fresh wind, the Pequod was now drawing nigh to these straits; Ahab[6] purposing to pass through them into the Javan sea, and thence, cruising northwards, over waters known to be frequented here and there by the Sperm Whale, sweep inshore by the Philippine Islands, and gain the far coast of Japan, in time for the great whaling season there. By these means, the circumnavigating Pequod would sweep almost all the known Sperm Whale cruising grounds of the world, previous to descending upon the Line[7] in the Pacific; where Ahab, though everywhere else foiled in his pursuit, firmly counted upon giving battle to Moby Dick, in the sea he was most known to frequent; and at a season when he might most reasonably be presumed to be haunting it.

But how now? in this zoned[8] quest, does Ahab touch no land? does his crew drink air? Surely, he will stop for water. Nay. For a long time, now, the circus-running sun has raced within his fiery ring, and needs no sustenance but what's in himself. So Ahab. Mark this, too, in the whaler. While other hulls are loaded down with alien stuff, to be transferred to foreign wharves; the world-wandering whale-ship carries no cargo but herself and crew, their weapons and their wants. She has a whole lake's contents bottled in her ample hold. She is ballasted with utilities; not altogether with unusable pig-lead and kentledge.[9] She carries years' water in her. Clear old prime Nantucket water; which, when three years afloat, the Nantucketer, in the Pacific, prefers to drink before the brackish fluid, but yesterday rafted off in casks, from the Peruvian or Indian streams. Hence it is, that, while other ships may have gone to China from New York, and back again, touching at a score of ports, the whale-ship, in all that interval, may not have sighted one grain of

---

[4] The Sea of Marmara, between the Black Sea and the Mediterranean. The other references are to Gibraltar and to "the isle fort at Cattegat." [Feidelson]

[5] large outrigger canoes with sails. [Feidelson]

[6] Captain of the whaleship Pequod, in search of a singular white whale (Moby Dick).

[7] the Equator.

[8] Many-zoned. [Feidelson]

[9] ballast, usually pig iron, at the bottom of the ship along the keelson. [Feidelson]

soil; her crew having seen no man but floating seamen like themselves. So that did you carry them the news that another flood had come; they would only answer — "Well, boys, here's the ark!"

Now, as many Sperm Whales had been captured off the western coast of Java, in the near vicinity of the Straits of Sunda; indeed, as most of the ground, roundabout, was generally recognised by the fishermen as an excellent spot for cruising; therefore, as the Pequod gained more and more upon Java Head, the look-outs were repeatedly hailed, and admonished to keep wide awake. But though the green palmy cliffs of the land soon loomed on the starboard bow, and with delighted nostrils the fresh cinnamon was snuffed in the air, yet not a single jet was descried. Almost renouncing all thought of falling in with any game hereabouts, the ship had well nigh entered the straits, when the customary cheering cry was heard from aloft, and ere long a spectacle of singular magnificence saluted us.

But here be it premised, that owing to the unwearied activity with which of late they have been hunted over all four oceans, the Sperm Whales, instead of almost invariably sailing in small detached companies, as in former times, are now frequently met with in extensive herds, sometimes embracing so great a multitude, that it would almost seem as if numerous nations of them had sworn solemn league and covenant for mutual assistance and protection. To this aggregation of the Sperm Whale into such immense caravans, may be imputed the circumstance that even in the best cruising grounds, you may now sometimes sail for weeks and months together, without being greeted by a single spout; and then be suddenly saluted by what sometimes seems thousands on thousands.

Broad on both bows, at the distance of some two or three miles, and forming a great semicircle, embracing one half of the level horizon, a continuous chain of whale-jets were up-playing and sparkling in the noon-day air. Unlike the straight perpendicular twin-jets of the Right Whale, which, dividing at top, fall over in two branches, like the cleft drooping boughs of a willow, the single forward-slanting spout of the Sperm Whale presents a thick curled bush of white mist, continually rising and falling away to leeward.

Seen from the Pequod's deck, then, as she would rise on a high hill of the sea, this host of vapory spouts, individually curling up into the air, and beheld through a blending atmosphere of bluish haze, showed like the thousand cheerful chimneys of some dense metropolis, descried of a balmy autumnal morning, by some horseman on a height.

As marching armies approaching an unfriendly defile in the mountains, accelerate their march, all eagerness to place that perilous passage in their rear, and once more expand in comparative security upon the plain; even so did this vast fleet of whales now seem hurrying forward through the straits; gradually contracting the wings of their semicircle, and swimming on, in one solid, but still crescentic[10] centre.

Crowding all sail the Pequod pressed after them; the harpooneers handling their weapons, and loudly cheering from the heads of their yet suspended

[10] crescent-like.

boats. If the wind only held, little doubt had they, that chased through these Straits of Sunda, the vast host would only deploy into the Oriental seas to witness the capture of not a few of their number. And who could tell whether, in that congregated caravan, Moby Dick himself might not temporarily be swimming, like the worshipped white-elephant in the coronation procession of the Siamese! So with stun-sail piled on stun-sail, we sailed along, driving these leviathans before us; when, of a sudden, the voice of Tashtego was heard, loudly directing attention to something in our wake.

Corresponding to the crescent in our van, we beheld another in our rear. It seemed formed of detached white vapors, rising and falling something like the spouts of the whales; only they did not so completely come and go; for they constantly hovered, without finally disappearing. Levelling his glass at this sight, Ahab quickly revolved in his pivot-hole, crying, "Aloft there, and rig whips and buckets to wet the sails; — Malays, sir, and after us!"

As if too long lurking behind the headlands, till the Pequod should fairly have entered the straits, these rascally Asiatics were now in hot pursuit, to make up for their over-cautious delay. But when the swift Pequod, with a fresh leading wind, was herself in hot chase; how very kind of these tawny philanthropists to assist in speeding her on to her own chosen pursuit, — mere riding-whips and rowels[11] to her, that they were. As with glass under arm, Ahab to-and-fro paced the deck; in his forward turn beholding the monsters he chased, and in the after one the bloodthirsty pirates chasing *him*; some such fancy as the above seemed his. And when he glanced upon the green walls of the watery defile in which the ship was then sailing, and bethought him that through that gate lay the route to his vengeance, and beheld, how that through that same gate he was now both chasing and being chased to his deadly end; and not only that, but a herd of remorseless wild pirates and in-human atheistical devils were infernally cheering him on with their curses; — when all these conceits had passed through his brain, Ahab's brow was left gaunt and ribbed, like the black sand beach after some stormy tide has been gnawing it, without being able to drag the firm thing from its place.

But thoughts like these troubled very few of the reckless crew; and when, after steadily dropping and dropping the pirates astern, the Pequod at last shot by the vivid green Cockatoo Point on the Sumatra side, emerging at last upon the broad waters beyond; then, the harpooneers seemed more to grieve that the swift whales had been gaining upon the ship, than to rejoice that the ship had so victoriously gained upon the Malays. But still driving on in the wake of the whales, at length they seemed abating their speed; gradually the ship neared them; and the wind now dying away, word was passed to spring to the boats. But no sooner did the herd, by some presumed wonderful instinct of the Sperm Whale, become notified of the three keels that were after them, — though as yet a mile in their rear, — than they rallied again, and forming in close ranks and battalions, so that their spouts all looked like flashing lines of stacked bayonets, moved on with redoubled velocity.

[11] spurs. [Feidelson]

Stripped to our shirts and drawers, we sprang to the white-ash,[12] and after several hours' pulling were almost disposed to renounce the chase, when a general pausing commotion among the whale gave animating token that they were now at last under the influence of that strange perplexity of inert irresolution, which, when the fishermen perceive it in the whale, they say he is gallied.* The compact martial columns in which they had been hitherto rapidly and steadily swimming, were now broken up in one measureless rout; and like King Porus' elephants in the Indian battle with Alexander,[13] they seemed going mad with consternation. In all directions expanding in vast irregular circles, and aimlessly swimming hither and thither, by their short thick spoutings, they plainly betrayed their distraction of panic. This was still more strangely evinced by those of their number, who, completely paralysed as it were, helplessly floated like water-logged dismantled ships on the sea. Had these leviathans been but a flock of simple sheep, pursued over the pasture by three fierce wolves, they could not possibly have evinced such excessive dismay. But this occasional timidity is characteristic of almost all herding creatures. Though banding together in tens of thousands, the lion-maned buffaloes of the West have fled before a solitary horseman. Witness, too, all human beings, how when herded together in the sheepfold of a theatre's pit, they will, at the slightest alarm of fire, rush helter-skelter for the outlets, crowding, trampling, jamming, and remorselessly dashing each other to death. Best, therefore, withhold any amazement at the strangely gallied whales before us, for there is no folly of the beasts of the earth which is not infinitely outdone by the madness of men.

Though many of the whales, as has been said, were in violent motion, yet it is to be observed that as a whole the herd neither advanced nor retreated, but collectively remained in one place. As is customary in those cases, the boats at once separated, each making for some one lone whale on the outskirts of the shoal. In about three minutes' time, Queequeg's harpoon was flung; the stricken fish darted blinding spray in our faces, and then running

---

* To *gally*, or *gallow*, is to frighten excessively, — to confound with fright. It is an old Saxon word. It occurs once in Shakespeare: —

> "The wrathful skies
> *Gallow* the very wanderers of the dark
> And make them keep their caves."
> *Lear*, Act iii, sc. ii

To common land usages, the word is now completely obsolete. When the polite landsman first hears it from the gaunt Nantucketer, he is apt to set it down as one of the whaleman's self-derived savageries. Much the same is it with many other sinewy Saxonisms of this sort, which emigrated to New England rocks with the noble brawn of the oldh English emigrants in the time of the Commonwealth. Thus, some of the best and furthest-descended English words — the etymological Howards and Percys[14] — are now democratised, plebeianised — so to speak — in the New World.[15] (Melville's note)

[12] oars of the whaleboat.
[13] Porus was defeated by Alexander the Great at the river Hydaspes in 327 B.C. [Feidelson]
[14] Aristocratic families of Britain. [Feidelson]
[15] This note appears only in the English first edition. [Feidelson]

away with us like light, steered straight for the heart of the herd. Though such a movement on the part of the whale struck under such circumstances, is in no wise unprecedented; and indeed is almost always more or less anticipated; yet does it present one of the more perilous vicissitudes of the fishery. For as the swift monster drags you deeper and deeper into the frantic shoal, you bid adieu to circumspect life and only exist in a delirious throb.

As, blind and deaf, the whale plunged forward, as if by sheer power of speed to rid himself of the iron leech that had fastened to him; as we thus tore a white gash in the sea, on all sides menaced as we flew, by the crazed creatures to and fro rushing about us; our beset boat was like a ship mobbed by ice-isles in a tempest, and striving to steer through their complicated channels and straits, knowing not at what moment it may be locked in and crushed.

But not a bit daunted, Queequeg[16] steered us manfully; now sheering off from this monster directly across our route in advance; now edging away from that, whose colossal flukes were suspended overhead, while all the time, Starbuck[17] stood up in the bows, lance in hand, pricking out of our way whatever whales he could reach by short darts, for there was no time to make long ones. Nor were the oarsmen quite idle, though their wonted duty was now altogether dispensed with. They chiefly attended to the shouting part of the business. "Out of the way, Commodore!" cried one, to a great dromedary[18] that of a sudden rose bodily to the surface, and for an instant threatened to swamp us. "Hard down with your tail, there!"[19] cried a second to another, which, close to our gunwale, seemed calmly cooling himself with his own fan-like extremity.

All whaleboats carry certain curious contrivances, originally invented by the Nantucket Indians, called druggs. Two thick squares of wood of equal size are stoutly clenched together, so that they cross each other's grain at right angles; a line of considerable length is then attached to the middle of this block, and the other end of the line being looped, it can in a moment be fastened to a harpoon. It is chiefly among gallied whales that this drugg is used. For then, more whales are close round you than you can possibly chase at one time. But sperm whales are not every day encountered; while you may, then, you must kill all you can. And if you cannot kill them all at once, you must wing them, so that they can be afterwards killed at your leisure. Hence it is, that at times like these the drugg comes into requisition. Our boat was furnished with three of them. The first and second were successfully darted, and we saw the whales staggeringly running off, fettered by the enormous sidelong resistance of the towing drugg. They were cramped like malefactors with the chain and ball. But upon flinging the third, in the act

---

[16] a Polynesian harpooner.
[17] first mate of the *Pequod*.
[18] referring to the whales' hump. [Feidelson]
[19] Turn yourself away from the wind, so as to get the wind behind you; in short, get out of our way. [Feidelson]

of tossing overboard the clumsy wooden block, it caught under one of the seats of the boat, and in an instant tore it out and carried it away, dropping the oarsman in the boat's bottom as the seat slid from under him. On both sides the sea came in at the wounded planks, but we stuffed two or three drawers and shirts in, and so stopped the leaks for the time.

It had been next to impossible to dart these drugged-harpoons, were it not that as we advanced into the herd, our whale's way greatly diminished; more-over, that as we went still further and further from the circumference of com-motion, the direful disorders seemed waning. So that when at last the jerking harpoon drew out, and the towing whale sideways vanished; then, with the tapering force of his parting momentum, we glided between two whales into the innermost heart of the shoal, as if from some mountain torrent we had slid into a serene valley lake. Here the storms in the roaring glens between the outermost whales, were heard but not felt. In this central expanse the sea presented that smooth satin-like surface, called a sleek, produced by the subtle moisture thrown off by the whale in his more quiet moods. Yes, we were now in that enchanted calm which they say lurks at the heart of every commotion. And still in the distracted distance we beheld the tumults of the outer concentric cirles, and saw successive pods[20] of whales, eight or ten in each, swiftly going round and round, like multiplied spans of horses in a ring; and so closely shoulder to shoulder, that a Titanic circus-rider might easily have overarched the middle ones, and so have gone round on their backs. Owing to the density of the crowd of reposing whales, more imme-diately surrounding the embayed axis of the herd, no possible chance of escape was at present afforded us. We must watch for a breach in the living wall that hemmed us in; the wall that had only admitted us in order to shut us up. Keeping at the centre of the lake, we were occasionally visited by small tame cows and calves; the women and children of this routed host.

Now, inclusive of the occasional wide intervals between the revolving outer circles, and inclusive of the spaces between the various pods in any one of those circles, the entire area at this juncture, embraced by the whole multi-tude, must have contained at least two or three square miles. At any rate — though indeed such a test at such a time might be deceptive — spoutings might be discovered from our low boat that seemed playing up almost from the rim of the horizon. I mention this circumstance, because, as if the cows and calves had been purposely locked up in this innermost fold; and as if the wide extent of the herd had hitherto prevented them from learning the pre-cise cause of its stopping; or, possibly, being so young, unsophisticated, and every way innocent and inexperienced; however it may have been, these smaller whales — now and then visting our becalmed boat from the margin of the lake — evinced a wondrous fearlessness and confidence, or else a still becharmed panic which it was impossible not to marvel at. Like household dogs they came snuffling round us, right up to our gunwales, and touching them; till it almost seemed that some spell had suddenly domesticated them.

---

[20] small herds or schools.

Queequeg patted their foreheads; Starbuck scratched their backs with his lance; but fearful of the consequences, for the time refrained from darting[21] it.

But far beneath this wondrous world upon the surface, another and still stranger world met our eyes as we gazed over the side. For, suspended in those watery vaults, floated the forms of the nursing mothers of the whales, and those that by their enormous girth seemed shortly to become mothers. The lake, as I have hinted, was to considerable depth exceedingly transparent; and as human infants while suckling will calmly and fixedly gaze away from the breast, as if leading two different lives at the time; and while yet drawing mortal nourishment, be still spiritually feasting upon some unearthly reminiscence; — even so did the young of these whales seem looking up towards us, but not at us, as if we were but a bit of Gulf-weed[22] in their new-born sight. Floating on their sides, the mothers also seemed quietly eyeing us. One of these little infants, that from certain queer tokens seemed hardly a day old, might have measured some fourteen feet in length, and some six feet in girth. He was a little frisky; though as yet his body seemed scarce yet recovered from that irksome position it had so lately occupied in the maternal reticule; where, tail to head, and all ready for the final spring, the unborn whale lies bent like a Tartar's bow. The delicate side-fins, and the palms of his flukes, still freshly retained the plaited crumpled appearance of a baby's ears newly arrived from foreign parts.

"Line! line!" cried Queequeg, looking over the gunwale; "him fast! him fast! — Who line him! Who struck? — Two whale; one big, one little!"

"What ails ye, man?" cried Starbuck.

"Look-e here," said Queequeg pointing down.

As when the stricken whale, that from the tub has reeled out hundreds of fathoms of rope; as, after deep sounding, he floats up again, and shows the slackened curling line buoyantly rising and spiralling towards the air; so now, Starbuck saw long coils of the umbilical cord of Madame Leviathan, by which the young cub seemed still tethered to its dam. Not seldom in the rapid vicissitudes of the chase, this natural line with the maternal end loose, becomes entangled with the hempen one, so that the cub is thereby trapped. Some of the subtlest secrets of the seas seemed divulged to us in this enchanted pond. We saw young Leviathan amours in the deep.*

* The sperm whale, as with all other species of the Leviathan, but unlike most other fish, breeds indifferently at all seasons; after a gestation which may probably be set down at nine months, producing but one at a time; though in some few known instances giving birth to an Esau and Jacob:[23] — a contingency provided for in suckling by two teats, curiously situated, one on each side of the anus; but the breasts themselves extend upwards from that. When by chance these precious parts in a nursing whale are cut by the hunter's lance, the mother's pouring milk and blood rivallingly discolor the sea for rods. The milk is very sweet and rich; it has been tasted by man; it might do well with strawberries. When overflowing with mutual esteem, the whales salute *more hominum*.[24] (Melville's note)

[21] initially wounding so as to incite.
[22] a branching seaweed with berrylike air vessels that keep it afloat. [Feidelson]
[23] twin sons of Isaac (*Genesis* 25:24–26). [Feidelson]
[24] in the manner of men. [Feidelson]

And thus, though surrounded by circle upon circle of consternations and affrights, did these inscrutable creatures at the centre freely and fearlessly indulge in all peaceful concernments; yea, serenely revelled in dalliance and delight. But even so, amid the tornadoed Atlantic of my being, do I myself still for ever centrally disport in mute calm; and while ponderous planets of unwaning woe revolve round me, deep down and deep inland there I still bathe me in eternal mildness of joy.

Meanwhile, as we thus lay entranced, the occasional sudden frantic spectacles in the distance evinced the activity of the other boats, still engaged in drugging the whales on the frontier of the host; or possibly carrying on the war within the first circle, where abundance of room and some convenient retreats were afforded them. But the sight of the enraged drugged whales now and then blindly darting to and fro across the circles, was nothing to what at last met our eyes. It is sometimes the custom when fast[25] to a whale more than commonly powerful and alert, to seek to hamstring him, as it were, by sundering or maiming his gigantic tail-tendon. It is done by darting a short-handled cutting-spade, to which is attached a rope for hauling it back again. A whale wounded (as we afterwards learned) in this part, but not effectually, as it seemed, had broken away from the boat, carrying along with him half of the harpoon line; and in the extraordinary agony of the wound, he was now dashing among the revolving circles like the lone mounted desperado Arnold, at the battle of Saratoga,[26] carrying dismay wherever he went.

But agonizing as was the wound of this whale, and an appalling spectacle enough, any way; yet the peculiar horror with which he seemed to inspire the rest of the herd, was owing to a cause which at first the intervening distance obscured from us. But at length we perceived that by one of the unimaginable accidents of the fishery, this whale had become entangled in the harpoon-line that he towed; he had also run away with the cutting-spade in him; and while the free end of the rope attached to that weapon, had permanently caught in the coils of the harpoon-line round his tail, the cutting-spade itself had worked loose from his flesh. So that tormented to madness, he was now churning through the water, violently flailing with his flexible tail, and tossing the keen spade about him, wounding and murdering his own comrades.

This terrific object seemed to recall the whole herd from their stationary fright. First, the whales forming the margin of our lake began to crowd a little, and tumble against each other, as if lifted by half spent billows from afar; then the lake itself began faintly to heave and swell; the submarine bridal-chambers and nurseries vanished; in more and more contracting orbits the whales in the more central circles began to swim in thickening clusters.

---

[25] fixed, joined.
[26] Benedict Arnold was officially without a command at the battle (October 7, 1777), but he appeared on the field mounted on a horse and galloped back and forth in the thick of the fight until, having collected some followers, he penetrated the British lines, had his horse shot from under him, and was himself wounded. [Feidelson]

Yes, the long calm was departing. A low advancing hum was soon heard; and then like to the tumultuous masses of block-ice when the great river Hudson breaks up in Spring, the entire host of whales came tumbling upon their inner centre, as if to pile themselves up in one common mountain. Instantly Starbuck and Queequeg changed places; Starbuck taking the stern.

"Oars! Oars!" he intensely whispered, seizing the helm — "gripe[27] your oars, and clutch your souls, now! My God, men, stand by! Shove him off, you Queequeg — the whale there! — prick him! — hit him! Stand up — stand up, and stay so! Spring, men — pull, men; never mind their backs — scrape them! — scrape away!"

The boat was now all but jammed between two vast black bulks, leaving a narrow Dardanelles[28] between their long lengths. But by desperate endeavor we at last shot into a temporary opening; then giving way rapidly, and at the same time earnestly watching for another outlet. After many similar hairbreadth escapes, we at last swiftly glided into what had just been one of the outer circles, but now crossed by random whales, all violently making for one centre. This lucky salvation was cheaply purchased by the loss of Queequeg's hat, who, while standing in the bows to prick the fugitive whales, had his hat taken clean from his head by the air-eddy made by the sudden tossing of a pair of broad flukes close by.

Riotous and disordered as the universal commotion now was, it soon resolved itself into what seemed a systematic movement; for having clumped together at last in one dense body, they then renewed their onward flight with augmented fleetness. Further pursuit was useless; but the boats still lingered in their wake to pick up what drugged whales might be dropped astern, and likewise to secure one which Flask had killed and waifed. The waif is a pennoned pole, two or three of which are carried by every boat; and which, when additional game is at hand, are inserted upright into the floating body of a dead whale, both to mark its place on the sea, and also as token of prior possession, should the boats of any other ship draw near.

The result of this lowering was somewhat illustrative of that sagacious saying in the Fishery, — the more whales the less fish. Of all the drugged whales, only one was captured. The rest contrived to escape for the time. . . .

---

[27] grip.
[28] strait between Europe and Asia Minor, connecting the Mediterranean to the Sea of Marmara. [Feidelson]

Emily Dickinson (1830–1886)

AMERICAN POET

I Taste a Liquor Never Brewed

I taste a liquor never brewed —
From Tankards scooped in Pearl —
Not all the Frankfort Berries
Yield such an Alcohol!

Inebriate of Air — am I —
And Debauchee of Dew —
Reeling — thro endless summer days —
From inns of Molten Blue —

When "Landlords" turn the drunken Bee
Out of the Foxgloves door —   10
When Butterflies — renounce their "drams" —
I shall but drink the more!

Till Seraphs swing their snowy Hats —
And Saints — to windows run —
To see the little Tippler
From Manzanilla[1] come!

Mark Twain (1835–1910)

AMERICAN NOVELIST

Huck's Island

The sun was up so high when I waked, that I judged it was after eight o'clock. I laid there in the grass and the cool shade, thinking about things and feeling rested and ruther comfortable and satisfied. I could see the sun

[1] a pale dry sherry produced in the Cadiz region of southern Spain; also, the name of a port in Trinidad, in the Caribbean.

out at one or two holes, but mostly it was big trees all about, and gloomy in there amongst them. There was freckled places on the ground where the light sifted down through the leaves, and the freckled places swapped about a little, showing there was a little breeze up there. A couple of squirrels set on a limb and jabbered at me very friendly.

I was powerful lazy and comfortable — didn't want to get up and cook breakfast. Well, I was dozing off again, when I thinks I hears a deep sound of "boom!" away up the river. I rouses up and rests on my elbow and listens; pretty soon I hears it again. I hopped up and went and looked out at a hole in the leaves, and I see a bunch of smoke laying on the water a long ways up — about abreast the ferry. And there was the ferry-boat full of people, floating along down. I knowed what was the matter, now. "Boom!" I see the white smoke squirt out of the ferry-boat's side. You see, they was firing cannon over the water, trying to make my carcass[1] come to the top.

I was pretty hungry, but it warn't going to do for me to start a fire, because they might see the smoke. So I set there and watched the cannon-smoke and listened to the boom. The river was a mile wide, there, and it always looks pretty on a summer morning — so I was having a good enough time seeing them hunt for my remainders, if I only had a bite to eat. Well, then I happened to think how they always put quicksilver in loaves of bread and float them off because they always go right to the drowned carcass and stop there. So says I, I'll keep a lookout, and if any of them's floating around after me, I'll give them a show. I changed to the Illinois edge of the island to see what luck I could have, and I warn't disappointed. A big double loaf come along, and I most got it, with a long stick, but my foot slipped and she floated out further. Of course I was where the current set in the closest to the shore — I knowed enough for that. But by-and-by along comes another one, and this time I won. I took out the plug and shook out the little dab of quicksilver, and set my teeth in. It was "baker's bread" — what the quality eat — none of your low-down corn-pone.

I got a good place amongst the leaves, and set there on a log, munching the bread and watching the ferry-boat, and very well satisfied. And then something struck me. I says, now I reckon the widow or the parson or somebody prayed that this bread would find me, and here it has gone and done it. So there ain't no doubt but there is something in that thing. That is, there's something in it when a body like the widow or the parson prays, but it don't work for me, and I reckon it don't work for only just the right kind.

I lit a pipe and had a good long smoke and went on watching. The ferry-boat was floating with the current, and I allowed I'd have a chance to see who was aboard when she come along, because she would come in close, where the bread did. When she'd got pretty well along down towards me, I put out my pipe and went to where I fished out the bread, and laid down behind a log on the bank in a little open place. Where the log forked I could peep through.

[1] Huck, who has run away from the confinements of society, is thought murdered.

By-and-by she come along, and she drifted in so close that they could a run out a plank and walked ashore. Most everybody was on the boat. Pap, and Judge Thatcher, and Bessie Thatcher, and Jo Harper, and Tom Sawyer, and his old Aunt Polly, and Sid and Mary, and plenty more. Everybody was talking about the murder, but the captain broke in and says:

"Look sharp, now; the current sets in the closest here, and maybe he's washed ashore and got tangled amongst the brush at the water's edge. I hope so, anyway."

I didn't hope so. They all crowded up and leaned over the rails, nearly in my face, and kept still, watching with all their might. I could see them first-rate, but they couldn't see me. Then the captain sung out:

"Stand away!" and the cannon let off such a blast right before me that it made me deef with the noise and pretty near blind with the smoke, and I judged I was gone. If they'd a had some bullets in, I reckon they'd a got the corpse they was after. Well, I see I warn't hurt, thanks to goodness. The boat floated on and went out of sight around the shoulder of the island. I could hear the booming, now and then, further and further off, and by-and-by after an hour, I didn't hear it no more. The island was three mile long. I judged they had got to the foot, and was giving it up. But they didn't yet a while. They turned around the foot of the island and started up the channel on the Missouri side, under steam, and booming once in a while as they went. I crossed over to that side and watched them. When they got abreast the head of the island they quit shooting and dropped over to the Missouri shore and went home to the town.

I knowed I was all right now. Nobody else would come a-hunting after me. I got my traps out of the canoe and made me a nice camp in the thick woods. I made a kind of a tent out of my blankets to put my things under so the rain couldn't get at them. I catched a catfish and haggled him open with my saw, and towards sundown I started my camp fire and had supper. Then I set out a line to catch some fish for breakfast.

When it was dark I set by my camp fire smoking, and feeling pretty satis-fied; but by-and-by it got sort of lonesome, and so I went and set on the bank and listened to the currents washing along, and counted the stars and drift-logs and rafts that come down, and then went to bed; there ain't no better way to put in time when you are lonesome; you can't stay so, you soon get over it.

And so for three days and nights. No difference — just the same thing. But the next day I went exploring around down through the island. I was boss of it; it all belonged to me, so to say, and I wanted to know all about it; but mainly I wanted to put in the time. I found plenty strawberries, ripe and prime; and green summer-grapes, and green razberries; and the green black-berries was just beginning to show. They would all come handy by-and-by, I judged.

Well, I went fooling along in the deep woods till I judged I warn't far from the foot of the island. I had my gun along, but I hadn't shot nothing;

it was for protection; thought I would kill some game nigh home. About this time I mighty near stepped on a good sized snake, and it went sliding off through the grass and flowers, and I after it, trying to get a shot at it. I clipped along, and all of a sudden I bounded right on to the ashes of a camp fire that was still smoking.

My heart jumped up amongst my lungs. I never waited for to look further, but uncocked my gun and went sneaking back on my tip-toes as fast as ever I could. Every now and then I stopped a second, amongst the thick leaves, and listened; but my breath come so hard I couldn't hear nothing else. I slunk along another piece further, then listened again; and so on, and so on; if I see a stump, I took it for a man; if I trod on a stick and broke it, it made me feel like a person had cut one of my breaths in two and I only got half, and the short half, too.

When I got to camp I warn't feeling very brash, there warn't much sand in my craw; but I says, this ain't no time to be fooling around. So I got all my traps into my canoe again so as to have them out of sight, and I put out the fire and scattered the ashes around to look like an old last year's camp, and then clumb a tree.

I reckon I was up in the tree two hours; but I didn't see nothing. I didn't hear nothing — I only *thought* I heard and seen as much as a thousand things. Well, I couldn't stay up there forever; so at last I got down, but I kept in the thick woods and on the lookout all the time. All I could get to eat was berries and what was left over from breakfast.

By the time it was night I was pretty hungry. So when it was good and dark, I slid out from shore before moonrise and paddled over to the Illinois bank — about a quarter of a mile. I went out in the woods and cooked a supper, and I had about made up my mind I would stay there all night, when I hear a *plunkety-plunk, plunkety-plunk*, and says to myself, horses coming; and next I hear people's voices. I got everything into the canoe as quick as I could, and then went creeping through the woods to see what I could find out. I hadn't got far when I hear a man say:

"We better camp here, if we can find a good place; the horses is about beat out. Let's look around."

I didn't wait, but shoved out and paddled away easy. I tied up in the old place, and reckoned I would sleep in the canoe.

I didn't sleep much. I couldn't, somehow, for thinking. And every time I waked up I thought somebody had me by the neck. So the sleep didn't do me no good. By-and-by I says to myself, I can't live this way; I'm agoing to find out who it is that's here on the island with me; I'll find it out or bust. Well, I felt better, right off.

So I took my paddle and slid out from shore just a step or two, and then let the canoe drop along down amongst the shadows. The moon was shining, and outside of the shadows it made it most as light as day. I poked along well onto an hour, everything still as rocks and sound asleep. Well by this time I was most down to the foot of the island. A little ripply, cool breeze begun to blow, and that was as good as saying the night was about done. I give her a turn with the paddle and brung her nose to shore; then I got my gun and slipped out and into the edge of the woods. I set down there on a log and looked out through the leaves. I see the moon go off watch and the darkness begin to blanket the river. But in a little while I see a pale streak over the tree-tops, and knowed the day was coming. So I took my gun and slipped off towards where I had run across that camp fire, stopping every minute or two to listen. But I hadn't no luck, somehow; I couldn't seem to find the place. But by-and-by, sure enough, I catched a glimpse of fire, away through the trees. I went for it, cautious and slow. By-and-by I was close enough to have a look, and there laid a man on the ground. It most give me the fan-tods.[2] He had a blanket around his head, and his head was nearly in the fire. I set there behind a clump of bushes, in about six foot of him, and kept my eyes on him steady. It was getting gray daylight, now. Pretty soon he gapped,[3] and stretched himself, and hove off the blanket, and it was Miss Watson's Jim! I bet I was glad to see him. I says:

"Hello, Jim!" and skipped out.

He bounced up and stared at me wild. Then he drops down on his knees, and puts his hands together and says:

"Doan' hurt me — don't! I hain't ever done no harm to a ghos'. I awluz liked dead people, en done all I could for 'em. You go en git in de river agin, whah you b'longs, en doan' do nuffn to Ole Jim, 'at 'uz awluz yo' fren'.'"

Well, I warn't long making him understand I warn't dead. I was ever so glad to see Jim. I warn't lonesome, now. I told him I warn't afraid of *him* telling the people where I was. I talked along, but he only set there and looked at me; never said nothing. Then I says:

"It's good daylight. Le's get breakfast. Make up your camp fire good."

"What's de use er makin' up de camp fire to cook strawbries en sich truck? But you got a gun, hain't you? Den we kin git sumfn better den strawbries."

"Strawberries and such truck," I says. "Is that what you live on?"

"I couldn' git nuffn else," he says.

"Why, how long you been on the island, Jim?"

"I come heah de night arter you's killed."

"What, all that time?"

"Yes-indeedy."

"And ain't you had nothing but that kind of rubbage to eat?"

"No, sah — nuffn else."

"Well, you must be most starved, ain't you?"

"I reck'n I could eat a hoss. I think I could. How long you ben on de islan'?"

"Since the night I got killed."

"No! W'y, what has you lived on? But you got a gun. Oh, yes, you got a gun. Dat's good. Now you kill sumfn en I'll make up de fire."

2 fidgets (colloquial).
3 yawned.

So we went over to where the canoe was, and while he built a fire in a grassy open place amongst the trees, I fetched meal and bacon and coffee, and coffee-pot and frying-pan, and sugar and tin cups, and the nigger was set back considerable, because he reckoned it was all done with witchcraft. I catched a good big cat-fish, too, and Jim cleaned him with his knife, and fried him.

When breakfast was ready, we lolled on the grass and eat it smoking hot. Jim laid it in with all his might, for he was most about starved. Then when we had got pretty well stuffed, we laid off and lazied. . . .

"How do you come to be here, Jim, and how'd you get here?"

He looked pretty uneasy, and didn't say nothing for a minute. Then he says:

"Maybe I better not tell."

"Why, Jim?"

"Well, dey's reasons. But you wouldn' tell on me ef I 'uz to tell you, would you, Huck?"

"Blamed if I would, Jim."

"Well, I b'lieve you, Huck. I — I *run off*."

"Jim!"

"But mind, you said you wouldn't tell — you know you said you wouldn't tell, Huck."

"Well, I did. I said I wouldn't, and I'll stick to it. Honest *injun* I will. People would call me a low down Abolitionist and despise me for keeping mum — but that don't make no difference. I ain't agoing to tell, and I ain't agoing back there anyways. So now, le's know all about it."

"Well, you see, it 'uz dis way. Ole Missus — dat's Miss Watson — she pecks on me all de time, en treats me pooty rough, but she awluz said she wouldn' sell me down to Orleans. But I noticed dey wuz a nigger trader roun' de place considable, lately, en I begin to git oneasy. Well, one night I creeps to de do', pooty late, en de do' warn't quite shet, en I hear ole missus tell de widder she gwyne to sell me down to Orleans, but she didn' want to, but she could git eight hund'd dollars for me, en it 'uz sich a big stack o' money she couldn' resis'. De widder she try to git her to say she wouldn' do it, but I never waited to hear de res'. I lit out mighty quick, I tell you.

"I tuck out en shin down de hill en 'spec to steal a skift 'long de sho' som'ers 'bove de town, but dey wuz people a-stirrin' yit, so I hid in de ole tumble-down cooper shop on de bank to wait for everybody to go 'way. Well, I wuz dah all night. Dey wuz somebody roun' all de time. 'Long 'bout six in de mawnin', skifts begin to go by, en 'bout eight er nine every skift dat went 'long wuz talkin' 'bout how yo' pap come over to de town en say you's killed. Dese las' skifts wuz full o' ladies en genlmen agoin' over for to see de place. Sometimes dey'd pull up at de sho' en take a res' b'fo' dey started acrost, so by de talk I got to know all 'bout de killin'. I 'uz powerful sorry you's killed, Huck, but I ain't no mo', now.

"I laid dah under de shavins all day. I 'uz hungry, but I warn't afeared; bekase I knowed ole missus en de widder wuz goin' to start to de camp-meetn' right arter breakfas' en be gone all day, en dey knows I goes off wid de cattle 'bout daylight, so dey wouldn' 'spec to see me roun' de place, en so dey wouldn' miss me tell arter dark in de evenin'. De yuther servants wouldn' miss me, kase dey'd shin out en take holiday, soon as de ole folks 'uz out'n de way.

"Well, when it come dark I tuck out up de river road, en went 'bout two miles er more to whah dey warn't no houses. I'd made up my mine 'bout what I's agwyne to do. You see ef I kep' on tryin' to git away afoot, de dogs 'ud track me; ef I stole a skift to cross over, dey'd miss dat skift, you see, en dey'd know 'bout whah I'd lan' on de yuther side en whah to pick up my track. So I says, a raff is what I's arter; it doan' *make* no track.

"I see a light a-comin' roun' de p'int, bymeby, so I wade' in en shove' a log ahead o' me, en swum more'n half-way acrost de river, en got in 'mongst de drift-wood, en kep' my head down low, en kinder swum agin de current tell de raff come along. Den I swum to de stern uv it, en tuck aholt. It clouded up en 'uz pooty dark for a little while. So I clumb up en laid down on de planks. De men 'uz all 'way yonder in de middle, whah de lantern wuz. De river wuz arisin' en dey wuz a good current; so I reck'n'd 'at by fo' in de mawnin' I'd be twenty-five mile down de river, en den I'd slip in, jis' b'fo' daylight, en swim asho' en take to de woods on de Illinoi side.[4]

"But I didn' have no luck. When we 'uz mos' down to de head er de islan', a man begin to come aft wid de lantern. I see it warn't no use fer to wait, so I slid overboad, en struck out fer de islan'. Well, I had a notion I could lan' mos' anywhers, but I couldn't — bank too bluff. I 'uz mos' to de foot er de islan' b'fo' I foun' a good place. I went into de woods en jedged I wouldn' fool wid raffs no mo' long as dey move de lantern roun' so. I had my pipe en a plug er dog-leg,[5] en some matches in my cap, en dey warn't wet, so I 'uz all right."

"And so you ain't had no meat nor bread to eat all this time? Why didn't you get mud-turkles?"

"How you gywne to git'm? You can't slip up on um en grab um; en how's a body gwyne to hit um wid a rock? How could a body do it in de night? en I warn't gwyne to show myself on de bank in de daytime."

"Well, that's so. You've had to keep in de woods all the time, of course. Did you hear 'em shooting the cannon?"

"Oh, yes. I knowed dey was arter you. I see um go by heah; watched um thoo de bushes."

Some young birds come along, flying a yard or two at a time and lighting. Jim said it was a sign it was going to rain. He said it was a sign when young chickens flew that way, and so he reckoned it was the same way when young birds done it. I was going to catch some of them, but Jim wouldn't let me.

---

[4] Illinois was legally free soil but was separated only by the Mississippi and Ohio Rivers from slave states. By state law, any Negro without freedom papers was subject to arrest and a system of indentured labor. Jim's most practical access to one of the northern states sympathetic to runaway slaves would be the Ohio River. [Eds.]

[5] a cheap tobacco. [Eds.]

He said it was death. He said his father laid mighty sick once, and some of them catched a bird, and his old granny said his father would die, and he did.

And Jim said you mustn't count the things you are going to cook for dinner, because that would bring bad luck. The same if you shook the table-cloth after sundown. And he said if a man owned a bee-hive, and that man died, the bees must be told about it before sun-up next morning, or else the bees would all weaken down and quit work and die. Jim said bees wouldn't sting idiots; but I didn't believe that, because I had tried them lots of times myself, and they wouldn't sting me.

I had heard about some of these things before, but not all of them. Jim knowed all kinds of signs. He said he knowed most everything. I said it looked to me like all the signs was about bad luck, and so I asked him if there warn't any good-luck signs. He says:

"Mighty few — an' *dey* ain' no use to a body. What you want to know when good luck's a-comin' for? want to keep it off?" And he said: "Ef you's got hairy arms en a hairy breas', it's a sign dat you's agwyne to be rich. Well, dey's some use in a sign like dat, 'kase it's so fur ahead. You see, maybe you's got to be po' a long time fust, en so you might git discourage' en kill yo'sef 'f you didn' know by de sign dat you gwyne to be rich bymeby."

"Have you got hairy arms and a hairy breast, Jim?"

"What's de use to ax dat question? don' you see I has?"

"Well, are you rich?"

"No, but I ben rich wunst, and gwyne to be rich agin. Wunst I had foteen dollars, but I tuck to specalat'n', en got busted out."

"What did you speculate in, Jim?"

"Well, fust I tackled stock."

"What kind of stock?"

"Why, live stock. Cattle, you know. I put ten dollars in a cow. But I ain't gwyne to resk no mo' money in stock. De cow up 'n' died on my han's."

"So you lost the ten dollars."

"No, I didn' lose it all. I on'y los' 'bout nine of it. I sole de hide en taller for a dollar en ten cents."

"You had five dollars and ten cents left. Did you speculate any more?"

"Yes. You know dat one-laigged nigger dat b'longs to old Misto Bradish? well, he sot up a bank, en say anybody dat put in a dollar would git fo' dollars mo' at de en' er de year. Well, all de niggers went in, but dey didn' have much. I wuz de on'y one dat had much. So I stuck out for mo' dan fo' dollars, en I said 'f I didn' git it I'd start a bank myself. Well o' course dat nigger want' to keep me out er de business, bekase he say dey warn't business 'nough for two banks, so he say I could put in my five dollars en he pay me thirty-five at de en' er de year.

"So I done it. Den I reck'n'd I'd inves' de thirty-five dollars right off en keep things a-movin'. Dey wuz a nigger name' Bob, dat had ketched a wood-flat,[6] en his marster didn' know it; en I bought it off'n him en told him to

---

[6] a flat-bottomed boat used for carrying timber. [Eds.]

take de thirty-five dollars when de en' er de year come; but somebody stole de wood-flat dat night, en nex' day de one-laigged nigger say de bank 's busted. So dey didn' none uv us git no money."

"What did you do with the ten cents, Jim?"

"Well, I 'uz gwyne to spen' it, but I had a dream, en de dream tole me to give it to a nigger name' Balum — Balum's Ass dey call him for short, he's one er dem chuckle-heads, you know. But hes lucky, dey say, en I see I warn't lucky. De dream say let Balum inves' de ten cents en he'd make a raise for me. Well, Balum he tuck de money, en when he wuz in church he hear de preacher say dat whoever give to de po' len' to de Lord, en boun' to git his money back a hund'd times. So Balum he tuck en give de ten cents to de po', en laid low to see what wuz gwyne to come of it."

"Well, what did come of it, Jim?"

"Nuffn' never come of it. I couldn' manage to k'leck dat money no way; en Balum he couldn'. I ain' gwyne to len' no mo' money 'dout I see de security. Boun' to git yo' money back a hund'd times, de preacher says! Ef I could git de ten *cents* back, I'd call it squah, en be glad er de chanst."

"Well, it's all right, anyway, Jim, long as you're going to be rich again some time or other."

"Yes — en I's rich now, come to look at it. I owns myself, en I's wuth eight hund'd dollars. I wisht I had de money, I wouldn' want no mo'."

₪

I wanted to go and look at a place right about the middle of the island, that I'd found when I was exploring; so we started, and soon got to it, because the island was only three miles long and a quarter of a mile wide.

This place was a tolerable long steep hill or ridge, about forty foot high. We had a rough time getting to the top, the sides was so steep and the bushes so thick. We tramped and clumb around all over it, and by-and-by found a good big cavern in the rock, most up to the top on the side towards Illinois. The cavern was as big as two or three rooms bunched together, and Jim could stand up straight in it. It was cool in there. Jim was for putting our traps in there, right away, but I said we didn't want to be climbing up and down there all the time.

Jim said if we had the canoe hid in a good place, and had all the traps in the cavern, we could rush there if anybody was to come to the island, and they would never find us without dogs. And besides, he said them little birds had said it was going to rain, and did I want the things to get wet?

So we went back and got the canoe and paddled up abreast the cavern, and lugged all the traps up there. Then we hunted up a place close by to hide the canoe in, amongst the thick willows. We took some fish off of the lines and set them again, and begun to get ready for dinner.

The door of the cavern was big enough to roll a hogshead in, and on one side of the door the floor stuck out a little bit and was flat and a good place to build a fire on. So we built it there and cooked dinner.

We spread the blankets inside for a carpet, and eat our dinner in there. We put all the other things handy at the back of the cavern. Pretty soon it darkened up and begun to thunder and lighten; so the birds was right about it. Directly it begun to rain, and it rained like all fury, too, and I never see the wind blow so. It was one of these regular summer storms. It would get so dark that it looked all blue-black outside, and lovely; and the rain would thrash along by so thick that the trees off a little ways looked dim and spider-webby; and here would come a blast of wind that would bend the trees down and turn up the pale underside of the leaves; and then a perfect ripper of a gust would follow along and set the branches to tossing their arms as if they was just wild; and next, when it was just about the bluest and blackest — *fst!* It was as bright as glory and you'd have a little glimpse of tree-tops a-plunging about, away off yonder in the storm, hundreds of yards further than you could see before; dark as sin again in a second, and now you'd hear the thunder let go with an awful crash and then go rumbling, grumbling, tumbling down the sky towards the under side of the world, like rolling empty barrels down stairs, where it's long stairs and they bounce a good deal, you know.

"Jim, this is nice," I says. "I wouldn't want to be nowhere else but here. Pass me along another hunk of fish and some hot cornbread."

"Well, you wouldn't a ben here, 'f it hadn't a ben for Jim. You'd a ben down dah in de woods widout any dinner, en gittn' mos' drownded, too, dat you would, honey. Chickens knows when its gwyne to rain, en so do de birds, chile. . . ."

Thomas Hardy (1840–1928)

ENGLISH NOVELIST, POET, and DRAMATIST

Egdon Heath

A Saturday afternoon in November was approaching the time of twilight, and the vast tract of unenclosed wild known as Egdon Heath embrowned itself moment by moment. Overhead the hollow stretch of whitish cloud shutting out the sky was as a tent which had the whole heath for its floor.

The heaven being spread with this pallid screen and the earth with the darkest vegetation, their meeting-line at the horizon was clearly marked. In such contrast the heath wore the appearance of an instalment of night which

Title supplied by editors. From *The Return of the Native* by Thomas Hardy (Wessex Edn.) in *The Works of Thomas Hardy in Prose and Verse*. Reprinted by permission of Harper & Row, Publishers, and Macmillan & Co. Ltd., London.

had taken up its place before its astronomical hour was come: darkness had
to a great extent arrived hereon, while day stood distinct in the sky. Looking
upwards, a furze-cutter would have been inclined to continue work; looking
down, he would have decided to finish his faggot and go home. The distant
rims of the world and of the firmament seemed to be a division in time no
less than a division in matter. The face of the heath by its mere complexion
added half an hour to evening; it could in like manner retard the dawn, sad-
den noon, anticipate the frowning of storms scarcely generated, and intensify
the opacity of a moonless midnight to a cause of shaking and dread.

In fact, precisely at this transitional point of its nightly roll into darkness
the great and particular glory of the Egdon waste began, and nobody could
be said to understand the heath who had not been there at such a time. It
could best be felt when it could not clearly be seen, its complete effect and
explanation lying in this and the succeeding hours before the next dawn:
then, and only then, did it tell its true tale. The spot was, indeed, a near
relation of night, and when night showed itself an apparent tendency to
gravitate together could be perceived in its shades and the scene. The sombre
stretch of rounds and hollows seemed to rise and meet the evening gloom in
pure sympathy, the heath exhaling darkness as rapidly as the heavens precipitated it. And so the obscurity in the air and the obscurity in the land
closed together in a black fraternization towards which each advanced half-
way.

The place became full of a watchful intentness now; for when other things
sank brooding to sleep the heath appeared slowly to awake and listen. Every
night its Titanic form seemed to await something; but it had waited thus,
unmoved, during so many centuries, through the crises of so many things,
that it could only be imagined to await one last crisis — the final overthrow.

It was a spot which returned upon the memory of those who loved it with
an aspect of peculiar and kindly congruity. Smiling champaigns of flowers
and fruit hardly do this, for they are permanently harmonious only with an
existence of better reputation as to its issues than the present. Twilight combined with the scenery of Egdon Heath to evolve a thing majestic without
severity, impressive without showiness, emphatic in its admonitions, grand in
its simplicity. The qualifications which frequently invest the façade of a
prison with far more dignity than is found in the façade of a palace double
its size lent to this heath a sublimity in which spots renowned for beauty
of the accepted kind are utterly wanting. Fair prospects wed happily with
fair times; but alas, if times be not fair! Men have oftener suffered from the
mockery of a place too smiling for their reason than from the oppression of
surroundings oversadly tinged. Haggard Egdon appealed to a subtler and
scarcer instinct, to a more recently learnt emotion, than that which responds
to the sort of beauty called charming and fair.

Indeed, it is a question if the exclusive reign of this orthodox beauty is
not approaching its last quarter. The new Vale of Tempe[1] may be a gaunt

[1] valley between Mounts Olympus and Ossa in Greece; sacred to Apollo.

waste in Thule[2]: human souls may find themselves in closer and closer harmony with external things wearing a sombreness distasteful to our race when it was young. The time seems near, if it has not actually arrived, when the chastened sublimity of a moor, a sea, or a mountain will be all of nature that is absolutely in keeping with the moods of the more thinking among mankind. And ultimately, to the commonest tourist, spots like Iceland may become what the vineyards and myrtle-gardens of South Europe are to him now; and Heidelberg and Baden be passed unheeded as he hastens from the Alps to the sand-dunes of Scheveningen.[3]

The most thorough-going ascetic could feel that he had a natural right to wander on Egdon: he was keeping within the line of legitimate indulgence when he laid himself open to influences such as these. Colours and beauties so far subdued were, at least, the birthright of all. Only in summer days of highest feather did its mood touch the level of gaiety. Intensity was more usually reached by way of the solemn than by way of the brilliant, and such a sort of intensity was often arrived at during winter darkness, tempests, and mists. Then Egdon was aroused to reciprocity; for the storm was its lover, and the wind its friend. Then it became the home of strange phantoms; and it was found to be the hitherto unrecognized original of those wild regions of obscurity which are vaguely felt to be compassing us about in midnight dreams of flight and disaster, and are never thought of after the dream till revived by scenes like this.

It was at present a place perfectly accordant with man's nature — neither ghastly, hateful, nor ugly: neither commonplace, unmeaning, nor tame; but, like man, slighted and enduring; and withal singularly colossal and mysterious in its swarthy monotony. As with some persons who have long lived apart, solitude seemed to look out of its countenance. It had a lonely face, suggesting tragical possibilities.

This obscure, obsolete, superseded country figures in Domesday. Its condition is recorded therein as that of heathy, furzy, briary wilderness — 'Bruaria.' Then follows the length and breadth in leagues; and, though some uncertainty exists as to the exact extent of this ancient lineal measure, it appears from the figures that the area of Egdon down to the present day has but little diminished. 'Turbaria Bruaria' — the right of cutting heath-turf — occurs in charters relating to the district. 'Overgrown with heth and mosse,' says Leland of the same dark sweep of country.

Here at least were intelligible facts regarding landscape — far-reaching proofs productive of genuine satisfaction. The untameable, Ishmaelitish[4] thing that Egdon now was it always had been. Civilization was its enemy; and ever since the beginning of vegetation its soil had worn the same antique brown dress, the natural and invariable garment of the particular formation. In its venerable one coat lay a certain vein of satire on human vanity in clothes. A person on a heath in raiment of modern cut and colours has more

[2] ancient Greek and Latin name for the most northerly region of the world.
[3] in the Netherlands.
[4] wild, outcast.

or less an anomalous look. We seem to want the oldest and simplest human clothing where the clothing of the earth is so primitive.

To recline on a stump of thorn in the central valley of Egdon, between afternoon and night, as now, where the eye could reach nothing of the world outside the summits and shoulders of heathland which filled the whole circumference of its glance, and to know that everything around and underneath had been from prehistoric times as unaltered as the stars overhead, gave ballast to the mind adrift on change, and harrassed by the irrespressible New. The great inviolate place had an ancient permanence which the sea cannot claim. Who can say of a particular sea that it is old? Distilled by the sun, kneaded by the moon, it is renewed in a year, in a day, or in an hour. The sea changed, the fields changed, the rivers, the villages, and the people changed, yet Egdon remained.

Gerard Manley Hopkins   (1844–1889)

ENGLISH POET and CLERGYMAN

Pied Beauty

Glory be to God for dappled things —
    For skies of couple-colour as a brinded cow;
      For rose-moles all in stipple upon trout that swim;
Fresh-firecoal chestnut-falls; finches' wings;
    Landscape plotted and pieced — fold, fallow, and plough;
      And áll trádes, their gear and tackle and trim.

All things counter, original, spare, strange;
    Whatever is fickle, freckled (who knows how?)
      With swift, slow; sweet, sour; adazzle, dim;
He fathers-forth whose beauty is past change: 10
                Praise him.

The Windhover:

TO CHRIST OUR LORD

I caught this morning morning's minion, king-
    dom of daylight's dauphin, dapple-dawn-drawn Falcon, in
        his riding
Of the rolling level underneath him steady air, and striding
High there, how he rung upon the rein of a wimpling wing
In his ecstasy! then off, off forth on swing,
    As a skate's heel sweeps smooth on a bow-bend: the hurl and
        gliding
Rebuffed the big wind. My heart in hiding
Stirred for a bird, — the achieve of, the mastery of the thing!

Brute beauty and valour and act, oh, air, pride, plume, here
    Buckle! AND the fire that breaks from thee then, a billion   10
Times told lovelier, more dangerous, O my chevalier!

No wonder of it: shéer plód makes plough down sillion[1]
Shine, and blue-bleak embers, ah my dear,
    Fall, gall themselves, and gash gold-vermilion.

Guy de Maupassant (1850–1893)

FRENCH SHORT STORY WRITER and NOVELIST

Love

THREE PAGES FROM A SPORTSMAN'S BOOK

I have just read among the general news in one of the papers a drama of passion. He killed her and then he killed himself, so he must have loved her. What matters He or She? Their love alone matters to me; and it does

---

[1] furrow in plowed land.

"The Windhover" by Gerard Manley Hopkins. From *Poems of Gerard Manley Hopkins,* Third Edition, edited by W. H. Gardner. Copyright 1948 by Oxford University Press, Inc. Reprinted by permission.

"Love: Three Pages from a Sportsman's Book" by Guy de Maupassant. From *The Complete Short Stories of Guy de Maupassant.*

not interest me because it moves me or astonishes me, or because it softens me or makes me think, but because it recalls to my mind a remembrance of my youth, a strange recollection of a hunting adventure where Love appeared to me, as the Cross appeared to the early Christians, in the midst of the heavens.

I was born with all the instincts and the senses of primitive man, tempered by the arguments and the restraints of a civilized being. I am passionately fond of shooting, yet the sight of the wounded animal, of the blood on its feathers and on my hands, affects my heart so as almost to make it stop.

That year the cold weather set in suddenly toward the end of autumn, and I was invited by one of my cousins, Karl de Rauville, to go with him and shoot ducks on the marshes, at daybreak.

My cousin was a jolly fellow of forty, with red hair, very stout and bearded, a country gentleman, an amiable semi-brute, of a happy disposition and endowed with that Gallic wit which makes even mediocrity agreeable. He lived in a house, half farm-house, half château, situated in a broad valley through which a river ran. The hills right and left were covered with woods, old manorial woods where magnificent trees still remained, and where the rarest feathered game in that part of France was to be found. Eagles were shot there occasionally, and birds of passage, such as rarely venture into our over-populated part of the country, invariably lighted amid these giant oaks, as if they knew or recognized some little corner of a primeval forest which had remained there to serve them as a shelter during their short nocturnal halt.

In the valley there were large meadows watered by trenches and separated by hedges; then, further on, the river, which up to that point had been kept between banks, expanded into a vast marsh. That marsh was the best shooting ground I ever saw. It was my cousin's chief care, and he kept it as a preserve. Through the rushes that covered it, and made it rustling and rough, narrow passages had been cut, through which the flat-bottomed boats, impelled and steered by poles, passed along silently over dead water, brushing up against the reeds and making the swift fish take refuge in the weeds, and the wild fowl, with their pointed, black heads, dive suddenly.

I am passionately fond of the water: of the sea, though it is too vast, too full of movement, impossible to hold; of the rivers which are so beautiful, but which pass on, and flee away; and above all of the marshes, where the whole unknown existence of aquatic animals palpitates. The marsh is an entire world in itself on the world of earth — a different world, which has its own life, its settled inhabitants and its passing travelers, its voices, its noises, and above all its mystery. Nothing is more impressive, nothing more disquieting, more terrifying occasionally, than a fen. Why should a vague terror hang over these low plains covered with water? Is it the low rustling of the rushes, the strange will-o'-the-wisp lights, the silence which prevails on calm nights, the still mists which hang over the surface like a shroud; or is it the almost inaudible splashing, so slight and so gentle, yet sometimes more terrifying than the cannons of men or the thunders of the skies, which make these marshes resemble countries one has dreamed of, terrible countries holding an unknown and dangerous secret?

No, something else belongs to it — another mystery, perhaps the mystery of the creation itself! For was it not in stagnant and muddy water, amid the heavy humidity of moist land under the heat of the sun, that the first germ of life pulsated and expanded to the day?

I arrived at my cousin's in the evening. It was freezing hard enough to split the stones.

During dinner, in the large room whose sideboards, walls, and ceiling were covered with stuffed birds, with wings extended or perched on branches to which they were nailed, — hawks, herons, owls, nightjars, buzzards, tiercels, vultures, falcons, — my cousin who, dressed in a sealskin jacket, himself resembled some strange animal from a cold country, told me what preparations he had made for that same night.

We were to start at half past three in the morning, so as to arrive at the place which he had chosen for our watching-place at about half past four. On that spot a hut had been built of lumps of ice, so as to shelter us somewhat from the trying wind which precedes daybreak, a wind so cold as to tear the flesh like a saw, cut it like the blade of a knife, prick it like a poisoned sting, twist it like a pair of pincers, and burn it like fire.

My cousin rubbed his hands: "I have never known such a frost," he said; "it is already twelve degrees below zero at six o'clock in the evening."

I threw myself on to my bed immediately after we had finished our meal, and went to sleep by the light of a bright fire burning in the grate.

At three o'clock he woke me. In my turn, I put on a sheepskin, and found my cousin Karl covered with a bearskin. After having each swallowed two cups of scalding coffee, followed by glasses of liqueur brandy, we started, accompanied by a gamekeeper and our dogs, Plongeon and Pierrot.

From the first moment that I got outside, I felt chilled to the very marrow. It was one of those nights on which the earth seems dead with cold. The frozen air becomes resisting and palpable, such pain does it cause; no breath of wind moves it, it is fixed and motionless; it bites you, pierces through you, dries you, kills the trees, the plants, the insects, the small birds themselves, who fall from the branches on to the hard ground, and become stiff themselves under the grip of the cold.

The moon, which was in her last quarter and was inclining all to one side, seemed fainting in the midst of space, so weak that she was unable to wane, forced to stay up yonder, seized and paralyzed by the severity of the weather. She shed a cold, mournful light over the world, that dying and wan light which she gives us every month, at the end of her period.

Karl and I walked side by side, our backs bent, our hands in our pockets and our guns under our arms. Our boots, which were wrapped in wool so that we might be able to walk without slipping on the frozen river, made no sound, and I looked at the white vapor which our dogs' breath made.

We were soon on the edge of the marsh, and entered one of the lanes of dry rushes which ran through the low forest.

Our elbows, which touched the long, ribbonlike leaves, left a slight noise behind us, and I was seized, as I had never been before, by the powerful and singular emotion which marshes cause in me. This one was dead, dead from cold, since we were walking on it, in the middle of its population of dried rushes.

Suddenly, at the turn of one of the lanes, I perceived the ice-hut which had been constructed to shelter us. I went in, and as we had nearly an hour to wait before the wandering birds would awake, I rolled myself up in my rug in order to try and get warm. Then, lying on my back, I began to look at the misshapen moon, which had four horns through the vaguely transparent walls of this polar house. But the frost of the frozen marshes, the cold of these walls, the cold from the firmament penetrated me so terribly that I began to cough. My cousin Karl became uneasy.

"No matter if we do not kill much today," he said: "I do not want you to catch cold; we will light a fire." And he told the gamekeeper to cut some rushes.

We made a pile in the middle of our hut which had a hole in the middle of the roof to let out the smoke, and when the red flames rose up to the clear, crystal blocks they began to melt, gently, imperceptibly, as if they were sweating. Karl, who had remained outside, called out to me: "Come and look here!" I went out of the hut and remained struck with astonishment. Our hut, in the shape of a cone, looked like an enormous diamond with a heart of fire, which had been suddenly planted there in the midst of the frozen water of the marsh. And inside, we saw two fantastic forms, those of our dogs, who were warming themselves at the fire.

But a peculiar cry, a lost, a wandering cry, passed over our heads, and the light from our hearth showed us the wild birds. Nothing moves one so much as the first clamor of a life which one does not see, which passes through the somber air so quickly and so far off, just before the first streak of a winter's day appears on the horizon. It seems to me, at this glacial hour of dawn, as if that passing cry which is carried away by the wings of a bird is the sigh of a soul from the world!

"Put out the fire," said Karl, "it is getting daylight."

The sky was, in fact, beginning to grow pale, and the flights of ducks made long, rapid streaks which were soon obliterated on the sky.

A stream of light burst out into the night; Karl had fired, and the two dogs ran forward.

And then, nearly every minute, now he, now I, aimed rapidly as soon as the shadow of a flying flock appeared above the rushes. And Pierrot and Plongeon, out of breath but happy, retrieved the bleeding birds, whose eyes still, occasionally, looked at us.

The sun had risen, and it was a bright day with a blue sky, and we were thinking of taking our departure, when two birds with extended necks and outstretched wings, glided rapidly over our heads. I fired, and one of them fell almost at my feet. It was a teal, with a silver breast, and then, in the blue space above me, I heard a voice, the voice of a bird. It was a short, repeated, heart-rending lament; and the bird, the little animal that had been spared began to turn round in the blue sky, over our heads, looking at its dead companion which I was holding in my hand.

Karl was on his knees, his gun to his shoulder watching it eagerly, until it should be within shot. "You have killed the duck," he said, "and the drake will not fly away."

He certainly did not fly away; he circled over our heads continually, and continued his cries. Never have any groans of suffering pained me so much as that desolate appeal, as that lamentable reproach of this poor bird which was lost in space.

Occasionally he took flight under the menace of the gun which followed his movements, and seemed ready to continue his flight alone, but as he could not make up his mind to this, he returned to find his mate.

"Leave her on the ground," Karl said to me, "he will come within shot by and by." And he did indeed come near us, careless of danger, infatuated by his animal love, by his affection for his mate, which I had just killed.

Karl fired, and it was as if somebody had cut the string which held the bird suspended. I saw something black descend, and I heard the noise of a fall among the rushes. And Pierrot brought it to me.

I put them — they were already cold — into the same game-bag, and I returned to Paris the same evening.

Stephen Crane (1870–1900)

AMERICAN SHORT STORY WRITER, NOVELIST, and JOURNALIST

The Open Boat

A TALE INTENDED TO BE AFTER THE FACT: BEING
THE EXPERIENCE OF FOUR MEN FROM THE
SUNK STEAMER *Commodore*

I

None of them knew the color of the sky. Their eyes glanced level, and were fastened upon the waves that swept toward them. These waves were of the hue of slate, save for the tops, which were of foaming white, and all

From *Stephen Crane: An Omnibus,* edited by Robert Wooster, published 1930, 1950 by Alfred A. Knopf, Inc. Reprinted courtesy of the publisher.

of the men knew the colors of the sea. The horizon narrowed and widened, and dipped and rose, and at all times its edge was jagged with waves that seemed thrust up in points like rocks.

Many a man ought to have a bathtub larger than the boat which here rode upon the sea. These waves were most wrongfully and barbarously abrupt and tall, and each froth-top was a problem in small-boat navigation.

The cook squatted in the bottom, and looked with both eyes at the six inches of gunwale which separated him from the ocean. His sleeves were rolled over his fat forearms, and the two flaps of his unbuttoned vest dangled as he bent to bail out the boat. Often he said, "Gawd! that was a narrow clip." As he remarked it he invariably gazed eastward over the broken sea.

The oiler, steering with one of the two oars in the boat, sometimes raised himself suddenly to keep clear of water that swirled in over the stern. It was a thin little oar, and it seemed often ready to snap.

The correspondent, pulling at the other oar, watched the waves and wondered why he was there.

The injured captain, lying in the bow, was at this time buried in that profound dejection and indifference which comes, temporarily at least, to even the bravest and most enduring when, willy-nilly, the firm fails, the army loses, the ship goes down. The mind of the master of a vessel is rooted deep in the timbers of her, though he command for a day or a decade; and this captain had on him the stern impression of a scene in the grays of dawn of seven turned faces, and later a stump of a topmast with a white ball on it, that slashed to and fro at the waves, went low and lower, and down. Thereafter there was something strange in his voice. Although steady, it was deep with mourning, and of a quality beyond oration or tears.

"Keep'er a little more south, Billie," said he.

"A little more south, sir," said the oiler in the stern.

A seat in this boat was not unlike a seat upon a bucking broncho, and by the same token a broncho is not much smaller. The craft pranced and reared and plunged like an animal. As each wave came, and she rose for it, she seemed like a horse making at a fence outrageously high. The manner of her scramble over these walls of water is a mystic thing, and, moreover, at the top of them were ordinarily these problems in white water, the foam racing down from the summit of each wave requiring a new leap, and a leap from the air. Then, after scornfully bumping a crest, she would slide and race and splash down a long incline, and arrive bobbing and nodding in front of the next menace.

A singular disadvantage of the sea lies in the fact that after successfully surmounting one wave you discover that there is another behind it just as important and just as nervously anxious to do something effective in the way of swamping boats. In a ten-foot dinghy one can get an idea of the resources of the sea in the line of waves that is not probable to the average experience, which is never at sea in a dinghy. As each slaty wall of water approached, it shut all else from the view of the men in the boat, and it was not difficult to imagine that this particular wave was the final outburst of the ocean, and the last effort of the grim water. There was a terrible grace in the move of the waves, and they came in silence, save for the snarling of the crests.

In the wan light the faces of the men must have been gray. Their eyes must have glinted in strange ways as they gazed steadily astern. Viewed from a balcony, the whole thing would doubtless have been weirdly picturesque. But the men in the boat had no time to see it, and if they had had leisure, there were other things to occupy their minds. The sun swung steadily up the sky, and they knew it was broad day because the color of the sea changed from slate to emerald-green streaked with amber lights, and the foam was like tumbling snow. The process of the breaking day was unknown to them. They were aware only of this effect upon the color of the waves that rolled toward them.

In disjointed sentences the cook and the correspondent argued as to the difference between a life-saving station and a house of refuge. The cook had said: "There's a house of refuge just north of the Mosquito Inlet Light, and as soon as they see us they'll come off in their boat and pick us up."

"As soon as who see us?" said the correspondent.

"The crew," said the cook.

"Houses of refuge don't have crews," said the correspondent. "As I understand them, they are only places where clothes and grub are stored for the benefit of shipwrecked people. They don't carry crews."

"Oh, yes, they do," said the cook.

"No, they don't," said the correspondent.

"Well, we're not there yet, anyhow," said the oiler, in the stern.

"Well," said the cook, "perhaps it's not a house of refuge that I'm thinking of as being near Mosquito Inlet Light; perhaps it's a lifesaving station."

"We're not there yet," said the oiler in the stern.

II

As the boat bounced from the top of each wave the wind tore through the hair of the hatless men, and as the craft plopped her stern down again the spray slashed past them. The crest of each of these waves was a hill, from the top of which the men surveyed for a moment a broad tumultuous expanse, shining and wind-riven. It was probably splendid, it was probably glorious, this play of the free sea, wild with lights of emerald and white and amber.

"Bully good thing it's an onshore wind," said the cook. "If not, where would we be? Wouldn't have a show."

"That's right," said the correspondent.

The busy oiler nodded his assent.

Then the captain, in the bow, chuckled in a way that expressed humor, contempt, tragedy, all in one. "Do you think we've got much of a show now, boys?" said he.

Whereupon the three were silent, save for a trifle of hemming and hawing.

To express any particular optimism at this time they felt to be childish and stupid, but they all doubtless possessed this sense of the situation in their minds. A young man thinks doggedly at such times. On the other hand, the ethics of their condition was decidedly against any open suggestion of hopelessness. So they were silent.

"Oh, well," said the captain, soothing his children, "we'll get ashore all right."

But there was that in his tone which made them think; so the oiler quoth, "Yes! if this wind holds."

The cook was bailing. "Yes! if we don't catch hell in the surf."

Canton-flannel gulls flew near and far. Sometimes they sat down on the sea, near patches of brown seaweed that rolled over the waves with a movement like carpets on a line in a gale. The birds sat comfortably in groups, and they were envied by some in the dinghy, for the wrath of the sea was no more to them than it was to a covey of prairie chickens a thousand miles inland. Often they came very close and stared at the men with black bead-like eyes. At these times they were uncanny and sinister in their unblinking scrutiny, and the men hooted angrily at them, telling them to be gone. One came, and evidently decided to alight on the top of the captain's head. The bird flew parallel to the boat and did not circle, but made short sidelong jumps in the air in chicken fashion. His black eyes were wistfully fixed upon the captain's head. "Ugly brute," said the oiler to the bird. "You look as if you were made with a jackknife." The cook and the correspondent swore darkly at the creature. The captain naturally wished to knock it away with the end of the heavy painter, but he did not dare do it, because anything resembling an emphatic gesture would have capsized this freighted boat; and so, with his open hand, the captain gently and carefully waved the gull away. After it had been discouraged from the pursuit the captain breathed easier on account of his hair, and others breathed easier because the bird struck their minds at this time as being somehow gruesome and ominous.

In the meantime the oiler and the correspondent rowed. And also they rowed. They sat together in the same seat, and each rowed an oar. Then the oiler took both oars; then the correspondent took both oars; then the oiler; then the correspondent. They rowed and they rowed. The very ticklish part of the business was when the time came for the reclining one in the stern to take his turn at the oars. By the very last star of truth, it is easier to steal eggs from under a hen than it was to change seats in the dinghy. First the man in the stern slid his hand along the thwart and moved with care, as if he were of Sèvres.[1] Then the man in the rowing-seat slid his hand along the other thwart. It was all done with the most extraordinary care. As the two sidled past each other, the whole party kept watchful eyes on the coming wave, and the captain cried: "Look out, now! Steady, there!"

The brown mats of seaweed that appeared from time to time were like islands, bits of earth. They were traveling, apparently, neither one way nor

---

[1] alluding to fine, delicate porcelain made in Sèvres, France.

the other. They were, to all intents, stationary. They informed the men in the boat that it was making progress slowly toward the land.

The captain, rearing cautiously in the bow after the dinghy soared on a great swell, said that he had seen the lighthouse at Mosquito Inlet. Presently the cook remarked that he had seen it. The correspondent was at the oars then, and for some reason he too wished to look at the lighthouse; but his back was toward the far shore, and the waves were important, and for some time he could not seize an opportunity to turn his head. But at last there came a wave more gentle than the others, and when at the crest of it he swiftly scoured the western horizon.

"See it?" said the captain.

"No," said the correspondent, slowly; "I didn't see anything."

"Look again," said the captain. He pointed. "It's exactly in that direction."

At the top of another wave the correspondent did as he was bid, and this time his eyes chanced on a small, still thing on the edge of the swaying horizon. It was precisely like the point of a pin. It took an anxious eye to find a lighthouse so tiny.

"Think we'll make it, Captain?"

"If this wind holds and the boat don't swamp, we can't do much else," said the captain.

The little boat, lifted by each towering sea and splashed viciously by the crests, made progress that in the absence of seaweed was not apparent to those in her. She seemed just a wee thing wallowing, miraculously top up, at the mercy of five oceans. Occasionally a great spread of water, like white flames, swarmed into her.

"Bail her, cook," said the captain, serenely.

"All right, Captain," said the cheerful cook.

III

It would be difficult to describe the subtle brotherhood of men that was here established on the seas. No one said that it was so. No one mentioned it. But it dwelt in the boat, and each man felt it warm him. They were a captain, an oiler, a cook, and a correspondent, and they were friends — friends in a more curiously ironbound degree than may be common. The hurt captain, lying against the water jar in the bow, spoke always in a low voice and calmly; but he could never command a more ready and swiftly obedient crew than the motley three of the dinghy. It was more than a mere recognition of what was best for the common safety. There was surely in it a quality that was personal and heartfelt. And after this devotion to the commander of the boat, there was this comradeship, that the correspondent, for instance, who had been taught to be cynical of men, knew even at the time was the best experience of his life. But no one said that it was so. No one mentioned it.

"I wish we had a sail," remarked the captain. "We might try my overcoat on the end of an oar, and give you two boys a chance to rest." So the cook and the correspondent held the mast and spread wide the overcoat; the oiler steered; and the little boat made good way with her new rig. Sometimes the oiler had to scull sharply to keep a sea from breaking into the boat, but otherwise sailing was a success.

Meanwhile the lighthouse had been growing slowly larger. It had now almost assumed color, and appeared like a little gray shadow on the sky. The man at the oars could not be prevented from turning his head rather often to try for a glimpse of this little gray shadow.

At last, from the top of each wave, the men in the tossing boat could see land. Even as the lighthouse was an upright shadow on the sky, this land seemed but a long black shadow on the sea. It certainly was thinner than paper. "We must be about opposite New Smyrna," said the cook, who had coasted this shore often in schooners. "Captain, by the way, I believe they abandoned that lifesaving station there about a year ago."

"Did they?" said the captain.

The wind slowly died away. The cook and the correspondent were not now obliged to slave in order to hold high the oar. But the waves continued their old impetuous swooping at the dinghy, and the little craft, no longer under way, struggled woundily over them. The oiler or the correspondent took the oars again.

Shipwrecks are *apropos* of nothing. If men could only train for them and have them occur when the men had reached pink condition, there would be less drowning at sea. Of the four in the dinghy none had slept any time worth mentioning for two days and two nights previous to embarking in the dinghy, and in the excitement of clambering about the deck of a foundering ship they had also forgotten to eat heartily.

For these reasons, and for others, neither the oiler nor the correspondent was fond of rowing at this time. The correspondent wondered ingenuously how in the name of all that was sane could there be people who thought it amusing to row a boat. It was not an amusement; it was a diabolical punishment, and even a genius of mental aberrations could never conclude that it was anything but a horror to the muscles and a crime against the back. He mentioned to the boat in general how the amusement of rowing struck him, and the weary-faced oiler smiled in full sympathy. Previously to the foundering, by the way, the oiler had worked a double watch in the engine room of the ship.

"Take her easy now, boys," said the captain. "Don't spend yourselves. If we have to run a surf you'll need all your strength, because we'll sure have to swim for it. Take your time."

Slowly the land arose from the sea. From a black line it became a line of black and a line of white — trees and sand. Finally the captain said that he could make out a house on the shore. "That's the house of refuge, sure," said the cook. "They'll see us before long, and come out after us."

The distant lighthouse reared high. "The keeper ought to be able to make us out now, if he's looking through a glass," said the captain. "He'll notify the lifesaving people."

"None of those other boats could have got ashore to give word of this wreck," said the oiler, in a low voice, "else the lifeboat would be out hunting us."

Slowly and beautifully the land loomed out of the sea. The wind came again. It had veered from the northeast to the southeast. Finally a new sound struck the ears of the men in the boat. It was the low thunder of the surf on the shore. "We'll never be able to make the lighthouse now," said the captain. "Swing her head a little more north, Billie."

"A little more north, sir," said the oiler.

Whereupon the little boat turned her nose once more down the wind, and all but the oarsman watched the shore grow. Under the influence of this expansion doubt and direful apprehension were leaving the minds of the men. The management of the boat was still most absorbing, but it could not prevent a quiet cheerfulness. In an hour, perhaps, they would be ashore.

Their backbones had become thoroughly used to balancing in the boat, and they now rode this wild colt of a dinghy like circus men. The correspondent thought that he had been drenched to the skin, but happening to feel in the top pocket of his coat, he found therein eight cigars. Four of them were soaked with seawater; four were perfectly scatheless. After 'a search, somebody produced three dry matches; and thereupon the four waifs rode impudently in their little boat and, with an assurance of an impending rescue shining in their eyes, puffed at the big cigars, and judged well and ill of all men. Everybody took a drink of water.

IV

"Cook," remarked the captain, "there don't seem to be any signs of life about your house of refuge."

"No," replied the cook. "Funny they don't see us!"

A broad stretch of lowly coast lay before the eyes of the men. It was of low dunes topped with dark vegetation. The roar of the surf was plain, and sometimes they could see the white lip of a wave as it spun up the beach. A tiny house was blocked out black upon the sky. Southward, the slim lighthouse lifted its little gray length.

Tide, wind, and waves were swinging the dinghy northward. "Funny they don't see us," said the men.

The surf's roar was here dulled, but its tone was nevertheless thunderous and mighty. As the boat swam over the great rollers the men sat listening to this roar. "We'll swamp sure," said everybody.

It is fair to say here that there was not a lifesaving station within twenty miles in either direction; but the men did not know this fact, and in consequence they made dark and opprobrious remarks concerning the eyesight of the nation's lifesavers. Four scowling men sat in the dinghy and surpassed records in the invention of epithets.

"Funny they don't see us."

The light-heartedness of a former time had completely faded. To their sharpened minds it was easy to conjure pictures of all kinds of incompetency and blindness and, indeed, cowardice. There was the shore of the populous land, and it was bitter and bitter to them that from it came no sign.

"Well," said the captain, ultimately, "I suppose we'll have to make a try for ourselves. If we stay out here too long, we'll none of us have strength left to swim after the boat swamps."

And so the oiler, who was at the oars, turned the boat straight for the shore. There was a sudden tightening of muscles. There was some thinking.

"If we don't all get ashore," said the captain — "if we don't all get ashore, I suppose you fellows know where to send news of my finish?"

They then briefly exchanged some addresses and admonitions. As for the reflections of the men, there was a great deal of rage in them. Perchance they might be formulated thus: "If I am going to be drowned — if I am going to be drowned — if I am going to be drowned, why, in the name of the seven mad gods who rule the sea, was I allowed to come thus far and contemplate sand and trees? Was I brought here merely to have my nose dragged away as I was about to nibble the sacred cheese of life? It is preposterous. If this old ninny-woman, Fate, cannot do better than this, she should be deprived of the management of men's fortunes. She is an old hen who knows not her intention. If she had decided to drown me, why did she not do it in the beginning and save me all this trouble? The whole affair is absurd. . . . But no; she cannot mean to drown me. She dare not drown me. She cannot drown me. Not after all this work." Afterward the man might have had an impulse to shake his fist at the clouds. "Just you drown me, now, and then hear what I call you!"

The billows that came at this time were more formidable. They seemed always just about to break and roll over the little boat in a turmoil of foam. There was a preparatory and long growl in the speech of them. No mind unused to the sea would have concluded that the dinghy could ascend these sheer heights in time. The shore was still afar. The oiler was a wily surfman. "Boys," he said swiftly, "she won't live three minutes more, and we're too far out to swim. Shall I take her to sea again, Captain?"

"Yes; go ahead!" said the captain.

This oiler, by a series of quick miracles and fast and steady oarsmanship, turned the boat in the middle of the surf and took her safely to sea again.

There was a considerable silence as the boat bumped over the furrowed sea to deeper water. Then somebody in gloom spoke: "Well, anyhow, they must have seen us from the shore by now."

The gulls went in slanting flight up the wind toward the gray, desolate east. A squall, marked by dingy clouds and clouds brick-red, like smoke from a burning building, appeared from the southeast.

"What do you think of those lifesaving people? Ain't they peaches?"

"Funny they haven't seen us."

"Maybe they think we're out here for sport! Maybe they think we're fishin'. Maybe they think we're damned fools."

It was a long afternoon. A changed tide tried to force them southward, but wind and wave said northward. Far ahead, where coastline, sea, and sky formed their mighty angle, there were little dots which seemed to indicate a city on the shore.

"St. Augustine?"

The captain shook his head. "Too near Mosquito Inlet."

And the oiler rowed, and then the correspondent rowed; then the oiler rowed. It was a weary business. The human back can become the seat of more aches and pains than are registered in books for the composite anatomy of a regiment. It is a limited area, but it can become the theater of innumerable muscular conflicts, tangles, wrenches, knots, and other comforts.

"Did you ever like to row, Billie?" asked the correspondent.

"No," said the oiler, "hang it!"

When one exchanged the rowing-seat for a place in the bottom of the boat, he suffered a bodily depression that caused him to be careless of everything save an obligation to wiggle one finger. There was cold seawater swashing to and fro in the boat, and he lay in it. His head, pillowed on a thwart, was within an inch of the swirl of a wave-crest, and sometimes a particularly obstreperous sea came inboard and drenched him once more. But these matters did not annoy him. It is almost certain that if the boat had capsized he would have tumbled comfortably out upon the ocean as if he felt sure that it was a great soft mattress.

"Look! There's a man on the shore!"

"Where?"

"There! See 'im? See 'im?"

"Yes, sure! He's walking along."

"Now he's stopped. Look! He's facing us!"

"He's waving at us!"

"So he is! By thunder!"

"Ah, now we're all right Now we're all right! There'll be a boat out here for us in half an hour."

"He's going on. He's running. He's going up to that house there."

The remote beach seemed lower than the sea, and it required a searching glance to discern the little black figure. The captain saw a floating stick, and they rowed to it. A bath towel was by some weird chance in the boat, and, tying this on the stick, the captain waved it. The oarsman did not dare turn his head, so he was obliged to ask questions.

"What's he doing now?"

"He's standing still again. He's looking, I think. . . . There he goes again — toward the house. . . . Now he's stopped again."

"Is he waving at us?"

"No, not now; he was, though."

"Look! There comes another man!"

"He's running."

"Look at him go, would you!"

"Why, he's on a bicycle. Now he's met the other man. They're both waving at us. Look!"

"There comes something up the beach."

"What the devil is that thing?"

"Why, it looks like a boat."

"Why, certainly, it's a boat."

"No; it's on wheels."

"Yes, so it is. Well, that must be the lifeboat. They drag them along shore on a wagon."

"That's the lifeboat, sure."

"No, by God, it's — it's an omnibus."

"I tell you it's a lifeboat."

"It is not! It's an omnibus. I can see it plain. See? One of these big hotel omnibuses."

"By thunder, you're right. It's an omnibus, sure as fate. What do you suppose they are doing with an omnibus? Maybe they are going around collecting the life-crew, hey?"

"That's it, likely. Look! There's a fellow waving a little black flag. He's standing on the steps of the omnibus. There come those other two fellows. Now they're all talking together. Look at the fellow with the flag. Maybe he ain't waving it!"

"That ain't a flag, is it? That's his coat. Why, certainly, that's his coat."

"So it is! it's his coat. He's taken it off and is waving it around his head. But would you look at him swing it!"

"Oh, say, there isn't any lifesaving station there. That's just a winter-resort hotel omnibus that has brought over some of the boarders to see us drown."

"What's that idiot with the coat mean? What's he signaling, anyhow?"

"It looks as if he were trying to tell us to go north. There must be a lifesaving station up there."

"No; he thinks we're fishing. Just giving us a merry hand. See? Ah, there, Willie!"

"Well, I wish I could make something out of those signals. What do you suppose he means?"

"He don't mean anything; he's just playing."

"Well, if he'd just signal us to try the surf again, or to go to sea and wait, or go north, or go south, or go to hell, there would be some reason in it. But look at him! He just stands there and keeps his coat revolving like a wheel. The ass!"

"There come more people."

"Now there's quite a mob. Look! Isn't that a boat?"

"Where? Oh, I see where you mean. No, that's no boat."

"That fellow is still waving his coat."

"He must think we like to see him do that. Why don't he quit it? It don't mean anything."

"I don't know. I think he is trying to make us go north. It must be that there's a lifesaving station there somewhere."

"Say, he ain't tired yet. Look at 'im wave!"

"Wonder how long he can keep that up. He's been revolving his coat ever since he caught sight of us. He's an idiot. Why aren't they getting men to bring a boat out? A fishing boat — one of those big yawls — could come out here all right. Why don't he do something?"

"Oh, it's all right now."

"They'll have a boat out here for us in less than no time, now that they've seen us."

A faint yellow tone came into the sky over the low land. The shadows on the sea slowly deepened. The wind bore coldness with it, and the men began to shiver.

"Holy smoke!" said one, allowing his voice to express his impious mood, "if we keep on monkeying out here! If we've got to flounder out here all night!"

"Oh, we'll never have to stay here all night! Don't you worry. They've seen us now, and it won't be long before they'll come chasing out after us."

The shore grew dusky. The man waving a coat blended gradually into this gloom, and it swallowed in the same manner the omnibus and the group of people. The spray, when it dashed uproariously over the side, made the voyagers shrink and swear like men who were being branded.

"I'd like to catch the chump who waved the coat. I feel like socking him one, just for luck."

"Why? What did he do?"

"Oh, nothing, but then he seemed so damned cheerful."

In the meantime the oiler rowed, and then the correspondent rowed, and then the oiler rowed. Gray-faced and bowed forward, they mechanically, turn by turn, plied the leaden oars. The form of the lighthouse had vanished from the southern horizon, but finally a pale star appeared, just lifting from the sea. The streaked saffron in the west passed before the all-merging darkness, and the sea to the east was black. The land had vanished, and was expressed only by the low and drear thunder of the surf.

"If I am going to be drowned — if I am going to be drowned — if I am going to be drowned, why, in the name of the seven mad gods who rule the sea, was I allowed to come thus far and contemplate sand and trees? Was I brought here merely to have my nose dragged away as I was about to nibble the sacred cheese of life?"

The patient captain, drooped over the water jar, was sometimes obliged to speak to the oarsman.

"Keep her head up! Keep her head up!"

"Keep her head up, sir." The voices were weary and low.

This was surely a quiet evening. All save the oarsman lay heavily and list-lessly in the boat's bottom. As for him, his eyes were just capable of noting the tall black waves that swept forward in a most sinister silence, save for an occasional subdued growl of a crest.

The cook's head was on a thwart, and he looked without interest at the water under his nose. He was deep in other scenes. Finally he spoke. "Billie," he murmured, dreamfully, "what kind of pie do you like best?"

V

"Pie!" said the oiler and the correspondent, agitatedly. "Don't talk about those things, blast you!"

"Well," said the cook, "I was just thinking about ham sandwiches, and — "

A night on the sea in an open boat is a long night. As darkness settled finally, the shine of the light, lifting from the sea in the south, changed to full gold. On the northern horizon a new light appeared, a small bluish gleam on the edge of the waters. These two lights were the furniture of the world. Otherwise there was nothing but waves.

Two men huddled in the stern, and distances were so magnificent in the dinghy that the rower was enabled to keep his feet partly warm by thrusting them under his companions. Their legs indeed extended far under the rowing-seat until they touched the feet of the captain forward. Sometimes, despite the efforts of the tired oarsman, a wave came piling into the boat, an icy wave of the night, and the chilling water soaked them anew. They would twist their bodies for a moment and groan, and sleep the dead sleep once more, while the water in the boat gurgled about them as the craft rocked.

The plan of the oiler and the correspondent was for one to row until he lost the ability, and then arouse the other from his sea-water couch in the bottom of the boat.

The oiler plied the oars until his head drooped forward and the over-power-ing sleep blinded him; and he rowed yet afterward. Then he touched a man in the bottom of the boat, and called his name. "Will you spell me for a little while?" he said meekly.

"Sure, Billie," said the correspondent, awaking and dragging himself to a sitting position. They exchanged places carefully, and the oiler, cuddling down in the seawater at the cook's side, seemed to go to sleep instantly.

The particular violence of the sea had ceased. The waves came without snarling. The obligation of the man at the oars was to keep the boat headed so that the tilt of the rollers would not capsize her, and to preserve her from filling when the crests rushed past. The black waves were silent and hard to be seen in the darkness. Often one was almost upon the boat before the oarsman was aware.

In a low voice the correspondent addressed the captain. He was not sure that the captain was awake, although this iron man seemed to be always awake. "Captain, shall I keep her making for that light north, sir?"

The same steady voice answered him. "Yes. Keep it about two points off the port bow."

The cook had tied a lifebelt around himself in order to get even the warmth which this clumsy cork contrivance could donate, and he seemed almost stove-like when a rower, whose teeth invariably chattered wildly as soon as he ceased his labor, dropped down to sleep.

The correspondent, as he rowed, looked down at the two men sleeping underfoot. The cook's arm was around the oiler's shoulders, and, with their fragmentary clothing and haggard faces, they were the babes of the sea — a grotesque rendering of the old babes in the wood.

Later he must have grown stupid at his work, for suddenly there was a growling of water, and a crest came with a roar and a swash into the boat, and it was a wonder that it did not set the cook afloat in his lifebelt. The cook continued to sleep, but the oiler sat up, blinking his eyes and shaking with the new cold.

"Oh, I'm awful sorry, Billie," said the correspondent, contritely.

"That's all right, old boy," said the oiler, and lay down again and was asleep.

Presently it seemed that even the captain dozed, and the correspondent thought that he was the one man afloat on all the oceans. The wind had a voice as it came over the waves, and it was sadder than the end.

There was a long, loud swishing astern of the boat, and a gleaming trail of phosphorescence, like blue flame, was furrowed on the black waters. It might have been made by a monstrous knife.

Then there came a stillness, while the correspondent breathed with open mouth and looked at the sea.

Suddenly there was another swish and another long flash of bluish light, and this time it was alongside the boat, and might almost have been reached with an oar. The correspondent saw an enormous fin speed like a shadow through the water, hurling the crystalline spray and leaving the long glowing trail.

The correspondent looked over his shoulder at the captain. His face was hidden, and he seemed to be asleep. He looked at the babes of the sea. They certainly were asleep. So, being bereft of sympathy, he leaned a little way to one side and swore softly into the sea.

But the thing did not then leave the vicinity of the boat. Ahead or astern, on one side or the other, at intervals long or short, fled the long sparkling streak, and there was to be heard the *whirroo* of the dark fin. The speed and power of the thing was greatly to be admired. It cut the water like a gigantic and keen projectile.

The presence of this biding thing did not affect the man with the same horror that it would if he had been a picnicker. He simply looked at the sea dully and swore in an undertone.

Nevertheless, it is true that he did not wish to be alone with the thing. He wished one of his companions to awake by chance and keep him company with it. But the captain hung motionless over the water jar, and the oiler and the cook in the bottom of the boat were plunged in slumber.

VI

"If I am going to be drowned — if I am going to be drowned — if I am going to be drowned, why, in the name of the seven mad gods who rule the sea, was I allowed to come thus far and contemplate sand and trees?"

During this dismal night, it may be remarked that a man would conclude that it was really the intention of the seven mad gods to drown him, despite the abominable injustice of it. For it was certainly an abominable injustice to drown a man who had worked so hard, so hard. The man felt it would be a crime most unnatural. Other people had drowned at sea since galleys swarmed with painted sails, but still —

When it occurs to a man that nature does not regard him as important, and that she feels she would not maim the universe by disposing of him, he at first wishes to throw bricks at the temple, and he hates deeply the fact that there are no bricks and no temples. Any visible expression of nature would surely be pelleted with his jeers.

Then, if there be no tangible thing to hoot, he feels, perhaps, the desire to confront a personification and indulge in pleas, bowed to one knee, and with hands supplicant, saying, "Yes, but I love myself."

A high cold star on a winter's night is the word he feels that she says to him. Thereafter he knows the pathos of his situation.

The men in the dinghy had not discussed these matters, but each had, no doubt, reflected upon them in silence and according to his mind. There was seldom any expression upon their faces save the general one of complete weariness. Speech was devoted to the business of the boat.

To chime the notes of his emotion, a verse mysteriously entered the correspondent's head. He had even forgotten that he had forgotten this verse, but it suddenly was in his mind.

> A soldier of the Legion lay dying in Algiers;
> There was lack of woman's nursing, there was dearth of woman's tears;
> But a comrade stood beside him, and he took that comrade's hand,
> And he said, "I never more shall see my own, my native land."[2]

In his childhood the correspondent had been made acquainted with the fact that a soldier of the Legion lay dying in Algiers, but he had never regarded the fact as important. Myriads of his schoolfellows had informed him of the soldier's plight, but the dinning had naturally ended by making him perfectly indifferent. He had never considered it his affair that a soldier of the Legion lay dying in Algiers, nor had it appeared to him as a matter for sorrow. It was less to him than the breaking of a pencil's point.

Now, however, it quaintly came to him as a human, living thing. It was no longer merely a picture of a few throes in the breast of a poet, meanwhile drinking tea and warming his feet at the grate; it was an actuality — stern, mournful, and fine.

The correspondent plainly saw the soldier. He lay on the sand with his feet out straight and still. While his pale left hand was upon his chest in an attempt to thwart the going of his life, the blood came between his fingers. In the far Algerian distance, a city of low square forms was set against a sky that was faint with the last sunset hues. The correspondent, plying the oars

2 from "Bingen on the Rhine" by Lady Maxwell, lines 1–4.

and dreaming of the slow and slower movements of the lips of the soldier, was moved by a profound and perfectly impersonal comprehension. He was sorry for the soldier of the Legion who lay dying in Algiers.

The thing which had followed the boat and waited had evidently grown bored at the delay. There was no longer to be heard the slash of the cut-water, and there was no longer the flame of the long trail. The light in the north still glimmered, but it was apparently no nearer to the boat. Sometimes the boom of the surf rang in the correspondent's ears, and he turned the craft seaward then and rowed harder. Southward, some one had evidently built a watch fire on the beach. It was too low and too far to be seen, but it made a shimmering, roseate reflection upon the bluff in back of it, and this could be discerned from the boat. The wind came stronger, and sometimes a wave suddenly raged out like a mountain cat, and there was to be seen the sheen and sparkle of a broken crest.

The captain, in the bow, moved on his water jar and sat erect. "Pretty long night," he observed to the correspondent. He looked at the shore. "Those lifesaving people take their time."

"Did you see that shark playing around?"

"Yes, I saw him. He was a big fellow, all right."

"Wish I had known you were awake."

Later the correspondent spoke into the bottom of the boat. "Billie!" There was a slow and gradual disentanglement. "Billie, will you spell me?"

"Sure," said the oiler.

As soon as the correspondent touched the cold, comfortable seawater in the bottom of the boat and had huddled close to the cook's lifebelt he was deep in sleep, despite the fact that his teeth played all the popular airs. This sleep was so good to him that it was but a moment before he heard a voice call his name in a tone that demonstrated the last stages of exhaustion. "Will you spell me?"

"Sure, Billie."

The light in the north had mysteriously vanished, but the correspondent took his course from the wide-awake captain.

Later in the night they took the boat farther out to sea, and the captain directed the cook to take one oar at the stern and keep the boat facing the seas. He was to call out if he should hear the thunder of the surf. This plan enabled the oiler and the correspondent to get respite together. "We'll give those boys a chance to get into shape again," said the captain. They curled down and, after a few preliminary chatterings and trembles, slept once more the dead sleep. Neither knew they had bequeathed to the cook the company of another shark, or perhaps the same shark.

As the boat caroused on the waves, spray occasionally bumped over the side and gave them a fresh soaking, but this had no power to break their repose. The ominous slash of the wind and the water affected them as it would have affected mummies.

"Boys," said the cook, with the notes of every reluctance in his voice, "she's

drifted in pretty close. I guess one of you had better take her to sea again."
The correspondent, aroused, heard the crash of the toppled crests.

As he was rowing, the captain gave him some whiskey-and-water, and this
steadied the chills out of him. "If I ever get ashore and anybody shows me
even a photograph of an oar — "

At last there was a short conversation.

"Billie! . . . Billie, will you spell me?"

"Sure," said the oiler.

VII

When the correspondent again opened his eyes, the sea and the sky were
each of the gray hue of the dawning. Later, carmine and gold was painted
upon the waters. The morning appeared finally, in its splendor, with a sky of
pure blue, and the sunlight flamed on the tips of the waves.

On the distant dunes were set many little black cottages, and a tall white
windmill reared above them. No man, nor dog, nor bicycle appeared on the
beach. The cottages might have formed a deserted village.

The voyagers scanned the shore. A conference was held in the boat.
"Well," said the captain, "if no help is coming, we might better try a run
through the surf right away. If we stay out here much longer we will be too
weak to do anything for ourselves at all." The others silently acquiesced in
this reasoning. The boat was headed for the beach. The correspondent wondered if none ever ascended the tall wind-tower, and if then they never looked
seaward. This tower was a giant, standing with its back to the plight of the
ants. It represented in a degree, to the correspondent, the serenity of nature
amid the struggles of the individual — nature in the wind, and nature in the
vision of men. She did not seem cruel to him then, nor beneficent, nor
treacherous, nor wise. But she was indifferent, flatly indifferent. It is, perhaps, plausible that a man in this situation, impressed with the unconcern
of the universe, should see the innumerable flaws of his life, and have them
taste wickedly in his mind, and wish for another chance. A distinction between right and wrong seems absurdly clear to him, then, in this new ignorance of the grave-edge, and he understands that if he were given another opportunity he would mend his conduct and his words, and be better and
brighter during an introduction or at a tea.

"Now, boys," said the captain, "she is going to swamp sure. All we can
do is to work her in as far as possible, and then when she swamps, pile out
and scramble for the beach. Keep cool now, and don't jump until she
swamps sure."

The oiler took the oars. Over his shoulders he scanned the surf. "Captain,"
he said, "I think I'd better bring her about and keep her head-on to the seas
and back her in."

"All right, Billie," said the captain. "Back her in." The oiler swung the
boat then, and, seated in the stern, the cook and the correspondent were

obliged to look over their shoulders to contemplate the lonely and indifferent shore.

The monstrous inshore rollers heaved the boat high until the men were again enabled to see the white sheets of water scudding up the slanted beach. "We won't get in very close," said the captain. Each time a man could wrest his attention from the rollers, he turned his glance toward the shore, and in the expression of the eyes during this contemplation there was a singular quality. The correspondent, observing the others, knew that they were not afraid, but the full meaning of their glances was shrouded.

As for himself, he was too tired to grapple fundamentally with the fact. He tried to coerce his mind into thinking of it, but the mind was dominated at this time by the muscles, and the muscles said they did not care. It merely occurred to him that if he should drown it would be a shame.

There were no hurried words, no pallor, no plain agitation. The men simply looked at the shore. "Now, remember to get well clear of the boat when you jump," said the captain.

Seaward the crest of a roller suddenly fell with a thunderous crash, and the long white comber came roaring down upon the boat.

"Steady now," said the captain. The men were silent. They turned their eyes from the shore to the comber and waited. The boat slid up the incline, leaped at the furious top, bounced over it, and swung down the long back of the wave. Some water had been shipped, and the cook bailed it out.

But the next crest crashed also. The tumbling, boiling flood of white water caught the boat and whirled it almost perpendicular. Water swarmed in from all sides. The correspondent had his hands on the gunwale at this time, and when the water entered at that place he swiftly withdrew his fingers, as if he objected to wetting them.

The little boat, drunken with this weight of water, reeled and snuggled deeper into the sea.

"Bail her out, cook! Bail her out!" said the captain.

"All right, Captain," said the cook.

"Now, boys, the next one will do for us sure," said the oiler. "Mind to jump clear of the boat."

The third wave moved forward, huge, furious, implacable. It fairly swallowed the dinghy, and almost simultaneously the men tumbled into the sea. A piece of lifebelt had lain in the bottom of the boat, and as the correspondent went overboard he held this to his chest with his left hand.

The January water was icy, and he reflected immediately that it was colder than he had expected to find it off the coast of Florida. This appeared to his dazed mind as a fact important enough to be noted at the time. The coldness of the water was sad; it was tragic. This fact was somehow mixed and confused with his opinion of his own situation, so that it seemed almost a proper reason for tears. The water was cold.

When he came to the surface he was conscious of little but the noisy water.

Afterward he saw his companions in the sea. The oiler was ahead in the race. He was swimming strongly and rapidly. Off to the correspondent's left, the cook's great white and corked back bulged out of the water; and in the rear the captain was hanging with his one good hand to the keel of the overturned dinghy.

There is a certain immovable quality to a shore, and the correspondent wondered at it amid the confusion of the sea.

It seemed also very attractive; but the correspondent knew that it was a long journey, and he paddled leisurely. The piece of life preserver lay under him, and sometimes he whirled down the incline of a wave as if he were on a hand-sled.

But finally he arrived at a place in the sea where travel was beset with difficulty. He did not pause swimming to inquire what manner of current had caught him, but there his progress ceased. The shore was set before him like a bit of scenery on a stage, and he looked at it and understood with his eyes each detail of it.

As the cook passed, much farther to the left, the captain was calling to him, "Turn over on your back, cook! Turn over on your back and use the oar."

"All right, sir." The cook turned on his back, and, paddling with an oar, went ahead as if he were a canoe.

Presently the boat also passed to the left of the correspondent, with the captain clinging with one hand to the keel. He would have appeared like a man raising himself to look over a board fence if it were not for the extraordinary gymnastics of the boat. The correspondent marveled that the captain could still hold to it.

They passed on nearer to shore — the oiler, the cook, the captain — and following them went the water jar, bouncing gaily over the seas.

The correspondent remained in the grip of this strange new enemy — a current. The shore, with its white slope of sand and its green bluff topped with little silent cottages, was spread like a picture before him. It was very near to him then, but he was impressed as one who, in a gallery, looks at a scene from Brittany or Algiers.

He thought: "I am going to drown? Can it be possible? Can it be possible? Can it be possible?" Perhaps an individual must consider his own death to be the final phenomenon of nature.

But later a wave perhaps whirled him out of this small deadly current, for he found suddenly that he could again make progress toward the shore. Later still he was aware that the captain, clinging with one hand to the keel of the dinghy, had his face turned away from the shore and toward him, and was calling his name. "Come to the boat! Come to the boat!"

In his struggle to reach the captain and the boat, he reflected that when one gets properly wearied drowning must really be a comfortable arrangement — a cessation of hostilities accompanied by a large degree of relief; and he was glad of it, for the main thing in his mind for some moments had been horror of the temporary agony. He did not wish to be hurt.

Presently he saw a man running along the shore. He was undressing with most remarkable speed. Coat, trousers, shirt, everything flew magically off him.

"Come to the boat!" called the captain.

"All right, Captain." As the correspondent paddled, he saw the captain let himself down to bottom and leave the boat. Then the correspondent performed his one little marvel of the voyage. A large wave caught him and flung him with ease and supreme speed completely over the boat and far beyond it. It struck him even then as an event in gymnastics and a true miracle of the sea. An overturned boat in the surf is not a plaything to a swimming man.

The correspondent arrived in water that reached only to his waist, but his condition did not enable him to stand for more than a moment. Each wave knocked him into a heap, and the undertow pulled at him.

Then he saw the man who had been running and undressing, and undressing and running, come bounding into the water. He dragged ashore the cook, and then waded toward the captain; but the captain waved him away and sent him to the correspondent. He was naked — naked as a tree in winter; but a halo was about his head, and he shone like a saint. He gave a strong pull, and a long drag, and a bully heave at the correspondent's hand. The correspondent, schooled in the minor formulae, said, "Thanks, old man." But suddenly the man cried, "What's that?" He pointed a swift finger. The correspondent said, "Go."

In the shallows, face downward, lay the oiler. His forehead touched sand that was periodically, between each wave, clear of the sea.

The correspondent did not know all that transpired afterward. When he achieved safe ground he fell, striking the sand with each particular part of his body. It was as if he had dropped from a roof, but the thud was grateful to him.

It seems that instantly the beach was populated with men with blankets, clothes, and flasks, and women with coffeepots and all the remedies sacred to their minds. The welcome of the land to the men from the sea was warm and generous; but a still and dripping shape was carried slowly up the beach, and the land's welcome for it could only be the different and sinister hospitality of the grave.

When it came night, the white waves paced to and fro in the moonlight, and the wind brought the sound of the great sea's voice to the men on the shore, and they felt that they could then be interpreters.

Robert Frost (1874–1963)

AMERICAN POET

Range-Finding

The battle rent a cobweb diamond-strung
And cut a flower beside a ground bird's nest
Before it stained a single human breast.
The stricken flower bent double and so hung.
And still the bird revisited her young.
A butterfly its fall had dispossessed
A moment sought in air his flower of rest,
Then lightly stooped to it and fluttering clung.

On the bare upland pasture there had spread
O'ernight 'twixt mullein stalks a wheel of thread   10
And straining cables wet with silver dew.
A sudden passing bullet shook it dry.
The indwelling spider ran to greet the fly,
But finding nothing, sullenly withdrew.

Come In

As I came to the edge of the woods,
Thrush music — hark!
Now if it was dusk outside,
Inside it was dark.

Too dark in the woods for a bird
By sleight of wing
To better its perch for the night,
Though it still could sing.

The last of the light of the sun
That had died in the west   10
Still lived for one song more
In a thrush's breast.

Far in the pillared dark
Thrush music went —
Almost like a call to come in
To the dark and lament.

But no, I was out for stars:
I would not come in.
I meant not even if asked,
And I hadn't been.   20

Thomas Mann (1875–1955)

AMERICAN NOVELIST, SHORT STORY WRITER,
and ESSAYIST (GERMAN-BORN)

Snow

Daily, five times a day, the guests expressed unanimous dissatisfaction with the kind of winter they were having. They felt it was not what they had a right to expect of these altitudes. It failed to deliver the renowned meteorological specific in anything like the quantity indicated by the prospectus, quoted by old inhabitants, or anticipated by new. There was a very great failure in the supply of sunshine, an element so important in the cures achieved up here that without it they were distinctly retarded. And whatever Herr Settembrini might think of the sincerity of the patients' desire to finish their cure, leave "home" and return to the flat-land, at any rate they insisted on their just dues. They wanted what they were entitled to, what their parents or husbands had paid for, and they grumbled unceasingly, at table, in lift, and in hall. The management showed a consciousness of what it owed them

Hans Castorp, a young provincial engineer, comes to the international tuberculosis sanatorium, Berghof, high in the Swiss Alps to visit his cousin. But his brief visit becomes a prolonged stay when it is discovered that he, too, has the disease. Set apart from the rest of the world, this "magic mountain" becomes a theater for the world of competing ideas, particularly the humanism and rationalism voiced by Herr Settembrini, an Italian writer and philosopher, as against the medieval mysticism and irrationality of Naphta, another patient. The sanatorium is also a microcosm of the world of emotions, contrasting Hans' sensual love for a Russian patient, Clavdia Chauchat, with flashbacks of his immature feelings for his classmate Pribislav Hippe. Thus isolated in a therapeutic context of a fight against death and disease — by fresh air "treatments," psychoanalytic lectures, and medical technology — Hans becomes aware of these worlds of ideas and feelings, and he begins "taking stock" of himself. The crucial incident of his development toward life occurs in this chapter.

by installing a new apparatus for heliotherapy. They had two already, but these did not suffice for the demands of those who wished to get sunburnt by electricity — it was so becoming to the ladies, young and old, and made all the men, though confirmed horizontallers, look irresistibly athletic. And the ladies, even though aware of the mechanico-cosmetical origin of this conquering-hero air, were foolish enough to be carried away by it. There was Frau Schönfeld, a red-haired, red-eyed patient from Berlin. In the salon she looked thirstily at a long-legged, sunken-chested gallant, who described himself on his visiting-card as "*Aviateur diplômé et Enseigne de la Marine allemande.*"[1] He was fitted out with the pneumothorax and wore "smoking" at the midday meal but not in the evening, saying this was their custom in the navy. "My God," breathed Frau Schönfeld at him, "what a tan this demon has — he gets it from the helio — it makes him look like a hunter of eagles!" "Just wait, nixie!" he whispered in her ear, in the lift, "I'll make you pay for looking at me like that!" It made goose-flesh and shivers run over her. And along the balconies, past the glass partitions, the demon eagle-hunter found his way to the nixie.

But the artificial sun was far from making up for the lack of the real one. Two or three days of full sunshine in the month — it was not good enough, gorgeous though these were, with deep, deep velvety blue sky behind the white mountain summits, a glitter as of diamonds and a fine hot glow on the face and the back of the neck, when they dawned resplendent from the prevailing thick mantle of grey mist. Two or three such days in the course of weeks could not satisfy people whose lot might be said to justify extraordinary demands from the external world. They had made an inward compact, by the terms of which they resigned the common joys and sorrows proper to flat-land humanity, and in exchange were made free of a life that was, to be sure, inactive, but on the other hand very lively and diverting, and care-free to the point of making one forget altogether the flight of time. Thus it was not much good for the Hofrat[2] to tell them how favourably the Berghof compared with a Siberian mine or a penal settlement, nor to sing the praises of the atmosphere, so thin and light, well-nigh as rare as the empty universal ether, free of earthly admixture whether good or bad, and even without actual sunshine to be preferred to the rank vapours of the plain. Despite all he could say, the gloomy disaffection gained ground, threats of unlicensed departure were the order of the day, were even put into execution, without regard for the warning afforded by the melancholy return of Frau Salomon to the fold, now a "life member," her tedious but not serious case having taken that turn by reason of her self-willed visit to her wet and windy Amsterdam.

But if they had no sun, they had snow. Such masses of snow as Hans Castorp had never till now in all his life beheld. The previous winter had done fairly well in that respect, but it had been as nothing compared to this one. The snow-fall was monstrous and immeasurable, it made one realize the

[1] certified aviator and sub-lieutenant in the German Navy.
[2] German Court Counselor.

extravagant, outlandish nature of the place. It snowed day in, day out, and all through the night. The few roads kept open were like tunnels, with towering walls of snow on either side, crystal and alabaster surfaces that were pleasant to look at, and on which the guests scribbled all sorts of messages, jokes and personalities. But even this path between walls was above the level of the pavement, and made of hard-packed snow, as one could tell by certain places where it gave way, and let one suddenly sink in up to the knee. One might, unless one were careful, break a leg. The benches had disappeared, except for the high back of one emerging here and there. In the town, the street level was so raised that the shops had become cellars, into which one descended by steps cut in the snow.

And on all these lying masses more snow fell, day in, day out. It fell silently, through air that was moderately cold, perhaps ten to fifteen degrees of frost. One did not feel the cold, it might have been much less, for the dryness and absence of wind deprived it of sting. The mornings were very dark, breakfast was taken by the light of the artificial moon that hung from the vaulted ceiling of the dining-room, above the gay stencilled border. Outside was the reeking void, the world enwrapped in grey-white cotton-wool, packed to the window-panes in snow and mist. No sight of the mountains; of the nearest evergreen now and again a glimpse through the fog, standing laden, and from time to time shaking free a bough of its heavy load, that flew into the air, and sent a cloud of white against the grey. At ten o'clock the sun, a wan wisp of light, came up behind its mountain, and gave the indistinguishable scene some shadowy hint of life, some sallow glimmer of reality; yet even so, it retained its delicate ghostliness, its lack of any definite line for the eye to follow. The contours of the peaks dissolved, disappeared, were dissipated in the mist, while the vision, led on from one pallidly gleaming slope of snow to another, lost itself in the void. Then a single cloud, like smoke, lighted up by the sun, might spread out before a wall of rock and hang there for long, motionless.

At midday the sun would half break through, and show signs of banishing the mist. In vain — yet a shred of blue would be visible, and suffice to make the scene, in its strangely falsified contours, sparkle marvellously far and wide. Usually, at this hour, the snowfall stopped, as though to have a look at what it had done; a like effect was produced by the rare days when the storm ceased, and the uninterrupted power of the sun sought to thaw away the pure and lovely surface from the new-fallen masses. The sight was at once fairylike and comic, an infantine fantasy. The thick light cushions plumped up on the boughs of trees, the humps and mounds of snow-covered rock-cropping or undergrowth, the droll, dwarfish, crouching disguise all ordinary objects wore, made of the scene a landscape in gnome-land, an illustration for a fairy-tale. Such was the immediate view — wearisome to move in, quaintly, roguishly stimulating to the fancy. But when one looked across the intervening space, at the towering marble statuary of the high Alps in full snow, one felt a quite different emotion, and that was awe of their majestic sublimity.

Afternoons between three and four, Hans Castorp lay in his balcony box, well wrapped, his head against the cushion, not too high or too low, of his excellent chair, and looked out at forest and mountain over his thick-upholstered balustrade. The snow-laden firs, dark-green to blackness, went marching up the sides of the valley, and beneath them the snow lay soft like down pillows. Above the tree line, the mountain walls reared themselves into the grey-white air: huge surfaces of snow, with softly veiled crests, and here and there a black jut of rock. The snow came silently down. The scene blurred more and more, it inclined the eye, gazing thus into woolly vacuity, to slumber. At the moment of slipping off one might give a start — yet what sleep could be purer than this in the icy air? It was dreamless. It was as free from the burden — even the unconscious burden — of organic life, as little aware of an effort to breathe this contentless, weightless, imperceptible air as is the breathless sleep of the dead. When Hans Castorp stirred again, the mountains would be wholly lost in a cloud of snow; only a pinnacle, a jutting rock, might show one instant, to be rapt away the next. It was absorbing to watch these ghostly pranks; one needed to keep alert to follow the transmutations, the veiling and unveiling. One moment a great space of snow-covered rock would reveal itself, standing out bold and free, though of base or peak naught was to be seen. But if one ceased to fix one's gaze upon it, it was gone, in a breath.

Then there were storms so violent as to prevent one's sitting on the balcony for the driven snow which blew in, in such quantity as to cover floor and chair with a thick mantle. Yes, even in this sheltered valley it knew how to storm. The thin air would be in a hurly-burly, so whirling full of snow one could not see a hand's breadth before one's face. Gusts strong enough to take one's breath away flung the snow about, drew it up cyclone-fashion from the valley floor to the upper air, whisked it about in the maddest dance; no longer a snow-storm, it was a blinding chaos, a white dark, a monstrous dereliction on the part of this inordinate and violent region; no living creature save the snow-bunting — which suddenly appeared in troops — could flourish in it.

And yet Hans Castorp loved this snowy world. He found it not unlike life at the sea-shore. The monotony of the scene was in both cases profound. The snow, so deep, so light, so dry and spotless, was the sand of down below. One was as clean as the other: you could shake the snow from boots and clothing, just as you could the fine-ground, dustless stone and shell, product of the sea's depth — neither left trace behind. And walking in the snow was a toilsome as on the dunes; unless, indeed, a crust had come upon it, by dint of thawing and freezing, when the going became easy and pleasant, like marching along the smooth, hard, wet, resilient strip of sand close to the edge of the sea.

But the storms and high-piled drifts of this year gave pedestrians small chance. They were favourable only for skiing. The snow-plough, labouring its best, barely kept free the main street of the settlement and the most indispensable paths. Thus the few short feasible stretches were always crowded with other walkers, ill and well: the native, the permanent guest, and the hotel population; and these in their turn were bumped by the sleds as they swung and swerved down the slopes, steered by men and women who leaned far back as they came on, and shouted importunately, being obsessed by the importance of their occupation. Once at the bottom they would turn and trundle their toy sledges uphill again.

Hans Castorp was thoroughly sick of all the walks. He had two desires: one of them, the stronger, was to be alone with his thoughts and his stock-taking projects; and this his balcony assured to him. But the other, allied unto it, was a lively craving to come into close and freer touch with the mountains, the mountains in their snowy desolation; toward them he was irresistibly drawn. Yet how could he, all unprovided and foot bound as he was, hope to gratify such a desire? He had only to step beyond the end of the shovelled paths — an end soon reached upon any of them — to plunge breast-high in the snowy element.

Thus it was Hans Castorp, on a day in his second winter with those up here, resolved to buy himself skis and learn to walk on them, enough, that is, for his purposes. He was no sportsman, had never been physically inclined to sport; and did not behave as though he were, as did many guests of the cure, dressing up to suit the mode and the spirit of the place. Hermine Kleefeld, for instance, among other females, though she was constantly blue in the face from lack of breath, loved to appear at luncheon in tweed knickers, and loll about after the meal in a basket-chair in the hall, with her legs sprawled out. Hans Castorp knew that he would meet with a refusal were he to ask the Hofrat to countenance his plan. Sports activities were unconditionally forbidden at the Berghof as in all other establishments of the kind. This atmosphere, which one seemed to breathe in so effortlessly, was a severe strain on the heart, and as for Hans Castorp personally, his lively comment on his own state, that "the getting used to being up here consisted in getting used to not getting used," had continued in force. His fever, which Rhadamanthus[3] ascribed to a moist spot, remained obstinate. Why else indeed should he be here? His desire, his present purpose was then clearly inconsistent and inadmissible. Yet we must be at the pains to understand him aright. He had no wish to imitate the fresh-air faddists and smart pseudo-sportsmen, who would have been equally eager to sit all day and play cards in a stuffy room, if only that had been interdicted by authority. He felt himself a member of another and closer community than this small tourist world; a new and a broader point of view, a dignity and restraint set him apart and made him conscious that it would be unfitting for him to emulate their rough-and-tumble in the snow. He had no escapade in view, his plans were so moderate that Rhadamanthus himself, had he known, might well have approved them. But the rules stood in the way, and Hans Castorp resolved to act behind his back.

He took occasion to speak to Herr Settembrini of his plan — who for sheer joy could have embraced him. "Si, si, si! Do so, do so, Engineer, do so with

[3] a son of Zeus who was made a judge in the underworld because of his great and unwavering justice.

the blessing of God! Ask after nobody's leave, but simply do it! Ah, your good angel must have whispered you the thought! Do it straightway, before the impulse leaves you. I'll go along, I'll go to the shop with you, and together we will acquire the instruments of this happy inspiration. I would go with you even into the mountains, I would be by your side, on winged feet, like Mercury's — but that I may not. May not! If that were all, how soon would I do it! That I cannot is the truth, I am a broken man. — But you — it will do you no harm, none at all, if you are sensible and do nothing rash. Even — even if it did you harm — just a little harm — it will still have been your good angel roused you to it. I say no more. Ah, what an unsurpassable plan! Two years up here, and still capable of such projects — ah, yes, your heart is sound, no need to despair of you. Bravo, bravo! By all means pull the wool over the eyes of your Prince of Shadows! Buy the snow-shoes, have them sent to me or Lukaçek, or the chandler below-stairs. You fetch them from here to go and practice, you go off on them — "

So it befell. Under Herr Settembrini's critical eye — he played the connoisseur, though innocent of sports — Hans Castorp acquired a pair of oaken skis, finished a light-brown, with tapering, pointed ends and the best quality of straps. He bought the iron-shod staff with the little wheel, as well, and was not content to have his purchases sent, but carried them on his shoulder to Settembrini's quarters, where he arranged with the grocer to take care of them for him. He had looked on enough at the sport to know the use of his tools; and choosing for his practice-ground an almost treeless slope not far behind the sanatorium, remote from the hubbub of the spot where other beginners learned the art, he began daily to make his first blundering attempts, watched by Herr Settembrini, who would stand at a little distance, leaning on his cane, with legs gracefully crossed, and greet his nursling's progress with applause. One day Hans Castorp, steering down the cleared drive toward the Dorf,[4] in act to take the skis back to the grocer's, ran into the Hofrat. Behrens never recognized him, though it was broad day, and our beginner had wellnigh collided with him. Shrouded in a haze of tobacco-smoke, he stalked past regardless.

Hans Castorp found that one quickly gets readiness in an art where strong desire comes in play. He was not ambitious for expert skill, and all he needed he acquired in a few days, without undue strain on wind or muscles. He learned to keep his feet tidily together and make parallel tracks; to avail himself of his stick in getting off; he learned how to take obstacles, such as small elevations of the ground, with a slight soaring motion, arms outspread, rising and falling like a ship on a billowy sea; learned, after the twentieth trial, not to trip and roll over when he braked at full speed, with the right Telemark turn, one leg forward, the other bent at the knee. Gradually he widened the sphere of his activities. One day it came to pass that Herr Settembrini saw him vanish in the far white mist; the Italian shouted a warning through cupped hands, and turned homewards, his pedagogic soul well-pleased.

[4] village.

It was beautiful here in these wintry heights: not mildly and ingratiatingly beautiful, more as the North Sea is beautiful in a westerly gale. There was no thunder of surf, a deathly stillness reigned, but roused similar feelings of awe. Hans Castorp's long, pliant soles carried him in all directions: along the left slope to Clavadel, on the right to Frauenkirch and Glaris, whence he could see the shadowy massif of the Amselfluh, ghostlike in the mist; into the Dischma valley, or up behind the Berghof in the direction of the wooded Seehorn, only the top of which, snow-covered, rose above the tree line, or the Drusatscha forest, with the pale outline of the Rhätikon looming behind it, smothered in snow. He took his skis and went up on the funicular to the Schatzalp; there, rapt six thousand feet above the sea, he revelled at will on the gleaming slopes of powdery snow — whence, in good weather, there was a view of majestic extent over all the surrounding territory.

He rejoiced in his new resource, before which all difficulties and hindrances to movement fell away. It gave him the utter solitude he craved, and filled his soul with impressions of the wild inhumanity, the precariousness of this region into which he had ventured. On his one hand he might have a precipitous, pine-clad declivity, falling away into the mists; on the other sheer rock might rise, with masses of snow, in monstrous, Cyclopean[5] forms, all domed and vaulted, swelling or cavernous. He would halt for a moment, to quench the sound of his own movement, when the silence about him would be absolute, complete, a wadded soundlessness, as it were, elsewhere all unknown. There was no stir of air, not so much as might even lightly sway the tree-boughs; there was not a rustle, nor the voice of a bird. It was primeval silence to which Hans Castorp hearkened, when he leaned thus on his staff, his head on one side, his mouth open. And always it snowed, snowed without pause, endlessly, gently, soundlessly falling.

No, this world of limitless silences had nothing hospitable; it received the visitor at his own risk, or rather it scarcely even received him, it tolerated his penetration into its fastnesses, in a manner that boded no good; it made him aware of the menace of the elemental, a menace not even hostile, but impersonally deadly. The child of civilization, remote from birth from wild nature and all her ways, is more susceptible to her grandeur than is her untutored son who has looked at her and lived close to her from childhood up, on terms of prosaic familiarity. The latter scarcely knows the religious awe with which the other regards her, that awe which conditions all his feeling for her, and is present, a constant, solemn thrill, in the profoundest depth of his soul. Hans Castorp, standing there in his puttees and long-sleeved camel's-hair waistcoat, on his skis *de luxe*, suddenly seemed to himself exceedingly presumptuous, to be thus listening to the primeval hush, the deathlike silence of these wintry fastnesses. He felt his breast lightened when, on his way home, the first chalets, the first abodes of human beings, loomed visible through the fog. Only then did he become aware that he had been for hours possessed by a secret awe and terror. On the island of Sylt he had stood by the edge of

---

[5] gigantic, referring to the Cyclops, a one-eyed giant.

the thundering surf. In his white flannels, elegant, self-assured, but most respectful, he had stood there as one stands before a lion's cage and looks deep into the yawning jaws of the beast, lined with murderous fangs. He had bathed in the surf, and heeded the blast of the coast-guard's horn, warning all and sundry not to venture rashly beyond the first line of billows, not to approach too nearly the oncoming tempest — the very last impulse of whose cataract, indeed, struck upon him like a blow from a lion's paw. From that experience our young man had learned the fearful pleasure of toying with forces so great that to approach them nearly is destruction. What he had not then felt was the temptation to come closer, to carry the thrilling contact with these deadly natural forces up to a point where the full embrace was imminent. Weak human being that he was — though tolerably well equipped with the weapons of civilization — what he at this moment knew was the fascination of venturing just so far into the monstrous unknown, or at least abstaining just so long from flight before it, that the adventure grazed the perilous, that it was just barely possible to put limits to it, before it became no longer a matter of toying with the foam and playfully dodging the ruthless paw — but the ultimate adventure, the billow, the lion's jaws, and the sea.

In a word, Hans Castorp was valorous up here — if by valour we mean not mere dull matter-of-factness in the face of nature, but conscious submission to her, the fear of death cast out by irresistible oneness. Yes, in his narrow, hypercivilized breast, Hans Castorp cherished a feeling of kinship with the elements, connected with the new sense of superiority he had lately felt at sight of the silly people on their little sleds; it had made him feel that a profounder, more spacious, less luxurious solitude than that afforded by his balcony chair would be beyond all price. He had sat there and looked abroad, at those mist-wreathed summits, at the carnival of snow, and blushed to be gaping thus from the breastwork of material well-being. This motive, and no momentary fad — no, nor yet any native love of bodily exertion — was what impelled him to learn the use of skis. If it was uncanny up there in the magnificence of the mountains, in the deathly silence of the snows — and uncanny it assuredly was, to our son of civilization — this was equally true, that in these months and years he had already drunk deep of the uncanny, in spirit and in sense. Even a colloquy with Naphta and Settembrini was not precisely the canniest thing in the world, it too led one on into uncharted and perilous regions. So if we can speak of Hans Castorp's feeling of kinship with the wild powers of the winter heights, it is in this sense, that despite his pious awe he felt these scenes to be a fitting theatre for the issue of his involved thoughts, a fitting stage for one to make who, scarcely knowing how, found it had devolved upon him to take stock of himself, in reference to the rank and status of the *Homo Dei*.[6]

No one was here to blow a warning to the rash one — unless, indeed, Herr Settembrini, with his farewell shout at Hans Castorp's disappearing back, had

---

[6] man of God.

been that man. But possessed by valorous desire, our youth had given the call no heed — as little as he had the steps behind him on a certain carnival night. "*Eh, Ingegnere, un po' di ragione, sa!*"[7] "Yes, yes, pedagogic Satana, with your *ragione*[8] and your *ribellione*,"[9] he thought. "But I'm rather fond of you. You are a wind-bag and a hand-organ man, to be sure. But you mean well, you mean much better, and more to my mind, than that knife-edged little Jesuit and Terrorist, apologist of the Inquisition and the knout, with his round eye-glasses — though he is nearly always right when you and he come to grips over my paltry soul, like God and the Devil in the mediæval legends."

He struggled, one day, powdered in snow to the waist, up a succession of snow-shrouded terraces, up and up, he knew not whither. Nowhither, per-haps; these upper regions blended with a sky no less misty-white than they, and where the two came together, it was hard to tell. No summit, no ridge was visible, it was a haze and a nothing, toward which Hans Castorp strove; while behind him the world, the inhabited valley, fell away swiftly from view, and no sound mounted to his ears. In a twinkling he was as solitary, he was as lost as heart could wish, his loneliness was profound enough to awake the fear which is the first stage of valour. "*Præterit figura huius mundi*,"[10] he said to himself, quoting Naphta, in a Latin hardly humanistic in spirit. He stopped and looked about. On all sides there was nothing to see, beyond small single flakes of snow, which came out of a white sky and sank to rest on the white earth. The silence about him refused to say aught to his spirit. His gaze was lost in the blind white void, he felt his heart pulse from the effort of the climb — that muscular organ whose animal-like shape and contracting motion he had watched, with a feeling of sacrilege, in the x-ray laboratory. A naïve reverence filled him for that organ of his, for the pulsating human heart, up here alone in the icy void, alone with its question and its riddle.

On he pressed; higher and higher toward the sky. Walking, he thrust the end of his stick in the snow and watched the blue light follow it out of the hole it made. That he liked; and stood for long at a time to test the little optical phenomenon. It was a strange, a subtle colour, this greenish-blue; colour of the heights and deeps, ice-clear, yet holding shadow in its depths, mysteriously exquisite. It reminded him of the colour of certain eyes, whose shape and glance had spelled his destiny; eyes to which Herr Settembrini, from his humanistic height, had referred with contempt as "Tartar slits" and "wolf's eyes" — eyes seen long ago and then found again, the eyes of Pribislav Hippe and Clavdia Chauchat. "With pleasure," he said aloud, in the pro-found stillness. "But don't break it — *c'est à visser, tu sais*."[11] And his spirit heard behind him words of warning in a mellifluous tongue.

A wood loomed, misty, far off to the right. He turned that way, to the end of having some goal before his eyes, instead of sheer white transcendence;

---

[7] "Hey, Engineer, a little reason (justice)!"
[8] reason, motive, right.
[9] rebellion.
[10] "The image of this world shall pass."
[11] "It's to be clamped (screwed) down, you know."

and made toward it with a dash, not remarking an intervening depression of the ground. He could not have seen it, in fact; everything swam before his eyes in the white mist, obliterating all contours. When he perceived it, he gave himself to the decline, unable to measure its steepness with his eye.

The grove that had attracted him lay the other side of the gully into which he had unintentionally steered. The trough, covered with fluffy snow, fell away on the side next the mountains, as he observed when he pursued it a little distance. It went downhill, the steep sides grew higher, this fold of the earth's surface seemed like a narrow passage leading into the mountain. Then the points of his skis turned up again, there began an incline, soon there were no more side walls; Hans Castorp's trackless course ran once more uphill along the mountain-side.

He saw the pine grove behind and below him, on his right, turned again toward it, and with a quick descent reached the laden trees; they stood in a wedge-shaped group, a vanguard thrust out from the mist-screened forests above. He rested beneath their boughs, and smoked a cigarette. The unnatural stillness, the monstrous solitude, still oppressed his spirit; yet he felt proud to have conquered them, brave in the pride of having measured to the height of surroundings such as these.

It was three in the afternoon. He had set out soon after luncheon, with the idea of cutting part of the long rest-cure, and tea as well, in order to be back before dark. He had brought some chocolate in his breeches pocket, and a small flask of wine; and told himself exultantly that he had still several hours to revel in all this grandeur.

The position of the sun was hard to recognize, veiled as it was in haze. Behind him, at the mouth of the valley, above that part of the mountains that was shut off from view, the clouds and mist seemed to thicken and move forward. They looked like snow — more snow — as though there were pressing demand for it! Like a good hard storm. Indeed, the little soundless flakes were coming down more quickly as he stood.

Hans Castorp put out his arm and let some of them come to rest on his sleeve; he viewed them with the knowing eye of the nature-lover. They looked mere shapeless morsels; but he had more than once had their like under his good lens, and was aware of the exquisite precision of form displayed by these little jewels, insignia, orders, agraffes — no jeweller, however skilled, could do finer, more minute work. Yes, he thought, there was a difference, after all, between this light, soft, white powder he trod with his skis, that weighed down the trees, and covered the open spaces, a difference between it and the sand on the beaches at home, to which he had likened it. For this powder was not made of tiny grains of stone; but of myriads of tiniest drops of water, which in freezing had darted together in symmetrical variation — parts, then, of the same anorganic substance which was the source of protoplasm, of plant life, of the human body. And among these myriads of enchanting little stars, in their hidden splendour that was too small for man's naked eye to see, there was not one like unto another; an endless inventiveness governed the development and unthinkable differentiation of one and the same basic scheme, the equilateral, equiangled hexagon. Yet each, in itself — this was the uncanny, the anti-organic, the life-denying character of them all — each of them was absolutely symmetrical, icily regular in form. They were too regular, as substance adapted to life never was to this degree — the living principle shuddered at this perfect precision, found it deathly, the very marrow of death — Hans Castorp felt he understood now the reason why the builders of antiquity purposely and secretly introduced minute variation from absolute symmetry in their columnar structures.

He pushed off again, shuffling through the deep snow on his flexible runners, along the edge of the wood, down the slope, up again at random, to his heart's content, about and into this lifeless land. Its empty, rolling spaces, its dried vegetation of single dwarf firs sticking up through the snow, bore a striking resemblance to a scene on the dunes. Hans Castorp nodded as he stood and fixed the likeness in his mind. Even his burning face, his trembling limbs, the peculiar and half-intoxicated mingled sensations of excitement and fatigue were pleasurable, reminding him as they did of that familiar feeling induced by the sea air, which could sting one like whips, and yet was so laden with sleepy essences. He rejoiced in his freedom of motion, his feet were like wings. He was bound to no path, none lay behind him to take him back whence he had come. At first there had been posts, staves set up as guides through the snow — but he had soon cut free from their tutelage, which recalled the coastguard with his horn, and seemed inconsistent with the attitude he had taken up toward the wild.

He pressed on, turning right and left among rocky, snow-clad elevations, and came behind them on an incline, then a level spot, then on the mountains themselves — how alluring and accessible seemed their softly covered gorges and defiles! His blood leaped at the strong allurement of the distance and the height, the ever profounder solitude. At risk of a late return he pressed on, deeper into the wild silence, the monstrous and the menacing, despite that gathering darkness was sinking down over the region like a veil, and heightening his inner apprehension until it presently passed into actual fear. It was this fear which first made him conscious that he had deliberately set out to lose his way and the direction in which valley and settlement lay — and had been as successful as heart could wish. Yet he knew that if he were to turn in his tracks and go downhill, he would reach the valley bottom — even if some distance from the Berghof — and that sooner than he had planned. He would come home too early, not have made full use of his time. On the other hand, if he were overtaken unawares by the storm, he would probably in any case not find his way home. But however genuine his fear of the elements, he refused to take premature flight; his being scarcely the sportsman's attitude, who only meddles with the elements so long as he knows himself their master, takes all precautions, and prudently yields when he must — whereas what went on in Hans Castorp's soul can only be described by the one word challenge. It was perhaps a blameworthy, presumptuous attitude, even united to such genuine awe. Yet this much is clear, to any human understanding: that when a young man has lived years long in the way this one had, something may gather — may accumulate, as our engineer might put it — in the depths of his soul, until one day it suddenly discharges itself, with a primitive exclamation of disgust, a mental "Oh, go to the devil!" a repudiation of all caution whatsoever, in short with a challenge. So on he went, in his seven-league slippers, glided down this slope too and pressed up the incline beyond, where stood a wooden hut that might be a hay-rick or shepherd's shelter, its roof weighted with flat stones. On past this to the nearest mountain ridge, bristling with forest, behind whose back the giant peaks towered upward in the mist. The wall before him, studded with single groups of trees, was steep, but looked as though one might wind to the right and get round it by climbing a little way up the slope. Once on the other side, he could see what lay beyond. Accordingly Hans Castorp set out on this tour of investigation, which began by descending from the meadow with the hut into another and rather deep gully that dropped off from right to left.

He had just begun to mount again when the expected happened, and the storm burst, the storm that had threatened so long. Or may one say "threatened" of the action of blind, nonsentient forces, which have no purpose to destroy us — that would be comforting by comparison — but are merely horribly indifferent to our fate should we become involved with them? "Hullo!" Hans Castorp thought, and stood still, as the first blast whirled through the densely falling snow and caught him. "That's a gentle zephyr — tells you what's coming." And truly this wind was savage. The air was in reality frightfully cold, probably some degrees below zero; but so long as it remained dry and still one almost found it balmy. It was when a wind came up that the cold began to cut into the flesh; and in a wind like the one that blew now, of which that first gust had been a forerunner, the furs were not bought that could protect the limbs from its icy rigours. And Hans Castorp wore no fur, only a woollen waistcoat, which he had found quite enough, or even, with the faintest gleam of sunshine, a burden. But the wind was at his back, a little sidewise; there was small inducement to turn and receive it in the face; so the mad youth, letting that fact reinforce the fundamental challenge of his attitude, pressed on among the single tree-trunks, and tried to outflank the mountain he had attacked.

It was no joke. There was almost nothing to be seen for swimming snow-flakes, that seemed without falling to fill the air to suffocation by their whirling dance. The icy gusts made his ears burn painfully, his limbs felt half paralysed, his hands were so numb he hardly knew if they held the staff. The snow blew inside his collar and melted down his back. It drifted on his shoulders and right side; he thought he should freeze as he stood into a snowman, with his staff stiff in his hands. And all this under relatively favouring circumstances; for let him turn his face to the storm and his situation would be still worse. Getting home would be no easy task — the harder, the longer he put it off.

At last he stopped, gave an angry shrug, and turned his skis the other way. Then the wind he faced took his breath on the spot, so that he was forced to go through the awkward process of turning round again to get it back, and collect his resolution to advance in the teeth of his ruthless foe. With bent head and cautious breathing he managed to get under way; but even thus forearmed, the slowness of his progress and the difficulty of seeing and breathing dismayed him. Every few minutes he had to stop, first to get his breath in the lee of the wind, and then because he saw next to nothing in the blinding whiteness, and moving as he did with head down, had to take care not to run against trees, or be flung headlong by unevennesses in the ground. Hosts of flakes flew into his face, melted there, and he anguished with the cold of them. They flew into his mouth, and died away with a weak, watery taste; flew against his eyelids so that he winked, overflowed his eyes and made seeing as difficult as it was now almost impossible for other reasons: namely, the dazzling effect of all that whiteness, and the veiling of his field of vision, so that his sense of sight was almost put out of action. It was nothingness, white, whirling nothingness, into which he looked when he forced himself to do so. Only at intervals did ghostly-seeming forms from the world of reality loom up before him: a stunted fir, a group of pines, even the pale silhouette of the hay-hut he had lately passed.

He left it behind, and sought his way back over the slope on which it stood. But there was no path. To keep direction, relatively speaking, into his own valley would be a question far more of luck than management; for while he could see his hand before his face, he could not see the ends of his skis. And even with better visibility, the host of difficulties must have combined to hinder his progress: the snow in his face, his adversary the storm, which hampered his breathing, made him fight both to take a breath and to exhale it, and constantly forced him to turn his head away to gasp. How could anyone — either Hans Castorp or another and much stronger than he — make head? He stopped, he blinked his lashes free of water drops, knocked off the snow that like a coat of mail was sheathing his body in front — and it struck him that progress, under the circumstances, was more than anyone could expect.

And yet Hans Castorp did progress. That is to say, he moved on. But whether in the right direction, whether it might not have been better to stand still, remained to be seen. Theoretically the chances were against it; and in practice he soon began to suspect something was wrong. This was not familiar ground beneath his feet, not the easy slope he had gained on mounting with such difficulty from the ravine, which had of course to be retraversed. The level distance was too short, he was already mounting again. It was plain that the storm, which came from the south-west, from the mouth of the valley, had with its violence driven him from his course. He had been exhausting himself, all this time, with a false start. Blindly, enveloped in white, whirling night, he laboured deeper and deeper into this grim and callous sphere.

"No, you don't," said he, suddenly, between his teeth, and halted. The words were not emotional, yet he felt for a second as though his heart had been clutched by an icy hand; it winced, and then knocked rapidly against his ribs, as it had the time Rhadamanthus found the moist cavity. Pathos in the grand manner was not in place, he knew, in one who had chosen defiance as his rôle, and was indebted to himself alone for all his present plight. "Not bad," he said, and discovered that his facial muscles were not his to command, that he could not express in his face any of his soul's emotions, for that it was stiff with cold. "What next? Down this slope; follow your nose home, I suppose, and keep your face to the wind — though that is a good deal easier said than done," he went on, panting with his efforts, yet actually speaking half aloud, as he tried to move on again: "but something has to happen, I can't sit down and wait, I should simply be buried in six-sided crystalline symmetricality, and Settembrini, when he came with his little horn to find me, would see me squatting here with a snow-cap over one ear." He realized that he was talking to himself, and not too sensibly — for which he took himself to task, and then continued on purpose, though his lips were so stiff he could not shape the labials, and so did without them, as he had on a certain other occasion that came to his mind. "Keep quiet, and get along with you out of here," he admonished himself, adding: "You seem to be wool-gathering, not quite right in your head, and that looks bad for you."

But this he only said with his reason — to some extent detached from the rest of him, though after all nearly concerned. As for his natural part, it felt only too much inclined to yield to the confusion which laid hold upon him with his growing fatigue. He even remarked this tendency and took thought to comment upon it. "Here," said he, "we have the typical reaction of a man who loses himself in the mountains in a snow-storm and never finds his way home." He gasped out other fragments of the same thought as he went, though he avoided giving it more specific expression. "Whoever hears about it afterwards, imagines it as horrible; but he forgets that disease — and the state I am in is, in a way of speaking, disease — so adjusts its man that it and he can come to terms; there are sensory appeasements, short circuits, a merciful narcosis — yes, oh yes, yes. But one must fight against them, after all, for they are two-faced, they are in the highest degree equivocal, everything depends upon the point of view. If you are not meant to get home, they are a benefaction, they are merciful; but if you mean to get home, they become sinister. I believe I still do. Certainly I don't intend — in this heart of mine so stormily beating it doesn't appeal to me in the least — to let myself be snowed under by this idiotically symmetrical crystallometry."

In truth, he was already affected, and his struggle against oncoming sensory confusion was feverish and abnormal. He should have been more alarmed on discovering that he had already declined from the level course — this time apparently on the other slope. For he had pushed off with the wind coming slantwise at him, which was ill-advised, though more convenient for the moment. "Never mind," he thought, "I'll get my direction again down below." Which he did, or thought he did — or, truth to tell, scarcely even thought so; worst of all, began to be indifferent whether he had done or no. Such was the effect of an insidious double attack, which he but weakly combated. Fatigue and excitement combined were a familiar state to our young man — whose acclimatization, as we know, still consisted in getting used to not getting used; and both fatigue and excitement were now present in such strength as to make impossible any thought of asserting his reason against them. He felt as often after a colloquy with Settembrini and Naphta, only to a far greater degree: dazed and tipsy, giddy, a-tremble with excitement. This was probably why he began to colour his lack of resistance to the stealing narcosis with half-maudlin references to the latest-aired complex of theories. Despite his scornful repudiation of the idea that he might lie down and be covered up with hexagonal symmetricality, something within him maundered on, sense or no sense: told him that the feeling of duty which bade him fight against insidious sensory appeasements was a purely ethical reaction, representing the sordid bourgeois view of life, irreligion, Philistinism; while the desire, nay, craving, to lie down and rest, whispered him in the guise of a comparison between this storm and a sand-storm on the desert, before which the Arab flings himself down and draws his burnous over his head. Only his lack of a burnous, the unfeasibility of drawing his woollen waistcoat over his head, prevented him from following suit — this although he was no longer a child, and pretty well aware of the conditions under which a man freezes to death.

There had been a rather steep declivity, then level ground, then again an ascent, a stiff one. This was not necessarily wrong; one must of course, on the way to the valley, traverse rising ground at times. The wind had turned capriciously round, for it was now at Hans Castorp's back, and that, taken by itself, was a blessing. Owing, perhaps, to the storm, or the soft whiteness of the incline before him, dim in the whirling air, drawing him toward it, he bent as he walked. Only a little further — supposing one were to give way to the temptation, and his temptation was great; it was so strong that it quite lived up to the many descriptions he had read of the "typical danger-state." It asserted itself, it refused to be classified with the general order of things, it insisted on being an exception, its very exigence challenged comparison — yet at the same time it never disguised its origin or aura, never denied that it was, so to speak, garbed in Spanish black, with snow-white, fluted ruff, and stood for ideas and fundamental conceptions that were characteristically gloomy, strongly Jesuitical and anti-human, for the rack-and-knout discipline which was the particular horror of Herr Settembrini, though he never opposed it without making himself ridiculous, like a hand-organ man for ever grinding out "*ragione*" to the same old tune.

And yet Hans Castorp did hold himself upright and resist his craving to lie down. He could see nothing, but he struggled, he came forward. Whether to the purpose or not, he could not tell; but he did his part, and moved on despite the weight the cold more and more laid upon his limbs. The present slope was too steep to ascend directly, so he slanted a little, and went on thus awhile without much heed whither. Even to lift his stiffened lids to peer before him was so great and so nearly useless an effort as to offer him small incentive. He merely caught glimpses: here clumps of pines that merged together; there a ditch or stream, a black line marked out between overhanging banks of snow. Now, for a change, he was going downhill, with the wind in his face, when, at some distance before him, and seeming to hang in the driving wind and mist, he saw the faint outline of a human habitation.

Ah, sweet and blessed sight! Verily he had done well, to march stoutly on despite all obstacles, until now human dwellings appeared, in sign that the inhabited valley was at hand. Perhaps there were even human beings, perhaps he might enter and abide the end of the storm under shelter, then get directions, or a guide if the dark should have fallen. He held toward this chimerical goal, that often quite vanished in mist, and took an exhausting climb against the wind before it was reached; finally drew near it — to discover, with what staggering astonishment and horror may be imagined, that it was only the hay-hut with the weighted roof, to which, after all his striving, by all his devious paths, he had come back.

That was the very devil. Hans Castorp gave vent to several heart-felt curses — of which his lips were too stiff to pronounce the labials. He examined the hut, to get his bearings, and came to the conclusion that he had approached it from the same direction as before — namely, from the rear; and therefore, what he had accomplished for the past hour — as he reckoned it — had been sheer waste of time and effort. But there it was, just as the books said. You went in a circle, gave yourself endless trouble under the delusion that you were accomplishing something, and all the time you were simply describing some great silly arc that would turn back to where it had its beginning, like the riddling year itself. You wandered about, without getting home. Hans Castorp recognized the traditional phenomenon with a certain grim satisfaction — and even slapped his thigh in astonishment at this punctual general law fulfilling itself in his particular case.

The lonely hut was barred, the door locked fast, no entrance possible. But Hans Castorp decided to stop for the present. The projecting roof gave the illusion of shelter, and the hut itself, on the side turned toward the mountains, afforded, he found, some little protection against the storm. He leaned his shoulder against the rough-hewn timber, since his long skis prevented him from leaning his back. And so he stood, obliquely to the wall, having thrust his staff in the snow; hands in pockets, his collar turned up as high as it would go, bracing himself on his outside leg, and leaning his dizzy head against the wood, his eyes closed, but opening them every now and then to look down his shoulder and across the gully to where the high mountain wall palely appeared and disappeared in mist.

His situation was comparatively comfortable. "I can stick it like this all night, if I have to," he thought, "if I change legs from time to time, lie on the other side, so to speak, and move about a bit between whiles, as of course I must. I'm rather stiff, naturally, but the effort I made has accumulated some inner warmth, so after all it was not quite in vain, that I have come round all this way. Come round — not coming round — that's the regular expression they use, of people drowned or frozen to death. — I suppose I used it because I am not quite so clear in the head as I might be. But it is a good thing I can stick it out here; for this frantic nuisance of a snow-storm can carry on until morning without a qualm, and if it only keeps up until dark it will be quite bad enough, for in the dark the danger of going round and round and *not* coming round is as great as in a storm. It must be toward evening already, about six o'clock, I should say, after all the time I wasted on my circular tour. Let's see, how late is it?" He felt for his watch; his numbed fingers could scarcely find and draw it from his pocket. Here it was, his gold hunting-watch, with his monogram on the lid, ticking faithfully away in this lonely waste, like Hans Castorp's own heart, that touching human heart that beat in the organic warmth of his interior man.

It was half past four. But deuce take it, it had been nearly as much before the storm burst. Was it possible his whole bewildered circuit had lasted scarcely a quarter of an hour? " 'Coming round' makes time seem long," he noted. "And when you *don't* 'come round' — does it seem longer? But the fact remains that at five or half past it will be regularly dark. Will the storm hold up in time to keep me from running in circles again? Suppose I take a sip of port — it might strengthen me."

He had brought with him a bottle of that amateurish drink, simply because it was always kept ready in flat bottles at the Berghof, for excursions — though not, of course, excursions like this unlawful escapade. It was not meant for people who went out in the snow and got lost and night-bound in the mountains. Had his senses been less befogged, he must have said to himself that if he were bent on getting home, it was almost the worst thing he could have done. He did say so, after he had drunk several swallows, for they took effect at once, and it was an effect much like that of the Kulmbacher beer on the evening of his arrival at the Berghof, when he had angered Settembrini by his ungoverned prattle anent fish-sauces and the like — Herr Ludovico, the pedagogue, the same who held madmen to their senses when they would give themselves rein. Hans Castorp heard through thin air the mellifluous sound of his horn; the orator and schoolmaster was nearing by forced marches, to rescue his troublesome nursling, life's delicate child, from his present desperate pass and lead him home. — All which was of course sheer rubbish, due to the Kulmbacher he had so foolishly drunk. For of course Herr Settembrini had no horn, how could he have? He had a hand-organ, propped by a sort of wooden leg against the pavement, and as he played a sprightly air, he flung his humanistic eyes up to the people in the houses. And furthermore he knew nothing whatever of what had happened, as he no longer lived in House Berghof, but with Lukaček the tailor, in his little attic room with the water-bottle, above Naphta's silken cell. Moreover, he would have nor right nor reason to interfere — no more than upon that carnival night on which Hans Castorp had found himself in a position quite as mad and bad as this one, when he gave the ailing Clavdia Chauchat back *son crayon* — his, Pribislav Hippe's, pencil. What position was that? What position could it be but the horizontal, literally and not metaphorically the position of all long-termers up here? Was not he himself used to lie long hours out of doors, in snow and frost, by night as well as day? And he was making ready to sink down when the idea seized him, took him as it were by the collar and fetched him up standing, that all this nonsense he was uttering was still inspired by the Kulmbacher beer and the impersonal, quite typical and traditional longing to lie down and sleep, of which he had always heard, and which would by quibbling and sophistry now betray him.

"That was the wrong way to go to work," he acknowledged to himself. "The port was not at all the right thing; just the few sips of it have made my head so heavy I cannot hold it up, and my thoughts are all just confused, stupid quibbling with words. I can't depend on them — not only the first thought that comes into my head, but even the second one, the correction which my reason tries to make upon the first — more's the pity. 'Son crayon!' That means her pencil, not his pencil, in this case; you only say son because crayon is masculine. The rest is just a pretty feeble play on words. Imagine stopping to talk about that when there is a much more important fact; namely, that my left leg, which I am using as a support, reminds me of the wooden leg on Settembrini's hand-organ, that he keeps jolting over the pavement with his knee, to get up close to the window and hold out his velvet hat for the girl up there to throw something into. And at the same time, I seem to be pulled, as though with hands, to lie down in the snow. The only thing to do is to move about. I must pay for the Kulmbacher, and limber up my wooden leg."

He pushed himself away from the wall with his shoulder. But one single pace forward, and the wind sliced at him like a scythe, and drove him back to the shelter of the wall. It was unquestionably the position indicated for the time; he might change it by turning his left shoulder to the wall and propping himself on the right leg, with sundry shakings of the left, to restore the circulation as much as might be. "Who leaves the house in weather like this?" he said. "Moderate activity is all right; but not too much craving for adventure, no coying with the bride of the storm. Quiet, quiet — if the head be heavy, let it droop. The wall is good, a certain warmth seems to come from the logs — probably the feeling is entirely subjective. — Ah, the trees, the trees! Oh, living climate of the living — how sweet it smells!"

It was a park. It lay beneath the terrace on which he seemed to stand — a spreading park of luxuriant green shade-trees, elms, planes, beeches, birches, oaks, all in the dappled light and shade of their fresh, full, shimmering foliage, and gently rustling tips. They breathed a deliciously moist, balsamic breath into the air. A warm shower passed over them, but the rain was sunlit. One could see high up in the sky the whole air filled with the bright ripple of raindrops. How lovely it was! Oh, breath of the homeland, oh, fragrance and abundance of the plain, so long foregone! The air was full of bird song — dainty, sweet, blithe fluting, piping, twittering, cooing, trilling, warbling, though not a single little creature could be seen. Hans Castorp smiled, breathing gratitude. But still more beauties were preparing. A rainbow flung its arc slanting across the scene, most bright and perfect, a sheer delight, all its rich glossy, banded colours moistly shimmering down into the thick, lustrous green. It was like music, like the sound of harps commingled with flutes and violins. The blue and the violet were transcendent. And they descended and magically blended, were transmuted and re-unfolded more lovely than before. Once, some years earlier, our young Hans Castorp had been privileged to hear a world-famous Italian tenor, from whose throat had gushed a glorious stream to witch the world with gracious art. The singer took a high note, exquisitely; then held it, while the passionate harmony swelled, unfolded, glowed from moment to moment with new radiance. Unsuspected veils dropped from before it one by one; the last one sank away, revealing what must surely be the ultimate tonal purity — yet no, for still another fell, and then a well-nigh incredible third and last, shaking into the air such an extravagance of tear-glistening splendour, that confused murmurs of protest rose from the audience, as though it could bear no more; and our young friend found that he was sobbing. — So now with the scene before him, constantly transformed and transfigured as it was before his eyes. The bright, rainy veil fell away; behind it stretched the sea, a southern sea of deep, deepest blue shot with silver lights, and a beautiful bay, on one side mistily open, on the other enclosed by mountains whose outline paled away into blue space. In the middle distance lay islands, where palms rose tall and small white houses gleamed among cypress groves. Ah, it was all too much, too blest for sinful mortals, that glory of light, that deep purity of the sky, that sunny freshness on the water! Such a scene Hans Castorp had never beheld, nor anything like it. On his holidays he had barely sipped at the south, the sea for him meant the colourless, tempestuous northern tides, to which he clung with inarticulate, childish love. Of the Mediterranean, Naples, Sicily, he knew nothing. And yet — he *remembered*. Yes, strangely enough, that was recognition which so moved him. "Yes, yes, its very image," he was crying out, as though in his heart he had always cherished a picture of this spacious, sunny bliss. Always — and that always went far, far, unthinkably far back, as far as the open sea there on the left where it ran out to the violet sky bent down to meet it.

The sky-line was high, the distance seemed to mount to Hans Castorp's view, looking down as he did from his elevation onto the spreading gulf beneath. The mountains held it embraced, their tree-clad foot-hills running down to the sea; they reached in half-circle from the middle distance to the point where he sat, and beyond. This was a mountainous littoral, at one point of which he was crouching upon a sun-warmed stone terrace, while before him the ground, descending among undergrowth, by moss-covered rocky steps, ran down to a level shore, where the reedy shingle formed little blue-dyed bays, minute archipelagoes and harbours. And all the sunny region, these open coastal heights and laughing rocky basins, even the sea itself out to the islands, where boats plied to and fro, was peopled far and wide. On every hand human beings, children of sun and sea, were stirring or sitting. Beautiful young human creatures, so blithe, so good and gay, so pleasing to see — at sight of them Hans Castorp's whole heart opened in a responsive love, keen almost to pain.

Youths were at work with horses, running hand on halter alongside their whinnying, head-tossing charges; pulling the refractory ones on a long rein, or else, seated bareback, striking the flanks of their mounts with naked heels, to drive them into the sea. The muscles of the riders' backs played beneath the sun-bronzed skin, and their voices were enchanting beyond words as they shouted to each other or to their steeds. A little bay ran deep into the coast line, mirroring the shore as does a mountain lake; about it girls were dancing. One of them sat with her back toward him, so that her neck, and the hair drawn to a knot above it smote him with loveliness. She sat with her feet in a depression of the rock, and played on a shepherd's pipe, her eyes roving above the stops to her companions, as in long, wide garments, smiling, with outstretched arms, alone, or in pairs swaying gently toward each other, they moved in the paces of the dance. Behind the flute-player — she too was white-clad, and her back was long and slender, laterally rounded by the movement of her arms — other maidens were sitting, or standing entwined to watch the dance, and quietly talking. Beyond them still, young men were practising archery. Lovely and pleasant it was to see the older ones show the younger, curly-locked novices, how to span the bow and take aim; draw with them, and laughing support them staggering back from the push of the arrow as it leaped from the bow. Others were fishing, lying prone on a jut of rock, waggling one leg in the air, holding the line out over the water, approaching their heads in talk. Others sat straining forward to fling the bait far out. A ship, with mast and yards, lying high out of the tide, was being eased, shoved, and steadied into the sea. Children played and exulted among the breaking waves. A young female, lying outstretched, drawing with one hand her flowered robe high between her breasts, reached with the other in the air after a twig bearing fruit and leaves, which a second, a slender-hipped creature, erect at her head, was playfully withholding. Young folk were sitting in nooks of the rocks, or hesitating at the water's edge, with crossed arms clutching either shoulder, as they tested the chill with their toes. Pairs strolled along the beach, close and confiding, at the maiden's ear the lips of the youth. Shaggy-haired goats leaped from ledge to ledge of the rocks, while the young goatherd, wearing perched on his brown curls a little hat with the brim turned up behind, stood watching them from a height, one hand on his hip, the other holding the long staff on which he leaned.

"Oh, lovely, lovely," Hans Castorp breathed. "How joyous and winning they are, how fresh and healthy, happy and clever they look! It is not alone the outward form, they seem to be wise and gentle through and through. That is what makes me in love with them, the spirit that speaks out of them, the sense, I might almost say, in which they live and play together." By which he meant the friendliness, the mutual courteous regard these children of the sun showed to each other, a calm, reciprocal reverence veiled in smiles, manifested almost imperceptibly, and yet possessing them all by the power of sense association and ingrained idea. A dignity, even a gravity, was held, as it were, in solution in their lightest mood, perceptible only as an ineffable spiritual influence, a high seriousness without austerity, a reasoned goodness conditioning every act. All this, indeed, was not without its ceremonial side. A young mother, in a brown robe loose at the shoulder, sat on a rounded mossy stone and suckled her child, saluted by all who passed with a characteristic gesture which seemed to comprehend all that lay implicit in their general bearing. The young men, as they approached, lightly and formally crossed their arms on their breasts, and smilingly bowed; the maidens shaped the suggestion of a curtsy, as the worshipper does when he passes the high altar, at the same time nodding repeatedly, blithely and heartily. This mixture of formal homage with lively friendliness, and the slow, mild mien of the mother as well, where she sat pressing her breast with her forefinger to ease the flow of milk to her babe, glancing up from it to acknowledge with a smile the reverence paid her — this sight thrilled Hans Castorp's heart with something very close akin to ecstasy. He could not get his fill of looking, yet asked himself in concern whether he had a right, whether it was not perhaps punishable, for him, an outsider, to be a party to the sunshine and gracious loveliness of all these happy folk. He felt common, clumsy-booted. It seemed unscrupulous.

A lovely boy, with full hair drawn sideways across his brow and falling on his temples, sat directly beneath him, apart from his companions, with arms folded on his breast — not sadly, not ill-naturedly, quite tranquilly on one side. This lad looked up, turned his gaze upward and looked at him, Hans Castorp, and his eyes went between the watcher and the scenes upon the strand, watching his watching, to and fro. But suddenly he looked past Hans Castorp into space, and that smile, common to them all, of polite and brotherly regard, disappeared in a moment from his lovely, purely cut, half-childish face. His brows did not darken, but in his gaze there came a solemnity that looked as though carven out of stone, inexpressive, unfathomable, a deathlike reserve, which gave the scarcely reassured Hans Castorp a thorough fright, not unaccompanied by a vague apprehension of its meaning.

He too looked in the same direction. Behind him rose towering columns, built of cylindrical blocks without bases, in the joinings of which moss had grown. They formed the façade of a temple gate, on whose foundations he was sitting, at the top of a double flight of steps with space between. Heavy of heart he rose, and, descending the stair on one side, passed through the high gate below, and along a flagged street, which soon brought him before other propylæa. He passed through these as well, and now stood facing the temple that lay before him, massy, weathered to a grey-green tone, on a foundation reached by a steep flight of steps. The broad brow of the temple rested on the capitals of powerful, almost stunted columns, tapering toward the top — sometimes a fluted block had been shoved out of line and projected a little in profile. Painfully, helping himself on with his hands, and sighing for the growing oppression of his heart, Hans Castorp mounted the high steps and gained the grove of columns. It was very deep, he moved in it as among the trunks in a forest of beeches by the pale northern sea. He purposely avoided the centre, yet for all that slanted back again, and presently stood before a group of statuary, two female figures carved in stone, on a high base: mother and daughter, it seemed; one of them sitting, older than the other, more dignified, right goddesslike and mild, yet with mourning brows above the lightless empty eye-sockets; clad in a flowing tunic and a mantle of many folds, her matronly brow with its waves of hair covered with a veil. The other figure stood in the protecting embrace of the first, with round, youthful face, and arms and hands wound and hidden in the folds of the mantle.

Hans Castorp stood looking at the group, and from some dark cause his laden heart grew heavier still, and more oppressed with its weight of dread and anguish. Scarcely daring to venture, but following an inner compulsion, he passed behind the statuary, and through the double row of columns beyond. The bronze door of the sanctuary stood open, and the poor soul's knees all but gave way beneath him at the sight within. Two grey old women, witchlike, with hanging breasts and dugs of finger-length, were busy there, between flaming braziers, most horribly. They were dismembering a child. In dreadful silence they tore it apart with their bare hands — Hans Castorp saw the bright hair blood-smeared — and cracked the tender bones between their jaws, their dreadful lips dripped blood. An icy coldness held him. He would have covered his eyes and fled, but could not. They at their gory business had already seen him, they shook their reeking fists and uttered curses — soundlessly, most vilely, with the last obscenity, and in the dialect of Hans Castorp's native Hamburg. It made him sick, sick as never before. He tried desperately to escape; knocked into a column with his shoulder — and found himself, with the sound of that dreadful whispered brawling still in his ears, still wrapped in the cold horror of it, lying by his hut, in the snow, leaning against one arm, with his head upon it, his legs in their skis stretched out before him.

It was no true awakening. He blinked his relief at being free from those execrable hags, but was not very clear, nor even greatly concerned, whether this was a hay-hut, or the column of a temple, against which he lay; and after a fashion continued to dream, no longer in pictures, but in thoughts hardly less involved and fantastic.

"I felt it was a dream, all along," he rambled. "A lovely and horrible dream. I knew all the time that I was making it myself — the park with the trees, the delicious moisture in the air, and all the rest, both dreadful and dear. In a way, I knew it all beforehand. But how is it a man can know all that and call it up to bring him bliss and terror both at once? Where did I get the beautiful bay with the islands, where the temple precincts, whither the eyes of that charming boy pointed me, as he stood there alone? Now I know that it is not out of our single souls we dream. We dream anonymously and communally, if each after his fashion. The great soul of which we are a part may dream through us, in our manner of dreaming, its own secret dreams, of its youth, its hope, its joy and peace — and its blood-sacrifice. Here I lie at my column and still feel in my body the actual remnant of my dream — the icy horror of the human sacrifice, but also the joy that had filled my heart to its very depths, born of the happiness and brave bearing of those human creatures in white. It is meet and proper, I hereby declare that I have a prescriptive right to lie here and dream these dreams. For in my life up here I have known reason and recklessness. I have wandered lost with Settembrini and Naphta in high and mortal places. I know all of man. I have known mankind's flesh and blood. I gave back to the ailing Clavdia Chauchat Pribislav Hippe's lead-pencil. But he who knows the body, life, knows death. And that is not all; it is, pedagogically speaking, only the beginning. One must have the other half of the story, the other side. For all interest in disease and death is only another expression of interest in life, as is proven by the humanistic faculty of medicine, that addresses life and its ails always so politely in Latin, and is only a division of the great and pressing concern which, in all sympathy, I now name by its name: the human being, the delicate child of life, man, his state and standing in the universe. I understand no little about him, I have learned much from 'those up here,' I have been driven up from the valley, so that the breath almost left my poor body. Yet now from the base of my column I have no meagre view. I have dreamed of man's state, of his cour-teous and enlightened social state; behind which, in the temple, the horrible blood-sacrifice was consummated. Were they, those children of the sun, so sweetly courteous to each other, in silent recognition of that horror? It would be a fine and right conclusion they drew. I will hold to them, in my soul, I will hold with them and not with Naphta, neither with Settembrini. They are both talkers; the one luxurious and spiteful, the other for ever blowing on his penny pipe of reason, even vainly imagining he can bring the mad to their senses. It is all Philistinism and morality, most certainly it is irreligious. Nor am I for little Naptha either, or his religion, that is only a *guazzabuglio*[12] of God and the Devil, good and evil, to the end that the individual soul shall plump into it head first, for the sake of mystic immersion in the universal. Pedagogues both! Their quarrels and counter-positions are just a *guazzabuglio* too, and a confused noise of battle, which need trouble nobody who keeps a little clear in his head and pious in his heart. Their aristocratic question! Disease, health! Spirit, nature! Are those contradictions? I ask, are they problems? No, they are no problems, neither is the problem of their aristoc-racy. The recklessness of death is in life, it would not be life without it — and in the centre is the position of the *Homo Dei*, between recklessness and reason, as his state is between mystic community and windy individualism. I, from my column, perceive all this. In this state he must live gallantly, asso-ciate in friendly reverence with himself, for only he is aristocratic, and the

12 medley, mixture.

counter-positions are not at all. Man is the lord of counter-positions, they can be only through him, and thus he is more aristocratic than they. More so than death, too aristocratic for death — that is the freedom of his mind. More aristocratic than life, too aristocratic for life, and that is the piety in his heart. There is both rhyme and reason in what I say, I have made a dream poem of humanity. I will cling to it. I will be good. I will let death have no mastery over my thoughts. For therein lies goodness and love of humankind, and in nothing else. Death is a great power. One takes off one's hat before him, and goes weavingly on tiptoe. He wears the stately ruff of the departed and we do him honour in solemn black. Reason stands simple before him, for reason is only virtue, while death is release, immensity, abandon, desire. Desire, says my dream. Lust, not love. Death and love — no, I cannot make a poem of them, they don't go together. Love stands opposed to death. It is love, not reason, that is stronger than death. Only love, not reason, gives sweet thoughts. And from love and sweetness alone can form come: form and civilization, friendly, enlightened, beautiful human intercourse — always in silent recognition of the blood-sacrifice. Ah, yes, it is well and truly dreamed. I have taken stock. I will remember. I will keep faith with death in my heart, yet well remember that faith with death and the dead is evil, is hostile to humankind, so soon as we give it power over thought and action. *For the sake of goodness and love, man shall let death have no sovereignty over his thoughts.* — And with this — I awake. or I have dreamed it out to the end, I have come to my goal. Long, long have I sought after this word, in the place where Hippe appeared to me, in my loggia, everywhere. Deep into the snow mountains my search has led me. Now I have it fast. My dream has given it me, in utter clearness, that I may know it for ever. Yes, I am in simple raptures, my body is warm, my heart beats high and knows why. It beats not solely on physical grounds, as finger-nails grow on a corpse; but humanly, on grounds of my joyful spirits. My dream word was a draught, better than port or ale, it streams through my veins like love and life, I tear myself from my dream and sleep, knowing as I do, perfectly well, that they are highly dangerous to my young life. Up, up! Open your eyes! These are your limbs, your legs here in the snow! Pull yourself together, and up! Look — fair weather!"

The bonds held fast that kept his limbs involved. He had a hard struggle to free himself — but the inner compulsion proved stronger. With a jerk he raised himself on his elbows, briskly drew up his knees, shoved, rolled, wrestled to his feet; stamped with his skis in the snow, flung his arms about his ribs and worked his shoulders violently, all the while casting strained, alert glances about him and above, where now a pale blue sky showed itself between grey-bluish clouds, and these presently drew away to discover a thin sickle of a moon. Early twilight reigned: no snowfall, no storm. The wall of the opposite mountain with its shaggy, tree-clad ridge stretched out before him plain and peaceful. Shadow lay on half its height, but the upper half was bathed in palest rosy light. How were things in the world? Was it morning? Had he, despite what the books said, lain all night in the snow and not frozen? Not a member was frost-bitten, nothing snapped when he stamped, shook and struck himself, as he did vigorously, all the time seeking to establish the facts of his situation. Ears, toes, finger-tips, were of course numb, but not more so than they had often been at night in his loggia. He could take his watch from his pocket — it was still going, it had not stopped, as it did if he forgot to wind it. It said not yet five — it was in fact considerably earlier, twelve, thirteen minutes. Preposterous! Could it be he had lain here in the snow only ten minutes or so, while all these scenes of horror and delight and those presumptuous thoughts had spun themselves in his brain, and the hexagonal hurly[13] vanished as it came? If that were true, then he must be grateful for his good fortune; that is, from the point of view of a safe home-coming. For twice such a turn had come, in his dream and fantasy, as had made him start up — once from horror, and again for rapture. It seemed, indeed, that life meant well by her lone-wandering delicate child.

Be all that as it might, and whether it was morning or afternoon — there could in fact be no doubt that it was still late afternoon — in any case, there was nothing in the circumstances or in his own condition to prevent his going home, which he accordingly did: descending in a fine sweep, as the crow flies, to the valley, where, as he reached it, lights were showing, though his way had been well enough lighted by reflection from the snow. He came down the Brehmenbühl, along the edge of the forest, and was in the Dorf by half past five. He left his skis at the grocer's, rested a little in Herr Settembrini's attic cell, and told him how the storm had overtaken him in the mountains. The horrified humanist scolded him roundly, and straightway lighted his spirit-kettle to brew coffee for the exhausted one — the strength of which did not prevent Hans Castorp from falling asleep as he sat.

An hour later the highly civilized atmosphere of the Berghof caressed him. He ate enormously at dinner. What he had dreamed was already fading from his mind. What he had thought — even that selfsame evening it was no longer so clear as it had been at first.

[13] commotion.

Sherwood Anderson (1876–1941)

AMERICAN SHORT STORY WRITER and NOVELIST

Death in the Woods

She was an old woman and lived on a farm near the town in which I lived. All country and small-town people have seen such old women, but no one knows much about them. Such an old woman comes into town driving an old worn-out horse or she comes afoot carrying a basket. She may own a few hens and have eggs to sell. She brings them in a basket and takes them to a grocer. There she trades them in. She gets some salt pork and some beans. Then she gets a pound or two of sugar and some flour.

Afterwards she goes to the butcher's and asks for some dog-meat. She may spend ten or fifteen cents, but when she does she asks for something. Formerly the butchers gave liver to any one who wanted to carry it away. In our family we were always having it. Once one of my brothers got a whole cow's liver at the slaughter-house near the fairgrounds in our town. We had it until we were sick of it. It never cost a cent. I have hated the thought of it ever since.

The old farm woman got some liver and a soup-bone. She never visited with any one, and as soon as she got what she wanted she lit out for home. It made quite a load for such an old body. No one gave her a lift. People drive right down a road and never notice an old woman like that.

There was such an old woman who used to come into town past our house one Summer and Fall when I was a young boy and was sick with what was called inflammatory rheumatism. She went home later carrying a heavy pack on her back. Two or three large gaunt-looking dogs followed at her heels.

The old woman was nothing special. She was one of the nameless ones that hardly any one knows, but she got into my thoughts. I have just suddenly now, after all these years, remembered her and what happened. It is a story. Her name was Grimes, and she lived with her husband and son in a small unpainted house on the bank of a small creek four miles from town.

The husband and son were a tough lot. Although the son was but twenty-one, he had already served a term in jail. It was whispered about that the woman's husband stole horses and ran them off to some other county. Now and then, when a horse turned up missing, the man had also disappeared. No one ever caught him. Once, when I was loafing at Tom Whitehead's livery-barn, the man came there and sat on the bench in front. Two or three other men were there, but no one spoke to him. He sat for a few minutes and then got up and went away. When he was leaving he turned around and stared at the men. There was a look of defiance in his eyes. "Well, I have tried to be friendly. You don't want to talk to me. It has been so wherever I have gone in this town. If, some day, one of your fine horses turns up missing, well, then what?" He did not say anything actually. "I'd like to bust one of you on the jaw," was about what his eyes said. I remember how the look in his eyes made me shiver.

The old man belonged to a family that had had money once. His name was Jake Grimes. It all comes back clearly now. His father, John Grimes, had owned a sawmill when the country was new, and had made money. Then he got to drinking and running after women. When he died there wasn't much left.

Jake blew in the rest. Pretty soon there wasn't any more lumber to cut and his land was nearly all gone.

He got his wife off a German farmer, for whom he went to work one June day in the wheat harvest. She was a young thing then and scared to death. You see, the farmer was up to something with the girl — she was, I think, a bound girl and his wife had her suspicions. She took it out on the girl when the man wasn't around. Then, when the wife had to go off to town for supplies, the farmer got after her. She told young Jake that nothing really ever happened, but he didn't know whether to believe it or not.

He got her pretty easy himself, the first time he was out with her. He wouldn't have married her if the German farmer hadn't tried to tell him where to get off. He got her to go riding with him in his buggy one night when he was threshing on the place, and then he came for her the next Sunday night.

She managed to get out of the house without her employer's seeing, but when she was getting into the buggy he showed up. It was almost dark, and he just popped up suddenly at the horse's head. He grabbed the horse by the bridle and Jake got out his buggy-whip.

They had it out all right! The German was a tough one. Maybe he didn't care whether his wife knew or not. Jake hit him over the face and shoulders with the buggy-whip, but the horse got to acting up and he had to get out.

Then the two men went for it. The girl didn't see it. The horse started to run away and went nearly a mile down the road before the girl got him stopped. Then she managed to tie him to a tree beside the road. (I wonder how I know all this. It must have stuck in my mind from small-town tales when I was a boy.) Jake found her there after he got through with the German. She was huddled up in the buggy seat, crying, scared to death. She told Jack a lot of stuff, how the German had tried to get her, how he chased her once into the barn, how another time, when they happened to be alone in the house together, he tore her dress open clear down the front. The German, she said, might have got her that time if he hadn't heard his old woman drive in at the gate. She had been off to town for supplies. Well, she would be putting the horse in the barn. The German managed to sneak off to the fields without his wife seeing. He told the girl he would kill her if she told. What could she do? She told a lie about ripping her dress in the barn when she was feeding the stock. I remember now that she was a bound girl and did not know where her father and mother were. Maybe she did not have any father. You know what I mean.

Such bound children were often enough cruelly treated. They were children who had no parents, slaves really. There were very few orphan homes then. They were legally bound into some home. It was a matter of pure luck how it came out.

II

She married Jake and had a son and daughter, but the daughter died.

Then she settled down to feed stock. That was her job. At the German's place she had cooked the food for the German and his wife. The wife was a strong woman with big hips and worked most of the time in the fields with her husband. She fed them and fed the cows in the barn, fed the pigs, the horses and the chickens. Every moment of every day, as a young girl, was spent feeding something.

Then she married Jake Grimes and he had to be fed. She was a slight thing, and when she had been married for three or four years, and after the two children were born, her slender shoulders became stooped.

Jake always had a lot of big dogs around the house, that stood near the unused sawmill near the creek. He was always trading horses when he wasn't stealing something and had a lot of poor bony ones about. Also he kept three or four pigs and a cow. They were all pastured in the few acres left of the Grimes place and Jake did little enough work.

He went into debt for a threshing outfit and ran it for several years, but it did not pay. People did not trust him. They were afraid he would steal the grain at night. He had to go a long way off to get work and it cost too much to get there. In the Winter he hunted and cut a little firewood, to be sold in some nearby town. When the son grew up he was just like the father. They got drunk together. If there wasn't anything to eat in the house when they came home the old man gave his old woman a cut over the head. She had a few chickens of her own and had to kill one of them in a hurry. When they were all killed she wouldn't have any eggs to sell when she went to town, and then what would she do?

She had to scheme all her life about getting things fed, getting the pigs fed so they would grow fat and could be butchered in the Fall. When they were butchered her husband took most of the meat off to town and sold it. If he did not do it first the boy did. They fought sometimes and when they fought the old woman stood aside trembling.

She had got the habit of silence anyway — that was fixed. Sometimes, when she began to look old — she wasn't forty yet — and when the husband and son were both off, trading horses or drinking or hunting or stealing, she went around the house and the barnyard muttering to herself.

How was she going to get everything fed? — that was her problem. The dogs had to be fed. There wasn't enough hay in the barn for the horses and the cow. If she didn't feed the chickens how could they lay eggs? Without eggs to sell how could she get things in town, things she had to have to keep the life of the farm going? Thank heaven, she did not have to feed her husband — in a certain way. That hadn't lasted long after their marriage and after the babies came. Where he went on his long trips she did not know. Sometimes he was gone from home for weeks, and after the boy grew up they went off together.

They left everything at home for her to manage and she had no money. She knew no one. No one ever talked to her in town. When it was Winter she had to gather sticks of wood for her fire, had to try to keep the stock fed with very little grain.

The stock in the barn cried to her hungrily, the dogs followed her about. In the Winter the hens laid few enough eggs. They huddled in the corners of the barn and she kept watching them. If a hen lays an egg in the barn in the Winter and you do not find it, it freezes and breaks.

One day in Winter the old woman went off to town with a few eggs and the dogs followed her. She did not get started until nearly three o'clock and the snow was heavy. She hadn't been feeling very well for several days and so she went muttering along, scantily clad, her shoulders stooped. She had an old grain bag in which she carried her eggs, tucked away down in the bottom. There weren't many of them, but in Winter the price of eggs is up. She would get a little meat in exchange for the eggs, some salt pork, a little sugar, and some coffee perhaps. It might be the butcher would give her a piece of liver.

When she had got to town and was trading in her eggs the dogs lay by the door outside. She did pretty well, got the things she needed, more than she had hoped. Then she went to the butcher and he gave her some liver and some dog-meat.

It was the first time any one had spoken to her in a friendly way for a long time. The butcher was alone in his shop when she came in and was annoyed by the thought of such a sick-looking old woman out on such a day. It was bitter cold and the snow, that had let up during the afternoon, was falling again. The butcher said something about her husband and her son, swore at them, and the old woman stared at him, a look of mild surprise in her eyes as he talked. He said that if either the husband or the son were going to get any of the liver or the heavy bones with scraps of meat hanging to them that he had put into the grain bag, he'd see him starve first.

Starve, eh? Well, things had to be fed. Men had to be fed, and the horses that weren't any good but maybe could be traded off, and the poor thin cow that hadn't given any milk for three months.

Horses, cows, pigs, dogs, men.

III

The old woman had to get back before darkness came if she could. The dogs followed at her heels, sniffing at the heavy grain bag she had fastened on her back. When she got to the edge of town she stopped by a fence and tied the bag on her back with a piece of rope she had carried in her dress-pocket for just that purpose. That was an easier way to carry it. Her arms ached. It was hard when she had to crawl over fences and once she fell over and landed in the snow. The dogs went frisking about. She had to struggle to get to her feet again, but she made it. The point of climbing over the fences was that there was a short cut over a hill and through a woods. She might have gone around by the road, but it was a mile farther that way. She was afraid she couldn't make it. And then, besides, the stock had to be fed. There was a little hay left and a little corn. Perhaps her husband and son would bring some home when they came. They had driven off in the only buggy the Grimes family had, a rickety thing, a rickety horse hitched to the buggy, two other rickety horses led by halters. They were going to trade horses, get a little money if they could. They might come home drunk. It would be well to have something in the house when they came back.

The son had an affair on with a woman at the county seat, fifteen miles away. She was a rough enough woman, a tough one. Once, in the Summer, the son had brought her to the house. Both she and the son had been drinking. Jack Grimes was away and the son and his woman ordered the old woman about like a servant. She didn't mind much; she was used to it. Whatever happened she never said anything. That was her way of getting along. She had managed that way when she was a young girl at the German's and ever since she had married Jake. That time her son brought his woman to the house they stayed all night, sleeping together just as though they were married. It hadn't shocked the old woman, not much. She had got past being shocked early in life.

With the pack on her back she went painfully along across an open field, wading in the deep snow, and got into the woods.

There was a path, but it was hard to follow. Just beyond the top of the hill, where the woods was thickest, there was a small clearing. Had some one once thought of building a house there? The clearing was as large as a building lot in town, large enough for a house and a garden. The path ran along the side of the clearing, and when she got there the old woman sat down to rest at the foot of a tree.

It was a foolish thing to do. When she got herself placed, the pack against the tree's trunk, it was nice, but what about getting up again? She worried about that for a moment and then quietly closed her eyes.

She must have slept for a time. When you are about so cold you can't get any colder. The afternoon grew a little warmer and the snow came thicker than ever. Then after a time the weather cleared. The moon even came out.

There were four Grimes dogs that had followed Mrs. Grimes into town, all tall gaunt fellows. Such men as Jake Grimes and his son always keep just such dogs. They kick and abuse them, but they stay. The Grimes dogs, in order to keep from starving, had to do a lot of foraging for themselves, and they had been at it while the old woman slept with her back to the tree at the side of the clearing. They had been chasing rabbits in the woods and in adjoining fields and in their ranging had picked up three other farm dogs.

After a time all the dogs came back to the clearing. They were excited about something. Such nights, cold and clear and with a moon, do things to dogs. It may be that some old instinct, come down from the time when they were wolves and ranged the woods in packs on Winter nights, comes back into them.

The dogs in the clearing, before the old woman, had caught two or three rabbits and their immediate hunger had been satisfied. They began to play, running in circles in the clearing. Round and round they ran, each dog's nose at the tail of the next dog. In the clearing, under the snow-laden trees and under the wintry moon they made a strange picture, running thus silently, in a circle their running had beaten in the soft snow. The dogs made no sound. They ran around and around in the circle.

It may have been that the old woman saw them doing that before she died. She may have awakened once or twice and looked at the strange sight with dim old eyes.

She wouldn't be very cold now, just drowsy. Life hangs on a long time. Perhaps the old woman was out of her head. She may have dreamed of her girlhood, at the German's, and before that, when she was a child and before her mother lit out and left her.

Her dreams couldn't have been very pleasant. Not many pleasant things had happened to her. Now and then one of the Grimes dogs left the running circle and came to stand before her. The dog thrust his face close to her face. His red tongue was hanging out.

The running of the dogs may have been a kind of death ceremony. It may have been that the primitive instinct of the wolf, having been aroused in the dogs by the night and the running, made them somehow afraid.

"Now we are no longer wolves. We are dogs, the servants of men. Keep alive, man! When man dies we becomes wolves again."

When one of the dogs came to where the old woman sat with her back against the tree and thrust his nose close to her face he seemed satisfied and went back to run with the pack. All the Grimes dogs did it at some time during the evening, before she died. I knew all about it afterward, when I grew to be a man, because once in a woods in Illinois, on another Winter night, I saw a pack of dogs act just like that. The dogs were waiting for me to die as they had waited for the old woman that night when I was a child, but when it happened to me I was a young man and had no intention whatever of dying.

The old woman died softly and quietly. When she was dead and when one of the Grimes dogs had come to her and had found her dead all the dogs stopped running.

They gathered about her.

Well, she was dead now. She had fed the Grimes dogs when she was alive, what about now?

There was the pack on her back, the grain bag containing the piece of salt pork, the liver the butcher had given her, the dog-meat, the soup bones. The butcher in town, having been suddenly overcome with a feeling of pity, had loaded her grain bag heavily. It had been a big haul for the old woman.

It was a big haul for the dogs now.

IV

One of the Grimes dogs sprang suddenly out from among the others and began worrying the pack on the old woman's back. Had the dogs really been wolves that one would have been the leader of the pack. What he did, all the others did.

All of them sank their teeth into the grain bag the old woman had fastened with ropes to her back.

They dragged the old woman's body out into the open clearing. The worn-out dress was quickly torn from her shoulders. When she was found, a day or two later, the dress had been torn from her body clear to the hips, but the dogs had not touched her body. They had got the meat out of the grain bag, that was all. Her body was frozen stiff when it was found, and the shoulders were so narrow and the body so slight that in death it looked like the body of some charming young girl.

Such things happened in towns of the Middle West, on farms near town, when I was a boy. A hunter out after rabbits found the old woman's body and did not touch it. Something, the beaten round path in the little snow-covered clearing, the silence of the place, the place where the dogs had worried the body trying to pull the grain bag away or tear it open — something startled the man and he hurried off to town.

I was in Main street with one of my brothers who was town newsboy and who was taking the afternoon papers to the stores. It was almost night.

The hunter came into a grocery and told his story. Then he went to a hardware-shop and into a drugstore. Men began to gather on the sidewalks. Then they started out along the road to the place in the woods.

My brother should have gone on about his business of distributing papers but he didn't. Every one was going to the woods. The undertaker went and the town marshal. Several men got on a dray and rode out to where the path left the road and went into the woods, but the horses weren't very sharply shod and slid about on the slippery roads. They made no better time than those of us who walked.

The town marshal was a large man whose leg had been injured in the Civil War. He carried a heavy cane and limped rapidly along the road. My brother and I followed at his heels, and as we went other men and boys joined the crowd.

It had grown dark by the time we got to where the old woman had left the road but the moon had come out. The marshal was thinking there might have been a murder. He kept asking the hunter questions. The hunter went along with his gun across his shoulders, a dog following at his heels. It isn't often a rabbit hunter has a chance to be so conspicuous. He was taking full advantage of it, leading the procession with the town marshal. "I didn't see any wounds. She was a beautiful young girl. Her face was buried in the snow. No, I didn't know her." As a matter of fact, the hunter had not looked closely at the body. He had been frightened. She might have been murdered and some one might spring out from behind a tree and murder him. In a woods, in the late afternoon, when the trees are all bare and there is white snow on the ground, when all is silent, something creepy steals over the mind and body. If something strange or uncanny has happened in the neighborhood all you think about is getting away from there as fast as you can.

The crowd of men and boys had got to where the old woman had crossed the field and went, following the marshal and the hunter, up the slight incline and into the woods.

My brother and I were silent. He had his bundle of papers in a bag slung across his shoulder. When he got back to town he would have to go on distributing his papers before he went home to supper. If I went along, as he had no doubt already determined I should, we would both be late. Either mother or our older sister would have to warm our supper.

Well, we would have something to tell. A boy did not get such a chance very often. It was lucky we just happened to go into the grocery when the hunter came in. The hunter was a country fellow. Neither of us had ever seen him before.

Now the crowd of men and boys had got to the clearing. Darkness comes quickly on such Winter nights, but the full moon made everything clear. My brother and I stood near the tree, beneath which the old woman had died.

She did not look old, lying there in that light, frozen and still. One of the men turned her over in the snow and I saw everything. My body trembled with some strange mystical feeling and so did my brother's. It might have been the cold.

Neither of us had ever seen a woman's body before. It may have been the snow, clinging to the frozen flesh, that made it look so white and lovely, so like marble. No woman had come with the party from town; but one of the men, he was the town blacksmith, took off his overcoat and spread it over her. Then he gathered her into his arms and started off to town, all the others following silently. At that time no one knew who she was.

v

I had seen everything, had seen the oval in the snow, like a miniature race-track, where the dogs had run, had seen how the men were mystified, had seen the white bare young-looking shoulders, had heard the whispered comments of the men.

The men were simply mystified. They took the body to the undertaker's, and when the blacksmith, the hunter, the marshal and several others had got inside they closed the door. If father had been there perhaps he could have got in, but we boys couldn't.

I went with my brother to distribute the rest of his papers and when we got home it was my brother who told the story.

I kept silent and went to bed early. It may have been I was not satisfied with the way he told it.

Later, in the town, I must have heard other fragments of the old woman's story. She was recognized the next day and there was an investigation.

The husband and son were found somewhere and brought to town and there was an attempt to connect them with the woman's death, but it did not work. They had perfect enough alibis.

However, the town was against them. They had to get out. Where they went I never heard.

I remember only the picture there in the forest, the men standing about, the naked girlish-looking figure, face down in the snow, the tracks made by the running dogs and the clear cold Winter sky above. White fragments of clouds were drifting across the sky. They went racing across the little open space among the trees.

The scene in the forest had become for me, without my knowing it, the foundation for the real story I am now trying to tell. The fragments, you see, had to be picked up slowly, long afterwards.

Things happened. When I was a young man I worked on the farm of a German. The hired-girl was afraid of her employer. The farmer's wife hated her.

I saw things at that place. Once later, I had a half-uncanny, mystical adventure with dogs in an Illinois forest on a clear, moon-lit Winter night. When I was a schoolboy, and on a Summer day, I went with a boy friend out along a creek some miles from town and came to the house where the old woman had lived. No one had lived in the house since her death. The doors were broken from the hinges; the window lights were all broken. As the boy and I stood in the road outside, two dogs, just roving farm dogs no doubt, came running around the corner of the house. The dogs were tall, gaunt fellows and came down to the fence and glared through at us, standing in the road.

The whole thing, the story of the old woman's death, was to me as I grew older like music heard from far off. The notes had to be picked up slowly one at a time. Something had to be understood.

The woman who died was one destined to feed animal life. Anyway, that is all she ever did. She was feeding animal life before she was born, as a child, as a young woman working on the farm of the German, after she married, when she grew old and when she died. She fed animal life in cows, in chickens, in pigs, in horses, in dogs, in men. Her daughter had died in childhood and with her one son she had no articulate relations. On the night when she died she was hurrying homeward, bearing on her body food for animal life.

She died in the clearing in the woods and even after her death continued feeding animal life.

You see it is likely that, when my brother told the story, that night when we got home and my mother and sister sat listening, I did not think he got the point. He was too young and so was I. A thing so complete has its own beauty.

I shall not try to emphasize the point. I am only explaining why I was dissatisfied then and have been ever since. I speak of that only that you may understand why I have been impelled to try to tell the simple story over again.

D. H. Lawrence (1885–1930)

ENGLISH POET, NOVELIST, ESSAYIST,
and SHORT STORY WRITER

Snake

A snake came to my water-trough
On a hot, hot day, and I in pyjamas for the heat,
To drink there.

In the deep, strange-scented shade of the great dark carob-tree
I came down the steps with my pitcher
And must wait, must stand and wait, for there he was at the trough before me.

He reached down from a fissure in the earth-wall in the gloom
And trailed his yellow-brown slackness soft-bellied down, over the edge of the stone
    trough
And rested his throat upon the stone bottom,
And where the water had dripped from the tap, in a small clearness,   10
He sipped with his straight mouth,
Softly drank through his straight gums, into his slack long body,
Silently.

Someone was before me at my water-trough,
And I, like a second comer, waiting.

He lifted his head from his drinking, as cattle do,
And looked at me vaguely, as drinking cattle do,
And flickered his two-forked tongue from his lips, and mused a moment,
And stooped and drank a little more,
Being earth-brown, earth-golden from the burning bowels of the earth   20
On the day of Sicilian July, with Etna smoking.

The voice of my education said to me
He must be killed,
For in Sicily the black, black snakes are innocent, the gold are venomous.

And voices in me said, If you were a man
You would take a stick and break him now, and finish him off.

But must I confess how I liked him,
How glad I was he had come like a guest in quiet, to drink at my water-trough
And depart peaceful, pacified, and thankless,
Into the burning bowels of this earth?   30

Was it cowardice, that I dared not kill him?
Was it perversity, that I longed to talk to him?
Was it humility, to feel so honoured?
I felt so honoured.

And yet those voices:
If you were not afraid, you would kill him!

And truly I was afraid, I was most afraid,
But even so, honoured still more
That he should seek my hospitality
From out the dark door of the secret earth.   40

He drank enough
And lifted his head, dreamily, as one who has drunken,
And flickered his tongue like a forked night on the air, so black;
Seeming to lick his lips,
And looked around like a god, unseeing, into the air,
And slowly turned his head,
And slowly, very slowly, as if thrice adream,
Proceeded to draw his slow length curving round
And climb again the broken bank of my wall-face.

And as he put his head into that dreadful hole,   50
And as he slowly drew up, snake-easing his shoulders, and entered farther,
A sort of horror, a sort of protest against his withdrawing into that horrid black
      hole,
Deliberately going into the blackness, and slowly drawing himself after,
Overcame me now his back was turned.

I looked round, I put down my pitcher,
I picked up a clumsy log
And threw it at the water-trough with a clatter.

I think it did not hit him,
But suddenly that part of him that was left behind convulsed in undignified haste,
Writhed like lightning, and was gone   60
Into the black hole, the earth-lipped fissure in the wall-front,
At which, in the intense still noon, I stared with fascination.

And immediately I regretted it.
I thought how paltry, how vulgar, what a mean act!
I despised myself and the voices of my accursed human education.

And I thought of the albatross,[1]
And I wished he would come back, my snake.

For he seemed to me again like a king,
Like a king in exile, uncrowned in the underworld,
Now due to be crowned again.   70

And so, I missed my chance with one of the lords
Of life.
And I have something to expiate;
A pettiness.

Ernest Hemingway (1898–1961)

AMERICAN SHORT STORY WRITER and NOVELIST

Indian Camp

At the lake shore there was another rowboat drawn up. The two Indians stood waiting.

Nick and his father got in the stern of the boat and the Indians shoved it off and one of them got in to row. Uncle George sat in the stern of the camp rowboat. The young Indian shoved the camp boat off and got in to row Uncle George.

The two boats started off in the dark. Nick heard the oarlocks of the other boat quite a way ahead of them in the mist. The Indians rowed with quick choppy strokes. Nick lay back with his father's arm around him. It was cold on the water. The Indian who was rowing them was working very hard, but the other boat moved further ahead in the mist all the time.

"Where are we going, Dad?" Nick asked. Separation

"Over to the Indian camp. There is an Indian lady very sick."

"Oh," said Nick.

Across the bay they found the other boat beached. Uncle George was smoking a cigar in the dark. The young Indian pulled the boat way up on the beach. Uncle George gave both the Indians cigars.

They walked up from the beach through a meadow that was soaking wet with dew, following the young Indian who carried a lantern. Then they went into the woods and followed a trail that led to the logging road that ran back into the hills. It was much lighter on the logging road as the

[1] large sea bird, symbol of good luck; reference to the bird in "The Rime of the Ancient Mariner" by Samuel Taylor Coleridge.

timber was cut away on both sides. The young Indian stopped and blew out his lantern and they all walked on along the road.

They came around a bend and a dog came out barking. Ahead were the lights of the shanties where the Indian bark-peelers lived. More dogs rushed out at them. The two Indians sent them back to the shanties. In the shanty nearest the road there was a light in the window. An old woman stood in the doorway holding a lamp.

Inside on a wooden bunk lay a young Indian woman. She had been trying to have her baby for two days. All the old women in the camp had been helping her. The men had moved off up the road to sit in the dark and smoke out of range of the noise she made. She screamed just as Nick and the two Indians followed his father and Uncle George into the shanty. She lay in the lower bunk, very big under a quilt. Her head was turned to one side. In the upper bunk was her husband. He had cut his foot very badly with an ax three days before. He was smoking a pipe. The room smelled very bad.

Nick's father ordered some water to be put on the stove, and while it was heating he spoke to Nick.

"This lady is going to have a baby, Nick," he said.

"I know," said Nick.

"You don't know," said his father. "Listen to me. What she is going through is called being in labor. The baby wants to be born and she wants it to be born. All her muscles are trying to get the baby born. That is what is happening when she screams."

"I see," Nick said.

Just then the woman cried out.

"Oh, Daddy, can't you give her something to make her stop screaming?" asked Nick.

"No. I haven't any anæsthetic," his father said. "But her screams are not important. I don't hear them because they are not important."

The husband in the upper bunk rolled over against the wall.

The woman in the kitchen motioned to the doctor that the water was hot. Nick's father went into the kitchen and poured about half of the water out of the big kettle into a basin. Into the water left in the kettle he put several things he unwrapped from a handkerchief.

"Those must boil," he said, and began to scrub his hands in the basin of hot water with a cake of soap he had brought from the camp. Nick watched his father's hands scrubbing each other with the soap. While his father washed his hands very carefully and thoroughly, he talked.

"You see, Nick, babies are supposed to be born head first but sometimes they're not. When they're not they make a lot of trouble for everybody. Maybe I'll have to operate on this lady. We'll know in a little while."

When he was satisfied with his hands he went in and went to work.

"Pull back that quilt, will you, George?" he said. "I'd rather not touch it."

Later when he started to operate Uncle George and three Indian men held the woman still. She bit Uncle George on the arm and Uncle George said, "Damn squaw bitch!" and the young Indian who had rowed Uncle George over laughed at him. Nick held the basin for his father. It all took a long time.

His father picked the baby up and slapped it to make it breathe and handed it to the old woman.

"See, it's a boy, Nick," he said. "How do you like being an interne?"

Nick said, "All right." He was looking away so as not to see what his father was doing.

"There. That gets it," said his father and put something into the basin.

Nick didn't look at it.

"Now," his father said, "there's some stitches to put in. You can watch this or not, Nick, just as you like. I'm going to sew up the incision I made."

Nick did not watch. His curiosity had been gone for a long time.

His father finished and stood up. Uncle George and the three Indian men stood up. Nick put the basin out in the kitchen.

Uncle George looked at his arm. The young Indian smiled reminiscently.

"I'll put some peroxide on that, George," the doctor said.

He bent over the Indian woman. She was quiet now and her eyes were closed. She looked very pale. She did not know what had become of the baby or anything.

"I'll be back in the morning," the doctor said, standing up. "The nurse should be here from St. Ignace[1] by noon and she'll bring everything we need."

He was feeling exalted and talkative as football players are in the dressing room after a game.

"That's one for the medical journal, George," he said. "Doing a Cæsarean with a jack-knife and sewing it up with nine-foot, tapered gut leaders."

Uncle George was standing against the wall, looking at his arm.

"Oh, you're a great man, all right," he said.

"Ought to have a look at the proud father. They're usually the worst sufferers in these little affairs," the doctor said. "I must say he took it all pretty quietly."

He pulled back the blanket from the Indian's head. His hand came away wet. He mounted on the edge of the lower bunk with the lamp in one hand and looked in. The Indian lay with his face toward the wall. His throat had been cut from ear to ear. The blood had flowed down into a pool where his body sagged the bunk. His head rested on his left arm. The open razor lay, edge up, in the blankets.

"Take Nick out of the shanty, George," the doctor said.

There was no need of that. Nick, standing in the door of the kitchen, had a good view of the upper bunk when his father, the lamp in one hand, tipped the Indian's head back.

[1] a town in northern Michigan.

It was just beginning to be daylight when they walked along the logging road back toward the lake.

"I'm terribly sorry I brought you along, Nickie," said his father, all his post-operative exhilaration gone. "It was an awful mess to put you through."

"Do ladies always have such a hard time having babies?" Nick asked.

"No, that was very, very exceptional."

"Why did he kill himself, Daddy?"

"I don't know, Nick. He couldn't stand things, I guess."

"Do many men kill themselves, Daddy?" *- needs assurance*

"Not very many, Nick."

"Do many women?"   *False assurance*

"Hardly ever."

"Don't they ever?"

"Oh, yes. They do sometimes."

"Daddy?"

"Yes."

"Where did Uncle George go?"

"He'll turn up all right."

"Is dying hard, Daddy?"

"No, I think it's pretty easy, Nick. It all depends."

They were seated in the boat, Nick in the stern, his father rowing. The sun was coming up over the hills. A bass jumped, making a circle in the water. Nick trailed his hand in the water. It felt warm in the sharp chill of the morning.

In the early morning on the lake sitting in the stern of the boat with his father rowing, he felt quite sure that he would never die.

Boy doesn't learn.   *Failure of initiation*

Loren Eiseley (b. 1907)

AMERICAN ZOOLOGIST and SCIENTIFIC WRITER

The Snout

I have long been an admirer of the octopus. The cephalopods are very old, and they have slipped, protean, through many shapes. They are the wisest of the mollusks, and I have always felt it to be just as well for us that they never came ashore, but — there are other things that have.

There is no need to be frightened. It is true some of the creatures are odd, but I find the situation rather heartening than otherwise. It gives one a feeling of confidence to see nature still busy with experiments, still dynamic, and not through nor satisfied because a Devonian fish managed to end as a two-legged character with a straw hat. There are other things brewing and growing in the oceanic vat. It pays to know this. It pays to know there is just as much future as there is past. The only thing that doesn't pay is to be sure of man's own part in it.

There are things down there still coming ashore. Never make the mistake of thinking life is now adjusted for eternity. It gets into your head — the certainty, I mean — the human certainty, and then you miss it all: the things on the tide flats and what they mean, and why, as my wife says, "they ought to be watched."

The trouble is we don't know what to watch for. I have a friend, one of these Explorers Club people, who drops in now and then between trips to tell me about the size of crocodile jaws in Uganda, or what happened on some back beach in Arnhem Land.[1]

"They fell out of the trees," he said. "Like rain. And into the boat."

"Uh?" I said, noncommittally.

"They did so," he protested, "and they were hard to catch."

"Really — " I said.

"We were pushing a dugout up one of the tidal creeks in northern Australia and going fast when *smacko* we jam this mangrove bush and the things come tumbling down.

"What were they doing sitting up there in bunches? I ask you. It's no place for a fish. Besides that they had a way of sidling off with those popeyes trained on you. I never liked it. Somebody ought to keep an eye on them."

"Why?" I asked.

"I don't know why," he said impatiently, running a rough, square hand through his hair and wrinkling his forehead. "I just mean they make you feel that way, is all. A fish belongs in the water. It ought to stay there—just as we live on land in houses. Things ought to know their place and stay in it, but those fish have got a way of sidling off. As though they had mental reservations and weren't keeping any contracts. See what I mean?"

"I see what you mean," I said gravely. "They ought to be watched. My wife thinks so too. About a lot of things."

"She does?" He brightened. "Then that's two of us. I don't know why, but they give you that feeling."

He didn't know why, but I thought that I did.

It began as such things always begin — in the ooze of unnoticed swamps, in the darkness of eclipsed moons. It began with a strangled gasping for air.

The pond was a place of reek and corruption, of fetid smells and of oxygen-starved fish breathing through laboring gills. At times the slowly contracting

---

[1] tropical region in northern Australia.

circle of the water left little windrows of minnows who skittered desperately to escape the sun, but who died, nevertheless, in the fat, warm mud. It was a place of low life. In it the human brain began.

There were strange snouts in those waters, strange barbels nuzzling the bottom ooze, and there was time — three hundred million years of it — but mostly, I think, it was the ooze. By day the temperature in the world outside the pond rose to a frightful intensity; at night the sun went down in smoking red. Dust storms marched in incessant progression across a wilderness whose plants were the plants of long ago. Leafless and weird and stiff they lingered by the water, while over vast areas of grassless uplands the winds blew until red stones took on the polish of reflecting mirrors. There was nothing to hold the land in place. Winds howled, dust clouds rolled, and brief erratic torrents choked with silt ran down to the sea. It was a time of dizzying contrasts, a time of change.

On the oily surface of the pond, from time to time a snout thrust upward, took in air with a queer grunting inspiration, and swirled back to the bottom. The pond was doomed, the water was foul, and the oxygen almost gone, but the creature would not die. It could breathe air direct through a little accessory lung, and it could walk. In all that weird and lifeless landscape, it was the only thing that could. It walked rarely and under protest, but that was not surprising. The creature was a fish.

In the passage of days the pond became a puddle, but the Snout survived. There was dew one dark night and a coolness in the empty stream bed. When the sun rose next morning the pond was an empty place of cracked mud, but the Snout did not lie there. He had gone. Down stream there were other ponds. He breathed air for a few hours and hobbled slowly along on the stumps of heavy fins.

It was an uncanny business if there had been anyone there to see. It was a journey best not observed in daylight, it was something that needed swamps and shadows and the touch of the night dew. It was a monstrous penetration of a forbidden element, and the Snout kept his face from the light. It was just as well, though the face should not be mocked. In three hundred million years it would be our own.

There was something fermenting in the brain of the Snout. He was no longer entirely a fish. The ooze had marked him. It takes a swamp-and-tide-flat zoologist to tell you about life; it is in this domain that the living suffer great extremes, it is here that the water-failures, driven to desperation, make starts in a new element. It is here that strange compromises are made and new senses are born. The Snout was no exception. Though he breathed and walked primarily in order to stay in the water, he was coming ashore.

He was not really a successful fish except that he was managing to stay alive in a noisome, uncomfortable, oxygen-starved environment. In fact the time was coming when the last of his kind, harried by more ferocious and speedier fishes, would slip off the edge of the continental shelf, to seek safety in the sunless abysses of the deep sea. But the Snout was a fresh-water Crossopterygian, to give him his true name, and cumbersome and plodding though he was, something had happened back of his eyes. The ooze had gotten in its work.

It is interesting to consider what sort of creatures we, the remote descendants of the Snout, might be, except for that green quagmire out of which he came. Mammalian insects perhaps we should have been — solid-brained, our neurones wired for mechanical responses, our lives running out with the perfection of beautiful, intricate, and mindless clocks. More likely we should never have existed at all. It was the Snout and the ooze that did it. Perhaps there also, among rotting fish heads and blue, night-burning bog lights, moved the eternal mystery, the careful finger of God. The increase was not much. It was two bubbles, two thin-walled little balloons at the end of the Snout's small brain. The cerebral hemispheres had appeared.

Among all the experiments in that dripping, ooze-filled world, one was vital: the brain had to be fed. The nerve tissues are insatiable devourers of oxygen. If they do not get it, life is gone. In stagnant swamp waters, only the development of a highly efficient blood supply to the brain can prevent disaster. And among those gasping, dying creatures, whose small brains winked out forever in the long Silurian drought, the Snout and his brethren survived.

Over the exterior surface of the Snout's tiny brain ran the myriad blood vessels that served it; through the greatly enlarged choroid plexuses,[2] other vessels pumped oxygen into the spinal fluid. The brain was a thin-walled tube fed from both surfaces. It could only exist as a thing of thin walls permeated with oxygen. To thicken, to lay down solid masses of nervous tissue such as exist among the fishes in oxygenated waters was to invite disaster. The Snout lived on a bubble, two bubbles in his brain.

It was not that his thinking was deep; it was only that it had to be thin. The little bubbles of the hemispheres helped to spread the area upon which higher correlation centers could be built, and yet preserve those areas from the disastrous thickenings which meant oxygen death to the swamp dweller. There is a mystery about those thickenings which culminate in the so-called solid brain. It is the brain of insects, of the modern fishes, of some reptiles and all birds. Always it marks the appearance of elaborate patterns of instinct and the end of thought. A road has been taken which, anatomically, is well-nigh irretraceable; it does not lead in the direction of a high order of consciousness.

Wherever, instead, the thin sheets of gray matter expand upward into the enormous hemispheres of the human brain, laughter, or it may be sorrow, enters in. Out of the choked Devonian waters emerged sight and sound and the music that rolls invisible through the composer's brain. They are there still in the ooze along the tideline, though no one notices. The world is fixed, we say: fish in the sea, birds in the air. But in the mangrove swamps by the

[2] network of membranous blood vessels.

Niger, fish climb trees and ogle uneasy naturalists who try unsuccessfully to chase them back to the water. There are things still coming ashore.

The door to the past is a strange door. It swings open and things pass through it, but they pass in one direction only. No man can return across that threshold, though he can look down still and see the green light waver in the water weeds.

There are two ways to seek the doorway: in the swamps of the inland waterways and along the tide flats of the estuaries where rivers come to the sea. By those two pathways life came ashore. It was not the magnificent march through the breakers and up the cliffs that we fondly imagine. It was a stealthy advance made in suffocation and terror, amidst the leaching bite of chemical discomfort. It was made by the failures of the sea.

Some creatures have slipped through the invisible chemical barrier between salt and fresh water into the tidal rivers, and later come ashore; some have crept upward from the salt. In all cases, however, the first adventure into the dreaded atmosphere seems to have been largely determined by the inexorable crowding of enemies and by the retreat further and further into marginal situations where the oxygen supply was depleted. Finally, in the ruthless selection of the swamp margins, or in the scramble for food on the tide flats, the land becomes home.

Not the least interesting feature of some of the tide-flat emergents is their definite antipathy for the full tide. It obstructs their food-collecting on the mud banks and brings their enemies. Only extremes of fright will drive them into the water for any period.

I think it was the great nineteenth-century paleontologist Cope[3] who first clearly enunciated what he called the "law of the unspecialized," the contention that it was not from the most highly organized and dominant forms of a given geological era that the master type of a succeeding period evolved, but that instead the dominant forms tended to arise from more lowly and generalized animals which were capable of making new adaptations, and which were not narrowly restricted to a given environment.

There is considerable truth to this observation, but, for all that, the idea is not simple. Who is to say without foreknowledge of the future which animal is specialized and which is not? We have only to consider our remote ancestor, the Snout, to see the intricacies into which the law of the unspecialized may lead us.

If we had been making zoological observations in the Paleozoic Age, with no knowledge of the strange realms life was to penetrate in the future, we would probably have regarded the Snout as specialized. We would have seen his air-bladder lung, his stubby, sluggish fins, and his odd ability to wriggle overland as specialized adaptations to a peculiarly restricted environmental

[3] Edward Drinker Cope (1840–1897).

niche in stagnant continental waters. We would have thought in water terms and we would have dismissed the Snout as an interesting failure off the main line of progressive evolution, escaping from his enemies and surviving success-fully only in the dreary and marginal surroundings scorned by the swift-finned teleost fishes who were destined to dominate the seas and all quick waters.

Yet it was this poor specialization — this bog-trapped failure — whose de-scendants, in three great movements, were to dominate the earth. It is only now, looking backward, that we dare to regard him as "generalized." The Snout was the first vetebrate to pop completely through the water membrane into a new dimension. His very specializations and failures, in a water sense, had preadapted him for a world he scarcely knew existed.

The day of the Snout was over three hundred million years ago. Not long since I read a book in which a prominent scientist spoke cheerfully of some ten billion years of future time remaining to us. He pointed out happily the things that man might do throughout that period. Fish in the sea, I thought again, birds in the air. The climb all far behind us, the species fixed and sure. No wonder my explorer friend had had a momentary qualm when he met the mudskippers with their mental reservations and lack of promises. There is something wrong with our world view. It is still Ptolemaic,[4] though the sun is no longer believed to revolve around the earth.

We teach the past, we see farther backward into time than any race before us, but we stop at the present, or, at best, we project far into the future ideal-ized versions of ourselves. All that long way behind us we see, perhaps inevi-tably, through human eyes alone. We see ourselves as the culmination and the end, and if we do indeed consider our passing, we think that sunlight will go with us and the earth be dark. We are the end. For us continents rose and fell, for us the waters and the air were mastered, for us the great living web has pulsated and grown more intricate.

To deny this, a man once told me, is to deny God. This puzzled me. I went back along the pathway to the marsh. I went, not in the past, not by the bones of dead things, not down the lost roadway of the Snout. I went instead in daylight, in the Now, to see if the door was still there, and to see what things passed through.

I found that the same experiments were brewing, that up out of that ancient well, fins were still scrambling toward the sunlight. They were small things, and which of them presaged the future I could not say. I saw only that they were many and that they had solved the oxygen death in many marvelous ways, not always ours.

I found that there were modern fishes who breathed air, not through a lung but through their stomachs or through strange chambers where their gills should be, or breathing as the Snout once breathed. I found that some

[4] cosmological system in which the earth was thought to stand at the center of the universe.

crawled in the fields at nightfall pursuing insects, or slept on the grass by pond sides and who drowned, if kept under water, as men themselves might drown.

Of all these fishes the mudskipper *Periophthalmus* is perhaps the strangest. He climbs trees with his fins and pursues insects; he snaps worms like a robin on the tide flats; he sees as land things see, and above all he dodges and evades with a curious popeyed insolence more suggestive of the land than of the sea. Of a different tribe and a different time he is, nevertheless, oddly reminiscent of the Snout.

But not the same. There lies the hope of life. The old ways are exploited and remain, but new things come, new senses try the unfamiliar air. There are small scuttlings and splashings in the dark, and out of it come the first croaking, illiterate voices of the things to be, just as man once croaked and dreamed darkly in that tiny vesicular forebrain.

Perpetually, now, we search and bicker and disagree. The eternal form eludes us — the shape we conceive as ours. Perhaps the old road through the marsh should tell us. We are one of many appearances of the thing called Life; we are not its perfect image, for it has no image except Life, and life is multitudinous and emergent in the stream of time.

SCIENCE

From morals he must be directed to the sciences and contemplate their beauty also, so that, having his eyes fixed upon beauty in the widest sense, he may no longer be the slave of a base and mean-spirited devotion to an individual example of beauty.

Diotima to Socrates, *Symposium*

SCIENCE has accustomed us to the miraculous. We accept heart transplants, outer space flights, and nuclear weapons almost as routinely as we accept electricity, airplanes and antibiotics. Seldom do we consider the social, political, or ethical consequences. Scientific and technological developments are enormously beneficial, but their full effects are, in many cases, incalculable; they produce new problems while solving the old.

In the natural world, insecticides destroy myriads of pests; and then their natural predators also die — of starvation. In education, science courses proliferate and scientists specialize ever more minutely, to the extent that they are often unable to communicate with other scientists, let alone laymen.

Technology also affects less obviously scientific areas of life with equal prominence and ambiguity. Justice may be aided or hindered by mass media which can influence every potential juror. The arts may be improved or impeded by electronic music and machine-made translations of literature. Love can be abetted or aborted by family planning. The conflict between science and religion continues unresolved: whose prerogative is the creation, control, and destruction of life — the scientist's or God's?

This symposium reveals similarities and differences between science and technology and between theoretical and applied science in various fields. The basic assumptions, beliefs, doubts, and superstitions of science are explored. Aristotle was one of the first to refer to science; he believed the study was "experience made art." For classical Greeks and Romans, science was a matter of precepts, often untested and learned by rote, handed down from one generation to another. The medieval scientist and scholar Roger Bacon distinguished between reason and experience for ascertaining and evaluating scientific data; since his time both concept and observations have encouraged scientific investigation. In their times, Benjamin Franklin demonstrated the pragmatic experimental method, while Thomas Henry Huxley defended the rationale and modes of scientific education.

Implicit in the consideration of scientific research and its limitations are ethical, moral, and philosophical questions. Because scientists seek to examine and understand the universe, do they therefore have the authority to try to create, control, improve upon — or even destroy — the world and its inhabitants? Is scientific research stimulated primarily by humanitarian, utilitarian, or economic motives? Or may it also be

788

governed by aesthetics, with elegance as a criterion for acceptable demonstrations and theories? To what extent can science be idealistic? If it can create a utopia, will that be the perverted realm of Swift's Lagado or Cheever's society where corrupt, uncontrollable technology controls corruptible human beings?

The complex relation of science to man is especially puzzling. Science can try to control human thought and behavior, much of which, as Freud realizes, seems governed by unconscious, irrational, idiosyncratic impulses. But are people sufficiently predictable and compliant to permit such control? Are investigators and experimenters sufficiently ethical to collect their data responsibly? May experimental subjects be sacrificed on the altar of science?

Although not all scientists may be uniformly aware of their moral responsibilities, Bronowski argues that they should be, through a self-imposed moral imperative; while Hawthorne, in presenting Rappaccini as an embodiment of the typical "mad scientist," sees the possibility of unethical, unscrupulous men who are not wholly aware of the consequences of their perspectives and procedures. Hawthorne also implies a fundamental mistrust of science.

But can the twentieth century, with its technological, mechanized, transistorized existence, really mistrust what it values? We often act as if we believe that progress is necessarily implied in the process of continual scientific investigation. Yet we realize that although scientific knowledge continually becomes more sophisticated, its users may not. The increase of scientific knowledge may present more problems for other scientists to try to solve. Therefore, we must examine thoroughly the province, methodology, and products of science, although we still risk being inundated by our own inventiveness and curiosity.

Aristotle (384–322 B.C.)

GREEK PHILOSOPHER, SCIENTIST, and PHYSICIAN

The Highest Wisdom

All men by nature desire to know. An indication of this is the delight we take in our senses; for even apart from their usefulness they are loved for themselves; and above all others the sense of sight. For not only with a view to action, but even when we are not going to do anything, we prefer sight to almost everything else. The reason is that this, most of all the senses, makes us know and brings to light many differences between things.

By nature animals are born with the faculty of sensation, and from sensation memory is produced in some of them, though not in others. And therefore the former are more intelligent and apt at learning than those which cannot remember; those which are incapable of hearing sounds are intelligent though they cannot be taught, e.g. the bee, and any other race of animals that may be like it; and those which besides memory have this sense of hearing, can be taught.

The animals other than man live by appearances and memories, and have but little of connected experience; but the human race lives also by art and reasonings. And from memory experience is produced in men; for many memories of the same thing produce finally the capacity for a single experience. Experience is almost identified with science and art, but really science and art come to men *through* experience; for 'experience made art', as Polus[1] says, and rightly, 'but inexperience luck.' And art arises, when from many notions gained by experience one universal judgement about a class of objects is produced. For to have a judgement that when Callias was ill of this disease this did him good, and similarly in the case of Socrates and in many individual cases, is a matter of experience; but to judge that it has done good to all persons of a certain constitution, marked off in one class, when they were ill of this disease, e.g. to phlegmatic or bilious people when burning with fever, — this is a matter of art.

With a view to action experience seems in no respect inferior to art, and we even see men of experience succeding more than those who have theory without experience. The reason is that experience is knowledge of individuals, art of universals, and actions and productions are all concerned with the individual; for the physician does not cure *man*, except in an incidental way, but

---

[1] Greek philosopher, a Sophist, somewhat younger than Socrates.

Title supplied by editors. From *Metaphysics*, Chs. I and II, in *The Works of Aristotle*, translated and edited by J. A. Smith and W. D. Ross. Reprinted by permission of the Clarendon Press, Oxford.

Callias or Socrates or some other called by some such individual name, who happens to be a man. If, then, a man has the theory without the experience, and knows the universal but does not know the individual included in this, he will often fail to cure; for it is the individual that is to be cured. But yet we think that *knowledge* and *understanding* belong to art rather than to experience, and we suppose artists to be wiser than men of experience (which implies that Wisdom depends in all cases rather on knowledge); and this because the former know the cause, but the latter do not. For men of experience know that the thing is so, but do not know why, while the others know the 'why' and the cause. Hence we think that the master-workers in each craft are more honourable and know in a truer sense and are wiser than the manual workers, because they know the causes of the things that are done [we think the manual workers are like certain lifeless things which act indeed, but act without knowing what they do, as fire burns, — but while the lifeless things perform each of their functions by a natural tendency, the labourers perform them through habit]²; thus we view them as being wiser not in virtue of being able to act, but of having the theory for themselves and knowing the causes. And in general it is a sign of the man who knows, that he can teach, and therefore we think art more truly knowledge than experience is; for artists can teach, and men of mere experience cannot.

Again, we do not regard any of the senses as Wisdom; yet surely these give the most authoritative knowledge of particulars. But they do not tell us the 'why' of anything — e.g. why fire is hot; they only say that it is hot.

At first he who invented any art that went beyond the common perceptions of man was naturally admired by men, not only because there was something useful in the inventions, but because he was thought wise and superior to the rest. But as more arts were invented, and some were directed to the necessities of life, others to its recreation, the inventors of the latter were naturally always regarded as wiser than the inventors of the former, because their branches of knowledge did not aim at utility. Hence when all such inventions were already established, the sciences which do not aim at giving pleasure or at the necessities of life were were discovered, and first in the places where men first began to have leisure. This is why the mathematical arts were founded in Egypt; for there the priestly caste was allowed to be at leisure.

We have said in the *Ethics* what the difference is between art and science and the other kindred faculties; but the point of our present discussion is this, that all men suppose what is called Wisdom to deal with the first causes and the principles of things. This is why, as has been said before, the man of experience is thought to be wiser than the possessors of any perception whatever, the artist wiser than the men of experience, the master-worker than the mechanic, and the theoretical kinds of knowledge to be more of the nature of Wisdom than the productive. Clearly then Wisdom is knowledge about certain causes and principles.

凸

² probably a later addition. [Smith and Ross]

Since we are seeking this knowledge, we must inquire of what kind are the causes and the principles, the knowledge of which is Wisdom. If we were to take the notions we have about the wise man, this might perhaps make the answer more evident. We suppose first, then, that the wise man knows all things, as far as possible, although he has not knowledge of each of them in detail; secondly, that he who can learn things that are difficult, and not easy for man to know, is wise (sense-perception is common to all, and therefore easy and no mark of Wisdom); again, he who is more exact and more capable of teaching the causes is wiser, in every branch of knowledge; and of the sciences, also, that which is desirable on its own account and for the sake of knowing it is more of the nature of Wisdom than that which is desirable on account of its results, and the superior science is more of the nature of Wisdom than the ancillary; for the wise man must not be ordered but must order, and he must not obey another, but the less wise must obey *him*.

Such and so many are the notions, then, which we have about Wisdom and the wise. Now of these characteristics that of knowing all things must belong to him who has in the highest degree universal knowledge; for he knows in a sense all the subordinate objects. And these things, the most universal, are on the whole the hardest for men to know; for they are furthest from the senses. And the most exact of the sciences are those which deal most with first principles; for those which involve fewer principles are more exact than those which involve additional principles, e.g. arithmetic than geometry. But the science which investigates causes is also the more communicable, for the people who teach are those who tell the causes of each thing. And understanding and knowledge pursued for their own sake are found most in the knowledge of that which is most knowable; for he who chooses to know for the sake of knowing will choose most readily that which is most truly knowledge, and such is the knowledge of that which is most knowable; and the first principles and the causes are most knowable; for by reason of these, and from these, all other things are known, but these are not known by means of the things subordinate to them. And the science which knows to what end each thing must be done is the most authoritative of the sciences, and more authoritative than any ancillary science; and this end is the good in each class, and in general the supreme good in the whole of nature. Judged by all the tests we have mentioned, then, the name in question ('Wisdom') falls to the same science; this must be a science that investigates the first principles and causes; for the good, i.e. the end and aim, is one of the causes.

That it is not a science of production is clear even from the history of the earliest philosophers. For it is owing to their wonder that men both now begin and at first began to philosophize; they wondered originally at the obvious difficulties, then advanced little by little and stated difficulties about the greater matters, e.g. about the phenomena of the moon and those of the sun, and about the stars and about the genesis of the universe. And a man who is puzzled and wonders thinks himself ignorant (whence even the lover of myth is in a sense a lover of Wisdom, for the myth is composed of wonders); therefore since they philosophized in order to escape from ignorance, evidently they were pursuing science in order to know, and not for any utilitarian end. And this is confirmed by the facts; for it was when almost all the necessities of life and the things that make for comfort and recreation were present, that such knowledge began to be sought. Evidently then we do not seek it for the sake of any other advantage; but as the man is free, we say, who exists for himself and not for another, so we pursue this as the only free science, for it alone exists for itself.

Hence the possession of it might be justly regarded as beyond human power; for in many ways human nature is in bondage, so that according to Simonides[3] 'God alone can have this privilege', and it is unfitting that man should not be content to seek the knowledge that is suited to him. If, then, there is something in what the poets say, and jealousy is natural to the divine power, it would probably occur in this case above all, and all who excelled in this knowledge would be unfortunate. But the divine power cannot be jealous (nay, according to the proverb, 'bards tell many a lie'), nor should any science be thought more honourable than one of this sort. For the most divine science is also most honourable; and this science alone is, in two ways, most divine. For the science which it would be most meet for God to have is a divine science, and so is any science that deals with divine objects; and this science alone has both these qualities; for (1) God is thought to be among the causes of all things and to be a first principle, and (2) such a science either God alone can have, or God above all others. All the sciences, indeed, are more necessary than this, but none is better.

Yet the acquisition of it must in a sense end in something which is the opposite of our original inquiries. For all men begin, as we said, by wondering that the matter is so (as those who have not yet perceived the explanation marvel at automatic marionettes) — whether the object of their wonder be the solstices or the incommensurability of the diagonal of a square with the side; for it seems wonderful to all men that there is a thing which cannot be measured even by the smallest unit. But we must end in the contrary and, according to the proverb, the better state, as is the case in these instances when men learn the cause; for there is nothing which would surprise a geometer so much as if the diagonal turned out to be commensurable.

We have stated, then, what is the nature of the science we are searching for, and what is the mark which our search and our whole investigation must reach.

---

[3] Greek lyric and elegaic poet (556–468 B.C.).

Lucretius (c. 99–55 B.C.)

ROMAN POET

On the Reliability of the Senses

Bodies that strike the eyes, awaking sight.
From certain things flow odours evermore,
As cold from rivers, heat from sun, and spray
From waves of ocean, eater-out of walls
Around the coasts. Nor ever cease to flit
The varied voices, sounds athrough the air.
Then too there comes into the mouth at times
The wet of a salt taste, when by the sea
We roam about; and so, whene'er we watch
The wormwood being mixed, its bitter stings.   10
To such degree from all things is each thing
Borne streamingly along, and sent about
To every region round; and nature grants
Nor rest nor respite of the onward flow,
Since 'tis incessantly we feeling have,
And all the time are suffered to descry
And smell all things at hand, and hear them sound.
Besides, since shape examined by our hands
Within the dark is known to be the same
As that by eyes perceived within the light   20
And lustrous day, both touch and sight must be
By one like cause aroused. So, if we test
A square and get its stimulus on us
Within the dark, within the light what square
Can fall upon our sight, except a square
That images the things? Wherefore it seems
The source of seeing is in images,
Nor without these can anything be viewed.

Now these same films I name are borne about
And tossed and scattered into regions all.   30
But since we do perceive alone through eyes,
It follows hence that whitherso we turn
Our sight, all things do strike against it there
With form and hue. And just how far from us
Each thing may be away, the image yields

**Title supplied by editors. From *Of the Nature of Things*
by Lucretius. Translated by W. E. Leonard. Everyman's
Library Edition. Reprinted by permission of E. P. Dutton & Co., Inc., and J. M. Dent & Sons Ltd., London.**

To us the power to see and chance to tell:
For when 'tis sent, at once it shoves ahead
And drives along the air that's in the space
Betwixt it and our eyes. And thus this air
All guides athrough our eyeballs, and, as 'twere,   40
Brushes athrough our pupils and thuswise
Passes across. Therefore it comes we see
How far from us each thing may be away,
And the more air there be that's driven before,
And too the longer be the brushing breeze
Against our eyes, the farther off removed
Each thing is seen to be: forsooth, this work
With mightily swift order all goes on,
So that upon one instant we may see
What kind the object and how far away.   50

Nor over-marvellous must this be deemed
In these affairs that, though the films which strike
Upon the eyes cannot be singly seen,
The things themselves may be perceived. For thus
When the wind beats upon us stroke by stroke
And when the sharp cold streams, 'tis not our wont
To feel each private particle of wind
Or of that cold, but rather all at once;
And so we see how blows affect our body,
As if one thing were beating on the same   60
And giving us the feel of its own body
Outside of us. Again, whene'er we thump
With finger-tip upon a stone, we touch
But the rock's surface and the outer hue,
Nor feel that hue by contact — rather feel
The very hardness deep within the rock.

Now come, and why beyond a looking-glass
An image may be seen, perceive. For seen
It soothly is, removèd far within.
'Tis the same sort as objects peered upon   70
Outside in their true shape, whene'er a door
Yields through itself an open peering-place,
And lets us see so many things outside
Beyond the house. Also that sight is made
By a twofold twin air: for first is seen
The air inside the door-posts; next the doors,
The twain to left and right; and afterwards
A light beyond comes brushing through our eyes,
Then other air, then objects peered upon
Outside in their true shape. And thus, when first   80
The image of the glass projects itself,
As to our gaze it comes, it shoves ahead

looking-glass: The Roman mirrors were of course of metal. [Leonard]

And drives along the air that's in the space
Betwixt it and our eyes, and brings to pass
That we perceive the air ere yet the glass.
But when we've also seen the glass itself,
Forthwith that image which from us is borne
Reaches the glass, and there thrown back again
Comes back unto our eyes, and driving rolls
Ahead of itself another air, that then   90
'Tis this we see before itself, and thus
It looks so far removed behind the glass.
Wherefore again, again, there's naught for wonder . . .

In those which render from the mirror's plane
A vision back, since each thing comes to pass
By means of the two airs. Now, in the glass
The right part of our members is observed
Upon the left, because, when comes the image
Hitting against the level of the glass,
'Tis not returned unshifted; but forced off   100
Backwards in line direct and not oblique, —
Exactly as whoso his plaster-mask
Should dash, before 'twere dry, on post or beam,
And it should straightway keep, at clinging there,
Its shape, reversèd, facing him who threw,
And so remould the features it gives back:
It comes that now the right eye is the left,
The left the right. An image too may be
From mirror into mirror handed on,
Until of idol-films even five or six   110   **idol-films:** images
Have thus been gendered. For whatever things
Shall hide back yonder in the house, the same,
However far removed in twisting ways,
May still be all brought forth through bending paths
And by these several mirrors seen to be
Within the house, since nature so compels
All things to be borne backward and spring off
At equal angles from all other things.   **At equal angles:** i.e. the angle of
To such degree the image gleams across   reflection equals the angle of inci-
From mirror unto mirror; where 'twas left   120   dence. [Leonard]
It comes to be the right, and then again
Returns and changes round unto the left.
Again, those little sides of mirrors curved
Proportionate to the bulge of our own flank
Send back to us their idols with the right
Upon the right; and this is so because
Either the image is passed on along
From mirror unto mirror, and thereafter,   **mirror unto mirror:** i.e. from one
When twice dashed off, flies back unto ourselves;   part to another of the same
Or else the image wheels itself around,   130   curved surface. [Leonard]

When once unto the mirror it has come,
Since the curved surface teaches it to turn
Toward us. Further, thou might'st well believe
That these film-idols step along with us
And set their feet in unison with ours
And imitate our carriage, since from that
Part of a mirror whence thou hast withdrawn
Straightway no images can be returned.

    Further, our eye-balls tend to flee the bright
And shun to gaze thereon; the sun even blinds,   140
If thou goest on to strain them unto him,
Because his strength is mighty, and the films
Heavily downward from on high are borne
Through the pure ether and the viewless winds,
And strike the eyes, disordering their joints.
So piercing lustre often burns the eyes,
Because it holdeth many seeds of fire
Which, working into eyes, engender pain.
Again, whatever jaundiced people view
Becomes wan-yellow, since from out their bodies   150
Flow many seeds wan-yellow forth to meet
The films of things, and many too are mixed
Within their eye, which by contagion paint
All things with sallowness. Again, we view
From dark recesses things that stand in light,
Because, when first has entered and possessed
The open eyes this nearer darkling air,
Swiftly the shining air and luminous
Followeth in, which purges then the eyes
And scatters asunder of that other air   160
The sable shadows, for in large degrees
This air is nimbler, nicer, and more strong.
And soon as ever 'thas filled and oped with light   **'thas: it has**
The pathways of the eyeballs, which before
Black air had blocked, there follow straightaway
Those films of things out-standing in the light,
Provoking vision — what we cannot do
From out the light with objects in the dark,
Because that denser darkling air behind
Followeth in, and fills each aperture   170
And thus blockades the pathways of the eyes
That there no images of any things
Can be thrown in and agitate the eyes.

    And when from far away we do behold
The squarèd towers of a city, oft
Rounded they seem, — on this account because
Each distant angle is perceived obtuse,

Or rather it is not perceived at all;
And perishes its blow nor to our gaze
Arrives its stroke, since through such length of air   180
Are borne along the idols that the air
Makes blunt the idol of the angle's point
By numerous collidings. When thuswise
The angles of the tower each and all
Have quite escaped the sense, the stones appear
As rubbed and rounded on a turner's wheel —
Yet not like objects near and truly round,
But with a semblance to them, shadowily.
Likewise, our shadow in the sun appears
To move along and follow our own steps   190
And imitate our carriage — if thou thinkest
Air that is thus bereft of light can walk,
Following the gait and motion of mankind.
For what we use to name a shadow, sure
Is naught but air deprived of light. No marvel:
Because the earth from spot to spot is reft
Progressively of light of sun, whenever
In moving round we get within its way,
While any spot of earth by us abandoned
Is filled with light again, on this account   200
It comes to pass that what was body's shadow
Seems still the same to follow after us
In one straight course. Since, evermore pour in
New lights of rays, and perish then the old,
Just like the wool that's drawn into the flame.
Therefore the earth is easily spoiled of light
And easily refilled and from herself
Washeth the black shadows quite away.

    And yet in this we don't at all concede
That eyes be cheated. For their task it is   210
To note in whatsoever place be light,
In what be shadow: whether or no the gleams
Be still the same, and whether the shadow which
Just now was here is that one passing thither,
Or whether the facts be what we said above,
'Tis after all the reasoning of mind
That must decide; nor can our eyeballs know
The nature of reality. And so
Attach thou not this fault of mind to eyes,
Nor lightly think our senses everywhere   220
Are tottering. The ship in which we sail
Is borne along, although it seems to stand;
The ship that bides in roadstead is supposed
There to be passing by. And hills and fields
Seem fleeing fast astern, past which we urge

The ship and fly under the bellying sails.
The stars, each one, do seem to pause, affixed
To the ethereal caverns, though they all
Forever are in motion, rising out
And thence revisiting their far descents   230
When they have measured with their bodies bright
The span of heaven. And likewise sun and moon
Seem biding in a roadstead, — objects which,
As plain fact proves, are really borne along.
Between two mountains far away aloft
From midst the whirl of waters open lies
A gaping exit for the fleet, and yet
They seem conjoinèd in a single isle.
When boys themselves have stopped their spinning
      round,
The halls still seem to whirl and posts to reel,   240
Until they now must almost think the roofs
Threaten to ruin down upon their heads.
And now, when nature begins to lift on high
The sun's red splendour and the tremulous fires,
And raise him o'er the mountain-tops, those moun-
      tains —
O'er which he seemeth then to thee to be,
His glowing self hard by atingeing them
With his own fire — are yet away from us
Scarcely two thousand arrow-shots, indeed
Oft scarce five hundred courses of a dart;   250
Although between those mountains and the sun
Lie the huge plains of ocean spread beneath
The vasty shores of ether, and intervene
A thousand lands, possessed by many a folk
And generations of wild beasts. Again,
A pool of water of but a finger's depth,
Which lies between the stones along the pave,
Offers a vision downward into earth
As far, as from the earth o'erspread on high
The gulfs of heaven; that thus thou seemest to
      view   260
Clouds down below and heavenly bodies plunged
Wondrously in heaven under earth.
Then too, when in the middle of the stream
Sticks fast our dashing horse, and down we gaze
Into the river's rapid waves, some force
Seems then to bear the body of the horse,
Though standing still, reversely from his course,
And swiftly push up-stream. And wheresoe'er
We cast our eyes across, all objects seem
Thus to be onward borne and flow along   270
In the same way as we. A portico,

though . . . motion: The stars and the sun, as well as the moon, were thought to rotate around the stationary earth.

Albeit it stands well propped from end to end
On equal columns, parallel and big,
Contracts by stages in a narrow cone,
When from one end the long, long whole is seen, —
Until, conjoining ceiling with the floor,
And the whole right side with the left, it draws
Together to a cone's nigh-viewless point.
To sailors on the main the sun he seems
From out the waves to rise, and in the waves   280
To set and bury his light — because indeed
They gaze on naught but water and the sky.
Again, to gazers ignorant of the sea,
Vessels in port seem, as with broken poops,
To lean upon the water, quite agog;
For any portion of the oars that's raised
Above the briny spray is straight, and straight
The rudders from above. But other parts,
Those sunk, immersed below the water-line,
Seem broken all and bended and inclined   290
Sloping to upwards, and turned back to float
Almost atop the water. And when the winds
Carry the scattered drifts along the sky
In the night-time, then seem to glide along
The radiant constellations 'gainst the clouds
And there on high to take far other course
From that whereon in truth they're borne. And then,
If haply our hand be set beneath one eye
And press below thereon, then to our gaze
Each object which we gaze on seems to be,   300
By some sensation twain — then twain the lights
Of lampions burgeoning in flowers of flame,
And twain the furniture in all the house,
Two-fold the visages of fellow-men,
And twain their bodies. And again, when sleep
Has bound our members down in slumber soft
And all the body lies in deep repose,
Yet then we seem to self to be awake
And move our members; and in night's blind gloom
We think to mark the daylight and the sun;   310
And, shut within a room, yet still we seem
To change our skies, our oceans, rivers, hills,
To cross the plains afoot, and hear new sounds,
Though still the austere silence of the night
Abides around us, and to speak replies,
Though voiceless. Other cases of the sort
Wondrously many do we see, which all
Seek, so to say, to injure faith in sense —
In vain, because the largest part of these
Deceives through mere opinions of the mind,   320

Again . . . water (283–92): referring to the phenomenon of the
refraction of light

lampions: oil lamps

Which we do add ourselves, feigning to see
What by the senses are not seen at all.
For naught is harder than to separate
Plain facts from dubious, which the mind forthwith
Adds by itself.
              Again, if one suppose
That naught is known, he knows not whether this
Itself is able to be known, since he
Confesses naught to know. Therefore with him
I waive discussion — who has set his head
Even where his feet should be. But let me grant   330
That this he knows, — I question: whence he knows
What 'tis to know and not-to-know in turn,
And what created concept of the truth,
And what device has proved the dubious
To differ from the certain? — since in things
He's heretofore seen naught of true. Thou'lt find
That from the senses first hath been create
Concept of truth, nor can the senses be
Rebutted. For criterion must be found
Worthy of greater trust, which shall defeat   340
Through own authority the false by true;
What, then, than these our senses must there be
Worthy a greater trust? Shall reason, sprung
From some false sense, prevail to contradict
Those senses, sprung as reason wholly is
From out the senses? — For lest *these* be true,
All reason also then is falsified.
Or shall the ears have power to blame the eyes,
Or yet the touch the ears? Again, shall taste
Accuse this touch or shall the nose confute   350
Or eyes defeat it? Methinks not so it is;
For unto each has been divided off
Its function quite apart, its power to each;
And thus we're still constrainèd to perceive
The soft, the cold, the hot apart, apart
All divers hues and whatso things there be
Conjoined with hues. Likewise the tasting tongue
Has its own power apart, and smells apart
And sounds apart are known. And thus it is
That no one sense can e'er convict another.   360
Nor shall one sense have power to blame itself,
Because it always must be deemed the same,
Worthy of equal trust. And therefore what
At any time unto these senses showed,
The same is true. And if the reason be
Unable to unravel us the cause
Why objects, which at hand were square, afar
Seemed rounded, yet it more availeth us,
Lacking the reason, to pretend a cause

For each configuration, than to let   370
From out our hands escape the obvious things
And injure primal faith in sense, and wreck
All those foundations upon which do rest
Our life and safety. For not only reason
Would topple down; but even our very life
Would collapse, unless we dared
To trust our senses and to keep away
From headlong heights and places to be shunned
Of a like peril, and to seek with speed
Their opposites! Again, as in a building,   380
If the first plumb-line be askew, and if
The square deceiving swerve from lines exact,
And if the level waver but the least
In any part, the whole construction then
Must turn out faulty — shelving and askew,
Leaning to back and front, incongruous,
That now some portions seem about to fall,
And falls the whole ere long — betrayed indeed
By first deceiving estimates: so too
Thy calculations in affairs of life   390
Must be askew and false, if sprung for thee
From senses false. So all that troop of words
Marshalled against the senses is quite vain. . . .

Ovid (43 B.C.–A.D. 17)

ROMAN POET

The Story of Daedalus and Icarus

Homesick for homeland, Daedalus hated Crete
And his long exile there, but the sea held him.
"Though Minos blocks escape[1] by land or water,"
Daedalus said, "surely the sky is open,
And that's the way we'll go. Minos' dominion
Does not include the air." He turned his thinking
Toward unknown arts, changing the laws of nature.
He laid out feathers in order, first the smallest,
A little larger next it, and so continued,
The way that pan-pipes rise in gradual sequence.   10
He fastened them with twine and wax, at middle,

[1] Daedalus and his son Icarus were imprisoned by Minos, King of Crete.

From *Metamorphoses* by Ovid, translated by Rolfe Humphries and published by Indiana University Press. Reprinted by permission.

At bottom, so, and bent them, gently curving,
So that they looked like wings of birds, most surely.
And Icarus, his son, stood by and watched him,
Not knowing he was dealing with his downfall,
Stood by and watched, and raised his shiny face
To let a feather, light as down, fall on it,
Or stuck his thumb into the yellow wax,
Fooling around, the way a boy will, always,
Whenever a father tries to get some work done.   20
Still, it was done at last, and the father hovered,
Poised, in the moving air, and taught his son:
"I warn you, Icarus, fly a middle course:
Don't go too low, or water will weigh the wings down;
Don't go too high, or the sun's fire will burn them.
Keep to the middle way. And one more thing,
No fancy steering by star or constellation,
Follow my lead!" That was the flying lesson,
And now to fit the wings to the boy's shoulders.
Between the work and warning the father found   30
His cheeks were wet with tears, and his hands trembled.
He kissed his son (*Good-bye*, if he had known it),
Rose on his wings, flew on ahead, as fearful
As any bird launching the little nestlings
Out of high nest into thin air. *Keep on,*
Keep on, he signals, *follow me!* He guides him
In flight — O fatal art! — and the wings move
And the father looks back to see the son's wings moving.
Far off, far down, some fisherman is watching
As the rod dips and trembles over the water,   40
Some shepherd rests his weight upon his crook,
Some ploughman on the handles of the ploughshare,
And all look up, in absolute amazement,
At those air-borne above. They must be gods!
They were over Samos, Juno's sacred island,
Delos and Paros toward the left, Lebinthus
Visible to the right, and another island,
Calymne, rich in honey. And the boy
Thought *This is wonderful!* and left his father,
Soared higher, higher, drawn to the vast heaven,   50
Nearer the sun, and the wax that held the wings
Melted in that fierce heat, and the bare arms
Beat up and down in air, and lacking oarage
Took hold of nothing. *Father!* he cried, and *Father!*
Until the blue sea hushed him, the dark water
Men call the Icarian now. And Daedalus,
Father no more, called "Icarus, where are you!
Where are you, Icarus? Tell me where to find you!"
And saw the wings on the waves, and cursed his talents,
Buried the body in a tomb, and the land   60
Was named for Icarus.

Roger Bacon (c. 1214–1292)

ENGLISH PHILOSOPHER

Experimental Science

. . . I now wish to unfold the principles of experimental science, since without experience nothing can be sufficiently known. For there are two modes of acquiring knowledge, namely, by reasoning and experience. Reasoning draws a conclusion and makes us grant the conclusion, but does not make the conclusion certain, nor does it remove doubt so that the mind may rest on the intuition of truth, unless the mind discovers it by the path of experience; since many have the arguments relating to what can be known, but because they lack experience they neglect the arguments, and neither avoid what is harmful nor follow what is good. For if a man who has never seen fire should prove by adequate reasoning that fire burns and injures things and destroys them, his mind would not be satisfied thereby, nor would he avoid fire, until he placed his hand or some combustible substance in the fire, so that he might prove by experience that which reasoning taught. But when he has had actual experience of combustion his mind is made certain and rests in the full light of truth. Therefore reasoning does not suffice, but experience does.

This is also evident in mathematics, where proof is most convincing. But the mind of one who has the most convincing proof in regard to the equilateral triangle will never cleave to the conclusion without experience, nor will he heed it, but will disregard it until experience is offered him by the intersection of two circles, from either intersection of which two lines may be drawn to the extremities of the given line; but then the man accepts the conclusion without any question. Aristotle's statement, then, that proof is reasoning that causes us to know is to be understood with the proviso that the proof is accompanied by its appropriate experience, and is not to be understood of the bare proof. His statement also in the first book of the Metaphysics that those who understand the reason and the cause are wiser than those who have empiric knowledge of a fact, is spoken of such as know only the bare truth without the cause. But I am here speaking of the man who knows the reason and the cause through experience. These men are perfect in their wisdom, as Aristotle maintains in the sixth book of the Ethics, whose simple statements must be accepted as if they offered proof, as he states in the same place.

He therefore who wishes to rejoice without doubt in regard to the truths underlying phenomena must know how to devote himself to experiment. For authors write many statements, and people believe them through reasoning which they formulate without experience. Their reasoning is wholly false. For it is generally believed that the diamond cannot be broken except by goat's blood, and philosophers and theologians misuse this idea. But fracture by means of blood of this kind has never been verified, although the effort has been made; and without that blood it can be broken easily. For I have seen this with my own eyes, and this is necessary, because gems cannot be carved except by fragments of this stone. Similarly it is generally believed that the castors employed by physicians are the testicles of the male animal. But this is not true, because the beaver has these under its breast, and both the male and female produce testicles of this kind. Besides these castors the male beaver has its testicles in their natural place; and therefore what is subjoined is a dreadful lie, namely, that when the hunters pursue the beaver, he himself knowing what they are seeking cuts out with his teeth these glands. Moreover, it is generally believed that hot water freezes more quickly than cold water in vessels, and the argument in support of this is advanced that contrary is excited by contrary, just like enemies meeting each other. But it is certain that cold water freezes more quickly for any one who makes the experiment. People attribute this to Aristotle in the second book of the Meteorologics; but he certainly does not make this statement, but he does make one like it, by which they have been deceived, namely, that if cold water and hot water are poured on a cold place, as upon ice, the hot water freezes more quickly, and this is true. But if hot water and cold are placed in two vessels, the cold will freeze more quickly. Therefore all things must be verified by experience.

But experience is of two kinds; one is gained through our external senses, and in this way we gain our experience of those things that are in the heavens by instruments made for this purpose, and of those things here below by means attested by our vision. Things that do not belong in our part of the world we know through other scientists who have had experience of them. As, for example, Aristotle on the authority of Alexander sent two thousand men through different parts of the world to gain experimental knowledge of all things that are on the surface of the earth, as Pliny[1] bears witness in his Natural History. This experience is both human and philosophical, as far as man can act in accordance with the grace given him; but this experience does not suffice him, because it does not give full attestation in regard to things corporeal owing to its difficulty, and does not touch at all on things spiritual. It is necessary, therefore, that the intellect of man should be otherwise aided, and for this reason the holy patriarchs and prophets, who first gave sciences to the world, received illumination within and were not dependent on sense alone. The same is true of many believers since the time of Christ. For the grace of faith illuminates greatly, as also do divine inspirations, not only in things spiritual, but in things corporeal and in the sciences of philosophy; as

---

[1] Pliny the Elder (23/4–79 A.D.), Roman writer and naturalist, was not a scientific observer but a rather uncritical encyclopedist.

Ptolemy[2] states in the Centilogium, namely, that there are two roads by which we arrive at the knowledge of facts, one through the experience of philosophy, the other through divine inspiration, which is far the better way, as he says. . . .

Since this Experimental Science is wholly unknown to the rank and file of students, I am therefore unable to convince people of its utility unless at the same time I disclose its excellence and its proper signification. This science alone, therefore, knows how to test perfectly what can be done by nature, what by the effort of art, what by trickery, what the incantations, conjurations, invocations, deprecations, sacrifices, that belong to magic, mean and dream of, and what is in them, so that all falsity may be removed and the truth alone of art and nature may be retained. This science alone teaches us how to view the mad acts of magicians, that they may be not ratified but shunned, just as logic considers sophistical reasoning.

This science . . . investigates by experiment the notable conclusions of all those sciences. For the other sciences know how to discover their principles by experiments, but their conclusions are reached by reasoning drawn from the principles discovered. But if they should have a particular and complete experience of their own conclusions, they must have it with the aid of this noble science. For it is true that mathematics has general experiments as regards its conclusions in its figures and calculations, which also are applied to all sciences and to this kind of experiment, because no science can be known without mathematics. But if we give our attention to particular and complete experiments and such as are attested wholly by the proper method, we must employ the principles of this science which is called experimental. I give as an example the rainbow and phenomena connected with it, of which nature are the circle around the sun and the stars, the streak [virga] also lying at the side of the sun or of a star, which is apparent to the eye in a straight line, and is called by Aristotle in the third book of the Meteorologics a perpendicular, but by Seneca a streak, and the circle is called a corona, phenomena which frequently have the colors of the rainbow. The natural philosopher discusses these phenomena, and the writer on Perspective has much to add pertaining to the mode of vision that is necessary in this case. But neither Aristotle nor Avicenna in their Natural Histories has given us a knowledge of phenomena of this kind, nor has Seneca, who composed a special book on them. But Experimental Science attests them.

Let the experimenter first, then, examine visible objects, in order that he may find colors arranged as in the phenomena mentioned above and also the same figure. For let him take hexagonal stones from Ireland or from India, which are called rainbows in Solinus on the Wonders of the World,[3] and let

---

2 Ptolemy of Alexandria, astronomer and geographer, made scientific observations between 121 and 151 A.D. and produced the most accurate of all ancient geographical works.
3 (c. 200 A.D.); author of *Collectanea Rerum Memorabilium*, which was a geographical summary of parts of the known world; practically the entire work was taken, without acknowledgment, from Pliny's *Natural History*.

him hold these in a solar ray falling through the window, so that he may find all the colors of the rainbow, arranged as in it, in the shadow near the ray. And further let the same experimenter turn to a somewhat dark place and apply the stone to one of his eyes which is almost closed, and we will see the colors of the rainbow clearly arranged just as in the bow. And since many employing these stones think that the phenomenon is due to the special virtue of those stones and to their hexagonal shape, therefore let the experimenter proceed further, and he will find this same peculiarity in crystalline stones correctly shaped, and in other transparent stones. Moreover, he will find this not only in white stones like the Irish crystals, but also in black ones, as is evident in the dark crystal[4] and in all stones of similar transparency. He will find it besides in crystals of a shape differing from the hexagonal, provided they have a roughened surface, like the Irish crystals, neither altogether smooth, nor rougher than they are. Nature produces some that have surfaces like the Irish crystals. For a difference in the corrugations causes a difference in the colors. And further let him observe rowers, and in the drops falling from the raised oars he finds the same colors when the solar rays penetrate drops of this kind. The same phenomenon is seen in water falling from the wheels of a mill; and likewise when one sees on a summer's morning the drops of dew on the grass in meadow or field, he will observe the colors. Likewise when it is raining, if he stands in a dark place and the rays beyond it pass through the falling rain, the colors will appear in the shadow near by; and frequently at night colors appear around a candle. Moreover, if a man in summer, when he rises from sleep and has his eyes only partly open, suddenly looks at a hole through which a ray of the sun enters, he will see colors. Moreover, if seated beyond the sun he draws his cap beyond his eyes, he will see colors; and similarly if he closes an eye the same thing happens under the shade of the eyebrows; and again the same phenomenon appears through a glass vessel filled with water and placed in the sun's rays. Or similarly if one having water in his mouth sprinkles it vigorously into the rays and stands at the side of the rays. So, too, if rays in the required position pass through an oil lamp hanging in the air so that the light falls on the surface of the oil, colors will be produced. Thus in an infinite number of ways colors of this kind appear, which the diligent experimenter knows how to discover. . . .

Another example can be given in the field of medicine in regard to the prolongation of human life, for which the medical art has nothing to offer except the regimen of health. But a far longer extension of life is possible. . . .

. . . Not only are remedies possible against the conditions of old age coming at the time of one's prime and before the time of old age, but also if the regimen of old age should be completed, the conditions of old age and senility can still be retarded, so that they do not arrive at their ordinary time, and when they do come they can be mitigated and moderated, so that both

[4] jet.

by retarding and mitigating them life may be prolonged beyond the limit. . . . And there is another farther limit, which has been set by God and nature, in accordance with the property of the remedies retarding the accidents of old age and senility and mitigating their evil. The first limit can be passed but the second cannot be. . . .

. . . Pliny, . . . in the twenty-second book of the Natural History states that a man stood in the presence of Augustus, who had prolonged his life beyond a hundred years. To the astonishment of the bystanders he was strong, robust, and active to such a degree that the emperor in wonder asked him what he did so as to live in this way. The man replied in a riddle, as Pliny says, that he had applied oil on the outside and mead on the inside. Moreover, as stated in the book on the Accidents of Old Age, in the time of King William of Sicily a man was found who renewed the period of his youth in strength and sense and sagacity beyond all human calculation for about sixty years, and from a rustic ploughman became a messenger of the king. While ploughing he found a golden vessel in the fields hidden in the earth, which contained an excellent liquor. Thinking the liquor was dew from the sky he drank it and washed his face, and was renewed in mind and body beyond measure. And in the book just mentioned it is recorded that a man anointed with an excellent unguent the whole surface of his body with the exception of the soles of his feet, and lived for several centuries without decay except in his soles, which he had neglected to anoint, and for this reason he nearly always rode. Moreover, the author of this book bore witness that he had seen a man, and had talked with him, who had lived for several centuries, because he took a medicine prepared by scientists for a great king, who lost hope for himself and wished the medicine to be tried on an ignorant person. Thus the man's life was prolonged, and he had official letters from the Pope of that time and from others in regard to this fact.

Therefore the excellent experimenter in the book on the Regimen of the Aged says that if what is tempered in the fourth degree, and what swims in the sea, and what grows in the air, and what is cast up by the sea, and a plant of India, and what is found in the vitals of a long-lived animal, and the two snakes which are the food of Tyrians and Aethiopians, be prepared and used in the proper way, and the *minera*[5] of the noble animal be present, the life of man could be greatly prolonged and the conditions of old age and senility could be retarded and mitigated. But that which is tempered in the fourth degree is gold, as is stated in the book on Spirits and Bodies,[6] which among all things is most friendly to nature. And if by a certain experiment gold should be made the best possible, or at any rate far better than nature and the art of alchemy can make it, as was the vessel found by the rustic, and it should be dissolved in such water as the ploughman drank, it would then produce a wonderful action on the body of man. And if there is added that which

[5] old French word meaning mine used here probably in the sense of blood. [Burke]
[6] *i.e.,* gases and solids. [Burke]

swims in the sea, namely, the pearl, which is a thing most efficacious for preserving life, and there is added also the thing that grows in the air.[7] This last is an *anthos* [flower] and is the flower of seadew, which possesses an ineffable virtue against the condition of old age. But the *dianthos* that is put in an electuary is not a flower, but is a mixture of leaves and fragments of wood and a small portion of flower. For the pure flower should be gathered in its proper season, and in many ways it is used in foods and drinks and electuaries. To these must be added what is cast up by the sea. This last is ambergris, which is spermaceti, a thing of wondrous virtue in this matter. The plant of India is similar to these, and is the excellent wood of the aloe, fresh and not seasoned. To these ingredients there is added that which is in the heart of a long-lived animal, namely, the stag. This is a bone growing in the stag's heart, which possesses great power against premature old age. The snake which is the food of the Tyrians is the Tyrian snake from which Tyriaca[8] is made, and whose flesh is properly prepared and eaten with spices. This is an excellent remedy for the condition of old age and for all the corruptions of the constitution, if it is taken with things suitable to one's constitution and condition, as we are taught in the book on the Regimen of the Aged. Aristotle, moreover, in the book of Secrets recommends strongly the flesh of the Tyrian snake for our ills. The snake that is the food of the Aethiopians is the dragon, as David says in the psalm, "Thou hast given it as food to the tribes of the Aethiopians." For it is certain that wise men of Aethiopia have come to Italy, Spain, France, England, and those lands of the Christians in which there are good flying dragons, and by the secret art they possess lure the dragons from their caverns. They have saddles and bridles in readiness, and they ride on these dragons and drive them in the air at high speed, so that the rigidity of their flesh may be overcome and its hardness tempered, just as in the case of boars and bears and bulls that are driven about by dogs and beaten in various ways before they are killed for food. After they have domesticated them in this way they have the art of preparing their flesh, similar to the art of preparing the flesh of the Tyrian snake, and they use the flesh against the accidents of old age, and they prolong life and sharpen their intellect beyond all conception. For no instruction that can be given by man can produce such wisdom as the eating of this flesh, as we have learned through men of proved reliability on whose word no doubt can be cast. . . .

If the elements should be prepared and purified in some mixture, so that there would be no action of one element on another, but so that they would be reduced to pure simplicity, the wisest have judged that they would have the most perfect medicine. . . .

. . . But owing to the difficulty of this very great experiment, and because few take an interest in experiments, since the labor involved is complicated and the expense very great, and because men pay no heed to the secrets of nature and the possibilities of art, it happens that very few have labored on

---

[7] Bacon does not complete these sentences, but the sense is clear enough. [Burke]
[8] antidote against poisonous bites. [Burke]

this very great secret of science, and still fewer have reached a laudable end.
... The formation of judgments, as I have said, is a function of this science,
in regard to what can happen by nature or be effected in art, and what not.
This science, moreover, knows how to separate the illusions of magic and to
detect all their errors in incantations, invocations, conjurations, sacrifices, and
cults. But unbelievers busy themselves in these mad acts and trust in them,
and have believed that the Christians used such means in working their
miracles. Wherefore this science is of the greatest advantage in persuading
men to accept the faith, since this branch alone of philosophy happens to
proceed in this way, because this is the only branch that considers matters
of this kind, and is able to overcome all falsehood and superstition and error
of unbelievers in regard to magic, such as incantations and the like already
mentioned. ...

Thomas More (1478–1535)

ENGLISH STATESMAN and HUMANIST

The Citizens of Utopia

But now, it seems, I must explain the behavior of the citizens toward one
another, the nature of their social relations, and the method of distribution
of goods. Since the city consists of households, households as a rule are made
up of those related by blood. Girls, upon reaching womanhood and upon
being settled in marriage, go to their husbands' domiciles. On the other hand,
male children and then grandchildren remain in the family and are subject
to the oldest parent, unless he has become a dotard with old age. In the
latter case the next oldest is put in his place.

But that the city neither be depopulated nor grow beyond measure, provision is made that no household shall have fewer than ten or more than sixteen adults; there are six thousand[1] such households in each city, apart from
its surrounding territory. Of children under age,[2] of course, no number can
be fixed. This limit is easily observed by transferring those who exceed the
number in larger families into those that are under the prescribed number.
Whenever all the families of a city reach their full quota, the adults in excess
of that number help to make up the deficient population of other cities.

[1] resulting in approximately 156,000 adults for the whole state (city and country). [Surtz]
[2] under marriageable age, 22 for men, 18 for women. [Surtz]

Title supplied by editors. From *Utopia* by Sir Thomas More, edited by Edward Surtz,
S.J. Copyright © 1964 by Yale University Press. Reprinted by permission of Yale University Press.

And if the population throughout the island should happen to swell above the fixed quotas, they enroll citizens out of every city and, on the mainland nearest them, wherever the natives have much unoccupied and uncultivated land, they found a colony under their own laws. They join with themselves the natives if they are willing to dwell with them. When such a union takes place, the two parties gradually and easily merge and together absorb the same way of life and the same customs, much to the great advantage of both peoples. By their procedures they make the land sufficient for both, which previously seemed poor and barren to the natives. The inhabitants who refuse to live according to their laws, they drive from the territory which they carve out for themselves. If they resist, they wage war against them. They consider it a most just cause for war when a people which does not use its soil but keeps it idle and waste nevertheless forbids the use and possession of it to others who by the rule of nature ought to be maintained by it.

If ever any misfortune so diminishes the number in any of their cities that it cannot be made up out of other parts of the island without bringing other cities below their proper strength (this has happened, they say, only twice in all the ages on account of the raging of a fierce pestilence), they are filled up by citizens returning from colonial territory. They would rather that the colonies should perish than that any of the cities of the island should be enfeebled.

But to return to the dealings of the citizens. The oldest, as I have said, rules the household. Wives wait on their husbands, children on their parents, and generally the younger on their elders.

Every city is divided into four equal districts. In the middle of each quarter is a market of all kinds of commodities. To designated market buildings the products of each family are conveyed. Each kind of goods is arranged separately in storehouses. From the latter any head of a household seeks what he and his require and, without money or any kind of compensation, carries off what he seeks. Why should anything be refused? First, there is a plentiful supply of all things and, secondly, there is no underlying fear that anyone will demand more than he needs. Why should there be any suspicion that someone may demand an excessive amount when he is certain of never being in want? No doubt about it, avarice and greed are aroused in every kind of living creature by the fear of want, but only in man are they motivated by pride alone — pride which counts it a personal glory to excel others by superfluous display of possessions. The latter vice can have no place at all in the Utopian scheme of things.

Next to the market place that I have mentioned are the food markets. Here are brought not only different kinds of vegetables, fruit, and bread but also fish and whatever is edible of bird and four-footed beast. Outside the city are designated places where all gore and offal may be washed away in running water. From these places they transport the carcasses of the animals slaughtered and cleaned by the hands of slaves. They do not allow their citizens to accustom themselves to the butchering of animals, by the practice of which they think that mercy, the finest feeling of our human nature, is gradually killed off. In addition, they do not permit to be brought inside the city anything filthy or unclean for fear that the air, tainted by putrefaction, should engender disease.

To continue, each street has spacious halls, located at equal distance from one another, each being known by a special name of its own. In these halls live the syphogrants.[3] To each hall are assigned thirty families, fifteen on either side, to take their meals in common. The managers of each hall meet at a fixed time in the market and get food according to the number of persons in their individual charge.

Special care is first taken of the sick who are looked after in public hospitals. They have four at the city limits, a little outside the walls. These are so roomy as to be comparable to as many small towns. The purpose is twofold: first, that the sick, however numerous, should not be packed too close together in consequent discomfort and, second, that those who have a contagious disease likely to pass from one to another may be isolated as much as possible from the rest. These hospitals are very well furnished and equipped with everything conducive to health. Besides, such tender and careful treatment and such constant attendance of expert physicians are provided that, though no one is sent to them against his will, there is hardly anybody in the whole city who, when suffering from illness, does not prefer to be nursed there rather than at home.

After the supervisor for the sick has received food as prescribed by the physicians, then the finest of everything is distributed equally among the halls according to the number in each, except that special regard is paid to the governor, the high priest, and the tranibors,[4] as well as to ambassadors and all foreigners (if there are any, but they are few and far between).[5] Yet the latter, too, when they are in Utopia, have definite homes got ready for them.

To these halls, at the hours fixed for dinner and supper, the entire syphograncy assembles, summoned by the blast of a brazen trumpet, excepting persons who are taking their meals either in the hospitals or at home. No one is forbidden, after the halls have been served, to fetch food from the market to his home: they realize that no one would do it without good reason. For, though nobody is forbidden to dine at home, yet no one does it willingly since the practice is considered not decent and since it is foolish to take the trouble of preparing an inferior dinner when an excellent and sumptuous one is ready at hand in the hall nearby.

In this hall all menial offices which to some degree involve heavy labor or soil the hands are performed by slaves. But the duty of cooking and preparing the food and, in fine, of arranging the whole meal is carried out by the women alone, taking turns for each family. Persons sit down at three or more tables according to the number of the company. The men sit with their backs

[3] annually elected governmental representatives for each thirty families.
[4] elected officials, each representing ten syphogrants.
[5] Utopians discourage any communication with other countries.

to the wall, the women on the outside, so that if they have any sudden pain or sickness, such as often happens to women with child, they may rise without disturbing the arrangements and go to the nurses.

The nurses sit separately with the infants in a dining room assigned for the purpose, never without a fire and a supply of clean water nor without cradles. Thus they can both lay the infants down and, when they wish, undo their wrappings and let them play freely by the fire. Each woman nurses her own offspring, unless prevented by either death or disease. When that happens, the wives of the syphogrants quickly provide a nurse and find no difficulty in doing so. The reason is that women who can do the service offer themselves with the greatest readiness since everybody praises this kind of pity and since the child who is thus fostered looks on his nurse as his natural mother. In the nurses' quarters are all children up to five years of age. All other minors, among whom they include all of both sexes below the age of marriage, either wait at table on the diners or, if they are not old and strong enough, stand by — and that in absolute silence. Both groups eat what is handed them from the table and have no other separate time for dining.

The syphogrant and his wife sit in the middle of the first table, which is the highest place and which allows them to have the whole company in view, for it stands crosswise at the farthest end of the dining room. Alongside them are two of the eldest, for they always sit four by four at all tables. But if there is a temple in the syphograncy, the priest and his wife so sit with the syphogrant as to preside. On both sides of them sit younger people, and next to them old people again, and so through the house those of the same age sit together and yet mingle with those of a different age. The reason for this practice, they say, is that the grave and reverend behavior of the old may restrain the younger people from mischievous freedom in word and gesture, since nothing can be done or said at table which escapes the notice of the old present on every side.

The trays of food are not served in order from the first place and so on, but all the old men, who are seated in conspicuous places, are served first with the best food, and then equal portions are given to the rest. The old men at their discretion give a share of their delicacies to their neighbors when there is not enough to go around to everybody in the house. Thus, due respect is paid to seniority, and yet all have an equal advantage.

They begin every dinner and supper with some reading which is conducive to morality but which is brief so as not to be tiresome. Taking their cue from the reading, the elders introduce approved subjects of conversation, neither somber nor dull. But they do not monopolize the whole dinner with long speeches: they are ready to hear the young men too, and indeed deliberately draw them out that they may test each one's ability and character, which are revealed in the relaxed atmosphere of a feast.

Their dinners are somewhat short, their suppers more prolonged, because the former are followed by labor, the latter by sleep and a night's rest. They think the night's rest to be more efficacious to wholesome digestion. No supper passes without music, nor does the dessert course lack delicacies. They burn spices and scatter perfumes and omit nothing that may cheer the company. For they are somewhat too much inclined to this attitude of mind: that no kind of pleasure is forbidden, provided no harm comes of it.

This is the common life they live in the city. In the country, however, since they are rather far removed from their neighbors, all take their meals in their own homes. No family lacks any kind of edible inasmuch as all the food eaten by the city dwellers comes from those who live in the country.

Francis Bacon (1561–1626)

ENGLISH PHILOSOPHER and STATESMAN

Idols of the Mind

The idols and false notions which are now in possession of the human understanding, and have taken deep root therein, not only so beset men's minds that truth can hardly find entrance, but even after entrance obtained, they will again in the very instauration of the sciences meet and trouble us, unless men being forewarned of the danger fortify themselves as far as may be against their assaults.

There are four classes of Idols which beset men's minds. To these for distinction's sake I have assigned names, — calling the first class *Idols of the Tribe*; the second, *Idols of the Cave*; the third, *Idols of the Market-place*; the fourth, *Idols of the Theatre*.

The formation of ideas and axioms by true induction is no doubt the proper remedy to be applied for the keeping off and clearing away of idols. To point them out, however, is of great use; for the doctrine of Idols is to the Interpretation of Nature what the doctrine of the refutation of Sophisms is to common Logic.

The Idols of the Tribe have their foundation in human nature itself, and in the tribe or race of men. For it is a false assertion that the sense of man is the

Title supplied by editors. From *Novum Organum* (xxxviii–lxi) in *The Works of Francis Bacon*, edited by James Spedding, Robert Ellis, and Douglas Heath.

measure of things. On the contrary, all perceptions as well of the sense as of the mind are according to the measure of the individual and not according to the measure of the universe. And the human understanding is like a false mirror, which, receiving rays irregularly, distorts and discolours the nature of things by mingling its own nature with it.

▣

The Idols of the Cave are the idols of the individual man. For every one (besides the errors common to human nature in general) has a cave or den of his own, which refracts and discolours the light of nature; owing either to his own proper and peculiar nature; or to his education and conversation with others; or to the reading of books, and the authority of those whom he esteems and admires; or to the differences of impressions, accordingly as they take place in a mind preoccupied and predisposed or in a mind indifferent and settled; or the like. So that the spirit of man (according as it is meted out to different individuals) is in fact a thing variable and full of perturbation, and governed as it were by chance. Whence it was well observed by Heraclitus[1] that men look for sciences in their own lesser worlds, and not in the greater or common world.

There are also Idols formed by the intercourse and association of men with each other, which I call Idols of the Market-place, on account of the commerce and consort of men there. For it is by discourse that men associate; and words are imposed according to the apprehension of the vulgar. And therefore the ill and unfit choice of words wonderfully obstructs the understanding. Nor do the definitions or explanations wherewith in some things learned men are wont to guard and defend themselves, by any means set the matter right. But words plainly force and overrule the understanding, and throw all into confusion, and lead men away into numberless empty controversies and idle fancies.

▣

Lastly, there are Idols which have immigrated into men's minds from the various dogmas of philosophies, and also from wrong laws of demonstration. These I call Idols of the Theatre; because in my judgment all the received systems are but so many stage-plays, representing worlds of their own creation after an unreal and scenic fashion. Nor is it only for the systems now in vogue, or only of the ancient sects and philosophies, that I speak; for many more plays of the same kind may yet be composed and in like artificial manner set forth; seeing that errors the most widely different have nevertheless causes for the most part alike. Neither again do I mean this only of entire systems, but also of many principles and axioms in science, which by tradition, credulity, and negligence have come to be received.

---

[1] first Greek philosopher (c. 500 B.C.) to explore the nature of knowledge and the soul.

But of these several kinds of Idols I must speak more largely and exactly, that the understanding may be duly cautioned.

〽

The human understanding is of its own nature prone to suppose the existence of more order and regularity in the world than it finds. And though there be many things in nature which are singular and unmatched, yet it devises for them parallels and conjugates and relatives which do not exist. Hence the fiction that all celestial bodies move in perfect circles; spirals and dragons[2] being (except in name) utterly rejected. Hence too the element of Fire with its orb is brought in, to make up the square with the other three which the sense perceives. Hence also the ratio of density of the so-called elements is arbitrarily fixed at ten to one. And so on of other dreams. And these fancies affect not dogmas only, but simple notions also.

〽

The human understanding when it has once adopted an opinion (either as being the received opinion or as being agreeable to itself) draws all things else to support and agree with it. And though there be a greater number and weight of instances to be found on the other side, yet these it either neglects and despises, or else by some distinction sets aside and rejects; in order that by this great and pernicious predetermination the authority of its former conclusions may remain inviolate. And therefore it was a good answer that was made by one who when they showed him hanging in a temple a picture of those who had paid their vows as having escaped shipwreck, and would have him say whether he did not now acknowledge the power of the gods, — "Aye," asked he again, "but where are they painted that were drowned after their vows?" And such is the way of all superstition, whether in astrology, dreams, omens, divine judgments, or the like; wherein men, having a delight in such vanities, mark the events where they are fulfilled, but where they fail, though this happen much oftener, neglect and pass them by. But with far more subtlety does this mischief insinuate itself into philosophy and the sciences; in which the first conclusion colours and brings into conformity with itself all that come after, though far sounder and better. Besides, independently of that delight and vanity which I have described, it is the peculiar and perpetual error of the human intellect to be more moved and excited by affirmatives than by negatives; whereas it ought properly to hold itself indifferently disposed towards both alike. Indeed in the establishment of any true axiom, the negative instance is the more forcible of the two.

〽

[2] perhaps a reference to the path followed by the moon and other planets; the ascending half of its path was called the dragon's head, the descending, the dragon's tail.

The human understanding is moved by those things most which strike and enter the mind simultaneously and suddenly, and so fill the imagination; and then it feigns and supposes all other things to be somehow, though it cannot see how, similar to those few things by which it is surrounded. But for that going to and fro to remote and heterogeneous instances, by which axioms are tried as in the fire, the intellect is altogether slow and unfit, unless it be forced thereto by severe laws and overruling authority.

卍

The human understanding is unquiet; it cannot stop or rest, and still presses onward, but in vain. Therefore it is that we cannot conceive of any end or limit to the world; but always as of necessity it occurs to us that there is something beyond. Neither again can it be conceived how eternity has flowed down to the present day; for that distinction which is commonly received of infinity in time past and in time to come can by no means hold; for it would thence follow that one infinity is greater than another, and that infinity is wasting away and tending to become finite. The like subtlety arises touching the infinite divisibility of lines, from the same inability of thought to stop. But this inability interferes more mischievously in the discovery of causes: for although the most general principles in nature ought to be held merely positive, as they are discovered, and cannot with truth be referred to a cause; nevertheless the human understanding being unable to rest still seeks something prior in the order of nature. And then it is that in struggling towards that which is further off it falls back upon that which is more nigh at hand; namely, on final causes: which have relation clearly to the nature of man rather than to the nature of the universe; and from this source have strangely defiled philosophy. But he is no less an unskilled and shallow philosopher who seeks causes of that which is most general, than he who in things subordinate and subaltern omits to do so.

卍

The human understanding is no dry light, but receives an infusion from the will and affections; whence proceed sciences which may be called "sciences as one would." For what a man had rather were true he more readily believes. Therefore he rejects difficult things from impatience of research; sober things, because they narrow hope; the deeper things of nature, from superstition; the light of experience, from arrogance and pride, lest his mind should seem to be occupied with things mean and transitory; things not commonly believed, out of deference to the opinion of the vulgar. Numberless in short are the ways, and sometimes imperceptible, in which the affections colour and infect the understanding.

卍

But by far the greatest hindrance and aberration of the human understanding proceeds from the dulness, incompetency, and deceptions of the senses;

in that things which strike the sense outweigh things which do not immediately strike it, though they be more important. Hence it is that speculation commonly ceases where sight ceases; insomuch that of things invisible there is little or no observation. Hence all the working of the spirits inclosed in tangible bodies lies hid and unobserved of men. So also all the more subtle changes of form in the parts of coarser substances (which they commonly call alteration, though it is in truth local motion through exceedingly small spaces) is in like manner unobserved. And yet unless these two things just mentioned be searched out and brought to light, nothing great can be achieved in nature, as far as the production of works is concerned. So again the essential nature of our common air, and of all bodies less dense than air (which are very many), is almost unknown. For the sense by itself is a thing infirm and erring; neither can instruments for enlarging or sharpening the senses do much; but all the truer kind of interpretation of nature is effected by instances and experiments fit and apposite; wherein the sense decides touching the experiment only, and the experiment touching the point in nature and the thing itself.

௵

The human understanding is of its own nature prone to abstractions and gives a substance and reality to things which are fleeting. But to resolve nature into abstractions is less to our purpose than to dissect her into parts; as did the school of Democritus,[3] which went further into nature than the rest. Matter rather than forms should be the object of our attention, its configurations and changes of configuration, and simple action, and law of action or motion; for forms are figments of the human mind, unless you will call those laws of action forms.

௵

Such then are the idols which I call *Idols of the Tribe*; and which take their rise either from the homogeneity of the substance of the human spirit, or from its preoccupation, or from its narrowness, or from its restless motion, or from an infusion of the affections, or from the incompetency of the senses, or from the mode of impression.

௵

The *Idols of the Cave* take their rise in the peculiar constitution, mental or bodily, of each individual; and also in education, habit, and accident. Of this kind there is a great number and variety; but I will instance those the pointing out of which contains the most important caution, and which have most effect in disturbing the clearness of the understanding.

௵

[3] Greek philosopher (c. 460–370 B.C.) who, with his teacher Leucippus, originated an atomic theory in which all matter consisted of different arrangements of ultimate tiny homogenous particles (atoms).

Men become attached to certain particular sciences and speculations, either because they fancy themselves the authors and inventors thereof, or because they have bestowed the greatest pains upon them and become most habituated to them. But men of this kind, if they betake themselves to philosophy and contemplations of a general character, distort and colour them in obedience to their former fancies; a thing especially to be noticed in Aristotle, who made his natural philosophy a mere bond-servant to his logic, thereby rendering it contentious and well nigh useless. The race of chemists again out of a few experiments of the furnace have built up a fantastic philosophy, framed with reference to a few things; and Gilbert[4] also, after he had employed himself most laboriously in the study and observation of the loadstone, proceeded at once to construct an entire system in accordance with his favourite subject.

〄

There is one principal and as it were radical distinction between different minds, in respect of philosophy and the sciences; which is this: that some minds are stronger and apter to mark the differences of things, others to mark their resemblances. The steady and acute mind can fix its contemplations and dwell and fasten on the subtlest distinctions: the lofty and discursive mind recognises and puts together the finest and most general resemblances. Both kinds however easily err in excess, by catching the one at gradations the other at shadows.

〄

There are found some minds given to an extreme admiration of antiquity, others to an extreme love and appetite for novelty; but few so duly tempered that they can hold the mean, neither carping at what has been well laid down by the ancients, nor despising what is well introduced by the moderns. This however turns to the great injury of the sciences and philosophy; since these affectations of antiquity and novelty are the humours of partisans rather than judgments; and truth is to be sought for not in the felicity of any age, which is an unstable thing, but in the light of nature and experience, which is eternal. These factions therefore must be abjured, and care must be taken that the intellect be not hurried by them into assent.

〄

Contemplations of nature and of bodies in their simple form break up and distract the understanding, while contemplations of nature and bodies in their composition and configuration overpower and dissolve the understanding: a distinction well seen in the school of Leucippus and Democritus as compared with the other philosophies. For that school is so busied with the particles that it hardly attends to the structure; while the others are so lost in

[4] William Gilbert (1540–1603), English physician and physicist, who established the magnetic nature of the earth.

admiration of the structure that they do not penetrate to the simplicity of nature. These kinds of contemplation should therefore be alternated and taken by turns; that so the understanding may be rendered at once penetrating and comprehensive, and the inconveniences above mentioned, with the idols which proceed from them, may be avoided.

Let such then be our provision and contemplative prudence for keeping off and dislodging the *Idols of the Cave*, which grow for the most part either out of the predominance of a favourite subject, or out of an excessive tendency to compare or to distinguish, or out of partiality for particular ages, or out of the largeness or minuteness of the objects contemplated. And generally let every student of nature take this as a rule, — that whatever his mind seizes and dwells upon with peculiar satisfaction is to be held in suspicion, and that so much the more care is to be taken in dealing with such questions to keep the understanding even and clear.

But the *Idols of the Market-place* are the most troublesome of all: idols which have crept into the understanding through the alliances of words and names. For men believe that their reason governs words; but it is also true that words react on the understanding; and this it is that has rendered philosophy and the sciences sophistical and inactive. Now words, being commonly framed and applied according to the capacity of the vulgar, follow those lines of division which are most obvious to the vulgar understanding. And whenever an understanding of greater acuteness or a more diligent observation would alter those lines to suit the true divisions of nature, words stand in the way and resist the change. Whence it comes to pass that the high and formal discussions of learned men end oftentimes in disputes about words and names; with which (according to the use and wisdom of the mathematicians) it would be more prudent to begin, and so by means of definitions reduce them to order. Yet even definitions cannot cure this evil in dealing with natural and material things; since the definitions themselves consist of words, and those words beget others: so that it is necessary to recur to individual instances, and those in due series and order. . . .

The idols imposed by words on the understanding are of two kinds. They are either names of things which do not exist (for as there are things left unnamed through lack of observation, so likewise are there names which result from fantastic suppositions and to which nothing in reality corresponds), or they are names of things which exist, but yet confused and ill-defined, and hastily and irregularly derived from realities. Of the former kind are Fortune, the Prime Mover, Planetary Orbits, Element of Fire, and like fictions which owe their origin to false and idle theories. And this class of idols is more easily expelled, because to get rid of them it is only necessary that all theories should be steadily rejected and dismissed as obsolete.

But the other class, which springs out of a faulty and unskilful abstraction, is intricate and deeply rooted. Let us take for example such a word as *humid*; and see how far the several things which the word is used to signify agree with each other; and we shall find the word *humid* to be nothing else than a mark loosely and confusedly applied to denote a variety of actions which will not bear to be reduced to any constant meaning. For it both signifies that which in itself is indeterminate and cannot solidise; and that which readily yields in every direction; and that which easily divides and scatters itself; and that which easily unites and collects itself; and that which readily flows and is put in motion; and that which readily clings to another body and wets it; and that which is easily reduced to a liquid, or being solid easily melts. Accordingly when you come to apply the word, — if you take it in one sense, flame is humid; if in another, air is not humid; if in another, fine dust is humid; if in another, glass is humid. So that it is easy to see that the notion is taken by abstraction only from water and common and ordinary liquids, without any due verification.

There are however in words certain degrees of distortion and error. One of the least faulty kinds is that of names of substances, especially of lowest species and well-deduced (for the notion of *chalk* and of *mud* is good, of *earth* bad); a more faulty kind is that of actions, as *to generate, to corrupt, to alter*; the most faulty is of qualities (except such as are the immediate objects of the sense) as *heavy, light, rare, dense,* and the like. Yet in all these cases some notions are of necessity a little better than others, in proportion to the greater variety of subjects that fall within the range of the human sense.

But the *Idols of the Theatre* are not innate, nor do they steal into the understanding secretly, but are plainly impressed and received into the mind from the play-books of philosophical systems and the perverted rules of demonstration. To attempt refutations in this case would be merely inconsistent with what I have already said: for since we agree neither upon principles nor upon demonstrations there is no place for argument. And this is so far well, inasmuch as it leaves the honour of the ancients untouched. For they are no wise disparaged — the question between them and me being only as to the way. For as the saying is, the lame man who keeps the right road outstrips the runner who takes a wrong one. Nay it is obvious that when a man runs the wrong way, the more active and swift he is the further he will go astray. . . .

John Locke (1632–1704)

ENGLISH PHILOSOPHER

An Essay Concerning Human Understanding

Every man being conscious to himself that he thinks, and that which his mind is applied about whilst thinking being the *ideas* that are there, it is past doubt that men have in their minds several *ideas* such as are those expressed by the words *whiteness, hardness, sweetness, thinking, motion, man, elephant, army, drunkenness* and others: it is in the first place then to be inquired, how he comes by them? I know it is a received doctrine that men have native *ideas* and original characters stamped upon their minds in their very first being. . . .

Let us then suppose the mind to be, as we say, white paper void of all characters, without any *ideas*. How comes it to be furnished? Whence comes it by that vast store which the busy and boundless fancy of man has painted on it with an almost endless variety? Whence has it all the materials of reason and knowledge? To this I answer, in one word, from *experience*; in that all our knowledge is founded, and from that it ultimately derives itself. Our observation, employed either about *external sensible objects, or about the internal operations of our minds perceived and reflected on by ourselves, is that which supplies our understandings with all the materials of thinking.* These two are the fountains of knowledge, from whence all the *ideas* we have, or can naturally have, do spring.

First, *our senses,* conversant about particular sensible objects, do *convey into the mind* several distinct *perceptions* of things, according to those various ways wherein those objects do affect them. And thus we come by those *ideas* we have of *yellow, white, heat, cold, soft, hard, bitter, sweet,* and all those which we call sensible qualities; which when I say the senses convey into the mind, I mean, they from external objects convey into the mind what produces there those *perceptions*. This great source of most of the *ideas* we have, depending wholly upon our senses, and derived by them to the understanding, I call SENSATION.

Secondly, the other fountain from which experience furnisheth the understanding with *ideas* is the *perception of the operations of our own minds* within us, as it is employed about the *ideas* it has got; which operations, when the soul comes to reflect on and consider, do furnish the understanding with another set of *ideas*, which could not be had from things without. And such are *perception, thinking, doubting, believing, reasoning, knowing, willing,* and all the different actings of our own minds; which we, being conscious of and observing in ourselves, do from these receive into our understandings as distinct *ideas* as we do from bodies affecting our senses. This source of *ideas* every man has wholly in himself; and though it be not sense, as having nothing to do with external objects, yet it is very like it, and might properly enough be called internal sense. But as I call the other *sensation*, so I call this REFLECTION, the *ideas* it affords being such only as the mind gets by reflecting on its own operations within itself. By REFLECTION then, in the following part of this discourse, I would be understood to mean that notice which the mind takes of its own operations, and the manner of them, by reason whereof there come to be *ideas* of these operations in the understanding. These two, I say, viz. external material things as the objects of SENSATION, and the operations of our own minds within as the objects of REFLECTION, are to me the only originals from whence all our *ideas* take their beginnings. The term *operations* here I use in a large sense, as comprehending not barely the actions of the mind about its *ideas*, but some sort of passions arising sometimes from them, such as is the satisfaction or uneasiness arising from any thought.

The understanding seems to me not to have the least glimmering of any *ideas* which it doth not receive from one of these two. *External objects furnish the mind with the* ideas *of sensible qualities,* which are all those different perceptions they produce in us; and the *mind furnishes the understanding with* ideas *of its own operations.*

These, when we have taken a full survey of them and their several modes, combinations, and relations, we shall find to contain all our whole stock of *ideas,* and that we have nothing in our minds which did not come in one of these two ways. Let anyone examine his own thoughts and thoroughly search into his understanding and then let him tell me whether all the original *ideas* he has there are any other than of the objects of his *senses,* or of the operations of his mind, considered as objects of his *reflection.* And how great a mass of knowledge soever he imagines to be lodged there, he will, upon taking a strict view, see that he has *not any* idea *in his mind but what one of these two have imprinted,* though perhaps, with infinite variety compounded and enlarged by the understanding, as we shall see hereafter.

He that attentively considers the state of a *child,* at his first coming into the world, will have little reason to think him stored with plenty of *ideas,* that are to be the matter of his future knowledge. It is by degrees he comes to be furnished with them. And though the *ideas* of obvious and familiar qualities imprint themselves before the memory begins to keep a register of time and order, yet it is often so late before some unusual qualities come in the way, that there are few men that cannot recollect the beginning of their acquaintance with them. And if it were worthwhile, no doubt a child might be so ordered as to have but a very few, even of the ordinary *ideas,* till he were grown up to a man. But all that are born into the world being surrounded with bodies that perpetually and diversely affect them, variety of *ideas,* whether care be taken about it or no, are imprinted on the minds of children. *Light* and *colours* are busy at hand everywhere when the eye is but open; *sounds* and some *tangible qualities* fail not to solicit their proper senses and force an entrance to the mind; but yet, I think it will be granted easily that, if a child were kept in a place where he never saw any other but black and white till he were a man, he would have no more *ideas* of scarlet or green than he that from his childhood never tasted an oyster or a pineapple has of those particular relishes.

Men then come to be furnished with fewer or more simple *ideas* from without, according as the *objects* they converse with afford greater or less variety; and from the operation of their minds within, according as they more or less *reflect* on them. For, though he that contemplates the operations of his mind cannot but have plain and clear *ideas* of them: yet, unless he turn his thoughts that way and consider them *attentively*, he will no more have clear and distinct *ideas* of all the *operations of his mind*, and all that may be observed therein, than he will have all the particular *ideas* of any landscape, or of the parts and motions of a clock, who will not turn his eyes to it and with attention heed all the parts of it. The picture or clock may be so placed that they may come in his way every day, but yet he will have but a confused *idea* of all the parts they are made up of, till he *applies himself with attention* to consider them each in particular.

And hence we see the reason why it is pretty late before most children get *ideas* of the operations of their own minds; and some have not any very clear or perfect *ideas* of the greatest part of them all their lives. Because, though they pass there continually, yet, like floating visions, they make not deep impressions enough to leave in the mind clear, distinct, lasting *ideas*, till the understanding turns inwards upon itself, *reflects* on its own *operations*, and makes them the object of its own contemplation. Children, when they come first into it, are surrounded with a world of new things which, by a constant solicitation of their senses, draw the mind constantly to them, forward to take notice of new and apt to be delighted with the variety of changing objects. Thus the first years are usually employed and diverted in looking abroad. Men's business in them is to acquaint themselves with what is to be found without; and so growing up in a constant attention to outward sensations, seldom make any considerable reflection on what passes within them, till they come to be of riper years; and some scarce ever at all.

Jonathan Swift (1667–1745)

ENGLISH SATIRIST and CLERGYMAN (IRISH-BORN)

The Academy of Lagado

This Academy is not an entire single Building, but a Continuation of several Houses on both Sides of a Street; which growing waste, was purchased and applyed to that Use.

I was received very kindly by the Warden, and went for many Days to the Academy. Every Room hath in it one or more Projectors; and I believe I could not be in fewer than five Hundred Rooms.

The first Man I saw was of a meagre Aspect, with sooty Hands and Face, his Hair and Beard long, ragged and singed in several Places. His Clothes, Shirt, and Skin were all of the same Colour. He had been Eight Years upon a Project for extracting Sun-Beams out of Cucumbers, which were to be put into Vials hermetically sealed, and let out to warm the Air in raw inclement Summers. He told me, he did not doubt in Eight Years more, that he should be able to supply the Governors Gardens with Sun-shine at a reasonable Rate; but he complained that his Stock was low, and intreated me to give him something as an Encouragement to Ingenuity, especially since this had been a very dear Season for Cucumbers. I made him a small Present, for my Lord had furnished me with Money on purpose, because he knew their Practice of begging from all who go to see them.

I went into another Chamber, but was ready to hasten back, being almost overcome with a horrible Stink. My Conductor pressed me forward, conjuring me in a Whisper to give no Offence, which would be highly resented; and therefore I durst not so much as stop my Nose. The Projector of this Cell was the most ancient Student of the Academy. His Face and Beard were of a pale Yellow; his Hands and Clothes dawbed over with Filth. When I was presented to him, he gave me a very close Embrace, (a Compliment I could well have excused.) His Employment from his first coming into the Academy, was an Operation to reduce human Excrement to its original Food, by separating the several Parts, removing the Tincture which it receives from the Gall, making the Odour exhale, and scumming off the Saliva. He had a weekly Allowance from the Society, of a Vessel filled with human Ordure, about the Bigness of a *Bristol* Barrel.

I saw another at work to calcine Ice into Gunpowder; who likewise shewed me a Treatise he had written concerning the Malleability of Fire, which he intended to publish.

Title supplied by editors. From *Gulliver's Travels*, Bk. III, Chs. 5 and 6, in *The Prose Works of Jonathan Swift*, edited by Herbert Davis. Reprinted by permission of Basil Blackwell, Publisher, Oxford.

There was a most ingenious Architect who had contrived a new Method for building Houses, by beginning at the Roof, and working downwards to the Foundation; which he justified to me by the like Practice of those two prudent Insects the Bee and the Spider.

There was a Man born blind, who had several Apprentices in his own Condition: Their Employment was to mix Colours for Painters, which their Master taught them to distinguish by feeling and smelling. It was indeed my Misfortune to find them at that Time not very perfect in their Lessons; and the Professor himself happened to be generally mistaken: This Artist is much encouraged and esteemed by the whole Fraternity.

In another Apartment I was highly pleased with a Projector, who had found a Device of plowing the Ground with Hogs, to save the Charges of Plows, Cattle, and Labour. The Method is this: In an Acre of Ground you bury at six Inches Distance, and eight deep, a Quantity of Acorns, Dates, Chesnuts, and other Masts or Vegetables whereof these Animals are fondest; then you drive six Hundred or more of them into the Field, where in a few Days they will root up the whole Ground in search of their Food, and make it fit for sowing, at the same time manuring it with their Dung. It is true, upon Experiment they found the Charge and Trouble very great, and they had little or no Crop. However, it is not doubted that this Invention may be capable of great Improvement.

I went into another Room, where the Walls and Ceiling were all hung round with Cobwebs, except a narrow Passage for the Artist to go in and out. At my Entrance he called aloud to me not to disturb his Webs. He lamented the fatal Mistake the World had been so long in of using Silk-Worms, while we had such plenty of domestick Insects, who infinitely excelled the former, because they understood how to weave as well as spin. And he proposed farther, that by employing Spiders, the Charge of dying Silks would be wholly saved; whereof I was fully convinced when he shewed me a vast Number of Flies most beautifully coloured, wherewith he fed his Spiders; assuring us, that the Webs would take a Tincture from them; and as he had them of all Hues, he hoped to fit every Body's Fancy, as soon as he could find proper Food for the Flies, of certain Gums, Oyls, and other glutinous Matter, to give a Strength and Consistence to the Threads.

There was an Astronomer who had undertaken to place a Sun-Dial upon the great Weather-Cock on the Town-House, by adjusting the annual and diurnal Motions of the Earth and Sun, so as to answer and coincide with all accidental Turnings of the Wind.

I was complaining of a small Fit of the Cholick; upon which my Conductor led me into a Room, where a great Physician resided, who was famous for curing that Disease by contrary Operations from the same Instrument. He had a large Pair of Bellows, with a long slender Muzzle of Ivory. This he conveyed eight Inches up the Anus, and drawing in the Wind, he affirmed he could make the Guts as lank as a dried Bladder. But when the Disease was more stubborn and violent, he let in the Muzzle while the Bellows was full of Wind, which he discharged into the Body of the Patient; then withdrew the Instrument to replenish it, clapping his Thumb strongly against the Orifice of the Fundament; and this being repeated three or four Times, the adventitious Wind would rush out, bringing the noxious along with it (like Water put into a Pump) and the Patient recovers. I saw him try both Experiments upon a Dog, but could not discern any Effect from the former. After the latter, the Animal was ready to burst, and made so violent a Discharge, as was very offensive to me and my Companions. The Dog died on the Spot, and we left the Doctor endeavouring to recover him by the same Operation.

I visited many other Apartments, but shall not trouble my Reader with all the Curiosities I observed, being studious of Brevity.

I had hitherto seen only one Side of the Academy, the other being appropriated to the Advancers of speculative Learning; of whom I shall say something when I have mentioned one illustrious Person more, who is called among them *the universal Artist*. He told us, he had been Thirty Years employing his Thoughts for the Improvement of human Life. He had two large Rooms full of wonderful Curiosities, and Fifty Men at work. Some were condensing Air into a dry tangible Substance, by extracting the Nitre, and letting the aqueous or fluid Particles percolate: Others softening Marble for Pillows and Pin-cushions; others petrifying the Hoofs of a living Horse to preserve them from foundring. The Artist himself was at that Time busy upon two great Designs: The first, to sow Land with Chaff, wherein he affirmed the true seminal Virtue to be contained, as he demonstrated by several Experiments which I was not skilful enough to comprehend. The other was, by a certain Composition of Gums, Minerals, and Vegetables outwardly applied, to prevent the Growth of Wool upon two young Lambs; and he hoped in a reasonable Time to propagate the Breed of naked Sheep all over the Kingdom.

We crossed a Walk to the other Part of the Academy, where, as I have already said, the Projectors in speculative Learning resided.

The first Professor I saw was in a very large Room, with Forty Pupils about him. After Salutation, observing me to look earnestly upon a Frame, which took up the greatest Part of both the Length and Breadth of the Room; he said, perhaps I might wonder to see him employed in a Project for improving speculative Knowledge by practical and mechanical Operations. But the World would soon be sensible of its Usefulness; and he flattered himself, that a more noble exalted Thought never sprang in any other Man's Head. Every one knew how laborious the usual Method is of attaining to Arts and Sciences; whereas by his Contrivance, the most ignorant Person at a reasonable Charge, and with a little bodily Labour, may write Books in Philosophy, Poetry, Politicks, Law, Mathematicks and Theology, without the least Assistance from Genius or Study. He then led me to the Frame, about the Sides whereof all his Pupils stood in Ranks. It was Twenty Foot square, placed in the Middle of the Room. The Superficies was composed of several Bits of Wood, about the Bigness of a Dye, but some larger than others. They were all linked together by slender Wires. These Bits of Wood were covered on every Square with Paper pasted on them; and on these Papers were written all the Words of their Language in their several Moods, Tenses, and Declensions, but without any Order. The Professor then desired me to observe, for he was going to set his Engine at work. The Pupils at his Command took each of them hold of an Iron Handle, whereof there were Forty fixed round the Edges of the Frame; and giving them a sudden Turn, the whole Disposition of the Words was entirely changed. He then commanded Six and Thirty of the Lads to read the several Lines softly as they appeared upon the Frame; and where they found three or four Words together that might make Part of a Sentence, they dictated to the four remaining Boys who were Scribes. This Work was repeated three or four Times, and at every Turn the Engine was so contrived, that the Words shifted into new Places, as the square Bits of Wood moved upside down.

Six Hours a-Day the young Students were employed in this Labour; and the Professor shewed me several Volumes in large Folios already collected, of broken Sentences, which he intended to piece together; and out of those rich Materials to give the World a compleat Body of all Arts and Sciences; which however might be still improved, and much expedited, if the Publick would raise a Fund for making and employing five Hundred such Frames in *Lagado*, and oblige the Managers to contribute in common their several Collections.

He assured me, that this Invention had employed all his Thoughts from his Youth; that he had emptyed the whole Vocabulary into his Frame, and made the strictest Computation of the general Proportion there is in Books between the Numbers of Particles, Nouns, and Verbs, and other Parts of Speech.

I made my humblest Acknowledgments to this illustrious Person for his great Communicativeness; and promised if ever I had the good Fortune to return to my native Country, that I would do him Justice, as the sole Inventer of this wonderful Machine; the Form and Contrivance of which I desired Leave to delineate upon Paper as in the Figure here annexed. I told him, although it were the Custom of our Learned in *Europe* to steal Inventions from each other, who had thereby at least this Advantage, that it became a Controversy which was the right Owner; yet I would take such Caution, that he should have the Honour entire without a Rival.

We next went to the School of Languages, where three Professors sat in Consultation upon improving that of their own Country.

The first Project was to shorten Discourse by cutting Polysyllables into one, and leaving out Verbs and Participles; because in Reality all things imaginable are but Nouns.

The other, was a Scheme for entirely abolishing all Words whatsoever: And this was urged as a great Advantage in Point of Health as well as Brevity. For, it is plain, that every Word we speak is in some Degree a Diminution of our Lungs by Corrosion; and consequently contributes to the shortening of our Lives. An Expedient was therefore offered, that since Words are only Names for *Things*, it would be more convenient for all Men to carry about them, such *Things* as were necessary to express the particular Business they are to

Plate 5 Part 3.

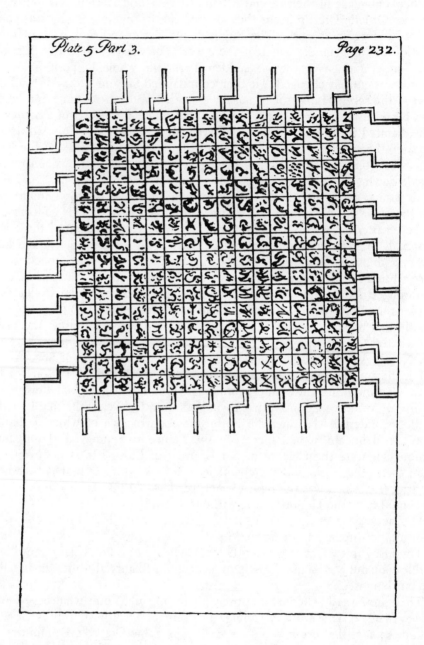

discourse on. And this Invention would certainly have taken Place, to the great Ease as well as Health of the Subject, if the Women in Conjunction with the Vulgar and Illiterate had not threatned to raise a Rebellion, unless they might be allowed the Liberty to speak with their Tongues, after the Manner of their Forefathers: Such constant irreconcileable Enemies to Science are the common People. However, many of the most Learned and Wise adhere to the new Scheme of expressing themselves by *Things*; which hath only this Inconvenience attending it; that if a Man's Business be very great, and of various Kinds, he must be obliged in Proportion to carry a greater Bundle of *Things* upon his Back, unless he can afford one or two strong Servants to attend him. I have often beheld two of those Sages almost sinking under the Weight of their Packs, like Pedlars among us; who when they met in the Streets would lay down their Loads, open their Sacks, and hold Conversation for an Hour together; then put up their Implements, help each other to resume their Burthens, and take their Leave.

But, for short Conversations a Man may carry Implements in his Pockets and under his Arms, enough to supply him, and in his House he cannot be at a Loss; therefore the Room where Company meet who practice this Art, is full of all *Things* ready at Hand, requisite to furnish Matter for this Kind of artificial Converse.

Another great Advantage proposed by this Invention, was, that it would serve as an universal Language to be understood in all civilized Nations, whose Goods and Utensils are generally of the same Kind, or nearly resembling, so that their Uses might easily be comprehended. And thus, Embassadors would be qualified to treat with foreign Princes or Ministers of State, to whose Tongues they were utter Strangers.

I was at the Mathematical School, where the Master taught his Pupils after a Method scarce imaginable to us in *Europe*. The Proposition and Demonstration were fairly written on a thin Wafer, with Ink composed of a Cephalick Tincture. This the Student was to swallow upon a fasting Stomach, and for three Days following eat nothing but Bread and Water. As the Wafer digested, the Tincture mounted to his Brain, bearing the Proposition along with it. But the Success hath not hitherto been answerable, partly by some Error in the *Quantum* or Composition, and partly by the Perverseness of Lads; to whom this Bolus is so nauseous, that they generally steal aside, and discharge it upwards before it can operate; neither have they been yet persuaded to use so long an Abstinence as the Prescription requires.

In the School of political Projectors I was but ill entertained; the Professors appearing in my Judgment wholly out of their Senses; which is a Scene that never fails to make me melancholy. These unhappy People were proposing Schemes for persuading Monarchs to chuse Favourites upon the Score of their Wisdom, Capacity and Virtue; of teaching Ministers to consult the publick Good; of rewarding Merit, great Abilities, and eminent Services; of instructing Princes to know their true Interest, by placing it on the same

Foundation with that of their People: Of chusing for Employments Persons qualified to exercise them; with many other wild impossible Chimæras, that never entered before into the Heart of Man to conceive; and confirmed in me the old Observation, that there is nothing so extravagant and irrational which some Philosophers have not maintained for Truth.

But, however I shall so far do Justice to this Part of the Academy, as to acknowledge that all of them were not so visionary. There was a most ingenious Doctor who seemed to be perfectly versed in the whole Nature and System of Government. This illustrious Person had very usefully employed his Studies in finding out effectual Remedies for all Diseases and Corruptions, to which the several Kinds of publick Administration are subject by the Vices or Infirmities of those who govern, as well as by the Licentiousness of those who are to obey. For Instance: Whereas all Writers and Reasoners have agreed, that there is a strict universal Resemblance between the natural and the political Body; can there be any thing more evident, than that the Health of both must be preserved, and the Diseases cured by the same Prescriptions? It is allowed, that Senates and great Councils are often troubled with redundant, ebullient, and other peccant Humours[1]; with many Diseases of the Head, and more of the Heart; with strong Convulsions, with grievous Contractions of the Nerves and Sinews in both Hands, but especially the Right: With Spleen, Flatus, Vertigoes and Deliriums; with scrophulous Tumours full of fœtid purulent Matter; with sower frothy Ructations; with Canine Appetites and Crudeness of Digestion; besides many others needless to mention. This Doctor therefore proposed, that upon the meeting of a Senate, certain Physicians should attend at the three first Days of their sitting, and at the Close of each Day's Debate, feel the Pulses of every Senator; after which having maturely considered, and consulted upon the Nature of the several Maladies, and the Methods of Cure; they should on the fourth Day return to the Senate-House, attended by their Apothecaries stored with proper Medicines; and before the Members sat, administer to each of them Lenitives, Aperitives, Abstersives, Corrosives, Restringents, Palliatives, Laxatives, Cephalalgicks, Ictericks, Apophlegmaticks, Acousticks, as their several Cases required; and according as these Medicines should operate, repeat, alter, or omit them at the next Meeting.

This Project could not be of any great Expence to the Publick; and might in my poor Opinion, be of much Use for the Dispatch of Business in those Countries where Senates have any Share in the legislative Power; beget Unanimity, shorten Debates, open a few Mouths which are now closed, and close many more which are now open; curb the Petulancy of the Young, and correct the Positiveness of the Old; rouze the Stupid, and damp the Pert.

Again; Because it is a general Complaint that the Favourites of Princes are troubled with short and weak Memories; the same Doctor proposed, that whoever attended a first Minister, after having told his Business with the

[1] Four humors — blood, choler (yellow bile), phlegm, and melancholy (black bile) — were thought to underlie human physiology; their relative proportion determined a man's general personality and constitution.

utmost Brevity, and in the plainest Words; should at his Departure give the
said Minister a Tweak by the Nose, or a Kick in the Belly, or tread on his
Corns, or lug him thrice by both Ears, or run a Pin into his Breech, or pinch
his Arm black and blue; to prevent Forgetfulness: And at every Levee Day
repeat the same Operation, till the Business were done or absolutely refused.

He likewise directed, that every Senator in the great Council of a Nation,
after he had delivered his Opinion, and argued in the Defence of it, should
be obliged to give his Vote directly contrary; because if that were done, the
Result would infallibly terminate in the Good of the Publick.

When Parties in a State are violent, he offered a wonderful Contrivance to
reconcile them. The Method is this. You take an Hundred Leaders of each
Party; you dispose them into Couples of such whose Heads are nearest of a
Size; then let two nice[2] Operators saw off the *Occiput* of each Couple at the
same Time, in such a Manner that the Brain may be equally divided. Let the
Occiputs thus cut off be interchanged, applying each to the Head of his
opposite Party-man. It seems indeed to be a Work that requireth some Exactness; but the Professor assured us, that if it were dextrously performed, the
Cure would be infallible. For he argued thus; that the two half Brains being
left to debate the Matter between themselves within the Space of one Scull,
would soon come to a good Understanding, and produce that Moderation as
well as Regularity of Thinking, so much to be wished for in the Heads of
those, who imagine they came into the World only to watch and govern its
Motion: And as to the Difference of Brains in Quantity or Quality, among
those who are Directors in Faction; the Doctor assured us from his own
Knowledge, that it was a perfect Trifle.

I heard a very warm Debate between two Professors, about the most com-
modious and effectual Ways and Means of raising Money without grieving
the Subject. The first affirmed, the justest Method would be to lay a certain
Tax upon Vices and Folly; and the Sum fixed upon every Man, to be rated
after the fairest Manner by a Jury of his Neighbours. The second was of an
Opinion directly contrary; to tax those Qualities of Body and Mind for which
Men chiefly value themselves; the Rate to be more or less according to the
Degrees of excelling; the Decision whereof should be left entirely to their own
Breast. The highest Tax was upon Men, who are the greatest Favourites of
the other Sex; and the Assessments according to the Number and Natures
of the Favours they have received; for which they are allowed to be their own
Vouchers. Wit, Valour, and Politeness were likewise proposed to be largely
taxed, and collected in the same Manner, by every Person giving his own
Word for the Quantum of what he possessed. But, as to Honour, Justice,
Wisdom and Learning, they should not be taxed at all; because, they are
Qualifications of so singular a Kind, that no Man will either allow them in his
Neighbour, or value them in himself.

The Women were proposed to be taxed according to their Beauty and
Skill in Dressing; wherein they had the same Privilege with the Men, to be

---

[2] careful.

determined by their own Judgment. But Constancy, Chastity, good Sense, and good Nature were not rated, because they would not bear the Charge of Collecting.

To keep Senators in the Interest of the Crown, it was proposed that the Members should raffle for Employments; every Man first taking an Oath, and giving Security that he would vote for the Court, whether he won or no; after which the Losers had in their Turn the Liberty of raffling upon the next Vacancy. Thus, Hope and Expectation would be kept alive; none would complain of broken Promises, but impute their Disappointments wholly to Fortune, whose Shoulders are broader and stronger than those of a Ministry.

Another Professor shewed me a large Paper of Instructions for discovering Plots and Conspiracies against the Government. He advised great Statesmen to examine into the Dyet of all suspected Persons; their Times of eating; upon which Side they lay in Bed; with which Hand they wiped their Posteriors; to take a strict View of their Excrements, and from the Colour, the Odour, the Taste, the Consistence, the Crudeness, or Maturity of Digestion, form a Judgment of their Thoughts and Designs: Because Men are never so serious, thoughtful, and intent, as when they are at Stool; which he found by frequent Experiment: For in such Conjunctures, when he used merely as a Trial to consider which was the best Way of murdering the King, his Ordure would have a Tincture of Green; but quite different when he thought only of raising an Insurrection, or burning the Metropolis.

The whole Discourse was written with great Acuteness, containing many Observations both curious and useful for Politicians, but as I conceived not altogether compleat. This I ventured to tell the Author, and offered if he pleased to supply him with some Additions. He received my Proposition with more Compliance than is usual among Writers, especially those of the Projecting Species; professing he would be glad to receive farther Information.

I told him, that in the Kingdom of *Tribnia*,[3] by the Natives called *Langden*,[4] where I had long sojourned, the Bulk of the People consisted wholly of Discoverers, Witnesses, Informers, Accusers, Prosecutors, Evidences, Swearers; together with their several subservient and subaltern Instruments; all under the Colours, the Conduct, and pay of Ministers and their Deputies. The Plots in that Kingdom are usually the Workmanship of those Persons who desire to raise their own Characters of profound Politicians; to restore new Vigour to a crazy Administration; to stifle or divert general Discontents; to fill their Coffers with Forfeitures; and raise or sink the Opinion of publick Credit, as either shall best answer their private Advantage. It is first agreed and settled among them, what suspected Persons shall be accused of a Plot: Then, effectual Care is taken to secure all their Letters and other Papers, and put the Owners in Chains. These Papers are delivered to a Set of Artists very dextrous in finding out the mysterious Meanings of Words, Syllables and Letters. For Instance, they can decypher a Close-stool to signify a Privy-Council; a Flock of Geese, a Senate; a lame Dog, an Invader; the Plague, a standing

[3] Britain (anagram).
[4] England (anagram).

Army; a Buzard, a Minister; the Gout, a High Priest; a Gibbet, a Secretary of State; a Chamber pot, a Committee of Grandees; a Sieve, a Court Lady; a Broom, a Revolution; a Mouse-trap, an Employment; a bottomless Pit, the Treasury; a Sink, a C—t; a Cap and Bells, a Favourite; a broken Reed, a Court of Justice; an empty Tun, a General; a running Sore, the Administration.

When this Method fails, they have two others more effectual; which the Learned among them call Acrosticks, and Anagrams. *First*, they can decypher all initial Letters into political Meanings: Thus, *N*, shall signify a Plot; *B*, a Regiment of Horse; *L*, a Fleet at Sea. Or, *secondly*, by transposing the Letters of the Alphabet, in any suspected Paper, they can lay open the deepest Designs of a discontented Party. So for Example, if I should say in a Letter to a Friend, *Our Brother* Tom *hath just got the Piles*; a Man of Skill in this Art would discover how the same Letters which compose that Sentence, may be analysed into the following Words; *Resist, —— a Plot is brought home —— The Tour*. And this is the Anagrammatick Method.

The Professor made me great Acknowledgments for communicating these Observations, and promised to make honourable mention of me in his Treatise.

I saw nothing in this Country that could invite me to a longer Continuance; and began to think of returning home to *England*.

Benjamin Franklin   (1706–1790)

AMERICAN STATESMAN and SCIENTIST

Invention and Experiment

. . . In Order of Time I should have mentioned before, that having in 1742 invented an open Stove, for the better warming of Rooms and at the same time saving Fuel, as the fresh Air admitted was warmed in Entring, I made a Present of the Model to Mr. Robert Grace, one of my early Friends, who having an Iron Furnace, found the Casting of the Plates for these Stoves a profitable Thing, as they were growing in Demand. To promote that Demand I wrote and published a Pamphlet Intitled, An Account of the New-Invented PENNSYLVANIA FIRE PLACES: *Wherein their Construction and manner of Operation is particularly explained; their Advantages above every other Method of warming Rooms demonstrated; and all Objections that have been*

Title supplied by editors. From *The Autobiography of Benjamin Franklin*, edited and annotated by Leonard W. Labaree *et al.*, based on *Benjamin Franklin's Memoirs Parallel Text Edition*, edited by Max Farrand. Reprinted by permission of the University of California Press and Yale University Press.

raised against the Use of them answered and obviated. &c.[1] This Pamphlet
had a good Effect, Govr. Thomas was so pleas'd with the Construction of this
Stove, as describ'd in it that he offer'd to give me a Patent for the sole Vend-
ing of them for a Term of Years; but I declin'd it from a Principle which has
ever weigh'd with me on such Occasions, viz. *That as we enjoy great Advantages from the Inventions of others, we should be glad of an Opportunity to
serve others by any Invention of ours, and this we should do freely and generously.* An Ironmonger in London, however, after assuming a good deal of
my Pamphlet, and working it up into his own, and making some small
Changes in the Machine, which rather hurt its Operation, got a Patent for it
there, and made as I was told a little Fortune by it. And this is not the only
Instance of Patents taken out for my Inventions by others, tho' not always
with the same Success: which I never contested, as having no Desire of
profiting by Patents my self, and hating Disputes. The Use of these Fire-
places in very many Houses both of this and the neighbouring Colonies, has
been and is a great Saving of Wood to the Inhabitants. . . .

In 1746 being at Boston, I met there with a Dr. Spence,[2] who was lately
arrived from Scotland, and show'd me some electric Experiments. They were
imperfectly perform'd, as he was not very expert; but being on a Subject quite
new to me, they equally surpriz'd and pleas'd me. Soon after my Return to
Philadelphia, our Library Company receiv'd from Mr. Peter Colinson, F.R.S.
of London a Present of a Glass Tube, with some Account of the Use of it in
making such Experiments. I eagerly seized the Opportunity of repeating
what I had seen at Boston, and by much Practice acquir'd great Readiness in
performing those also which we had an Account of from England, adding a
Number of new Ones. I say much Practice, for my House was continually
full for some time, with People who came to see these new Wonders. To
divide a little this Incumbrance among my Friends, I caused a Number of
similar Tubes to be blown at our Glass-House, with which they furnish'd
themselves, so that we had at length several Performers. Among these the
principal was Mr. Kinnersley, an ingenious Neighbour, who being out of
Business, I encouraged to undertake showing the Experiments for Money,
and drew up for him two Lectures, in which the Experiments were rang'd
in such Order and accompanied with Explanations in such Method, as that
the foregoing should assist in Comprehending the following. He procur'd an
elegant Apparatus for the purpose, in which all the little Machines that I
had roughly made for myself, were nicely form'd by Instrument-makers. His

---

1 Though Franklin used his invention as early as the winter of 1739–40, he first advertised
this pamphlet for sale Nov. 14, 1744. . . . The stove sharply reduced the heat wasted up
the fireplace chimney and distributed warmth by convection as well as by radiation and
conduction. With it, he asserted, the common room was "twice as warm as it used to
be, with a quarter of the Wood I formerly consum'd there." None of his original stoves
is known to have survived; the "Franklin stove" as now known is a great modification,
since it does not use convection — the drawing in of a current of air to be heated and
then circulated. [abridged]
2 Archibald Spencer; the year was actually 1743.

Lectures were well attended and gave great Satisfaction; and after some time he went thro' the Colonies exhibiting them in every capital Town, and pick'd up some Money. In the West India Islands indeed it was with Difficulty the Experiments could be made, from the general Moisture of the Air.

Oblig'd as we were to Mr. Colinson for his Present of the Tube, &c. I thought it right he should be inform'd of our Success in using it, and wrote him several Letters containing Accounts of our Experiments. He got them read in the Royal Society, where they were not at first thought worth so much Notice as to be printed in their Transactions. One Paper which I wrote for Mr. Kinnersley, on the Sameness of Lightning with Electricity, I sent to Dr. Mitchel, an Acquaintance of mine, and one of the Members also of that Society; who wrote me word that it had been read but was laught at by the Connoisseurs: The Papers however being shown to Dr. Fothergill, he thought them of too much value to be stifled, and advis'd the Printing of them. Mr. Collinson then gave them to Cave for publication in his Gentleman's Magazine; but he chose to print them separately in a Pamphlet, and Dr. Fothergill wrote the Preface.[3] Cave it seems judg'd rightly for his Profit; for by the Additions that arriv'd afterwards they swell'd to a Quarto Volume, which has had five Editions, and cost him nothing for Copy-money. . . .

Samuel Johnson (1709–1784)

ENGLISH CRITIC, POET, and LEXICOGRAPHER

In Praise of Curiosity

. . . But, although this general desire of aggrandizing themselves by raising their profession, betrays men to a thousand ridiculous and mischievous acts of supplantation and detraction, yet as almost all passions have their good as well as bad effects, it likewise excites ingenuity, and sometimes raises an honest and useful emulation of diligence. It may be observed in general, that no trade had ever reached the excellence to which it is now improved, had its professors looked upon it with the eyes of indifferent spectators; the ad-

[3] In fact, many scientists in England recognized from the beginning that Franklin's experiments were important. Extracts from his 1747 letters were printed in the Royal Society's *Philosophical Transactions*, . . . and the letter to Mitchell, read before the Royal Society and "Deservedly admired not only for the Clear Intelligent Stile, but also for the Novelty of the Subjects," was cited importantly. . . . With one exception . . . all his major letters on electricity, 1747–53, were printed. [abridged]

Title supplied by editors. From *The Rambler*, IX, for Tuesday, April 17, 1750, corrected and edited by Alexander Chalmers.

vances, from the first rude essays, must have been made by men who valued themselves for performances, for which scarce any other would be persuaded to esteem them.

It is pleasing to contemplate a manufacture rising gradually from its first mean state by the successive labours of innumerable minds; to consider the first hollow trunk of an oak, in which perhaps, the shepherd could scarce venture to cross a brook swelled with a shower, enlarged at last into a ship of war, attacking fortresses, terrifying nations, setting storms and billows at defiance, and visiting the remotest parts of the globe. And it might contribute to dispose us to a kinder regard for the labours of one another, if we were to consider from what unpromising beginnings the most useful productions of art have probably arisen. Who, when he saw the first sand or ashes, by a casual intenseness of heat melted into a metalline form, rugged with excrescences, and clouded with impurities, would have imagined, that in this shapeless lump lay concealed so many conveniences of life, as would in time constitute a great part of the happiness of the world? Yet by some such fortuitous liquefaction was mankind taught to procure a body at once in a high degree solid and transparent, which might admit the light of the sun, and exclude the violence of the wind; which might extend the sight of the philosopher to new ranges of existence, and charm him at one time with the unbounded extent of the material creation, and at another with the endless subordination of animal life; and, what is yet of more importance, might supply the decays of nature, and succour old age with subsidiary sight. Thus was the first artificer in glass employed, though without his own knowledge or expectation. He was facilitating and prolonging the enjoyment of light, enlarging the avenues of science, and conferring the highest and most lasting pleasures; he was enabling the student to contemplate nature, and the beauty to behold herself.

This passion for the honour of a profession, like that for the grandeur of our own country, is to be regulated, not extinguished. Every man, from the highest to the lowest station, ought to warm his heart and animate his endeavours with the hopes of being useful to the world, by advancing the art which it is his lot to exercise; and for that end he must necessarily consider the whole extent of its application, and the whole weight of its importance. But let him not too readily imagine that another is ill employed, because for want of fuller knowledge of his business, he is not able to comprehend its dignity. Every man ought to endeavour at eminence, not by pulling others down, but by raising himself, and enjoy the pleasure of his own superiority, whether imaginary or real, without interrupting others in the same felicity. The philosopher may very justly be delighted with the extent of his views, and the artificer with the readiness of his hands; but let the one remember, that, without mechanical performances, refined speculation is an empty dream, and the other, that, without theoretical reasoning, dexterity is little more than a brute instinct.

Nathaniel Hawthorne (1804–1864)

AMERICAN NOVELIST and SHORT STORY WRITER

Rappaccini's Daughter

[FROM THE WRITINGS OF AUBÉPINE]

A young man, named Giovanni Guasconti, came, very long ago, from the more southern region of Italy, to pursue his studies at the University of Padua. Giovanni, who had but a scanty supply of gold ducats in his pocket, took lodgings in a high and gloomy chamber of an old edifice which looked not unworthy to have been the palace of a Paduan noble, and which, in fact, exhibited over its entrance the armorial bearings of a family long since extinct. The young stranger, who was not unstudied in the great poem of his country,[1] recollected that one of the ancestors of this family, and perhaps an occupant of this very mansion, had been pictured by Dante as a partaker of the immortal agonies of his Inferno. These reminiscences and associations, together with the tendency to heartbreak natural to a young man for the first time out of his native sphere, caused Giovanni to sigh heavily as he looked around the desolate and ill-furnished apartment.

"Holy Virgin, signor!" cried old Dame Lisabetta, who, won by the youth's remarkable beauty of person, was kindly endeavoring to give the chamber a habitable air, "what a sigh was that to come out of a young man's heart! Do you find this old mansion gloomy? For the love of Heaven, then, put your head out of the window, and you will see as bright sunshine as you have left in Naples."

Guasconti mechanically did as the old woman advised, but could not quite agree with her that the Paduan sunshine was as cheerful as that of southern Italy. Such as it was, however, it fell upon a garden beneath the window and expended its fostering influences on a variety of plants, which seemed to have been cultivated with exceeding care.

"Does this garden belong to the house?" asked Giovanni.

"Heaven forbid, signor, unless it were fruitful of better pot herbs than any that grow there now," answered old Lisabetta. "No; that garden is cultivated by the own hands of Signor Giacomo Rappaccini, the famous doctor, who, I warrant him, has been heard of as far as Naples. It is said that he distils these plants into medicines that are as potent as a charm. Oftentimes you may see

---

[1] *The Divine Comedy* by Dante Alighieri (1265–1321), Italian poet.

From *Mosses from an Old Manse* in the *Complete Works of Nathaniel Hawthorne*, Vol. II, edited by George Parsons Lathrop. Reprinted by permission of Houghton Mifflin Company.

the signor doctor at work, and perchance the signora, his daughter, too, gathering the strange flowers that grow in the garden."

The old woman had now done what she could for the aspect of the chamber; and, commending the young man to the protection of the saints, took
her departure.

Giovanni still found no better occupation than to look down into the garden beneath his window. From its appearance, he judged it to be one of those
botanic gardens which were of earlier date in Padua than elsewhere in Italy
or in the world. Or, not improbably, it might once have been the pleasure-
place of an opulent family; for there was the ruin of a marble fountain in the
centre, sculptured with rare art, but so wofully shattered that it was impossible to trace the original design from the chaos of remaining fragments. The
water, however, continued to gush and sparkle into the sunbeams as cheerfully as ever. A little gurgling sound ascended to the young man's window,
and made him feel as if the fountain were an immortal spirit that sung its
song unceasingly and without heeding the vicissitudes around it, while one
century imbodied it in marble and another scattered the perishable garniture
on the soil. All about the pool into which the water subsided grew various
plants, that seemed to require a plentiful supply of moisture for the nourishment of gigantic leaves, and, in some instances, flowers gorgeously magnificent. There was one shrub in particular, set in a marble vase in the midst
of the pool, that bore a profusion of purple blossoms, each of which had the
lustre and richness of a gem; and the whole together made a show so resplendent that it seemed enough to illuminate the garden, even had there been no
sunshine. Every portion of the soil was peopled with plants and herbs, which,
if less beautiful, still bore tokens of assiduous care, as if all had their individual
virtues, known to the scientific mind that fostered them. Some were placed
in urns, rich with old carving, and others in common garden pots; some crept
serpent-like along the ground or climbed on high, using whatever means of
ascent was offered them. One plant had wreathed itself round a statue of
Vertumnus, which was thus quite veiled and shrouded in a drapery of hanging foliage, so happily arranged that it might have served a sculptor for a study.

While Giovanni stood at the window he heard a rustling behind a screen
of leaves, and became aware that a person was at work in the garden. His
figure soon emerged into view, and showed itself to be that of no common
laborer, but a tall, emaciated, sallow, and sickly-looking man, dressed in a
scholar's garb of black. He was beyond the middle term of life, with gray hair,
a thin, gray beard, and a face singularly marked with intellect and cultivation,
but which could never, even in his more youthful days, have expressed much
warmth of heart.

Nothing could exceed the intentness with which this scientific gardener
examined every shrub which grew in his path: it seemed as if he was looking
into their inmost nature, making observations in regard to their creative essence, and discovering why one leaf grew in this shape and another in that,

and wherefore such and such flowers differed among themselves in hue and perfume. Nevertheless, in spite of this deep intelligence on his part, there was no approach to intimacy between himself and these vegetable existences. On the contrary, he avoided their actual touch or the direct inhaling of their odors with a caution that impressed Giovanni most disagreeably; for the man's demeanor was that of one walking among malignant influences, such as savage beasts, or deadly snakes, or evil spirits, which, should he allow them one moment of license, would wreak upon him some terrible fatality. It was strangely frightful to the young man's imagination to see this air of insecurity in a person cultivating a garden, that most simple and innocent of human toils, and which had been alike the joy and labor of the unfallen parents of the race. Was this garden, then, the Eden of the present world? And this man, with such a perception of harm in what his own hands caused to grow, — was he the Adam?

The distrustful gardener, while plucking away the dead leaves or pruning the too luxuriant growth of the shrubs, defended his hands with a pair of thick gloves. Nor were these his only armor. When, in his walk through the garden, he came to the magnificent plant that hung its purple gems beside the marble fountain, he placed a kind of mask over his mouth and nostrils, as if all this beauty did but conceal a deadlier malice; but, finding his task still too dangerous, he drew back, removed the mask, and called loudly, but in the infirm voice of a person affected with inward disease, —

"Beatrice! Beatrice!"

"Here am I, my father. What would you?" cried a rich and youthful voice from the window of the opposite house — a voice as rich as a tropical sunset, and which made Giovanni, though he knew not why, think of deep hues of purple or crimson and of perfumes heavily delectable. "Are you in the garden?"

"Yes, Beatrice," answered the gardener, "and I need your help."

Soon there emerged from under a sculptured portal the figure of a young girl, arrayed with as much richness of taste as the most splendid of the flowers, beautiful as the day, and with a bloom so deep and vivid that one shade more would have been too much. She looked redundant with life, health, and energy; all of which attributes were bound down and compressed, as it were, and girdled tensely, in their luxuriance, by her virgin zone. Yet Giovanni's fancy must have grown morbid while he looked down into the garden; for the impression which the fair stranger made upon him was as if here were another flower, the human sister of those vegetable ones, as beautiful as they, more beautiful than the richest of them, but still to be touched only with a glove, nor to be approached without a mask. As Beatrice came down the garden path, it was observable that she handled and inhaled the odor of several of the plants which her father had most sedulously avoided.

"Here, Beatrice," said the latter, "see how many needful offices require to be done to our chief treasure. Yet, shattered as I am, my life might pay the penalty of approaching it so closely as circumstances demand. Henceforth, I fear, this plant must be consigned to your sole charge."

"And gladly will I undertake it," cried again the rich tones of the young lady, as she bent towards the magnificent plant and opened her arms as if to embrace it. "Yes, my sister, my splendor, it shall be Beatrice's task to nurse and serve thee; and thou shalt reward her with thy kisses and perfumed breath, which to her is as the breath of life."

Then, with all the tenderness in her manner that was so strikingly expressed in her words, she busied herself with such attentions as the plant seemed to require; and Giovanni, at his lofty window, rubbed his eyes and almost doubted whether it were a girl tending her favorite flower, or one sister performing the duties of affection to another. The scene soon terminated. Whether Dr. Rappaccini had finished his labors in the garden, or that his watchful eye had caught the stranger's face, he now took his daughter's arm and retired. Night was already closing in; oppressive exhalations seemed to proceed from the plants and steal upward past the open window; and Giovanni, closing the lattice, went to his couch and dreamed of a rich flower and beautiful girl. Flower and maiden were different, and yet the same, and fraught with some strange peril in either shape.

But there is an influence in the light of morning that tends to rectify whatever errors of fancy, or even of judgment, we may have incurred during the sun's decline, or among the shadows of the night, or in the less wholesome glow of moonshine. Giovanni's first movement, on starting from sleep, was to throw open the window and gaze down into the garden which his dreams had made so fertile of mysteries. He was surprised and a little ashamed to find how real and matter-of-fact an affair it proved to be, in the first rays of the sun which gilded the dew-drops that hung upon leaf and blossom, and, while giving a brighter beauty to each rare flower, brought everything within the limits of ordinary experience. The young man rejoiced that, in the heart of the barren city, he had the privilege of overlooking this spot of lovely and luxuriant vegetation. It would serve, he said to himself, as a symbolic language to keep him in communion with Nature. Neither the sickly and thoughtworn Dr. Giacomo Rappaccini, it is true, nor his brilliant daughter, were now visible; so that Giovanni could not determine how much of the singularity which he attributed to both was due to their own qualities and how much to his wonder-working fancy; but he was inclined to take a most rational view of the whole matter.

In the course of the day he paid his respects to Signor Pietro Baglioni, professor of medicine in the university, a physician of eminent repute, to whom Giovanni had brought a letter of introduction. The professor was an elderly personage, apparently of genial nature, and habits that might almost be called jovial. He kept the young man to dinner, and made himself very agreeable by the freedom and liveliness of his conversation, especially when warmed by a flask or two of Tuscan wine. Giovanni, conceiving that men of science, inhabitants of the same city, must needs be on familiar terms with one another, took an opportunity to mention the name of Dr. Rappaccini. But the professor did not respond with so much cordiality as he had anticipated.

"Ill would it become a teacher of the divine art of medicine," said Professor Pietro Baglioni, in answer to a question of Giovanni, "to withhold due and well-considered praise of a physician so eminently skilled as Rappaccini; but, on the other hand, I should answer it but scantily to my conscience were I to permit a worthy youth like yourself, Signor Giovanni, the son of an ancient friend, to imbibe erroneous ideas respecting a man who might hereafter chance to hold your life and death in his hands. The truth is, our worshipful Dr. Rappaccini has as much science as any member of the faculty — with perhaps one single exception — in Padua, or all Italy; but there are certain grave objections to his professional character."

"And what are they?" asked the young man.

"Has my friend Giovanni any disease of body or heart, that he is so inquisitive about physicians?" said the professor, with a smile. "But as for Rappaccini, it is said of him — and I, who know the man well, can answer for its truth — that he cares infinitely more for science than for mankind. His patients are interesting to him only as subjects for some new experiment. He would sacrifice human life, his own among the rest, or whatever else was dearest to him, for the sake of adding so much as a grain of mustard seed to the great heap of his accumulated knowledge."

"Methinks he is an awful man indeed," remarked Guasconti, mentally recalling the cold and purely intellectual aspect of Rappaccini. "And yet, worshipful professor, is it not a noble spirit? Are there many men capable of so spiritual a love of science?"

"God forbid," answered the professor, somewhat testily; "at least, unless they take sounder views of the healing art than those adopted by Rappaccini. It is his theory that all medicinal virtues are comprised within those substances which we term vegetable poisons. These he cultivates with his own hands, and is said even to have produced new varieties of poison, more horribly deleterious than Nature, without the assistance of this learned person, would ever have plagued the world withal. That the signor doctor does less mischief than might be expected with such dangerous substances is undeniable. Now and then, it must be owned, he has effected, or seemed to effect, a marvellous cure; but, to tell you my private mind, Signor Giovanni, he should receive little credit for such instances of success, — they being probably the work of chance, — but should be held strictly accountable for his failures, which may justly be considered his own work."

The youth might have taken Baglioni's opinions with many grains of allowance had he known that there was a professional warfare of long continuance between him and Dr. Rappaccini, in which the latter was generally thought to have gained the advantage. If the reader be inclined to judge for himself, we refer him to certain black-letter tracts on both sides, preserved in the medical department of the University of Padua.

"I know not, most learned professor," returned Giovanni, after musing on what had been said of Rappaccini's exclusive zeal for science, — "I know not how dearly this physician may love his art; but surely there is one object more dear to him. He has a daughter."

"Aha!" cried the professor, with a laugh. "So now our friend Giovanni's secret is out. You have heard of this daughter, whom all the young men in Padua are wild about, though not half a dozen have ever had the good hap to see her face. I know little of the Signora Beatrice save that Rappaccini is said to have instructed her deeply in his science, and that, young and beautiful as fame reports her, she is already qualified to fill a professor's chair. Perchance her father destines her for mine! Other absurd rumors there be, not worth talking about or listening to. So now, Signor Giovanni, drink off your glass of lachryma."[2]

Guasconti returned to his lodgings somewhat heated with the wine he had quaffed, and which caused his brain to swim with strange fantasies in reference to Dr. Rappaccini and the beautiful Beatrice. On his way, happening to pass by a florist's, he bought a fresh bouquet of flowers.

Ascending to his chamber, he seated himself near the window, but within the shadow thrown by the depth of the wall, so that he could look down into the garden with little risk of being discovered. All beneath his eye was a solitude. The strange plants were basking in the sunshine, and now and then nodding gently to one another, as if in acknowledgment of sympathy and kindred. In the midst, by the shattered fountain, grew the magnificent shrub, with its purple gems clustering all over it; they glowed in the air, and gleamed back again out of the depths of the pool, which thus seemed to overflow with colored radiance from the rich reflection that was steeped in it. At first, as we have said, the garden was a solitude. Soon, however, — as Giovanni had half hoped, half feared, would be the case, — a figure appeared beneath the antique sculptured portal, and came down between the rows of plants, inhaling their various perfumes as if she were one of those beings of old classic fable that lived upon sweet odors. On again beholding Beatrice, the young man was even startled to perceive how much her beauty exceeded his recollection of it; so brilliant, so vivid, was its character, that she glowed amid the sunlight, and, as Giovanni whispered to himself, positively illuminated the more shadowy intervals of the garden path. Her face being now more revealed than on the former occasion, he was struck by its expression of simplicity and sweetness, — qualities that had not entered into his idea of her character, and which made him ask anew what manner of mortal she might be. Nor did he fail again to observe, or imagine, an analogy between the beautiful girl and the gorgeous shrub that hung its gemlike flowers over the fountain, — a resemblance which Beatrice seemed to have indulged a fantastic humor in heightening, both by the arrangement of her dress and the selection of its hues.

Approaching the shrub, she threw open her arms, as with a passionate ardor, and drew its branches into an intimate embrace — so intimate that her

2 a kind of wine; also tears, moroseness.

features were hidden in its leafy bosom and her glistening ringlets all intermingled with the flowers.

"Give me thy breath, my sister," exclaimed Beatrice; "for I am faint with common air. And give me this flower of thine, which I separate with gentlest fingers from the stem and place it close beside my heart."

With these words the beautiful daughter of Rappaccini plucked one of the richest blossoms of the shrub, and was about to fasten it in her bosom. But now, unless Giovanni's draughts of wine had bewildered his senses, a singular incident occurred. A small orange-colored reptile, of the lizard or chameleon species, chanced to be creeping along the path, just at the feet of Beatrice. It appeared to Giovanni, — but, at the distance from which he gazed, he could scarcely have seen anything so minute, — it appeared to him, however, that a drop or two of moisture from the broken stem of the flower descended upon the lizard's head. For an instant the reptile contorted itself violently, and then lay motionless in the sunshine. Beatrice observed this remarkable phenomenon, and crossed herself, sadly, but without surprise; nor did she therefore hesitate to arrange the fatal flower in her bosom. There it blushed, and almost glimmered with the dazzling effect of a precious stone, adding to her dress and aspect the one appropriate charm which nothing else in the world could have supplied. But Giovanni, out of the shadow of his window, bent forward and shrank back, and murmured and trembled.

"Am I awake? Have I my senses?" said he to himself. "What is this being? Beautiful shall I call her, or inexpressibly terrible?"

Beatrice now strayed carelessly through the garden, approaching closer beneath Giovanni's window, so that he was compelled to thrust his head quite out of its concealment in order to gratify the intense and painful curiosity which she excited. At this moment there came a beautiful insect over the garden wall; it had, perhaps, wandered through the city, and found no flowers or verdure among those antique haunts of men until the heavy perfumes of Dr. Rappaccini's shrubs had lured it from afar. Without alighting on the flowers, this winged brightness seemed to be attracted by Beatrice, and lingered in the air and fluttered about her head. Now, here it could not be but that Giovanni Guasconti's eyes deceived him. Be that as it might, he fancied that, while Beatrice was gazing at the insect with childish delight, it grew faint and fell at her feet; its bright wings shivered; it was dead — from no cause that he could discern, unless it were the atmosphere of her breath. Again Beatrice crossed herself and sighed heavily as she bent over the dead insect.

An impulsive movement of Giovanni drew her eyes to the window. There she beheld the beautiful head of the young man — rather a Grecian than an Italian head, with fair, regular features, and a glistening of gold among his ringlets — gazing down upon her like a being that hovered in mid air. Scarcely knowing what he did, Giovanni threw down the bouquet which he had hitherto held in his hand.

"Signora," said he, "there are pure and healthful flowers. Wear them for the sake of Giovanni Guasconti."

"Thanks, signor," replied Beatrice, with her rich voice, that came forth as it were like a gush of music, and with a mirthful expression half childish and half woman-like. "I accept your gift, and would fain recompense it with this precious purple flower; but if I toss it into the air it will not reach you. So Signor Guasconti must even content himself with my thanks."

She lifted the bouquet from the ground, and then, as if inwardly ashamed at having stepped aside from her maidenly reserve to respond to a stranger's greeting, passed swiftly homeward through the garden. But few as the moments were, it seemed to Giovanni, when she was on the point of vanishing beneath the sculptured portal, that his beautiful bouquet was already beginning to wither in her grasp. It was an idle thought; there could be no possibility of distinguishing a faded flower from a fresh one at so great a distance.

For many days after this incident the young man avoided the window that looked into Dr. Rappaccini's garden, as if something ugly and monstrous would have blasted his eyesight had he been betrayed into a glance. He felt conscious of having put himself, to a certain extent, within the influence of an unintelligible power by the communication which he had opened with Beatrice. The wisest course would have been, if his heart were in any real danger, to quit his lodgings and Padua itself at once; the next wiser, to have accustomed himself, as far as possible, to the familiar and daylight view of Beatrice — thus bringing her rigidly and systematically within the limits of ordinary experience. Least of all, while avoiding her sight, ought Giovanni to have remained so near this extraordinary being that the proximity and possibility even of intercourse should give a kind of substance and reality to the wild vagaries which his imagination ran riot continually in producing. Guasconti had not a deep heart — or, at all events, its depths were not sounded now; but he had a quick fancy, and an ardent southern temperament, which rose every instant to a higher fever pitch. Whether or no Beatrice possessed those terrible attributes, that fatal breath, the affinity with those so beautiful and deadly flowers which were indicated by what Giovanni had witnessed, she had at least instilled a fierce and subtle poison into his system. It was not love, although her rich beauty was a madness to him; nor horror, even while he fancied her spirit to be imbued with the same baneful essence that seemed to pervade her physical frame; but a wild off-spring of both love and horror that had each parent in it, and burned like one and shivered like the other. Giovanni knew not what to dread; still less did he know what to hope; yet hope and dread kept a continual warfare in his breast, alternately vanquishing one another and starting up afresh to renew the contest. Blessed are all simple emotions, be they dark or bright! It is the lurid intermixture of the two that produces the illuminating blaze of the infernal regions.

Sometimes he endeavored to assuage the fever of his spirit by a rapid walk through the streets of Padua or beyond its gates: his footsteps kept time with the throbbings of his brain, so that the walk was apt to accelerate itself to a race. One day he found himself arrested; his arm was seized by a portly personage, who had turned back on recognizing the young man and expended much breath in overtaking him.

"Signor Giovanni! Stay, my young friend!" cried he. "Have you forgotten me? That might well be the case if I were as much altered as yourself."

It was Baglioni, whom Giovanni had avoided ever since their first meeting, from a doubt that the professor's sagacity would look too deeply into his secrets. Endeavoring to recover himself, he stared forth wildly from his inner world into the outer one and spoke like a man in a dream.

"Yes; I am Giovanni Guasconti. You are Professor Pietro Baglioni. Now let me pass!"

"Not yet, not yet, Signor Giovanni Guasconti," said the professor, smiling, but at the same time scrutinizing the youth with an earnest glance. "What! did I grow up side by side with your father? and shall his son pass me like a stranger in these old streets of Padua? Stand still, Signor Giovanni; for we must have a word or two before we part."

"Speedily, then, most worshipful professor, speedily," said Giovanni, with feverish impatience. "Does not your worship see that I am in haste?"

Now, while he was speaking there came a man in black along the street, stooping and moving feebly like a person in inferior health. His face was all over-spread with a most sickly and sallow hue, but yet so pervaded with an expression of piercing and active intellect that an observer might easily have overlooked the merely physical attributes and have seen only this wonderful energy. As he passed, this person exchanged a cold and distant salutation with Baglioni, but fixed his eyes upon Giovanni with an intentness that seemed to bring out whatever was within him worthy of notice. Nevertheless, there was a peculiar quietness in the look, as if taking merely a speculative, not a human, interest in the young man.

"It is Dr. Rappaccini!" whispered the professor when the stranger had passed. "Has he ever seen your face before?"

"Not that I know," answered Giovanni, starting at the name.

"He *has* seen you! he must have seen you!" said Baglioni, hastily. "For some purpose or other, this man of science is making a study of you. I know that look of his! It is the same that coldly illuminates his face as he bends over a bird, a mouse, or a butterfly, which, in pursuance of some experiment, he has killed by the perfume of a flower; a look as deep as Nature itself, but without Nature's warmth of love. Signor Giovanni, I will stake my life upon it, you are the subject of one of Rappaccini's experiments!"

"Will you make a fool of me?" cried Giovanni, passionately. "*That*, signor professor, were an untoward experiment."

"Patience! patience!" replied the imperturbable professor. "I tell thee, my poor Giovanni, that Rappaccini has a scientific interest in thee. Thou hast fallen into fearful hands! And the Signora Beatrice, — what part does she act in this mystery?"

But Guasconti, finding Baglioni's pertinacity intolerable, here broke away, and was gone before the professor could again seize his arm. He looked after the young man intently and shook his head.

"This must not be," said Baglioni to himself. "The youth is the son of my old friend, and shall not come to any harm from which the arcana of medical science can preserve him. Besides, it is too insufferable an impertinence in Rappaccini, thus to snatch the lad out of my own hands, as I may say, and make use of him for his infernal experiments. This daughter of his! It shall be looked to. Perchance, most learned Rappaccini, I may foil you where you little dream of it!"

Meanwhile Giovanni had pursued a circuitous route, and at length found himself at the door of his lodgings. As he crossed the threshold he was met by old Lisabetta, who smirked and smiled, and was evidently desirous to attract his attention; vainly, however, as the ebullition of his feelings had momentarily subsided into a cold and dull vacuity. He turned his eyes full upon the withered face that was puckering itself into a smile, but seemed to behold it not. The old dame, therefore, laid her grasp upon his cloak.

"Signor! signor!" whispered she, still with a smile over the whole breadth of her visage, so that it looked not unlike a grotesque carving in wood, darkened by centuries. "Listen, signor! There is a private entrance into the garden!"

"What do you say?" exclaimed Giovanni, turning quickly about, as if an inanimate thing should start into feverish life. "A private entrance into Dr. Rappaccini's garden?"

"Hush! hush! not so loud!" whispered Lisabetta, putting her hand over his mouth. "Yes; into the worshipful doctor's garden, where you may see all his fine shrubbery. Many a young man in Padua would give gold to be admitted among those flowers."

Giovanni put a piece of gold into her hand.

"Show me the way," said he.

A surmise, probably excited by his conversation with Baglioni, crossed his mind, that this interposition of old Lisabetta might perchance be connected with the intrigue, whatever were its nature, in which the professor seemed to suppose that Dr. Rappaccini was involving him. But such a suspicion, though it disturbed Giovanni, was inadequate to restrain him. The instant that he was aware of the possibility of approaching Beatrice, it seemed an absolute necessity of his existence to do so. It mattered not whether she were angel or demon; he was irrevocably within her sphere, and must obey the law that whirled him onward, in ever-lessening circles, towards a result which he did not attempt to foreshadow; and yet, strange to say, there came across him a sudden doubt whether this intense interest on his part were not delusory; whether it were really of so deep and positive a nature as to justify him in now thrusting himself into an incalculable position; whether it were not merely the fantasy of a young man's brain, only slightly or not at all connected with his heart.

He paused, hesitated, turned half about, but again went on. His withered guide led him along several obscure passages, and finally undid a door, through which, as it was opened, there came the sight and sound of rustling leaves, with the broken sunshine glimmering among them. Giovanni stepped forth, and, forcing himself through the entanglement of a shrub that wreathed its tendrils over the hidden entrance, stood beneath his own window in the open area of Dr. Rappaccini's garden.

How often is it the case that, when impossibilities have come to pass and dreams have condensed their misty substance into tangible realities, we find ourselves calm, and even coldly self-possessed, amid circumstances which it would have been a delirium of joy or agony to anticipate! Fate delights to thwart us thus. Passion will choose his own time to rush upon the scene, and lingers sluggishly behind when an appropriate adjustment of events would seem to summon his appearance. So was it now with Giovanni. Day after day his pulses had throbbed with feverish blood at the improbable idea of an interview with Beatrice, and of standing with her, face to face, in this very garden, basking in the Oriental sunshine of her beauty, and snatching from her full gaze the mystery which he deemed the riddle of his own existence. But now there was a singular and untimely equanimity within his breast. He threw a glance around the garden to discover if Beatrice or her father were present, and, perceiving that he was alone, began a critical observation of the plants.

The aspect of one and all of them dissatisfied him; their gorgeousness seemed fierce, passionate, and even unnatural. There was hardly an individual shrub which a wanderer, straying by himself through a forest, would not have been startled to find growing wild, as if an unearthly face had glared at him out of the thicket. Several also would have shocked a delicate instinct by an appearance of artificialness indicating that there had been such commixture, and, as it were, adultery, of various vegetable species, that the production was no longer of God's making, but the monstrous offspring of man's depraved fancy, glowing with only an evil mockery of beauty. They were probably the result of experiment, which in one or two cases had succeeded in mingling plants individually lovely into a compound possessing the questionable and ominous character that distinguished the whole growth of the garden. In fine, Giovanni recognized but two or three plants in the collection, and those of a kind that he well knew to be poisonous. While busy with these contemplations he heard the rustling of a silken garment, and, turning, beheld Beatrice emerging from beneath the sculptured portal.

Giovanni had not considered with himself what should be his deportment; whether he should apologize for his intrusion into the garden, or assume that he was there with the privity at least, if not by the desire, of Dr. Rappaccini or his daughter; but Beatrice's manner placed him at his ease, though leaving him still in doubt by what agency he had gained admittance. She came lightly along the path and met him near the broken fountain. There was surprise in her face, but brightened by a simple and kind expression of pleasure.

"You are a connoisseur in flowers, signor," said Beatrice, with a smile, alluding to the bouquet which he had flung her from the window. "It is no marvel, therefore, if the sight of my father's rare collection has tempted you to take a nearer view. If he were here, he could tell you many strange and interesting facts as to the nature and habits of these shrubs; for he has spent a lifetime in such studies, and this garden is his world."

"And yourself, lady," observed Giovanni, "if fame says true, — you likewise are deeply skilled in the virtues indicated by these rich blossoms and these spicy perfumes. Would you deign to be my instructress, I should prove an apter scholar than if taught by Signor Rappaccini himself."

"Are there such idle rumors?" asked Beatrice, with the music of a pleasant laugh. "Do people say that I am skilled in my father's science of plants? What a jest is there! No; though I have grown up among these flowers, I know no more of them than their hues and perfume; and sometimes methinks I would fain rid myself of even that small knowledge. There are many flowers here, and those not the least brilliant, that shock and offend me when they meet my eye. But pray, signor, do not believe these stories about my science. Believe nothing of me save what you see with your own eyes."

"And must I believe all that I have seen with my own eyes?" asked Giovanni, pointedly, while the recollection of former scenes made him shrink. "No, signora; you demand too little of me. Bid me believe nothing save what comes from your own lips."

It would appear that Beatrice understood him. There came a deep flush to her cheek; but she looked full into Giovanni's eyes, and responded to his gaze of uneasy suspicion with a queenlike haughtiness.

"I do so bid you, signor," she replied. "Forget whatever you may have fancied in regard to me. If true to the outward senses, still it may be false in its essence; but the words of Beatrice Rappaccini's lips are true from the depths of the heart outward. Those you may believe."

A fervor glowed in her whole aspect and beamed upon Giovanni's consciousness like the light of truth itself; but while she spoke there was a fragrance in the atmosphere around her, rich and delightful, though evanescent, yet which the young man, from an indefinable reluctance, scarcely dared to draw into his lungs. It might be the odor of the flowers. Could it be Beatrice's breath which thus embalmed her words with a strange richness, as if by steeping them in her heart? A faintness passed like a shadow over Giovanni and flitted away; he seemed to gaze through the beautiful girl's eyes into her transparent soul, and felt no more doubt or fear.

The tinge of passion that had colored Beatrice's manner vanished; she became gay, and appeared to derive a pure delight from her communion with the youth not unlike what the maiden of a lonely island might have felt conversing with a voyager from the civilized world. Evidently her experience of life had been confined within the limits of that garden. She talked now about matters as simple as the daylight or summer clouds, and now asked questions in reference to the city, or Giovanni's distant home, his friends, his mother, and his sisters — questions indicating such seclusion, and such lack of familiarity with modes and forms, that Giovanni responded as if to an infant. Her spirit gushed out before him like a fresh rill that was just catching its first glimpse of the sunlight and wondering at the reflections of earth and sky which were flung into its bosom. There came thoughts, too, from a deep source, and fantasies of a gemlike brilliancy, as if diamonds and rubies sparkled upward among the bubbles of the fountain. Ever and anon there gleamed across the young man's mind a sense of wonder that he should be walking side by side with the being who had so wrought upon his imagination, whom he had idealized in such hues of terror, in whom he had positively witnessed such manifestations of dreadful attributes, — that he should be conversing with Beatrice like a brother, and should find her so human and so maidenlike. But such reflections were only momentary; the effect of her character was too real not to make itself familiar at once.

In this free intercourse they had strayed through the garden, and now, after many turns among its avenues, were come to the shattered fountain, beside which grew the magnificent shrub, with its treasury of glowing blossoms. A fragrance was diffused from it which Giovanni recognized as identical with that which he had attributed to Beatrice's breath, but incomparably more powerful. As her eyes fell upon it, Giovanni beheld her press her hand to her bosom as if her heart were throbbing suddenly and painfully.

"For the first time in my life," murmured she, addressing the shrub, "I had forgotten thee."

"I remember, signora," said Giovanni, "that you once promised to reward me with one of these living gems for the bouquet which I had the happy boldness to fling to your feet. Permit me now to pluck it as a memorial of this interview."

He made a step towards the shrub with extended hand; but Beatrice darted forward, uttering a shriek that went through his heart like a dagger. She caught his hand and drew it back with the whole force of her slender figure. Giovanni felt her touch thrilling through his fibres.

"Touch it not!" exclaimed she, in a voice of agony. "Not for thy life! It is fatal!"

Then, hiding her face, she fled from him and vanished beneath the sculptured portal. As Giovanni followed her with his eyes, he beheld the emaciated figure and pale intelligence of Dr. Rappaccini, who had been watching the scene, he knew not how long, within the shadow of the entrance.

No sooner was Guasconti alone in his chamber than the image of Beatrice came back to his passionate musings, invested with all the witchery that had been gathering around it ever since his first glimpse of her, and now likewise imbued with a tender warmth of girlish womanhood. She was human; her nature was endowed with all gentle and feminine qualities; she was worthiest to be worshipped; she was capable, surely, on her part, of the height and heroism of love. Those tokens which he had hitherto considered as proofs of a frightful peculiarity in her physical and moral system were now either forgotten, or, by the subtle sophistry of passion transmitted into a golden crown of enchantment, rendering Beatrice the more admirable by so much as she was the more unique. Whatever had looked ugly was now beautiful; or, if incapable of such a change, it stole away and hid itself among those shapeless half ideas which throng the dim region beyond the daylight of our perfect consciousness. Thus did he spent the night, nor fell asleep until the dawn had begun to awake the slumbering flowers in Dr. Rappaccini's garden, whither Giovanni's dreams doubtless led him. Up rose the sun in his due season, and, flinging his beams upon the young man's eyelids, awoke him to a sense of pain. When thoroughly aroused, he became sensible of a burning and tingling agony in his hand — in his right hand — the very hand which Beatrice had grasped in her own when he was on the point of plucking one of the gemlike flowers. On the back of that hand there was now a purple print like that of four small fingers, and the likeness of a slender thumb upon his wrist.

Oh, how stubbornly does love, — or even that cunning semblance of love which flourishes in the imagination, but strikes no depth of root into the heart, — how stubbornly does it hold its faith until the moment comes when it is doomed to vanish into thin mist! Giovanni wrapped a handkerchief about his hand and wondered what evil thing had stung him, and soon forgot his pain in a reverie of Beatrice.

After the first interview, a second was in the inevitable course of what we call fate. A third; a fourth; and a meeting with Beatrice in the garden was no longer an incident in Giovanni's daily life, but the whole space in which he might be said to live; for the anticipation and memory of that ecstatic hour made up the remainder. Nor was it otherwise with the daughter of Rappaccini. She watched for the youth's appearance, and flew to his side with confidence as unreserved as if they had been playmates from early infancy — as if they were such playmates still. If, by any unwonted chance, he failed to come at the appointed moment, she stood beneath the window and sent up the rich sweetness of her tones to float around him in his chamber and echo and reverberate throughout his heart: "Giovanni! Giovanni! Why tarriest thou? Come down!" And down he hastened into that Eden of poisonous flowers.

But, with all this intimate familiarity, there was still a reserve in Beatrice's demeanor, so rigidly and invariably sustained that the idea of infringing it scarcely occurred to his imagination. By all appreciable signs, they loved; they had looked love with eyes that conveyed the holy secret from the depths of one soul into the depths of the other, as if it were too sacred to be whispered by the way; they had even spoken love in those gushes of passion when their spirits darted forth in articulated breath like tongues of long-hidden flame; and yet there had been no seal of lips, no clasp of hands, nor any slightest caress such as love claims and hallows. He had never touched one of the gleaming ringlets of her hair; her garment — so marked was the physical barrier between them — had never been waved against him by a breeze. On the few occasions when Giovanni had seemed tempted to overstep the limit, Beatrice grew so sad, so stern, and [withal wore] such a look of desolate separation, shuddering at itself, that not a spoken word was requisite to repel him. At such times he was startled at the horrible suspicions that rose, monster-like, out of the caverns of his heart and stared him in the face; his love grew thin and faint as the morning mist; his doubts alone had substance. But, when Beatrice's face brightened again after the momentary shadow, she was transformed at once from the mysterious, questionable being whom he had watched with so much awe and horror; she was now the beautiful and unsophisticated girl whom he felt that his spirit knew with a certainty beyond all other knowledge.

A considerable time had now passed since Giovanni's last meeting with Baglioni. One morning, however, he was disagreeably surprised by a visit from the professor, whom he had scarcely thought of for whole weeks, and would willingly have forgotten still longer. Given up as he had long been to a pervading excitement, he could tolerate no companions except upon condition of their perfect sympathy with his present state of feeling. Such sympathy was not to be expected from Professor Baglioni.

The visitor chatted carelessly for a few moments about the gossip of the city and the university, and then took up another topic.

"I have been reading an old classic author lately," said he, "and met with a story that strangely interested me. Possibly you may remember it. It is of an Indian prince, who sent a beautiful woman as a present to Alexander the Great. She was as lovely as the dawn and gorgeous as the sunset; but what especially distinguished her was a certain rich perfume in her breath — richer than a garden of Persian roses. Alexander, as was natural to a youthful conqueror, fell in love at first sight with this magnificent stranger; but a certain sage physician, happening to be present, discovered a terrible secret in regard to her."

"And what was that?" asked Giovanni, turning his eyes downward to avoid those of the professor.

"That this lovely woman," continued Baglioni, with emphasis, "had been nourished with poisons from her birth upward, until her whole nature was so imbued with them that she herself had become the deadliest poison in existence. Poison was her element of life. With that rich perfume of her breath she blasted the very air. Her love would have been poison — her embrace death. Is not this a marvellous tale?"

"A childish fable," answered Giovanni, nervously starting from his chair. "I marvel how your worship finds time to read such nonsense among your graver studies."

"By the by," said the professor, looking uneasily about him, "what singular fragrance is this in your apartment? Is it the perfume of your gloves? It is faint, but delicious; and yet, after all, by no means agreeable. Were I to breathe it long, methinks it would make me ill. It is like the breath of a flower; but I see no flowers in the chamber."

"Nor are there any," replied Giovanni, who had turned pale as the professor spoke; "nor, I think, is there any fragrance except in your worship's imagination. Odors, being a sort of element combined of the sensual and the spiritual, are apt to deceive us in this manner. The recollection of a perfume, the bare idea of it, may easily be mistaken for a present reality."

"Ay; but my sober imagination does not often play such tricks," said Baglioni; "and, were I to fancy any kind of odor; it would be that of some vile apothecary drug, wherewith my fingers are likely enough to be imbued. Our worshipful friend Rappaccini, as I have heard, tinctures his medicaments with odors richer than those of Araby. Doubtless, likewise, the fair and learned Signora Beatrice would minister to her patients with draughts as sweet as a maiden's breath; but woe to him that sips them!"

Giovanni's face evinced many contending emotions. The tone in which the professor alluded to the pure and lovely daughter of Rappaccini was a torture to his soul; and yet the intimation of a view of her character, opposite to his own, gave instantaneous distinctness to a thousand dim suspicions, which now grinned at him like so many demons. But he strove hard to quell them and to respond to Baglioni with a true lover's perfect faith.

"Signor professor," said he, "you were my father's friend; perchance, too, it is your purpose to act a friendly part towards his son. I would fain feel nothing towards you save respect and deference; but I pray you to observe, signor, that there is one subject on which we must not speak. You know not the Signora Beatrice. You cannot, therefore, estimate the wrong — the blasphemy, I may even say — that is offered to her character by a light or injurious word."

"Giovanni! my poor Giovanni!" answered the professor, with a calm expression of pity, "I know this wretched girl far better than yourself. You shall hear the truth in respect to the poisoner Rappaccini and his poisonous daughter; yes, poisonous as she is beautiful. Listen; for, even should you do violence to my gray hairs, it shall not silence me. That old fable of the Indian woman has become a truth by the deep and deadly science of Rappaccini and in the person of the lovely Beatrice."

Giovanni groaned and hid his face.

"Her father," continued Baglioni, "was not restrained by natural affection from offering up his child in this horrible manner as the victim of his insane zeal for science; for, let us do him justice, he is as true a man of science as ever distilled his own heart in an alembic. What, then, will be your fate? Beyond a doubt you are selected as the material of some new experiment. Perhaps the result is to be death; perhaps a fate more awful still. Rappaccini, with what he calls the interest of science before his eyes, will hesitate at nothing."

"It is a dream," muttered Giovanni to himself; "surely it is a dream."

"But," resumed the professor, "be of good cheer, son of my friend. It is not yet too late for the rescue. Possibly we may even succeed in bringing back this miserable child within the limits of ordinary nature, from which her father's madness has estranged her. Behold this little silver vase! It was wrought by the hands of the renowned Benvenuto Cellini, and is well worthy to be a love gift to the fairest dame in Italy. But its contents are invaluable. One little sip of this antidote would have rendered the most virulent poisons of the Borgias innocuous. Doubt not that it will be as efficacious against those of Rappaccini. Bestow the vase, and the precious liquid within it, on your Beatrice, and hopefully await the result."

Baglioni laid a small, exquisitely wrought silver vial on the table and withdrew, leaving what he had said to produce its effect upon the young man's mind.

"We will thwart Rappaccini yet," thought he, chuckling to himself, as he descended the stairs; "but, let us confess the truth of him, he is a wonderful man — a wonderful man indeed; a vile empiric, however, in his practice, and therefore not to be tolerated by those who respect the good old rules of the medical profession."

Throughout Giovanni's whole acquaintance with Beatrice, he had occasionally, as we have said, been haunted by dark surmises as to her character; yet so thoroughly had she made herself felt by him as a simple, natural, most affectionate, and guileless creature, that the image now held up by Professor Baglioni looked as strange and incredible as if it were not in accordance with his own original conception. True, there were ugly recollections connected with his first glimpses of the beautiful girl; he could not quite forget the bouquet that withered in her grasp, and the insect that perished amid the sunny air, by no ostensible agency save the fragrance of her breath. These incidents, however, dissolving in the pure light of her character, had no longer the efficacy of facts, but were acknowledged as mistaken fantasies, by whatever testimony of the senses they might appear to be substantiated. There is something truer and more real than what we can see with the eyes and touch with the finger. On such better evidence had Giovanni founded his confidence in Beatrice, though rather by the necessary force of her high attributes than by any deep and generous faith on his part. But now his spirit was incapable of sustaining itself at the height to which the early enthusiasm of passion had exalted it; he fell down, grovelling among earthly doubts, and defiled therewith the pure whiteness of Beatrice's image. Not that he gave her up; he did but distrust. He resolved to institute some decisive test that should satisfy him, once for all, whether there were those dreadful peculiarities in her physical nature which could not be supposed to exist without some corresponding monstrosity of soul. His eyes, gazing down afar, might have deceived him as to the lizard, the insect, and the flowers; but if he could witness, at the distance of a few paces, the sudden blight of one fresh and healthful flower in Beatrice's hand, there would be room for no further question. With this idea he hastened to the florist's and purchased a bouquet that was still gemmed with the morning dew-drops.

It was now the customary hour of his daily interview with Beatrice. Before descending into the garden, Giovanni failed not to look at his figure in the mirror, — a vanity to be expected in a beautiful young man, yet, as displaying itself at that troubled and feverish moment, the token of a certain shallowness of feeling and insincerity of character. He did gaze, however, and said to himself that his features had never before possessed so rich a grace, nor his eyes such vivacity, nor his cheeks so warm a hue of superabundant life.

"At least," thought he, "her poison has not yet insinuated itself into my system. I am no flower to perish in her grasp."

With that thought he turned his eyes on the bouquet, which he had never once laid aside from his hand. A thrill of indefinable horror shot through his frame on perceiving that those dewy flowers were already beginning to droop; they wore the aspect of things that had been fresh and lovely yesterday. Giovanni grew white as marble, and stood motionless before the mirror, staring at his own reflection there as at the likeness of something frightful. He remembered Baglioni's remark about the fragrance that seemed to pervade the chamber. It must have been the poison in his breath! Then he shuddered — shuddered at himself. Recovering from his stupor, he began to watch with curious eye a spider that was busily at work hanging its web from the antique cornice of the apartment, crossing and recrossing the artful system of interwoven lines — as vigorous and active a spider as ever dangled from an old ceiling. Giovanni bent towards the insect, and emitted a deep, long breath. The spider suddenly ceased its toil; the web vibrated with a tremor originating in the body of the small artisan. Again Giovanni sent forth a breath, deeper, longer, and imbued with a venomous feeling out of his heart: he knew not whether he were wicked, or only desperate. The spider made a convulsive gripe with his limbs and hung dead across the window.

"Accursed! accursed!" muttered Giovanni, addressing himself. "Hast thou grown so poisonous that this deadly insect perishes by thy breath?"

At that moment a rich, sweet voice came floating up from the garden.

"Giovanni! Giovanni! It is past the hour! Why tarriest thou? Come down!"

"Yes," muttered Giovanni again. "She is the only being whom my breath may not slay! Would that it might!"

He rushed down, and in an instant was standing before the bright and loving eyes of Beatrice. A moment ago his wrath and despair had been so fierce that he could have desired nothing so much as to wither her by a glance; but with her actual presence there came influences which had too real an existence to be at once shaken off: recollections of the delicate and benign power of her feminine nature, which had so often enveloped him in a religious calm; recollections of many a holy and passionate outgush of her heart, when the pure fountain had been unsealed from its depths and made visible in its transparency to his mental eye; recollections which, had Giovanni known how to estimate them, would have assured him that all this ugly mystery was but an earthly illusion, and that, whatever mist of evil might seem to have gathered over her, the real Beatrice was a heavenly angel. Incapable as he was of such high faith, still her presence had not utterly lost its magic. Giovanni's rage was quelled into an aspect of sullen insensibility. Beatrice, with a quick spiritual sense, immediately felt that there was a gulf of blackness between them which neither he nor she could pass. They walked on together, sad and silent, and came thus to the marble fountain and to its pool of water on the ground, in the midst of which grew the shrub that bore gem-like blossoms. Giovanni was affrighted at the eager enjoyment — the appetite, as it were — with which he found himself inhaling the fragrance of the flowers.

"Beatrice," asked he, abruptly, "whence came this shrub?"

"My father created it," answered she, with simplicity.

"Created it! created it!" repeated Giovanni. "What mean you, Beatrice?"

"He is a man fearfully acquainted with the secrets of Nature," replied Beatrice; "and, at the hour when I first drew breath, this plant sprang from the soil, the offspring of his science, of his intellect, while I was but his earthly child. Approach it not!" continued she, observing with terror that Giovanni was drawing nearer to the shrub. "It has qualities that you little dream of. But I, dearest Giovanni, — I grew up and blossomed with the plant and was nourished with its breath. It was my sister, and I loved it with a human affection; for, alas! — hast thou not suspected it? — there was an awful doom."

Here Giovanni frowned so darkly upon her that Beatrice paused and trembled. But her faith in his tenderness reassured her, and made her blush that she had doubted for an instant.

"There was an awful doom," she continued, "the effect of my father's fatal love of science, which estranged me from all society of my kind. Until Heaven sent thee, dearest Giovanni, oh, how lonely was thy poor Beatrice!"

"Was it a hard doom?" asked Giovanni, fixing his eyes upon her.

"Only of late have I known how hard it was," answered she, tenderly. "Oh, yes; but my heart was torpid, and therefore quiet."

Giovanni's rage broke forth from his sullen gloom like a lightning flash out of a dark cloud.

"Accursed one!" cried he, with venomous scorn and anger. "And, finding thy solitude wearisome, thou hast severed me likewise from all the warmth of life and enticed me into thy region of unspeakable horror!"

"Giovanni!" exclaimed Beatrice, turning her large bright eyes upon his face. The force of his words had not found its way into her mind; she was merely thunderstruck.

"Yes, poisonous thing!" repeated Giovanni, beside himself with passion. "Thou hast done it! Thou hast blasted me! Thou hast filled my veins with poison! Thou hast made me as hateful, as ugly, as loathsome and deadly a creature as thyself — a world's wonder of hideous monstrosity! Now, if our breath be happily as fatal to ourselves as to all others, let us join our lips in one kiss of unutterable hatred, and so die!"

"What has befallen me?" murmured Beatrice, with a low moan out of her heart. "Holy Virgin, pity me, a poor heart-broken child!"

"Thou, — dost thou pray?" cried Giovanni, still with the same fiendish scorn. "Thy very prayers, as they come from thy lips, taint the atmosphere with death. Yes, yes; let us pray! Let us to church and dip our fingers in the holy water at the portal! They that come after us will perish as by a pestilence! Let us sign crosses in the air! It will be scattering curses abroad in the likeness of holy symbols!"

"Giovanni," said Beatrice, calmly, for her grief was beyond passion, "why dost thou join thyself with me in those terrible words? I, it is true, am the horrible thing thou namest me. But thou, — what hast thou to do, save with one other shudder at my hideous misery to go forth out of the garden and mingle with thy race, and forget that there ever crawled on earth such a monster as poor Beatrice?"

"Dost thou pretend ignorance?" asked Giovanni, scowling upon her. "Behold! this power have I gained from the pure daughter of Rappaccini."

There was a swarm of summer insects flitting through the air in search of the food promised by the flower odors of the fatal garden. They circled round Giovanni's head, and were evidently attracted towards him by the same influence which had drawn them for an instant within the sphere of several of the shrubs. He sent forth a breath among them, and smiled bitterly at Beatrice as at least a score of the insects fell dead upon the ground.

"I see it! I see it!" shrieked Beatrice. "It is my father's fatal science! No, no, Giovanni; it was not I! Never! never! I dreamed only to love thee and be with thee a little time, and so to let thee pass away, leaving but thine image in mine heart; for, Giovanni, believe it, though my body be nourished with poison, my spirit is God's creature, and craves love as its daily food. But my father, — he has united us in this fearful sympathy. Yes; spurn me, tread upon me, kill me! Oh, what is death after such words as thine? But it was not I. Not for a world of bliss would I have done it."

Giovanni's passion had exhausted itself in its outburst from his lips. There now came across him a sense, mournful, and not without tenderness, of the intimate and peculiar relationship between Beatrice and himself. They stood, as it were, in an utter solitude, which would be made none the less solitary by the densest throng of human life. Ought not, then, the desert of humanity around them to press this insulated pair closer together? If they should be cruel to one another, who was there to be kind to them? Besides, thought Giovanni, might there not still be a hope of his returning within the limits of ordinary nature, and leading Beatrice, the redeemed Beatrice, by the hand? O, weak, and selfish, and unworthy spirit, that could dream of an earthly union and earthly happiness as possible, after such deep love had been so bitterly wronged as was Beatrice's love by Giovanni's blighting words! No, no; there could be no such hope. She must pass heavily, with that broken heart, across the borders of Time — she must bathe her hurts in some fount of paradise, and forget her grief in the light of immortality, and *there* be well.

But Giovanni did not know it.

"Dear Beatrice," said he, approaching her, while she shrank away as always at his approach, but now with a different impulse, "dearest Beatrice, our fate is not yet so desperate. Behold! there is a medicine, potent, as a wise physician has assured me, and almost divine in its efficacy. It is composed of ingredients the most opposite to those by which thy awful father has brought this calamity upon thee and me. It is distilled of blessed herbs. Shall we not quaff it together, and thus be purified from evil?"

"Give it me!" said Beatrice, extending her hand to receive the little silver vial which Giovanni took from his bosom. She added, with a peculiar emphasis, "I will drink; but do thou await the result."

She put Baglioni's antidote to her lips; and, at the same moment, the figure of Rappaccini emerged from the portal and came slowly towards the marble fountain. As he drew near, the pale man of science seemed to gaze with a triumphant expression at the beautiful youth and maiden, as might an artist who should spend his life in achieving a picture or a group of statuary and finally be satisfied with his success. He paused; his bent form grew erect with conscious power; he spread out his hands over them in the attitude of a father imploring a blessing upon his children; but those were the same hands that had thrown poison into the stream of their lives. Giovanni trembled. Beatrice shuddered nervously, and pressed her hand upon her heart.

"My daughter," said Rappaccini, "thou art no longer lonely in the world. Pluck one of those precious gems from thy sister shrub and bid thy bridegroom wear it in his bosom. It will not harm him now. My science and the sympathy between thee and him have so wrought within his system that he now stands apart from common men, as thou dost, daughter of my pride and triumph, from ordinary women. Pass on, then, through the world, most dear to one another and dreadful to all besides!"

"My father," said Beatrice, feebly, — and still as she spoke she kept her hand upon her heart, — "wherefore didst thou inflict this miserable doom upon thy child?"

"Miserable!" exclaimed Rappaccini. "What mean you, foolish girl? Dost thou deem it misery to be endowed with marvellous gifts against which no power nor strength could avail an enemy — misery, to be able to quell the mightiest with a breath — misery, to be as terrible as thou art beautiful? Wouldst thou, then, have preferred the condition of a weak woman, exposed to all evil and capable of none?"

"I would fain have been loved, not feared," murmured Beatrice, sinking down upon the ground. "But now it matters not. I am going, father, where the evil which thou hast striven to mingle with my being will pass away like a dream — like the fragrance of these poisonous flowers, which will no longer taint my breath among the flowers of Eden. Farewell, Giovanni! Thy words of hatred are like lead within my heart; but they, too, will fall away as I ascend. Oh, was there not, from the first, more poison in thy nature than in mine?"

To Beatrice, — so radically had her earthly part been wrought upon by Rappaccini's skill, — as poison had been life, so the powerful antidote was death; and thus the poor victim of man's ingenuity and of thwarted nature, and of the fatality that attends all such efforts of perverted wisdom, perished

there, at the feet of her father and Giovanni. Just at that moment Professor
Pietro Baglioni looked forth from the window, and called loudly, in a tone
of triumph mixed with horror, to the thunderstricken man of science, —
    "Rappaccini! Rappaccini! and is *this* the upshot of your experiment!"

Edgar Allan Poe   (1809–1849)

AMERICAN POET and SHORT STORY WRITER

Sonnet — To Science

Science! true daughter of Old Time thou art!
    Who alterest all things with thy peering eyes.
Why preyest thou thus upon the poet's heart,
    Vulture, whose wings are dull realities?
How should he love thee? or how deem thee wise,
    Who wouldst not leave him in his wandering
To seek for treasure in the jewelled skies,
    Albeit he soared with an undaunted wing?
Hast thou not dragged Diana from her car,
    And driven the Hamadryad from the wood   10
To seek a shelter in some happier star?
    Hast thou not torn the Naiad from her flood,
The Elfin from the green grass, and from me
The summer dream beneath the tamarind tree?

Charles Dickens   (1812–1870)

ENGLISH NOVELIST

Fact and Fancy

"Now, what I want is, Facts. Teach these boys and girls nothing but Facts.
Facts alone are wanted in life. Plant nothing else, and root out everything
else. You can only form the minds of reasoning animals upon Facts; nothing

"Sonnet — to Science" by Edgar Allan Poe. From *The Poems of Edgar Allan Poe,*
Edited with an Introduction, Notes, Variant Readings and Appendix by Killis Campbell
[1917]. New York: Russell & Russell, 1966. Reprinted by permission.

Title supplied by editors. "Fact and Fancy" by Charles Dickens. From *Hard Times,*
Bk. I, by Charles Dickens (Norton Critical Edition, edited and annotated by George H.
Ford and Sylvere Monod). Reprinted by permission of W. W. Norton & Company, Inc.

else will ever be of any service to them. This is the principle on which I bring up my own children, and this is the principle on which I bring up these children. Stick to Facts, sir!"

The scene was a plain, bare, monotonous vault of a schoolroom, and the speaker's square forefinger emphasized his observations by underscoring every sentence with a line on the schoolmaster's sleeve. The emphasis was helped by the speaker's square wall of a forehead, which had his eyebrows for its base, while his eyes found commodious cellarage in two dark caves, overshadowed by the wall. The emphasis was helped by the speaker's mouth, which was wide, thin, and hard set. The emphasis was helped by the speaker's voice, which was inflexible, dry, and dictatorial. The emphasis was helped by the speaker's hair, which bristled on the skirts of his bald head, a plantation of firs to keep the wind from its shining surface, all covered with knobs, like the crust of a plum pie, as if the head had scarcely warehouse-room for the hard facts stored inside. The speaker's obstinate carriage, square coat, square legs, square shoulders — nay, his very neckcloth, trained to take him by the throat with an unaccommodating grasp, like a stubborn fact, as it was — all helped the emphasis.

"In this life, we want nothing but Facts, sir; nothing but Facts!"

The speaker, and the schoolmaster, and the third grown person present, all backed a little, and swept with their eyes the inclined plane of little vessels then and there arranged in order, ready to have imperial gallons of facts poured into them until they were full to the brim.

回

Thomas Gradgrind, sir. A man of realities. A man of facts and calculations. A man who proceeds upon the principle that two and two are four, and nothing over, and who is not to be talked into allowing for anything over. Thomas Gradgrind, sir — peremptorily Thomas — Thomas Gradgrind. With a rule and a pair of scales, and the multiplication table always in his pocket, sir, ready to weigh and measure any parcel of human nature, and tell you exactly what it comes to. It is a mere question of figures, a case of simple arithmetic. You might hope to get some other nonsensical belief into the head of George Gradgrind, or Augustus Gradgrind, or John Gradgrind, or Joseph Gradgrind (all supposititious, non-existent persons), but into the head of Thomas Gradgrind — no, sir!

In such terms Mr. Gradgrind always mentally introduced himself, whether to his private circle of acquaintance, or to the public in general. In such terms, no doubt, substituting the words "boys and girls" for "sir", Thomas Gradgrind now presented Thomas Gradgrind to the little pitchers before him, who were to be filled so full of facts.

Indeed, as he eagerly sparkled at them from the cellarage before mentioned, he seemed a kind of cannon loaded to the muzzle with facts, and prepared to blow them clean out of the regions of childhood at one discharge. He seemed a galvanizing apparatus, too, charged with a grim mechanical substitute for the tender young imaginations that were to be stormed away.

"Girl number twenty," said Mr. Gradgrind, squarely pointing with his square forefinger, "I don't know that girl. Who is that girl?"

"Sissy Jupe, sir," explained number twenty, blushing, standing up, and curtseying.

"Sissy is not a name," said Mr. Gradgrind. "Don't call yourself Sissy. Call yourself Cecilia."

"It's father as calls me Sissy, sir," returned the young girl in a trembling voice, and with another curtsey.

"Then he has no business to do it," said Mr. Gradgrind. "Tell him he mustn't. Cecilia Jupe. Let me see. What is your father?"

"He belongs to the horse-riding, if you please, sir."

Mr. Gradgrind frowned, and waved off the objectionable calling with his hand.

"We don't want to know anything about that, here. You mustn't tell us about that, here. Your father breaks horses, don't he?"

"If you please, sir, when they can get any to break, they do break horses in the ring, sir."

"You mustn't tell us about the ring here. Very well, then. Describe your father as a horsebreaker. He doctors sick horses, I dare say?"

"Oh, yes, sir."

"Very well, then. He is a veterinary surgeon, a farrier, and horsebreaker. Give me your definition of a horse."

(Sissy Jupe thrown into the greatest alarm by this demand.)

"Girl number twenty unable to define a horse!" said Mr. Gradgrind, for the general behoof of all the little pitchers. "Girl number twenty possessed of no facts in reference to one of the commonest of animals! Some boy's definition of a horse. Bitzer, yours."

The square finger, moving here and there, lighted suddenly on Bitzer, perhaps because he chanced to sit in the same ray of sunlight which, darting in at one of the bare windows of the intensely whitewashed room, irradiated Sissy. For, the boys and girls sat on the face of the inclined plane in two compact bodies, divided up the centre by a narrow interval; and Sissy, being at the corner of a row on the sunny side, came in for the beginning of a sunbeam, of which Bitzer, being at the corner of a row on the other side, a few rows in advance, caught the end. But, whereas the girl was so dark-eyed and dark-haired that she seemed to receive a deeper and more lustrous colour from the sun, when it shone upon her, the boy was so light-eyed and light-haired that the self-same rays appeared to draw out of him what little colour he ever possessed. His cold eyes would hardly have been eyes, but for the short ends of lashes which, by bringing them into immediate contrast with something paler than themselves, expressed their form. His short-cropped hair might have been a mere continuation of the sandy freckles on his forehead and face. His skin was so unwholesomely deficient in the natural tinge, that he looked as though, if he were cut, he would bleed white.

"Bitzer," said Thomas Gradgrind. "Your definition of a horse."

"Quadruped. Graminivorous.[1] Forty teeth, namely twenty-four grinders, four eye-teeth, and twelve incisive. Sheds coat in the spring; in marshy countries, sheds hoofs, too. Hoofs hard, but requiring to be shod with iron. Age known by marks in mouth." Thus (and much more) Bitzer.

"Now, girl number twenty," said Mr. Gradgrind, "you know what a horse is."

She curtseyed again, and would have blushed deeper, if she could have blushed deeper than she had blushed all this time. Bitzer, after rapidly blinking at Thomas Gradgrind with both eyes at once, and so catching the light upon his quivering ends of lashes that they looked like the antennae of busy insects, put his knuckles to his freckled forehead, and sat down again.

The third gentleman now stepped forth. A mighty man at cutting and drying, he was; a government officer; in his way (and in most other people's too), a professed pugilist; always in training, always with a system to force down the general throat like a bolus,[2] always to be heard of at the bar of his little Public-office, ready to fight all England. To continue in the fistic phraseology, he had a genius for coming up to the scratch,[3] wherever and whatever it was, and proving himself an ugly customer. He would go in an damage any subject whatever with his right, follow up with his left, stop, exchange, counter, bore his opponent (he always fought All England)[4] to the ropes, and fall upon him neatly. He was certain to knock the wind out of common sense, and render that unlucky adversary deaf to the call of time. And he had it in charge from high authority to bring about the great Public-office Millennium, when Commissioners[5] should reign upon earth.

"Very well," said this gentleman, briskly smiling, and folding his arms. "That's a horse. Now, let me ask you, girls and boys, Would you paper a room with representations of horses?"

After a pause, one half of the children cried in chorus, "Yes, sir!" Upon which the other half, seeing in the gentleman's face that Yes was wrong, cried out in chorus, "No, sir!" — as the custom is, in these examinations.

"Of course, No. Why wouldn't you?"

A pause. One corpulent slow boy, with a wheezy manner of breathing, ventured the answer, Because he wouldn't paper a room at all, but would paint it.

"You *must* paper it," said the gentleman, rather warmly.

"You must paper it," said Thomas Gradgrind, "whether you like it or not. Don't tell *us* you wouldn't paper it. What do you mean, boy?"

---

[1] grass-feeding. [eds.]

[2] a large pill.

[3] a line drawn across the center of the ring in the early days of prize-fighting. Contestants would commence a match by stepping up to opposite sides of this line, and the match would end when one of the two could no longer come up to the scratch line at the beginning of a new round.

[4] fighting according to a national code of rules for the prize-ring — one of the codes superseded by the adoption of the Marquis of Queensberry's rules in 1866.

[5] administrative officials in various departments of government such as Customs or Income Taxes.

"I'll explain to you, then," said the gentleman, after another and a dismal pause, "why you wouldn't paper a room with representations of horses. Do you ever see horses walking up and down the sides of rooms in reality — in fact? Do you?"

"Yes, sir!" from one half. "No, sir!" from the other.

"Of course, No," said the gentleman, with an indignant look at the wrong half. "Why, then, you are not to see anywhere what you don't see in fact; you are not to have anywhere what you don't have in fact. What is called Taste, is only another name for Fact."

Thomas Gradgrind nodded his approbation.

"This is a new principle, a discovery, a great discovery," said the gentleman. "Now I'll try you again. Suppose you were going to carpet a room. Would you use a carpet having a representation of flowers upon it?"

There being a general conviction by this time that "No, sir!" was always the right answer to this gentleman, the chorus of No was very strong. Only a few feeble stragglers said Yes; among them Sissy Jupe.

"Girl number twenty," said the gentleman, smiling in the calm strength of knowledge.

Sissy blushed, and stood up.

"So you would carpet your room — or your husband's room, if you were a grown woman, and had a husband — with representations of flowers, would you," said the gentleman. "Why would you?"

"If you please, sir, I am very fond of flowers," returned the girl.

"And is that why you would put tables and chairs upon them, and have people walking over them with heavy boots?"

"It wouldn't hurt them, sir. They wouldn't crush and wither if you please, sir. They would be the pictures of what was very pretty and pleasant, and I would fancy —"

"Ay, ay, ay! But you mustn't fancy," cried the gentleman, quite elated by coming so happily to his point. "That's it! You are never to fancy."

"You are not, Cecilia Jupe," Thomas Gradgrind solemnly repeated, "to do anything of that kind."

"Fact, fact, fact!" said the gentleman. And "Fact, fact, fact!" repeated Thomas Gradgrind.

"You are to be in all things regulated and governed," said the gentleman, "by fact. We hope to have before long, a board of fact, composed of commissioners of fact, who will force the people to be a people of fact, and of nothing but fact. You must discard the word Fancy altogether. You have nothing to do with it. You are not to have, in any object of use or ornament, what would be a contradiction in fact. You don't walk upon flowers in fact; you cannot be allowed to walk upon flowers in carpets. You don't find that foreign birds and butterflies come and perch upon your crockery; you cannot be permitted to paint foreign birds and butterflies upon your crockery. You never meet with quadrupeds going up and down walls; you must not have quadrupeds represented upon walls. You must use," said the gentleman, "for all these purposes, combinations and modifications (in primary colours) of mathematical figures which are susceptible of proof and demonstration. This is the new discovery. This is Fact. This is taste."

The girl curtseyed and sat down. She was very young, and she looked as if she were frightened by the matter of fact prospect the world afforded.

"Now, if Mr. M'Choakumchild," said the gentleman, "will proceed to give his first lesson here, Mr. Gradgrind, I shall be happy, at your request, to observe his mode of procedure."

Mr. Gradgrind was much obliged. "Mr. M'Choakumchild, we only wait for you."

So, Mr. M'Choakumchild began in his best manner. He and some one hundred and forty other schoolmasters had been lately turned at the same time, in the same factory, on the same principles, like so many pianoforte legs. He had been put through an immense variety of paces, and had answered volumes of headbreaking questions. Orthography, etymology, syntax, and prosody, biography, astronomy, geography, and general cosmography, the sciences of compound proportion, algebra, land-surveying and levelling, vocal music and drawing from models, were all at the ends of his ten chilled fingers. He had worked his stony way into Her Majesty's most Honourable Privy Council's Schedule B,[6] and had taken the bloom off the higher branches of mathematics and physical science, French, German, Latin, and Greek. He knew all about all the Water Sheds of all the world (whatever they are), and all the histories of all the peoples, and all the names of all the rivers and mountains, and all the productions, manners, and customs of all the countries, and all their boundaries and bearings on the two-and-thirty points of the compass. Ah, rather overdone, M'Choakumchild. If he had only learnt a little less, how infinitely better he might have taught much more!

He went to work, in this preparatory lesson, not unlike Morgiana[7] in the Forty Thieves; looking into all the vessels ranged before him, one after another, to see what they contained. Say, good M'Choakumchild. When from thy boiling store thou shalt fill each jar brimful by-and-by, dost thou think that thou wilt always kill outright the robber Fancy lurking within — or sometimes only maim him and distort him? . . .

---

[6] a syllabus established in 1846 specifying what subjects were to be mastered by candidates training to become teachers. Schedule B was drawn up by a sub-Committee of the Privy Council.
[7] Ali Baba's slave in the *Arabian Nights' Entertainments* who killed forty thieves by pouring boiling oil into the jars in which they were hiding.

Walt Whitman (1819–1892)

AMERICAN POET and JOURNALIST

When I Heard the Learn'd Astronomer

When I heard the learn'd astronomer,
When the proofs, the figures, were ranged in columns before me,
When I was shown the charts and diagrams, to add, divide, and measure them,
When I sitting heard the astronomer where he lectured with much applause in the
    lecture-room,
How soon unaccountable I became tired and sick,
Till rising and gliding out I wander'd off by myself,
In the mystical moist night air, and from time to time,
Look'd up in perfect silence at the stars.

Thomas Henry Huxley (1825–1895)

ENGLISH BIOLOGIST and ESSAYIST

Science and Culture

This distinctive character of our own times lies in the vast and constantly
increasing part which is played by natural knowledge. Not only is our daily
life shaped by it, not only does the prosperity of millions of men depend
upon it, but our whole theory of life has long been influenced, consciously or
unconsciously, by the general conceptions of the universe, which have been
forced upon us by physical science.

In fact, the most elementary acquaintance with the results of scientific
investigation shows us that they offer a broad and striking contradiction to
the opinion so implicitly credited and taught in the middle ages.

The notions of the beginning and the end of the world entertained by our
forefathers are no longer credible. It is very certain that the earth is not the
chief body in the material universe, and that the world is not subordinated

"When I Heard the Learn'd Astronomer" by Walt Whitman. From *Complete Poetry and Selected Prose* by Walt Whitman, edited by James E. Miller, Jr. (Riverside Edition). Reprinted by permission of Houghton Mifflin Company.

"Science and Culture" by Thomas Henry Huxley. From *Animal Automatism and Other Essays*.

to man's use. It is even more certain that nature is the expression of a definite order with which nothing interferes, and that the chief business of mankind is to learn that order and govern themselves accordingly. Moreover this scientific "criticism of life"[1] presents itself to us with different credentials from any other. It appeals not to authority, nor to what anybody may have thought or said, but to nature. It admits that all our interpretations of natural fact are more or less imperfect and symbolic, and bids the learner seek for truth not among words but among things. It warns us that the assertion which outstrips evidence is not only a blunder but a crime.

The purely classical education advocated by the representatives of the Humanists in our day, gives no inkling of all this. A man may be a better scholar than Erasmus,[2] and know no more of the chief causes of the present intellectual fermentation than Erasmus did. Scholarly and pious persons, worthy of all respect, favour us with allocutions upon the sadness of the antagonism of science to their mediæval way of thinking, which betray an ignorance of the first principles of scientific investigation, an incapacity for understanding what a man of science means by veracity, and an unconsciousness of the weight of established scientific truths, which is almost comical.

There is no great force in the *tu quoque*[3] argument, or else the advocates of scientific education might fairly enough retort upon the modern Humanists that they may be learned specialists, but that they possess no such sound foundation for a criticism of life as deserves the name of culture. And, indeed, if we were disposed to be cruel, we might urge that the Humanists have brought this reproach upon themselves, not because they are too full of the spirit of the ancient Greek, but because they lack it.

The period of the Renascence is commonly called that of the "Revival of Letters," as if the influences then brought to bear upon the mind of Western Europe had been wholly exhausted in the field of literature. I think it is very commonly forgotten that the revival of science, effected by the same agency, although less conspicuous, was not less momentous.

In fact, the few and scattered students of nature of that day picked up the clue to her secrets exactly as it fell from the hands of the Greeks a thousand years before. The foundations of mathematics were so well laid by them, that our children learn their geometry from a book written for the schools of Alexandria two thousand years ago.[4] Modern astronomy is the natural continuation and development of the work of Hipparchus and of Ptolemy; modern physics of that of Democritus and of Archimedes; it was long before modern biological science outgrew the knowledge bequeathed to us by Aristotle, by Theophrastus, and by Galen.

---

[1] The phrase is from Matthew Arnold, who applied it to humanistic study. This lecture of Huxley's is, in part, a response to the concept expressed in Arnold's phrase.
[2] Dutch humanist, scholar and theologian (1466–1536), who largely ignored contemporary developments in the arts and sciences.
[3] you also.
[4] The propositions of Euclid (c. 323–285 B.C.), Greek mathematician and physicist at Alexandria, are being questioned today for the first time.

We cannot know all the best thoughts and sayings[5] of the Greeks unless we know what they thought about natural phænomena. We cannot fully apprehend their criticism of life unless we understand the extent to which that criticism was affected by scientific conceptions. We falsely pretend to be the inheritors of their culture, unless we are penetrated, as the best minds among them were, with an unhesitating faith that the free employment of reason, in accordance with scientific method, is the sole method of reaching truth.

Thus I venture to think that the pretensions of our modern Humanists to the possession of the monopoly of culture and to the exclusive inheritance of the spirit of antiquity must be abated, if not abandoned. But I should be very sorry that anything I have said should be taken to imply a desire on my part to depreciate the value of classical education, as it might be and as it sometimes is. The native capacities of mankind vary no less than their opportunities; and while culture is one, the road by which one man may best reach it is widely different from that which is most advantageous to another. Again, while scientific education is yet inchoate and tentative, classical education is thoroughly well organised upon the practical experience of generations of teachers. So that, given ample time for learning and destination for ordinary life, or for a literary career, I do not think that a young Englishman in search of culture can do better than follow the course usually marked out for him, supplementing its deficiencies by his own efforts.

But for those who mean to make science their serious occupation; or who intend to follow the profession of medicine; or who have to enter early upon the business of life; for all these, in my opinion, classical education is a mistake; and it is for this reason that I am glad to see "mere literary education and instruction" shut out from the curriculum of Sir Josiah Mason's College,[6] seeing that its inclusion would probably lead to the introduction of the ordinary smattering of Latin and Greek.

Nevertheless, I am the last person to question the importance of genuine literary education, or to suppose that intellectual culture can be complete without it. An exclusively scientific training will bring about a mental twist as surely as an exclusively literary training. The value of the cargo does not compensate for a ship's being out of trim; and I should be very sorry to think that the Scientific College would turn out none but lop-sided men.

There is no need, however, that such a catastrophe should happen. Instruction in English, French, and German is provided, and thus the three greatest literatures of the modern world are made accessible to the student.

French and German, and especially the latter language, are absolutely indispensable to those who desire full knowledge in any department of science. But even supposing that the knowledge of these languages acquired is not more than sufficient for purely scientific purposes, every Englishman has,

[5] Arnold's definition of culture.
[6] a college of science in Birmingham, England, at which Huxley delivered this dedicatory speech in 1880.

in his native tongue, an almost perfect instrument of literary expression; and, in his own literature, models of every kind of literary excellence. If an Englishman cannot get literary culture out of his Bible, his Shakespeare, his Milton, neither, in my belief, will the profoundest study of Homer and Sophocles, Virgil and Horace, give it to him.

Thus, since the constitution of the College makes sufficient provision for literary as well as for scientific education, and since artistic instruction is also contemplated, it seems to me that a fairly complete culture is offered to all who are willing to take advantage of it.

But I am not sure that at this point the "practical" man, scotched but not slain, may ask what all this talk about culture has to do with an Institution, the object of which is defined to be "to promote the prosperity of the manufactures and the industry of the country." He may suggest that what is wanted for this end is not culture, nor even a purely scientific discipline, but simply a knowledge of applied science.

I often wish that this phrase, "applied science," had never been invented. For it suggests that there is a sort of scientific knowledge of direct practical use, which can be studied apart from another sort of scientific knowledge, which is of no practical utility, and which is termed "pure science." But there is no more complete fallacy than this. What people call applied science is nothing but the application of pure science to particular classes of problems. It consists of deductions from those general principles, established by reasoning and observation, which constitute pure science. No one can safely make these deductions until he has a firm grasp of the principles; and he can obtain that grasp only by personal experience of the operations of observation and of reasoning on which they are founded.

Almost all the processes employed in the arts and manufactures fall within the range either of physics or of chemistry. In order to improve them, one must thoroughly understand them; and no one has a chance of really understanding them, unless he has obtained that mastery of principles and that habit of dealing with facts, which is given by long-continued and well-directed purely scientific training in the physical and the chemical laboratory. So that there really is no question as to the necessity of purely scientific discipline, even if the work of the College were limited by the narrowest interpretation of its stated aims.

And, as to the desirableness of a wider culture than that yielded by science alone, it is to be recollected that the improvement of manufacturing processes is only one of the conditions which contribute to the prosperity of industry. Industry is a means and not an end; and mankind work only to get something which they want. What that something is depends partly on their innate, and partly on their acquired, desires.

If the wealth resulting from prosperous industry is to be spent upon the gratification of unworthy desires, if the increasing perfection of manufacturing processes is to be accompanied by an increasing debasement of those who carry them on, I do not see the good of industry and prosperity.

Now it is perfectly true that men's views of what is desirable depend upon their characters; and that the innate proclivities to which we give that name are not touched by any amount of instruction. But it does not follow that even mere intellectual education may not, to an indefinite extent, modify the practical manifestation of the characters of men in their actions, by supplying them with motives unknown to the ignorant. A pleasure-loving character will have pleasure of some sort; but, if you give him the choice, he may prefer pleasures which do not degrade him to those which do. And this choice is offered to every man, who possesses in literary or artistic culture a never-failing source of pleasures, which are neither withered by age, nor staled by custom, nor embittered in the recollection by the pangs of self-reproach.

If the Institution opened to-day fulfils the intention of its founder, the picked intelligences among all classes of the population of this district will pass through it. No child born in Birmingham, henceforward, if he have the capacity to profit by the opportunities offered to him, first in the primary and other schools, and afterwards in the Scientific College, need fail to obtain, not merely the instruction, but the culture most appropriate to the conditions of his life.

Within these walls, the future employer and the future artisan may sojourn together for a while, and carry, through all their lives, the stamp of the influences then brought to bear upon them. Hence, it is not beside the mark to remind you, that the prosperity of industry depends not merely upon the improvement of manufacturing processes, not merely upon the ennobling of the individual character, but upon a third condition, namely, a clear understanding of the conditions of social life, on the part of both the capitalist and the operative, and their agreement upon common principles of social action. They must learn that social phænomena are as much the expression of natural laws as any others; that no social arrangements can be permanent unless they harmonise with the requirements of social statics and dynamics; and that, in the nature of things, there is an arbiter whose decisions execute themselves.

But this knowledge is only to be obtained by the application of the methods of investigation adopted in physical researches to the investigation of the phænomena of society. . . .

Sigmund Freud (1856–1939)

AUSTRIAN PSYCHOLOGIST and FOUNDER of PSYCHOANALYSIS

The Psychology of Resistance

Ladies and Gentlemen, — Before we can make any further progress in our understanding of the neuroses, we stand in need of some fresh observations. Here we have two such, both of which are very remarkable and at the time when they were made were very surprising. Our discussions of last year will, it is true, have prepared you for both of them.

In the first place, then, when we undertake to restore a patient to health, to relieve him of the symptoms of his illness, he meets us with a violent and tenacious resistance, which persists throughout the whole length of the treatment. This is such a strange fact that we cannot expect it to find much credence. It is best to say nothing about it to the patient's relatives, for they invariably regard it as an excuse on our part for the length or failure of our treatment. The patient, too, produces all the phenomena of this resistance without recognizing it as such, and if we can induce him to take our view of it and to reckon with its existence, that already counts as a great success. Only think of it! The patient, who is suffering so much from his symptoms and is causing those about him to share his sufferings, who is ready to undertake so many sacrifices in time, money, effort and self-discipline in order to be freed from those symptoms — we are to believe that this same patient puts up a struggle in the interest of his illness against the person who is helping him. How improbable such an assertion must sound! Yet it is true; and when its improbability is pointed out to us, we need only reply that it is not without analogies. A man who has gone to the dentist because of an unbearable toothache will nevertheless try to hold the dentist back when he approaches the sick tooth with a pair of forceps.

The patient's resistance is of very many sorts, extremely subtle and often hard to detect; and it exhibits protean changes in the forms in which it manifests itself. The doctor must be distrustful and remain on his guard against it.

In psycho-analytic therapy we make use of the same technique that is familiar to you from dream-interpretation. We instruct the patient to put himself into a state of quiet, unreflecting self-observation, and to report to us whatever internal perceptions he is able to make — feelings, thoughts, memories — in the order in which they occur to him. At the same time we warn him expressly against giving way to any motive which would lead him to make a selection among these associations or to exclude any of them, whether

Title supplied by editors. From **The Complete Introductory Lectures on Psychoanalysis** by Sigmund Freud, trans. and ed. James Strachey. Permission by Liveright, Publishers, New York, and George Allen & Unwin Ltd., London.

on the ground that it is too *disagreeable* or too *indiscreet* to say, or that it is too *unimportant* or *irrelevant*, or that it is *nonsensical* and need not be said. We urge him always to follow only the surface of his consciousness and to leave aside any criticism of what he finds, whatever shape that criticism may take; and we assure him that the success of the treatment, and above all its duration, depends on the conscientiousness with which he obeys this fundamental technical rule of analysis. We already know from the technique of dream-interpretation that the associations giving rise to the doubts and objections I have just enumerated are precisely the ones that invariably contain the material which leads to the uncovering of the unconscious.

The first thing we achieve by setting up this fundamental technical rule is that it becomes the target for the attacks of the resistance. The patient endeavours in every sort of way to extricate himself from its provisions. At one moment he declares that nothing occurs to him, at the next that so many things are crowding in on him that he cannot get hold of anything. Presently we observe with pained astonishment that he has given way first to one and then to another critical objection: he betrays this to us by the long pauses that he introduces into his remarks. He then admits that there is something he really cannot say — he would be ashamed to; and he allows this reason to prevail against his promise. Or he says that something has occurred to him, but it concerns another person and not himself and is therefore exempt from being reported. Or, what has now occurred to him is really too unimportant, too silly and senseless: I cannot possibly have meant him to enter into thoughts like that. So it goes on in innumerable variations, and one can only reply that 'to say everything' really does mean 'to say everything'.

One hardly comes across a single patient who does not make an attempt at reserving some region or other for himself so as to prevent the treatment from having access to it. A man, whom I can only describe as of the highest intelligence, kept silence in this way for weeks on end about an intimate love-affair, and, when he was called to account for having broken the sacred rule, defended himself with the argument that he thought this particular story was his private business. Analytic treatment does not, of course, recognize any such right of asylum. Suppose that in a town like Vienna the experiment was made of treating a square such as the Hohe Markt, or a church like St. Stephen's, as places where no arrests might be made, and suppose we then wanted to watch a particular criminal. We could be quite sure of finding him in the sanctuary. I once decided to allow a man, on whose efficiency much depended in the external world, the right to make an exception of this kind because he was bound under his oath of office not to make communications about certain things to another person. He, it is true, was satisfied with the outcome; but I was not. I determined not to repeat an attempt under such conditions.

Obsessional neurotics understand perfectly how to make the technical rule almost useless by applying their over-conscientiousness and doubts to it. Patients suffering from anxiety hysteria occasionally succeed in carrying the rule *ad absurdum* by producing only associations which are so remote from what we are in search of that they contribute nothing to the analysis. But it is not my intention to induct you into the handling of these technical difficulties. It is enough to say that in the end, through resolution and perseverance, we succeed in extorting a certain amount of obedience to the fundamental technical rule from the resistance — which thereupon jumps over to another sphere.

It now appears as an *intellectual* resistance, it fights by means of arguments and exploits all the difficulties and improbabilities which normal but uninstructed thinking finds in the theories of analysis. It is now our fate to hear from this single voice all the criticisms and objections which assail our ears in a chorus in the scientific literature of the subject. And for this reason none of the shouts that reach us from outside sound unfamiliar. It is a regular storm in a tea-cup. But the patient is willing to be argued with; he is anxious to get us to instruct him, teach him, contradict him, introduce him to the literature, so that he can find further instruction. He is quite ready to become an adherent of psycho-analysis — on condition that analysis spares him personally. But we recognize this curiosity as a resistance, as a diversion from our particular tasks, and we repel it. In the case of an obsessional neurotic we have to expect special tactics of resistance. He will often allow the analysis to proceed on its way uninhibited, so that it is able to shed an ever-increasing light upon the riddle of his illness. We begin to wonder in the end, however, why this enlightenment is accompanied by no practical advance, no diminution of the symptoms. We are then able to realize that resistance has withdrawn on to the doubt belonging to the obsessional neurosis and from that position is successfuly defying us. It is as though the patient were saying: 'Yes, that's all very nice and interesting, and I'll be very glad to go on with it further. It would change my illness a lot if it were true. But I don't in the least believe that it *is* true; and, so long as I don't believe it, it makes no difference to my illness.' Things can proceed like this for a long time, till finally one comes up against this uncommitted attitude itself, and the decisive struggle then breaks out.

Intellectual resistances are not the worst: one always remains superior to them. But the patient also knows how to put up resistances, without going outside the framework of the analysis, the overcoming of which is among the most difficult of technical problems. Instead of remembering, he *repeats* attitudes and emotional impulses from his early life which can be used as a resistance against the doctor and the treatment by means of what is known as 'transference'. If the patient is a man, he usually extracts this material from his relation to his father, into whose place he fits the doctor, and in that way he makes resistances out of his efforts to become independent in himself and in his judgements, out of his ambition, the first aim of which was to do things as well as his father or to get the better of him, or out of his unwillingness to burden himself for the second time in his life with a load of gratitude. Thus at times one has an impression that the patient has entirely replaced his better intention of making an end to his illness by the alternative one of putting the doctor in the wrong, of making him realize his impotence and of triumphing over him. Women have a masterly gift for exploiting an affectionate, erotically tinged transference to the doctor for the purposes of resistance. If this attachment reaches a certain height, all their interest in the immediate situation in the treatment and all the obligations they undertook at its commencement vanish; their jealousy, which is never absent, and their exasperation at their inevitable rejection, however considerately expressed, are bound to have a damaging effect on their personal understanding with the doctor and so to put out of operation one of the most powerful motive forces of the analysis.

Resistances of this kind should not be one-sidedly condemned. They include so much of the most important material from the patient's past and bring it back in so convincing a fashion that they become some of the best supports of the analysis if a skilful technique knows how to give them the right turn. Nevertheless, it remains a remarkable fact that this material is always in the service of the resistance to begin with and brings to the fore a *façade* that is hostile to the treatment. It may also be said that what is being mobilized for fighting against the alterations we are striving for are character-traits, attitudes of the ego. In this connection we discover that these character-traits were formed in relation to the determinants of the neurosis and in reaction against its demands, and we come upon traits which cannot normally emerge, or not to the same extent, and which may be described as latent. Nor must you get an impression that we regard the appearance of these resistances as an unforeseen risk to analytic influence. No, we are aware that these resistances are bound to come to light; in fact we are dissatisfied if we cannot provoke them clearly enough and are unable to demonstate them to the patient. Indeed we come finally to understand that the overcoming of these resistances is the essential function of analysis and is the only part of our work which gives us an assurance that we have achieved something with the patient.

If you further consider that the patient makes all the chance events that occur during his analysis into interferences with it, that he uses as reasons for slackening his efforts every diversion outside the analysis, every comment by a person of authority in his environment who is hostile to analysis, any chance organic illness or any that complicates his neurosis and, even, indeed, every improvement in his condition — if you consider all this, you will have obtained an approximate, though still incomplete, picture of the forms and methods of the resistance, the struggle against which accompanies every analysis. . . .

Albert Einstein (1879–1955)

SWISS MATHEMATICAL PHYSICIST (GERMAN-BORN)

On the Production of Nuclear Weapons

August 2, 1939

F. D. Roosevelt
President of the United States
White House
Washington, D.C.

SIR:

Some recent work by E. Fermi and L. Szilard,[1] which has been communicated to me in manuscript, leads me to expect that the element uranium may be turned into a new and important source of energy in the immediate future. Certain aspects of the situation which has arisen seem to call for watchfulness and, if necessary, quick action on the part of the Administration. I believe therefore that it is my duty to bring to your attention the following facts and recommendations:

In the course of the last four months it has been made probable — through the work of Joliot[2] in France as well as Fermi and Szilard in America — that it may become possible to set up a nuclear chain reaction in a large mass of uranium, by which vast amounts of power and large quantities of new radium-like elements would be generated. Now it appears almost certain that this could be achieved in the immediate future.

This new phenomenon would also lead to the construction of bombs, and it is conceivable — though much less certain — that extremely powerful bombs of a new type may thus be constructed. A single bomb of this type, carried by boat and exploded in a port, might very well destroy the whole port together with some of the surrounding territory. However, such bombs might very well prove to be too heavy for transportation by air.

The United States has only very poor ores of uranium in moderate quantities. There is some good ore in Canada and the former Czechoslovakia, while the most important source of uranium is Belgian Congo.

In view of this situation you may think it desirable to have some permanent contact maintained between the Administration and the group of physicists

---

[1] nuclear physicists.
[2] French physicist (1900–1958), who discovered new radioactive elements produced artificially.

Title supplied by editors. Letter by Albert Einstein to President Roosevelt — August 2, 1939. Reprinted by permission as found in *The Atomic Age*, edited by Morton Grodzins and Eugene Rabinowitch, © 1963 by Basic Books, Inc., Publishers, New York.

working on chain reactions in America. One possible way of achieving this might be for you to entrust with this task a person who has your confidence and who could perhaps serve in an inofficial capacity. His task might comprise the following:

a) to approach Government Departments, keep them informed of the further development, and put forward recommendations for Government action, giving particular attention to the problem of securing a supply of uranium ore for the United States;

b) to speed up the experimental work, which is at present being carried on within the limits of the budgets of University laboratories, by providing funds, if such funds be required, through his contacts with private persons who are willing to make contributions for this cause, and perhaps also by obtaining the co-operation of industrial laboratories which have the necessary equipment.

I understand that Germany has actually stopped the sale of uranium from the Czechoslovakian mines which she has taken over. That she should have taken such early action might perhaps be understood on the ground that the son of the German Under-Secretary of State, von Weizsäcker, is attached to the Kaiser-Wilhelm-Institut in Berlin where some of the American work on uranium is now being repeated.

Yours very truly,

(signed) ALBERT EINSTEIN

Leo Szilard   (1898–1964)

AMERICAN PHYSICIST (HUNGARIAN-BORN)

The Implications of Nuclear Warfare

July 17, 1945

Discoveries of which the people of the United States are not aware may affect the welfare of this nation in the near future. The liberation of atomic power which has been achieved places atomic bombs in the hands of the Army. It places in your hands, as Commander-in-Chief, the fateful decision whether or not to sanction the use of such bombs in the present phase of the war against Japan.

We, the undersigned scientists, have been working in the field of atomic

Title supplied by editors. "A Petition to the President of the United States" by Leo Szilard, dated July 17, 1945. Reprinted by permission as found in *The Atomic Age*, edited by Morton Grodzins and Eugene Rabinowitch, © 1963 by Basic Books, Inc., Publishers, New York.

power. Until recently we have had to fear that the United States might be attacked by atomic bombs during this war and that her only defense might lie in a counterattack by the same means. Today, with the defeat of Germany, this danger is averted and we feel impelled to say what follows:

The war has to be brought speedily to a successful conclusion and attacks by atomic bombs may very well be an effective method of warfare. We feel, however, that such attacks on Japan could not be justified, at least not unless the terms which will be imposed after the war on Japan were made public in detail and Japan were given an opportunity to surrender.

If such public announcement gave assurance to the Japanese that they could look forward to a life devoted to peaceful pursuits in their homeland and if Japan still refused to surrender, our nation might then, in certain circumstances, find itself forced to resort to the use of atomic bombs. Such a step, however, ought not to be made at any time without seriously considering the moral responsibilities which are involved.

The development of atomic power will provide the nations with new means of destruction. The atomic bombs at our disposal represent only the first step in this direction and there is almost no limit to the destructive power which will become available in the course of their future development. Thus a nation which sets the precedent of using these newly liberated forces of nature for purposes of destruction may have to bear the responsibility of opening the door to an era of devastation on an unimaginable scale.

If after this war a situation is allowed to develop in the world which permits rival powers to be in uncontrolled possession of these new means of destruction, the cities of the United States as well as the cities of other nations will be in continuous danger of sudden annihilation. All the resources of the United States, moral and material, may have to be mobilized to prevent the advent of such a world situation. Its prevention is at present the solemn responsibility of the United States — singled out by virtue of her lead in the field of atomic power.

The added material strength which this lead gives to the United States brings with it the obligation of restraint, and if we were to violate this obligation our moral position would be weakened in the eyes of the world and in our own eyes. It would then be more difficult for us to live up to our responsibility of bringing the unloosened forces of destruction under control.

In view of the foregoing, we, the undersigned,[1] respectfully petition: first, that you exercise your power as Commander-in-Chief to rule that the United States shall not resort to the use of atomic bombs in this war unless the terms which will be imposed upon Japan have been made public in detail and Japan, knowing these terms, has refused to surrender; second, that in such an event the question whether or not to use atomic bombs be decided by you in the light of the considerations presented in this petition as well as all the other moral responsibilities which are involved.

[1] The signatures are held by the United States government as classified information; the original petition is on file in the Manhattan District Files of the Atomic Energy Commission. Authorities have disagreed about whether there are 63 or 70 signatures.

Norbert Wiener (1894–1964)

AMERICAN MATHEMATICAL LOGICIAN
and FOUNDER OF CYBERNETICS

A Scientist Rebels

SIR: —

I have received from you a note in which you state that you are engaged in a project concerning controlled missiles, and in which you request a copy of a paper which I wrote for the National Defense Research Committee during the war.

As the paper is the property of a government organization, you are of course at complete liberty to turn to that government organization for such information as I could give you. If it is out of print as you say, and they desire to make it available for you, there are doubtless proper avenues of approach to them.

When, however, you turn to me for information concerning controlled missiles, there are several considerations which determine my reply. In the past, the comity of scholars has made it a custom to furnish scientific information to any person seriously seeking it. However, we must face these facts: The policy of the government itself during and after the war, say in the bombing of Hiroshima and Nagasaki, has made it clear that to provide scientific information is not a necessarily innocent act, and may entail the gravest consequences. One therefore cannot escape reconsidering the established custom of the scientist to give information to every person who may inquire of him. The interchange of ideas which is one of the great traditions of science must of course receive certain limitations when the scientist becomes an arbiter of life and death.

For the sake, however, of the scientist and the public, these limitations should be as intelligent as possible. The measures taken during the war by our military agencies, in restricting the free intercourse among scientists on related projects or even on the same project, have gone so far that it is clear that if continued in time of peace this policy will lead to the total irresponsibility of the scientist, and ultimately to the death of science. Both of these are disastrous for our civilization, and entail grave and immediate peril for the public.

I realize, of course, that I am acting as the censor of my own ideas, and it may sound arbitrary, but I will not accept a censorship in which I do not participate. The experience of the scientists who have worked on the atomic bomb has indicated that in any investigation of this kind the scientist ends by putting unlimited powers in the hands of the people whom he is least in-

"A Scientist Rebels" by Norbert Wiener appeared as an open letter to a research scientist of an aircraft corporation. From *The Atlantic Monthly* (January, 1947). Reprinted by permission.

clined to trust with their use. It is perfectly clear also that to disseminate information about a weapon in the present state of our civilization is to make it practically certain that that weapon will be used. In that respect the controlled missile represents the still imperfect supplement to the atom bomb and to bacterial warfare.

The practical use of guided missiles can only be to kill foreign civilians indiscriminately, and it furnishes no protection whatsoever to civilians in this country. I cannot conceive a situation in which such weapons can produce any effect other than extending the kamikaze way of fighting to whole nations. Their possession can do nothing but endanger us by encouraging the tragic insolence of the military mind.

If therefore I do not desire to participate in the bombing or poisoning of defenseless peoples — and I most certainly do not — I must take a serious responsibility as to those to whom I disclose my scientific ideas. Since it is obvious that with sufficient effort you can obtain my material, even though it is out of print, I can only protest *pro forma* in refusing to give you any information concerning my past work. However, I rejoice at the fact that my material is not readily available, inasmuch as it gives me the opportunity to raise this serious moral issue. I do not expect to publish any future work of mine which may do damage in the hands of irresponsible militarists.

I am taking the liberty of calling this letter to the attention of other people in scientific work. I believe it is only proper that they should know of it in order to make their own independent decisions, if similar situations should confront them.

NORBERT WIENER

Hart Crane (1899–1932)

AMERICAN POET

One Arc Synoptic

Through the bound cable strands, the arching path
Upward, veering with light, the flight of strings, —
Taut miles of shuttling moonlight syncopate
The whispered rush, telepathy of wires.
Up the index of night, granite and steel —
Transparent meshes — fleckless the gleaming staves —
Sibylline voices flicker, waveringly stream
As though a god were issue of the strings. . . .

And through that cordage, threading with its call
One arc synoptic of all tides below —   10
Their labyrinthine mouths of history
Pouring reply as though all ships at sea
Complighted in one vibrant breath made cry, —
"Make thy love sure — to weave whose song we ply!"
— From black embankments, moveless soundings hailed,
So seven oceans answer from their dream.

And on, obliquely up bright carrier bars
New octaves trestle the twin monoliths
Beyond whose frosted capes the moon bequeaths
Two worlds of sleep (O arching strands of song!) —   20
Onward and up the crystal-flooded aisle
White tempest nets file upward, upward ring
With silver terraces the humming spars,
The loft of vision, palladium helm of stars.

Sheerly the eyes, like seagulls stung with rime —
Slit and propelled by glistening fins of light —
Pick biting way up towering looms that press
Sidelong with flight of blade on tendon blade
— Tomorrows into yesteryear — and link
What cipher-script of time no traveller reads   30
But who, through smoking pyres of love and death,
Searches the timeless laugh of mythic spears.

Like hails, farewells — up planet-sequined heights
Some trillion whispering hammers glimmer Tyre:
Serenely, sharply up the long anvil cry
Of inchling æons silence rivets Troy.
And you, aloft there — Jason! hesting Shout!
Still wrapping harness to the swarming air!
Silvery the rushing wake, surpassing call,
Beams yelling Æolus! splintered in the straits!   40

From gulfs unfolding, terrible of drums,
Tall Vision-of-the-Voyage, tensely spare —
Bridge, lifting night to cycloramic crest
Of deepest day — O Choir, translating time
Into what multitudinous Verb the suns
And synergy of water ever fuse, recast
In myriad syllables, — Psalm of Cathay!
O Love, thy white, pervasive Paradigm . . . !

E. B. White (b. 1899)

AMERICAN ESSAYIST

The Door

Everything (he kept saying) is something it isn't. And everybody is always somewhere else. Maybe it was the city, being in the city, that made him feel how queer everything was and that it was something else. Maybe (he kept thinking) it was the names of the things. The names were tex and frequently koid. Or they were flex and oid or they were duroid (sani) or flexsan (duro), but everything was glass (but not quite glass) and the thing that you touched (the surface, washable, crease-resistant) was rubber, only it wasn't quite rubber and you didn't quite touch it but almost. The wall, which was glass but thrutex, turned out on being approached not to be a wall, it was something else, it was an opening or doorway — and the doorway (through which he saw himself approaching) turned out to be something else, it was a wall. And what he had eaten not having agreed with him.

He was in a washable house, but he wasn't sure. Now about those rats, he kept saying to himself. He meant the rats that the Professor had driven crazy by forcing them to deal with problems which were beyond the scope of rats, the insoluble problems. He meant the rats that had been trained to jump at the square card with the circle in the middle, and the card (because it was something it wasn't) would give way and let the rat into a place where the food was, but then one day it would be a trick played on the rat, and the card would be changed, and the rat would jump but the card wouldn't give way, and it was an impossible situation (for a rat) and the rat would go insane and into its eyes would come the unspeakably bright imploring look of the frustrated, and after the convulsions were over and the frantic racing around, then the passive stage would set in and the willingness to let anything be done to it, even if it was something else.

He didn't know which door (or wall) or opening in the house to jump at, to get through, because one was an opening that wasn't a door (it was a void, or koid) and the other was a wall that wasn't an opening, it was a sanitary cupboard of the same color. He caught a glimpse of his eyes staring into his eyes, in the thrutex, and in them was the expression he had seen in the picture of the rats — weary after convulsions and the frantic racing around, when they were willing and did not mind having anything done to them. More and more (he kept saying) I am confronted by a problem which is incapable of solution (for this time even if he chose the right door, there would be no food behind it) and that is what madness is, and things seeming different from what they are. He heard, in the house where he was, in the city to which he had gone (as toward a door which might, or might not, give way), a noise — not a loud noise but more of a low prefabricated humming. It came from a place in the base of the wall (or stat) where the flue carrying the filterable air was, and not far from the Minipiano, which was made of the same material nailbrushes are made of, and which was under the stairs. "This, too, has been tested," she said, pointing, but not at it, "and found viable." It wasn't a loud noise, he kept thinking, sorry that he had seen his eyes, even though it was through his own eyes that he had seen them.

First will come the convulsions (he said), then the exhaustion, then the willingness to let anything be done. "And you better believe it *will* be."

All his life he had been confronted by situations which were incapable of being solved, and there was a deliberateness behind all this, behind this changing of the card (or door), because they would always wait till you had learned to jump at the certain card (or door) — the one with the circle — and then they would change it on you. There have been so many doors changed on me, he said, in the last twenty years, but it is now becoming clear that it is an impossible situation, and the question is whether to jump again, even though they ruffle you in the rump with a blast of air — to make you jump. He wished he wasn't standing by the Minipiano. First they would teach you the prayers and the Psalms, and that would be the right door (the one with the circle), and the long sweet words with the holy sound, and that would be the one to jump at to get where the food was. Then one day you jumped and it didn't give way, so that all you got was the bump on the nose, and the first bewilderment, the first young bewilderment.

I don't know whether to tell her about the door they substituted or not, he said, the one with the equation on it and the picture of the amoeba reproducing itself by division. Or the one with the photostatic copy of the check for thirty-two dollars and fifty cents: But the jumping was so long ago, although the bump is . . . how those old wounds hurt! Being crazy this way wouldn't be so bad if only, if only. If only when you put your foot forward to take a step, the ground wouldn't come up to meet your foot the way it does. And the same way in the street (only I may never get back to the street unless I jump at the right door), the curb coming up to meet your foot, anticipating ever so delicately the weight of the body, which is somewhere else. "We could take your name," she said, "and send it to you." And it wouldn't be so bad if only you could read a sentence all the way through without jumping (your eye) to something else on the same page; and then (he kept thinking) there was that man out in Jersey, the one who started to chop his trees down, one by one, the man who began talking about how he would take his house to pieces, brick by brick, because he faced a problem incapable of solution, probably, so he began to hack at the trees in the yard, began to pluck with trembling fingers at the bricks in the house. Even if a house is not washable, it is worth taking down. It is not till later that the exhaustion sets in.

But it is inevitable that they will keep changing the doors on you, he said, because that is what they are for; and the thing is to get used to it and not let it unsettle the mind. But that would mean not jumping, and you can't. Nobody can not jump. There will be no not-jumping. Among rats, perhaps, but among people never. Everybody has to keep jumping at a door (the one with the circle on it) because that is the way everybody is, specially some people. You wouldn't want me, standing here, to tell you, would you, about my friend the poet (deceased) who said, "My heart has followed all my days something I cannot name"? (It had the circle on it.) And like many poets, although few so beloved, he is gone. It killed him, the jumping. First, of course, there were the preliminary bouts, the convulsions, and the calm and the willingness.

I remember the door with the picture of the girl on it (only it was spring), her arms outstretched in loveliness, her dress (it was the one with the circle on it) uncaught, beginning the slow, clear, blinding cascáde — and I guess we would all like to try that door again, for it seemed like the way and for a while it was the way, the door would open and you would go through winged and exalted (like any rat) and the food would be there, the way the Professor had it arranged, everything O.K., and you had chosen the right door for the world was young. The time they changed that door on me, my nose bled for a hundred hours — how do you like that, Madam? Or would you prefer to show me further through this so strange house, or you could take my name and send it to me, for although my heart has followed all my days something I cannot name, I am tired of the jumping and I do not know which way to go, Madam, and I am not even sure that I am not tried beyond the endurance of man (rat, if you will) and have taken leave of sanity. What are you following these days, old friend, after your recovery from the last bump? What is the name, or is it something you cannot name? The rats have a name for it by this time, perhaps, but I don't know what they call it. I call it plexikoid and it comes in sheets, something like insulating board, unattainable and ugli-proof.

And there was the man out in Jersey, because I keep thinking about his terrible necessity and the passion and trouble he had gone to all those years in the indescribable abundance of a householder's detail, building the estate and the planting of the trees and in spring the lawn-dressing and in fall the bulbs for the spring burgeoning, and the watering of the grass on the long light evenings in summer and the gravel for the driveway (all had to be thought out, planned) and the decorative borders, probably, the perennials and the bug spray, and the building of the house from plans of the architect, first the sills, then the studs, then the full corn in the ear, the floors laid on the floor timbers, smoothed, and then the carpets upon the smooth floors and the curtains and the rods therefor. And then, almost without warning, he would be jumping at the same old door and it wouldn't give: they had changed it on him, making life no longer supportable under the elms in the elm shade, under the maples in the maple shade.

"Here you have the maximum of openness in a small room."

It was impossible to say (maybe it was the city) what made him feel the way he did, and I am not the only one either, he kept thinking — ask any doctor if I am. The doctors, they know how many there are, they even know where the trouble is only they don't like to tell you about the prefrontal lobe because that means making a hole in your skull and removing the work of centuries. It took so long coming, this lobe, so many, many years. (Is it something you read in the paper, perhaps?) And now, the strain being so great, the door having been changed by the Professor once too often . . . but it only means a whiff of either, a few deft strokes, and the higher animal becomes a little easier in his mind and more like the lower one. From now on, you see, that's the way it will be, the ones with the small prefrontal lobes[1] will win because the other ones are hurt too much by this incessant bumping. They can stand just so much, eh, Doctor? (And what is that, pray, that you have in your hand?) Still, you never can tell, eh, Madam?

He crossed (carefully) the room, the thick carpet under him softly, and went toward the door carefully, which was glass and he could see himself in it, and which, at his approach, opened to allow him to pass through; and beyond he half expected to find one of the old doors that he had known, perhaps the one with the circle, the one with the girl her arms outstretched in loveliness and beauty before him. But he saw instead a moving stairway, and descended in light (he kept thinking) to the street below and to the other people. As he stepped off, the ground came up slightly, to meet his foot.

Herbert J. Muller (b. 1905)

AMERICAN ESSAYIST

The Scientific Method

Let us admit the case of the conservative: if we once start thinking no one can guarantee where we shall come out, except that many objects, ends, and institutions are doomed. Every thinker puts some portion of an apparently stable world in peril and no one can wholly predict what will emerge in its place.

JOHN DEWEY

SCIENCE AND THE TRADITION

Although science is no doubt the Jehovah of the modern world, there is considerable doubt about the glory of its handiwork. Apart from such downright heretics as D. H. Lawrence, there is a growing distrust of science, a

---

[1] the part of the brain most closely associated with psychical and intellectual processes.

growing anxiety to minimize and localize it. A large company will tolerate it only on its best behavior, and only for the hewing and hauling, the provision of the material means of life. They will have none of it in the matters of ideals or ends, which they hand over to religion, philosophy, and art. And they resent science because it has confused these high matters. Howard Dykema Roelofs expresses a common sentiment: "Religion can produce on occasion what science never does, namely, saints. Today we have science and scientists aplenty. We lack saints."

Now the easy answer is that religion has been on the job for some thousands of years, and that its record does not inspire confidence. The saints have rarely had much to do with the administration of society; there is some question whether they compensate for all the obscurantism, the intolerance of doubt and dissent, the justification of barbarous means by holy ends, the bigotry, hatred, and tyranny that have always flourished under religion, and often been fostered by it. But such tit for tat gets us nowhere with the real problem. Science has introduced very grave complications into the drama of civilization. The miracles it has worked become means of broadcasting and amplifying vulgarity, greed, and stupidity; worse, they include high-powered engines for wholesale slaughter; and their sum is the problem of managing an immensely complex industrial society. For better or worse, however, science is plainly here to stay — at least as long as our civilization. As plainly, then, the sensible policy is to make its stay for better. And the first move is to drop all invidious comparisons and take an easy look at it. To resent so remarkable a power because men abuse it is as illogical as to resent language because men speak error and evil.

Men rarely marvel at all their practical knowledge. They take it for granted because it always works; they are more struck by the talisman that occasionally seems to work, the prayer that seems to be granted. This attitude is understandable, given all the contingencies and uncertainties of life, but it is also a hangover from primitive times, when nature held many more mysteries and terrors. The philosopher who answers the extraordinary questions inherits the prestige of the witch doctor; the priest who calls for prayer invokes the *feeling* of security that men especially needed when they had so little knowledge or power of control. But the more particular reason why science is held in relatively low esteem is the persistence of an ancient aristocratic tradition.

John Crowe Ransom[1] refers approvingly to the "secret notion" of most art lovers, that art distinguishes Man from animals in kind, science only in degree of efficiency. This is scarcely a secret; artists have long been free enough in announcing that their activity is higher and holier. They can appeal, moreover, to the "inveterate conceit" remarked by Bacon: "that the dignity of the human mind is lowered by long and frequent intercourse with experiments and particulars, which are the objects of sense, and confined to matter." This conceit is in turn, as Dewey[2] has pointed out, the historic product of class

[1] American poet (b. 1888).
[2] John Dewey (1859–1952), American philosopher.

relations. In Greek and Oriental cultures, practical activities were the business of artisans and traders, when not of slaves; the exercise of pure reason, all transactions with the rulers of the universe, were the exclusive privilege of the higher class, and were accordingly made independent of the vulgar operations of doing and making. "Theoretical kinds of knowledge," Aristotle said, are "more of the nature of Wisdom than the productive." Ransom clearly has this patrician attitude; throughout *The World's Body* he refers to science as something that is "merely" useful, that "belongs to the economic impulse and does not free the spirit." And a host of literary men are much more supercilious about the wealth and power that enable them to contemplate their inability to live on bread alone.

This tradition explains the curious fact that an advance in knowledge is generally viewed as a "problem." Offhand, one would expect men to welcome science as a means of securing their values; it seems a threat because the official custodians of values have kept them in an unearthly realm of their own. In general, the source of all confusion and distrust is that science, the author of our world, is still a stranger here itself. Its findings have yet to become really absorbed in the tissue of common knowledge, its methods really naturalized in everyday habits of thought. Simple men play gladly with its by-products, but they have not caught on to the changes in the rules of the whole game; intellectuals still approach it like youngsters learning the facts of life, and like the bright youngsters often need to know a little more or very much less. Because old ways of looking at things seem more natural and necessary, and old habits like essential ingredients of human nature, new ways and new conditions of life are regarded as outrages upon human nature, defiances of its constitutional rights; and all present disharmonies look like permanent incompatibilities. Hence science is considered a fearful hazard, if not a blight. Its method seems somehow more "inhuman" than the rationalism of philosophers and theologians; its electrons and fields of force seem more remote from living reality than abstractions like "substance" and "essence"; its theories seem more dangerous than the absurdities men have lived by for centuries; its offspring, the Machine, is simply a monster.[3] And so men try to solve the problems science has raised, not by a thorough assimilation of it, but by an anxious restriction of it to the "material" or "economic" realm — a kind of ghetto where it cannot contaminate the pure Aryan blood of their values and ideals.

---

[3] *The Grapes of Wrath* is a striking example of this neopathetic fallacy. A leading villain in Steinbeck's novel is the Tractor, ruthlessly ploughing up the lands and lives of poor farmers and then standing cold, dead — altogether a sorry successor to that willing servant and noble friend of man, the Horse. Steinbeck has told magnificently the terrible story of the many people who are left out of the abstractions of long-view economists; we need more novelists to deal concretely with the tragic dislocations that are the price of industrial "progress." But he also creates his own abstractions, interrupts his story to write essays in competition with the economists; and his generalizations are sometimes shallow and sentimental. To attack one efficient machine in a machine civilization is simply futile. At that, Steinbeck falsifies even concrete, individual experience. Actually, men do not regard their machines as soulless; they fondle them as they do all their tools, keep them sleek, call them "beauties." (Muller's note)

Unquestionably, science is dangerous. So are all adventures in thought, all dealings with the world; so is the whole experiment of civilization. In periods of crisis, moreover, all ideal instruments are abused. Men go to war equipped with the terrible weapons now provided by science; but they still go in a religious spirit, following the gleam, living the myth. At any rate the basic fact remains that science has come to stay and is in a position to give rather than take orders. If it has yet to become naturalized, it is nevertheless omnipresent as Jehovah never was, at once a spirit moving upon the face of the waters and a man walking in the garden in the cool of day. We therefore need to see just what it is, what it can and cannot do, and then to feel at home with it. We finally need to bring it into harmonious relation with the other values by which we live. For the split between our intellectual habits and our patterns of living, Hogben[4] remarked, can easily be fatal to both.

What Science Is

Roughly stated, the scientific method is to go and look, and then look again. The most elaborate experiments and abstruse equations are designed to answer the simple question, "What are the facts?" Today this question seems so natural and obviously sensible that it is hard to understand how for centuries men could repeat Pliny's[5] statement, that the blood of a goat would shatter a diamond, when a simple test would have disproved it. Yet it seems that they did not perform the test; and the explanation is that the basis of their thought was not empirical but "rational." Although Aristotle went to nature, he returned for authority to pure reason. He simply asserted that heavy bodies must fall faster than light ones, just as he asserted that planets move in circles because the circle is the only perfect figure. Hence Galileo's Pisa experiment[6] marked a real revolution in thought. It marked, Dewey summarizes:

> a change from the qualitative to the quantitative or metric; from the heterogeneous to the homogeneous; from intrinsic form to relations; from esthetic harmonies to mathematical formulae; from contemplative enjoyment to active manipulation and control; from rest to change; from eternal objects to temporal sequence.

In this summary, science already begins to look strange to the plain man; and of course it is strange. Even as roughly stated, its method is still not generally applied to moral, political, or other problems. For science is not, strictly, "organized common sense." Common sense is not only much vaguer and more cocksure but in a way, curiously, more practical. It deals with the

---

[4] Lancelot Hogben (b. 1895), English physiologist.
[5] Pliny the Elder (23/4–79 A.D.), Roman naturalist and encyclopedist.
[6] Galileo (1564–1642), according to legend, dropped two spheres of different weights from the top of the tower of Pisa; they took the same amount of time to reach the ground, thus disproving the widely-held theory that the weight of an object determines the speed of its descent.

total concrete situation, takes life as it comes. Science always abstracts for a very limited purpose, makes up fictions. Especially in late years, it has left common sense far behind. When scientists try to speak the plain man's language, they tell him that the quantum theory may be understood by the analogy of a clock whose mechanism had vanished, leaving only the ticks, and that if he still doesn't understand, the point is that the universe is "not only queerer than we suppose, but queerer than we *can* suppose."

Yet science does remain simply a form of organized intelligence; to become oriented to it, we again do well to begin with the obvious. Although men talk as if the object of intelligence were the discovery and contemplation of eternal truths, actually they employ it chiefly to handle the new situations that are always arising even in a routine life. In daily experience they are continually experimenting, reconstructing, adjusting themselves to a continually changing environment; otherwise there could be no consciousness, no real experience at all. The scientific method is a systematic extension of this behavior. George H. Mead[7] therefore described it as "only the evolutionary process grown self-conscious." Biologically, it is an advance in the natural direction: more differentiation, finer adaptation to environment, greater control over environment.

Similarly the basic interests of science, the concern with the "material" world, are not actually newfangled or alien. Men often feel that nature is hostile to them, at best very careless, at worst unfathomably cruel; in their philosophies they have represented it as a show of illusory or accidental appearances, in their religions as a mess of devil's pottage. Nevertheless they also feel a deep and constant kinship. They naturally personify the world about them and draw from it their metaphors for human life: they bud and bloom in youth, they ripen like fruit on the bough, they fall into the sere, the yellow leaf. The rhythms of nature are in their blood. Like poetry, science explores and articulates these relations; it realizes our rich heritage as children of this earth. Like Christian theology, moreover, it assumes that the heritage is lawful. Science grew out of the medieval faith that the world is orderly and rational, and that all happenings in it could be explained. Scientists now consider this a postulate, not a fact, and their explanations are usually offensive to orthodox theologians; nevertheless they have the same working faith as the theologians. Thus Newton could lay the foundations of the mechanistic universe in a spirit of extreme piety, and be applauded by other devout Christians; he was simply clarifying the ways of God to man. Thus agnostic scientists still admire all the evidence of uniformity, regularity, harmony in the universe. They admire the most wonderful of miracles, that there are not incessant miracles.

In other words, they are not really so inhuman as they are reputed to be. Whereas the man on the street sees only the gadgetry of science, intellectuals are prone to the other extreme of viewing it always in the abstract. They

[7] American philosopher (1863–1931).

dwell upon its remorseless impersonality, the coldness of its truth; they forget its personal satisfactions, the imaginative value of its truths. For to scientists truth is indeed beauty. Mathematicians exclaim over the "elegance" of their demonstrations, Einstein delights in the "pre-established harmonies" that physicists discover, J. W. N. Sullivan is struck by the "astonishing beauty and symmetry" that Minkowski[8] gave the theory of relativity by adding the notion of a four-dimensional continuum. On the other hand, they are displeased by unsightly gaps or bulges in their theory-patterns, dislike the messiness of quantum physics even when its theories seem to fit the facts. Their effort is always to get all their facts to fall into a shape, and their preference among theories, when the experimental test has yet to decide, appears to be determined chiefly by the esthetic quality of the shape. Thus Sullivan notes the comments of Einstein and Eddington[9] on each other's attempt to reduce the laws of electromagnetism to geometry: Einstein said he simply did not "like" Eddington's theory, though he could not disprove it, and Eddington said Einstein's theory was a matter of "taste." Altogether, the generic motive of science is no doubt utilitarian — "service to mankind," if one likes more exalted terms; but the individual scientist, like the individual artist, does his work for the simple, unexalted reason that he likes it, and when it turns out right he feels a comparable lift and glow.

The simple answer to Ransom, then, is that science does "free the spirit." He has forced a narrow view of utility upon it, just as moralists and scientists often do upon art. Like thought itself, science has become a passion and a luxury. It follows the gleam, it stirs hopes too wildly dear. It is indeed often not utilitarian enough: science for science's sake is as much a cult as art for art's sake, and can carry one as far from the actualities of purposeful living. Yet this same passion calls out the plain answer to Roelofs. Science does produce saints. Not to go down the long list of heroes and martyrs, Mme. Curie[10] will do as an example of simple, noble goodness. Such idealism is not itself scientific, to be sure, and may be called religious. Nevertheless the fact remains that science can inspire it without benefit of clergy.

This demonstration that even the scientist is human may seem inconsequential. It finally leads, however, to the heart of the problem of what science is. The recent developments in its philosophy may be summed up in precisely this recognition of the "human element," the human "standpoint" that is literally involved in all statements. Scientific laws are not chips off the old block Reality; as interpretations of sense impressions, they take after the human mind as well. All knowledge is a joint enterprise, an affair whose conditions are both inside and outside the organism. It is the offspring of the marriage of man and nature, a union in which the older partner may be

[8] Hermann Minkowski (1864–1909), Russian-German mathematician and teacher of Einstein. He wrote on the theory of numbers and on space and time.
[9] Sir Arthur Stanley Eddington (1882–1944), British astronomer, physicist, and author.
[10] Pierre and Marie (1867–1934) Curie, French physicists, were the discoverers of radium; their work on radioactivity laid the foundation for much later research in nuclear physics and chemistry.

expected to outlive the younger but which is indissoluble during the life of man.

. . . Einstein tells us how to understand the scientist's method: "Don't listen to his words, examine his achievements." Still better, watch him at work, examine the actual operations by which he gets his knowledge; and here an excellent guide is William H. George's *The Scientist in Action*. Whatever it may become in theory, George points out, a scientific fact is in practice an observation of coincidences. Although products of sensory impression, facts are impersonal in that they are independent of the judgment of any one man; they are statements of coincidences that can be observed under the same conditions by all men. The scientist can therefore gather and test them without bothering about such philosophical problems as whether there really is an external world; "real" is not an observable property. He does have to bother, however, with the problem of classifying and interpreting his facts, fitting them into patterns called theories and laws. The more comprehensive these are, the better he is pleased; but the most comprehensive is still tentative and does not "reduce by one the number of absolute truths to be discovered." Newton's great laws were patterns into which hitherto unconnected facts could be fitted; Einstein devised a different pattern that could accommodate all these and other facts; and we may expect that more inclusive but still different patterns will be devised by Zweistein, Dreistein, etc.

In other words, facts and figures do *not* speak for themselves. For all their stubbornness, they are accommodating enough to allow a number of different interpretations — and there are always enough of them around to support almost any theory. Moreover, the facts are not simply there, waiting in line to be discovered. The scientist selects from a host of possibilities, he looks *for* as well as *at*, he may accordingly *overlook* — as Grimaldi's[11] experiments on the path of light were long neglected because they did not fit in with Newton's corpuscular theory. Hence the advance of science has not been automatic or really systematic, and it has not been in a straight line. Science is first of all the creation of scientists, who are also men with temperaments, special interests, predispositions. (Bertrand Russell has noted, for example, the divergent developments in animal psychology under Thorndike and Koehler:[12] "Animals studied by Americans rush about frantically, with an incredible display of hustle and pep, and at last achieve the desired result by chance. Animals observed by Germans sit still and think, and at last evolve the solution out of their inner consciousness.") More significantly, science is the creation of a definite type of mentality, which has been interested in certain kinds of phenomena but notoriously indifferent to others, averse to the seeming "wild data." Most significantly, it is the creation of a culture, a

[11] Francesco Maria Grimaldi (1618–1663), Italian physicist who discovered diffraction of light and was one of the first to postulate a wave theory of light.
[12] Edward Lee Thorndike (1874–1949) was an American psychologist who formulated important theories of educational psychology. Wolfgang Köhler (b. 1887), German psychologist, was one of the developers of the Gestalt theory in psychology.

society with special interests. Even physics, which seems wholly impersonal and autonomous, has been influenced by vested social interests. The concept of energy was developed to meet the manufacturers' need of a bookkeeping device, a way of measuring the efficiency of machines in units of work; in general there is an obvious correspondence between the long reign of classical mechanics and the needs of industry. Today, when science has developed a highly specialized technique, language, and subject matter of its own, it is still dependent upon the greater society for its privileges. It is the more profoundly a fashion of the times.

This view is not designed to humble or discredit the scientist. Rather it relieves him of the awful responsibility of speaking absolute truth. It stresses his continuity with the organic processes of evolution, the tremendous adventure of civilization, the vital needs and purposes of society; the scientist no more than the poet can afford the illusion that his activity is pure or priestly. It makes clearer the cultural pattern of science today: the concept itself of patterns, fields, organic wholes, which . . . has become important in all the sciences, and which parallels the collectivistic trend in the world of affairs. And it enables a more realistic approach, specifically, to the difficult issue of just where science properly begins and ends.

The popular notion is that science necessarily involves the use of instruments in a laboratory. Knowledge cannot be really scientific unless men have got it out of a test tube, taken an X-ray picture of it, or tried it out on some guinea pigs. Such methods are very well for dealings with sticks and stones, animal life, or the human body; but it follows that they cannot apply to the motions of mind or spirit. Laboratory workers themselves are often contemptuous of the social sciences, and of psychology when it leaves the laboratory and deals with such immeasurables as "consciousness" and "insight." They distrust any statement that cannot be put into an equation. And so the critic is warned off the sciences of man, which are naturally closest to his interests. He is left with the problem of determining just where, then, the sciences stop and the humanities begin, and just what use he can make of the power that has in any event so thoroughly made over the world in which the humanities have their being.

To begin with, there are important distinctions that should remain distinct. Some generous philosophers identify science with all disciplined thought, uniting all the humanities and the sciences in one big happy family. Thus Cassius J. Keyser defines science as any work that aims to establish by legitimate means a body of categorical propositions about the actual world; he therefore accepts as science the work of Plato and Aristotle — and blurs the fundamental difference between their thought and the thought of Galileo or Darwin. Moreover, there are important differences between the sciences. The physicist and the chemist have the adventitious advantage of large subsidies (capitalism has been a generous if not a disinterested patron) and now of relative freedom from personal prejudice or official interference; the psychologist and the sociologist are at any moment likely to tread on the corns of public opinion or get mixed up in some live social issue. But the former also have the intrinsic advantage of a subject matter that lends itself to the extremely helpful devices of mathematical measurement and controlled experiment. The experimental test is especially important, as the ultimate criterion for distinguishing scientific knowledge from philosophic speculation.

Nevertheless most distinguished scientists appear to agree with Max Planck,[13] that from physics to sociology there is a continuous chain; and I can see no practical or logical reason for choosing to break the chain. On practical grounds, it would seem desirable to give science as much scope as possible, and not to discourage important social inquiries by verbal quibbles or qualms about their scientific chastity; it would seem foolish to demand complete, positive knowledge or none. On logical grounds, any sharp break in the chain is not only arbitrary but inconsistent with the basic scientific assumption of natural continuity. That the physical sciences are more objective and more exact than the sciences of man makes them neither more fundamental nor fundamentally different. The differences are in degree, not in kind.

Ultimately the unity of science lies in the logic, not the materials or the specific techniques of its inquiry. As formulated by Dewey in his monumental work, this is a logic of discovery and invention. Its forms are not a priori but postulational and operational; they are not absolute modes of pure reason but generalizations drawn from previous inquiry and liable to modification by subsequent discoveries. Indeed, scientists object to any theory, such as vitalism in biology, which is complete and therefore offers no possibility of advance; their curious objection, J. H. Woodger observes, is that it is *too* successful, *too* perfect. They demand that all theories live dangerously. But this experimental logic does not absolutely require the specific technique of laboratory experiment. It requires primarily that theories be so formulated as to leave room for future discoveries and almost certain modifications. It thereby exposes, indeed, the essential weakness of the sciences of man today, which is not so much the jungle growth of theory as the attitude toward this theory. As scientists, psychologists and sociologists are still very young, and like youngsters much too cocky — few physicists speak with quite the assurance of John B. Watson or Pareto.[14] More specifically, they are seldom content with mere postulates and approximates; they set up some explanatory principle as necessary and sufficient, the one positive truth by which all the other little truths must be sired or certified. Yet their attitude is quite gratuitous. This very criticism of it implies that an experimental logic can be applied to these problems too.

"Wherever there is the slightest possibility of the human mind to *know*," wrote Karl Pearson, "there is a legitimate problem of science." If men have "known" all sorts of absurdities, there can be no question about a fact, strictly

---

[13] German physicist (1858–1947) who developed the quantum theory.
[14] John Watson (1878–1958), American psychologist, codified and publicized the theory of behaviorism; Vilfredo Pareto (1848–1923), Italian economist and sociologist, developed several theories of social and economic change.

defined, and such facts are available in all spheres of interest. Observation, not measurement of coincidences, is their criterion. If it is clearly more difficult to classify and interpret them in the sciences of man, it is not clearly impossible; important relations have already been established and systematically formulated. Students of the humanities who deny that there are fundamental laws in their province necessarily think in a way that presupposes such laws — else their thought would be pointless. In sum, only by divorcing human affairs from natural processes can they be shut off from scientific inquiry; and this ancient expedient disposes of the problem by creating two more.

The Use and Abuse of Science

The practical uses and abuses of science are generally conspicuous enough. They have alike, however, confused the issue of its value. Men consider chiefly the *results* of scientific inquiry, and build their philosophies on current theories as if all thought labeled scientific were necessarily valid. They neglect the logic of inquiry, the *method* that has produced all the dazzling results and that will survive all the current theories. The disciples of science are therefore apt to become only another species of theologian. Still more superficial, however, is the view that science is useful only for menial work, the chores of society, and should be shut off from spiritual matters. This aristocratic division of labor is in effect a return to mumbo jumbo. Its advocates are trying to achieve ends without a realistic study of means, and ultimately they divorce ends and means. In placing mind or spirit in an unearthly realm of its own, they do not actually elevate it; they leave it up a creek.

To begin with, the findings of science are clearly relevant to spiritual interests. There can be no sound judgment of any values without a knowledge of actual conditions, the nature and possibilities of man and his environment; about such matters the scientist has a great deal to say. Grant that his primary interest is in processes, apart from all considerations of value, and that the critic's primary interest is in outcomes, in which considerations of value are central; still a knowledge of processes is always helpful in a study of outcomes.

Even more pertinent is the method of science. Theoretically it is depressing, because it assumes determinism. Actually it gives us freedom, freedom where we want it and can do something with it — freedom, as Dewey says, not apart from natural events but in and among them. It is the philosophers and theologians who have characteristically restricted both our thought and our action; setting out from fixed truths instead of hypotheses, they permitted less freedom than the experimental method, which may imply determinism but which remains *experimental*. Science, therefore, not only has proved an efficient instrument of human purposes but has created new purposes, liberated purposefulness from the ends arbitrarily fixed by ancient high priests of thought. Likewise its method is fundamentally more humane. The philosophers and theologians have characteristically set up absolute antitheses, of right and wrong, good and evil, and conceived their first duty to be the annihilation of most other thinkers. Scientists work more by assimilation, a reconciliation of opposites that are more apparent than real. Each new theory recaptures from a higher level the elements of truth in previous theories, and is in turn due to be included in a still higher synthesis; Newton's great contributions remain solid after Einstein devised a larger pattern. In short, despite its supposed inhumanity, science exemplifies the humanistic ideal.

Also pertinent here is the moral value of science, which is so apparent that it is often overlooked. In no other human activity is a higher premium placed upon truthfulness, or is the ideal of truthfulness more fully realized. Success in science is possible only on these terms. The eminent statesman or businessman may be unscrupulous, and indeed cannot afford too many or too fine scruples; the passionate sincerity of artists and other intellectuals may still be warped by wishful preferences, and their fervor and eloquence come by more easily because of the wishfulness; but no scientist can ever hope to succeed by misrepresenting, or by remolding according to his heart's desire. (Paul Kammerer, the well-known biologist who did fake his results, was driven to suicide by the disgrace of exposure.) His hard-won success, moreover, cannot be exploited for private gain, at least if he is to retain his professional standing. Outside his profession, needless to add, the scientist is no paragon of selfless virtue and wisdom, and within it he will cherish his brain child, hold out for his own theory as long as the facts permit. Yet the scientific community as a whole is the most impressive example history has yet known of a disinterested, coöperative enterprise, international in scope, directed toward impersonal ends and by impersonal standards. It is the most impressive demonstration of the actual possibility of "supra-personal, supra-partisan, supra-racial standards and values."

In such ways, to repeat, science can free the spirit. So can its tremendous revelations, which have also been considered alien to the human spirit. Astronomy is the striking example. Men are often depressed by the immensities it reveals: How insignificant is man, how transient his life in the perspective of the stars! Such reflections may induce a becoming humility. But neither can man lick a gorilla, or outrun an antelope, and this popular habit of measuring him by astronomical coördinates is also pointless. We may as reasonably look down on the stars, for they cannot contemplate either themselves or us. Meanwhile astronomy has other meanings for us. The stars were the first clear evidence of uniformity, regularity, harmony in the world; man might never have achieved any science at all, Poincaré remarked, had clouds always hid them. They have as well a clear imaginative or spiritual value. The spectacle lifts us out of ourselves; and if it shows how little man is, it also shows how great is his spirit, which can enjoy the immense harmony and embrace the immense mystery.

In general, science has unquestionably widened and enriched the whole context of thought, the whole background of immediate experience. The issue of whether or not to use its findings is in the end academic. Try as we will, we cannot escape its influence. We cannot walk abroad except in its shadow; it is in the air we breathe, the language we use as unconsciously. The student of esthetics, for example, may rebel against the excesses of "psychological" investigation and try once more to take his beauty straight. Nevertheless his main terms — imagination, emotion, sensation, will, intuition, expression, etc. — are charged with some kind of psychological theory. That it is usually a vague or dubious theory only emphasizes the need of his realizing what he is about. And the moment he leaves esthetics to generalize about the relation of art to other interests and purposes, he is up to his neck in matters about which scientists have had much to say. He is perforce a kind of psychologist and social scientist. He might better be an informed one.

Unhappily, however, we cannot escape the influence of pseudo-science either; and so we must go back to the beginning. The extraordinary success of scientific inquiry has also stimulated a busy shopping around to pick up some scientific dress at bargain rates. The most obvious bargains are in technical jargon, which may then clutter up not only a man's prose style but his thinking; he is apt to think that he has solved a problem when he has merely located it, as in the Unconscious, or given it a new name, such as "sublimation." But the general reason for all the awed misunderstanding is again that laymen usually pick up only the latest findings, not the logic of inquiry. With its elaborate system of fictions and symbols, which may or may not stand for something "real," science might be defined as madness with a method. To miss the method is to be left simply with madness.

Perhaps the most common and dangerous fallacy is the assumption that science tells us "all that matters." Max Eastman stated it baldly when he insisted that poets must stop "trying to tell us anything about life," because as poets they know nothing about it. This is a hard thing to tell an earnest man. It is also a very silly thing, and should embarrass scientists as much as it distresses poets; the exclusive right to say something about life is a terrible responsibility. Yet scientists, too, often talk carelessly in this way. Physicists will say that a table is "really" only a swarm of particles, or biochemists that man is "nothing but" a parcel of chemicals worth about a dollar. All that is of no value for their limited purposes — the distinctive qualities of human experience, the extraordinarily rich variety of sensation and emotion in a world of shape and color, fruit and flower, dream and song — they may then dismiss as merely "subjective," beneath the dignity of knowledge. They forget that they are always abstracting, and that their abstractions are also fictions. "It is the Nemesis of the struggle for exactitude by the man of science," writes H. S. Jennings,[15] "that it leads him to present a mutilated, merely fractional account of the world as a true and complete picture."

The greatest victories of science have in a sense been cheap victories, for they have been won by a careful refusal to engage the more difficult, certainly no less important problems of ethics, politics, and the humanities generally.

---

[15] Herbert Spencer Jennings (1868–1947), American zoologist.

The physicist rules out all that he cannot rule, reduces what is left to the simplest possible terms. It is an excellent policy — for his purposes. But he may then forget that what cannot be measured or calculated may nevertheless be immeasurably important, have incalculable consequences, and that the terms of life as it is lived are not simple. Take even the unanswerable questions, the metaphysical questions that it is now fashionable to dismiss as meaningless. "All problems are artificial," Dewey wrote in a careless moment, "which do not grow, even if indirectly, out of the conditions under which life . . . is carried on." Roelofs answers rightly that *all* problems grow out of these conditions. Where else could they come from? Metaphysical speculation may be unproductive of strict knowledge, and is often a dangerous nuisance because it is mistaken for knowledge. Its high imaginings may also be a source of inspiration and strength. In either event the fact remains that men naturally wonder about the ultimate mysteries, give rich meaning to meaningless questions, and behave in accordance with the answers they have given the unanswerable. And so they must, for many indispensable meanings and purposes outrun all evidence.

At most, science gives us certain directions for dealing with certain things. Its abstractions are like paper money, facilitating commerce with actuality so that every transaction need not be an exchange of cows. Its abstractions are a necessary evil; and they become simply an evil if men hoard them for their own sake, forget their instrumental function and their arbitrary value. But it is especially important for the literary critic to remember that science never tells us everything about anything — that, in fact, it tells us very little about any *thing*. It leaves out of its abstractions all the unique particulars, the concrete qualities, the substantial body of direct experience that is the primary subject matter of art. The scientist's apple suggested the law of gravitation and as happily obeys the laws of biology. The apple of our experience is a unique object that may please the palate and the eye, evoke the emotions appropriate to autumn, symbolize the plight of the unemployed, enable an archer to become a national hero. Our apple is no less significant than its better behaved symbol.

Similarly the critic in particular needs to guard against the confusion commonly inspired by scientific analysis. Analysis can reduce all human behavior to its biological origins and these in turn to their physical basis; then men believe that they have completely "explained" behavior, proved that it is "simply" physical. A great deal of emotion has been generated by the elementary fallacy pointed out by Broad: because B grows out of A and C grows out of B, C is nothing but A in disguise. Scientists know that organic life is qualitatively different from inorganic matter, the conscious life of man qualitatively different from other forms of life; they may nevertheless forget that what matters most to us as men is not the common beginnings but the unique ends. Critics fall into the same fallacy when they confine science to the "economic impulse" because it is rooted there. But they also fall into it when they describe art as "merely" a compensation for some psychic maladjustment, or "essentially" an expression of class interest. They confuse the conditions of something with its cause, and both with the thing itself.

The gist of all these extravagances is that science has suffered as much from its disciples as has any faith. For it is indeed a faith, and often a very naïve one. Apart from the gross worship of time-saving and time-killing devices as ends in themselves, the disciples have displayed the artless optimism of prophets and crusaders through the centuries, based on the illusion that men always welcome light and once brought to see the truth will act upon it. They have displayed as well the frequent arrogance, intolerance, and inhumanity of the prophets and crusaders. Thomas Huxley, who declared that faith is "the one unpardonable sin," had through all his career an absolute faith in the religion of science, accepting as gospel not only its method but its current assumptions, and on the basis of these questionable assumptions erecting an often harsh philosophy. Others have been contemptuous of values other than their own devotion to verifiable knowledge, contemptuous even of the vital needs they were presumably serving. Until recently, "purpose" and "value" were the most horrid words a scientist could hear.

All in all, science is a means to a better life on earth, but cannot alone secure this end. The most that one can argue for it is that it is an indispensable means, the best investment for hope. Yet this is a sound argument; and with it I should end. Philosophy, religion, and art provide valuable experiences and suggest valuable ways of dealing with the world; science provides the most certain knowledge, the most certain means of generating more knowledge, the most certain means of manipulating this knowledge to control the natural world. Hence the necessary postscript even to preliminary discussion is that scientists now tend increasingly to think scientifically about their own activity. They are examining the implications and facing the responsibilities of the enormous power they wield. They are subjecting science to the same ruthless analysis that religion has had to endure since the eighteenth century, conducting a searching inquiry into their basic assumptions and their logic, systematically formulating the philosophy that in their naïve, exuberant youth they did not realize was a philosophy. Poincaré, Whitehead, Planck, Einstein, Jennings, Woodger, Koehler, Mannheim — such men offer a profounder criticism of science than one gets from most thinkers who are jealously defending their values from its encroachment. They are less ignorant of their ignorance.

Jacob Bronowski (b. 1908)

ENGLISH MATHEMATICIAN and WRITER (POLISH-BORN)

The Dilemma of the Scientist

I

We live in times of difficult decisions for scientists, for statesmen and for the lay public. Many of these decisions are forced on us by new scientific discoveries, and the difficulties in making them are created by the distance between the scientist and the public. (Indeed, there is a frightening distance even between scientists in one field and those in another.) This sense of distance is, I think, a grave threat to the survival of the kind of society in which science can flourish at all.

People hate scientists. There is no use in beating about the bush here. The scientist is in danger of becoming the scapegoat for the helplessness which the public feels. And if an immense revulsion of public feeling does lead to the destruction of the scientific tradition, then the world may again enter a dark age as it did after the Goths destroyed Rome. It is not impossible that the whole mechanical and intellectual society which we know could be abolished by a great wave of fanaticism.

That is the danger which faces us, because people hate scientists. But even if this danger does not come to pass, something as terrible can happen — and is happening. This is that the scientist is forced, by the hatred of public opinion, to side with established authority and government. He becomes a prisoner of the hatred of the lay public, and by that becomes the tool of authority.

My purpose today is not to underline these obvious dangers, which we may hide from ourselves but which in our hearts we all know to exist. My purpose is to try and give a picture, as I see it, of the real responsibilities of scientists, government and public, in order that, beginning from this diagnosis, we may begin to cure the great and threatening division between them.

II

What the lay public does when it hates the scientist is what it does also when it hates policemen and ministers of state and all symbols of authority. It tries to shift the responsibility for decisions from its own shoulders to the shoulders of other people. "They have done this", it says. And "They" is always the law, the government — or in this case the scientist.

Title supplied by editors. Text of a speech delivered to the Association of Atomic Scientists in London on 9 July 1955. Address given at the annual conference of the International Liaison Committee of Organisations for Peace at Oosterbeek, The Netherlands, on August 25, 1955. Reprinted by permission of the author.

You must allow me here to make a digression which is not strictly part of my theme, but which I think needs saying. It is this: that we must not forget that scientists do bear a heavy responsibility. I am, of course, about to explain that really the public and governments bear the main responsibility. But this does not shift from us, the scientists, the grave onus of having acquiesced in the abuse of science. We have contrived weapons and policies with our public conscience, which each of us individually would never have undertaken with his private conscience. Men are only murderers in large groups. They do not individually go out and strangle their neighbour. And scientists are only murderers in large groups — collectively. For scientists are very ordinary human beings. Any collection of people in any laboratory contains good and bad, people with conscience and without, and what we have allowed to happen is the conquest of science by the minority without conscience which exists in every group.

It is sad that scientists have been exceptionally corruptible. Look into your own experience. Most of us have come from poor parents. We have worked our own way up. The practice of science has enabled us to earn salaries which would be unthinkable to us if we had stayed peddling whatever our fathers peddled. Quite suddenly, the possession of a special skill has opened to us a blue door into the ante-chambers of prime ministers. We sit at conference tables, we have become important people, because we happen to be able to be murderers. And therefore scientists have been bought with large salaries and fellowships and rewards quite inappropriate to their merits, because a policy was furthered by their techniques. The scientist has proved to be the easiest of all men to blind with the attractions of public life.

Having said this, I now propose to stop abusing the scientist. I think it is right that we should all make this confession of guilt — I have been as guilty as anyone else — but this is all spilt milk, this is all water over the dam. We must now look towards what we can do to remedy what has happened. And it certainly cannot be remedied by a gigantic strike of scientists, who will suddenly refuse to have anything to do with commercial or war research; because the society of scientists contains too many fallible human beings to make this practicable.

III

When the public dreams of such a strike, when it says "scientists ought not to have invented this or disclosed that secret", it is already demanding something of the individual scientist which lies beyond his personal responsibility.

The voters of Great Britain elect for the purpose of making their policy 630 members of Parliament. They do not elect the people who go to Harwell or the people who go to my own research laboratory. That is: we have already deputed to those whom we elect the responsibility for framing policy in peace and war, and it is quite wrong to ask a body of professional experts like the scientists to take this responsibility from the men whom our society has named.

The individual scientist is not the keeper of the public conscience, because that is not what he was chosen for. The population at large, through its deputed ministers, has chosen scientists to execute certain public orders which are thought to represent the public will. And you cannot ask the scientist to be executioner of this will, and judge as well. If you have given a body of scientists this particular hangman's task, you cannot ask them also to form a collective opposition to it. The collective responsibility belongs to the lay public and, through that, to those who were elected by the public to carry it out.

Thus when Einstein, on the 2nd August, 1939, wrote a letter to President Roosevelt, in order to draw his attention to the possibility of an atomic bomb, he was acting with exemplary correctness. He was disclosing to the elected head of government a matter of public importance on which the decision was not his, the writer's, but was the President's to make.

We must explain to people that they are asking of scientists quite the wrong collective decisions when they say "you should not have invented this" or "you should not have disclosed that". This is asking us all to betray the public in the same way as Dr. Klaus Fuchs[1] did, by asking scientists to make decisions which are for the nation to make. The only man who ever, on his own responsibility, was willing to shoulder public responsibility in this way was Dr. Fuchs. But so far from being hailed as the only sane scientist, he was treated as quite the opposite — as of course he was, since scientists have no right to betray the will of the nation. Yet Fuchs did just what the public asks of every scientist — he decided what to do with a scientific invention.

IV

Very well. We will agree that the scientist is not the keeper of the nation's policy. Then what is he the keeper of? He is the keeper of his own private conscience. His responsibility is not to be seduced as a person. He has the right to act individually as a conscientious objector. Indeed, I believe he has the duty to act as a conscientious objector. I would like to repeat this point. It is in this country an offence to betray the armed forces or to seduce their members from their allegiance. It is not an offence to refuse to be a soldier. And I believe that this is exactly like the position of the scientist. He has no business to act as if he commands the army, but he has a business to settle with his own conscience: the serious business whether he personally will engage in forms of research of which he does not morally approve.

My claim then is that the individual scientist should exercise his own personal conscience. This is his duty. What is the duty of governments in this respect? It is to make it possible for him to exercise his conscience. The responsibility of governments in this is to create the conditions in which a scientist can say: "No!" to projects in which he does not want to take part. He must even be able to give advice which is distasteful to those in authority,

[1] Born in Germany in 1912, Fuchs was naturalized as a British citizen in 1942. In 1950 he was sentenced to imprisonment for disclosing nuclear secrets to the Russians.

and still must not be hounded out of public life, or prevented from making a living.

In all countries the serious threat to scientists who have once touched the fringes of secret subjects is, that they are then caught in something from which they can never escape again. They do not get a passport, in case somebody captures them. They cannot get a job because, if they do not want to do this, then they are too dangerous or awkward to be trusted with anything else. This is what we must prevent governments from doing, and this can only be prevented by the opinion of quite ordinary citizens. This is the duty which citizens owe to scientists, to insist that governments shall make it possible for scientists to be conscientious objectors if they wish.

V

I have explored this subject in general terms, and I would now like to be specific. I would like to tell you precisely what I think is the responsibility of the public, of the scientist, and of governments.

The responsibility of the public is to make the decisions of policy on which their future depends, and to make them themselves. And in a democracy the apparatus for this is to elect those people in whose judgment you have confidence — and to elect them on the issues which in fact face the world. Now you can only elect such people, you can only put pressure on them about public issues, if you are well informed. The greatest lack in public opinion today is lack of information about what is possible and not possible in science. This sets my teeth on edge every time I read a scientific newsflash. I will quote one of many instances, which I find distasteful: the use of the phrase "cobalt bomb". This is a technical term for a piece of medical equipment, but has suddenly become transformed into something to describe how a hydrogen bomb might be clothed. As a result, of the fifty million people in this country, forty-nine million nine hundred odd thousand have heard the words "cobalt bomb", but are helplessly confused between radio-active treatment and something that you blow people up with.

The public must be well informed; and the public gets not only the government it deserves, but the newspapers it deserves.

If this is once granted, the next step I think is simple. If it is once granted that we believe in democratic election, and that in our generation this can only be carried out by a public informed on the scientific issues on which the fate of nations hangs, then the duty of the scientist is clear. The duty of the scientist is to inform the public. The duty of the scientist is to create the public opinion for right policies, and this he can only create if the public shares his knowledge.

My generation has a heavy task here because it ought to spend the bulk of its time — alas — not in laboratories at all, but in explaining to the voting public what is going on in laboratories. What are the choices which face us? What could be done with antibiotics, with new materials, with coal (if you like) and with alternative forms of energy? These are urgent questions and yet, however many times we raise them, the layman still does not understand the scale of the changes which our work is making, and on which the answers must hang.

VI

Let me tell you a slightly irreverent story about this. At the time the Smyth Report[2] was published in America, there was published in this country a White Paper on the British contribution to atomic energy. One of the documents in it is the directive which Mr. Winston Churchill, as he then was, gave about the setting up of an atomic energy project. This directive begins with the words, "Though personally satisfied with the power of existing explosives . . ." This bland phrase is a monument to a non-scientific education. For it could only have been written by a man, an intelligent man, who simply does not understand how big a million is. The difference between atomic explosives and ordinary explosives is the difference between the length of a nuclear bond and a molecular bond; and this is a factor of more than a million. To suppose somehow that in multiplying the energy of an explosive by a million, you are doing nothing very different from multiplying it by two, or five, or ten — this is simply not to grasp the scale of the world.

And the public just does not grasp it. To say "ten to the sixth" to anybody today, however educated, is still to invite the reproof that one is stressing mere numerical details. One of our tasks, as scientists, must be to educate people in the scale of things.

While I am telling improper stories — improper in the only amusing sense — I will tell you that everybody who works in industrial research has this trouble all the time when he discusses the economics of new processes. We put forward the result of research, or we simply estimate what would happen if a piece of research proved successful. And at once we get back a balance sheet from the finance department, which says: the current process makes a profit of 2/2d. a ton, and what you have in mind might make a loss of 8d. a ton; it is therefore not worth pursuing. This, if you please, is the comment on a piece of research which, if it works on the full scale, might cut costs by a factor of five. But no accountant understands a factor of five; he budgets in shillings and pence, and what is liable to lose is to him as good as lost. One cannot explain a factor of five, or a factor of a million, to people who have not been brought up in a scientific tradition. This is what I mean when I say that the scientist has a duty to become a teacher to the public in understanding the pace, the nature, the scale of the changes which are possible in our lifetime.

VII

I have detailed the duties of the public and of the scientist. What are the duties of government? The duties of government are to give the public the

[2] Henry D. Smyth, *A General Account of the Development of Methods of Using Atomic Energy for Military Purposes* (U.S. Government Printing Office, 1945).

opportunity to learn, and therefore to give scientists the opportunity to teach. And I have already suggested that these duties are twofold. One is to give scientists freedom to live their own lives if they do not want to go on with research projects which seem to them without conscience. The other is the duty to allow scientists to speak freely on subjects of world importance.

As for the second, everyone who has ever been connected with the Atomic Energy projects knows how it is met today. We spend our time waiting for some American journalist to publish some piece of information which we know to be accurate, so that we may then quote it as being the opinion of the *New York Times*. I am being frank about this: I do it all the time. I read what the great indiscreet senator said to the small indiscreet reporters, and I know that nine statements are nonsense and one statement is accurate. Then I quote the one that is accurate — but not as my opinion.

Of course it is natural that governments resist the explosive opinions of scientists. All governments, all societies are resistant to change. Rather over two thousand years ago, Plato was anxious to exile poets from his society; and in our lifetime, for the same reason, governments are in effect anxious to exile or at least silence scientists. They are anxious to exile all dissidents, because dissidents are the people who will change society.

There is a simple difference between governments and scientists. Governments believe that society ought to stay the way it is for good — and particularly that there ought to be no more elections. Scientists believe that society ought to be stable, but this does not mean the same thing to them as being static. We scientists want to see an *evolving* society, because when the physical world is evolving (and we are helping to evolve it) the forms of society and government cannot be kept the same.

VIII

Having described the duties of the public, of scientists and of governments, let me now underline what I have said by describing what happens in all three cases if these duties are not kept. If governments do not allow scientists freedom of conscience to work at what they like and to refuse to work at what they do not like, and to speak freely about why they do so, then you get the gravest of all disasters — the disaster of state intolerance. This is a disaster because it saps both sides of the moral contract. For there is a moral contract between society and its individuals which allows the individual to be a dissident; and if the state breaks this moral contract, then it leaves the individual no alternative but to become a terrorist. I do not know whether the great state trials in Russia were just or were false. But I know that if they were just, if men like Radek and Trotsky and Zinoviev[3] really committed those enormities, then this in itself condemns the system of government which does not allow any other form of protest than such a form. The grave danger to

[3] Karl Radek (1855–1939?), Soviet propagandist, and Grigan Zinoviev (1883–1936), Soviet statesman, were victims of Stalin's purges. Leon Trotsky (1879–1940), Soviet political leader and Marxist theoretician, was expelled from the U.S.S.R. by Stalin in 1929.

our society, too, is that this becomes the only choice which is left open to scientists, if state intolerance imprisons them and tries to turn them into a secret Egyptian priestcraft.

The great sin of the public is acquiescence in this secrecy. I am horrified by the feeling that I get, from such trifling things as American advertisements, that people really enjoy the sense that they are not to be trusted. There is an advertisement running in the "New Yorker" at the moment (I think for a clothing firm) which shows a man who has just got out of an aeroplane. He has a face like a prize-fighter, he is well-dressed and wears what in New York is called a sharp hat, and he carries a bag in one hand which is chained to his wrist. He is carrying secret documents. This is the holy of holies. This is what we are to admire — the man with his mouth shut tight who is not trusting you and me, because of course you and I are not to be trusted. When people come to believe this, when they themselves believe that it is better for them not to know, then totalitarianism is on the doorstep. Then you are ready for Hitler to get up and say, "I am the man who will take your communal responsibilities. I will make your decisions for you."

And the third in our scheme, the scientist, must preserve the tradition of quarrelling, of questioning and of dissent on which science (and I believe all post-Renaissance civilisation) has been built. He must do this for two reasons. First, there is the mundane reason which is obvious in the failure of German research after Hitler took power. It is this: that you do not get good science as soon as you have reduced the scientists to yes-men. It is the nature of scientists to be thoroughly contrary people — let us own up to that. It is the nature of science as an activity to doubt your word and mine. . . . As soon as you get a science, such as atomic energy research in totalitarian Germany, in which the young men are no longer allowed to question what the great men have said, then that science is dead. You can find in the files of the German Atomic Energy Commission that several young men made what I suppose must be called very good suggestions, but they were not followed because (such is the influence of totalitarianism) Heisenberg always knew the answers already.

This does not happen in English laboratories yet. Mr. Churchill begins by saying that he is satisfied with existing explosives, but after the comma he does give young scientists the opportunity to be dissatisfied. This tradition, this independence and tolerance, is I believe the base of all our values; and this is what we as scientists must preserve.

IX

I have given you the simple practical grounds for allowing scientists to be awkward, but I believe also that imaginatively and intellectually this is equally important. The sense of intellectual heresy is the life-blood of our civilisation. And the heresy of scientists cannot be confined to their science. Newton was thoroughly and rightly contrary in science, and he was also a thorough heretic in religious matters. For the same reason, people like Oppenheimer and Einstein are found to associate with such unreliable characters. You cannot say to scientists, "When you get into the laboratory at nine in the morning, you are going to be a dissenter; and when you go out at five-thirty you are going to become a citizen who touches his cap and who is politically sound". The intellect is not divided into these simple categories.

I have said that the duty of the scientist is today publicly to become a teacher. Let me end by saying something of what he is to teach. There is, of course, the scientific method. There are things about the scale and order of size of which I have spoken. There are the possibilities which are open to us in controlling nature and ourselves. Above all, he can teach men to ask whether the distance between promise and achievement in our age need be quite so large; whether there must be such a gap between what society is capable of doing and what it does. All this, every scientist can teach.

But every scientist can also teach something deeper. He can teach men to resist all forms of acquiescence, of indifference and imposition of secrecy and denial. We must resist the attitude of officials, that there ought to be a good reason why something should be published before you allow it. We must teach even officials that there will have to be a very good reason indeed before anyone is silenced by secrecy.

Mr. Gordon Dean, the late Chairman of the American Atomic Energy Commission, has just been complaining against secrecy on practical grounds. He says that both the commercial reactors which are being built in America are still on the secret list, and that this is handicapping American business in its competition with English business for world reactor markets. God works in a mysterious way, and it may be that science will be liberated by this anxiety to sell atomic power. At any rate, let us not look askance at any ally in the drive against silence. My message today, in this and in all else, has been the scientist's duty to speak. There is one thing above all others that the scientist has a duty to teach to the public and to governments: it is the duty of heresy.

Stephen Spender (b. 1909)

ENGLISH POET and CRITIC

The Express

After the first powerful, plain manifesto
The black statement of pistons, without more fuss
But gliding like a queen, she leaves the station.
Without bowing and with restrained unconcern
She passes the houses which humbly crowd outside,
The gasworks, and at last the heavy page
Of death, printed by gravestones in the cemetery.
Beyond the town, there lies the open country
Where, gathering speed, she acquires mystery,
The luminous self-possession of ships on ocean.   10
It is now she begins to sing — at first quite low
Then loud, and at last with a jazzy madness —
The song of her whistle screaming at curves,
Of deafening tunnels, brakes, innumerable bolts.
And always light, aerial, underneath,
Retreats the elate metre of her wheels.
Steaming through metal landscape on her lines,
She plunges new eras of white happiness,
Where speed throws up strange shapes, broad curves
And parallels clean like trajectories from guns.   20
At last, further than Edinburgh or Rome,
Beyond the crest of the world, she reaches night
Where only a low stream-line brightness
Of phosphorus on the tossing hills is light.
Ah, like a comet through flame, she moves entranced,
Wrapt in her music no bird song, no, nor bough
Breaking with honey buds, shall ever equal.

Louis N. Ridenour (1911–1959)

AMERICAN PHYSICIST and MILITARY ADVISER

The Responsibility of the Scientist

Now that the war is officially over, everyone seems to be trying to guarantee the peace in his own individual way. The wrangles and name-calling among the various peace-lovers parallel some of the worst features of a war, though they stop short of bloodletting.

I am sure that there are few people who love peace more devoutly, or who wish more profoundly to guarantee and preserve it, than Norbert Wiener. Yet I find myself in violent disagreement with his views as stated in his letter, "A Scientist Rebels." The issues involved are so important that the point of view of a scientist opposed to Wiener should be clearly stated.

Fundamentally, our disagreement turns on two points.

The first concerns the social responsibility of the scientist. Wiener clearly believes that the scientist is the armorer of modern war, and as such holds a responsibility of unique importance. I feel that the social responsibility of the scientist is unique in no important way. It is identical with the social responsibility of every other thinking man, except for one special and temporary thing. It is necessary today to educate the non-scientific public to the Promethean nature of atomic energy and the true character of science (for example, that it contains no secrets). This education must be done, so that all the people can participate in the decisions they will have to make concerning the organization of society in such a form that wars become less likely.

This educational job was splendidly begun by our government with the publication of the Smyth Report[1] — a step that has recently been criticized by men who do not understand the meaning and the scope of the stupendous educational enterprise we have only just begun. Such an attitude toward the publication of the Smyth Report is the best possible evidence that, if the instruction of all people in these matters is not done promptly and well, we shall continue to wriggle out of the thinking that is demanded of us, using the well-worn old loopholes: "Not such a terrible weapon"; "Every offensive weapon brings a countermeasure"; "We'll keep the secret"; "We'll keep ahead in armaments"; "Let's have a cheap preventive war"; and so on.

Secondly, Wiener wishes to dissociate himself utterly from any activity connected with preparation for war, even to the extent of doing everything

[1] Henry D. Smyth, *A General Account of the Development of Methods of Using Atomic Energy for Military Purposes* (U.S. Government Printing Office, 1945).

he can to make those preparations ineffective. I regard it as deplorable that our nation is preparing for war, and I prefer to leave to others the actual work involved; but so long as it is the policy of our nation to prepare for war, I shall certainly not attempt to impede such preparations. In fact, I have tried to help them by pointing out a way in which our anxiety to increase our military strength is harming our potential military performance: the hysterical insistence on secrecy in nuclear physics is slowing our progress in that field. I conceive the duty of the peace-lover to be that of working for a world in which national arms are no longer desired by a majority of the people of this country or of the world. Meanwhile, I do not believe in the wisdom, propriety, or effectiveness of attempts to sabotage the preparation of arms when these arms are as widely believed to be necessary as they are today.

Wiener's views in these matters are best stated in his own words. The occasion for the letter that was printed in the January *Atlantic* was that Wiener had been asked, by an employee of an aircraft company engaged in work on guided missiles, for a copy of a National Defense Research Committee report he had written during the war. This report was out of print, and Wiener's correspondent had assumed that the simplest way to get a copy was to appeal to the author. In denying the request, Wiener said: —

> The policy of the government itself during and after the war . . . has made it clear that to provide scientific information is not a necessarily innocent act. . . . The interchange of ideas which is one of the great traditions of science must of course receive certain limitations when the scientist becomes an arbiter of life and death. . . .
>
> The measures taken during the war by our military agencies, in restricting the free intercourse among scientists . . . [will] if continued in time of peace . . . lead to the total irresponsibility of the scientist, and ultimately to the death of science. Both of these are disastrous for our civilization, and entail grave and immediate peril for the public. . . .
>
> I will not accept a censorship in which I do not participate. . . . To disseminate information about a weapon in the present state of our civilization is to make it practically certain that that weapon will be used. . . .
>
> The practical use of guided missiles can only be to kill foreign civilians indiscriminately. . . . Their possession can do nothing but endanger us by encouraging the tragic insolence of the military mind. . . .
>
> I do not expect to publish any future work of mine which may do damage in the hands of irresponsible militarists.

No doubt Wiener's letter sounded eminently sensible, and even lofty, to many who read it. The motives that lie back of it are certainly lofty, and with them I have no quarrel. But the assumptions on which it rests are open to the gravest question. Wiener encourages his readers to believe that, since technology is the daughter of science, and war is increasingly shaped by technology, the scientist has a unique moral and social responsibility. He must guide his work along peaceful channels; he must suppress such of his findings as apply to war.

This simply does not fit with the basic character of science. By definition, science consists of a completely open-minded probing into the unknown. No man can say what will be found as the result of a given investigation; and certainly no man can predict the nature of the practical engineering outcome of a given scientific investigation. Lee De Forest, the inventor of the three-electrode vacuum tube that is the basis of all present-day electronics, is said to be appalled at the babel and cacophony his invention has loosed upon the world. But De Forest was an inventor, not a scientist. The inventor or the engineer knows the goal of his work; the scientist has no goal but truth. He may have a preconception, based on existing theory, of what he will find in a given experiment, but he is ready to discard this in a moment if his results fail to bear it out.

To continue with our example, then: if De Forest is amazed at the results his invention has brought, imagine how Clerk Maxwell and Heinrich Hertz would feel if they could spend a day with the networks. Before Maxwell, the notion of electromagnetic radiation — radio waves — had never been conceived; before Hertz, radio waves had never knowingly been generated by man. With sufficient imagination, De Forest might have foreseen mass entertainment as the result of his improvement in the existing wireless communication art. It is altogether unthinkable that either Maxwell or Hertz could have had the slightest notion that he was providing a medium for the advertising of soap.

This essential unknowability of the practical ends of scientific investigation makes it senseless to speak, as some do, of "the planning of science for human betterment." This bit of Marxist doctrine is widely met nowadays, even in the best circles, and Professor Wiener does himself and his colleagues a disservice by embracing it. Since we cannot guess how technology will use the still unknown results of a proposed scientific investigation, we must therefore conclude that either science as a whole is good for mankind or it is not. We can "plan" science only to the extent of turning it off or on. Since science, through technology, really means material civilization, the question becomes: Is material civilization good for mankind or is it not? There are arguments on both sides of that question, but clearly its resolution is by no means the concern of the scientist alone.

Other meaningless phrases are finding their way into conversation and the public prints. According to this country's announced policy for the international control of atomic energy, we desire "the interchange of scientific information for peaceful purposes." What can this possibly mean? Either scientific information is exchanged or it is not. No man can say what the practical effect of such interchange will be, and the nature of that effect depends fundamentally upon political and social factors, not upon the nature of the scientific information that is exchanged.

What I have said thus far about the unknowability of goal applies to science. What of technology, which by definition has a definable goal? Should an effort be made to guide technology toward peaceful ends? Professor Wiener thinks that it should. While objecting to the military interference with scientific publication that took place during the war and is still going on, he himself feels competent to perform intelligent censorship. He proposes to perform this censorship on the basis of the practical use that is contemplated for his own ideas. He states flatly, for example, that the only possible use of guided missiles is to murder foreign civilians indiscriminately.

Overlooking the astonishing lack of logic that is involved in imposing one's own censorship while simultaneously rejecting that of others, I feel that Wiener is wrong in this attitude. In a peaceful world, work even on guided missiles would proceed, though not on the same scale or with such desperate intensity as now. Guided missiles would be developed for a wholly peaceful and scientific purpose, not a military one. Given peace, they will carry man's instruments, and finally man himself, through outer space to the planets and the stars.

Here, as before — here even in the branch of engineering that Wiener regards as the farthest-north of militarism — here still the principle holds. If the world is "postured for peace," as the Senators say (some of them say it in a way which implies that the posture involves a barrel), science, technology, and the useful arts contribute to the enrichment and the improvement of peaceful life. If the world is racked with suspicion, preparing for war, or in the throes of combat, the identical arts, techniques, skills, and individuals will contribute to the frightfulness and the horror of war. The decision rests on the contemporary character of world thought and world organization.

This is the basis for my assertion that the "social responsibility of the scientist" is identical with the social responsibility of every thinking man. Each must do his best to make sure that science, the canning industry, young men, the railroads — in short, the entire rubric of our society — are used for harmless and laudable purposes, and not for war. This desirable end can be attained only in a world where measures short of war are applied to solve international frictions. The scientist can no more choose whether he works for war or for peace than the Western Electric Company can choose whether the telephone instruments it manufactures are used on domestic circuits or as Army phones on a field of battle. The scientist does science, and Western Electric makes telephones. The use of either product is determined by society as a whole.

Anyone who feels a *special* sense of guilt because he helped create an atomic bomb, or anyone who believes that the creators of the atomic bomb should feel so, is confusing two quite different things. He is identifying the profound immorality of murder with the relatively insignificant matter of improving the means of murder. God told Moses, "Thou shalt not kill" — not "Thou shalt not kill with atomic energy, for that is so effective as to be sinful." The immorality of war is shared by all. Technical improvements in weapons can influence only the logistics and the strategy of any war that may occur; whether a war occurs or not is the crucial matter, and this is determined by the current "posture" of the world.

Among the social and political factors that influence the posture of the world at any given time, the state of armament of the nations is of great importance. So is the rate at which this state of armament is increasing or decreasing. There is some evidence to suggest that arms beget war, and presumably this is what causes Wiener and others of similar views to do personally whatever they can to retard the arming of our nation. Wiener's refusal to supply the report for which he was asked, though a purely formal matter, can only be regarded as an action taken in the belief that arms are bad in themselves, and that the more feebly this nation is armed, the less likely is war. Such a belief may be partly or entirely correct. I simply do not know whether, in a feral world, it is wiser for a nation to be strong or to be weak. And since I do not know, I do not feel it my privilege, much less my duty, to challenge by individual action the clear decision in favor of armaments that has been made by our government.

By coincidence, Wiener's position in this particular matter bears a very close relationship to an important misconception widely held among those having no knowledge of science. The latter view can be called, for short, the small-war philosophy. The small-war men desire to restrain technology (which they often miscall "science") with a view to making the next war as much like the last as possible. The bombs that dropped on North America in World War II were few and small, the reasoning runs. If we can only stop weapon development at its present level, the coming war will leave our children the chance to live it through.

There are two important defects in this reasoning. First, it cannot work. Under present political arrangements, the only weapon development it lies in our power to stop is that of our own country, and stopping this could in no way guarantee that World War III would resemble World War II. Second, the small-war philosophy entirely misses the moral point; one war differs from another by not one whit of principle. The effectiveness of the weapons used in a war in no way increases or diminishes the moral guilt of murder.

I am dubious of proposals for instant unilateral disarmament and uncompromising individual pacifism. It seems to me that this country offers the best current approximation to freedom of the individual, under law, that can be found anywhere in our admittedly imperfect world. The status of the individual in our society contrasts markedly with the freedom that the individual is said to enjoy in Russia. I recognize fully that most of the desirable freedoms of the individual would be submerged, even in this country, if we had another war; but I feel that the tradition of their former existence would bring them back, if we had a succeeding peace. Given lasting peace, I am sure that the freedom of the individual would emerge everywhere in the world, under any form of government whatever; because the craving for this freedom is one of the basic human hungers, and our present peaceful technology is so abundant that we can fill even this expensive appetite, if war can be avoided. Even though I am thus convinced that freedom of the individual will appear eventually under any form of government, I am interested in preserving the form that has so far afforded the greatest freedom: our own.

Thus it seems to me deplorable but understandable that this country, while desiring and working toward peace, feels it necessary to be strong in a military sense. I shall be seriously worried about our arms only if we commence to put reliance in them as our guarantee of peace. Armaments are neither designed for this role nor useful in it. So long as we continue in a sincere effort to create a successful world organization by participation in and modification of the United Nations, it is idle to object to our possession of arms in a world of the present sort. Worse, it may be dangerous as well. I am sure that we should be regarded as a nation of lunatics if we engaged today in any thorough unilateral disarmament.

The scientist, on whom so much attention has focused for the past year and a half, is in a difficult position at the present time. Because he wishes to re-establish the traditional internationalism of his profession, he is a Communist. Because he served his country well in the war just past, he is an irresponsible armsmonger, with a childish delight in frightful new technical weapons. Because he is concerned over the damage that an uncritical policy of continued secrecy can do to our scientific and technological progress as a nation — whether for peace or war — he is an idealist who wants to give the bomb to Russia, and he "nauseates" Mr. Baruch.[2] Because some scientists, such as Wiener, are devout pacifists, the scientist is an un-American fellow who cannot be trusted. Because certain other scientists are still working for the Army and Navy, helping to arm our nation in accordance with the overwhelmingly expressed desire of the people of the country, science is the whore of the military. Because, among the perhaps ten thousand scientists and engineers who had contact with the atomic energy project, one has been convicted of a breach of secrecy, scientists are Red spies.

What I am claiming here is that scientists are people like everybody else. In common with all other citizens of the world, they have a heavy responsibility to work toward a world-wide political organization, social philosophy, and public morality that can be adequate to prevent wars between nations. To suggest that the scientist has an outstanding responsibility in terms of this entirely unscientific problem is misleading and harmful, for it encourages the lazy to fob their own responsibility off onto someone else. Wiener, in the name of science, is cheerfully accepting a unique social responsibility, while lasting peace demands that the responsibility be shared by all.

Finally, I reject the defeatist withdrawal from the world as it is, that is implicit in Wiener's letter. The only hope for man today is to work for a better world within the framework of what we have, imperfect as this is. It *can* be improved, and such improvement must arise not from withdrawal, but from intelligent and vigorous participation in existing affairs. Most scientists stand ready to do their part.

[2] Bernard Baruch (1870–1965), American stock broker, presidential adviser, holder of various appointive public offices, and expert in wartime economic mobilization. He was the United States representative to the U.N. Atomic Energy Commission (1946–47), and the American plan ('Baruch' plan) for control of atomic weapons was the subject of much debate in both the U.S. and the U.N.

John Cheever (b. 1912)

AMERICAN NOVELIST and SHORT STORY WRITER

The Enormous Radio

Jim and Irene Westcott were the kind of people who seem to strike that satisfactory average of income, endeavor, and respectability that is reached by the statistical reports in college alumni bulletins. They were the parents of two young children, they had been married nine years, they lived on the twelfth floor of an apartment house near Sutton Place,[1] they went to the theatre on an average of 10.3 times a year, and they hoped someday to live in Westchester. Irene Westcott was a pleasant, rather plain girl with soft brown hair and a wide, fine forehead upon which nothing at all had been written, and in the cold weather she wore a coat of fitch skins dyed to resemble mink. You could not say that Jim Westcott looked younger than he was, but you could at least say of him that he seemed to feel younger. He wore his graying hair cut very short, he dressed in the kind of clothes his class had worn at Andover, and his manner was earnest, vehement, and intentionally naïve. The Westcotts differed from their friends, their classmates, and their neighbors only in an interest they shared in serious music. They went to a great many concerts — although they seldom mentioned this to anyone — and they spent a good deal of time listening to music on the radio.

Their radio was an old instrument, sensitive, unpredictable, and beyond repair. Neither of them understood the mechanics of radio — or of any of the other appliances that surrounded them — and when the instrument faltered, Jim would strike the side of the cabinet with his hand. This sometimes helped. One Sunday afternoon, in the middle of a Schubert quartet, the music faded away altogether. Jim struck the cabinet repeatedly, but there was no response; the Schubert was lost to them forever. He promised to buy Irene a new radio, and on Monday when he came home from work he told her that he had got one. He refused to describe it, and said it would be a surprise for her when it came.

The radio was delivered at the kitchen door the following afternoon, and with the assistance of her maid and the handyman Irene uncrated it and brought it into the living room. She was struck at once with the physical ugliness of the large gumwood cabinet. Irene was proud of her living room, she had chosen its furnishings and colors as carefully as she chose her clothes, and now it seemed to her that the new radio stood among her intimate pos-

[1] a small, upper Manhattan street inhabited by particularly wealthy residents.

sessions like an aggressive intruder. She was confounded by the number of dials and switches on the instrument panel, and she studied them thoroughly before she put the plug into a wall socket and turned the radio on. The dials flooded with a malevolent green light, and in the distance she heard the music of a piano quintet. The quintet was in the distance for only an instant; it bore down upon her with a speed greater than light and filled the apartment with the noise of music amplified so mightily that it knocked a china ornament from a table to the floor. She rushed to the instrument and reduced the volume. The violent forces that were snared in the ugly gumwood cabinet made her uneasy. Her children came home from school then, and she took them to the Park. It was not until later in the afternoon that she was able to return to the radio.

The maid had given the children their suppers and was supervising their baths when Irene turned on the radio, reduced the volume, and sat down to listen to a Mozart quintet that she knew and enjoyed. The music came through clearly. The new instrument had a much purer tone, she thought, than the old one. She decided that tone was most important and that she could conceal the cabinet behind a sofa. But as soon as she had made her peace with the radio, the interference began. A crackling sound like the noise of a burning powder fuse began to accompany the singing of the strings. Beyond the music, there was a rustling that reminded Irene unpleasantly of the sea, and as the quintet progressed, these noises were joined by many others. She tried all the dials and switches but nothing dimmed the interference, and she sat down, disappointed and bewildered, and tried to trace the flight of the melody. The elevator shaft in her building ran beside the living-room wall, and it was the noise of the elevator that gave her a clue to the character of the static. The rattling of the elevator cables and the opening and closing of the elevator doors were reproduced in her loud-speaker, and, realizing that the radio was sensitive to electrical currents of all sorts, she began to discern through the Mozart the ringing of telephone bells, the dialing of phones, and the lamentation of a vacuum cleaner. By listening more carefully, she was able to distinguish doorbells, elevator bells, electric razors, and Waring mixers, whose sounds had been picked up from the apartments that surrounded hers and transmitted through her loudspeaker. The powerful and ugly instrument, with its mistaken sensitivity to discord, was more than she could hope to master, so she turned the thing off and went into the nursery to see her children.

When Jim Westcott came home that night, he went to the radio confidently and worked the controls. He had the same sort of experience Irene had had. A man was speaking on the station Jim had chosen, and his voice swung instantly from the distance into a force so powerful that it shook the apartment. Jim turned the volume control and reduced the voice. Then, a minute or two later, the interference began. The ringing of telephones and doorbells set in, joined by the rasp of the elevator doors and the whir of cooking appliances. The character of the noise had changed since Irene had tried the radio earlier; the last of the electric razors was being unplugged, the vacuum cleaners had all been returned to their closets, and the static reflected that change in pace that overtakes the city after the sun goes down. He fiddled with the knobs but couldn't get rid of the noises, so he turned the radio off and told Irene that in the morning he'd call the people who had sold it to him and give them hell.

The following afternoon, when Irene returned to the apartment from a luncheon date, the maid told her that a man had come and fixed the radio. Irene went into the living room before she took off her hat or her furs and tried the instrument. From the loudspeaker came a recording of the "Missouri Waltz." It reminded her of the thin, scratchy music from an old-fashioned phonograph that she sometimes heard across the lake where she spent her summers. She waited until the waltz had finished, expecting an explanation of the recording, but there was none. The music was followed by silence, and then the plaintive and scratchy record was repeated. She turned the dial and got a satisfactory burst of Caucasian music — the thump of bare feet in the dust and the rattle of coin jewelry — but in the background she could hear the ringing of bells and a confusion of voices. Her children came home from school then, and she turned off the radio and went to the nursery.

When Jim came home that night, he was tired, and he took a bath and changed his clothes. Then he joined Irene in the living room. He had just turned on the radio when the maid announced dinner, so he left it on, and he and Irene went to the table.

Jim was too tired to make even a pretense of sociability, and there was nothing about the dinner to hold Irene's interest, so her attention wandered from the food to the deposits of silver polish on the candlesticks and from there to the music in the other room. She listened for a few moments to a Chopin prelude and then was surprised to hear a man's voice break in. "For Christ's sake, Kathy," he said, "do you always have to play the piano when I get home?" The music stopped abruptly. "It's the only chance I have," a woman said. "I'm at the office all day." "So am I," the man said. He added something obscene about an upright piano, and slammed a door. The passionate and melancholy music began again.

"Did you hear that?" Irene asked.

"What?" Jim was eating his dessert.

"The radio. A man said something while the music was still going on — something dirty."

"It's probably a play."

"I don't think it *is* a play," Irene said.

They left the table and took their coffee into the living room. Irene asked Jim to try another station. He turned the knob. "Have you seen my garters?" a man asked. "Button me up," a woman said. "Have you seen my garters?" the man said again. "Just button me up and I'll find your garters," the woman said. Jim shifted to another station. "I wish you wouldn't leave apple cores in the ashtrays," a man said. "I hate the smell."

"This is strange," Jim said.

"Isn't it?" Irene said.

Jim turned the knob again. " 'On the coast of Coromandel where the early pumpkins blow,' " a woman with a pronounced English accent said, "in the middle of the woods lived the Yonghy-Bonghy-Bò. Two old chairs, and half a candle, one old jug without a handle . . .' "

"My God!" Irene cried. "That's the Sweeney's nurse."

" 'These were all his worldly goods,' " the British voice continued.

"Turn that thing off," Irene said. "Maybe they can hear *us*." Jim switched the radio off. "That was Miss Armstrong, the Sweeneys' nurse," Irene said. "She must be reading to the little girl. They live in 17-B. I've talked with Miss Armstrong in the Park. I know her voice very well. We must be getting other people's apartments."

"That's impossible," Jim said.

"Well, that was the Sweeneys' nurse," Irene said hotly. "I know her voice. I know it very well. I'm wondering if they can hear us."

Jim turned the switch. First from a distance and then nearer, nearer, as if borne on the wind, came the pure accents of the Sweeneys' nurse again: " *'Lady Jingly! Lady Jingly!'* " she said, " *'Sitting where the pumpkins blow, will you come and be my wife, said the Yonghy-Bonghy-Bò . . .'* "

Jim went over to the radio and said "Hello" loudly into the speaker.

" *'I am tired of living singly,'* " the nurse went on, " *'on this coast so wild and shingly, I'm a-weary of my life; if you'll come and be my wife, quite serene would be my life . . .'* "

"I guess she can't hear us," Irene said. "Try something else."

Jim turned to another station, and the living room was filled with the uproar of a cocktail party that had overshot its mark. Someone was playing the piano and singing the Whiffenpoof Song, and the voices that surrounded the piano were vehement and happy. "Eat some more sandwiches," a woman shrieked. There were screams of laughter and a dish of some sort crashed to the floor.

"Those must be the Fullers, in 11-E," Irene said. "I knew they were giving a party this afternoon. I saw her in the liquor store. Isn't this too divine? Try something else. See if you can get those people in 18-C."

The Westcotts overheard that evening a monologue on salmon fishing in Canada, a bridge game, running comments on home movies of what had apparently been a fortnight at Sea Island, and a bitter family quarrel about an overdraft at the bank. They turned off their radio at midnight and went to bed, weak with laughter. Sometime in the night, their son began to call for a glass of water and Irene got one and took it to his room. It was very early. All the lights in the neighborhood were extinguished, and from the boy's window she could see the empty street. She went into the living room and tried the radio. There was some faint coughing, a moan, and then a man spoke. "Are you all right, darling?" he asked. "Yes," a woman said wearily. "Yes, I'm all right, I guess," and then she added with great feeling, "but, you know, Charlie,

I don't feel like myself any more. Sometimes there are about fifteen or twenty minutes in the week when I feel like myself. I don't like to go to another doctor, because the doctor's bills are so awful already, but I just don't feel like myself, Charlie. I just never feel like myself." They were not young, Irene thought. She guessed from the timbre of their voices that they were middle-aged. The restrained melancholy of the dialogue and the draft from the bedroom window made her shiver, and she went back to bed.

The following morning, Irene cooked breakfast for the family — the maid didn't come up from her room in the basement until ten — braided her daughter's hair, and waited at the door until her children and her husband had been carried away in the elevator. Then she went into the living room and tried the radio. "I don't want to go to school," a child screamed. "I hate school. I won't go to school. I hate school." "You will go to school," an enraged woman said. "We paid eight hundred dollars to get you into that school and you'll go if it kills you." The next number on the dial produced the worn record of the "Missouri Waltz." Irene shifted the control and invaded the privacy of several breakfast tables. She overheard demonstrations of indigestion, carnal love, abysmal vanity, faith, and despair. Irene's life was nearly as simple and sheltered as it appeared to be, and the forthright and sometimes brutal language that came from the loudspeaker that morning astonished and troubled her. She continued to listen until her maid came in. Then she turned off the radio quickly, since this insight, she realized, was a furtive one.

Irene had a luncheon date with a friend that day, and she left her apartment at a little after twelve. There were a number of women in the elevator when it stopped at her floor. She stared at their handsome and impassive faces, their furs, and the cloth flowers in their hats. Which one of them had been to Sea Island, she wondered. Which one had overdrawn her bank account? The elevator stopped at the tenth floor and a woman with a pair of Skye terriers joined them. Her hair was rigged high on her head and she wore a mink cape. She was humming the "Missouri Waltz."

Irene had two Martinis at lunch, and she looked searchingly at her friend and wondered what her secrets were. They had intended to go shopping after lunch, but Irene excused herself and went home. She told the maid that she was not to be disturbed; then she went into the living room, closed the doors, and switched on the radio. She heard, in the course of the afternoon, the halting conversation of a woman entertaining her aunt, the hysterical conclusion of a luncheon party, and a hostess briefing her maid about some cocktail guests. "Don't give the best Scotch to anyone who hasn't white hair," the hostess said. "See if you can get rid of that liver paste before you pass those hot things, and could you lend me five dollars? I want to tip the elevator man."

As the afternoon waned, the conversations increased in intensity. From where Irene sat, she could see the open sky above the East River. There were hundreds of clouds in the sky, as though the south wind had broken the winter into pieces and were blowing it north, and on her radio she could hear the arrival of cocktail guests and the return of children and businessmen from their schools and offices. "I found a good-sized diamond on the bathroom floor this morning," a woman said. "It must have fallen out of that bracelet Mrs. Dunston was wearing last night." "We'll sell it," a man said. "Take it down to the jeweller on Madison Avenue and sell it. Mrs. Dunston won't know the difference, and we could use a couple of hundred bucks . . ." " 'Oranges and lemons, say the bells of St. Clement's,' " the Sweeneys' nurse sang. "Half-pence and farthings, say the bells of St. Martin's. When will you pay me? say the bells at old Bailey . . .' " "It's not a hat," a woman cried, and at her back roared a cocktail party. "It's not a hat, it's a love affair. That's what Walter Florell said. He said it's not a hat, it's a love affair," and then, in a lower voice, the same woman added, "Talk to somebody, for Christ's sake, honey, talk to somebody. If she catches you standing here not talking to anybody, she'll take us off her invitation list, and I love these parties."

The Westcotts were going out for dinner that night, and when Jim came home, Irene was dressing. She seemed sad and vague, and he brought her a drink. They were dining with friends in the neighborhood, and they walked to where they were going. The sky was broad and filled with light. It was one of those splendid spring evenings that excite memory and desire, and the air that touched their hands and faces felt very soft. A Salvation Army band was on the corner playing "Jesus Is Sweeter." Irene drew on her husband's arm and held him there for a minute, to hear the music. "They're really such nice people, aren't they?" she said. "They have such nice faces. Actually, they're so much nicer than a lot of the people we know." She took a bill from her purse and walked over and dropped it into the tambourine. There was in her face, when she returned to her husband, a look of radiant melancholy that he was not familiar with. And her conduct at the dinner party that night seemed strange to him, too. She interrupted her hostess rudely and stared at the people across the table from her with an intensity for which she would have punished her children.

It was still mild when they walked home from the party, and Irene looked up at the spring stars. " 'How far that little candle throws its beams,' " she exclaimed. " 'So shines a good deed in a naughty world.' " She waited that night until Jim had fallen asleep, and then went into the living room and turned on the radio.

Jim came home at about six the next night. Emma, the maid, let him in, and he had taken off his hat and was taking off his coat when Irene ran into the hall. Her face was shining with tears and her hair was disordered. "Go up to 16-C, Jim!" she screamed. "Don't take off your coat. Go up to 16-C. Mr. Osborn's beating his wife. They've been quarrelling since four o'clock, and now he's hitting her. Go up there and stop him."

From the radio in the living room, Jim heard screams, obscenities, and thuds. "You know you don't have to listen to this sort of thing," he said. He strode into the living room and turned the switch. "It's indecent," he said. "It's like looking in windows. You know you don't have to listen to this sort of thing. You can turn it off."

"Oh, it's so horrible, it's so dreadful," Irene was sobbing. "I've been listening all day, and it's so depressing."

"Well, if it's so depressing, why do you listen to it? I bought this damned radio to give you some pleasure," he said. "I paid a great deal of money for it. I thought it might make you happy. I wanted to make you happy."

"Don't, don't, don't, don't quarrel with me," she moaned, and laid her head on his shoulder. "All the others have been quarrelling all day. Everybody's been quarrelling. They're all worried about money. Mrs. Hutchinson's mother is dying of cancer in Florida and they don't have enough money to send her to the Mayo Clinic. At least, Mr. Hutchinson says they don't have enough money. And some woman in this building is having an affair with the handyman — with that hideous handyman. It's too disgusting. And Mrs. Melville has heart trouble and Mr. Hendricks is going to lose his job in April and Mrs. Hendricks is horrid about the whole thing and that girl who plays the 'Missouri Waltz' is a whore, a common whore, and the elevator man has tuberculosis and Mr. Osborn has been beating Mrs. Osborn." She wailed, she trembled with grief and checked the stream of tears down her face with the heel of her palm.

"Well, why do you have to listen?" Jim asked again. "Why do you have to listen to this stuff if it makes you so miserable?"

"Oh, don't, don't, don't," she cried. "Life is too terrible, too sordid and awful. But we've never been like that, have we, darling? Have we? I mean we've always been good and decent and loving to one another, haven't we? And we have two children, two beautiful children. Our lives aren't sordid, are they, darling? Are they?" She flung her arms around his neck and drew his face down to hers. "We're happy, aren't we, darling? We are happy, aren't we?"

"Of course we're happy," he said tiredly. He began to surrender his resentment. "Of course we're happy. I'll have that damned radio fixed or taken away tomorrow." He stroked her soft hair. "My poor girl," he said.

"You love me, don't you?" she asked. "And we're not hypocritical or worried about money or dishonest, are we?"

"No, darling," he said.

A man came in the morning and fixed the radio. Irene turned it on cautiously and was happy to hear a California-wine commercial and a recording of Beethoven's Ninth Symphony, including Schiller's "Ode to Joy." She kept the radio on all day and nothing untoward came from the speaker.

A Spanish suite was being played when Jim came home. "Is everything all right?" he asked. His face was pale, she thought. They had some cocktails and went in to dinner to the "Anvil Chorus" from "Il Trovatore." This was followed by Debussy's "La Mer."

"I paid the bill for the radio today," Jim said. "It cost four hundred dollars. I hope you'll get some enjoyment out of it."

"Oh, I'm sure I will," Irene said.

"Four hundred dollars is a good deal more than I can afford," he went on. "I wanted to get something that you'd enjoy. It's the last extravagance we'll be able to indulge in this year. I see that you haven't paid your clothing bills yet. I saw them on your dressing table." He looked directly at her. "Why did you tell me you'd paid them? Why did you lie to me?"

"I just didn't want you to worry, Jim," she said. She drank some water. "I'll be able to pay my bills out of this month's allowance. There were the slipcovers last month, and that party."

"You've got to learn to handle the money I give you a little more intelligently, Irene," he said. "You've got to understand that we won't have as much money this year as we had last. I had a very sobering talk with Mitchell today. No one is buying anything. We're spending all our time promoting new issues, and you know how long that takes. I'm not getting any younger, you know. I'm thirty-seven. My hair will be gray next year. I haven't done as well as I'd hoped to do. And I don't suppose things will get any better."

"Yes, dear," she said.

"We've got to start cutting down," Jim said. "We've got to think of the children. To be perfectly frank with you, I worry about money a great deal. I'm not at all sure of the future. No one is. If anything should happen to me, there's the insurance, but that wouldn't go very far today. I've worked awfully hard to give you and the children a comfortable life," he said bitterly. "I don't like to see all of my energies, all of my youth, wasted in fur coats and radios and slipcovers and — "

"Please, Jim," she said. "Please. They'll hear us."

"*Who'll hear us?* Emma can't hear us."

"The radio."

"Oh, I'm sick!" he shouted. "I'm sick to death of your apprehensiveness. The radio can't hear us. Nobody can hear us. And what if they can hear us? Who cares?"

Irene got up from the table and went into the living room. Jim went to the door and shouted at her from there. "Why are you so Christly all of a sudden? What's turned you overnight into a convent girl? You stole your mother's jewelry before they probated her will. You never gave your sister a cent of that money that was intended for her — not even when she needed it. You made Grace Howland's life miserable, and where was all your piety and your virtue when you went to that abortionist? I'll never forget how cool you were. You packed your bag and went off to have that child murdered as if you were going to Nassau. If you'd had any reasons, if you'd had any good reasons — "

Irene stood for a minute before the hideous cabinet, disgraced and sickened, but she held her hand on the switch before she extinguished the music and the voices, hoping that the instrument might speak to her kindly, that she might hear the Sweeneys' nurse. Jim continued to shout at her from the door. The voice on the radio was suave and noncommittal. "An early-morning railroad disaster in Tokyo," the loudspeaker said, "killed twenty-nine people. A fire in a Catholic hospital near Buffalo for the care of blind children was extinguished early this morning by nuns. The temperature is forty-seven. The humidity is eighty-nine."

John Updike (b. 1932)

AMERICAN POET, NOVELIST, and SHORT STORY WRITER

Vibration

The world vibrates, my sleepless nights
discovered. The air conditioner hummed;
I turned it off. The plumbing
in the next apartment sang;
I moved away, and found a town
whose factories shuddered as they worked
all night. The wires on the poles
outside my windows quivered in an ecstasy
stretched thin between horizons.
I went to where no wires were; and there,   10
as I lay still, a dragon tremor
seized my darkened body, gnawed
my heart, and murmured, *I am you.*

"Vibration" by John Updike. © Copyright 1963 by John Updike. Reprinted from *Telephone Poles and Other Poems*, by John Updike, by permission of Alfred A. Knopf, Inc. Originally appeared in *The New Yorker*.

THE ARTS

*By its original meaning poetry means
simply creation, and creation, as you know,
can take very various forms. Any action
which is the cause of a thing emerging
from non-existence into existence might
be called poetry, and all the processes in all
the crafts are kinds of poetry, and all those
who are engaged in them poets.*

DIOTIMA TO SOCRATES, *Symposium*

THE ARTS today bask in popularity. Many campuses boast writers-in-residence; pop art decorates wastebaskets; and yesterday's trash is today's Tiffany glass or tomorrow's *objet d'art*. Still, the nation spends more money at racetracks than on paintings and grants draft deferments more readily to students of veterinary science than to students of architecture.

Despite our ostensible enthusiasm for the arts, we tend to regard poets, painters, and their products as somewhat suspect. Perhaps we *should* be suspicious of what we have to be taught in school to "appreciate." Perhaps we should enjoy the arts spontaneously, as children do.

Yet to react to the arts with utter spontaneity is to react naively to complex media whose very complexity demands some understanding. Art imposes form and organization upon the apparent haphazardness of nature and life. But by what means? And through what sort of form and organization? Imposing order implies artificiality. An artifact may be a lifeless abstraction, but it can also give us otherwise unobtainable insights into nature and life.

What, then, is the relation of art to reality? How does an artist transform historical data into drama, random sounds into a symphony, wood and stone into a dwelling? Perhaps he should remain faithful to his raw materials and medium, making few changes or none. Or he may wish to take liberties and alter his materials, but if he does, how much of the artist's personality may justifiably remain in his completed work? To what extent is he influenced by his era and milieu? To what extent can and should he be an innovator? What is the most effective source of inspiration: other works of art, the common experiences of life, natural phenomena, the gods — or drugs? Does the artist's intention matter, or his skill, or the amount of effort he expends?

Historically, there have been various definitions of art. Plato believed that art is inspired communication which includes an attempt to reproduce the source of inspiration. Aristotle, replying in the *Poetics* to Plato, maintained that art involves an aesthetic: an ordering, proportioning, and regulating of the experiences and emotions it represents. Others have equated art with inspiration, be it divine, demonic, or terrestrial. The distinction which emerged between inspiration and direction, art and craft, exists today, although the Renaissance attempted to reconcile the two ideas, particularly through Sidney's concept of the "golden world of art."

In the following symposium on the arts, only Plato insists on art as direct, unadorned communication; the other contributors, implicitly or openly, value some artistic shaping of the raw materials. Indeed, much art depends on indirect communication through symbols, a technique that Eisenstein explains and Marianne Moore employs. Susanne Langer considers whether such symbols — and language and art in general — may ever be used, legitimately or unscrupulously, to move or otherwise manipulate an audience.

The arts are seen to have other functions. Wright believes art should accommodate human personalities and experiences. Carroll uses it to entertain and to teach, much as Horace proposes. Grass regards the arts as a vehicle of social and political commentary and criticism. Other contributors to this symposium suggest that art may be used to shock, to reveal, to inspire, to persuade, or even to propagandize.

It is not surprising that conceptions of the relative merits of the arts — of *Tartuffe* or *King Lear*, or of pop or op — vary. For each person who responds to the arts becomes a critic, with his own criteria and his own notion of the functions of criticism. Criticism is valid only to the extent that one medium or technique can be discussed in terms of another; whether or not one can ever *write* meaningfully about music or verbally dissect a symbol is a matter of individual judgment. Moreover, criticism is valid only to the extent that the critic's personal responses and tastes can be depersonalized, made general and meaningful to the tastes of others. Yet the fundamental issue remains: has anyone at all the right to brand some work of art "good" or "bad," and to expect others to accept his judgment?

These issues are relevant even if we are neither artists nor critics, for the arts continually impinge on our daily existence — from the style of our clothes, to the mode of our worship, to the choice of what we read and say of the movies or music we claim to enjoy. Consequently, we need to satisfy ourselves with answers to at least some of these questions in order to define the basis for our own tastes. The points of view which follow provide a means to some of the answers. The arts, rather than being apart from life, are a part of life; and in responding to them we see ourselves and our world with a greater degree of clarity and compassion.

Plato (c. 427–c. 347 B.C.)

GREEK PHILOSOPHER

Art and Truth

Indeed, I continued,[1] our commonwealth has many features which make me think it was based on very sound principles, especially our rule not on any account to admit the poetry of dramatic representation. Now that we have distinguished the several parts of the soul, it seems to me clearer than ever that such poetry must be firmly excluded.

What makes you say so?

Between ourselves — for you will not denounce me to the tragedians and the other dramatists — poetry of that sort seems to be injurious to minds which do not possess the antidote in a knowledge of its real nature.

What have you in mind?

I must speak out, in spite of a certain affection and reverence I have had from a child for Homer, who seems to have been the original master and guide of all this imposing company of tragic poets.[2] However, no man must be honoured above the truth; so, as I say, I must speak my mind.

Do, by all means.

Listen then, or rather let me ask you a question. Can you tell me what is meant by representation in general? I have no very clear notion myself.

So you expect me to have one!

Why not? It is not always the keenest eye that is the first to see something.

True; but when you are there I should not be very desirous to tell what I saw, however plainly. You must use your own eyes.

Well then, shall we proceed as usual and begin by assuming the existence of a single essential nature or Form for every set of things which we call by the same name? Do you understand?

I do.

Then let us take any set of things you choose. For instance there are any number of beds or of tables, but only two Forms, one of Bed and one of Table.

Yes.

And we are in the habit of saying that the craftsman, when he makes the beds or tables we use or whatever it may be, has before his mind the Form[3]

---

[1] Socrates is addressing his pupil Glaucon.

[2] The plots of Greek tragedy were normally stories borrowed from epic poetry. Hence Homer was spoken of as the first tragic poet. [Cornford]

[3] "Form" does not mean "shape," but the essential properties which constitute what the thing, by definition, is. [Cornford]

Title supplied by editors. From *The Republic of Plato*, translated by **F. M. Cornford.** First American edition, 1945. Reprinted by permission of Oxford University Press.

of one or other of these pieces of furniture. The Form itself is, of course, not the work of any craftsman. How could it be?

It could not.

Now what name would you give to a craftsman who can produce all the things made by every sort of workman?

He would need to have very remarkable powers!

Wait a moment, and you will have even better reason to say so. For, besides producing any kind of artificial thing, this same craftsman can create all plants and animals, himself included, and earth and sky and gods and the heavenly bodies and all the things under the earth in Hades.

That sounds like a miraculous feat of virtuosity.

Are you incredulous? Tell me, do you think there could be no such craftsman at all, or that there might be someone who could create all these things in one sense, though not in another? Do you not see that you could do it yourself, in a way?

In what way, I should like to know.

There is no difficulty; in fact there are several ways in which the thing can be done quite quickly. The quickest perhaps would be to take a mirror and turn it round in all directions. In a very short time you could produce sun and stars and earth and yourself and all the other animals and plants and lifeless objects which we mentioned just now.

Yes, in appearance, but not the actual things.

Quite so; you are helping out my argument. My notion is that a painter is a craftsman of that kind. You may say that the things he produces are not real; but there is a sense in which he too does produce a bed.

Yes, the appearance of one.

And what of the carpenter? Were you not saying just now that he only makes a particular bed, not what we call the Form or essential nature of Bed?

Yes, I was.

If so, what he makes is not the reality, but only something that resembles it. It would not be right to call the work of a carpenter or of any other handicraftsman a perfectly real thing, would it?

Not in the view of people accustomed to thinking on these lines.[4]

We must not be surprised, then, if even an actual bed is a somewhat shadowy thing as compared with reality.

True.

Now shall we make use of this example to throw light on our question as to the true nature of this artist who represents things? We have here three sorts of bed: one which exists in the nature of things and which, I imagine, we could only describe as a product of divine workmanship; another made by the carpenter; and a third by the painter. So the three kinds of bed belong respectively to the domains of these three: painter, carpenter, and god.

---

[4] Familiar with the Platonic doctrine, as opposed to current materialism, which regards the beds we sleep on as real things and the Platonic Form as a mere 'abstraction' or notion existing only in our minds. [Cornford]

Yes.

Now the god made only one ideal or essential Bed, whether by choice or because he was under some necessity not to make more than one; at any rate two or more were not created, or could they possibly come into being.

Why not?

Because, if he made even so many as two, then once more a single ideal Bed would make its appearance, whose character those two would share; and that one, not the two, would be the essential Bed. Knowing this, the god, wishing to be the real maker of a real Bed, not a particular manufacturer of one particular bed, created one which is essentially unique.

So it appears.

Shall we call him, then, the author of the true nature of Bed, or something of that sort?

Certainly he deserves the name, since all his works constitute the real nature of things.

And we may call the carpenter the manufacturer of a bed?

Yes.

Can we say the same of the painter?

Certainly not.

Then what is he, with reference to a bed?

I think it would be fairest to describe him as the artist who represents the things which the other two make.

Very well, said I; so the work of the artist is at the third remove from the essential nature of the thing?

Exactly.

The tragic poet, too, is an artist who represents things; so this will apply to him: he and all other artists are, as it were, third in succession from the throne of truth.

Just so.

We are in agreement, then, about the artist. But now tell me about our painter: which do you think he is trying to represent — the reality that exists in the nature of things, or the products of the craftsman?

The products of the craftsman.

As they are, or as they appear? You have still to draw that distinction.

How do you mean?

I mean: you may look at a bed or any other object from straight in front or slantwise or at any angle. Is there then any difference in the bed itself, or does it merely look different?

It only looks different.

Well, that is the point. Does painting aim at reproducing any actual object as it is, or the appearance of it as it looks? In other words, is it a representation of the truth or of a semblance?

Of a semblance.

The art of representation, then, is a long way from reality; and apparently the reason why there is nothing it cannot reproduce is that it grasps only a small part of any object, and that only an image. Your painter, for example, will paint us a shoemaker, a carpenter, or other workman, without understanding any one of their crafts; and yet, if he were a good painter, he might deceive a child or a simple-minded person into thinking his picture was a real carpenter, if he showed it them at some distance.

No doubt.

But I think there is one view we should take in all such cases. Whenever someone announces that he has met with a person who is master of every trade and knows more about every subject than any specialist, we should reply that he is a simple fellow who has apparently fallen in with some illusionist and been tricked into thinking him omniscient, because of his own inability to discriminate between knowledge and ignorance and the representation of appearances.

Quite true.

Then it is now time to consider the tragic poets and their master, Homer, because we are sometimes told that they understand not only all technical matters but also all about human conduct, good or bad, and about religion; for, to write well, a good poet, so they say, must know his subject; otherwise he could not write about it. We must ask whether these people have not been deluded by meeting with artists who can represent appearances, and in contemplating the poets' work have failed to see that it is at the third remove from reality, nothing more than semblances, easy to produce with no knowledge of the truth. Or is there something in what they say? Have the good poets a real mastery of the matters on which the public thinks they discourse so well?

It is a question we ought to look into.

Well then, if a man were able actually to do the things he represents as well as to produce images of them, do you believe he would seriously give himself up to making these images and take that as a completely satisfying object in life? I should imagine that, if he had a real understanding of the actions he represents, he would far sooner devote himself to performing them in fact. The memorials he would try to leave after him would be noble deeds, and he would be more eager to be the hero whose praises are sung than the poet who sings them.

Yes, I agree; he would do more good in that way and win a greater name.

Here is a question, then, that we may fairly put to Homer or to any other poet. We will leave out of account all mere matters of technical skill: we will not ask them to explain, for instance, why it is that, if they have a knowledge of medicine and not merely the art of reproducing the way physicians talk, there is no record of any poet, ancient or modern, curing patients and bequeathing his knowledge to a school of medicine, as Asclepius[5] did. But when Homer undertakes to tell us about matters of the highest importance, such as the conduct of war, statesmanship, or education, we have a right to

[5] Greek god of healing; he was originally a mortal who was elevated to divinity.

inquire into his competence. 'Dear Homer,' we shall say, 'we have defined the artist as one who produces images at the third remove from reality. If your knowledge of all that concerns human excellence was really such as to raise you above him to the second rank, and you could tell what courses of conduct will make men better or worse as individuals or as citizens, can you name any country which was better governed thanks to your efforts? Many states, great and small, have owed much to a good lawgiver, such as Lycurgus at Sparta, Charondas in Italy and Sicily, and our own Solon.[6] Can you tell us of any that acknowledges a like debt to you?'

I should say not, Glaucon replied. The most devout admirers of Homer make no such claim.

Well, do we hear of any war in Homer's day being won under his command or thanks to his advice?

No.

Or of a number of ingenious inventions and technical contrivances, which would show that he was a man of practical ability like Thales of Miletus or Anacharsis the Scythian?[7]

Nothing of the sort.

Well, if there is no mention of public services, do we hear of Homer in his own lifetime presiding, like Pythagoras, over a band of intimate disciples who loved him for the inspiration of his society and handed down a Homeric way of life, like the way of life which the Pythagoreans called after their founder and which to this day distinguishes them from the rest of the world?

No; on the contrary, Homer's friend with the absurd name, Creophlyus,[8] would look even more absurd when considered as a product of the poet's training, if the story is true that he completely neglected Homer during his lifetime.

Yes, so they say. But what do you think, Glaucon? If Homer had really possessed the knowledge qualifying him to educate people and make them better men, instead of merely giving us a poetical representation of such matters, would he not have attracted a host of disciples to love and revere him? After all, any number of private teachers like Protagoras of Abdera and Prodicus of Ceos[9] have succeeded in convincing their contemporaries that they will never be fit to manage affairs of state or their own households unless these masters superintend their education; and for this wisdom they are so pas-

---

[6] Lycurgus (c. 9th century B.C.) was the traditional founder of the Spartan constitution; Charondas (c. 5th century B.C.) was the lawgiver of his native town, Catana; and Solon (638?–?559 B.C.) was an Athenian statesman who reformed the constitution to give all citizens some share in the government.

[7] Thales (early sixth cent.) made a fortune out of a corner in oil-mills when his knowledge of the stars enabled him to predict a large olive harvest, thus proving that wise men could be rich if they chose (Aristotle, *Politics*, i, 11). Anacharsis was said to have invented the anchor and the potter's wheel (Diogenes, Laertes, i. 105). [Cornford]

[8] Creophylus' name is supposed to be derived from two words meaning 'flesh' and 'tribe.' He is said to have been an epic poet from Chios. [Cornford]

[9] Two of the most famous Sophists of the fifth century. Plato's *Protagoras* gives a vivid picture of them on a visit to a rich patron at Athens. [Cornford]

sionately admired that their pupils are all but ready to carry them about on their shoulders. Can we suppose that Homer's contemporaries, or Hesiod's,[10] would have left them to wander about reciting their poems, if they had really been capable of helping their hearers to be better men? Surely they would sooner have parted with their money and tried to make the poets settle down at home; or failing that, they would have danced attendance on them wherever they went, until they had learnt from them all they could.

I believe you are quite right, Socrates.

We may conclude, then, that all poetry, from Homer onwards, consists in representing a semblance of its subject, whatever it may be, including any kind of human excellence, with no grasp of the reality. We were speaking just now of the painter who can produce what looks like a shoemaker to the spectator who, being as ignorant of shoemaking as he is himself, judges only by form and colour. In the same way the poet, knowing nothing more than how to represent appearances, can paint in words his picture of any craftsman so as to impress an audience which is equally ignorant and judges only by the form of expression; the inherent charm of metre, rhythm, and musical setting is enough to make them think he has discoursed admirably about generalship or shoemaking or any other technical subject. Strip what the poet has to say of its poetical colouring, and I think you must have seen what it comes to in plain prose. It is like a face which was never really handsome, when it has lost the fresh bloom of youth.

Quite so.

Here is a further point, then. The artist, we say, this maker of images, knows nothing of the reality, but only the appearance. But that is only half the story. An artist can paint a bit and bridle, while the smith and the leatherworker can make them. Does the painter understand the proper form which bit and bridle ought to have? Is it not rather true that not even the craftsmen who make them know that, but only the horseman who understands their use?

Quite true.

May we not say generally that there are three arts concerned with any object — the art of using it, the art of making it, and the art of representing it?

Yes.

And that the excellence or beauty or rightness of any implement or living creature or action has reference to the use for which it is made or designed by nature?

Yes.

It follows, then, that the user must know most about the performance of the thing he uses and must report on its good or bad points to the maker. The flute-player, for example, will tell the instrument-maker how well his flutes serve the player's purpose, and the other will submit to be instructed about how they should be made. So the man who uses any implement will

[10] (c. 8th century B.C.); author of *The Works and Days*, a series of moral admonitions in verse, and the *Theogony*, which recounts the story of Zeus' assumption of the kingship of the gods.

speak of its merits and defects with knowledge, whereas the maker will take his word and possess no more than a correct belief, which he is obliged to obtain by listening to the man who knows.

Quite so.

But what of the artist? Has he either knowledge or correct belief? Does he know from direct experience of the subjects he portrays whether his representations are good and right or not? Has he even gained a correct belief by being obliged to listen to someone who does know and can tell him how they ought to be represented?

No, he has neither.

If the artist, then, has neither knowledge nor even a correct belief about the soundness of his work, what becomes of the poet's wisdom in respect of the subjects of his poetry?

It will not amount to much.

And yet he will go on with his work, without knowing in what way any of his representations is sound or unsound. He must, apparently, be reproducing only what pleases the taste or wins the approval of the ignorant multitude.

Yes, what else can he do?

We seem, then, so far to be pretty well agreed that the artist knows nothing worth mentioning about the subjects he represents, and that art is a form of play, not to be taken seriously. This description, moreover, applies above all to tragic poetry, whether in epic or dramatic form.

Exactly.

Aristotle (384–322 B.C.)

GREEK PHILOSOPHER, SCIENTIST, and PHYSICIAN

The Essence of Drama

The Origins of Poetry

In general, two causes, both inherent in man's nature, seem to have led to the birth of poetry. Imitation is natural to man from childhood; he differs from the other animals in that he is the most imitative: the first things he learns come to him through imitation. Then, too, all men take pleasure in imitative representations. Actual experience gives proof of this: the sight of

Title supplied by editors. From the *Poetics* in Aristotle: *On Poetry and Style*, translated by G. M. A. Grube, copyright ©, 1958, by The Liberal Arts Press, Inc., reprinted by permission of the Liberal Arts Press Division of The Bobbs-Merrill Company, Inc.

certain things gives us pain, but we enjoy looking at the most exact images of them, whether the forms of animals which we greatly despise or of corpses. The reason is that learning things is most enjoyable, not only for philosophers but for others equally, though they have but little experience of it. Hence they enjoy the sight of images because they learn as they look; they reason what each image is, that there, for example, is that man whom we know. If a man does not know the original, the imitation as such gives him no pleasure; his pleasure is then derived from its workmanship, its color, or some similar reason.

Next, imitation and melody and rhythm are ours by nature (meter being clearly a part of rhythm); so men were naturally gifted from the beginning, and, progressing step by step, they created poetry out of their random utterances.

Poetry developed in different ways according to men's characters. The more serious-minded imitated the noble deeds of noble men; the more common imitated the actions of meaner men; the latter wrote satiric verse while the former wrote hymns and encomia. We cannot mention any satiric work before Homer, though there were probably many, but we can begin with his *Margites*[1] and other things of the kind. The iambic meter was introduced because it was particularly suitable to this type of poetry, and such a poem is called *iambeion* to this day, because men used to satirize each other in this meter. . . .

Tragedy first arose without deliberate intent, as did comedy also. The former originated with the leaders of the dithyramb, the latter with the leaders of the phallic songs[2] which even today remain customary in many cities. Tragedy developed little by little as men improved whatever part of it became distinct. Many changes were introduced into tragedy, but these ceased when it found its true nature. Aeschylus with the first to introduce a second actor; he also made the chorus less important and gave first place to the spoken parts. Sophocles added both a third actor and painted scenery. It is only at a late date that short incidents and the language of ridicule developed in length and dignity as the satyr-play changed into tragedy. The iambic trimeter replaced the trochaic tetrameter which had been used at first because the poetry was then satyric[3] and more closely related to the dance.

When spoken parts came in, nature herself found the appropriate meter, as the iambic is of all meters most like ordinary speech. This is proved by the fact that iambic lines occur most frequently in ordinary conversation, whereas hexameters occur but rarely, and then only when we abandon conversational

---

[1] "The Booby;" a Greek comic poem with a fool for a hero.
[2] songs at fertility rites for Dionysius or the daimon (spirit or lesser god) Phales, a personification of the phallus.
[3] Satyric poetry is that of the satyr-play previously mentioned, which usually had a chorus of satyrs, and has nothing to do with satire. [Grube]

cadences. As for the number of *epeisodia*[4] and the way the other features of tragedy are said to have been elaborated, let us consider these also to have been dealt with, for to discuss them one by one would surely be a lengthy task.

回

The History of Comedy

Comedy is, as we said, an imitation of men who are inferior but not altogether vicious. The ludicrous is a species of ugliness; it is a sort of flaw and ugliness which is not painful or injurious. An obvious example is the comic mask, ugly and twisted but not painful to look at.

We know how tragedy changed and who made the changes, but comedy was not seriously pursued at first and its development is obscure. Only in more recent times was comedy produced at public expense;[5] before that it was performed by volunteers, and its various forms had developed before the time of those who are called comic writers and are remembered. We do not know who introduced the masks, the prologues, the several actors and the rest. Comic plots originated in Sicily (Epicharmus and Phormis), while at Athens it was Crates[6] who first abandoned the lampoon to write comic works with stories and plots of general interest.

Epic and Tragedy: Unity of Time

Epic poetry resembles tragedy in so far as it is an imitation in verse of what is morally worthy; they differ in that the epic has only one meter and is narrative in form. They also differ in length, for tragedy tries to confine itself, as much as possible, within one revolution of the sun or a little more, whereas the time of an epic is unlimited. This, however, was at first true also of tragedy.[7]

Some parts are common to both; others are peculiar to tragedy. It follows that anyone who knows good tragedy from bad also knows about the epic, as the elements of the epic are present in tragedy, though not all the elements of tragedy are to be found in the epic.

回

[4] An *epeisodion* is any part of a tragedy which stands between two choral odes. We may translate it by "act" as the nearest equivalent. [Grube]
[5] Greek dramas were performed at public festivals in the public theater, with chorus and actors equipped at public expense. [Grube, abridged]
[6] Epicharmus was a Greek comic poet (c. 540 B.C.) from whom Plato allegedly learned dialogue; Phormis, a Syracusan comic poet (5th century B.C.), wrote on historio-mythological plots; Crates, a Greek comic poet (5th century B.C.), was characterized by Aristotle as a neat, finished writer drawing on limited resources.
[7] This is the only reference in the *Poetics* to the famous "unity of time." It is not a precept. Aristotle simply recognizes the fact that "as far as possible" tragedy "tries" to restrict itself to one day. To unity of place there is no reference at all. He does insist on unity of action. [Grube, abridged]

The Definition of Tragedy

Epic poetry and comedy will be discussed later. Let us now take up the definition of tragedy which emerges from what has been said. Tragedy, then, is the imitation of a good action, which is complete and of a certain length, by means of language made pleasing for each part separately; it relies in its various elements not on narrative but on acting; through pity and fear[8] it achieves the purgation (catharsis) of such emotions.

By "language made pleasing" I mean language which has rhythm, melody, and music. By "separately for the parts" I mean that some parts use only meter while others also have music. And as it is through acting that the poets present their imitation, one first and necessary element of a tragedy is the arranging of the spectacle. Then come music and diction, for these are the means used in the imitation. By diction I mean the actual composition of the verses, while the effect of music is clear to all.

The Six Elements or Aspects of Tragedy

Since it is an action which is imitated, it is performed by persons who must have qualities of character and mind, and from them we transfer these predicates to the actions also. Character and thought are the two natural causes of action; through actions men succeed or fail. The imitation of the action is the plot, for this is what I mean by plot, namely, the arrangement of the incidents. Character, on the other hand, is that which leads us to attribute certain qualities to the persons who act. Thought is present in all they say to prove a point or to express an opinion. Every tragedy, therefore, has these six necessary elements which make it what it is: plot, character, diction, thought, spectacle, and music. Two of these elements are the means of imitation, one is the manner, three belong to the objects imitated,[9] and besides these there are no others. We may say that most poets use these elements; every tragedy, in much the same manner, has spectacle, character, plot, diction, music, and thought.

Plot and Character

The most important of these is the arrangement of incidents, for tragedy is an imitation, not of men but of action and life, of happiness and misfortune. These are to be found in action, and the goal of life is a certain kind of activity, not a quality. Men are what they are because of their characters, but it is in action that they find happiness or the reverse. The purpose of

[8] The exact meaning of *phobos* lies probably somewhere between "fear" and "terror." [Grube, abridged]

[9] Clearly, music and diction (language) are the means of imitation; the three elements which belong to the model are the plot, character, and thought. Spectacle belongs to the manner of imitation. [Grube, abridged]

action on the stage is not to imitate character, but character is a by-product of the action. It follows that the incidents and the plot are the end which tragedy has in view, and the end is in all things the most important. Without action there could be no tragedy, whereas a tragedy without characterization is possible.

The tragedies of most of our recent poets have no characterization and, generally speaking, there are many such poets. This is the difference, among painters, between Zeuxis and Polygnotus, for Polygnotus expresses character very well, while Zeuxis does not express it at all.[10] Moreover, a series of speeches expressing character, well written and well thought-out though they might be, would not fulfill the essential function of a tragedy; this would be better achieved by a play which had a plot and structure of incidents, even though deficient in respect to character. Besides, the most important means by which a tragedy stirs the emotions reside in the plot, namely Reversals and Recognitions. Another argument is that those who begin to write poetry attain mastery in diction and characterization before they attain it in plot structure. Nearly all our early poets are examples of this.

The plot is the first essential and the soul of a tragedy; character comes second. Pretty much the same is true of painting: the most beautiful colors, laid on at random, give less pleasure than a black-and-white drawing. It is the action which is the object of the imitation; the individual characters are subsidiary to it.

Thought and Character

Thought is the third element in tragedy. It is the capacity to express what is involved in, or suitable to, a situation. In prose this is the function of statesmanship and rhetoric. Earlier writers made their characters speak like statesmen; our contemporaries make them speak like rhetoricians. A person's character makes clear what course of action he will choose or reject where this is not clear. Speeches, therefore, which do not make this choice clear, or in which the speaker does not choose or reject any course of action at all, do not express character. Thought comes in where something is proved or disproved, or where some general opinion is expressed.

Diction, Music, Spectacle

Diction is the fourth of the elements we mentioned. By diction I mean, as I said before, the use of words to express one's meaning. Its function is the same in verse and prose. Of the remaining elements, music is most important among the features of tragedy which give pleasure. As for the spectacle, it stirs the emotions, but it is less a matter of art than the others, and

---

[10] Polygnotus (5th century B.C.), considered the first great painter, represented men of high moral purpose; Zeuxis' art (later 5th century B.C.) was less moral and technically more sophisticated.

has least to do with poetry, for a tragedy can achieve its effect even apart from the performance and the actors. Indeed, spectacular effects belong to the craft of the property man[11] rather than to that of the poet.

◫

Plot: Beginning, Middle, and End

Having now defined these elements, our next point is what the plot structure should be, as this is the first and most important part of a tragedy. We have established that a tragedy is the imitation of an action which is whole and complete, and also of a certain length, for a thing can be whole without being of any particular size. "Whole" means having a beginning, a middle, and an end. The beginning, while not necessarily following something else, is, by definition, followed by something else. The end, on the contrary, follows something else by definition, either always or in most cases, but nothing else comes after it. The middle both itself follows something else and is followed by something else. To construct a good plot, one must neither begin nor end haphazardly but make a proper use of these three parts.

Size or Length

However, an animal, or indeed anything which has parts, must, to be beautiful, not only have these parts in the right order but must also be of a definite size. Beauty is a matter of size and order. An extraordinarily small animal would not be beautiful, nor an extraordinarily large one. Our view of the first is confused because it occupies only an all but imperceptible time, while we cannot view the second all at once, so that the unity of the whole would escape us if, for example, it were a thousand miles long. It follows that, as bodies and animals must have a size that can easily be perceived as a whole, so plots must have a length which can easily be remembered. However, the limit set to length by the circumstances of the dramatic presentation or by the perceptive capacity of the audience is not a matter of dramatic art. If a hundred tragedies were competing at once, the poets would compete with their eye on the water clock, and this they say happened at one time. What is a matter of art is the limit set by the very nature of the action, namely, that the longer is always the more beautiful, provided that the unity of the whole is clearly perceived. A simple and sufficient definition is: such length as will allow a sequence of events to result in a change from bad to good fortune or from good fortune to bad in accordance with what is probable or inevitable.

◫

Unity of Plot

A story does not achieve unity, as some people think, merely by being about one person. Many things, indeed an infinite number of things, happen to the

[11] The best modern equivalent is probably "the producer." [Grube, abridged]

same individual, some of which have no unity at all. In the same way one individual performs many actions which do not combine into one action. . . . As in other kinds of imitative art each imitation must have one object, so with the plot: since it is the imitation of an action, this must be one action and the whole of it; the various incidents must be so constructed that, if any part is displaced or deleted, the whole plot is disturbed and dislocated. For if any part can be inserted or omitted without manifest alteration, it is no true part of the whole.

罔

Tragedy and History[12]

It also follows from what has been said that it is not the poet's business to relate actual events, but such things as might or could happen in accordance with probability or necessity. A poet differs from a historian, not because one writes verse and the other prose (the work of Herodotus[13] could be put into verse, but it would still remain a history, whether in verse or prose), but because the historian relates what happened, the poet what might happen. That is why poetry is more akin to philosophy and is a better thing than history; poetry deals with general truths, history with specific events. The latter are, for example, what Alcibiades[14] did or suffered, while general truths are the kind of thing which a certain type of person would probably or inevitably do or say. Poetry aims to do this by its choice of names; this is clearly seen in comedy, for when the writers of comedy have constructed their plots in accordance with probability, they give their characters typical names, nor are they, like the writers of iambic lampoons, concerned with a particular individual.

Names of Characters: Traditional Legends

The tragedians cling to the names of historical persons. The reason is that what is possible is convincing, and we are apt to distrust what has not yet happened as not possible, whereas what has happened is obviously possible, else it could not have happened. However, there are tragedies which use only one or two of the well-known names, the others being fictitious. . . . It is not, therefore, absolutely necessary to cling to the traditional stories which are the usual subjects of tragedy. In fact, it is absurd to strive to do so, for even the familiar stories are familiar only to a few, yet are enjoyed by all. All this shows that it is the plot, rather than the verse, which makes a (tragic) poet, for he is a poet in virtue of his imitation, and he imitates actions. He is no less a poet if he happens to tell a true story, for nothing prevents some actual events from being probable or possible, and it is this probability or possibility that makes the (tragic) poet. . . .

[12] Aristotle fails to distinguish history from chronicle. [Grube, modified]
[13] Greek historian (5th century B.C.), who wrote with great charm, wit, and literary skill.
[14] Athenian general and statesman (c. 450–404 B.C.).

Types of Plots

The episodic are the worst of all plots and actions; and by an episodic plot I mean one in which the episodes have no probable or inevitable connection. Poor poets compose such plots through lack of talent, good poets do it to please the actors. As they write in competition and stretch the plot too far, they are thereby compelled to distort the sequence of events.

The object of the imitation is not only a complete action but such things as stir up pity and fear, and this is best achieved when the events are unexpectedly interconnected. This, more than what happens accidentally and by chance, will arouse wonder. Even chance events arouse most wonder when they have the appearance of purpose, as in the story of the man who was responsible for the death of Mitys and was watching a festival at Argos when the statue of his victim fell upon him and killed him. Things like that do not seem to happen without purpose, and plots of this kind are necessarily better.

Simple and Complex Plots

Some plots are simple, others are complex, just as the actions which they imitate are clearly one or the other. I call simple an action which is one and continuous, as defined above, and in the course of which the change of fortune occurs without recognition or reversal. A complex action is one wherein the change of fortune is accompanied either by recognition or reversal, or by both. These must emerge from the plot structure itself so that they are connected with what has gone before as the inevitable or probable outcome. It makes all the difference whether one incident is caused by another or merely follows it.

Reversals and Recognitions

Reversal (*peripeteia*) is a change of the situation into its opposite, and this too must accord with the probable or the inevitable. So in the *Oedipus* the man comes to cheer Oedipus and to rid him of his fear concerning his mother; then, by showing him who he is, he does the opposite; also in the *Lynceus* the hero is brought in to die and Danaus follows, intending to kill him, but in the event it is Danaus who dies and the other who is saved.

Recognition (*anagnorisis*), as the names implies, is a change from ignorance to knowledge of a bond of love or hate between persons who are destined for good fortune or the reverse. The finest kind of recognition is accompanied by simultaneous reversals, as in the *Oedipus*. There are, to be sure, other forms of recognition: the knowledge acquired may be of inanimate objects, indeed of anything; one may recognize that someone has, or has not, done something. But the recognition which is most fully part of the plot and of the action is the kind we noted first. This kind of recognition and reversal will evoke pity or fear. Tragedy is the imitation of such actions, and good or ill fortune results from them.

This recognition is between persons. Sometimes the identity of one person is known, and then only one person is recognized by the other; at other times both have to be recognized, as when Iphigenia is recognized by Orestes as soon as she sends the letter, but another recognition scene is necessary for her to recognize Orestes.[15]

These things, reversal and recognition, are two parts of the plot. A third is suffering. We have discussed two of the three, namely reversal and recognition. Suffering (*pathos*) is a fatal or painful action like death on the stage, violent physical pain, wounds, and everything of that kind.

卐

The Sections of a Tragedy

We have previously mentioned the parts of tragedy in the sense of its qualitative parts. The quantitative sections, on the other hand, into which a tragedy is divided are the following: *prologos, epeisodion, exodus,* and the choral part, itself subdivided into *parodos* and *stasima.* These occur in all tragedies; there may also be actors' songs and *kommoi.*

The *prologos* is that whole section which precedes the entrance of the chorus; the *epeisodion* is a whole section between complete choral odes; the *exodos* is that whole section of a tragedy which is not followed by a choral ode. In the choral part, the entrance song (*parados*) is the first complete statement of the chorus, a *stasimon* is a song of the chorus without anapaests or trochees; a *kommos* is a dirge in which actors and chorus join.

We spoke previously of the parts which must be considered as qualitative elements of tragedy; these are the quantitative parts.

卐

Possible Changes of Fortune

We must discuss next what a writer should aim at and what he should avoid in constructing his plot, how tragedy will come to fulfill its proper function. As already stated, the plot of the finest tragedies must not be simple but complex;[16] it must also represent what is fearful or pitiful, as this is characteristic of tragic imitation. It clearly follows that, in the first place, good men must not be seen suffering a change from prosperity to misfortune; this is not fearful or pitiful but shocking. Nor must the wicked pass from

[15] The incident is from Euripides' *Iphigenia in Tauris* when Iphigenia, rescued from death by her father's hand, is reunited with her brother Orestes through the intervention of Apollo and Artemis.
[16] Complex plots have reversal and recognition. [Grube, abridged]

misfortune to prosperity; this, of all things, is the least tragic; nothing happens as it should, it is neither humane nor fearful nor pitiful. A thoroughly wicked man must not pass from prosperity to misfortune either; such a plot may satisfy our feeling of humanity, but it does not arouse pity or fear. We feel pity for a man who does not deserve his misfortune; we fear for someone like ourselves; neither feeling is here involved.

The Tragic Character

We are left with a character in between the other two; a man who is neither outstanding in virtue and righteousness, nor is it through wickedness and vice that he falls into misfortune, but through some flaw.[17] He should also be famous or prosperous, like Oedipus, Thyestes,[18] and the noted men of such noble families.

The Best Plots

A good plot must consist of a single and not, as some people say, of a double story; the change of fortune should not be from misfortune to prosperity but, on the contrary, from prosperity to misfortune. This change should not be caused by outright wickedness but by a serious flaw in a character such as we have just described, or one better rather than worse. This is proved by what has happened: at first tragic poets related any kind of story, but now the best tragedies are constructed around the fortunes of a few families, and are concerned with Alcmaeon, Oedipus, Orestes, Meleager, Thyestes, Telephus, and any other such men who have endured or done terrible things. The best products of the tragic art have this kind of plot structure.

People are therefore mistaken when they criticize Euripides on this very point, because his tragedies are of this kind and many of them end unhappily, for this, as I said, is right. There is convincing proof of this; in the theater and in dramatic contests such dramas are seen to be the most tragic if they are well performed, and even though Euripides manages his plays badly in other respects, he obviously is the most tragic of the poets.

The Double Plot of Comedy

The double plot, such as we find in the Odyssey, where, at the end, the good are rewarded and the bad punished, is thought by some to be the best, but in fact it holds only second place. It is the weakness of our audiences that places it first, and the poets seek to please the spectators. The pleasure

---

[17] The "flaw" is a moral or intellectual weakness. [Grube]

[18] the brother of Atreus, who was Agamemnon's father, and King of Mycenae. The two brothers quarreled, and Atreus, having banished Thyestes, then pretended to be reconciled with him and served him the flesh of his own children at a banquet. Thyestes' son Aegisthus later revenged his father by inciting Agamemnon's wife, Clytemnestra, to kill her husband.

provided in this way, however, belongs to comedy rather than to tragedy: it is in comedy that those who, in the story, are the greatest enemies, like Orestes and Aegisthus, are reconciled in the end, walk off the stage as friends, and no one kills anybody.

卍

Pity and Fear should be due to Plot, not to Spectacle

Fear and pity can be caused by the spectacle or by the plot structure itself. The latter way is better and argues a better poet. The story should be so constructed that the events make anyone who hears the story shudder and feel pity even without seeing the play. The story of Oedipus has this effect. To arouse pity and fear by means of the spectacle requires less art and a costly performance. And those plays which, by means of the spectacle, arouse not fear but only amazement have nothing in common with tragedy. We should not require from tragedy every kind of pleasure, but only its own peculiar kind.

The Tragic Situation

As the tragic poet must aim to produce by his imitation the kind of pleasure which results from fear and pity, he must do so through the plot. We must therefore investigate what sort of incidents are terrible or pitiful. Such actions must necessarily occur between people who are friends, enemies, or neither. Between enemies neither the action itself nor the intention excites pity, except is so far as suffering is pitiful in itself. The same is true between people who are neither friends nor enemies. When, however, suffering is inflicted upon each other by people whose relationship implies affection, as when a brother kills, or intends to kill, his brother, a son his father, a mother her son, a son his mother, or some other such action takes place — those are the situations to look for.

卍

Four Aims in Characterization

In expressing character there are four things to aim at. Of these the first and foremost is that the characters should be good. Words and action express character, as we stated, if they bring out a moral choice, and the character is good if the choice is right. This applies to every type: even a woman or a slave can be good, though the former of these is a weaker being and the slave is altogether inferior. In the second place, characters must be appropriate or true to type: there is a manly character, but it is not appropriate for a woman to be manly or a clever speaker. The third aim is to be true to life, and this is different from being good or true to type. The fourth is consistency. Even if the character represented displays inconsistency as a character trait, he must be consistent in his inconsistency. . . .

In characterization as in plot structure, one must always aim at either what is probable or what is inevitable, so that a certain character will say or do certain things in a way that is probable or inevitable, and one incident will follow the other in the same way.

The Supernatural

The solution of the plot should also emerge from the story itself; it should not require the use of the supernatural, as it does in the *Medea* and in the threatened departure of the Greeks in the *Iliad*.[19] The supernatural should be used only in connection with events that lie outside the play itself, things that have happened long ago beyond the knowledge of men, or future events which need to be foretold and revealed, for we attribute to the gods the power of seeing all things. In the incidents of the play there should be nothing inexplicable or, if there is, it should be outside the actual play, as in the *Oedipus* of Sophocles.

Characterization

Since tragedy is the imitation of characters better than those we know in life, we should imitate good portrait painters. They too render the characteristic appearance of their subject in a good likeness which is yet more beautiful than the original. So when the poet is imitating men who are given to anger, indolence, and other faults of character, he should represent them as they are, and yet make them worthy. As such an example of violent temper we have the Achilles of Agathon[20] and Homer.

Care for Details of Presentation

These things the poet must keep in mind. Besides these, he must also pay attention to the visual and other impressions which, apart from its essential effects, a poetic presentation inevitably makes upon the audience, for frequent errors are possible here also. These are adequately dealt with in my published works.

▣

Kinds of Recognition

What recognition is has already been stated. As to its different kinds, the first, least artistic but most frequently used through lack of talent, is recognition by tokens or signs. Some of these signs are congenital, like the spear-shaped birthmark of the Sons of Earth, or the stars which Carcinus used in

[19] The Greek expression ἀπὸ μηχανῆς, translated "the supernatural," refers to the "machine" by which the gods were made to appear on the roof of the scene building, or to such similar devices as the "Chariot of the Sun" sent to save Medea in Euripides' play. Aristotle does not condemn the epiphanies of the gods, but would restrict them to revealing the past or future. [Grube, abridged]
[20] Athenian tragic poet (c. 450–c. 400 B.C.) at whose home Plato's *Symposium* is held; his play of *Achilles* is lost.

his *Thyestes*; others are acquired, whether marks on the body like wounds, external possessions like necklaces, or the skiff which was the means of recognition in the *Tyro*. There is a better and a worse way of using these signs; both his old nurse and the swineherds recognize Odysseus by his scar, but the manner of their recognition is quite different. Recognitions deliberately brought about to prove one's identity are less artistic, as are all recognitions of this kind; but those that emerge from the circumstances of the reversal are better, as in the bath scene with Odysseus' old nurse.[21]

The second kind of recognition is that contrived by the poet; it is inartistic for this very reason, as Orestes in the *Iphigenia* brings about the recognition that he is Orestes. The recognition of Iphigenia follows from the letter, but Orestes says himself what the poet, not the plot, requires him to say. This is why it comes very close to the fault mentioned above in the case of Odysseus and the swineherds, for Orestes too could have had some tokens with him. The cry of the shuttle in the *Tyreus* of Sophocles also belongs here.

The third kind of recognition is through memory: we see one thing and recall another, as a character in the *Cyprians* of Dicaeogenes saw the picture and wept, or the recognition scene in the lay of Antinous, where Odysseus listens to the bard and weeps at his memories, and this leads to the recognition.

Recognition of the fourth kind is by inference, as in the *Choephori*:[22] someone like me has come, there is no one like me except Orestes, therefore Orestes has come. . . .

There is a further kind of composite recognition based upon a wrong inference by one of the two parties involved, as in *Odysseus the False Messenger*, where one said he would know the bow he had never seen, and the other understood him to say he would recognize it, and thus made a false inference.

Of all these, the best recognition is that which emerges from the events themselves, where the amazement and the surprise are caused by probable means, as in the *Oedipus* of Sophocles and the *Iphigenia*, for it was probable that Iphigenia should wish to send a letter. This is the only kind of recognition which dispenses with contrived tokens and necklaces. The second best is recognition based on a correct inference. . . .

Epic and Tragic Plots

It is necessary to remember what has already often been mentioned, and not to compose a tragedy with an epic plot structure, by which I mean a plot with many stories, as would be the case if someone were to make the whole

---

[21] While Odysseus, still believed to be a beggar, is in his palace, his old nurse is told by Penelope to wash his feet (which is a natural proceeding arising out of the plot) and she recognizes the scar. This is the bath scene of *Odyssey* 19. Later, Odysseus, choosing his own time, makes himself known to Eumaeus and Philoetius and shows them the scar to convince them (*Odyssey* 21. 221–2). This [recognition] does not emerge from the circumstances so naturally. [Grube, abridged]

[22] *The Libation Bearers* by Aeschylus, second part of the *Oresteia*, a trilogy about Orestes.

story of the *Iliad* into a tragedy. In the *Iliad*, because of its magnitude, the different parts adopt a length appropriate to each, but in tragedies such length is contrary to the concept of the drama. One may prove this by referring to those who have made the whole story of the fall of Troy into a tragedy, and not, like Euripides,[23] parts of that story only, or to those who wrote a tragedy on Niobe, but not in the way Aeschylus did. These writers have been hissed off the stage or at least been unsuccessful, for even Agathon was hissed off the stage for this reason alone.

Defective Plots

Yet in their handling of reversals and in simple plots these poets wonderfully achieve the effect they aim at, for indeed this sort of thing is tragic and satisfies our humane feelings, that is, when a clever but wicked man like Sisyphus[24] is deceived, or a brave criminal is defeated. This is probable in Agathon's sense when he said that many unlikely things are likely to happen.

Horace   (65–8 B.C.)

ROMAN POET, SATIRIST, and CRITIC

On the Art of Poetry

Should some painter take the fancy to draw the neck of a horse joined to a human head, and to overlay with varicolored plumage limbs gathered from anywhere and everywhere, making what appeared at the top a beautiful woman to end below as a foul fish, when you were admitted to the spectacle, should you, even though his friends, restrain your laughter? Believe me, dear Pisos, most similar to such a picture would be a book which figured forth, like the dreams of one in a fever, mad imaginings wherein neither foot nor head could be attributed to any one shape.

"But to painters and to poets the right has always been conceded of daring what they willed." Granted, and this privilege we ask for ourselves and allow to others: but not to the extent that wild animals should unite with tame, that serpents should be mated with birds, or lambs with tigers.

Poems very often begin sonorously, making great promises; then, as they proceed, one widely gleaming purple patch after another is sewn on, when

---

[23] as in *The Trojan Women* and *Iphigenia in Tauris*.
[24] For an offense against Zeus, Sisyphus was condemned to roll a rock eternally up a hill in Hades; when he reaches the top, the rock always rolls down again.

there are described the grove and altar of Diana and the winding stream that rushes through the goodly fields, or the River Rhine, or the rainbow. But here was not the place for these descriptions. Furthermore, perhaps you (a painter) are particularly adept at sketching a cypress tree: what of it, if he who pays you to paint him is to be represented swimming in despair from a wrecked fleet? When a wine jar has been begun, on what excuse is a small pitcher brought from the potter's wheel? In short, whatever you design, let it have, if nothing else, simplicity and unity.

Noble sire and worthy sons, most of us poets are deceived by the semblance of excellence. I endeavor to be brief and become obscure; sinew and spirit desert the searcher after polish; one striving for grandeur becomes bombastic; whatsoever is excessively cautious and fearful of the tempest crawls along the ground; and he who yearns after too prodigal a variety in his theme — he paints a dolphin in the forest, or a wild boar amid the waves. If the poet not have genuine artistry, the effort to avoid an imperfection leads him into graver botchery.

The poorest artificer who dwells near the Aemelian School will model the nails and imitate the flowing hair in bronze, but he will fail in the prime essential of his work, because he will not know how to order it as a whole. If I were taking pains to compose anything, I should no more wish to be this fellow than I should to go through life with a misshapen nose, at the same time much admired for comely black eyes and hair.

Choose material proportionate to your powers, you who write, and long consider what your shoulders can carry, what they cannot. Neither command of language nor perspicuous arrangement will fail the author who has chosen his subject wisely. The excellence and charm of arrangement, if I be not much mistaken, consists in this, — to say at each and every time just what should at that time be said, and to defer a very great part of what might be said, and for the nonce omit it. The author must choose and reject as he pushes forward with his poem. . . .

It is not enough that poems be beautiful: they must be charming too, and must lead the hearer's mind in whatsoever direction they will. As human countenances smile on those who are smiling, so too they show sympathy with those who weep. If you wish me to weep, you must first grieve yourself. . . . If you speak your part badly, I shall either go to sleep or laugh. Sad words become the sad face, threatening words the angry one, sportive jests the frolicsome, grave precepts the mien of austerity. For nature fashions us within to the various states of fortune: she makes us glad, drives us to anger, tortures and bends us to the ground under weighty sorrow; then she publishes in our speech the passions of our spirits. If the actor's words be not in keeping with his fortune, the Roman gentry will laugh jeeringly, and the commoners too.

It will make a great difference whether a god is speaking or a hero, whether a seasoned old man or a hot-headed, impetuous youth, whether an influential matron or an officious nurse, whether a wandering merchant or the farmer of a small, flourishing estate, whether a Colchian or an Assyrian, a Theban or an Argive.

Either follow established tradition or make your invention consistent. . . .

If you introduce into your scene anything not previously tried, and presume to create a new character, keep him to the very end as he was at the beginning, and make him consistent. . . . What is public property will become your private own if you not linger upon the trite, commonly trodden path, nor take pains to be an overly careful, word-for-word translator, nor plunge head-long into narrow straits of imitation, to take one step out of which, shame or the rules of the work will prevent. . . .

The aim of poets is either to be beneficial or to delight, or in their phrases to combine charm and high applicability to life. Be brief about whatever precepts you give, that receptive minds may readily take them in and faith-fully retain them: whatever is to no purpose flows away from the full mind. Whatever you invent for the sake of pleasing, let it be not too distant from truth, and do not in your drama call for belief of just anything you fancy. . . . The elders' class scorn poetry devoid of useful precept; the knightly caste have little regard for what is austere. By at once delighting and teaching the reader, the poet who mixes the sweet with the useful has everybody's approval. His book earns money for the booksellers' firm of the Sosii; it crosses seas; it extends the literary life of its author.

There are faults, however, for which we wish to make allowance; for the string does not always give back the tone which the mind and hand had willed, and the effort to strike bass very often results in treble; the archer cannot always hit what he aims at. Indeed, when there is much that shines in a poem, I shall not be offended by a few blemishes, which either negligence permitted or human frailty could not avoid. . . . Indeed, in a long work occasional sleep is bound to creep upon one. As with painting, so with poetry: one picture you will find more captivating the nearer you stand, another, the farther away; one is preferable in shadow, another, for which the acute keen-ness of the critic need not be feared, wants to be viewed in the light. This one pleases once; that, visited ten times, will still please.

Elder youth, although I am aware that you have been guided in the way of rectitude by your father's counsel, and that you have good discernment of your own, heed and keep ever in mind this concept: in certain fields of endeavor, moderately good, passable achievement may properly be granted recognition. . . . but that poets may be mediocre neither man, nor gods, nor booksellers have granted.

Offensive, between the enjoyable courses of a banquet, are discordant music, heavy perfume, and poppy-seed with Sardinian honey, since the feast could have dispensed with these: likewise a poem, which is brought into being and designed for the delight of the spirit, if it depart ever so little from the highest in quality, sinks toward the lowest.

One who is ignorant about sports lets athletic equipment alone, and if he has no skill with quoits, balls, or trundling hoops he takes no part in the games, lest throngs of spectators indulge in justifiable laughter; but the ignoramus about poetry composes verses. Why not? He is freeborn and gentle, and, more to the point, has knightly rank, money, and a character above suspicion! But as for you, you will not speak or perform anything which is contrary to the natural bent of your own mind; such is your judgment, such your intelligence. If at any future time you write something, bring it to the attention of the critic Maecus, to your father's, to mine; and put your manuscript away and keep it for nine years. You can always destroy what you have not published; there is no art to unsay what you have once let go of.

　　　　　　　　　　回

The savage dwellers in the woods were deterred from slaughter and foul living by Orpheus, the priest and messenger of the gods, on which account it was fabled that he tamed tigers and ferocious lions; likewise Amphion, the founder of Thebes, was bruited[1] to move rocks by the sound of his lyre, and with soft entreaty to lead them where he wished. It was the office of wisdom, in that former time, to set the bounds of public and private property, and the limits of the sacred and the secular, tó prohibit promiscuous concubinage, and found the rite of marriage; to establish the civic order and record the laws: it was in these performances that the honor and renown of the divine bards and poems came into being. Following these, Homer achieved distinction and Tyrtaeus[2] inspired masculine minds to war with his verses; prophecies were told in verse, the course of life taught, the good will of kings cultivated, and diversion and the victorious achievement of great tasks unfolded: so you need not feel shame for the Muse skillful at the lyre and for Apollo, the god of singers.

　　　　　　　　　　回

It has been questioned whether a poem achieves worthy distinction through nature or through art. I do not see that either avails alone, application without abundant natural bent or genius untrained, so much does each demand the help of the other, and amicably combine with it. He who yearns to reach the desired goal as a runner takes great pains and does much work as a boy, recoils not from sweat or from cold, abstains from wine and women; any flutist who plays at the Pythian games[3] has first bowed to and trembled under a master. And it is not pardonable to take such an attitude as this: "A marvelous poet am I; [and in our little game] 'scurf take the hindmost'; to me it is disgraceful to be last, and is especially so to admit ignorance of whatever I do not know."

---

[1] reputed.
[2] Greek elegiac poet (7th century B.C.), who wrote war songs and exhortations in epic language.
[3] festival at Delphi in honor of Apollo, with musical competitions and athletic contests.

Plutarch (c. A.D. 46–c. 120)

GREEK HISTORIAN, BIOGRAPHER, and PHILOSOPHER

Marc Antony's Funeral Oration

. . . Caesar fell in the Senate-house. Antony immediately disguised himself as a slave and went into hiding. But when he learned that the conspirators had merely assembled on the Capitol and had no further designs against anyone, he persuaded them to come down into the city and sent them his son as a hostage. He even went so far as to entertain Cassius in his house, and Lepidus did the same for Brutus. He also arranged a meeting of the Senate, at which he moved that an amnesty should be declared and that provinces should be allotted to Brutus and Cassius and their supporters. The Senate passed this proposal, and also voted that no change should be made in the measures which Caesar had taken. So when Antony left the Senate on this occasion, his reputation had never stood higher, for it was felt that he had delivered Rome from civil war and had succeeded in resolving an exceptionally difficult and confused situation in a most prudent and statesmanlike fashion.

However, these counsels of moderation were soon swept away by the tide of popular feeling which was now running in Antony's favour, and which inspired him with the hope that if Brutus could be overthrown, he himself would be sure to become the first man in Rome. It so happened that when Caesar's body was carried out for burial, Antony delivered the customary eulogy over it in the Forum. When he saw that his oratory had cast a spell over the people and that they were deeply stirred by his words, he began to introduce into his praises a note of pity and of indignation at Caesar's fate. Finally, at the close of his speech, he snatched up the dead man's robe and brandished it aloft, all bloodstained as it was and stabbed through in many places, and called those who had done the deed murderers and villains. This appeal had such an effect upon the people that they piled up benches and tables and burned Caesar's body in the Forum, and then, snatching up firebrands from the pyre, they ran to the houses of his assassins and attacked them.

Title supplied by editors. "Marc Antony's Funeral Oration" by Plutarch. From "The Life of Marc Antony" in *Parallel Lives* by Plutarch. Reprinted from *Makers of Rome,* translated by Ian Scott-Kilvert and published by Penguin Books Ltd. Reprinted by permission.

Augustine (353–430)

EARLY CHRISTIAN CHURCH FATHER and PHILOSOPHER

The Rapture of the Theater

The theater enraptured me, for its shows were filled with pictures of my own miseries and with tinder for my fires. Why is it that a man likes to grieve over doleful and tragic events which he would not want to happen to himself? The spectator likes to experience grief at such scenes, and this very sorrow is a pleasure to him. What is this but a pitiable folly? For the more a man is moved by these things, the less free is he from such passions. However, when he himself experiences it, it is usually called misery; when he experiences it with regard to others, it is called mercy. But what sort of mercy is to be shown to these unreal things upon the stage? The auditor is not aroused to go to the aid of the others; he is only asked to grieve over them. Moreover, he will show greater approval of the author of such representations, the greater the grief he feels. But if men's misfortunes, whether fictitious or of ancient times, are put on in such manner that the spectator does not feel sorrow, then he leaves in disgust and with disapproval. If grief is aroused in him, he remains in the theater, full of attention and enjoying himself.

Tears and sorrow, therefore, are objects of love. Certainly, every man likes to enjoy himself. But while no man wants to be wretched, does he nevertheless want to be merciful? Now since mercy cannot exist apart from grief, is it for this sole reason that grief is loved? This also has friendship as its source and channel. But where does it go? Where does it flow? Why does it run down into a torrent of boiling pitch, into those immense surges of loathsome lusts? For into these it is changed, and by its own choice it is turned from the purity of heaven into something distorted and base. Shall mercy, therefore, be cast aside? By no means. At certain times, therefore, sorrows may be loved. But shun uncleanness, O my soul! With God as my keeper, the God of our fathers, worthy to be praised and exalted above all forever, shun uncleanness!

Today still I feel compassion, but in those days at the theater I felt joy together with the lovers when by shameful means they had joy in one another, although those things were only pretended in the show, and when they lost each other, I became sad like one who feels compassion. Both situations gave me delight. But now I have more pity for one who rejoices in a shameful deed than for one who has suffered, so to speak, damage to a pernicious pleasure or loss of some vile joy. This is surely the truer mercy, and sorrow finds no delight in it. Although any man who sorrows over a sinner is commended for his act of charity, yet one who shows fraternal mercy prefers rather that there be no occasion for his sorrow. If there is a good will that is at the same time bad-willed, which cannot be, then only a truly and sincerely merciful man can wish that there might be some unfortunates, so that he could show mercy to them. Hence, a certain kind of sorrow can be commended, but none can be loved. Such mercy is yours, O Lord God, for you love our souls with a purity of love more deep and wide than that we have for ourselves, and you are unalterably merciful, because you suffer no wound from sorrow. "And for these things who is sufficient."

But in my wretchedness at that time I loved to feel sorrow, and I sought out opportunities for sorrow. In the false misery of another man as it was mimicked on the stage, that actor's playing pleased me most and had the strongest attraction for me which struck tears from my eyes. What wonder was it that I, an unhappy sheep straying from your flock and impatient of your protection, should be infected with loathsome sores? Hence came my love for such sorrows, by which I was not pierced deep down — for I did not like to suffer such things, but only to look at them — and by which, when they were heard and performed, I was scratched lightly, as it were. As a result, as though from scratches made by fingernails, there followed a burning tumor and horrid pus and wasting away. Such was my life, but was it truly life, my God?

Giraldus Cambrensis   (c. 1147–c. 1223)

WELSH HISTORIAN and CLERGYMAN

The Effects of Music

It appears, then, that music acts in contrary ways; when employed to give intensity to the feelings, it inflames, when to abate them, it lulls. Hence the Irish and Spaniards, and some other nations, mix plaintive music with their funeral wailings, giving poignancy to their present grief, as well as, perhaps, tranquillizing the mind when the worst is past. Music also alleviates toil, and in labour of various kinds the fatigue is cheered by sounds uttered in measured time. Hence, artificers of all sorts relieve the weariness of their tasks by songs. The very beasts, not to speak of serpents, and birds, and porpoises, are attracted by musical harmony to listen to its melody; and what is still more

Title supplied by editors. "The Effects of Music" by Giraldus Cambrensis. From *Topography of Ireland*, translated by T. Wright, in *The Portable Medieval Reader*, edited by James Bruce Ross and Mary Martin McLaughlin.

remarkable, swarms of bees are recalled to their hives, and induced to settle, by musical sounds. I have sometimes observed, when on a voyage, shoals of porpoises long following in the wake of the ship when she was pursuing her course, and how they leaped above the surface, and erected their ears to listen to the tones of the harp or the trumpet.

Moreover, as Isidore[1] remarks, "No teaching can be perfect without harmony. Indeed, there is nothing in which it is not found. The world itself is said to be harmoniously formed, and the very heavens revolve amidst the harmony of the spheres. Sounds, the materials of which melodies are composed, are threefold: first they are harmonic, being produced by the voices of singers; secondly, they are organic, being produced by wind; thirdly, they are rhythmical, produced by the touch of the fingers. For sounds are either produced by the voice, through the throat; or by wind, as a trumpet or pipe; or by the touch, as by the harp, or any other instrument the melody of which is produced by the finger."

Cennino Cennini (c. 1370–c. 1440)

ITALIAN PAINTER

A Painter on His Craft

It is not without the impulse of a lofty spirit that some are moved to enter this profession, attractive to them through natural enthusiasm. Their intellect will take delight in drawing, provided their nature attracts them to it of themselves, without any master's guidance, out of loftiness of spirit. And then, through this delight, they come to want to find a master; and they bind themselves to him with respect for authority, undergoing an apprenticeship in order to achieve perfection in all this. There are those who pursue it, because of poverty and domestic need, for profit and enthusiasm for the profession too; but above all these are to be extolled the ones who enter the profession through a sense of enthusiasm and exaltation. . . .

The basis of the profession, the very beginning of all these manual operations, is drawing and painting. These two sections call for a knowledge of the

[1] possibly Isidore of Alexandria (5th century), Greek Neoplatonist philosopher; or Isidore of Seville (c. 560–636), Spanish encyclopedist and historian who condensed and reproduced many works of Latin and Christian literature. These works helped keep alive antique learning in the Dark Ages.

Title supplied by editors. "A Painter on His Craft" by Cennino Cennini. From *The Craftsman's Handbook* by Cennino Cennini (translated by D. V. Thompson). Dover Publications, Inc., New York, 1952. Reprinted through permission of the publisher.

following: how to work up or grind, how to apply size, to put on cloth, to gesso, to scrape the gessos and smooth them down, to model with gesso, to lay bole,[1] to gild, to burnish; to temper, to lay in; to pounce, to scrape through, to stamp or punch; to mark out, to paint, to embellish, and to varnish, on panel or ancona.[2] To work on a wall you have to wet down, to plaster, to true up, to smooth off, to draw, to paint in fresco. To carry to completion in secco:[3] to temper, to embellish, to finish on the wall. And let this be the schedule of the aforesaid stages which I, with what little knowledge I have acquired, will expound, section by section. . . .

Now you must forge ahead again, so that you may pursue the course of this theory. You have made your tinted papers; the next thing is to draw. You should adopt this method. Having first practised drawing for a while as I have taught you above, that is, on a little panel, take pains and pleasure in constantly copying the best things which you can find done by the hand of great masters. And if you are in a place where many good masters have been, so much the better for you. But I give you this advice: take care to select the best one every time, and the one who has the greatest reputation. And, as you go on from day to day, it will be against nature if you do not get some grasp of his style and of his spirit. For if you undertake to copy after one master today and after another one tomorrow, you will not acquire the style of either one or the other, and you will inevitably, through enthusiasm, become capricious, because each style will be distracting your mind. You will try to work in this man's way today, and in the other's tomorrow, and so you will not get either of them right. If you follow the course of one man through constant practice, your intelligence would have to be crude indeed for you not to get some nourishment from it. Then you will find, if nature has granted you any imagination at all, that you will eventually acquire a style individual to yourself, and it cannot help being good; because your hand and your mind, being always accustomed to gather flowers, would ill know how to pluck thorns.

Mind you, the most perfect steersman that you can have, and the best helm lie in the triumphal gateway of copying from nature. And this outdoes all other models; and always rely on this with a stout heart, especially as you begin to gain some judgment in draughtsmanship. Do not fail, as you go on, to draw something every day, for no matter how little it is it will be well worth while, and will do you a world of good.

Your life should always be arranged just as if you were studying theology, or philosophy, or other theories, that is to say, eating and drinking moderately, at least twice a day, electing digestible and wholesome dishes, and light wines; saving and sparing your hand, preserving it from such strains as heaving stones, crowbars, and many other things which are bad for your hand, from giving them a chance to weary it. There is another cause which, if you indulge it,

[1] yellowish clay.
[2] corner of a wall, or truss supporting a cornice.
[3] dry (as opposed to fresco, fresh, i.e. wet).

can make your hand so unsteady that it will waver more, and flutter far more, than leaves do in the wind, and this is indulging too much in the company of women. Let us get back to our subject. Have a sort of pouch made of pasteboard, or just thin wood, made large enough in every dimension for you to put in a royal folio, that is, a half; and this is good for you to keep your drawings in, and likewise to hold the paper on for drawing. Then always go out alone, or in such company as will be inclined to do as you do, and not apt to disturb you. And the more understanding this company displays, the better it is for you. When you are in churches or chapels, and beginning to draw, consider, in the first place, from what section you think you wish to copy a scene or figure; and notice where its darks and half tones and high lights come; and this means that you have to apply your shadow with washes of ink; to leave the natural ground in the half tones; and to apply the high lights with white lead. . . .

If you want to get the effect of a velvet, do the drapery with any colour you wish, tempered with yolk of egg. Then make the cut threads, as the velvet requires, with a miniver brush, in a colour tempered with oil; and make the cut threads rather coarse. And you may make black velvets in this way, and red ones, and any coloured ones, tempering in this way. . . .

If you happen to have to work on woollen cloth, on account of tourneys or jousts, for gentlemen or great lords sometimes teem with desire for distinctive things, and want their arms in gold or silver on this sort of cloth: first, according to the colour of the stuff or cloth, select the crayon which it requires for drawing; and fix it with a pen, just as you did on the velvet. Then take white of egg, well beaten as I taught you before, and an equal amount of size,[4] in the usual way; and put it on the nap of this cloth, on the part where you have to do gilding. Then when it is dry take a crook, and burnish over this cloth; then apply two more coats of this tempera. When it is quite dry, apply your mordant[5] so as not to go outside the tempered part, and lay whatever gold or silver you think fit.

[4] glue-like substance for coating paper or cloth.
[5] acid for etching; substance used to fix dye.

Leonardo da Vinci (1452–1519)

ITALIAN PAINTER, SCULPTOR,
ARCHITECT, and ENGINEER

Nature as the Supreme Authority

How from age to age the art of painting continually declines and deteriorates when painters have no other standard than work already done:

The painter will produce pictures of little merit if he takes the works of others as his standard; but if he will apply himself to learn from the objects of nature he will produce good results. This we see was the case with the painters who came after the time of the Romans, for they continually imitated each other, and from age to age their art steadily declined.

After these came Giotto the Florentine, and he — reared in mountain solitudes, inhabited only by goats and suchlike beasts — turning straight from nature to his art, began to draw on the rocks the movements of the goats which he was tending, and so began to draw the figures of all the animals which were to be found in the country, in such a way that after much study he not only surpassed the masters of his own time but all those of many preceding centuries. After him art again declined, because all were imitating paintings already done; and so for centuries it continued to decline until such time as Tommaso the Florentine, nicknamed Masaccio, showed by the perfection of his work how those who took as their standard anything other than nature, the supreme guide of all the masters, were wearying themselves in vain. Similarly I would say about these mathematical subjects, that those who study only the authorities and not the works of nature are in art the grandsons and not the sons of nature, which is the supreme guide of the good authorities.

Mark the supreme folly of those who censure such as learn from nature, leaving uncensured the authorities who were themselves the disciples of this same nature!

Title supplied by editors. "Nature as the Supreme Authority" by Leonardo da Vinci. From *The Notebooks of Leonardo da Vinci*, translated by Edward MacCurdy. Reprinted by permission of Harcourt, Brace & World, Inc.

Philip Sidney (1554–1586)

ENGLISH POET, COURTIER, and SOLDIER

The Golden World of Art

... Since the authors of most of our sciences were the Romans, and before them the Greeks, let us a little stand upon their authorities, but even[1] so far as to see what names they have given unto this now scorned skill. Among the Romans a poet was called *vates*, which is as much as a diviner, foreseer, or prophet, ... so heavenly a title did that excellent people bestow upon this heart-ravishing knowledge. And so far were they carried into the admiration thereof, that they thought in the chanceable hitting upon any such verses great foretokens of their following fortunes were placed; whereupon grew the word of *Sortes Virgilianæ*, when by sudden opening of Virgil's book they lighted upon some verse of his making. Whereof the Histories of the Emperors' Lives[2] are full: as of Albinus,[3] the governor of our island, who in his childhood met with this verse,

Arma amens capio, nec sat rationis in armis,[4]

and in his age performed it. Although it were a very vain and godless superstition, as also it was to think that spirits were commanded by such verses — whereupon this word charms, derived of *carmina*, cometh — so yet serveth it to show the great reverence those wits were held in, and altogether not without ground, since both the oracles of Delphos and Sibylla's prophecies were wholly delivered in verses; for that same exquisite observing of number[5] and measure in words, and that high-flying liberty of conceit[6] proper to the poet, did seem to have some divine force in it.

And may not I presume a little further to show the reasonableness of this word *vates*, and say that the holy David's Psalms are a divine poem? If I do, I shall not do it without the testimony of great learned men, both ancient and modern. But even the name of Psalms will speak for me, which, being

---

[1] only.
[2] the *Augustan Histories*, a collection of lives of the Roman Emperors from 117 to 284 A.D., by Aelius Spartianus, Vulcacius Gallicanus, Trebellius Pollio, Julius Capitolinus, Flavius Vospiscus, and Aelius Lampridius.
[3] Albinus, who was governor of Britain in Roman times, led an army over to Lyons against his rival, Septimus Severus, and was there slain. [Cook, abridged]
[4] "To arms I rush in frenzy — not that good cause is shown for arms." (*Aeneid*, II, 314).
[5] meter.
[6] imagination.

Title supplied by editors. "The Golden World of Art" by Philip Sidney. From *Defense of Poesy* by Philip Sidney, edited by Albert S. Cook and published by Ginn and Company. Reprinted by permission.

interpreted, is nothing but Songs; then, that it is fully written in metre, as all learned Hebricians agree, although the rules be not yet fully found; lastly and principally, his handling his prophecy, which is merely poetical. For what else is the awaking his musical instruments, the often and free changing of persons, his notable prosopopœias, when he maketh you, as it were, see God coming in His majesty, his telling of the beasts' joyfulness and hills' leaping, but a heavenly poesy, wherein almost he showeth himself a passionate lover of that unspeakable and everlasting beauty to be seen by the eyes of the mind, only cleared by faith? But truly now having named him, I fear I seem to profane that holy name, applying it to poetry, which is among us thrown down to so ridiculous an estimation. But they that with quiet judgments will look a little deeper into it, shall find the end and working of it such as, being rightly applied, deserveth not to be scourged out of the church of God.

But now let us see how the Greeks named it and how they deemed of it. The Greeks called him ποιητήν,[7] which name hath, as the most excellent, gone through other languages. It cometh of this word ποιεῖν, which is "to make"; wherein I know not whether by luck or wisdom we Englishmen have met with the Greeks in calling him a maker. Which name how high and incomparable a title it is, I had rather were known by marking the scope of other sciences than by any partial allegation. There is no art delivered unto mankind that hath not the works of nature for his principal object, without which they could not consist, and on which they so depend as they become actors and players, as it were, of what nature will have set forth. So doth the astronomer look upon the stars, and, by that he seeth, set down what order nature hath taken therein. So do the geometrician and arithmetician in their divers sorts of quantities. So doth the musician in times tell you which by nature agree, which not. The natural philosopher thereon hath his name, and the moral philosopher standeth upon the natural virtues, vices, and passions of man; and "follow nature," saith he, "therein, and thou shalt not err." The lawyer saith what men have determined, the historian what men have done. The grammarian speaketh only of the rules of speech, and the rhetorician and logician, considering what in nature will soonest prove and persuade, thereon give artificial rules, which still are compassed within the circle of a question, according to the proposed matter. The physician weigheth the nature of man's body, and the nature of things helpful or hurtful unto it. And the metaphysic, though it be in the second and abstract notions, and therefore be counted supernatural, yet doth he, indeed, build upon the depth of nature.

Only the poet, disdaining to be tied to any such subjection, lifted up with the vigor of his own invention, doth grow, in effect, into another nature, in making things either better than nature bringeth forth, or, quite anew, forms such as never were in nature, as the heroes, demi-gods, cyclops, chimeras, furies, and such like; so as he goeth hand in hand with nature, not enclosed

---

[7] maker.

within the narrow warrant of her gifts, but freely ranging within the zodiac of his own wit. Nature never set forth the earth in so rich tapestry as divers poets have done; neither with pleasant rivers, fruitful trees, sweet-smelling flowers, nor whatsoever else may make the too-much-loved earth more lovely; her world is brazen, the poets only deliver a golden.

But let those things alone, and go to man — for whom as the other things are, so it seemeth in him her uttermost cunning is employed — and know whether she have brought forth so true a lover as Theagenes;[8] so constant a friend as Pylades;[9] so valiant a man as Orlando;[10] so right a prince as Xenophon's Cyrus,[11] so excellent a man every way as Virgil's Æneas? Neither let this be jestingly conceived, because the works of the one be essential, the other in imitation or fiction; for any understanding knoweth the skill of each artificer standeth in that idea, or fore-conceit of the work, and not in the work itself. And that the poet hath that idea is manifest, by delivering them forth in such excellency as he hath imagined them. Which delivering forth, also, is not wholly imaginative, as we are wont to say by them that build castles in the air; but so far substantially it worketh, not only to make a Cyrus, which had been but a particular excellency, as nature might have done, but to bestow a Cyrus upon the world to make many Cyruses, if they will learn aright why and how that maker made him. Neither let it be deemed too saucy a comparison to balance the highest point of man's wit with the efficacy of nature; but rather give right honor to the Heavenly Maker of that maker, who, having made man to His own likeness, set him beyond and over all the works of that second nature. Which in nothing he showeth so much as in poetry, when with the force of a divine breath he bringeth things forth far surpassing her doings, with no small argument to the incredulous of that first accursed fall of Adam, — since our erected wit maketh us know what perfection is, and yet our infected will keepeth us from reaching unto it. But these arguments will by few be understood, and by fewer granted; thus much I hope will be given me, that the Greeks with some probability of reason gave him the name above all names of learning.

---

[8] the hero of Heliodorus' *Aethiopica*, one of Sidney's favorite Greek romances.
[9] the close friend of Orestes in Euripides' *Iphigenia in Tauris*.
[10] hero of Ariosto's *Orlando Furioso*, based on the *Song of Roland*.
[11] protagonist of Xenophon's *Cyrapoedia*, a historical romance; he served the Renaissance as a model hero.

William Shakespeare (1564–1616)

ENGLISH DRAMATIST and POET

An Honourable Man

[SCENE II. *The Forum*]

Enter BRUTUS *and* CASSIUS, *with the* PLEBEIANS

PLEBEIANS. We will be satisfied! Let us be satisfied! — will be satisfied: demand an explanation

BRUTUS. Then follow me, and give me audience, friends.

Cassius, go you into the other street,

And part the numbers. — numbers: crowd

Those that will hear me speak, let 'em stay here;

Those that will follow Cassius, go with him; — Cassius: co-leader of the conspiracy against Caesar; he persuaded Brutus to join in the assassination.

And public reasons shall be rendered

Of Cæsar's death.

1 PLEBEIAN. I will hear Brutus speak.

2 PLEBEIAN. I will hear Cassius; and compare their reasons

When severally we hear them rendered. 10 — severally: separately

[*Exit Cassius, with some of the Plebeians.*]
Brutus goes into the pulpit.

3 PLEBEIAN. The noble Brutus is ascended; silence!

BRUTUS. Be patient till the last. — last: end of the speech

Romans, countrymen and lovers! hear me for my — lovers: dear friends
cause, and be silent, that you may hear; believe
me for mine honour, and have respect to mine
honour, that you may believe; censure me in your — censure: judge
wisdom, and awake your senses, that you may the
better judge. If there be any in this assembly, any
dear friend of Cæsar's, to him I say, that Brutus'
love to Cæsar was no less than his. If then that 20
friend demand why Brutus rose against Cæsar, this
is my answer: Not that I lov'd Cæsar less, but
that I lov'd Rome more. Had you rather Cæsar

Title supplied by editors. From Act III, scene ii of
Julius Caesar in *The Complete Plays and Poems of William Shakespeare*, edited by William Allan Neilson and
Charles Jarvis Hill (New Cambridge Edition). Brackets
indicate emended readings; minor textual revisions by
Arthur F. Kinney. Reprinted by permission of Houghton
Mifflin Company.

were living and die all slaves, than that Cæsar were
dead, to live all free men? As Cæsar lov'd me,
I weep for him; as he was fortunate, I rejoice at
it; as he was valiant, I honour him; but, as he was
ambitious, I slew him. There is tears for his love;
joy for his fortune; honour for his valour; and
death for his ambition. Who is here so base 30
that would be a bondman? If any, speak; for
him have I offended. Who is here so rude that
would not be a Roman? If any, speak; for him
have I offended. Who is here so vile that will not
love his country? If any, speak; for him have I
offended. I pause for a reply.

rude: barbarous

ALL.   None, Brutus, none.

BRUTUS.   Then none have I offended. I have done
no more to Cæsar than you shall do to Brutus. 39
The question of his death is enroll'd in the Capitol;
his glory not extenuated, wherein he was worthy,
nor his offences enforc'd, for which he suffered
death.

shall: would

question . . . enroll'd: justification for his death is on record

enforc'd: exaggerated

Enter ANTONY [*and others*], *with Cæsar's body*

Here comes his body, mourn'd by Mark Antony;
who, though he had no hand in his death, shall
receive the benefit of his dying, a place in the commonwealth; as which of you shall not? With this
I depart, that, as I slew my best lover for the good
of Rome, I have the same dagger for myself, when
it shall please my country to need my death. 50

ALL.   Live, Brutus! live, live!

1 PLEBEIAN.   Bring him with triumph home unto
his house.

2 PLEBEIAN.   Give him a statue with his ancestors.

3 PLEBEIAN.   Let him be Cæsar.

4 PLEBEIAN.   Cæsar's better parts
Shall be crown'd in Brutus.

parts: qualities

1 PLEBEIAN.   We'll bring him to his house
With shouts and clamours.

BRUTUS.   My countrymen, —

2 PLEBEIAN.   Peace! Silence! Brutus speaks.

1 PLEBEIAN.   Peace, ho!

BRUTUS.   Good countrymen, let me depart
alone,
And, for my sake, stay here with Antony.
Do grace to Cæsar's corpse, and grace his speech 60
Tending to Cæsar's glories, which Mark Antony,
By our permission, is allow'd to make.
I do entreat you, not a man depart
Save I alone, till Antony have spoke.   [*Exit*

1 PLEBEIAN.   Stay, ho! and let us hear Mark
Antony.

3 PLEBEIAN.   Let him go up into the public chair;
We'll hear him. Noble Antony, go up.

ANTONY.   For Brutus' sake, I am beholding to   beholding: indebted
you.   [*Goes into the pulpit*]

4 PLEBEIAN.   What does he say of Brutus?

3 PLEBEIAN.   He says, for Brutus' sake
He finds himself beholding to us all.   70

4 PLEBEIAN.   'Twere best he speak no harm of
Brutus here.

1 PLEBEIAN.   This Cæsar was a tyrant.

3 PLEBEIAN.   Nay, that's certain:
We are blest that Rome is rid of him.

2 PLEBEIAN.   Peace! let us hear what Antony can
say.

ANTONY.   You gentle Romans, —

ALL.   Peace, ho! let us hear him.

ANTONY.   Friends, Romans, countrymen, lend me
your ears!
I come to bury Cæsar, not to praise him.
The evil that men do lives after them,
The good is oft interred with their bones;
So let it be with Cæsar. The noble Brutus   80
Hath told you Cæsar was ambitious;
If it were so, it was a grievous fault,
And grievously hath Cæsar answer'd it.   answer'd: paid for
Here, under leave of Brutus and the rest —
For Brutus is an honourable man;
So are they all, all honourable men —
Come I to speak in Cæsar's funeral.
He was my friend, faithful and just to me;
But Brutus says he was ambitious,
And Brutus is an honourable man.   90
He hath brought many captives home to Rome,
Whose ransoms did the general coffers fill;   general: public
Did this in Cæsar seem ambitious?
When that the poor have cried, Cæsar hath wept;
Ambition should be made of sterner stuff:
Yet Brutus says he was ambitious,
And Brutus is an honourable man.
You all did see that on the Lupercal
I thrice presented him a kingly crown,
Which he did thrice refuse. Was this ambition? 100
Yet Brutus says he was ambitious,
And, sure, he is an honourable man.
I speak not to disprove what Brutus spoke,
But here I am to speak what I do know.
You all did love him once, not without cause;
What cause witholds you then to mourn for him?

O judgement! thou art fled to brutish beasts,
And men have lost their reason. Bear with me;
My heart is in the coffin there with Cæsar,
And I must pause till it come back to me.   110

    1 PLEBEIAN. Methinks there is much reason in
      his sayings.
    2 PLEBEIAN. If thou consider rightly of the
      matter,
Cæsar has had great wrong.
    3 PLEBEIAN.   Has he, masters?
I fear there will a worse come in his place.
    4 PLEBEIAN. Mark'd ye his words? He would
      not take the crown;
Therefore 'tis certain he was not ambitious.
    1 PLEBEIAN. If it be found so, some will dear
      abide it.   **abide: pay for**
    2 PLEBEIAN. Poor soul! his eyes are red as fire
      with weeping.
    3 PLEBEIAN. There's not a nobler man in Rome
      than Antony.
    4 PLEBEIAN. Now mark him, he begins again to
      speak.   120
    ANTONY. But yesterday the word of Cæsar might
Have stood against the world; now lies he there,
And none so poor to do him reverence.   **poor: of low social status**
O masters, if I were dispos'd to stir
Your hearts and minds to mutiny and rage,
I should do Brutus wrong, and Cassius wrong,
Who, you all know, are honourable men.
I will not do them wrong; I rather choose
To wrong the dead, to wrong myself and you,
Than I will wrong such honourable men.   130
But here's a parchment with the seal of Cæsar;
I found it in his closet; 'tis his will.   **closet: chamber**
Let but the commons hear this testament —   **commons: common people**
Which, pardon me, I do not mean to read —
And they would go and kiss dead Cæsar's wounds
And dip their napkins in his sacred blood,   **napkins: handkerchiefs**
Yea, beg a hair of him for memory,
And, dying, mention it within their wills,
Bequeathing it as a rich legacy
Unto their issue.   140
    4 PLEBEIAN. We'll hear the will. Read it, Mark
      Antony.
    ALL. The will, the will! we will hear Cæsar's will!
    ANTONY. Have patience, gentle friends, I must
      not read it;
It is not meet you know how Cæsar lov'd you.   **meet: proper**
You are not wood, you are not stones, but men;
And, being men, hearing the will of Cæsar,

It will inflame you, it will make you mad.
'Tis good you know not that you are his heirs;
For, if you should, O, what would come of it!   149
   4 PLEBEIAN.   Read the will; we'll hear it, Antony.
You shall read us the will, Cæsar's will.
   ANTONY.   Will you be patient? Will you stay a
     while?
I have o'ershot myself to tell you of it.   **o'ershot myself:** spoken too openly
I fear I wrong the honourable men.
Whose daggers have stabb'd Cæsar; I do fear it.
   4 PLEBEIAN.   They were traitors. Honourable
     men!
   ALL.   The will! the testament!
   2 PLEBEIAN.   They were villains, murderers. The
     will! Read the will!
   ANTONY.   You will compel me, then, to read the
     will?
Then make a ring about the corpse of Cæsar,   160
And let me show you him that made the will.
Shall I descend? and will you give me leave?
   ALL.   Come down.
   2 PLEBEIAN.   Descend.
   3 PLEBEIAN.   You shall have leave.
            [*Antony comes down from the pulpit.*]
   4 PLEBEIAN.   A ring; stand round.
   1 PLEBEIAN.   Stand from the hearse! Stand from   **hearse:** bier
     the body.
   2 PLEBEIAN.   Room for Antony, most noble
     Antony.
   ANTONY.   Nay, press not so upon me; stand far off.
   ALL.   Stand back! Room! Bear back!   170
   ANTONY.   If you have tears, prepare to shed them
     now.
You all do know this mantle; I remember   **mantle:** toga
The first time ever Cæsar put it on.
'Twas on a summer's evening, in his tent,
That day he overcame the Nervii.   **Nervii:** a Belgian tribe
Look, in this place ran Cassius' dagger through;
See what a rent the envious Casca made;
Through this the well-beloved Brutus stabb'd,
And as he pluck'd his cursed steel away,
Mark how the blood of Cæsar followed it,   180
As rushing out of doors to be resolv'd   **As:** as though
If Brutus so unkindly knock'd or no;   **unkindly:** (1) cruelly, (2) unnatu-
For Brutus, as you know, was Cæsar's angel.   rally
Judge, O you gods, how dearly Cæsar lov'd him!
This was the most unkindest cut of all;
For when the noble Cæsar saw him stab,
Ingratitude, more strong than traitors' arms,

Quite vanquish'd him. Then burst his mighty
    heart;
And, in his mantle muffling up his face,
Even at the base of Pompey's statuë,   190
Which all the while ran blood, great Cæsar fell.
O, what a fall was there, my countrymen!
Then I, and you, and all of us fell down,
Whilst bloody treason flourish'd over us.
O, now you weep, and I perceive you feel
The dint of pity. These are gracious drops.
Kind souls, what, weep you when you but behold
Our Cæsar's vesture wounded? Look you here:
                [*Lifting Cæsar's mantle*]
Here is himself, marr'd, as you see, with traitors.

1 PLEBEIAN. O piteous spectacle!   200
2 PLEBEIAN. O noble Cæsar!
3 PLEBEIAN. O woeful day!
4 PLEBEIAN. O traitors, villains!
1 PLEBEIAN. O most bloody sight!
2 PLEBEIAN. We will be reveng'd!
[ALL.]   Revenge! About!
Seek! Burn! Fire! Kill! Slay!
Let not a traitor live!
ANTONY.   Stay, countrymen.
1 PLEBEIAN. Peace there! hear the noble Antony.
2 PLEBEIAN. We'll hear him, we'll follow him,
    we'll die with him.
ANTONY. Good friends, sweet friends, let me not
    stir you up   210
To such a sudden flood of mutiny.
They that have done this deed are honourable.
What private griefs they have, alas, I know not,
That made them do it; they are wise and honourable
And will, no doubt, with reasons answer you.
I come not, friends, to steal away your hearts.
I am no orator, as Brutus is;
But, as you know me all, a plain blunt man
That love my friend; and that they know full well
That gave me public leave to speak of him;   220
For I have neither [wit], nor words, nor worth,
Action, nor utterance, nor the power of speech
To stir men's blood; I only speak right on.
I tell you that which you yourselves do know;
Show you sweet Cæsar's wounds, poor, poor, dumb
    mouths,
And bid them speak for me. But were I Brutus,
And Brutus Antony, there were an Antony
Would ruffle up your spirits, and put a tongue
In every wound of Cæsar, that should move

wit: intellectual capacity
utterance: eloquence
right on: directly

ruffle: rouse

The stones of Rome to rise and mutiny.   230
    ALL. We'll mutiny.
    1 PLEBEIAN. We'll burn the house of Brutus.
    3 PLEBEIAN. Away, then! come, seek the con-
      spirators.
    ANTONY. Yet hear me, countrymen; yet hear me
      speak.
    ALL. Peace, ho! hear Antony, most noble Antony!
    ANTONY. Why, friends, you go to do you know
      not what.
Wherein hath Cæsar thus deserv'd your loves?
Alas, you know not; I must tell you, then.
You have forgot the will I told you of.
    ALL. Most true. The will! Let's stay and hear
      the will.   240
    ANTONY. Here is the will, and under Cæsar's seal.
To every Roman citizen he gives,
To every several man, seventy-five drachmas.
    2 PLEBEIAN. Most noble Cæsar! We'll revenge
      his death.
    3 PLEBEIAN. O Royal Cæsar!   **Royal: generous**
    ANTONY. Hear me with patience.
    ALL. Peace, ho!
    ANTONY. Moreover, he hath left you all his walks,
His private arbours and new-planted orchards,
On this side Tiber; he hath left them you   250
And to your heirs forever, common pleasures,   **pleasures: pleasure grounds**
To walk abroad and recreate yourselves.
Here was a Cæsar! When comes such another?
    1 PLEBEIAN. Never, never! Come, away, away!
We'll burn his body in the holy place,
And with the brands fire the traitors' houses.
Take up the body.
    2 PLEBEIAN. Go fetch fire.
    3 PLEBEIAN. Pluck down benches.   259
    4 PLEBEIAN. Pluck down forms, windows, any-
      thing.   [*Exeunt Plebeians [with the body*]
    ANTONY. Now let it work. Mischief, thou art   **Mischief: evil**
      afoot,
Take thou what course thou wilt!

John Dryden (1631–1700)

ENGLISH POET and DRAMATIST

A Song for St. Cecilia's Day, 1687

I

From Harmony, from heav'nly Harmony
 This universal Frame began.
  When Nature underneath a heap
  Of jarring Atomes lay,
  And cou'd not heave her Head,
The tuneful Voice was heard from high,
  Arise ye more than dead.
Then cold, and hot, and moist, and dry,
In order to their stations leap,
  And Musick's pow'r obey.   10
From Harmony, from heav'nly Harmony
 This universal Frame began:
  From Harmony to Harmony
Through all the compass of the Notes it ran,
The Diapason closing full in Man.

universal Frame: world

cold . . . dry: the only possible properties of matter, according to Renaissance theory

heav'nly Harmony: The spheres, when correctly in orbit, made sweet music scarcely audible to men.

II

What Passion cannot Musick raise and quell!
  When *Jubal* struck the corded Shell,
  His list'ning Brethren stood around
  And wond'ring, on their Faces fell
  To worship that Celestial Sound.   20
Less than a God they thought there cou'd not dwell
  Within the hollow of that Shell
  That spoke so sweetly and so well.
What Passion cannot Musick raise and quell!

Jubal: legendary inventor of harp and organ

III

 The Trumpets loud Clangor
  Excites us to Arms
 With shrill Notes of Anger
  And mortal Alarms.

St. Cecilia, a Roman martyr of the early church, was, according to legend, interested in music and became the patroness of church music. She was often represented as playing the organ. A musical society formed in London to perform compositions in her honor asked Dryden to write this poem (to be set to music) in 1687.

From *The Poems of John Dryden,* edited by James Kinsley. Reprinted by permission of the Clarendon Press, Oxford.

The double double double beat
  Of the thundring DRUM   30
Cryes, heark the Foes come;
Charge, Charge, 'tis too late to retreat.

IV

The soft complaining FLUTE
In dying Notes discovers
The Woes of hopeless Lovers,
Whose Dirge is whisper'd by the warbling LUTE.

V

Sharp VIOLINS proclaim
Their jealous Pangs, and Desperation,
Fury, frantick Indignation,
Depth of Pains, and height of Passion,   40
  For the fair, disdainful Dame.

VI

But oh! what Art can teach
  What human Voice can reach
The sacred ORGANS praise?
Notes inspiring holy Love,
Notes that wing their heav'nly ways
  To mend the Choires above.

mend: free from sin, make better
Choires: (1) singers (2) sanctuaries

VII

Orpheus cou'd lead the savage race;
And Trees unrooted left their place;
  Sequacious of the Lyre: 50
But bright CECILIA rais'd the wonder high'r;
When to her ORGAN, vocal Breath was giv'n
An Angel heard, and straight appear'd
  Mistaking Earth for Heaven.

Orpheus: a legendary singer and
harpist whose music charmed and
tamed wild beasts and caused
trees to follow him in servitude

Grand CHORUS

As from the pow'r of sacred Lays
  The Spheres began to move,
And sung the great Creator's praise
  To all the bless'd above;
So when the last and dreadful hour
This crumbling Pageant shall devour,   60
The TRUMPET *shall be heard on high,*
The Dead shall live, the Living die,
And MUSICK *shall untune the Sky.*

Johann Wolfgang von Goethe (1749–1832)

GERMAN DRAMATIST, POET, SCIENTIST,
and COURT-OFFICIAL

On the Inspiration of the Poet

You come back, wavering shapes, out of the past
In which you first appeared to clouded eyes.
Should I attempt this time to hold you fast?
Does this old dream still thrill a heart so wise?
You crowd? You press? Have, then, your way at last.
As from the mist around me you arise;
My breast is stirred and feels with youthful pain
The magic breath that hovers round your train.

With you return pictures of joyous days,
Shadows that I once loved again draw near;   10
Like a primeval tale, half lost in haze,
First love and friendship also reappear;
Grief is renewed, laments retrace the maze
Of Life's strange labyrinthian career,
Recalling dear ones who, by fortune's treason
Robbed of fair hours, passed before my season.

They will not hear me as I sing these songs,
The parted souls to whom I sang the first;
Gone is that first response, in vain one longs
For friendly crowds that have long been dispersed.   20
My grief resounds to strangers, unknown throngs
Applaud it, and my anxious heart would burst.
Whoever used to praise my poem's worth,
If they still live, stray scattered through the earth.

And I am seized by long forgotten yearning
For that kingdom of spirits, still and grave;
To flowing song I see my feelings turning,
As from aeolian harps, wave upon wave;
A shudder grips me, tear on tear falls burning,
Soft grows my heart, once so severe and brave;   30
What I possess, seems far away to me,
And what is gone becomes reality.

Wolfgang Amadeus Mozart (1756–1791)

AUSTRIAN COMPOSER

The Act of Creating

When I am, as it were, completely myself, entirely alone, and of good cheer — say, travelling in a carriage, or walking after a good meal, or during the night when I cannot sleep; it is on such occasions that my ideas flow best and most abundantly. *Whence* and *how* they come, I know not; nor can I force them. Those ideas that please me I retain in memory, and am accustomed, as I have been told, to hum them to myself. If I continue in this way, it soon occurs to me how I may turn this or that morsel to account, so as to make a good dish of it, that is to say, agreeably to the rules of counterpoint, to the peculiarities of the various instruments, etc.

All this fires my soul, and, provided I am not disturbed, my subject enlarges itself, becomes methodised and defined, and the whole, though it be long, stands almost complete and finished in my mind, so that I can survey it, like a fine picture or a beautiful statue, at a glance. Nor do I hear in my imagination the parts *successively*, but I hear them, as it were, all at once.... What a delight this is I cannot tell! All this inventing, this producing, takes place in a pleasing lively dream. Still the actual hearing of the *tout ensemble* is after all the best. What has been thus produced I do not easily forget, and this is perhaps the best gift I have my Divine Maker to thank for.

When I proceed to write down my ideas, I take out of the bag of my memory, if I may use that phrase, what has been previously collected into it in the way I have mentioned. For this reason the committing to paper is done quickly enough, for everything is, as I said before, already finished; and it rarely differs on paper from what it was in my imagination. At this occupation I can therefore suffer myself to be disturbed; for whatever may be going on around me, I write, and even talk, but only of fowls and geese, or of Gretel or Bärbel,[1] or some such matters. But why my productions take from my hand that particular form and style that makes them *Mozartish,* and different from the works of other composers, is probably owing to the same cause which renders my nose so large or so aquiline, or, in short, makes it Mozart's, and different from those of other people. For I really do not study or aim at any originality.

[1] probably a reference to characters in Mozart's "The Marriage of Figaro."

Title supplied by editors. "The Act of Creating" by Wolfgang Amadeus Mozart. Although the authenticity of this letter is in doubt, it has been attributed to Mozart. From *The Life of Mozart* by Edward Holmes. Everyman's Library Edition. Reprinted by permission of E. P. Dutton & Co., Inc., and J. M. Dent & Sons Ltd., London.

Samuel Taylor Coleridge (1772–1834)

ENGLISH POET and CRITIC

Kubla Khan

OR, A VISION IN A DREAM. A FRAGMENT.

The following fragment is here published at the request of a poet of great and deserved celebrity [Lord Byron], and, as far as the Author's own opinions are concerned, rather as a psychological curiosity, than on the ground of any supposed *poetic* merits.

In the summer of the year 1797, the Author, then in ill health, had retired to a lonely farm-house between Porlock and Linton, on the Exmoor confines of Somerset and Devonshire. In consequence of a slight indisposition, an anodyne had been prescribed, from the effects of which he fell asleep in his chair at the moment that he was reading the following sentence, or words of the same substance, in 'Purchas's Pilgrimage': 'Here the Khan Kubla commanded a palace to be built, and a stately garden thereunto. And thus ten miles of fertile ground were inclosed with a wall.' The Author continued for about three hours in a profound sleep, at least of the external senses, during which time he has the most vivid confidence, that he could not have composed less than from two to three hundred lines; if that indeed can be called composition in which all the images rose up before him as *things*, with a parallel production of the correspondent expressions, without any sensation or consciousness of effort. On awaking he appeared to himself to have a distinct recollection of the whole, and taking his pen, ink, and paper, instantly and eagerly wrote down the lines that are here preserved. At this moment he was unfortunately called out by a person on business from Porlock, and detained by him above an hour, and on his return to his room, found, to his no small surprise and mortification, that though he still retained some vague and dim recollection of the general purport of the vision, yet, with the exception of some eight or ten scattered lines and images, all the rest had passed away like the images on the surface of a stream into which a stone has been cast, but, alas! without the after restoration of the latter!

> Then all the charm
> Is broken — all that phantom-world so fair
> Vanishes, and a thousand circlets spread,
> And each mis-shape['s] the other. Stay awhile,

"Kubla Khan" by Samuel Taylor Coleridge. From *The Complete Poetical Works of S. T. Coleridge*, edited by Ernest Hartley Coleridge. Reprinted by permission of the Clarendon Press, Oxford.

Poor youth! who scarcely dar'st lift up thine eyes —
The stream will soon renew its smoothness, soon
The visions will return! And lo, he stays,
And soon the fragments dim of lovely forms
Come trembling back, unite, and now once more
The pool becomes a mirror.

[From *The Picture; or, the Lover's Resolution*, ll. 91–100.]

Yet from the still surviving recollections in his mind, the Author has frequently purposed to finish for himself what had been originally, as it were, given to him. Σαμερον αδιον ασω [Αὔριον ἄδιον ἄοω 1834]:[1] but the tomorrow is yet to come.

As a contrast to this vision, I have annexed a fragment of a very different character, describing with equal fidelity the dream of pain and disease.

In Xanadu did Kubla Khan
A stately pleasure-dome decree:
Where Alph, the sacred river, ran
Through caverns measureless to man
    Down to a sunless sea.
So twice five miles of fertile ground
With walls and towers were girdled round:
And there were gardens bright with sinuous rills,
Where blossomed many an incense-bearing tree;
And here were forests ancient as the hills,   10
Enfolding sunny spots of greenery.

But oh! that deep romantic chasm which slanted
Down the green hill athwart a cedarn cover!
A savage place! as holy and enchanted
As e'er beneath a waning moon was haunted
By woman wailing for her demon-lover!
And from this chasm, with ceaseless turmoil seething,
As if this earth in fast thick pants were breathing,
A mighty fountain momently was forced:
Amid whose swift half-intermitted burst   20
Huge fragments vaulted like rebounding hail,
Or chaffy grain beneath the thresher's flail:
And 'mid these dancing rocks at once and ever
It flung up momently the sacred river.
Five miles meandering with a mazy motion
Through wood and dale the sacred river ran,
Then reached the caverns measureless to man,
And sank in tumult to a lifeless ocean:
And 'mid this tumult Kubla heard from far
Ancestral voices prophesying war!   30

[1] "Today I shall sing more sweetly. [Tomorrow I shall sing more sweetly.]"

The shadow of the dome of pleasure
　　Floated midway on the waves;
　　Where was heard the mingled measure
　　From the fountain and the caves.
It was a miracle of rare device,
A sunny pleasure-dome with caves of ice!

　　A damsel with a dulcimer
　　In a vision once I saw:
　　It was an Abyssinian maid,
　　And on her dulcimer she played,   40
　　Singing of Mount Abora.
　　Could I revive within me
　　Her symphony and song,
　　To such a deep delight 'twould win me,
That with music loud and long,
I would build that dome in air,
That sunny dome! those caves of ice!
And all who heard should see them there,
And all should cry, Beware! Beware!
His flashing eyes, his floating hair!   50
Weave a circle round him thrice,
And close your eyes with holy dread,
For he on honey-dew hath fed,
And drunk the milk of Paradise.

John Keats (1795–1821)

ENGLISH POET

Ode on a Grecian Urn

I

Thou still unravish'd bride of quietness,
　　Thou foster-child of silence and slow time,
Sylvan historian, who canst thus express
　　A flowery tale more sweetly than our rhyme:
What leaf-fring'd legend haunts about thy shape
　　Of deities or mortals, or of both,
　　　　In Tempe or the dales of Arcady?
　　What men or gods are these? What maidens loth?
What mad pursuit? What struggle to escape?
　　　　What pipes and timbrels? What wild ecstasy?   10

Tempe: valley in Greece near Mount Olympus, home of the gods
Arcady: rustic area in Greece which became a symbol in later literature for peaceful pastoral existence

From *John Keats: Selected Poems and Letters*, edited by Douglas Bush (Riverside Edition). Reprinted by permission of Houghton Mifflin Company.

II

Heard melodies are sweet, but those unheard
   Are sweeter; therefore, ye soft pipes, play on;
Not to the sensual ear, but, more endear'd,
   Pipe to the spirit ditties of no tone:
Fair youth, beneath the trees, thou canst not leave
   Thy song, nor ever can those trees be bare;
     Bold Lover, never, never canst thou kiss,
Though winning near the goal — yet, do not grieve;
   She cannot fade, though thou hast not thy bliss,
     For ever wilt thou love, and she be fair!   20

III

Ah, happy, happy boughs! that cannot shed
   Your leaves, nor ever bid the Spring adieu;
And, happy melodist, unwearied,
   For ever piping songs for ever new;
More happy love! more happy, happy love!
   For ever warm and still to be enjoy'd,
     For ever panting, and for ever young;
All breathing human passion far above,
   That leaves a heart high-sorrowful and cloy'd,
     A burning forehead, and a parching tongue.   30

IV

Who are these coming to the sacrifice?
   To what green altar, O mysterious priest,
Lead'st thou that heifer lowing at the skies,
   And all her silken flanks with garlands drest?
What little town by river or sea shore,
   Or mountain-built with peaceful citadel,
     Is emptied of this folk, this pious morn?
And, little town, thy streets for evermore
   Will silent be; and not a soul to tell
     Why thou art desolate, can e'er return.   40

V

O Attic shape! Fair attitude! with brede
   Of marble men and maidens overwrought,
With forest branches and the trodden weed;
   Thou, silent form, dost tease us out of thought
As doth eternity: Cold Pastoral!
   When old age shall this generation waste,
     Thou shalt remain, in midst of other woe
Than ours, a friend to man, to whom thou say'st,
   "Beauty is truth, truth beauty, — that is all
     Ye know on earth, and all ye need to know."   50

Charles Baudelaire (1821–1867)

FRENCH POET

The Sun

Along old terraces where blinds tent the masonry
Each one a separate shelter for private luxury,
When the cruel sun redoubles its sharp stroke
On street and hedgerow, on rooftop and brake,
I walk alone, absorbed in my curious exercise,
Duelling with words that dodge in corners and byways;
Stumbling on rhymes as on crooked setts, colliding
With a sudden clear line which dreams were past finding.

The all-satisfying sun, anaemia's enemy,
Gives life to the worm and the rose impartially;   10
Evaporating care and sending it skywards
He brings honey to the hive, and to the mute mind words.
It is he who makes the ancient cripples young again
With the gaiety and gentleness of young children;
He orders the harvest to increase and flourish
In that old heart where life is the perpetual wish.

When he comes down into the city like a poet
Transfiguring the values of things the most abject,
He enters like royalty, unaccompanied by officials,
All the palatial hotels and all the hospitals.   20

Lewis Carroll (1832–1898)

ENGLISH MATHEMATICIAN and WRITER

Jabberwocky

'Twas brillig, and the slithy toves
    Did gyre and gimble in the wabe:
All mimsy were the borogoves,
    And the mome raths outgrabe.

"The Sun" from *Les Fleurs du Mal* by Charles Baudelaire. Translated by David Paul and reprinted with his permission.

"Jabberwocky" and "Humpty Dumpty" by Lewis Carroll. From *Through the Looking-Glass and What Alice Found There.*

975

"Beware the Jabberwock, my son!
   The jaws that bite, the claws that catch!
Beware the Jubjub bird, and shun
   The frumious Bandersnatch!"

He took his vorpal sword in hand:
   Long time the manxome foe he sought —   10
So rested he by the Tumtum tree,
   And stood awhile in thought.

And, as in uffish thought he stood,
   The Jabberwock, with eyes of flame,
Came whiffling through the tulgey wood,
   And burbled as it came!

One, two! One, two! And through and through
   The vorpal blade went snicker-snack!
He left it dead, and with its head
   He went galumphing back.   20

"And hast thou slain the Jabberwock?
   Come to my arms, my beamish boy!
O frabjous day! Callooh! Callay!"
   He chortled in his joy.

'Twas brillig, and the slithy toves
   Did gyre and gimble in the wabe:
All mimsy were the borogoves,
   And the mome raths outgrabe.

Humpty Dumpty

. . . "That shows that there are three hundred and sixty-four days when you might get unbirthday presents —— "

"Certainly," said Alice.

"And only *one* for birthday presents, you know. There's glory for you!"

"I don't know what you mean by 'glory,'" Alice said.

Humpty Dumpty smiled contemptuously. "Of course you don't — till I tell you. I meant 'there's a nice knock-down argument for you!'"

"But 'glory' doesn't mean 'a nice knockdown argument,'" Alice objected.

"When *I* use a word," Humpty Dumpty said, in rather a scornful tone, "it means just what I choose it to mean — neither more nor less."

"The question is," said Alice, "whether you *can* make words mean so many different things."

"The question is," said Humpty Dumpty, "which is to be master —— that's all."

Alice was too much puzzled to say anything; so after a minute Humpty Dumpty began again. "They've a temper, some of them — particularly verbs: they're the proudest — adjectives you can do anything with, but not verbs — however, I can manage the whole lot of them! Impenetrability! That's what I say!"

"Would you tell me, please," said Alice, "what that means?"

"Now you talk like a reasonable child," said Humpty Dumpty, looking very much pleased. "I meant by 'impenetrability' that we've had enough of that subject, and it would be just as well if you'd mention what you mean to do next, as I suppose you don't mean to stop here all the rest of your life."

"That's a great deal to make one word mean," Alice said in a thoughtful tone.

"When I make a word do a lot of work like that," said Humpty Dumpty, "I always pay it extra."

"Oh!" said Alice. She was too much puzzled to make any other remark.

"Ah, you should see 'em come round me of a Saturday night," Humpty Dumpty went on, wagging his head gravely from side to side, "for to get their wages, you know."

(Alice didn't venture to ask what he paid them with; and so you see I ca'n't tell *you*.)

"You seem very clever at explaining words, Sir," said Alice. "Would you kindly tell me the meaning of the poem called 'Jabberwocky'?"

"Let's hear it," said Humpty Dumpty. "I can explain all the poems that ever were invented — and a good many that haven't been invented just yet."

This sounded very hopeful, so Alice repeated the first verse: —

> " 'Twas brillig, and the slithy toves
>   Did gyre and gimble in the wabe:
> All mimsy were the borogoves,
>   And the mome raths outgrabe."

"That's enough to begin with," Humpty Dumpty interrupted: "there are plenty of hard words there. 'Brillig' means four o'clock in the afternoon — the time when you begin *broiling* things for dinner."

"That'll do very well," said Alice: "and 'slithy'?"

"Well, 'slithy' means 'lithe and slimy.' 'Lithe' is the same as 'active.' You see it's like a portmanteau — there are two meanings packed up into one word."

"I see it now," Alice remarked thoughtfully: "and what are 'toves'?"

"Well, 'toves' are something like badgers — they're something like lizards — and they're something like corkscrews."

"They must be very curious-looking creatures."

"They are that," said Humpty Dumpty: "also they make their nests under sun-dials — also they live on cheese."

"And what's to 'gyre' and to 'gimble'?"

"To 'gyre' is to go round and round like a gyroscope. To 'gimble' is to make holes like a gimblet."

"And '*the wabe*' is the grass-plot round a sun-dial, I suppose?" said Alice, surprised at her own ingenuity.

"Of course it is. It's called '*wabe*,' you know, because it goes a long way before it, and a long way behind it —— "

"And a long way beyond it on each side," Alice added.

"Exactly so. Well then, '*mimsy*' is 'flimsy and miserable' (there's another portmanteau for you). And a '*borogove*' is a thin shabby-looking bird with its feathers sticking out all round — something like a live mop."

"And then '*mome raths*'?" said Alice. "I'm afraid I'm giving you a great deal of trouble."

"Well, a '*rath*' is a sort of green pig: but '*mome*' I'm not certain about. I think it's short for 'from home' — meaning that they'd lost their way, you know."

"And what does '*outgrabe*' mean?"

"Well, '*outgribing*' is something between bellowing and whistling, with a kind of sneeze in the middle: however, you'll hear it done, maybe — down in the wood yonder — and, when you've once heard it, you'll be *quite* content. Who's been repeating all that hard stuff to you?"

Vincent van Gogh   (1853–1890)

DUTCH PAINTER

From Idea into Art

I have been working very hard. I had not made many compositions or studies for a long time, so when I once got started, I became so eager that many a morning I got up at four o'clock. . . .

It must not surprise you that some of my figures are so entirely different from those I make at times when I use models.

I *seldom work from memory* — I do not practice that kind of thing very much. Besides, I am so used to work with the natural form now and can keep my personal feeling out of it much better than I could at first. I waver less — and just because I am sitting opposite the model, SOMETIMES I FEEL MORE LIKE MYSELF. When I have a model who is quiet and steady and with whom I am acquainted, then I draw repeatedly till there is one drawing that is different from the rest, which does not look like an ordinary study, but more typical and with more feeling. All the same it was made under circumstances similar to those of the others, yet the latter are just studies with less feeling

Title supplied by editors. From *Letters to an Artist: from Vincent van Gogh to Anton van Rappard* translated by Rela van Messel. Copyright 1936, © 1964 by The Viking Press, Inc. Reprinted by permission of The Viking Press, Inc.

and life in them. This manner of working is like another one, just as plausible. As to *The Little Winter Gardens*, for example, you said yourself they had so much feeling; all right, but that was not accidental — I drew them several times and there was no feeling in them. Then afterwards — after I had done the ones that were so stiff — came the others. It is the same with the clumsy and awkward things. HOW IT HAPPENS THAT I CAN EXPRESS SOMETHING OF THAT KIND? Because the thing has already taken form in my mind before I start on it. The first attempts are absolutely unbearable. I say this because I want you to know that if you see something worth while in what I am doing, it is not by accident but because of real intention and purpose.

I am very much pleased to have you notice that of late I have been trying to express the values of crowds, and that I try to separate things in the dizzy whirl and chaos one can see in each little corner of Nature.

Formerly the light and shade in my studies were mostly arbitrary, at least they were not put down logically, and so they were colder and flatter. When I once get *the feeling of my subject*, and get to know it, I usually draw it in three or more variations — be it a figure or landscape — only I always refer to Nature for every one of them and then I do my best not to put in *any detail*, as the dream quality would then be lost. When Tersteeg[1] or my brother then says to me: "What is that, grass or coal?" I answer: "Glad to hear that you cannot see what it is."

Still it is enough like Nature for the simple peasants of this part of the country. They say: "Yes, that's the hedge of Juffrouw Renese," and: "There are the beanpoles of van der Louw."

William Butler Yeats (1865–1939)

IRISH POET and DRAMATIST

Adam's Curse

We sat together at one summer's end,
That beautiful mild woman, your close friend,
And you and I,[1] and talked of poetry.
I said: 'A line will take us hours maybe;

[1] a family friend who bought and freely criticized van Gogh's work.

[1] Yeats, Maud Gonne (Yeats' beloved), and Maud Gonne's sister.

Yet if it does not seem a moment's thought,
Our stitching and unstitching has been naught.
Better go down upon your marrow-bones
And scrub a kitchen pavement, or break stones
Like an old pauper, in all kinds of weather;
For to articulate sweet sounds together 10
Is to work harder than all these, and yet
Be thought an idler by the noisy set
Of bankers, schoolmasters, and clergymen
The martyrs call the world.'

       And thereupon
That beautiful mild woman for whose sake
There's many a one shall find out all heartache
On finding that her voice is sweet and low
Replied: 'To be born woman is to know —
Although they do not talk of it at school — 20
That we must labour to be beautiful.'

I said: 'It's certain there is no fine thing
Since Adam's fall but needs much labouring.
There have been lovers who thought love should be
So much compounded of high courtesy
That they would sigh and quote with learned looks
Precedents out of beautiful old books;
Yet now it seems an idle trade enough.'

We sat grown quiet at the name of love;
We saw the last embers of daylight die, 30
And in the trembling blue-green of the sky
A moon, worn as if it had been a shell
Washed by time's waters as they rose and fell
About the stars and broke in days and years.

I had a thought for no one's but your ears:
That you were beautiful, and that I strove
To love you in the old high way of love;
That it had all seemed happy, and yet we'd grown
As weary-hearted as that hollow moon.

Sailing to Byzantium

I

That is no country for old men. The young
In one another's arms, birds in the trees
— Those dying generations — at their song,
The salmon-falls, the mackerel-crowded seas,
Fish, flesh, or fowl, commend all summer long
Whatever is begotten, born, and dies.
Caught in that sensual music all neglect
Monuments of unageing intellect.

II

An aged man is but a paltry thing,
A tattered coat upon a stick, unless   10
Soul clap its hands and sing, and louder sing
For every tatter in its mortal dress,
Nor is there singing school but studying
Monuments of its own magnificence;
And therefore I have sailed the seas and come
To the holy city of Byzantium.

> **Byzantium:** holy city of Eastern Christianity

III

O sages standing in God's holy fire
As in the gold mosaic of a wall,
Come from the holy fire, perne in a gyre,
And be the singing-masters of my soul.   20
Consume my heart away; sick with desire
And fastened to a dying animal
It knows not what it is; and gather me
Into the artifice of eternity.

> **As:** as if
>
> **perne in a gyre:** spin out and back to form intersecting cones (spirals) of movement

IV

Once out of nature I shall never take
My bodily form from any natural thing,
But such a form as Grecian goldsmiths make
Of hammered gold and gold enamelling
To keep a drowsy Emperor awake;
Or set upon a golden bough to sing   30
To lords and ladies of Byzantium
Of what is past, or passing, or to come.

Luigi Pirandello (1867–1936)

ITALIAN DRAMATIST, NOVELIST,
and SHORT STORY WRITER

Six Characters in Search of an Author

CHARACTERS OF THE COMEDY IN THE MAKING

THE FATHER

THE MOTHER

THE STEPDAUGHTER

THE SON

MADAME PACE

THE BOY ⎫

THE CHILD ⎭ *(These two do not speak)*

ACTORS OF THE COMPANY

THE MANAGER

LEADING LADY

LEADING MAN

SECOND LADY LEAD

L'INGÉNUE

JUVENILE LEAD

OTHER ACTORS AND ACTRESSES

PROPERTY MAN

PROMPTER

MACHINIST

MANAGER'S SECRETARY

DOOR-KEEPER

SCENE-SHIFTERS

Scene: Daytime, the stage of a theater

ACT I

N.B. *The Comedy is without acts or scenes. The performance is interrupted once, without the curtain being lowered, when* THE MANAGER *and the chief characters withdraw to arrange the scenario. A second interruption of the action takes place when, by mistake, the stage hands let the curtain down.*

The spectators will find the curtain raised and the stage as it usually is during the daytime. It will be half dark, and empty, so that from the beginning the public may have the impression of an impromptu performance.

PROMPTER'S *box and a small table and chair for* THE MANAGER.

Two other small tables and several chairs scattered about as during rehearsals.

The ACTORS *and* ACTRESSES *of the company enter from the back of the stage: First one, then another, then two together: nine or ten in all. They are about to rehearse a Pirandello play:* Mixing It Up. *Some of the company move off towards their dressing rooms. The* PROMPTER, *who has the "book" under his arm, is waiting for* THE MANAGER *in order to begin the rehearsal.*

The ACTORS *and* ACTRESSES, *some standing, some sitting, chat and smoke. One perhaps reads a paper; another cons his part.*

From the book *Naked Masks: Five Plays* by Luigi Pirandello. Edited by Eric Bentley. Copyright, 1922, 1952, by E. P. Dutton & Co., Inc. Renewal, 1950, by Stefano, Fausto and Lietta Pirandello. Dutton Paperback Series. Reprinted by permission of E. P. Dutton & Co., Inc.

982

Finally, THE MANAGER *enters and goes to the table prepared for him. His* SECRETARY *brings him his mail, through which he glances. The* PROMPTER *takes his seat, turns on a light, and opens the "book."*

THE MANAGER (*Throwing a letter down on the table*). I can't see. (*To* PROPERTY MAN) Let's have a little light, please!

PROPERTY MAN. Yes sir, yes, at once. (*A light comes down on to the stage*)

THE MANAGER (*Clapping his hands*). Come along! Come along! Second act of *Mixing it Up*. (*Sits down*)

(*The* ACTORS *and* ACTRESSES *go from the front of the stage to the wings, all except the three who are to begin the rehearsal*)

THE PROMPTER (*Reading the "book"*). "Leo Gala's house. A curious room serving as dining-room and study."

THE MANAGER (*To* PROPERTY MAN). Fix up the old red room.

PROPERTY MAN (*Noting it down*). Red set. All right!

THE PROMPTER (*Continuing to read from the "book"*). "Table already laid and writing desk with books and papers. Bookshelves. Exit rear to Leo's bed-room. Exit left to kitchen. Principal exit to right."

THE MANAGER (*Energetically*). Well, you understand: The principal exit over there; here, the kitchen. (*Turning to* ACTOR *who is to play the part of Socrates*) You make your entrances and exits here. (*To* PROPERTY MAN) The baize doors at the rear, and curtains.

PROPERTY MAN (*Noting it down*). Right-o!

PROMPTER (*Reading as before*). "When the curtain rises, Leo Gala, dressed in cook's cap and apron is busy beating an egg in a cup. Philip, also dressed as a cook, is beating another egg. Guido Venanzi is seated and listening."

LEADING MAN (*To* MANAGER). Excuse me, but must I absolutely wear a cook's cap?

THE MANAGER (*Annoyed*). I imagine so. It says so there anyway. (*Pointing to the "book"*)

LEADING MAN. But it's ridiculous!

THE MANAGER. Ridiculous? Ridiculous? Is it my fault if France won't send us any more good comedies, and we are reduced to putting on Pirandello's works where nobody understands anything, and where the author plays the fool with us all? (*The* ACTORS *grin.* THE MANAGER *goes to* LEADING MAN *and shouts*) Yes sir, you put on the cook's cap and beat eggs. Do you suppose that with all this egg-beating business you are on an ordinary stage? Get that out of your head. You represent the shell of the eggs you are beating! (*Laughter and comments among the* ACTORS) Silence! and listen to my explanations, please! (*To* LEADING MAN): "The empty form of reason without the fullness of instinct, which is blind" — You stand for reason, your wife is instinct. It's a mixing up of the parts, according to which you who act your own part become the puppet of yourself. Do you understand?

LEADING MAN. I'm hanged if I do.

THE MANAGER. Neither do I. But let's get on with it. It's sure to be a glorious failure anyway. (*Confidentially*): But I say, please face three-quarters. Otherwise, what with the abstruseness of the dialogue, and the public that won't be able to hear you, the whole thing will go to hell. Come on! come on!

PROMPTER. Pardon sir, may I get into my box? There's a bit of a draught.

THE MANAGER. Yes, yes, of course!

At this point, the DOOR-KEEPER *has entered from the stage door and advances towards* THE MANAGER'*s table, taking off his braided cap. During this ma-nœuver, the* SIX CHARACTERS *enter, and stop by the door at back of stage, so that when the* DOOR-KEEPER *is about to announce their coming to* THE MAN-AGER, *they are already on the stage. A tenuous light surrounds them, almost as if irradiated by them — the faint breath of their fantastic reality.*

This light will disappear when they come forward towards the ACTORS. *They preserve, however, something of the dream lightness in which they seem almost suspended; but this does not detract from the essential reality of their forms and expressions.*

He who is known as THE FATHER *is a man of about 50: hair, reddish in color, thin at the temples; he is not bald, however; thick moustaches, falling over his still fresh mouth, which often opens in an empty and uncertain smile. He is fattish, pale; with an especially wide forehead. He has blue, oval-shaped eyes, very clear and piercing. Wears light trousers and a dark jacket. He is alter-natively mellifluous and violent in his manner.*

THE MOTHER *seems crushed and terrified as if by an intolerable weight of shame and abasement. She is dressed in modest black and wears a thick widow's veil of crêpe. When she lifts this, she reveals a wax-like face. She always keeps her eyes downcast.*

THE STEPDAUGHTER *is dashing, almost impudent, beautiful. She wears mourning too, but with great elegance. She shows contempt for the timid half-frightened manner of the wretched* BOY (14 *years old, and also dressed in black); on the other hand, she displays a lively tenderness for her little sister,* THE CHILD (*about four*), *who is dressed in white, with a black silk sash at the waist.*

THE SON (22) *tall, severe in his attitude of contempt for* THE FATHER, *super-cilious and indifferent to* THE MOTHER. *He looks as if he had come on the stage against his will.*

DOORKEEPER (*Cap in hand*). Excuse me, sir. . . .

THE MANAGER (*Rudely*). Eh? What is it?

DOORKEEPER (*Timidly*). These people are asking for you, sir.

THE MANAGER (*Furious*). I am rehearsing, and you know perfectly well no one's allowed to come in during rehearsals! (*Turning to the* CHARACTERS): Who are you, please? What do you want?

THE FATHER (*Coming forward a little, followed by the others, who seem embarrassed*). As a matter of fact . . . we have come here in search of an author. . . .

THE MANAGER (*Half angry, half amazed*). An author? What author?

THE FATHER. Any author, sir.

THE MANAGER. But there's no author here. We are not rehearsing a new piece.

THE STEPDAUGHTER (*Vivaciously*). So much the better, so much the better! We can be your new piece.

AN ACTOR (*Coming forward from the others*). Oh, do you hear that?

THE FATHER (*To* STEPDAUGHTER). Yes, but if the author isn't here . . . (*To* MANAGER) . . . unless you would be willing. . . .

THE MANAGER. You are trying to be funny.

THE FATHER. No, for Heaven's sake, what are you saying? We bring you a drama, sir.

THE STEPDAUGHTER. We may be your fortune.

THE MANAGER. Will you oblige me by going away? We haven't time to waste with mad people.

THE FATHER (*Mellifluously*). Oh sir, you know well that life is full of infinite absurdities, which, strangely enough, do not even need to appear plausible, since they are true.

THE MANAGER. What the devil is he talking about?

THE FATHER. I say that to reverse the ordinary process may well be considered a madness: that is, to create credible situations, in order that they may appear true. But permit me to observe that if this be madness, it is the sole *raison d'être* of your profession, gentlemen. (*The* ACTORS *look hurt and perplexed*)

THE MANAGER (*Getting up and looking at him*) So our profession seems to you one worthy of madmen then?

THE FATHER. Well, to make seem true that which isn't true . . . without any need . . . for a joke as it were . . . Isn't that your mission, gentlemen: to give life to fantastic characters on the stage?

THE MANAGER (*Interpreting the rising anger of the* COMPANY). But I would beg you to believe, my dear sir, that the profession of the comedian is a noble one. If today, as things go, the playwrights give us stupid comedies to play and puppets to represent instead of men, remember we are proud to have given life to immortal works here on these very boards! (*The* ACTORS, *satisfied, applaud their* MANAGER)

THE FATHER (*Interrupting furiously*). Exactly, perfectly, to living beings more alive than those who breathe and wear clothes: being less real perhaps, but truer! I agree with you entirely. (*The* ACTORS *look at one another in amazement*)

THE MANAGER. But what do you mean? Before, you said . . .

THE FATHER. No, excuse me, I meant it for you, sir, who were crying out that you had no time to lose with madmen, while no one better than yourself knows that nature uses the instrument of human fantasy in order to pursue her high creative purpose.

THE MANAGER. Very well — but where does all this take us?

THE FATHER. Nowhere! It is merely to show you that one is born to life in many forms, in many shapes, as tree, or as stone, as water, as butterfly, or as woman. So one may also be born a character in a play.

THE MANAGER (*With feigned comic dismay*). So you and these other friends of yours have been born characters?

THE FATHER. Exactly, and alive as you see! (MANAGER *and* ACTORS *burst out laughing*)

THE FATHER (*Hurt*). I am sorry you laugh, because we carry in us a drama, as you can guess from this woman here, veiled in black.

THE MANAGER (*Losing patience at last and almost indignant*). Oh, chuck it! Get away please! Clear out of here! (*To* PROPERTY MAN) For Heaven's sake, turn them out!

THE FATHER (*Resisting*). No, no, look here, we. . . .

THE MANAGER (*Roaring*). We come here to work, you know.

LEADING ACTOR. One cannot let oneself be made such a fool of.

THE FATHER (*Determined, coming forward*). I marvel at your incredulity, gentlemen. Are you not accustomed to see the characters created by an author spring to life in yourselves and face each other? Just because there is no "book" (*Pointing to the* PROMPTER'S *box*) which contains us, you refuse to believe. . . .

THE STEPDAUGHTER (*Advances towards* MANAGER, *smiling and coquettish*). Believe me, we are really six most interesting characters, sir; side-tracked however.

THE FATHER. Yes, that is the word! (*To* MANAGER *all at once*) In the sense, that is, that the author who created us alive no longer wished, or was no longer able, materially to put us into a work of art. And this was a real crime, sir; because he who has had the luck to be born a character can laugh even at death. He cannot die. The man, the writer, the instrument of the creation will die, but his creation does not die. And to live for ever, it does not need to have extraordinary gifts or to be able to work wonders. Who was Sancho Panza? Who was Don Abbondio? Yet they live eternally because — live germs as they were — they had the fortune to find a fecundating matrix, a fantasy which could raise and nourish them: make them live for ever!

THE MANAGER. That is quite all right. But what do you want here, all of you?

THE FATHER. We want to live.

THE MANAGER (*Ironically*). For Eternity?

THE FATHER. No, sir, only for a moment . . . in you.

AN ACTOR. Just listen to him!

LEADING LADY. They want to live, in us! . . .

JUVENILE LEAD (*Pointing to the* STEPDAUGHTER). I've no objection, as far as that one is concerned!

THE FATHER. Look here! Look here! The comedy has to be made. (*To the* MANAGER) But if you and your actors are willing, we can soon concert it among ourselves.

THE MANAGER (*Annoyed*). But what do you want to concert? We don't go in for concerts here. Here we play dramas and comedies!

THE FATHER. Exactly! That is just why we have come to you.

THE MANAGER. And where is the "book"?

THE FATHER. It is in us! (*The* ACTORS *laugh*) The drama is in us, and we are the drama. We are impatient to play it. Our inner passion drives us on to this.

THE STEPDAUGHTER (*Disdainful, alluring, treacherous, full of impudence*). My passion, sir! Ah, if you only knew! My passion for him! (*Points to the* FATHER *and makes a pretence of embracing him. Then she breaks out into a loud laugh*)

THE FATHER (*Angrily*). Behave yourself! And please don't laugh in that fashion.

THE STEPDAUGHTER. With your permission, gentlemen, I, who am a two months' orphan, will show you how I can dance and sing. (*Sings and then dances* Prenez garde à Tchou-Tchin-Tchou)

> Les chinois sont un peuple malin,
> De Shanghaï à Pékin,
> Ils ont mis des écriteaux partout:
> Prenez garde à Tchou-Tchin-Tchou.[1]

ACTORS *and* ACTRESSES. Bravo! Well done! Tip-top!

THE MANAGER. Silence! This isn't a café concert, you know! (*Turning to the* FATHER *in consternation*) Is she mad?

THE FATHER. Mad? No, she's worse than mad.

THE STEPDAUGHTER (*To* MANAGER). Worse? Worse? Listen! Stage this drama for us at once! Then you will see that at a certain moment I . . . when this little darling here . . . (*Takes the* CHILD *by the hand and leads her to the* MANAGER) isn't she a dear? (*Takes her up and kisses her*) Darling! Darling! (*Puts her down again and adds feelingly*) Well, when God suddenly takes this dear little child away from that poor mother there; and this imbecile here (*seizing hold of the* BOY *roughly and pushing him forward*) does the stupidest things, like the fool he is, you will see me run away. Yes, gentlemen, I shall be off. But the moment hasn't arrived yet. After what has taken place between him and me (*indicates the* FATHER *with a horrible wink*) I can't remain any longer in this society, to have to witness the anguish of this mother here for that fool . . . (*Indicates the* SON) Look at him! Look at him! See how indifferent, how frigid he is, because he is the legitimate son. He despises me, despises him (*pointing to the* BOY), despises this baby here; because . . . we are bastards. (*Goes to the* MOTHER *and embraces her*) And he doesn't want to recognize her as his mother — she who is the common mother of us all. He looks down upon her as if she were only the mother of us three bastards. Wretch! (*She says all this very rapidly, excitedly. At the word* "bastards" *she raises her voice, and almost spits out the final* "Wretch!")

[1] *The Chinese are a cunning people,*
From Shanghai to Peking,
They have put posters everywhere:
Beware of Tchou-Tchin-Tchou.

THE MOTHER (*To the* MANAGER, *in anguish*). In the name of these two little children, I beg you . . . (*She grows faint and is about to fall*) Oh God!

THE FATHER (*Coming forward to support her as do some of the* ACTORS). Quick, a chair, a chair for this poor widow!

THE ACTORS. Is it true? Has she really fainted?

THE MANAGER. Quick, a chair! Here!

(*One of the* ACTORS *brings a chair, the others proffer assistance. The* MOTHER *tries to prevent the* FATHER *from lifting the veil which covers her face*)

THE FATHER. Look at her! Look at her!

THE MOTHER. No, stop; stop it please!

THE FATHER (*Raising her veil*). Let them see you!

THE MOTHER (*Rising and covering her face with her hands, in desperation*). I beg you, sir, to prevent this man from carrying out his plan which is loathsome to me.

THE MANAGER (*Dumbfounded*). I don't understand at all. What is the situation? Is this lady your wife? (*To the* FATHER)

THE FATHER. Yes, gentlemen: my wife!

THE MANAGER. But how can she be a widow if you are alive? (*The* ACTORS *find relief for their astonishment in a loud laugh*)

THE FATHER. Don't laugh! Don't laugh like that, for Heaven's sake. Her drama lies just here in this: she has had a lover, a man who ought to be here.

THE MOTHER (*With a cry*). No! No!

THE STEPDAUGHTER. Fortunately for her, he is dead. Two months ago as I said. We are mourning, as you see.

THE FATHER. He isn't here you see, not because he is dead. He isn't here — look at her a moment and you will understand — because her drama isn't a drama of the love of two men for whom she was incapable of feeling anything except possibly a little gratitude — gratitude not for me but for the other. She isn't a woman, she is a mother, and her drama — powerful, sir, I assure you — lies, as a matter of fact, all in these four children she has had by two men.

THE MOTHER. I had them? Have you got the courage to say that I wanted them? (*To the* COMPANY) It was his doing. It was he who gave me that other man, who forced me to go away with him.

THE STEPDAUGHTER. It isn't true.

THE MOTHER (*Startled*). Not true, isn't it?

THE STEPDAUGHTER. No, it isn't true, it just isn't true.

THE MOTHER. And what can you know about it?

THE STEPDAUGHTER. It isn't true. Don't believe it. (*To* MANAGER) Do you know why she says so? For that fellow there. (*Indicates the* SON) She tortures herself, destroys herself on account of the neglect of that son there; and she wants him to believe that if she abandoned him when he was only two years old, it was because he (*indicates the* FATHER) made her do so.

THE MOTHER (*Vigorously*). He forced me to it, and I call God to witness it.

(*To the* MANAGER) Ask him (*indicates* the FATHER) if it isn't true. Let him speak. You (*to* DAUGHTER) are not in a position to know anything about it.

THE STEPDAUGHTER. I know you lived in peace and happiness with my father while he lived. Can you deny it?

THE MOTHER. No, I don't deny it . . .

THE STEPDAUGHTER. He was always full of affection and kindness for you. (*To the* BOY, *angrily*) It's true, isn't it? Tell them! Why don't you speak, you little fool?

THE MOTHER. Leave the poor boy alone. Why do you want to make me appear ungrateful, daughter? I don't want to offend your father. I have answered him that I didn't abandon my house and my son through any fault of mine, nor from any wilful passion.

THE FATHER. It is true. It was my doing.

LEADING MAN (*To the* COMPANY). What a spectacle!

LEADING LADY. We are the audience this time.

JUVENILE LEAD. For once, in a way.

THE MANAGER (*Beginning to get really interested*). Let's hear them out. Listen!

THE SON. Oh yes, you're going to hear a fine bit now. He will talk to you of the Demon of Experiment.

THE FATHER. You are a cynical imbecile. I've told you so already a hundred times. (*To the* MANAGER) He tries to make fun of me on account of this expression which I have found to excuse myself with.

THE SON (*With disgust*). Yes, phrases! phrases!

THE FATHER. Phrases! Isn't everyone consoled when faced with a trouble or fact he doesn't understand, by a word, some simple word, which tells us nothing and yet calms us?

THE STEPDAUGHTER. Even in the case of remorse. In fact, especially then.

THE FATHER. Remorse? No, that isn't true. I've done more than use words to quieten the remorse in me.

THE STEPDAUGHTER. Yes, there was a bit of money too. Yes, yes, a bit of money. There were the hundred lire he was about to offer me in payment, gentlemen. . . . (*Sensation of horror among the* ACTORS)

THE SON (*To the* STEPDAUGHTER). This is vile.

THE STEPDAUGHTER. Vile? There they were in a pale blue envelope on a little mahogany table in the back of Madame Pace's shop. You know Madame Pace — one of those ladies who attract poor girls of good family into their ateliers, under the pretext of their selling *robes et manteaux*.[2]

THE SON. And he thinks he has bought the right to tyrannize over us all with those hundred lire he was going to pay; but which, fortunately — note this, gentlemen — he had no chance of paying.

THE STEPDAUGHTER. It was a near thing, though, you know! (*Laughs ironically*)

THE MOTHER (*Protesting*). Shame, my daughter, shame!

[2] dresses and coats.

THE STEPDAUGHTER. Shame indeed! This is my revenge! I am dying to live that scene. . . . The room . . . I see it. . . . Here is the window with the mantles exposed, there the divan, the looking-glass, a screen, there in front of the window the little mahogany table with the blue envelope containing one hundred lire. I see it. I see it. I could take hold of it. . . . But you, gentlemen, you ought to turn your backs now: I am almost nude, you know. But I don't blush: I leave that to him. (*Indicating* FATHER)

THE MANAGER. I don't understand this at all.

THE FATHER. Naturally enough. I would ask you, sir, to exercise your authority a little here, and let me speak before you believe all she is trying to blame me with. Let me explain.

THE STEPDAUGHTER. Ah yes, explain it in your own way.

THE FATHER. But don't you see that the whole trouble lies here. In words, words. Each one of us has within him a whole world of things, each man of us his own special world. And how can we ever come to an understanding if I put in the words I utter the sense and value of things as I see them; while you who listen to me must inevitably translate them according to the conception of things each one of you has within himself. We think we understand each other, but we never really do. Look here! This woman (*indicating the* MOTHER) takes all my pity for her as a specially ferocious form of cruelty.

THE MOTHER. But you drove me away.

THE FATHER. Do you hear her? I drove her away! She believes I really sent her away.

THE MOTHER. You know how to talk, and I don't; but, believe me sir (*To* MANAGER), after he had married me . . . who knows why? . . . I was a poor insignificant woman. . . .

THE FATHER. But, good Heaven! it was just for your humility that I married you. I loved this simplicity in you. (*He stops when he sees she makes signs to contradict him, opens his arms wide in sign of desperation, seeing how hopeless it is to make himself understood*) You see she denies it. Her mental deafness, believe me, is phenomenal, the limit (*touches his forehead*): deaf, deaf, mentally deaf! She had plenty of feeling. Oh yes, a good heart for the children; but the brain — deaf, to the point of desperation—!

THE STEPDAUGHTER. Yes, but ask him how his intelligence has helped us.

THE FATHER. If we could see all the evil that may spring from good, what should we do? (*At this point the* LEADING LADY *who is biting her lips with rage at seeing the* LEADING MAN *flirting with the* STEPDAUGHTER, *comes forward and says to the* MANAGER)

LEADING LADY. Excuse me, but are we going to rehearse today?

MANAGER. Of course, of course; but let's hear them out.

JUVENILE LEAD. This is something quite new.

L'INGÉNUE. Most interesting!

LEADING LADY. Yes, for the people who like that kind of thing. (*Casts a glance at* LEADING MAN)

THE MANAGER (*To* FATHER). You must please explain yourself quite clearly. (*Sits down*)

THE FATHER. Very well then: listen! I had in my service a poor man, a clerk, a secretary of mine, full of devotion, who became friends with her. (*Indicating the* MOTHER) They understood one another, were kindred souls in fact, without, however, the least suspicion of any evil existing. They were incapable even of thinking of it.

THE STEPDAUGHTER. So he thought of it — for them!

THE FATHER. That's not true. I meant to do good to them — and to myself, I confess, at the same time. Things had come to the point that I could not say a word to either of them without their making a mute appeal, one to the other, with their eyes. I could see them silently asking each other how I was to be kept in countenance, how I was to be kept quiet. And this, believe me, was just about enough of itself to keep me in a constant rage, to exasperate me beyond measure.

THE MANAGER. And why didn't you send him away then — this secretary of yours?

THE FATHER. Precisely what I did, sir. And then I had to watch this poor woman drifting forlornly about the house like an animal without a master, like an animal one has taken in out of pity.

THE MOTHER. Ah, yes! . . .

THE FATHER (*Suddenly turning to the* MOTHER). It's true about the son anyway, isn't it?

THE MOTHER. He took my son away from me first of all.

THE FATHER. But not from cruelty. I did it so that he should grow up healthy and strong by living in the country.

THE STEPDAUGHTER (*Pointing to him ironically*). As one can see.

THE FATHER (*Quickly*). Is it my fault if he has grown up like this? I sent him to a wet nurse in the country, a peasant, as *she* did not seem to me strong enough, though she is of humble origin. That was, anyway, the reason I married her. Unpleasant all this may be, but how can it be helped? My mistake possibly, but there we are! All my life I have had these confounded aspirations towards a certain moral sanity. (*At this point the* STEPDAUGHTER *bursts out into a noisy laugh*) Oh, stop it! Stop it! I can't stand it.

THE MANAGER. Yes, please stop it, for Heaven's sake.

THE STEPDAUGHTER. But imagine moral sanity from him, if you please — the client of certain ateliers like that of Madame Pace!

THE FATHER. Fool! That is the proof that I am a man. This seeming contradiction, gentlemen, is the strongest proof that I stand here a live man before you. Why, it is just for this very incongruity in my nature that I have had to suffer what I have. I could not live by the side of that woman (*indicating the* MOTHER) any longer; but not so much for the boredom she inspired me with as for the pity I felt for her.

THE MOTHER. And so he turned me out —.

THE FATHER. — well provided for! Yes, I sent her to that man, gentlemen . . . to let her go free of me.

THE MOTHER. And to free himself.

THE FATHER. Yes, I admit it. It was also a liberation for me. But great evil has come of it. I meant well when I did it; and I did it more for her sake than mine. I swear it. (*Crosses his arms on his chest; then turns suddenly to the* MOTHER) Did I ever lose sight of you until that other man carried you off to another town, like the angry fool he was? And on account of my pure interest in you . . . my pure interest, I repeat, that had no base motive in it . . . I watched with the tenderest concern the new family that grew up around her. She can bear witness to this. (*Points to the* STEPDAUGHTER)

THE STEPDAUGHTER. Oh yes, that's true enough. Whèn I was a kiddie, so so high, you know, with plaits over my shoulders and knickers longer than my skirts, I used to see him waiting outside the school for me to come out. He came to see how I was growing up.

THE FATHER. This is infamous, shameful!

THE STEPDAUGHTER. No. Why?

THE FATHER. Infamous! Infamous! (*Then excitedly to* MANAGER, *explaining*) After she (*indicating* MOTHER) went away, my house seemed suddenly empty. She was my incubus, but she filled my house. I was like a dazed fly alone in the empty rooms. This boy here (*indicating the* SON) was educated away from home, and when he came back, he seemed to me to be no more mine. With no mother to stand between him and me, he grew up entirely for himself, on his own, apart, with no tie of intellect or affection binding him to me. And then — strange but true — I was driven, by curiosity at first and then by some tender sentiment, towards her family, which had come into being through my will. The thought of her began gradually to fill up the emptiness I felt all around me. I wanted to know if she were happy in living out the simple daily duties of life. I wanted to think of her as fortunate and happy because far away from the complicated torments of my spirit. And so, to have proof of this, I used to watch that child coming out of school.

THE STEPDAUGHTER. Yes, yes. True. He used to follow me in the street and smiled at me, waved his hand, like this. I would look at him with interest, wondering who he might be. I told my mother, who guessed at once. (*The* MOTHER *agrees with a nod*) Then she didn't want to send me to school for some days; and when I finally went back, there he was again — looking so ridiculous — with a paper parcel in his hands. He came close to me, caressed me, and drew out a fine straw hat from the parcel, with a bouquet of flowers — all for me!

THE MANAGER. A bit discursive this, you know!

THE SON (*Contemptuously*). Literature! Literature!

THE FATHER. Literature indeed! This is life, this is passion!

THE MANAGER. It may be, but it won't act.

THE FATHER. I agree. This is only the part leading up. I don't suggest this should be staged. She (*pointing to the* STEPDAUGHTER), as you see, is no longer the flapper with plaits down her back —.

THE STEPDAUGHTER. — and the knickers showing below the skirt!

THE FATHER. The drama is coming now, sir; something new, complex, most interesting.

THE STEPDAUGHTER. As soon as my father died. . . .

THE FATHER. — there was absolute misery for them. They came back here, unknown to me. Through her stupidity! (*Pointing to the* MOTHER) It is true she can barely write her own name; but she could anyhow have got her daughter to write to me that they were in need. . . .

THE MOTHER. And how was I to divine all this sentiment in him?

THE FATHER. That is exactly your mistake, never to have guessed any of my sentiments.

THE MOTHER. After so many years apart, and all that had happened. . . .

THE FATHER. Was it my fault if that fellow carried you away? It happened quite suddenly; for after he had obtained some job or other, I could find no trace of them; and so, not unnaturally, my interest in them dwindled. But the drama culminated unforeseen and violent on their return, when I was impelled by my miserable flesh that still lives. . . . Ah! what misery, what wretchedness is that of the man who is alone and disdains debasing *liaisons!* Not old enough to do without women, and not young enough to go and look for one without shame. Misery? It's worse than misery; it's a horror; for no woman can any longer give him love; and when a man feels this. . . . One ought to do without, you say? Yes, yes, I know. Each of us when he appears before his fellows is clothed in a certain dignity. But every man knows what unconfessable things pass within the secrecy of his own heart. One gives way to the temptation, only to rise from it again, afterwards, with a great eagerness to reestablish one's dignity, as if it were a tombstone to place on the grave of one's shame, and a monument to hide and sign the memory of our weaknesses. Everybody's in the same case. Some folks haven't the courage to say certain things, that's all!

THE STEPDAUGHTER. All appear to have the courage to do them though.

THE FATHER. Yes, but in secret. Therefore, you want more courage to say these things. Let a man but speak these things out, and folks at once label him a cynic. But it isn't true. He is like all the others, better indeed, because he isn't afraid to reveal with the light of the intelligence the red shame of human bestiality on which most men close their eyes so as not to see it. Woman — for example, look at her case! She turns tantalizing inviting glances on you. You seize her. No sooner does she feel herself in your grasp than she closes her eyes. It is the sign of her mission, the sign by which she says to man: "Blind yourself, for I am blind."

THE STEPDAUGHTER. Sometimes she can close them no more: when she no longer feels the need of hiding her shame to herself, but dry-eyed and dispassionately, sees only that of the man who has blinded himself without love. Oh, all these intellectual complications make me sick, disgust me — all this philosophy that uncovers the beast in man, and then seeks to save him, excuse him . . . I can't stand it, sir. When a man seeks to "simplify" life bestially, throwing aside every relic of humanity, every chaste aspiration, every pure feeling, all sense of ideality, duty, modesty, shame . . . then nothing is more revolting and nauseous than a certain kind of remorse — crocodiles' tears, that's what it is.

THE MANAGER. Let's come to the point. This is only discussion.

THE FATHER. Very good, sir! But a fact is like a sack which won't stand up when it is empty. In order that it may stand up, one has to put into it the reason and sentiment which have caused it to exist. I couldn't possibly know that after the death of that man, they had decided to return here, that they were in misery, and that she (*pointing to the* MOTHER) had gone to work as a modiste, and at a shop of the type of that of Madame Pace.

THE STEPDAUGHTER. A real high-class modiste, you must know, gentlemen. In appearance, she works for the leaders of the best society; but she arranges matters so that these elegant ladies serve her purpose . . . without prejudice to other ladies who are . . . well . . . only so so.

THE MOTHER. You will believe me, gentlemen, that it never entered my mind that the old hag offered me work because she had her eye on my daughter.

THE STEPDAUGHTER. Poor mamma! Do you know, sir, what that woman did when I brought her back the work my mother had finished? She would point out to me that I had torn one of my frocks, and she would give it back to my mother to mend. It was I who paid for it, always I; while this poor creature here believed she was sacrificing herself for me and these two children here, sitting up at night sewing Madame Pace's robes.

THE MANAGER. And one day you met there. . . .

THE STEPDAUGHTER. Him, him. Yes, sir, an old client. There's a scene for you to play! Superb!

THE FATHER. She, the Mother arrived just then. . . .

THE STEPDAUGHTER (*Treacherously*). Almost in time!

THE FATHER (*Crying out*). No, in time! in time! Fortunately I recognized her . . . in time. And I took them back home with me to my house. You can imagine now her position and mine: she, as you see her; and I who cannot look her in the face.

THE STEPDAUGHTER. Absurd! How can I possibly be expected — after that — to be a modest young miss, a fit person to go with his confounded aspirations for "a solid moral sanity"?

THE FATHER. For the drama lies all in this — in the conscience that I have, that each one of us has. We believe this conscience to be a single thing, but it is many-sided. There is one for this person, and another for that. Diverse consciences. So we have this illusion of being one person for all, of having a personality that is unique in all our acts. But it isn't true. We perceive this when, tragically perhaps, in something we do, we are, as it were, suspended, caught up in the air on a kind of hook. Then we perceive that all of us was not in that act, and that it would be an atrocious injustice to judge us by that action alone, as if all our existence were summed up in that one deed. Now do you understand the perfidy of this girl? She surprised me in a place where she ought not to have known me, just as I could not exist for her; and she now seeks to attach to me a reality such as I could never suppose I should have to assume for her in a shameful and fleeting moment of my life. I feel this above all else. And the drama, you will see, acquires a tremendous value from this point. Then there is the position of the others ... his ... (*Indicating the* SON)

THE SON (*Shrugging his shoulders scornfully*). Leave me alone! I don't come into this.

THE FATHER. What? You don't come into this?

THE SON. I've got nothing to do with it, and don't want to have; because you know well enough I wasn't made to be mixed up in all this with the rest of you.

THE STEPDAUGHTER. We are only vulgar folk! He is the fine gentleman. You may have noticed, Mr. Manager, that I fix him now and again with a look of scorn while he lowers his eyes — for he knows the evil he has done me.

THE SON (*Scarcely looking at her*). I?

THE STEPDAUGHTER. You! you! I owe my life on the streets to you. Did you or did you not deny us, with your behavior, I won't say the intimacy of home, but even that mere hospitality which makes guests feel at their ease? We were intruders who had come to disturb the kingdom of your legitimacy. I should like to have you witness, Mr. Manager, certain scenes between him and me. He says I have tyrannized over everyone. But it was just his behavior which made me insist on the reason for which I had come into the house — this reason he calls "vile" — into his house, with my mother, who is his mother too. And I came as mistress of the house.

THE SON. It's easy for them to put me always in the wrong. But imagine, gentlemen, the position of a son, whose fate it is to see arrive one day at his home a young woman of impudent bearing, a young woman who inquires for his father, with whom who knows what business she has. This young man has then to witness her return bolder than ever, accompanied by that child there. He is obliged to watch her treat his father in an equivocal and confidential manner. She asks money of him in a way that lets one suppose he must give it her, *must*, do you understand, because he has every obligation to do so.

THE FATHER. But I have, as a matter of fact, this obligation. I owe it to your mother.

THE SON. How should I know? When had I ever seen or heard of her? One day there arrive with her (*indicating* STEPDAUGHTER) that lad and this baby here. I am told: "This is *your* mother too, you know." I divine from her manner (*indicating* STEPDAUGHTER *again*) why it is they have come home. I had rather not say what I feel and think about it. I shouldn't even care to confess to myself. No action can therefore be hoped for from me in this affair. Believe me, Mr. Manager, I am an "unrealized" character, dramatically speaking; and I find myself not at all at ease in their company. Leave me out of it, I beg you.

THE FATHER. What? It is just because you are so that ...

THE SON. How do you know what I am like? When did you ever bother your head about me?

THE FATHER. I admit it. I admit it. But isn't that a situation in itself?

This aloofness of yours which is so cruel to me and to your mother, who returns home and see you almost for the first time grown up, who doesn't recognize you but knows you are her son . . . (*Pointing out the* MOTHER *to the* MANAGER) See, she's crying!

THE STEPDAUGHTER (*Angrily, stamping her foot*). Like a fool!

THE FATHER (*Indicating* STEPDAUGHTER). She can't stand him, you know. (*Then referring again to the* SON): He says he doesn't come into the affair, whereas he is really the hinge of the whole action. Look at that lad who is always clinging to his mother, frightened and humiliated. It is on account of this fellow here. Possibly his situation is the most painful of all. He feels himself a stranger more than the others. The poor little chap feels mortified, humiliated at being brought into a home out of charity as it were. (*In confidence*) —: He is the image of his father. Hardly talks at all. Humble and quiet.

THE MANAGER. Oh, we'll cut him out. You've no notion what a nuisance boys are on the stage . . .

THE FATHER. He disappears soon, you know. And the baby too. She is the first to vanish from the scene. The drama consists finally in this: when that mother re-enters my house, her family born outside of it, and shall we say superimposed on the original, ends with the death of the little girl, the tragedy of the boy and the flight of the elder daughter. It cannot go on, because it is foreign to its surroundings. So after much torment, we three remain: I, the mother, that son. Then, owing to the disappearance of that extraneous family, we too find ourselves strange to one another. We find we are living in an atmosphere of moral desolation which is the revenge, as he (*indicating* SON) scornfully said of the Demon of Experiment, that unfortunately hides in me. Thus, sir, you see when faith is lacking, it becomes impossible to create certain states of happiness, for we lack the necessary humility. Vaingloriously, we try to substitute ourselves for this faith, creating thus for the rest of the world a reality which we believe after their fashion, while, actually, it doesn't exist. For each one of us has his own reality to be respected before God, even when it is harmful to one's very self.

THE MANAGER. There is something in what you say. I assure you all this interests me very much. I begin to think there's the stuff for a drama in all this, and not a bad drama either.

THE STEPDAUGHTER (*Coming forward*). When you've got a character like me.

THE FATHER (*Shutting her up, all excited to learn the decision of the* MANAGER). You be quiet!

THE MANAGER (*Reflecting, heedless of interruption*). It's new . . . hem . . . yes . . .

THE FATHER. Absolutely new!

THE MANAGER. You've got a nerve though, I must say, to come here and fling it at me like this . . .

THE FATHER. You will understand, sir, born as we are for the stage . . .

THE MANAGER. Are you amateur actors then?

THE FATHER. No, I say born for the stage, because . . .

THE MANAGER. Oh, nonsense. You're an old hand, you know.

THE FATHER. No sir, no. We act that rôle for which we have been cast, that rôle which we are given in life. And in my own case, passion itself, as usually happens, becomes a trifle theatrical when it is exalted.

THE MANAGER. Well, well, that will do. But you see, without an author . . . I could give you the address of an author if you like . . .

THE FATHER. No, no. Look here! You must be the author.

THE MANAGER. I? What are you talking about?

THE FATHER. Yes, you, you! Why not?

THE MANAGER. Because I have never been an author: that's why.

THE FATHER. Then why not turn author now? Everybody does it. You don't want any special qualities. Your task is made much easier by the fact that we are all here alive before you . . .

THE MANAGER. It won't do.

THE FATHER. What? When you see us live our drama . . .

THE MANAGER. Yes, that's all right. But you want someone to write it.

THE FATHER. No, no. Someone to take it down, possibly, while we play it, scene by scene! It will be enough to sketch it out at first, and then try it over.

THE MANAGER. Well . . . I am almost tempted. It's a bit of an idea. One might have a shot at it.

THE FATHER. Of course. You'll see what scenes will come out of it. I can give you one, at once . . .

THE MANAGER. By Jove, it tempts me. I'd like to have a go at it. Let's try it out. Come with me to my office. (*Turning to the* ACTORS) You are at liberty for a bit, but don't stop out of the theater for long. In a quarter of an hour, twenty minutes, all back here again! (*To the* FATHER) We'll see what can be done. Who knows if we don't get something really extraordinary out of it?

THE FATHER. There's no doubt about it. They (*indicating the* CHARACTERS) had better come with us too, hadn't they?

THE MANAGER. Yes, yes. Come on! come on! (*Moves away and then turning to the* ACTORS). Be punctual, please!

(MANAGER *and the* SIX CHARACTERS *cross the stage and go off. The other* ACTORS *remain, looking at one another in astonishment*)

LEADING MAN. Is he serious? What the devil does he want to do?

JUVENILE LEAD. This is rank madness.

THIRD ACTOR. Does he expect to knock up a drama in five minutes?

JUVENILE LEAD. Like the improvisers!

LEADING LADY. If he thinks I'm going to take part in a joke like this . . .

JUVENILE LEAD. I'm out of it anyway.

FOURTH ACTOR. I should like to know who they are. (*Alludes to* CHARACTERS)

THIRD ACTOR. What do you suppose? Madmen or rascals!

JUVENILE LEAD. And he takes them seriously!

L'INGÉNUE. Vanity! He fancies himself as an author now.

LEADING MAN. It's absolutely unheard of. If the stage has come to this . . . well, I'm . . .

FIFTH ACTOR. It's rather a joke.

THIRD ACTOR. Well, we'll see what's going to happen next.

(*Thus talking, the* ACTORS *leave the stage; some going out by the little door at the back; others retiring to their dressing-rooms.*
The curtain remains up.
The action of the play is suspended for twenty minutes)

ACT II

The stage call-bells ring to warn the company that the play is about to begin again.

The STEPDAUGHTER *comes out of the* MANAGER's *office along with the* CHILD *and the* BOY. *As she comes out of the office, she cries:*

Nonsense! Nonsense! Do it yourselves! I'm not going to mix myself up in this mess. (*Turning to the* CHILD *and coming quickly with her on to the stage*) Come on, Rosetta, let's run!

(THE BOY *follows them slowly, remaining a little behind and seeming perplexed*)

THE STEPDAUGHTER (*Stops, bends over the* CHILD *and takes the latter's face between her hands*). My little darling! You're frightened, aren't you? You don't know where we are, do you? (*Pretending to reply to a question of the* CHILD) What is the stage? It's a place, baby, you know, where people play at being serious, a place where they act comedies. We've got to act a comedy now, dead serious, you know; and you're in it also, little one. (*Embraces her, pressing the little head to her breast, and rocking the* CHILD *for a moment*) Oh darling, darling, what a horrid comedy you've got to play! What a wretched part they've found for you! A garden . . . a fountain . . . look . . . just suppose, kiddie, it's here. Where, you say? Why, right here in the middle. It's all pretence you know. That's the trouble, my pet: it's all make-believe here. It's better to imagine it though, because if they fix it up for you, it'll only be painted cardboard, painted cardboard for the rockery, the water, the plants . . . Ah, but I think a baby like this one would sooner have a make-believe fountain than a real one, so she could play with it. What a joke it'll be for the others! But for you, alas! not quite such a joke: you who are real, baby dear, and really play by a real fountain that is big and green and beautiful, with ever so many bamboos around it that are reflected in the water, and a whole lot of little ducks swimming about . . . No, Rosetta, no, your mother doesn't bother about you on account of that wretch of a son there. I'm in the devil of a temper, and as for that lad . . . (*Seizes* BOY *by the arm to force him o take one of his hands out of his pockets*) What have you got there? What are you hiding? (*Pulls his hand out of his pocket, looks into it and catches the glint of a revolver*) Ah, where did you get this?

(THE BOY, *very pale in the face, looks at her, but does not answer*)

Idiot! If I'd been in your place, instead of killing myself, I'd have shot one of those two, or both of them: father and son.

(THE FATHER *enters from the office, all excited from his work.* THE MANAGER *follows him*)

THE FATHER. Come on, come on, dear! Come here for a minute! We've arranged everything. It's all fixed up.

THE MANAGER (*Also excited*). If you please, young lady, there are one or two points to settle still. Will you come along?

THE STEPDAUGHTER (*Following him towards the office*). Ouff! what's the good, if you've arranged everything.

(THE FATHER, MANAGER *and* STEPDAUGHTER *go back into the office again* [*off*] *for a moment. At the same time,* THE SON, *followed by* THE MOTHER, *comes out*)

THE SON (*Looking at the three entering office*). Oh this is fine, fine! And to think I can't even get away!

(THE MOTHER *attempts to look at him, but lowers her eyes immediately when he turns away from her. She then sits down.* THE BOY *and* THE CHILD *approach her. She casts a glance again at* THE SON, *and speaks with humble tones, trying to draw him into conversation*)

THE MOTHER. And isn't my punishment the worst of all? (*Then seeing from the* SON'S *manner that he will not bother himself about her*) My God! Why are you so cruel? Isn't it enough for one person to support all this torment? Must you then insist on others seeing it also?

THE SON (*Half to himself, meaning* THE MOTHER *to hear, however*). And they want to put it on the stage! If there was at least a reason for it! He thinks he has got at the meaning of it all. Just as if each one of us in every circumstance of life couldn't find his own explanation of it! (*Pauses*) He complains he was discovered in a place where he ought not to have been seen, in a moment of his life which ought to have remained hidden and kept out of the reach of that convention which he has to maintain for other people. And what about my case? Haven't I had to reveal what no son ought ever to reveal: how father and mother live and are man and wife for themselves quite apart from that idea of father and mother which we give them? When this idea is revealed, our life is then linked at one point only to that man and that woman; and as such it should shame them, shouldn't it?

(THE MOTHER *hides her face in her hands. From the dressing-rooms and the little door at the back of the stage the* ACTORS *and* STAGE MANAGER *return, followed by the* PROPERTY MAN, *and the* PROMPTER. *At the same moment,* THE MANAGER *comes out of his office, accompanied by the* FATHER *and the* STEPDAUGHTER)

THE MANAGER. Come on, come on, ladies and gentlemen! Heh! you there, machinist!

MACHINIST. Yes sir?

THE MANAGER. Fix up the white parlor with the floral decorations. Two wings and a drop with a door will do. Hurry up!

(*The* MACHINIST *runs off at once to prepare the scene, and arranges it while* THE MANAGER *talks with the* STAGE MANAGER, *the* PROPERTY MAN, *and the* PROMPTER *on matters of detail*).

THE MANAGER (*To* PROPERTY MAN). Just have a look, and see if there isn't a sofa or divan in the wardrobe . . .

PROPERTY MAN. There's the green one.

THE STEPDAUGHTER. No, no! Green won't do. It was yellow, ornamented with flowers — very large! and most comfortable!

PROPERTY MAN. There isn't one like that.

THE MANAGER. It doesn't matter. Use the one we've got.

THE STEPDAUGHTER. Doesn't matter? It's most important!

THE MANAGER. We're only trying it now. Please don't interfere. (*To* PROPERTY MAN) See if we've got a shop window — long and narrowish.

THE STEPDAUGHTER. And the little table! The little mahogany table for the pale blue envelope!

PROPERTY MAN (*To* MANAGER). There's that little gilt one.

THE MANAGER. That'll do fine.

THE FATHER. A mirror.

THE STEPDAUGHTER. And the screen! We must have a screen. Otherwise how can I manage?

PROPERTY MAN. That's all right, Miss. We've got any amount of them.

THE MANAGER (*To the* STEPDAUGHTER). We want some clothes pegs too, don't we?

THE STEPDAUGHTER. Yes, several, several!

THE MANAGER. See how many we've got and bring them all.

PROPERTY MAN. All right!

(*The* PROPERTY MAN *hurries off to obey his orders. While he is putting the things in their places, the* MANAGER *talks to the* PROMPTER *and then with the* CHARACTERS *and the* ACTORS)

THE MANAGER (*To* PROMPTER). Take your seat. Look here: this is the outline of the scenes, act by act. (*Hands him some sheets of paper*) And now I'm going to ask you to do something out of the ordinary.

PROMPTER. Take it down in shorthand?

THE MANAGER (*Pleasantly surprised*). Exactly! Can you do shorthand?

PROMPTER. Yes, a little.

MANAGER. Good! (*Turning to a stage hand*) Go and get some paper from my office, plenty, as much as you can find.

(*The* STAGE HAND *goes off, and soon returns with a handful of paper which he gives to the* PROMPTER)

THE MANAGER (*To* PROMPTER). You follow the scenes as we play them, and try and get the points down, at any rate the most important ones. (*Then addressing the* ACTORS) Clear the stage, ladies and gentlemen! Come over here (*Pointing to the Left*) and listen attentively.

LEADING LADY. But, excuse me, we . . .

THE MANAGER. (*Guessing her thought*). Don't worry! You won't have to improvise.

LEADING MAN. What have we to do then?

THE MANAGER. Nothing. For the moment you just watch and listen. Everybody will get his part written out afterwards. At present we're going to try the thing as best we can. They're going to act now.

THE FATHER (*As if fallen from the clouds into the confusion of the stage*). We? What do you mean, if you please, by a rehearsal?

THE MANAGER. A rehearsal for them. (*Points to the* ACTORS)

THE FATHER. But since we are the characters . . .

THE MANAGER. All right: "characters" then, if you insist on calling yourselves such. But here, my dear sir, the characters don't act. Here the actors do the acting. The characters are there, in the "book" — (*Pointing towards* PROMPTER's *box*) when there is a "book"!

THE FATHER. I won't contradict you; but excuse me, the actors aren't the characters. They want to be, they pretend to be, don't they? Now if these gentlemen here are fortunate enough to have us alive before them . . .

THE MANAGER. Oh this is grand! You want to come before the public yourselves then?

THE FATHER. As we are . . .

THE MANAGER. I can assure you it would be a magnificent spectacle!

LEADING MAN. What's the use of us here anyway then?

THE MANAGER. You're not going to pretend that you can act? It makes me laugh! (*The* ACTORS *laugh*) There, you see, they are laughing at the notion. But, by the way, I must cast the parts. That won't be difficult. They cast themselves. (*To the* SECOND LADY LEAD) You play the Mother. (*To the* FATHER) We must find her a name.

THE FATHER. Amalia, sir.

THE MANAGER. But that is the real name of your wife. We don't want to call her by her real name.

THE FATHER. Why ever not, if it is her name? . . . Still, perhaps, if that lady must . . . (*Makes a slight motion of the hand to indicate the* SECOND LADY LEAD) I see this woman here (*means the* MOTHER) as Amalia. But do as you like. (*Gets more and more confused*) I don't know what to say to you. Already, I begin to hear my own words ring false, as if they had another sound . . .

THE MANAGER. Don't you worry about it. It'll be our job to find the right tones. And as for her name, if you want her Amalia, Amalia it shall be; and if you don't like it, we'll find another! For the moment though, we'll call the characters in this way: (*to* JUVENILE LEAD) You are the Son; (*to the* LEADING LADY) You naturally are the Stepdaughter . . .

THE STEPDAUGHTER (*Excitedly*). What? what? I, that woman there? (*Bursts out laughing*)

THE MANAGER (*Angry*). What is there to laugh at?

LEADING LADY (*Indignant*). Nobody has ever dared to laugh at me. I insist on being treated with respect; otherwise I go away.

THE STEPDAUGHTER. No, no, excuse me . . . I am not laughing at you . . .

THE MANAGER (*To* STEPDAUGHTER). You ought to feel honored to be played by . . .

LEADING LADY (*At once, contemptuously*). "That woman there" . . .

THE STEPDAUGHTER. But I wasn't speaking of you, you know. I was speaking of myself — whom I can't see at all in you! That is all. I don't know . . . but . . . you . . . aren't in the least like me . . .

THE FATHER. True. Here's the point. Look here, sir, our temperaments, our souls . . .

THE MANAGER. Temperament, soul, be hanged. Do you suppose the spirit of the piece is in you? Nothing of the kind!

THE FATHER. What, haven't we our own temperaments, our own souls?

THE MANAGER. Not at all. Your soul or whatever you like to call it takes shape here. The actors give body and form to it, voice and gesture. And my actors — I may tell you — have given expression to much more lofty material than this little drama of yours, which may or may not hold up on the stage. But if it does, the merit of it, believe me, will be due to my actors.

THE FATHER. I don't dare contradict you, sir; but, believe me, it is a terrible suffering for us who are as we are, with these bodies of ours, these features to see . . .

THE MANAGER (*Cutting him short and out of patience*). Good heavens! The make-up will remedy all that, man, the make-up . . .

THE FATHER. Maybe. But the voice, the gestures . . .

THE MANAGER. Now, look here! On the stage, you as yourself, cannot exist. The actor here acts you, and that's an end to it!

THE FATHER. I understand. And now I think I see why our author who conceived us as we are, all alive, didn't want to put us on the stage after all. I haven't the least desire to offend your actors. Far from it! But when I think that I am to be acted by . . . I don't know by whom . . .

LEADING MAN (*On his dignity*). By me, if you've no objection!

THE FATHER (*Humbly, mellifluously*). Honored, I assure you, sir. (*Bows*)

Still, I must say that try as this gentleman may, with all his good will and wonderful art, to absorb me into himself . . .

LEADING MAN. Oh chuck it! "Wonderful art!" Withdraw that, please!

THE FATHER. The performance he will give, even doing his best with make-up to look like me . . .

LEADING MAN. It will certainly be a bit difficult! (*The* ACTORS *laugh*)

THE FATHER. Exactly! It will be difficult to act me as I really am. The effect will be rather — apart from the make-up — according as to how he supposes I am, as he senses me — if he does sense me — and not as I inside of myself feel myself to be. It seems to me then that account should be taken of this by everyone whose duty it may become to criticize us . . .

THE MANAGER. Heavens! The man's starting to think about the critics now! Let them say what they like. It's up to us to put on the play if we can. (*Looking around*) Come on! come on! Is the stage set? (*To the* ACTORS *and* CHARACTERS) Stand back — stand back! Let me see, and don't let's lose any more time! (*To the* STEPDAUGHTER) Is it all right as it is now?

THE STEPDAUGHTER. Well, to tell the truth, I don't recognize the scene.

THE MANAGER. My dear lady, you can't possibly suppose that we can construct that shop of Madame Pace piece by piece here? (*To the* FATHER) You said a white room with flowered wall paper, didn't you?

THE FATHER. Yes.

THE MANAGER. Well then. We've got the furniture right, more or less. Bring that little table a bit further forward. (*The* STAGE HANDS *obey the order. To* PROPERTY MAN) You go and find an envelope, if possible, a pale blue one; and give it to that gentleman. (*Indicates* FATHER)

PROPERTY MAN. An ordinary envelope?

MANAGER *and* FATHER. Yes, yes, an ordinary envelope.

PROPERTY MAN. At once, sir. (*Exit*)

THE MANAGER. Ready, everyone! First scene — the Young Lady. (*The* LEADING LADY *comes forward*) No, no, you must wait. I meant her. (*Indicating the* STEPDAUGHTER) You just watch —

THE STEPDAUGHTER (*Adding at once*). How I shall play it, how I shall live it! . . .

LEADING LADY (*Offended*). I shall live it also, you may be sure, as soon as I begin!

THE MANAGER (*With his hands to his head*). Ladies and gentlemen, if you please! No more useless discussions! Scene I: the young lady with Madame Pace: Oh! (*Looks around as if lost*) And this Madame Pace, where is she?

THE FATHER. She isn't with us, sir.

THE MANAGER. Then what the devil's to be done?

THE FATHER. But she is alive too.

THE MANAGER. Yes, but where is she?

THE FATHER. One minute. Let me speak! (*Turning to the* ACTRESSES) If these ladies would be so good as to give me their hats for a moment . . .

THE ACTRESSES (*Half surprised, half laughing, in chorus*). What?
Why?
Our hats?
What does he say?

THE MANAGER. What are you going to do with the ladies' hats? (*The AC-
TORS laugh*)

THE FATHER. Oh nothing. I just want to put them on these pegs for a
moment. And one of the ladies will be so kind as to take off her mantle . . .

THE ACTORS. Oh, what d'you think of that? Only the mantle?
He must be mad.

SOME ACTRESSES. But why?
Mantles as well?

THE FATHER. To hang them up here for a moment. Please be so kind, will
you?

THE ACTRESSES. (*Taking off their hats, one or two also their cloaks, and
going to hang them on the racks*) After all, why not?
There you are!
This is really funny.
We've got to put them on show.

THE FATHER. Exactly; just like that, on show.

THE MANAGER. May we know why?

THE FATHER. I'll tell you. Who knows if, by arranging the stage for her, she
does not come here herself, attracted by the very articles of her trade? (*Inviting the* ACTORS *to look towards the exit at back of stage*) Look! Look!

(*The door at the back of stage opens and* MADAME PACE *enters and takes a
few steps forward. She is a fat, oldish woman with puffy oxygenated hair. She
is rouged and powdered, dressed with a comical elegance in black silk.
Round her waist is a long silver chain from which hangs a pair of scissors. The*
STEPDAUGHTER *runs over to her at once amid the stupor of the* ACTORS)

THE STEPDAUGHTER (*Turning towards her*). There she is! There she is!

THE FATHER (*Radiant*). It's she! I said so, didn't I? There she is!

THE MANAGER (*Conquering his surprise, and then becoming indignant*).
What sort of a trick is this?

LEADING MAN (*Almost at the same time*). What's going to happen next?

JUVENILE LEAD. Where does *she* come from?

L'INGÉNUE. They've been holding her in reserve, I guess.

LEADING LADY. A vulgar trick!

THE FATHER (*Dominating the protests*). Excuse me, all of you! Why are
you so anxious to destroy in the name of a vulgar, commonplace sense of truth,
this reality which comes to birth attracted and formed by the magic of the
stage itself, which has indeed more right to live here than you, since it is
much truer than you — if you don't mind my saying so? Which is the actress
among you who is to play Madame Pace? Well, here is Madame Pace herself.
And you will allow, I fancy, that the actress who acts her will be less true than

this woman here, who is herself in person. You see my daughter recognized her and went over to her at once. Now you're going to witness the scene!

(*But the scene between* THE STEPDAUGHTER *and* MADAME PACE *has already begun despite the protest of the* ACTORS *and the reply of* THE FATHER. *It has begun quietly, naturally, in a manner impossible for the stage. So when the* ACTORS, *called to attention by* THE FATHER, *turn round and see* MADAME PACE, *who has placed one hand under* THE STEPDAUGHTER'S *chin to raise her head, they observe her at first with great attention, but hearing her speak in an unintelligible manner their interest begins to wane*)

THE MANAGER. Well? well?

LEADING MAN. What does she say?

LEADING LADY. One can't hear a word.

JUVENILE LEAD. Louder! Louder please!

THE STEPDAUGHTER (*Leaving* MADAME PACE, *who smiles a Sphinx-like smile, and advancing towards the* ACTORS). Louder? Louder? What are you talking about? These aren't matters which can be shouted at the top of one's voice. If I have spoken them out loud, it was to shame him and have my revenge. (*Indicates* FATHER) But for Madame it's quite a different matter.

THE MANAGER. Indeed? indeed? But here, you know, people have got to make themselves heard, my dear. Even we who are on the stage can't hear you. What will it be when the public's in the theater? And anyway, you can very well speak up now among yourselves, since we shan't be present to listen to you as we are now. You've got to pretend to be alone in a room at the back of a shop where no one can hear you.

(THE STEPDAUGHTER *coquettishly and with a touch of malice makes a sign of disagreement two or three times with her finger*)

THE MANAGER. What do you mean by no?

THE STEPDAUGHTER (*Sotto voce, mysteriously*). There's someone who will hear us if she (*indicating* MADAME PACE) speaks out loud.

THE MANAGER (*In consternation*). What? Have you got someone else to spring on us now? (*The* ACTORS *burst out laughing*)

THE FATHER. No, no sir. She is alluding to me. I've got to be here — there behind that door, in waiting; and Madame Pace knows it. In fact, if you will allow me, I'll go there at once, so I can be quite ready. (*Moves away*)

THE MANAGER (*Stopping him*). No! wait! wait! We must observe the conventions of the theater. Before you are ready . . .

THE STEPDAUGHTER (*Interrupting him*). No, get on with it at once! I'm just dying, I tell you, to act this scene. If he's ready, I'm more than ready.

THE MANAGER (*Shouting*). But, my dear young lady, first of all, we must have the scene between you and this lady . . . (*Indicates* MADAME PACE) Do you understand? . . .

THE STEPDAUGHTER. Good Heavens! She's been telling me what you know already: that Mamma's work is badly done again, that the material's ruined;

and that if I want her to continue to help us in our misery I must be patient . . .

MADAME PACE (*Coming forward with an air of great importance*). Yes indeed, sir, I no wanta take advantage of her, I no wanta be hard . . .

(*Note:* MADAME PACE *is supposed to talk in a jargon half Italian, half English*)

THE MANAGER (*Alarmed*). What? What? she talks like that? (*The* ACTORS *burst out laughing again*)

THE STEPDAUGHTER (*Also laughing*). Yes, yes, that's the way she talks, half English, half Italian! Most comical it is!

MADAME PACE. Itta seem not verra polite gentlemen laugha atta me eef I trya best speaka English.

THE MANAGER. *Diamine!* Of course! Of course! Let her talk like that! Just what we want. Talk just like that, Madame, if you please! The effect will be certain. Exactly what was wanted to put a little comic relief into the crudity of the situation. Of course she talks like that! Magnificent!

THE STEPDAUGHTER. Magnificent? Certainly! When certain suggestions are made to one in language of that kind, the effect is certain, since it seems almost a joke. One feels inclined to laugh when one hears her talk about an "old signore" "who wanta talka nicely with you." Nice old signore, eh, Madame?

MADAME PACE. Not so old, my dear, not so old! And even if you no lika him, he won't make any scandal!

THE MOTHER (*Jumping up amid the amazement and consternation of the* ACTORS *who had not been noticing her. They move to restrain her*). You old devil! You murderess!

THE STEPDAUGHTER (*Running over to calm her* MOTHER). Calm yourself, mother, calm yourself! Please don't . . .

THE FATHER (*Going to her also at the same time*). Calm yourself! Don't get excited! Sit down now!

THE MOTHER. Well then, take that woman away out of my sight!

THE STEPDAUGHTER (*To* MANAGER). It is impossible for my mother to remain here.

THE FATHER (*To* MANAGER). They can't be here together. And for this reason, you see: that woman there was not with us when we came . . . If they are on together, the whole thing is given away inevitably, as you see.

THE MANAGER. It doesn't matter. This is only a first rough sketch — just to get an idea of the various points of the scene, even confusedly . . . (*Turning to* the MOTHER *and leading her to her chair*) Come along, my dear lady, sit down now, and let's get on with the scene . . .

(*Meanwhile, the* STEPDAUGHTER, *coming forward again, turns to* MADAME PACE)

THE STEPDAUGHTER. Come on, Madame, come on!

MADAME PACE (*Offended*). No, no, *grazie*. I not do anything witha your mother present.

THE STEPDAUGHTER. Nonsense! Introduce this "old signore" who wants to talk nicely to me. (*Addressing the company imperiously*) We've got to do this scene one way or another, haven't we? Come on! (*To* MADAME PACE) You can go!

MADAME PACE. Ah yes! I go'way! I go'way! Certainly! (*Exits furious*)

THE STEPDAUGHTER (*To the* FATHER). Now you make your entry. No, you needn't go over there. Come here. Let's suppose you've already come in. Like that, yes! I'm here with bowed head, modest-like. Come on! Out with your voice! Say "Good morning, Miss" in that peculiar tone, that special tone . . .

THE MANAGER. Excuse me, but are you the Manager, or am I? (*To the* FATHER, *who looks undecided and perplexed*) Get on with it, man! Go down there to the back of the stage. You needn't go off. Then come right forward here.

(THE FATHER *does as he is told, looking troubled and perplexed at first. But as soon as he begins to move, the reality of the action affects him, and he begins to smile and to be more natural. The* ACTORS *watch intently*)

THE MANAGER (*Sotto voce, quickly to the* PROMPTER *in his box*). Ready! ready? Get ready to write now.

THE FATHER (*Coming forward and speaking in a different tone*). Good afternoon, Miss!

THE STEPDAUGHTER (*Head bowed down slightly, with restrained disgust*). Good afternoon!

THE FATHER (*Looks under her hat which partly covers her face. Perceiving she is very young, he makes an exclamation, partly of surprise, partly of fear lest he compromise himself in a risky adventure*). Ah . . . but . . . ah . . . I say . . . this is not the first time that you have come here, is it?

THE STEPDAUGHTER (*Modestly*). No sir.

THE FATHER. You've been here before, eh? (*Then seeing her nod agreement*) More than once? (*Waits for her to answer, looks under her hat, smiles, and then says*) Well then, there's no need to be so shy, is there? May I take off your hat?

THE STEPDAUGHTER (*Anticipating him and with veiled disgust*). No sir . . . I'll do it myself. (*Takes it off quickly*)

(THE MOTHER, *who watches the progress of the scene with* THE SON *and the other two* CHILDREN *who cling to her, is on thorns; and follows with varying expressions of sorrow, indignation, anxiety, and horror the words and actions of the other two. From time to time she hides her face in her hands and sobs*)

THE MOTHER. Oh, my God, my God!

THE FATHER (*Playing his part with a touch of gallantry*). Give it to me! I'll put it down. (*Takes hat from her hands*) But a dear little head like yours ought to have a smarter hat. Come and help me choose one from the stock, won't you?

L'INGÉNUE (*Interrupting*). I say . . . those are our hats, you know.

THE MANAGER (*Furious*). Silence! silence! Don't try and be funny, if you please . . . We're playing the scene now, I'd have you notice. (*To the* STEP-DAUGHTER) Begin again, please!

THE STEPDAUGHTER (*Continuing*). No thank you, sir.

THE FATHER. Oh, come now. Don't talk like that. You must take it. I shall be upset if you don't. There are some lovely little hats here; and then — Madame will be pleased. She expects it, anyway, you know.

THE STEPDAUGHTER. No, no! I couldn't wear it!

THE FATHER. Oh, you're thinking about what they'd say at home if they saw you come in with a new hat? My dear girl, there's always a way round these little matters, you know.

THE STEPDAUGHTER (*All keyed up*). No, it's not that. I couldn't wear it because I am . . . as you see . . . you might have noticed . . . (*Showing her black dress*)

THE FATHER. . . . in mourning! Of course: I beg your pardon: I'm frightfully sorry . . .

THE STEPDAUGHTER (*Forcing herself to conquer her indignation and nausea*). Stop! Stop! It's I who must thank you. There's no need for you to feel mortified or specially sorry. Don't think any more of what I've said. (*Tries to smile*) I must forget that I am dressed so . . .

THE MANAGER (*Interrupting and turning to the* PROMPTER). Stop a minute! Stop! Don't write that down. Cut out that last bit. (*Then to the* FATHER *and* STEPDAUGHTER) Fine! it's going fine! (*To the* FATHER *only*) And now you can go on as we arranged. (*To the* ACTORS) Pretty good that scene, where he offers her the hat, eh?

THE STEPDAUGHTER. The best's coming now. Why can't we go on?

THE MANAGER. Have a little patience! (*To the* ACTORS) Of course, it must be treated rather lightly.

LEADING MAN. Still, with a bit of go in it!

LEADING LADY. Of course! It's easy enough! (*To* LEADING MAN) Shall you and I try it now?

LEADING MAN. Why, yes! I'll prepare my entrance. (*Exit in order to make his entrance*)

THE MANAGER (*To* LEADING LADY). See here! The scene between you and Madame Pace is finished. I'll have it written out properly after. You remain here . . . oh, where are you going?

LEADING LADY. One minute. I want to put my hat on again. (*Goes over to hat-rack and puts her hat on her head*).

THE MANAGER. Good! You stay here with your head bowed a bit.

THE STEPDAUGHTER. But she isn't dressed in black.

LEADING LADY. But I shall be, and much more effectively than you.

THE MANAGER (*To* STEPDAUGHTER). Be quiet please, and watch! You'll be able to learn something. (*Clapping his hands*) Come on! come on! Entrance, please!

(*The door at rear of stage opens, and the* LEADING MAN *enters with the lively manner of an old gallant. The rendering of the scene by the* ACTORS *from the very first words is seen to be quite a different thing, though it has not in any way the air of a parody. Naturally, the* STEPDAUGHTER *and the* FATHER, *not being able to recognize themselves in the* LEADING LADY *and the* LEADING MAN, *who deliver their words in different tones and with a different psychology, express, sometimes with smiles, sometimes with gestures, the impression they receive*)

LEADING MAN. Good afternoon, Miss . . .

THE FATHER (*At once unable to contain himself*). No! no!

(THE STEPDAUGHTER, *noticing the way the* LEADING MAN *enters, bursts out laughing*)

THE MANAGER (*Furious*). Silence! And you, please, just stop that laughing. If we go on like this, we shall never finish.

THE STEPDAUGHTER. Forgive me, sir, but it's natural enough. This lady (*indicating* LEADING LADY) stands there still; but if she is supposed to be me, I can assure you that if I heard anyone say "Good afternoon" in that manner and in that tone, I should burst out laughing as I did.

THE FATHER. Yes, yes, the manner, the tone . . .

THE MANAGER. Nonsense! Rubbish! Stand aside and let me see the action.

LEADING MAN. If I've got to represent an old fellow who's coming into a house of an equivocal character . . .

THE MANAGER. Don't listen to them, for Heaven's sake! Do it again! It goes fine. (*Waiting for the* ACTORS *to begin again*) Well?

LEADING MAN. Good afternoon, Miss.

LEADING LADY. Good afternoon.

LEADING MAN (*Imitating the gesture of the* FATHER *when he looked under the hat, and then expressing quite clearly first satisfaction and then fear*). Ah, but . . . I say . . . this is not the first time that you have come here, is it?

THE MANAGER. Good, but not quite so heavily. Like this. (*Acts himself*) "This isn't the first time that you have come here" . . . (*To* LEADING LADY) And you say: "No, sir."

LEADING LADY. No, sir.

LEADING MAN. You've been here before, more than once.

THE MANAGER. No, no, stop! Let her nod "yes" first. "You've been here before, eh?" (*The* LEADING LADY *lifts up her head slightly and closes her eyes as though in disgust. Then she inclines her head twice*)

THE STEPDAUGHTER (*Unable to contain herself*) Oh my God! (*Puts a hand to her mouth to prevent herself from laughing*)

THE MANAGER (*Turning round*). What's the matter?

THE STEPDAUGHTER. Nothing, nothing!

THE MANAGER (*To* LEADING MAN). Go on!

LEADING MAN. You've been here before, eh? Well then, there's no need to be so shy, is there? May I take off your hat?

(*The* LEADING MAN *says this last speech in such a tone and with such gestures that the* STEPDAUGHTER, *though she has her hand to her mouth, cannot keep from laughing*)

LEADING LADY (*Indignant*). I'm not going to stop here to be made a fool of by that woman there.

LEADING MAN. Neither am I! I'm through with it!

THE MANAGER (*Shouting to* STEPDAUGHTER). Silence! for once and all, I tell you!

THE STEPDAUGHTER. Forgive me! forgive me!

THE MANAGER. You haven't any manners: that's what it is! You go too far.

THE FATHER (*Endeavoring to intervene*). Yes, it's true, but excuse her . . .

THE MANAGER. Excuse what? It's absolutely disgusting.

THE FATHER. Yes, sir, but believe me, it has such a strange effect when . . .

THE MANAGER. Strange? Why strange? Where is it strange?

THE FATHER. No, sir; I admire your actors — this gentleman here, this lady; but they are certainly not us!

THE MANAGER. I should hope not. Evidently they cannot be you, if they are actors.

THE FATHER. Just so: actors! Both of them act our parts exceedingly well. But, believe me, it produces quite a different effect on us. They want to be us, but they aren't, all the same.

THE MANAGER. What is it then anyway?

THE FATHER. Something that is . . . that is theirs — and no longer ours . . .

THE MANAGER. But naturally, inevitably. I've told you so already.

THE FATHER. Yes, I understand . . . I understand . . .

THE MANAGER. Well then, let's have no more of it! (*Turning to the* ACTORS) We'll have the rehearsals by ourselves, afterwards, in the ordinary way. I never could stand rehearsing with the author present. He's never satisfied! (*Turning to* FATHER *and* STEPDAUGHTER) Come on! Let's get on with it again; and try and see if you can't keep from laughing.

THE STEPDAUGHTER. Oh, I shan't laugh any more. There's a nice little bit coming from me now: you'll see.

THE MANAGER. Well then: when she says "Don't think any more of what I've said. I must forget, etc.," you (*addressing the* FATHER) come in sharp with "I understand, I understand"; and then you ask her . . .

THE STEPDAUGHTER (*Interrupting*). What?

THE MANAGER. Why she is in mourning.

THE STEPDAUGHTER. Not at all! See here: when I told him that it was useless for me to be thinking about my wearing mourning, do you know how he answered me? "Ah well," he said, "then let's take off this little frock."

THE MANAGER. Great! Just what we want, to make a riot in the theater!

THE STEPDAUGHTER. But it's the truth!

THE MANAGER. What does that matter? Acting is our business here. Truth up to a certain point, but no further.

THE STEPDAUGHTER. What do you want to do then?

THE MANAGER. You'll see, you'll see! Leave it to me.

THE STEPDAUGHTER. No sir! What you want to do is to piece together a little romantic sentimental scene out of my disgust, out of all the reasons, each more cruel and viler than the other, why I am what I am. He is to ask me why I'm in mourning; and I'm to answer with tears in my eyes, that it is just two months since papa died. No sir, no! He's got to say to me; as he did say: "Well, let's take off this little dress at once." And I; with my two months' mourning in my heart, went there behind that screen, and with these fingers tingling with shame . . .

THE MANAGER (*Running his hands through his hair*). For Heaven's sake! What are you saying?

THE STEPDAUGHTER (*Crying out excitedly*). The truth! The truth!

THE MANAGER. It may be. I don't deny it, and I can understand all your horror; but you must surely see that you can't have this kind of thing on the stage. It won't go.

THE STEPDAUGHTER. Not possible, eh? Very well! I'm much obliged to you — but I'm off!

THE MANAGER. Now be reasonable! Don't lose your temper!

THE STEPDAUGHTER. I won't stop here! I won't! I can see you've fixed it all up with him in your office. All this talk about what is possible for the stage . . . I understand! He wants to get at his complicated "cerebral drama," to have his famous remorses and torments acted; but I want to act my part, *my part!*

THE MANAGER (*Annoyed, shaking his shoulders*) Ah! Just *your* part! But, if you will pardon me, there are other parts than yours: his (*indicating the* FATHER) and hers! (*Indicating the* MOTHER) On the stage you can't have a character becoming too prominent and overshadowing all the others. The thing is to pack them all into a neat little framework and then act what is actable. I am aware of the fact that everyone has his own interior life which he wants very much to put forward. But the difficulty lies in this fact: to set out just so much as is necessary for the stage, taking the other characters into consideration, and at the same time hint at the unrevealed interior life of each. I am willing to admit, my dear young lady, that from your point of view it would be a fine idea if each character could tell the public all his troubles in a nice monologue or a regular one-hour lecture (*Good-humoredly*) You must restrain yourself, my dear, and in your own interest, too; because this fury of yours, this exaggerated disgust you show, may make a bad impression, you know. After you have confessed to me that there were others before him at Madame Pace's and more than once . . .

THE STEPDAUGHTER (*Bowing her head, impressed*). It's true. But remember those others mean him for me all the same.

THE MANAGER (*Not understanding*). What? The others? What do you mean?

THE STEPDAUGHTER. For one who has gone wrong, sir, he who was responsible for the first fault is responsible for all that follow. He is responsible for my faults, was, even before I was born. Look at him, and see if it isn't true!

THE MANAGER. Well, well! And does the weight of so much responsibility seem nothing to you? Give him a chance to act it, to get it over!

THE STEPDAUGHTER. How? How can he act all his "noble remorses," all his "moral torments," if you want to spare him the horror of being discovered one day — after he had asked her what he did ask her — in the arms of her, that already fallen woman, that child, sir, that child he used to watch come out of school? (*She is moved*)

(THE MOTHER *at this point is overcome with emotion, and breaks out into a fit of crying.*

All are touched. A long pause)

THE STEPDAUGHTER (*As soon as the* MOTHER *becomes a little quieter, adds resolutely and gravely*). At present, we are unknown to the public. Tomorrow, you will act us as you wish, treating us in your own manner. But do you really want to see drama, do you want to see it flash out as it really did?

THE MANAGER. Of course! That's just what I do want, so I can use as much of it as is possible.

THE STEPDAUGHTER. Well then, ask that Mother there to leave us.

THE MOTHER (*Changing her low plaint into a sharp cry*). No! No! Don't permit it, sir, don't permit it!

THE MANAGER. But it's only to try it.

THE MOTHER. I can't bear it. I can't.

THE MANAGER. But since it has happened already . . . I don't understand!

THE MOTHER. It's taking place now. It happens all the time. My torment isn't a pretended one. I live and feel every minute of my torture. Those two children there — have you heard them speak? They can't speak any more. They cling to me to keep my torment actual and vivid for me. But for themselves, they do not exist, they aren't any more. And she (*indicating* STEPDAUGHTER) has run away, she has left me, and is lost. If I now see her here before me, it is only to renew for me the tortures I have suffered for her too.

THE FATHER. The eternal moment! She (*indicating the* STEPDAUGHTER) is here to catch me, fix me, and hold me eternally in the stocks for that one fleeting and shameful moment of my life. She can't give it up! And you sir, cannot either fairly spare me it.

THE MANAGER. I never said I didn't want to act it. It will form, as a matter of fact, the nucleus of the whole first act right up to her surprise. (*Indicating the* MOTHER)

THE FATHER. Just so! This is my punishment: the passion in all of us that must culminate in her final cry.

THE STEPDAUGHTER. I can hear it still in my ears. It's driven me mad, that cry — You can put me on as you like; it doesn't matter. Fully dressed, if you like — provided I have at least the arm bare; because, standing like this (*she goes close to the* FATHER *and leans her head on his breast*) with my head so, and my arms round his neck, I saw a vein pulsing in my arm here; and then, as if that live vein had awakened disgust in me, I closed my eyes like this, and let my head sink on his breast. (*Turning to the* MOTHER) Cry out, mother! Cry out! (*Buries head in* FATHER's *breast, and with her shoulders raised as if to prevent her hearing the cry, adds in tones of intense emotion*) Cry out as you did then!

THE MOTHER (*Coming forward to separate them*). No! My daughter, my daughter! (*And after having pulled her away from him*) You brute! you brute! She is my daughter! Don't you see she's my daughter?

THE MANAGER (*Walking backwards towards footlights*). Fine! fine! Damned good! And then, of course — curtain!

THE FATHER (*Going towards him excitedly*). Yes, of course, because that's the way it really happened.

THE MANAGER (*Convinced and pleased*). Oh, yes, no doubt about it. Curtain here, curtain!

(*At the reiterated cry of* THE MANAGER, THE MACHINIST *lets the curtain down, leaving* THE MANAGER *and* THE FATHER *in front of it before the footlights*)

THE MANAGER. The darned idiot! I said "curtain" to show the act should end there, and he goes and lets it down in earnest. (*To the* FATHER, *while he pulls the curtain back to go onto the stage again*) Yes, yes, it's all right. Effect certain! That's the right ending. I'll guarantee the first act, at any rate.

ACT III

When the curtain goes up again, it is seen that the stage hands have shifted the bit of scenery used in the last part, and have. rigged up instead at the back of the stage a drop, with some trees, and one or two wings. A portion of a fountain basin is visible. THE MOTHER *is sitting on the Right with the two children by her side.* THE SON *is on the same side, but away from the others. He seems bored, angry, and full of shame.* THE FATHER *and* THE STEPDAUGHTER *are also seated towards the Right front. On the other side (Left) are the* ACTORS, *much in the positions they occupied before the curtain was lowered. Only* THE MANAGER *is standing up in the middle of the stage, with his hand closed over his mouth, in the act of meditating.*

THE MANAGER (*Shaking his shoulders after a brief pause*). Ah yes: the second act! Leave it to me, leave it all to me as we arranged, and you'll see! It'll go fine!

THE STEPDAUGHTER. Our entry into his house (*indicates* FATHER) in spite of him . . . (*indicates the* SON)

THE MANAGER (*Out of patience*). Leave it to me, I tell you!

THE STEPDAUGHTER. Do let it be clear, at any rate, that it is in spite of my wishes.

THE MOTHER (*From her corner, shaking her head*). For all the good that's come of it . . .

THE STEPDAUGHTER (*Turning towards her quickly*). It doesn't matter. The more harm done us, the more remorse for him.

THE MANAGER (*Impatiently*). I understand! Good Heavens! I understand! I'm taking it into account.

THE MOTHER (*Supplicatingly*). I beg you, sir, to let it appear quite plain that for conscience' sake I did try in every way . . .

THE STEPDAUGHTER (*Interrupting indignantly and continuing for the* MOTHER). . . . to pacify me, to dissuade me from spiting him. (*To* MANAGER) Do as she wants: satisfy her, because it is true! I enjoy it immensely. Anyhow, as you can see, the meeker she is, the more she tries to get at his heart, the more distant and aloof does he become.

THE MANAGER. Are we going to begin this second act or not?

THE STEPDAUGHTER. I'm not going to talk any more now. But I must tell you this: you can't have the whole action take place in the garden, as you suggest. It isn't possible!

THE MANAGER. Why not?

THE STEPDAUGHTER. Because he (*indicates the* SON *again*) is always shut up alone in his room. And then there's all the part of that poor dazed-looking boy there which takes place indoors.

THE MANAGER. Maybe! On the other hand, you will understand — we can't change scenes three or four times in one act.

THE LEADING MAN. They used to once.

THE MANAGER. Yes, when the public was up to the level of that child there.

THE LEADING LADY. It makes the illusion easier.

THE FATHER (*Irritated*). The illusion! For Heaven's sake, don't say illusion. Please don't use that word, which is particularly painful for us.

THE MANAGER (*Astounded*). And why, if you please?

THE FATHER. It's painful, cruel, really cruel; and you ought to understand that.

THE MANAGER. But why? What ought we to say then? The illusion, I tell you, sir, which we've got to create for the audience . . .

THE LEADING MAN. With our acting.

THE MANAGER. The illusion of a reality.

THE FATHER. I understand; but you, perhaps, do not understand us. Forgive me! You see . . . here for you and your actors, the thing is only — and rightly so . . . a kind of game . . .

THE LEADING LADY (*Interrupting indignantly*). A game! We're not children here, if you please! We are serious actors.

THE FATHER. I don't deny it. What I mean is the game, or play, of your art, which has to give, as the gentleman says, a perfect illusion of reality.

THE MANAGER. Precisely —!

THE FATHER. Now, if you consider the fact that we (*indicates himself and the other five* CHARACTERS), as we are, have no other reality outside of this illusion . . .

THE MANAGER (*Astonished, looking at his* ACTORS, *who are also amazed*). And what does that mean?

THE FATHER (*After watching them for a moment with a wan smile*). As I say, sir, that which is a game of art for you is our sole reality. (*Brief pause. He goes a step or two nearer the* MANAGER *and adds*) But not only for us, you know, by the way. Just you think it over well. (*Looks him in the eyes*) Can you tell me who you are?

THE MANAGER (*Perplexed, half smiling*). What? Who am I? I am myself.

THE FATHER. And if I were to tell you that that isn't true, because you are I? . . .

THE MANAGER. I should say you were mad —! (*The* ACTORS *laugh*)

THE FATHER. You're quite right to laugh: because we are all making believe here. (*To* MANAGER) And you can therefore object that it's only for a joke that that gentleman there (*indicates the* LEADING MAN), who naturally is himself, has to be me, who am on the contrary myself — this thing you see here. You see I've caught you in a trap! (*The* ACTORS *laugh*)

THE MANAGER (*Annoyed*). But we've had all this over once before. Do you want to begin again?

THE FATHER. No, no! that wasn't my meaning! In fact, I should like to request you to abandon this game of art (*Looking at the* LEADING LADY *as if anticipating her*) which you are accustomed to play here with your actors, and to ask you seriously once again: who are you?

THE MANAGER (*Astonished and irritated, turning to his* ACTORS). If this fellow here hasn't got a nerve! A man who calls himself a character comes and asks me who I am!

THE FATHER (*With dignity, but not offended*). A character, sir, may always ask a man who he is. Because a character has really a life of his own, marked with his especial characteristics; for which reason he is always "somebody." But a man — I'm not speaking of you now — may very well be "nobody."

THE MANAGER. Yes, but you are asking these questions of me, the boss, the manager! Do you understand?

THE FATHER. But only in order to know if you, as you really are now, see yourself as you once were with all the illusions that were yours then, with all the things both inside and outside of you as they seemed to you — as they were then indeed for you. Well, sir, if you think of all those illusions that mean nothing to you now, of all those things which don't even *seem* to you to exist any more, while once they *were* for you, don't you feel that — I won't say these boards — but the very earth under your feet is sinking away from you when you reflect that in the same way this *you* as you feel it today — all this present reality of yours — is fated to seem a mere illusion to you tomorrow?

THE MANAGER (*Without having understood much, but astonished by the specious argument*). Well, well! And where does all this take us anyway?

THE FATHER. Oh, nowhere! It's only to show you that if we (*indicating the* CHARACTERS) have no other reality beyond your illusion, you too must not count overmuch on your reality as you feel it today, since, like that of yesterday, it may prove an illusion for you tomorrow.

THE MANAGER (*Determining to make fun of him*). Ah, excellent! Then you'll be saying next that you, with this comedy of yours that you brought here to act, are truer and more real than I am.

THE FATHER (*With the greatest seriousness*). But of course; without doubt!

THE MANAGER. Ah, really?

THE FATHER. Why, I thought you'd understand that from the beginning.

THE MANAGER. More real than I?

THE FATHER. If your reality can change from one day to another . . .

THE MANAGER. But everyone knows it can change. It is always changing, the same as anyone else's.

THE FATHER (*With a cry*). No, sir, not ours! Look here! That is the very difference! Our reality doesn't change: it can't change! It can't be other than what it is, because it is already fixed for ever. It's terrible. Ours is an immutable reality which should make you shudder when you approach us if you are really conscious of the fact that your reality is a mere transitory and fleeting illusion, taking this form today and that tomorrow, according to the conditions, according to your will, your sentiments, which in turn are controlled by an intellect that shows them to you today in one manner and tomorrow . . . who knows how? . . . Illusions of reality represented in this fatuous comedy of life that never ends, nor can ever end! Because if tomorrow it were to end . . . then why, all would be finished.

THE MANAGER. Oh for God's sake, will you *at least* finish with this philosophizing and let us try and shape this comedy which you yourself have brought me here? You argue and philosophize a bit too much, my dear sir. You know you seem to me almost, almost . . . (*Stops and looks him over from head to foot*) Ah, by the way, I think you introduced yourself to me as a — what shall . . . we say — a "character," created by an author who did not afterwards care to make a drama of his own creations.

THE FATHER. It is the simple truth, sir.

THE MANAGER. Nonsense! Cut that out, please! None of us believes it, because it isn't a thing, as you must recognize yourself, which one can believe seriously. If you want to know, it seems to me you are trying to imitate the manner of a certain author whom I heartily detest — I warn you — although I have unfortunately bound myself to put on one of his works. As a matter of fact, I was just starting to rehearse it, when you arrived. (*Turning to the* ACTORS) And this is what we've gained — out of the frying pan into the fire!

THE FATHER. I don't know to what author you may be alluding, but believe me I feel what I think; and I seem to be philosophizing only for those who do not think what they feel, because they blind themselves with their own sentiment. I know that for many people this self-blinding seems much more "human"; but the contrary is really true. For man never reasons so much and becomes so introspective as when he suffers; since he is anxious to get at the cause of his sufferings, to learn who has produced them, and whether it is just or unjust that he should have to bear them. On the other hand, when he is happy, he takes his happiness as it comes and doesn't analyze it, just as if happiness were his right. The animals suffer without reasoning about their sufferings. But take the case of a man who suffers and begins to reason about it. Oh no! it can't be allowed! Let him suffer like an animal, and then — ah yes, he is "human!"

THE MANAGER. Look here! Look here! You're off again, philosophizing worse than ever.

THE FATHER. Because I suffer, sir! I'm not philosophizing: I'm crying aloud the reason of my sufferings.

THE MANAGER (*Makes brusque movement as he is taken with a new idea*). I should like to know if anyone has ever heard of a character who gets right out of his part and perorates and speechifies as you do. Have you ever heard of a case? I haven't.

THE FATHER. You have never met such a case, sir, because authors, as a rule, hide the labor of their creations. When the characters are really alive before their author, the latter does nothing but follow them in their action, in their words, in the situations which they suggest to him; and he has to will them the way they will themselves — for there's trouble if he doesn't. When a character is born, he acquires at once such an independence, even of his own author, that he can be imagined by everybody even in many other situations where the author never dreamed of placing him; and so he acquires for himself a meaning which the author never thought of giving him.

THE MANAGER. Yes, yes, I know this.

THE FATHER. What is there then to marvel at in us? Imagine such a misfortune for characters as I have described to you: to be born of an author's fantasy, and be denied life by him; and then answer me if these characters left alive, and yet without life, weren't right in doing what they did do and are doing now, after they have attempted everything in their power to persuade him to give them their stage life. We've all tried him in turn, I, she (*indicating the* STEPDAUGHTER) and she. (*Indicating the* MOTHER)

THE STEPDAUGHTER. It's true. I too have sought to tempt him, many, many times, when he had been sitting at his writing table, feeling a bit melancholy, at the twilight hour. He would sit in his armchair too lazy to switch on the light, and all the shadows that crept into his room were full of our presence coming to tempt him. (*As if she saw herself still there by the writing table, and was annoyed by the presence of the* ACTORS) Oh, if you would only go away, go away and leave us alone — mother here with that son of hers — I with that Child — that Boy there always alone — and then I with him — (*just hints at the* FATHER) — and then I alone, alone . . . in those shadows! (*Makes a sudden movement as if in the vision she has of herself illuminating those shadows she wanted to seize hold of herself*) Ah! my life! my life! Oh, what scenes we proposed to him — and I tempted him more than any of the others!

THE FATHER. Maybe. But perhaps it was your fault that he refused to give us life: because you were too insistent, too troublesome.

THE STEPDAUGHTER. Nonsense! Didn't he make me so himself? (*Goes close to the* MANAGER *to tell him as if in confidence*) In my opinion he abandoned us in a fit of depression, of disgust for the ordinary theater as the public knows it and likes it.

THE SON. Exactly what it was, sir; exactly that!

THE FATHER. Not at all! Don't believe it for a minute. Listen to me! You'll be doing quite right to modify, as you suggest, the excesses both of this girl here, who wants to do too much, and of this young man, who won't do anything at all.

THE SON. No, nothing!

THE MANAGER. You too get over the mark occasionally, my dear sir, if I may say so.

THE FATHER. I? When? Where?

THE MANAGER. Always! Continuously! Then there's this insistence of yours in trying to make us believe you are a character. And then too, you must really argue and philosophize less, you know, much less.

THE FATHER. Well, if you want to take away from me the possibility of representing the torment of my spirit which never gives me peace, you will be suppressing me: that's all. Every true man, sir, who is a little above the level of the beasts and plants does not live for the sake of living, without knowing how to live; but he lives so as to give a meaning and a value of his own to life. For me this is *everything*. I cannot give up this, just to represent a mere fact as she (*indicating the* STEPDAUGHTER) wants. It's all very well for her, since her "vendetta" lies in the "fact." I'm not going to do it. It destroys my *raison d'être*.

THE MANAGER. Your *raison d'être*! Oh, we're going ahead fine! First she starts off, and then you jump in. At this rate, we'll never finish.

THE FATHER. Now, don't be offended! Have it your own way — provided, however, that within the limits of the parts you assign us each one's sacrifice isn't too great.

THE MANAGER. You've got to understand that you can't go on arguing at your own pleasure. Drama is action, sir, action and not confounded philosophy.

THE FATHER. All right. I'll do just as much arguing and philosophizing as everybody does when he is considering his own torments.

THE MANAGER. If the drama permits! But for Heaven's sake, man, let's get along and come to the scene.

THE STEPDAUGHTER. It seems to me we've got too much action with our coming into his house. (*Indicating* FATHER) You said, before, you couldn't change the scene every five minutes.

THE MANAGER. Of course not. What we've got to do is to combine and group up all the facts in one simultaneous, close-knit action. We can't have it as you want, with your little brother wandering like a ghost from room to room, hiding behind doors and meditating a project which — what did you say it did to him?

THE STEPDAUGHTER. Consumes him, sir, wastes him away!

THE MANAGER. Well, it may be. And then at the same time, you want the little girl there to be playing in the garden . . . one in the house, and the other in the garden: isn't that it?

THE STEPDAUGHTER. Yes, in the sun, in the sun! That is my only pleasure: to see her happy and careless in the garden after the misery and squalor of the horrible room where we all four slept together. And I had to sleep with her — I, do you understand? — with my vile contaminated body next to hers; with her folding me fast in her loving little arms. In the garden, whenever she spied me, she would run to take me by the hand. She didn't care for the big flowers, only the little ones; and she loved to show me them and pet me.

THE MANAGER. Well then, we'll have it in the garden. Everything shall happen in the garden; and we'll group the other scenes there. (*Calls a* STAGE HAND) Here, a back-cloth with trees and something to do as a fountain basin. (*Turning round to look at the back of the stage*) Ah, you've fixed it up. Good! (*To* STEPDAUGHTER) This is just to give an idea, of course. The Boy, instead of hiding behind the doors, will wander about here in the garden, hiding behind the trees. But it's going to be rather difficult to find a child to do that scene with you where she shows you the flowers. (*Turning to the* YOUTH) Come forward a little, will you please? Let's try it now! Come along! come along! (*Then seeing him come shyly forward, full of fear and looking lost*) It's a nice business, this lad here. What's the matter with him? We'll have to give him a word or two to say. (*Goes close to him, puts a hand on his shoulders, and leads him behind one of the trees*) Come on! come on! Let me see you a little! Hide here . . . yes, like that. Try and show your head just a little as if you were looking for someone . . . (*Goes back to observe the effect, when the* BOY *at once goes through the action*) Excellent! fine! (*Turning to* STEPDAUGHTER) Suppose the little girl there were to surprise him as he looks round, and run over to him, so we could give him a word or two to say?

THE STEPDAUGHTER. It's useless to hope he will speak, as long as that fellow there is here . . . (*Indicates the* SON) You must send him away first.

THE SON (*Jumping up*). Delighted! delighted! I don't ask for anything better. (*Begins to move away*)

THE MANAGER (*At once stopping him*) No! No! Where are you going? Wait a bit!

(*The* MOTHER *gets up, alarmed and terrified at the thought that he is really about to go away. Instinctively she lifts her arms to prevent him, without, however, leaving her seat*)

THE SON (*To* MANAGER, *who stops him*). I've got nothing to do with this affair. Let me go please! Let me go!

THE MANAGER. What do you mean by saying you've got nothing to do with this?

THE STEPDAUGHTER (*Calmly, with irony*). Don't bother to stop him: he won't go away.

THE FATHER. He has to act the terrible scene in the garden with his mother.

THE SON (*Suddenly resolute and with dignity*). I shall act nothing at all. I've said so from the very beginning. (*To the* MANAGER) Let me go!

THE STEPDAUGHTER (*Going over to the* MANAGER) Allow me? (*Puts down the* MANAGER's *arm which is restraining the* SON) Well, go away then, if you want to! (*The* SON *looks at her with contempt and hatred. She laughs and says*) You see, he can't, he can't go away! He is obliged to stay here, indissolubly bound to the chain. If I, who fly off when that happens which has to happen, because I can't bear him — if I am still here and support that face and expression of his, you can well imagine that he is unable to move. He has to remain here, has to stop with that nice father of his, and that mother whose only son he is. (*Turning to the* MOTHER) Come on, mother, come along! (*Turning to* MANAGER *to indicate her*) You see, she was getting up to keep him back. (*To the* MOTHER, *beckoning her with her hand*) Come on! come on! (*Then to* MANAGER) You can imagine how little she wants to show these actors of yours what she really feels; but so eager is she to get near him that . . . There, you see? She is willing to act her part. (*And in fact, the* MOTHER *approaches him; and as soon as the* STEPDAUGHTER *has finished speaking, opens her arms to signify that she consents*)

THE SON (*Suddenly*). No! No! If I can't go away, then I'll stop here; but I repeat: I act nothing!

THE FATHER (*To* MANAGER *excitedly*). You can force him, sir.

THE SON. Nobody can force me.

THE FATHER. I can.

THE STEPDAUGHTER. Wait a minute, wait . . . First of all, the baby has to go to the fountain . . . (*Runs to take the* CHILD *and leads her to the fountain*)

THE MANAGER. Yes, yes of course; that's it. Both at the same time.

(*The* SECOND LADY LEAD *and the* JUVENILE LEAD *at this point separate themselves from the group of* ACTORS. *One watches the* MOTHER *attentively; the other moves about studying the movements and manner of the* SON *whom he will have to act*)

THE SON (*To* MANAGER). What do you mean by both at the same time? It isn't right. There was no scene between me and her. (*Indicates the* MOTHER) Ask her how it was!

THE MOTHER. Yes, it's true. I had come into his room . . .

THE SON. Into my room, do you understand? Nothing to do with the garden.

THE MANAGER. It doesn't matter. Haven't I told you we've got to group the action?

THE SON (*Observing the* JUVENILE LEAD *studying him*). What do you want?

THE JUVENILE LEAD. Nothing! I was just looking at you.

THE SON (*Turning towards the* SECOND LADY LEAD). Ah! she's at it too: to re-act her part! (*Indicating the* MOTHER)

THE MANAGER. Exactly! And it seems to me that you ought to be grateful to them for their interest.

THE SON. Yes, but haven't you yet perceived that it isn't possible to live in front of a mirror which not only freezes us with the image of ourselves, but throws our likeness back at us with a horrible grimace?

THE FATHER. That is true, absolutely true. You must see that.

THE MANAGER (*To* SECOND LADY LEAD *and* JUVENILE LEAD). He's right! Move away from them!

THE SON. Do as you like. I'm out of this!

THE MANAGER. Be quiet, you, will you? And let me hear your mother! (*To* MOTHER) You were saying you had entered . . .

THE MOTHER. Yes, into his room, because I couldn't stand it any longer. I went to empty my heart to him of all the anguish that tortures me . . . But as soon as he saw me come in . . .

THE SON. Nothing happened! There was no scene. I went away, that's all! I don't care for scenes!

THE MOTHER. It's true, true. That's how it was.

THE MANAGER. Well now, we've got to do this bit between you and him. It's indispensable.

THE MOTHER. I'm ready . . . when you are ready. If you could only find a chance for me to tell him what I feel here in my heart.

THE FATHER (*Going to* SON *in a great rage*). You'll do this for your mother, for your mother, do you understand?

THE SON (*Quite determined*). I do nothing!

THE FATHER (*Taking hold of him and shaking him*). For God's sake, do as I tell you! Don't you hear your mother asking you for a favor? Haven't you even got the guts to be a son?

THE SON (*Taking hold of the* FATHER). No! No! And for God's sake stop it, or else . . . (*General agitation. The* MOTHER, *frightened, tries to separate them*)

THE MOTHER (*Pleading*). Please! please!

THE FATHER (*Not leaving hold of the* SON). You've got to obey, do you hear?

THE SON (*Almost crying from rage*). What does it mean, this madness you've got? (*They separate*) Have you no decency, that you insist on showing everyone our shame? I won't do it! I won't! And I stand for the will of our author in this. He didn't want to put us on the stage, after all!

THE MANAGER. Man alive! You came here . . .

THE SON (*Indicating* FATHER). He did! I didn't!

THE MANAGER. Aren't you here now?

THE SON. It was his wish, and he dragged us along with him. He's told you not only the things that did happen, but also things that have never happened at all.

THE MANAGER. Well, tell me then what did happen. You went out of your room without saying a word?

THE SON. Without a word, so as to avoid a scene!

THE MANAGER. And then what did you do?

THE SON. Nothing . . . walking in the garden . . . (*Hesitates for a moment with expression of gloom*)

THE MANAGER (*Coming closer to him, interested by his extraordinary reserve*). Well, well . . . walking in the garden . . .

THE SON (*Exasperated*). Why on earth do you insist? It's horrible! (*The* MOTHER *trembles, sobs, and looks towards the fountain*)

THE MANAGER (*Slowly observing the glance and turning towards the* SON *with increasing apprehension*). The baby?

THE SON. There in the fountain . . .

THE FATHER (*Pointing with tender pity to the* MOTHER). She was following him at the moment . . .

THE MANAGER (*To the* SON, *anxiously*). And then you . . .

THE SON. I ran over to her; I was jumping in to drag her out when I saw something that froze my blood . . . the boy there, standing stock still, with eyes like a madman's, watching his little drowned sister, in the fountain! (*The* STEPDAUGHTER *bends over the fountain to hide the* CHILD. *She sobs*) Then . . . (*A revolver shot rings out behind the trees where the* BOY *is hidden*)

THE MOTHER (*With a cry of terror runs over in that direction together with several of the* ACTORS *amid general confusion*). My son! My son! (*Then amid the cries and exclamations one hears her voice*) Help! Help!

THE MANAGER (*Pushing the* ACTORS *aside while they lift up the* BOY *and carry him off*). Is he really wounded?

SOME ACTORS. He's dead! dead!

OTHER ACTORS. No, no, it's only make believe, it's only pretence!

THE FATHER (*With a terrible cry*). Pretence? Reality, sir, reality!

THE MANAGER. Pretence? Reality? To hell with it all! Never in my life has such a thing happened to me. I've lost a whole day over these people, a whole day!

Curtain

Frank Lloyd Wright (1869–1959)

AMERICAN ARCHITECT

Modern Architecture: The Cardboard House

Let us take for text . . . the greatest of all references to simplicity, the inspired admonition: "*Consider the lilies of the field — they toil not, neither do they spin, yet verily I say unto thee — Solomon in all his glory was not arrayed like one of these.* An inspired saying — attributed to an humble Architect in ancient times, called Carpenter, who gave up Architecture nearly two thousand years ago to go to work upon its Source.

And if the text should seem to you too far away from our subject this afternoon —

The Cardboard House

— consider that for that very reason the text has been chosen. The cardboard house needs an antidote. The antidote is far more important than the house. As antidote — and as practical example, too, of the working out of an ideal of organic simplicity that has taken place here on American soil, step by step, under conditions that are your own — could I do better than to take apart for your benefit the buildings I have tried to build, to show you how they were, long ago, dedicated to the Ideal of Organic Simplicity? It seems to me that while another might do better than that, I certainly could not — for that is, truest and best, what I know about the Subject. What a man *does, that* he has.

When, "in the cause of Architecture," in 1893, I first began to build the houses, sometimes referred to by the thoughtless as "The New School of the Middle West" (some advertiser's slogan comes along to label everything in this our busy woman's country), the only way to simplify the awful building in vogue at the time was to conceive a finer entity — a better building — and get it built. The buildings standing then were all tall and all tight. Chimneys were lean and taller still, sooty fingers threatening the sky. And beside them, sticking up by way of dormers through the cruelly sharp, saw-tooth roofs, were the attics for "help" to swelter in. Dormers were elaborate devices, cunning little buildings complete in themselves, stuck to the main roof slopes to let "help" poke heads out of the attic for air.

Invariably the damp sticky clay of the prairie was dug out for a basement under the whole house, and the rubblestone walls of this dank basement always stuck up above the ground a foot or more and blinked, with half-windows. So the universal "cellar" showed itself as a bank of some kind of masonry running around the whole house, for the house to sit up on — like a chair. The lean, upper house-walls of the usual two floors above this stone or brick basement were wood, set on top of this masonry-chair, clapboarded and painted, or else shingled and stained, preferably shingled and mixed, up and down, all together with mouldings crosswise. These overdressed wood house-walls had, cut in them — or cut out of them, to be precise — big holes for the big cat and little holes for the little cat to get in and out or for ulterior purposes of light and air. The house-walls were be-corniced or bracketed up at the top into the tall, purposely profusely complicated roof, dormers plus. The whole roof, as well as the roof as a whole, was scalloped and ridged and tipped and swanked and gabled to madness before they would allow it to be either shingled or slated. The whole exterior was be-deviled — that is to say, mixed to puzzle-pieces, with corner boards, panel-boards, window-frames, corner-blocks, plinth-blocks, rosettes, fantails, ingenious and jigger work in general. This was the only way they seemed to have, then, of "putting on style." The scroll-saw and turning-lathe were at the moment the honest means of this fashionable mongering by the wood-butcher and to this entirely "moral" end. Unless the householder of the period were poor indeed, usually an ingenious corner-tower on his house eventuated into a candle-snuffer dome, a spire, an inverted rutabaga or radish or onion or — what is your favorite vegetable? Always elaborate bay-windows and fancy porches played "ring around a rosy" on this "imaginative" corner feature. And all this the building of the period could do equally well in brick or stone. It was an impartial society. All material looked pretty much alike in that day.

Simplicity was as far from all this scrap-pile as the pandemonium of the barn-yard is far from music. But it was easy for the Architect. All he had to do was to call: "Boy, take down No. 37, and put a bay-window on it for the lady!"

So — the first thing to do was to get rid of the attic and, therefore, of the dormer and of the useless "heights" below it. And next, get rid of the unwholesome basement, entirely — yes, absolutely — in any house built on the prairie. Instead of lean, brick chimneys, bristling up from steep roofs to hint at "judgment" everywhere, I could see necessity for one only, a broad generous one, or at most, for two, these kept low down on gently sloping roofs or perhaps flat roofs. The big fireplace below, inside, became now a place for a real fire, justified the great size of this chimney outside. A real fireplace at that time was extraordinary. There were then "mantels" instead. A mantel was a marble frame for a few coals, or a piece of wooden furniture with tiles stuck in it and a "grate," the whole set slam up against the wall. The "mantel" was an insult to comfort, but the *integral* fireplace became an important part of the building itself in the houses I was allowed to build out there on the prairie. It refreshed me to see the fire burning deep in the masonry of the house itself.

Taking a human being for my scale, I brought the whole house down in height to fit a normal man; believing in no other scale, I broadened the mass out, all I possibly could, as I brought it down into spaciousness. It has been said that were I three inches taller (I am 5 feet 8½ inches tall), all my houses would have been quite different in proportion. Perhaps.

House-walls were now to be started at the ground on a cement or stone water-table that looked like a low platform under the building, which it usually was, but the house-walls were stopped at the second story window-sill level, to let the rooms above come through in a continuous window-series, under the broad eaves of a gently sloping, overhanging roof. This made enclosing screens out of the lower walls as well as light screens out of the second story walls. Here was true *enclosure of interior space*. A new sense of building, it seems.

The climate, being what it was, a matter of violent extremes of heat and cold, damp and dry, dark and bright, I gave broad protecting roof-shelter to the whole, getting back to the original purpose of the "Cornice." The undersides of the roof projections were flat and light in color to create a glow of reflected light that made the upper rooms not dark, but delightful. The over-hangs had double value, shelter and preservation. for the walls of the house as well as diffusion of reflected light for the upper story, through the "light screens" that took the place of the walls and were the windows.

At this time, a house to me was obvious primarily as interior space under fine shelter. I liked the sense of *shelter*. I liked the sense of shelter in the "look of the building." I achieved it, I believe. I then went after the varie-gated bands of material in the old walls to eliminate odds and ends in favor of one material and a single surface from grade to eaves, or grade to second story sill-cope, treated as simple enclosing screens, — or else made a plain screen band around the second story above the window-sills, turned up over on to the ceiling beneath the eaves. This screen band was of the same material as the under side of the eaves themselves, or what architects call the "soffit." The planes of the building parallel to the ground were all stressed, to grip the whole to earth. Sometimes it was possible to make the enclosing wall below this upper band of the second story, from the second story window-sill clear down to the ground, a heavy "wainscot" of fine masonry material resting on the cement or stone platform laid on the foundation. I liked that wainscot to be of masonry material when my clients felt they could afford it.

As a matter of form, too, I liked to see the projecting base, or water-table, set out over the foundation walls themselves — as a substantial preparation for the building. This was managed by setting the studs of the walls to the inside of the foundation walls, instead of to the outside. All door and window tops were now brought into line with each other with only comfort-able head-clearance for the average human being. Eliminating the sufferers from the "attic" enabled the roofs to lie low. The house began to associate with the ground and become natural to its prairie site. And would the young man in architecture ever believe that this was all "new" then? Not only new, but destructive heresy — or ridiculous eccentricity. So New that what little prospect I had of ever earning a livelihood by making houses was nearly wrecked. At first, "they" called the houses "dress-reform" houses, because Society was just then excited about that particular "reform." This simplifica-tion looked like some kind of "reform" to them. Oh, they called them all sorts of names that cannot be repeated, but "they" never found a better term for the work unless it was "Horizontal Gothic," "Temperance Architecture" (with a sneer), etc., etc. I don't know how I escaped the accusation of an-other "Renaissance."

What I have just described was all on the *outside* of the house and was there chiefly because of what had happened *inside*. Dwellings of that period were "cut-up," advisedly and completely, with the grim determination that should go with any cutting process. The "interiors" consisted of boxes beside or inside other boxes, called *rooms*. All boxes inside a complicated boxing. Each domestic "function" was properly box to box. I could see little sense in this inhibition, this cellular sequestration that implied ancestors familiar with the cells of penal institutions, except for the privacy of bed-rooms on the upper floor. They were perhaps all right as "sleeping boxes." So I declared the whole lower floor as one room, cutting off the kitchen as a laboratory, putting servants' sleeping and living quarters next to it, semi-detached, on the ground floor, screening various portions in the big room, for certain domestic purposes — like dining or reading, or receiving a formal caller. There were no plans like these in existence at the time and my clients were pushed toward these ideas as helpful to a solution of the vexed servant-problem. Scores of doors disappeared and no end of partition. They liked it, both clients and servants. The house became more free as "space" and more liveable, too. Interior spaciousness began to dawn.

Having got what windows and doors that were left lined up and lowered to convenient human height, the ceilings of the rooms, too, could be brought over on to the walls, by way of the horizontal, broad bands of plaster on the walls above the windows, the plaster colored the same as the room ceilings. This would bring the ceiling-surface down to the very window tops. The ceilings thus expanded, by extending them downward as the wall band above the windows, gave a generous overhead to even small rooms. The sense of the whole was broadened and made plastic, too, by this expedient. The enclosing walls and ceilings were thus made to flow together.

Here entered the important element of Plasticity — indispensable to successful use of the Machine, for true expression of Modernity. The outswinging windows were fought for because the casement window associated the house with out-of-doors — gave free openings, outward. In other words the so-called "casement" was simple and more human. In use and effect, more natural. If it had not existed I should have invented it. It was not used at that time in America, so I lost many clients because I insisted upon it when they wanted the "guillotine" or "double-hung" window then in use. The Guillotine was not simple nor human. It was only expedient. I used it once in the Winslow House — my first house — and rejected it thereafter — forever. Nor at that time did I entirely eliminate the wooden trim. I did make it "plastic," that is, light and continuously flowing instead of the heavy "cut and butt" of the usual carpenter work. No longer did the "trim," so-called, look like carpenter work. The machine could do it perfectly well as I laid it out. It was all after "quiet." This plastic trim, too, with its running "back-hand" enabled poor workmanship to be concealed. It was necessary with the field resources at hand at that time to conceal much. Machinery versus the union had already demoralized the workmen. The Machine resources were so little understood that extensive drawings had to be made merely to show the "mill-man" what to leave off. But the "trim" finally became only a single, flat, narrow, horizontal wood-band running around the room, one at the top of the windows and doors and another next to the floors, both connected with narrow, vertical, thin wood-bands that were used to divide the wall-surfaces of the whole room smoothly and flatly into folded color planes. The trim merely completed the window and door openings in this same plastic sense. When the interior had thus become wholly plastic, instead of structural, a New element, as I have said, had entered Architecture. Strangely enough an element that had not existed in Architectural History before. Not alone in the trim, but in numerous ways too tedious to describe in words, this revolutionary sense of the plastic whole, an instinct with me at first, began to work more and more intelligently and have fascinating, unforeseen consequences. Here was something that began to organize itself. When several houses had been finished and compared with the house of the period, there was very little of that house left standing. Nearly every one had stood the house of the period as long as he could stand it, judging by appreciation of the change. Now all this probably tedious description is intended to indicate directly in bare outline how thus early there *was* an ideal of organic simplicity put to work, with historical consequences, here in your own country. The main motives and indications were (and I enjoyed them all):

First — To reduce the number of necessary parts of the house and the separate rooms to a minimum, and make all come together as enclosed space — so divided that light, air and vista permeated the whole with a sense of unity.

Second — To associate the building as a whole with its site by extension and emphasis of the planes parallel to the ground, but keeping the floors off the best part of the site, thus leaving that better part for use in connection with the life of the house. Extended level planes were found useful in this connection.

Third — To eliminate the room as a box and the house as another by making all walls enclosing screens — the ceilings and floors and enclosing screens to flow into each other as one large enclosure of space, with minor subdivisions only.

Make all house proportions more liberally human, with less wasted space in structure, and structure more appropriate to material, and so the whole more liveable. *Liberal* is the best word. Extended straight lines or streamlines were useful in this.

Fourth — To get the unwholesome basement up out of the ground, entirely above it, as a low pedestal for the living-portion of the home, making the foundation itself visible as a low masonry platform, on which the building should stand.

Fifth — To harmonize all necessary openings to "outside" or to "inside" with good human proportions and make them occur naturally — singly or as a series in the scheme of the whole building. Usually they appeared as "light-screens" instead of walls, because all the "Architecture" of the house was chiefly the way these openings came in such walls as were grouped about the rooms as enclosing screens. The *room* as such was now the essential architectural expression, and there were to be no holes cut in the walls as holes are cut in a box, because this was not in keeping with the ideal of "plastic." Cutting holes was violent.

Sixth — To eliminate combinations of different materials in favor of mono-material so far as possible; to use no ornament that did not come out of the nature of materials to make the whole building clearer and more expressive as a place to live in, and give the conception of the building appropriate revealing emphasis. Geometrical or straight lines were natural to the machinery at work in the building trades then, so the interiors took on this character naturally.

Seventh — To incorporate all heating, lighting, plumbing so that these systems became constituent parts of the building itself. These service features became architectural and in this attempt the ideal of an organic architecture was at work.

Eighth — To incorporate as organic Architecture — so far as possible — furnishings, making them all one with the building and designing them in simple terms for machine work. Again straight lines and rectilinear forms.

Ninth — Eliminate the Decorator. He was all curves and all efflorescence, if not all "period."

This was all rational enough so far as the thought of an organic architecture went. The particular forms this thought took in the feeling of it all could only be personal. There was nothing whatever at this time to help make them what they were. All seemed to be the most natural thing in the world and grew up out of the circumstances of the moment. Whatever they may be worth in the long run is all they are worth.

Now *simplicity* being the point in question in this early constructive effort, organic simplicity I soon found to be a matter of true coordination. And Beauty I soon felt to be a matter of the sympathy with which such coordination was affected. Plainness was not necessarily simplicity. Crude furniture of the Roycroft-Stickley-Mission Style, which came along later, was offensively plain, plain as a barn door — but never was simple in any true sense. Nor, I found, were merely machine-made things in themselves simple. To think "in simple," is to deal in simples, and that means with an eye single to the altogether. This, I believe, is the secret of simplicity. Perhaps we may truly regard nothing at all as simple in itself. I believe that no one thing in itself is ever so, but must achieve simplicity (as an Artist should use the term) as a perfectly realized part of some organic whole. Only as a feature or any part becomes an harmonious element in the harmonious whole does it arrive at the estate of simplicity. Any wild flower is truly simple, but double the same wild flower by cultivation, it ceases to be so. The *scheme* of the original is no longer clear. Clarity of design and perfect significance both are first essentials of the spontaneously born simplicity of the lilies of the field who neither toil nor spin, as contrasted with Solomon who had "toiled and spun" — that is to say, no doubt had put on himself and had put on his temple, properly "composed," everything in the category of good things but the cookstove.

Five lines where three are enough is stupidity. Nine pounds where three are sufficient is stupidity. But to eliminate expressive words that intensify or vivify meaning in speaking or writing is not simplicity; nor is similar elimination in Architecture simplicity — it, too, may be stupidity. In Architecture, expressive changes of surface, emphasis of line and especially textures of material, may go to make facts eloquent, forms more significant. Elimination, therefore, may be just as meaningless as elaboration, perhaps more often so. I offer any fool, for an example.

To know what to leave out and what to put in, just where and just how — Ah, *that* is to have been educated in knowledge of SIMPLICITY.

As for Objects of Art in the house even in that early day they were the "bête noir" of the new simplicity. If well chosen, well enough in the house, but only if each was properly digested by the whole. Antique or modern sculpture, paintings, pottery, might become objectives in the Architectural scheme and I accepted them, aimed at them, and assimilated them. Such things may take their places as elements in the design of any house. They are then precious things, gracious and good to live with. But it is difficult to do this well. Better, if it may be done, to design all features together. At that time, too, I tried to make my clients see that furniture and furnishings, not built in as integral features of the building, should be designed as attributes of whatever furniture was built in and should be seen as minor parts of the building itself, even if detached or kept aside to be employed on occasion. But when the building itself was finished, the old furniture the clients already possessed went in with them to await the time when the interior might be completed. Very few of the houses were, therefore, anything but painful to me after the clients moved in and, helplessly, dragged the horrors of the old order along after them.

But I soon found it difficult, anyway, to make some of the furniture in the "abstract"; that is, to design it as architecture and make it "human" at the same time — fit for human use. I have been black and blue in some spot, somewhere, almost all my life from too intimate contacts with my own furniture. Human beings must group, sit or recline — confound them — and they must dine, but dining is much easier to manage and always was a great artistic opportunity. Arrangements for the informality of sitting comfortably, singly or in groups, where it is desirable or natural to sit, and still to belong in disarray to the scheme as a whole — that is a matter difficult to accomplish. But it can be done now, and should be done, because only those attributes of human comfort and convenience, made to belong in this digested or integrated sense to the architecture of the home as a whole, should be there at all, in Modern Architecture. For that matter about four-fifths of the contents of nearly every home could be given away with good effect to that home. But the things given away might go on to poison some other home. So why not at once destroy undesirable things . . . make an end of them?

Here then, in foregoing outline, is the gist of America's contribution to Modern American Architecture as it was already under way in 1893. But the gospel of elimination is one never preached enough. No matter how much preached, Simplicity is a spiritual ideal seldom organically reached. Nevertheless, by assuming the virtue by imitation — or by increasing structural makeshifts to get superficial simplicity — the effects may cultivate a taste that will demand the reality in course of time, but it may also destroy all hope of the real thing.

Standing here, with the perspective of long persistent effort in the direction of an organic Architecture in view, I can again assure you out of this initial experience that Repose is the reward of true simplicity and that organic simplicity is sure of Repose. Repose is the highest quality in the Art of Architecture, next to integrity, and a reward for integrity. Simplicity may well be held to the fore as a spiritual ideal, but when actually achieved, as in the "lilies of the field," it is something that comes of itself, something spontaneously born out of the nature of the doing whatever it is that is to be done. Simplicity, too, is a reward for fine feeling and straight thinking in working a principle well in hand, to a consistent end. Solomon knew nothing about it, for he was only wise. And this, I think, is what Jesus meant by the text we have chosen for this discourse — "Consider the lilies of the field," as contrasted, for beauty, with Solomon.

Now, a chair *is* a machine to sit in.

A home *is* a machine to live in.

The human body *is* a machine to be worked by will.

A tree *is* a machine to bear fruit.

A plant *is* a machine to bear flowers and seeds.

And, as I've admitted before somewhere, a heart *is* a suction-pump. Does that idea thrill you?

Trite as it is, it may be as well to think it over because the *least* any of these things may be, *is* just that. All of them are that before they are anything else. And to violate that mechanical requirement in any of them is to finish before anything of higher purpose can happen. To ignore the fact is either sentimentality or the prevalent insanity. Let us acknowledge in this respect, that this matter of mechanics is just as true of the work of Art as it is true of anything else. But, were we to stop with that trite acknowledgment, we should only be living in a low, rudimentary sense. This skeleton rudiment accepted, *understood*, is the first condition of any fruit or flower we may hope to get from ourselves. Let us continue to call this flower and fruit of ourselves, even in this Machine Age, ART. Some Architects, as we may see, now consciously acknowledge this "Machine" rudiment. Some will eventually get to it by circuitous mental labor. Some *are* the thing itself without question and already in need of "treatment." But "Americans" (I prefer to be more specific and say "Usonians") have been educated "blind" to the higher human uses of it all — while actually in sight of this higher human use all the while.

Therefore, now let the declaration that "all is machinery" stand nobly forth for what it is worth. But why not more profoundly declare that "Form follows Function" and let it go at that? Saying, "Form follows Function," is not only deeper, it is clearer, and it goes further in a more comprehensive way to say the thing to be said, because the implication of this saying includes the heart of the whole matter. It may be that Function follows Form, as, or if, you prefer, but it is easier thinking with the first proposition just as it is easier to stand on your feet and nod your head than it would be to stand on your head and nod your feet. Let us not forget that Simplicity of the Universe is very different from the Simplicity of a Machine.

New significance in Architecture implies new materials qualifying form and textures, requires fresh feeling, which will eventually qualify both as "ornament." But "Decoration" must be sent on its way or now be given the meaning that it has lost, if it is to stay. Since "Decoration" became acknowledged as such, and ambitiously set up for itself as Decoration, it has been a makeshift, in the light of this ideal of Organic Architecture. Any House Decoration, as such, is an architectural makeshift, however well it may be done, unless the decoration, so called, is part of the Architect's design in both concept and execution.

Since Architecture in the old sense died and Decoration has had to shift for itself more and more, all so-called Decoration has become *ornamental,* therefore no longer *integral.* There can be no true simplicity in either Architecture or Decoration under any such condition. Let Decoration, therefore, die for Architecture, and the Decorator become an Architect, but not an "Interior Architect."

Ornament can never be applied to Architecture any more than Architecture should ever be applied to Decoration. All ornament, if not developed within the nature of Architecture and as organic part of such expression, vitiates the whole fabric no matter how clever or beautiful it may be as something in itself.

Yes — for a century or more Decoration has been setting up for itself, and in our prosperous country has come pretty near to doing very well, thank you. I think we may say that it is pretty much all we have now to show as Domestic Architecture, as Domestic Architecture still goes with us at the present time. But we may as well face it. The Interior Decorator thrives with us because we have no Architecture. Any Decorator is the natural enemy of organic simplicity in Architecture. He, persuasive Doctor-of-Appearances that he *must* be when he becomes Architectural substitute, will give you an imitation of anything, even an imitation of imitative simplicity. Just at the moment, May 1930, he is expert in this imitation. France, the born Decorator, is now engaged with "Madame," owing to the good fortune of the French market, in selling us this ready-made or made-to-order simplicity. Yes, Imitation Simplicity is the latest addition to imported "stock." The Decorators of America are now equipped to furnish *especially* this. Observe. And how very charming the suggestions conveyed by these imitations sometimes are!

Would you have again the general principles of the spiritual-ideal of organic simplicity at work in our Culture? If so, then let us reiterate: First, Simplicity is Constitutional Order. And it is worthy of note in this connection that 9 times 9 equals 81 is just as simple as 2 plus 2 equals 4. Nor is the obvious more simple necessarily than the occult. The obvious is obvious simply because it falls within our special horizon, is therefore easier for us to *see;* that is all. Yet all simplicity near or far has a countenance, a visage, that is characteristic. But this countenance is visible only to those who can grasp the whole and enjoy the significance of the minor part, as such, in relation to the whole when in flower. This is for the critics.

This characteristic visage may be simulated — the real complication glossed over, the internal conflict hidden by surface and belied by mass. The internal complication may be and usually is increased to create the semblance of and get credit for — simplicity. This is the Simplicity-lie usually achieved by most of the "surface and mass" architects. This is for the young architect.

Truly ordered simplicity in the hands of the great artist may flower into a bewildering profusion, exquisitely exuberant, and render all more clear than ever. Good William Blake says exuberance is *beauty*, meaning that it is so in this very sense. This is for the Modern Artist with the Machine in his hands. False Simplicity — Simplicity as an affectation, that is Simplicity constructed as a Decorator's outside put upon a complicated, wasteful engineer's or carpenter's "Structure," outside or inside — is not good enough Simplicity. It cannot be simple at all. But that is what passes for Simplicity, now that startling Simplicity-effects are becoming the *fashion*. That kind of Simplicity is *violent*. This is for "Art and Decoration."

Soon we shall want Simplicity inviolate. There is one way to get that Simplicity. My guess is, there is *only* one way really to get it. And that way is, on principle, by way of *Construction* developed as Architecture. That is for us, one and all.

Wallace Stevens (1879–1955)

AMERICAN POET and INSURANCE EXECUTIVE

Thirteen Ways of Looking at a Blackbird

I

Among twenty snowy mountains,
The only moving thing
Was the eye of the blackbird.

II

I was of three minds,
Like a tree
In which there are three blackbirds.

III

The blackbird whirled in the autumn winds.
It was a small part of the pantomime.

IV

A man and a woman
Are one.   10
A man and a woman and a blackbird
Are one.

V

I do not know which to prefer,
The beauty of inflections
Or the beauty of innuendoes,
The blackbird whistling
Or just after.

VI

Icicles filled the long window
With barbaric glass.
The shadow of the blackbird   20
Crossed it, to and fro.
The mood
Traced in the shadow
An indecipherable cause.

VII

O thin men of Haddam,
Why do you imagine golden birds?
Do you not see how the blackbird
Walks around the feet
Of the women about you?

VIII

I know noble accents   30
And lucid, inescapable rhythms;
But I know, too,
That the blackbird is involved
In what I know.

IX

When the blackbird flew out of sight,
It marked the edge
Of one of many circles.

X

At the sight of blackbirds
Flying in a green light,
Even the bawds of euphony   40
Would cry out sharply.

XI

He rode over Connecticut
In a glass coach.
Once, a fear pierced him,
In that he mistook
The shadow of his equipage
For blackbirds.

XII

The river is moving.
The blackbird must be flying.

XIII

It was evening all afternoon.   50
It was snowing
And it was going to snow.
The blackbird sat
In the cedar-limbs.

Igor Stravinsky (b. 1882)

RUSSIAN COMPOSER (IN AMERICA)

The Performance of Music

It is necessary to distinguish two moments, or rather two states of music: potential music and actual music. Having been fixed on paper or retained in the memory, music exists already prior to its actual performance, differing in this respect from all the other arts, just as it differs from them, as we have seen, in the categories that determine its perception.

The musical entity thus presents the remarkable singularity of embodying two aspects, of existing successively and distinctly in two forms separated from each other by the hiatus of silence. This peculiar nature of music determines its very life as well as its repercussions in the social world, for it presupposes two kinds of musicians: the creator and the performer.

Let us note in passing that the art of the theater which requires the com-

This essay is adapted from one of Stravinsky's Charles Eliot Norton Lectures at Harvard. Reprinted by permission of the publishers from Igor Stravinsky, *The Poetics of Music*. Cambridge, Mass.: Harvard University Press, Copyright, 1947, by the President and Fellows of Harvard College.

position of a text and its translation into oral and visual terms, poses a similar, if not absolutely identical, problem; for there is a distinction that cannot be ignored: the theater appeals to our understanding by addressing itself simultaneously to sight and hearing. Now of all our senses sight is the most closely allied to the intellect, and hearing is appealed to in this case through articulated language, the vehicle for images and concepts. So the reader of a dramatic work can more easily imagine what its actual presentation would be like than the reader of a musical score can imagine how the actual instrumental playing of the score would sound. And it is easy to see why there are far fewer readers of orchestral scores than there are readers of books about music.

In addition, the language of music is strictly limited by its notation. The dramatic actor thus finds he has much more latitude in regard to *chronos*[1] and intonation than does the singer who is tightly bound to *tempo*[2] and *melos*.[3]

This subjection, which is often so trying to the exhibitionism of certain soloists, is at the very heart of the question that we propose to take up now: the question of the executant and the interpreter.

The idea of interpretation implies the limitations imposed upon the performer or those which the performer imposes upon himself in his proper function, which is to transmit music to the listener.

The idea of execution implies the strict putting into effect of an explicit will that contains nothing beyond what it specifically commands.

The conflict of these two principles — execution and interpretation — is at the root of all the errors, all the sins, all the misunderstandings that interpose themselves between the musical work and the listener and prevent a faithful transmission of its message.

Every interpreter is also of necessity an executant. The reverse is not true. Following the order of succession rather than of precedence, we shall first consider the executant.

It is taken for granted that I place before the performer written music wherein the composer's will is explicit and easily discernible from a correctly established text. But no matter how scrupulously a piece of music may be notated, no matter how carefully it may be insured against every possible ambiguity through the indications of *tempo*, shading, phrasing, accentuation, and so on, it always contains hidden elements that defy definition because verbal dialectic is powerless to define musical dialectic in its totality. The realization of these elements is thus a matter of experience and intuition, in a word, of the talent of the person who is called upon to present the music.

Thus, in contrast to the craftsman of the plastic arts, whose finished work is presented to the public eye in an always identical form, the composer runs a perilous risk every time his music is played, as the competent presentation of his work each time depends on the unforeseeable and imponderable factors

[1] time; quantity of time-interval.
[2] speed at which sounds are made; rate of movement.
[3] arrangement of sound, sequence of pitches.

that go to make up the virtues of fidelity and sympathy, without which the work will be unrecognizable on one occasion, inert on another, and in any case betrayed.

Between the executant pure and simple and the interpreter in the strict sense of the word, there exists a difference in make-up that is of an ethical rather than of an aesthetic order, a difference that presents a point of conscience: theoretically, one can only require of the executant the translation into sound of his musical part, which he may do willingly or grudgingly, whereas one has the right to seek from the interpreter, in addition to the perfection of this translation into sound, a loving care — which does not mean, be it surreptitious or openly affirmed, a recomposition.

The sin against the spirit of the work always begins with a sin against its letter and leads to the endless follies which an ever-flourishing literature in the worst taste does its best to sanction. Thus it follows that a *crescendo*, as we all know, is always accompanied by a speeding up of movement, while a slowing down never fails to accompany a *diminuendo*. The superfluous is refined upon; a *piano, piano pianissimo* is delicately sought after; great pride is taken in perfecting useless nuances — a concern that usually goes hand in hand with inaccurate rhythm . . .

These are just so many practices dear to superficial minds forever avid for, and satisfied with, an immediate and facile success that flatters the vanity of the person who obtains it and perverts the taste of those who applaud it. How many remunerative careers have been launched by such practices! How many times have I been the victim of these misdirected attentions from abstractors of quintessences who waste time splitting hairs over a *pianissimo*, without so much as noticing egregious blunders of rendition! Exceptions, you may say. Bad interpreters should not make us forget the good ones. I agree — noting, however, that the bad ones are in the majority and that the virtuosos who serve music faithfully and loyally are much rarer than those who, in order to get settled in the comfortable berth of a career, make music serve them.

The widespread principles that govern the interpretation of the romantic masters in particular make these composers the predestined victims of the criminal assaults we are speaking about. The interpretation of their works is governed by extra-musical considerations based on the loves and misfortunes of the victim. The title of a piece becomes an excuse for gratuitous hind-thought. If the piece has none, a title is thrust upon it for wildly fanciful reasons. I am thinking of the Beethoven sonata that is never designated otherwise than by the title of "The Moonlight Sonata" without anyone ever knowing why; of the waltz in which it is mandatory to find Frédéric Chopin's "Farewell."

Obviously, it is not without a reason that the worst interpreters usually tackle the Romantics. The musically extraneous elements that are strewn throughout their works invite betrayal, whereas a page in which music seeks to express nothing outside of itself better resists attempts at literary deformation. It is not easy to conceive how a pianist could establish his reputation by taking Haydn as his war-horse. That is undoubtedly the reason why that great musician has not won among our interpreters a renown that is in keeping with his true worth.

In regard to interpretation, the last century left us in its ponderous heritage a curious and peculiar species of soloist without precedent in the distant past — a soloist called the orchestra leader.

It was romantic music that unduly inflated the personality of the *Kapell-meister*,[4] even to the point of conferring upon him — along with the prestige that he today enjoys on his podium, which in itself concentrates attention upon him — the discretionary power that he exerts over the music committed to his care. Perched on his sibylline tripod, he imposes his own movements, his own particular shadings upon the compositions he conducts, and he even reaches the point of talking with a naïve impudence of his specialities, of *his* fifth, of *his* seventh, the way a chef boasts of a dish of his own concoction. Hearing him speak, one thinks of the billboards that recommend eating places to automobilists: "At so-and-so's restaurant, his wines, his special dishes."

There was never anything like it in the past, in times that nevertheless already knew as well as our time go-getting and tyrannical virtuosos, whether instrumentalists or prima donnas. But those times did not yet suffer from the competition and plethora of conductors, who almost to a man aspire to set up a dictatorship over music.

Do not think I am exaggerating. A quip that was passed on to me some years ago clearly shows the importance which the conductor has come to take on in the preoccupations of the musical world. One day a person who presides over the fortunes of a big concert agency was being told about the success obtained in Soviet Russia by that famous conductorless orchestra of which we have already spoken: "That doesn't make much sense," declared the person in question, "and it doesn't interest me. What I'd really be interested in is not an orchestra without a conductor, but a conductor without an orchestra."

To speak of an interpreter means to speak of a translator. And it is not without reason that a well-known Italian proverb, which takes the form of a play on words, equates translation with betrayal.

Conductors, singers, pianists, all virtuosos should know or recall that the first condition that must be fulfilled by anyone who aspires to the imposing title of interpreter, is that he be first of all a flawless executant. The secret of perfection lies above all in his consciousness of the law imposed upon him by the work he is performing. And here we are back at the great principle of submission that we have so often invoked in the course of our lessons. This submission demands a flexibility that itself requires, along with technical mastery, a sense of tradition and, commanding the whole, an aristocratic culture that is not merely a question of acquired learning.

This submissiveness and culture that we require of the creator, we should

---

[4] bandmaster.

justly and naturally require of the interpreter as well. Both will find therein freedom in extreme rigor and, in the final analysis, if not in the first instance, success — true success, the legitimate reward of the interpreters who in the expression of their most brilliant virtuosity preserve that modesty of movement and that sobriety of expression which is the mark of thoroughbred artists.

I said somewhere that it was not enough to hear music, but that it must also be seen. What shall we say of the ill-breeding of those grimacers who too often take it upon themselves to deliver the "inner meaning" of music by disfiguring it with their affected airs? For, I repeat, one sees music. An experienced eye follows and judges, sometimes unconsciously, the performer's least gesture. From this point of view one might conceive the process of performance as the creation of new values that call for the solution of problems similar to those which arise in the realm of choreography. In both cases we give special attention to the control of gestures. The dancer is an orator who speaks a mute language. The instumentalist is an orator who speaks an unarticulated language. Upon one, just as upon the other, music imposes a strict bearing. For music does not move in the abstract. Its translation into plastic terms requires exactitude and beauty: the exhibitionists know this only too well.

The beautiful presentation that makes the harmony of what is seen correspond to the play of sounds demands not only good musical instruction on the part of the performer, but also requires a complete familiarity on his part, whether singer, instrumentalist, or conductor, with the style of the works entrusted to him; a very sure taste for expressive values and for their limitations, a secure sense for that which may be taken for granted — in a word, an education not only of the ear, but of the mind.

Such an education cannot be acquired in the schools of music and the conservatories, for the teaching of fine manners is not their object: very rarely does a violin teacher even point out to his pupils that it is ill-becoming, when playing, to spread one's legs too far apart.

It is nonetheless strange that such an educational program is nowhere put into effect. Whereas all social activities are regulated by rules of etiquette and good breeding, performers are still in most cases entirely unaware of the elementary precepts of musical civility, that is to say of *musical good breeding* — a matter of common decency that a child may learn . . .

The *Saint Matthew Passion* of Johann Sebastian Bach is written for a chamber-music ensemble. Its first performance in Bach's lifetime was perfectly realized by a total force of thirty-four musicians, including soloists and chorus. That is known. And nevertheless in our day one does not hesitate to present the work, in complete disregard of the composer's wishes, with hundreds of performers, sometimes almost a thousand. This lack of understanding of the interpreter's obligations, this arrogant pride in numbers, this concupiscence of the many, betrays a complete lack of musical education.

The absurdity of such a practice is in point of fact glaring in every respect, and above all from the acoustic point of view. For it is not enough that the sound reach the ear of the public; one must also consider in what condition, in what state, the sound is received. When the music was not conceived for a huge mass of performers, when its composer did not want to produce massive dynamic effects, when the frame is all out of proportion to the dimensions of the work, multiplication of the number of participant performers can produce only disastrous effects.

Sound, exactly like light, acts differently according to the distance that separates the point of emission from the point of reception. A mass of performers situated on a platform occupies a surface that becomes proportionately larger as the mass becomes more sizeable. By increasing the number of points of emission one increases the distances that separate these points from one another and from the hearer. So that the more one multiplies the points of emission, the more blurred reception will be.

In every case the doubling of parts weighs down the music and constitutes a peril that can be avoided only by proceeding with infinite tact. Such additions call for a subtle and delicate proportioning that itself presupposes the surest of tastes and a discriminating culture.

It is often believed that power can be increased indefinitely by multiplying the doubling of orchestral parts — a belief that is completely false: thickening is not strengthening. In a certain measure and up to a certain point, doubling may give the illusion of strength by effecting a reaction of a psychological order on the listener. The sensation of shock simulates the effect of power and helps to establish an illusion of balance among the sounding tonal masses. A good deal might be said in this connection about the balance of forces in the modern orchestra, a balance more easily explained by our aural habits than justified by exactness of proportions.

It is a positive fact that beyond a certain degree of extension the impression of intensity diminishes instead of increases and succeeds only in dulling the sensation.

Musicians should come to realize that for their art the same holds true as for the art of the billboard: that the blowing-up of sound does not hold the ear's attention — just as the advertising expert knows that letters which are too large do not attract the eye.

A work of art cannot contain itself. Once the creator has completed his work, he necessarily feels the need to share his joy. He quite naturally seeks to establish contact with his fellow man, who in this case becomes his listener. The listener reacts and becomes a partner in the game initiated by the creator. Nothing less, nothing more. The fact that the partner is free to accept or to refuse participation in the game does not automatically invest him with the authority of a judge.

The judicial function presupposes a code of sanctions which mere opinion does not have at its disposal. And it is quite illicit, to my way of thinking, to set the public up as a jury by entrusting to it the task of rendering a verdict on the value of a work. It is already quite enough that the public is called upon to decide its ultimate fate.

The fate of a work, of course, depends in the final analysis on the public's taste, on the variations of its humor and habits; in a word, on its preferences. But the fate of a work does not depend upon the public's judgment as if it were a sentence without appeal.

I call your attention to this all-important point: consider on the one hand the conscious effort and patient organization that the composing of a work of art requires, and on the other hand the judgment — which is at least hasty and of necessity improvised — that follows the presentation of the work. The disproportion between the duties of the person who composes and the rights of those who judge him is glaring, since the work offered to the public, whatever its value may be, is always the fruit of study, reasoning, and calculation that imply exactly the converse of improvisation.

I have expatiated at some length on this theme in order to make you see more clearly where the true relations between the composer and the public lie, with the performer acting as an intermediary. You will thereby realize more fully the performer's moral responsibility.

For only through the performer is the listener brought in contact with the musical work. In order that the public may know what a work is like and what its value is, the public must first be assured of the merit of the person who presents the work to it and of the conformity of that presentation to the composer's will.

The listener's task becomes especially harrowing when a first hearing is concerned; for the listener in this case has no point of reference and possesses no basis for comparison.

And so it comes about that the first impression, which is so important, the first contact of the new-born work with the public, is completely dependent upon the validity of a presentation that eludes all controls.

Such, then, is our situation before an unpublished work when the quality of the performers before us does not guarantee that the composer will not be betrayed and that we shall not be cheated.

In every period the forming of an elite has given us that advance assurance in matters of social relations which permits us to have full confidence in the unknown performers who appear before us under the aegis of that flawless bearing which education bestows. Lacking a guarantee of this kind, our relations with music would always be unsatisfactory. You will understand, the situation being what it is, why we have stressed at such length the importance of education in musical matters.

We have said previously that the listener was, in a way, called upon to become the composer's partner. This presupposes that the listener's musical instruction and education are sufficiently extensive so that he may not grasp the main features of the work as they emerge, but also may even follow to some degree the changing aspects of its unfolding.

As a matter of fact, such active participation is an unquestionably rare thing, just as the creator is a rare occurrence in the mass of humanity. This exceptional participation gives the partner such lively pleasure that it unites him in a certain measure with the mind that conceived and realized the work to which he is listening, giving him the illusion of identifying himself with the creator. That is the meaning of Raphael's famous adage: To understand is to equal.

But such understanding is the exception; the ordinary run of listeners, no matter how attentive to the musical process one supposes them to be, enjoy music only in a passive way.

Unfortunately, there exists still another attitude toward music which differs from both that of the listener who gives himself up to the working out of the music — participating in and following it step by step — and from the attitude of the listener who tries docilely to go along with the music: for we must now speak of indifference and apathy. Such is the attitude of snobs, of false enthusiasts who see in a concert or a performance only the opportunity to applaud a great conductor or an acclaimed virtuoso. One has only to look for a moment at those "faces gray with boredom," as Claude Debussy put it, to measure the power music has of inducing a sort of stupidity in those unfortunate persons who listen to it without hearing it. Those of you who have done me the honor of reading the *Chronicles of My Life* perhaps recall that I stress this matter in regard to mechanically reproduced music.

The propagation of music by all possible means is in itself an excellent thing; but by spreading it abroad without taking precautions, by offering it willy-nilly to the general public which is not prepared to hear it, one lays this public open to the most deadly saturation.

The time is no more when Johann Sebastian Bach gladly traveled a long way on foot to hear Buxtehude.[5] Today radio brings music into the home at all hours of the day and night. It relieves the listener of all effort except that of turning a dial. Now the musical sense cannot be acquired or developed without exercise. In music, as in everything else, inactivity leads gradually to the paralysis, to the atrophying of faculties. Understood in this way, music becomes a sort of drug which, far from stimulating the mind, paralyzes and stultifies it. So it comes about that the very undertaking which seeks to make people like music by giving it a wider and wider diffusion, very often only achieves the result of making the very people lose their appetite for music whose interest was to be aroused and whose taste was to be developed.

[5] Dietrich Buxtehude (c. 1637–1707), Danish organist and composer of church music.

D. H. Lawrence (1885–1930)

ENGLISH POET, NOVELIST, ESSAYIST,
and SHORT STORY WRITER

Christs in the Tirol

The real Tirol does not seem to extend far south of the Brenner, and northward it goes right to the Starnberger See. Even at Sterzing the rather gloomy atmosphere of the Tirolese Alps is being dispersed by the approach of the South. And, strangely enough, the roadside crucifixes become less and less interesting after Sterzing. Walking down from Munich to Italy, I have stood in front of hundreds of *Martertafeln*[1]; and now I miss them; these painted shrines by the Garda See are not the same.

I, who see a tragedy in every cow, began by suffering from the Secession pictures[2] in Munich. All these new paintings seemed so shrill and restless. Those that were meant for joy shrieked and pranced for joy, and sorrow was a sensation to be relished, curiously; as if we were epicures in suffering, keen on a new flavour. I thought with kindliness of England, whose artists so often suck their sadness like a lollipop, mournfully, and comfortably.

Then one must walk, as it seems, for miles and endless miles past crucifixes, avenues of them. At first they were mostly factory made, so that I did not notice them, any more than I noticed the boards with warnings, except just to observe they were there. But coming among the Christs carved in wood by the peasant artists, I began to feel them. Now, it seems to me, they create almost an atmosphere over the northern Tirol, an atmosphere of pain.

I was going along a marshy place at the foot of the mountains, at evening, when the sky was a pale, dead colour and the hills were nearly black. At a meeting of the paths was a crucifix, and between the feet of the Christ a little red patch of dead poppies. So I looked at him. It was an old shrine, and the Christus was nearly like a man. He seemed to me to be real. In front of me hung a Bavarian peasant, a Christus, staring across at the evening and the black hills. He had broad cheek-bones and sturdy limbs, and he hung doggedly on the cross, hating it. He reminded me of a peasant farmer, fighting slowly and meanly, but not giving in. His plain, rudimentary face stared stubbornly at the hills, and his neck was stiffened, as if even yet he were struggling away from the cross he resented. He would not yield to it. I stood

[1] figures of the Passion erected along the roadside to mark places where wayfarers have met with fatal accidents.

[2] Secession pictures were those painted by a group of *art nouveau* artists in Austria (1890–1905) and considered at the time daring and advanced.

in front of him, and realized him. He might have said, "Yes, here I am, and it's bad enough, and it's suffering, and it doesn't come to an end. *Perhaps* something will happen, will help. If it doesn't, I s'll have to go on with it." He seemed stubborn and struggling from the root of his soul, his human soul. No Godship had been thrust upon him. He was human clay, a peasant Prometheus-Christ, his poor soul bound in him, blind, but struggling stubbornly against the fact of the nails. And I looked across at the tiny square of orange light, the window of a farmhouse on the marsh. And, thinking of the other little farms, of how the man and his wife and his children worked on till dark, intent and silent, carrying the hay in their arms out of the streaming thunder-rain which soaked them through, I understood how the Christus was made.

And after him, when I saw the Christs posing on the Cross, à la Guido Reni,[3] I recognized them as the mere conventional symbol, meaning no more Christ than St. George and the Dragon on a five-shilling-piece means England.

There are so many Christs carved by men who have carved to get at the meaning of their own soul's anguish. Often, I can distinguish one man's work in a district. In the Zemm valley, right in the middle of the Tirol, there are some half-dozen crucifixes by the same worker, who has whittled away in torment to see himself emerge out of the piece of timber, so that he can understand his own suffering, and see it take on itself the distinctness of an eternal thing, so that he can go on further, leaving it. The chief of these crucifixes is a very large one, deep in the Klamm, where it is always gloomy and damp. The river roars below, the rock wall opposite reaches high overhead, pushing back the sky. And by the track where the pack-horses go, in the cold gloom, hangs the large, pale Christ. He has fallen forward, just dead, and the weight of his full-grown, mature body is on the nails of the hands. So he drops, as if his hands would tear away, and he would fall to earth. The face is strangely brutal, and is set with an ache of weariness and pain and bitterness, and his rather ugly, passionate mouth is shut with bitter despair. After all, he had wanted to live and to enjoy his manhood. But fools had ruined his body, and thrown his life away, when he wanted it. No one had helped. His youth and health and vigour, all his life, and himself, were just thrown away as waste. He had died in bitterness. It is sombre and damp, silent save for the roar of water. There hangs the falling body of the man who had died in bitterness of spirit, and the driver of the pack-horses takes off his hat, cringing in his sturdy cheerfulness as he goes beneath.

He is afraid. I think of the carver of the crucifix. He also was more or less afraid. They all, when they carved or erected these crucifixes, had fear at the bottom of their hearts. And so the monuments to physical pain are found everywhere in the mountain gloom. By the same hand that carved the big, pale Christ I found another crucifix, a little one, at the end of a bridge. This Christ had a fair beard instead of a black one, and his body was hanging differently. But there was about him the same bitterness, the same despair, even

[3] an Italian painter (1575–1642), whose work was characterized often by insipid sentiment and a lack of vitality.

a touch of cynicism. Evidently the artist could not get beyond the tragedy that tormented him. No wonder the peasants are afraid, as they take off their hats in passing up the valley.

They are afraid of physical pain. It terrifies them. Then they raise, in their startled helplessness of suffering, these Christs, these human attempts at deciphering the riddle of pain. In the same way they paint the humorous little pictures of some calamity — a man drowned in a stream or killed by a falling tree — and nail it up near the scene of the accident. "*Memento mori*,"[4] they say everywhere. And so they try to get used to the idea of death and suffering, to rid themselves of some of the fear thereof. And all tragic art is part of the same attempt.

But some of the Christs are quaint. One I know is very elegant, brushed and combed. "I'm glad I am no lady," I say to him. For he is a pure lady-killer. But he ignores me utterly, the exquisite. The man who made him must have been dying to become a gentleman.

And a fair number are miserable fellows. They put up their eyebrows plaintively, and pull down the corners of their mouths. Sometimes they gaze heavenwards. They are quite sorry for themselves.

"Never mind," I say to them. "It'll be worst yet, before you've done."

Some of them look pale and done-for. They didn't make much fight; they hadn't much pluck in them. They make me sorry.

"It's a pity you hadn't got a bit more kick in you," I say to them. And I wonder why in England one sees always this pale, pitiful Christ with no "go" in him. Is it because our national brutality is so strong and deep that we must create for ourselves an anæmic Christus, for ever on the whine; either that, or one of those strange neutrals with long hair, that are supposed to represent to our children the Jesus of the New Testament.

In a tiny glass case beside the high-road where the Isar is a very small stream, sits another Christ that makes me want to laugh, and makes me want to weep also. His little head rests on his hand, his elbow on his knee, and he meditates, half-wearily. I am strongly reminded of Walther von Vogelweide[5] and the German medieval spirit. Detached, he sits, and dreams, and broods, in his little golden crown of thorns, and his little cloak of red flannel, that some peasant woman has stitched for him.

"*Couvre-toi de gloire, Tartarin — couvre-toi de flanelle*,"[6] I think to myself.

But he sits, a queer little man, fretted, plunged in anxiety of thought, and yet dreaming rather pleasantly at the same time. I think he is the forefather of the warm-hearted German philosopher and professor.

He is the last of the remarkable Christs of the peasants that I have seen. Beyond the Brenner an element of unreality seems to creep in. The Christs are

[4] "Remember that thou must die."
[5] the leading poet and minnesinger of medieval Germany (1170–1230).
[6] "Cover thyself with glory, Tartarin — cover thyself with flannel," two injunctions addressed to the comic hero of the 19th century French novel *Tartarin de Tarascon* by Alphonse Daudet, in order to suggest the dual nature of man: the aspiring, heroic soul and the reluctant, earthbound body.

given great gashes in the breast and knees, and from the brow and breast and hands and knees streams of blood trickle down, so that one sees a weird striped thing in red and white that is not at all a Christus. And the same red that is used for the blood serves also to mark the path, so that one comes to associate the *Martertafeln* and their mess of red stripes with the stones smeared with scarlet paint for guidance. The wayside chapels, going south, become fearfully florid and ornate, though still one finds in them the little wooden limbs, arms and legs and feet, and little wooden cows or horses, hung up by the altar, to signify a cure in these parts. But there is a tendency for the Christs themselves to become either neuter or else sensational. In a chapel near St. Jakob, a long way from the railway, sat the most ghastly Christus I can imagine. He is seated, after the crucifixion. His eyes, which are turned slightly to look at you, are bloodshot till they glisten scarlet, and even the iris seems purpled. And the misery, the almost criminal look of hate and misery on the bloody, disfigured face is shocking. I was amazed at the ghastly thing: moreover, it was fairly new.

South of the Brenner again, in the Austrian Tirol, I have not seen anyone salute the Christus: not even the guides. As one goes higher the crucifixes get smaller and smaller. The wind blows the snow under the tiny shed of a tiny Christ: the guides tramp stolidly by, ignoring the holy thing. That surprised me. But perhaps these were particularly unholy men. One does not expect a great deal of an Austrian, except real pleasantness.

So, in Austria, I have seen a fallen Christus. It was on the Jaufen, not very far from Meran. I was looking at all the snowpeaks all around, and hurrying downhill, trying to get out of a piercing wind, when I almost ran into a very old *Martertafel*. The wooden shed was silver-grey with age, and covered on the top with a thicket of lichen, weird, grey-green, sticking up its tufts. But on the rocks at the foot of the cross was the armless Christ, who had tumbled down and lay on his back in a weird attitude. It was one of the old, peasant Christs, carved out of wood, and having the long, wedge-shaped shins and thin legs that are almost characteristic. Considering the great sturdiness of a mountaineer's calves, these thin, flat legs are interesting. The arms of the fallen Christ had broken off at the shoulders, and they hung on their nails, as *ex voto*[7] limbs hang in the shrines. But these arms dangled from their palms, one at each end of the cross, the muscles, carved in wood, looking startling, upside down. And the icy wind blew them backwards and forwards. There, in that bleak place among the stones, they looked horrible. Yet I dared not touch either them or the fallen image. I wish some priest would go along and take the broken thing away.

So many Christs there seem to be: one in rebellion against his cross, to which he was nailed; one bitter with the agony of knowing he must die, his heart-beatings all futile; one who felt sentimental; one who gave in to his misery; one who was a sensationalist; one who dreamed and fretted with thought.

[7] votive.

Perhaps the peasant carvers of crucifixes are right, and all these were found on the same cross. And perhaps there were others too: one who waited for the end, his soul still with a sense of right and hope; one ashamed to see the crowd make beasts of themselves, ashamed that he should provide for their sport; one who looked at them and thought: "And I am of you. I might be among you, yelling at myself in that way. But I am not, I am here. And so —"

All those Christs, like a populace, hang in the mountains under their little sheds. And perhaps they are falling, one by one. And I suppose we have carved no Christs, afraid lest they should be too like men, too like ourselves. What we worship must have exotic form.

Marianne Moore (b. 1887)

AMERICAN POET

Poetry

I, too, dislike it: there are things that are important beyond all this fiddle.
   Reading it, however, with a perfect contempt for it, one discovers in
     it after all, a place for the genuine.
         Hands that can grasp, eyes
         that can dilate, hair that can rise
           if it must, these things are important not because a

high-sounding interpretation can be put upon them but because they are
   useful. When they become so derivative as to become unintelligible,
     the same thing may be said for all of us, that we
         do not admire what
         we cannot understand: the bat
           holding on upside down or in quest of something to   **10**

eat, elephants pushing, a wild horse taking a roll, a tireless wolf under
   a tree, the immovable critic twitching his skin like a horse that feels a flea,
     the base-
   ball fan, the statistician —
     nor is it valid
         to discriminate against 'business documents and

school-books'; all these phenomena are important. One must make a distinction
   however: when dragged into prominence by half poets, the result is not poetry,
    nor till the poets among us can be   20
       'literalists of
       the imagination' — above
          insolence and triviality and can present

for inspection, 'imaginary gardens with real toads in them', shall we have
   it. In the meantime, if you demand on the one hand,
    the raw material of poetry in
      all its rawness and
      that which is on the other hand
         genuine, you are interested in poetry.

Archibald MacLeish (b. 1892)

AMERICAN POET, DRAMATIST, and CRITIC

Ars Poetica

A poem should be palpable and mute
As a globed fruit,

Dumb
As old medallions to the thumb,

Silent as the sleeve-worn stone
Of casement ledges where the moss has grown —

A poem should be wordless
As the flight of birds.

                 𝄞

A poem should be motionless in time
As the moon climbs,   10

Leaving, as the moon releases
Twig by twig the night-entangled trees,

Leaving, as the moon behind the winter leaves,
Memory by memory the mind —

A poem should be motionless in time
As the moon climbs.

卍

A poem should be equal to:
Not true.

For all the history of grief
An empty doorway and a maple leaf.   20

For love
The leaning grasses and two lights above the sea —

A poem should not mean
But be.

Susanne K. Langer   (b. 1895)

AMERICAN PHILOSOPHER

The Lord of Creation

The world is aflame with man-made public disasters, artificial rains of brimstone and fire, planned earthquakes, cleverly staged famines and floods. The Lord of Creation is destroying himself. He is throwing down the cities he has built, the works of his own hand, the wealth of many thousand years in his frenzy of destruction, as a child knocks down its own handiwork, the whole day's achievement, in a tantrum of tears and rage.

What has displeased the royal child? What has incurred his world-shattering tantrum?

The bafflement of the magnificent game he is playing. Its rules and its symbols, his divine toys, have taken possession of the player. For this global war is not the old, hard, personal fight for the means of life, *bellum omnium contra omnes*,[1] which animals perpetually wage; this is a war of monsters. Not mere men but great superpersonal giants, the national states, are met in combat.

[1] the war of all against all.

From *Fortune* magazine (January, 1944). Reprinted by permission of *Fortune* and the author.

They do not hate and attack and wrestle as injured physical creatures do; they move heavily, inexorably, by strategy and necessity, to each other's destruction. The game of national states has come to this pass, and the desperate players ride their careening animated toys to a furious suicide.

These moloch[2] gods, these monstrous states, are not natural beings; they are man's own work, products of the power that makes him lord over all other living things — his mind. They are not of the earth, earthy, as families and herds, hives and colonies are, whose members move and fight as one by instinct and habit until a physical disturbance splits them and the severed parts reconstitute themselves as new organized groups. The national states are not physical groups; they are social symbols, profound and terrible.

They are symbols of the new way of life, which the past two centuries have given us. For thousands of years, the pattern of daily life — working, praying, building, fighting, and raising new generations — repeated itself with only slow or unessential changes. The social symbols expressive of this life were ancient and familiar. Tribal gods or local saints, patriarchs, squires, or feudal lords, princes and bishops, raised to the highest power in the persons of emperors and popes — they were all expressions of needs and duties and opinions grounded in an immemorial way of life. The average man's horizon was not much greater than his valley, his town, or whatever geographical ramparts bounded his community. Economic areas were small, and economic problems essentially local. Naturally in his conception the powers governing the world were local, patriarchal, and reverently familiar.

Then suddenly, within some two hundred years, and for many places far less than that, the whole world has been transformed. Communities of different tongues and faiths and physiognomies have mingled; not as of old in wars of conquest, invading lords and conquered population gradually mixing their two stocks, but by a new process of foot-loose travel and trade, dominated by great centers of activity that bring individuals from near and far promiscuously together as a magnet draws filings from many heaps into close but quite accidental contact. Technology has made old horizons meaningless and localities indefinite. For goods and their destinies determine the structure of human societies. This is a new world, a world of persons, not of families and clans, or parishes and manors. The proletarian order is not founded on a hearth and its history. It does not express itself in a dialect, a local costume, a rite, a patron saint. All such traditions by mingling have canceled each other, and disappeared.

Most of us feel that since the old controlling ideas of faith and custom are gone, mankind is left without anchorage of any sort. None of the old social symbols fit this modern reality, this shrunken and undifferentiated world in which we lead a purely economic, secular, essentially homeless life.

But mankind is never without its social symbols; when old ones die, new ones are already in process of birth; and the new gods that have superseded

[2] requiring frightful sacrifice. Moloch was a god whose cult demanded the burning of children.

all faiths are the great national states. The conception of them is mystical and moral, personal and devotional; they conjure with names and emblems, and demand our constant profession and practice of the new orthodoxy called "Patriotism."

Of all born creatures, man is the only one that cannot live by bread alone. He lives as much by symbols as by sense report, in a realm compounded of tangible things and virtual images, of actual events and ominous portents, always between fact and fiction. For he sees not only actualities but meanings. He has, indeed, all the impulses and interests of animal nature; he eats, sleeps, mates, seeks comfort and safety, flees pain, falls sick and dies, just as cats and bears and fishes and butterflies do. But he has something more in his repertoire, too — he has laws and religions, theories and dogmas, because he lives not only through sense but through symbols. That is the special asset of his mind, which makes him the master of earth and all its progeny.

By the agency of symbols — marks, words, mental images, and icons of all sorts — he can hold his ideas for contemplation long after their original causes have passed away. Therefore, he can think of things that are not presented or even suggested by his actual environment. By associating symbols in his mind, he combines things and events that were never together in the real world. This gives him the power we call imagination. Further, he can symbolize only part of an idea and let the rest go out of consciousness; this gives him the faculty that has been his pride throughout the ages — the power of abstraction. The combined effect of these two powers is inestimable. They are the roots of his supreme talent, the gift of reason.

In the war of each against all, which is the course of nature, man has an unfair advantage over his animal brethren; for he can see what is not yet there to be seen, know events that happened before his birth, and take possession of more than he actually eats; he can kill at a distance; and by rational design he can enslave other creatures to live and act for him instead of for themselves.

Yet this mastermind has strange aberrations. For in the whole animal kingdom there is no such unreason, no such folly and impracticality as man displays. He alone is hounded by imaginary fears, beset by ghosts and devils, frightened by mere images of things. No other creature wastes time in unprofitable ritual or builds nests for dead specimens of its race. Animals are always realists. They have intelligence in varying degrees — chickens are stupid, elephants are said to be very clever — but, bright or foolish, animals react only to reality. They may be fooled by appearance, by pictures or reflections, but once they know them as such, they promptly lose interest. Distance and darkness and silence are not fearful to them, filled with voices or forms, or invisible presences. Sheep in the pasture do not seem to fear phantom sheep beyond the fence, mice don't look for mouse goblins in the clock, birds do not worship a divine thunderbird.

But oddly enough, men do. They think of all these things and guard against them, worshiping animals and monsters even before they conceive of divinities in their own image. Men are essentially unrealistic. With all their extraordinary intelligence, they alone go in for patently impractical actions — magic and exorcism and holocausts — rites that have no connection with common-sense methods of self-preservation, such as a highly intelligent animal might use. In fact, the rites and sacrifices by which primitive man claims to control nature are sometimes fatal to the performers. Indian puberty rites are almost always intensely painful, and African natives have sometimes died during initiations into honorary societies.

We usually assume that very primitive tribes of men are closer to animal estate than highly civilized races; but in respect of practical attitudes, this is not true. The more primitive man's mind, the more fantastic it seems to be; only with high intellectual discipline do we gradually approach the realistic outlook of intelligent animals.

Yet this human mind, so beclouded by phantoms and superstitions, is probably the only mind on earth that can reach out to an awareness of things beyond its practical environment and can also conceive of such notions as truth, beauty, justice, majesty, space and time and creation.

There is another paradox in man's relationship with other creatures: namely, that those very qualities he calls animalian — "brutal," "bestial," "inhuman" — are peculiarly his own. No other animal is so deliberately cruel as man. No other creature intentionally imprisons its own kind, or invents special instruments of torture such as racks and thumbscrews for the sole purpose of punishment. No other animal keeps its own brethren in slavery; so far as we know, the lower animals do not commit anything like the acts of pure sadism that figure rather largely in our newspapers. There is no torment, spite, or cruelty for its own sake among beasts, as there is among men. A cat plays with its prey, but does not conquer and torture smaller cats. But man, who knows good and evil, is cruel for cruelty's sake; he who has a moral law is more brutal than the brutes, who have none; he alone inflicts suffering on his fellows with malice aforethought.

If man's mind is really a higher form of the animal mind, his morality a specialized form of herd instinct, then where in the course of evolution did he lose the realism of a clever animal and fall prey to subjective fears? And why should he take pleasure in torturing helpless members of his own race?

The answer is, I think, that man's mind is *not* a direct evolution from the beast's mind, but is a unique variant and therefore has had a meteoric and startling career very different from any other animal history. The trait that sets human mentality apart from every other is its preoccupation with symbols, with images and names that *mean* things, rather than with things themselves. This trait may have been a mere sport of nature once upon a time. Certain creatures do develop tricks and interests that seem biologically unimportant. Pack rats, for instance, and some birds of the crow family take a capricious pleasure in bright objects and carry away such things for which they have, presumably, no earthly use. Perhaps man's tendency to see certain forms as *images*, to hear certain sounds not only as signals but as expressive tones, and to be excited by sunset colors or starlight, was originally just a peculiar sensitivity in a rather highly developed brain. But whatever its cause, the ultimate destiny of this trait was momentous; for all human activity is based on the appreciation and use of symbols. Language, religion, mathematics, all learning, all science and superstition, even right and wrong, are products of symbolic expression rather than direct experience. Our commonest words such as "house" and "red" and "walking," are symbols; the pyramids of Egypt and the mysterious circles of Stonehenge are symbols; so are dominions and empires and astronomical universes. We live in a mind-made-world, where the things of prime importance are images or words that embody ideas and feelings and attitudes.

The animal mind is like a telephone exchange; it receives stimuli from outside through the sense organs and sends out appropriate responses through the nerves that govern muscles, glands, and other parts of the body. The organism is constantly interacting with its surroundings, receiving messages and acting on the new state of affairs that the messages signify.

But the human mind is not a simple transmitter like a telephone exchange. It is more like a great projector; for instead of merely mediating between an event in the outer world and a creature's responsive action, it transforms or, if you will, distorts the event into an image to be looked at, retained, and contemplated. For the images of things that we remember are not exact and faithful transcriptions even of our actual sense impressions. They are made as much by what we think as by what we see. It is a well-known fact that if you ask several people the size of the moon's disk as they look at it, their estimates will vary from the area of a dime to that of a barrel top. Like a magic lantern, the mind projects its ideas of things on the screen of what we call "memory"; but like all projections, these ideas are transformations of actual things. They are, in fact, *symbols* of reality, not pieces of it.

A symbol is not the same thing as a sign: that is a fact that psychologists and philosophers often overlook. All intelligent animals use signs; so do we. To them as well as to us sounds and smells and motions are signs of food, danger, the presence of other beings, or of rain or storm. Furthermore, some animals not only attend to signs but produce them for the benefit of others. Dogs bark at the door to be let in; rabbits thump to call each other; the cooing of doves and the growl of a wolf defending his kill are unequivocal signs of feelings and intentions to be reckoned with by other creatures.

We use signs just as animals do, though with considerable more elaboration. We stop at red lights and go on green; we answer calls and bells, watch the sky for coming storms, read trouble or promise or anger in each other's eyes. That is animal intelligence raised to the human level. Those of us who are dog lovers can probably all tell wonderful stories of how high our dogs have sometimes risen in the scale of clever sign interpretation and sign using.

A sign is anything that announces the existence or the imminence of some event, the presence of a thing or a person, or a change in a state of affairs. There are signs of the weather, signs of danger, signs of future good or evil, signs of what the past has been. In every case a sign is closely bound up with something to be noted or expected in experience. It is always a part of the situation to which it refers, though the reference may be remote in space and time. In so far as we are led to note or expect the signified event we are making correct use of a sign. This is the essence of rational behavior, which animals show in varying degrees. It is entirely realistic, being closely bound up with the actual objective course of history — learned by experience, and cashed in or voided by further experience.

If man had kept to the straight and narrow path of sign using, he would be like the other animals, though perhaps a little brighter. He would not talk, but grunt and gesticulate and point. He would make his wishes known, give warnings, perhaps develop a social system like that of bees and ants, with such a wonderful efficiency of communal enterprise that all men would have plenty to eat, warm apartments — all exactly alike and perfectly convenient — to live in, and everybody could and would sit in the sun or by the fire, as the climate demanded, not talking but just basking, with every want satisfied, most of his life. The young would romp and make love, the old would sleep, the middle-aged would do the routine work almost unconsciously and eat a great deal. But that would be the life of a social, superintelligent, purely sign-using animal.

To us who are human, it does not sound very glorious. We want to go places and do things, own all sorts of gadgets that we do not absolutely need, and when we sit down to take it easy we want to talk. Rights and property, social position, special talents and virtues, and above all our ideas, are what we live for. We have gone off on a tangent that takes us far away from the mere biological cycle that animal generations accomplish; and that is because we can use not only signs but symbols.

A symbol differs from a sign in that it does not announce the presence of the object, the being, condition, or what not, which is its meaning, but merely *brings this thing to mind*. It is not a mere "substitute sign" to which we react as though it were the object itself. The fact is that our reaction to hearing a person's name is quite different from our reaction to the person himself. There are certain rare cases where a symbol stands directly for its meaning: in religious experience, for instance, the Host is not only a symbol but a Presence. But symbols in the ordinary sense are not mystic. They are the same sort of thing that ordinary signs are; only they do not call our attention to something necessarily present or to be physically dealt with — they call up merely a conception of the thing they "mean."

The difference between a sign and a symbol is, in brief, that a sign causes us to think or act *in face of* the thing signified, whereas a symbol causes us to think *about* the thing symbolized. Therein lies the great importance of symbolism for human life, its power to make this life so different from any other animal biography that generations of men have found it incredible to suppose that they were of purely zoological origin. A sign is always embedded in reality, in a present that emerges from the actual past and stretches to the future; but a symbol may be divorced from reality altogether. It may refer to what is *not* the case, to a mere idea, a figment, a dream. It serves, therefore, to liberate thought from the immediate stimuli of a physically present world; and that liberation marks the essential difference between human and non-human mentality. Animals think, but they think *of* and *at* things; men think primarily *about* things. Words, pictures, and memory images are symbols that may be combined and varied in a thousand ways. The result is a symbolic structure whose meaning is a complex of all their respective meanings, and this kaleidoscope of *ideas* is the typical product of the human brain that we call the "stream of thought."

The process of transforming all direct experience into imagery or into that supreme mode of symbolic expression, language, has so completely taken possession of the human mind that it is not only a special talent but a dominant, organic need. All our sense impressions leave their traces in our memory not only as signs disposing our practical reactions in the future but also as symbols, images representing our *ideas* of things; and the tendency to manipulate ideas, to combine and abstract, mix and extend them by playing with symbols, is man's outstanding characteristic. It seems to be what his brain most naturally and spontaneously does. Therefore his primitive mental function is not judging reality, but *dreaming his desires*.

Dreaming is apparently a basic function of human brains, for it is free and unexhausting like our metabolism, heartbeat, and breath. It is easier to breathe than to refrain from breathing. The symbolic character of dreams is fairly well established. Symbol mongering, on this ineffectual, uncritical level, seems to be instinctive, the fulfillment of an elementary need rather than the purposeful exercise of a high and difficult talent.

The special power of man's mind rests on the evolution of this special activity, not on any transcendently high development of animal intelligence. We are not immeasurably higher than other animals; we are different. We have a biological need and with it a biological gift that they do not share.

Because man has not only the ability but the constant need of *conceiving* what has happened to him, what surrounds him, what is demanded of him — in short, of symbolizing nature, himself, and his hopes and fears — he has a constant and crying need of *expression*. What he cannot express, he cannot *conceive*; what he cannot conceive is chaos, and fills him with terror.

If we bear in mind this all-important craving for expression we get a new picture of man's behaviour; for from this trait spring his power and his weaknesses. The process of symbolic transformation that all our experiences undergo is nothing more nor less than the process of *conception*, which underlies the human faculties of abstraction and imagination.

When we are faced with a strange or difficult situation, we cannot react directly, as other creatures do, with flight, aggression, or any such simple instinctive pattern. Our whole reaction depends on how we manage to conceive the situation — whether we cast it in a definite dramatic form, whether we see it as a disaster, a challenge, a fulfillment of doom, or a fiat of the Divine Will. In words of dreamlike images, in artistic or religious or even in cynical form, we must *construe* the events of life. There is great virtue in the figure of speech, "I can *make* nothing of it," to express a failure to understand something. Thought and memory are processes of *making* the thought content and the memory image; the pattern of our ideas is given by the symbols through which we express them. And in the course of manipulating those symbols we inevitably distort the original experience, as we abstract certain features of it, embroider and reinforce those features with other ideas, until the conception we project on the screen of memory is quite different from anything in our real history.

Conception is a necessary and elementary process; what we do with our conception is another story. That is the entire history of human culture — of intelligence and morality, folly and superstition, ritual, language, and the arts — all the phenomena that set man apart from, and above, the rest of the animal kingdom. As the religious mind has to make all human history a drama of sin and salvation in order to define its own moral attitudes, so a scientist wrestles with the mere presentation of "the facts" before he can reason about them. The process of *envisaging* facts, values, hopes, and fears underlies our whole behavior pattern; and this process is reflected in the evolution of an extraordinary phenomenon found always, and only, in human societies — the phenomenon of language.

Language is the highest and most amazing achievement of the symbolistic human mind. The power it bestows is almost inestimable, for without it anything properly called "thought" is impossible. The birth of language is the dawn of humanity. The line between man and beast — between the highest ape and the lowest savage — is the language line. Whether the primitive Neanderthal man was anthropoid or human depends less on his cranial capacity, his upright posture, or even his use of tools and fire, than on one issue we shall probably never be able to settle — whether or not he spoke.

In all physical traits and practical responses, such as skills and visual judgments, we can find a certain continuity between animal and human mentality. Sign using is an ever evolving, ever improving function throughout the whole animal kingdom, from the lowly worm that shrinks into his hole at the sound of an approaching foot, to the dog obeying his master's command, and even to the learned scientist who watches the movements of an index needle.

This continuity of the sign-using talent has led psychologists to the belief that language is evolved from the vocal expressions, grunts and coos and cries, whereby animals vent their feelings or signal their fellows; that man has elaborated this sort of communion to the point where it makes a perfect exchange of ideas possible.

I do not believe that this doctrine of the origin of language is correct. The essence of language is symbolic, not signific; we use it first and most vitally to formulate and hold ideas in our own minds. Conception, not social control, is its first and foremost benefit.

Watch a young child that is just learning to speak play with a toy; he says the name of the object, e.g.: "Horsey! horsey! horsey!" over and over again, looks at the object, moves it, always saying the name to himself or to the world at large. It is quite a time before he talks to anyone in particular; he talks first of all to himself. This is his way of forming and fixing the *conception* of the object in his mind, and around this conception all his knowledge of it grows. Names are the essence of language; for the *name* is what abstracts the conception of the horse from the horse itself, and lets the mere idea recur at the speaking of the name. This permits the conception gathered from one horse experience to be exemplified again by another instance of a horse, so that the notion embodied in the name is a general notion.

To this end, the baby uses a word long before he asks for the object; when he wants his horsey he is likely to cry and fret, because he is reacting to an actual environment, not forming ideas. He uses the animal language of *signs* for his wants; talking is still a purely symbolic process — its practical value has not really impressed him yet.

Language need not be vocal; it may be purely visual, like written language, or even tactual, like the deaf-mute system of speech; but it *must be denotative.* The sounds, intended or unintended, whereby animals communicate do not constitute a language, because they are signs, not names. They never fall into an organic pattern, a meaningful syntax of even the most rudimentary sort, as all language seems to do with a sort of driving necessity. That is because signs refer to actual situations, in which things have obvious relations to each other that require only to be noted; but symbols refer to ideas, which are not physically there for inspection, so their connections and features have to be represented. This gives all true language a natural tendency toward growth and development, which seems almost like a life of its own. Languages are not invented; they grow with our need for expression.

In contrast, animal "speech" never has a structure. It is merely an emotional response. Apes may greet their ration of yams with a shout of "Nga!" But they do not say "Nga" between meals. If they could *talk* about their yams instead of just saluting them, they would be the most primitive men instead of the most anthropoid of beasts. They would have ideas, and tell each other things true or false, rational or irrational; they would make plans and invent laws and sing their own praises, as men do.

The history of speech is the history of our human descent. Yet the habit of transforming morality into symbols, of contemplating and combining and distorting symbols, goes beyond the confines of language. All *images* are symbols, which make us think about the things they mean.

This is the source of man's great interest in "graven images," and in *mere appearances* like the face of the moon or the human profiles he sees in rocks and trees. There is no limit to the meanings he can read into natural phenomena. As long as this power is undisciplined, the sheer enjoyment of finding meanings in everything, the elaboration of concepts without any regard to truth and usefulness seems to run riot; superstition and ritual in their pristine strength go through what some anthropologists have called a "vegetative" stage, where the dream-like symbols, gods and ghouls and rites, multiply like the overgrown masses of life in a jungle. From this welter of symbolic forms emerge the images that finally govern a civilization; the great symbols of religion, society, and selfhood.

What does an image "mean"? Anything it is thought to resemble. It is only because we can abstract quite unobvious forms from the actual appearance of things that we see line drawings in two dimensions as images of colored, three-dimensional objects, find the likeness of a dipper in a constellation of seven stars, or see a face on a pansy. Any circle may represent the sun or moon; an upright monolith may be a man.

Whenever we can fancy a similarity we tend to see something represented. The first thing we do, upon seeing a new shape, is to assimilate it to our own idea of something that it resembles, something that is known and important to us. Our most elementary concepts are of our own actions, and the limbs or organs that perform them; other things are named by comparison with them. The opening of a cave is its mouth, the divisions of a river its arms. Language, and with it all articulate thought, grows by this process of unconscious metaphor. Every new idea urgently demands a word; if we lack a name for it, we call it after the first namable thing seen to bear even a remote analogy to it. Thus all the subtle and variegated vocabulary of a living language grows up from a few roots of very general application; words as various in meaning as "gentle" and "ingenious" and "general" spring from the one root "ge" meaning "to give life."

Yet there are conceptions that language is constitutionally unfit to express. The reason for this limitation of our verbal powers is a subject for logicians and need not concern us here. The point of interest to us is that, just as rational, discursive thought is bound up with language, so the life of feeling, of direct personal and social consciousness, the emotional stability of man and his sense of orientation in the world are bound up with images directly given to his senses. Fire and water, noise and silence, high mountains and deep caverns, the brief beauty of flowers, the persistent grin of a skull. These seem to be irresistible parallels to the expressive forms we find in nature and the forms of our inner life; thus the use of light to represent all things good, joyful, comforting, and of darkness to express all sorts of sorrow, despair, or horror, is so primitive as to be well-nigh unconscious.

A flame is a soul; a star is a hope; the silence of winter is death. All such images, which serve the purpose of metaphorical thinking, are *natural symbols*. They have not conventionally assigned meanings, like words, but recommend themselves even to a perfectly untutored mind, a child's or a savage's, because they are definitely articulated *forms*, and to see something expressed in such forms is a universal human talent. We do not have to learn to use natural symbols; it is one of our primitive activities.

The fact that sensuous forms of natural processes have a significance beyond themselves makes the range of our symbolism, and with it the horizon of our consciousness, much wider and deeper than language. This is the source of ritual, mythology, and art. Ritual is a symbolic rendering of certain emotional *attitudes*, which have become articulate and fixed by being constantly expressed. Mythology is man's image of his world, and of himself in the world. Art is the exposition of his own subjective history, the life of feeling, the human spirit in all its adventures.

Yet this power of envisagement, which natural symbolism bestows, is a dangerous one; for human beings can envisage things that do not exist, and create horrible worlds, insupportable duties, monstrous gods and ancestors. The mind that can see past and future, the poles and the antipodes, and guess at obscure mechanisms of nature, is ever in danger of seeing what is not there, imagining false and fantastic causes, and courting death instead of life. Because man can play with ideas, he is unrealistic; he is inclined to neglect the all-important interpretation of signs for a rapt contemplation of symbols.

Some twenty years ago, Ernst Cassirer[3] set forth a theory of human mentality that goes far toward explaining the vagaries of savage religions and the ineradicable presence of superstition even in civilized societies: a symbol, he observed, is the embodiment of an idea; it is at once an abstract and a physical fact. Now its great emotive value lies in the concept it conveys; this inspires our reverent attitude, the attention and awe with which we view it. But man's untutored thought always tends to lose its way between the symbol and the fact. A skull represents death; but to a primitive mind the skull *is* death. To have it in the house is not unpleasant but dangerous. Even in civilized societies, symbolic objects — figures of saints, relics, crucifixes — are revered for their supposed efficacy. Their actual power is a power of *expression*, of embodying and thus revealing the greatest concepts humanity has reached; these concepts are the commanding forces that change our estate from a brute existence to the transcendent life of the spirit. But the symbol-loving mind of man reveres the meaning not *through* the articulating form but *in* the form so that the image appears to be the actual object of love and fear, supplication and praise.

Because of this constant identification of concepts with their expressions, our world is crowded with unreal beings. Some societies have actually realized that these beings do not belong to nature, and have postulated a so-called "other world" where they have their normal existence and from which they are said to descend, or arise, into our physical realm. For savages it is chiefly a nether world that sends up spooks; for more advanced cults it is from the heavens that supernatural beings, the embodiments of human ideas — of virtue, triumph, immortality — descend to the mundane realm. But from this source emanates also a terrible world government, with heavy commands and sanctions. Strange worship and terrible sacrifices may be the tithes exacted by the beings that embody our knowledge of nonanimalian human nature.

So the gift of symbolism, which is the gift of reason, is at the same time the seat of man's peculiar weakness — the danger of lunacy. Animals go mad with hydrophobia or head injuries, but purely mental aberrations are rare; beasts are not generally subject to insanity except through a confusion

---

[3] German Jewish philosopher (1874–1945), who analyzed cultural values.

of signs, such as the experimentally produced "nervous breakdown" in rats.[4] It is man who hears voices and sees ghosts in the dark, feels irrational compulsions and holds fixed ideas. All these phantasms are symbolic forms that have acquired a false factual status. It has been truly said that everybody has some streak of insanity; i.e., the threat of madness is the price of reason.

Because we can think of things potential as well as actual, we can be held in nonphysical bondage by laws and prohibitions and commands and by images of a governing power. This makes men tyrants over their own kind. Animals control each other's actions by immediate threats, growls and snarls and passes; but when the bully is roving elsewhere, his former domain is free of him. We control our inferiors by setting up symbols of our power, and the mere idea that words or images convey stands there to hold our fellows in subjection even when we cannot lay our hands on them. There is no flag over the country where a wolf is king; he is king where he happens to prowl, so long as he is there. But men, who can embody ideas and set them up to view, oppress each other by symbols of might.

The envisagements of good and evil, which make man a moral agent, make him also a conscript, a prisoner, and a slave. His constant problem is to escape the tyrannies he has created. Primitive societies are almost entirely tyrannical, symbol-bound, coercive organizations; civilized governments are so many conscious schemes to justify or else to disguise man's inevitable bondage to law and conscience.

Slowly, through ages and centuries, we have evolved a picture of the world we live in; we have made a drama of the earth's history and enhanced it with a backdrop of divinely ordered, star-filled space. And all this structure of infinity and eternity against which we watch the pageant of life and death, and all the moral melodrama itself, we have wrought by a gradual articulation of such vast ideas in symbols — symbols of good and evil, triumph and failure, birth and maturity and death. Long before the beginning of any known history, people saw in the heavenly bodies, in the changes of day and night or of the seasons, and in great beasts, symbolic forms to express those ultimate concepts that are the very frame of human existence. So gods, fates, the cohorts of good and evil were conceived. Their myths were the first formulations of cosmic ideas. Gradually the figures and traditions of religion emerged; ritual, the overt expression of our mental attitudes, became more and more intimately bound to definite and elaborate concepts of the creative and destructive powers that seem to control our lives.

Such beings and stories and rites are sacred because they are the great symbols by which the human mind orients itself in the world. To a creature that lives by reason, nothing is more terrible than what is formless and meaningless; one of our primary fears is fear of chaos. And it is the fight against chaos that has produced our most profound and indispensable images — the

---

[4] by building up their expectations through positive reinforcement and then frustrating them.

myths of light and darkness, of creation and passion, the symbols of the altar flame, the daystar, and the cross.

For thousands of years people lived by the symbols that nature presented to them. Close contact with earth and its seasons, intimate knowledge of stars and tides, made them feel the significance of natural phenomena and gave them a poetic, unquestioning sense of orientation. Generations of erudite and pious men elaborated the picture of the temporal and spiritual realms in which each individual was a pilgrim soul.

Then came the unprecedented change, the almost instantaneous leap of history from the immemorial tradition of the plow and the anvil to the new age of the machine, the factory, and the ticker tape. Often in no more than the length of a life-time the shift from handwork to mass production, and with it from poetry to science and from faith to nihilism, has taken place. The old nature symbols have become remote and have lost their meanings; in the clatter of gears and the confusion of gadgets that fill the new world, there will not be any obvious and rich and sacred meanings for centuries to come. All the accumulated creeds and rites of men are suddenly in the melting pot. There is no fixed community, no dynasty, no family inheritance — only the one huge world of men, vast millions of men, still looking on each other in hostile amazement.

A sane, intelligent animal should have invented, in the course of ten thousand years or more, some sure and obvious way of accommodating indefinite numbers of its own kind on the face of a fairly spacious earth. Modern civilization has achieved the highest triumphs of knowledge, skill, ingenuity, theory; yet all around its citadels, engulfing and demolishing them, rages the maddest war and confusion, inspired by symbols and slogans as riotous and irrational as anything the "vegetative" stage of savage phantasy could provide. How shall we reconcile this primitive nightmare excitement with the achievements of our high, rational, scientific culture?

The answer is, I think, that we are no longer in possession of a definite, established culture; we live in a period between an exhausted age — the European civilization of the white race — and an age still unborn, of which we can say nothing as yet. We do not know what races shall inherit the earth. We do not know what even the next few centuries may bring. But it is quite evident, I think, that we live in an age of transition, and that before many more generations have passed, mankind will make a new beginning and build itself a different world. Whether it will be a "brave, new world," or whether it will start all over with an unchronicled "state of nature" such as Thomas Hobbes described, wherein the individual's life is "nasty, brutish, and short," we simply cannot tell. All we know is that every tradition, every institution, every tribe is gradually becoming uprooted and upset, and we are waiting in a sort of theatrical darkness between the acts.

Because we are at a new beginning, our imaginations tend to a wild, "vegetative" overgrowth. The political upheavals of our time are marked, therefore, by a veritable devil dance of mystical ideologies, vaguely conceived, passionately declared, holding out fanatic hopes of mass redemption and mass beatitudes. Governments vie with each other in proclaiming social plans, social aims, social enterprises, and demanding bloody sacrifices in the name of social achievements.

New conceptions are always clothed in an extravagant metaphorical form, for there is no language to express genuinely new ideas. And in their pristine strength they imbue the symbols that express them with their own mystery and power and holiness. It is impossible to disengage the welter of ideas embodied in a swastika, a secret sign, or a conjuring word from the physical presence of the symbol itself; hence the apparently nonsensical symbol worship and mysticism that go with new movements and visions. This identification of symbolic form and half-articulate meaning is the essence of all mythmaking. Of course the emotive value is incomprehensible to anyone who does not see such figments as expressive forms. So an age of vigorous new conception and incomplete formulation always has a certain air of madness about it. But it is really a fecund and exciting period in the life of reason. Such is our present age. Its apparent unreason is a tremendous unbalance and headiness of the human spirit, a conflict not only of selfish wills but of vast ideas in the metaphorical state of emergence.

The change from fixed community life and ancient local custom to the mass of unpedigreed human specimens that actually constitutes the world in our industrial and commercial age had been too sudden for the mind of man to negotiate. Some transitional form of life had to mediate between those extremes. And so the idol of nationality arose from the wreckage of tribal organization. The concept of the national state is really the old tribe concept applied to millions of persons, unrelated and different creatures gathered under the banner of a government. Neither birth nor language nor even religion holds such masses together, but a mystic bond is postulated even where no actual bond of race, creed, or color may ever have existed.

At first glance it seems odd that the concept of nationality should reach its highest development just as all actual marks of national origins — language, dress, physiognomy, and religion — are becoming mixed and obliterated by our new mobility and cosmopolitan traffic. But it is just the loss of these things that inspires this hungry seeking for something like the old egocentric pattern in the vast and formless brotherhood of the whole earth. While mass production and universal communication clearly portend a culture of world citizenship, we cling desperately to our nationalism, a more and more attenuated version of the old clan civilization. We fight passionate and horrible wars for the symbols of our nations, we make a virtue of self-glorification and exclusiveness and invent strange anthropologies to keep us at least theoretically set apart from other men.

Nationalism is a transition between an old and a new human order. But even now we are not really fighting a war of nations; we are fighting a war of fictions, from which a new vision of the order of nature will someday emerge. The future, just now, lies wide open — open and dark, like interstellar space; but in that emptiness there is room for new gods, new cultures, mysterious now and nameless as an unborn child.

Sergei Eisenstein (1898–1948)

RUSSIAN FILM DIRECTOR

Film as Metaphor, Film as Form

... Inner speech, the flow and sequence of thinking unformulated into the logical constructions in which uttered, formulated thoughts are expressed, has a special structure of its own. This structure is based on a quite distinct series of laws. What is remarkable therein, and why I am discussing it, is that the laws of construction of inner speech turn out to be precisely those *laws which lie at the foundation of the whole variety of laws governing the construction of the form and composition of art-works.* And there is not one formal method that does not prove the spit and image of one or another law governing the construction of inner speech, as distinct from the logic of uttered speech. It could not be otherwise.

We know that at the basis of the creation of form lie sensual and imagist thought processes. Inner speech is precisely at the stage of image-sensual structure, not yet having attained that logical formulation with which speech clothes itself before stepping out into the open. It is noteworthy that, just as logic obeys a whole series of laws in its constructions, so, equally, this inner speech, this sensual thinking, is subject to no less clear-cut laws and structural peculiarities. These are known and, in the light of the considerations here set out, represent an inexhaustible storehouse, as it were, of laws for the construction of form, the study and analysis of which have immense importance in the task of mastering the "mysteries" of the technique of form.

For the first time we are placed in possession of a firm storehouse of postulates, bearing on what happens to the initial thesis of the theme when it is translated into a chain of sensory images. The field for study in this direction is colossal. The point is that the forms of sensual, pre-logical thinking, which are preserved in the shape of inner speech among the peoples who have reached an adequate level of social and cultural development, at the same time also represent in mankind at the dawn of cultural development norms of conduct in general, i.e., the laws according to which flow the processes of sensual thought are equivalent for them to a "habit logic" of the future. In accordance with these laws they construct norms of behavior, ceremonials, customs, speech, expressions, etc., and, if we turn to the immeasurable treasury of folklore, of outlived and still living norms and forms of behavior preserved by societies still at the dawn of their development, we find that, what for them has been or still is a norm of behavior and custom-wisdom, turns out to be at the same time precisely what we employ as "artistic methods" and "technique of embodiment" in our art-works. I have no space to discuss in detail the question of the early forms of thought process. I have no opportunity here to picture for you its basic specific characteristics, which are a reflection of the exact form of the early social organization of the communal structures. This is no time to pursue the manner in which, from these general postulates, are worked out the separate characteristic marks and forms of the construction of representations. I will limit myself to quoting two or three instances exemplifying this principle, that one or other given moment in the practice of form-creation is at the same time a moment of custom-practice from the stage of development at which representations are still constructed in accordance with the laws of sensual thinking. I emphasize here, however, that such construction is not of course in any sense exclusive. On the contrary, from the very earliest period there obtains simultaneously a flow of practical and logical experiences, deriving from practical labor processes; a flow that gradually increases on the basis of them, discarding these earlier forms of thinking and embracing gradually all the spheres not only of labor, but also of other intellectual activities, abandoning the earlier forms to the sphere of sensual manifestations.

Consider, for example, that most popular of artistic methods, the so-called *pars pro toto*.[1] The power of its effectiveness is known to everyone. The pince-nez of the surgeon in *Potemkin*[2] are firmly embedded in the memory of anyone who saw the film. The method consisted in substituting the whole (the surgeon) by a part (the pince-nez), which played his rôle, and, it so happened, played it much more sensual-intensively that it could have been played even by the re-appearance of the surgeon. It so happens that this method is the most typical example of a thinking form from the arsenal of early thought processes. At that stage we were still without the unity of the whole and the part as we now understand it. At that stage of non-differentiated thinking the part is *at* one and the same time also the whole. There is not unity of part and whole, but instead obtains an objective identity in representation of whole and part. It is immaterial whether it be part or whole — it plays invariably the rôle of aggregate and whole. This takes place not only in the simplest practical fields and actions, but immediately appears as soon as you emerge from the limits of the simplest "objective" practice. Thus, for example, if you receive an ornament made of a bear's tooth, it signifies that the whole bear has been given to you, or, what in these conditions signifies the same thing, the strength of the bear as a whole. In the conditions of modern practice such a proceeding would be absurd. No one, having received a button off a suit, would imagine himself to be dressed in

[1] a part [standing] for the whole.
[2] Eisenstein's famous film, about revolution and the relations between oppressors and the oppressed.

the complete suit. But as soon even as we move over into the sphere in which sensual and image constructions play the decisive rôle, into the sphere of artistic constructions, the same *pars pro toto* begins immediately to play a tremendous part for us as well. The pince-nez, taking the place of a whole surgeon, not only completely fills his rôle and place, but does so with a huge sensual-emotional increase in the intensity of the impression, to an extent considerably greater than could have been obtained by the reappearance of the surgeon-character himself.

As you perceive, for the purposes of a sensual artistic impression, we have used, as a compositional method, one of those laws of early thinking which, at appropriate stages, appear as the norms and practice of everyday behavior. We made use of a construction of a sensual thinking type, and as a result, instead of a "logico-informative" effect, we receive from the construction actually an emotional sensual effect. We do not register the fact that the surgeon has drowned, we emotionally react to the fact through a definite compositional presentation of this fact.

It is important to note here that what we have analyzed in respect to the use of the close-up, in our example of the surgeon's pince-nez, is not a method of characteristic solely of the cinema alone and specific to it. It equally has a methodological place and is employed in, for example, literature. "*Pars pro toto*" in the field of literary forms is what is known to us under the term synecdoche.

Let us indeed recall the definition of the two kinds of synecdoche. The first kind: this kind consists in that one receives *a presentation of the part instead of the whole*. This in turn has a series of sorts:

1. Singular instead of plural. ("The Son of Albion reaching for freedom" instead of "The sons of, etc.")
2. Collective instead of composition of the clan. ("Mexico enslaved by Spain" instead of "The Mexicans enslaved.")
3. Part instead of whole. ("Under the master's eye.")
4. Definite instead of indefinite. ("A hundred times we've said . . .")
5. Species instead of genus.

The second series of synecdoches consists in *the whole instead of the part*. But, as you perceive, both series and all their several subdivisions are subject to one and the same basic condition. Which condition is: the identity of the part and the whole and hence the "equivalence," the equal significance in replacing one by the other.

No less striking examples of the same occur in paintings and drawings, where two color spots and a flowing curve give a complete sensual replacement of the whole object.

What is of interest here is not this list itself, but the fact that is confirmed by the list. Namely, that we are dealing here not with specific methods, peculiar to this or that art-medium, but first and foremost with a specific course and condition of embodied thinking — with sensual thinking, for which a given structure is a law. In this special, synecdochic, use of the "close-up," in the color-spot and curve, we have but particular instances of the operation of this law of *pars pro toto*, characteristic of sensual thinking, dependent upon whatever art-medium in which it happens to be functioning for its purpose of embodiment of the basic creative scheme.

Another example. We are well aware that every embodiment must be in strict artistic accord with the story situation being embodied. We know that this concerns costume, setting, accompanying music, light, color. We know that this accord concerns not only the demands made by naturalistic conviction, but also, and perhaps to a greater degree, the demands of sustaining the emotional expression. If a dramatist's scene "sounds" a certain key, then all elements of its embodiment must sound the same key. There is an unsurpassed classical example of this in *King Lear*, whose inner tempest echoes the tempest on the moor, raging round him on the stage. We can also find examples of a reverse construction — for purposes of contrast: say that a maximum raging of passion is to be resolved by an intentional static and immobile quality. Here, too, all elements of the embodiment would be realized with just as strict a sustaining and accord with the theme, though in this case with opposite indications, as well.

Such a demand also spreads over into the shot and the montage, whose means must likewise compositionally echo and respond to the basic compositional key for the treatment of the entire work and of each scene in it.[3]

It appears that this element, sufficiently recognized and universal in art, can be found on a certain level of development in similar inevitable and obligatory modes of behavior in life. Here is an example from Polynesian practice — a practice that is preserved in customs today with little change. When any Polynesian woman is in confinement, there is a peremptory rule that all gates in the settlement must be opened, all doors thrown open, that everyone (including men, as well) is to remove any sashes, aprons, headbands, that all tied knots are to be untied, and so forth; that is, all circumstances, all concomitant details, must be arranged in a character exactly corresponding to the basic theme of what is occurring: everything must be opened, untied, to give maximum ease to the appearance in the world of the new child!

Let us now turn to another medium. Let us take a case where the material of the form-creation turns out to be the artist himself. This also confirms the truth of our thesis. Even more: in this instance the structure of the finished composition not only reproduces, as it were, a reprint of the structure of the laws along which flow sensual thought-processes. In this instance the circumstance itself, here united with the object-subject of creation, as a whole duplicates a picture of the psychic state and representation corresponding to the early forms of thought. Let us look once more at two examples. All investigators and travelers are invariably somewhat astonished at one char-

---

[3] The considerable skill achieved in this field by our silent cinema fell perceptibly from the moment of transition to sound-film — for evidence, see most of our sound-films. (Eisenstein's note)

acteristic of early forms of thought quite incomprehensible to a human being accustomed to think in the categories of current logic. It is the characteristic involving the conception that a human being, while being himself and conscious of himself as such, yet simultaneously considers himself to be also some other person or thing, and, further, to be so, just as definitely and just as concretely, materially. In the specialized literature on this subject there is the particularly popular example of one of the Indian tribes of Northern Brazil.

The Indians of this tribe — the Bororo — maintain that, while human beings, they are none the less at the same time also a special kind of red parakeet common in Brazil. Note that by this they do not in any way mean that they will become these birds after death, or that their ancestors were such in the remote past. Not at all. They directly maintain that they are in reality these actual birds. It is not here a matter of identity of names or relationship; they mean a complete simultaneous identity of both.

However strange and unusual this may sound to us, it is nevertheless possible to quote from artistic practice quantities of instances which would sound almost word for word like the Bororo idea concerning simultaneous double existence of two completely different and separate and, none the less, real images. It is enough only to touch on the question of the self-feeling of the actor during his creation or performance of a rôle. Here, immediately, arises the problem of "I" and "him." Where "I" is the individuality of the performer, and "he" the individuality of the performed image of the rôle. This problem of the simultaneity of "I" and "not I" in the creation and performance of a rôle is one of the central "mysteries" of acting creation. The solution of it wavers between complete subordination of "him" to "I" — and "he" (complete trans-substantiation). While the contemporary attitude to this problem in its formulation approaches the clear enough dialectic formula of the "unity of inter-penetrating opposites," and "I" of the actor and the "he" of the image, the leading opposite being the image, nevertheless in concrete self-feeling the matter is by a long way not always so clear and definite for the actor. In one way or another, "I" and "he," "their" inter-relationship, "their" connections, "their" interactions inevitably figure at every stage in the working out of the rôle. . . .

No less revealing are descriptions in the memoirs of a whole series of actors of their behavior at the moment of putting on make-up or their costume, which they accompany by a complete "magic" operation of "transformation" with whisperings, such as "I am already not me," "I am already so-and-so," "See, I'm beginning to be him," and so on.

In one way or another, more or less controlled, simultaneous actuality in the playing of the rôle is bound to be present in the creative process of even, albeit, the most inveterate supporter of complete "trans-substantiation." There are, in fact, too few cases known in the history of the theater of an actor leaning on the "fourth [non-existent] wall!"

It is characteristic that a similarly fluctuating dual apprehension of stage action as both a reality of theater and a reality of representation exists also with the spectator. Here too, correct apprehension is a united duality, on the one hand preventing the spectator from killing the villain, in that he remembers the latter is not a reality, while on the other giving him the occasion for laughter or tears, in that he forgets that he is witnessing a representation, a play-acting. . . .

🏮

We shall find that a . . . crowd of pictures, carefully selected and reduced to the extreme laconism of two or three details, is to be found in the finest examples of literature.

Take Pushkin's narrative poem, *Poltava*[4] — the scene of Kochubei's execution. In this scene the theme of "Kochubei's end" is expressed with unusual vividness in the image of "the end of Kochubei's execution." But the actual image of this end of the execution arises and grows out of the juxtaposition of three almost "documentarily" selected representations of three detail incidents from the episode:

> "Too late," someone then said to them,
> And pointed finger to the field.
> There the fatal scaffold was dismantled,
> A priest in cassock black was praying,
> And onto a wagon was being lifted
> By two cossacks an oaken coffin. . . .

It would be difficult to find a more effective selection of details to convey the sensation of the image of death in all its horror, than these from the conclusion of the execution scene.

The validity of choosing a realistic method to produce and achieve an emotional quality can be confirmed by some very curious examples. Here, for instance, is another scene from Pushkin's *Poltava*, in which the poet magically causes the image of a nocturnal flight to rise before the reader in all its picturesque and emotional possibilities:

> But no one knew just how or when
> She vanished. A lone fisherman
> In that night heard the clack of horses' hoofs,
> Cossack speech and a woman's whisper. . . .

Three shots:

1. Clack of horses' hoofs.
2. Cossack speech.
3. A woman's whisper.

Once more three objectively expressed representations (in sound!) come together in an emotionally expressed unifying image, distinct from the per-

---

[4] Aleksandr Pushkin (1799–1837), the greatest Russian poet. *Poltava* is a historical poem about Peter the Great, tsar of Russia from 1682 and emperor from 1721 to 1725, and one of Russia's greatest statesmen, organizers and reformers.

ception of the separate phenomena if encountered apart from their association
with each other. The method is used solely for the purpose of evoking the
necessary emotional experience in the reader. The emotional experience only,
because the information that Marya has vanished has been given in a previous
single line ("*She vanished. A lone fisherman*"). Having told the reader that
she had vanished, the author wanted to give him the experience as well. To
achieve this, he turns to montage. With three details selected from all the
elements of flight, his image of nocturnal flight emerges in montage fashion,
imparting the experience of the action to the senses.

To the three sound pictures he adds a fourth picture. It has the effect of a
full stop. To attain this effect he chooses his fourth picture from another
sense. This last "close-up" is not in sound, but in sight:

> . . . And eight horseshoes had left their traces
> Over the meadow morning dew. . . .

Thus Pushkin uses montage in creating the images of a work of art. But
Pushkin uses montage just as skillfully when he creates the image of a character, or of an entire *dramatis personae*. With a superlative combination of
various aspects (i.e., "camera set-ups") and of different elements (i.e., montage pieces of pictorially represented things, clarified by the framing of the
shot) Pushkin gains astonishing reality in his delineations. Man, indeed,
complete and feeling, emerges from the pages of Pushkin's poems.

When Pushkin works with a large quantity of montage pieces, his use of
montage grows more intricate. Rhythm, constructed with successive long
phrases and phrases as short as a single word, introduces a dynamic characteristic to the image of the montage construction. This rhythm serves to
establish the actual temperament of the character being depicted, giving us
a dynamic characterization of his behavior.

One can also learn from Pushkin how an orderly succession in transmitting
and disclosing a man's characteristics and personality can heighten the total
value of the image. An excellent example in this connection is his description
of Peter the Great in *Poltava*:

> I. . . . And then with highest exaltation
> II. There sounded, ringing, Peter's voice:
> III. "To arms, God with us!" From the tent,
> IV. By crowding favorites surrounded,
> V. Peter emerges. His eyes
> VI. Are flashing. His look is terrible.
> VII. His movements swift. Magnificent he,
> VIII. In all his aspect, wrath divine.
> IX. He goes. His charger is led him.
> X. Fiery and docile faithful steed.
> XI. Scenting the fray's fire
> XII. It quivers. It turns its eyes aslant
> XIII. And dashes into the fight's dust,
> XIV. Proud of its mighty rider.

The above numbering is of the poem's lines. Now we shall write out this same passage again as a shooting-script, numbering the "shots" as edited by Pushkin:

1. And then with highest exaltation there sounded, ringing, Peter's voice: "To arms, God with us!"
2. From the tent, by crowding favorites surrounded,
3. Peter emerges.
4. His eyes are flashing.
5. His look is terrible.
6. His movements swift.
7. Magnificent he,
8. In all his aspect, wrath divine.
9. He goes.
10. His charger is led him.
11. Fiery and docile faithful steed.
12. Scenting the fray's fire it quivers.
13. It turns its eyes aslant
14. And dashes into the fight's dust, proud of its mighty rider.

The number of *lines* and the number of *shots* prove to be *identical*, fourteen in each case. But there is almost no internal congruence between the lay-out of the lines and the lay-out of the shots; such congruence occurs only twice in the entire fourteen lines: VIII = 8 and X = 11. Furthermore the content of a shot varies as much as two complete lines (1, 14) and as little as a single word (9).[5]

This is very instructive for film-workers, particularly those specializing in sound.

Let us examine how Peter is "edited":

Shots 1, 2, 3 contain an excellent example of the *significant* presentation of a figure in action. Here three degrees, three stages of his appearance, are absolutely distinct: (1) Peter is not yet shown, but is introduced in sound — his voice. (2) Peter has emerged from the tent, but he is not yet visible. All we can see is the group of favorites surrounding his emergence from the tent. (3) At last, only in a third stage, is Peter actually seen as he comes from the tent.

These are followed by *flashing eyes*, as the most important detail in his general appearance (4). And then — the whole face (5). Only then his full figure is displayed (although very likely cut at the knees by the lower frame-line of a traveling shot) to show his movements, their swiftness and brusqueness. The rhythm of the movement and the character it illuminates are expressed "impetuously" by the clash of short phrases. The full display of the full figure is given only in Shot 7, and now in a manner beyond the conveyance of information — vividly, as an image: "Magnificent he." In the following shot this description is strengthened and heightened: "In all his aspect,

---

[5] In Russian "he goes" is a single word, *idët* (phonetically, "id-yót"). [Leyda]

wrath divine." Only in this eighth shot does Pushkin reveal Peter with the full power of a plastic representation. This eighth shot, obviously, contains Peter at full height, emphasized by all the resources of shot composition, with a crown of clouds above him, with tents and people surrounding him at his feet. After this broad shot the poet at once returns us to the realm of movement and action with the single word: "He goes" (*idët*). It would be difficult to seize more vividly Peter's second decisive characteristic: Peter's stride — the most important since the "flashing eyes." The laconic "He goes," completely conveys the feeling of that enormous, elemental, impetuous stride of Peter, who always made such difficulties for his suite in keeping up with him. It was in as masterly a manner that Valentin Serov seized and impressed that "stride of Peter" in his celebrated picture of Peter at the construction of St. Petersburg.[6]

I believe that the presentation above is a correct film reading of the passage. In the first place, such an "introduction" of a Pushkin character is generally typical of his style. . . . A second proof of the correctness of the above reading is the determination of the order of the words that, with absolute exactitude, in turn *order the successive appearance* of each element, all of which finally fuse into the image of the character, plastically "revealing" it.

Shots 2 and 3 would be constructed quite differently if, instead of:

> . . . From the tent,
> By crowding favorites surrounded,
> Peter emerges. . . .

the text had read:

> . . . Peter emerges,
> By crowding favorites surrounded,
> From the tent. . . .

If the emergence had begun with, instead of leading up to, Peter, the impression would have been quite different. As Pushkin wrote it, it is a model of expressiveness, achieved by a purely montage method and with purely montage means. For every instance there is available a different expressive construction. But the expressive construction chosen for each instance prescribes and outlines in advance that "only right arrangement of the only suitable words," about which Tolstoy wrote in *What Is Art?*

The sound of Peter's voice and his words are arranged with just the same quality of logical succession that pervades the pictorial images (see Shot 1). For Pushkin did not write:

> . . . "To arms, God with us!"
> Sounded Peter's voice, ringing,
> And with highest exaltation.

---

[6] St. Petersburg, now Leningrad, was built at the direction of Peter and in 1712 was made the capital of Russia.

but:

> And then with highest exaltation
> There sounded, ringing, Peter's voice:
> "To arms, God with us!" . . .

If we, as film-makers, should be faced with the task of building up the expressiveness of such an exclamation, we, too, must transmit it so that there is an ordered succession, revealing first its *exaltation*, then its ringing quality, followed by our *recognition of the voice* as Peter's, and finally, to distinguish *the words* that this exalted, ringing voice of Peter *utters:* "To arms, God with us!" It seems clearly evident that in "staging" such a passage, the solution of the opening could simply be resolved by hearing first a phrase of exclamation coming from the tent, in which the words could not be distinguished, but which would already resound the exalted and ringing qualities which we would later recognize as characteristic of Peter's voice.

As we see, this has enormous importance in connection with the problem of enriching the expressive resources of film.

The example is a model of the most complex type of sound-picture, or audio-visual composition. It seems amazing that there are those who think it hardly necessary to seek assistance from such media, and that one can accumulate quite enough experience in the study of co-ordination of music and action exclusively from the opera or ballet! . . .

Henry Moore (b. 1898)

ENGLISH SCULPTOR

The Sculptor Speaks

It is a mistake for a sculptor or a painter to speak or write very often about his job. It releases tension needed for his work. By trying to express his aims with rounded-off logical exactness, he can easily become a theorist whose actual work is only a caged-in exposition of conceptions evolved in terms of logic and words.

But though the non-logical, instinctive, subconscious part of the mind must play its part in his work, he also has a conscious mind which is not inactive. The artist works with a concentration of his whole personality, and the conscious part of it resolves conflicts, organises memories, and prevents him from trying to walk in two directions at the same time.

It is likely, then, that a sculptor can give, from his own conscious experience, clues which will help others in their approach to sculpture, and this article tries to do this, and no more. It is not a general survey of sculpture, or of my own development, but a few notes on some of the problems that have concerned me from time to time.

Appreciation of sculpture depends upon the ability to respond to form in three dimensions. That is perhaps why sculpture has been described as the most difficult of all arts; certainly it is more difficult than the arts which involve appreciation of flat forms, shape in only two dimensions. Many more people are 'form-blind' than colour-blind. The child learning to see, first distinguishes only two-dimensional shape; it cannot judge distances, depths. Later, for its personal safety and practical needs, it has to develop (partly by means of touch) the ability to judge roughly three dimensional distances. But having satisfied the requirements of practical necessity, most people go no farther. Though they may attain considerable accuracy in the perception of flat form, they do not make the further intellectual and emotional effort needed to comprehend form in its full spatial existence.

This is what the sculptor must do. He must strive continually to think of, and use, form in its full spatial completeness. He gets the solid shape, as it were, inside his head — he thinks of it, whatever its size, as if he were holding it completely enclosed in the hollow of his hand. He mentally visualises a complex form from all round itself; he knows while he looks at one side what the other side is like; he identifies himself with its centre of gravity, its mass, its weight; he realises its volume, as the space that the shape displaces in the air.

And the sensitive observer of sculpture must also learn to feel shape simply as shape, not as description or reminiscence. He must, for example, perceive an egg as a simple single solid shape, quite apart from its significance as food, or from the literary idea that it will become a bird. And so with solids such as a shell, a nut, a plum, a pear, a tadpole, a mushroom, a mountain peak, a kidney, a carrot, a tree-trunk, a bird, a bud, a lark, a lady-bird, a bulrush, a bone. From these he can go on to appreciate more complex forms or combinations of several forms.

Since the Gothic, European sculpture had become overgrown with moss, weeds — all sorts of surface excrescences which completely concealed shape. It has been Brancusi's special mission to get rid of this overgrowth, and to make us once more shape-conscious. To do this he has had to concentrate on very simple direct shapes, to keep his sculpture, as it were, one-cylindered, to refine and polish a single shape to a degree almost too precious. Brancusi's work, apart from its individual value, has been of historical importance in the development of contemporary sculpture. But it may now be no longer necessary to close down and restrict sculpture to the single (static) form unit. We can now begin to open out. To relate and combine together several forms of varied sizes, sections and directions into one organic whole.

Although it is the human figure which interests me most deeply, I have always paid great attention to natural forms, such as bones, shells, and pebbles, etc. Sometimes for several years running I have been to the same part of the sea-shore — but each year a new shape of pebble has caught my eye, which the year before, though it was there in hundreds, I never saw. Out of the millions of pebbles passed in walking along the shore, I choose out to see with excitement only those which fit in with my existing form-interest at the time. A different thing happens if I sit down and examine a handful one by one. I may then extend my form-experience more, by giving my mind time to become conditioned to a new shape.

There are universal shapes to which everybody is sub-consciously conditioned and to which they can respond if their conscious control does not shut them off.

Pebbles show nature's way of working stone. Some of the pebbles I pick up have holes right through them.

When first working direct in a hard and brittle material like stone, the lack of experience and great respect for the material, the fear of ill-treating it, too often result in relief surface carving, with no sculptural power.

But with more experience the completed work in stone can be kept within the limitations of its material, that is, not be weakened beyond its natural constructive build, and yet be turned from an inert mass into a composition which has a full form existence, with masses of varied sizes and sections working together in spatial relationship.

A piece of stone can have a hole through it and not be weakened — if the hole is of studied size, shape and direction. On the principle of the arch, it can remain just as strong.

The first hole made through a piece of stone is a revelation.

The hole connects one side to the other, making it immediately more three-dimensional.

A hole can itself have as much shape-meaning as a solid mass.

Sculpture in air is possible, where the stone contains only the hole, which is the intended and considered form.

The mystery of the hole — the mysterious fascination of caves in hillsides and cliffs.

There is a right physical size for every idea.

Pieces of good stone have stood about my studio for long periods, because though I've had ideas which would fit their proportions and materials perfectly, their size was wrong.

There is a size to scale not to do with its actual physical size, its measurement in feet and inches — but connected with vision.

A carving might be several times over life size and yet be petty and small in feeling — and a small carving only a few inches in height can give the feeling of huge size and monumental grandeur, because the vision behind it is big. Example, Michelangelo's drawings or a Masaccio madonna — and the Albert Memorial.[1]

Yet actual physical size has an emotional meaning. We relate everything to our own size, and our emotional response to size is controlled by the fact that men on the average are between five and six feet high.

[1] a massive, highly ornate monument in London erected under Queen Victoria's auspices to commemorate her deceased consort, Prince Albert (1819–1861).

An exact model to 1/10 scale of Stonehenge, where the stones would be less than us, would lose all its impressiveness.

Sculpture is more affected by actual size considerations than painting. A painting is isolated by a frame from its surroundings (unless it serves just a decorative purpose) and so retains more easily its own imaginary scale.

If practical considerations allowed me, cost of material, of transport etc., I should like to work on large carvings more often than I do. The average in-between size does not disconnect an idea enough from prosaic everyday life. The very small or the very big takes on an added size emotion.

Recently I have been working in the country, where, carving in the open air, I find sculpture more natural than in a London studio, but it needs bigger dimensions. A large piece of stone or wood placed almost anywhere at random in a field, orchard or garden immediately looks right and inspiring.

My drawings are done mainly as a help towards making sculpture — as a means of generating ideas for sculpture, tapping oneself for the initial idea; and as a way of sorting out ideas and developing them.

Also, sculpture compared with drawing is a slow means of expression, and I find drawing a useful outlet for ideas which there is not time enough to realise as sculpture. And I use drawings as a methods of study and observation of natural forms (drawings from life, drawings of bones, shells etc.).

And I sometimes draw just for its own enjoyment.

Experience, though, has taught me that the difference there is between drawing and sculpture should not be forgotten. A sculptural idea which may be satisfactory as a drawing always needs some alteration when translated into sculpture.

At one time whenever I made drawings for sculpture I tried to give them as much the illusion of real sculpture as I could — that is, I drew by the method of illusion, of light falling on a solid subject. But I now find that carrying a drawing so far that it becomes a substitute for the sculpture, either weakens the desire to do the sculpture, or is likely to make the sculpture only a dead realisation of the drawing.

I now leave a wider latitude in the interpretation of the drawings I make for sculpture, and draw often in line and flat tones without the light and shade illusion of three dimensions; but this does not mean that the vision behind the drawing is only two dimensional.

The violent quarrel between the abstractionists and the surrealists seems to me quite unnecessary. All good art has contained both abstract and surrealist elements, just as it has contained both classical and romantic elements — order and surprise, intellect and imagination, conscious and unconscious. Both sides of the artist's personality must play their part. And I think the first inception of a painting or a sculpture may begin from either end. As far as my own experience is concerned, I sometimes begin a drawing with no preconceived problem to solve, with only the desire to use pencil on paper, and make lines, tones and shapes with no conscious aim; but as my mind takes in what is so produced, a point arrives where some idea becomes conscious and crystallises, and then a control and ordering begin to take place.

Or sometimes I start with a set subject; or to solve, in a block of stone of known dimensions, a sculptural problem I've given myself, and then consciously attempt to build an ordered relationship of forms, which shall express my idea. But if the work is to be more than just a sculptural exercise, unexplainable jumps in the process of thought occur; and the imagination plays its part.

It might seem from what I have said of shape and form that I regard them as ends in themselves. Far from it. I am very much aware that associational, psychological factors play a large part in sculpture. The meaning and significance of form itself probably depends on the countless associations of man's history. For example, rounded forms convey an idea of fruitfulness, maturity, probably because the earth, women's breasts, and most fruits are rounded, and these shapes are important because they have this background in our habits of perception. I think the humanist organic element will always be for me of fundamental importance in sculpture, giving sculpture its vitality. Each particular carving I make takes on in my mind a human or occasionally animal, character and personality, and this personality controls its design and formal qualities, and makes me satisfied or dissatisfied with the work as it develops.

My own aim and direction seems to be consistent with these beliefs, though it does not depend upon them. My sculpture is becoming less representational, less an outward visual copy, and so what some people would call more abstract; but only because I believe that in this way I can present the human psychological content of my work with the greatest directness and intensity.

Robert Francis (b. 1901)

AMERICAN POET

Catch

Two boys uncoached are tossing a poem together,
Overhand, underhand, backhand, sleight of hand, every hand,
Teasing with attitudes, latitudes, interludes, altitudes,
High, make him fly off the ground for it, low, make him stoop,
Make him scoop it up, make him as-almost-as-possible miss it,
Fast, let him sting from it, now, now fool him slowly,
Anything, everything tricky, risky, nonchalant,
Anything under the sun to outwit the prosy,
Over the tree and the long sweet cadence down,
Over his head, make him scramble to pick up the meaning,   10
And now, like a posy, a pretty one plump in his hands.

George Orwell (1903–1950)

ENGLISH ESSAYIST and NOVELIST

Politics and the English Language

Most people who bother with the matter at all would admit that the English language is in a bad way, but it is generally assumed that we cannot by conscious action do anything about it. Our civilization is decadent and our language — so the argument runs — must inevitably share in the general collapse. It follows that any struggle against the abuse of language is a sentimental archaism, like preferring candles to electric light or hansom cabs to aeroplanes. Underneath this lies the half-conscious belief that language is a natural growth and not an instrument which we shape for our own purposes.

Now, it is clear that the decline of a language must ultimately have political and economic causes: it is not due simply to the bad influence of this or that individual writer. But an effect can become a cause, reinforcing the original cause and producing the same effect in an intensified form, and so on indefinitely. A man may take to drink because he feels himself to be a failure, and then fail all the more completely because he drinks. It is rather the same thing that is happening to the English language. It becomes ugly and inaccurate because our thoughts are foolish, but the slovenliness of our language makes it easier for us to have foolish thoughts. The point is that the process is reversible. Modern English, especially written English, is full of bad habits which spread by imitation and which can be avoided if one is willing to take the necessary trouble. If one gets rid of these habits one can think more clearly, and to think clearly is a necessary first step towards political regeneration: so that the fight against bad English is not frivolous and is not the exclusive concern of professional writers. I will come back to this presently, and I hope that by that time the meaning of what I have said here will have become clearer. Meanwhile, here are five specimens of the English language as it is now habitually written.

These five passages have not been picked out because they are especially bad — I could have quoted far worse if I had chosen — but because they illustrate various of the mental vices from which we now suffer. They are a little below the average, but are fairly representative samples. I number them so that I can refer back to them when necessary:

(1) I am not, indeed, sure whether it is not true to say that the Milton who once seemed not unlike a seventeenth-century Shelley had not become, out of an experience ever more bitter in each year, more alien [*sic*] to the founder of that Jesuit sect which nothing could induce him to tolerate.

PROFESSOR HAROLD LASKI (Essay in *Freedom of Expression*)

(2) Above all, we cannot play ducks and drakes with a native battery of idioms which prescribes such egregious collocations of vocables as the Basic *put up with* for *tolerate* or *put at a loss* for *bewilder*.

PROFESSOR LANCELOT HOGBEN (*Interglossa*)

(3) On the one side we have the free personality: by definition it is not neurotic, for it has neither conflict nor dream. Its desires, such as they are, are transparent, for they are just what institutional approval keeps in the forefront of consciousness; another institutional pattern would alter their number and intensity; there is little in them that is natural, irreducible, or culturally dangerous. But *on the other side*, the social bond itself is nothing but the mutual reflection of these self-secure integrities. Recall the definition of love. Is not this the very picture of a small academic? Where is there a place in this hall of mirrors for either personality or fraternity?

Essay on psychology in *Politics* (New York)

(4) All the "best people" from the gentlemen's clubs, and all the frantic fascist captains, united in common hatred of Socialism and bestial horror of the rising tide of the mass revolutionary movement, have turned to acts of provocation, to foul incendiarism, to medieval legends of poisoned wells, to legalize their own destruction of proletarian organizations, and rouse the agitated petty-bourgeoisie to chauvinistic fervour on behalf of the fight against the revolutionary way out of the crisis.

Communist pamphlet

(5) If a new spirit *is* to be infused into this old country, there is one thorny and contentious reform which must be tackled, and that is the humanization and galvanization of the B.B.C. Timidity here will bespeak canker and atrophy of the soul. The heart of Britain may be sound and of strong beat, for instance, but the British lion's roar at present is like that of Bottom in Shakespeare's *Midsummer Night's Dream* — as gentle as any sucking dove. A virile new Britain cannot continue indefinitely to be traduced in the eyes or rather ears, of the world by the effete languors of Langham Place, brazenly masquerading as "standard English." When the Voice of Britain is heard at nine o'clock, better far and infinitely less ludicrous to hear aitches honestly dropped than the present priggish, inflated, inhibited, school-ma'amish arch braying of blameless bashful mewing maidens!

Letter in *Tribune*

Each of these passages has faults of its own, but, quite apart from avoidable ugliness, two qualities are common to all of them. The first is staleness of imagery: the other is lack of precision. The writer either has a meaning and cannot express it, or he inadvertently says something else, or he is almost indifferent as to whether his words mean anything or not. This mixture of vagueness and sheer incompetence is the most marked characteristic of modern English prose, and especially of any kind of political writing. As soon as certain topics are raised, the concrete melts into the abstract and no one seems able to think of turns of speech that are not hackneyed: prose consists less and less of *words* chosen for the sake of their meaning, and more and more of *phrases* tacked together like the sections of a prefabricated hen-house. I list below, with notes and examples, various of the tricks by means of which the work of prose-construction is habitually dodged:

DYING METAPHORS. A newly invented metaphor assists thought by evoking a visual image, while on the other hand a metaphor which is technically "dead" (e.g. *iron resolution*) has in effect reverted to being an ordinary word and can generally be used without loss of vividness. But in between these two classes there is a huge dump of worn-out metaphors which have lost all evocative power and are merely used because they save people the trouble of inventing phrases for themselves. Examples are: *Ring the changes on, take up the cudgels for, toe the line, ride roughshod over, stand shoulder to shoulder with, play into the hands of, no axe to grind, grist to the mill, fishing in troubled waters, on the order of the day, Achilles' heel, swan song, hotbed.* Many of these are used without knowledge of their meaning (what is a "rift," for instance?), and incompatible metaphors are frequently mixed, a sure sign that the writer is not interested in what he is saying. Some metaphors now current have been twisted out of their original meaning without those who use them even being aware of the fact. For example, *toe the line* is sometimes written *tow the line.* Another example is *the hammer and the anvil,* now always used with the implication that the anvil gets the worst of it. In real life it is always the anvil that breaks the hammer, never the other way about: a writer who stopped to think what he was saying would be aware of this, and would avoid perverting the original phrase.

OPERATORS or VERBAL FALSE LIMBS. These save the trouble of picking out appropriate verbs and nouns, and at the same time pad each sentence with extra syllables which give it an appearance of symmetry. Characteristic phrases are: *render inoperative, militate against, make contact with, be subjected to, give rise to, give grounds for, have the effect of, play a leading part (role) in, make itself felt, take effect, exhibit a tendency to, serve the purpose of, etc., etc.* The keynote is the elimination of simple verbs. Instead of being a single word, such as *break, stop, spoil, mend, kill,* a verb becomes a *phrase,* made up of a noun or adjective tacked on to some general-purposes verb such as *prove, serve, form, play, render.* In addition, the passive voice is wherever possible used in preference to the active, and noun constructions are used instead of gerunds (*by examination of* instead of *by examining*). The range of verbs is further cut down by means of the *-ize* and *de-* formations, and the banal statements are given an appearance of profundity by means of the *not un-* formation. Simple conjunctions and prepositions are replaced by such phrases as *with respect to, having regard to, the fact that, by dint of, in view of, in the interests of, on the hypothesis that;* and the ends of sentences are saved from anticlimax by such resounding commonplaces as *greatly to be desired, cannot be left out of account, a development to be expected in the near future, deserving of serious consideration, brought to a satisfactory conclusion,* and so on and so forth.

PRETENTIOUS DICTION. Words like *phenomenon, element, individual* (as noun), *objective, categorical, effective, virtual, basic, primary, promote, constitute, exhibit, exploit, utilize, eliminate, liquidate,* are used to dress up simple statement and give an air of scientific impartiality to biased judgments. Adjectives like *epoch-making, epic, historic, unforgettable, triumphant, age-old, inevitable, inexorable, veritable,* are used to dignify the sordid processes of international politics, while writing that aims at glorifying war usually takes on an archaic colour, its characteristic words being: *realm, throne, chariot, mailed fist, trident, sword, shield, buckler, banner, jackboot, clarion.* Foreign words and expressions such as *cul de sac, ancien régime, deus ex machina, mutatis mutandis, status quo, gleichschaltung, weltanschauung,* are used to give an air of culture and elegance. Except for the useful abbreviations *i.e., e.g.,* and *etc.,* there is no real need for any of the hundreds of foreign phrases now current in English. Bad writers, and especially scientific, political and sociological writers, are nearly always haunted by the notion that Latin or Greek words are grander than Saxon ones, and unnecessary words like *expedite, ameliorate, predict, extraneous, deracinated, clandestine, subaqueous* and hundreds of others constantly gain ground from their Anglo-Saxon opposite numbers.[1] The jargon peculiar to Marxist writing (*hyena, hangman, cannibal, petty bourgeois, these gentry, lacquey, flunkey, mad dog, White Guard,* etc.) consists largely of words and phrases translated from Russian, German or French; but the normal way of coining a new word is to use a Latin or Greek root with the appropriate affix and, where necessary, the *-ize* formation. It is often easier to make up words of this kind (*deregionalize, impermissible, extramarital, non-fragmentatory* and so forth) than to think up the English words that will cover one's meaning. The result, in general, is an increase in slovenliness and vagueness.

MEANINGLESS WORDS. In certain kinds of writing, particularly in art criticism and literary criticism, it is normal to come across long passages which are almost completely lacking in meaning.[2] Words like *romantic, plastic, values,*

[1] An interesting illustration of this is the way in which the English flower names which were in use till very recently are being ousted by Greek ones, *snapdragon* becoming *antirrhinum, forget-me-not* becoming *myosotis,* etc. It is hard to see any practical reason for this change of fashion: it is probably due to an instinctive turning-away from the more homely word and a vague feeling that the Greek word is scientific. (Orwell's note)

[2] Example: "Comfort's catholicity of perception and image, strangely Whitmanesque in range, almost the exact opposite in aesthetic compulsion, continues to evoke that trembling atmospheric accumulative hinting at a cruel, an inexorably serene timelessness . . . Wrey Gardiner scores by aiming at simple bull's-eyes with precision. Only they are not so simple, and through this contented sadness runs more than the surface bitter-sweet of resignation." (*Poetry Quarterly.*) (Orwell's note)

human, dead, sentimental, natural, vitality, as used in art criticism, are strictly meaningless, in the sense that they not only do not point to any discoverable object, but are hardly ever expected to do so by the reader. When one critic writes, "The outstanding feature of Mr. X's work is its living quality," while another writes, "The immediately striking thing about Mr. X's work is its peculiar deadness," the reader accepts this as a simple difference of opinion. If words like *black* and *white* were involved, instead of the jargon words *dead* and *living,* he would see at once that language was being used in an improper way. Many political words are similarly abused. The word *Fascism* has now no meaning except in so far as it signifies "something not desirable." The words *democracy, socialism, freedom, patriotic, realistic, justice,* have each of them several different meanings which cannot be reconciled with one another. In the case of a word like *democracy,* not only is there no agreed definition, but the attempt to make one is resisted from all sides. It is almost universally felt that when we call a country democratic we are praising it: consequently the defenders of every kind of régime claim that it is a democracy, and fear that they might have to stop using the word if it were tied down to any one meaning. Words of this kind are often used in a consciously dishonest way. That is, the person who uses them has his own private definition, but allows his hearer to think he means something quite different. Statements like *Marshal Pétain was a true patriot, The Soviet Press is the freest in the world, The Catholic Church is opposed to persecution,* are almost always made with intent to deceive. Other words used in variable meanings, in most cases more or less dishonestly, are: *class, totalitarian, science, progressive, reactionary, bourgeois, equality.*

Now that I have made this catalogue of swindles and perversions, let me give another example of the kind of writing that they lead to. This time it must of its nature be an imaginary one. I am going to translate a passage of good English into modern English of the worst sort. Here is a well-known verse from *Ecclesiastes*:

> "I returned and saw under the sun, that the race is not to the swift, nor the battle to the strong, neither yet bread to the wise, nor yet riches to men of understanding, nor yet favour to men of skill; but time and chance happeneth to them all."

Here it is in modern English.

> "Objective consideration of contemporary phenomena compels the conclusion that success or failure in competitive activities exhibits no tendency to be commensurate with innate capacity, but that a considerable element of the unpredictable must invariably be taken into account."

This is a parody, but not a very gross one. Exhibit (3), above, for instance, contains several patches of the same kind of English. It will be seen that I have not made a full translation. The beginning and ending of the sentence follow the original meaning fairly closely, but in the middle the concrete illustrations — race, battle, bread — dissolve into the vague phrase "success or failure in competitive activities." This had to be so, because no modern writer of the kind I am discussing — no one capable of using phrases like "objective consideration of contemporary phenomena" — would ever tabulate his thoughts in that precise and detailed way. The whole tendency of modern prose is away from concreteness. Now analyse these two sentences a little more closely. The first contains forty-nine words but only sixty syllables, and all its words are those of everyday life. The second contains thirty-eight words of ninety syllables: eighteen of its words are from Latin roots, and one from Greek. The first sentence contains six vivid images, and only one phrase ("time and chance") that could be called vague. The second contains not a single fresh, arresting phrase, and in spite of its ninety syllables it gives only a shortened version of the meaning contained in the first. Yet without a doubt it is the second kind of sentence that is gaining ground in modern English. I do not want to exaggerate. This kind of writing is not yet universal, and outcrops of simplicity will occur here and there in the worst-written page. Still, if you or I were told to write a few lines on the uncertainty of human fortunes, we should probably come much nearer to my imaginary sentence than to the one from *Ecclesiastes*.

As I have tried to show, modern writing at its worst does not consist in picking out words for the sake of their meaning and inventing images in order to make the meaning clearer. It consists in gumming together long strips of words which have already been set in order by someone else, and making the results presentable by sheer humbug. The attraction of this way of writing is that it is easy. It is easier — even quicker, once you have the habit — to say *In my opinion it is a not unjustifiable assumption that* than to say *I think*. If you use ready-made phrases, you not only don't have to hunt about for words; you also don't have to bother with the rhythms of your sentences, since these phrases are generally so arranged as to be more or less euphonious. When you are composing in a hurry — when you are dictating to a stenographer, for instance, or making a public speech — it is natural to fall into a pretentious, Latinized style. Tags like *a consideration which we should do well to bear in mind* or *a conclusion to which all of us would readily assent* will save many a sentence from coming down with a bump. By using stale metaphors, similes and idioms, you save much mental effort, at the cost of leaving your meaning vague, not only for your reader but for yourself. This is the significance of mixed metaphors. The sole aim of a metaphor is to call up a visual image. When these images clash — as in *The Fascist octopus has sung its swan song, the jackboot is thrown into the melting pot* — it can be taken as certain that the writer is not seeing a mental image of the objects he is naming; in other words he is not really thinking. Look again at the examples I gave at the beginning of this essay. Professor Laski (1) uses five negatives in fifty-three words. One of these is superfluous, making nonsense of the whole passage, and in addition there is the slip *alien* for akin, making further nonsense, and several avoidable pieces of clumsiness which increase the general vagueness. Professor Hogben (2) plays ducks and drakes with a battery which is able to write prescriptions, and, while disapproving of the everyday phrase *put up with*, is unwilling to look *egregious* up in the dictionary and see what it means. (3), if one takes an uncharitable attitude towards it, is simply meaningless: probably one could work out its intended meaning by reading the whole of the article in which it occurs. In (4), the writer knows more or less what he wants to say, but an accumulation of stale phrases chokes him like tea leaves blocking a sink. In (5), words and meaning have almost parted company. People who write in this manner usually have a general emotional meaning — they dislike one thing and want to express solidarity with another — but they are not interested in the detail of what they are saying. A scrupulous writer, in every sentence that he writes, will ask himself at least four questions, thus: What am I trying to say? What words will express it? What image or idiom will make it clearer? Is this image fresh enough to have an effect? And he will probably ask himself two more: Could I put it more shortly? Have I said anything that is avoidably ugly? But you are not obliged to go to all this trouble. You can shirk it by simply throwing your mind open and letting the ready-made phrases come crowding in. They will construct your sentences for you — even think your thoughts for you, to a certain extent — and at need they will perform the important service of partially concealing your meaning even from yourself. It is at this point that the special connection between politics and the debasement of language becomes clear.

In our time it is broadly true that political writing is bad writing. Where it is not true, it will generally be found that the writer is some kind of rebel, expressing his private opinions and not a "party line." Orthodoxy, of whatever colour, seems to demand a lifeless, imitative style. The political dialects to be found in pamphlets, leading articles, manifestos, White Papers and the speeches of under-secretaries do, of course, vary from party to party, but they are all alike in that one almost never finds in them a fresh, vivid, home-made turn of speech. When one watches some tired hack on the platform mechanically repeating the familiar phrases — *bestial atrocities, iron heel, blood-stained tyranny, free peoples of the world, stand shoulder to shoulder* — one often has a curious feeling that one is not watching a live human being but some kind of dummy: a feeling which suddenly becomes stronger at moments when the light catches the speaker's spectacles and turns them into blank discs which seem to have no eyes behind them. And this is not altogether fanciful. A speaker who uses that kind of phraseology has gone some distance towards turning himself into a machine. The appropriate noises are coming out of his larynx, but his brain is not involved as it would be if he were choosing his words for himself. If the speech he is making is one that he is accustomed to make over and over again, he may be almost unconscious of what he is saying, as one is when one utters the responses in church. And this reduced state of consciousness, if not indispensable, is at any rate favourable to political conformity.

In our time, political speech and writing are largely the defence of the indefensible. Things like the continuance of British rule in India, the Russian purges and deportations, the dropping of the atom bombs on Japan, can indeed be defended, but only by arguments which are too brutal for most people to face, and which do not square with the professed aims of political parties. Thus political language has to consist largely of euphemism, question-begging and sheer cloudy vagueness. Defenceless villages are bombarded from the air, the inhabitants driven out into the countryside, the cattle machine-gunned, the huts set on fire with incendiary bullets: this is called *pacification*. Millions of peasants are robbed of their farms and sent trudging along the roads with no more than they can carry: this is called *transfer of population* or *rectification of frontiers*. People are imprisoned for years without trial, or shot in the back of the neck or sent to die of scurvy in Arctic lumber camps: this is called *elimination of unreliable elements*. Such phraseology is needed if one wants to name things without calling up mental pictures of them. Consider for instance some comfortable English professor defending Russian totalitarianism. He cannot say outright, "I believe in killing off your opponents when you can get good results by doing so." Probably, therefore, he will say something like this:

"While freely conceding that the Soviet régime exhibits certain features which the humanitarian may be inclined to deplore, we must, I think, agree that a certain curtailment of the right to political opposition is an unavoidable concomitant of transitional periods, and that the rigours which the Russian people have been called upon to undergo have been amply justified in the sphere of concrete achievement."

The inflated style is itself a kind of euphemism. A mass of Latin words falls upon the facts like soft snow, blurring the outlines and covering up all the details. The great enemy of clear language is insincerity. When there is a gap between one's real and one's declared aims, one turns as it were instinctively to long words and exhausted idioms, like a cuttlefish squirting out ink. In our age there is no such thing as "keeping out of politics." All issues are political issues, and politics itself is a mass of lies, evasions, folly, hatred and schizophrenia. When the general atmosphere is bad, language must suffer. I should expect to find — this is a guess which I have not sufficient knowledge to verify — that the German, Russian and Italian languages have all deteriorated in the last ten or fifteen years, as a result of dictatorship.

But if thought corrupts language, language can also corrupt thought. A bad usage can spread by tradition and imitation, even among people who should and do know better. The debased language that I have been discussing is in some ways very convenient. Phrases like *a not unjustifiable assumption, leaves much to be desired, would serve no good purpose, a consideration which we should do well to bear in mind,* are a continuous temptation, a packet of aspirins always at one's elbow. Look back through this essay, and for certain you will find that I have again and again committed the very faults I am protesting against. By this morning's post I have received a pamphlet dealing with conditions in Germany. The author tells me that he "felt impelled" to write it. I open it at random, and here is almost the first sentence that I see: "(The Allies) have an opportunity not only of achieving a radical transformation of Germany's social and political structure in such a way as to avoid a nationalistic reaction in Germany itself, but at the same time of laying the foundations of a cooperative and unified Europe." You see, he "feels impelled" to write — feels, presumably, that he has something new to say — and yet his words, like cavalry horses answering the bugle, group themselves automatically into the familiar dreary pattern. This invasion of one's mind by ready-made phrases (*lay the foundations, achieve a radical transformation*) can only be prevented if one is constantly on guard against them, and every such phrase anaesthetizes a portion of one's brain.

I said earlier that the decadence of our language is probably curable. Those who deny this would argue, if they produced an argument at all, that language merely reflects existing social conditions, and that we cannot influence its development by any direct tinkering with words and constructions. So far as the general tone or spirit of a language goes, this may be true, but it is not true in detail. Silly words and expressions have often disappeared, not through any evolutionary process but owing to the conscious action of a minority. Two recent examples were *explore every avenue* and *leave no stone unturned,* which were killed by the jeers of a few journalists. There is a long list of fly-blown metaphors which could similarly be got rid of if enough people would interest themselves in the job; and it should also be possible to laugh the *not un-* formation out of existence,[3] reduce the amount of Latin and Greek in the average sentence, to drive out foreign phrases and strayed scientific words, and, in general, to make pretentiousness unfashionable. But all these are minor points. The defence of the English language implies more than this, and perhaps it is best to start by saying what it does *not* imply.

To begin with it has nothing to do with archaism, with the salvaging of obsolete words and turns of speech, or with the setting up of a "standard English" which must never be departed from. On the contrary, it is especially concerned with the scrapping of every word or idiom which has outworn its usefulness. It has nothing to do with correct grammar and syntax, which are of no importance so long as one makes one's meaning clear, or with the avoidance of Americanisms, or with having what is called a "good prose style." On the other hand it is not concerned with fake simplicity and the attempt to make written English colloquial. Nor does it even imply in every case preferring the Saxon word to the Latin one, though it does imply using the fewest and shortest words that will cover one's meaning. What is above all needed is to let the meaning choose the word, and not the other way about. In prose, the worst thing one can do with words is to surrender to them. When you think of a concrete object, you think wordlessly, and then, if you want to describe the thing you have been visualizing you probably hunt about till you

[3] One can cure oneself of the *not un-* formation by memorizing this sentence: *A not unblack dog was chasing a not unsmall rabbit across a not ungreen field.* (Orwell's note)

find the exact words that seem to fit it. When you think of something abstract you are more inclined to use words from the start, and unless you make a conscious effort to prevent it, the existing dialect will come rushing in and do the job for you, at the expense of blurring or even changing your meaning. Probably it is better to put off using words as long as possible and get one's meaning as clear as one can through pictures or sensations. Afterwards one can choose — not simply *accept* — the phrases that will best cover the meaning, and then switch round and decide what impression one's words are likely to make on another person. This last effort of the mind cuts out all stale or mixed images, all prefabricated phrases, needless repetitions, and humbug and vagueness generally. But one can often be in doubt about the effect of a word or a phrase, and one needs rules that one can rely on when instinct fails. I think the following rules will cover most cases:

(i) Never use a metaphor, simile or other figure of speech which you are used to seeing in print.

(ii) Never use a long word where a short one will do.

(iii) If it is possible to cut a word out, always cut it out.

(iv) Never use the passive where you can use the active.

(v) Never use a foreign phrase, a scientific word or a jargon word if you can think of an everyday English equivalent.

(vi) Break any of these rules sooner than say anything outright barbarous.

These rules sound elementary, and so they are, but they demand a deep change of attitude in anyone who has grown used to writing in the style now fashionable. One could keep all of them and still write bad English, but one could not write the kind of stuff that I quoted in those five specimens at the beginning of this article.

I have not here been considering the literary use of language, but merely language as an instrument for expressing and not for concealing or preventing thought. Stuart Chase and others have come near to claiming that all abstract words are meaningless, and have used this as a pretext for advocating a kind of political quietism. Since you don't know what Fascism is, how can you struggle against Fascism? One need not swallow such absurdities as this, but one ought to recognize that the present political chaos is connected with the decay of language, and that one can probably bring about some improvement by starting at the verbal end. If you simplify your English, you are freed from the worst follies of orthodoxy. You cannot speak any of the necessary dialects, and when you make a stupid remark its stupidity will be obvious, even to yourself. Political language — and with variations this is true of all political parties, from Conservatives to Anarchists — is designed to make lies sound truthful and murder respectable, and to give an appearance of solidity to pure wind. One cannot change this all in a moment, but one can at least change one's own habits, and from time to time one can even, if one jeers loudly enough, send some worn-out and useless phrase — some *jackboot, Achilles' heel, hotbed, melting pot, acid test, veritable inferno* or other lump of verbal refuse — into the dustbin where it belongs.

W. H. Auden (b. 1907)

AMERICAN POET (ENGLISH-BORN)

Musée des Beaux Arts

About suffering they were never wrong,
The Old Masters: how well they understood
Its human position; how it takes place
While someone else is eating or opening a window or
    just walking dully along;
How, when the aged are reverently, passionately
    waiting
For the miraculous birth, there always must be
Children who did not specially want it to happen,
    skating
On a pond at the edge of the wood:
They never forgot
That even the dreadful martyrdom must run its
    course   10
Anyhow in a corner, some untidy spot
Where the dogs go on with their doggy life and the
    torturer's horse
Scratches its innocent behind on a tree.

In Brueghel's *Icarus*, for instance: how everything
    turns away
Quite leisurely from the disaster; the ploughman may
Have heard the splash, the forsaken cry,
But for him it was not an important failure; the sun
    shone
As it had to on the white legs disappearing into the
    green
Water; and the expensive delicate ship that must
    have seen
Something amazing, a boy falling out of the sky,   20
Had somewhere to get to and sailed calmly on.

Old Masters: 16th/17th century Dutch and Flemish painters whose large genre scenes of everyday life include references to suffering and tragedy (usually from the Bible or mythology)

Brueghel's Icarus: reference to Pieter Brueghel the Elder's painting "The Fall of Icarus"

Musée des Beaux Arts: the Fine Arts Museum, Brussels. From *Collected Shorter Poems 1927–1957*, by W. H. Auden. © Copyright 1966 by W. H. Auden. Reprinted by permission of Random House, Inc., and Faber and Faber Ltd., London.

Dylan Thomas (1914–1953)

WELSH POET

In My Craft or Sullen Art

In my craft or sullen art
Exercised in the still night
When only the moon rages
And the lovers lie abed
With all their griefs in their arms,
I labour by singing light
Not for ambition or bread
Or the strut and trade of charms
On the ivory stages
But for the common wages   10
Of their most secret heart.

Not for the proud man apart
From the raging moon I write
On these spindrift pages
Nor for the towering dead
With their nightingales and psalms
But for the lovers, their arms
Round the griefs of the ages,
Who pay no praise or wages
Nor heed my craft or art.   20

Ingmar Bergman (b. 1918)

SWEDISH FILM DIRECTOR

The Magic of Film

My association with film goes back to the world of childhood.

My grandmother had a very large old apartment in Uppsala. I used to sit under the dining-room table there, "listening" to the sunshine which came in through the gigantic windows. The cathedral bells went ding-dong, and the sunlight moved about and "sounded" in a special way. One day, when winter was giving way to spring and I was five years old, a piano was being played in the next apartment. It played waltzes, nothing but waltzes. On the wall hung a large picture of Venice. As the sunlight moved across the picture the water in the canal began to flow, the pigeons flew up from the square, people talked and gesticulated. Bells sounded, not those of Uppsala Cathedral but from the picture itself. And the piano music also came from that remarkable picture of Venice.

A child who is born and brought up in a vicarage acquires an early familiarity with life and death behind the scenes. Father performed funerals, marriages, baptisms, gave advice and prepared sermons. The devil was an early acquaintance, and in the child's mind there was a need to personify him. This is where my magic lantern came in. It consisted of a small metal box with a carbide lamp — I can still remember the smell of the hot metal — and colored glass slides: Red Riding Hood and the Wolf, and all the others. And the Wolf was the Devil, without horns but with a tail and a gaping red mouth, strangely real yet incomprehensible, a picture of wickedness and temptation on the flowered wall of the nursery.

When I was ten years old I received my first, rattling film projector, with its chimney and lamp. I found it both mystifying and fascinating. The first film I had was nine feet long and brown in color. It showed a girl lying asleep in a meadow, who woke up and stretched out her arms, then disappeared to the right. That was all there was to it. The film was a great success and was projected every night until it broke and could not be mended any more.

This little rickety machine was my first conjuring set. And even today I remind myself with childish excitement that I am really a conjurer, since cinematography is based on deception of the human eye. I have worked it out that if I see a film which has a running time of one hour, I sit through twenty-seven minutes of complete darkness — the blankness between frames. When I show a film I am guilty of deceit. I use an apparatus which is constructed to take advantage of a certain human weakness, an apparatus with which I can sway my audience in a highly emotional manner — make them laugh, scream with fright, smile, believe in fairy stories, become indignant, feel shocked, charmed, deeply moved or perhaps yawn with boredom. Thus I am either an impostor or, when the audience is willing to be taken in, a conjurer. I perform conjuring tricks with apparatus so expensive and so wonderful that any entertainer in history would have given anything to have it.

A film for me begins with something very vague — a chance remark or a bit of conversation, a hazy but agreeable event unrelated to any particular situation. It can be a few bars of music, a shaft of light across the street. Sometimes in my work at the theater I have envisioned actors made up for yet unplayed roles.

These are split-second impressions that disappear as quickly as they come, yet leave behind a mood — like pleasant dreams. It is a mental state, not an actual story, but one abounding in fertile associations and images. Most of all, it is a brightly colored thread sticking out of the dark sack of the unconscious. If I begin to wind up this thread, and do it carefully, a complete film will emerge.

This primitive nucleus strives to achieve definite form, moving in a way that may be lazy and half asleep at first. Its stirring is accompanied by vibrations and rhythms which are very special and unique to each film. The picture sequences then assume a pattern in accordance with these rhythms, obeying laws born out of and conditioned by my original stimulus.

If that embryonic substance seems to have enough strength to be made into a film, I decide to materialize it. Then comes something very complicated and difficult: the transformation of rhythms, moods, atmosphere, tensions, sequences, tones and scents into words and sentences, into an understandable screenplay.

This is an almost impossible task.

The only thing that can be satisfactorily transferred from that original complex of rhythms and moods is the dialogue, and even dialogue is a sensitive substance which may offer resistance. Written dialogue is like a musical score, almost incomprehensible to the average person. Its interpretation demands a technical knack plus a certain kind of imagination and feeling — qualities which are so often lacking, even among actors. One can write dialogue, but how it should be delivered, its rhythm and tempo, what is to take place between lines — all this must be omitted for practical reasons. Such a detailed script would be unreadable. I try to squeeze instructions as to location, characterization and atmosphere into my screenplays in understandable terms, but the success of this depends on my writing ability and the perceptiveness of the reader, which are not always predictable.

Now we come to essentials, by which I mean montage, rhythm and the relation of one picture to another — the vital third dimension without which the film is merely a dead product from a factory. Here I cannot clearly give a key, as in a musical score, nor a specific idea of the tempo which determines the relationship of the elements involved. It is quite impossible for me to indicate the way in which the film "breathes" and pulsates.

I have often wished for a kind of notation which would enable me to put on paper all the shades and tones of my vision, to record distinctly the inner structure of a film. For when I stand in the artistically devastating atmosphere of the studio, my hands and head full of all the trivial and irritating details that go with motion-picture production, it often takes a tremendous effort to remember how I originally saw and thought out this or that sequence, or what was the relation between the scene of four weeks ago and that of today. If I could express myself clearly, in explicit symbols, then this problem would be almost eliminated and I could work with absolute confidence that whenever I liked I could prove the relationship between the part and the whole and put my finger on the rhythm, the continuity of the film.

Thus the script is a very imperfect *technical* basis for a film. And there is another important point in this connection which I should like to mention.

Film has nothing to do with literature; the character and substance of the two art forms are usually in conflict. This probably has something to do with the receptive process of the mind. The written word is read and assimilated by a conscious act of the will in alliance with the intellect; little by little it affects the imagination and the emotions. The process is different with a motion picture. When we experience a film, we consciously prime ourselves for illusion. Putting aside will and intellect, we make way for it in our imagination. The sequence of pictures plays directly on our feelings.

Music works in the same fashion; I would say that there is no art form that has so much in common with film as music. Both affect our emotions directly, not via the intellect. And film is mainly rhythm; it is inhalation and exhalation in continuous sequence. Ever since childhood, music has been my great source of recreation and stimulation, and I often experience a film or play musically.

It is mainly because of this difference between film and literature that we should avoid making films out of books. The irrational dimension of a literary work, the germ of its existence, is often untranslatable into visual terms —and it, in turn, destroys the special, irrational dimension of the film. If, despite this, we wish to translate something literary into film terms, we must make an infinite number of complicated adjustments which often bear little or no fruit in proportion to the effort expended.

I myself have never had any ambition to be an author. I do not want to write novels, short stories, essays, biographies, or even plays for the theater. I only want to make films — films about conditions, tensions, pictures, rhythms and characters which are in one way or another important to me. The motion picture, with its complicated process of birth, is my method of saying what I want to my fellow men. I am a film-maker, not an author.

Thus the writing of the script is a difficult period but a useful one, for it compels me to prove logically the validity of my ideas. In doing this, I am caught in a conflict — a conflict between my need to transmit a complicated situation through visual images, and my desire for absolute clarity. I do not intend my work to be solely for the benefit of myself or the few, but for the entertainment of the general public. The wishes of the public are imperative. But sometimes I risk following my own impulse, and it has been shown that the public can respond with surprising sensitivity to the most unconventional line of development.

When shooting begins, the most important thing is that those who work with me feel a definite contact, that all of us somehow cancel out our conflicts through working together. We must pull in one direction for the sake of the work at hand. Sometimes this leads to dispute, but the more definite and clear the "marching orders," the easier it is to reach the goal which has been set. This is the basis for my conduct as director, and perhaps the explanation of much of the nonsense that has been written about me.

While I cannot let myself be concerned with what people think and say about me personally, I believe that reviewers and critics have every right to interpret my films as they like. I refuse to interpret my work to others, and I cannot tell the critic what to think; each person has the right to understand a film as he sees it. Either he is attracted or repelled. A film is made to create reaction. If the audience does not react one way or another, it is an indifferent work and worthless.

I do not mean by this that I believe in being "different" at any price. A lot has been said about the value of originality, and I find this foolish. Either you are original or you are not. It is completely natural for artists to take from and give to each other, to borrow from and experience one another. In my own life, my great literary experience was Strindberg. There are works of his which can still make my hair stand on end — *The People of Hemsö*, for example. And it is my dream to produce *Dream Play* some day. Olof Molander's production of it in 1934 was for me a fundamental dramatic experience.

On a personal level, there are many people who have meant a great deal to me. My father and mother were certainly of vital importance, not only in themselves but because they created a world for me to revolt against. In my family there was an atmosphere of hearty wholesomeness which I, a sensitive young plant, scorned and rebelled against. But that strict middle-class home gave me a wall to pound on, something to sharpen myself against. At the same time they taught me a number of values — efficiency, punctuality, a sense of financial responsibility — which may be "bourgeois" but are nevertheless important to the artist. They are part of the process of setting oneself severe standards. Today as a film-maker I am conscientious, hard-working and extremely careful; my films involve good craftsmanship, and my pride is the pride of a good craftsman.

Among the people who have meant something in my professional development is Torsten Hammaren of Gothenburg. I went there from Hälsingborg, where I had been head of the municipal theater for two years. I had no conception of what theater was; Hammaren taught me during the four years I stayed in Gothenburg. Then, when I made my first attempts at film, Alf Sjöberg — who directed *Torment* — taught me a great deal. And there was Lorens Marmstedt, who really taught me film-making from scratch after my first unsuccessful movie. Among other things I learned from Marmstedt is the one unbreakable rule: you must look at your own work very coldly and clearly; you must be a devil to yourself in the screening room when watching the day's rushes. Then there is Herbert Grevenius, one of the few who believed in me as a writer. I had trouble with script-writing, and was reaching out more and more to the drama, to dialogue, as a means of expression. He gave me great encouragement.

Finally, there is Carl Anders Dymling, my producer. He is crazy enough to place more faith in the sense of responsibility of a creative artist than in calculations of profit and loss. I am thus able to work with an integrity that has become the very air I breathe, and one of the main reasons I do not want to work outside of Sweden. The moment I lose this freedom I will cease to be a film-maker, because I have no skill in the art of compromise. My only significance in the world of film lies in the freedom of my creativity.

Today, the ambitious film-maker is obliged to walk a tightrope without a net. He may be a conjurer, but no one conjures the producer, the bank director or the theater owners when the public refuses to go see a film and lay down the money by which producer, bank director, theater owner and conjurer can live. The conjurer may then be deprived of his magic wand; I would like to be able to measure the amount of talent, initiative and creative ability which has been destroyed by the film industry in its ruthlessly efficient sausage machine. What was play to me once has now become a struggle. Failure, criticism, public indifference all hurt more today than yesterday. The brutality of the industry is undisguised — yet that can be an advantage.

So much for people and the film business. I have been asked, as a clergyman's son, about the role of religion in my thinking and film-making. To me, religious problems are continuously alive. I never cease to concern myself with them; it goes on every hour of every day. Yet this does not take place on the emotional level, but on an intellectual one. Religious emotion, religious sentimentality, is something I got rid of long ago — I hope. The religious problem is an intellectual one to me; the relationship of my mind to my intuition. The result of this conflict is usually some kind of tower of Babel.

Philosophically, there is a book which was a tremendous experience for me: Eiono Kaila's *Psychology of the Personality*. His thesis that man lives strictly according to his needs — negative and positive — was shattering to me, but terribly true. And I built on this ground.

People ask what are my intentions with my films — my aims. It is a difficult and dangerous question, and I usually give an evasive answer: I try to tell the truth about the human condition, the truth as I see it. This answer seems to satisfy everyone, but it is not quite correct. I prefer to describe what I *would like* my aim to be.

There is an old story of how the cathedral of Chartres was struck by lightning and burned to the ground. Then thousands of people came from all points of the compass, like a giant procession of ants, and together they began to rebuild the cathedral on its old site. They worked until the building was completed — master builders, artists, laborers, clowns, noblemen, priests, burghers. But they all remained anonymous, and no one knows to this day who built the cathedral of Chartres.

Regardless of my own beliefs and my own doubts, which are unimportant in this connection, it is my opinion that art lost its basic creative drive the moment it was separated from worship. It severed an umbilical cord and now lives its own sterile life, generating and degenerating itself. In former days the artist remained unknown and his work was to the glory of God. He lived and died without being more or less important than other artisans; "eternal values," "immortality" and "masterpiece" were terms not applicable in his

ase. The ability to create was a gift. In such a world flourished invulnerable
ssurance and natural humility.

Today the individual has become the highest form and the greatest bane
of artistic creation. The smallest wound or pain of the ego is examined under
a microscope as if it were of eternal importance. The artist considers his
isolation, his subjectivity, his individualism almost holy. Thus we finally
gather in one large pen, where we stand and bleat about our loneliness without
listening to each other and without realizing that we are smothering each
other to death. The individualists stare into each other's eyes and yet deny
the existence of each other. We walk in circles, so limited by our own
anxieties that we can no longer distinguish between true and false, between
the gangster's whim and the purest ideal.

Thus if I am asked what I would like the general purpose of my films to
be, I would reply that I want to be one of the artists in the cathedral on the
great plain. I want to make a dragon's head, an angel, a devil — or perhaps
a saint — out of stone. It does not matter which; it is the sense of satisfaction
that counts. Regardless of whether I believe or not, whether I am a Christian
or not, I would play my part in the collective building of the cathedral.

Günter Grass (b. 1927)

GERMAN NOVELIST, POET, DRAMATIST, and ARTIST

The Onion Cellar

Seen from the street, the Onion Cellar looked like many of the newer night
clubs which are distinguished from the older bars and cabarets by, among
other things, their higher prices. The higher prices were justified by the
outlandish decoration of these night spots, many of which termed themselves
"Artists' clubs" and also by their names. There was "The Ravioli Room"
(discreet and refined), "The Taboo" (mysterious and existentialist), "The
Paprika" (spicy and high-spirited). And of course there was "The Onion
Cellar".

The words "Onion Cellar" and a poignantly naïve likeness of an onion had
been painted with deliberate awkwardness on an enamel sign which hung in
the old German manner from elaborate wrought-iron gallows in front of the
house. The one and only window was glassed with bottle-green bull's-eye

From *The Tin Drum*, by Günter Grass, translated by Ralph Manheim. © Copyright
1961, 1962 by Pantheon Books, a Division of Random House, Inc. Reprinted by permission.

panes. The iron door, painted with red lead, had no doubt seen service outside an air-raid shelter in the war years. Outside it stood the doorman in a rustic sheepskin. Not everyone was allowed in the Onion Cellar. Especially on Fridays, when wages turn to beer, it was the doorman's business to turn away certain Old City characters, for whom the Onion Cellar was too expensive in the first place. Behind the red-lead door, those who were allowed in found five concrete steps. You went down, found yourself on a landing some three feet square, to which a poster for a Picasso show lent an original, artistic turn. Four more steps took you to the checkroom. "Please pay later," said a little cardboard sign, and indeed, the young man at the counter, usually an art student with a beard, refused to take money in advance, because the Onion Cellar was not only expensive but also and nevertheless high class.

The owner in person welcomed every single guest with elaborate gestures and mobile, expressive eyebrows, as though initiating him into a secret rite. As we know, the owner's name was Ferdinand Schmuh; he was a man who shot sparrows now and then, and had a keen eye for the society which had sprung up in Düsseldorf (and elsewhere, though not quite so quickly) since the currency reform.

The Onion Cellar — and here we see the note of authenticity essential to a successful night club — was a real cellar; in fact, it was quite damp and chilly under foot. Tubular in shape, it measured roughly thirteen by sixty, and was heated by two authentic cast-iron stoves. Yet in one respect the Cellar wasn't a cellar after all. The ceiling had been taken off, so that the club actually included the former ground-floor apartment. The one and only window was not a real cellar window, but the former window of the ground-floor apartment. However, since one might have looked out of the window if not for its opaque bull's-eye panes; since there was a gallery that one reached by a highly original and highly precipitous staircase, the Onion Cellar can reasonably be termed "authentic", even if it was not a real cellar — and besides, why should it have been?

Oskar[1] has forgotten to tell you that the staircase leading to the gallery was not a real staircase but more like a companionway, because on either side of its dangerously steep steps there were two extremely original clotheslines to hold on to; the staircase swayed a bit, making you think of an ocean voyage and adding to the price.

The Onion Cellar was lighted by acetylene lamps such as miners carry, which broadcast a smell of carbide — again adding to the price — and transported the customer unto the gallery of a mine, a potash mine for instance, three thousand feet below the surface of the earth: cutters bare to the waist hack away at the rock, opening up a vein; the scraper hauls out the salt, the windlass roars as it fills the cars; far behind, where the gallery turns off to Friedrichshall Two, a swaying light; that's the head foreman and here he

[1] a midget who is the protagonist of Grass's novel.

comes with a cheery hello, swinging a carbide lamp that looks exactly like the carbide lamps that hung from the unadorned, slapdashly whitewashed walls of the Onion Cellar, casting their light and smell, adding to the prices, and creating an original atmosphere.

The customers were uncomfortably seated on common crates covered with onion sacks, yet the plank tables scrubbed and spotless, recalled the guests from the mine to a peaceful peasant inn such as we sometimes see in the movies.

That was all! But what about the bar? No bar. Waiter, the menu please! Neither waiter nor menu. In fact, there was no one else but ourselves, the Rhine River Three. Klepp, Scholle, and Oskar sat beneath the staircase that was really a companionway. We arrived at nine, unpacked our instruments, and began to play at about ten. But for the present it is only a quarter past nine and I won't be able to speak about us until later. Right now let us keep an eye on Schmuh, who occasionally spot sparrows with a small-caliber rifle.

As soon as the Onion Cellar had filled up — half-full was regarded as full — Schmuh, the host, donned his shawl. This shawl had been specially made for him. It was cobalt-blue silk, printed with a golden-yellow pattern. I mention all this because the donning of the shawl was significant. The pattern printed on the shawl was made up of golden-yellow onions. The Onion Cellar was not really "open" until Schmuh had put on his shawl.

The customers — businessmen, doctors, lawyers, artists, journalists, theater and movie people, well-known figures from the sporting world, officials in the provincial and municipal government, in short, a cross section of the world which nowadays calls itself intellectual — came with wives, mistresses, secretaries, interior decorators, and occasional male mistresses, to sit on crates covered with burlap. Until Schmuh put on his golden-yellow onions, the conversation was subdued, forced, dispirited. These people wanted to talk, to unburden themselves, but they couldn't seem to get started; despite all their efforts, they left the essential unsaid, talked around it. Yet how eager they were to spill their guts, to talk from their hearts, their bowels, their entrails, to forget about their brains just this once, to lay bare the raw, unvarnished truth, the man within. Here and there a stifled remark about a botched career, a broken marriage. One gathers that the gentleman over there with the massive head, the intelligent face and soft, almost delicate hands, is having trouble with his son, who is displeased about his father's past. Those two ladies in mink, who still look quite attractive in the light of the carbide lamp, claim to have lost their faith, but they don't say in what. So far we know nothing about the past of the gentleman with the massive head, nor have we the slightest idea what sort of trouble his son is making for him on account of this unknown past; if you'll forgive Oskar a crude metaphor, it was like laying eggs; you push and push . . .

The pushing in the Onion Cellar brought meager results until Schmuh appeared in his special shawl. Having been welcomed with a joyful "Ah!"

for which he thanked his kind guests, he vanished for a few minutes behind a curtain at the end of the Onion Cellar, where the toilets and storeroom were situated.

But why did a still more joyous "Ah", an "Ah" of relief and release, welcome the host on his reappearance? The proprietor of a successful nightclub disappears behind a curtain, takes something from the storeroom, flings a choice selection of insults in an undertone at the washroom attendant who is sitting there reading an illustrated weekly, reappears in front of the curtain and is welcomed like the Saviour, like the legendary uncle from Australia!

Schmuh came back with a little basket on his arm and moved among the guests. The basket was covered with a blue-and-yellow checkered napkin. On the cloth lay a considerable number of little wooden boards, shaped like pigs or fish. There he handed out to his guests with little bows and compliments which showed, beyond the shadow of a doubt, that he had grown up in Budapest and Vienna; Schmuh's smile was like the smile on a copy of a copy of the supposedly authentic Mona Lisa.

The guests, however, looked very serious as they took their little boards. Some exchanged boards with their neighbors, for some preferred the silhouette of a pig, while others preferred the more mysterious fish. They sniffed at the pieces of wood and moved them about. Schmuh, after serving the customers in the gallery, waited until all the little boards had come to rest.

Then — and every heart was waiting — he removed the napkin, very much in the manner of a magician: beneath it lay still another napkin, upon which, almost unrecognizable at first glance, lay the paring knives.

These too he proceeded to hand out. But this time he made his rounds more quickly, whipping up the tension that permitted him to raise his prices; he paid no more compliments, and left no time for any exchanges of knives; a calculated haste entered into his movements. "On your mark, get set," he shouted. At "Go" he tore the napkin off the basket, reached into the basket and handed out, dispensed, distributed among the multitude . . . onions — onions such as were represented, golden-yellow and slightly stylized, on his shawl, plain ordinary onions, not tulip bulbs, but onions such as women buy in the market, such as the vegetable woman sells, such as the peasant, the peasant's wife, or the hired girl plants and harvests, onions such as may be seen, more or less faithfully portrayed in the still lifes of the lesser Dutch masters. Such onions, then, Schmuh dispensed among his guests until each had an onion and no sound could be heard but the purring of the stoves and the whistling of the carbide lamps. For the grand distribution of onions was followed by silence. Into which Ferdinand Schmuh cried: "Ladies and gentlemen, help yourselves." And he tossed one end of his shawl over his left shoulder like a skier just before the start. This was the signal.

The guests peeled the onions. Onions are said to have seven skins. The ladies and gentlemen peeled the onions with the paring knives. They removed the first, third, blond, golden-yellow, rust-brown, or better still, onion-colored skin, they peeled until the onion became glassy, green, whitish, damp.

and watery-sticky, until it smelled, smelled like an onion. Then they cut it as one cuts onions, deftly or clumsily, on the little chopping boards shaped like pigs or fish; they cut in one direction and another until the juice spurted or turned to vapor — the older gentlemen were not very handy with paring knives and had to be careful not to cut their fingers; some cut themselves even so, but didn't notice it — the ladies were more skillful, not all of them, but those at least who were housewives at home, who knew how one cuts up onions for hash-brown potatoes, or for liver with apples and onion rings; but in Schmuh's onion cellar there was neither, there was nothing whatever to eat, and anyone who wanted to eat had to go elsewhere, to the "Fischl", for instance, for at the Onion Cellar onions were only cut. Why all these onions? For one thing, because of the name. The Onion Cellar had its specialty: onions. And moreover, the onion, the cut onion, when you look at it closely . . . but enough of that, Schmuh's guests had stopped looking, they could see nothing more, because their eyes were running over and not because their hearts were so full; for it is not true that when the heart is full the eyes necessarily overflow, some people can never manage it, especially in our century, which in spite of all the suffering and sorrow will surely be known to posterity as the tearless century. It was this drought, this tearlessness that brought those who could afford it to Schmuh's Onion Cellar, where the host handed them a little chopping board — pig or fish — a paring knife for eighty pfennigs, and for twelve marks an ordinary field-, garden-, and kitchen-variety onion, and induced them to cut their onions smaller and smaller until the juice — what did the onion juice do? It did what the world and the sorrows of the world could not do: it brought forth a round, human tear. It made them cry. At last they were able to cry again. To cry properly, without restraint, to cry like mad. The tears flowed and washed everything away. The rain came. The dew. Oskar has a vision of floodgates opening. Of dams bursting in the spring floods. What is the name of that river that overflows every spring and the government does nothing to stop it?

After this cataclysm at twelve marks eighty, human beings who have had a good cry open their mouths to speak. Still hesitant, startled by the nakedness of their own words, the weepers poured out their hearts to their neighbors on the uncomfortable, burlap-covered crates, submitted to questioning, let themselves be turned inside-out like overcoats. But Oskar, who with Klepp and Scholle sat tearless behind the staircase or companionway, will be discreet; from among all the disclosures, self-accusations, confessions that fell on his ears, he will relate only the story of Miss Pioch, who lost her Mr. Vollmer many times over, so acquiring a strong heart and a tearless eye, which necessitated frequent visits to Schmuh's Onion Cellar.

We met, said Miss Pioch when she had finished crying, in the streetcar. I had just come from the store — she owns and operates an excellent bookstore. The car was full and Willy — that's Mr. Vollmer — stepped on my right foot. He stepped so hard that I couldn't stand on it any more, and we loved each other at first sight. I couldn't walk either, so he offered me his arm, escorted, or rather carried, me home, and from that day on he took loving care of the toenail which had turned black and blue under his heel. He loved me, not just my toe, until the toenail came loose from its toe — the right big toe — and there was nothing to prevent a new toenail from growing in. The day the dead toenail fell, his love began to cool. Both of us were miserable about it. It was then that Willy — he still cared for me in a way and, besides, we had so much in common — had his terrible idea. Let me, he pleaded, trample your left big toe until the nail turns a light, then a darker purple. I consented and he trampled. Again he loved me with his whole being, and his love endured until my big toenail, the left one it was, fell away like a withered leaf; and then it was autumn again for our love. Willy wanted to start in again on my right big toe, the nail had meanwhile grown in again. But I wouldn't let him. If your love for me is really so overpowering, I said, it ought to outlast a toenail. He couldn't seem to understand. He left me. Months later, we met at a concert. The seat beside me happened to be unoccupied and after the intermission he sat down in it. They were doing the *Ninth Symphony*. When the chorus started up, I removed the shoe from my right foot and held the foot out in front of him. He stepped on it with might and main, but I didn't do anything to interfere with the concert. Seven weeks later Willy left me again. We had two more brief reprieves; twice more I held out my toe, first the left one, then the right one. Today both my toes are maimed. The nails won't grow in again. From time to time Willy comes to see me; shaken, full of pity for me and for himself, he sits at my feet on the rug and stares, unloving and unweeping, at the two nailless victims of our love. Sometimes I say: Come along Willy, let's go to Schmuh's Onion Cellar and have a good cry. But so far he has refused to come. What the poor soul must suffer without the consolation of tears!

Later — this Oskar relates only to satisfy the curious among you — Mr. Vollmer (he sold radios, I might mention in passing) did come to our Cellar. They cried together and it seems, as Klepp told me yesterday in visiting hour,[2] that they have just been married.

It was from Tuesday to Saturday — the Onion Cellar was closed on Sunday — that the onion brought the more basic tragedies of human existence welling to the surface. But the most violent weeping was done on Mondays, when our cellar was patronized by the younger set. On Monday Schmuh served onions to students at half-price. The most frequent guests were medical and pre-medical students — of both sexes. Quite a few art students as well, particularly among those who were planning to teach drawing later on, spent a portion of their stipends on onions. But where, I have wondered ever since, did the boys and girls in their last year of high school get the money for onions?

Young people have a different way of crying. They have entirely different problems from their elders, but this doesn't mean that examinations are their only source of anguish. Oh, what conflicts between father and son, mother

[2] Oskar is in a mental hospital.

and daughter, were aired in the Onion Cellar! A good many of the young people felt that they were not understood, but most of them were used to it; nothing to cry about. Oskar was glad to see that love, and not just sexual frustration, could still wring tears from the young folks. Gerhard and Gudrun for instance.

At first they sat downstairs; it was only later that they wept side by side in the gallery. She, large and muscular, a handball player and student of chemistry. She wore her hair over her neck in a big bun. Most of the time she looked straight ahead of her out of grey, motherly eyes, a clean forthright gaze that reminded me of the Women's Association posters during the war.

In spite of her fine forehead, smooth, milky-white, and radiant with health, her face was her misfortune. Her cheeks and her round, firm chin down to her Adam's apple bore the distressing traces of a vigorous growth of beard that the poor thing kept trying in vain to shave off. Her sensitive skin reacted violently to the razor blade. Gudrun wept for her red, cracked, pimply complexion, she wept for the beard that kept growing back in. They had not met in the streetcar like Miss Pioch and Mr. Vollmer, but in the train. He was sitting opposite her, they were both on their way back from their between-semesters vacation. He loved her instantly in spite of the beard. She, because of her beard, was afraid to love him, but was full of admiration for what to him was his misfortune, his chin, which was as smooth and beardless as a baby's bottom, and made him bashful in the presence of girls. Nevertheless, Gerhard spoke to Gudrun, and by the time they left the train at the Düsseldorf station, they were friends at least. After that they saw each other every day. They spoke of this and that, and shared a good part of their thoughts, but never alluded to the beard that was missing or the beard that was all too present. Gerhard was considerate of Gudrun; knowing that her skin was sensitive, he never kissed her. Their love remained chaste, though neither of them set much store by chastity, for she was interested in chemistry while he was studying medicine. When a friend suggested the Onion Cellar, they smiled contemptuously with the skepticism characteristic of chemists and medical men. But finally they went, for purposes of documentation, as they assured each other. Never has Oskar seen young people cry so. They came time and time again; they went without food to save up the six marks forty it cost them, and wept about the beard that was absent and the beard that devastated the soft, maidenly skin. Sometimes they tried to stay away from the Onion Cellar. One Monday they didn't come, but the following Monday they were back again. Rubbing the chopped onion between their fingers, they admitted that they had tried to save the six marks forty; they had tried doing it by themselves in her room with a cheap onion, but it wasn't the same. You needed an audience. It was so much easier to cry in company. It gave you a real sense of brotherhood in sorrow when to the right and left of you and in the gallery overhead your fellow students were all crying their hearts out.

This was another case in which the Onion Cellar bestowed not only tears but also, little by little, a cure. Apparently the tears washed away their inhibitions and brought them, as the saying goes, closer together. He kissed her tortured cheeks, she fondled his smooth chin, and one day they stopped coming to the Onion Cellar; they didn't need it any more. Oskar met them months later in Königs-Allee. He didn't recognize them at first. He, the glabrous Gerhard, sported a waving, reddish-blond beard; she, the prickly Gudrun, had barely a slight dark fuzz on her upper lip, very becoming to her. Her chin and cheeks were smooth, radiant, free from vegetation. Still studying but happily married, a student couple. Oskar can hear them in fifty years talking to their grandchildren. She, Gudrun: "That was long ago, before Grandpa had his beard." And he, Gerhard: "That was in the days when your Grandma was having trouble with her beard and we went to the Onion Cellar every Monday."

But to what purpose, you may ask, are three musicians still sitting under the companionway or staircase? What use had the onion shop, what with all this weeping, wailing, and gnashing of teeth, for a regular, and regularly paid, band?

Once the customers had finished crying and unburdening themselves, we took up our instruments and provided a musical transition to normal, everyday conversation. We made it easy for the guests to leave the Onion Cellar and make room for more guests. Klepp, Scholle, and Oskar were not personally lovers of onions. Besides, there was a clause in our contract forbidding us to "use" onions in the same way as the guests. We had no need of them anyway. Scholle, the guitarist, had no ground for sorrow, he always seemed happy and contented, even when two strings on his banjo snapped at once in the middle of a rag. As to Klepp, the very concepts of crying and laughing are to this day unclear to him. Tears make him laugh; I have never seen anyone laugh as hard as Klepp did at the funeral of the aunt who used to wash his shirts and socks before he got married. But what of Oskar? Oskar had plenty of ground for tears. Mightn't he have used a few tears to wash away Sister Dorothea and that long, futile night spent on a still longer coconut-fiber runner? And my Maria? There is no doubt that she gave me cause enough for grief. Didn't Stenzel, her boss, come and go as he pleased in the flat in Bilk? Hadn't Kurt, my son, taken to calling the grocery-store-owner first "Uncle Stenzel" and then "Papa Stenzel"? And what of those who lay in the faraway sand of Saspe Cemetery or in the clay at Brenntau: my poor mama, the foolish and lovable Jan Bronski, and Matzerath, the cook who knew how to transform feelings into soups? All of them needed to be wept for. But Oskar was one of the fortunate who could still weep without onions. My drum helped me. Just a few very special measures were all it took to make Oskar melt into tears that were no better or worse than the expensive tears of the Onion Cellar.

As for Schmuh, the proprietor, he never touched his onions either. In his case the sparrows he shot out of hedges and bushes in his free time filled the bill. Sometimes, after shooting, Schmuh would line up his twelve dead sparrows on a newspaper, shed tears over the little bundles of feathers before they even had time to grow cold, and, still weeping, strew bird food over the Rhine

meadows and the pebbles by the water. In the Cellar he had still another
outlet for his sorrow. He has gotten into the habit of giving the washroom
attendant a ferocious tongue-lashing once a week, making more and more use
of archaic expressions like "slut", "miserable strumpet", "blasted old har-
ridan". "Out of my sight!" we could hear him below, "Despicable monster!
You're fired!" He would dismiss his victim without notice and hire a new
one. But soon he ran into difficulty, there were no washroom attendants left.
There was nothing for it but to hire back those he had previously fired. They
were only too glad to accept; most of Schmuh's insults didn't mean much to
them anyway, and they made good money. The guests at the Onion Cellar —
an effect of so much weeping no doubt — made exorbitant use of the facilities,
and moreover Homo lacrimans[3] tends to be more generous than his dry-
eyed counterpart. Especially the gentlemen, who, after begging leave in voices
choked with tears to step out for a minute, could be counted on to reach
deep into their purses. Another source of income for the washroom attendant
was the sale of the famous onion-print handkerchiefs inscribed with the
legend: "In the Onion Cellar". They sold like hotcakes, for when they were
no longer needed to wipe the eyes with they made attractive souvenirs and
could be worn on the head. They could also be made into pennants which
the habitués of the Onion Cellar would hang in the rear windows of their
cars, so bearing the fame of Schmuh's Onion Cellar, in vacation time, to
Paris, the Côte d'Azur, Rome, Ravenna, Rimini, and even remote Spain.

We musicians and our music had still another function. Occasionally
some of the guests would partake of two onions in quick succession; the result
was an outbreak that might easily have degenerated into an orgy. Schmuh
insisted on a certain restraint; when gentlemen began taking off their ties and
ladies undoing their blouses, he would order us to step in with our music and
counteract the stirrings of lewdness. However, Schumuh himself was largely
responsible for these ticklish situations, what with his insidious habit of
serving up a second onion to particularly vulnerable customers.

The most spectacular outburst I can recall was to influence Oskar's whole
career, though I shall not go so far as to speak of a crucial turning point.
Schmuh's wife, the vivacious Billy, did not come to the Cellar very often, and
when she did, it was in the company of friends to whom Schmuh was far from
partial. One night she turned up with Woode, the music critic, and Wackerlei, the architect and pipe-smoker. Both of them were regular customers,
but their sorrows were of the most boring variety. Woode wept for religious
reasons — he was always being converted or reconverted to something or
other; as for Wackerlei, the pipe-smoker, he was still bewailing a professorship
he had turned down in the twenties for the sake of a little Danish fly-by-night
who had gone and married a South American and had six children by him,
which was still a source of grief to Wackerlei and made his pipe go out year
after year. It was the somewhat malicious Woode who persuaded Madame

[3] man crying.

Schmuh to cut into an onion. She cut, the tears flowed, and she began to spill. She laid Schmuh bare, told stories about him that Oskar will tactfully pass over in silence; it took several of the more powerful customers to prevent Schmuh from flinging himself on his spouse; don't forget that there were paring knives on every table. In any case, Schmuh was forcibly restrained until the indiscreet Billy could slip away with her friends Woode and Wackerlei.

Schmuh was very upset. I could see that by the way his hands flew about arranging and rearranging his onion shawl. Several times he vanished behind the curtain and reviled the washroom attendant. Finally he came back with a full basket and informed his guests in a tone of hysterical glee that he, Schmuh, was in a generous mood and was going to hand out a free round of onions. Which he proceeded to do.

Every human situation, however painful, strikes Klepp as a terrific joke, but on this occasion he was tense and held his flute at the ready. For we knew how dangerous it was to offer these high-strung people a double portion of tears, of the tears that wash away barriers.

Schmuh saw that we were holding our instruments in readiness and forbade us to play. At the tables the paring knives were at work. The beautiful outer skins, colored like rosewood, were thrust heedlessly aside. The knives bit into vitreous onion flesh with pale-green stripes. Oddly enough, the weeping did not begin with the ladies. Gentlemen in their prime — the owner of a large flour mill, a hotel-owner with his slightly rouged young friend, a nobleman high in the councils of an important business firm, a whole tableful of men's clothing manufacturers who were in town for a board meeting, the bald actor who was known in the Cellar as the Gnasher, because he gnashed his teeth when he wept — all were in tears before the ladies joined in. But neither the ladies nor the gentlemen wept the tears of deliverance and release that the first onion had called forth; this was a frantic, convulsive crying jag. The Gnasher gnashed his teeth blood-curdlingly; had he been on the stage, the whole audience would have joined in; the mill-owner banged his carefully groomed grey head on the table top; the hotel-owner mingled his convulsions with those of his delicate young friend. Schmuh, who stood by the stairs, let his shawl droop and peered with malicious satisfaction at the near-unleashed company. Suddenly, a lady of ripe years tore off her blouse before the eyes of her son-in-law. The hotel-owner's young friend, whose slightly exotic look had already been remarked on, bared his swarthy torso, and leaping from table top to table top performed a dance which exists perhaps somewhere in the Orient. The orgy was under way. But despite the violence with which it began, it was a dull, uninspired affair, hardly worth describing in detail.

Schmuh was disappointed; even Oskar lifted his eyebrows in disgust. One or two cute strip tease acts; men appeared in ladies' underwear, Amazons donned ties and suspenders; a couple or two disappeared under the table; the Gnasher chewed up a brassiere and apparently swallowed some of it.

The hubbub was frightful, wows and yippees with next to nothing behind them. At length Schmuh, disgusted and maybe fearing the police, left his

post by the stairs, bent down over us, gave first Klepp, then me a poke, and
hissed: "Music! Play something, for God's sake. Make them stop."

But it turned out that Klepp, who was easy to please, was enjoying himself.
Shaking with laughter, he couldn't do a thing with his flute. Scholle, who
looked on Klepp as his master, imitated everything Klepp did, including his
laughter. Only Oskar was left — but Schmuh could rely on me. I pulled my
drum from under the bench, nonchalantly lit a cigarette, and began to drum.

Without any notion of what I was going to do, I made myself understood.
I forgot all about the usual café concert routine. Nor did Oskar play jazz.
For one thing I didn't like to be taken for a percussion maniac. All right, I
was a good drummer, but not a hepcat. Sure, I like jazz, but I like Viennese
waltzes too. I could play both, but I didn't have to. When Schmuh asked
me to step in with my drum, I didn't play anything I had ever learned, I
played with my heart. It was a three-year-old Oskar who picked up those
drumsticks. I drummed my way back, I drummed up the world as a three-
year-old[4] sees it. And the first thing I did to these postwar humans incapable
of a real orgy was to put a harness on them: I led them to Posadowski-Weg,
to Auntie Kauer's kindergarten. Soon I had their jaws hanging down; they
took each other by the hands, turned their toes in, and waited for me, their
Pied Piper. I left my post under the staircase and took the lead. "Bake, bake,
bake a cake": that was my first sample. When I had registered my success —
childlike merriment on every hand — I decided to scare them out of their
wits. "Where's the Witch, black as pitch?" I drummed. And I drummed up
the wicked black Witch who gave me an occasional fright in my childhood
days and in recent years has terrified me more and more; I made her rage
through the Onion Cellar in all her gigantic, coal-black frightfulness, so
obtaining the results for which Schmuh required onions; the ladies and
gentlemen wept great round, childlike tears, the ladies and gentlemen were
scared pink and green; their teeth chattered, they begged me to have mercy.
And so, to comfort them, and in part to help them back into their outer and
undergarments, their silks and satins, I drummed: "Green, green, green is my
raiment" and "Red, red, red is my raiment", not to mention "Blue, blue,
blue . . ." and "Yellow, yellow, yellow". By the time I had gone through all
the more familiar colors, my charges were all properly dressed. Thereupon I
formed them into a procession, led them through the Onion Cellar as though
it were Jeschkentaler-Weg. I led them up the Erbsberg, round the hideous
Gutenberg Monument, and on the Johannis-Wiese grew daisies which they,
the ladies and gentlemen, were free to pick in innocent merriment. Then,
at last, wishing to give all those present, including Schmuh the head man,
something by which to remember their day in kindergarten, I gave them all
permission to do number one. We were approaching Devil's Gulch, a sinister
place it was, gathering beechnuts, when I said on my drum: now, children,
you may go. And they availed themselves of the opportunity. All the ladies
and gentlemen, Schmuh the host, even the far-off washroom attendant, all

---

4 Oskar received his first drum when he was three years old.

the little children wet themselves, psss, psss they went, they all crouched down and listened to the sound they were making and they all wet their pants. It was only when the music had died down — Oskar had left the infant sound effects to themselves except for a soft distant roll — that I ushered in unrestrained merriment with one loud, emphatic boom. All about me the company roared, tittered, babbled childish nonsense:

> Smash a little windowpane
> Put sugar in your beer,
> Mrs. Biddle plays the fiddle,
> Dear, dear, dear.

I led them to the cloakroom, where a bewildered student gave Schmuh's kindergarteners their wraps; then, with the familiar ditty "Hard-working washerwoman scrubbing out the clothes," I drummed them up the concrete steps, past the doorman in the rustic sheepskin. I dismissed the kindergarten beneath the night sky of spring, 1950, a trifle cool perhaps, but studded with fairy-tale stars, as though made to order for the occasion. Forgetful of home, they continued for quite some time to make childish mischief in the Old City, until at length the police helped them to remember their age, social position, and telephone number.

As for me, I giggled and caressed my drum as I went back to the Onion Cellar, where Schmuh was still clapping his hands, still standing bowlegged and wet beside the staircase, seemingly as happy in Auntie Kauer's kindergarten as on the Rhine meadows when a grown-up Schmuh went shooting sparrows.

X. J. Kennedy (b. 1929)

AMERICAN POET

Ars Poetica

> The goose that laid the golden egg
> Died looking up its crotch
> To find out how its sphincter worked.
>
> Would you lay well? Don't watch.

GLOSSARY OF LITERARY TERMS

Words which appear in *italics* within a definition are themselves defined in their proper alphabetical position.

Abstract Words: words which deal with general classifications as opposed to specific and individual instances; words representing ideals, classes, conditions or qualities of being which express a quality apart from an object. "Truth" and "justice" are abstract, as are general allegorical names such as "Everyman" and "Good Report." "Beauty" is an abstract word, whereas "rosebud" is the opposite, a *concrete word*.

Aesthetic Distance: the detachment between an author and his work which suggests to the reader that the author is reacting objectively to the incidents or emotions described in the work.

Allegory: a formally extended *metaphor* in which the *characters*, objects, and *setting* of a prose or verse *narrative* have a comprehensible meaning within the work as the story but also represent abstract ideas and their relationships to provide another, more general, meaning. Frequently the abstract or generalized significance of an allegory deals with a moral question. "The Lion" (p. 640) and "Rappaccini's Daughter" (p. 839) are allegorical.

Alliteration: the repetition of an initial sound in words of close proximity. The line "Five miles meandering with a mazy motion" provides an example of alliteration.

Allusion: a reference to a fictitious or historic person, event, or work outside or within the literary work. T. S. Eliot's "The Love Song of J. Alfred Prufrock" (p. 189) contains numerous allusions, including those to the Italian artist Michelangelo, to Hesiod's *The Works and Days* (1. 29), to Marvell's "To His Coy Mistress" (1. 92), and to Shakespeare's *Hamlet* (1. 112).

Ambiguity: a word or statement that conveys more than one possible meaning and leaves uncertain precisely what the author means. Ambiguity in literature may be intentional or unintentional; "deliberate ambiguity" in a poem is created in such a way that the plural meanings contribute to one total meaning.

Anachronism: the chronologically incorrect use of a person, event, scene, situation, or language. A clock striking in *Oedipus the King* would be an anachronism.

Analogue: a word, *character*, *setting*, or situation used implicitly or explicitly to resemble another word, character, setting, or situation usually outside the work. Franz Kafka's hunter Gracchus is analogous to Christ. (See "The Hunter Gracchus," p. 365.)

Analogy: a comparison of two or more things with some (although not necessarily many) common qualities; used in literature to define, to clarify, or to demonstrate a point.

Anecdote: a short narrative episode, frequently based in fact and meant to be informative, amusing, or of biographical interest.

Antagonist: the *character* in a literary work who opposes the chief character, or *protagonist*.

Anticlimax: a conclusion of a sentence, passage, or work which is weaker or less emphatic than the preceding material has led the reader to anticipate. Occasionally anticlimax is deliberately used for comic effect, as in Orgon's comic refrain, "And Tartuffe?" (Molière's *Tartuffe*, I, iii).

Antithesis: the rhetorical technique which uses pairs of opposing syntactic elements or ideas, such as old age versus youth or generosity versus greed. Petrarch's "Laura Rules Me Still" (p. 46) provides a good example of the use of antithesis: "Here she was humble, there she walked in pride,/Now harsh, now gentle; pitiful, pitiless;" etc.

Apostrophe: a direct address to an absent person, thing, or abstract quality. An example is Milton's address in "Lycidas" (p. 658): "Yet once more, O ye Laurels, . . ." (11. 1–2).

Archaism: obsolete words, phrases, or syntax often deliberately used to evoke a sense of the past.

Archetype: in literature, a pattern of human behavior or experience that recurs throughout history, within and outside of works of literature. The theme of the life cycle in Agee's "A Visit to Grandma's" (p. 202) is archetypal.

Assonance: the repetition of identical or similar vowel sounds, usually in stressed syllables of close proximity. The vowel sounds are followed by different consonant sounds, as in the words "ride" and "time," and "went" and "send."

Atmosphere: the predominant mood of a work, usually evoked by description and physical *setting*.

Ballad: a narrative song evolved from an oral tradition of recitation or song. Ballads frequently make use of *colloquial* language, *dialect*, *incremental repetition*, and, in the *refrain* or chorus, *nonsense words*. Some ballads are the work of a single poet or composer, but many are the result of communal invention. The ballad *stanza* is a quatrain of alternating four- and three-stress lines rhyming *abcb*. "Edward" (p. 487) and "Skipper Ireson's Ride" (p. 526) are ballads.

Bestiary: a primarily fabulous account of animal habits, often presented through *allegory* or *analogy* in order to draw a moral lesson or to expound church doctrine. Bestiaries were extremely popular in medieval Europe. "The Lion" (p. 640) is an extract from a medieval bestiary.

Bombast: flamboyant and extravagant words and expressions. See Tartuffe's remarks in Molière's *Tartuffe* (p. 251).

Burlesque: comic writing which mocks social customs, persons, or works of art by treating the petty with apparent seriousness ("high burlesque") or the serious with irreverent lightheartedness (*travesty*, or "low burlesque"). Burlesque may include the use of *parody* or *caricature* to achieve comic effect.

Cadence: the rhythmic movement created by the arrangement of *stressed* and unstressed syllables in lines of poetry and prose.

Caesura: a noticeable pause, determined by punctuation or *rhetoric*, in a line of verse. The caesura in the following line is indicated by slash marks: "Loving in truth, // and faine in verse my love to show."

Canon: the body of writing authoritatively attributed to a single author.

Caricature: an artistic or literary portrait which ridicules its subject by exaggerating significant features. Dickens employs caricature in "Fact and Fancy" (p. 860).

Catastrophe: (also *denouement* or "resolution") the conclusion of a play which incorporates all the actions resulting from the *climax*. The term is commonly applied to *tragedy*.

Catharsis: according to Aristotle, an audience's release of the emotions of pity and fear which are evoked by great *tragedy*. See Aristotle's "The Essence of Drama" (p. 933).

Cause and Effect: a common rhetorical means of defining a word or an idea by discussing its origin and its end.

Character: generally, any person in a work of literature. Also, a form of literature which consists of a brief *sketch* of a "type" of person or a way of life; the form is used to illustrate a particular quality such as honesty or to describe a class of persons such as innkeepers. See Overbury's "A Good Wife" (p. 148).

Chorus: in classical Greek drama, the group of singers and dancers which is interested in the destiny of principal *characters* and comments on the action and its moral significance. The chorus functions as an ideal spectator, establishing the proper reactions to events and actions. Note the role of the chorus in *Oedipus the King* (p. 433).

Cliché: a stereotyped, unimaginative phrase or sentiment. Polly Espy (in Shulman's "Love Is a Fallacy," p. 212) speaks in clichés, and the selection contains numerous *parodies* of clichés.

Climax: the turning point in the *plot* of a literary work; the climax is marked by a crisis or confrontation of opposing forces, ideas, or *characters*. The term is generally used in reference to drama.

Colloquialism: an informal, conversational expression which is more elevated than slang and more casual than formal, written speech. For examples of colloquialisms see "Huck's Island" by Mark Twain (p. 704): Huck uses expressions such as "when it was good and dark" and "I had about made up my mind."

Comedy: a mode of writing which is amusing and in which the *protagonist* resolves his difficulties happily. Comedy attains its impact through devices of *wit* and humor which vary from verbal play (*puns*, jokes, "double entendre"), physical humor (slapstick, pratfalls, pantomime), or satirical allusion, to overall *plot* structure. In a "comedy of intrigue," one character manipulates the others; in a "comedy of manners," social customs are ridiculed; in a "situation comedy," coincidences and twists of the plot are paramount. See Aristotle's discussion of comedy in "The Essence of Drama" (p. 933).

Conceit: an intellectually ingenious *metaphor* which compares two apparently dissimilar objects or situations, usually developing the comparison through many lines or through an entire poem. A famous example is Donne's comparison of lovers to a compass in "A Valediction: forbidding Mourning" (p. 147).

Concrete Words: words which refer to specific things or situations, or to qualities perceptible to the senses; words used in precise description; the opposite of *abstract words*.

Connotation: the associated meanings or attitudes, often emotional, suggested by a particular word or expression; the opposite of *denotation*.

Consonance: the repetition of consonant sounds with changes in the intervening vowel sounds: "pitter:patter" and "will:well" are examples of consonance.

Contrast: the opposition of objects, ideas, or incidents to clarify or to emphasize.

Couplet: two consecutive *rhyming* lines of poetry. For example: "Had we but World enough, and Time,/This coyness Lady were no crime." A couplet may also be a *stanza* of two lines, usually, but not necessarily, with end rhymes. See also *heroic couplet*.

Decorum: congruity of the parts of a literary work. Aristotle most specifically referred to decorum as the appropriateness of language to *character* (e.g., a king must speak in elevated language, while a peasant should speak in *slang*), but from Cicero's time through the 18th century decorum signified fitness or congruence of *character, setting,* and action.

Denotation: the precise, literal meaning of a word independent of its possible associations; the opposite of *connotation*.

Denouement: (also *catastrophe*) the resolution or untangling of a *plot*. Sometimes, especially in classical drama, the denouement involves a discovery or revelation of facts previously unknown to the *protagonist*; it also may include *peripeteia*, a reversal of the protagonist's fortunes.

Deus ex Machina: an unanticipated or unlikely occurrence which helps to solve apparently insoluble problems and thus to conclude a *plot*. The term literally means "a god from a machine;" it originated when the ancient Greeks had a character dressed as a god descend by stage machinery to end the play. The resolution of Molière's *Tartuffe* (p. 251) is an example of the use of *deus ex machina*.

Dialect: a regional variation of a language distinguished by certain expressions and pronunciation common to a group. In "Skipper Ireson's Ride" (p. 526), Whittier includes the dialect of the people of Marblehead: " 'Here's Flud Oirson, fur his horrd horrt,/Torr'd an' furtherr'd an' corr'd in a corrt/By the women o' Morble'ead!' "

Dialogue: conversation or thought of two or more persons which is expressed in writing. Also, a work of literature in the form of a conversation. For example, Plato's "Symposium: On Love" (p. 5) is a dialogue between Diotima and Socrates.

Diction: the choice of words in writing and speech. Also, the level of language used in writing; the four most common levels of language are formal, informal, *colloquial,* and *slang*.

Didacticism: that quality of a literary work which conveys the author's explicit intention to instruct and improve the reader; the lesson is often a moral one. Ovid's "The Art of Loving" (p. 30) is didactic, as is Lucretius' "On the Reliability of the Senses" (p. 795).

Digression: a temporary departure from the subject; a passage irrelevant or only distantly related to the forward movement of the work in which it occurs.

Dramatic Monologue: a poem in which a single *character* (who is not the poet) is speaking to one or more people who are silent or absent. The speaker exposes his own ideas or emotions during a critical moment; only his comments indicate the presence or presumed responses of his listener. Browning's "The

Bishop Orders His Tomb at Saint Praxed's Church" (p. 338) is a dramatic monologue; Eliot's "The Love Song of J. Alfred Prufrock" (p. 189) is a variation of the form.

Elegy: a personal, mournful, and contemplative poem, usually written in elevated language, which meditates on death. Milton's "Lycidas" (p. 658) is an example of an elegy which was inspired by the death of a specific person.

Elision: the omission or suppression of a syllable or vowel to facilitate pronunciation or accomodate the *meter* in a poem. Some elisions in Donne's "Batter My Heart, Three Person'd God" (p. 148) are: "o'erthrow;" "to'another;" "to'admit;" "captiv'd;" "dearely'I love you;" "mee,'untie;" and "you'enthrall."

Ellipsis: the omission of one or more words which are understood in context. Ellipsis is commonly used in poetry to achieve a terse or emphatic effect or to maintain *meter*. An example of ellipsis in Hopkins "Pied Beauty" (p. 716) may be found in the phrase "Landscape plotted and pieced:" the words "which is" are omitted and understood. The term ellipsis is also used in connection with any omitted material, which is designated by the marks ". . ."

Empathy: the total projection of the reader's personality and emotions into a *character* or situation in a literary work.

End-stopped Line: (also "closed line") a single line of poetry containing an idea expressed in a complete grammatical unit; the opposite of *run-on lines*. These lines from Yeats' "The Second Coming" (p. 360) are end-stopped lines: "Surely some revelation is at hand;/Surely the Second Coming is at hand."

Enjambment: (also *run-on*) the running-over of poetic meaning and syntax from one line of poetry to the next. The following lines from Arnold's "Dover Beach" (p. 358) demonstrate enjambment: "Ah, love, let us be true/To one another! for the world, which seems/To lie before us like a land of dreams, . . ."

Epic: a long narrative poem, written in elevated style, celebrating a traditional, historical, or national hero whose actions are momentous in effect and scope. Superhuman beings frequently intervene in the action of an epic, and there are certain formal characteristics of the *structure* (*invocations* of the muse, a beginning "in medias res," *epic similes*). Some epics belong to an oral tradition and are composed by an impersonal poet to be sung or recited. Homer's *Odyssey* ("Poseidon's Revenge," p. 619) is this type of epic. Other epics, like Vergil's *Aeneid* ("Dido and Aeneas," p. 14) are composed by a poet with more individuality and are meant to be read.

Epic Simile: an extended, elevated, and intricate comparison which is so elaborate that it temporarily focuses attention exclusively on itself rather than on the object of the comparison; characteristic of *epic* poetry. The passage "Dido wandered wild . . . like a doe trailing an arrow . . ." (11. 69–73) from Vergil's "Dido and Aeneas" is an epic simile, as are the following passages from Dante's "Paolo and Francesca:" "As the wings of wintering starlings . . ." (11. 1–3); "As cranes go over . . ." (11. 7–9); and "As mating doves that love calls . . ." (11. 43–45).

Epigram: a terse statement, often witty or satirical. Martial's "I Do Not Love You" (p. 40) is an epigram.

Epilogue: a final statement, concluding section, or appendix to a literary work. Also, in a play, the actor who delivers the concluding statement.

Episode: a discrete portion of a *narrative*, based on a self-contained incident in the *plot*. Also, in classical Greek *tragedy*, the part of the play between two choral *odes*.

Epitaph: commemorative poetry meant for tombstone inscription or written as if so intended. The epitaph which Swift wrote for his own grave and Yeats' version of that inscription appear on page 168.

Epithet: a single adjective or apt phrase characterizing a person or thing. Epithets are characteristic elements of epics. Homer's *Odyssey* ("Poseidon's Revenge," p. 619) contains such epithets as "great-hearted hero," "lovely nymph Kalypso," and "grey-eyed Athena."

Eulogy: an elevated speech in praise of a person, thing, or incident. See Antony's eulogy for Caesar in Shakespeare's "An Honourable Man" (p. 960), though his use here is *ironic*.

Euphemism: a vague or elevated word or phrase used to avoid directness which may be considered indelicate or offensive. "Passed away" is a euphemism for "died," and "elderly" is a euphemism for "old."

Exemplum: a *parable* or *tale* in a medieval sermon, used to illustrate a moral. "The Lion" (p. 640) from a medieval *bestiary* is an exemplum.

Expressionism: a form of art which employs *symbols*, abstractions, and stylization and thus distorts reality in order to convey objectively an author's or character's subjective attitudes or experience.

Fable: a brief moral tale, often involving uncommon incidents and having as characters animals who speak and act like human beings. For an example of a fable, see Rabelais' "The Fable of the Horse and the Ass" (p. 645).

Familiar Essay: a personal essay which reveals the author's impressions and attitudes. Addison's "The Aesthetics of Nature" (p. 667) is a familiar essay.

Fantasy: a literary work which contains obviously imaginary, dreamlike incidents or settings. Malamud's "Angel Levine" (p. 412) is a fantasy.

Flashback: an interruption in the chronological sequence of a plot due to the presentation of an episode which occurs earlier in time than the action of the narrative in which it appears.

Free Verse: poetry in which the lines are of varying lengths and do not follow a predetermined metrical pattern. Whitman's "When I Heard the Learn'd Astronomer" (p. 866) is written in free verse.

Genre: a major category of literary works: for example, *comedy, tragedy, lyric, epic, novel,* short story, essay, drama.

Gothic: a mode of writing which emphasizes horror, mystery, desolation, and the supernatural. Among its conventions are ghosts, crumbling graveyards, deserted castles, and mysterious disappearances. The style of writing is frequently ornate.

Haiku: a form of Japanese *lyric* which has three lines of five, seven, and five syllables respectively and focuses on an emotional or spiritual response to one or two natural *images*. The haiku poem distills thought and feeling to nearly pure suggestion. (See "A Garland of Haiku," p. 665.)

Hamartia: in classical Greek *tragedy* the hero's weakness of character, misjudgment, or "tragic flaw" which brings about his downfall.

Heroic Couplet: two rhymed lines of iambic pentameter which often contain a complete thought (are "closed") and often also contain *antithesis* or *parallelism*. The following heroic couplet is from Pope's "Nature and the Social State of Man" (p. 670): "The creature had his feast of life before;/Thou too must perish, when thy feast is o'er!"

Hybris: (also "hubris") usually taken to be pride, but more precisely an act of blasphemy, the flaw of the classical Greek tragic hero who places his own will or ideas above those of the gods or fate and thus brings about his own suffering and destruction.

Hymn: originally a general song of praise and glorification. Since the establishment of the Christian church, the term usually refers to religious *lyric* poems which praise God and are meant to be sung. An example is Watts' "The Hazard of Loving the Creatures" (p. 151).

Hyperbole: an expression characterized by conscious, obvious exaggeration and overstatement. The narrator in Marvell's "To His Coy Mistress" (p. 150) uses such hyperboles as: "An hundred years should go to praise/Thine Eyes, and on thy Forehead Gaze./Two hundred to adore each Breast:/But thirty thousand to the rest."

Idiom: a phrase or expression which, because of its syntactical or metaphorical peculiarities, has an actual meaning somewhat different from the literal meanings of its component words. The statement "if you were out of the picture, the field would be open" from Shulman's "Love Is a Fallacy" (p. 212) is idiomatic.

Image: a vivid and particular representation which involves any — or all — of the senses to convey the essence of an object, sensation, or experience. Also, a figure of speech, especially a *simile* or *metaphor*. Images in Hopkins' "Pied Beauty" (p. 716) include "skies of couple-colour as a brinded cow," "Fresh-firecoal chestnut-falls," and "Landscape plotted and pieced." Yevtushenko's "Party Card" (p. 221) contains good examples of different types of images: "Mind-crushing explosions," "The rain of July lightly falling," "the flushed and smoking dark," "Child crying," "Horse whinnying."

Impressionism: a style of writing which stresses the author's or a character's immediate, overall impressions and feelings about a reality which may be fleetingly experienced. Minute, selective details are combined to provide a mosaic picture suggestive of a more comprehensive whole.

Incremental Repetition: in a *ballad*, repetition, with slight variation, of a line or stanza for emphasis, emotional effect, or advancement of the narrative. The *refrains* of "Edward" (p. 487) contain incremental repetition: " 'O I hae killed my hauke sae guid,' " " 'O I hae killed my reid-roan steid,' " " 'O I hae killed my fadir deir,' " etc.

Induction: a process of reasoning which draws general conclusions from a number of particular facts and related and specific instances. The method of reasoning in Plato's "Symposium: On Love" (p. 5) is inductive.

Interior Monologue: in a novel, the recording of a character's inner thoughts and feelings, apparently random, illogical, and freely associative, but actually artistically arranged to allow the reader to follow and to understand the activity of the character's mind and the stream of his thought.

Invective: a harsh, insulting, direct attack on a person or idea. Albany delivers a series of invectives at Goneril, including such statements as "You are not worth the dust which the rude wind/Blows in your face," "Tigers, not daughters," "Most barbarous, most degenerate!," "thou art a fiend,/A woman's shape doth shield thee" (*King Lear*, IV,ii).

Invocation: an appeal to a muse or god for inspiration or assistance; invocations are characteristic of *epics*. In "Lycidas" (p. 658), Milton evokes the "Sisters of the sacred well."

Irony: an arrangement of words in which the literal statement expresses a contrast to or the opposite of its intended, implicit meaning. Examples of "verbal irony" are seen in Swift's "An Argument against Abolishing Christianity" (p. 308) and "The Acadamy of Lagado" (p. 826). An "ironic situation" is the opposite of what might have been expected, as in Robinson's "Richard Cory" (p. 543). "Dramatic irony" occurs when the reader or spectator realizes what the characters do not — that the consequences of their actions will be contrary to their expectations. For an example of dramatic irony, see *Oedipus the King* (p. 433).

Jargon: the specialized language of an identifiable group or profession. "Politics and the English Language" by Orwell (p. 1076) includes a discussion of jargon.

Kenning: in Old English poetry, a metaphorical or otherwise figurative phrase used as a *synonym* for a noun. "Seafarer" is a kenning for "ship" or "sailor."

Legend: a tradition or story, derived from history but not actually verifiable, which originates in oral, folk culture.

Lyric: a short subjective poem expressing intense attitudes, beliefs, emotions, or reasoning of the poet. *Songs, odes, sonnets, elegies,* and *hymns* are all types of lyric poetry.

Melodrama: a work which seeks to arouse violent emotions through sensational incidents and a clear-cut struggle between good and evil; the forces of good generally triumph. The characters of a melodrama are "types" such as the innocent girl, the villain, and the hero.

Metaphor: an implicit comparison, applying to one thing characteristics and associations usually attributed to another. In Eliot's "The Love Song of J. Alfred Prufrock" (p. 189), the fog appears as an animal — a cat: "The yellow fog that rubs its back upon the window-panes,/The yellow smoke that rubs its muzzle on the window-panes/Licked its tongue into the corners of the evening." In Poe's "Sonnet — To Science" (p. 860), science is presented as a "Vulture" who "preyest . . . upon the poet's heart."

Meter: in poetry, the recurrence of a regular or nearly regular rhythmic unit. The most common type of meter in English verse is "accentual-syllabic," based on a fixed number of *stressed* and unstressed syllables. Purely "accentual" meter predetermines only the number of stresses in a line, while the number of syllables may vary. "Syllabic" meter, on the other hand, has a fixed number of syllables, although the number of stresses may vary. The meter of Greek and Latin poetry is *quantitative,* based on a recurring pattern of long and short syllables. The smallest recurring metrical unit is called a "foot;" the line itself is called a *verse.* A line of poetry may have one foot ("monometer"), two feet ("dimeter"), three feet ("trimeter"), four feet ("tetrameter"), five feet ("pentameter"), or six feet ("hexameter"). The most common types of feet are "iambic" (unstressed syllable followed by a stressed syllable), "trochaic" (stress/ unstress), "anapestic" (unstress/ unstress/ stress), "dactyllic" (stress/ unstress/ stress), "spondaic" (stress/ stress), and "pyrrhic" (unstress/ unstress).

Metonymy: the replacement of the name of one thing with the name of another, closely associated, thing. Thus the army may be referred to as "the sword."

Mood: the predominant emotional atmosphere of a literary work.

Motif: in a literary work, a repeated idea, word, *image*, phrase, or situation which is usually clearly related to and expressive of the central *theme*. The term is also used to denote a conventional situation in literature, such as the estrangement of young lovers or the discovery of birthmarks which identify a prince.

Myth: a fictitious story which expresses symbolically the deepest beliefs or world view of a culture and serves to explain historical or natural phenomena. In his *Metamorphoses*, Ovid created myths like "Echo and Narcissus" (p. 634) and "The Story of Daedalus and Icarus" (p. 803).

Narrative: a story; a tale; a recounting of fictional or nonfictional events, often in chronological order. Types of narratives are the *epic*, the short story, and the *novel*.

Narrator: the person, or "voice," which tells a story.

Naturalism: a philosophic outlook which views man wholly as the product of natural processes. In literary history, naturalism most specifically refers to novelists of the late 19th and early 20th centuries who believed that the writer or artist should treat life with scientific objectivity and precision and should not impose value judgments. In their effort to show how natural forces mold human character and action, these novelists stressed material environment, which was generally presented as sordid and oppressive. Guy de Maupassant ("Love: Three Pages from a Sportsman's Book," p. 717) is a representative of the naturalistic movement in literature.

Neoclassicism: a movement of the 18th century which advocated respect for antiquity and for discipline and strict conformity to the forms and rules of Greek and Roman classical art and literature. *Satire, heroic couplets*, formal symmetry and regularity, logic, "correctness," polish, and *decorum* are all characteristics of neoclassical literature. In neoclassical drama, the three *unities* (of action, time, and place) are carefully observed. Examples of neoclassical writers are Voltaire ("Candide Meets the Oreillons," p. 513), Addison ("The Aesthetics of Nature," p. 667), Swift ("An Argument against Abolishing Christianity," p. 308, "The Academy of Lagado," p. 826), and Pope ("Nature and the Social State of Man," p. 670).

Nonsense Verse: rhythmic, humorous *verse* featuring nonexistent words, absurdities, or non sequiturs. See Carroll's "Jabberwocky" (p. 975).

Novel: a fictional prose *narrative*, usually of substantial length.

Novelette: a piece of fiction shorter than a *novel*, but longer than a short story: for example, Trilling's "Of This Time, Of That Place" (p. 561).

Novella: a short prose *narrative* with a satirical or realistic *plot* and usually containing a moral. Boccaccio's "The Clever Monk" (p. 488) is a novella.

Ode: a formal *lyric* characterized by elevated language and a dignified *theme*. A "Pindaric ode," originally a choral celebration and thus usually ecstatic or passionate in tone, is divided into *strophe*, "antistrophe," and "epode;" in such classical Greek dramas as *Oedipus the King* (p. 433), dancers move forward on the strophe, backward during the antistrophe, and sing the epode without moving. The "Horatian (or "homostrophic") ode" is more personal in subject and quieter in tone and uses a consistent stanzaic form throughout (with variations by individual poets). Keats' "Ode on a Grecian Urn" (p. 973) is a Horatian ode. The "Cowleyan ("irregular" or "false Pindaric") ode" has no consistent stanzaic form.

Onomatopoeia: the use of words whose sounds suggest their meanings and imitate the natural sound associated with the object or action involved. Examples: "buzz," "crunch," "hiss," "splash." The term may be extended to cover the acoustical suggestions of phrases or lines of poetry: notice Arnold's use of sound in lines 10–14 of "Dover Beach" (p. 358) to suggest the sound of the action of the waves against the shore.

Oxymoron: a paradoxical figure of speech which unites two opposing or incongruous terms. In "Ode on a Grecian Urn" (p. 973), Keats speaks of "unheard" melodies and "ditties of no tone."

Panegyric: a eulogistic formal speech or piece of writing praising a person or event.

Parable: a brief *narrative* from which a moral lesson may be drawn. A parable may be an *allegory*. The best examples of parables are found in the teachings of Christ. (See the parable of the Good Samaritan, *Luke* 10: 30–37.)

Paradox: an apparently contradictory statement or situation which is in fact true. The following lines of Donne's "Batter My Heart, Three Person'd God" (p. 148) are paradoxical: "Take mee to you, imprison mee, for I/Except you'enthrall mee, never shall be free,/Nor ever chast, except you ravish mee."

Parallelism: the technique which develops corresponding phrases, passages, incidents, or ideas in a similar or repetitive way.

Paraphrase: the rewording of a statement, attempting to keep the original meaning while changing the manner of expression; usually used for summary or clarification.

Parody: an imitation of the style of a serious composition or type of composition for the purposes of amusement, ridicule, or reform.

Pastoral: a composition dealing with the idealized life or activity of shepherds and shepherdesses, generally emphasizing and praising the values of a simple rural life. Theocritus ("The Harvest Home: Idyll VII," p. 628) is considered the first writer of pastoral poetry, and later poets imitated some of his themes and conventions: a singing contest between peasants; a lament for a dead shepherd (see Milton's "Lycidas," p. 658); a song of courtship; or a eulogy. A pastoral poem may also be called a "bucolic," an "eclogue," or an "idyll."

Pathetic Fallacy: a literary device, a form of *personification*, which attributes human emotions to natural phenomena or inanimate objects. For example, in "Stanzas to Augusta" (p. 155) Byron speaks of "Nature" as "smiling," and in Milton's "Lycidas" (p. 658) the youth's death causes cowslips to "hang the pensive head," flowers to wear "sad embroidery," and daffodils to "fill their cups with tears."

Pathos: in a literary work, that quality intended to arouse the reader's sympathy, tenderness, sorrow, and pity for a passive, innocent character who is in no way responsible for his suffering. Cordelia is a "pathetic" character in *King Lear* (p. 59).

Peripeteia: a reversal of the hero's fortune; traditionally part of the crisis of classical tragedy, but also used in reference to comedy, where the change would be from bad fortune to good. See Aristotle's definition in "The Essence of Drama" (p. 933).

Peroration: the conclusion of a formal speech, including a summary and a recapitulation.

Persona: historically, the mask worn by a *character* in Roman drama. In modern critical usage, the term has come to mean the character or personality projected by the poet or *narrator*. The Bishop, not the poet, is the *persona* of Browning's "The Bishop Orders His Tomb at Saint Praxed's Church" (p. 338), and Gulliver is the *persona* of Swift's *Gulliver's Travels* ("The Academy of Lagado," p. 826).

Personification: the attribution of human characteristics to nonhuman ideas, objects, or creatures. In the second *stanza* of Keats' "To Autumn" (p. 684), autumn is personified as a woman.

Plot: a sequence of events as they are narrated and dramatized by an author, usually with emphasis on causal relationships and usually involving a conflict of *characters*, forces, or qualities.

Poetic Justice: an ideal system in which rewards and punishments are exactly appropriate to virtue or vice.

Poetic License: the freedom claimed by some writers to depart from an accepted standard and to suspend logic or formal literary conventions or metrics.

Poetic Prose: prose writing which demonstrates self-conscious cultivation of *cadence* and figurative language.

Poetics: a systematic theory about the nature of poetry, or a group of precepts about the composition of poetry. A famous example is Horace's "On the Art of Poetry" (p. 946).

Point of View: the perspective from which events are narrated. If the narrative voice presents the author's own awareness and is not limited to a single *character's* observations or to a point in time, the point of view is "omniscient." If events are presented through the observation and understanding of a single character, the point of view is "first person." The first person point of view may be "naïve" (if the character is not aware of implications) or merely "limited" (if he understands the meaning of all he is able to observe and hear). If events and characters are related as though by a camera, the point of view is "objective."

Portmanteau Words: a term originated by Lewis Carroll to distinguish a new word ("neologism"), sometimes humorously ambiguous, which is made by condensing two well-known words. For example, "slithy," made from "lithe" and "slimy," is a portmanteau word, as is "smog," a collapsing of "smoke" and "fog." (See "Jabberwocky," p. 975, and "Humpty Dumpty," p. 976.)

Primitivism: a philosophy which holds that natural man, who is more open to his natural and inherent instincts and less apt to be corrupted by social conventions and impositions, is superior to socialized or civilized man. An example of writing which illustrates primitivism is "Huck's Island" by Mark Twain (p. 704).

Prologue: the introduction or preface to a literary work, particularly to a drama.

Protagonist: the central *character*, or "hero," in a literary work.

Psalm: a sacred *lyric* or song of praise. See Psalm 23 by David ("The Lord Is My Shepherd: three versions," p. 228).

Pseudonym: a name invented by an author to conceal his own identity. "George Orwell" is the pseudonym, or pen name, of Eric Blair, and "Lewis Carroll" is the pseudonym of Charles Dodgson.

Pun: a humorous play on words which suggests simultaneously different meanings or applications for one word or for words having similar sounds but different meanings. Puns are characteristic of Shakespearean language: for example, the Fool's lines "But, for all this, thou shalt have as many dolours for thy daughters as thou canst tell in a year" (II, iv, 54–55) contain a pun on the word "dolours" (sorrows, dollars).

Putative Author: the fictional author of a work which is presented as autobiographical. The use of such authors, particularly in 18th century novels, allowed *satire* without endangering the safety of the actual writer and helped to create an illusion of historical truth. "Lemuel Gulliver" is the putative author of *Gulliver's Travels* by Jonathan Swift. (See "The Academy of Lagado," p. 826.)

Quantitative Verse: poetry whose rhythmic patterns of sound are based on syllables of varying temporal duration. In classical Greek and Latin poetry certain syllables were actually held for a longer period of time than others; but in English verse the duration of syllables rarely differs so much as the *stress*, or force with which they are spoken.

Realism: the detailed presentation of the external world or reality as it appears. Realism is primarily concerned with facts, and the subject matter is usually commonplace, everyday characters, experiences, or circumstances. Realism should not be confused with *naturalism*, which involves a philosophic (somewhat deterministic) view.

Reductio ad absurdum: literally, "reduction to an absurdity." A method of argument in which a position is shown to be absurd by the use of extreme, though logical, instances of that position.

Refrain: recurring words or lines, usually in a poem at the end of stanzas. Refrains, often containing *incremental repetition*, are characteristic of *ballads*.

Renaissance: literally, "rebirth." A period in which art and learning were "reborn" in Europe: the Continental Renaissance occurred in the 14th and 15th centuries, the English Renaissance in the 16th century. During the Renaissance, classical forms and ideas were revived and assimilated with contemporary native ideas and traditions. The result was usually the replacement of a medieval, religious world view by a humanistic world view.

Repartee: a rapid and witty retort or an exchange of witty remarks.

Resolution: the final outcome of a conflict; the *denouement*.

Reversal: the climactic change in a character's fortunes; the *peripeteia*.

Rhetoric: the art of speaking or writing clearly or persuasively. Rhetoric is dependent on principles of organization, presentation, and delivery. The term "rhetorical" implies a primary concern with the effects of discourse.

Rhetorical Question: a question which implies its own answer. Since a reply is not intended, the device is used to persuade. Examples of rhetorical questions may be found in Faulkner's "Dry September" (p. 552): "'Wont you take a white woman's word before a nigger's?'" and "'Do you accuse a white woman of lying?'"

Rhyme: association by similarity of sound. When the consonant and vowel sounds of two or more words are identical, the rhyme is "perfect" (run: sun). If the similarity of sounds is in the final stressed syllable of a pair of words, the rhyme is called "masculine" (confide: inside); if the words are of two or more syllables and the similarity of sound occurs in the last two syllables in the pair, the rhyme is called "feminine" or "double" (removal: approval). If the similarity occurs in three consecutive syllables in a pair of words, the rhyme is called "triple" (sickening: quickening). If the similarity occurs in a pair of words which do not come at the ends of lines, the rhyme is called "internal." "End rhyme," employing a pair of similar sounding words at the close of poetic lines, is the most common; "beginning rhyme," using the first words of lines of verse, is relatively uncommon. *Verse* which makes no patterned use of sound repetition is called "blank verse" if *meter* is maintained; it is called *free verse* if neither meter nor rhyme is maintained. "Slant rhyme" employs similar but not identical sounds and frequently depends on the use of *assonance* or *consonance* (high: slide).

Rhyme Scheme: the pattern of "end rhymes" in poetry. *Rhymes* are designated by identical letters: if a stanza has a rhyme scheme of *ababcc*, it means that the first and third lines rhyme with each other, the second and fourth lines rhyme with each other, and the final two lines are connected by a different rhyme.

Rhythm: the recurrence of sounds or emphasis at equal time intervals. Prose as well as *verse* may contain rhythm; the preconceived rhythmic pattern of poetry is *meter*.

Rising Action: the complication of a *plot* in a literary work; the events which precede the *climax*.

Romantic: a type of literature which places primary emphasis on emotions or on the emotional apprehension of events; the chief Romantic Period in English and American literature occurred during the late 18th and early 19th centuries. In this period, the highest values were the individual, the self, the spontaneous, the past, the primitive, the natural, and the imaginative or fantastic. Wordsworth ("Lines Composed a Few Miles above Tintern Abbey," p. 680), Byron ("Stanzas to Augusta," p. 155), Coleridge ("Kubla Khan," p. 971), and Keats ("To Autumn," p. 684, and "Ode on a Grecian Urn," p. 973) are known as romantic poets.

Run-on Lines: consecutive lines of poetry which separately do not contain a single grammatical construction or idea. The technical term for the process which results in run-on lines is *enjambment*.

Sarcasm: a form of *irony* in which sharp disapproval masquerades as praise.

Satire: a form of writing which uses humor to criticize vice or folly in people or institutions and which evokes a response of scorn, condemnation, or desire to improve. If the intention is to correct existing faults, the work is known as "Horatian" satire (after the Roman satirist Horace); if the work is only a detailed attack, bitter in tone and without hope for reform, the work is called either *invective* or "Juvenalian" satire (after the Roman satirist Juvenal). In "The Academy of Lagado" (p. 826), Swift satirizes the absurd results of scientific investigation when goals are not clearly evaluated.

Scansion: the act of determining the *meter* of a poem by dividing the lines into feet and identifying the kind of feet by locating the *stressed* and unstressed syllables.

Sensibility: in its 20th century sense, the characteristic emotional and intellectual responses of a writer, a character, or the reader toward sensory experience.

Sentimentalism: self-indulgence in emotions of pity or sympathy. The term, synonymous with "sentimentality," may also refer to a belief in the natural and absolute goodness of humanity.

Setting: the physical and chronological location of a literary work.

Simile: a direct and explicit comparison between two apparently unlike things, usually introduced by "as," "like," "than," or "seems." Examples of similes are: "Blind eyes could blaze like meteors" and "gliding like a queen." See also *epic simile*.

Sketch: a concise literary work, resembling the short story or the essay, which focuses on a description of a single *character*, scene, or incident.

Slang: colloquial language outside standard or formal usage, usually consisting of coined words and expressions or humorous metaphorical extensions of the meaning of accepted words. Slang falls out of use rapidly unless adopted as part of a more fixed, standard usage. Much of the language in Shulman's "Love Is a Fallacy" (p. 212) is slang: for example, " 'If you don't want to be in the swim,' " and " 'Oh, it just knocked me out. That Walter Pidgeon is so dreamy. I mean he fractures me.' "

Soliloquy: a monologue, found most frequently in drama, in which a character who is alone expresses aloud his thoughts about himself or others or about incidents which he has observed. The soliloquy is generally used to characterize a person or to reveal certain facts to an otherwise unknowing reader or audience. Edgar speaks a soliloquy in II, iii of *King Lear*.

Song: a short, emotional *lyric* composed to be sung.

Sonnet: a fourteen-line *lyric* poem which is usually in iambic pentameter and of a standard design: the "Italian" ("Petrarchan") sonnet is divided into an octet (8 lines) and a sestet (6 lines), and the "English" ("Shakespearean" or "Spenserian") sonnet is divided into three quatrains (4 lines) and a couplet. The rhyming pattern of the Italian sonnet is: *abba/abba//cde/cde* (or *cdc/dcd*; or *cdc/ddc*; or *cdc/ede*). The rhyme schemes of the English sonnet are: *abab/cdcd/efef/gg* (Shakespearean) and *abab/bcbc/cdcd/ee* (Spenserian). The development of thought in the sonnet corresponds with the form: the first part raises a problem or doubt which is resolved by the second part. Sonnets, which originated as the lover's adoration of an inaccessible mistress, are traditionally of a personal nature and are used for formal communication between private parties (lovers, a man to God, etc.).

Sprung Rhythm: a term originated by Gerard Manley Hopkins to describe his own use of stressed syllables. The term is used in reference to the *meter* of a poem; sprung rhythm allows any number of syllables in a single foot and requires only that the first syllable of the foot be accented.

Stanza: a formal unit of lines in a poem. Stanzas are generally repeated throughout a poem in a consistent pattern of *meter*, length, and (usually) *rhyme*. Stanzas of two lines are called *couplets;* of three lines, "triplets" or "tercets;" of four lines, "quatrains;" of six lines, "sestets;" of eight lines, "octets." A "rhyme royal" is a seven-line stanza of iambic pentameter, rhyming *ababbcc.* "Ottava rima" is an eight-line stanza of iambic pentameter, rhyming *abababcc.* The "Spenserian stanza" consists of nine lines, the first eight of iambic pentameter and the ninth of iambic hexameter, rhyming *ababbcbcc.* "Terza rima" is a series of three-line stanzas with interlocking rhymes, thus rhyming *aba, bcb, cdc, ded,* etc. A variant form of stanza is the *strophe,* a unit of the *ode.*

Stichomythia: a *dialogue* composed of alternating single lines of two characters. Stichomythia is used especially in classical drama to show extreme tension or strong argument, heightening the drama by accelerating its pace. The exchange between Oedipus and Creon, beginning with line 602 of *Oedipus the King,* is an example of stichomythia.

Stock Character: a conventional character; a "type," often identified by name (such as "Good Report") or traditional role. Stocks characters are common in 18th century drama. An example is Tartuffe — the hypocrite, the imposter — in Molière's *Tartuffe* (p. 251).

Stream of Consciousness: a method of narration which records the continuous flow of a *character's* (or characters') thoughts in a range from full consciousness to subconsciousness and pure psychological reaction. It attempts to reproduce the complexity of mental activity, fusing, by association, thought, perception, observation, memory, and reflection.

Stress: accent or emphasis on a single syllable in *verse.* The pattern of stressed and unstressed syllables in a line of poetry is its *meter.*

Strophe: a stanzaic division of an *ode* which indicates a change in speaker, subject, manner, or mood. For example, see the divisions of Keats' "To Autumn" (p. 684).

Structure: the arrangement of events, images, and ideas in a literary work. Often the ordering of the parts provides a clue to the meaning of the work itself.

Style: the distinctive qualities of an author; specifically, his characteristic mode of expression, his selection and arrangement of words and the devices he uses in his writing. Because an author's choices of vocabulary, syntax, or *images* are determined by his purposes, his personal attitudes, and his central vision, his style is an important key to the meaning of his work.

Subplot: the secondary or minor *plot* in a literary work; it may parallel the main plot, oppose it, comment on it, serve as relief from it, or be totally unrelated to it. The Gloucester plot parallels the main plot in *King Lear* (p. 59).

Suspense: uncertainty, often characterized by anxiety, about the outcome of a *plot.* Suspense is created to provoke the reader's interest or excitement.

Syllogism: a pattern for logical argument in which a generalization (the "major premise") followed by a specific example (the "minor premise") leads to a "conclusion." Thus the statement "All men are mortal" is a major premise; "Sam is a man" is a minor premise; and the conclusion is that "Sam is mortal."

Symbol: a word, character, situation, or scene used in such a way that it conveys not only its literal meaning but a connotative, and often thematic, meaning as well. A symbol is distinct from an *image* in that it suggests a meaning beyond itself as well as its literal, concrete meaning.

Symbolism: the use of *symbols* in a literary work to evoke personal, emotional responses and to express ideal, immaterial, or otherwise intangible truths or states. The writers of the Symbolist Movement, which originated in France in the late 19th century, employed symbolism in a reaction against *realism*, the literal and the rational. Yeats, who developed his own esoteric system of symbols — including "gyres" and many other kinds of spirals — was greatly influenced by this school. (See "The Second Coming," p. 360, and "Sailing to Byzantium," p. 981.)

Syncopation: a temporary displacement of metrical accent, occurring most obviously in poetry when the *meter* and the rhetorical accent differ. The line "And all is seared with trade; bleared, smeared with toil" is an example of syncopation in Hopkins' "God's Grandeur" (p. 360).

Syncope: the abbreviation of a word by omitting a sound or letter; most frequently used in poetry to aid in keeping the *meter*. For example, "mem'ry" for "memory," "ev'ry" for "every," and "Heav'n" for "Heaven."

Synecdoche: a figure of speech in which a part represents the whole or the whole stands for one of its parts: for example, "three sails" used for "three ships."

Synesthesia: the use of *images* of one sense to express the experience of another sense: for example, "warm color," "musty silence."

Synonym: words having the same or similar meanings. Words having opposite or nearly opposite meanings are known as "antonyms."

Synopsis: a summary or condensed statement of a *narrative* or argument.

Tale: an imaginative *narrative* which stresses events rather than *character*. The term also connotes the narration of a strange or impossible story or incident in a simple and realistic manner.

Tension: a high degree of intensity produced by the balancing of opposing *characters*, ideas, *images*, or levels or language in a literary work.

Texture: the combination of literary techniques and *tones* which distinguishes and characterizes a particular work.

Theme: a dominant idea or "message" in a literary work. In *didactic* literature it is called the author's "thesis."

Tone: an author's emotional attitudes toward his subject and his intended audience. Tone is often extended in meaning to refer to all those stylistic characteristics, such as *diction* and *symbolism*, which help to demonstrate this attitude.

Tragedy: a mode of writing which evokes fear, pity, or sadness and in which difficulties cannot be resolved without great suffering, pain, or death to the hero or to many of the *characters* involved. So serious is the crisis that the old order disintegrates or is destroyed and replaced by a new order. Generally tragedy combines a vision of the limitations of the human condition with a sense of man's ultimate dignity. The *style* and language of tragedies are traditionally elevated and characterized by dignity and seriousness. See Aristotle's definition of tragedy in "The Essence of Drama" (p. 933) and the tragedies of *Oedipus the King* (p. 433) and *King Lear* (p. 59).

Transcendentalism: a philosophic movement emphasizing that man can transcend empirical knowledge to intuit directly a spiritual reality.

Travesty: (also "low burlesque") a *parody* of an intrinsically dignified subject, usually through an incongruous, undignified *style*.

Trope: any figure of speech expressing a meaning other than its customary or literal one. *Similes* and *metaphors* are common tropes.

Ubi Sunt: literally, "Where are they?," from a Latin phrase meaning "Where are those who were before us?" A conventional *theme* in literature, emphasizing the transcience of human life and the futility of worldly achievement.

Understatement: an *ironic* assertion which deliberately represents something as less than is the actual case.

Unities: in drama, the "unity of action," the "unity of time," and the "unity of place." A play should have a single *plot* line revolving around a single crisis, in a single locale, and should cover no more than twenty-four hours. The "three unities" are commonly (though not always correctly) attributed to Aristotle. (See "The Essence of Drama," p. 933.)

Unity: the wholeness of a literary work whose diverse elements work together to effect a totality.

Universality: a characteristic of the themes, ideas, or characters in a literary work which suggests that they are applicable everywhere and under all conditions.

Verisimilitude: apparent actuality or truth of a literary work, usually provided by a credible combination of realistic events, motivation, and circumstances.

Verse: a poem, poetry; a single line of metrical writing, a line of poetry. Also, metrical writing which is less intense, less inspired, and more mechanically composed than poetry.

Versification: the writing of *verse*; metrical structure.

Victorian: a period of English literature extending through the reign of Queen Victoria (1837–1901) which is generally characterized by serious concern with moral issues and an interest in the economic and social welfare of the people. In a narrow and pejorative sense, the term applies to literature which is highly conventional or complacent in matters of religion and philosophy or austere in matters of morality.

Wit: that quality of a writer which produces ingenious expressions or writing which is amusing because of clever perceptions. Wit is usually highly verbal and intellectually subtle and is often expressed in such figures as *puns*, *conceits*, and *paradoxes*.

INDEX of Authors, Titles, and First Lines of Poetry

Names of authors appear in **boldface**; titles appear in *italics*. When the title and the first line of a poem are the same, the poem is indexed by its first line.

1123